# THE LEGAL ENVIRONMENT OF BUSINESS

## McGraw-Hill Publishing Company

New York
St. Louis
San Francisco
Auckland
Bogotá
Caracas
Hamburg
Lisbon
London
Madrid
Mexico
Milan
Montreal
New Delhi
Oklahoma City
Paris
San Juan
São Paulo
Singapore
Sydney
Tokyo
Toronto

*Eighth Edition*

# THE LEGAL ENVIRONMENT OF BUSINESS

## Robert N. Corley

Distinguished Professor of Legal Studies Emeritus
University of Georgia

## O. Lee Reed

Professor of Legal Studies
University of Georgia

## Peter J. Shedd

Professor of Legal Studies
University of Georgia

With the assistance of
**Jere W. Morehead**
Assistant Professor of Legal Studies
University of Georgia

This book was set in Baskerville by the College Composition Unit
in cooperation with Ruttle Shaw & Wetherill, Inc.
The editor was Johanna Schmid;
the production supervisor was Leroy A. Young.
The cover was designed by Joan Greenfield.
Project supervision was done by The Total Book.
R. R. Donnelley & Sons Company was printer and binder.

# THE LEGAL ENVIRONMENT OF BUSINESS

**Library of Congress Cataloging-in-Publication Data**

Corley, Robert Neil.
   The legal environment of business/Robert N. Corley, O. Lee Reed, Jr.,
   Peter J. Shedd; with the assistance of Jere Morehead.—8th ed.

p.      cm.
Includes index.
ISBN 0-07-013287-9
   1. Trade regulation—United States.     I. Reed, O. Lee (Omer Lee)
II. Shedd, Peter J.    III. Title.
KF1600.C6     1990
346. 73'07—dc20
[347.3067]                          89-8025

1 2 3 4 5 6 7 8 9 0 D O C D O C 8 9 4 3 2 1 0 9

ISBN 0-07-013287-9

# ABOUT THE
# AUTHORS

**Robert N. Corley** is a Distinguished Professor of Legal Studies Emeritus of the University of Georgia. He received his J.D. and B.S. degrees from the University of Illinois, where he taught for eighteen years. He was admitted to the Illinois Bar in 1956. Professor Corley is past president of the American Business Law Association and a past member of the editorial board of the *American Business Law Journal.* In 1985 he was awarded the Senior Faculty Award of Excellence by the American Business Law Association. Winner of numerous teaching awards at both the undergraduate and graduate levels, he has also taught in several national executive development programs. Since 1964 he has been senior author of *The Legal Environment of Business.* His contributions have shaped the content of the entire legal environment of business field.

**O. Lee Reed** holds a J.D. degree from the University of Chicago and a B.A. degree from Birmingham-Southern College. Presently, he is Professor of Legal Studies at the University of Georgia. The author of many scholarly articles, he is former editor-in-chief of the *American Business Law Journal.* He also has served as president of the Southeastern Regional Business Law Association. Professor Reed has received teacher-of-the-year awards from both undergraduate and graduate student organizations. He has been co-author of *The Legal Environment of Business* since 1977.

**Peter J. Shedd** is a Professor of Legal Studies at the University of Georgia where he received J.D. and B.B.A. degrees. Professor Shedd has extensive experience as a teacher, researcher, and author of business-related texts. He also has been an active member in the American Business Law Association and the Southeastern Regional Business Law Association. Professor Shedd has served as a staff editor of the *American Business Law Journal.* In 1980, he was recognized as the first recipient of the ABLA Faculty Award of Excellence for younger teachers in the business law and legal studies discipline.

# CONTENTS

# PART THREE
# CONTRACTS AND TORTS

# PART FOUR
## CONDUCTING BUSINESS

**Chapter 14**   INTERNATIONAL BUSINESS TRANSACTIONS                                     409

# PART FIVE
# PROTECTING EMPLOYEES

# PART SIX
## PROTECTING PARTIES TO TRANSACTIONS

## Chapter 19   INVESTOR PROTECTION   576

# LIST OF CASES

# PREFACE

Over a quarter of a century ago, Professor Robert L. Black of the University of Illinois and I believed that the traditional business law course would not adequately educate business students about the law. It seemed to us that issues relating to government regulation of business were more relevant than were many issues of private law such as the holder-in-due-course concept. This was because new legal theories had brought expanded rights to employees, consumers, investors, and others. These new rights imposed corollary duties on business which were often enforced by government regulatory agencies at all levels.

Although no university offered such a course, we prepared a text to emphasize public law areas rather than private ones and legal relationship rather than legal transactions. We called our text *The Legal Environment of Business* and suggested it as the title of a new course. With pride we note that many, if not most, accredited schools of business now offer such a course. With mixed emotions we note that many competing texts have been written using the same title, content, and basic approach. It is clearly the growth area of the business law discipline.

As we enter the last decade of the twentieth century, most business educators believe that courses about the role of law in business decisions are of paramount importance. These courses must cover both public law and private law subjects. Public law issues such as those relating to white-collar crime, insider trading, affirmative action, and billion-dollar mergers are leading news stories. The private law of contracts and agency is of concern to all businesses because of issues such as the right of an employer to terminate an employee whose contract is terminable at the will of the employer at any time without liability. The law of torts, especially product liability, is the subject of a highly emotional debate. Thus it is important that today's courses cover these relevant areas of the law and that they create an awareness of contemporary legal issues.

The trend toward coverage of both public law and private law issues is part of an evolutionary process in our discipline. The seven previous editions of this text were part of this process. The coverage has been expanded in some areas and reduced in others. What has evolved is the table of contents for this eighth edition which we believe includes discussion of those issues which will be most relevant to business school graduates in the years ahead.

## GUIDING PRINCIPLES

In preparing this eighth edition, four basic principles have guided us: (1) The materials should actively prepare students for decision making in business rather than merely summarize for them the course content of various law school subjects: (2) Law is information that serves as a tool for generating policy and for making business decisions; (3) The law is only one influence on business decisions. Ethical considerations also play a major role in defining appropriate business conduct; and (4) Substantive rules of law are important and should be a part of the learning process.

## CASE TREATMENT

The materials in this book include text discussions, summaries of important legislation, articles, and decided cases. We have deleted most of the procedural issues from the cases and have omitted case references and footnotes. Since we believe that students should be required to study judicial language and reasoning on substantive issues, we include those portions of each case that show the arguments of the parties and the court's resolution of the issues raised. We have shortened long cases without deleting the heart of the opinions.

## FEATURES

This edition of *The Legal Environment of Business* contains many noteworthy features. Among the more important are:

**1** *Clear, straightforward writing style.* We believe that the study of law is difficult enough without burdening students additionally by a complex writing style. The publisher has also aided readability by using color, large type, wide margins, and many headings throughout the text.

**2** *Cases.* Each chapter contains several cases illustrating the text. Special pains have been taken throughout the book to include recent cases of interest to the business community. There are 62 cases new to this edition; each chapter contains one or more new cases. Thirty-five cases were decided in 1987 and 1988.

**3** *Text in seven parts.* The seven parts each consist of three or four chapters. The instructor can therefore select the subjects to be covered and the order of coverage. The last three parts deal with the law in its role of protecting employees, the general public, and society from harmful business activities.

**4** *New chapters.* There are two new chapters. Chapter 5 is devoted to arbitration as a substitute for litigation. Arbitration is of growing significance to all business transactions, especially in international affairs. The second new chapter is a result of dividing Chapter 15 of the Seventh Edition (Consumer Protection) into two chapters—one dealing with consumer protection, the other with debtor protection.

**5** *International business.* The topic of international business is of growing importance in the business curriculum. We are indebted to Professor Jere Morehead of the University of Georgia for preparing this chapter of the book. He brings to this chapter a background of dealing with these issues at the Justice Department and teaching a course in international business.

**6** *Appropriate private law coverage.* Although this text primarily deals with public law issues, part three contains appropriate private law coverage as well. For instance, product liability and business-related accidents make it necessary for students to understand the tort system, which is the subject of two chapters. Since contracts form the basis for economic exchanges, and much government regulation affects contracts, one chapter is devoted to principles of contract law. This coverage also introduces contracts to students who will not take additional, specialized courses in private law subjects. Agency and suretyship are also discussed in parts of chapters.

**7** *Treatment of ethical issues.* Many chapters discuss ethical issues of public and social policy which underlie legal rules. The text contains several references to the Caterpillar Tractor Company Code of Worldwide Business Conduct and Operating Principles, which are used to illustrate the approach of a major corporation to current ethical issues.

**8** *Chapter preview.* Each chapter begins with a preview of the material covered in the chapter. This feature will help students relate their reading to key chapter concepts.

## STUDENT AIDS

The text continues to include a glossary that defines legal terms used throughout the text so that students will not need access to a legal dictionary. The appendixes include the United States Constitution and excerpts from the antitrust laws and labor laws. We believe that students often benefit from reading the exact language of the Constitution and some of the major statutes that furnish the basic legal principles for substantial portions of the text.

Following this preface, there is a special section addressed to students. In this section we provide step-by-step instructions on how to study this textbook. We include as a part of the instructions a written example of the case briefing system so that students will know how to brief a case if the instructor asks them to do so.

## SUPPLEMENTARY MATERIALS

To supplement the textbook coverage, a comprehensive instructor's manual and test bank are available to adopters. The instructor's manual was prepared by the textbook authors. The test bank was prepared by Daphyne Saunders Thomas, James Madison University.

For students there is a study guide prepared by Professor O. Lee Reed. As one of the coauthors of the text, his special insight has enabled him to prepare a study guide that complements the text. As a learning tool, it should help students understand the more difficult subjects of the text. If the study guide is not available to students, it may be ordered for them by their bookstores on a rush basis directly from the publisher.

## NEW COAUTHOR

I am pleased that Professor Peter J. Shedd of the University of Georgia is willing to join the Legal Environment team. He brings to the project a record of significant accomplishments in teaching, research, service, and university administration. As the first recipient of the American Business Law Association Award of Excellence for Junior Faculty, he established his national leadership in our discipline early in his career. He brings new ideas, enthusiasm, and superior writing and research skills to our text. For this edition he devoted his efforts to the chapters on business organization and securities regulation. I look forward to work with him in the years ahead and greatly appreciate his willingness to assume these added duties.

## ACKNOWLEDGMENTS

The authors are grateful to the Caterpillar Tractor Company of Peoria, Illinois, for permission to quote extensively through the text from its Code of Worldwide Business Conduct and Operating Principles.

The authors also acknowledge the assistance of the following professors who reviewed the manuscript and provided many helpful suggestions: Edward Kaminsky, University of Central Florida; Lee J. Ness, University of North Dakota; Daphyne Saunders Thomas, James Madison University; and Burke T. Ward, Villanova University.

Finally, we wish a special note of gratitude to Annette Bodzin who once again has been everything that any author could ask for in a production editor.

**Robert N. Corley**

# TO THE STUDENT

## How to Study *The Legal Environment of Business*

To gain the most from this textbook, you should learn how to study written material effectively. You can achieve effective study through use of the SQ3R method, a method widely taught by study-skills psychologists for learning textual material.

SQ3R stands for **survey, question, read, recite,** and **review.** As a study method, it has dramatically improved the grade-point averages of most students who have practiced it. It is based upon the concept that active study of written material improves memory and comprehension of information far better than passive reading. Unfortunately, many students have not recognized the difference between active study and mere passive reading.

Students often read a textbook chapter exactly as they would read a novel or a magazine article. They begin with the first sentence of the chapter and read straight through the material, pausing only to underline occasionally. This way of reading may be suitable for a novel, but it is quite inappropriate for a textbook. Psychologists insist that an active study method must begin with a **survey** of the material to be read. If you plan to spend two hours studying a thirty-page chapter, take three to five minutes in the beginning and survey the chapter. First, read the boldtype section headings; (each chapter of this book is divided into numbered sections). Second, read a sentence or two from the text of each section. The purpose of this survey is to familiarize you with the topics covered in the chapter. Fight the tendency to stop your surveying process in order to comprehend all of the concepts you are surveying. Comprehension is not the goal of surveying.

Following the survey of all the sections, go back to the beginning of the chapter. Ask yourself a **question** before reading each section. Ask it aloud, if possible, but silently if circumstances demand. The important thing is actually to "talk to yourself." Normally, each section heading can easily be turned into a question. If the section heading reads **Stare Decisis,** ask yourself the question, "What does stare decisis mean?"

Only after asking a question are you finally ready to **read** a chapter section. In reading keep your question in mind. By so doing you will be reading for a purpose: to discover the answer to your question.

Upon finishing each section, stop and **recite** the answer to your question.

As an example, at the end of the section on stare decisis say to yourself, "Stare decisis refers to the legal tradition that a judge in a given case will follow the precedent established in similar cases decided by courts in that jurisdiction." According to psychologists, to recite this way greatly aids memory. Recitation also lets you know whether or not you have understood the material just read.

The last step of the SQ3R method is **review.** When devoting two hours to the study of a chapter, take the final fifteen minutes of that time to review the material. Review the questions taken from the headings of each chapter section and recite the answers to them, rereading material if necessary to answer accurately.

While the SQ3R method may be used effectively to study any subject, the **case briefing system** is uniquely designed to aid in the study of court decisions. In studying law, students frequently write up case briefs of each decision they read. Whether you are required to write up every decision is up to your individual instructor. However, the case briefing system provides an excellent framework for comprehending complicated judicial reasoning processes, and you should brief cases whether required to do so or not.

To avoid getting lost in a maze of judicial terminology, you should ask yourself a standard set of questions about each case decision and read to discover the answers to these questions. These standard questions lie at the heart of the case briefing system. They are:

**1** Who is the plaintiff and who is the defendant?

**2** What are the facts of the case? (Who did what to whom? What is the behavior complained of?)

**3** Did the plaintiff or the defendant win in the lower court(s), and which party is appealing? (All decisions in this textbook come from appellate courts.)

**4** What was the legal issue or issues appealed?

**5** Does the plaintiff or the defendant win on the appeal?

**6** What rules of law and reasoning does the appellate court use in deciding the issue?

Here is an illustration of a written case brief. It is a brief of the first case in the book, which is found on page 52. Before looking at the brief you should now read that case. To understand the case you need to know that a "summary judgment" occurs when a court determines that no genuine factual dispute exists and that either the plaintiff or the defendant is entitled to judgment as a matter of law. No evidence is presented before a jury. The court (judge) rules in favor of the plaintiff or the defendant on the basis of what the law is rather than on which facts (who did what to whom, etc.) are believed.

**Case Brief**

WOODRUFF v. GEORGIA STATE UNIVERSITY, 394 S.E.2d 697 (Ga. 1983) [The notation following the name of the case indicates that the case may be found in volume 394 of the *Southeastern Reporter*, second series, starting at page 697. The Supreme Court of Georgia decided the case in 1983.]

**Plaintiff and Defendant**

The plaintiff (who brings the lawsuit against the defendants by filing a complaint) is Woodruff, a student. The defendants are the Georgia Board of Regents, Georgia State University, and certain Georgia State professors.

**Facts**

Woodruff was pursuing a master's degree program in the music department. She received an "F" on the basis of plagiarism, appealed that grade to a university appeals committee, and got the grade changed to "incomplete." Thereafter, she claims, her music department professors were "hostile and sarcastic" to her. When she finally received her master's degree and sought to enter the doctoral program at another university, none of her Georgia State music professors would give her the recommendations required by the other university. She sued the defendants in state court, alleging constitutional violations, tort, and breach of contract claims.

**Lower Court**

The trial court granted summary judgment in favor of the defendants. The plaintiff appealed. The case is now before the Supreme Court of Georgia.

**Issue Appealed**

Is a dispute concerning academic decisions of a public university a justiciable controversy, i.e., will a court decide the merits of such a dispute?

**Who Wins**

The defendants.

**Reasoning**

Judges are "ill-equipped" to make policy decisions that belong properly to other public officials. In particular, judges should not review a teacher's academic assessment of a student's work. This protects teachers and the school system from the "unbearable burden of continuous legal turmoil." It also shields the courts from "an incalculable new potential for lawsuits...."

As with the SQ3R method, the case briefing system assists you best when you pause after reading each case to recite answers to the questions raised by the system. These questions should either be memorized or written down for easy reference while reading case material.

Regular use of the SQ3R method and the case briefing system will substantially raise the grades of most students. The secret to your own success, however, is for you to continue to practice these methods despite an initial awkwardness in their use. The temptation to slide back into a passive reading of the material must be overcome.

**Robert N. Corley**
**O. Lee Reed**
**Peter J. Shedd**

# THE LEGAL ENVIRONMENT OF BUSINESS

# *Part One*
# INTRODUCTION

# Chapter

## *1*

# The Law and Lawyers

## CHAPTER PREVIEW

This chapter introduces you to law, lawyers, and legal terminology. The various classifications of legal subjects, such as private law versus public law and substance versus procedure, are illustrated. Other influences on behavior, such as ethical considerations, are discussed. This text primarily deals with law that relates to the business environment and the ways in which it affects business decisions. The law is one of the means for controlling the conduct of businesses.

In reading this chapter, give special attention to the following legal terms: administrative law, felony, fixture, misdemeanor, negligence, procedural law, stare decisis, substantive law, tort, and white-collar crime.

### 1. The Law and Business

The subject matter of this text is the law as it defines and prescribes the environment in which business is conducted in the United States. Since the focus of the book is law, much of the discussion concerns litigation and lawyers. In a real sense, litigation has replaced baseball as our national pastime. Today, our courts are filled with cases involving every conceivable controversy that may arise. Whenever people have a disagreement, there is a distinct possibility that they may resolve it with a lawsuit.

We are the most litigious society in history. We protect our rights by litigating. We change society through litigation. Every year several million lawsuits are filed. The issues include questions of broad public policy, such as the use of nuclear power or the right to life in the abortion cases. The range of cases includes such issues as liability for injuries caused by defective products or medical practice, and liability to a victim of discrimination in employment. Many cases, such as those dealing with couples seeking a divorce, involve issues of importance to the litigants only. Many cases are actually frivolous and of importance to no one. Thus, the range of litigation runs from the most serious and important issues to issues of no importance at all.

Whether it is a cause or an effect of our litigious society, a significant development in recent years is the explosion in the number of lawyers in this country. In 1970 there were about 350,000 lawyers. By the mid-1980s, there were 650,000, and in the 1990s the number will reach 1 million. Two-thirds of the world's lawyers practice in the United States. Law and lawyers are involved in almost every aspect of our daily lives and in almost every business decision. In 1987 the 100 biggest law firms in the United States billed their clients $8.6 billion, a 20 percent increase from 1986. These legal costs are significant to most businesses. An understanding of the law and the role of lawyers in conducting business is essential to an understanding of the legal environment of business.

The increase in the amount of litigation and in the number of lawyers is consistent with another trend in our society—increased regulation of business. Although enforcement varies from time to time, there has been increased regulation of business in the post-World War II period. This has been in response to public demands for protection from an unhealthy environment, for safer products and workplaces, and for equal employment opportunity. This text discusses these regulatory laws as a major component of the legal environment of business.

The basic role of law in business decisions is readily apparent. It constrains business in its decisions and in its selection of alternative courses of action. Certain conduct is illegal, and individuals or businesses who commit acts or omissions declared to be illegal are subject to sanctions. There may be fines or imprisonment if the conduct is declared a crime. The sanctions may include liability for dollar damages if the conduct is tortious (involving a wrongful act) or a breach of contract. In addition, the law and legal sanctions may be used to prevent certain conduct or to require that certain things be done. Business decisions must be made within the law, or sanctions will be imposed. The law is the foundation for the regulation of all business conduct and decisions. Throughout this text, we will attempt to acquaint you with some of the more important laws controlling business decisions and individual behavior.

## 2. Definitions of Law

Before we classify various legal subjects, you should recognize several definitions of the word "law." No word of such common usage is so hard to define precisely or is used to express a variety of concepts as is the word "law." For example, "law" is used to describe specific statutory enactments and also to denote a general system of rules for governing conduct. Popular uses of the terms "law," "legal," and "illegal" are limitless. The meaning of these words in any particular situation must be determined from the context in which they are used. For example, the use of "illegal" to describe a forward pass in a football game differs significantly from the use of "illegal" to describe a contract. The force of the law generally is not involved in a football game, but since the game must be played by rules, the use of legal terminology is to be expected. An illegal contract is similar to an illegal forward pass in that both may result in penalties. However, the legality of a contract is determined by our courts and the legal system. To date, the legality of a forward pass has been left up to the game's referees to decide.

Law is often considered to be a command: You shall do this or you shall not do that. As a command, it is prescribed by a superior, and the inferior is bound to obey. Law is a rule of conduct commanding what is right and prohibiting what is wrong. The criminal law is essentially a body of commands flowing from the people as a whole to people as individuals telling them what they may or may not do.

Many areas of our law, such as those involving contracts and torts, do not "command compliance" in the technical sense. They are so constructed that an aggrieved party is given a remedy against one who violates accepted legal principles in these areas. Civil courts, except in unusual situations, do not require compliance but instead impose liability for noncompliance.

### LAW AS PRINCIPLES USED BY COURTS

Law has also been defined as the body of principles and rules which the courts apply in the decision of controversies. Law is made up of three elements: (1) formulated legislation, including constitutions, statutes, treaties, ordinances, and codes; (2) rules of law announced by the courts in deciding cases; and (3) the system of legal concepts and techniques which forms the basis of judicial action.

Justice Oliver Wendell Holmes said, "Law is a statement of the circumstances in which the public force will be brought to bear through courts." Law is simply what the courts will or will not order in any particular case. Other judges have stated that law is "a rule of reason applied to existing conditions," that "it is an expression of the public will," and it is "that which must be obeyed and followed by citizens subject to sanctions or legal consequences."

## LAW AS A SCHEME OF SOCIAL CONTROL

Law is a scheme for controlling the conduct of people; it deals with social interests. Whereby social interests recognize a right in one person, courts create machinery to assist the person with this right in obtaining redress against the person with the duty or obligation if the duty is not performed or if the obligation is unfulfilled. By this concept, law has four characteristics:

**1** It is a scheme of social control.

**2** It protects social interests.

**3** It accomplishes its purpose by recognizing a capacity in persons to influence the conduct of others.

**4** It provides courts and legal procedures to help the person with this capacity.

This definition of law supports the position of judges as social engineers. This role is present in decisions such as those allowing abortions, prohibiting prayer in school, and requiring busing of school children to achieve racial balance in education.

## LAW AS JUSTICE

All the foregoing definitions convey the concept that law regulates human conduct and that through courts it resolves controversies. The goal of law is justice, but law and justice are not synonymous, just as legal justice and social justice are not synonymous. Justice has been defined as that which is founded in equity, honesty, and righteousness. It is the attempt of honorable persons to do that which is fair. Justice is the purpose and end of government and civil society. Apparently, the achievement of justice depends upon the concept of right and wrong in the society involved. The purpose of justice in our society, as stated in the Declaration of Independence, is to secure for all "life, liberty, and the pursuit of happiness."

Social justice recognizes more rights and duties than does legal justice, although the trend of the law is toward equating these concepts. Perfect justice would require that all persons discharge all their obligations and duties so that all other persons may enjoy all their rights and privileges. Our society through law determines which rights and duties will be protected and strives through its judicial system for perfect justice. Of course, the law is incapable of perfect justice because it is in the hands of imperfect people and operates with imperfect procedures. As law approaches perfect justice, legal justice and social justice tend to merge.

Dean Roscoe Pound of the Harvard Law School attempted to define law in terms of justice when he said that the science of law is "that organized body of knowledge that has to do with the administration of justice by public or regular tribunals in accordance with principles or rules of general character and more or less uniform application."

## 3. Schools of Legal Thought

Closely allied to these definitions of law are schools of legal thought which help us understand the various uses of the words "law" and "illegal." They also identify the different influences which help to shape the development of legal principles. Among the more generally recognized schools of legal thought are the historical, the analytical, the natural, the sociological, and the realist.

The historical school gives great weight to custom and history as a source of law. Law comes from the habits and traditions of people. For example, conduct such as taking the life of another has traditionally been considered wrongful by all civilized peoples, and therefore we have laws relating to homicide. Similarly, the laws relating to business transactions have developed out of the manner of doing business and customary business practices. According to this school of legal thought, human actions and beliefs have formed the law, and not vice versa.

The analytical school of legal thought is based upon a belief and reliance on logic as the basis of law. Under this philosophy, law is conceived by reason and logic. Law comes from the sovereign or government because of the need for order and a system of known rules to follow. Social order logically requires definite rules for governing human conduct.

The natural school of legal thought gives great weight to the influence of religion and divine principles in developing the law. Law arises from right, reason, and the intelligence of man as derived from his Creator. Law distinguishes right from wrong. The natural law philosophy has given us courts of equity and, indeed, much of our constitutional theory. Such concepts as due process of law and equal protection of the laws have come from the natural law philosophy.

The sociological school of legal thought gives recognition to the law as a scheme of social control. It is consistent with the definition of law given on page 5. This legal philosophy considers the law to be the result of competing social forces and values. Law results from the purposes that are to be accomplished. The sociologist uses facts and economic and social theory in developing the law, and he or she views the law as the means of resolving disputes and conflicts between different groups and interests in society.

The realist school of legal thought is a development of this century. The realist takes a very pragmatic approach to law. Law comes from experience. Holmes's definition of law is an example of realist reasoning. Realists are impressed with the role of facts and are willing to recognize exceptions to almost every general rule of law. Realists recognize that law is constantly changing.

These schools of legal thought further demonstrate the difficulty of defining "law" and of understanding its sources, uses, and development. It will be helpful to keep the various philosophies in mind as the subject matter of this text is studied.

## 4. The Rule of Law

Justice Felix Frankfurter in his opinion in *United States v. Mine Workers*, 330 U.S. 258 (1947), began with these words: "The historic phrase 'a government of laws and not of men' epitomizes the distinguishing character of our political society. When John Adams put that phrase into the Massachusetts Declaration of Rights, he was not indulging a rhetorical flourish. He was expressing the aim of those who, with him, framed the Declaration of Independence and founded the Republic." Adams's statement, which recognizes the role of the rule of law in our society, had its origin in England prior to the Magna Charta. The Magna Charta used the term *"per legem terrae"*—the law of the land. English history is filled with numerous statements proclaiming that even the royal power is subject to the rule of law.

The concept of the rule of law has been the cornerstone of our society and government from the beginning, and it is simply accepted as part of our heritage. As President Lincoln said, it is the "political religion" of the country.

In our society, it is the law which is used to decide disputes, not the wishes or ideas of any mere mortal, irrespective of his or her position. Moreover, the parties for the most part accept the fact that the dispute will be decided by a rule of law and that the winner and the loser alike will accept the determination without resorting to another method of resolution, such as force.

The role of the rule of law as the basic ingredient in ordered liberty is obvious from even a cursory examination of the matters before the Supreme Court in any term. The issues presented involve **due process** of law, **equal protection** of the laws, and the power of the governors over the governed. To a substantial extent, the failures of our society can be directly attributed to the failure of people to accept and abide by the application of rules of law. In a real sense, the subject matter of this text is the rule of law as it applies to business.

The study of law essentially concerns "rules of law." A rule of law, using Holmes's definition, is a statement that if certain facts exist, then the judicial branch of government will take certain action or refuse to take certain action at the request of someone involved. In other words, a rule of law is a prediction as to what a court will or will not do in a given factual situation. It is then obvious that facts create legal issues which are resolved by using rules of law. You should therefore be aware of the tremendous importance of facts to the law. A majority of our legal procedures are designed to discover the facts. For instance, the function of the jury is fact finding.

## 5. Lawyers

Before we begin our examination of various legal topics, it is helpful to have an understanding of lawyers and the legal profession. As members of the legal profession, lawyers usually play a major role in the application of rules of law and legal principles. Liberty and justice are abstractions that can only be realized when individuals operate a system in such a manner as to achieve them. The law can only work through individuals; it is not self-enforcing. Although courts and juries constitute the decision makers in our judicial system, lawyers play an integral role in our legal system.

The practice of law is a profession. It involves a dedication to society in which the service performed is more important than any remuneration received for the service. The individual practitioner assumes duties and responsibilities which extend to the courts, to the public, and to the client.

A lawyer's first duty is to the administration of justice. As an officer of the court, he or she should see that proceedings are conducted in a dignified and orderly manner and that issues are tried on their merits only. The practice of law is not a game or mere battle of wits, but a means to promote justice. The lawyer's duties to each client require the highest degree of fidelity, loyalty, and integrity.

To engage in the practice of law is not a natural or constitutional right but a privilege conferred because one knows the law and possesses good moral character. The latter involves a proper conception of the nature and duties of the office of attorney and also of the ethics of the profession. It has sometimes been described as absolute obedience to the unenforceable. Absolute honesty and integrity are minimum standards for the profession.

Sometimes the conduct of some lawyers has not met the high professional standards of the profession. Conflicts of interest and activities such as "ambulance chasing" have occurred, contrary to professional ethics. The courts and bar associations try to eliminate such activities by disbarring or suspending such persons from the practice of law. The code of ethical standards for lawyers undergoes periodic review and updating in order that the profession may effectively serve the public interest.

A lawyer serves in essentially three capacities—counselor, advocate, and public servant. As a counselor, a lawyer by the very nature of the profession knows his or her client's most important secrets and affairs. A lawyer is often actively involved in the personal decisions of clients, ranging from their business affairs and family matters such as divorce to their alleged violations of the criminal law. These relationships dictate that a lawyer meet the highest standards of professional and ethical conduct.

As an advocate, a lawyer is not only a "fighter" in court but a negotiator of compromise. Lawyers spend most of their efforts seeking solutions to differences between adversaries. Advocacy is practiced not only before courts and juries but also before opposing counsel and with one's own client as well.

As public servants, lawyers serve in all capacities at all levels of organized society. Their formal education, training, and experience leave them better equipped than most to render valuable public service.

It is obvious that if a lawyer is to give competent advice and adequate representation, he or she must know to the fullest extent possible all the facts involved in any legal problem presented by the client. In attempting to ensure that a lawyer may be fully advised of a client's problems and all matters affecting them, the rules of evidence provide that confidential communications to a lawyer are privileged. The law does not permit a lawyer to reveal such facts and testify against a client, even if called to the stand to do so at a trial. This is called the attorney-client privilege, and it may extend to communications made to the lawyer's employees in certain cases. This is especially important today because law firms frequently use paralegals to gather facts and assist attorneys. This privilege extends to corporations as well as to individuals. The corporate privilege protects communications by corporate employees with corporate counsel.

## 6.   General Classifications of Legal Subjects

The law has often been described as "a seamless web" in which principles of law are hopelessly and endlessly intertwined with each other. For this reason, any attempted classification or description of the many and varied legal subjects is necessarily inaccurate.

One means of classifying the law is to divide it into matters of public law and matters of private law. *Public law* includes **constitutional law, administrative law,** and **criminal law.** In each of these areas, society or "the people" are directly involved. Their interests are represented by a governmental agency, officer, or official whose obligation it is to see that justice is accomplished and the ends of society fulfilled. Public law provides a major portion of the legal environment of business. For this reason, much of the material in subsequent chapters deals with constitutional and administrative areas of public law and their application to business.

*Private law* encompasses those legal problems and relationships which exist between individuals, as contrasted with those in which society is involved. Private law is traditionally separated into **the law of contracts, the law of torts,** and **the law of property.** See Table 1-1.

Another important classification or distinction in law is the one between substance and procedure. **Substantive law** defines the legal relationship of people with other people, or as between them and the state. Thus, the rules of contract law are substantive in nature. **Procedural law** deals with the method and means by which substantive law is made and administered. In other words, substantive rules of law define rights and duties, while procedural rules of law provide the machinery for enforcing those rights and duties. Every social institution has rules by which it conducts its affairs or

**TABLE 1-1**  Subdivisions of the Classifications of Legal Subjects

| The Law of Contracts | The Law of Property | Procedural Law |
| --- | --- | --- |
| Sales of goods | Real property | Pleadings |
| Commercial paper | Personal property | Evidence |
| Secured transactions | Leases | Trials |
| Bank deposits and collections | Bailments | Appeals |
| Creditors' rights | Wills | Civil procedure |
| Consumer protection | Trusts and estates | Criminal procedure |
| Debtor protection | Mortgages | Probate procedure |

"proceeds." There are rules of law relating to legislative procedure which govern the steps that must be taken for a statute to be valid. A typical rule of legislative procedure might require that all bills be read to the assembly twice before adoption. Failure to follow this rule of procedure might void the legislature's attempt to create rights or duties in the statute.

Judicial procedures involve the method of conducting lawsuits, appeals, and the enforcement of judgments. The rules for conducting civil trials are different from those for criminal trials. For example, each party may call the other party to the witness stand for cross-examination in a civil trial, but the defendant may not be required to testify in a criminal case. Procedural problems sometimes arise concerning papers filed in lawsuits, the admission of evidence, and various other techniques involved in trying the case. They are the rules of the game. Many rules classified as procedural in character might be just as easily classified as substantive because they actually affect rights and duties. Chapter 4 deals with the procedural aspects of law in greater depth.

A classification similar to that of public versus private contrasts civil law cases with criminal cases. For administrative purposes courts usually separate criminal actions from other lawsuits, with the latter known as civil cases. Such cases include (1) suits for breach of contract, (2) **torts,** and (3) other actions in which the remedy sought is not punishment of the defendant but a remedy such as dollar damages.

The sections that follow provide a brief introduction to four of the basic legal subjects. The first, criminal law, is a public law subject and the remainder are private law topics.

### 7.  The Criminal Law

A crime is a public wrong against society. Criminal cases are brought by the government on behalf of the people. When a person is convicted of a crime, one of the following punishments may be imposed: (1) death, (2) imprisonment, (3) fine, (4) removal from office, or (5) disqualification from holding and enjoying any office or from voting. Among the purposes of such punishment are to protect the public and to deter persons from wrongful conduct. Conduct involved in murder and kidnapping is considered criminal in order to protect individuals from harm. Arson and embezzlement are terms used to describe crimes relating to the protection of property. Some conduct is criminal in order to protect government and the public interest. For example, bribery of a public official is a wrong against society as is price-fixing or selling pornography. Punishment is also imposed simply for the sake of punishment, as well as the isolation and suppression of the criminal element of society.

Although criminal conduct often or usually involves acts of violence or the wrongful use of physical force, other criminal conduct involves nonviolent, illegal acts committed by guile, deceit, or concealment, or through simple contracts. Such wrongful conduct as obtaining money by false pretenses or obtaining a business advantage by agreeing with a competitor to fix the price of goods or services is criminal.

Although business crime does not depend on force or violence, physical injury and even death can be caused by it. Defective products sold in violation of applicable statutes frequently cause injuries. Building code violations may result in fire and injury to persons and property. Some businesses, in order to compete, buy stolen merchandise or employ illegal aliens. The maintenance of a dangerous workplace may be a crime. In one recent case, for example, three executives of a corporation were sentenced to twenty-five years in prison because one of their employees died from work-connected cyanide poisoning.

Criminal law is generally subdivided into **felonies** and **misdemeanors.** This classification is based on the punishment imposed in the event of a conviction. Felonies are punishable by fine or imprisonment in a penitentiary for a period of one year or more, whereas misdemeanors are punishable by a fine or a jail sentence of less than one year. Table 1-2 lists typical offenses under each classification.

Violations of traffic ordinances, building codes, and similar municipal ordinances are sometimes termed *petty offenses*. A person guilty of such an offense may be fined or put in jail or both. Punishment is imposed for petty offenses to deter others from similar conduct as well as punish the guilty party.

## WHITE-COLLAR CRIME

Criminal law includes many crimes that may be committed by a business enterprise as well as those that may be committed by individuals. Some business crimes, such as violating antitrust laws and laws on insider trading of securities, will be discussed later in this book. These crimes are often referred to as **white-collar crimes.** The amount of white-collar crime greatly concerns the business community. Losses from embezzlement and employee theft, including theft through manipulation of computers, not only exceed losses from burglary and larceny but also are growing at an alarming rate.

**TABLE 1-2**  Criminal Offenses

| Typical Felonies (Imprisonment for More than One Year and/or Fine) | Typical Misdemeanors (Jail for Less than One Year and/or Fine) |
| --- | --- |
| Aggravated assault | Battery |
| Arson | Gambling |
| Bribery | Larceny (petty) |
| Burglary | Littering |
| Embezzlement | Prostitution |
| Forgery | Public disturbance |
| Kidnapping | Simple assault |
| Larceny (grand) | Traffic offenses |
| Manslaughter | Trespass |
| Mayhem | |
| Murder | |
| Price-fixing | |
| Rape | |
| Robbery | |

The Bureau of National Affairs estimates that employee theft costs companies at least $15 billion and perhaps as much as $25 billion each year.

Hundreds of millions of dollars were involved in illegal insider-trading cases in the mid-1980s. A recent study found that from 1976 to 1985 the number of women arrested for embezzlement increased 55 percent. Fraud arrests among women rose 84 percent during the same period. As the makeup of the work force has changed, it has become clear that white-collar crime is committed by both men and women and is a major problem facing business and society.

There is evidence that losses from shoplifting by employees exceed losses from shoplifting by customers. The cost of crime is a cost of doing business, which results in higher prices for consumers. Costs include higher insurance premiums as well as the cost of the property stolen. The total cost of business-related crime amounts to several billion dollars annually.

One reason sometimes advanced for the increase in white-collar crime is that historically the risk of being caught and sent to prison has been slight. For example, bribery of local officials frequently was considered a legitimate cost of doing business, especially overseas. In addition, employers are often hesitant to prosecute employees for crimes such as embezzlement because disclosure would adversely affect the image of the business. Discharge without prosecution has been a common action taken against employees committing such crimes.

Legal scholars are suggesting new approaches in an attempt to reverse the trend. The most common suggestion is to impose stiff penalties for white-collar crime. Another is to improve the internal controls of businesses so that internal theft and wrongdoing are more likely to be discovered. Finally, there is a trend toward punishing corporate officials for the crimes of their corporations. A corporate official who fixes prices with competitors in violation of the Sherman Antitrust Act is more likely to go to jail now than in the past, and the fine for such conduct has been greatly increased. For example, two former top executives of Beech-Nut Nutrition Corporation were sentenced to a year and a day in prison and fined $100,000 for their roles in selling phony apple juice for infants.

### RICO

There is a growing tendency to combine suits for dollar damages with criminal law, especially when the violations are considered to be white-collar crimes. In 1970, Congress enacted a statute entitled the Racketeer Influenced and Corrupt Organizations Act, commonly known as RICO. It was intended to combat organized crime by encouraging private parties to join the battle. It did so by giving private parties the right to file suits for triple damages and attorneys' fees when federal laws dealing with various forms of fraud have been violated by an individual or a business twice within a ten-year period. The illegal acts are any indictable federal crime, including wire and mail fraud.

The law has not had its intended impact. Rather than encouraging suits against organized crime, RICO has encouraged suits against accounting firms, brokerage houses, banks, and other businesses. A recent survey found that over 75 percent of all RICO suits involve securities frauds or other types of business fraud and less than 10 percent involve criminal activity generally associated with organized crime. When you consider that RICO cases constitute almost 10 percent of the case load in federal courts, the impact of the law is obvious.

RICO has converted cases where recovery had been limited to actual damages to cases where triple damages now may be collected. Under this law, two violations in a ten-year period establish racketeering even though there are no criminal convictions. The use of mail or the telephone makes access to RICO very easy for any plaintiff alleging fraud in a business transaction. A plaintiff need not prove a racketeering injury—only an injury resulting from the illegal act.

There are many threatened or filed RICO suits that lack merit. However, many defendants settle such suits and pay substantial sums to do so. The threat of triple damages and of being labeled a racketeer encourages settlement by people who are, in fact, innocent of criminal conduct.

RICO cases often involve routine commercial transactions and business disputes that generally are not considered to be criminal. For example, RICO has been used by the Federal Deposit Insurance Corporation (FDIC) to recover funds lost in a bank failure. RICO cases have arisen in landlord-tenant disputes, labor relations cases, the sale of land, and, of course, the sale of securities.

There are numerous proposals before Congress to change RICO. The sponsors want to require that a pattern of racketeering be evident before anyone can collect triple damages, and many would not allow a suit for damages in the absence of a criminal conviction. In this important area of business criminal law, new developments are likely. In the meantime, all business people should recognize the great risks inherent in RICO.

### PROBLEMS

The criminal justice system is a subject of great debate today. For example, the acquittal of former President Reagan's attempted assassin on the ground of temporary insanity has prompted a reexamination of the insanity defense. The public attitude that "justice" was not achieved in so significant a case has fueled the continuing debate about an individual's responsibility for his or her conduct. In addition, the dockets of the criminal courts are overcrowded in many areas of the country. Many persons convicted of criminal conduct appeal their convictions to higher courts, creating a heavy case load and congestion in those courts. Although the number of judges hearing criminal cases has been greatly increased in recent years, delay and the many problems associated with it still exist.

The criminal law system in this country often fails to provide swift and sure punishment of criminals. It has apparently failed to deter many criminal acts or to rehabilitate a significant portion of those persons convicted of crimes. We have overcrowded jails and unworkable probation systems. As a result, many experts are seeking changes in our criminal law system. For example, some people propose eliminating many offenses commonly regarded as victimless crimes. Alcoholism and drug addiction, for example, would no longer be considered wrongs against society if such people had their way. The same may be true of adultery, sodomy, and other sex crimes between consenting adults, as well as many forms of gambling. Those who propose these changes contend that far too much police effort is spent on these nonviolent crimes, which became part of criminal law in an earlier era when there were different views on morality.

In late 1981, a federal task force on violent crime made sixty-four recommendations to improve the criminal justice system. Among the more significant suggested changes were to:

1  Permit judges to deny bail to persons rated a danger to the community.

2  Eliminate parole of federal inmates, forcing them to serve the entire sentence imposed.

3  Allow verdicts of "guilty but mentally ill," thus blocking release of many now considered not guilty because of insanity.

4  Make illegally seized evidence admissible in trials if police thought they were complying with the law.

5  Bar lawsuits challenging convictions unless filed within three years.

As a result of these and other recommendations, it is likely that there will be major changes in the criminal justice system in the future. For example, in 1987 the Supreme Court upheld the constitutionality of the Bail Reform Act of 1984, which permits judges to jail defendants awaiting trial if the defendants are found to be likely hazards to the community. Thus, preventive detention now is constitutional.

## 8. The Law of Contracts

Contract law concerns the legal relationships created between individuals by their own agreement. The purpose of contract law is to make promises enforceable by courts. It contains several subbodies of law which are frequently treated as separate legal subjects. For example, there is a special body of law relating to contracts for the sale of goods, and there is another covering the subject of commercial paper such as checks and notes. Although the general principles of contract law developed in the common law in case-by-case decisions, the specialized areas are usually covered to a substantial degree by a statute known as the Uniform Commercial Code.

The detailed subject matter of contracts is covered in Chapter 9. Throughout this text we refer to contracts and to contractual obligations. Many of the chapters contain discussions directly related to contracts. For example, most of the laws that protect consumers relate to the contractual obligations of consumers. Debtor protection, a part of contract law, protects debtors in their borrowing contracts. Much of the discussion about business organizations finds its basis in the law of contracts. The conduct of business is primarily a series of contracts, and one of the major functions of lawyers is to assist with these contracts. Lawyers draft contracts and review those drafted by others prior to their execution. These duties are a part of the "preventive law" function of attorneys—to avoid disputes and controversies through legal advice. Large corporations usually retain "house counsel" to perform these functions, and other businesses frequently retain outside counsel for this purpose.

As we refer to contracts throughout this text, remember that the law of contracts provides the basis whereby persons can create legal rights and impose legal duties on themselves by their own agreement. Such agreements may be expressed orally or in writing, or they may be implied from the conduct of the parties. The force of organized society, exerted by the courts and the appropriate executive agencies, stands behind a valid contract and provides machinery for its enforcement. Whenever a contract is breached, the injured party can obtain money damages equivalent to the economic loss which he or she can prove was suffered because of the breach. If a breach by one party is serious enough, the other party may be permitted to rescind or cancel the contract. In some circumstances, the remedy of an injured party may be a decree of specific performance—an order of a court of equity commanding the defendant actually to perform the bargain as agreed.

Many of the legal problems arising in contract law can be described as language issues. Such cases involve "contract interpretation," or a search for the intention of the parties. This is especially true in contracts drafted by the parties themselves without the assistance of legal counsel.

## 9. The Law of Torts

A tort is a wrong other than a breach of contract committed against persons or their property for which the law gives a right to recover damages. It differs from a crime, which is a wrong against society, although the same act may be both a wrong against a person and against society, as for example, an assault.

Tort liability is based on two premises: that in a civilized society persons will not intentionally injure others or their property, and that all persons will exercise reasonable care and caution in their activities. The first premise has resulted in a group of torts usually labeled *intentional torts*. These include such traditional wrongs as assault and battery, false imprisonment, libel, slander, trespass, and conversion of personal property. It also includes relatively new torts such as interference with contractual relationships and invasion of privacy. The second premise has led to the general field of tort liability known as **negligence.** Negligence is frequently further broken down into degrees, depending on the extent of carelessness involved and the extent of the duty owed. For example, a grocery store's operator owes a higher standard of care to customers than to trespassers.

Each of these premises creates liability for wrongful conduct because a party is at fault. Our legal system in effect says: "If you are at *fault* and cause injury to another or his property, you shall compensate the injured party for the loss with money."

A major area of tort litigation today deals with malpractice suits against professionals such as physicians, dentists, accountants, lawyers, architects, and engineers. Malpractice actions are a special form of negligence action based on the alleged failure of the professional person to perform services in accordance with professional standards. The law of torts is covered in detail in Chapter 10.

For many years tort claims have been the single largest source of civil litigation in this country. Most of these controversies have resulted from automobile collisions. In addition to automobile accident and other negligence cases, business is often involved in tort actions arising out of the sale of a product which has caused harm. Product liability suits involve injuries such as those resulting from deleterious food or defective drugs. Although such suits have contractual aspects, they usually seek damages for injuries caused by the product. Therefore, *product liability*, a major subject of the law of torts, is covered in a separate chapter—Chapter 11.

## 10. The Law of Property

The law of property concerns the rights and duties of ownership and possession of real estate and personal property. These rights and duties are frequently created by contract and enforced by the law of contracts and torts. Thus, some legal scholars do not consider property to be a separate classification. Perhaps no legal concept has been as important in American history, and as significant for our cultural and economic development, as that of private property. As one might expect, the vast majority of statutes and decisions rendered by both the courts and administrative agencies deals in some way with issues involving the ultimate determination of property rights.

Property is usually classified, according to the nature of the subject matter which is owned, as **real** or **personal property,** and the latter is further classified as **tangible** or **intangible.** Real property is land or any interest in land and includes things permanently attached thereto, such as timber and buildings, which are called **fixtures.** Personal property encompasses chattels or things such as livestock, an automobile, clothing, or a television set. These and real property are referred to as tangible property because the property owned has physical existence. Personal property also includes intangible property such as stocks, bonds, accounts receivable, and patent rights. Frequently intangible property is associated with a document, such as a stock certificate. The document itself is not the property interest, or rights owned, but merely evidence of them. Even if the document is destroyed, the property may still exist.

The concept of property is frequently described in terms of ownership, title to, and possession of corporeal objects. Ownership has to do with the extent of a person's rights in property and is usually synonymous with *title*. Title itself is a confusing term because it is frequently associated with a document of title, such as that to an automobile. Because of this, people frequently think of title in terms of a document labeled "title." Yet persons usually have "title" to the clothes they wear and to their other property without a document of title. Possession is a term which often indicates physical control or dominion. However, in law, possession must be defined in terms of the assistance that the law gives a person in controlling property. For example, it is easy to physically possess a book, but impossible to physically possess a 1,000-acre tract of land. However, one may be in legal possession of a 1,000-acre tract because of sanctions provided by law to keep others out.

The term **ownership** includes, besides the right to possess objects, the right to dispose of them by sale, gift, or will; the right to use, possess, and enjoy them; the right to change their nature; and probably the right to destroy them. These rights are creatures of the law which are backed by legal sanctions. Thus, without law, property is nonexistent. Although most people tend to think of property as the thing owned itself, this approach is inaccurate. More correctly, it consists of a bundle of legal rights, such as those listed previously, with respect to a thing. The bundle of rights theory expands the limits of property rights beyond the physical. For example, a court in a recent divorce case ruled that "celebrity status" was property and had to be divided with the celebrity's former spouse by assigning a dollar value to it. With this concept of property, it is viewed as a series of legal relationships between the owner and all other persons in which the owner has many rights, and the others, each individually, owe him or her many duties which are often negative in character. There is, for example, a duty not to take or use another's property.

Ownership also encompasses a series of limitations imposed by law on the owner and often carries with it duties owed by the owner to other persons. Ownership does not include a complete bundle of rights. It is always subject to the rights of government such as the right of government to take private property for public purposes (**eminent domain**), the power to tax, and so on. When it is viewed in this manner, technically all property is intangible, consisting of specific legal rights and duties that may exist *with regard to* a physical, tangible object. Nevertheless, it is generally accepted in legal terminology to refer to the property rights associated with corporeal things as being tangible property.

Everyone knows the more common rights associated with ownership. Clearly, the owner of farmland generally has the right to sow crops on it, harvest and sell them, and keep the proceeds for personal use (unless, of course, the owner has contracted that right away by leasing the land to a tenant). Also, the owner of a farm has the right, as a rule, to sell it and then use the proceeds of sale as he or she sees fit. And, by a properly executed will, the owner can, subject to some limitations, dispose of the farm at death as he or she wishes. Fundamental to the concept of property are the rights to exclude others from its possession and use.

## 11. Sources of Law

The total body of law by which we are governed comes from four basic sources: (1) constitutions, (2) legislation, (3) judicial decisions, and (4) the rules, regulations, and decisions of administrative agencies. If it is assumed that administrative agencies are part of the executive branch of government, then our body of law comes from all three branches.

Under our constitutional system, the constitution of the governmental unit is its basic and supreme law. All other laws, written or unwritten, must be in harmony with it, or they are void. By and large, state constitutions are modeled after the federal Constitution and, as such, provide the same general organization for government, dividing it into executive, legislative, and judicial branches, giving each branch checks and balances on the others. In addition to providing a government's organization, constitutions define the powers and functions of the various branches. Historically, there was a distinction in this respect between the federal and state constitutions. The federal Constitution when ratified was a delegation of authority from the states, which were the basic sovereigns, to the federal government. All powers not contained therein were retained by the states. In other words, the federal Constitution contains grants of power to the federal government, which was established by the states. On the other hand, state governments have all other powers not denied them by the federal or their own constitution. State constitutions, therefore, generally contain limitations on the power of state government.

Most of our laws are found in some form of legislation. Legislative bodies exist at all levels of government, as the term includes not only Congress but also state general assemblies, city councils, and many other local government bodies that adopt or enact laws. The term *legislation* in its broad sense includes treaties entered into by the executive branch of government and ratified by the Senate.

Legislation enacted by Congress or a state legislature is usually referred to as a **statute.** Laws passed by local governments are frequently called **ordinances.** Compilations of legislation at all levels of government are called **codes.** For example, we have local traffic codes covering such matters as speed limits, and state laws such as the Uniform Commercial Code which covers all aspects of commercial transactions. The statutes of the United States are known as the U.S. Code.

Judicial decisions provide us with our third major source of laws, often referred to as the common law. Courts "make law" as part of the process of deciding cases and controversies before them. The case law created in this process is based on a doctrine known as stare decisis, the principle that prior decisions provide precedents which should be followed in subsequent cases involving the same question of law. In other words, where a rule of law has been announced and followed by courts so that the rule has become settled by judicial decision, a precedent is established for future cases. Judicial decisions create precedent where there is no legislation as well as by interpreting legislation. This precedent is found by studying cases.

When a court decides a case, particularly upon an appeal from a lower court decision, the court writes an opinion setting forth, among other things, the reasons for its decision. From these written opinions, rules of law can be deduced, and these make up the body of what is called case law or common law. The decisions set forth later in the text are cases that have been decided by courts of review. All cases that have been decided are available to interested persons for use in legal research, as are the statutory enactments of legislatures.

The common law system, which originated in England, is contrasted with civil law systems such as those in France and Spain. Civil law systems rely primarily on statutes for the law. Issues not covered by specific statutes are decided by courts on their merits in civil law systems without the use of precedent. With the exception of Louisiana, the states of the United States have used the common law system rather than the civil law system as a model. Many state constitutions specifically adopt the common law of England except where changed by statute.

Stare decisis arose from the desire of courts as well as society for certainty and predictability in the law. In addition, following precedent was expedient. The common law, through precedent, settled many legal issues and brought stability into many areas of the law, such as contracts. Individuals could then act in reliance upon prior decisions with reasonable certainty as to the results of their conduct.

As you read further, remember that the judicial system has established a general priority among the various sources of law. Constitutions prevail over statutes, and statutes prevail over common law principles established in court decisions. Courts will not turn to case decisions for law if a statute is directly in point.

The fourth source of law is generally referred to as administrative law. This source gives us rules and regulations similar to statutes as well as case decisions. Administrative law will be discussed in detail in Chapter 8. The role of courts in interpreting legislation and the problems associated with case law are discussed in the next chapter.

## 12.   Other Influences on Behavior

One definition of law noted in the previous section is a scheme of social control. Law is not the only method of controlling society, however. Factors other than law influence and regulate the behavior of individuals and business organizations. Among the more important are economic principles, individual and institutional ethical standards, and a company's or firm's view of its responsibility to society. The law interacts with economics, ethics, and social responsibility to influence decisions.

The forces or factors which influence business decisions and individual conduct are often compatible and consistent with each other. The law provides the foundation for ethical standards in that it often distinguishes right from wrong. However, the goals and principles of law and economics, of law and ethical standards, or of economics and ethical standards are sometimes in conflict. For example, the economics of a situation may indicate that a price-fixing agreement among competitors would be desirable, but the law and perhaps ethical values would dictate that such an agreement not be made. These factors have different weights at different times and under different conditions. The law is often said to provide the foundation for the operation of the other factors.

It is apparent that our competitive economic system provides both incentives and constraints on individual and business decisions and the conduct that flows from them. Indeed, most decisions to do or not to do a certain thing are based on the economic consequences of the contemplated course of action. The profit motive and cost considerations play as great a role in most decisions as do legal aspects. Our competitive economic system is based upon millions of people and thousands of businesses making numerous daily decisions in their own self-interest. Indeed, there are those who believe that economic considerations and the profit motive are the best means of regulating business conduct.

Ethical standards are also very important in business decision making and in controlling human behavior. *Ethics* has been defined as the name given to our concern for good behavior. It is our commitment to what is right and our rejection of what is wrong. Ethics provides a system of values beyond what the law requires or prohibits. Ethical values are required if people are to live together in a free society. It is not enough to have laws. People and businesses must have values because a free society depends upon the trust and confidence of people. High ethical standards are the foundation upon which trust and confidence are built.

Today, many business associations as well as professional groups such as the American Bar Association or the American Institute of Certified Public Accountants have adopted ethics codes. In addition, many companies have established their own codes of ethics. There is also a federal ethics code for government service. Although these codes do not have the force of law, employees of these firms and members of the professions and government employees are expected to obey them. This "obedience to the legally unenforceable" in a real sense is the hallmark of a profession. If business persons desire professional status, a commitment to a positive code of ethical values is essential.

Although most of this text concerns laws and the legal environment in which business operates, it also deals with several aspects of economics and with business ethics and social responsibility. For example, the material on antitrust laws is the portion that deals most heavily with economic theory. The legal environment is so closely interconnected with our economic system that one of its major concerns is ensuring that our competitive economic system actually works. Materials on business ethics and businesses' responsibility to society are discussed throughout the text where appropriate because ethical standards which become generally accepted frequently are enacted into law. In a sense, the law follows society's view of what is right and wrong. Any examination of trends in the law requires reference to contemporary ethical standards that may become law.

## 13.   Law and Ethics

Defining ethics as "good behavior" and "a recognition of the rights and interests of others as well as society as a whole" means that ethical standards go beyond the law. It is often said that ethics leads the law and is ahead of or above the law. Morality must exist above the law if it is to advance. If the goal of the law is justice, including social justice, then the ethics of society plays a major role in the search for that goal.

The basis of most ethical standards is honesty. Honesty is also required in our legal system. Witnesses testify under oath and are cross-examined as a part of the search for truth. We assume that juries will be able to ascertain the truth. Thus, both the law and ethics are founded on the same fundamental principles and goals. Yet their standards are not always the same.

Although the law and ethics are not identical, each influences the other. Traditional ethical values have often changed the law as moral standards usually are developed and generally accepted prior to becoming law. The law also influences ethical values as it provides a sense of what is right and what is wrong. Ethical values are also affected by economic considerations. Economic principles and ethics are compatible most of the time. Profits cannot be considered unethical most of the time if our competitive system is to survive.

As previously noted, all professions, government, and many businesses have adopted codes of ethics. These value systems of the organizations serve as internal laws for persons subject to them. These codes of ethics are codes of conscience based on fairness, honesty, courtesy, self-restraint, and consideration for others. Such codes may only require disclosure of facts to superiors in certain situations. At other times they may dictate decisions and conduct. They are based on a collective sense of right and wrong. This in turn is influenced by the time frame and by the cultural background of society with special input from religions and philosophy. Many codes are general statements, because the more specific the code, the more difficult it is to obtain agreement to the principles. Most codes are written in positive rather than negative terms.

Ethical business conduct often requires behavior at a level well above the minimum required by law. Ethical conduct may be thought of as doing more than the law requires or less than it allows. An individual's or society's sense of ethics may actually condemn that which the law allows. Ethical codes often recognize that the interests of society are paramount to those of the individual.

For purposes of illustrating a typical code of business conduct we have selected the one developed by the Caterpillar Tractor Company of Peoria, Illinois. Its code was selected because Caterpillar is a company conducting business worldwide in a basic industry employing thousands of people. The company has been very successful in obtaining acceptance of and compliance with its operating principles and ethical standards. Excerpts from its

"Code of Worldwide Business Conduct and Operating Principles" will be found throughout this text to demonstrate the close connection between law, ethics, and corporate responsibility.

Caterpillar's code recognizes that the company is subject to the law of many countries and that what is legal in some countries may be illegal in others. Its code requires adherence to local laws but goes further and contains a commitment to work for constructive change where desirable. The code states:

## OBSERVANCE OF LOCAL LAWS

A basic requirement levied against any business enterprise is that it know and obey the law. This is rightfully required by those who govern; and it is well understood by business managers.

However, a corporation operating on a global scale will inevitably encounter laws which vary widely from country to country. They may even conflict with each other. And laws in some countries may encourage or require business practices which—based on experience elsewhere in the world—we believe to be wasteful or unfair. Under such conditions it scarcely seems sufficient for a business manager merely to say; we obey the law, whatever it may be!

We are guided by the belief that the law is not an end but a means to an end—the end presumably being order, justice, and, not infrequently, strengthening of the governmental unit involved. If it is to achieve these ends in changing times and circumstances, law itself cannot be insusceptible to change or free of criticism. The law can benefit from both.

Therefore, in a world characterized by a multiplicity of divergent laws at international, national, state, and local levels, Caterpillar's intentions fall in two parts: (1) to obey the law; and (2) to offer, where appropriate, constructive ideas for change in the law.

The "Caterpillar Code's Statement on Business Ethics" also recognizes that complying with the law is only the beginning of what is necessary for ethical business conduct. Its comment on business ethics provides:

## BUSINESS ETHICS

The law is a floor. Ethical business conduct should normally exist at a level well above the minimum required by the law.

One of a company's most valuable assets is a reputation for integrity. If that be tarnished, customers, investors, suppliers, employees, and those who sell our products will seek affiliation with other, more attractive companies. We intend to hold to a single high standard of integrity everywhere. We will keep our word. We won't promise more than we can reasonably expect to deliver; nor will we make commitments we don't intend to keep.

The goal of corporate communication is the truth—well and persuasively told. In our advertising and other public communications, we will avoid not only untruths, but also exaggeration, overstatement, and boastfulness.

Caterpillar employees shall not accept costly entertainment or gifts (excepting mementos and novelties of nominal value) from dealers, suppliers, and others with whom we do business. And we won't tolerate circumstances that produce, or reasonably appear to produce, conflict between personal interests of an employee and interests of the company.

We seek long-lasting relationships—based on integrity—with all whose activities touch upon our own.

The ethical performance of the enterprise is the sum of the ethics of the men and women who work here. Thus, we are all expected to adhere to high standards of personal integrity. For example, perjury or any other illegal act ostensibly taken to "protect" the company is wrong. A sale made because of deception is wrong. A production quota achieved through questionable means or figures is wrong. The end doesn't justify the means.

---

Finally, the code acknowledges the importance of employees' compliance by requiring regular reporting. Note the specific request that the reports go to the legal counsel:

## REPORTING CODE COMPLIANCES

Each officer, subsidiary head, plant or parts department manager, and department head shall prepare a memorandum by the close of each year: (1) affirming a full knowledge and understanding of this Code; and (2) reporting any events or activities which might cause an impartial observer to conclude that the Code hasn't been fully followed. These reports should be sent directly to the company's General Counsel; General Offices; Peoria, Illinois.

---

## REVIEW QUESTIONS

**1**  Name the five schools of legal thought discussed in section 3 and give an example of a legal area or principle that was developed because of each school or philosophy.

**2**  Compare and contrast the following:
  **a** Public law and private law
  **b** Civil law and criminal law
  **c** Tort and crime
  **d** Felony and misdemeanor
  **e** Substance and procedure
  **f** Personal property and real property
  **g** Title to property and possession of property

**3**  Which of the following are generally considered to be white-collar crimes?
  **a** Arson
  **b** Bribery
  **c** Burglary
  **d** Embezzlement
  **e** Forgery

**f** Obstruction of justice
**g** Price-fixing
**h** Rape
**i** Robbery
**j** Securities fraud

**4** A Belgian company believed that it was a victim of overbilling by a New York supplier of aviation parts. It sued for triple damages, alleging that the bills had been submitted by mail and were fraudulent. No criminal case had been brought against the supplier. Is the plaintiff entitled to triple damages? Explain.

**5** Jones, a stockbroker, called two customers on the telephone and attempted to sell them stock. Assume that his statements constitute securities fraud. What action are the customers likely to take if the fraud is discovered? Explain.

**6** List three of the changes in the criminal law system that have been proposed by the federal task force on violent crime and give the common thread of each proposal.

**7** Which body of civil law results in the most litigation in the United States? What is the usual legal theory asserted in such cases? Why did the law develop this theory?

**8** Ranch owners in West Texas brought suit against the owners and operators of airplanes and equipment used in a "weather modification program" by which they engaged in cloud seeding. The trial court issued an injunction commanding the defendants to refrain from seeding the clouds or in any way interfering with the natural conditions of the air, atmosphere, and air space over and in the area of plaintiff's lands, and to refrain from affecting or modifying the weather conditions on or about said lands in any degree or way. What theory of property was used by the court?

**9** In which of the following events is a successful lawsuit likely? What theory would be used by the plaintiff? Explain.
   **a** A man attempted suicide by jumping in front of a subway train.
   **b** A burglar fell through a skylight while attempting to steal lights from the roof of a public school.
   **c** An overweight man had a heart attack while starting his lawn mower.
   **d** A man was injured in a telephone booth when a drunken driver rammed the booth.

**10** Different terminology is used to describe legislation. List three terms which describe the product of the legislative process.

**11** Name four factors other than the law which have significant influence on individual and business behavior.

**12** A worker was killed when a trench collapsed. An investigation revealed that the trench was 27 feet deep and was without shoring, which is in violation of safety standards. The president of the corporation was charged with negligent homicide. Is a finding of guilty possible?

**13** Lawyers serve in three capacities and owe duties and obligations to three groups or institutions. Identify the three capacities and groups.

**14** What is the relationship between law and ethics?

# Chapter
# 2

# The Powers and Functions of Courts

## CHAPTER PREVIEW

This chapter discusses the powers and functions of courts. There are three basic powers: (1) judicial review, (2) interpretation of the Constitution and legislation, and (3) the making of law in the process of deciding cases (stare decisis). Judicial review is the power to decide if a statute passed by the legislative branch or an action by the executive branch violates the Constitution. Those involved in the process of interpretation apply the general language of a statute to a specific controversy. Judicial interpretation helps "fill out" legislation, and thus courts have a "legislative" function to perform. Case law gives us our common law system and all of the problems inherent in it. The chapter will also discuss the fact-finding function of the jury in our court system.

The following legal terms and concepts are of special importance in this chapter: conflict-of-laws principles, dicta, judicial activism, judicial restraint, judicial review, legislative history, precedent, procedural law, remedial statutes, and substantive law.

## 1. Introduction

As was noted before, law comes from constitutions, legislation, decided cases, and administrative rulings. Courts play a major role in the development of the law as it comes from each of these sources. Courts not only have the function to interpret the Constitution but also to decide whether a law is in violation of the Constitution. This latter function is known as the power of judicial review.

When legislation is enacted, courts are frequently called upon to interpret its language and to apply it to a specific controversy. Statutes usually are written in general language. Since cases deal with specific problems, interpretation is necessary to fill in the gaps of the legislation and to eliminate the ambiguities caused by the general language used in statutes. Judicial interpretation gives much of the substance to legislation, and thus courts have a "legislative" function to perform.

The common law system has several aspects which tend to increase the cost of litigation and which fail to give it the desired level of certainty and predictability. Case law is sometimes difficult to find, and it is not always followed. The sections which follow discuss the doctrine of judicial review, the interpretation of legislation, and the problems of the common law system. Chapter 8 discusses administrative law, including the role of courts in reviewing decisions of administrative agencies. As you study this chapter, keep in mind the distinction between questions of law and questions of fact.

## 2.   Judges and Justices

Before we look at the powers and functions of courts, some background and understanding of the people who operate our courts are helpful. The people who operate our courts are usually called judges. In some reviewing courts, such as the U.S. Supreme Court, jurists are called justices. In this discussion, we will refer to trial court persons as judges and reviewing court persons as justices.

In all cases being tried before a judge, the function of the court is to determine the applicable rules of law to be used to decide the case before it. Such rules may be **procedural** or **substantive.** In cases tried without a jury, the court is also responsible for finding the facts. In cases tried before a jury, the function of the jury is to decide questions of fact.

Trial judges are the main link between the law and the citizens it serves. The trial judge renders decisions which deal directly with people in conflict. These judges bear the burden of upholding the dignity of the courts and maintaining respect for the law. They have the primary duty to observe and to apply constitutional limitations and guarantees. They should not be swayed by public clamor or consideration of personal popularity nor fear unjust criticism. They should not improperly interfere in the conduct of a trial. They should be mindful of the general law and administer justice with due regard for the integrity of the legal system. Trial judges are responsible for conducting the "search for truth."

The roles of justice and judge differ substantially. Whereas a trial judge has direct contact with the litigation and litigants, a justice rarely has any contact with them. Justices do more than simply decide an appeal—they give reasons for their decisions in written form so that they will become **precedent** and a part of our body of law. Thus, decisions by justices may affect society as a whole as well as the litigants. In deciding cases before them, justices must consider not only the result between the parties but also the total effect of the decision on the law. In this sense, their role is similar to that of legislators. On review, justices are essentially concerned with issues of *law*. Issues of *fact* are resolved at the trial court level.

For the foregoing reasons, the personal characteristics required for a justice are somewhat different from those of a trial judge. The manner of performing duties and the methodology also vary between trial and reviewing courts. A trial judge who has observed the witnesses is able to use knowledge gained from participation as an essential ingredient in his or her decision. A justice must spend most of the time in the library studying the briefs, the record of proceedings, and the law in reaching decisions.

The judicial power is perhaps the most extensive power possessed by any branch of government. Lower court judges may be reviewed by a reviewing court, but they have almost absolute personal immunity from legal actions against them based on their judicial acts. They do not have absolute immunity for nonjudicial acts such as hiring personnel. A judge may have liability for violating the laws against discrimination in employment. Judicial immunity extends to court personnel such as prosecutors and police officers who testify, as well. The system works only if such persons can act without fear of reprisal. The judicial immunity of judges applies even when the judge acts maliciously, exceeds his or her authority, or commits grave procedural errors. A judge can be sued only if he or she acts in clear absence of jurisdiction or is to be prevented from doing so. For example, the Supreme Court in 1984 held that a judge may be enjoined by another court from doing an illegal act, but even then, he or she has no liability for damages flowing from the illegal act. In such cases, the only liability is for the attorney's fees and court costs involved in the injunction suit.

## 3.   The Jury

Before we turn to a discussion of the judicial functions, we should understand the role of the jury as a fact-finding body. Since litigation involves questions of law and fact, the distinction between such questions and the limited role of the courts in cases tried before a jury must be recognized.

The function of the jury in criminal cases is to prevent government oppression and, in both criminal and civil cases, to ascertain the facts. This contrasts with the function of the court, which is to ascertain the law applicable to a case. Remember that in cases tried without a jury, the court also is the finder of the facts.

The jury system was adopted as a matter of right in the Constitution of the United States. The Sixth and Seventh Amendments to the U.S. Constitution guarantee the right of trial by jury in both criminal and civil cases. The Fifth Amendment provides for indictment by a grand jury for capital offenses and infamous crimes. A *grand jury* differs from a petit jury. A grand jury determines whether there is sufficient evidence of guilt to warrant a trial. The *petit jury* is the jury that determines actual guilt or innocence. **Indictment** is the term used to describe the decision of a grand jury. In civil cases the right to trial by a jury is preserved in suits at common law when the amount in controversy exceeds $20. State constitutions have like provisions guaranteeing the right of trial by jury in state courts.

Historically, a jury consisted of twelve persons. Today many states and some federal courts have rules of procedure which provide for smaller juries in both criminal and civil cases. Such provisions are constitutional since the Constitution does not specify the *number* of jurors—only the *types* of cases which may be brought to trial before a jury at common law. There is no discernible difference between results reached by a six-person jury and those reached by a twelve-person jury. As a result, many cases are tried before six-person juries today.

In most states, a jury's decision must be unanimous, or a total assertion. It is believed that the truth is more nearly to be found and justice rendered if the jury acts only on one common conscience. Statutes and constitutions specify the number of jurors who must concur for a verdict. In some states less than a unanimous verdict is constitutionally permissible for a jury of twelve. However, less than unanimous verdicts are not permissible for six-person juries.

Recognizing that a jury's function is to determine the facts, a relatively new technique of a "mock" trial is being used by attorneys in some very significant cases. The attorneys assemble a group of citizens and present their evidence. The jury then deliberates and makes findings. This dress rehearsal gives attorneys insight on jury reaction to the evidence and points up weaknesses in the case. Sometimes issues are tested without introducing evidence. Lawyers argue the case on the basis of assumed facts to "the jury" for a few hours and the jury returns a verdict. The verdicts often cause plaintiffs to take a more realistic view of their damages and almost always prompt a negotiated settlement.

The jury system has been subject to much criticism. It has been contended that many jurors are not qualified to distinguish fact from fiction, that they vote their prejudices, and that their emotions are too easily swayed by skillful trial lawyers. However, most members of the bench and bar feel the "right to be tried by a jury of his peers" in criminal cases is as fair and effective a method of ascertaining the truth and giving an accused his or her "day in court" as has been devised.

As Jeremiah Black, the attorney for the defendant in the famous case of *Ex Parte Milligan*, said:

I do not assert that the jury trial is an infallible mode of ascertaining truth. Like everything human, it has its imperfection. I only say, that it is the best protection for innocence and the surest mode of punishing guilt that has yet been discovered. It has borne the test of longer experience, and borne it better than any other legal institution that ever existed among men.

Jurors do not take notes as a general rule and do not give reasons for their decision. Judges often feel that a jury does not understand the court's instructions on the law of the case to be decided. Actually, it would be almost impossible for the jury to agree as to the reasons for its verdict. A jury may agree as to the result but disagree on some of the facts, and different jurors may have different ideas on the significance of various items of testimony.

Many people attempt to avoid jury duty. Some lose money because of time away from a job or profession. Others may feel great "pressure" in helping to make important decisions affecting the lives of many people. As a result of people coming forth with multiple excuses for avoiding jury duty, courts are often forced either to go with juries consisting of the unemployed and retired, or they must excuse only a few persons from jury duty. Because of the desire to have juries that are a cross-section of society, most courts tend toward the latter and refuse to accept most excuses that are advanced to avoid jury duty. Today there is a strong trend toward requiring jury duty of all citizens, irrespective of any hardship that such service may entail.

To alleviate problems associated with jury service, many states are expanding the rolls of people eligible for service and are reducing the list of occupations that exempt a person from jury duty. For example, lawyers and the police are exempt in many states, but firefighters usually are not. In addition some states are limiting the service of each juror to one case, and if a juror is called for duty but not assigned to a case, that juror is excused for at least one year.

One of the most difficult issues facing the judicial system is the right to a trial by jury in very complex and complicated cases which frequently take a long time to try. For example, many antitrust cases involve economic issues that baffle economists, and such cases may last for several months or even years. The average juror cannot comprehend the meaning of much of the evidence, let alone remember it when the time to reach a verdict arrives. Long trials also may cause financial hardship for many jurors. As a practical matter, many persons cannot serve on a jury for several weeks or months. For these and other reasons, some people recommend that the right to a trial by jury be abolished in very complex and time-consuming cases.

## 4.  Judicial Review

The most significant of the powers of the judiciary is known as **judicial review.** The doctrine of judicial review empowers courts to review laws passed by the legislative body and to declare them to be unconstitutional and thus void. It also allows the courts to review actions taken by the executive branch and to declare them to be unconstitutional. Although the Constitution does not expressly provide that the judiciary shall be the overseer of the government, the net effect of this doctrine is to make it so. Chief Justice John Marshall in *Marbury v. Madison*[1] announced the doctrine of judicial review, using the following language and reasoning:

> The question, whether an act, repugnant to the constitution, can become the law of the land, is a question deeply interesting to the United States; but, happily, not of an intricacy proportioned to its interest....
>
> It is a proposition too plain to be contested, that the constitution controls any legislative act repugnant to it; or that the legislature may not alter the constitution by an ordinary act....
>
> Certainly, all those who have framed written constitutions contemplate them as forming the fundamental and paramount law of the nation, and consequently, the theory of every such government must be, that an act of the legislature, repugnant to the constitution, is void....
>
> If an act of the legislature, repugnant to the constitution, is void, does it, notwithstanding its invalidity, bind the courts, and oblige them to give it effect? Or, in other words, though it be not law, does it constitute a rule as operative as if it was a law? This would be to overthrow, in fact, what was established in theory; and would seem, at first view, an absurdity too gross to be insisted on. It shall, however, receive a more attentive consideration.
>
> It is, emphatically, the province and duty of the judicial department, to say what the law is. Those who apply the rule to particular cases, must of necessity expound and interpret that rule. If two laws conflict with each other, the courts must decide on the operation of each. So, if a law be in opposition to the constitution; if both the law and the constitution apply to a particular case, so that the court must either decide that case, conformable to the law, disregarding the constitution; or conformable to the constitution, disregarding the law; the court must determine which of these conflicting rules governs the case: this is of the very essence of judicial duty. If then, the courts are to regard the constitution, and the constitution is superior to any ordinary act of the legislature, the constitution, and not such ordinary act, must govern the case to which they both apply.

The doctrine of judicial review as a component of the concept of separation of powers was subjected to a severe test during the mid-1970s. As a part of the so-called "Watergate affair," a special prosecutor sought to subpoena certain documents and tape recordings from the President of the United States. The President claimed executive privilege and stated that he was the final authority on the issue. The application of judicial review to the executive branch was the basic issue in this historic confrontation. Chief Jus-

---

[1] U.S. (1 Cranch) 137 (1803).

tice Warren Burger, in speaking for a unanimous court in the case of *United States v. Nixon,* stated in part:[2]

> ...[W]e turn to the claim that the subpoena should be quashed because it demands "confidential conversations between a President and his close advisors that it would be inconsistent with the public interest to produce." The first contention is a broad claim that the separation of powers doctrine precludes judicial review of a President's claim of privilege....
>
> In the performance of assigned constitutional duties each branch of the Government must initially interpret the Constitution, and the interpretation of its powers by any branch is due great respect from the others. The President's counsel...reads the Constitution as providing an absolute privilege of confidentiality for all presidential communications. Many decisions of this Court, however, have unequivocally reaffirmed the holding of *Marbury v. Madison,* that "it is emphatically the province and duty of the judicial department to say what the law is."...
>
> Our system of government "requires that federal courts on occasion interpret the Constitution in a manner at variance with the construction given the document by another branch."...Notwithstanding the deference each branch must accord the others, the "judicial power of the United States" vested in the federal courts by Art. III, § 1 of the Constitution can no more be shared with the Executive Branch than the Chief Executive, for example, can share with the Judiciary the veto power, or the Congress share with the Judiciary the power to override a presidential veto. Any other conclusion would be contrary to the basic concept of separation of powers and the checks and balances that flow from the scheme of a tripartite government. We therefore reaffirm that it is "emphatically the province and the duty" of this Court "to say what the law is" with respect to the claim of privilege presented in this case.

## 5. Attitudes toward Judicial Review

As individual jurists exercise the power of judicial review, they do so with varying attitudes and philosophies. Some judges believe that the power should be used very sparingly, although others are willing to use it more often. Those who believe that the power should not be used except in unusual cases are said to believe in **judicial restraint.** Those who think that the power should be used whenever the needs of society justify its use believe in **judicial activism.** All members of the judiciary believe in judicial restraint and all are activists to some extent. Often a jurist may be an activist in one area of the law and a firm believer in judicial restraint in another. Both judicial restraint and judicial activism describe attitudes or tendencies by matters of degree. Both terms also are used to describe general attitudes toward the exercise of the power of judicial review.

---

[2] 94 S.Ct. 3090 (1974).

## JUDICIAL RESTRAINT

The philosophy of judicial restraint developed naturally from the recognition that, in exercising the power of judicial review, the courts are overseeing their co-equal branches of government. When the power of judicial review is used to set aside decisions by the other branches of government, the courts are wielding great power. It followed that logic and a commitment to the constitutional system dictate that this almost unlimited power be exercised with great restraint.

Those who believe in this philosophy think that constitutional issues are too important to be decided unless absolutely necessary and are to be avoided if there is another legal basis for a decision. They believe that the proper use of judicial power demands that courts refrain from determining the constitutionality of an act of Congress unless it is absolutely necessary to a decision of a case. This modest view of the role of the judiciary is based upon the belief that litigation is not the appropriate technique for bringing about social, political, and economic change.

The philosophy of judicial restraint is sometimes referred to as *judicial abstention* or *strict construction*. Strict constructionists believe that the Constitution should be interpreted in light of what the Founding Fathers intended. They place great weight on the debates of the Constitutional Convention and in the language of the Constitution. "Judicial abstention" means that courts will decide only those matters which they must in order to resolve actual cases and controversies before them. Courts should abstain from deciding issues whenever possible, and doubts about the constitutionality of legislation should be resolved in favor of the statute. Cases should be decided on the facts if possible and on the narrowest possible grounds.

Those who believe in judicial restraint feel that social, political, and economic change in society should result from the political process rather than from court action. Justice John Marshall Harlan in *Reynolds v. Sims*, 84 S.Ct. 1362 (1964), epitomized this philosophy when, in dissenting from a reapportionment decision, he stated in part:

> The vitality of our political system, on which in the last analysis all else depends, is weakened by reliance on the judiciary for political reform....These decisions give support to a current mistaken view of the Constitution and the constitutional function of this Court. This view, in a nutshell, is that every major social ill in the country can find its cure in some constitutional 'principle,' and that this Court should 'take the lead' in promoting reform when other branches of government fail to act. The Constitution is not a panacea for every blot upon the public welfare, nor should this Court, ordained as a judicial body, be thought of as a general haven for reform movements. The Constitution is an instrument of government, fundamental to which is the premise that in a diffusion of governmental authority lies the greatest promise that this nation will realize liberty for all its citizens. This Court, limited in function in accordance with that premise, does not serve its high purpose when it exceeds its

authority, even to satisfy justified impatience with the slow working of the political process.

Judges who identify with judicial restraint give great deference to the political process and to the other branches of government. They believe that the courts, especially the federal courts, ought to defer to the actions of the states and of the coordinate branches of government unless these actions are clearly unconstitutional. They allow the states and the federal legislative and executive branches wide latitude in finding solutions to the nation's problems.

Judicial restraint jurists have a deep commitment to precedent. They overrule cases only when the prior decision is clearly wrong. Persons who follow this belief do not believe that they should attempt to write their own personal convictions into the law. They do not view the role of the lawyer and the practice of law as that of social reform. To them, this is the function of the political process.

Followers of judicial restraint often take a pragmatic approach to litigation. Whenever possible, decisions are based on the facts rather than a principle of law. Reviewing courts exercising judicial restraint tend to accept the trial court decisions unless they are clearly wrong on the facts or the law. If there is any reasonable basis for the lower court decision, it will not be reversed if this philosophy dominates the thinking of the reviewing court. Such courts often engage in a balancing approach to their decisions. They weigh competing interests. For example, justices who adhere to judicial restraint often weigh the rights of the person accused of crime with the interests of the victim and of society in determining the extent of the rights of the accused in criminal cases.

### JUDICIAL ACTIVISM

Throughout most of our history, judicial restraint has been the dominant philosophy. Today, a slight majority of the justices of the U.S. Supreme Court usually follow this philosophy, but all courts to some degree are activists. Indeed, many argue that today's Supreme Court is significantly activist. They point to decisions such as those allowing abortions to prove their point.

Those who believe in the philosophy of judicial activism believe that courts have a major role to play in correcting wrongs in our society. To them, courts must provide leadership in bringing about social, political, and economic change because the political system is often too slow or unable to bring about those changes which are necessary to improve society. Activists tend to be innovative and less dependent on precedent for their decisions. They are value-oriented and policy-directed. Activist jurists believe that constitutional issues must be decided within the context of contemporary society and that the meaning of the Constitution is relative to the times in which it is being interpreted. To activists, the courts, and especially the Supreme

Court, sit as a continuing Constitutional Convention to meet the needs of today.

During the 1950s and 1960s, there was an activist majority on the Supreme Court. This activist majority brought about substantial changes in the law, especially in such areas as civil rights, reapportionment, and the criminal law. For example, the activist court of this period ordered desegregation of public schools and gave us the one-man, one-vote concept in the distributing of legislative bodies. Earl Warren, Chief Justice during this period, used to request that lawyers appearing before the Court address themselves to the effect of their clients' positions on society. "Tell me why your position is 'right' and that of your opponent is 'wrong' from the standpoint of society," was a common request to lawyers arguing cases before him.

Activist courts tend to be more result-conscious and to place less reliance on precedent. Activists are often referred to as liberals, but that description is too narrow to explain their belief in the role of the judiciary as an instrument of change. They also believe that justices must examine for themselves the great issues facing society and then decide these issues in light of contemporary standards. Otherwise, we are governed by the dead or by people who were not aware of all of the complexities of today's problems.

Tables 2-1 and 2-2 illustrate typical judicial restraint and activist decisions. Those labeled "judicial restraint" have been decided by other branches of government and the political process. Those labeled "activist" are examples of decisions in which the judiciary has imposed its will on society.

The importance of judicial philosophy and ideology was never more apparent to the public than in the 1987 hearings on the nomination of Justice Robert H. Bork of the Washington, D.C., Court of Appeals to be a member of the Supreme Court. Justice Bork had been confirmed unanimously by the Senate to serve on the Court of Appeals. Yet when his nomination was announced, violent opposition to the appointment surfaced.

**TABLE 2-1**  Typical Judicial Restraint Decisions

1  Male-only draft is not a denial of equal protection of the law.
2  States can regulate nuclear power.
3  States can tax the foreign income of multinational corporations.
4  Prayer in the legislature does not violate the First Amendment.
5  Unanimous verdicts are not required, and juries may consist of fewer than twelve persons.
6  Communal living may be prohibited.
7  Homosexuality can be a crime.
8  Class action suits require actual notice to members of the class.
9  Plaintiffs must have direct interest in a lawsuit to have standing to sue.
10  Seniority has preference over affirmative action in layoffs.
11  A federal law that allows judges to deny bail to accused criminals who may pose a threat to society is constitutional.
12  State and local employees are subject to the Federal Fair Labor Standards Act.

**TABLE 2-2** Typical Activist Decisions

1  Busing is a valid technique to achieve school desegregation.
2  Legislative apportionment must be based on population and not area.
3  No prayer is to be permitted in school.
4  The *Miranda* warning shall be given to all criminal suspects prior to interrogation.
5  Abortion is not a crime.
6  Female pensions must be the same as male pensions, even though, on average, females live longer.
7  There shall be equal pay for comparable worth.
8  Legislative veto of decisions of governmental agencies is unconstitutional.
9  Residency requirement for public assistance violates equal protection.
10 OSHA inspectors must have a search warrant if a business objects to inspection.
11 State laws that require teaching "Creation Science" as well as evolution are unconstitutional.
12 Certain public employees, such as a public defender, cannot be fired because of political affiliation.

Few, if any, challenged his impressive legal credentials which included a professorship in constitutional law at Yale University and publication of numerous scholarly articles.

Why was there so much opposition to Justice Bork? It was simply because the Supreme Court in 1987 was closely divided between advocates of judicial restraint and advocates of judicial activism. Many people believed that four of the sitting justices could qualify as followers of judicial restraint and the other four could correctly be labeled as activists. Some court watchers found three activists (Brennan, Marshall, and Blackman), three strong followers of judicial restraint (Rehnquist, O'Connor, and Scalia), and two with swing votes (Stevens tending toward judicial activism and White toward judicial restraint). In any event, it was believed by many senators that Justice Bork would tilt the court toward conservatism. It was assumed that he would vote to reverse the decisions legalizing abortion and would favor free markets over government regulation of business. As a result, senators who agreed with his perceived views strongly backed his appointment and those with differing views sought to prevent his confirmation. Although Bork did not receive Senate approval, the country as a whole became aware of the importance of the judicial philosophy of each member of the Supreme Court.

## 6. The Interpretation of Legislation

The second major function of the courts is to interpret legislation. Most legislation is by its very nature stated in general language. It usually purports to cover a multitude of factual situations and is often ambiguous and imprecise. It is up to the judiciary to find the meaning of general language in a statute and apply it to the limited facts of a case. The purpose of statutory construction is to determine the intent of the legislature when the statute was enacted.

One technique of statutory interpretation is to examine the **legislative history** of an act to determine the purpose of the legislation or the evil it was designed to correct. Courts try to find the legislative intent by examining the debates of the legislative body, the committee reports, amendments that were rejected, and other matters that transpired prior to the adoption of the statute. Legislative history may supply the legislative intent, but many of the questions of interpretation which confront courts were never even visualized by the legislature. The real problem often is to determine what the legislature *would have* intended had it considered the question.

Resort to legislative history is not the only means for ascertaining the legislative intent. Courts have developed rules of statutory construction which are frequently followed in determining the legislative intent. These rules in effect recognize that the courts do not actually know what the legislature intended. Therefore, by following the rule of construction it is assumed that the legislature intended a certain meaning. Many of these rules are based on the type of law being interpreted. For example:

1   Taxing laws shall be **strictly** construed.

2   Criminal laws shall be **strictly** construed.

3   Statutes in derogation of the common law shall be **strictly** construed.

4   Remedial statutes shall be **liberally** construed.

The first two rules mean that doubts about the applicability of a taxing law or criminal law will be resolved in favor of the taxpayer or the defendant, respectively. The third rule means that statutes which change the common law will be interpreted as doing so only to the extent that the lawmakers intended and specified. Such a statute will change the common law only to the extent necessary to carry out legislative intent. The fourth rule recognizes that many laws provide a legal remedy for victims of a violation of the law. Such statutes are described as remedial because of the remedy given. As a general rule, a *remedial* statute is given a broad or liberal interpretation. Doubts about meaning are usually resolved in favor of the remedy created for the injured party. What happens if a remedial statute is in derogation of the common law? Courts have an obvious choice of alternative rules that allow the desired interpretation.

There are rules of law which aid in finding the meaning of words used in statutes. Some words are simply given their plain or usual meaning. Technical words are usually given their technical meaning. Others are interpreted by the context in which they are used. For example, if a general word in a statute follows particular and specific words of the same nature, the general words take their meaning from the specific words and are presumed to be restricted to the same genus as those words. A statute that said that indigent persons were not required to pay filing fees, sheriff's fees, or "other court costs" was construed to include the cost of publishing notice of a lawsuit in the newspaper. The language "other court costs" takes its meaning from the words preceding it.

There are other rules of statutory construction that are not based on the type of statute of the words used. If a statute, for example, contains both specific and general provisions, the specific provisions control. However, courts also attempt to give effect to all the provisions of a statute, if possible, so the purpose of the act will be accomplished. Exemptions from statutes are construed strictly against the party claiming the exemption. Repeal by implication is not favored. If two statutes purport to cover the same topic, they will be construed as consistent with each other if possible, and effect will be given to both. However, if two statutes so clearly conflict that they cannot stand together upon any reasonable construction of both, the legislature is presumed to have repealed the earlier statute while it enacted the latter one.

A frequently cited rule provides: "A thing may be within the letter of the statute and yet not within the statute because it is not within its spirit nor within the intention of the makers." This rule allows a court to have a great deal of flexibility and to give an interpretation contrary to the plain meaning.

The meaning of a statute may also be established indirectly. A legislative body may fail to act in an area in which the meaning of a law has already been established. The meaning may have been based on judicial decision or on interpretation by the executive branch of government charged with its administration. When an established interpretation is present and not changed, it becomes the accepted one because it is presumed the legislature would pass a new law if the meaning were not correct. Many people question the validity of this reasoning.

The role of courts in interpreting statutes is very important. The power of courts to interpret legislation means that, in the final analysis, what the court says a statute means determines its effect.

## 7. Uniform Statutes

Each state has its own constitution, statutes, and body of case law. As a result, there are substantial differences in the law among the various states. In many cases, it does not matter that the law is not uniform. If the parties to a dispute are citizens of the same state and if the controversy has all of its contacts with that state, the law of that state is used to resolve the dispute. However, if citizens of different states are involved in a transaction (perhaps a buyer in one state contracts with a seller in another), many difficult questions may arise if the law in one state differs from the law in another. Although a body of law called "conflict of laws" (see page 44) has been developed to cover such cases, more uniformity may be desirable.

Uniformity in the law may be achieved either by federal legislation or by the enactment of the same law by all states. The latter method has been attempted by a legislative drafting group known as the National Conference of Commissioners on Uniform State Laws. These commissioners endeavor to promote uniformity by drafting model acts. When approved by the National Conference, proposed uniform acts are recommended to the state legislatures for adoption.

More than 100 uniform laws have been drafted and presented to the various state legislatures. Most of these relate to business; the response has varied. A few of the uniform laws have been adopted by all the states. Sometimes a state adopts the uniform law in principle but changes some of the provisions to meet local needs. As a result, we often have "nonuniform uniform state laws."

The most significant uniform law for business is the Uniform Commercial Code. It was prepared for the stated purpose of collecting in one body the law that "deals with all the phases which may ordinarily arise in the handling of a commercial transaction from start to finish...." Thus it covers the law as it relates to the sale of goods, the use of commercial paper to pay for them, and the giving of security to ensure that the purchase price will be paid. The Uniform Commercial Code is not applicable to contracts for the sale of real estate or to contracts for personal services. It is limited to commercial transactions involving personal property.

## CASE LAW

### 8.  Inherent Problems

The third major function of courts is to create law when deciding cases and controversies. Precedent is a byproduct of judicial decisions. Several aspects of case law must be understood if we are to understand the role of law and lawyers in the decision-making process. First, notwithstanding the fact that common law arose out of a desire for certainty, and is designed to create it, common law creates a great deal of uncertainty in the law. The sheer volume of judicial decisions, each possibly creating precedent, makes "the law" beyond the comprehension of lawyers and judges, let alone the rest of us. Large law firms employ lawyers whose sole task is to search the case reports for "the law" to be used in lawsuits and in advising clients. Access to hundreds of volumes of cases is required. Since the total body of ruling case law is beyond the grasp of lawyers, it is obvious that laypersons who are supposed to know the law and govern their conduct accordingly do not know the law and are somewhat bewildered by it. Case law does not give the level of certainty and predictability intended by its creators. Moreover, in many cases the law is not clear. It is not found by searching cases. The law used to decide many cases is being made in the deciding process. Many years ago a legal scholar in discussing this aspect of case law observed:

> It is the judges that make the common law. Do you know how they make it? Just as a man makes laws for his dog. When your dog does anything you want to break him of, you wait till he does it, and then beat him for it. This is the way you make laws for your dog: and this is the way the judges make laws for you and me. They won't tell a man beforehand what it is he should not do—they won't so much as allow of his being told: they lie by till he has done something which they say he should not have done, and then they hang him for it. What way, then, has any man of coming at this dog-law? Only by watching their proceedings: by observing in what cases they have hanged a man, in what cases they have sent him to jail, in what cases they have seized his goods, and so forth.[3]

The common law system of reliance on precedent is not very efficient. Conflicting precedents are frequently cited to a court by the parties of litigation. One of the major tasks of the courts in such cases is to determine which of the precedents cited is applicable. In addition, even today, many questions of law arise on which there has been no prior decision, or in areas where the only authority is by implication.

The problem of finding the law in a case law system is compounded in a country which consists of fifty sovereign states, because each of these creates its own body of common law. The law as it develops on a case-by-case basis in different states varies from state to state. Moreover, the federal legal system is superimposed on the state systems, thus creating additional bodies of judge-made laws. The methods of determining the applicable precedent where conflicts exist between the laws of different jurisdictions are discussed later in section 10.

There is an important distinction between precedent and mere dicta. A judicial decision, as authority for future cases, is limited by the facts upon which it is founded and the rules of law upon which the decision actually is based. Frequently courts make comments on matters not necessary to the decision reached. Such expressions, called "dicta," lack the force of a judicial settlement; they, strictly speaking, are not precedent which courts will be required to follow within the rule of stare decisis. However, dicta may be followed if sound and just, and dicta which have been repeated frequently are often given the force of precedent. Moreover, even though a statement by a court is not pure precedent, it does express the court's opinion, and to the

---

[3]5 Bentham, *Works* 235, quoted in 1 Steffen and Levi, *Cases and Materials on the Elements of the Law* 207 (3d ed., 1946).

extent that the court is knowledgeable about the subject matter, the court's opinion is entitled to some weight.

One of the major reasons that the case law system leads to uncertainty is that a precedent may be changed or reversed. Since case law is susceptible to change, absolute reliance on it is not possible. This problem is discussed further in the next section.

## 9.  The Weight to Be Given Precedent

Case law created by the judiciary can be changed by the judiciary. The common law is not set in stone to be left unchanged for decades and centuries. As Justice William O. Douglas observed:

> Inherent in the common law is a dynamic principle which allows it to grow and to tailor itself to meet changing needs within the doctrine of stare decisis, which, if correctly understood, was not static and did not forever prevent the courts from reversing themselves or from applying principles of common law to new situations as the need arose. If this were not so, we must succumb to a rule that a judge should let others "long dead and unaware of the problems of the age in which he lives, do his thinking for him."

Courts usually hesitate to reject a precedent or to change case law. The assumption is made that a principle or rule of law announced in a former judicial decision, if unfair or contrary to public policy, will be changed by legislation. Precedent has more force in trial courts than in courts of review, which have the power to make precedent in the first instance. However, stare decisis does not mean that former decisions *always* will be followed, even by trial courts. A former ruling may have been erroneous, or the conditions upon which it was based may have changed or may no longer exist. The doctrine does not require courts to multiply their errors by using former mistakes as authority and support for new errors. Thus just as legislatures change the law by new legislation, courts change the law, from time to time, by reversing or modifying former precedents.

Justice White, dissenting in one of the cases subsequent to *Roe v. Wade*, 93 S.Ct. 705 (1973), which legalized abortions, had occasion to discuss the rule of stare decisis and the deference which ought to be given precedent. He observed:

> The rule of *stare decisis* is essential if case-by-case judicial decisionmaking is to be reconciled with the principle of the rule of law, for when governing legal standards are open to revision in every case, deciding cases becomes a mere exercise of judicial will, with arbitrary and unpredictable results. But *stare decisis* is not the only constraint upon judicial decisionmaking. Cases—like this one— that involve our assumed power to set aside on grounds of unconstitutionality a State or federal statute representing the democratically expressed will of the

people call other considerations into play. Because the Constitution itself is ordained and established by the people of the United States, constitutional adjudication by this Court does not, in theory at any rate, frustrate the authority of the people to govern themselves through institutions of their own devising and in accordance with principles of their own choosing. But decisions that find in the Constitution principles or values that cannot fairly be read into that document usurp the people's authority, for such decisions represent choices that the people have never made and that they cannot disavow through corrective legislation. For this reason, it is essential that this Court maintain the power to restore authority to its proper possessors by correcting constitutional decisions that, on reconsideration, are found to be mistaken.

The Court has therefore adhered to the rule that *stare decisis* is not rigidly applied in cases involving constitutional issues, and has not hesitated to overrule decisions, or even whole lines of cases, where experience, scholarship, and reflection demonstrated that their fundamental premises were not to be found in the Constitution. *Stare decisis* did not stand in the way of the Justices who, in the late 1930s, swept away constitutional doctrines that had placed unwarranted restrictions on the power of the State and Federal Governments to enact social and economic legislation. Nor did *stare decisis* deter a different set of Justices, some fifteen years later, from rejecting the theretofore prevailing view that the Fourteenth Amendment permitted the States to maintain the system of racial segregation. In both instances, history has been far kinder to those who departed from precedent than to those who would have blindly followed the rule of *stare decisis*."[4]

Justice Stevens, in response to Justice White, wrote:

Justice White…is of course correct in pointing out that the Court "has not hesitated to overrule decisions, or even whole lines of cases, where experience, scholarship, and reflection demonstrated that their fundamental premises were not to be found in the Constitution." But Justice White has not disavowed the "fundamental premises" on which the decision in *Roe v. Wade* rests. He has not disavowed the Court's prior approach to the interpretation of the word "liberty" or, more narrowly, the line of cases that culminated in the unequivocal holding, applied to unmarried persons and married persons alike, "that the Constitution protects individual decisions in matters of childbearing from unjustified intrusion by the State."

Nor does the fact that the doctrine of *stare decisis* is not an absolute bar to the reexamination of past interpretations of the Constitution mean that the values underlying that doctrine may be summarily put to one side. There is a strong public interest in stability, and in the orderly conduct of our affairs, that is served by a consistent course of constitutional adjudication.

Thus it can be seen that the amount of deference to be given stare decisis often depends on the conclusion that a justice may desire to reach. Justices agree on the abstract principle of commitment to precedent except where the rule of law is wrong. Disagreement is likely to arise, however, on the

---

[4]*Thornburgh v. American College of Obstetricians*, 106 S.Ct, 2169, 2192 (1986).

issue of correctness of a legal rule or principle and whether it should continue to be followed.

Judges are subject to social forces and changing circumstances just as are legislatures. The personnel of courts changes, and each new generation of judges has a responsibility to reexamine precedents and to adapt them to changing conditions. This responsibility is especially present in cases involving constitutional issues. A doctrine known as "constitutional relativity" stands for the proposition that the meaning of the language found in the Constitution is relative to the time in which it is being interpreted. The doctrine has been used rather frequently by the Supreme Court to give effect to society's attitudes. Under this concept great weight is attached to social forces and needs, as the court sees them, in formulating judicial decisions. As the attitudes and problems of society change, precedent changes.

Some quotes from justices indicate their attitude toward precedent. For example, Justice Wanamaker in the case of *Adams Express Co. v. Beckwith*, 100 Ohio St. 348, said that "A decided case is worth as much as it weighs in reason and righteousness, and no more. It is not enough to say 'thus saith the court.' It must prove its right to control in any given situation by the degree in which it supports the rights of a party violated and serves the cause of justice as to all parties concerned." Or as Justice Musmanno stated in the case of *Bosley v. Andrews*, 393 Pa. 161 (1958):

> Stare decisis is the viaduct over which the law travels in transporting the precious cargo of justice. Prudence and a sense of safety dictate that the piers of that viaduct should be examined and tested from time to time to make certain that they are sound, strong and capable of supporting the weight above....A precedent, in law, in order to be binding, should appeal to logic and a genuine sense of justice. What lends dignity to the law founded on precedent is that, if analyzed, the particularly cited case wields authority by the sheer force of its self-integrated honesty, integrity, and rationale. A precedent cannot, and should not, control, if its strength depends alone on the fact that it is old, but may crumble at the slightest probing touch of instinctive reason and natural justice.

The extent to which precedent is followed varies a great deal depending on the subject matter of the litigation. If the dispute involves subject areas of private law, such as torts, contracts, or property, there is much greater deference to precedent than if the subject area is constitutional law. The fact that precedent is to be given great weight in the areas of private law does not mean that courts will continue to follow a rule of private law where the reasoning behind the rule no longer exists. Even here, precedents are reversed as the needs of society change. The belief that the meaning of the Constitution is relative to the times in which it is being interpreted results in less deference to precedent in constitutional law cases. To the extent that courts provide leadership in bringing about social, political, and economic change, they are likely to give less weight to precedent and more weight to other factors which influence judicial decisions.

## 10.   Selecting the Applicable Case Law

Each state has its own statutory laws and its own body of judge-made precedent. These laws cover both matters of substance and matters of procedure. Generally, the decisions of one state are considered to be applicable precedent only in that state. The decisions of other states, however, may be considered by way of analogy when there are no previous decisions on the point in question in the state where a case is being heard. For example, precedent of other states is frequently referred to in cases involving the construction of statutes such as the Uniform Acts, where each state has adopted the same statute. Where there is no precedent, a case is one of "first impression." In such cases, each state is free to decide for itself questions concerning its common law and interpretation of its own constitution and statutes.

In addition to this system of fifty distinct bodies of state precedent, there is the federal legal system. The federal courts have their own body of procedural law and substantive law on questions arising under the federal Constitution, codes, statutes, or treaties. Decisions of the federal courts are binding on state courts in federal question cases. In federal court suits based on diversity of citizenship, the federal courts use the substantive law of the states in which they are sitting to determine the rights and duties of the parties. However, in such cases, the federal courts use their own rules of procedure. Thus, just as state courts are bound by federal precedent in certain situations, so also are federal courts bound by state precedent in others.

The problem of determining the applicable case law is sometimes difficult because of conflicting precedents within the same court system. When a case or controversy involves more than one state, the difficulty is compounded when the precedents of each state differ. In case law, differences between the states are quite common. The law of torts varies from state to state as does the law of contracts. For example, in some states the plaintiff in an auto accident case must allege and prove freedom from negligence that contributed to the accident. In other states, a defendant must prove that the accident was the fault of the plaintiff if liability is to be avoided. Similar differences exist in every area of the law because there is no uniformity in case law.

In cases involving transactions or occurrences with contact with more than one state, the question must always be asked: Which state law applies? To answer this question a body of law has developed primarily through judicial decisions, which is generally referred to as **"conflict of laws."** The decisions that comprise this body of law simply determine which state's substantive law is applicable to any given question when more than one state is involved. This usually arises where all or some of the facts occur in one state and the trial is held in another. For example, the conflict-of-laws rules for tort actions are, in most cases, that the law of the place of injury is applicable. Thus, if a car accident occurred in Missouri but suit was brought in an

Illinois state court, the judge would apply the law of Missouri in determining the rights of the parties. There are several different views held by courts about which law to select in resolving issues involving contracts. Some favor the law of the state where the contract was made, others the law of the place of performance, and still others have adopted the "grouping of contacts" theory which uses the law of the state with the most substantial contact with the contract. This latter theory has also been applied in a few tort cases. In the criminal law, the law of the place of the crime is the applicable substantive law. Table 2-3 illustrates typical conflict-of-laws principles.

In a multistate situation, the first problem confronting the court is, therefore, to select the appropriate state to turn to for legal precedent on substantive issues. Once a determination has been made of which state is appropriate, the court's business then is to review the citations of authority advanced by the opposing attorneys to determine which of that state's case decisions to apply in following the doctrine of stare decisis.

Therefore, it must be recognized that there is a body of law used to decide conflicts between the precedent of the various states. This is especially significant in our modern society with its ease of communication and transportation. The trend toward uniform statutes and codes has tended to decrease these conflicts, but many of them still exist. So long as we have a federal system and fifty separate state bodies of substantive law, the area of conflict of laws will continue to be of substantial importance in the application of the doctrine of stare decisis.

**TABLE 2-3**  Sample Conflict-of-Laws Principles

| Substantive Law Issue | Law to Be Applied |
| --- | --- |
| 1  Liability for injury caused by tortious conduct | 1  State in which injury was inflicted |
| 2  Validity of a contract | 2  State in which contract was made<br>or<br>State in which it is to be performed<br>or<br>State with most significant contacts with the contract<br>or<br>State specified in the contract |
| 3  Inheritance of real property | 3  State of situs of real property |
| 4  Inheritance of tangible personal property | 4  State of domicile of deceased |
| 5  Validity of a marriage | 5  State of celebration |
| 6  Child custody | 6  State of domicile of child |
| 7  Workers' compensation | 7  State of employment or<br>State in which injury was received |

## 11.   The Judicial Process

In deciding cases and in examining the powers discussed in the prior sections, courts are often faced with several alternatives. They may decide the case by use of existing statutes and precedents. This will often be the case as courts must have a deep commitment to the common law system. However, as previously noted, they may refuse to apply existing case law or may declare a statute to be void as unconstitutional. Also, if there is no statute or case law, the court may decide the case and create law in the process. However, case law as a basis for deciding controversies often provides only the point of departure from which the difficult labor of the courts begins. Courts must examine and compare cases cited as authority to them, to determine not only which is correct, but whether the principles or rules of law contained there should be followed or rejected as no longer valid. In reaching and preparing its decision, the court must consider whether the law as announced will provide justice in the particular case and whether it will establish sound precedent for future cases involving similar issues.

The foregoing alternatives raise several questions: Why do courts reach one conclusion rather than another in any given case? What formula, if any, is used in deciding cases and in determining the direction of the law? What forces tend to influence judicial decisions when the public interest is involved?

There is, obviously, no simple answer to these questions. Many persons assume that logic is the basic tool of the judicial decision. But Justice Holmes stated "the life of the law has not been logic; it has been experience."[5] Other persons argue that courts merely reflect the predominant attitude of the times and that they simply follow the more popular course in decisions where the public is involved.

Justice Benjamin Cardozo, in a series of lectures on the judicial process[6] discussed the sources of information judges utilize in deciding cases. He stated that if the answer were not clearly established by statute or by unquestioned precedent, the problem was twofold: "He [the judge] must first extract from the precedents the underlying principle, the *ratio decidendi;* he must then determine the path or direction along which the principle is to work and develop, if it is not to wither and die."[7] The first part of the problem is separating legal principles from dicta so that the actual precedent is clear. Commenting on the second aspect of the problem, Cardozo said: "The directive force of a principle may be exerted along the line of logical progression; this I will call the rule of analogy or the method of philosophy; along the line of historical development; this I will call the method of evolution; along the lines of the customs of the community; this I will call the

---

[5]Holmes, *The Common Law* 1 (1938).

[6]Cardozo, *The Nature of the Judicial Process* (1921). Excerpts are used by permission from the Yale University Press.

[7]Id. at 28.

method of tradition; along the lines of justice, morals and social welfare, the *mores* of the day; and this I will call the method of sociology."[8]

In Cardozo's judgment, the rule of analogy was entitled to certain presumptions and should be followed if possible. He believed that the judge who molds the law by the method of philosophy is satisfying humanity's deepseated desire for certainty. History, in indicating the direction of precedent, often illuminates the path of logic and plays an important part in decisions in areas such as real property. Custom or trade practice has supplied much of the direction of the law in the area of business. All judicial decisions are at least in part directed by the judge's viewpoint on the welfare of society. The end served by law must dictate the administration of justice, and ethical considerations, if ignored, will ultimately overturn a principle of law.

Noting the psychological aspects of judges' decisions, Cardozo observed that it is the subconscious forces which keep judges consistent with one another. In so recognizing that all persons, including judges, have a philosophy which gives coherence and direction to their thought and actions whether they admit it or not, he stated:[9]

> All their lives, forces which they do not recognize and cannot name, have been tugging at them—inherited instincts, traditional beliefs, acquired conviction; and the resultant is an outlook on life, a conception of social needs,...which when reasons are nicely balanced, must determine where choice shall fall. In this mental background every problem finds its setting. We may try to see things as objectively as we please. None the less, we can never see them with any eyes except our own. To that test they are all brought—a form of pleading or an act of parliament, the wrongs of paupers or the rights of princes, a village ordinance or a nation's charter.

In the following comments, Cardozo summarized his view of the judicial process.

# FROM THE NATURE OF THE JUDICIAL PROCESS[10]
Benjamin N. Cardozo

...My analysis of the judicial process comes then to this, and little more: logic, and history, and custom, and utility, and the accepted standards of right conduct are the forces which singly or in combination shape the progress of the law. Which of these forces

[8]Id. at 30–31.
[9]Id. at 12–13.
[10]Id. at 112–115.

shall dominate in any case must depend largely upon the comparative impor-tance or value of the social interests that will be thereby promoted or impaired. One of the most fundamental social interests is that law shall be uniform and impartial. There must be nothing in its action that savors of prejudice or favor or even arbitrary whim or fitfulness. Therefore in the main there shall be adherence to precedent. There shall be symmetrical development, consistently with history or custom when history or custom has been the motive force, or the chief one, in giving shape to existing rules, and with logic or philosophy when the motive power has been theirs. But symmetrical development may be bought at too high a price. Uniformity ceases to be a good when it becomes uniformity of oppression. The social interest served by symmetry or certainty must then be balanced against the social interest served by equity and fairness or other elements of social welfare. These may enjoin upon the judge the duty of drawing the line at another angle, or staking the path along new courses, of marking a new point of departure from which others who come after him will set out upon their journey.

If you ask how he is to know when one interest outweighs another, I can only answer that he must get his knowledge just as the legislator gets it, from experience and study and reflection; in brief, from life itself. Here, indeed, is the point of contact between the legislator's work and his. The choice of methods, the appraisement of values, must in the end be guided by like considerations for the one as for the other. Each indeed is legislating within the limits of his competence. No doubt the limits for the judge are narrower. He legislates only between gaps. He fills the open spaces in the law. How far he can go without traveling beyond the walls of the interstices cannot be staked out for him upon a chart. He must learn it for himself as he gains the sense of fitness and proportion that comes with years of habitude in the practice of an art. Even within the gaps, restrictions not easy to define, but felt, however impalpable they may be, by every judge and lawyer, hedge and circumscribe his action. They are established by the traditions of the centuries, by the example of other judges, his predecessors and his colleagues, by the collective judgment of the profession, and by the duty of adherence to the pervading spirit of the law....None the less, within the confines of these open spaces and those of precedent and tradition, choice moves with a freedom which stamps its action as creative. The law which is the resulting product is not found, but made. The process, being legislative, demands the legislator's wisdom....

## REVIEW QUESTIONS

1 Contrast the functions of the following:
   **a** A trial judge and a reviewing court justice
   **b** A grand jury and a petit jury
   **c** Judge and jury
   **d** Uniform statutes and federal laws

2 The Supreme Court held that the Selective Service law is constitutional, notwithstanding the fact that only males are subject to the draft. It also allowed courts in the state of Florida to televise criminal proceedings, over the objection of defendants. What judicial philosophy is reflected in these decisions? Explain.

**3**   The jury system is frequently criticized by litigants and jurists. List four reasons for much of the criticism.

**4**   A government employee who had been fired by the President of the United States sued the President for wrongful discharge. The defendant contended that he could not be sued for actions performed as part of his official duties. Who decides this issue? Why?

**5**   At the hearings on his confirmation, one Supreme Court Justice laid out his judicial philosophy as follows:

It is the business of a judge to decide cases on the narrowest grounds possible and not to reach out for constitutional questions. As a judge, you can't have the freedom to substitute your own views for the law.
  A judge should try to obey and not go beyond the intent of Congress in interpreting federal laws. A judge must be most reluctant to depart from prior precedent. A judge is not a legislator and the Supreme Court should not be used as an instrument of policy.

Which judicial philosophy is expressed by the foregoing summary?

**6**   In recent years, courts have halted construction of a dam to preserve an endangered species of fish, ruled that females must be allowed to compete with males in athletics, banned school dress codes, and blocked suspension of public school students without a hearing. Courts have operated the schools in Boston, Massachusetts, and the prisons in Alabama. Which judicial philosophy is present in these decisions? Explain.

**7**   Courts are frequently called upon to interpret the Constitution and legislation. This function is performed in the context of applying legislation to a factual situation. Answer the following questions relative to statutory interpretation.

**a** Why is it necessary for courts to interpret legislation?
**b** List two techniques that are used to perform this function.
**c** List three rules of statutory construction based on the type of law involved.
**d** List two rules of statutory construction based on the words used in the statute.

**8**   A state statute provided that "every person who, at the request of the owner of any real property…rents, leases or otherwise supplies equipment…for clearing, grading, filling in, or otherwise improving any real property…has a lien upon such real property for the value of the services rendered for such purposes."
  A wrecking company supplied trucks and drivers for removal of debris, which resulted from the demolition of a building on certain premises. The owner failed to pay the cost of removal, and the wrecking company filed a lien under the statute mentioned above. There was no such lien at common law. What rules of statutory construction could be used by a court to decide the validity of the lien?

**9**   What are some of the advantages of a precedent-oriented legal system? What are some of the disadvantages?

**10**   Ann, a resident of Iowa, purchased some auto parts by mail from RST Company in Illinois. The contract called for the seller to deliver the parts to Ann. Ann wishes to return some of the parts she received, but RST refuses to accept returns. Iowa has a law requiring sellers of consumer goods to refund the purchase price if the goods are returned within ten days. Illinois has no such law. What law will be applied regarding the return of the merchandise? Explain.

**11**  George was on a coast-to-coast trip by automobile. While passing through Ohio, he had a flat tire. It was fixed by Al's Turnpike Service Station, and later, while George was driving in Indiana, the tire came off and George was injured. George was hospitalized in Indiana, so he sued Al in Indiana for his injuries. What rules of substantive law will the Indiana court use to determine if Al is at fault? Explain.

**12**  Justice Cardozo, in his comments about the judicial process, described four forces which, singly or in combination, shaped the progress of the law. Name or describe these four forces, and give an example of each.

**13**  Stare decisis is less likely to be followed in the area of public law than in the area of private law. Why?

*Chapter*

# 3

# Court Systems

## CHAPTER PREVIEW

This chapter examines the state and federal court systems. It demonstrates the difference between trial courts and reviewing courts. It also distinguishes between courts of law and courts of equity. Finally, it identifies some of the problems with the court systems.

The following terms are introduced: clean-hands doctrine, certiorari, chancery, diversity of citizenship, doctrine of abstention, equity, federal questions jurisdiction, small-claims court.

## 1. Introduction

The court system at the federal level and in most states contains three levels—trial courts, intermediate reviewing courts, and final reviewing courts. Lawsuits are commenced at the trial court level, and the results are reviewed at one or more of the other two levels.

For a court to hear and decide a case at any level it must have **jurisdiction.** Jurisdiction is power over the subject matter of the case and over the parties. Some state trial courts have general jurisdiction; others have limited jurisdiction. They may be limited as to subject matter, amount in controversy, or area in which the parties live. For example, small-claims courts have jurisdiction only if the amount in controversy does not exceed a certain sum. Even a court of general jurisdiction has geographical limitations. As we shall see in this chapter, all federal courts have limited jurisdiction.

Courts, especially those of limited jurisdiction, may be named according to the subject matter with which they deal. Probate courts deal with wills and the estates of deceased persons; juvenile courts with juvenile crime and dependent children; criminal and police courts with violators of state laws and municipal ordinances; and traffic courts with traffic violations. For an accurate classification of the courts of any state, the statutes of that state must be examined.

Even courts of general jurisdiction cannot attempt to resolve every dispute or controversy that may arise. Some issues are simply nonjusticiable as the following case illustrates.

# WOODRUFF v. GEORGIA STATE UNIVERSITY
304 S.E.2d 697 (Ga. 1983)

WELTNER, J.: Woodruff brought this action against the Board of Regents, Georgia State University and certain Georgia State University professors alleging state and federal constitutional violations, tort, and breach of contract claims. The trial court granted summary judgment and Woodruff appeals.

Woodruff was admitted to a master's degree program in the music department of Georgia State University in 1972. In the fall of 1973, she received an "F" on the basis of plagiarism, and appealed that grade to an appeals committee within the university. The committee changed the grade to an "incomplete." She alleges that thereafter her professors were "hostile and sarcastic" to her, refusing to help her with course work and thesis preparation, changing course requirements prior to graduation, placing damaging information about her in an open file, and giving her undeservedly low grades in an attempt to block her graduation.

In 1979, after seven years in a program which normally takes two or three years to complete, Woodruff was awarded the de-

gree of Master of Arts in Music. She then applied for admittance into a doctoral program at the University of Georgia in Athens, which required recommendations from former professors. Woodruff's former professors either refused or ignored her request for recommendations. In their depositions, several professors testified that Woodruff was an "argumentative and troublesome" student who was erratic in her studies and not academically qualified to proceed to a doctoral program. They offered academic reasons for withholding their recommendations....

...[T]he central issue is whether or not a dispute concerning academic decisions of a public educational institution is a justiciable controversy.

In the general realm of educational institutions, we have reviewed standards of dismissals and student discipline. We have examined the denial of student eligibility to participate in sports, and we have refused to permit the judiciary to referee high school football games. The Court of Appeals has upheld the authority of a local board of education to impose proficiency requirements as a prerequisite to graduation from high school. School financing was considered in *Deriso v. Cooper,* 246 Ga. 540 (1970). *Deriso v. Cooper* raised, as well, questions concerning the adequacy of school curriculum and physical facilities, "and various others relating to the manner in which educational services shall be provided and student progress shall be monitored."

We have not thus far, however, entertained an individual student's complaint seeking money damages for alleged impropriety in academic assessment of her work.

"This court traditionally has been reluctant to embark upon courses of judicial action which would require continuing supervision of the official conduct of public officers....Courts are ill-equipped to make such fundamental, legislative and administrative policy decisions as how much local supplement to teachers' salaries should be paid in order to attract qualified teachers, how many levels of English or math should be taught, whether a system of pupil ability grouping shall or shall not be used, whether buildings shall be constructed and, if so, where, and the myriad other matters involved in the everyday administration of a public school system which the courts would face were they to embark upon the course of judicial activism desired by the school patrons. *Resolutions of these discretionary policy de-*

*terminations best can be made by other branches of government*" (Emphasis supplied).

In *McDaniel v. Thomas,* we declined to tell the General Assembly precisely how it must allocate state funds among school systems. In *Deriso v. Cooper,* we declined to tell a local school board the manner in which it must perform its responsibilities. In *Georgia High School Assn. v. Waddell,* we declined to review the call of a football referee.

We now decline to review a teacher's academic assessment of a student's work.

This is clearly consistent with the authorities we have mentioned. It is restraint which stems from confidence that school authorities are able to discharge their academic duties in fairness and with competence. It is born alike of the necessity for shielding the courts from an incalculable new potential for lawsuits, testing every Latin grade and every selection for the Safety Patrol.

It protects every teacher from the cost and agony of litigation initiated by pupils and their parents who would rely upon the legal process rather than the learning process.

It protects every school system—all of them laboring under pressures of financing, personnel problems and student discipline, academic performance, taxpayer revolt and patron unrest, and a rising tide of recalls—from an added and unbearable burden of continuous legal turmoil....[*Judgment affirmed.*]

## THE STATE COURT SYSTEM

### 2. Governing Principles

Government in the United States is based on dual sovereignty; that is, the judicial branch is an essential element of government at both the state and federal levels. Both the state and federal court systems are created and their operations governed from three sources. First, constitutions provide the general framework for the court system. Second, the legislature, pursuant to constitutional authority, enacts statutes which add body to the framework. This legislation provides for various courts; establishes their jurisdiction, or an area of authority; and deals with such problems as the tenure, selection, and duties of judges. Other legislation may establish the general rules of procedure to be used by these courts. Finally, each court sets forth its own rules of procedure within the statutory bounds set. These rules are detailed and may specify, for example, the form of a summons or the times when various documents must be filed with the court clerk. Thus, a study of the court system for any particular state must refer to its constitution, such legislation as Civil Practice Acts, and the rules of the various courts. Each state has its own terminology and arrangement for its courts. Figure 3-1 is representative of the courts of a typical state.

**FIGURE 3-1**
Typical State Court System.

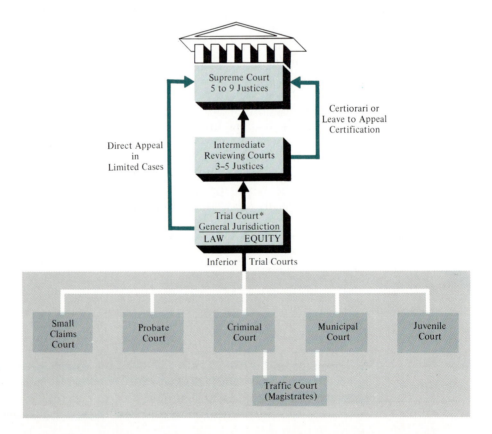

### 3. Trial Courts

The general jurisdiction trial court is frequently known as the "circuit court," deriving its name from earlier times when the judge "rode the circuit," or in other words traveled from town to town in a certain territory over which his court had jurisdiction, hearing and deciding cases. Some states call the basic trial court the "superior court," while others call it the "district court" or "court of common pleas." In New York it is known as the "supreme court." The term "general jurisdiction" means that the court has the power to hear any type of case. The courts below this trial court in Figure 3-1 are limited to the types of cases which they may hear and thus are referred to as "inferior courts," or courts of limited jurisdiction. For example, probate courts are involved with the administration of the estates of deceased persons or those of incompetents. Juvenile courts deal with criminal offenses committed by children below a stated age.

At one time the basic trial courts were divided into two branches, one known as a "court of law" and the other a "court of chancery or equity," but this is no longer the case in most states. The distinction between law and equity is discussed in section 11 of this chapter.

Some states do not have intermediate reviewing courts between the trial court and the court of final resort; however, intermediate reviewing courts are usually found in the more heavily populated states. Some states call their court of last resort "Supreme Court of Appeals" or "Court of Appeals."

### 4. Reviewing Courts

In states with two levels of reviewing courts, most appeals are taken to the lower of the two courts, and the highest court of the state will review only very important cases. Courts of review are essentially concerned with questions of law. Although a party is entitled to one trial and one appeal, he or she may obtain a second review if the higher reviewing court, in the exercise of its discretion, agrees to such a review. The procedure for requesting a second review is to file what is called in some states a "petition for leave to appeal" and in others a "petition for a writ of certiorari."

Since this request for a second review must be acted upon by the higher court, the party requesting it actually obtains a second review, although it is a limited one. The case is examined to see whether it is one that the highest court wishes to hear. Deciding such requests is a major function of the Supreme Court of the United States and of the highest court in each state. As a practical matter, less than 5 percent of all such requests are granted.

### 5. Small-Claims Courts

One court of limited jurisdiction is especially important to the business community. This court, usually known as **small-claims court,** handles the majority of litigation between business and its customers. Small-claims courts are used by businesses to collect accounts and by customers to settle disputes with the business community that are relatively minor from a financial standpoint. Such suits are often quite important from the standpoint of principle, however. For example, many persons use small-claims courts to sue for damages caused by defective merchandise or by services poorly performed. Landlord-tenant disputes are another example of controversies decided in these courts.

Small-claims courts have low court costs and simplified procedures. The informality of the proceedings speeds up the flow of cases. The services of a lawyer are not usually required, but if one side uses a lawyer, the other side probably needs one also. Some states do not allow lawyers to participate in these proceedings. Such courts usually are subject to a dollar limitation over the suits which may be filed. In some states this amount may be as low as $500, whereas in others it may be as high as $5,000. A typical jurisdictional amount is $2,000. Most states have raised this jurisdictional limitation, as inflation has taken its toll here.

As small-claims courts have grown in number and their case loads have expanded, numerous problems have arisen. In large cities, there is often a need for a bilingual court. In addition, night sessions are frequently required so that litigants need not miss work. As a practical matter, the judge often serves as mediator of the dispute, and many cases are settled by agreement with the court. For many people, the chance to complain to some third party is all they really seek in filing a lawsuit. Any financial recovery is secondary. One continuing problem, however, is that many successful litigants are unable to collect their judgments because the decision of the small-claims court is not self-enforcing. A recent study in New York City found that 44 percent of successful litigants in small-claims court did not collect any of the money due to them.

## THE FEDERAL COURT SYSTEM

### 6.  Jurisdiction

Article III of the Constitution (see Appendix 1) provides that judicial power be vested in the Supreme Court and such lower courts as Congress may create. The judicial power of the federal courts is limited. Essentially, it extends to matters involving questions of federal law (federal question cases), to matters in which the United States is a party, to controversies among the states, and to cases involving *diversity of citizenship* (suits between citizens of different states). The federal judicial power does not extend to cases involving a state law between citizens of the same state. Such cases will be dismissed by federal courts because they lack the power to hear them.

In order for a claim to arise under the Constitution, laws, or treaties of the United States (federal question), a right or immunity created by said Constitution or laws must be an essential element of the plaintiff's cause of action. Thus, federal question cases may be based on issues arising out of the U.S. Constitution or out of federal statutes. Any amount of money may be involved in such a case, and it need not be a suit for damages. For example, a suit to enjoin a violation of a constitutional right can be filed in the federal courts as a federal question case. These civil actions may involve matters such as bankruptcy or suits based on patents, copyrights, trademarks, taxes, elections, the rights guaranteed by the Bill of Rights, and those rights secured to individual citizens by the Fourteenth Amendment. In addition, by statute the federal district courts have original jurisdiction to try tort cases involving citizens who suffer damages caused by officers or agents of the federal government.

The district courts are the trial courts of the federal judicial system. They have original jurisdiction, exclusive of the courts of the states, over all federal crimes; that is, all offenses against the laws of the United States. The accused is entitled to a trial by jury in the state and district where the crime was committed.

If a case affects ambassadors or other public ministers and consuls, or is one in which a state is a party, the Supreme Court has original jurisdiction. In all other cases, the Supreme Court has appellate jurisdiction unless Congress creates an exception.

Under its constitutional authorization, Congress has enacted legislation providing for various inferior federal courts; it has also defined their jurisdiction. Congress has created twelve U.S. Courts of Appeals plus a special Court of Appeals for the Federal Circuit. This special reviewing court, located in Washington, D.C., hears appeals from special courts such as the U.S. Claims Court and Contract Appeals, as well as from administrative decisions such as those by the Patent and Trademark Office. Congress has also created the U.S. district courts (at least one in each state) and other courts, such as the Court of Military Appeals, to handle special subject matter. Figure 3-2 illustrates the federal court system and shows the relationship of state courts and administrative agencies for review purposes. The U.S. Code also contains provisions concerning such matters as appellate procedure and the review of actions by administrative agencies. The Federal Rules of Civil Procedure provide the details concerning procedures to be followed in federal court litigation.

## 7. Diversity of Citizenship Cases

There are several problems related to the jurisdiction of federal courts based on diversity of citizenship. Diversity of citizenship does not extend to domestic relations cases. The fact that a husband and wife may live in different states does not justify the federal courts to hear their divorce case. In

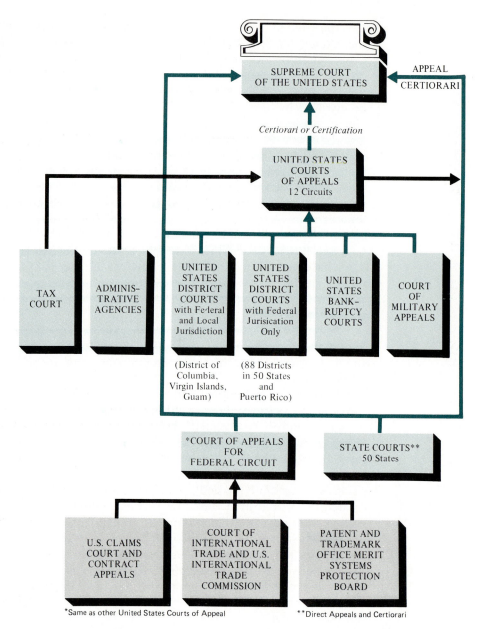

**FIGURE 3-2**
The Federal Court System.

addition, diversity of citizenship requires that all plaintiffs be citizens of different states from all defendants. If a case involves several parties on one or more sides of the case, and if a party on one side is a citizen of the same state as a party on the other, there will then be no diversity of citizenship and thus no federal jurisdiction. In some types of cases where some parties actually represent others, deciding if total diversity exists is sometimes difficult.

---

# NAVARRO SAV. ASS'N v. LEE
100 S.CT. 1779 (1980)

---

POWELL, J.: The question is whether the trustees of a business trust may invoke the diversity jurisdiction of the federal courts on the basis of their own citizenship, rather than that of the trust's beneficial shareholders.

The respondents are eight individual trustees of Fidelity Mortgage Investors, a business trust organized under Massachusetts law. They hold title to real estate investments in trust for the benefit of Fidelity's shareholders. The declaration of trust gives the respondents exclusive authority over this property "free from any power and control of the Shareholders, to the same extent as if the Trustees were the sole owners of the Trust Estate in their own right...." The respondents have power to transact Fidelity's business, execute documents, and "sue and be sued in the name of the Trust or in their names as Trustees of the Trust." They may invest the funds of the trust, lend money, and initiate or compromise lawsuits relating to the trust's affairs.

In 1971, respondents lent $850,000 to a Texas firm in return for a promissory note payable to themselves as trustees. The note was secured in part by a commitment letter in which petitioner Navarro Savings and Loan Association agreed to lend the Texas firm $850,000 to cover its obligation to the respondents. In 1973, respondents called upon Navarro to make the "takeout" loan. Navarro refused, and this action followed....

Federal jurisdiction was premised upon diversity of citizenship. The complaint asserted—and the parties agree—that Navarro was a Texas citizen and that each respondent was a citizen of another State. The parties have stipulated, however, that some of Fidelity's beneficial shareholders were Texas residents.

The District Court dismissed the action for want of subject matter jurisdiction. Concluding that a business trust is a citizen of every State in which its shareholders reside, the court held that the parties lacked the complete diversity.... The Court of Appeals for the Fifth Circuit reversed. It held that the respondent trustees were real parties in interest because they had full power to manage and control the trust and to sue on its behalf. Since complete diversity existed among the actual parties to the controversy, the Court of Appeals directed the District Court to proceed to trial on the merits. We granted certiorari....

Federal courts have jurisdiction over controversies between "citizens of different States" by virtue of 28 U.S.C. § 1332(a)(1) and U.S. Const., Art. III, § 2. Early in its history, this Court established that the "citizens" upon whose diversity a plaintiff grounds jurisdiction must be real and substantial parties to the controversy. Thus, a federal court must disregard nominal or formal parties and rest jurisdiction only upon the citizenship of real parties to the controversy.

The early cases held that only persons

could be real parties to the controversy. Artificial or "invisible" legal creatures were not citizens of any State. Although corporations suing in diversity long have been "deemed" citizens, unincorporated associations remain more collections of individuals. When the "persons composing such association" sue in their collective name, they are the parties whose citizenship determines the diversity jurisdiction of a federal court.

Navarro contends that Fidelity's trust form masks an unincorporated association of individuals who make joint real estate investments. Navarro observes that certain features of the trust's operations also characterize the operations of an association: centralized management, continuity of enterprise, and unlimited duration. Arguing that this trust is in substance an association, Navarro reasons that the real parties to the lawsuit are Fidelity's beneficial shareholders.

We need not reject the argument that Fidelity shares some attributes of an association. In certain respects, a business trust also resembles a corporation. But this case involves neither an association nor a corporation. Fidelity is an express trust, and the question is whether its trustees are real parties to this controversy for purposes of a federal court's diversity jurisdiction.

As early as 1808, this Court stated that trustees of an express trust are entitled to bring diversity actions in their own names and upon the basis of their own citizenship. Fed. Rule Civ. Proc. 17(a) now provides that such trustees are real parties in interest for procedural purposes. Yet similar principles governed diversity jurisdiction long before the advent of uniform rules of procedure. In 1870, the Court declared that jurisdiction properly founded upon the diverse citizenship of individual trustees "is not defeated by the fact that the parties whom they represent may be disqualified." "[T]he citizen-ship of those who may have the equitable interest" is simply irrelevant....A trustee is a real party to the controversy for purposes of diversity jurisdiction when he possesses certain customary powers to hold, manage, and dispose of assets for the benefit of others. The trustees in this case have such powers. At all relevant times, Fidelity operated under a declaration of trust that authorized the trustees to take legal title to trust assets, to invest those assets for the benefit of the shareholders, and to sue and be sued in their capacity as trustees. Respondents filed this lawsuit in that capacity. They seek damages for breach of an obligation running to the holder of a promissory note held in their own names. Fidelity's 9,500 beneficial shareholders had no voice in the initial investment decision. They can neither control the disposition of this action nor intervene in the affairs of the trust except in the most extraordinary situations.

We conclude that these respondents are active trustees whose control over the assets held in their names is real and substantial. That the trust may depart from conventional forms in other respects has no bearing upon this determination. Nor does Fidelity's resemblance to a business enterprise alter the distinctive rights and duties of the trustees. There is no allegation of sham or collusion. The respondents are not "naked trustees" who act as "mere conduits" for a remedy flowing to others. They have legal title; they manage the assets; they control the litigation. In short, they are real parties to the controversy. For more than 150 years, the law has permitted trustees who meet this standard to sue in their own right, without regard to the citizenship of the trust beneficiaries. We find no reason to forsake that principle today. [*The judgment of the Court of Appeals is affirmed.*]

The fact that business corporations are frequently incorporated in one state and have their principal place of business in another state also causes problems in determining when diversity of citizenship exists. A corporation is a citizen of the state of incorporation and also a citizen of the state in which it has its principal place of business, for purposes of diversity jurisdiction. Thus, a Delaware corporation with its principal place of business in Illinois is a citizen of both Delaware and Illinois for purposes of diversity. If any party on the other side of a lawsuit with such a corporation is a citizen of either Illinois or Delaware, there is then no diversity and no federal jurisdiction. Questions as to the state in which a corporation has its principal place of business often arise. The total activity of the corporation is examined to determine its principal place of business. This test incorporates both the "place of activities" and the "nerve center" tests. The nerve center test places general emphasis on the locus of the managerial and policy-making functions of the corporations. The place of activities test focuses on production or sales activities. The "total activity" test is not an equation that can provide a simple answer to the question of a corporation's principal place of business. Each case necessarily involves somewhat subjective analysis.

In diversity of citizenship cases, the federal courts have a jurisdictional amount of more than $50,000. If a case involves multiple plaintiffs with separate and distinct claims, *each* claim must satisfy the jurisdictional amount. Thus, in a class action suit, the claim of each plaintiff must meet the $50,000 minimum, unless changed by statute.

## 8.   Federal Reviewing Courts

Like most state court systems, the federal court system has both courts of appeal and a supreme court. Typically, litigants who wish to have the legal rulings of a federal district court judge reviewed appeal to one of the thirteen federal circuit courts of appeal. Because the litigants are entitled to only one review, or appeal as a matter of right, a subsequent review by the United States Supreme Court must be obtained through a petition for a writ of **certiorari** by the Supreme Court.

A petition for a writ of certiorari is a request by the losing party to a higher court for permission to file an additional appeal. In such cases, the Supreme Court has discretion as to whether or not it will grant the petition and allow another review. The review is not a matter of right. Writs of certiorari are granted only in cases of substantial federal importance or where there is an obvious conflict between decisions of two or more Circuit Courts of Appeals in an area of the law which needs clarification. Certiorari may be granted before or after the decision of the Circuit Court of Appeals. When the Supreme Court of the United States reviews petitions for a writ of certiorari, the writ is granted if four of the nine justices vote to take the case. The net result of this procedure is that the Supreme Court spends a great deal of time and effort in deciding which cases it will hear. It is able to pick and choose those issues with which it will be involved.

Most of the cases previously decided by the United States Supreme Court came before it on a petition for a writ of certiorari. In addition to these cases, the Supreme Court historically heard a number of cases that were directly appealed to the Supreme Court, bypassing the court of appeals. In an attempt to allow the Supreme Court to manage its case load more efficiently, in 1988 Congress passed and President Reagan signed legislation that essentially removes most mandatory appeals to the Supreme Court. This legislation should allow the justices to limit its case load through the granting or denying of writs of certiorari.

In addition to accepting cases through certiorari, the Supreme Court will review questions of federal law certified to it for decision by the federal courts of appeals. Furthermore, the U.S. district courts and the Courts of Appeals cannot review, retry, or correct the judicial errors charged against a state court. Final judgments or decrees rendered by the highest court of a state are reviewed only by the Supreme Court of the United States. State cases reviewed by the U.S. Supreme Court must concern the validity of a treaty or statute of the United States or must present a question involving the validity of a state statute on the grounds that the statute is repugnant to the Constitution, treaties, or laws of the United States and that the state decision is in favor of the statute's validity. When a case involves the constitutionality of a state statute or treaty or when a citizen's rights, privileges, or immunities under the constitution or laws are impaired, the case may be brought to the Supreme Court by writ of certiorari. In all other cases the decision of the highest state court is not subject to review.

### 9. Transfer from the States to the Federal System

A case may be transferred from the state court system to the federal court system. First, a defendant sued in a state court may have the case removed to the federal system if it meets the requirements of those cases which first could have been brought into the federal system. In other words, if the case involves a *federal question*, or if there is diversity of citizenship and the requisite amount is involved, the case may be transferred by a defendant to the federal district court.

In addition, there is a special statute dealing with civil rights cases. If a defendant is denied or cannot enforce in the courts of a state a right under any law providing for the equal civil rights of citizens of the United States, the case may be removed from the state courts to the appropriate federal district court. This statute makes it clear that such cases involve a federal question.

Whenever a separate and independent claim or cause of action, which would be removable if sued upon alone, is joined with one or more otherwise nonremovable claims or causes of action, the entire case may be removed. The district court may determine all issues in the case, or, in its discretion, may send all matters not otherwise within its original jurisdiction back to the state court. Or the case may be sent back after the federal issues are decided and only state issues remain. In exercising its discretion, the court considers judicial economy, convenience, fairness, and comity.

Second, a party may seek review of the decision of a state's highest court by writ of certiorari where a federal question is involved. Each year there are several thousand such petitions filed; almost all of them are denied.

## 10. The Law in the Federal Courts

As a general proposition, each court system uses its own rules of procedure. Thus, in the federal courts, the Federal Rules of Procedure (both civil and criminal) are followed. For state court proceedings, each state has adopted applicable rules of procedure.

The problem as to the applicable substantive law is far more complex. In federal question cases, the controlling statutes and judicial decisions are those of the federal courts by definition. However, if the case is in the federal courts because of diversity of citizenship, what is the applicable substantive law? Is there a federal common law? The case which follows is a landmark decision answering these questions.

---

# ERIE RAILROAD v. TOMPKINS
304 U.S. 64 (1938)

---

BRANDEIS, J.: The question for decision is whether the oft-challenged doctrine of *Swift v. Tyson* shall now be disapproved.

Tompkins, a citizen of Pennsylvania, was injured on a dark night by a passing freight train of the Erie Railroad Company while walking along its right of way at Hughestown in that state. He claimed the accident occurred through negligence in the operation, or maintenance, of the train; that he was rightfully on the premises as a licensee because he was on a commonly used beaten footpath which ran for a short distance alongside the tracks; and that he was struck by something which looked like a door projecting from one of the moving cars. To enforce that claim he brought an action in the federal court for Southern New York, which has jurisdiction because the company is a corporation of that state. It denied liability; and the case was tried by a jury.

The Erie insisted that its duty to Tompkins was no greater than that owed to a trespasser. It contended, among other things, that its duty to Tompkins, and hence its liability, should be determined in accordance with the Pennsylvania law; that under the law of Pennsylvania, as declared by its highest court, persons who use pathways along the railroad right of way—that is, a longitudinal pathway as distinguished from a crossing—are to be deemed trespassers; and that the railroad is not liable for injuries to undiscovered trespassers resulting from its negligence, unless it be wanton or willful. Tompkins denied that any such rule had been established by the decisions of the Pennsylvania courts; and contended that, since there was no statute of the state on the subject, the railroad's duty and liability is to be determined in federal courts as a matter of general law.

The trial judge refused to rule that the applicable law precluded recovery. The jury brought in a verdict of $30,000; and the judgment entered thereon was affirmed by the Circuit Court of Appeals, which held that it was unnecessary to consider whether the law of Pennsylvania was as contended, because the question was one not of local but of general law, and that

**...upon questions of general law the federal courts are free, in absence of a local statute, to exercise their independent judgment as to what the law is; and it is well settled that the question of the responsibility of a railroad for injuries caused by its servants is one of general law....Where the public has made open and notorious use of a railroad right of way for a long period of time and without objection, the company owes to persons on such permissive pathway a duty of care in the operation of its trains....It is likewise generally recognized law that a jury may find that negligence exists toward a pedestrian using a permissive path on the railroad right of way if he is hit by some object projecting from the side of the train.**

The Erie had contended that application of the Pennsylvania rule was required, among other things, by section 34 of the Federal Judiciary Act which provides: "The laws of the several States, except where the Constitution, treaties, or statutes of the United States otherwise require or provide, shall be regarded as rules of decision in trials at common law, in the courts of the United States, in cases where they apply."

Because of the importance of the question whether the federal court was free to disregard the alleged rule of the Pennsylvania common law, we granted certiorari....

First. *Swift v. Tyson,* 16 Pet. 1, 18, 10 L.Ed. 865, held that federal courts exercising jurisdiction on the ground of diversity of citizenship need not, in matters of general jurisprudence, apply the unwritten law of the state as declared by its highest court; that they are free to exercise an independent judgment as to what the common law of the state is—or should be....

Doubt was repeatedly expressed as to the correctness of the construction given section 34, and as to the soundness of the rule which it introduced. But it was the more recent research of a competent scholar, who examined the original document, which established that the construction given to it by the Court was erroneous; and that the purpose of the section was merely to make certain that, in all matters except those in which some federal law is controlling, the federal courts exercising jurisdiction in diversity of citizenship cases would apply as their rules of decision the law of the state, unwritten as well as written....

Second. Experience in applying the doctrine of *Swift v. Tyson* had revealed its defects, political and social; and the benefits expected to flow from the rule did not accrue. Persistence of state courts in their own opinions on questions of common law prevented uniformity, and the impossibility of discovering a satisfactory line of demarcation between the province of general law and that of local law developed a new well of uncertainties.

On the other hand, the mischievous results of the doctrine had become apparent. Diversity of citizenship jurisdiction was conferred in order to prevent apprehended discrimination in state courts against those not citizens of the state. *Swift v. Tyson* introduced grave discrimination by noncitizens against citizens. It made rights enjoyed under the unwritten "general law" vary according to whether enforcement was sought in the state or in the federal court; and the privilege of selecting the court in which the right should be determined was conferred upon the noncitizen. Thus, the doctrine rendered impossible equal protection of the law. In attempting to promote uniformity of law throughout the United States, the doctrine had prevented uniformity in the administration of the law of the state....

Third. Except in matters governed by the Federal Constitution or by acts of Congress, the law to be applied in any case is the law of the state. And whether the law of the state shall be declared by its Legislature in a statute or by its highest court in a decision is not a matter of federal concern. There is no federal general common law. Congress has no power to declare substantive rules of common law applicable in a state whether they be local in their nature or "general," whether they be commercial law or a part of the law of torts. And there is no clause in the Constitution that purports to confer such a power upon the federal courts....

The fallacy underlying the rule declared in *Swift v. Tyson* is made clear by Mr. Justice Holmes. The doctrine rests upon the assumption that there is "a transcendental body of law outside of any particular State but obligatory that federal courts have the power to use their judgment as to what the rules of common law are; and that in the federal courts "the parties are entitled to an independent judgment on matters of general law":

**...But law in the sense in which courts speak of it today does not exist without some definite authority behind it. The common law so far as it is enforced in a State, whether called common law or not, is not the common law generally but the law of that State existing by the authority of that State without regard to what it may have been in England or anywhere else....**

**The authority and only authority is the State, and if that be so, the voice adopted by the State as its own (whether it be of its Legislature or of its Supreme Court) should utter the last word.**

Thus the doctrine of *Swift v. Tyson* is, as Mr. Justice Holmes said, "an unconstitutional assumption of powers by the Courts of the United States which no lapse of time or respectable array of opinion should make us hesitate to correct." In disapproving that doctrine we do not hold unconstitutional section 34 of the Federal Judiciary Act of 1789 or any other act of Congress. We merely declare that in applying the doctrine this Court and the lower courts have invaded rights which in our opinion are reserved by the Constitution to the several states.

Fourth. The defendant contended that by common law of Pennsylvania as declared by its highest court, the only duty owed to the plaintiff was to refrain from willful or wanton injury. The plaintiff denied that such is the Pennsylvania law. In support of their respective contentions the parties discussed and cited many decisions of the Supreme Court of the state. The Circuit Court of Appeals ruled that the question of liability is one of general law; and on that ground declined to decide the issue of state law. As we hold this was error, the judgment is reversed and the case remanded to it for further proceedings in conformity with our opinion. [*Reversed.*]

In following the law of the state where the court sits in diversity of citizenship cases, the federal court will examine the total body of law of the state in which it is sitting, including the state's conflict-of-laws principles. Thus, in using the law of state X, it may, in turn, look to the law of some other state for the actual precedent. For example, assume that a citizen of the state of Illinois sues a citizen of the state of Indiana in the federal district court in Indiana for personal injuries received in an automobile accident which occurred in the state of Kentucky. The federal district court sitting in Indiana uses federal procedure and the substantive law of the state of Indiana. The substantive law of the state of Indiana includes the conflict of laws principle that the applicable tort law is the law of the place of injury. The federal court in Indiana, therefore, will use the Kentucky tort law since that is the law which would be used by the Indiana state court.

Since federal courts use federal procedure and state substantive law in diversity cases, many decisions are concerned with whether a given issue is one of substantive law or one of procedure. If the state rule of law, whether created by statute or case decision, will affect the result of the controversy, the rule is treated as substantive and will be followed by the federal court in diversity cases. This is true even if the state law is considered wrong by the federal judges. As one federal judge noted, "Federal judges are bound by state court precedents when interpreting state law, no matter how awful, until the precedents are changed."

As a result of the doctrine of *Erie Railroad v. Tompkins*, federal courts are sometimes presented with a dilemma when there is no state decision or statute on the issue involved in a diversity case. In such situations, the federal court under a doctrine known as **abstention** may hold its case in abeyance and direct the litigants to try their case in the state court. This is also true if a federal question is involved with a question of state law. The doctrine is invoked to allow the state to decide state issues prior to the federal court's deciding federal issues, especially where the state decision may end the litigation. The doctrine allows federal courts to eliminate guesswork on the meaning of local laws and is designed to further harmonious relations between state and federal courts. The state court may decide the federal question if the parties so desire, or it may leave the federal question to the federal courts. In the event the state court decides the federal question, the losing party may seek review by the U.S. Supreme Court.

## 11.  Courts of Equity Contrasted with Courts of Law

Courts having general jurisdiction in the United States have traditionally been divided into courts of law and courts of equity. Some states historically had two separate courts, and others simply had one court with one side known as law and the other side known as **equity** or chancery.

Courts of law were developed early in English jurisprudence to handle cases such as the various forms of trespass, other torts, and breach of contract. These courts dealt with legal disputes where one party was seeking money damages from another. Courts of law were not equipped to give remedies such as requiring a person to do or not to do something.

When courts of law were inadequate to furnish the desired relief, a practice developed of petitioning the king of England for such relief. As the number of such petitions grew, the king delegated his authority in granting or denying petitions to his chancellor. The name **chancery** is derived from this practice. Since the action taken was originally taken by the king, results were not a matter of right but in each case rested in the grace and favor of the king; or, by modern terminology, the decisions were strictly discretionary.

The concept of equity did not originate in England, however. Aristotle had defined equity as the "correction of the law, where, by reason of its universality, it is deficient." The purpose of equity has always been to remedy defects in the law. As courts of chancery grew and developed in England, the need for supplemental legal procedures where courts of law were inadequate assisted the steady growth of equity, although the courts of law strenuously objected.

Courts of chancery or equity were firmly entrenched in English jurisprudence by the time the American court system was developed. Those who established our courts recognized the need for resort to natural principles to define and interpret positive law and to remedy its defects, and they therefore provided for equity jurisprudence.

In recent years, federal law and many state laws have attempted to abolish the distinctions between law and equity. These attempts have affected procedural aspects of the distinction but have not changed its substantive aspects. These attempts have combined the procedures of law and equity into one action known as a "civil action." In civil actions, equitable concepts have been generally utilized and adopted for actions at law. The influence of equity has predominated over law where the procedures have been combined.

Notwithstanding statements that the distinctions between law and equity have been abolished, since the historical substantive distinctions are still important, it is usually necessary to decide whether an action would have been "at law" or "in chancery." Many states require that the pleading so indicate.

Many matters depend on whether an action is legal or equitable in nature. For example, cases in chancery, with a few exceptions such as will contests, are not tried before a jury. The court, or in a few states a person appointed by it, known as a "master in chancery," serves as the trier and finder of the facts. Thus, whether a party has a right to a trial by jury depends on the nature of the action.

Equity jurisdiction is used in cases where the remedy at law is deemed inadequate. That is, where dollar damages are not an adequate remedy, a court of chancery will hear the case. Such cases as suits for an accounting;

cancellation, rescission, or reformation of a contract; injunctions; partition suits; suits to quiet title; and suits for specific performance are litigated in chancery. If a case is filed in equity and if the remedy at law, such as dollar damages for breach of contract, is an adequate remedy, the suit in equity will be dismissed.

---

# BECKMAN v. VASSALL-DILLWORTH LINCOLN-MERCURY
468 A.2d 784 (Pa. Super. 1983)

---

On December 14, 1978, Beckman signed a contract with the Vassall-Dillworth Lincoln-Mercury dealership for the purchase of a 1979 Lincoln Continental. Four weeks later Beckman inquired about the car. He was told that the purchase order agreement was lost, so no car was ordered. The dealer offered to order a 1979 Lincoln Continental, but at a price higher than the price originally agreed upon. Beckman sued the dealership for specific performance of the original contract. The trial court dismissed the suit.

MONTGOMERY, J....Beckman contends the trial court incorrectly held he was not entitled to specific performance because he failed to show that he had no adequate remedy at law. It is clear that an order for specific performance is inappropriate where the moving party has an adequate remedy at law. Our Court has held that specific performance is a proper remedy when the subject matter of an agreement is an asset that is unique or one such that its equivalent cannot be purchased on the open market. In this case, the record shows that the Appellant was given an opportunity by the dealer to purchase the automobile he wanted, but at a higher price. It may not be ignored that the Appellant could also have sought to purchase the same vehicle from another source. His remedy in such circumstances was to seek damages for any difference between the original order price and the actual purchase price he paid. Because the subject matter of the contract was not unique, and because it is obvious that an adequate remedy at law was available, we agree with the lower court's rejection of the Appellant's demand for specific performance. [*Affirmed.*]

---

## 12.   Equitable Procedures

Courts of equity use *maxims* instead of rules of law. Strictly speaking, there are no legal rights in equity, for the decision is based on moral rights and natural justice. A court of equity is a court of conscience in which precedent is secondary to natural justice.

Some of the typical maxims of equity are:

1 "Equity will not suffer a right to exist without a remedy."

2 "Equity regards as done that which ought to be done."

3 "Where there is equal equity, the law must prevail."

4 "He who comes into equity must do so with clean hands."

5 "He who seeks equity must do equity."

6 "Equity aids the vigilant."

7 "Equality is equity."

These maxims serve as guides for the chancellor to use in exercising his or her discretion. For example, the **clean-hands doctrine** (no. 4) prohibits a party who is guilty of misconduct in the matter in litigation from receiving the aid of a court of equity. Many cases simply involve a balancing of the equities in order to achieve justice. Notice how obvious the equities were in the case which follows.

---

# TUDOR ENGINEERING CO. v. MOUW
709 P.2d 146 (Idaho 1985)

---

Plaintiff, Tudor Engineering Company, sued the defendant, Mouw, for $291.97 for professional land surveying services. Ultimately plaintiff received a judgment for $304.22. When the defendant failed to pay the judgment, plaintiff instituted proceedings to have defendant's home sold at a judicial sale. The defendant was not served with actual notice of the impending sale. Plaintiff was the only bidder at the sale and purchased the home for $385.65. After the statutory period during which the defendant could pay off the debt and regain his home (period of redemption) had expired, plaintiff was given a sheriff's deed to the home.

After receipt of the deed, plaintiff advertised the property for sale for $49,000. The defendant then asked the court to set aside the sale or in the alternative to allow him to redeem the property equitably. The trial court vacated the sheriff's sale and gave

Mouw a right to redeem the property by paying the judgment and court costs.

DONALDSON, J.:...Idaho, like many states, recognizes the existence of an equitable right to redeem property.

**"Courts of equity...may, upon a proper bill declaring...fraud, mistake or other circumstances appealing to the discretion of the chancellor, relieve a debtor whose property has been sold from failure to redeem within the statutory period....The court cannot award the right to redeem under the statute, but merely refuses to allow a party with unclean hands to benefit from his wrongful induction of a debtor into a trap from which the law cannot extricate him, and strips the wrongdoer of the title which the debtor intended to and would have otherwise redeemed; the debtor being required to pay at a later date what he would have paid at the time demanded by law."** *Southern Idaho Production Credit Ass'n v. Ruiz,*

**666 P.2d 1151, 1155 (1983), quoting *Steinour v. Oakley State Bank*, 262 P. 1052, 1053 (1928).**

In *Steinour,* the purchaser mislead [sic] the debtor into believing that the statutory period of redemption would be extended. The Court found that an equitable right to relief might exist based upon the purchaser's allegedly wrongful conduct. In *Ruiz,* the parties stipulated that the debtor was incompetent at all times following the filing of the original action. We held that such incompetence was an "other circumstance" within the meaning of the rule set out in *Steinour* sufficient to justify examining the transaction to determine whether equitable relief was appropriate.

As we stated in *Ruiz,* "A granting of an equitable right of redemption is, in effect, a balancing of the equities that exist on either side of the dispute." The trial court must weigh the various equitable considerations and determine whether, in its discretion, the debtor is entitled to an equitable right of redemption. The trial court's decision will not be disturbed on appeal where it is supported by substantial, competent evidence.

In the present case, the trial court listed the following...equitable considerations which, in its view, justified a grant of equitable relief. First, the gross inadequacy of the purchase price at execution. Tudor purchased the property for $385.65 and shortly thereafter advertised it for sale for $49,000.00. In *Ruiz,* we noted that the adequacy of the sale price at foreclosure, while not conclusive, is an important factor in determining whether an equitable right of redemption should be granted. Second,... Tudor failed to provide any of the interested parties with actual notice of the execution sale....

After reviewing the record we conclude that the factors outlined above constitute substantial, competent evidence in support of the trial court's decision. Accordingly, we affirm...the district court's decision granting Mouw an equitable right of redemption.... [*Affirmed.*]

---

The decision of the court of equity is called a *decree,* as contrasted with a *judgment* in a court of law which is measured in damages. A decree of a court of equity is said to be in personam; that is, it directs the defendant to do or not to do some specific thing.

Decrees are either final or interlocutory. A decree is final when it disposes of the issues in the case, reserving no question to be decided in the future. A decree is interlocutory when it reserves some question to be determined in the future. A decree granting a temporary injunction would be interlocutory.

Failure of the defendant to obey a decree of a court of equity is contempt of court. Any person in contempt of court may be placed in jail or fined.

Equity has played a significant role in our system of jurisprudence, and it will continue to do so. In moving toward social justice the courts will rely more on equitable maxims and less on rigid rules of law. This will also contribute further to the decay of the doctrine of stare decisis.

## 13.   Contemporary Problems

A headline in *The Wall Street Journal* read "Too Much Law, Too Many Lawyers, Not Enough Justice." The president of Harvard, Derek Bok, observed that "there is far too much law for those who can afford it and far too little for those who cannot." Such articles and observations are strong evidence that there are numerous problems facing the court system. Delay and the high cost of operating the system are two major problems. Court dockets have expanded with resultant delays in recent years because of the litigious nature of our society and increases in population. The high cost of litigation has priced most minor disputes either out of the court system or to small-claims court, where the matter can be resolved without legal counsel. It is no longer economically feasible to litigate such matters as consumer claims for shoddy merchandise or poor services with the aid of an attorney. The costs of transmitting property on death are unsatisfactorily high for many Americans. It has been estimated that it costs up to 100 times as much to transfer property on death in this country as it does in England. Probate costs often run 2½ to 3 times funeral expenses.

"Justice delayed is justice denied." That often-quoted cliché sums up the most obvious defect in our court system—court congestion and the delay that results therefrom. In many large cities, the backlog of civil cases is so great that a period of five or more years elapses between the transaction or occurrence in question and a jury trial. Such delays tend to force unsatisfactory settlements upon many plaintiffs. They also cause other serious problems for the parties and adversely affect the search for truth. The thousands of criminal cases awaiting trials or pending on appeal at all times raise many serious consequences for society. Not the least of these is that an accused person free on bond is free to commit more crimes while the case is awaiting trial.

The high cost of legal services, especially of litigation, greatly concerns clients and the organized bar. Litigation is expensive, not only for the parties to the dispute, but also for society as a whole. Society pays the cost of providing judges, court officials, and juries. The current trend is to have more and longer jury trials, thus greatly increasing the cost of the system. Much of jurors' time is unproductively spent, since they must frequently wait for the lawyers and the court to proceed. Since jurors are paid by the day, inefficiency adds to society's costs.

The price of adequate legal advice is out of the reach of many low- and middle-income persons. The wealthy can afford the best legal talent. Public defender programs provide free legal service to indigents charged with crime, and legal aid projects have generally made legal service available to poor persons with civil problems. However, the cost of legal services for the average person is often prohibitive. As a result, many people either do not have legal advice when it is needed or often turn to other laypersons for legal advice. Although the increase in the number of lawyers and the resulting competition have helped alleviate this problem, the cost of adequate legal assistance has made it unavailable to many Americans.

However, adequate legal services are usually available to personal-injury and other damage claim litigants, irrespective of the client's ability to pay. The poorest person in the country can obtain the best legal talent in a personal-injury case because of a method of compensation known as the *contingent fee system.* In cases handled under the contingent fee arrangement, the attorney's fee is a fixed percentage of the total recovery. In a typical case, the attorney receives one-third of the net amount collected for the client.

The contingent fee system gives everyone equal access to the courts and to legal talent, although it often does so at a high cost to the client. Assume that a person loses both legs as the result of the negligent conduct of another, and that the issue of negligence is not debatable. Assume that the jury awards the victim $3 million as damages. It is difficult to believe that the attorney earned a fee of $1 million in such a case. Of course, if the liability or the extent of injury is not clear, then the attorney certainly would earn more of the fee for his or her efforts.

## 14.   Delay: Some Solutions

Many state legislatures and court authorities are implementing several changes designed to eliminate and reduce court congestion and the backlog of court cases. Among the changes to reduce court congestion which have partial acceptance to date are: (1) six-person juries instead of twelve; (2) requiring only majority verdicts instead of unanimous ones; (3) elimination of oral argument on appeal whenever possible; (4) application of management techniques to the system by designating someone other than a judge to assign cases, court rooms, and juries so that all judicial personnel are utilized more effectively; and (5) elimination of jury trials in certain types of cases. In addition, the number of judges has been expanded in many jurisdictions.

Several suggestions have been made to reduce the case load of the federal courts. Perhaps the most radical idea is to abolish diversity of citizenship jurisdiction in the federal courts or to deny jurisdiction if the plaintiff is from the same state as the court in which the case is filed. It is argued that there is no rational basis today for putting an automobile accident case in a federal court simply because litigants are citizens of different states, especially if the plaintiff is from the state from which the jury will be selected. A similar proposal previously adoted raised the jurisdictional amount to $50,000.

It has also been proposed that a special court be created to hear petitions for writs of certiorari. This would enable the Supreme Court to spend its time deciding cases before it rather than requiring it to spend a significant portion of its time deciding which cases it wants to hear. Each year the Supreme Court must review over 5,000 petitions for writs of certiorari. This new court would probably consist of courts of appeals justices on a rotating basis.

## REVIEW QUESTIONS

**1** An attorney filed a $10 million class action suit against the National Football League for allowing a players' strike. He alleged a denial of the pursuit of happiness. Is this suit a proper suit?

**2** Answer the following questions about the jurisdiction of federal courts:
   **a** Over what type of cases do federal courts have jurisdiction?
   **b** What is the jurisdictional amount in the federal courts?
   **c** For diversity-of-citizenship purposes, a corporation is a citizen of two states. Name them.

**3** Pat sues Mike in a state court, seeking damages for breach of contract. The trial court finds for Mike. Pat announces that she will appeal "all the way to the Supreme Court of the United States if necessary" to change the decision. Assuming that Pat has the money to do so, will she be able to obtain review by the Supreme Court of the United States? Explain.

**4** Paula, a citizen of Georgia, was crossing a street in New Orleans when she was struck by a car driven by David, a citizen of Texas. The car was owned by David's employer, a Delaware corporation, which has its principal place of business in Atlanta, Georgia. Paula sues both David and the corporation in the federal district court in New Orleans. Paula's complaint alleges damages in the amount of $100,000. Does this court have jurisdiction? Why, or why not?

**5** Henry, a citizen of Illinois, was driving in downtown Keokuk, Iowa, when his automobile was struck by a truck owned by XYZ Corporation and operated by Daniel, an employee of XYZ. XYZ is a Delaware corporation with its principal place of business in Madison, Wisconsin. Daniel resides in Green Bay, Wisconsin. Henry suffered serious injuries resulting in damages of approximately $55,000. Henry sues Daniel and XYZ Corporation in the federal district court in Keokuk, Iowa. Does the court have jurisdiction? Why, or why not?

**6** Use the same facts as in question 5, except assume that XYZ's principal place of business is Moline, Illinois. Does the federal district court have jurisdiction? Why, or why not?

**7** Peter agreed to sell the Blackacre property to Paul. Prior to closing the transaction, oil was discovered on Blackacre, and Peter refused to complete the contract. Paul sues Peter to require performance of the contract. In what court should he sue? Explain.

**8** Adam and Eve were not married. By contract they had agreed to live together and to divide all property evenly on death of either party or on separation. They separated and began to live in separate states. Adam sued Eve in federal court to collect all of the proceeds of the sale of their apartment. Eve moved to dismiss, alleging it was a domestic relations suit and thus an exception to diversity jurisdiction. What was the result? Why?

**9** A tort action was filed in the state court of Illinois by an Illinois limited partnership. The general partner was a citizen of Illinois, and the limited partners were citizens of Illinois and a Delaware corporation. The defendant was a Delaware corporation. The defendant requests that the case be removed from the Illinois court to a federal district court. Should it be? Explain.

**10** Joe College deposited $300 with his landlord to secure his lease and pay for any damages to the apartment which he had rented. At the end of the school year, he vacated the apartment and requested the return of his deposit. Although the landlord admitted that the apartment was in good shape, she refused to return the deposit. What should Joe College do? Explain.

**11** Plaintiff, a shareholder of Defendant Corporation, sought dissolution of the corporation. He alleged that the acts of those in control of the corporation were illegal, fraudulent, or both, and corporation assetswere being misapplied. Plaintiff admit-

ted to participating in some of the illegal acts. Is plaintiff entitled to equitable relief? Why, or why not?

**12** Plaintiff, a Pennsylvania citizen, filed suit for personal injuries against defendant, a Delaware corporation. After the state statute of limitations had run, the defendant filed a motion to dismiss and proved that its principal place of business is Pennsylvania. Will plaintiff's case be dismissed? Explain.

# Chapter

# *4*

# Litigation

## CHAPTER PREVIEW

This chapter is concerned with litigation as the most important means of finally resolving disputes. It traces a lawsuit through its four stages—pleading, discovery, the trial, and review.

The following legal terms are introduced in this chapter: appellant, appellee, brief, burden of proof, class action suit, clear and convincing proof, deposition, directed verdict, forum non conveniens, hearsay rule, in personam, in rem, jury instruction, long-arm statute, motion, peremptory challenge, pleadings, preponderance of evidence, privilege, res judicata, standing to sue, summary judgment, summons, venue, and voir dire.

## 1. Introduction

The law as a means to an ordered and civilized society seeks to avoid controversy and disputes. It also provides techniques for resolving them when they arise. The most obvious legal technique for resolving disputes is a judicial decision ending litigation among the parties to a controversy. This has replaced naked force as a solution to controversy.

Although statistics are not kept which would prove the point, it is generally accepted that most disputes in our society are resolved by mutual agreement without resort to litigation. In addition, more than 90 percent of all lawsuits filed are settled by the parties and their attorneys without a court decision.

The law plays a major role in encouraging such settlements. It is the framework within which the parties evaluate their positions and contains many procedures designed to encourage settlement. The high cost of litigation, both financial and in time, is a major force in many settlements. Since both parties are usually required to pay their own attorneys (the losing party usually pays court costs only), financial considerations weigh heavily even for wealthy parties and large corporations. The high cost of litigation often results in payments to plaintiffs with very weak cases because such cases have nuisance value. The amount of the nuisance value is often the cost of a successful defense.

# PRETRIAL

## 2.   Parties to Litigation

In a criminal case the people of the state or the people of the United States, depending on whether or not the alleged crime is a state offense or a federal offense, bring action against the named defendant. Whereas most civil cases use the term **plaintiff** to describe the party bringing the lawsuit, and the term **defendant** to describe the party against whom it is brought, there are some cases, especially in courts of equity, in which the parties are described as the **petitioner** and the **respondent.** When a counterclaim is filed, most jurisdictions use the term *counter-plaintiff* and *counter-defendant* to describe the parties to the counterclaim. Thus, the plaintiff also becomes a counter-defendant and the defendant also becomes a counter-plaintiff when a counterclaim is filed.

When the result at the trial court level is appealed, the party appealing is usually referred to as the **appellant,** and the successful party in the trial court is called the **appellee.** Most jurisdictions, in publishing decisions of reviewing courts, list the appellant first and the appellee second, even though the appellant may have been the defendant in the trial court. As a result, the names used in a case are somewhat misleading. Since the party first named is not always the plaintiff, in studying cases in this text it should be recognized that the first-named party in the case title may be the defendant-appellant.

In most state jurisdictions and in federal courts, the law allows all persons to join in one lawsuit as plaintiffs if the causes of action arise out of the same transaction or series of transactions and involve common questions of law or fact. In addition, plaintiffs may join as defendants all persons who are necessary to a complete determination or settlement of the questions involved. It is not necessary that each defendant be interested in every claim. In addition, if a defendant alleges that there cannot be a complete determination of a controversy without the presence of other parties, such a defendant may bring in new third parties as third-party defendants. This procedure is usually followed when there is someone who may have liability to a defendant if the defendant has liability to the plaintiff.

There are two problem areas or issues relating to the parties to a lawsuit which frequently arise in litigation. The first of these issues is generally described as "standing to sue," which is discussed in the next section. The second problem area relating to the parties is class action suits. These suits, which involve one or more individuals suing on behalf of all who may have the same grounds for suit, are discussed more fully in section 4.

## 3. Standing to Sue

The question in **standing to sue** is whether a litigant is entitled to have the court decide the dispute. This issue has two aspects: (1) Does the court have jurisdiction, and (2) if the answer is yes, should the court in the exercise of its discretion assume jurisdiction? Both questions recognize the limited role of courts in our society.

The Constitution requires that a plaintiff must allege a case or controversy between himself or herself and the defendant if the court is to have jurisdiction. The "standing" question is whether the plaintiff has alleged such a personal stake in the outcome of the controversy to warrant his or her invocation of the court's jurisdiction and to justify its exercise in his or her behalf.

Standing requires an allegation of a present or immediate injury in fact; the party requesting standing must allege such a personal stake in the outcome of the controversy as to assure concrete adverseness, which sharpens the presentation of issues. There must be some causal connection between the asserted injury and the challenged action, and the injury must be of the type likely to be redressed by a favorable decision.

Additional limitations on standing may exist even though the foregoing requirements are met, because the judiciary seeks to avoid deciding questions of broad social import where no individual rights would be vindicated; it also seeks to limit access to the court system to those litigants best suited to assert a particular claim. One of these limits on standing is that a litigant must normally assert his or her own legal interests rather than those of third parties. Without the requirement of standing, courts would be called upon to decide abstract questions of wide public significance. Such questions are best resolved by the political process.

When the asserted harm is a generalized grievance shared in substantially equal measure by all or a large class of citizens, that harm alone normally does not warrant the exercise of jurisdiction by a court. For example, individual radio listeners do not have standing to obtain review of a decision canceling a radio station's license. Likewise, a plaintiff must assert his or her own legal rights and not those of a third party. For example, a citizen objected to surveillance of civilians by the Army. The case was dismissed without a showing that the plaintiff was one of the civilians under surveillance.

Standing to sue is often an issue in cases brought by organizations on behalf of their members. An association may have standing to assert claims for its members even if it suffers no injury. Representational standing requires that: (1) the association have members with standing to sue in their own right; (2) the interest the association seeks to protect must be fundamental to the organization's purpose; and (3) the claim asserted and the relief requested must not require individual participation in the litigation. This last requirement was used to prevent a college-student organization from challenging the constitutionality of the Selective Service Act provision making students who failed to register for the draft ineligible for federal financial assistance. The court held that there was no organizational standing because individual participation is required. It held that it is in the financial interests of many students to defend the constitutionality of the statute and their individual participation is required.

Standing to sue does not depend upon the merits of the plaintiff's contention that particular conduct is illegal. The presence of standing is determined by the nature and source of the plaintiff's claim. The basic question in such a case is whether the constitutional or statutory provision on which the claim rests can be understood as granting the plaintiff a right to judicial relief. Congress may grant an express right of action to persons who otherwise would lack standing if the plaintiff has sustained a personal injury, even if the injury is shared by a large class.

As a general rule, "standing" requires that a complaining party have a very personal stake in the outcome of the controversy to ensure adversity in the proceedings, that will result in all aspects of the issues being presented for decision. A complainant must present facts showing that his or her individual needs require the remedy being sought. A plaintiff must show that he or she has sustained or is immediately in danger of sustaining a direct injury as a result of a governmental action involved in the lawsuit. In civil rights cases and in cases involving environmental threats, the courts have been rather liberal in finding a personal stake in a plaintiff bringing an action. In such cases, standing to sue still requires a specific injury in fact to the plaintiff.

# HAVENS REALTY CORP. v. COLEMAN

102 S.Ct. 1114 (1982)

The Fair Housing Act of 1968 outlaws discrimination in housing and Section 812 authorizes civil suits to enforce the law. Suit was filed against the defendant operator of two apartment complexes alleging "racial steering" in violation of the law. The suit was filed by a black tester (Coleman) and a white tester (Willis). The black plaintiff was told that no apartments were available but the white tester was told that there were vacancies. The District Court held that the plaintiffs lacked standing and dismissed the suit. The Court of Appeals reversed.

BRENNAN, J.:…Our inquiry with respect to the standing issues raised in this case is guided by our decision in *Gladstone Realtors v. Village of Bellwood,* 441 U.S. 91 (1979). There we considered whether six individuals and the Village of Bellwood had standing to sue under the Fair Housing Act, to redress injuries allegedly caused by the racial steering practices of two real estate brokerage firms. Based on the complaints, we concluded that the Village and four of the individual plaintiffs did have standing to sue under the Fair Housing Act. In reaching that conclusion, we held that…the sole requirement for standing to sue under § 812 is the Article III minima of injury-in-fact: that the plaintiff alleges that as a result of the defendant's actions he had suffered "a distinct and palpable injury." With this understanding, we proceed to determine whether each of the respondents in the present case has the requisite standing.

The Court of Appeals held that Coleman and Willis have standing to sue… as "testers."

In the present context, "testers" are individuals who, without an intent to rent or purchase a home or apartment pose as renters or purchasers for the purpose of collecting evidence of unlawful steering practices. Section 804(d) states that it is unlawful for an individual or firm covered by the Act "[t]o represent to *any person* because of race, color, religion, sex, or national origin that any dwelling is not available for inspection, sale, or rental when such dwelling is in fact so available," a prohibition made enforceable through the creation of an explicit cause of action in § 812(a) of the Act. Congress has thus conferred on all "persons" a legal right to truthful information about available housing.

This congressional intention cannot be overlooked in determining whether testers have standing to sue. As we have previously recognized, "[t]he actual or threatened injury required by Art. III may exist solely by virtue of 'statutes creating legal rights, the invasion of which creates standing.…'" Section 804(d), which, in terms, establishes an enforceable right to truthful information concerning the availability of housing, is such an enactment. A tester who has been the object of a misrepresentation made unlawful under § 804(d) has suffered injury in precisely the form the statute was intended to guard against, and therefore has standing to maintain a claim for damages under the Act's provisions. That the tester may have approached the real estate agent fully expecting that he would receive false information, and without any intention of buying or renting a home, does not negate the simple fact of injury within the meaning of § 804(d)....

In the instant case, respondent Coleman—the black tester—alleged injury to her statutorily created right to truthful housing information. As part of the complaint, she averred that petitioners told her on four different occasions that apartments were not available in the Henrico County complexes while informing white testers that apartments were available. If the facts are as alleged, then respondent has suffered "specific injury" from the challenged acts of petitioners and the Article III requirement of injury-in-fact is satisfied.

Respondent Willis' situation is different. He made no allegation that petitioners misrepresented to him that apartments were

unavailable in the two apartment complexes. To the contrary, Willis alleged that on each occasion that he inquired he was informed that apartments were available. As such, Willis has alleged no injury to his statutory right to accurate information concerning the availability of housing. We thus discern no support for the Court of Appeals' holding that Willis has standing to sue in his capacity as a tester. More to the point, because Willis does not allege that he was a victim of a discriminatory misrepresentation, he has not pleaded a cause of action under § 804(d). We must therefore reverse the Court of Appeals' judgment insofar as it reversed the District Court's dismissal of Willis' "tester" claims. [*So ordered.*]

### 4.   Class Action Suits

A **class action suit** is one in which a person files suit on his or her own behalf and on behalf of all other persons who may have a similar claim. For example, all sellers of real estate through a broker were certified as a class in an antitrust suit against Atlanta, Georgia, realtors. All persons suing a drug company, alleging injuries from a product, constituted a class for a tort action. Class action suits may also be filed on behalf of all shareholders of a named corporation. The number of people comprising a class is frequently quite large. Class action suits are popular because they often involve matters in which no one member of the class would have a sufficient financial interest to warrant litigation. However, the combined interest of all members of the class not only makes litigation feasible, it quite often makes it very profitable for the lawyer who brings the suit. In addition, such litigation avoids a multiplicity of suits involving the same issue, especially when the issues are complex and the cost of preparation and defense is very substantial. Many of the cases involve millions of dollars. In one recent case, the recovery was $310 million and the attorney's fees were $25 million.

Class action suits are often considered a form of harassment by many defendants. It has been alleged that some lawyers have on occasion sought out a member of a class and encouraged him or her to file suit. Courts cannot prevent lawyers for a class from contacting members of the class even though this increases the danger of abuse.

At the federal level, the Supreme Court has tended to discourage class action suits. First, federal cases require that members of the class be given notice of the lawsuit—actual notice and not merely notice by newspaper publication is usually required. This notice must be given to all members of the class whose names and addresses can be found through reasonable efforts. In addition, those plaintiffs seeking to bring the class action suit must pay all court costs of the action, including the cost of compiling the names and addresses of those in the class. If the trial court denies the plaintiff a right to represent the class, that decision cannot be appealed until a final decision in the lawsuit itself. Denial of class action status making it impractical to continue the litigation does not give grounds for an immediate appeal of the denial.

If a class action suit is in federal court because of diversity of citizenship, the claim of each member of the class must meet the jurisdictional amount of $50,000. This requirement, together with the requirement of notice to each member of the class, has greatly reduced the number of class action suits in federal courts. However, the practice of consumers' and plaintiffs' lawyers of combining a single grievance into a lawsuit on behalf of every possible litigant is quite common in state courts. There are numerous state class action statutes which allow consumers and others to file suit in state courts on behalf of all citizens of that state. For some claims suitable to class action, there may be as many as fifty class action suits at once. Although the Supreme Court has attempted to reduce class action cases, it is apparent that public companies are still subject to this type of claim.

The notice in class action suits typically includes a form for persons to sign indicating that they desire to be a part of the class. However, some state procedures are "opt-out" rather than "opt-in." In these states, a person is a member of the class unless affirmative action is taken to be excluded. Either procedure satisfies due process, as the case which follows illustrates.

---

# PHILLIPS PETROLEUM CO. v. SHUTTS
105 S.Ct. 2965 (1985)

---

During the 1970s, Phillips Petroleum Co., petitioner, produced or purchased natural gas from leased land located in eleven states. Respondents, royalty owners possessing rights to leases from which petitioner produced the gas, brought a class action suit against petitioner in a Kansas state court, seeking to recover interest on royalty payments that had been delayed by petitioner.

The trial court certified a class consisting of 33,000 royalty owners. Respondents provided each class member with a notice by first-class mail describing the action and informing each member that he or she could appear in person or by counsel, that otherwise they would be represented by respondents, and that class members would be included in the class and bound by the judgment unless they "opted out" of the action by returning a "request for exclusion." The final class consisted of some 28,000 members, who reside in all fifty states, the District of Columbia, and several foreign countries. The average claim of each member of the class was $100.

Petitioner asserted that the Kansas trial court did not possess personal jurisdiction over absent plaintiff class members as required by *International Shoe Co. v. Washington*, 326 U.S. 310, (1945), and similar cases. Related to this first claim was petitioner's contention that the "opt-out" notice to absent class members, which forced them to return the request for exclusion in order to avoid the suit, was insufficient to bind class members who were not residents of Kansas or who did not possess "minimum contacts" with Kansas.

The Supreme Court of Kansas held that the absent class members were plaintiffs, not defendants, and thus the traditional minimum contacts test of *International Shoe* did not apply. The court held that nonresident class action plaintiffs were only entitled to adequate notice, an opportunity to be heard, an opportunity to opt out of the case, and adequate representation by the named plaintiffs.

REHNQUIST, J.:…Reduced to its essentials, petitioner's argument is that unless out-of-state plaintiffs affirmatively consent, the Kansas courts may not exert jurisdiction over their claims. Petitioner claims that failure to execute and return the "request for exclusion" provided with the class notice cannot constitute consent of the out-of-state plaintiffs; thus Kansas courts may exercise jurisdiction over these plaintiffs only if the plaintiffs possess the sufficient "minimum contacts" with Kansas as that term is used in cases involving personal jurisdiction over out-of-state defendants. Since Kansas had no prelitigation contact with many of the plaintiffs and leases involved, petitioner

claims that Kansas has exceeded its jurisdictional reach and thereby violated the due process rights of the absent plaintiffs.

In *International Shoe* we were faced with an out-of-state corporation which sought to avoid the exercise of personal jurisdiction over it as a defendant by Washington state court. We held that…the Due Process Clause did not permit a State to make a binding judgment against a person with whom the State had no contacts, ties, or relations. If the defendant possessed certain minimum contacts with the State, so that it was "reasonable and just, according to our traditional conception of fair play and substantial justice" for a State to exercise personal jurisdiction, the State could force the defendant to defend himself in the forum, upon pain of default, and could bind him to a judgment….[P]etitioner claims that the same analysis must apply to absent class-action plaintiffs….

We think petitioner's premise is in error. The burdens placed by a State upon an absent class-action plaintiff are not of the same order or magnitude as those it places upon an absent defendant. An out-of-state defendant summoned by a plaintiff is faced with the full powers of the forum State to render judgment *against* it. The defendant must generally hire counsel and travel to the forum to defend itself from the plaintiff's claim, or suffer a default judgment. The defendant may be forced to participate in extended and often costly discovery, and will be forced to respond in damages or to comply with some other form of remedy imposed by the court should it lose the suit. The defendant may also face liability for court costs and attorney's fees. These burdens are substantial and the minimum contacts requirement of the Due Process Clause prevents the forum State from unfairly imposing them upon the defendant.

A class-action plaintiff, however, is in quite a different posture….The class action was an invention of equity to enable it to proceed to a decree in suits where the number of those interested in the litigation was too great to permit joinder. The absent parties would be bound by the decree so long as the named parties adequately represented the absent class and the prosecution of the litigation was within the common interest.

Modern plaintiff class actions follow the same goals, permitting litigation of a suit involving common questions when there are too many plaintiffs for proper joinder. Class actions also may permit the plaintiffs to pool claims which would be uneconomical to litigate individually. For example, this lawsuit involves claims averaging about $100 per plaintiff; most of the plaintiffs would have no realistic day in court if a class action were not available.

In sharp contrast to the predicament of a defendant haled into an out-of-state forum, the plaintiffs in this suit were not haled anywhere to defend themselves upon pain of a default judgment....Unlike a defendant in a civil suit, a class-action plaintiff is not required to fend for himself. The court and named plaintiffs protect his interests....

Besides this continuing solicitude for their rights, absent plaintiff class members are not subject to other burdens imposed upon defendants. They need not hire counsel or appear. They are almost never subject to counterclaims or cross-claims, or liability for fees or costs. Absent plaintiff class members are not subject to coercive or punitive remedies. Nor will an adverse judgment typically bind an absent plaintiff for any damages, although a valid adverse judgment may extinguish any of the plaintiff's claim which was litigated.

Unlike a defendant in a normal civil suit, an absent class-action plaintiff is not required to do anything. He may sit back and allow the litigation to run its course, content in knowing that there are safeguards provided for his protection.

Petitioner contends, however, that the "opt out" procedure provided by Kansas is not good enough, and that an "opt in" procedure is required to satisfy the Due Process Clause of the Fourteenth Amendment. Insofar as plaintiffs who have no minimum contacts with the forum State are concerned, an "opt in" provision would require that each class member affirmatively consent to his inclusion within the class.

...In this case we hold that a forum State may exercise jurisdiction over the claim of an absent class-action plaintiff, even though that plaintiff may not possess the minimum contacts with the forum which would support personal jurisdiction over a defendant....The plaintiff must receive notice....The notice should describe the action and the plaintiff's rights in it. Additionally, we hold that due process requires at a minimum that an absent plaintiff be provided with an opportunity to remove himself from the class by executing and returning an "opt out" or "request for exclusion" form to the court....

We reject petitioner's contention that the Due Process Clause of the Fourteenth Amendment requires that absent plaintiffs affirmatively "opt in" to the class, rather than be deemed members of the class if they do not "opt out."...

We therefore hold that the protection afforded the plaintiff class members by the Kansas statute satisfies the Due Process Clause....

We conclude that the Kansas court properly asserted personal jurisdiction over the absent plaintiffs and their claims against petitioner....[*Affirmed*]

## 5.  Jurisdiction of Courts

Jurisdiction refers to the power of a court to hear a case. To have the power
to hear a case, the court must have jurisdiction over the subject matter of
the case and the parties to the case. Jurisdiction over the subject matter exists if the case is of the type which the court is authorized to hear. This is
not a problem with state courts of general jurisdiction. It may be in cases
before the inferior state courts and can be an issue in all federal cases, because, as previously noted, all federal courts are courts of limited jurisdiction. For example, a federal court would not have jurisdiction over a breach
of contract suit for $40,000 damages between citizens of different states
because it doesn't meet the jurisdictional amount. If the amount were
$55,000 and the parties were citizens of the same state, the federal court
would still have no power to hear the case because of lack of diversity of
citizenship. Similarly, a state probate court would lack the power to hear
a murder case.

Jurisdiction over the plaintiff is obtained by plaintiff's filing the suit.
Such action indicates voluntary submission to the power of the court. Jurisdiction over the defendant is usually obtained by the service of a **summons,**
or notice to appear in court, although in some cases it is obtained by the
publication of notice and mailing a summons to the last known address. Service of summons on the defendant usually is valid if it is served upon any
member of the household above a specified age, and if another copy addressed to the defendant is mailed to the home. This procedure recognizes
the practical difficulties which may exist in finding the defendant, and at
the same time accomplishes the goal of the summons, which is simply to
give the defendant fair notice of the suit.

For many years, it was felt that a summons could not be properly
served beyond the borders of the state in which it was issued. However, this
concept has changed, and most states now have **long-arm statutes** which
provide for the service of process beyond their boundaries. Such statutes
are valid and constitutional if they provide a defendant with due process of
law. Due process requires only that if a defendant is not present within the
forum state, he or she must have certain minimum contacts with it so that
maintenance of the suit does not offend "traditional notions of fair play and
substantial justice."

The typical long-arm statute allows a court to obtain jurisdiction over a
defendant even though the process is served beyond its borders if the defendant has (1) committed a tort within the state; (2) owns property within
the state, which property is the subject matter of the lawsuit; or (3) entered
into a contract within the state or transacted the business which is the subject matter of the lawsuit within the state.

Long-arm statutes do not authorize extraterritorial service of process in
all cases. It is only where requiring a defendant to appear and defend does
not violate due process that jurisdiction is obtained under long-arm statutes.
The case which follows illustrates the extent of constitutional limitations on

modern long-arm statutes which allow extraterritorial service of process to obtain jurisdiction.

---

# WORLD-WIDE VOLKSWAGEN CORP. v. WOODSON
## 100 S.Ct. 559 (1980)

Plaintiff-respondent filed a product liability suit in a state court of Oklahoma to recover for personal injuries sustained in an automobile accident. The automobile had been purchased from the defendants in the state of New York. The defendants were a New York corporation that did no business in Oklahoma. They were served under the Oklahoma long-arm statute and they objected to the Court's jurisdiction.

WHITE, J.:...The issue before us is whether, consistently with the Due Process Clause of the Fourteenth Amendment, an Oklahoma court may exercise in personam jurisdiction over a nonresident automobile retailer and its wholesale distributor in a products liability action, when the defendants' only connection with Oklahoma is the fact that an automobile sold in New York to New York residents became involved in an accident in Oklahoma....

As has long been settled, and as we re-affirm today, a state court may exercise personal jurisdiction over a nonresident defendant only so long as there exist "minimum contacts" between the defendant and the forum State. The concept of minimum contacts, in turn, can be seen to perform two related, but distinguishable, functions. It protects the defendant against the burdens of litigating in a distant or inconvenient forum. And it acts to ensure that the States through their courts, do not reach out beyond the limits imposed on them by their status as coequal sovereigns in a federal system.

The protection against inconvenient litigation is typically described in terms of "reasonableness" or "fairness." We have said that the defendant's contacts with the forum State must be such that maintenance of the suit "does not offend 'traditional notions of fair play and substantial justice.'" The relationship between the defendant and the forum must be such that it is reasonable...to require the corporation to defend the particular suit which is brought there. Implicit in this emphasis on reasonableness is the understanding that the burden on the defendant, while always a primary concern, will in an appropriate case be considered in light of other relevant factors, including the forum State's interest in adjudicating the dispute, the plaintiff's interest in obtaining convenient and effective relief,...the interstate judicial system's interest in obtaining the most efficient resolution of controversies; and the shared interest of the several States in furthering fundamental substantive social policies.

The limits imposed on state jurisdiction by the Due Process Clause, in its role as a guarantor against inconvenient litigation, have been substantially relaxed over the years....

Nevertheless, we have never accepted the proposition that state lines are irrelevant for jurisdictional purposes, nor could we and remain faithful to the principles of interstate federalism embodied in the Constitution....

Hence, even while abandoning the shibboleth that "[t]he authority of every tribunal is necessarily restricted by the territorial limits of the State in which it is established," we emphasized that the reasonableness of asserting jurisdiction over the defendant must be assessed "in the context of our federal system of government," and stressed that the Due Process Clause ensures, not only fairness, but also the "orderly administration of the laws."

Thus, the Due Process Clause "does not contemplate that a state may make binding a judgment in personam against an individual or corporate defendant with which the state has no contacts, ties, or relations." Even if the defendant would suffer minimal or no inconvenience from being forced to litigate before the tribunals of another State; even if the forum State has a strong interest in applying its law to the controversy; even if the forum State is the most convenient location for litigation, the Due Process Clause, acting as an instrument of interstate federalism, may sometimes act to divest the State of its power to render a valid judgment.

Applying these principles to the case at hand, we find in the record before us a total absence of those affiliating circumstances that are a necessary predicate to any exercise of state-court jurisdiction. Petitioners carry on no activity whatsoever in Oklahoma. They close no sales and perform no services there. They avail themselves of none of the privileges and benefits of Oklahoma law. They solicit no business there either through salespersons or through advertising reasonably calculated to reach the State. Nor does the record show that they regularly sell cars at wholesale or retail to Oklahoma customers or residents or that they indirectly, through others, serve or seek to serve the Oklahoma market. In short, respondents seek to base jurisdiction on one, isolated occurrence and whatever inferences can be drawn therefrom: the fortuitous circumstance that a single Audi automobile, sold in New York to New York res-

idents, happened to suffer an accident while passing through Oklahoma.

It is argued, however, that because an automobile is mobile by its very design and purpose it was "foreseeable" that the Robinsons' Audi would cause injury in Oklahoma. Yet "foreseeability" alone has never been a sufficient benchmark for personal jurisdiction under the Due Process Clause....

If foreseeability were the criterion,... every seller of chattels would in effect appoint the chattel his agent for service of process. His amenability to suit would travel with the chattel....This is not to say, of course, that foreseeability is wholly irrelevant. But the foreseeability that is critical to due process analysis is not the mere likelihood that a product will find its way into the forum State. Rather, it is that the defendant's conduct and connection with the forum State are such that he should reasonably anticipate being haled into court there. The Due Process Clause, by ensuring the "orderly administration of the laws," gives a degree of predictability to the legal system that allows potential defendants to structure their primary conduct with some minimum assurance as to where that conduct will and will not render them liable to suit.

When a corporation "purposefully avails itself of the privilege of conducting activities within the forum State," it has clear notice that it is subject to suit there, and can act to alleviate the risk of burdensome litigation by procuring insurance, passing the expected costs on to customers, or, if the risks are too great, severing its connection with the State. Hence if the sale of a product of a manufacturer or distributor such as Audi or Volkswagen is not simply an isolated occurrence, but arises from the efforts of the manufacturer or distributor to serve directly or indirectly, the market for its product in other States, it is not unreasonable to subject it to suit in one of those States if its allegedly defective merchandise has there been the source of injury to its owner or to others. The forum State does not exceed its powers under the Due Process Clause if it asserts personal jurisdiction over a corporation that delivers its products into the stream of commerce with the expectation that they will be purchased by consumers in the forum State.

But there is no such or similar basis for Oklahoma jurisdiction over World-Wide or Seaway in this case....[*Because we find that petitioners have no "contacts, ties, or relations" with the State of Oklahoma, the judgment of the Supreme Court of Oklahoma is Reversed.*]

---

Occasionally, process may be served upon a defendant who has no minimum contacts with the state in which a court sits. For example, a bankruptcy court may order process served nationwide. It may be required to do so in order to settle the affairs of a bankrupt corporation. All citizens of the United States have sufficient contact to justify this jurisdiction by United States courts.

It was previously noted that jurisdiction may sometimes be obtained by publication of notice of the suit in a general circulation newspaper and by mailing a copy of the summons to the defendant. This method is often used in cases involving title to real estate and in divorce actions. Such cases proceed **in rem** (against the thing) rather than **in personam** (against the person). The judgments or decrees in such cases affect the property involved or the status (marriage) but do not operate against the defendant individually. Marital status or title to property may be changed, but no personal liability results. Service by publication must also meet due process standards. For example, a Kentucky law which authorized posting of a notice of eviction of a tenant on the premises rather than by mail was held to be a denial of due process. Notice by publication must be reasonably calculated to ensure that the defendant learns of the suit.

The foregoing discussion of jurisdiction related to civil suits. In criminal suits, the crime must have been committed within the state for the court to have jurisdiction of the case. Jurisdiction of the person of the defendant is obtained by arrest. In the event of arrest in a state other than that in which the crime was committed, extradition is necessary. This is obtained by the governor of the state of arrest voluntarily turning the prisoner over to the governor of the requesting state.

### 6. Venue

A question similar to jurisdiction refers to the place or court in which the lawsuit should be brought, or what is the proper **venue.** Although jurisdiction determines if a court has the *power* to hear a case, venue determines whether a court *should* hear the case when any one of several courts technically might have jurisdiction. A typical venue statute specifies that suit must be brought in the county of residence of any defendant who is joined in good faith and not solely for the purpose of fixing venue in that county. Suits may also be brought in the county where the transaction or some part thereof occurred out of which the cause of action arose. Actions against nonresidents can usually be commenced in any county which has jurisdiction, with jurisdiction being obtained under a long-arm statute. Corporations are usually considered to be residents of any county in which they have a registered office or are doing business. Corporations not authorized to do business in a state are usually treated as nonresidents. Similar rules usually exist for partnerships. They are generally considered to be residents of any county in which a partner resides, in which there is a partnership office, or in which the partnership does business. Thus, venue statutes provide, as one of two possibilities for the proper forum for a lawsuit, the place of residence of the defendant, and define where this is.

Most venue statutes have special provisions for suits involving real estate which require the suit to be brought in the county where the real estate is located. Special provisions frequently allow suits against insurance companies in the county where the plaintiff resides.

A defendant may object to the venue for several reasons. First of all, he or she may complain that the requirements of the venue statute as discussed above are not met. This will not usually be the case because, as noted, the statutes are specific and relatively clear. Venue may also be objected to because of prejudice of either the judge or, in some cases, the probable jury to be selected. The latter objection is frequently made in a criminal trial which has had substantial publicity. Motions for a change of venue based on the prejudice of the trial judge must usually be supported by affidavit but are granted as a matter of right if in proper form. Failure to object to the venue is a **waiver,** and the trial may proceed if the court where the suit was brought has jurisdiction, in spite of the provisions of the venue statute, or constitutional requirements of due process.

Another ground for a change of venue is the doctrine of **forum non conveniens,** which literally means that the place of trial is not convenient. The defendant may attempt to invoke this principle in cases in which the plaintiff has attempted to have the suit tried in a country which produces juries known for large verdicts. For example, a plane crash killed a citizen of Scotland. The crash was in Scotland. When suit was filed in the United States, the case was dismissed for being brought in the wrong venue. The plaintiff had filed in the United States expecting a larger verdict.

## 7.  Pleadings

Most lawsuits begin by a plaintiff's filing a pleading called a "complaint" with the court clerk. (In this section, for convenience, we refer to judge, plaintiff, and defendant as if they are male; obviously, however, both sexes may be represented by these terms.) The complaint contains allegations by the plaintiff and a statement of the relief sought. The clerk issues a summons which, together with a copy of the complaint, is served on the defendant by leaving it either with him personally or with some member of his family, if the law so provides. The summons provides notice of the date the defendant is required to file his **pleading,** usually called an "answer," or his appearance in the suit.

Failure to file an appearance is considered a default, which may result in the court's awarding the plaintiff the relief sought. The defendant's answer will either admit or deny each allegation of the plaintiff's complaint and may contain affirmative defenses, such as payment of the obligation, which will defeat the plaintiff's claim. The answer may also contain causes of action the defendant has against the plaintiff, called **counterclaims.**

After receiving the defendant's answer, the plaintiff will, unless the applicable rules of procedure do not so require, file a reply which specifically admits or denies each allegation of the defendant's answer. The factual issues of a lawsuit are thus formed by one party making an allegation and the other party either admitting it or denying it. Pleadings give notice of each party's contentions and serve to set the boundary lines of the litigation.

## 8. Motions Before Trial

Not all lawsuits involve questions of fact. In many cases the parties may be in complete agreement as to the facts, in which case the issue to be decided is the legal effect of these facts. Such cases involve only questions of law. Questions of law may be raised at several stages of the lawsuit.

First of all, the defendant may, instead of filing an answer, file a pleading which at common law was called a "general demurrer." Today we usually call this a "**motion** to dismiss for failure to state a cause of action or a claim for relief." By this pleading the defendant, in effect, says to the court: "Even if everything the plaintiff says in his complaint is true, he is not entitled to the relief he seeks." For example, in a state where mental cruelty is not a ground for divorce, a complaint seeking a divorce on such grounds would be dismissed. The litigation would end unless the plaintiff then filed an amended complaint. It would have to properly allege a ground on which a divorce might be granted.

In addition, a defendant may also move to dismiss a suit for reasons which as a matter of law prevent the plaintiff from winning his suit. Such matters as a discharge in bankruptcy, lack of jurisdiction of the court to hear the suit, or expiration of the time limit during which the defendant is subject to suit may be raised by such a motion. This latter ground is usually referred to as the "statute of limitations." Each state has proscribed a time limit after which you cannot file suit. For example, suits for breach of a contract for the sale of goods must be filed within four years of the breach. These are matters of a technical nature which raise questions of law for the court's decision.

Most states and the federal courts will allow either party to submit a case for final decision through procedures known as "motions for **summary judgment**" or "motions for judgment on the pleadings." In such hearings, the court examines all papers on file in the case, including affidavits that may have been filed with the motion or in opposition to it, to see if a genuine material issue of fact remains. If there is no such question of fact, the court will then decide the legal question raised by the facts and find in favor of one party or the other.

## 9.   Discovery Procedures

Modern law has procedures commonly referred to as **discovery procedures.** These are used when the parties are filing their pleadings and before the trial itself. These procedures are designed to take the "sporting aspect" out of litigation and ensure that the results of lawsuits are based on the merits of the controversy and not on the ability, skill, or cunning of counsel. Historically, an attorney who had no case on the facts or law could win a lawsuit through surprise by keeping silent about a fact or by concealing his or her true case until the trial. Verdicts should not be based on the skill or lack thereof of counsel, but on the relative merits of the controversy. Discovery practice is designed to ensure that each side is fully aware of all the facts involved in the case and of the intentions of the parties, prior to trial. One of its purposes is to encourage settlement of suits, avoiding actual trial. Another is to aid trial preparation by providing the likely answers in advance of the questioning of witnesses at the trial. Discovery, in this way, provides a "dress rehearsal" for the trial.

Discovery practices include the taking of the **deposition** of other parties and witnesses, the serving of written questions to be answered under oath by the opposite party, compulsory physical examinations by doctors chosen by the other party, orders requiring the production of exhibits, documents, maps, photographs, and so on, and the serving by one party on another of demands to admit facts under oath. (Some courts, those of Illinois for example, have even allowed the discovery of the amount of insurance coverage possessed by the defendant in a personal injury case.) These procedures allow a party to learn not only about matters that may be used as evidence, but also about matters that may lead to the discovery of evidence.

Just prior to the trial, a pretrial conference between the lawyers and the judge will be held in states with modern rules of procedure. At this conference the pleadings, results of the discovery process, and probable evidence are reviewed in an attempt to settle the suit. The issues may be further narrowed, and the judge may even predict the outcome in order to encourage settlement.

On occasion, a party may fail to comply with the discovery rules. When this occurs, a party may actually lose a case or facts sought may be considered proved.

# THE TRIAL

### 10. Jury Selection

In addition to questions of law, most lawsuits involve questions of fact. Such a case as an automobile negligence action or a criminal proceeding is essentially a question of fact. Suits at law and criminal actions have traditionally been tried before a jury, while suits in equity have been considered too complicated for juries; as a general rule these questions of fact have been found by the courts. It should be noted, however, that a jury is sometimes used in chancery cases to serve as the trier of the facts.

For purposes of examining a trial, we shall use a typical suit for dollar damages either in tort or contract being tried before a jury. As the case is called, the first order of business is to select a jury. Prior to the calling of the case, the court clerk will have summoned prospective jurors. Their names will have been drawn at random from lists of eligible citizens, and the number of jurors required, six or twelve, will be selected or called into the jury box for the conduct of **voir dire** examination. Voir dire examination is simply a method by which the court and often the attorneys for each party examine each juror as to his or her qualification and ability to be fair and impartial. A party to a lawsuit is entitled to fair and impartial jurors in both civil and criminal cases. Due process requires that a party be allowed to inquire into a prospective juror's biases and prejudices either through questions asked by the judge or by counsel.

Each side in the lawsuit may challenge or excuse a prospective juror for cause. In addition, each side will be given a certain number of challenges known as **peremptory challenges** for which no cause need be given. Each side has an opportunity to evaluate the jurors and either to accept them or to reject them until the challenges are exhausted. Prospective jurors are sworn to give truthful answers to the questions on voir dire. The processes continue until the full jury is selected.

### 11. Opening Statements

After selecting jurors to hear the case, the attorneys then make their opening statements. An opening statement is not evidence but is used to familiarize the jury with the essential facts which each side expects to prove. It functions as a preface to a book. In order that the jury may understand the overall picture of the case and the relevancy of each bit of evidence as presented, each side informs the jury of the facts she or he expects to prove and of the witnesses she or he expects to call to make such proof. After the opening statements are made, the party with the **burden of proof,** which is usually the plaintiff, presents his or her evidence. The term burden of proof is explained more fully in section 15.

## 12.   Introducing Evidence

Evidence is normally presented in open court by the examination of witnesses and production of documents and other exhibits. The person calling a witness has a right to examine that witness and ask questions to establish the facts about the case with which the witness is familiar. As a general rule, a party calling a witness is not permitted to ask "leading questions." After the party calling the witness has completed direct examination, the other party is given the opportunity to cross-examine the witness. Matters inquired into on cross-examination are limited to those matters raised on direct examination. Cross-examination is an art, and the well-prepared lawyer will usually not ask a question on cross-examination to which he or she does not already know the answer.

After the cross-examination, the party calling the witness again has the opportunity of examining the witness. This examination is called "redirect examination." It is limited to those matters gone into on cross-examination and is used to clarify matters raised on cross-examination. After redirect examination, the opposing party is allowed recross-examination, with the corresponding limitation as to the scope of the questions. Witnesses may be asked to identify exhibits. Expert witnesses may be asked to give their opinions, within certain limitations, about the case. Sometimes, experts are allowed to answer hypothetical questions. For example, a doctor in a personal injury case may be given all the evidence surrounding the accident and then be asked hypothetically whether such an occurrence might have or could have caused the injury which the plaintiff suffered. Expert testimony is required whenever special knowledge is necessary to help resolve a dispute. Specialists who testify for a fee are numerous, and the fees are usually substantial. Nevertheless, the winning party is only entitled to collect the statutory witness fee from the losing party as the Supreme Court held in the case which follows.

# CRAWFORD FITTING CO. v J.T. GIBBONS, INC.
107 S.Ct. 2494 (1987)

The U.S. Code, § 1920, provides that a federal court "may tax" witness fees as costs against the losing party. It also states in § 1821 that a witness "shall be paid" a fee of $30 per day for court attendance. In one antitrust case the winning party was awarded $86,480.70 for expert witness fees. In a discrimination case the winning party sought $11,807 in expert witness fees which request was denied. The cases are consolidated in this appeal.

REHNQUIST, J.:...In these two consolidated cases we address the power of federal courts to require a losing party to pay the compensation of the winner's expert witnesses. We…hold that when a prevailing party seeks reimbursement for fees paid to its own expert witnesses, a federal court is bound by the limits of § 1821, absent contract or explicit statutory authority to the contrary.…Federal Rule of Civil Procedure 54(d) provides in part: "Except when express provision therefore is made either in a statute of the United States or in these rules, costs shall be allowed as of course to the prevailing party unless the court otherwise directs." The logical conclusion from the language and interrelation of these provisions is that § 1821 specifies the amount of the fee that must be tendered to a witness, § 1920 provides that the fee may be taxed as a cost, and Rule 54(d) provides that the cost shall be taxed against the losing party unless the court otherwise directs.

Petitioners argue that § 1920 does not preclude taxation of…amounts in excess of the § 1821 fee. Thus, the discretion granted by Rule 54(d) is a separate source of power to tax as costs expenses not enumerated in § 1920. We think, however, that no reasonable reading of these provisions together can lead to this conclusion, for petitioners' view renders § 1920 superfluous. If Rule 54(d) grants courts discretion to tax whatever costs may seem appropriate, then § 1920, which enumerates the costs that may be taxed, serves no role whatsoever. We think the better view is that § 1920 defines the term "costs" as used in Rule 54(d). Section 1920 enumerates expenses that a federal court may tax as a cost under the discretionary authority found in Rule 54(d). It is phrased permissively because Rule 54(d) generally grants a federal court discretion to refuse to tax costs in favor of the prevailing party. One of the items enumerated in § 1920 is the witness fee, set by § 1821 at $30 per day.

We cannot accept an interpretation of Rule 54(d) that would render any of these specific statutory provisions entirely without meaning. Repeals by implication are not favored, and petitioners proffer the ultimate in implication, for Rule 54(d) and §§ 1920 and 1821 are not even inconsistent. We think that it is clear that in §§ 1920 and 1821, Congress comprehensively addressed the taxation of fees for litigants' witnesses. This conclusion is all the more compelling when we consider that § 1920(6) allows the taxation, as a cost, of the compensation of court-appointed expert witnesses. There is no provision that sets a limit on the compensation for court-appointed expert witnesses in the way that § 1821 sets a limit for litigants' witnesses. It is therefore clear that when Congress meant to set a limit on fees, it knew how to do so. We think that the inescapable effect of these sections in combination is that a federal court may tax expert witness fees in excess of the $30-per-day limit set out in § 1821 only when the witness is court-appointed. The discretion granted by Rule 54(d) is not a power to evade this specific congressional command. Rather, it is solely a power to decline to tax, as costs, the items enumerated in § 1920.…

We hold that absent explicit statutory or contractual authorization for the taxation of the expenses of a litigant's witness as costs, federal courts are bound by the limitations set out in 28 U.S.C. § 1821 and § 1920. [*It is so ordered.*]

---

After the party with the burden of proof has presented his or her evidence, the opposing party usually makes a motion for a **directed verdict.** This motion asks the court to decide the case as a matter of law and to, in effect, tell the jury that the facts are not in dispute.

The court can only direct a verdict for one party if the evidence, taken in the light most favorable to the other party, establishes as a matter of law that the party moving is entitled to a verdict. Either party may make such a motion, although it is usually used by defendants to argue that the plaintiff has failed to prove each allegation of his complaint. Just as a plaintiff must *allege* certain facts or have the complaint dismissed by motion to dismiss, he must have some *proof* of each essential allegation or lose the case on a motion for a directed verdict, as the following case illustrates.

---

# SAFEWAY STORES, INC. v. WILLMON

708 S.W.2d 623 (Ark. 1986)

---

DUDLEY, J.: The appellee, the plaintiff below, was a customer in the Safeway Store in Malvern and, while pushing a shopping cart down an aisle, slipped on a liquid substance and fell. At trial, the court overruled appellant's motions for a directed verdict, both at the close of the case-in-chief and at the close of all evidence. Appellant contends that the trial court erred in submitting the issue of negligence to the jury. The argument is well taken. We reverse and dismiss.

The law governing the liability of a store owner for injuries to a business invitee who slips and falls on a foreign substance on the premises is well settled. To establish liability of the store owner to the invitee, the invitee must prove that the presence of the foreign substance on the floor was the result of negligence on the part of the store owner, or that the substance had been on the floor for such a length of time that the storekeeper knew, or reasonably should have known, of its presence and failed to use ordinary care to remove it. The mere fact that a patron slips and falls in a store does not raise an inference of negligence....

Appellee slipped on a substance which was specifically identified as clear water by two of appellant's employees who made an inspection of the liquid. The only evidence indicating the foreign substance might be something other than plain water was when the appellee testified that some unknown store employee told him it looked like soapy water.

None of the witnesses knew the origin of the water. Appellee called the store manager as his witness, and the manager speculated that it might have been brought from the water fountain at the rear of the store to the place of the spill, or that someone could have spilled a soft drink cup filled with ice. A store employee testified that he at first guessed it came from one of the one gallon plastic jugs of distilled water which was shelved nearby. However, inspection of the jugs showed that none of them leaked. There simply was no substantial evidence about how the water came to be on the floor. There was only sheer speculation and rank conjecture. There was no proof that the water was on the floor as the result of negligence on the part of the storekeeper.

Similarly, there was no proof that the water had been on the floor for such a length of time that the storekeeper knew, or should have known of its presence and failed to use ordinary care to remove it. Appellant's records show that the aisle where the fall occurred had been swept an hour and fifteen minutes before the fall. Employees had been up and down the aisle in the interval between the time of sweeping and the time of the fall. There was no evidence that any employee knew of the spill or reasonably should have known of it. There was only evidence that if an employee had been working at the checkout counter at the end of the aisle, that employee would have been within fifteen feet of the spill.

Possible causes of a fall, as opposed to probable causes, do not constitute substantial evidence of negligence. [*Reversed and dismissed.*]

---

In cases tried without a jury, either party may move for a finding in his favor. Such a motion will be allowed during the course of the trial if the result is not in doubt. Although judges on such motions weigh the evidence, they may end the trial only if there is no room for a fair difference of opinion as to the result.

If the motion for directed verdict is overruled, the defendant then presents his or her evidence. The order of examination of these witnesses is the same as those for the plaintiff. Historically, the party calling a witness vouched for his or her credibility. The party was not allowed to impeach the witnesses he or she had called. Today in the federal courts and in many states, a party may impeach the testimony of any witness if it can be shown that the witness may not be telling the truth. After the defendant has presented all his or her evidence, the original party may bring in rebuttal evidence. When neither party has any additional evidence, the attorneys and the judge retire for a conference to consider the instructions to be given the jury.

## 13. Jury Instructions

**Jury instructions** serve to acquaint the jury with the law applicable to the case. As previously stated, the function of the jury is to find the facts, and the function of the court is to determine the applicable law. The purpose of jury instructions is to bring the facts and the law together in an orderly manner that will result in a decision. At the conference, each attorney submits to the court instructions which he or she feels should be given to the jury. The court examines these instructions and confers with the attorneys, then decides which instructions will be given to the jury. A typical jury instruction follows:

> The plaintiff in his complaint has alleged that he was injured as the proximate cause of the negligence of the defendant. If you find from the evidence that the defendant was guilty of negligence, which proximately caused plaintiff's injuries, then your verdict should be for the plaintiff.

In this instruction, the court is in effect saying that the plaintiff must prove that the defendant was at fault. Thus, the jury is instructed as to the result to be returned if they find certain facts.

## 14.   Deciding the Case

After the conference on jury instructions, the attorneys argue the case to the jury. The party with the burden of proof, usually the plaintiff, is given an opportunity to open the argument and to close it. The defendant's attorney is only allowed to argue after the plaintiff's argument and is only allowed to argue once. After the arguments are completed, the court reads the instructions to the jury, and the jury retires to deliberate. Upon reaching a verdict, the jury returns from the jury room and announces its verdict, and judgment is entered.

Then the losing party may file a posttrial motion. This motion raises questions of law by seeking a new trial or a judgment notwithstanding the verdict of the jury. A motion seeking a new trial may be granted if the judge decides that the jury's verdict is contrary to the manifest weight of the evidence. The court may enter a judgment opposite to that of the jury verdict if the judge finds that the jury verdict is, as a matter of law, erroneous. This is the same test as the one used for a directed verdict. To reach such a conclusion, the court must find that reasonable persons viewing the evidence could not have reached the jury verdict returned. For example, a verdict for the plaintiff may be based on sympathy instead of evidence. It is from the ruling on the posttrial motion that the losing party may appeal.

## 15.   The Burden of Proof

The term burden of proof has two distinct meanings depending on the context in which it is used. It may describe the person with the burden of coming forward with evidence on a particular issue. The party alleging the existence of a certain fact usually has the burden of coming forward with evidence to establish the fact.

The more common usage of the term is to identify the party with the *burden of persuasion.* The party with this burden must convince the trier of fact on the issue involved. If a party with the burden of persuasion fails to do so, that party loses the lawsuit.

The extent of proof required to satisfy the burden of persuasion varies, depending upon the issue and the type of case. There are three distinct levels of proof recognized by the law. For criminal cases, the burden of proof is described as "beyond a reasonable doubt." This means that the prosecution in a criminal case has the burden of convincing the trier of fact, usually a jury, that the defendant is guilty of the crime charged and that the jury has no reasonable doubt about the defendant's guilt. This burden of proof does not require evidence beyond any doubt, but only beyond a reasonable doubt. A reasonable doubt is one that a reasonable person viewing the evidence might reasonably entertain. This standard is not used in civil cases.

In civil cases the party with the burden of proof will be subject to one of two standards—the **clear and convincing proof** standard, or the **preponderance of the evidence** standard. The latter standard is used most frequently. It requires that a party convince the jury by a preponderance of evidence that the facts are as he or she contends. By preponderance of evidence we mean there is greater weight of evidence in support of the proposition than there is against it. In terms of the scales of justice, it means that they tilt more one way than the other.

The clear and convincing proof requirement is used in certain situations where the law requires more than a simple preponderance of the evidence but less than proof beyond a reasonable doubt. For example, in a securities law case, proof of fraud usually requires clear and convincing evidence if a plaintiff is to succeed. The scales of justice must tilt heavily one way. A slight preponderance of evidence in favor of the party asserting the truth of a proposition is not enough. Unless the evidence clearly establishes the proposition, the party with the burden of proof fails to sustain it and loses the lawsuit.

## 16.  Rules of Evidence

In the conduct of a trial, the rules of evidence govern the admissibility of testimony and exhibits and establish which facts may be presented to the jury and which facts may not. The lawyer is concerned with specific rules of evidence, but an understanding of the areas in which these rules operate will give us some insight into the workings of our judicial system.

### PRIVILEGED COMMUNICATIONS

One of the major rules for excluding evidence is based on what the law calls "privileged communications" or **privilege.** Nearly everyone is aware that the Fifth Amendment contains a privilege against compulsory self-incrimination. In addition, communications between an attorney and client are considered privileged by the law in order that such communications can be made without fear of their subsequent use against the client. Fair play requires that an attorney not be required to testify as to matters told in confidence by a client. Some matters are privileged, such as the existence of insurance coverage of a party, because of the great effect that knowledge of the existence of insurance would have on a jury. Matters which are privileged are matters which by the rules of fair play should not be admitted into evidence.

## HEARSAY RULE

Another basic concept of our judicial system is the right of confrontation, or the right to be confronted by the witnesses against you and to cross-examine them about their allegations or contentions. Cross-examination in open court, as a fundamental right, provides the background for the rule of evidence known as the **hearsay rule.** Hearsay is an out-of-court statement which is being offered to prove the truth of the matter contained in the statement. For example, if the issue of the case was whether certain stock had been purchased, the testimony of a witness that her broker had *told* her the stock had been purchased would be hearsay. The statement is offered to prove the purchase of the stock when the *broker* is not available for cross-examination. The lack of cross-examination establishes that hearsay evidence should not be admitted. There are many exceptions to the hearsay rule. For example, if the party *herself* had made the statement, she could hardly object to the fact that she was not able to cross-examine herself, and thus we have the exception for admissions against interest by a party to the suit. Testimony at a former trial at which the party was able to cross-examine and subsequent unavailability of the witness create another exception to the hearsay rule. Business entries made in the ordinary course of business constitute still another exception. They may be introduced as evidence of the facts they represent. In a criminal case a dying declaration by the victim of murder is an exception, because the effect of impending death is considered by the courts to give sufficient credibility to the truthfulness of the testimony to eliminate the need for cross-examination. There are many other exceptions to the hearsay rule, but each of them is based on the fact that cross-examination has either been had at a former time or is not required for a fair trial in the present case.

## RELEVANCY

There are other rules of evidence, such as the rule requiring that all evidence be relevant to the matter involved in the litigation. If a person is involved in a suit for breach of contract for the sale of goods, wares, or merchandise, the fact that he has been divorced five times should have no effect on the litigation and would not be admissible evidence. It might, if presented, influence some member of the jury who particularly disliked divorced persons. In cases where direct testimony as to what happened is not available, evidence of habit or practice is sometimes admitted to show what probably happened, and this is considered relevant.

## DOCUMENTS

Another rule of evidence concerns the requirement of producing the best evidence available as proof in a lawsuit. The "best evidence rule," as it is commonly called, pertains only to written documents. There are many other rules of evidence concerning written documents, such as the "parol evidence rule," which prevents the proof of modification or change of a written document by the use of oral evidence.

It can be seen from this short examination of these elementary rules of evidence that they specify the rules of the game, so to speak, to ensure a fair trial and that each party has ample opportunity to present his or her contentions and case without unduly taking advantage of the other party. These rules were not created to serve as a stumbling block to meritorious litigants or to create unwarranted roadblocks to justice. On the contrary, the rules of evidence were created and should be applied to ensure fair play and to aid in the goal of having controversies determined on their merits.

### FEDERAL RULES

In order to reduce the cost of litigation and to speed up the search for truth, the Supreme Court has adopted rules of evidence for civil and criminal trials in the federal courts which greatly expand the admissibility of evidence and eliminate many of the traditional technical rules of evidence. For example, (1) cross-examination of a witness is not limited to the scope of direct examination; (2) a lawyer calling a witness does not vouch for the witness's credibility, which may be attacked by any party, including the party calling the witness; (3) expert testimony requires much less groundwork in that the facts or data upon which an expert bases his or her opinion need not be admissible in evidence; (4) opinion testimony on the ultimate issue to be decided by the jury is admissible; and (5) an expanded list of exceptions may be applied to the hearsay rule. This list of hearsay exceptions includes any statement having some inherent guarantee of trustworthiness if the statement has more bearing on the point for which it is offered than the other evidence reasonably available.

These rules of evidence have reduced the expense of litigation and, as well, have sped up the trial process. In addition, more evidence is presented to juries for their factual determination. As a result of these rules, evidence is often admissible in federal cases that would not be admissible if the case were tried in state courts.

## 17. Appellate Procedure

The previous chapter discussed the structure of the court system, including courts of review. Each state prescribes its own appellate procedure and determines the jurisdiction of its various reviewing courts. Although the procedure followed in an appeal is essentially a problem for the lawyer, certain aspects of this procedure assist us in understanding our judicial system.

Courts of review deal with the record of the proceedings in lower court. All the pleadings, testimony, and motions are reduced to a written record, which is filed with the court of review. The court of review studies the issues, testimony, and proceedings to determine whether prejudicial errors occurred or whether the lower court reached an erroneous result. In addition to the record, each party files a **brief** (the appellant may file a reply brief on receipt of the appellee's brief) which contains a short description of the nature of the case, the factual situation, the points and authorities on which the party relies, and his or her argument for reversing or affirming the decision of the lower court, depending on whether the party is an appellant or appellee. The points and authorities contain the statutes and judicial decisions relied upon as precedent in the argument.

In addition to the brief, the reviewing court is often given the benefit of oral argument in deciding the case. The attorneys are given a specified amount of time to explain orally to the court their position in the case. This also gives the court of review an opportunity to question the attorneys about various aspects of the case.

After oral argument, an impression vote is usually taken, and the case is assigned to one justice to prepare an opinion. Each justice has a staff of clerks assisting in the preparation of opinions. The intellectual backgrounds of these clerks have some influence on the decisions. The opinion as prepared by the clerks and the justice may not follow the impression vote. After the opinion is prepared, it will be circulated among the other members of the court. If a majority approve the opinion, it is adopted. Those who disagree may prepare a dissenting opinion. Thereafter the opinion is announced, and the losing party may ask for a rehearing on points stated in the opinion which he or she believes to be erroneous. Such rehearings are rarely granted. If the rehearing is denied or none is requested, the decision then becomes final. The mandate of the reviewing court is then forwarded to the trial court for appropriate proceedings either by way of enforcement of the decision or new proceedings, if required.

Courts of review are essentially concerned with questions of law. However, a reviewing court may be asked to grant a new trial on the ground that the decision in the lower court is contrary to the manifest weight of the evidence found in the record. Thus, questions of fact may be examined. In the federal courts and in many states, reviewing courts are not allowed to disturb factual findings unless they are clearly erroneous. This limitation recognizes the unique opportunity afforded the trial judge in evaluating the credibility of witnesses and weighing the evidence. Because of the deference due the trial judge, unless an appellate court is left with the "definite and firm conviction that a mistake has been committed," the reviewing court must accept the trial court's findings of fact. Determining the weight and credibility of the evidence is the special province of the trial court. An appellate court cannot substitute its interpretation of the evidence for that of the trial court simply because the reviewing court might give the facts another construction or resolve the ambiguities differently.

The case which follows illustrates the deference that must be given the trial judge by appellate courts. This deference is especially important when a decision rests heavily on the credibility of the witnesses. Only the trial judge can be aware of the variations in demeanor and tone of voice that bear so heavily on the listener's understanding of and belief in what is said.

# ANDERSON v. CITY OF BESSEMER CITY, N.C.
105 S.Ct. 1504 (1985)

Bessemer City (respondent) decided in 1975 to hire a new recreation director. A committee of four men and one woman was responsible for choosing the director. Eight persons applied for the position, including Anderson (petitioner), the only woman applicant. At the time, she was a 39-year-old schoolteacher with college degrees in social studies and education. The committee chose a 24-year-old male applicant, who had recently graduated from college with a degree in physical education. The four men voted to offer the job to him, and only the woman voted for petitioner. Petitioner then filed discrimination charges with the Equal Employment Opportunity Commission (EEOC). When conciliation efforts failed, Anderson filed suit under Title VII of the Civil Rights Act of 1964. After a trial in which testimony from petitioner, the applicant who was hired, and members of the selection committee was heard, the court issued a memorandum announcing its finding that petitioner was entitled to judgment because she had been denied the position on account of her sex. The court's finding that petitioner had been denied employment because of her sex was based on findings of fact that petitioner was the most qualified candidate, that she had been asked questions during her interview regarding her spouse's feelings about her application for the position that other applicants were not asked, and that the male committee members were biased against hiring a woman. The reasons given for the decisions were a pretext. The

Court of Appeals reversed, holding that the district court's findings were clearly erroneous and that the court had therefore erred in finding that petitioner had been discriminated against on account of sex.

WHITE, J.:...Because a finding of intentional discrimination is a finding of fact, the standard governing appellate review of a district court's finding of discrimination is that set forth in Federal Rule of Civil Procedure 52(a): "Findings of fact shall not be set aside unless clearly erroneous, and due regard shall be given to the opportunity of the trial court to judge of the credibility of the witnesses." The question before us, then, is whether the Court of Appeals erred in holding the District Court's finding of discrimination to be clearly erroneous.

Although the meaning of the phrase "clearly erroneous" is not immediately apparent, certain general principles governing the exercise of the appellate court's power to overturn findings of a district court may be derived from our cases. The foremost of these principles...is that "a finding is 'clearly erroneous' when although there is evidence to support it, the reviewing court on the entire evidence is left with the definite and firm conviction that a mistake has been committed." This standard plainly does not entitle a reviewing court to reverse the finding of the trier of fact simply because it is convinced that it would have decided the case differently. The reviewing court oversteps the bounds of its duty under Rule 52 if it undertakes to duplicate the role of the lower court. In applying the clearly erroneous standard to the findings of a district court sitting without a jury, appellate courts must constantly have in mind that their function is not to decide factual issues *de novo*. If the District Court's account of the evidence is plausible in light of the record viewed in its entirety, the court of appeals may not reverse it even though convinced that had it been sitting as the trier of fact, it would have weighed the evidence differently. Where there are two permissible views of the evidence, the fact-finder's choice between them cannot be clearly erroneous....

The rationale for deference to the original finder of fact is not limited to the superiority of the trial judge's position to make determinations of credibility. The trial judge's major role is the determination of fact, and with experience in fulfilling that role comes expertise....

In addition, the parties to a case on appeal have already been forced to concentrate their energies and resources on persuading the trial judge that their account of the facts is the correct one; requiring them to persuade three more judges at the appellate level is requiring too much. As the Court has stated in a different context, the trial on the merits should be "the 'main event'...rather than a 'tryout on the road.'" For these reasons, review of factual findings under the clearly-erroneous standard—with its deference to the trier of fact—is the rule, not the exception.

When findings are based on determinations regarding the credibility of witnesses, Rule 52 demands even greater deference to the trial court's findings; for only the trial judge can be aware of the variations in demeanor and tone of voice that bear so heavily on the listener's understanding of and belief in what is said. This is not to suggest that the trial judge may insulate his findings from review by denominating them

credibility determinations, for factors other than demeanor and inflection go into the decision whether or not to believe a witness. Documents or objective evidence may contradict the witness' story; or the story itself may be so internally inconsistent or implausible on its face that a reasonable factfinder would not credit it. Where such factors are present, the court of appeals may well find clear error even in a finding purportedly based on a credibility determination. But when a trial judge's finding is based on his decision to credit the testimony of one of two or more witnesses, each of whom has told a coherent and facially plausible story that is not contradicted by extrinsic evidence, that finding, if not internally inconsistent, can virtually never be clear error.

Application of the foregoing principles to the facts of the case lays bare the errors committed by the Fourth Circuit in its employment of the clearly-erroneous standard. In detecting clear error in the District Court's finding that petitioner was better qualified than Mr. Kincaid, the Fourth Circuit improperly conducted what amounted to a *de novo* weighing of the evidence in the record. The District Court's finding was based on essentially undisputed evidence regarding the respective backgrounds of petitioner and Mr. Kincaid and the duties that went with the position of Recreation Director. The District Court, after considering the evidence, concluded that the position of Recreation Director in Bessemer City carried with it broad responsibilities for creating and managing a recreation program involving not only athletics, but also other activities for citizens of all ages and interests. The court determined that petitioner's more varied educational and employment background and her extensive involvement in a variety of civic activities left her better qualified to implement such a rounded program than Mr. Kincaid, whose background was more narrowly focused on athletics.

The Fourth Circuit, reading the same record, concluded that the basic duty of the Recreation Director was to implement an athletic program, and that the essential qualification for a successful applicant would be either education or experience specifically related to athletics. Accordingly, it seemed evident to the Court of Appeals that Mr. Kincaid was in fact better qualified than petitioner.

Based on our own reading of the record, we cannot say that either interpretation of the facts is illogical or implausible. Each has support in inferences that may be drawn from the facts in the record; and if either interpretation had been drawn by a district court on the record before us, we would not be inclined to find it clearly erroneous. The question we must answer, however, is not whether the Fourth Circuit's interpretation of the facts was clearly erroneous, but whether the District Court's finding was clearly erroneous. The District Court determined that petitioner was better qualified, and, as we have stated above, such

a finding is entitled to deference notwithstanding that it is not based on credibility determinations. When the record is examined in light of the appropriately deferential standard, it is apparent that it contains nothing that mandates a finding that the District Court's conclusion was clearly erroneous....

Our determination that the findings of the District Court regarding petitioner's qualifications, the conduct of her interview, and the bias of the male committee members were not clearly erroneous leads us to conclude that the court's finding that petitioner was discriminated against on account of her sex was also not clearly erroneous. The District Court's findings regarding petitioner's superior qualifications and the bias of the selection committee are sufficient to support the inference that petitioner was denied the position of Recreation Director on account of her sex. Accordingly, we hold that the Fourth Circuit erred in denying petitioner relief under Title VII....

Accordingly, the judgment of the Court of Appeals is....[*Reversed.*]

---

## 18. Enforcement of Judgments and Decrees

After a judgment in a court of law or a decree in a court of equity has become final, either because of the decision on appeal or because the losing party failed to perfect an appeal within the proper time, it may become necessary for the successful party to obtain judicial assistance in enforcing the court decision. For example, the judgment debtor may not voluntarily pay the amount of the judgment to the judgment creditor.

In such a case, the judgment creditor may levy execution on the property of the judgment debtor, cause any property which is not exempt from execution by statute to be sold at public sale, and have the proceeds applied on the judgment. The judgment creditor may also garnishee the wages of the judgment debtor, subject to the amount that is exempt, or attach any property which may be due him or her. Modern statutes give the judgment creditor the right to question the judgment debtor in open court to discover assets that might be applied to the debt. All states allow a debtor to keep certain items of property and a certain amount of wages free from his or her debts. In addition, the federal bankruptcy law provides exemptions. The debtor may exempt significant amounts of property from the proceedings. The net effect of this law is to allow bankrupt judgment debtors to avoid the judgment and at the same time retain many of their assets.

## 19.  Res Judicata

Once a decision of the court has become final, it is said to be **res judicata**—"the thing has been decided"—meaning that a final decision is conclusive on all issues between the parties whether raised in the litigation or not. Res judicata means that a cause of action finally determined by a competent court cannot be litigated by the parties in a new proceeding by the same court or in any other court. By final decision, we mean that either the case has been finally decided on appeal or that the time for appeal has expired. This prevents successive suits involving the same question between the same parties and brings disputes to a final conclusion. A matter once litigated and legally determined is conclusive between the parties in all subsequent proceedings. The case which follows illustrates this concept.

# CUMMINGS v. DRESHER
218 N.E.2d 688 (N.Y. 1966)

DESMOND, J.: There was a collision between an automobile owned by Martin Cummings and driven by Mary Cummings and an automobile driven by Bernard Dresher. The car driven by Bernard Dresher was owned by Standard Electric Co., Inc., and in it Henry Dresher was a passenger. Driver Bernard Dresher and passenger Henry Dresher as coplaintiffs sued driver Mary Cummings and owner Martin Cummings in the Federal District Court for damages for personal injuries sustained by the two Dresher brothers. The issues up for determination in that *Dresher v. Cummings* suit included, therefore, questions as to the negligence of either or both the Dreshers and either or both of the defendants Cummings. Returning their verdict, the jury told the Federal Judge that it found in favor of the passenger Henry Dresher against defendants Cummings and found also that Mrs. Cummings was "guilty of negligence" and the "plaintiff" (apparently meaning driver Bernard Dresher) "was guilty" of contributory negligence to a very minor degree. The Judge, to "complete" the verdict, instructed the Clerk to ask the jury whether it intended a verdict of no cause of action in Bernard Dresher's suit. The jurors replied that such was their intention. Judgment was thereupon entered in favor of Mr. and Mrs. Cummings dismissing the complaint of Bernard Dresher, and the judgment was affirmed by the Federal Court of Appeals 325 F.2d 156 (2d Cir.). At the close of these Federal court proceedings it was completely clear that the jury had found that driver Mary Cummings had been found guilty of negligence and that, therefore, she as driver and her husband as owner had to pay damages to passenger Henry Dresher. Equally clear was the Federal court jury's finding that driver Bernard Dresher had been guilty of contributory negligence and so, notwithstanding the found negligence of driver Mary Cummings, Bernard Dresher could not recover against the defendants Cummings.

Despite this definite and unmistakable Federal court jury finding as to both drivers being at fault, driver Mary Cummings and her husband brought the present suit against driver Dresher and the corporate owner of the Dresher car. The courts below, for inscrutable reasons, held that the Federal court judgment was not determinative here. We do not understand why in a reasonable, prompt and nonrepetitious judicial system the negligence or not of these two drivers must be decided all over again, after having once been settled after a jury trial in which all these same people were parties and all the same issues tried and decided. "One who has had his day in court should not be permitted to litigate the question anew...." Under such circumstances the judgment is held to be conclusive upon those who were parties to the action in which the judgment was rendered. Where a full opportunity has been afforded to a party to the prior action and he has failed to prove his freedom from liability or to establish liability or culpability on the part of another, there is no reason for retrying these issues.... [*Reversed.*]

## REVIEW QUESTIONS

**1** For each term in the left-hand column, match the most appropriate description in the right-hand column:

(1) Best evidence rule

(2) Beyond a reasonable doubt

(3) Brief

(4) Opening statement

(5) Attorney-client privilege

(a) The burden-of-proof standard in criminal cases

(b) The usual burden-of-proof standard in civil cases

(c) A rule of evidence which prevents lawyers from testifying against their clients

(d) A document used in the appeal process to set forth the grounds on which the appeal is based

(e) A factual summary as to what each party expects to prove in a jury trial

(6) Preponderance of the evidence

(7) Hearsay

(8) Voir dire examination

(9) Res judicata

(10) Peremptory challenge

(11) Clear-and-convincing-proof standard

(12) Jury instruction

(f) A rule of evidence that requires that a document be presented as evidence; it does not permit oral testimony as to the contents of the document

(g) A principle that gives finality to legal disputes

(h) The removal of a prospective juror for which no cause need be given

(i) An out-of-court statement offered to prove a point which is not subject to cross-examination

(j) The questioning of prospective jurors as to their qualifications to be fair and impartial

(k) A method of informing the jury as to the law applicable to the case

(l) A burden-of-proof standard used in limited situations in which the law requires more proof than usual

**2** Kay was injured when a pool table collapsed on her foot. The manufacturer was a Missouri corporation which sold the pool table to a wholesaler in Nebraska. The wholesaler sold to an Iowa pool hall where the injury occurred. Kay sued the manufacturer in Iowa, and summons was served on the manufacturer in Missouri. The defendant challenged the jurisdiction of the court. Decide the challenge. Give reasons for your answer.

**3** The Minnesota Public Interest Research Group is a college-student-directed, non-profit corporation. It purports to represent the interests of college students on issues of public importance. This group filed suit to challenge the constitutionality of the Selective Service Act provision making students who failed to register for the draft ineligible for federal financial assistance. The government moved to have the suit dismissed. Rule on the motion, and give reasons for your ruling.

**4** Plaintiff, a resident of New York, brought a libel suit against defendant magazine publisher, an Ohio corporation, in federal district court in New Hampshire alleging jurisdiction by reason of diversity of citizenship. The statute of limitations had run out in all other states. Defendant's contacts with New Hampshire consist of monthly sales of some 10,000 to 15,000 copies of its nationally published magazine. Defendant moved to dismiss because the plaintiff had never been to New Hampshire. What was the result? Why?

**5** The plaintiff alleged that the defendant caused pharmacists to mislabel drugs by marketing drugs with the similar appearance to those sold by the plaintiff. The trial court found for the defendant. It found that a technical violation of federal law had occurred but found no proof of intent. The Court of Appeals reversed, holding that the trial court failed to give sufficient weight to the evidence of a violation. Did the reviewing court act within its proper role? Explain.

**6** An action was brought in federal court by a realtor against the Real Estate Commission challenging a regulation relating to advertising by real estate dealers. The court found for the defendants. A subsequent action was brought in state court by the same plaintiff against the same defendants. They moved to dismiss the suit. How should the court rule on the motion? Explain.

**7** A class action suit was filed on behalf of certain odd-lot traders against brokerage firms and a stock exchange for alleged violations of the antitrust and securities laws. Plaintiffs asked the court to order defendants to furnish the names and addresses of all members of the class because defendants could easily gather the information and because plaintiffs had limited funds. Should the court grant the plaintiffs' request? Explain.

**8** A paving contractor, incorporated in Delaware with its principal place of business being in Georgia, was hired to oil and chip streets in a mobile-home park located in Florida. Heavy winds developed during the spraying of oil on the street, and a light film of oil was sprayed on ninety-six mobile homes, doing approximately $600 damage to each. A class action suit was filed in federal court seeking $57,000 damages. Does the court have jurisdiction? Explain.

**9** Geraldine's car had been illegally repossessed in Texas by the Baker Bank, a federally chartered national bank located in the state of Tennessee. The National Bank Act requires that suits against national banks be brought in the county in which the bank is located. Geraldine sued the bank in Texas, and the bank moved to dismiss. What was the result? Why?

**10** Mincey was injured by a steel drum which he was cutting with a circular saw. He sued the manufacturer of the saw, and the manufacturer, in turn, served interrogatories upon the plaintiff. The interrogatories requested information about the defendant's medical history, work history, and educational background. In addition, the defendant then requested the identities of expert witnesses to be called by the plaintiff and the substance of their testimony. Must the plaintiff answer the questions? Why, or why not?

**11** A Japanese manufacturer of valve stems for tires sold its product to a Taiwanese company; the Taiwanese company assembled the valve stems into its tires, which were sold worldwide. Twenty percent of the tires were sold in California. In that state, an accident occurred in which a motorcycle tire blew out, injuring the rider. Is the Japanese manufacturer subject to suit in California by the Taiwanese manufacturer that settled the product liability suit? Why, or why not?

**12** Burger King, a Florida-based corporation, granted a twenty-year franchise to a franchisee in Michigan. The franchisee provides that it is established in Miami and governed by Florida law. All payments of fees and reports are to be made in Florida. The franchisor sued the franchisee in Florida and sought jurisdiction under Florida's long-arm statute. Must the franchisee defend the case in Florida? Explain.

**13** A group of employees sued their employer to recover benefits under the Fair Labor Standards Act. The federal district court found that the employees were seamen because they worked on navigable waters; thus they were not covered by the overtime law. The Court of Appeals reviewed the evidence and found that the employees were primarily maintenance employees who spent only a small portion of their time on "maritime work." It therefore found that the employees were not seamen and as such were entitled to overtime payments. Upon further review by the Supreme Court, what result would you expect? Why?

**14**   A products liability suit for personal injuries was filed in which it was alleged that a carlift manufactured by the defendant was defective. Plaintiffs sought a complete list of the defendant's customers so that each of them could be contacted to determine if any other carlifts had failed to function properly. Is this proper discovery? Why or why not?

# *Chapter*

# 5

# Arbitration

## CHAPTER PREVIEW

This chapter examines the use of arbitration as a substitute for litigation. Arbitration is the submission of a dispute to a third party, called an arbitrator, to obtain a binding decision resolving the controversy. Historically, the law has favored litigation over arbitration. Today, public policy favors arbitration over litigation for several reasons which are discussed in this chapter.

The finality of arbitration and the difficulty of challenging the decision of the arbitrator are emphasized. Special attention is paid to the Federal Arbitration Act which covers all agreements to arbitrate when the subject matter involves interstate commerce. The trend toward compulsory arbitration for certain dollar levels of disputes is also covered.

The following terms are introduced: arbitrator, award, de novo hearing, mediation, and submission.

## 1. Introduction

Litigation is not the only method used for resolving conflicts and disputes. Most disputes are settled by the parties themselves, frequently with the assistance of legal counsel. Of the numerous reasons for settling disputes, many are economic because of the high cost of litigation in time and money. As long as each party must pay his or her own lawyer, the cost of litigation will be a driving force toward settlement. A major role of lawyers is to negotiate settlements of potential and existing lawsuits.

The law also contains other procedures and techniques for settling disputes without formal litigation. Many of these techniques are included within the body of law known as administrative law, the subject matter of Chapter 8. As a practical matter, more problems and controversies are submitted to administrative agencies for decision than are submitted to courts. (Several later chapters deal more specifically with the role of these administrative agencies, including the National Labor Relations Board and the Federal Trade Commission.)

**Arbitration** is a substitute for litigation that is very important to business, especially in international transaction and in labor-management relations. In international business transactions, an arbitration clause in a contract determines the person or persons called the **arbitrator**(s) who will resolve any controversies before they arise; the parties have thereby avoided litigation of issues relating to their contract in the courts of any one country.

Arbitration as a substitute for litigation must be contrasted with **mediation,** a process in which a third party is asked to help settle the dispute. The mediator provides an unbiased viewpoint and skill in effecting compromise. Although a mediator cannot impose a solution upon the parties, his or her viewpoint of a fair and reasonable settlement is usually given significant weight. This is especially true in labor-management disputes, because the public usually accepts the mediator's viewpoint as a reasonable solution.

On the other hand, arbitration proceedings are a nonjudicial means for submitting a controversy to a third person or persons for a *binding* decision. Arbitration may result either from agreement of the parties to the controversy or from legislation which requires that certain disputes be decided by that process. Courts may be involved in the arbitration process if a party refuses to arbitrate a dispute that is covered by an agreement to arbitrate or if the losing party decides to challenge the decision of the arbitrators.

## 2.  Reasons for Arbitration

The fundamental premise upon which the policy of the law favoring arbitration is grounded is the laudable goal of providing a relatively quick and inexpensive resolution of contractual disputes by avoiding the expense and delay of extended court proceedings. It provides a means of avoiding the formalities and vexation of ordinary litigation. For example, formal pleadings and other technical steps are usually not required.

Arbitration also serves to help ease congested court dockets. A primary function of arbitration is to serve as a substitute for and not a prelude to litigation. It is a private proceeding with no public record available to the press and others. Thus, by keeping their dispute private, adversaries may be more likely to preserve their business relationships.

Arbitration also has the advantage of submitting many disputes to experts for solutions. For example, if the issue involves whether or not a building has been properly constructed, the matter could be submitted to an architect for resolution. If it involves a technical accounting problem, it could be submitted to a certified public accountant. The Securities and Exchange Commission (SEC) has approved an arrangement where investors with complaints against securities dealers must submit them for arbitration. The arbitration is handled by arbitrators assigned by the various stock exchanges and the National Association of Securities Dealers. They possess the special knowledge required to determine if a customer of a brokerage house has a legitimate complaint.

Arbitration is of special importance in labor relations where it provides the grievance procedures under collective bargaining contracts. It provides the means for industrial self-government, a system of private law for all problems that may arise in the workplace. No other system is as capable of expeditiously resolving so many disputes.

## 3. Arbitration Proceedings

The term **submission** is used to describe the act of referring a matter to the arbitration process. Submission is covered in section 4 of this chapter. A submission to arbitration usually results from the voluntary agreement of the parties. However, it may result from legislation, in which case it is compulsory arbitration.

After the submission, a hearing is conducted by the arbitrator or arbitrators. Both parties are allowed to present evidence and to argue their own points of view. Then a decision known as an **award** is handed down.

In most states the arbitrator's award must be in writing. The award need not, and generally does not, set forth findings of fact, conclusions of law, or the reasons for it. The award is valid as long as it settles the entire controversy and states which party is to pay the other a sum of money.

When the arbitrator provides the basis for decision in the form of an opinion or letter, that document becomes a part of the award. A disclosure of findings and the reasons therefore must be given if the applicable statute, arbitration agreement, or submission so requires.

Because the parties themselves, by virtue of the submission, frame the issues to be resolved and define the scope of the arbitrator's powers, the parties generally are bound by the resulting award. A court will make every reasonable presumption in favor of the arbitration award and the arbitrator's acts and proceedings since the parties have usually consented to arbitration. An award is final on all issues submitted, and it will be enforced by the courts as if it were a judgment of the court. As will be discussed in detail later in this chapter, awards are not subject to judicial review on the merits of the decision.

After the award is made by the arbitrator, it is usually filed with the clerk of an appropriate court. If no objections to the award are filed within a statutory period, it becomes final and a judgment.

Most states and the Congress have enacted statutes covering voluntary arbitration. These statutes cover all aspects of the submission, the award, and its enforcement. Under voluntary statutory arbitration, an agreement to submit an issue to arbitration is irrevocable, and a party who senses that the process is not going well cannot withdraw and resort to litigation. At common law such a withdrawal was permitted.

## 4.  The Submission

The issues submitted to arbitration, as framed in the submission, may be questions of fact, questions of law, or mixed questions of fact and law. They may include the interpretation of the arbitration agreement. The submission may be the result of a contract or it may be a requirement by statute. Doubts concerning the arbitrability of an issue are usually resolved in favor of arbitration. When courts are called upon to determine arbitrability, arbitration will not be denied unless it may be said with positive assurance that the arbitration agreement does not cover the asserted dispute.

Submission by contract occurs if the parties enter into an agreement to arbitrate an existing dispute. The arbitration agreement is the submission in this case. In addition, the parties may contractually agree to submit to arbitration all issues that *may* arise in the future, or they may agree that either party *may* demand arbitration of any issue that may arise. Submission in these circumstances occurs when a demand to arbitrate is served on the other party. This demand is either a notice that a matter is being referred to the arbitrator agreed upon by the parties, or a demand that the matter be referred to arbitration.

Most state statutes authorizing arbitration require the agreement to be in writing. Since the goal of arbitration is to obtain a quick resolution of disputes, most statutes require submission within a stated time period, usually six months, after the dispute arises.

In the absence of a statute, the rights and duties of the parties to a submission are described and limited by their agreement. Parties who have contracted to arbitrate are not required to arbitrate any matters other than those which they previously had agreed to arbitrate. Whether a particular dispute is arbitrable is a question for the court, although the parties may agree to arbitrate additional questions.

Sometimes a dispute arises as to whether or not the parties have agreed to submit an issue to arbitration. In such a case, one party refuses to arbitrate and the other files suit to compel arbitration. The court hearing the case decides the issue of arbitrability but does not decide the basic issue between the parties. The case which follows explains the role of courts when the issue of arbitrability arises.

# AT&T TECH., INC. v. COMMUNICATIONS WORKERS
106 S.Ct. 1415 (1986)

A collective-bargaining agreement covering telephone equipment installation workers provided for arbitration of differences arising over interpretation of the agreement. Article 9 provided that the employer was free to exercise certain management functions, including the hiring, placement, and termination of employees. Such issues were excluded from the arbitration clause, but Article 20 prescribed the order in which employees would be laid off when lack of work necessitated layoff.

The employer laid off seventy-nine installers, and the union filed a grievance claiming that there was no lack of work and, therefore, that the layoffs violated Article 20. The employer refused to submit the grievance to arbitration on the ground that under Article 9 the layoffs were not arbitrable. The union then sought to compel arbitration by filing suit in federal district court. That court found that the union's interpretation of Article 20 was at least "arguable" and that it was for the arbitrator, not the court, to decide whether that interpretation had merit; accordingly, it ordered the petitioner to arbitrate. The court of appeals affirmed.

WHITE, J.:...The issue presented in this case is whether a court asked to order arbitration of a grievance filed under a collective-bargaining agreement must first determine that the parties intended to arbitrate the dispute, or whether that determination is properly left to the arbitrator.

The principles necessary to decide this case are not new. They were set out by this Court over 25 years ago in a series of cases known as the *Steelworkers Trilogy*. These precepts have served the industrial relations community well, and have led to continued reliance on arbitration, rather than strikes or lockouts, as the preferred method of resolving disputes arising during the term of a collective-bargaining agreement. We see no reason either to question their continuing validity, or to eviscerate their meaning by creating an exception to their general applicability.

The first principle gleaned from the *Trilogy* is that "arbitration is a matter of contract and a party cannot be required to submit to arbitration any dispute which he has not agreed so to submit." This axiom recognizes the fact that arbitrators derive their authority to resolve disputes only because the parties have agreed in advance to submit such grievances to arbitration.

The second rule, which follows inexorably from the first, is that the question of arbitrability—whether a collective-bargaining agreement creates a duty for the parties to arbitrate the particular grievance—is undeniably an issue for judicial determination. Unless the parties clearly and unmistakably provide otherwise, the question of whether the parties agreed to arbitrate is to be decided by the court, not the arbitrator.

...The duty to arbitrate being of contractual origin, a compulsory submission to arbitration cannot precede judicial determination that the collective bargaining agreement does in fact create such a duty.

The third principle derived from our prior cases is that, in deciding whether the parties have agreed to submit a particular grievance to arbitration, a court is not to rule on the potential merits of the underlying claims. Whether "arguable" or not, indeed even if it appears to the court to be frivolous, the union's claim that the employer has violated the collective-bargaining agreement is to be decided, not by the court asked to order arbitration, but as the parties have agreed, by the arbitrator. "The courts, therefore, have no business weighing the merits of the grievance, considering whether there is equity in a particular claim, or determining whether there is particular language in the written instrument which will support the claim. The agreement is to submit all grievances to arbitration, not merely those which the court will deem meritorious."

Finally, where it has been established that where the contract contains an arbitration clause, there is a presumption of arbitrability in the sense that "[a]n order to arbitrate the particular grievance should not be denied unless it may be said with positive assurance that the arbitration clause is not susceptible of an interpretation that covers the asserted dispute. Doubts should be resolved in favor of coverage." Such a presumption is particularly applicable where the clause is as broad as the one employed in this case, which provides for arbitration of "any differences arising with respect to the interpretation of this contract or the performance of any obligation hereunder...." In such cases, "[i]n the absence of any express provision excluding a particular grievance from arbitration, we think only the most forceful evidence of a purpose to exclude the claim from arbitration can prevail."

This presumption of arbitrability for labor disputes recognizes the greater institutional competence of arbitrators in interpreting collective bargaining agreements, furthers the national labor policy of peaceful resolution of labor disputes and thus best accords with the parties' presumed objec-

tives in pursuing collective bargaining. The willingness of parties to enter into agreements that provide for arbitration of specified disputes would be "drastically reduced," however, if a labor arbitrator had the "power to determine his own jurisdiction...." Were this the applicable rule, an arbitrator would not be constrained to resolve only those disputes that the parties have agreed in advance to settle by arbitration, but instead, would be empowered "to impose obligations outside the contract limited only by his understanding and conscience." This result undercuts the longstanding federal policy of promoting industrial harmony through the use of collective-bargaining agreements, and is antithetical to the function of a collective-bargaining agreement as setting out the rights and duties of the parties.

With these principles in mind, it is evident that the Seventh Circuit erred in ordering the parties to arbitrate the arbitrability question. It is the court's duty to interpret the agreement and to determine whether the parties intended to arbitrate grievances concerning layoffs predicated on a "lack of work" determination by the Company. If the court determines that the agreement so provides, then it is for the arbitrator to determine the relative merits of the parties' substantive interpretations of the agreement. It was for the court, not the arbitrator, to decide in the first instance whether the dispute was to be resolved through arbitration.

The Union does not contest the application of these principles to the present case. Instead, it urges the Court to examine the specific provisions of the agreement for itself and to affirm the Court of Appeals on the ground that the parties had agreed to arbitrate the dispute over the layoffs at issue here. But it is usually not our function in the first instance to construe collective-bargaining contracts and arbitration clauses, or to consider any other evidence that might unmistakably demonstrate that a particular grievance was not to be subject to arbitration. The issue in the case is whether, because of express exclusion or other forceful evidence, the dispute over the interpretation of Article 20 of the contract, the layoff provision, is not subject to the arbitration clause. That issue should have been decided by the District Court and reviewed by the Court of Appeals; it should not have been referred to the arbitrator.

The judgment of the Court of Appeals is vacated, and the case is remanded for proceedings in conformity with this opinion. [*It is so ordered.*]

## 5. The Arbitrators

One of the reasons that arbitration is frequently preferable to litigation is that the dispute can be submitted to an expert for decision. Architects can be used to decide disputes about construction, medical doctors can be used to decide health care disputes, and academicians can be used to decide issues within their area of expertise.

This use of experts is especially important in labor-management relations. Arbitration is the technique used in collective-bargaining contracts to settle grievances of employees against their employers. Arbitration is able to resolve disputes arising out of labor contracts without resorting to judicial intervention. It is quick and efficient and minimizes disruption in the workplace. Labor arbitration has attracted a large number of experts—both lawyers and academicians.

Arbitration provides for decision making by experts with experience in the particular industry and with knowledge of the customs and practices of the particular work site. Parties often choose arbitrators based on their knowledge of the "common law of the shop." They expect the arbitrator to look beyond strictly legal criteria to other factors that bear on the proper resolution of a dispute. These factors may include "the effect upon productivity of a particular result, its consequence to the morale of the shop and whether tensions will be heightened or diminished." The ablest judge cannot be expected to bring the same experience and competence to bear upon the determination of a grievance, because he cannot be similarly informed.

Another issue relates to the number of arbitrators to hear a dispute. It is common to use one arbitrator who is considered objective and impartial. Such arbitrators are often chosen from a list of qualified arbitrators provided by the American Arbitration Association.

It is also common to have a panel of three arbitrators. In such cases each party selects an arbitrator and the two so selected choose a third. It is not surprising that when this procedure is used, allegations of bias are often made by the losing party. The case which follows discusses this problem and expresses the usual attitude toward such challenges.

# ANDERSON v. NICHOLS

359 E.E.2d 117 (W.Va. 1987)

Anderson (appellee) leased land to Nichols (appellant) to mine coal. The lease provides that Nichols would pay an $8,750 minimum royalty and that Nichols would continue mining until all of the coal was mined. Nichols ceased mining operations and Anderson demanded arbitration as provided in the contract. By a 2 to 1 vote, the panel awarded Anderson $105,000 in damages. The dissenting member of the panel voted to limit the damages to $52,000. Nichols challenged the award in court alleging, among other grounds, that the arbitrator selected by Anderson was biased.

The arbitration provision provided that "one arbitrator shall be selected by lessors and one by lessee within ten days after notice in writing from either party to the other specifying the need for arbitration and the issue or issues to be arbitrated; the two so selected shall select a third arbitrator within five days after their selection. The decision or award of the arbitrators, or a majority of them shall be binding upon the parties and shall be the exclusive means of settling all claims, disputes, or actions growing herefrom or involved herein."

NEELY, J.:…The primary complaint of the appellants…is that arbitrator Fish was biased on behalf of the appellees. Appellants ground this complaint upon an affidavit of arbitrator Tucker which said: That in the course of the arbitrators' deliberation Mr. Fish stated that prior to his having been selected as an arbitrator he had visited the coal mine involved in the arbitration at the request of Mr. Anderson in anticipation of being an expert engineering witness on behalf of Mr. Anderson in the arbitration proceed-

ings, that he had formed an opinion based upon his view of the coal mine that Cecil Nichols and N.F. Mining Company had not recovered all the merchantable and minable coal from the leased premises, and that he had conveyed that opinion to Mr. Anderson.

That in the course of the arbitrators' deliberations, Mr. Fish undertook to influence the arbitrators' decision by stating that based upon his visit to the coal mine Nichols and N.F. Mining Company could have found merchantable and minable coal had they driven entries to the right of the main entries. Thus we are squarely presented with a recurring problem in arbitration law—namely, how to handle an allegation of partiality when an arbitrator is selected under a standard arbitration clause that provides that each party shall name one arbitrator and the two so named shall then agree upon a third….

It has been this Court's policy to encourage arbitration among commercial parties as an alternative to litigation. Furthermore, to the maximum extent possible we have attempted to avoid exactly the type of problem that has arisen in this case. Here the award of the arbitrators was eminently fair; a just conclusion was reached expeditiously, economically, and without the technical constraints of complex legal rules. Yet the payment of the award in this case has been delayed by imaginative challenges in both the trial and appellate courts.

The appellants allege lack of fairness because the arbitrator appointed by the appellees had prior business dealings with the appellees; yet, the record discloses that the appellants' arbitrator, Mr. Tucker, is a signatory upon the appeal bond filed to perfect the appellants' appeal to this Court and that appellants have an ongoing financial relationship with Mr. Tucker's bank. Thus, from the conduct of both parties it appears reasonable to infer that when they entered into their agreement to arbitrate they envisaged that each side would name an arbitrator friendly to that side and that those two arbitrators would then name an impartial umpire.

One of the leading cases on arbitration in the United States is *Commonwealth Corp. v. Casualty Co.*, 89 S.Ct. 337, (1968), where the Supreme Court of the United States set aside an arbitration agreement because the third arbitrator (impartial umpire) under an arbitration clause similar to the one in the case before us had an undisclosed relationship as an engineering consultant with one of the parties.... It [is] obvious that the Supreme Court of the United States, under the United States Arbitration Act, will look only at the impartiality of the neutral umpire.

The U.S. Supreme Court seems willing to accept the obvious, namely that under the standard arbitration clause where each party selects one arbitrator and the two so selected choose a third, the parties expect their personally-named arbitrators to be advocates for each respective position. In this regard, Mr. Justice White said in his concurring opinion:

**The Court does not decide today that arbitrators are to be held to the standards of judicial decorum of Article III judges, or indeed of any judges. It is often because they are men of affairs, not apart from but of the marketplace, that they are effective in their adjudicatory function. This does not mean the judiciary must overlook outright chicanery in giving effect to their awards; that would be an abdication of our responsibility. But it does mean that arbitrators are not automatically disqualified by a business relationship with the parties before them if both parties are informed of the relationship in ad-**

**vance, or if they are unaware of the facts but the relationship is trivial.**

The New York Court of Appeals, a court particularly expert in commercial matters, has gone even further in recognizing that under a standard tripartite arbitration clause the arbitrators named by the parties will inevitably be individuals that the parties believe are favorably disposed to their side....

In fact, the right to appoint one's own arbitrator is a "valuable" contractual right:

**"The right to appoint one's own arbitrator, which is the essence of tripartite arbitration... would be of little moment were it to comprehend solely the choice of a 'neutral.' It becomes a valued right, which parties will bargain for and litigate over, only if it involves a choice of one believed to be sympathetic to his position or favorably disposed to him."...**

Accordingly, it has been held, seemingly without exception, that—absent overt corruption or misconduct in the arbitration itself, which is not alleged here—no arbitrator appointed by a party may be challenged on the ground of his relationship to that party.

In the case before us there is no allegation of "outright chicanery," "overt corruption," or "misconduct in the arbitration itself." As the record amply reveals, both parties appointed arbitrators who were favorably disposed to them, and that is what both had envisaged in the arbitration provision of the lease when they entered into it. Indeed, had Mr. Fish accepted a bribe for endorsing a favorable report, or had Mr. Morton, the neutral umpire, enjoyed a substantial, undisclosed business relationship with the appellees, then the threshold of actual fraud would have been reached. Under the facts of this case, however, we find that the arbitrators behaved properly and that the award in this case was exemplary....[*Affirmed.*]

## 6.  Court-annexed Mandatory Arbitration

About one-third of the states have adopted mandatory arbitration as a means of reducing court congestion. In these states, statutes are enacted which are supplemented by court rules that set forth the manner of conducting such arbitration. These statutes have resulted from studies which show that a dispute that would require three days if resolved by a 12-person jury trial can be decided in two or three hours by an arbitrator.

Mandatory arbitration statutes cover only a few types of cases. A typical statute applies the procedure to claims exclusively for money in an amount not exceeding $15,000, not including interest and costs. Most jurisdictions expressly exclude actions involving real estate titles and equitable issues. In addition, arbitration is required only in those cases in which a party has demanded a jury trial. This is based on the assumption that a judge hearing a case is almost as efficient as an arbitrator hearing one. The time saved in jury trials include not only the judge's time but the jury's as well.

Mandatory arbitration, while requiring substantially less time than litigation, does not provide speedy justice. The usual procedure for a claim filed in court that is covered by the mandatory arbitration law is to place the claim in the arbitration track at time of filing. At this time the date and time of hearing is assigned, typically eight months from the date of filing. If the claim is undervalued at the time of filing or by the court in diverting the claim to arbitration, the claimant is not precluded from the opportunity to realize his claim's full, potential value. No party need accept the award of the arbitrators as final, and any party may reject the award and proceed to trial where no monetary limit would apply.

The arbitrators in the mandatory arbitration process are retired judges and practicing lawyers, usually experienced trial attorneys. The panel will consist of three members appointed from a list of available arbitrators although the parties may agree on a lesser number. Arbitrators are paid a daily per diem usually around $200 per day.

Discovery procedures may be used prior to the hearing on arbitration. Since no discovery is permitted after the hearing without permission of the court, an early and thorough degree of preparation is necessary to achieve a full hearing on the merits of the controversy. This also prevents the hearing from being used as an opportunity to discover the adversary's case en route to an eventual trial. Most discovery is by interrogatory rather than by deposition.

The arbitrators have the power to determine the admissibility of evidence and to decide the law and the facts of the case. Rulings on objections to evidence or on other issues which arise during the hearing are made by the chairperson of the panel. States have different rules relating to the admissibility of evidence. In most states the established rules of evidence must be followed by the arbitrators. For example, most states would admit documents into evidence as long as the other party has been given a copy of the document in advance of the hearing. There are, however, several jurisdictions which do not require hearings to be conducted according to the established rules of evidence. For example, New Jersey law provides: "The arbitrator shall admit all relevant evidence and shall not be bound by the rules of evidence." Other states, such as the state of Washington, leave to the discretion of the arbitrator the extent to which the rules of evidence will apply.

The award which decides in favor of the plaintiff or the defendant is filed with the clerk of the court promptly upon termination of the hearing. It disposes of all issues but usually does not include findings of fact or conclusions of law. In the event that neither of the parties files a notice of rejection of the award or requests to proceed to trial within the stated time limits, either party may move for a judgment on the award.

As previously noted, any party who was present at the arbitration hearing, either in person or by counsel, may file a written notice of rejection of the award and request to proceed to trial. The filing of a single rejection shall be sufficient to enable all parties to proceed to trial on all issues of the case without filing a separate rejection. The failure of a party to be present, either in person or by counsel, at an arbitration hearing constitutes a waiver of the right to reject the award. In essence, a party's lack of participation operates as a consent to the entry by the court of a judgment on the award. Since the procedure of mandatory court-annexed arbitration is an integral part of the judicial process of dispute resolution, its process must be utilized either to finally resolve the dispute or as the obligatory step prior to resolution by trial. To allow any party to ignore the arbitration hearing would permit a mockery of this deliberate attempt to achieve an expeditious and less costly resolution of private controversies.

The rejection procedure is probably required for the laws requiring arbitration to be constitutional. (See section 11 on the judicial review of mandatory arbitrations statutes.) The right to reject the award and to proceed to trial is the sole remedy of a party dissatisfied with the award. In a sense the award is an intermediate step in resolving the dispute if the trial itself is desired. The right to reject the award exists without regard to the basis for the rejection. Many jurisdictions authorize fee and cost sanctions to be imposed on parties who fail to improve their positions at the trial after hearing. It is hoped that the quality of the arbitrators, the integrity of the hearings, and the fairness of the awards will keep to a minimum the number of rejections.

## THE FEDERAL ARBITRATION ACT

### 7. Impact on Federal Statutes

The Federal Arbitration Act covers any arbitration clause in a contract that involves interstate commerce. Under it, courts are to "rigorously" enforce arbitration agreements. A court assumes arbitration was intended unless it can say with positive assurance that the arbitration clause was not intended to include the particular dispute. The federal policy clearly favors arbitration of commercial disputes. The Federal Arbitration Act provides that arbitration agreements "shall be valid, irrevocable, and enforceable, save upon such grounds as exist at law or in equity for the revocation of any contract." The rights granted by this law are not dependent upon the forum, whether federal or state, in which they are asserted.

The attitude of the federal courts toward arbitration as it affects federal statutes is explained by the case which follows. It involves the Securities Exchange Act of 1934 and the Racketeer Influenced and Corrupt Organizations Act (RICO), both of which are of extreme importance to the business community today.

---

# SHEARSON/AMERICAN EXPRESS, INC. v. McMAHON
107 S.Ct. 2332, (1987)

---

Customers of a stock brokerage firm registered with the Securities and Exchange Commission (SEC) signed agreements providing for arbitration of any controversy relating to their accounts. Later they filed suit against the firm alleging violations of the securities laws and of the Racketeer Influenced and Corrupt Organizations Act (RICO). The brokerage firm petitioned to compel arbitration of the controversy. The District Court held that the securities law issues were arbitrable but that the RICO claim was not. The Court of Appeals held that neither was arbitrable.

O'CONNOR, J.:...This case presents two questions regarding the enforceability of predispute arbitration agreements between brokerage firms and their customers. The first is whether a claim brought under § 10(b) of the Securities Exchange Act of 1934 (Exchange Act), must be sent to arbitration in accordance with the terms of an arbitration agreement. The second is whether a claim brought under the Racketeer Influenced and Corrupt Organizations Act

(RICO), must be arbitrated in accordance with the terms of such an agreement.

The Federal Arbitration Act provides the starting point for answering the questions raised in this case. The Act was intended to reverse centuries of judicial hostility to arbitration agreements by placing arbitration agreements upon the same footing as other contracts. The Arbitration Act accomplishes this purpose by providing that arbitration agreements "shall be valid irrevocable, and enforceable, save upon such grounds as exist at law or in equity for the revocation of any contract." The Act also provides that a court must stay its proceedings if it is satisfied that an issue before it is arbitrable under the agreement, § 3; and it authorizes a federal district court to issue an order compelling arbitration if there has been a "failure, neglect, or refusal" to comply with the arbitration agreement, §4.

The Arbitration Act thus establishes a federal policy favoring arbitration, requiring that we rigorously enforce agreements to arbitrate. This duty to enforce arbitration agreements is not diminished when a party bound by an agreement raises a claim founded on statutory rights. As we observed in *Mitsubishi Motors Corp. v. Soler-Chrysler-Plymouth, Inc.,* "we are well past the time when judicial suspicion of the desirability of arbitration and of the competence of arbitral tribunals" should inhibit enforcement of the Act "in controversies based on statutes." Absent a well-founded claim that an arbitration agreement resulted from the sort of fraud or excessive economic power that "would provide grounds 'for the revocation of any contract,'" the Arbitration Act "provides no basis for disfavoring agreements to arbitrate statutory claims by skewing the otherwise hospitable inquiry into arbitrability."

The Arbitration Act, standing alone, therefore mandates enforcement of agreements to arbitrate statutory claims. Like any statutory directive, the Arbitration Act's mandate may be overridden by a contrary congressional command. The burden is on the party opposing arbitration, however, to show that Congress intended to preclude a waiver of judicial remedies for the statutory rights at issue.

If Congress did intend to limit or prohibit waiver of a judicial forum for a particular claim, such an intent "will be deducible from the statute's text or legislative history, or from an inherent conflict between arbitration and the statute's underlying purposes.

To defeat application of the Arbitration Act in this case, therefore, the McMahons must demonstrate that Congress intended to make an exception to the Arbitration Act for claims arising under RICO and the Exchange Act, an intention discernible from the text, history, or purposes of the statute....

[The Court then found that the Exchange Act of 1934 did not specifically address the question of the arbitrability of § 10(b) claims but that arbitration was a suitable means for enforcing rights under the Act. It distinguished earlier decisions and

held that—here the SEC has sufficient statutory authority to ensure that arbitration is adequate to vindicate Exchange Act rights—enforcement of the arbitration agreement does not effect a waiver of "compliance with any provision" of the Exchange Act.]

Unlike the Exchange Act, there is nothing in the text of the RICO statute that even arguably evinces congressional intent to exclude civil RICO claims from the dictates of the Arbitration Act. This silence in the text is matched by silence in the statute's legislative history....There is no hint in these legislative debates that Congress intended for RICO treble-damages claims to be excluded from the ambit of the Arbitration Act.

Because RICO's text and legislative history fail to reveal any intent to override the provisions of the Arbitration Act, the McMahons must argue that there is an irreconcilable conflict between arbitration and RICO's underlying purposes....The McMahons have argued that RICO claims are too complex to be subject to arbitration. We determined in *Mitsubishi,* however, that "potential complexity should not suffice to ward off arbitration." Antitrust matters are every bit as complex as RICO claims, but we found that the "adaptability and access to expertise" characteristic of arbitration rebutted the view "that an arbitral tribunal could not properly handle an antitrust matter."

Likewise, the McMahons contend that the "overlap" between RICO's civil and criminal provisions renders § 1964(c) claims nonarbitrable....*Mitsubishi* recognized that treble-damages suits for claims arising under §1 of the Sherman Act may be subject to arbitration, even though such conduct may also give rise to claims of criminal liability. We similarly find that the criminal provisions of RICO do not preclude arbitration of bona fide civil actions brought under § 1964(c).

The McMahons' final argument is that the public interest in the enforcement of

RICO precludes its submission to arbitration. *Mitsubishi* again is relevant to the question. In that case we thoroughly examined the legislative intent behind §4 of the Clayton Act in assaying whether the importance of the private treble-damages remedy in enforcing the antitrust laws precluded arbitration of §4 claims. We found that "[n]otwithstanding its important incidental policing function, the treble-damages cause of action...seeks primarily to enable an injured competitor to gain compensation for that injury." Emphasizing the priority of the compensatory function of §4 over its deterrent function, *Mitsubishi* concluded that "so long as the prospective litigant effectively may vindicate its statutory cause of action in the arbitral forum, the statute will continue to serve both its remedial and deterrent function."

The legislative history of §1964(c) reveals the same emphasis on the remedial role of the treble-damages provision....This focus on the remedial function...is reinforced by the recurrent references in the legislative debates to §4 of the Clayton Act as the model for the RICO treble-damages provision....

Not only does *Mitsubishi* support the arbitrability of RICO claims, but there is even more reason to suppose that arbitration will adequately serve the purposes of RICO than that it will adequately protect private enforcement of the antitrust laws. Antitrust violations generally have a widespread impact on national markets as a whole, and the antitrust treble-damages provision gives private parties an incentive to bring civil suits that serve to advance the na-

tional interest in a competitive economy. RICO's drafters likewise sought to provide vigorous incentives for plaintiffs to pursue RICO claims that would advance society's fight against organized crime. But in fact RICO actions are seldom asserted "against the archetypal, intimidating mobster." ("only 9% of all civil RICO cases have involved allegations of criminal activity normally associated with professional criminals.") The special incentives necessary to encourage civil enforcement actions against organized crime do not support nonarbitrability of run-of-the-mill civil RICO claims brought against legitimate enterprises. The private attorney general role for the typical RICO plaintiff is simply less plausible than it is for the typical antitrust plaintiff, and does not support a finding that there is an irreconcilable conflict between arbitration and enforcement of the RICO statute.

In sum, we find no basis for concluding that Congress intended to prevent enforcement of agreements to arbitrate RICO claims. The McMahons may effectively vindicate their RICO claim in an arbitral forum, and therefore there is no inherent conflict between arbitration and the purposes underlying § 1964(c). Moreover, nothing in RICO's text or legislative history otherwise demonstrates congressional intent to make an exception to the Arbitration Act for RICO claims. Accordingly, the McMahons, "having made the bargain to arbitrate," will be held to their bargain. Their RICO claim is arbitrable under the terms of the Arbitration Act. [*Reversed and remanded.*]

## 8.  Impact on State Laws

The federal policy favoring arbitration frequently conflicts with state laws favoring litigation as the means to resolve a dispute. Sometimes a state law specifically provides that designated matters are not to be submitted to arbitration. Are these state laws constitutional when applied to businesses engaged in interstate commerce? The Commerce Clause and the Supremacy Clause of the United States Constitution are often used to set aside such state laws that deny arbitration of certain disputes. The case which follows is typical of those addressing the validity of state laws seeking to prevent arbitration.

# SOUTHLAND CORP. v. KEATING
104 S.Ct. 852 (1984)

BURGER, C.J.:…We noted probable jurisdiction to consider whether the California Franchise Investment Law, which invalidates certain arbitration agreements covered by the Federal Arbitration Act, violates the Supremacy Clause.…

Appellant The Southland Corporation is the owner and franchisor of 7-Eleven convenience stores. Southland's standard franchise agreement provides each franchisee with a license to use certain registered trademarks, a lease or sublease of a convenience store owned or leased by Southland, inventory financing, and assistance in advertising and merchandising. The franchisees operate the stores, supply bookkeeping data, and pay Southland a fixed percentage of gross profits. The franchise agreement also contains the following provision requiring arbitration:

**Any controversy of claim arising out of or relating to this Agreement or the breach thereof shall be settled by arbitration in accordance with the Rules of the American Arbitration Association…and judgment upon any award rendered by the arbitrator may be entered in any court having jurisdiction thereof.**

Appellees are 7-Eleven franchisees. Between September 1975 and January 1977, several appellees filed individual actions against Southland in California Superior Court alleging, among other things, fraud, oral misrepresentation, breach of contract, breach of fiduciary duty, and violation of the disclosure requirements of the California Franchise Investment Law. Southland's answer…included the affirmative defense of failure to arbitrate.…

The California Court of Appeals… interpreted the arbitration clause to require arbitration of all claims asserted under the Franchise Investment Law, and construed the Franchise Investment Law not to invalidate such agreements to arbitrate. Alternatively, the court concluded that if the Franchise Investment Law rendered arbitration agreements involving commerce unenforceable, it would conflict with § 2 of the Federal Arbitration Act and therefore be invalid under the Supremacy Clause…The California Supreme Court interpreted the Franchise Investment Law to require judicial consideration of claims brought under that statute and concluded that the California statute did not contravene the federal Act.…

The California Franchise Investment Law provides: "Any condition, stipulation or provision purporting to bind any person acquiring any franchise to waive compliance with any provision of this law or any rule or order hereunder is void." The California

Supreme Court interpreted this statute to require judicial consideration of claims brought under the State statute and accordingly refused to enforce the parties' contract to arbitrate such claims. So interpreted, the California Franchise Investment Law directly conflicts with § 2 of the Federal Arbitration Act and violates the Supremacy Clause.

In enacting § 2 of the federal Act, Congress declared a national policy favoring arbitration and withdrew the power of the states to require a judicial forum for the resolution of claims which the contracting parties agreed to resolve by arbitration....

The Federal Arbitration Act rests on the authority of Congress to enact substantive rules under the Commerce Clause....The Arbitration Act creates a body of federal substantive law (which is)...applicable in state and federal courts....The problems Congress faced were...twofold: the old common law hostility toward arbitration, and the failure of state arbitration statutes to mandate enforcement of arbitration agreements. To confine the scope of the Act to arbitrations sought to be enforced in federal courts would frustrate what we believe Congress intended to be a broad enactment appropriate in scope to meet the large problems Congress was addressing....

We are unwilling to attribute to Congress the intent, in drawing on the comprehensive powers of the Commerce Clause, to create a right to enforce an arbitration contract and yet make the right dependent for its enforcement on the particular forum in which it is asserted. And since the overwhelming proportion of all civil litigation in this country is in the state courts, we cannot believe Congress intended to limit the Arbitration Act to disputes subject only to *federal* court jurisdiction. Such an interpretation would frustrate Congressional intent to place an arbitration agreement upon the same footing as other contracts, where it belongs.

In creating a substantive rule applicable in state as well as federal courts, Congress intended to foreclose state legislative attempts to undercut the enforceability of arbitration agreements. We hold that § 31512 of the California Franchise Investment Law violates the Supremacy Clause....[*Reversed.*]

---

Sometimes the state law does not directly attack the policy of arbitration but only conflicts with it. Note that the case which follows also arose in California and that the statute involved probably was not intended to conflict with the federal policy.

---

# PERRY v. THOMAS
107 S.Ct. 2520 (1987)

---

Thomas brought suit in the state court of California against his former employer alleging breach of his employment contract because of the employer's failure to pay commissions on securities sales. The employment contract contained a provision whereby Thomas had agreed to submit any dispute with his employer to arbitration.

Perry filed a petition to compel Thomas to submit the dispute to arbitration under the Federal Arbitration Act.

Thomas opposed arbitration on the ground that his suit was authorized by California Labor Code § 229, which provides that wage collection actions may be maintained without regard to the existence of any private agreement to arbitrate. The California courts refused to compel arbitration.

MARSHALL, J.... In this appeal we decide whether § 2 of the Federal Arbitration Act (Act), 9 U.S.C. § 1 et seq., which mandates enforcement of arbitration agreements, preempts § 229 of the California Labor Code, which provides that actions for the collection of wages may be maintained "without regard to the existence of any private agreement to arbitrate."

Section 2 is a congressional declaration of a liberal federal policy favoring arbitration agreements, notwithstanding any state substantive or procedural policies to the contrary. The effect of the section is to create a body of federal substantive law of arbitrability, applicable to any arbitration agreement within the coverage of the Act. Enacted pursuant to the Commerce Clause, U.S. Const. Art. I, § 8, cl. 3, this body of substantive law is enforceable in both state and federal courts.... In enacting § 2 of the federal Act, Congress declared a national policy favoring arbitration and withdrew the power of the states to require a judicial forum for the resolution of claims which the contracting parties agreed to resolve by arbitration. Congress intended to foreclose state legislative attempts to undercut the enforceability of arbitration agreements. Section 2, therefore, embodies a clear federal policy of requiring arbitration unless the agreement to arbitrate is not part of a contract evidencing interstate commerce or is revocable upon such grounds as exist at law or in equity for the revocation of any contract. We see nothing in the Act indicating that the broad principle of enforceability is subject to any additional limitations under state law....

The present appeal addresses the preemptive effect of the Federal Arbitration Act, a statute that embodies Congress's intent to provide for the enforcement of arbitration agreements within the full reach of the Commerce Clause. Its general applicability reflects that the preeminent concern of Congress in passing the Act was to enforce private agreements into which parties had entered. We have accordingly held that these agreements must be rigorously enforced. This clear federal policy places § 2 of the Act in unmistakable conflict with California's § 229 requirement that litigants be provided a judicial forum for resolving wage disputes. Therefore, under the Supremacy Clause, the state statute must give way.... [*Reversed and remanded.*]

## JUDICIAL REVIEW OF AWARDS

### 9. General Principles

Since the object of arbitration is to avoid the formalities, delay, and expense of litigation in court, judicial review of an arbitrator's award is quite restricted. The review is more limited than appellate review of a trial court's decision. The arbitrator's findings on questions of both law and fact are conclusive.

Arbitration clauses are liberally interpreted when the issue contested is the scope of the clause. If the scope of an arbitration clause is debatable or reasonably in doubt, the clause is construed in favor of arbitration.

The fact that the arbitrator made erroneous rulings during the hearing, or reached erroneous findings of fact from the evidence, is no ground for setting aside the award because the parties have agreed that he should be the judge of the facts. An erroneous view of the law no matter how egregious is binding because the parties have agreed to accept his view of the law. Error of law renders the award void only when it would require the parties to commit a crime or otherwise to violate a positive mandate of the law. Courts do not interfere with an award by examining the merits of the controversy, the sufficiency of the evidence supporting the award, or the reasoning supporting the decision. Were it otherwise, arbitration would fail of its chief purpose; instead of being a substitute for litigation, it would merely be the beginning of litigation. Broad judicial review on the merits would render arbitration wasteful and superfluous.

Courts of review are sometimes called upon to set aside an award when the decision is allegedly against public policy. The case which follows addresses the power of courts to set aside awards to uphold public policy.

---

# UNITED PAPERWORKERS INTERN. UNION v. MISCO, INC.
108 S.Ct. 364 (1987)

---

A collective-bargaining agreement authorized the submission to binding arbitration of any grievance that arose from the interpretation or application of the agreement's terms. It reserved to management (respondent) the right to establish and enforce rules regulating employee discharge and discipline. One of management's rules listed as a cause for discharge the possession or use of controlled substances on company property. Cooper, an employee who operated a hazardous machine, was apprehended by police in the backseat of someone else's car in the company parking lot with marijuana smoke in the air and a lighted marijuana cigarette in the front-seat ashtray.

The company discharged Cooper for violation of the disciplinary rule. He then filed a grievance which proceeded to arbitration on the issue of whether there was just cause for the discharge. The arbitrator upheld the grievance and ordered Cooper's reinstatement with back pay, finding that the cigarette incident was insufficient proof that Cooper was using or possessed marijuana on company property. The District Court vacated the arbitration award and the Court of Appeals affirmed, ruling that reinstatement would violate the public policy "against the operation of dangerous machinery by persons under the influence of drugs or alcohol." The court held that the cigarette incident and the finding of marijuana in Cooper's car established a violation of the disciplinary rule that gave respondent just cause for discharge.

WHITE, J....The issue for decision involves several aspects of when a federal court may refuse to enforce an arbitration award rendered under a collective-bargaining agreement....The Union asserts that an arbitral award may not be set aside on public policy grounds unless the award orders conduct that violates the positive law, which is not the case here....Respondent, on the other hand, defends the public policy decision of the Court of Appeals....

Collective-bargaining agreements commonly provide grievance procedures to settle disputes between union and employer with respect to the interpretation and application of the agreement and require binding arbitration for unsettled grievances. In such cases,...the courts play only a limited role when asked to review the decision of an arbitrator. The courts are not authorized to reconsider the merits of an award even though the parties may allege that the award rests on errors of fact or on misinterpretation of the contract. The refusal of courts to review the merits of an arbitration award is the proper approach to arbitration under collective bargaining agreements. The federal policy of settling labor disputes by arbitration would be undermined if courts had the final say on the merits of the awards. As long as the arbitrator's award draws its essence from the collective-bargaining agreement, and is not merely his own brand of industrial justice, the award is legitimate.

The function of the court is very limited when the parties have agreed to submit all questions of contract interpretation to the arbitrator. It is confined to ascertaining whether the party seeking arbitration is making a claim which on its face is governed by the contract. Whether the moving party is right or wrong is a question of contract interpretation for the arbitrator. In these circumstances the moving party should not be deprived of the arbitrator's judgment, when it was his judgment and all that it connotes that was bargained for.

The courts, therefore, have no business weighing the merits of the grievance, considering whether there is equity in a particular claim, or determining whether there is particular language in the written instrument which will support the claim.

The reasons for insulating arbitral decisions from judicial review are grounded in the federal statutes regulating labor-management relations. These statutes reflect a decided preference for private settlement of labor disputes without the intervention of government....

The courts have jurisdiction to enforce collective-bargaining contracts; but where the contract provides grievance and arbitration procedures, those procedures must first be exhausted and courts must order resort to the private settlement mechanisms without dealing with the merits of the dispute. Because the parties have contracted to have disputes settled by an arbitrator chosen by them rather than by a judge, it is the arbitrator's view of the facts and of the meaning of the contract that they have agreed to accept. Courts thus do not sit to hear claims of factual or legal error by an arbitrator as an appellate court does in reviewing decisions of lower courts. To resolve disputes about the application of a collective-bargaining agreement, an arbitrator must find facts and a court may not reject those findings simply because it disagrees with them. The same is true of the arbitrator's interpretation of the contract. The arbitrator may not ignore the plain language of the contract; but the parties having authorized the arbitrator to give meaning to the language of the agreement, a court should not reject an award on the ground that the arbitrator misread the contract. So, too, where it is contemplated that the arbitrator will determine remedies for contract violations that he finds, courts have no authority to disagree with his honest judgment in that respect. If the courts were free to intervene on these grounds, the speedy resolution of grievances by private mechanisms would be greatly undermined. Furthermore, it must be remembered that grievance and arbitration procedures are part and parcel of the ongoing process of collective bargaining. It is through these processes that the supplementary rules of the plant are established. As the Court has said, the arbitrator's award settling a dispute with respect to the interpretation or application of a labor agreement must draw its essence from the contract and cannot simply reflect the arbitrator's own notions of industrial justice. But as long as the arbitrator is even arguably construing or applying the contract and acting within the scope of his authority, that a court is convinced he committed serious error does not suffice to overturn his decision. Of course, decisions procured by the parties through fraud or through the arbitrator's dishonesty need not be enforced. But there is nothing of that sort involved in this case.

The Company's position, simply put, is that the arbitrator committed grievous error in finding that the evidence was insufficient to prove that Cooper had possessed or used marijuana on company property. But the Court of Appeals, although it took a distinctly jaundiced view of the arbitrator's decision in this regard, was not free to refuse enforcement because it considered Cooper's presence in the white Cutlass, in the circumstances, to be ample proof that Rule II.1 was violated. No dishonesty is alleged; only improvident, even silly, factfinding is claimed. This is hardly sufficient basis for disregarding what the agent appointed by the parties determined to be the historical facts.

The Court of Appeals held that the evidence of marijuana in Cooper's car required that the award be set aside because to reinstate a person who had brought drugs onto the property was contrary to the public policy "against the operation of dangerous machinery by persons under the influence of drugs or alcohol." We cannot affirm that judgment.

A court's refusal to enforce an arbitrator's award under a collective-bargaining agreement because it is contrary to public policy is a specific application of the more general doctrine, rooted in the common law, that a court may refuse to enforce contracts that violate law or public policy. That doctrine derives from the basic notion that no court will lend its aid to one who founds a cause of action upon an immoral or illegal act, and is further justified by the observation that the public's interests in confining the scope of private agreements to which it is not a party will go unrepresented unless the judiciary takes account of those interests when it considers whether to enforce such agreements. In the common law of contracts, this doctrine has served as the foundation for occasional exercises of judicial power to abrogate private agreements.

In *W.R. Grace*, we recognized that "a court may not enforce a collective-bargaining agreement that is contrary to public policy," and stated that "the question of public policy is ultimately one for resolution by the courts." We cautioned, however, that a court's refusal to enforce an arbitrator's *interpretation* of such contracts is limited to situations where the contract as interpreted would violate "some explicit public policy" that is "well defined and dominant, and is to be ascertained by reference to the laws and legal precedents and not from general considerations of supposed public interests.…"

Two points follow from our decision in *W.R. Grace*. First, a court may refuse to enforce a collective-bargaining agreement when the specific terms contained in that agreement violate public policy. Second, it is apparent that our decision in that case does not otherwise sanction a broad judicial power to set aside arbitration awards as against public policy. Although we discussed the effect of that award on two broad areas of public policy, our decision turned on our examination of whether the award created any explicit conflict with other "laws and legal precedents" rather than an assessment of "general considerations of supposed public interests." At the very least, an alleged public policy must be properly framed under the approach set out in *W.R. Grace,* and the violation of such a policy must be clearly shown if an award is not to be enforced.

As we see it, the formulation of public policy set out by the Court of Appeals did not comply with the statement that such a policy must be ascertained by reference to the laws and legal precedents and not from general considerations of supposed public interests. The Court of Appeals made no attempt to review existing laws and legal precedents in order to demonstrate that they establish a "well defined and dominant" policy against the operation of dangerous machinery while under the influence of drugs. Although certainly such a judgment is firmly rooted in common sense, we explicitly held in *W.R. Grace* that a formulation of public policy based only on "general considerations of supposed public interests" is not the sort that permits a court to set aside an arbitration award that was entered in accordance with a valid collective-bargaining agreement....[*Reversed.*]

Correction of an award is likewise restricted to any statutory grounds. The arbitrator, like the court of review, is limited by statute to correct an award. Many states allow an arbitrator to correct an "evident miscalculation of figures." There are two elements to satisfy the condition for correction: there must be a miscalculation, and the miscalculation must be "evident."

### 10. Review Under Federal Law

Judicial review of an award is limited to the issues set forth in the applicable statute and to the scope of the submission. If the arbitration is conducted pursuant to state statute, that statute must be consulted to determine what, if any, grounds are available to challenge an award in court. In cases which are subject to the Federal Arbitration Act because they involve interstate commerce, its provisions control.

Section 10 of the Federal Arbitration Act provides that an arbitration award may be vacated on four grounds: (a) Where the award was procured by corruption, fraud, or other undue means; (b) Where there was evident partiality or corruption in the arbitrators, or either of them; (c) Where the arbitrators were guilty of misconduct in refusing to postpone the hearing, upon sufficient cause shown, or in refusing to hear evidence pertinent and material to the controversy; or of any other misbehavior by which the rights of any party have been prejudiced; and (d) Where the arbitrators exceeded their powers, or so imperfectly executed them that a mutual, final, and definite award upon the subject matter submitted was not made.

These grounds must be construed in light of the rule that the Court's function in vacating, or confirming, an arbitration award is severely limited. As a general rule, the decision of the arbitration board on all questions of law and fact is conclusive. Courts confirm awards unless grounds are established to support vacating or modifying them. As set forth in subsection (a) above, the Federal Arbitration provides that an award can be vacated if it can be proved that it was procured by "corruption, fraud, or other undue means." "Undue means" is defined as something akin to fraud and corruption. "Undue means" goes beyond the merely inappropriate or inadequate nature of the evidence and refers to some aspect of the arbitrator's decision or decision-making process obtained in some manner that was unfair and beyond the normal process contemplated by the arbitration act. The courts tend to interpret "undue means" in conjunction with terms "corruption" and "fraud" which precede it, and thus, "undue means" requires some type of bad faith in the procurement of the award.

Subsection (c) above covers arbitral misconduct. The concept of arbitral "misconduct" does not lend itself to a precise definition. Among the actions that have been found to constitute such misconduct on the part of an arbitrator as would warrant vacating an arbitration award are the following: participation in ex parte communications with a party or a witness, without the knowledge or consent of the other party; ex parte receipt of evidence as to a material fact, without notice to a party; holding hearings or conducting deliberations in the absence of a member of an arbitration panel, or rendering an award without consulting a panel member; undertaking an independent investigation into a material matter after the close of hearings and without notice to the parties; and accepting gifts or other hospitality from a party during the proceedings.

An award may likewise be set aside on the basis of procedural error by an arbitration panel if, for instance, the panel arbitrarily denies a reasonable request for postponement of a hearing, or commits an egregious evidentiary error, such as refusing to hear material evidence or precluding a party's efforts to develop a full record.

Finally, subsection (d) involving the question of whether the arbitrators exceeded their power relates to the arbitrability of the underlying dispute. An arbitrator exceeds his powers and authority when he attempts to resolve an issue that is not arbitrable because it is outside the scope of the arbitration agreement. Conversely, if the issues presented to the arbitrators are within the scope of the arbitration agreement, subsection (d) does not require the court to "review the merits of every construction of the contract."

### 11. Judicial Review—Statutory Arbitration

Ordinarily arbitration is the result of a contract. The parties agree to arbitrate certain matters, and without a statute, they cannot be required to arbitrate other matters. The scope of any judicial review of arbitration awards has previously been discussed and the very limited role of courts in reviewing such awards emphasized. Parties to a contract are bound by the award even if it is unwise and wrong on the facts or law. Such is not the case with statutorily mandated or compulsory arbitration. Voluntary arbitration and compulsory arbitration are fundamentally different because a party may consent to almost any restriction upon or deprivation of a right, but a similar restriction or deprivation, if compelled by government, must accord with procedural and substantive due process of law. Therefore, a higher level of judicial review of an arbitration award is warranted where the arbitration is statutorily mandated.

Laws providing for compulsory arbitration are subject to numerous constitutional challenges. Many courts have generally held that compulsory arbitration statutes that effectively close the courts to the litigants by compelling them to resort to arbitrators for a final and binding determination are void as against public policy and are unconstitutional in that (1) they deprive one of his property and liberty of contract without due process of the law; (2) they violate the litigant's seventh amendment right to a jury trial and/or the state's constitutional access to courts provisions; and (3) they result in the unconstitutional delegation of legislative or judicial power in violation of state constitutional separation of powers provisions.

Compulsory arbitration may be constitutional, however, if fair procedures are provided by the legislature and ultimate judicial review is available. Courts throughout the United States have uniformly upheld compulsory arbitration statutory schemes as against the constitutional challenges previously mentioned where **de novo judicial review** of the arbitrator's award is available to either party. De novo review means that the court tries the issues anew or for a second time. See section 6 for an explanation of court-annexed mandatory arbitration.

In mandatory proceedings a record of proceedings is required. Also, findings of fact and conclusions of law are essential if there is to be enough judicial review to satisfy due process. Judicial review of compulsory arbitration requires a de novo review of the interpretation and application of the law by the arbitrators.

## 12. Policy Trends and Ethical Considerations

An important element of any process of resolving disputes is its fairness to the parties involved. The legitimacy and usefulness of any such process will greatly depend on the equitable treatment of the parties and the impartiality of any decisions or recommendations by judge, jury, arbitrator, mediator, or others.

A growing area for increased arbitration and mediation is consumer complaints. Most consumer complaints do not involve enough money to warrant litigation other than through small-claims courts or class action suits. Except for small-claims litigation, consumer lawsuits against a company tend to be very costly, not only in money, but in goodwill for the corporation. As a result, many corporations desire to settle such complaints quickly and easily through some kind of arbitration or mediation process.

To build consumer confidence and goodwill, many corporations have established arbitration or mediation procedures to handle customer complaints. A Better Business Bureau frequently serves as arbitrator or mediator in such cases. In this case, the submission is made to an expert with a general reputation for fairness to both sides. The disadvantage to the consumer in using the Better Business Bureau to arbitrate is that the decision, as with traditional commercial arbitration, is binding on both parties and cannot normally be appealed to a court. Other third-party arbitration services often reach decisions which are binding on the manufacturer or dealer only if the consumer is satisfied with the decision and elects to accept it. If dissatisfied, the consumer is free to sue in court. This is also the case with arbitration panels established by manufacturers or trade associations.

For example, defective automobiles have been the focus of innumerable consumer complaints. Several U.S. manufacturers have recently experimented with panels to handle consumer complaints on a voluntary basis. Often called AUTOCAPs (Automobile Consumer Action Programs), the panels attempt to resolve disputes involving both sales and service. They are composed of industry members and a majority of consumer representatives. A panel's decision in any dispute, while binding on the dealer or manufacturer if the consumer accepts it, may be rejected by the consumer. Although the companies say the panels have worked well, consumer groups have complained of delays, difficult access, and general dissatisfaction. At least one company has been criticized by a consumer representative for not heeding the advice of consumer members in creating a program truly fair to consumers. An industry-sponsored program does run a greater risk of being partial to the industry, especially if the industry chooses the consumer representatives. The ethical dangers and practical disadvantages of any voluntary process stacked against the consumer would ultimately undermine it, throwing the consumer back to more traditional litigation or arbitration.

Connecticut and California have passed automobile "lemon laws" requiring a consumer to use any mediation or nonbinding arbitration procedures established by auto manufacturers to try to settle complaints before going to court to seek a refund or replacement. If such laws become common throughout the country, the impartiality and fairness of such dispute resolution procedures would be crucial, as the consumer would be required to use them before seeking certain remedies in court. The California law, for example, ensures that these informal dispute settlement procedures will be impartial. The law requires that the procedures meet the Federal Trade Commission's minimum fairness standards, including the consumer's right to make an informal settlement binding only if he or she is satisfied.

Some critics favor using governmental agencies for mediation rather than industry-run or industry-sponsored groups. Local and state consumer protection offices and special agencies such as state motor vehicle bureaus have become more involved in mediation but normally lack the power to force a settlement or to arbitrate. Private or industry-supported mediation and arbitration can be effective if precautions are taken to ensure objectivity and fair treatment.

## REVIEW QUESTIONS

**1**   There was a dispute between an insurance company and an insured party concerning value on the loss of a diamond ring. The insurance policy required arbitration of disputes. Each party selected an arbitrator and the two selected a third. The third, without consulting the other two or receiving any testimony, fixed the value of the loss. Will the court set aside this award? Why or why not?

**2**   A dispute arose between partners. The partnership agreement provided that if the parties were unable to agree on any matter, it would be submitted to arbitration. One partner filed suit asking a court to appoint a receiver for the business. The other insisted on arbitration. How will the dispute be resolved? Why?

**3**   While conducting a hearing, an arbitrator allowed hearsay evidence and allowed opinions to be given as to the cause of an injury by laypersons. May the losing party have the award set aside on these grounds? Why or why not?

**4**   Give four reasons why public policy today prefers arbitration over litigation for resolving disputes.

**5**   Plaintiffs and defendant were parties to a lease which contained a provision requiring arbitration of all disputes. A dispute arose, and the matter was submitted to arbitration before three arbitrators. By a 2 to 1

vote, the arbitrators found for the plaintiffs. In a suit brought to enforce the decision, the defendant contended that the award was unlawful because it was not unanimous. Is he correct? Why or why not?

**6**   Two parties had a dispute over the amount of money due as "minimum royalties" under a mineral lease. They submitted the dispute to arbitration and the arbitrators awarded the lessor $37,214.67. The Court held that there was no substantial evidence in the record to support an award of less than the minimum royalty of $75,000 and directed entry of a judgment for that amount. Was it proper for the court to increase the award? Why or why not?

**7**   Condominium owners brought suit against a contractor for breach and negligent performance of a contract to construct condominium buildings. The contractor made a demand that the claims be submitted to arbitration pursuant to the sales contract which contained an arbitration clause. He moved for stay of the court proceedings and an order compelling arbitration. The judge refused and said that after he had decided the case, the reviewing courts could decide if he was correct. Should the contractor be allowed to appeal this order, or should the trial be held before any appeal? Explain.

**8**   An employee was discharged for "gross negligence" in the performance of his duties. He filed a grievance and demanded arbitration as provided in the collective-bargaining agreement with his union. At the hearing the arbitrator limited the testimony to evidence directly related to one incident. The employee wanted to introduce evidence of other events which tended to show a pattern of discrimination against the employee but this evidence was not admitted. The arbitrator upheld the discharge. Will a court reverse this decision? Why or why not?

**9**   A state statute required that claims for wrongful discharge by state-employed college professors be submitted to arbitration. It also prohibited suits against any state university for breach of contract and made arbitration the exclusive remedy. Is the state law constitutional? Why or why not?

**10**   Consider the same facts as in question 9. What could be done, if anything, to make the law constitutional while still favoring arbitration of such disputes?

**11**   Byrd invested $164,000 with a stock brokerage firm. The parties had a written agreement to arbitrate any disputes that might arise out of the account. When the value of the account declined to $50,000 Byrd filed suit in federal court, alleging violations of the Securities Exchange Act of 1934 and of various state-law provisions. The firm filed a motion to compel arbitration of the claims under the parties' agreement. What was the result? Why?

**12**   A publicly held corporation sued its former president for waste of corporate assets. He filed a demand for arbitration pursuant to his employment agreement seeking back salary. There were several issues common to both matters and the corporation sought to delay the arbitration proceeding until the lawsuit was completed. Is the lawsuit a valid ground for denying arbitration? Why or why not?

**13**   A bank fired a head teller for cashing a forged check of $3,500. A union filed a grievance and demanded arbitration. Rather than order the employee rehired or affirm the discharge, the arbitration ordered the teller rehired upon reimbursement of the bank for its loss. The collective bargaining agreement was silent on the issue of reimbursement. Is this a proper award? Explain.

# *Part Two*
# CONSTITUTIONAL AND ADMINISTRATIVE LAW

# Chapter

# *6*

# The Constitution and Business

## CHAPTER PREVIEW

The Constitution of the United States provides the foundation for the legal system. This chapter covers some of the provisions of the original Constitution which are of special significance to the business community. The next chapter is devoted to amendments to the Constitution and their role in the legal environment of business.

This chapter gives special attention to the commerce clause. As interpreted, this clause grants certain powers to the federal government and also limits the regulatory powers of state and local governments. Since taxation is a form of regulation, the commerce clause has a significant impact on state and local taxation of business.

In addition to the commerce clause, this chapter introduces the supremacy clause, the import-export clause, the contract clause, and the privileges and immunities clause. The complete United States Constitution is given in Appendix 1 on page 813. Refer to it as this chapter and the next one are studied.

The following terms are important in this chapter: apportionment, commerce clause, contract clause, federalism, full faith and credit clause, import-export clause, nexus, police power, preemption, privileges and immunities clause, separation of powers, and supremacy clause.

## 1. Organization

The Constitution, as originally enacted, contained seven articles and a preamble. The Preamble sets forth the purposes of the Constitution, which include such general goals as the establishment of justice and the promotion of general welfare.

Article I establishes the legislative branch of government and defines its functions, powers, method of conducting business, and limitations on its powers, as well as the manner of election and removal of its members. Section 8 of Article I grants Congress numerous powers, including the power to tax and the power to regulate commerce. These powers will be discussed later in this chapter. Some of the other enumerated powers relate to external affairs and the power to wage war. Of special importance to business is the power to enact uniform laws on the subject of bankruptcy and laws that promote the progress of science and useful arts, by securing for limited times to authors and inventors the exclusive right to their writings and discoveries.

Article II vests the executive power in the President. It defines his term of office, qualifications for office, and manner of election. This latter provision, together with the Twelfth Amendment, which concerns the electoral college, is currently the subject of much criticism, with many people advocating election by popular vote. Article II also makes the President the Commander in Chief of the Armed Forces and authorizes him to enter into treaties with the advice and consent of the Senate. It is this article that requires the annual State of the Union message by the President.

Article III creates the judicial branch of government. It defines the original jurisdiction of the Supreme Court and authorizes Congress to create other federal court systems as discussed in Chapter 3. This provision underlies recent attempts to deny courts the power to decide cases involving abortions, school prayer, and busing to achieve integration. Article III also defines treason.

Article IV contains several provisions dealing with relationships between the states. It is often referred to as "the states' relation article," and is discussed in section 8 of this chapter.

Article V sets forth methods for amending the Constitution. To date, there have been twenty-six amendments approved by one of the authorized methods. The proposed equal rights for women amendment was adopted by Congress and ratified by thirty-five states before the time for ratification expired. A proposed amendment on abortion is pending.

Article VI contains the supremacy clause, which means that federal laws and treaties are the supreme law of the land. The supremacy clause frequently comes into play when states attempt to regulate a business activity that the federal government also regulates. It will be discussed further in section 3 of this chapter.

## 2.   Separation of Powers

One of the most important of our constitutional law concepts is the doctrine of **separation of powers.** It arose out of the strong fear the founders of this country had that too much power might be concentrated in one branch of government. This doctrine has both horizontal and vertical aspects. First, the horizontal aspect describes the theory that each of three branches of government (executive, legislative, and judicial) has a separate function to perform. Each is not to perform the functions of the others because no one person may exercise the powers of more than one branch at the same time. As the Supreme Court has stated in several cases:

> Each branch shall by the law of its creation be limited to the exercise of the powers appropriate to its own department and no other...As a general rule...the powers confided by the Constitution to one of these departments cannot be exercised by another.

One facet of this functional aspect of separation of powers is that each branch has the capacity or power to limit the other branches in the performance of their respective functions. For example, courts exercising the power of judicial review may limit the actions of the executive and the legislative branches of government. The legislative branch may determine the jurisdiction of federal courts and may limit the powers of the executive. The executive appoints the judiciary with the advice and consent of the Senate. Therefore, although each branch of government has a separate function to perform, these branches are closely interrelated and each has some control over the others. No branch of government is free to act with total independence of the others. Although the separation of powers concept admits that each branch has some control and influence over the others, it recognizes that each branch of government is to be free from the *coercive* influence of the others. Congress should not interfere with the President as he carries out his duty to "take care that the Laws be faithfully executed." The converse is also true. The President should not interfere with Congress as it performs its constitutional responsibilities.

The vertical aspect of separation of powers is **federalism** or dual federalism. This aspect recognizes that we have two levels of government—a federal level and a state and local level. Each has a separate and distinct role to play. The federal government must recognize that it was created by the states and that states have some sovereignty. The Tenth Amendment reserves some powers to the states and to the people. Congress may not impair the ability of state government to function in the federal system. Likewise, state government may not curtail in any substantial manner the exercise of powers granted by states to the federal government.

Thus, the doctrine of separation of powers has both vertical and horizontal aspects.

Former Justice John M. Harlan, in discussing the reasons for our government of divided powers, concluded that in such a government lay the best promise for realizing a free society. In explaining the doctrine of separation of powers he observed:

> The matter has a double aspect: *first*, the division of governmental authority between the states and the central government; *second*, the distribution of power within the federal establishment itself. The former, doubtless born not so much of political principle as of the necessity for achieving a more perfect union than had proved possible under the Articles of Confederation, was solved by making the authority of the Federal Government supreme within the sphere of powers expressly or impliedly delegated to it and reserving to the states all other powers—a reservation which subsequently found express protection in the Bill of Rights through the provisions of the Tenth Amendment. The second aspect of the governmental structure was solved, purely as a matter of political theory, by distributing the totality of federal power among the legislative, executive and judicial branches of the government, each having defined functions. Thus eventuated the two great constitutional doctrines of federalism—often inaccurately referred to as the doctrine of states' rights—and separation of powers.

### 3.  The Supremacy Clause

Closely related to the doctrine of separation of powers is the **supremacy clause.** This clause makes the federal law supreme over a state law. The supremacy clause invalidates all state laws that conflict or interfere with an act of Congress. This specific clause guarantees federal supremacy even though the states created the federal government. When courts are called upon to decide if a state law is invalid under the supremacy clause because it conflicts with a federal law, they must construe or interpret the two laws to see if they are in conflict. A conflict exists if the state statute would prevent or interfere with the accomplishment and execution of the full purposes and objectives of Congress. It is immaterial that a state did not intend to frustrate the federal law if the state law in fact does so.

Sometimes a federal law is said to **preempt** an area of law. If a federal law preempts a subject, then any state law is unconstitutional under the supremacy clause. The conflict is apparent, and the evidence of it is conclusive. This applies not only to federal statutes but also to the rules and regulations of federal administrative agencies, as the case which follows illustrates.

# FIDELITY FEDERAL SAVINGS AND LOAN ASSOCIATION v. REGINALD D. DE LA CUESTA
102 S.Ct. 3014 (1982)

The Federal Home Loan Bank Board (Board) regulates federal savings and loan associations. In 1976, the Board became concerned about the increasing controversy over "due-on-sale" clauses in mortgages. A due-on-sale clause permits a lender to declare the entire balance of a loan immediately due and payable if the property securing the loan is sold or otherwise transferred. The controversy had arisen because the courts of several states including California had declared such clauses to be illegal as against public policy unless a transfer had impaired the security for a loan. If the reason for acceleration was simply to increase the rate of interest, the clause was illegal.

To end the controversy, the Board issued a regulation which provided:

**[A federal savings and loan] association continues to have the power to include, as a matter of contract between it and the borrower, a provision in its loan instrument whereby the association may, at its option, declare immediately due and payable sums secured by the association's security instrument if all or any part of the real property securing the loan is sold or transferred by the borrower without the association's prior written consent. Except as [otherwise] provided in...this section..., exercise by the association of such option (hereafter called a due-on-sale clause) shall be exclusively governed by the terms of the loan contract, and all rights and remedies of the association and borrower shall be fixed and governed by that contract.**

In the preamble of the due-on-sale regulation, the Board explained its intent that the due-on-sale practices of federal savings and loans be governed "exclusively by Federal law." The Board emphasized that "[f]ederal associations shall not be bound by or subject to any conflicting State law which imposes different...due-on-sale requirements."

A federal savings and loan association in California sought to enforce its due-on-sale clause. The mortgagor contended that under California law the clause was unenforceable. The trial court upheld the clause and the California Court of Appeals reversed, finding no intent to supersede state law.

BLACKMUN, J.:...At issue in this case is the pre-emptive effect of a regulation, issued by the Federal Home Loan Bank Board (Board), permitting federal savings and loan associations to use "due-on-sale" clauses in their mortgage contracts. Appellees dispute both the Board's intent and its statutory authority to displace restrictions imposed by the California Supreme Court on the exercise of these clauses.

The pre-emption doctrine, which has its roots in the Supremacy Clause, requires us to examine congressional intent. Preemption may be either express or implied, and "is compelled whether Congress' command is explicitly stated in the statute's language or implicitly contained in its structure and purpose." Absent explicit pre-emptive language, Congress' intent to supersede state law altogether may be inferred because "[t]he scheme of federal regulation may be so pervasive as to make reasonable the inference that Congress left no room for the States to supplement it," because "the Act of Congress may touch a field in which the federal interest is so dominant that the federal system will be assumed to preclude enforcement of state laws on the same subject," or because "the object sought to be obtained by federal law and the character of obligations imposed by it may reveal the same purpose."

Even where Congress has not completely displaced state regulation in a specific area, state law is nullified to the extent that it actually conflicts with federal law. Such a conflict arises when "compliance with both federal and state regulations is a physical impossibility," or when state law "stands as an obstacle to the accomplishment and execution of the full purposes and objectives of Congress." These principles are not inapplicable here simply because real property law is a matter of special concern to the States: "The relative importance to the State of its own law is not material when there is a conflict with a valid federal law, for the Framers of our Constitution provided that the federal law must prevail."

Federal regulations have no less preemptive effect than federal statutes. Where Congress has directed an administrator to exercise his discretion, his judgments are subject to judicial review only to determine whether he has exceeded his statutory authority or acted arbitrarily. When the administrator promulgates regulations intended to preempt state law, the court's inquiry is similarly limited:

**If [h]is choice represents a reasonable accommodation of conflicting policies that were committed to the agency's care by the statute, we should not disturb it unless it appears from the statute or its legislative history that the accommodation is not one that Congress would have sanctioned....**

A pre-emptive regulation's force does not depend on express congressional authorization to displace state law; moreover, whether the administrator failed to exercise an option to promulgate regulations which did not disturb state law is not dispositive. Thus, the Court of Appeal's narrow focus on Congress' intent to supersede state law was misdirected. Rather, the questions upon which resolution of this case rests are whether the Board meant to pre-empt California's due-on-sale law, and, if so, whether that action is within the scope of the Board's delegated authority....

(The court then found a clear intent to preempt state law on the part of the Board. Such clauses were declared to be legal if a Federal Savings & Loan Association wanted to use them. The preamble made it clear that such clauses were to be governed *exclusively* by Federal law without regard to any limitations imposed by state law.)

The question remains whether the Board acted within its statutory authority in issuing the pre-emptive due-on-sale regulation. The language and history of the Home Owner's Loan Act convince us that Congress delegated to the Board ample authority to regulate the lending practices of federal savings and loans so as to further the Act's purposes, and that (this regulation) is consistent with those purposes. Accordingly, we hold that the Board's due-on-sale regulation bars application of the (state law) to federal savings and loan associations. The judgment of the Court of Appeals is reversed. [*It is so ordered.*]

Thus, the first question in preemption cases is whether Congress intended to displace state law. Congress sometimes specifically provides for preemption. If it does not do so, a state statute is preempted only where compliance with both the federal law and the state law is a physical impossibility or where the state law stands as an obstacle to the accomplishment and execution of the full purposes and objectives of Congress. Where there is no actual conflict between a federal law and a state law, there must be provable congressional intent to preempt. In evaluating the impact of a state law, courts usually examine the purposes of both laws. If the objectives are virtually identical, then the courts attempt to reconcile the laws and enforce both. If the purposes are in conflict, chances are that the state law cannot be enforced and the court will find an intent to preempt. Table 6-1 lists several examples of cases in which the preemption issue has been litigated in recent years.

Many of the cases involving preemption and the supremacy clause involve conflicts that are not readily apparent. Arizona had a statute which provided for the suspension of licenses of drivers who could not satisfy judgments arising out of auto accidents, even if the driver was bankrupt. The statute was unconstitutional since it was in conflict with the federal law on bankruptcy. The purpose of the Bankruptcy Act is to give debtors new opportunity unhampered by the pressure and discouragement of pre-existing debt. The challenged state statute hampers the accomplishment and execution of the full purposes and objectives of the Bankruptcy Act enacted by Congress.

### 4.   External Affairs

The President has the power to make treaties, with the advice and consent of the Senate, as is stated in Article II, Section 2 of the Constitution. This power has grown in its importance to the economic life and defense of the nation, as the United States has become a leader in world affairs.

The treaties of most countries affect only their external relations with other countries. The United States is unique in that its treaties are part of the "supreme Law of the Land," and thus have the internal force of the Constitution and laws enacted by Congress. Article VI of the Constitution provides in part: "This Constitution, and the Laws of the United States which shall be made in Pursuance thereof; and all Treaties made, or which shall be made, under the Authority of the United States, shall be the supreme Law of the Land; and the Judges in every State shall be bound thereby, any Thing in the Constitution or Laws of any State to the Contrary notwithstanding." Note that the language employed makes the laws enacted by Congress binding only if made within the limitations of the Constitution. It apparently provides no such restriction on the effect of treaties made "under the Authority of the United States." Therefore, business is subject to

**TABLE 6-1**   Examples of State Laws Challenged as Preempted by Federal Law

| State or Local Law | Federal Law | Preemption Yes | Preemption No |
|---|---|:---:|:---:|
| 1 A state law conditions the construction of nuclear power plants on the existence of adequate storage facilities and the means of disposal. | Atomic Energy Act | | X |
| 2 A city conditions renewal of taxicab franchise on settlement of a labor dispute. | National Labor Relations Act | X | |
| 3 A state statute provides that a employee is ineligible for unemployment compensation if employee is provided "financing," by means other than payment of regular union dues, for strike that has caused his unemployment. (Financing of strike by national union prevents unemployment compensation.) | National Labor Relations Act | | X |
| 4 A state statute permits indirect purchasers to collect damages for overcharges resulting from price-fixing conspiracies. | Sherman Antitrust Act | X | |
| 5 A state law authorizes a tort claim by workers that a union has breached its duty to ensure a safe workplace. | Labor-Management Relations Act (Landrum-Griffin) | X | |
| 6 A state statute requires employers to allow up to four months' unpaid pregnancy leave and reinstatement. | Pregnancy Discrimination Act | | X |
| 7 A state imposes permit requirements on mining operations located on federal forest lands. | Forest Service Statutes and Regulations | | X |
| 8 A state law prohibits repeat violators of labor laws from doing business with the state. | National Labor Relations Act | X | |
| 9 A state statute attempts to control share acquisitions in state companies. The statute withholds voting rights from an acquiror of a controlling share of an Indiana corporation until a majority of the company's pre-existing, disinterested shareholders approves the acquisition. | Williams Act (governs hostile corporate stock tender-offers) | | X |
| 10 A Vermont nuisance law purports to cover out-of-state sources of water pollution. | Clean Water Act | X | |
| 11 State criminal prosecution for aggravated battery is filed against corporate officials because of unsafe workplace conditions. | Occupational Safety and Health Act | X | |

the provisions of all treaties entered into by the President which are ratified by the Senate. They are the supreme Law of the Land.

### 5.   The Contract Clause

Section 10 of Article I of the United States Constitution says in part that no state shall pass any law impairing the obligation of contracts. This provision does not apply to the federal government, which does in fact frequently enact laws and adopt regulations that affect existing contracts. For example, the Department of Agriculture from time to time embargoes grain sales to foreign countries, usually as a result of problems in foreign affairs.

The limitation on state action impairing contracts has not been given a literal application. As a result of judicial interpretation, some state laws which affect existing contracts have been approved, especially when the law is passed to deal with a specific emergency situation. On the other hand, this constitutional provision does generally limit alternatives available to state government and prevents the enactment of legislation that changes vested contract rights. The case that follows, while declaring a state statute unconstitutional for violating the contract clause, does indicate those areas in which a literal application will not result.

---

## ALLIED STRUCTURAL STEEL CO. v. SPANNAUS

98 S.Ct. 2716 (1978)

Plaintiff, an Illinois corporation, maintained an office in Minnesota with thirty employees. It had a pension plan, adopted in 1963 and qualified under Section 401 of the Internal Revenue Code, under which employees were entitled to retire and receive a pension at age 65 regardless of length of service. An employee's pension right became vested if he or she satisfied certain conditions as to length of service and age. Plaintiff, the sole contributor to the pension trust fund, each year made contributions to the fund based on actuarial predictions of eventual payout needs. The plan neither required contributions nor imposed any sanction on it for failure to make adequate contributions. Plaintiff retained not only a right to amend the plan but also to terminate it any time and for any reason.

In 1974, Minnesota enacted the Private Pension Benefits Protection Act (Act), under which a private employer of 100 employees or more (at least one of whom was a Minnesota resident) who provided pension benefits under a plan meeting the qualifications of Section 401 of the Internal Revenue Code, was subject to a "pension funding charge" if he terminated the plan or closed a Minnesota office. The charge was assessed if the pension funds were insufficient to cover full pensions for all employees who had worked at least 20 years, and if periods of employment prior to the effective date of the Act were to be included in the 20-year employment criterion. Shortly thereafter, in a move planned before passage of the Act, plaintiff closed its Minnesota office, and several of its employees, who were then discharged, had no vested pension rights even though they had worked for 20 years or more, thus qualifying as pension obligees under the Act. Subsequently, the State sought to collect a pension funding charge of $185,000.

Plaintiff then brought suit in Federal District Court for injunction and declaratory relief, claiming that the Act unconstitutionally impaired its contractual obligations to its employees under its pension plan. The lower court upheld the state law and the plaintiff appealed.

STEWART, J.:...The issue in this case is whether the application of Minnesota's Private Pension Benefits Protection Act to the appellant violates the Contract Clause of the United States Constitution....

There can be no question of the impact of the Minnesota Private Pension Benefits Protection Act upon the company's contractual relationships with its employees. The Act substantially altered those relationships by superimposing pension obligations upon the company conspicuously beyond those that it had voluntarily agreed to undertake. But it does not inexorably follow that the Act, as applied to the company, violates the Contract Clause of the Constitution.

The language of the Contract Clause appears unambiguously absolute: "No state shall...pass any...Law impairing the Obligation of Contracts." The Clause is not, however, the draconian provision that its words might seem to imply. As the Court has recognized, "literalism in the construction of the contract clause...would make it destructive of the public interest by depriving the State of its prerogative of self-protection."...

First of all, it is to be accepted as a commonplace that the Contract Clause does not operate to obliterate the police power of the states....

If the Contract Clause is to retain any meaning at all, however, it must be understood to impose some limits upon the power of a State to abridge existing contractual relationships, even in the exercise of its otherwise legitimate police power. The existence and nature of those limits were clearly indicated in a series of cases in this Court arising from the efforts of the States to deal with the unprecedented emergencies brought on by the severe economic depression of the early 1930's.

In *Home Building & Loan Assn. v. Blaisdell*, 290 U.S. 398, the Court upheld against a Contract Clause attack a mortgage moratorium law that Minnesota had enacted to provide relief for homeowners threatened with foreclosure. Although the legislation conflicted directly with lenders' contractual foreclosure rights, the Court there acknowledged that, despite the Contract Clause, the States retain residual authority to enact laws "to safeguard the vital interests of (their) people." In upholding the state mortgage moratorium law, the Court found five factors significant. First, the state legislature had declared in the Act itself that an emergency need for the protection of homeowners existed. Second, the state law was enacted to protect a basic societal interest, not a favored group. Third, the relief was appropriately tailored to the emergency that it was designed to meet. Fourth, the imposed conditions were reasonable. And, finally, the legislation was limited to the duration of the emergency.

The *Blaisdell* opinion thus clearly implied that if the Minnesota moratorium legislation had not possessed the characteristics attributed to it by the Court, it would have been invalid under the Contract Clause of the Constitution....

In applying these principles to the present case, the first inquiry must be whether the state law has, in fact, operated as a substantial impairment of a contractual relationship. The severity of the impairment measures the height of the hurdle the state legislation must clear. Minimal alteration of contractual obligations may end the inquiry at its first stage. Severe impairment, on the other hand, will push the inquiry to a careful examination of the nature and purpose of the state legislation.

The severity of an impairment of contractual obligations can be measured by the factors that reflect the high value the Framers placed on the protection of private contracts. Contracts enable individuals to order their personal and business affairs according to their particular needs and interests. Once arranged, those rights and obligations are binding under the law, and the parties are entitled to rely on them.

[The court then reviewed the effect of the state law on the pension plan.] Thus, the statute in question here nullifies express terms of the company's contractual obligations and imposes a completely unexpected liability in potentially disabling amounts.... Yet there is no showing in the record before us that this severe disruption of contractual expectations was necessary to meet an important general social problem....This law can hardly be characterized, as one enacted to protect a broad societal interest rather than a narrow class.

Moreover, in at least one other important respect the Act does not resemble the mortgage moratorium legislation whose constitutionality was upheld in the *Blaisdell* case. This legislation, imposing a sudden totally unanticipated, and substantial retroactive obligation upon the company to its employees, was not enacted to deal with a situation remotely approaching the broad and desperate emergency economic conditions of the early 1930's—conditions of which the Court in *Blaisdell* took judicial notice.

Entering a field it had never before sought to regulate, the Minnesota Legislature grossly distorted the company's existing contractual relationships with its employees by superimposing retroactive obligations upon the company substantially beyond the terms of its employment contracts. And that burden was imposed upon the company only because it closed its office in the State.

This Minnesota law simply does not possess the attributes of those state laws that in the past have survived challenge under the Contract Clause of the Constitution. The law was not even purportedly enacted to deal with a broad, generalized economic or social problem. It did not operate in an area already subject to state regulation at the time the company's contractual obligations were originally undertaken, but invaded an area never before subject to regulation by the State. It did not effect simply a temporary alteration of the contractual relationships of those within its coverage, but worked a severe, permanent, and immediate change in those relationships—irrevocably and retroactively. And its narrow aim was levelled not at every Minnesota employer, not even at every Minnesota employer who left the State, but only at those who had in the past been sufficiently enlightened as voluntarily to agree to establish pension plans for their employees....

We do hold that if the Contract Clause means anything at all, it means that Minnesota could not constitutionally do what it tried to do to the company in this case. [*Reversed.*]

## 6.   The Taxing Power

The taxing power is the power by which government raises revenue to defray its expenses. It apportions the cost of government among those who receive its benefits. The purpose of taxation and the purposes and function of government are coextensive, in that the taxing power, in the broad sense, includes all charges and burdens imposed by government upon persons or property for the use and support of government.

The taxing power can be exercised only for public purposes. A tax is not a contract based on assent but is a statutory liability based on force and authority. A tax is not a debt in the usual sense of the word, and the constitutional prohibitions against imprisonment for debt are not applicable.

The theory supporting taxation is that since governmental functions are a necessity, the government has the right to compel persons and property within its jurisdiction to defray the costs of these functions. The payment of taxes gives no right to the taxpayer. The privilege of enjoying the protection and services of government is not based on taxes paid. As a matter of fact, there are many examples which illustrate that those who receive the most from the government pay the fewest taxes.

Taxes are paid by those able to do so, in order that all persons may share in the general benefits resulting from government. Thus, property can be taxed without an obvious personal benefit to the property owner.

The power of taxation is in theory exclusively exercised by the legislative branch of the government. The only limitations on the exercise of the taxing power are found in federal and state constitutions and the political power of the electorate to replace the legislators. Since the power of taxation is a legislative function, statutes dealing with taxation must be complete as to both the method of ascertaining the tax and its collection. The fact that a tax may destroy a business or the value of property is no basis for a judicial determination that the tax is unconstitutional. The court must find that the tax violates some specific provision of the Constitution before it can be held invalid. The decision as to the wisdom or propriety of the tax is left to the legislature.

The taxing power is used to accomplish many goals other than raising revenue. Taxation is a very important form of regulation. Tax policy is a major ingredient in government efforts to regulate the economy. Tax laws are also used by the federal government to equalize competition among different businesses. For example, the gasoline tax is an important part of the equalization of costs between truckers and other forms of transportation. The taxing power has been used to encourage uniform legislation among the states. States were encouraged to adopt unemployment compensation benefits because the federal tax allows, as a credit, a certain portion of the tax paid to states.

The federal taxing power is also used to implement social policies. For example, the federal estate tax and the graduated income tax were in part adopted to break up large accumulations of wealth. In addition, the federal government pays money to the states to encourage certain activities such as education, road building, and raising the drinking age. That the spending power is the ultimate use of the tax power to advance a social agenda is illustrated by the following case. Persons in one part of the country pay for social improvements in another as a direct result of the exercise of the taxing and spending power of the federal government.

# SOUTH DAKOTA v. DOLE

107 S.Ct. 2793 (1987)

The U.S. Code (Title 23 § 158) directs the Secretary of Transportation to withhold a percentage of allocable federal highway funds from states "in which the purchase or public possession...of any alcoholic beverage by a person who is less than twenty-one years of age is lawful." South Dakota, which permits persons 19 years old or older to purchase beer containing up to 3.2% alcohol, sued in Federal District Court for a declaratory judgment that § 158 violates the constitutional limitations on congressional exercise of the spending power under Art. I, § 8, cl. 1, of the Constitution. The lower courts held the law constitutional.

REHNQUIST, J.:...The Constitution empowers Congress to "lay and collect Taxes, Duties, Imposts, and Excises, to pay the Debts and provide for the common Defence and general Welfare of the United States." Art. I, § 8, cl. 1. Incident to this power, Congress may attach conditions on the receipt of federal funds, and has repeatedly employed the power to further broad policy objectives by conditioning receipt of federal moneys upon compliance by the recipient with federal statutory and administrative directives.

The breadth of this power was made clear in *United States v. Butler,* 56 S.Ct. 312 (1936), where the Court, resolving a longstanding debate over the scope of the Spending Clause, determined that "the power of Congress to authorize expenditure of public moneys for public purposes is not limited by the direct grants of legislative power found in the Constitution." Thus, objectives not thought to be within Article I's "enumerated legislative fields" may nevertheless be attained through the use of the spending power and the conditional grant of federal funds.

The spending power is of course not unlimited, but is instead subject to several general restrictions articulated in our cases. The first of these limitations is derived from the language of the Constitution itself: the exercise of the spending power must be in pursuit of "the general welfare." In considering whether a particular expenditure is intended to serve general public purposes, courts should defer substantially to the judgment of Congress. Second, we have required that if Congress desires to condition the States' receipt of federal funds, it must do so unambiguously enabling the States to exercise their choice knowingly, cognizant of the consequences of their participation. Third, our cases have suggested (without significant elaboration) that conditions on federal grants might be illegitimate if they are unrelated to the federal interest in particular national projects or programs. Finally, we have noted that other constitutional provisions may provide an independent bar to the conditional grant of federal funds.

South Dakota does not seriously claim that § 158 is inconsistent with any of the first three restrictions mentioned above. We can readily conclude that the provision is designed to serve the general welfare, especially in light of the fact that the concept of welfare or the opposite is shaped by Congress. Congress found that the differing drinking ages in the States created particular incentives for young persons to combine their desire to drink with their ability to drive, and that this interstate problem required a national solution. The means it chose to address this dangerous situation were reasonably calculated to advance the general welfare. The conditions upon which States receive the funds, moreover, could not be more clearly stated by Congress. And the State itself, rather than challenging the germaneness of the condition to federal purposes, admits that it has never contended that the congressional action was unrelated to a national concern in the absence of the Twenty-first Amendment. Indeed, the condition imposed by Congress is directly related to one of the main purposes for which highway funds are expended—safe interstate travel. This goal of the interstate highway system had been frustrated by varying drinking ages among the States. A presidential commission appointed to study alcohol-related accidents and fatalities on the Nation's highways concluded that the lack of uniformity in the States' drinking

ages created "an incentive to drink and drive" because "young persons commut[e] to border States where the drinking age is lower." Presidential Commission on Drunk Driving, Final Report 11 (1983). By enacting § 158, Congress conditioned the receipt of federal funds in a way reasonably calculated to address this particular impediment to a purpose for which the funds are expended.

The remaining question about the validity of § 158—and the basic point of disagreement between the parties—is whether the Twenty-first Amendment constitutes an "independent constitutional bar" to the conditional grant of federal funds....

The "independent constitutional bar" limitation on the spending power is not, as petitioner suggests, a prohibition on the indirect achievement of objectives which Congress is not empowered to achieve directly. Instead, we think that the language in our earlier opinions stands for the unexceptionable proposition that the power may not be used to induce the States to engage in activities that would themselves be unconstitutional. Thus, for example, a grant of federal funds conditioned on invidiously discriminatory state action or the infliction of cruel and unusual punishment would be an illegitimate exercise of the Congress' broad spending power. But no such claim can be or is made here. Were South Dakota to succumb to the blandishments offered by Congress and raise its drinking age to 21, the State's action in so doing would not violate the constitutional rights of anyone.

Our decisions have recognized that in some circumstances the financial inducement offered by Congress might be so coercive as to pass the point at which "pressure turns into compulsion." Here, however, Congress has directed only that a State desiring to establish a minimum drinking age lower than 21 lose a relatively small percentage of certain federal highway funds. Petitioner contends that the coercive nature of this program is evident from the degree of success it has achieved. We cannot conclude, however, that a conditional grant of federal money of this sort is unconstitutional simply by reason of its success in achieving the congressional objective.

When we consider, for a moment, that all South Dakota would lose if she adheres to her chosen course as to a suitable minimum drinking age is 5% of the funds otherwise obtainable under specified highway grant programs, the argument as to coercion is shown to be more rhetoric than fact....

Here Congress has offered relatively mild encouragement to the States to enact higher minimum drinking ages than they would otherwise choose. But the enactment of such laws remains the prerogative of the States not merely in theory but in fact. Even if Congress might lack the power to impose a national minimum drinking age directly, we conclude that encouragement to state action found in § 158 is a valid use of the spending power....[*Affirmed.*]

Few questions are raised today concerning the *validity* of a federally imposed tax. The Sixteenth Amendment to the Constitution and the broad scope of the federal taxing power which has been approved by the courts eliminates most such issues. Of course, there is a considerable amount of litigation involving the *interpretation* and *application* of the federal tax laws and regulations. Great deference is given to the position taken by the Commissioner of Internal Revenue in such cases. Courts tend to hold that federal taxing laws are valid unless there is some clear constitutional infirmity in them.

### 7. The Import-Export Clause

A provision closely connected with the taxing power is the **Import-Export Clause.** This clause prohibits states from taxing imports. It prohibits both the federal and state governments from directly taxing exports. The Clause seeks to alleviate three main concerns by committing sole power to lay imposts and duties on imports in the federal government, with no concurrent state power. First, the federal government must speak with one voice when regulating commercial relations with foreign governments; and tariffs, which might affect foreign relations, could not be implemented by the states consistently with that exclusive power. Second, import revenues were to be the major source of revenue of the federal government and should not be diverted to the states. Third, harmony among the states might be disturbed unless seaboard states, with their crucial ports of entry, were prohibited from levying taxes on citizens of other states by taxing goods merely flowing through their ports to the inland states not situated as favorably geographically.

Difficult questions often arise regarding the point when property ceases to be an import or when it becomes an export and thus comes within the protection of the constitutional guarantee. At one time it was thought that goods remained imports as long as they were in their original packages. Today, the original-package doctrine is not followed. If goods have lost their status as imports, the clause no longer prevents state taxation of them. A nondiscriminatory ad valorem property tax on goods no longer in transit does not hamper commerce or constitute a form of tribute by seaboard states to the disadvantage of the interior states. Such a tax cannot have any impact whatsoever on the federal government's exclusive regulation of foreign commerce, probably the most important purpose of the clause's prohibition. By definition, such a tax does not fall on imports as such because of their place of origin. Nor will such taxation deprive the federal government of the exclusive right to all revenues from imposts and duties on imports and exports, since that right by definition only extends to revenues from exactions of a particular category. Unlike imposts and duties, which are essentially taxes on the commercial privilege of bringing goods into a country, property taxes are taxes by which a state apportions the cost of such services as police and fire protection among the beneficiaries according to their respective wealth; there is no reason why an importer should not bear his share of these costs along with his competitors who handle only domestic goods. The Import-Export Clause clearly prohibits state taxation based on the foreign origin of the imported goods, but it cannot be read to accord imported goods preferential treatment that permits escape from uniform taxes imposed without regard to foreign origin for services which the state supplies.

## 8. States' Relation Article

Article IV is sometimes referred to as the *states' relation article*. It contains provisions for the admission of new states and authorizes Congress to make rules governing territories and property of the United States. Section 4 of the article guarantees every state a republican form of government and imposes upon the federal government the duty to protect the states from invasion. It also guarantees each state protection against domestic violence.

Section 2 of Article IV contains the so-called **privileges and immunities clause.** This clause provides that "the Citizens of each State shall be entitled to all Privileges and Immunities of Citizens in the several States." This clause assures equality of treatment for all citizens. The clause places the citizens of each state on the same footing as citizens of other states concerning the advantages of citizenship. It relieves them from the disabilities of alienage in other states. It inhibits discriminating legislation against them by other states; it gives them the right of free ingress into other states, and egress from them; it ensures to them while in other states the same freedom possessed by the citizens of those states in acquisition and enjoyment of property and in the pursuit of happiness; and it secures to them while in other states equal protection of their laws. No provision in the Constitution so strongly tends to constitute the citizens of the United States as one people as this provision, because it prevents a state from discriminating against citizens of other states in favor of its own. A municipality is a subdivision of the state, and municipal ordinances may be challenged as a violation of the privileges and immunities clause.

Many attempts to favor local citizens over citizens of other states arise from attempts to benefit local residents economically. For example, Alaska passed a local hire act that required oil and gas leases to which the state was a party contain a provision requiring the employment of qualified Alaskan residents in preference to nonresidents. The act violated the privileges and immunities clause. Alaska's ownership of the oil and gas was insufficient justification for the discrimination.

The case which follows is typical of those dealing with attempts to favor citizens of one state over the citizens of another state. Notice that in this case, however, the courts attempted to do so.

---

# SUPREME COURT OF N.H. v. PIPER
105 S.Ct. 1272 (1985)

---

POWELL, J.:...The Rules of the Supreme Court of New Hampshire limit bar admission to state residents. We here consider whether this restriction violates the Privileges and Immunities Clause of the United States Constitution, Art. IV, § 2.

Kathryn Piper lives in Lower Waterford, Vermont, about 400 yards from the New Hampshire border. In 1979, she applied to take the February 1980 New Hampshire bar examination. Piper submitted with her application a statement of intent to become a New Hampshire resident. Following an investigation, the Board of Bar Examiners found that Piper was of good moral character and met the other requirements for admission. She was allowed to take, and passed, the examination. Piper was informed by the Board that she would have to establish a home address in New Hampshire prior to being sworn in.

On May 7, 1980, Piper requested from the Clerk of the New Hampshire Supreme Court a dispensation from the residency requirement. Although she had a "possible job" with a lawyer in Littleton, New Hampshire, Piper stated that becoming a resident of New Hampshire would be inconvenient. Her house in Vermont was secured by a mortgage with a favorable interest rate, and she and her husband recently had become parents. According to Piper, these "problems peculiar to [her] situation...warrant[ed] that an exception be made."

On May 13, 1980, the Clerk informed Piper that her request had been denied. She then formally petitioned the New Hampshire Supreme Court for permission to become a member of the bar. She asserted that she was well qualified and that her "situation [was] sufficiently unique that the granting of an exception…[would] not result in the setting of any undesired precedent."

The Supreme Court denied Piper's formal request on December 31, 1980.

On March 22, 1982, Piper filed this action in the United States District Court for the District of New Hampshire. She named as defendants the State Supreme Court, its five Justices, and its Clerk. She alleged that Rule 42 of the New Hampshire Supreme Court, that excludes nonresidents from the bar, violates the Privileges and Immunities Clause of the United States Constitution, Art. IV, § 2.…

Article IV, § 2 of the Constitution provides that the "citizens of each State shall be entitled to all Privileges and Immunities of Citizens in the several States." This clause was intended to "fuse into one Nation a collection of independent, sovereign States." Recognizing this purpose, we have held that it is "[o]nly with respect to those 'privileges' and 'immunities' bearing on the vitality of the nation as a single entity" that a State must accord residents and nonresidents equal treatment. In *Baldwin*, for example, we concluded that a State may charge a nonresident more than it charges a resident for the same elk-hunting license. Because elk-hunting is "recreation" rather than a "means of a livelihood," we found that the right to a hunting license was not "fundamental" to the promotion of interstate harmony.

Derived, like the Commerce Clause, from the fourth of the Articles of Confederation, the Privileges and Immunities Clause was intended to create a national economic union. It is therefore not surprising that this Court repeatedly has found that one of the privileges which the Clause guarantees to citizens of State A is that of doing business in State B on terms of substantial equality with the citizens of that State.

In *Ward v. Maryland*, 12 Wall. 418, 449 (1871), the Court invalidated a statute under which nonresidents were required to pay $300 per year for a license to trade in goods not manufactured in Maryland, while resident traders paid a fee varying from $12 to $150. Similarly, in *Toomer*, the Court held that nonresident fishermen could not be required to pay a license fee of $2,500 for each shrimp boat owned when residents were charged only $25 per boat. Finally, in *Hicklin v. Orbeck*, 437 U.S. 518,397 (1978), we found violative of the Privileges and Immunities Clause a statute containing a resident hiring preference for all employment related to the development of the State's oil and gas resources.

There is nothing in *Ward, Toomer,* or *Hicklin* suggesting that the practice of law should not be viewed as a "privilege" under Article IV, § 2. Like the occupations considered in our earlier cases, the practice of law is important to the national economy. As the Court noted in *Goldfarb*, the "activities of lawyers play an important part in commercial intercourse."

The lawyer's role in the national economy is not the only reason that the opportunity to practice law should be considered a "fundamental right." We believe that the legal profession has a noncommercial role and duty that reinforce the view that the practice of law falls within the ambit of the Privileges and Immunities Clause. Out-of-state lawyers may—and often do—represent persons who raise unpopular federal claims. In some cases, representation by nonresident counsel may be the only means available for the vindication of federal rights. The lawyer who champions unpopular causes surely is as important to the "maintenance of well-being of the Union," as was the shrimp fisherman in *Toomer,* or the pipeline worker in *Hicklin.…*

We therefore conclude that the right to practice law is protected by the Privileges and Immunities Clause.

The conclusion that Rule 42 deprives nonresidents of a protected privilege does not end our inquiry. The Court has stated that "[l]ike many other constitutional provisions, the Privileges and Immunities Clause is not an absolute." The Clause does not preclude discrimination against nonresidents where: (i) there is a substantial reason for the difference in treatment; and (ii) the discrimination practiced against nonresidents bears a substantial relationship to the State's objective. In deciding whether the discrimination bears a close or substantial relationship to the State's objective, the Court has considered the availability of less restrictive means.

The Supreme Court of New Hampshire offers several justifications for its refusal to admit nonresidents to the bar. It asserts that nonresident members would be less likely: (i) to become, and remain, familiar with local rules and procedures; (ii) to behave ethically; (iii) to be available for court proceedings; and (iv) to do *pro bono* and other volunteer work in the State. We find that none of these reasons meets the test of "substantiality," and that the means chosen do not bear the necessary relationship to the State's objectives....

We conclude that New Hampshire's bar residency requirement violates Art. IV, § 2, of the United States Constitution. The nonresident's interest in practicing law is a "privilege" protected by the Clause. Although the lawyer is an officer of the court, he does not hold a position that can be entrusted only to a full-fledged member of the political community. A State may discriminate against nonresidents only where its reasons are "substantial," and the difference in treatment bears a close or substantial relation to those reasons. No such showing has been made in this case. Accordingly, we affirm the judgment of the Court of Appeals. [*It is so ordered.*]

---

In a similar case, the courts held invalid a Virginia bar admission rule that waived the bar examination for applicants who have been admitted to another state's bar for five years and intend to practice full-time in Virginia, but only if they are also residents of Virginia.

The clause does not prevent state citizenship from being used to distinguish among persons, however. A state may limit the right to vote and to hold office to its citizens. The same is true of the right to pay resident tuition to a state university. It is only with respect to those privileges and immunities bearing upon the vitality of the nation as a single entity that the state must treat all citizens, resident and nonresident, equally.

Article IV also contains the so-called **full faith and credit clause.** It provides that "Full Faith and Credit shall be given in each State to the public Acts, Records, and judicial proceedings of every other State...." This does not mean that the precedent in one state is binding in other states, but only that final decisions or judgments rendered in any given state shall be enforced as between the original parties in other states. Full faith and credit applies to a specific decision as it affects the rights of the parties, and not to the reasons or principles upon which it was based. A court judgment in one state is conclusive upon the merits of the issues in another state only if the court in the first state had power to pass on the merits—that is, had jurisdiction over the subject matter and the relevant parties. The first court's decision on jurisdiction, if that is an issue, is res judicata if the issue of jurisdiction was fully considered by the first court deciding the controversy. A party with a judgment or decree from the courts of one state may obtain enforcement through proper proceedings in other states without relitigating the issues of the original case.

Finally, the states' relation article provides for extradition of those accused of crime from one state to another. This is accomplished by judicial proceedings with the consent of the governor of the surrendering state.

## THE COMMERCE CLAUSE

### 9. Introduction

The power of the federal government to regulate business activity is found in the so-called **commerce clause** of the Constitution. The commerce clause states: "Congress shall have power...to regulate Commerce with foreign Nations, and among the several States, and with the Indian Tribes...." This grant of power has been broadly interpreted to give the federal government broad power to regulate business. This power to regulate is the power to prescribe the rules by which commerce is to be conducted. The actual extent of this power will be discussed in subsequent sections.

The commerce clause has been interpreted as imposing limitations on the power of state government to regulate business under the state police power. The **police power** of state and local governments is the inherent power to control persons and property within the jurisdiction of the state to promote the general welfare. General welfare includes the public health, safety, and morals. The inherent police power of the states was reserved to them by the Constitution. The effect of the commerce clause on the police power will be discussed in section 12 of this chapter.

### 10. Foreign Commerce

The commerce clause has three parts. The first grants the federal government power to regulate foreign commerce. The power to regulate foreign commerce is vested exclusively in the federal government, and it extends to all aspects of foreign trade. In other words, the power to regulate foreign commerce is total. The federal government can prohibit foreign commerce entirely. For example, in recent years the federal government has imposed trade embargoes on countries such as South Africa. It can also allow commerce with restrictions.

To state that federal power to regulate foreign commerce is exclusive means that state and local governments may not regulate such commerce. However, state and local governments sometimes attempt directly or indirectly to regulate imports or exports to some degree. Such attempts are unconstitutional. State or local laws which regulate or interfere with federal regulation of commerce with foreign nations are invalid as violations of the commerce and supremacy clauses.

The right to import includes the right to sell goods imported. States may not prohibit the sale of imported goods any more than they can prohibit their import. The exclusive federal power over imported goods continues until the goods are mingled with and become a part of the general property of the country, so that for all purposes the imported product is given similar treatment with other property. In most cases, imported goods become a part of internal commerce when the importer or wholesaler disposes of them to retail dealers in local communities. However, if a state or local law tends to continue to distinguish the goods from a point of origin, the foreign-commerce aspect continues, and the law is invalid. For example, a city required that all goods sold at retail originating behind the Iron Curtain be so labeled. This law was unconstitutional.

## 11.   Interstate Commerce

The second component of the commerce clause is the power to regulate commerce "among the several states." At first, this phrase was interpreted to mean interstate commerce as contrasted with intrastate commerce. Later, in a long series of judicial decisions, the power was expanded through interpretation to include not only the channels and instrumentalities of interstate commerce but also activities affecting interstate commerce.

The power of Congress over commerce being plenary, it extends to all commerce, be it great or small. Labeling an activity a "local" or "intrastate" activity does not resolve the question of whether Congress may regulate it under the commerce clause. The commerce power extends to those intrastate activities which so affect interstate commerce, or the exertion of the power of Congress over it, as to make regulation of them appropriate. Regulation is appropriate if it aids in the effective regulation of interstate commerce. Even activity that is purely intrastate in character may be regulated by Congress, when the activity, combined with like conduct by others similarly situated, substantially affects commerce among the states or with foreign nations.

Interstate commerce may be affected positively or negatively in the sense that regulated economic activity may encourage commerce or hinder it. The nature of the activity itself and its effect on interstate commerce may warrant the application of federal law. Such activity need not result from a violation of the law. The unlawful conduct itself need not have an effect on interstate commerce.

Today, legislative acts adjusting the benefits and burdens of economic life are presumed to be constitutional. A court may invalidate legislation enacted under the commerce clause only if there is clearly no rational basis for a congressional finding that the regulated activity affects interstate commerce, or if there is no reasonable connection between the regulatory means selected and the asserted ends. The judicial task ends once the court determines that Congress acted rationally in adopting a particular regulatory scheme.

The case which follows traces the history of the expansion of the commerce clause and its extension to activities beyond interstate commerce.

# PEREZ v. UNITED STATES
91 S.Ct. 1357 (1971)

The defendant was convicted of violating the "loan sharking" provisions of the Federal Consumer Credit Protection Act. It was proved beyond any doubt that the defendant as a part of organized crime had used extortion in collecting illegal rates of interest. He challenged the constitutionality of the statute on the ground that Congress has no power to control the local activity of loan sharking.

DOUGLAS, J.:...The constitutional question is a substantial one....

The Commerce Clause reaches in the main three categories of problems. First, the use of channels of interstate or foreign commerce which Congress deems are being misused, as for example, the shipment of stolen goods or of persons who have been kidnapped. Second, protection of the instrumentalities of interstate commerce, as for example, the destruction of an aircraft, or persons or things in commerce, as for example, thefts from interstate shipments. Third,

those activities affecting commerce. It is with this last category that we are here concerned.

Chief Justice Marshall in *Gibbons v. Ogden*, 9 Wheat. 1, 195, 6 L.Ed. 23, said:

**The genius and character of the whole government seems to be, that its action is to be applied to all the external concerns of the nation, and to those internal concerns which affect the states generally; but not to those which are completely within a particular state, which do not affect other states, and with which it is not necessary to interfere, for the purpose of executing some of the general powers of the government. The completely internal commerce of a state, then, may be considered as reserved for the state itself....**

Chief Justice Stone wrote for a unanimous Court in 1942 that Congress could provide for the regulation of the price of intrastate milk, the sale of which, in competition with interstate milk, affects the price structure and federal regulation of the latter. The commerce power, he said, "extends to those activities intrastate which so affect interstate commerce, or the exertion of the power of Congress over it, as to make regulation of them an appropriate means to the attainment of a legitimate end, the effective execution of the granted power to regulate interstate commerce."

*Wickard v. Filburn*, 317 U.S. 111, soon followed in which a unanimous Court held that wheat grown wholly for home consumption was constitutionally within the scope of federal regulation of wheat production because, though never marketed interstate, it supplied the need of the grower which otherwise would be satisfied by his purchases in the open market. We said:

> ...even if appellee's activity be local and though it may not be regarded as commerce, it may still, whatever its nature, be reached by Congress if it exerts a substantial economic effect on interstate commerce, and this irrespective of whether such effect is what might at some earlier time have been defined as 'direct' or 'indirect.'

As pointed out in *United States v. Darby*, 312 U.S. 100, the decision sustaining an Act of Congress which prohibited the employment of workers in the production of goods "for interstate commerce" at other than prescribed wages and hours—a *class of activities*—was held properly regulated by Congress without proof that the particular intrastate activity against which a sanction was laid had an effect on commerce. A unanimous Court said:

> ...Congress has sometimes left it to the courts to determine whether the intrastate activities have the prohibited effect on the commerce, as in the Sherman Act. It has sometimes left it to an administrative board or agency to determine whether the activities sought to be regulated or prohibited have such effect, as in the case of the Interstate Commerce Act, and the National Labor Relations Act, or whether they come within the statutory definition of the prohibited Act, as in the Federal Trade Commission Act. And sometimes Congress itself has said that a partic-

ular activity affects the commerce, as it did in the present Act, the Safety Appliance Act and the Railway Labor Act. In passing on the validity of legislation of the class last mentioned the only function of courts is to determine whether the particular activity regulated or prohibited is within the reach of the federal power.

That case is particularly relevant here because it involved a criminal prosecution, a unanimous Court holding that the Act was "sufficiently definite to meet constitutional demands." Petitioner is clearly a *member of the class* which engages in "extortionate credit transactions" as defined by Congress and the description of that class has the required definiteness.

It was the "class of activities" test which we employed in *Heart of Atlanta Motel, Inc. v. United States*, 379 U.S. 241, to sustain an Act of Congress requiring hotel or motel accommodations for Negro guests. The Act declared that "any inn, hotel, motel, or other establishment which provides lodging to transient guests affects commerce *per se*." That exercise of power under the Commerce Clause was sustained....In a companion case, *Katzenbach v. McClung*, 379 U.S. 294, we ruled on the constitutionality of the restaurant provision of the same Civil Rights Act which regulated the restaurant "if...it serves or offers to serve interstate travelers or a substantial portion of the food which it serves...has moved in commerce." Apart from the effect on the flow of food in commerce to restaurants, we spoke of the restrictive effect of the exclusion of Negroes from restaurants on interstate travel by Negroes. In emphasis of our position that it was the *class of activities* regulated that was the measure, we acknowledged that Congress appropriately considered the "total incidence" of the practice on commerce.

Where the *class of activities* is regulated and that *class* is within the reach of federal power, the courts have no power "to excise, as trivial, individual instances" of the class.

Extortionate credit transactions, though purely intrastate, may in the judgment of Congress affect interstate commerce. In an analogous situation, Mr. Justice Holmes, speaking for a unanimous Court, said "...when it is necessary in order to prevent an evil to make the law embrace more than the precise thing to be prevented it may do so."...

In the setting of the present case there is a tie-in between local loan sharks and interstate crime.

The findings by Congress are quite adequate on that ground...

"Even where extortionate credit transactions are purely intrastate in character, they nevertheless directly affect interstate and foreign commerce."...

It appears...that loan sharking in its national setting is one way organized interstate crime holds its guns to the heads of the poor and the rich alike and syphons funds from numerous localities to finance its national operations. [*Affirmed.*]

---

The power of Congress under the commerce clause is subject to other constitutional limitations such as those contained in the Bill of Rights. The effect of the commerce clause on the rights of state and local government as protected by the Tenth Amendment has caused the courts a great deal of difficulty. For example, prior to 1976, the Supreme Court held that the commerce clause allowed Congress to regulate the wages of employees of state and local government. From 1976 to 1985, the Court held that Congress could not regulate employees who were engaged in areas of traditional governmental functions. This later decision was reversed in 1985 when the court recognized the inherent difficulty in separating traditional functions from nontraditional ones.

The commerce clause by its specific language does not provide any special limitation on Congress' action with respect to the states. However, the Constitution precludes the national government from devouring the essentials of state sovereignty. There is general reliance on the political process to protect the states from such action by the federal government. The judicial process is used only as a last resort to protect the states as states.

In summary, the states occupy a special and specific position in our constitutional system. The scope of Congress' authority under the commerce clause must reflect that position. But the principal and basic limit on the federal commerce power is that inherent in all congressional action—the built-in restraints that our system provides through state participation in federal governmental action. The political process ensures that laws that unduly burden the states will not be promulgated. If laws are passed under the commerce clause that apply to state government, they are presumed to be constitutional.

Keep in mind that although Congress has the power to regulate certain activities, it may decide not to exercise it. There are activities that the federal government could regulate but has chosen not to. Also keep in mind that not all business or commercial activity is commerce. For example, it has been held that the activity of accrediting institutions of higher learning is not commerce. Professional baseball has repeatedly been held to be a "sport" and not a business. As a practical matter, the trend is to consider that almost every business activity is a part of commerce, but there are still some noncommercial pursuits.

## 12. The Commerce Clause and the State Police Power

The grant of power to Congress over commerce does not contain any provision which expressly excludes states from exercising authority over commerce. The Supreme Court in *Cooley v. The Board of Wardens of Port of Philadelphia*[1] held that the nature of the commerce power did not by *implication* prohibit state action and that some state power over commerce is compatible with the federal power. Nevertheless, there are definite limitations on the state powers over commerce because of the commerce clause. This is sometimes called the dominant commerce clause concept.

The decisions of the Court have established three distinct subject areas of governmental regulation of commerce, as shown in Table 6-2. Some areas are exclusively federal, some are said to be exclusively local, and still others are such that regulation of them may be dual.

The subject area which is exclusively federal, in addition to foreign commerce, concerns those internal matters where uniformity on a nationwide basis is essential. Any state regulation of such subjects is void whether Congress has entered the field or not.

In theory, those matters which are exclusively within the states' power are intrastate activities which do not have a substantial effect on interstate commerce. As noted in the previous section, it is becoming more and more difficult, if not impossible, to find a subject matter which is truly exclusively local in the sense that it does not affect interstate commerce.

The third subject area between the above two extremes, where joint regulation is permissible, can be divided into three subparts. The first concerns those subjects over which the federal government has preempted the field. By express language or by comprehensive regulation Congress has shown that it intends to exercise exclusive dominion over the subject matter. When a federal statute has thus preempted the field, *any* state or local law pertaining to the same subject matter is unconstitutional under the commerce clause and the supremacy clause, and the state regulation is void. The net effect of a law that preempts the field makes the subject matter of the law exclusively federal. The subject of preemption was discussed in section 3 under "The Supremacy Clause."

The second division of the area of possible joint regulation includes situations in which the federal regulation of a subject matter is not comprehensive enough to preempt the field. Here state regulation is permitted, but when state law is inconsistent or conflicts irreconcilably with the federal stat-

---

[1]53 U.S. 299 (1851).

**TABLE 6-2**   Possible Subjects for Government Regulation

| Exclusively Federal Subjects | Possible Dual Regulation Subjects | Exclusively Local Subjects |
|---|---|---|
| I.<br>Any state regulatory law is unconstitutional under supremacy and commerce clauses. | II.<br>Federal law preempts the field—moves the subject matter to area No. I.<br><br>III.<br>Federal law does not preempt the field. A state law is unconstitutional if it:<br>1  Is in irreconcilable conflict with federal law<br>2  Constitutes an *undue* burden on interstate commerce<br>3  Discriminates against interstate commerce in favor of intrastate commerce<br><br>IV.<br>No federal law/state law is unconstitutional if it:<br>1  Constitutes an undue burden on interstate commerce<br>2  Discriminates against interstate commerce in favor of intrastate commerce | V.<br>The impact on state and local government of laws based on the commerce clause is very limited. Very few subjects are exclusively local. |

ute, it is unconstitutional and void. Irreconcilable conflicts exist when it is not possible for a business to comply with both statutes. If compliance with both is not possible, the state law must fall under the supremacy clause and the commerce clause. If compliance with both is reasonably possible, dual compliance is required. This usually has the effect of forcing business to meet the requirements of the law with the greatest burden. For example, if the state minimum wage is $5.00 per hour and the federal is $4.25, employers would be required to pay $5.00 since the conflict can be reconciled.

The commerce clause also invalidates state laws imposing an undue burden on interstate commerce. The commerce clause does not prohibit the imposing of burdens on interstate commerce—only the imposition of *undue* burdens. The states have the authority under the police power to regulate matters of legitimate local concern, even though interstate commerce may be affected.

State statutes fall into two categories: those that burden interstate commerce only incidentally, and those that affirmatively discriminate against such transactions. For cases in the first category, courts weigh the burdens against the benefits and find undue burdens only if they clearly exceed the local benefits. Cases in the second category are subject to more demanding scrutiny. If a state law either in substance or in practical effect discriminates against interstate commerce, the state must not only prove that the law has a legitimate purpose but also that the purpose cannot be achieved by a non-discriminatory means. If a state law is pure economic protectionism, the courts apply a virtual per se rule of invalidity.

In deciding cases that are concerned with state legislation that may or may not burden interstate commerce without discrimination against it, the courts are involved in a "weighing" process, or a balancing of competing interests. However, in many cases incomparables exist that cannot be weighed. In the weighing process, the court examines the goal of the state legislation and weighs it against the burden imposed on business. Although doubts are resolved in favor of state laws, many are held to be unconstitutional, such as the one in the case which follows.

# KASSEL v. CONSOLIDATED FREIGHTWAYS CORP., ETC.

101 S.Ct. 1309 (1981)

POWELL, J.: The question is whether an Iowa statute that prohibits the use of certain large trucks within the State unconstitutionally burdens interstate commerce.

Respondent, Consolidated Freightways Corporation of Delaware (Consolidated) is one of the largest common carriers in the country. It offers service in 48 states. Among other routes, Consolidated carries commodities through Iowa on Interstate 80, the principal east-west route linking New York, Chicago, and the West Coast, and on Interstate 35, a major north-south route.

Consolidated mainly uses two kinds of trucks. One consists of a three-axle tractor pulling a 40-foot two-axle trailer. This unit, commonly called a single, or "semi" is 55 feet in length overall. Consolidated also uses a two-axle tractor pulling a single-axle trailer which, in turn, pulls a single-axle dolly and a second single-axle trailer. This combination, known as a double, or twin, is 65 feet long overall. Many trucking companies, including Consolidated, increasingly prefer to use doubles to ship certain kinds of commodities. Doubles have larger capacities, and the trailers can be detached and routed separately if necessary. Consolidated would like to use 65-foot doubles on many of its trips through Iowa.

The State of Iowa, however, by statute restricts the length of vehicles that may use its highways. Unlike all other States in the West and Midwest, Iowa generally prohibits the use of 65-foot doubles within its borders. Instead, most truck combinations are restricted to 55 feet in length. Doubles, mobile homes, trucks carrying vehicles such as tractors and other farm equipment, and singles hauling livestock, are permitted to be as long as 60 feet....

Because of Iowa's statutory scheme, Consolidated cannot use its 65-foot doubles to move commodities through the State. Instead, the company must do one of four things: (i) use 55-foot singles; (ii) use 60-foot doubles; (iii) detach the trailers of a 65-foot and shuttle each through the State separately; or (iv) divert 65-foot doubles around Iowa.

Dissatisfied with these options, Consolidated filed this suit in the District court averring that Iowa's statutory scheme unconstitutionally burdens interstate commerce. Iowa defended the law as a reasonable safety measure enacted pursuant to its police power. The State asserted that 65-foot doubles are more dangerous than 55-foot singles and, in any event, that the law promotes safety and reduces road wear within the State by diverting much truck traffic to other States.

In a 14-day trial, both sides adduced evidence on safety, and on the burden on interstate commerce imposed by Iowa's law. On the question of safety, the District Court found that the "evidence clearly establishes that the twin is as safe as the semi."

"There is no valid safety reason for barring twins from Iowa's highways because of their configuration.

"The evidence convincingly, if not overwhelmingly, establishes that the 65-foot twin is as safe as, if not safer than, the 60-foot twin and the 55-foot semi....

"Twins and semis have different characteristics. Twins are more maneuverable, are less sensitive to wind, and create less splash and spray. However, they are more likely than semis to jackknife or upset. They can be backed only for a short distance. The negative characteristics are not such that they render the twin less safe than semis overall. Semis are more stable but are more likely to rear end another vehicle."

The District Court...concluded that the state law impermissibly burdened interstate commerce....The Court of Appeals for the Eighth Circuit affirmed.

It is unnecessary to review in detail the evolution of the principles of Commerce Clause adjudication. The Clause is both a "prolific source of national power and an equally prolific source of conflict with legislation of the state(s)." The Clause permits Congress to legislate when it perceives that the national welfare is not furthered by the independent actions of the States. It is now well established, also, that the Clause itself is a limitation upon state power even without congressional implementation. The Clause requires that some aspects of trade generally must remain free from interference by the States. When a state ventures excessively into the regulation of these aspects of commerce, it "trespasses upon national interests," and the courts will hold the state regulation invalid under the Clause alone.

The Commerce Clause does not, of course, invalidate all state restrictions on commerce. It has long been recognized that, "in the absence of conflicting legislation by Congress, there is a residuum of power in the State to make laws governing matters of local concern which nevertheless in some measure affect interstate commerce or even, to some extent, regulate it." The extent of permissible state regulation is not always easy to measure. It may be said with confidence, however, that a State's power to regulate commerce is never greater than in matters traditionally of local concern. For example, regulations that touch upon safety—especially highway safety—are those that "the Court has been most reluctant to invalidate." Indeed, "if safety justifications are not illusory, the Court will not second guess legislative judgment about their importance in comparison with related burdens on interstate commerce." Those who would challenge such bona fide safety regulations must overcome a "strong presumption of validity."

But the incantation of a purpose to promote the public health or safety does not insulate a state law from Commerce Clause attack. Regulations designed for that salutary purpose nevertheless may further the purpose so marginally, and interfere with commerce so substantially, as to be invalid under the Commerce Clause. In the Court's recent unanimous decision in *Raymond,* we declined to "accept the State's contention that the inquiry under the Commerce Clause is ended without a weighing of the asserted safety purpose against the degree of interference with interstate commerce." This "weighing" by a court requires—and indeed the constitutionality of the state regulation depends on—"a sensitive consideration of the weight and nature of the state regulatory concern in light of the extent of the burden imposed on the course of interstate commerce."

The State failed to present any persuasive evidence that 65-foot doubles are less safe than 55-foot singles. Moreover, Iowa's law is now out of step with the laws of all other midwestern and western States. Iowa thus substantially burdens the interstate flow of goods by truck. In the absence of con-

gressional action to set uniform standards, some burdens associated with state safety regulations must be tolerated. But where, as here, the State's safety interest has been found to be illusory, and its regulations impair significantly the federal interest in efficient and safe interstate transportation, the state law cannot be harmonized with the Commerce Clause....

Consolidated, meanwhile, demonstrated that Iowa's law substantially burdens interstate commerce. Trucking companies that wish to continue to use 65-foot doubles must route them around Iowa or detach the trailers of the doubles and ship them through separately. Alternatively, trucking companies must use the smaller 55-foot singles or 60-foot doubles permitted under Iowa law. Each of these options engenders inefficiency and added expense. The record shows that Iowa's law added about $12.6 million each year to the costs of trucking companies. Consolidated alone incurred about $2 million per year in increased costs....

Because Iowa has imposed this burden without any significant countervailing safety interest, its statute violates the Commerce Clause. The judgment of the Court of Appeals is affirmed. [*Affirmed.*]

---

Among examples of state laws found to be constitutional through the balancing or weighing process are (1) a Minnesota law which banned retail sale of milk in plastic, nonreturnable and nonrefillable containers, but permitted such sale in other nonreturnable, nonrefillable containers such as paperboard milk cartons; (2) a New Hampshire law requiring aircraft used for hunting to display large registration numbers; and (3) a Virginia statute which required all stockbrokers to register with the state. In all three cases the court held that the burden was not excessive in relation to the local benefits.

Finally, the commerce clause has been construed as prohibiting discrimination against interstate commerce in favor of intrastate commerce. State and local governments frequently attempt by legislation to aid local business in its competition with interstate business. The commerce clause requires that all taxes and regulations be the same for local businesses as for businesses engaged in interstate commerce. While interstate commerce is required to pay its fair share of all taxes, it must be placed on a plane of equality with local trade or commerce. A state may not place itself in a position of economic isolation from other states.

The third area of possible joint regulation exists where there is no federal law at all. When there is no federal regulation of a subject, state regulation of interstate commerce is permissible, providing, of course, that it does not discriminate against interstate commerce in favor of local business and does not impose an undue burden on interstate commerce.

### 13. The Commerce Clause and Taxation

Taxation is a primary form of regulation. Therefore, taxes imposed by state and local governments are subject to the limitations imposed by the commerce clause. The commerce clause limits property taxes, income taxes, and sales or use taxes levied by state and local governments on interstate commerce. Since taxation distributes the cost of government among those who receive its benefits, interstate commerce is not exempt from state and local taxes. The purpose of the commerce clause is to ensure that it only pays its fair share.

Several distinct constitutional problems exist when a state seeks to tax businesses engaged in interstate commerce. These issues are: (1) Is the tax properly apportioned? (2) Is there a sufficient minimum connection (**nexus**) between the activity being taxed and the tax to satisfy due process? (3) Does the tax discriminate against interstate commerce? And (4) does the tax impose an unconstitutional burden on interstate commerce? This latter issue relates to the question of whether the tax is fairly related to services provided by the state.

The concept of **apportionment** is used to prevent multiple taxation of the same property or income of interstate businesses. Apportionment formulas are used to allocate the tax burden of an interstate business among the states entitled to tax it. The commerce clause requires states to use reasonable formulas when more than one state is taxing the same thing.

The term *nexus* describes the requirement of some sufficient contact, connection, tie, or link to the taxing state to justify the tax. In other words, there must be sufficient local activities to justify the tax in a constitutional sense. A business operating in a state directly benefits from its police and fire protection, the use of its roads, and the like. Indirectly, it will be able to recruit employees more easily if they have easy access to good schools, parks, and civic centers. If the state gives anything for which it can reasonably expect payment, then the tax has a sufficient nexus. In cases involving property taxes, the term *taxable situs* is used in place of nexus, but each is concerned with the adequacy of local activities to support the tax.

The concepts of undue burdens against interstate commerce and discrimination against interstate commerce through taxation are the same as these concepts as applied to other forms of regulation. Taxes which differ from those levied on intrastate commerce cannot be levied on interstate commerce. This case which follows illustrates the tests used to decide if a state tax violates the commerce clause.

# D.H. HOLMES CO. LTD. v. McNAMARA
108 S.Ct. 1619 (1988)

Appellant operates 13 department stores in Louisiana. It contracted with out-of-state companies to design, print, and distribute merchandise catalogs. Appellant paid for the catalogs, which were shipped primarily to addressees in Louisiana. Undeliverable catalogs were returned to its New Orleans store. The distribution was designed to improve its sales and name-recognition among Louisiana residents.

Appellant did not pay any sales taxes where the catalogs were printed. The Louisiana Department of Revenue and Taxation assessed taxes on the catalogs' value under a statute imposing a 3 percent use tax on all tangible personal property used in Louisiana. "Use" was defined as the exercise of any right or power over such property incident to ownership, including distribution.

The lower courts held that appellant owed the tax notwithstanding a commerce clause challenge.

REHNQUIST, J.:...The Commerce Clause of the Constitution, Art. I, § 8, cl. 3, provides that Congress shall have the power "[t]o regulate Commerce with foreign Nations, and among the several States, and with the Indian Tribes." Even where Congress has not acted affirmatively to protect interstate commerce, the Clause prevents States from discriminating against that commerce. The distinction between the power of the State to shelter its people from menaces to their health or safety and from fraud, even when those dangers emanate from interstate commerce, and its lack of power to retard, burden or constrict the flow of such commerce for their economic advantage, is one deeply rooted in both our history and our law.

One frequent source of conflict of this kind occurs when a State seeks to tax the sale or use of goods within its borders. This recurring dilemma is exemplified in what has come to be the leading case in the area, *Complete Auto Transit, Inc. v. Brady*, 97 S.Ct. 1076 (1977). In *Complete Auto*, Mississippi imposed a tax on appellant's business of in-state transportation of motor vehicles manufactured outside the State. We found that the State's tax did not violate the Commerce Clause, because appellant's activity had a substantial nexus with Mississippi, and the tax was fairly apportioned, did not discriminate against interstate commerce, and was fairly related to benefits provided by the State....

*Complete Auto* abandoned the abstract notion that interstate commerce "itself" cannot be taxed by the States. We recognized that, with certain restrictions, interstate commerce may be required to pay its fair share of State taxes. Accordingly, in the present case, it really makes little difference for Commerce Clause purposes whether appellant's catalogs "came to rest" in the mailboxes of its Louisiana customers or whether they were still considered in the stream of interstate commerce....

In the case before us, then, the application of Louisiana's use tax to Holmes' catalogs does not violate the Commerce Clause if the tax complies with the four prongs of *Complete Auto*. We have no doubt that the second and third elements of the test are satisfied. The Louisiana taxing scheme is fairly apportioned, for it provides a credit against its use tax for sales taxes that have been paid in other States. Holmes paid no sales tax for the catalogs where they were designed or printed; if it had, it would have been eligible for a credit against the use tax exacted. Similarly, Louisiana imposed its use tax only on the 82% of the catalogs distributed in-state; it did not attempt to tax that portion of the catalogs that went to out-of-state customers.

The Louisiana tax structure likewise does not discriminate against interstate commerce. The use tax is designed to compensate the state for revenue lost when residents purchase out-of-state goods for use within the State. It is equal to the sales tax applicable to the same tangible personal property purchased in-state; in fact, both taxes are set forth in the same sections of the Louisiana statutes.

*Complete Auto* requires that the tax be fairly related to benefits provided by the State, but that condition is also met here. Louisiana provides a number of services that facilitate Holmes' sale of merchandise within the State: It provides fire and police protection for Holmes' stores, runs mass transit and maintains public roads which benefit appellant's customers, and supplies a number of other civic services from which Holmes profits. To be sure, many others in the State benefit from the same services; but that does not alter the fact that the use tax paid by Holmes, on catalogs designed to increase sales, is related to the advantages provided by the State which aid appellant's business.

Finally, we believe that Holmes' distribution of its catalogs reflects a substantial nexus with Louisiana. To begin with, Holmes' contention that it lacked sufficient control over the catalogs' distribution in Louisiana to be subject to the use tax verges on the nonsensical. Holmes ordered and paid for the catalogs and supplied the list of customers to whom the catalogs were sent; any catalogs that could not be delivered were returned to it. Holmes admits that it initiated the distribution to improve its sales and name-recognition among Louisiana residents. Holmes also has a significant presence in Louisiana, with 13 stores and over $100,000,000 in annual sales in the State. The distribution of catalogs to approximately 400,000 Louisiana customers was directly aimed at expanding and enhancing its Louisiana business. There is "nexus" aplenty here....

Because Louisiana's imposition of its use tax on Holmes does not violate the Commerce Clause, the judgment of the Louisiana Court of Appeal is [*Affirmed.*]

# REVIEW QUESTIONS

**1**  Goldkist had entered into a contract to sell 50 million chickens to Russia. When the Russians invaded Afghanistan, President Carter imposed an embargo on the sale of food to Russia. Did his action violate the contract clause? Explain.

**2**  A class action suit was filed that charged two real estate trade associations and six named real estate firms with violating the federal antitrust laws. It alleged a conspiracy to fix prices in the purchase and sale of residential real estate by the systematic use of fixed commission rates, widespread fee splitting, and the suppression of market information from buyers and sellers. The defendants contended that the law could not cover their activities, which were local and not in interstate commerce. Does the power of the federal government extend to this local activity? Explain.

**3**  The federal government enacted a statute requiring all automobiles sold in interstate commerce to be equipped with "air bags" in the front passenger compartment. A state has a statute requiring all motor vehicles sold in the state to be equipped with three sets of seat belts in the front seat. The auto manufacturers indicate that they can comply with both laws, but only at extra expense to the manufacturer. Are both laws enforceable? Explain.

**4**  A Florida statute prohibits out-of-state banks from owning or controlling a business in Florida that sells investment advisory services. Another statute prohibits all corporations except state-chartered banks and national banks located in Florida from performing certain trust and fiduciary functions. An Illinois bank sought to operate an investment management subsidiary in Florida. It

challenged the constitutionality of these statutes. What was the result? Why?

**5**  Illinois enacted a statute which prohibited transporting into the state for purposes of disposal or storage spent nuclear fuel that was used by out-of-state electric utilities. Illinois has the only away-from-site facility in the U.S. that is accepting spent fuel for storage. Is this statute constitutional? Why, or why not?

**6**  A manufacturer of rope, in filing its Ohio personal-property tax return, deducted from the total value of its inventory the value of imported fibers. These were stored in their original packages for future use in the manufacturing process. Are goods exempt from state taxation so long as they remain in the original package? Explain.

**7**  A Virginia statute prohibited nonresidents of Virginia from catching certain fish in the Virginia portion of Chesapeake Bay and obtaining commercial fishing licenses. There was a federal enrollment and licensing law which authorized federal licensing of fishing boats. Is the Virginia law constitutional? Why, or why not?

**8**  A federal law provides for a $50,000 payment to the survivors of a state police officer who dies as a result of job-related injuries. It also provides that the benefit shall be in addition to any other benefit that may be due from any other source. The Arkansas Worker's Compensation law provided that its death benefit would be reduced to the extent of any federal benefits. Is the Arkansas law constitutional? Why or why not?

**9**  A federal statute known as the "Surface Mining and Reclamation Act" regulated surface mining of coal on prime farm land. Several coal companies challenged the power of Congress to regulate this activity. What result? Why?

**10**  North Carolina imposed an ad valorem tax on imported tobacco held in custom-bonded warehouses prior to domestic manufacture and sale. The tobacco was usually held for two years as part of the aging process. Customs duties were paid to the federal government when the tobacco was taken from the warehouse. Does the North Carolina tax violate the import-export clause? Why, or why not?

**11**  The city of Camden, New Jersey, adopted an ordinance requiring that at least 40 percent of the employees of contractors working on city construction projects be Camden residents. The constitutionality of the ordinance was challenged under the privileges and immunities clause of Article IV of the United States Constitution. The city contended that the clause only applies to state laws and not to local ordinances. Is the city correct? Explain.

**12**  The Montana statutory elk-hunting-license scheme imposed substantially higher (seven-and-a-half times) license fees on nonresidents of the state than on residents. It also required nonresidents, but not residents, to purchase a "combination" license to be able to obtain any number of elks, even one. Out-of-state hunters challenged the constitutionality of the Montana

hunting license law. What was the result? Why?

**13**  A Rhode Island statute defined debt collection as the practice of law; it limited the activity to licensed attorneys. A nationwide debt-collection corporation challenged the constitutionality of the state statute, pointing out that debt collection includes activities that fall short of court proceedings. Is the state law constitutional? Why, or why not?

**14**  A private landfill for solid waste in New Jersey was prohibited by court order from accepting waste from Philadelphia, Pennsylvania. The landfill was almost full, but New Jersey communities were allowed to continue its use. Did the court decision violate the commerce clause? Explain.

**15**  New York's Alcoholic Beverage Control Law required every distiller selling to wholesalers in the state to affirm that they will sell liquor at a price that is no higher than the lowest price they will charge wholesalers anywhere else in the United States during the next month. Is this law constitutional? Why, or why not?

**16**  An Ohio statute awards a tax credit against the motor fuel sales tax for ethanol, but only if it is produced in Ohio or in a state which grants tax advantages to ethanol produced in Ohio. Is the statute constitutional? Why or why not?

*Chapter*

# 7

# The Bill of Rights and Business

## CHAPTER PREVIEW

This chapter discusses the protections of the Bill of Rights as they relate to business. It also covers the Fourteenth Amendment to the United States Constitution. Courts use this amendment to make the provisions of the Bill of Rights applicable to state and local governments. Special attention is given to the protection of commercial speech. As you study the material, keep in mind that even our basic constitutional rights are limited and that they change over time.

The following legal terms are introduced in this chapter: commercial speech, double jeopardy, procedural and substantive due process, equal protection clause, establishment clause, free exercise clause, grand jury, libel, malice, and prior restraint.

## 1. Introduction

Perhaps no part of the U.S. Constitution is so well known or held as sacred as the so-called Bill of Rights, the first ten amendments to the Constitution. Most of us are acquainted to some degree with the freedoms of speech, press, religion, and assembly. Usually we do not think of these matters in a business context; we think of them more as dealing with personal rights of individuals in a free society. There are, however, very important aspects of these freedoms relating to economic opportunity and business activity.

As the materials dealing with the Bill of Rights are studied, four important aspects should be kept in mind. First of all, constitutional rights are not absolutes. They are limited to some degree. Mr. Justice Black, dissenting in *Tinker v. Des Moines Independent Community School Dist.*, 89 S.Ct. 733 (1969), noted this fact when he stated:

> The truth is that a teacher of kindergarten, grammar school, or high school pupils no more carries into a school with him a complete right to freedom of speech and expression than an anti-Catholic or anti-Semitic carries with him a complete freedom of speech and religion into a Catholic church or Jewish synagogue. Nor does a person carry with him into the United States Senate or House, or to the Supreme Court, or any other court, a complete constitutional right to go into those places contrary to their rules and speak his mind on any subject he pleases. It is a myth to say that any person has a constitutional right to say what he pleases, where he pleases, and when he pleases.

The same sense of limitation applies to all basic constitutional protections, although certain people (including some Supreme Court justices) from time to time contend to the contrary.

Second, the extent of any limitation on a basic constitutional guarantee depends upon the nature of the competing public policy in a given case. Cases involving the Bill of Rights almost always require courts to strike a balance either between some goal or policy of society and the constitutional protection involved or between competing constitutional guarantees. For example, such cases may involve conflict between the goal of deterring or preventing crime and the rights of the accused, or between freedom of the press and the rights of one on trial. The courts are continually involved in a weighing process to determine the extent of constitutional protections.

Third, constitutional guarantees exist in order to remove certain issues from the political process and the ballot box. They exist to protect the minority from the majority. Freedom of expression (press and speech) protects the unpopular idea or viewpoint. Freedom of assembly allows groups with ideologies foreign to most of us to meet and express their philosophy. Even the most dangerous criminal is entitled to an attorney and is protected from illegal searches and seizures of evidence. The Bill of Rights protects the "worst" among us even more than it does the "best."

Finally, as previously noted, constitutional rights vary from time to time. The doctrine of constitutional relativity especially applies to the Bill of

Rights. Not only do the rights change, they are affected by emergencies such as war or civil strife. Constitutional principles are constantly reapplied and reexamined.

# THE FIRST AMENDMENT

## 2.   Freedom of Religion

The First Amendment gives us our basic freedoms, commonly known as (1) freedom of religion, (2) freedom of speech, (3) freedom of the press, (4) freedom of assembly, and (5) the right to petition the government for a redress of grievances. These freedoms are intimately connected with the conduct of business as well as with all other aspects of our daily lives.

Freedom of religion is sometimes referred to as the separation of church and state. The First Amendment provisions on freedom of religion have two aspects or are based on two clauses. The First Amendment bans any law "respecting an establishment of religion" (the **establishment clause**) or prohibiting the free exercise thereof (the **free exercise clause**). Cases involving school prayer and tax aid to parochial schools are examples of cases arising under the establishment clause. Cases under this clause usually involve aid to religious organizations or the intrusion of religion into government activities.

Most business-related freedom of religion cases involve the free exercise clause. Religious principles are cited in attempts to prevent the application of a state law or regulation to religious organizations; thus, religion is often asserted as the basis for an exemption to a law. In such cases, courts are called upon to weigh the free exercise of religion against a compelling state interest. Religious liberty may be limited if the limitation proves to be essential to accomplish an overriding governmental interest. A burden upon religion exists where the state makes receipt of an important benefit conditioned upon conduct proscribed by a religious belief, or where it denies such a benefit because of conduct mandated by religious belief, thereby putting substantial pressure on an adherent to modify his or her behavior and to violate his or her beliefs. The state may justify an inroad on religious liberty by showing that it is the least restrictive means of achieving a compelling state interest. However, only those interests of the highest order can overbalance legitimate claims to the free exercise of religion. In the case which follows, notice that the person asserting religious beliefs acquired these beliefs after being employed.

# HOBBIE v. UNEMPLOYMENT APPEALS COM'N OF FLORIDA

107 S.Ct. 1046 (1987)

After two-and-a-half years of employment, Hobbie informed her employer that she was joining the Seventh-Day Adventist Church and that, for religious reasons, she would no longer be able to work at the employer's jewelry store on her Sabbath. When she refused to work scheduled shifts on Friday evenings and Saturdays, she was discharged. She then filed a claim for unemployment compensation which was denied for "misconduct connected with her work." Under Florida law, unemployment compensation benefits are available to persons who become "unemployed through no fault of their own." This denial was upheld by the courts of Florida.

BRENNAN, J....The question to be decided is whether Florida's denial of unemployment compensation benefits to appellant violates the Free Exercise Clause of the First Amendment of the Constitution, as applied to the States through the Fourteenth Amentment....

Under our precedents, the Appeals Commission's disqualification of appellant from receipt of benefits violates the Free Exercise Clause of the First Amendment, applicable to the States through the Fourteenth Amendment. *Sherbert v. Verner*, 83 S.Ct. 1790 (1963); *Thomas v. Review Board of the Indiana Employment Security Div.*, 101 S.Ct. 1425 (1981). In *Sherbert* we considered South Carolina's denial of unemployment compensation benefits to a Sabbatarian who, like Hobbie, refused to work on Saturdays. The Court held that the State's disqualification of Sherbert:

**forced her to choose between following the precepts of her religion and forfeiting benefits, on the one hand, and abandoning one of the precepts of her religion in order to accept work, on the other hand. Governmental imposition of such a choice puts the same kind of burden upon the free exercise of religion as would a fine imposed against her for her Saturday worship.**

We concluded that the State had imposed a burden upon Sherbert's free exercise rights that had not been justified by compelling state interest.

In *Thomas* too, the Court held that a State's denial of unemployment benefits unlawfully burdened an employee's right to free exercise of religion. Thomas, a Jehovah's Witness, held religious beliefs that forbade his participation in the production of armaments. He was forced to leave his job when the employer closed his department and transferred him to a division that fabricated turrets for tanks. Indiana then denied Thomas unemployment compensation benefits. The Court found that the employee had been "put to a choice between fidelity to religious belief or cessation of work" and that the coercive impact of the forfeiture of benefits in this situation was undeniable:

**Not only is it apparent that appellant's declared ineligibility for benefits derives solely from the practice of...religion, but the pressure upon the employee to forego that practice is unmistakable.**

We see no meaningful distinction among the situation of Sherbert, Thomas, and Hobbie. We again affirm, as stated in *Thomas*:

**Where the state conditions receipt of an important benefit upon conduct proscribed by a religious faith, or where it denies such a benefit because of conduct mandated by religious belief, thereby putting substantial pressure on an adherent to modify his behavior and to violate his beliefs, a burden upon religion exists. While the compulsion may be indirect, the infringement upon free exercise is nonetheless substantial....**

The Appeals Commission also attempts to distinguish this case by arguing that, unlike the employees in *Sherbert* and *Thomas,* Hobbie was the "agent of change" and is therefore responsible for the consequences of the conflict between her job and her religious beliefs. In *Sherbert* and *Thomas,* the employees held their respective religious beliefs at the time of hire; subsequent changes in the conditions of employment made *by the employer* caused the conflict between work and belief. In this case, Hobbie's beliefs changed during the course of her employment, creating a conflict between job and faith that had not previously existed. The Appeals Commission contends that "it is...unfair for an employee to adopt religious beliefs that conflict with existing employment and expect to continue the employment without compromising those beliefs" and that this "intentional disregard

of the employer's interests...constitutes misconduct."

In effect, the Appeals Commission asks us to single out the religious convert for different, less favorable treatment than that given an individual whose adherence to his or her faith precedes employment. We decline to do so. The First Amendment protects the free exercise rights of employees who adopt religious beliefs or convert from one faith to another after they are hired. The timing of Hobbie's conversion is immaterial to our determination that her free exercise rights have been burdened; the salient inquiry under the Free Exercise Clause is the burden involved. In *Sherbert, Thomas,* and the present case, the employee was forced to choose between fidelity to religious belief and continued employment; the forfeiture of unemployment benefits for choosing the former over the latter brings unlawful coercion to bear on the employee's choice....

We conclude that Florida's refusal to award unemployment compensation benefits to appellant violated the Free Exercise Clause of the First Amendment. Here, as in *Sherbert* and *Thomas,* the State may not force an employee "to choose between following the precepts of her religion and forfeiting benefits,...and abandoning one of the precepts of her religion in order to accept work." The judgment of the Florida Fifth District Court of Appeal is therefore [*Reversed.*]

---

Freedom of religion has been used to challenge legislation requiring the closing of business establishments on Sunday. Although the motive for such legislation may be, in part, religious, there are also economic reasons for such legislation. As a result, if law is based on economic considerations, it may be upheld if its classifications are reasonable and in the public interest.

However, many such laws have been held invalid as a violation of the First Amendment.

There are other examples of freedom-of-religion cases that concern business. Some of them are summarized in Table 7-1.

## 3. Freedom of the Press

The publishing business is the only organized private business given explicit constitutional protection. Freedom of the press as guaranteed by the First Amendment authorizes a private business to provide organized scrutiny of government.

Freedom of the press means more than just the right to print and to publish. It essentially means that this right must exist without governmental interference. Interference may take many forms, including taxation. One state tried to tax printer's ink used by large newspapers. Another applied a sales tax to general-interest magazines, but the law exempted newspapers and certain magazines that qualify as "religious, professional, trade newspapers" and certain magazines that qualify as "religious, professional, trade and sports journals." Both were found to violate the First Amendment's protection of the press.

Freedom of the press is not absolute. The press is not free to print anything it wants without liability. Rather, freedom of the press is usually construed to prohibit **prior restraints** on publications. If the press publishes that which is illegal or libelous, it has liability for doing so. This liability for damages may be either criminal or civil.

**TABLE 7-1**    Examples of Freedom-of-Religion Issues Affecting Business

| | | Answer | |
|---|---|:---:|:---:|
| | | Yes | No |
| 1 | Is it constitutional to apply the Fair Labor Standards Act (minimum-wage law) to a nonprofit religious organization? | X | |
| 2 | Is it constitutional to apply the labor laws relating to union elections to parochial school teachers? | | X |
| 3 | Is a state law constitutional which provides Sabbath observers with an absolute and unqualified right not to work on their Sabbath? | | X |
| 4 | Is religious belief justification for refusing to participate in the Social Security system? | | X |
| 5 | Does the 1964 Civil Rights Act, which obligates employers to make reasonable accommodations of employees' religious beliefs, violate the First Amendment's establishment clause? | | X |
| 6 | A provision of the Civil Rights Act exempts religious organizations from the provisions against discrimination based on religion; does it cover secular, nonprofit activities as well as religious ones? | X | |

There are many examples of limitations on freedom of the press. For example, courts have allowed the Federal Communications Commission to censor "filthy" words on television. The power of the Commission extends to upholding the public's interest in responsible broadcasting. Freedom of the press does not create an absolute right to know and a concomitant governmental duty to disclose. Thus, the press may not always have access to government records in the absence of a statute such as the Freedom of Information Act.

Do members of the media have greater rights than other citizens? The press frequently asserts that it does. For example, members of the press frequently assert the existence of privileged communications between themselves and informants. They contend that there is a constitutional right to protect the confidential identity of sources of information. The courts have held that no such privileged communication exists. The Constitution does not create such a privileged communication. Unless a statute creates a "shield" for reporters, none exists. There is no federal "shield" law, but some states have enacted them. Even where a statute creates such a privilege, the rights of the press must be balanced with the rights of others, and the shield law may or may not protect reporters who wish to keep their sources confidential.

When the special status of the press has been at issue, the courts have usually held that the press has no special status. For example, a reporter's telephone records may be subpoenaed from the telephone company the same as those of anyone else. A newspaper may be searched pursuant to a search warrant the same as any other business. Newspapers have tort liability for invasion of privacy the same as other defendants.

A major area of litigation involving freedom of the press is defamation. The tort theory known as **libel** is used to recover damages as a result of printed defamation of character. Libel cases compensate individuals for harm inflicted by defamatory printed falsehoods. Since the threat of a libel suit could have a chilling effect on freedom of the press and on the public's rights to information, the law has a different standard for imposing liability when the printed matter concerns an issue of public interest and concern. If the person involved is a public official or figure, a plaintiff seeking damages for emotional distress caused by offensive publications must prove actual **malice** in order to recover. "Actual malice" includes knowledge that the printed statements were false or circumstances showing a reckless disregard for whether they were true or not. If the plaintiff is not a public figure or public official, there is liability for libelous statements without a proof of malice.

The gist of a libel suit is a false statement. At common law, there was a presumption that a defamatory statement was false. This presumption has been changed in most states. Even if it has not been changed, the Supreme Court has held that a plaintiff who is a public figure must always prove falsity of the media's statements. Also, a plaintiff who is a private figure must prove falsity if the subject matter of the statement is of public concern. When the statement is of public concern, the constitutional protections of free speech and free press supplant the common-law presumption.

In a landmark decision concerning the rights of journalist-defendants in libel cases, a plaintiff sought by use of discovery techniques to ascertain the state of mind of the journalist at the time of publication. Since the plaintiff was required to prove malice, he sought to do so with the defendant's own testimony obtained by deposition. The journalist claimed that the First Amendment prohibited such questioning and that discovery procedures could not be used to ascertain the state of mind of a journalist. In rejecting the contentions of the defendant-journalist, the court held that the First Amendment does not protect journalists from having to testify on opinions, judgments, and convictions they held while preparing stories. As a result of this and other decisions, it seems clear that freedom of the press allows the publication of almost anything. However, liability may result if the published matter should not have been published, and the press as a defendant usually has no special status.

## 4. Freedom of Speech

Freedom of speech is sometimes referred to as freedom of expression. This freedom covers both verbal and written communications. In addition, it covers conduct or actions considered symbolic speech. Although freedom of speech is not absolute, it is as close to being absolute as any constitutional guarantee. It exists to protect the minority from the majority. It means freedom to express ideas antagonistic to those of the majority. Freedom of speech exists for thoughts many of us hate and for ideas that may be foreign to us. It means freedom to express the unorthodox, and it recognizes that there is no such thing as a false idea.

Freedom of speech protects corporations as well as individuals. The public interests served by freedom of expression protect the listener as well as the speaker. Freedom of expression includes freedom of information or the rights of the public to be informed. Since corporations may add to the public's knowledge and information, they also have the right to free speech. Although it may not be coextensive with the right of an individual, it may not be limited without a compelling state interest in doing so. State regulatory commissions often seek to limit the activities of public utilities. Such attempts may run afoul of the First Amendment, as occurred in the following case.

# CONSOL. EDISON v. PUBLIC SERVICE COM'N.

100 S.Ct. 2326 (1980)

POWELL, J.:...The question in this case is whether the First Amendment, as incorporated by the Fourteenth Amendment, is violated by an order of the Public Service Commission of the State of New York that prohibits the inclusion in monthly electric bills of inserts discussing controversial issues of public policy.

The Consolidated Edison Company of New York...placed written material entitled "Independence Is Still a Goal, and Nuclear Power Is Needed To Win The Battle" in its January 1976 billing envelope. The bill insert stated Consolidated Edison's views on "the benefits of nuclear power," saying that they "far outweigh any potential risk" and that nuclear power plants are safe, economical, and clean. The utility also contended that increased use of nuclear energy would further this country's independence from foreign energy sources.

[In 1977 the Public Service Commission of the State of New York issued an order which]...prohibited "utilities from using bill inserts to discuss political matters, including the desirability of future development of nuclear power."...The Commission concluded that Consolidated Edison customers who receive bills containing inserts are a captive audience of diverse views who should not be subjected to the utility's beliefs. Accordingly, the Commission barred utility companies from including bill inserts that express "their opinions or viewpoints on controversial issues of public policy." The Commission did not, however, bar utilities from sending bill inserts discussing topics that are not "controversial issues of public policy."...

Consolidated Edison sought review of the Commission's order in the New York state courts....The Court of Appeals held that the order did not violate the Constitution because it was a valid time, place, and manner regulation designed to protect the privacy of Consolidated Edison's customers....

The First and Fourteenth Amendments guarantee that no State shall abridge the freedom of speech. Freedom of speech is indispensable to the discovery and spread of political truth and the best test of truth is the power of the thought to get itself accepted in the competition of the market. The First and Fourteenth Amendments remove governmental restraints from the arena of public discussion, putting the decision as to what views shall be voiced largely into the hands of each of us, in the hope that use of such freedom will ultimately produce a more capable citizenry and more perfect polity.

This Court has emphasized that the First Amendment embraces at the least the liberty to discuss publicly and truthfully all matters of public concern. In the mailing that triggered the regulation at issue, Consolidated Edison advocated the use of nuclear power. The Commission has limited the means by which Consolidated Edison may participate in the public debate on this question and other controversial issues of national interest and importance. Thus, the Commission's prohibition of discussion of controversial issues strikes at the heart of the freedom to speak.

The Commission's ban on bill inserts is not, of course, invalid merely because it imposes a limitation upon speech. We must consider whether the State can demonstrate that its regulation is constitutionally permissible....(as) a reasonable time, place, or manner restriction...or a narrowly tailored means of serving a compelling state interest.

This Court has recognized the validity of reasonable time, place, or manner regulations that serve a significant governmental interest and leave ample alternative channels for communication....Various methods of speech, regardless of their content, may frustrate legitimate governmental goals. No matter what its message, a roving soundtrack that blares at 2 A.M. disturbs neighborhood tranquility.

A restriction that regulates only the time, place or manner of speech may be imposed so long as it's reasonable. But when regulation is based on the content of speech, governmental action must be scrutinized more carefully to ensure that communication has not been prohibited merely because public officials disapprove the speaker's views.

As a consequence, we have emphasized that time, place, and manner regulations must be applicable to all speech irrespective of content. Governmental action that regulates speech on the basis of its subject matter "slips from the neutrality of time, place, and circumstance into a concern about content." Therefore, a constitutionally permissible time, place, or manner restriction may not be based upon either the content or subject matter of speech.

The Commission does not pretend that its action is unrelated to the content or subject matter of bill inserts. Indeed, it has undertaken to suppress certain bill inserts precisely because they address controversial issues of public policy. The Commission allows inserts that present information to consumers on certain subjects, such as energy conservation measures, but it forbids the use of inserts that discuss public controversies. The Commission, with commendable candor, justifies its ban on the ground that consumers will benefit from receiving "useful" information, but not from the prohibited information. The Commission's own rationale demonstrates that its action cannot be upheld as a content-neutral time, place, or manner regulation.

Where a government restricts the speech of a private person, the state action may be sustained only if the government can show that the regulation is a precisely drawn means of serving a compelling state interest.

...The Commission argues that its prohibition is necessary (i) to avoid forcing Consolidated Edison's views on a captive audience, (ii) to allocate limited resources in the public interest, and (iii) to ensure that ratepayers do not subsidize the cost of the bill inserts.

Even if a short exposure to Consolidated Edison's views may offend the sensibilities of some consumers, the ability of government to shut off discourse solely to protect others from hearing it is dependent upon a showing that substantial privacy interests are being invaded in an essentially intolerable manner. A less stringent analysis would permit a government to slight the First Amendment's role in affording the public access to discussion, debate and the dissemination of information and ideas. Where a single speaker communicates to many listeners, the First Amendment does not permit the government to prohibit speech as intrusive unless the captive audience cannot avoid objectional speech.

Passengers on public transportation or residents of a neighborhood disturbed by the raucous broadcasts from a passing soundtruck, may well be unable to escape an unwanted message. But customers who encounter an objectionable billing insert may effectively avoid further bombardment of their sensibilities simply by averting their eyes. The customer of Consolidated Edison may escape exposure to objectionable material simply by transferring the bill insert from envelope to wastebasket....

The Commission's suppression of bill inserts that discuss controversial issues of public policy directly infringes the freedom of speech protected by the First and Fourteenth Amendments. The state action is neither a valid time, place, or manner restriction,...nor a narrowly drawn prohibition justified by a compelling state interest. Accordingly, the regulation is invalid. [*Reversed.*]

---

The issue of freedom of speech arises in many business situations. For example, cases involving picketing, especially with unions, often are concerned with this issue. The right to picket peacefully for a lawful purpose is well-recognized. A state or local law that prohibits all picketing would be unconstitutional since picketing per se is a valuable form of communication. However, a state law that limits picketing or other First Amendment freedoms may be constitutional if: (1) the regulation is within the constitutional power of government, (2) it furthers an important or substantial governmental interest, (3) it is unrelated to suppression of free expression, and (4) the incidental restriction on First Amendment freedoms is no greater than is essential to further the government's interest. Under these principles, laws that prevent pickets from obstructing traffic and those designed to prevent violence would be constitutional. For example, a Texas statute that prohibits "mass picketing," defined as picketing by more than two persons within 50 feet of any entrance or of one another, does not violate the First Amendment. In 1988 the Supreme Court held that a city ordinance prohibiting picketing in front of an individual residence was constitutional. It did not ban all residential picketing and met the four tests previously noted. It was enacted to prevent picketing of the homes of doctors who perform abortions.

Courts may limit the number of pickets to preserve order and promote safety, but they will not deny pickets the right to express opinions in a picket line. For example, a court order preventing a client from picketing her lawyer was held to be a violation of the First Amendment. Freedom of speech even extends to boycotts of a business for a valid public purpose such as the elimination of discrimination.

Freedom of expression does not protect obscene materials. In the case of pornography involving children, the material is not protected by the First Amendment, even if it is not legally obscene. The community's interest in banning such material outweighs any First Amendment interests. People who sell obscene materials or child pornography are frequently prosecuted for doing so. The difficult issues in obscenity cases are defining obscenity and determining whether or not items involved are obscene.

A movie, book, or magazine is obscene and subject to state regulation if it violates a three-part test: (1) if it, taken as a whole, appeals to a prurient interest in sex; (2) if it portrays, in a patently offensive way, sexual conduct specifically defined by the applicable state law; and, (3) if it, taken as a whole, does not have serious literary, artistic, political, or scientific value. In deciding whether allegedly obscene work has "literary, artistic, political, or scientific value," a court must determine not whether an ordinary member of any given community would find serious literary, artistic, political, or scientific value in a work, but whether a reasonable person would find such value in the material taken as whole. The mere fact that a minority of a population believes that work has serious value does not mean that the "reasonable person" would not find that it has such value. At one time, if a work had any redeeming social value or if it were of social importance, it was not obscene. This test of obscenity has been rejected.

Obscenity cases based on past conduct are much less difficult than those involving a prior restraint. Although freedom of speech does not protect obscenity, it does prevent most attempts to censor speech in advance. Prior restraints, while not illegal per se, must have safeguards to protect First Amendment rights. Courts will seldom enjoin obscenity and will leave law enforcement to deal with actual violations.

In some free-speech cases, an individual whose own speech or conduct may not be prohibited is nevertheless permitted to challenge a statute limiting speech because it also threatens other people not before the court. The person is allowed to challenge the statute because others who may desire to engage in legally protected expression may refrain from doing so. They may fear the risk of prosecution, or they may not want to risk having a law declared to be only partially invalid. This is known as the *overbreadth doctrine.* It means that the legislators have gone too far in seeking to achieve a goal.

For example, an airport authority resolution declared the central terminal area "not open for First Amendment activities." The resolution was unconstitutional under the First Amendment overbreadth doctrine. The resolution reached the "universe of expressive activity" and in effect created a "First-Amendment-Free Zone" at the airport. Nearly every person who entered the airport would violate the resolution, since it bars all First Amendment activities, including talking and reading.

## 5.  Commercial Speech

Historically, commercial speech was not protected by the First Amendment. However, in the 1970s the Supreme Court began to recognize that free commercial speech was essential to the public's right to know. Several cases established that commercial speech was protected.

# VA. ST. BD. OF PHARM. v. VA. CIT. CONS. COUNCIL

96 S.Ct. 1817 (1976)

The plaintiffs were consumers of prescription drugs who claimed that they would benefit from advertising of prescription drugs. They brought suit against the Virginia State Board of Pharmacy challenging the constitutionality of a Virginia statute declaring it unprofessional conduct for a licensed pharmacist to advertise the price of prescription drugs. The Board was empowered to revoke a license for a violation as well as to impose monetary penalties. As a result of the statute, all advertising of the price of prescription drugs was effectively forbidden. The lower court held the law to be in violation of the First and Fourteenth Amendments. The Board appealed.

BLACKMUN, J.:...Freedom of speech presupposes a willing speaker. But where a speaker exists, as is the case here, the protection afforded is to the communication, to its source and to its recipients both....If there is a right to advertise, there is a reciprocal right to receive the advertising, and it may be asserted by these appellees....The appellants contend that the advertisement of prescription drug prices is outside the protection of the First Amendment because it is "commercial speech."...

Last term, in *Bigelow v. Virginia*, 421 U.S. 809 (1975), the notion of unprotected "commercial speech" all but passed from the scene. We reversed a conviction for violation of a Virginia statute that made the circulation of any publication to encourage or promote the processing of an abortion in Virginia a misdemeanor....We rejected the contention that the publication was unprotected because it was commercial....We concluded that "the Virginia courts erred in

their assumptions that advertising, as such, was entitled to no First Amendment protection," and we observed that the "relationship of speech to the marketplace of products or of services does not make it valueless in the marketplace of ideas."...

Here,...the question whether there is a First Amendment exception for "commercial speech" is squarely before us. Our pharmacist does not wish to editorialize on any subject, cultural, philosophical, or political. He does not wish to report any particular newsworthy fact, or to make generalized observations even about commercial matters. The "idea" he wishes to communicate is simply this: "I will sell you the X prescription drug at the Y price." Our question, then, is whether this communication is wholly outside the protection of the First Amendment.

We begin with several propositions that already are settled or beyond serious dispute. It is clear, for example, that speech does not lose its First Amendment protection because money is spent to protect it, as in a paid advertisement of one form or another. Speech likewise is protected even though it may involve a solicitation to purchase or otherwise pay or contribute money....

Our question is whether speech which does "no more than propose a commercial transaction," is so removed from any "exposition of ideas," and from "'truth, science, morality, and arts in general, in its diffusion of liberal sentiments on the administration of Government,'" that it lacks all protection. Our answer is that it is not.

Focusing first on the individual parties to the transaction that is proposed in the commercial advertisement, we may assume that the advertiser's interest is a purely economic one. That hardly disqualifies him from protection under the First Amendment....

As to the particular consumer's interest in the free flow of commercial information that interest may be as keen, if not keener by far, than his interest in the day's most urgent political debate. Appellees' case in this respect is a convincing one. Those whom the suppression of prescription drug price information hits the hardest are the poor, the sick, and particularly the aged. A disproportionate amount of their income tends to be spent on prescription drugs; yet they are the least able to learn, by shopping from pharmacist to pharmacist, where their scarce dollars are best spent. When drug prices vary as strikingly as they do, information as to who is charging what becomes more than a convenience. It could mean the alleviation of physical pain or the enjoyment of the basic necessities.

Generalizing, society also may have a strong interest in the free flow of commercial information. Even an individual advertisement, though entirely "commercial," may be of general public interest....Obviously, not all commercial messages contain the same or even a very great public interest element. There are few to which such an element, however, could not be added. Our pharmacist, for example, could cast himself as a commentator on store-to-store disparities in drug prices, giving his own and those of a competitor as proof. We see little point in requiring him to do so, and little difference if he does not.

Moreover, there is another consideration that suggests that no line between publicly "interesting" or "important" commercial advertising and the opposite kind could ever be drawn. Advertising, however tasteless and excessive it sometimes may seem, is nonetheless dissemination of information as to who is producing and selling what product, for what reason, and at what price. So long as we preserve a predominately free enterprise economy, the allocation of our resources in large measure will be made through numerous private economic decisions. It is a matter of public interest that those decisions, in the aggregate, be intelligent and well informed. To this end, the free flow of commercial information is indispensable. And if it is indispensable to the proper allocation of resources in a free enterprise system, it is also indispensable to the formation of intelligent opinions as to how that system ought to be regulated or altered. Therefore, even if the First Amendment were thought to be primarily an instrument to enlighten public decision making in a democracy, we could not say that the free flow of information does not serve that goal....

In concluding that commercial speech, like other varieties, is protected, we of course do not hold that it can never be regulated in any way. Some forms of commercial speech regulation are surely permissible....[For example] untruthful speech, commercial or otherwise, has never been protected for its own sake....The First Amendment as we construe it today, does not prohibit the State from insuring that the stream of commercial information flow cleanly as well as freely....

What is at issue is whether a State may completely suppress the dissemination of concededly truthful information about entirely lawful activity, fearful of that information's effect upon its disseminators and its recipients. Reserving other questions, we conclude that the answer to this one is in the negative. [*Affirmed.*]

Commercial speech is not protected to the same extent as noncommercial speech. In a case involving a billboard ordinance which banned all billboards, the Supreme Court held the law unconstitutional because it banned noncommercial billboards. The court stated that the Constitution accords a lesser protection to commercial speech than to other forms of speech. Commercial speech is protected only if it concerns a lawful activity and is not misleading. A restriction on commercial speech is valid if it seeks to implement a substantial governmental interest, directly advances that interest, and reaches no farther than necessary to accomplish the objective. For example, a state may restrict some advertising that is designed to promote products that, though legal, are considered undesirable by the legislature. Such limitations might cover prostitution, gambling, alcohol, smoking, or chewing tobacco. It is up to the states to decide how to regulate legal but potentially harmful businesses.

In commercial speech cases, the courts are involved in the weighing process previously noted. "For sale" signs cannot be banned in residential areas, but "adult entertainment" businesses may be restricted to certain areas. Universities may ban sales by outsiders in residence halls, but all live entertainment may not be banned from a community. Many commercial speech cases involve attempts by government to regulate morality. These attempts often fail in the weighing process because of the overwhelming importance of freedom of speech, although some are successful.

### 6.   Other First Amendment Freedoms

First Amendment freedoms also include the right to assemble and associate, and the right to petition the government for a redress of grievances. In addition, the specifics of the Bill of Rights have additional implied rights, such as the right of privacy, the right to knowledge, and the right to one's beliefs. These rights were derived from the others actually specified. For example, the right of freedom of speech and press has been held to include not only the right to utter or to print but the right to distribute, the right to receive, and the right to read. Freedom of expression includes freedom of inquiry, freedom of thought, and freedom to teach. Moreover, the right of association is more than the right to attend a meeting or to join a group. It also includes the right *not* to join a group. For example, lack of political party affiliation may not be a ground for discharging certain employees.

The freedom of assembly and protection of association is relevant to many cases involving unpopular groups such as Nazis and Communists. For example, some cases concern the issuance of passports to Communists, and others involve laws prohibiting Communists from holding certain positions such as offices in labor unions or jobs in defense plants. Such laws have been held as unconstitutional as a result of the First Amendment. On the other hand, the First Amendment does not prevent laws designed to change the conduct of traditional mainstream groups such as the International Rotary or the United States Jaycees. The Constitution is no bar to state laws requiring that these organizations admit women to membership. While such organizations and their members have a First Amendment right of expressive association, there is no evidence to suggest that admitting women will affect, in any significant way, the existing members' ability to carry out their various purposes. Thus, it can be seen that the Constitution is designed to protect minorities more than the majority.

The guarantee of freedom of assembly and association prevents guilt by association. It also ensures privacy in one's association. For example, it has been held that state law may not compel the disclosure of membership lists of a constitutionally valid association. Such a disclosure implies likelihood of a substantial restraint upon the member's right to freedom of association. Protection also extends to forms of association that are not political, such as the social, legal, and economic benefits of membership in groups. For example, the First Amendment right to associate and to assemble prevents a state from denying a license to practice law to a Communist. It also prevents a state from denying a group such as the South African rugby team the right to play a match in the United States. However, keep in mind that the right to associate and to express collective opinions does not mean that government or anyone else must follow those opinions.

## OTHER PROVISIONS

### 7.  The Fourth Amendment

The Fourth Amendment protects individuals and corporations from unreasonable searches and seizures. It primarily protects persons from unwarranted intrusions into their individual privacy.

Fourth Amendment issues usually arise in criminal cases. Among typical issues are (1) the validity of searches incident to an arrest, (2) the validity of search warrants—the presence of probable cause to issue the warrant, (3) the validity of consents to searches, and (4) the extent to which property such as automobiles may be searched without a warrant. In addition, electronic surveillance often raises Fourth Amendment issues. For example, the Omnibus Crime Control and Safe Streets Act authorizes the electronic interception of communications pursuant to a court-authorized order. A "bug" was placed in a building by covert entry.

The Supreme Court held that such surveillance does not violate the Fourth Amendment.

In recent years, the protection of the Fourth Amendment has been narrowed by court decisions. To protect police officers, courts have held that officers may search someone being arrested and the immediate area around him or her for weapons. Officers searching an automobile are given far more latitude than when searching a person, a home, or a building. Persons lawfully arrested may be convicted of other crimes with evidence obtained as the result of valid searches. The right to search for evidence extends to the premises of persons not suspected of criminal conduct. Such premises may include offices of operating newspapers and attorneys. In addition, one who does not own a vehicle may not object to its search even if that person has property in the vehicle.

In 1987, the court continued to narrow the protection of the Fourth Amendment. It held that public employers may search a government worker's office without a search warrant if they have reason to suspect wrongdoing. Only a reasonable suspicion of wrongdoing, not probable cause, is required. Government employees do have some expectation of privacy, and this issue will be litigated further as government attempts to deal with problems such as drug abuse and AIDS.

Fourth Amendment protection extends to civil matters as well as to criminal cases. For example, in a case involving the right of a counselor to visit the home of a welfare recipient, it was held that such home visits did not violate the Fourth Amendment. In another case, it was held that building inspectors do not have the right to inspect for building code violations without a warrant, if the owner of the premises objects. The Fourth Amendment has been used to prevent the Securities and Exchange Commission (SEC) from using confidential reports obtained in the course of its function to establish a violation of federal law. The reports cannot be required for one purpose and then used for another without running afoul of the Fourth Amendment.

Legislative bodies frequently provide for inspections of businesses without a search warrant. For example, the Occupational Safety and Health Act (OSHA) authorizes agents of the secretary of labor to conduct unannounced searches of the work area of any employment facility to inspect for safety hazards and violations of OSHA regulations. The Supreme Court in 1978 held this federal law to be unconstitutional under the Fourth Amendment. If an owner of a business objects to an inspection, inspectors must go to court and obtain a search warrant. To obtain this warrant inspectors must show that the standards for conducting an inspection are satisfied; they do not need to show probable cause.

In 1987, the Supreme Court reviewed a state law that authorizes warrantless searches of junkyards. A divided court (5 to 4) in the case which follows said that warrantless searches of junkyards are constitutional.

# NEW YORK v. BURGER

107 S.Ct. 2636 (1987)

Burger's junkyard business consists of dismantling automobiles and selling their parts. A New York statute authorized warrantless inspections of automobile junkyards. Police officers entered his junkyard and asked to see his license and records of automobiles and vehicle parts in his possession. He replied that he did not have such documents which are required by the statute. After announcing their intention to conduct an inspection of the junkyard pursuant to the statute, the officers, without objection by respondent, conducted the inspection and discovered stolen vehicles and parts. Burger, who was charged with possession of stolen property, moved to suppress the evidence obtained as a result of the inspection. He contended that the administrative inspection statute is unconstitutional when it authorizes warrantless searches. After the trial court denied his motion, Burger was convicted. His conviction was reversed on appeal when the New York Court of Appeals held the statute to be unconstitutional.

BLACKMUN, J.:...This case presents the question whether the warrantless search of an automobile junkyard, conducted pursuant to a statute authorizing such a search, falls within the exception to the warrant requirement for administrative inspections of pervasively regulated industries....

The Court long has recognized that the Fourth Amendment's prohibition on unreasonable searches and seizures is applicable to commercial premises, as well as to private homes. An owner or operator of a business thus has an expectation of privacy in commercial property, which society is prepared to consider to be reasonable. This expectation exists not only with respect to traditional police searches conducted for the gathering of criminal evidence but also with respect to administrative inspections designed to enforce regulatory statutes. An expectation of privacy in commercial premises, however, is different from, and indeed less than, a similar expectation in an individual's home. This expectation is particularly attenuated in commercial property employed in "closely regulated" industries....Certain industries have such a history of government oversight that no reasonable expectation of privacy could exist for a proprietor over the stock of such an enterprise.

Because the owner or operator of commercial premises in a "closely regulated" industry has a reduced expectation of privacy, the warrant and probable-cause requirements, which fulfill the traditional Fourth Amendment standard of reasonableness for a government search have lessened application in his context. Rather, we conclude that, as in other situations of special need, where privacy interests of the owner are weakened and the government interests in regulating particular businesses are concomitantly heightened, a warrantless inspection of commercial premises may well be reasonable within the meaning of the Fourth Amendment.

This warrantless inspection, however, even in the context of a pervasively regulated business, will be deemed to be reasonable only so long as three criteria are met. First, there must be a "substantial" government interest that informs the regulatory scheme pursuant to which the inspection is made....

Second, the warrantless inspections must be necessary to further the regulatory scheme. For example, in *Dewey* we recognized that forcing mine inspectors to obtain a warrant before every inspection might alert mine owners or operators to the impending inspection, thereby frustrating the purposes of the Mine Safety and Health Act—to detect and thus to deter safety and health violations.

Finally, the statute's inspection program, in terms of the certainty and regularity of its application, must provide a constitutionally adequate substitute for a warrant. In other words, the regulatory statute must perform the two basic functions of a warrant: it must advise the owner of the commercial premises that the search is being made pursuant to the law and has a properly defined scope, and it must limit the discretion of the inspecting officers. To perform this first function, the statute must be sufficiently comprehensive and defined that the owner of commercial property cannot help but be aware that his property will be subject to periodic inspections undertaken for specific purposes. In addition, in defining how a statute limits the discretion of the inspectors, we have observed that it must be carefully limited in time, place, and scope.

Searches made pursuant to...(this law) clearly fall within this established exception to the warrant requirement for administrative inspections in closely regulated businesses. First, the nature of the regulatory statute reveals that the operation of a junkyard, part of which is devoted to vehicle dismantling, is a "closely regulated" business in the State of New York. The provisions regulating the activity of vehicle dismantling are extensive....This history of government regulation of junk-related activities argues

strongly in favor of the "closely regulated" status of the automobile junkyard.

Accordingly, in light of the regulatory framework governing his business and the history of regulation of related industries, an operator of a junkyard engaging in vehicle dismantling has a reduced expectation of privacy in this "closely regulated" business.

The New York regulatory scheme satisfied the three criteria necessary to make reasonable warrantless inspection....First, the State has a substantial interest in regulating the vehicle-dismantling and automobile-junkyard industry because motor vehicle theft has increased in the State and because the problem of theft is associated with this industry....

Second, regulation of the vehicle-dismantling industry reasonably serves the State's substantial interest in eradicating automobile theft. It is well established that the theft problem can be addressed effectively by controlling the receiver of, or market in, stolen property. Automobile junkyards and vehicle dismantlers provide the major market for stolen vehicles and vehicle parts.

Thus, the State rationally may believe that it will reduce car theft by regulations that prevent automobile junkyards from becoming markets for stolen vehicles and that help trace the origin and destination of vehicle parts.

Moreover, the warrantless administrative inspections...are necessary to further the regulatory scheme....Because stolen cars and parts often pass quickly through an automobile junkyard, "frequent" and "unannounced" inspections are necessary in order to detect them. In sum, surprise is crucial if the regulatory scheme aimed at remedying this major social problem is to function at all.

Third, § 415-a5 provides a "constitutionally adequate substitute for a warrant." The statute informs the operator of a vehicle dismantling business that inspections will be made on a regular basis. Thus, the vehicle dismantler knows that the inspections to which he is subject do not constitute discretionary acts by a government official but are conducted pursuant to statute....

Finally, the "time, place, and scope" of the inspection is limited to place appropriate restraints upon the discretion of the inspecting officers. The officers are allowed to conduct an inspection only during the regular and usual business hours. The inspections can be made only of vehicle-dismantling and re-lated industries. And the permissible scope of these searches is narrowly defined: the inspectors may examine the records, as well as "any vehicles or parts of vehicles which are subject to the record keeping requirements of this section and which are on the premises."

A search conducted pursuant to §415-a5, therefore, clearly falls within the well-established exception to the warrant requirement for administrative inspections of "closely regulated" businesses....[*Reversed and remanded.*]

---

### 8.   The Fifth Amendment

The Fifth Amendment is best known for its protection against compulsory self-incrimination. People frequently plead "the Fifth," and almost everyone knows they are exercising their right to its protection. The Fifth Amendment goes much further, however. It contains other protections, and, more specifically, it (1) requires indictment by a **grand jury** for a capital offense or infamous crime, (2) prohibits **double jeopardy,** (3) requires just compensation in eminent domain proceedings, and (4) contains a due process clause.

A grand jury must decide whether there is sufficient evidence of guilt to justify the accused's standing trial. Grand juries are usually made up of twenty-three persons, and it takes a majority vote to indict a defendant. It takes less proof to indict a person and to require him or her to stand trial than it does to convict. The grand jury provision contains an exception for court-martial proceedings.

Proper functioning of the grand jury system depends upon secrecy of the proceedings. This secrecy protects the innocent accused from disclosure of the accusations made against him or her before the grand jury. However, transcripts of grand jury proceedings may be obtained if necessary to avoid possible injustice in judicial proceedings. For example, a litigant may use a grand jury transcript at a trial to impeach a witness, to refresh the witness's recollection, to test his or her credibility, and the like. The disclosure of a grand jury transcript is appropriate only in those cases where the need for it outweighs the public interest in secrecy, and the burden of demonstrating this balance rests upon a private party seeking disclosure.

Protection against double jeopardy means that a person cannot be tried twice by the same governmental body for the same offense. The double jeopardy clause protects corporations as well as individuals.

The Fifth Amendment protects life, liberty, and property from deprivation by the federal government without due process of law. The Fourteenth Amendment contains an identical provision which applies to the states. Although due process is difficult to define, it basically amounts to "fundamental fairness." Since interpretations of the due process clauses of the Fifth and Fourteenth Amendments are for all practical purposes identical, the discussion of due process later in this chapter under the Fourteenth Amendment and the case included there also illustrate due process under the Fifth Amendment.

## 9. Eminent Domain

Eminent domain is used by the government to acquire real property for public purposes. The Fifth Amendment requires the government to provide just compensation. This is a question of fact for a jury if the property owner and the condemning governmental unit cannot agree on a fair market value of the property taken.

In 1987, the Supreme Court gave new vigor to the rights of property owners. For several decades the courts had approved land-use regulations and held that they did not require just compensation. In two cases that year, the court retreated from this proposition. In the first case, it held that any temporary acquisition of property required just compensation. If the state occupies someone's property, even for a short period, it must pay rental. The case involved a church summer camp whose buildings were destroyed by a flood. The state restricted all use of the land because it was in a flood plain. A state court lifted the restriction but denied compensation to the owners for the loss of use prior to the decision. The Supreme Court said that the state had to pay for the time the restriction was in effect. According to the Fifth Amendment, any governmental action that even temporarily denies a landowner use of land is a taking. The fact that it lessens government flexibility in land-use regulation is immaterial.

The second case involved access to public beaches. A landowner sought a building permit. The state conditioned granting it on the owners granting an easement to the public to pass across their private property to reach the public beach. The case which follows applies the Fifth Amendment to this state action. It is important to note that the government's power to forbid a particular land use includes the power to condition such use on some concession by the owner; however, the condition must further the same governmental purpose advanced as justification for prohibiting the use.

# NOLLAN v. CALIFORNIA COASTAL COM'N

107 S.Ct. 3141 (1987)

James and Mary Nollan own a beachfront lot in Ventura County, California. A quarter-mile north of their property is Faria County Park, an oceanside public park with a public beach and recreation area. Another public beach area, known locally as "the Cove," lies 1,800 feet south of their lot. A concrete seawall approximately eight feet high separates the beach portion of the Nollans' property from the rest of the lot. The historic mean tide line determines the lot's oceanside boundary.

The California Coastal Commission granted a permit to the Nollans to replace a small bungalow on their beachfront lot with a larger house upon the condition that they allow the public an easement to pass across their beach to the other beaches previously referred to.

The Nollans objected to the condition and contended that imposition of the access condition violated the Takings Clause of the Fifth Amendment, as incorporated against the states by the Fourteenth Amendment. The California courts held that the Constitution did not require payment for the easement.

SCALIA, J.:...Had California simply required the Nollans to make an easement across their beachfront available to the public on a permanent basis in order to increase public access to the beach, rather than conditioning their permit to rebuild their house on their agreeing to do so, we have no doubt there would have been a taking.... Indeed, one of the principal uses of the eminent domain power is to assure that the government be able to require conveyance of just such interests, so long as it pays for them....

We have repeatedly held that as to property reserved by its owner for private use, the right to exclude others is one of the most essential sticks in the bundle of rights that are commonly characterized as property.... Where governmental action results in a permanent physical occupation of the property, by the government itself or by others, our cases uniformly have found a taking to the extent of the occupation, without regard to whether the action achieves an important public benefit or has only minimal economic impact on the owner. We think a "permanent physical occupation" has occurred, for purposes of that rule, where individuals are given a permanent and continuous right to pass to and fro, so that the real property may continuously be traversed, even though no particular individual is permitted to station himself permanently upon the premises.

Given, then, that requiring uncompensated conveyance of the easement outright would violate the Fourteenth Amendment, the question becomes whether requiring it to be conveyed as a condition for issuing a land use permit alters the outcome. We have long recognized that land use regulation does not effect a taking if it substantially advances legitimate state interests and does not deny an owner economically viable use of his land. Our cases have not elaborated on the standards for determining what constitutes a "legitimate state interest" or what type of connection between the regulation and the state interest satisfies the requirement that the former "substantially advance" the latter. They have made clear, however, that a broad range of governmental purposes and regulations satisfies these requirements.

The Commission argues that among these permissible purposes are protecting the public's ability to see the beach, assisting the public in overcoming the "psychological barrier" to using the beach created by a developed shorefront, and preventing congestion on the public beaches. We assume, without deciding, that this is so—in which case the Commission unquestionably would be able to deny the Nollans their permit outright if their new house (alone, or by reason of the cumulative impact produced in conjunction with other construction) would substantially impede these purposes, unless the denial would interfere so drastically with the Nollans' use of their property as to constitute a taking.

The Commission argues that a permit condition that serves the same legitimate police-power purpose as a refusal to issue the permit should not be found to be a taking if the refusal to issue the permit would not constitute a taking. We agree. Thus, if the Commission attached to the permit some condition that would have protected the public's ability to see the beach notwithstanding construction of the new house—for example, a height limitation, a width restriction, or a ban on fences—so long as the Commission could have exercised its police power (as we have assumed it could) to forbid construction of the house altogether, imposition of the condition would also be constitutional. Moreover (and here we come closer to the facts of the present case), the condition would be constitutional even if it consisted of the requirement that the Nollans provide a viewing spot on their property for passersby with whose sighting of the ocean their new house would interfere. Although such a requirement, constituting a permanent grant of continuous access to the property, would have to be considered a taking if it were not attached to a development permit, the Commission's assumed power to forbid construction of the house in order to protect the public's view of the beach must surely include the power to condition construction upon some concession by the owner, even a concession of property rights, that serves the same end. If a prohibition designed to accomplish that purpose would be a legitimate exercise of the police power rather than a taking, it would be strange to conclude that providing the owner an alternative to that prohibition which accomplishes the same purpose is not.

The evident constitutional propriety disappears, however, if the condition substituted for the prohibition utterly fails to further the end advanced as the justification for the prohibition. When that essential nexus is eliminated, the situation becomes the same as if California law forbade shouting fire in a crowded theater, but granted dispensations to those willing to contribute $100 to the state treasury. While a ban on shouting fire can be a core exercise of the State's police power to protect the public safety, and can thus meet even our stringent standards for regulation of speech, adding the unrelated condition alters the purpose to one which, while it may be legitimate, is inadequate to sustain the ban. Therefore, even though, in a sense, requiring a $100 tax contribution in order to shout fire is a lesser restriction on speech than an outright ban, it would not pass constitutional muster. Similarly here, the lack of nexus between the condition and the original purpose of the building restriction converts that purpose to something other than what it was. The purpose then becomes, quite simply, the obtaining of an easement to serve some valid governmental purpose, but without payment of compensation. Whatever may be the outer limits of "legitimate state interests" in the takings and land use context, this is not one of them. In short, unless the permit condition serves the same governmental purpose as the development ban, the building restriction is not a valid regulation of land use but "an out-and-out plan of extortion."...

We therefore find that the Commission's imposition of the permit condition cannot be treated as an exercise of its land use power for any of these purposes.... California is free to advance its comprehensive program, if it wishes, by using its power of eminent doman for this "public purpose," but if it wants an easement across the Nollans' property, it must pay for it. [*Reversed.*]

## 10. Self-incrimination

Issues concerning the Fifth Amendment protection against compulsory self-incrimination as it relates to a business may arise when a person is called to testify in court or when a businessperson is served with a subpoena requiring the production of records. Unless a person has been granted immunity from prosecution, no one may be called upon to testify against himself or herself in any governmental hearing such as a congressional proceeding.

The protection against compulsory self-incrimination does not protect one from such voluntary acts as the preparation of records in the ordinary course of business. Since the production of records does not compel oral testimony, the Fifth Amendment does not prevent the use of written evidence including documents either in the hands of the accused or of someone else such as an accountant. All that is protected is the extortion of information from the accused. Therefore business records can be obtained even if they are incriminating.

It is obvious that a corporation or other collective entity cannot be called upon to testify: only individuals can do so. Therefore, it is often observed that the protection against compulsory self-incrimination does not apply to corporations. Although corporations are citizens for most purposes, they are not citizens for this purpose. In addition, collective entities such as labor unions and partnerships have no privilege against self-incrimination. The privilege belongs to individuals and not to groups which individuals may represent. Corporations, unions, and partnerships also have no right to refuse to submit their books and records in response to a subpoena; such records clearly are not protected by the Fifth Amendment. The only business protected by the Fifth Amendment privilege against compulsory self-incrimination is a sole proprietorship. Of course corporate officials, union officials, and partners cannot be required to give oral testimony even though they must produce subpoenaed documents if that oral testimony may tend to incriminate them.

When business records are subpoenaed, it is often contended that the act of producing the records is itself incriminating. The argument is made that compliance with the subpoena tacitly concedes the existence of the papers demanded and their control by the person served. It also would indicate the taxpayer's belief that the papers are those described in the subpoena. The court has indicated that each case depends on its own set of facts, and the act of answering a subpoena may or may not be privileged, depending on those facts. As the following case illustrates, the most important fact is the form of business organization whose records are being sought. If the business is a corporation, then the individual required to supply the records cannot use the Fifth Amendment to avoid producing them.

# BRASWELL v. U.S.
108 S.Ct. 2284 (1988)

A federal grand jury issued a subpoena to "Randy Braswell (Petitioner) as the President" of two corporations, requiring him to produce corporate records. The subpoena provided that petitioner could deliver the records to the agent serving the subpoena, and did not require petitioner to testify. The corporations involved were incorporated by Braswell in Mississippi and he is the sole shareholder. Braswell's wife and mother are the directors and officers of both corporations but neither has any authority over the corporations' business affairs. The District Court denied the motion and the Court of Appeals affirmed.

REHNQUIST, J.:...This case presents the question whether the custodian of corporate records may resist a subpoena for such records on the ground that the act of production would incriminate him in violation of the Fifth Amendment. We conclude that he may not.

There is no question but that the contents of the subpoenaed business records are not privileged. Similarly, petitioner asserts no self-incrimination claim on behalf of the corporation; it is well established that such artificial entities are not protected by the Fifth Amendment. Petitioner instead relies solely upon the argument that his act of producing the documents has independent testimonial significance, which would incriminate him individually, and that the Fifth Amendment prohibits government compulsion of that act. The bases for this argument are extrapolated from the decisions of this Court in *Fisher* and *Doe*.

In *Fisher*, the Court rejected the argument that the contents of the subpoenaed records were protected. The Court, however, went on to observe:

**The act of producing evidence in response to a subpoena nevertheless has communicative aspects of its own, wholly aside from the contents of the papers produced. Compliance with the subpoena tacitly concedes the existence of the papers demanded and their possession or control by the taxpayer. It also would indicate the taxpayer's belief that the papers are those described in the subpoena. The elements of compulsion are clearly present, but the more difficult issues are whether the tacit averments of the taxpayer are both 'testimonial' and 'incriminating' for purposes of applying the Fifth Amendment. These questions perhaps do not lend themselves to categorical answers; their resolution may instead depend on the facts and**

**circumstances of particular cases or classes thereof.**

The Court concluded that under the "facts and circumstances" there presented, the act of producing the accountants' papers would not involve testimonial self-incrimination.

Eight years later, in *United States v. Doe,* the Court revisited the question, this time in the context of a claim by a sole proprietor that the compelled production of business records would run afoul of the Fifth Amendment. After rejecting the contention that the contents of the records were themselves protected, the Court proceeded to address whether respondent's act of producing the records would constitute protected testimonial incrimination. The Court concluded that respondent had established a valid Fifth Amendment claim. It deferred to the lower courts, which had found that enforcing the subpoenas at issue would provide the Government valuable information: By producing the records, respondent would admit that the records existed, were in his possession, and were authentic.

Had petitioner conducted his business as a sole proprietorship, *Doe* would require that he be provided the opportunity to show that his act of production would entail testimonial self-incrimination. But petitioner has operated his business through the corporate form, and we have long recognized that for purposes of the Fifth Amendment, corporations and other collective entities are treated differently from individuals. This doctrine—known as the collective entity rule—has a lengthy and distinguished pedigree.

[The court then reviewed the cases which have held (1) that there is a clear distinction between an individual and a corporation, and the latter has no right to refuse to submit its books and papers for an examination at the suit of the State, (2) that officers of corporations could not refuse to deliver corporate records because of possible personal incrimination, (3) that labor unions are collective entities unprotected by the Fifth Amendment, and (4) that partners cannot refuse to produce partnership records because they are held in a representative capacity.]

The plain mandate of these decisions is that without regard to whether the subpoena is addressed to the corporation, or as here, to the individual in his capacity as a custodian, a corporate custodian such as petitioner may not resist a subpoena for corporate records on Fifth Amendment grounds. Petitioner argues, however, that…the collective entity decisions were concerned with the contents of the documents subpoenaed, however, and not with the act of production. In *Fisher* and *Doe,* the Court moved away from the privacy based collective entity rule, replacing it with a compelled testimony standard under which the contents of business documents are never privileged but the act of producing the documents may be. Under this new regime, the act of production privilege is available without regard to the entity whose records are being sought.…

To be sure, the holding in *Fisher*—later reaffirmed in *Doe*—embarked upon a new course of Fifth Amendment analysis. We cannot agree, however, that it rendered the collective entity rule obsolete. The agency rationale undergirding the collective entity decisions, in which custodians asserted that production of entity records would incriminate them personally, survives.…The Court has consistently recognized that the custodian of corporate or entity records holds those documents in a representative rather than a personal capacity. Artificial entities such as corporations may act only through their agents, and a custodian's assumption of his representative capacity leads to certain obligations, including the duty to produce corporate records on proper demand by the

Government. Under those circumstances, the custodian's act of production is not deemed a personal act, but rather an act of the corporation. Any claim of Fifth Amendment privilege asserted by the agent would be tantamount to a claim of privilege by the corporation—which of course possesses no such privilege....

Indeed, the opinion in *Fisher*—upon which petitioner places primary reliance—indicates that the custodian of corporate records may not interpose a Fifth Amendment objection to the compelled production of corporate records, even though the act of production may prove personally incriminating....The Court observed: "This Court has...time and again allowed subpoenas against the custodian of corporate documents or those belonging to other collective entities such as unions and partnerships and those of bankrupt businesses over claims that the documents will incriminate the custodian despite the fact that producing the documents tacitly admits their existence and their location in the hands of their possessor."...

Thus, whether one concludes—as did the Court—that a custodian's production of corporate records is deemed not to constitute testimonial self-incrimination, or instead that a custodian waives the right to exercise the privilege, the lesson of *Fisher* is clear: A custodian may not resist a subpoena for corporate records on Fifth Amendment grounds....

We note further that recognizing a Fifth Amendment privilege on behalf of the records custodians of collective entities would have a detrimental impact on the Government's efforts to prosecute "white-collar crime," one of the most serious problems confronting law enforcement authorities. The greater portion of evidence of wrongdoing by an organization or its representatives is usually found in the official records and documents of that organization.

Were the cloak of the privilege to be thrown around these impersonal records and documents, effective enforcement of many federal and state laws would be impossible. If custodians could assert a privilege, authorities would be stymied not only in their enforcement efforts against those individuals but also in their prosecutions of organizations....

Although a corporate custodian is not entitled to resist a subpoena on the ground that his act of production will be personally incriminating, we do think certain consequences flow from the fact that the custodian's act of production is one in his representative rather than personal capacity. Because the custodian acts as a representative, the act is deemed one of the corporation and not the individual. Therefore, the Government concedes, as it must, that it may make no evidentiary use of the "individual act" against the individual. For example, in a criminal prosecution against the custodian, the Government may not introduce into evidence before the jury the fact that the subpoena was served upon and the corporation's documents were delivered by one particular individual, the custodian. The Government has the right, however, to use the corporation's act of production against the custodian. The Government may offer testimony—for example, from the process server who delivered the subpoena and from the individual who received the records—establishing that the corporation produced the records subpoenaed. The jury may draw from the corporation's act of production the conclusion that the records in question are authentic corporate records, which the corporation possessed, and which it produced in response to the subpoena. And if the defendant held a prominent position within the corporation that produced the records, the jury may, just as it would had someone else produced the documents, reasonably infer that he had possession of the documents or knowledge of their contents. Because the jury is not told that the defendant produced the records, any nexus between the defendant and the documents results solely from the corporation's act of production and other evidence in the case.... [*Affirmed.*]

## 11. The Sixth Amendment

The Sixth Amendment, like the Fifth, provides multiple protection in criminal cases. Essentially, its protections give one the right (1) to a speedy and public trial, (2) to a trial by jury, (3) to be informed of the charge against him or her, (4) to confront one's accuser, (5) to subpoena witnesses in one's favor, and (6) to have the assistance of an attorney.

The American concept of a jury trial contemplates a jury drawn from a fair cross section of the community. The jury guards against the exercise of arbitrary power by using the commonsense judgment of the community as a hedge against the overzealous or mistaken prosecutor. The jury's perspective of facts is used in preference to the professional or perhaps overconditioned, or biased response of a judge.

Community participation in administering criminal law is not only consistent with our democratic heritage, it is also critical to public confidence in the fairness of the criminal justice system. Therefore, a state may not restrict jury service only to special groups or exclude identifiable segments playing major roles in the community. For example, a Missouri law which excluded females who requested an automatic exemption from jury duty was unconstitutional as violating the "cross-section" concept. Likewise, minorities may not be systematically excluded from jury duty.

The right to a trial by jury does not require twelve-person juries nor does it require unanimous verdicts. However, if the jury is less than twelve, the verdict must be unanimous. A person may not be convicted by a nonunanimous six-person jury.

The right to a jury trial does not extend to state juvenile court delinquency proceedings because they are not criminal prosecutions. However, juveniles do have the right to counsel, to confront the witnesses against them, and to cross-examine them.

The right to an attorney exists in any cases where incarceration is a possible punishment. It exists at every stage of the proceeding, commencing with an investigation that centers on a person as the accused. Thus, it can be seen that there are many technical aspects to the Sixth Amendment, and numerous cases still arise concerning it.

### 12. The Seventh Amendment

The Seventh Amendment guarantees the right to a trial by jury in suits at common law where the amount in controversy exceeds $20. (This amount obviously has not been changed to keep up with inflation.) There is no right to a trial by jury in suits in equity or chancery. Likewise, there is no right to a trial by jury when the proceedings did not exist at common law but where they have been created by legislation. For example, in suits against the United States where Congress has waived governmental immunity, there is no right to a trial by jury unless the statute waiving the immunity specifically grants it. This concept was recently reaffirmed in a suit by a government employee alleging age discrimination. There is a right to trial by jury in age discrimination cases against private employers, but no such right exists in cases against the government, because the Seventh Amendment does not apply in suits against the government.

There is also no right to a jury trial in cases brought before administrative agencies. These agencies did not exist at common law. The Seventh Amendment does not prohibit Congress from assigning the fact-finding function and initial judicial decision to an administrative forum. The jury would be incompatible with this. Fact finding was never the exclusive province of the jury. The Seventh Amendment does not make the jury the exclusive mechanism for fact finding. Much of it is done by administrative agencies such as the National Labor Relations Board, the Equal Employment Opportunity Commission, and the Occupational Health and Safety Administration. The case which finally established this important principle is a part of the next chapter on Administrative Agencies.

## THE FOURTEENTH AMENDMENT

### 13. Introduction

Section 1 of the Fourteenth Amendment contains four provisions. First, it establishes that all persons born or naturalized in the United States are citizens of both the United States and of the state in which they reside. This provision was designed to establish state citizenship as well as United States citizenship for the slaves freed by the Emancipation Proclamation and by the Thirteenth Amendment.

To further establish rights of all citizens, including freed slaves, the Fourteenth Amendment contains three clauses commonly referred to as (1) the privileges and immunities clause, (2) the due process clause, and (3) the equal protection clause. The exact language is as follows:

No State shall make or enforce any law which shall abridge the privileges or immunities of citizens of the United States; nor shall any State deprive any person of life, liberty or property, without due process of law, nor deny to any person within its jurisdiction the equal protection of the laws.

While all three clauses play a significant role in constitutional law, the due process clause and the equal protection clause have been involved in more significant litigation than has the privileges and immunities clause. The due process clause has played a unique role in constitutional development—one that was probably not anticipated at the time of its ratification. This significant role has been to make most of the provisions of the Bill of Rights applicable to the states. The first phrase of Article I of the Bill of Rights commences: "*Congress* shall make no law...." How then are state and local governments prohibited from making such a law? Some jurists have argued that the due process clause of the Fourteenth Amendment "incorporates" or "carries over" the Bill of Rights and makes its provisions applicable to the states. Starting in 1925, a majority of the Supreme Court started applying various portions of the first eight amendments to the states using the due process clause of the Fourteenth Amendment as the vehicle establishing applicability.

Some justices have argued that all the provisions of the Bill of Rights are incorporated, while others have strongly rejected the incorporation theory. In 1937, Justice Benjamin Cardozo contended that those basic human rights "implicit in the concept of ordered liberty" were incorporated by the due process clause, but all other rights were not. In the latter group at that time were such protections as the Fifth Amendment's safeguard against double jeopardy. As time went by, piecemeal incorporation or absorption of the Bill of Rights continued. For example, the doctrine of separation of church and state was picked up in 1947; the requirement of public trials, in 1948; the Fourth Amendment protection against unreasonable searches and seizures, in 1961; the Eighth Amendment's guarantee against cruel and unusual punishment, in 1962; the Sixth Amendment's right to counsel, in 1963; and the Fifth Amendment's safeguard against compulsory self-incrimination, in 1964. Although justices used different theories and argued about the wisdom of allowing federal courts to use the due process clause to invalidate any state legislative act which they found offensive, the steady march of incorporation continued in the 1960s and 1970s. Cases have held that the Fourteenth Amendment incorporated the right to trial by an impartial jury, the right to a speedy trial, and the protection against double jeopardy. Only a few provisions of the first ten amendments, such as a grand jury indictment, a jury trial in civil cases, and excessive bail, are not yet picked up or incorporated by the due process clause.

The following sections discuss the other aspects of due process and the meaning of the equal protection clause.

## 14.   Due Process of Law

The term *due process of law*, which is probably involved in more litigation than any other constitutional phrase, cannot be narrowly defined. The term describes fundamental principles of liberty and justice. Simply stated, due process means "fundamental fairness and decency." It means that *government* may not act in a manner that is arbitrary, capricious, or unreasonable. The clause does not prevent private individuals or corporations, including public utilities, from acting in an arbitrary or unreasonable manner. The due process clause only applies to state action.

The issues in due process cases are usually divided into questions of **procedural due process** and **substantive due process.** Substantive due process issues arise when property or other rights are directly affected by governmental action. Procedural due process cases often are concerned with whether proper notice has been given and a proper hearing has been conducted. Such cases frequently involve procedures established by state statute. However, many cases involve procedures which are not created by statute. For example, the due process clause has been used to challenge the procedure used in the dismissal of a student from a university medical school.

Due process issues have been discussed previously in other chapters. For example, the validity of long-arm statutes and the minimum contact required is a due process issue. The clause is invoked any time procedures are questioned. The case which follows typifies those challenging state procedures as a denial of due process of law.

# PERALTA v. HEIGHTS MEDICAL CENTER, INC.
108 S.Ct. 896 (1988)

Peralta, the appellant, guaranteed a hospital debt incurred by one of his employees. So it was filed but Peralta was not served properly and he did not appear or answer the complaint. A default judgment was entered and property belonging to Peralta was sold, unbeknownst to him, to pay the debt.

Two years later, Peralta filed a Bill of Review to set aside the judgment and the sale of his property. The hospital admitted the improper service but contended that the judgment should stand because Peralta admitted that he had no defense to the original suit. The Texas courts held that there must be proof of a meritorious defense before a judgment will be set aside in a Bill of Review.

WHITE, J.:....In opposition to summary judgment, appellant denied that he had been personally served and that he had notice of the judgment. The case proceeded through the Texas courts on that basis, and it is not denied by appellee that under our cases, a judgment entered without notice or service is constitutionally infirm. An elementary and fundamental requirement of due process in any proceeding which is to be accorded finality is notice reasonably calculated, under the circumstances, to apprise interested parties of the pendency of the action and afford them the opportunity to present their objections. Failure to give notice violates the most rudimentary demands of due process of law.

The Texas courts nevertheless held, as appellee urged them to do, that to have the judgment set aside, appellant was required to show that he had a meritorious defense, apparently on the ground that without a defense, the same judgment would again be entered on retrial and hence appellant had suffered no harm from the judgment entered without notice. But this reasoning is untenable. As appellant asserts, had he had notice of the suit, he might have impleaded the employee whose debt had been guaranteed, worked out a settlement, or paid the debt. He would also have preferred to sell his property himself in order to raise funds rather than to suffer it sold at a constable's auction.

Nor is there any doubt that the entry of the judgment itself had serious consequences. It is not denied that the judgment was entered on the county records, became a lien on appellant's property, and was the basis for issuance of a writ of execution under which appellant's property was promptly sold, without notice. Even if no execution sale had yet occurred, the lien encumbered the property and impaired appellant's ability to mortgage or alienate it; and state procedures for creating and enforcing such liens are subject to the strictures of due process. Here, we assume that the judgment against him and the ensuing consequences occurred without notice to appellant, notice at a meaningful time and in a meaningful manner that would have given him an opportunity to be heard....

The Texas court held that the default judgment must stand absent a showing of a meritorious defense to the action in which judgment was entered without proper notice to appellant, a judgment that had substantial adverse consequences to appellant. By reason of the Due Process Clause of the Fourteenth Amendment, that holding is plainly infirm.

Where a person has been deprived of property in a manner contrary to the most basic tenets of due process, it is no answer to say that in his particular case due process of law would have led to the same result because he had no adequate defense upon the merits. As we observed in *Armstrong v. Manzo*, only "wip[ing] the slate clean...would have restored the petitioner to the position he would have occupied had due process of law been accorded to him in the first place." The Due Process Clause demands no less in this case.

The judgment below is [*Reversed.*]

During the early part of this century, the due process clauses of the Fifth and the Fourteenth Amendments were used by the Supreme Court to guard the sanctity of private property. Legislative attempts to regulate the economy by laws such as those imposing minimum wages or maximum hours for women and children were held to be unconstitutional as a denial of "substantive due process of law." During this period, if the substance of a law deprived persons of property, the law usually would be declared unconstitutional by the courts as a denial of "due process." If a federal law were under attack, the Fifth Amendment was cited as the ground; and if a state law were involved, the protection of the Fourteenth was invoked.

After the mid-1930s and President Roosevelt's attempt to pack the Supreme Court, the judicial attitude toward the application of the due process clause to economic legislation changed dramatically. The Supreme Court refused to find such legislation unconstitutional on the ground of infringement of "substantive due process," and substantive due process as a bar to economic legislation tended to pass into oblivion.

After the 1930s, the due process clause was most frequently invoked in cases involving individual liberties and civil rights. In the latter area, it was used by courts in seeking a balance between the basic civil rights of individuals and the interests of society as a whole. These cases frequently dealt with "procedural" issues rather than with "substantive" issues. Many of the "non-economic" issues were raised in criminal cases, while others concerned state action that affected such basic rights as freedom of speech, press, and religion.

Since the change of attitude by at least a majority of the court toward the "due process clause," there is in effect a double standard in the application of the clause. Legislation in the economic sector is presumed to be constitutional, and few challenges on the due process ground can expect to be successful. On the other hand, when basic human freedoms are involved, the courts regard any legislation tending to curb or limit them to be suspect. As a result courts do not hesitate to declare legislation dealing with fundamental human rights such as freedom of speech, press, assembly, worship, or petition to be unconstitutional as a denial of due process of law. In other words, today there is a presumption of constitutionality of economic legislation, but legislation which tends to restrict fundamental rights is suspect and subject to more exacting judicial scrutiny under the Fourteenth Amendment. This double standard is often justified because of the crucial importance of these basic freedoms, which must be protected by the judiciary from the "vicissitudes" of political action. As a result, the due process clause prohibits experimentation with the basic fundamental liberties by the legislative and executive branches of government. It places the judiciary in the role of guarding these rights. Courts are thus the guardians of fundamental liberty; but, at least today, they are not significant players in the administration of our economic system.

## 15. Equal Protection

Almost no law treats all persons equally. Laws draw lines and treat people differently. Therefore, almost any state or local law imaginable can be challenged under the equal protection clause. It is obvious that the equal protection clause does not always deny states the power to treat different persons in different ways. Yet the equal protection clause embodies the ethical idea that law should not treat people differently without a satisfactory reason making such treatment fair under the circumstances. In deciding cases using that clause to challenge state and local laws, courts use two distinct approaches. One is the traditional or *minimum rationality* approach, and the other is called the *strict scrutiny* approach. (See Table 7-2.)

Whether the approach determines the result of a case or whether the desired result dictates the approach to be used is not always clear. As a practical matter, if the traditional (minimum rationality) approach is used, the challenged law and its classifications are usually found *not* to be a violation of equal protection. On the other hand, if the "strict scrutiny" test is used, the classifications are usually found to be unconstitutional under the equal protection clause.

Under the minimum rationality approach, a classification will survive an equal protection challenge if it has a *rational* connection to a *permissible* state end. A permissible state end is one that is not prohibited by another provision of the Constitution. It qualifies as a legitimate goal of government. The classification must have a reasonable basis (not wholly arbitrary), and the courts will assume any state of facts that can be used to justify the classification. These laws often involve economic issues such as mandatory retirement ages or social legislation such as welfare laws.

Such laws are presumed to be constitutional because courts recognize that the legislature must draw lines creating distinctions and that such tasks cannot be avoided. Further, courts in applying this standard admit that perfection in making classifications is neither possible nor necessary. Only when no rational basis for the classification exists is it unconstitutional under the

**TABLE 7-2**   Equal Protection Analysis

| Standard | Minimum Rationality | Quasi-Strict Scrutiny | Strict Scrutiny |
|---|---|---|---|
| Classifications must be | Rationally connected to a permissible or legitimate government objective | Substantially related to an important government interest | Necessary to a compelling state interest |
| Examples | **Presumed Valid**<br>Height<br>Weight<br>Age<br>Testing<br>School desegregation<br>Veteran's preference<br>Marriage | **Quasi-Suspect Classes**<br>Sex<br>Gender<br>Legitimacy<br>Affirmative action | **Suspect Classes**<br>Race<br>National origin<br>Alienage<br><br>**Fundamental Rights**<br>To vote<br>To travel |

equal protection clause. A classification judged by this standard must be rationally related to the state's objectives. The classification may be imperfect and may not be the best to accomplish the purpose, yet it is still constitutional if there is a rational basis for the classification. For example, a state law imposing mandatory retirement of police at age fifty was held valid when the rational basis test was applied to it.

Under the strict scrutiny test, a classification will be a denial of equal protection unless the classification is necessary to a *compelling* state end. It is not enough that a classification be rational, it must be necessary. It is not enough that a classification be permissible to a state end, it must be a compelling state objective. To withstand constitutional challenge when this test is used, the law must serve important governmental objectives and the classification must be substantially related to achieving these objectives.

The strict scrutiny test is used if the classification involves either (1) a suspect class, or (2) a fundamental constitutional right. A suspect class is one that has such disabilities, has been subjected to such a history of purposeful unequal treatment, or has been relegated to such a position of political powerlessness that it commands extraordinary protection from the political process of the majority. For example, classifications directed at race, national origin, and alienage are clearly suspect. As a result, the judiciary strictly scrutinizes laws directed at them. Unless the state can prove that its statutory classifications have a compelling state interest as a basis, the classifications will be considered a denial of equal protection. Classifications which are subject to strict judicial scrutiny are presumed to be unconstitutional. The state must convince the court that the classification is fair, reasonable, and necessary to accomplish the objective of legislation that is compelling to a state interest.

Strict judicial scrutiny is applied to a second group of cases, those which involve classifications directed at fundamental rights. If a classification unduly burdens or penalizes the exercise of a constitutional right, it will be stricken unless it is found to be necessary to a compelling state interest. Among such rights are the right to vote and the right to travel. Doubts about such laws result in their being stricken by the courts as a denial of equal protection.

Some cases actually fall between the two tests previously discussed. These cases use what is sometimes called "quasi strict scrutiny" tests because the classifications are only partially suspect or the rights involved are not quite fundamental. For example, classifications directed at sex and legitimacy are partially suspect. In cases involving classifications based on sex or gender, the courts have taken this position between the two tests or at least have modified the strict scrutiny approach. Such classifications are unconstitutional unless they are *substantially* related to an *important* government objective. This modified version of strict scrutiny has resulted in holdings which find laws to be valid as well as unconstitutional.

Equal protection cases run the whole spectrum of legislative attempts to solve society's problems. For example, a major use of the equal protection clause by courts has been to require the integration of public schools. In addition, the meaning and application of the equal protection clause have been central issues in cases involving (1) apportionment of legislative bodies, (2) racial segregation in the sale and rental of real estate, (3) laws distinguishing between the rights of legitimates and illegitimates, (4) the makeup of juries, (5) voting requirements, (6) welfare residency requirements, (7) rights of aliens, and (8) the use of property taxes as the means of financing public schools. The equal protection clause is the means to the end, or goal, of equality of opportunity. As such, it may be utilized by anyone claiming unequal treatment in any case. At the same time the clause will not prevent states from remedying the effects of past discrimination. For example, a court required that 50 percent of all promotions in a state police department go to black officers until either 25 percent of all corporals were black or until other legal procedures were developed and approved. The Supreme Court in 1987 held that the 50 percent promotion requirement was permissible under the equal protection clause of the Fourteenth Amendment: it was justified for compelling governmental interest in eradicating discriminatory exclusion of blacks from higher level positions and was narrowly tailored to serve this purpose.

## REVIEW QUESTIONS

**1** The New York Constitution grants a civil service employment preference to certain veterans in the form of points added to examination scores. To qualify, they must (1) be New York residents who are honorably discharged veterans of the armed forces, (2) have served during a time of war, and (3) have been New York residents when they entered military service. Some were denied the veterans' preference because they were not New York residents when they joined the Army. Is this a denial of equal protection? Why or why not?

**2** Mike Love, a truck driver, had his Illinois driver's license revoked after he was convicted of three traffic offenses within twelve months. The revocation was based on administrative regulations which did not require a hearing prior to revocation. But they did make a hearing available after revocation. Love challenged this as a denial of due process. Was he correct? Why or why not?

**3** Doe is the owner of several sole proprietorships. A grand jury, during the course of an investigation of corruption in the awarding of county and municipal contracts, served five subpoenas on Doe seeking his business records, including telephone calls, bank accounts, and checks.

    **(a)** Are the records privileged under the Fifth Amendment? Why or why not?

    **(b)** Is there any ground for refusing to deliver the records? Explain.

**4** After the control of the county legislature had shifted to the Democratic Party, the newly appointed county public defender, a Democrat, notified the Republican assistant public defenders that their employment was to be terminated. They brought suit based on the allegation that they were discharged solely because they were Republicans and that such a discharge was unconstitutional. Decide the case and give reasons for your decision.

**5** A restaurant was refused a liquor license because of opposition by a church located within 10 feet of the restaurant. A state statute gives churches and schools veto power over liquor licenses if the church is within 100 feet of the establishment seeking the license. Is the state law constitutional? Why, or why not?

**6** Charges were filed against a judge by a commission on judicial conduct. The judge sought to take the deposition of a newspaper reporter to question him about persons he had interviewed and the information obtained. The newspaper reporter claimed a privilege of confidential communications to a reporter and refused to reveal his sources. He was held in contempt on appeal. What was the result? Why?

**7** A Florida statute required newspapers that assail the character of political candidates to afford free space to the candidate for reply. Is the law constitutional? Why, or why not?

**8** A Maine statute has prohibited roadside billboards except for signs announcing the time and place of religious or civic events, election campaign signs, and signs erected by historic and cultural institutions. A suit is filed challenging the constitutionality of the statute. What will be the result? Why?

**9** A Pennsylvania Bar Association rule prohibited direct-mail solicitation by attorneys. A Pennsylvania attorney who was a certified pilot with a master's degree in computer science used direct mail to solicit clients among aircraft owners and computer users. When the bar association sought to discipline the attorney, he contended that the rule was unconstitutional. What was the result? Why?

**10** OSHA inspectors arrived at Barlow's Factory to conduct a safety inspection. Barlow's administrators refused to allow them to enter the plant and then filed suit for an injunction to prevent any inspections without a search warrant. Section 8(a) of the Occupational Safety and Health Act empowers agents of the secretary of labor to conduct unannounced searches of the work area of any employment facility for safety hazards and violations of OSHA regulations. Is Barlow's entitled to the injunction? Why, or why not?

**11** Thornton, a manager of a department store, refused to work on Sundays. A state statute provided Sabbath observers with an absolute and unqualified right not to work on their Sabbath. Is the state law constitutional? Why, or why not?

**12** P brought suit against D, a privately owned and operated public utility, for damages. D had terminated P's electric service because she failed to pay her bills. P alleged that she had not been given any notice and that there was no hearing before her service was discontinued; therefore, she contended, there was a denial of property without due process of law, contrary to the Fourteenth Amendment. D contended that its action was not "state action," and therefore the traditional requirements of due process did not need to be met. What was the result? Why?

**13** Under a state workers' compensation law, a widower is denied benefits for his wife's work-related death unless he is mentally or physically incapacitated or proves dependence on his wife's earnings. However, the statute grants death benefits to a widow without such restrictions. When

Wengler's wife died in a work-related accident, a claim for death benefits was denied. He contended that the statute was unconstitutional. What was the result? Why?

**14** The state of Virginia followed the common law doctrine of necessaries under which a husband was liable for necessaries such as food, lodging, and medical care furnished the wife, but a wife did not have a similar obligation on behalf of the husband. A hospital sought to collect from a husband for his wife's hospital bill. He contended that the doctrine violated the equal protection clause of the Fourteenth Amendment. Was he correct? Why, or why not?

# Chapter

# 8

# Administrative Law

## CHAPTER PREVIEW

This chapter concerns the legal principles and problems relating to what is sometimes called the fourth branch of government—the regulatory agencies, bureaus, and commissions. The fourth branch of government creates laws when it adopts rules and regulations to regulate business activity. It investigates business to determine if laws have been violated, and it prosecutes violations. Finally, it holds hearings to determine questions of fact and of law. The direct day-to-day legal impact on business of the rules and regulations adopted and enforced by these agencies is probably greater than the impact of the courts or other branches of government. Administrative agencies create and enforce the majority of all laws constituting the legal environment of business. Almost every business activity is regulated to some degree by the administrative process at either the state or federal level.

This chapter will discuss administrative powers and those situations in which courts will set regulatory decisions or the rules aside. It will also discuss regulations adopted by agencies. Special emphasis will be placed on the problems that business encounters as a result of the administrative process.

The following terms are of special importance in this chapter: administrative law judge, cease and desist order, consent order, exhaustion of remedies, general counsel, immunity, peter principle, quasi-judicial function, and quasi-legislative function.

## 1. Introduction

As our industrial society grows and becomes more complex, the social and economic problems that confront society multiply fantastically. Not only do these issues increase in number, but interrelationships and conflicting social goals complicate their solution. Also, advances in technology require special training and experience for us to attempt an intelligent solution of problems in many areas.

To solve these problems our society turns to the methodology referred to as the **administrative process.** This administrative process relies upon independent regulatory agencies, bureaus, and commissions to develop laws and enforce them. In a real sense, these independent regulatory agencies constitute a fourth branch of government.

Table 8-1 lists several of the more important federal agencies and briefly describes their functions. Many of these agencies will be discussed in detail in later chapters. For example, the Equal Employment Opportunity Commission is discussed in Chapter 16, the National Labor Relations Board in Chapters 17 and 18, the Securities and Exchange Commission in Chapter 19, the Federal Trade Commission in Chapters 22 to 24, and the Environmental Protection Agency in Chapter 25.

Although we focus on federal agencies in this chapter, keep in mind that state and local governments also have many agencies. For example, cases involving industrial accidents and injuries to employees are heard by state workers' compensation boards, and most local governments have zoning boards which make recommendations on zoning laws. State governments usually license and regulate intrastate transportation in a manner similar to the Interstate Commerce Commission's (ICC) regulation of interstate ground transportation. In addition, state boards usually set rates for local utilities supplying gas and electricity. The principles and problems discussed in this chapter generally apply to the state and local administrative process as well as to the federal. It is clear that almost every aspect of our daily lives is regulated to a substantial degree by the administrative process.

## 2. Reasons for the Use of Administrative Agencies

Early in our history it was necessary to create a fourth branch of government possessing the powers and functions of the other three branches. There are many reasons why we needed to create administrative agencies to have a more effective government. First, the legislative branch apparently could not legislate in sufficient detail to cover all aspects of a problem. Congress cannot possibly legislate in minute detail and, as a consequence, it uses more and more general language in stating its regulatory aims and purposes. For example, Congress cannot enact a tax law that would cover every possible issue that might arise. Therefore, it delegates to the Internal Rev-

**TABLE 8-1**   Major Federal Agencies

| Name | Functions |
| --- | --- |
| Consumer Product Safety Commission (CPSC) | Protects the public against unreasonable risks of injury associated with consumer products |
| Environmental Protection Agency (EPA) | Administers all laws relating to the environment, including laws on water pollution, air pollution, solid wastes, pesticides, toxic substances, etc. |
| Federal Aviation Administration (FAA) (part of the Dept. of Transportation) | Regulates civil aviation to provide safe and efficient use of airspace |
| Federal Communications Commission (FCC) | Regulates interstate and foreign communications by means of radio, television, wire, cable, and satellite |
| Federal Reserve Board (FRB) | Regulates the availability and cost of money and credit; the nation's central bank |
| Federal Trade Commission (FTC) | Protects the public from anticompetitive behavior and unfair and deceptive business practices |
| Food and Drug Administration (FDA) | Administers laws to prohibit distribution of adulterated, misbranded, or unsafe food and drugs |
| Equal Employment Opportunity Commission (EEOC) | Seeks to prevent discrimination in employment based on race, color, religion, sex, or national origin and other unlawful employment practices |
| Interstate Commerce Commission (ICC) | Regulates interstate surface transportation |
| National Labor Relations Board (NLRB) | Conducts union certification elections and holds hearings on unfair labor practice complaints |
| Nuclear Regulatory Commission (NRC) | Licenses and regulates the nuclear energy industry |
| Occupational Safety and Health Administration (OSHA) | Ensures all workers a safe and healthy work environment |
| Securities and Exchange Commission (SEC) | Enforces the federal securities laws which regulate sale of securities to the investing public |

enue Service (IRS) the power to make rules and regulations to fill in the gaps and create the necessary details to make tax laws workable. In many areas an agency has had to develop detailed rules and regulations to carry out a legislative policy.

Courts also cannot handle all disputes and controversies that may arise. For example, each year tens of thousands of industrial accidents cause injury or death to workers. If each of these industrial accidents resulted in traditional litigation, the courts simply would not have the time nor the personnel to handle the multitude of cases. Therefore, workers' compensation boards decide such claims. Likewise, most cases involving alleged discrimination in employment are turned over to agencies for decision.

Another reason many agencies are created is to refer a problem or area to experts for solution and management. The Federal Reserve Board (FRB), the Nuclear Regulatory Commission (NRC), and the Food and Drug Administration (FDA) are examples of agencies with expertise beyond that of Congress or the executive branch. The development of sound policies and proper decisions in many areas requires expertise, and thus we tend to resort to administrative agencies for this expertise. Similarly, administrative agencies are often desirable because they provide needed continuity and consistency in the formulation, application, and enforcement of rules and regulations governing business.

Many governmental agencies exist to protect the public, especially from the business community. Business has often failed to regulate itself, and the lack of self-regulation has often been contrary to the public interest. For example, the failure of business to voluntarily refrain from polluting many streams and rivers as well as the air led to the creation of the Environmental Protection Agency (EPA). The sale of worthless securities to the investing public was a major force behind the creation of the Securities and Exchange Commission (SEC). The manufacture and the sale of dangerous products led to the creation of the Consumer Product Safety Commission (CPSC). It is our practice to turn to a governmental agency for assistance whenever a business or business practice may injure significant numbers of the general public. The prevailing attitude is that the government's duty is to protect the public from harm.

Agencies are often created to replace competition with regulation. When a firm is given monopoly power, it loses its freedom of contract, and a governmental body is given the power to determine the provisions of its contracts. For example, electric utility companies are usually given a monopoly in the geographic area in which they serve. A state agency such as a public service commission then has the power to set the rate structure for the utility. Similar agencies have regulated transportation and banking because of the disparity of bargaining power between the business and the public. Regulation is often a substitute for competition.

Of course, many agencies were created simply out of necessity. If we are to have a mail service, a post office is necessary. Welfare programs require government personnel to administer them. The Social Security concept dictates that there be a federal agency to determine eligibility and pay benefits. The mere existence of most government programs automatically creates a new agency or expands the functions of an existing one.

Almost every governmental agency has been created because of a recognized problem in society and from the belief that an agency may be able to help solve the problem. Governmental agencies usually have laudable goals and noble purposes, such as the elimination of discrimination, the providing of a safe and healthy workplace, or the protection of consumers. These agencies allow other branches of government to determine policy while giving those carrying out the policy a significant degree of flexibility and discretion.

### 3.   Functions

As previously noted, administrative agencies tend to possess functions of the other three branches of government. These functions are generally described as (1) rule making, (2) adjudicating, (3) prosecuting, (4) advising, (5) supervising, and (6) investigating. These functions do not concern all administrative agencies to the same degree. Some agencies are primarily adjudicating bodies, such as industrial commissions that rule on workers' compensation claims. Others are primarily supervisory, such as the SEC, which oversees the issue and sale of investment securities. To be sure, most agencies perform all the foregoing functions to some degree in carrying out their responsibilities. Figure 8-1 explains how these functions have been delegated to these agencies.

Agencies exercise their quasi-legislative power by issuing rules and regulations that have the force and effect of law. These rules and regulations may be used to resolve an issue if they are relevant to any issue involved in an adjudicative proceeding. Before rules and regulations are adopted, interested parties are given an opportunity to be heard on the desirability and legality of the proposals.

Guidelines are also issued by agencies to supplement rules. Guidelines are administrative interpretations of the statutes which a commission is responsible for enforcing, and they provide guidance in evaluating the legality of certain practices. They deal with a particular practice and may cut across industry lines.

Rules and regulations may apply to a business practice irrespective of the industry involved, or they may apply only to an industry. For example, Occupational Safety and Health Administration (OSHA) rules may cover

**FIGURE 8-1**
Administrative Agencies.

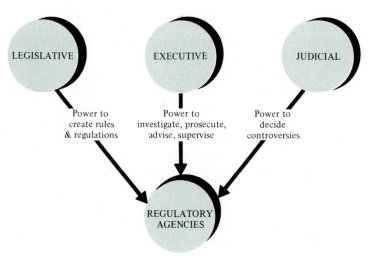

anyone using certain equipment, or a rule may be drafted so that its coverage is limited to an industry such as drug manufacturing.

The advisory function may be accomplished by making reports to the President or to Congress. For example, the FTC may propose new legislation to Congress, or it may inform the Attorney General of the need for judicial action due to violations of the law. Agencies also report information to the general public that should be known in the public interest, and they publish advisory opinions. For example, a commission may give advice as to whether a firm's proposed course of action might violate any of the laws which that commission administers. Advisory opinions are not as binding as formal rulings, but they do give a business an indication of the view an agency would take if the practice in question were challenged formally. The advisory opinion is a unique device generally not available in the judicial system, as courts deal only with actual cases and controversies.

One of the major functions of all agencies is to investigate activities and practices that may be illegal. Because of this investigative power, agencies can gather and compile information concerning the organization and business practices of any corporation or industry engaged in commerce to determine whether there has been a violation of any law. In exercising their investigative functions, agencies may utilize the subpoena power and require reports, examine witnesses under oath, and examine and copy documents, or they may obtain information from other governmental offices. This power of investigation complements the exercise of the other powers such as giving advice, prosecuting violations, issuing rules, and entering **cease and desist orders.**

There is a federal law which makes it a crime to make any false or fraudulent statement in any matter within the jurisdiction of a federal agency. A person may be guilty of a violation without proof that he or she had knowledge that the matter was within the jurisdiction of a federal agency, as happened in the following case.

# UNITED STATES v. YERMIAN
104 S.Ct. 2936 (1984)

POWELL, J.:…It is a federal crime under 18 U.S.C. § 1001 to make any false or fraudulent statement in any matter within the jurisdiction of a federal agency. To establish a violation of § 1001, the Government must prove beyond a reasonable doubt that the statement was made with knowledge of its falsity. This case presents the question whether the Government also must prove that the false statement was made with actual knowledge of federal agency jurisdiction.

Respondent Esmail Yermian was convicted…on three counts of making false statements in a matter within the jurisdiction of a federal agency, in violation of § 1001. The convictions were based on false statements respondent supplied his employer in connection with a Department of Defense security questionnaire. Respondent was hired in 1979 by Gulton Industries, a defense contractor. Because respondent was to have access to classified material in the course of his employment, he was required to obtain a Department of Defense Security Clearance. To this end, Gulton's security officer asked respondent to fill out a "Worksheet For Preparation of Personnel Security Questionnaire."

In response to a question on the worksheet asking whether he had ever been charged with any violation of law, respondent failed to disclose that in 1978 he had been convicted of mail fraud, in violation of 18 U.S.C. § 1341. In describing his employment history, respondent falsely stated that he had been employed by two companies that had in fact never employed him. The Gulton security officer typed these false representations onto a form entitled "Department of Defense Personnel Security Questionnaire." Respondent reviewed the typed document for errors and signed a certification stating that his answers were "true, complete, and correct to the best of [his] knowledge" and that he understood "that any misrepresentation or false statement... may subject [him] to prosecution under section 1001 of the United States Criminal Code."

After witnessing respondent's signature, Gulton's security officer mailed the typed form to the Defense Industrial Security Clearance Office for processing. Government investigators subsequently discovered that respondent had submitted false statements on the security questionnaire. Confronted with this discovery, respondent acknowledged that he had responded falsely to questions regarding his criminal record and employment history. On the basis of these false statements, respondent was charged with three counts in violation of § 1001.

At trial, respondent admitted to having actual knowledge of the falsity of the statements he had submitted in response to the Department of Defense Security Questionnaire. He explained that he had made the false statements so that information on the security questionnaire would be consistent with similar fabrications he had submitted to Gulton in his employment application. Respondent's sole defense at trial was that he had no actual knowledge that his false statements would be transmitted to a federal agency.

Consistent with this defense, respondent requested a jury instruction requiring the Government to prove not only that he had actual knowledge that his statements were false at the time they were made, but also that he had actual knowledge that those statements were made in a matter within the jurisdiction of a federal agency. The District Court rejected that request and instead instructed the jury that the Government must prove that respondent "knew or should have known that the information was to be submitted to a government agency." Respondent's objection to this instruction was overruled, and the jury returned convictions on all three counts charged in the indictment.

The Court of Appeals for the Ninth Circuit reversed, holding that...the government must prove beyond a reasonable doubt that the defendant knew at the time he made the false statement that it was made in a matter within the jurisdiction of a federal agency....

The only issue presented in this case is whether Congress intended the terms "knowingly and willfully" in § 1001 to modify the statute's jurisdictional language, thereby requiring the Government to prove that false statements were made with actual knowledge of federal agency jurisdiction. The issue thus presented is one of statutory interpretation. Accordingly, we turn first to the language of the statute.

The relevant language of § 1001 provides:

**Whoever, in any matter within the jurisdiction of any department or agency of the United States knowingly and willfully...makes any false, fictitious or fraudulent statements or representations,...shall be fined....**

The statutory language requiring that knowingly false statements be made "in any matter within the jurisdiction of any department or agency of the United States" is a jurisdictional requirement. Its primary purpose is to identify the factor that makes the false statement an appropriate subject for federal concern. Jurisdictional language need not contain the same culpability requirement as other elements of the offense. Indeed, we have held that "the existence of the fact that confers federal jurisdiction need not be one in the mind of the actor at the time he perpetrates the act made criminal by the federal statute." Certainly in this case, the statutory language makes clear that Congress did not intend the terms "knowingly and willfully" to establish the standard of culpability for the jurisdictional element of § 1001. The jurisdictional language appears in a phrase separate from the prohibited conduct modified by the terms "knowingly and willfully." Any natural reading of § 1001, therefore, establishes that the terms

"knowingly and willfully" modify only the making of "false, fictitious or fraudulent statements," and not the predicate circumstance that those statements be made in a matter within the jurisdiction of a federal agency. Once this is clear, there is no basis for requiring proof that the defendant had actual knowledge of federal agency jurisdiction. The statute contains no language suggesting any additional element of intent, such as a requirement that false statements be "knowingly made in a matter within federal agency jurisdiction," or "with the intent to deceive the federal government." On its face, therefore, § 1001 requires that the Government prove that false statements were made knowingly and willfully, and it unambiguously dispenses with any requirement that the Government also prove that those statements were made with actual knowledge of federal agency jurisdiction. Respondent's argument that the legislative history of the statute supports a contrary interpretation is unpersuasive....

There is no support in the legislative history for respondent's argument that the terms "knowingly and willfully" modify the phrase "in any matter within the jurisdiction of a federal agency."

Both the plain language and the legislative history establish that proof of actual knowledge of federal agency jurisdiction is not required under § 1001. Accordingly, we reverse the decision of the Court of Appeals to the contrary. [*It is so ordered.*]

---

The **quasi-judicial function** involves both fact finding and applying law to the facts. If violations of the law are found, sanctions, such as a fine or other penalty, may be imposed. In addition, an agency may issue a cease and desist order to prevent further violations. Violations of cease and desist orders are punishable by fine.

Quasi-judicial proceedings usually begin with a complaint filed by the agency. The complaint contains allegations of fact concerning the alleged illegal conduct. After the formal complaint is served, the respondent files an answer to the charges and allegations. The case is then assigned to an administrative law judge. At the hearing, counsel for the agency and the respondent produce evidence to prove or disprove the allegations of fact in the complaint and answer. The judge rules on the admissibility of evidence, rules on motions made by counsel, and renders an initial decision that includes a statement of findings and conclusions, along with reasons for them, as to all material issues of fact and law. The ruling also includes an order the judge deems appropriate in view of the evidence in the record. This order becomes final if not challenged within thirty days after it is filed. On the appeal, the agency, board, or commission reviews the record of the initial decision and has all the powers it could have exercised if it had rendered that decision itself.

In reviewing the evidence, the agency uses the preponderance of the evidence standard rather than the clear and convincing proof or beyond a reasonable doubt standard of the criminal law. (Refer to the discussions of burden of proof in Chapter 4.)

Many cases before agencies are settled by agreement before a final decision, just as most lawsuits are settled. Such a settlement results in the issuance of a **consent order** which states that the respondent admits to the jurisdiction of the agency and waives all rights to seek a judicial review. However, a respondent does not have to admit that the business has been guilty of a violation of the law; but the respondent does agree not to engage in the business activities which were the subject of the complaint. A consent order saves considerable expense and has the same legal force and effect as a final cease and desist order issued after a full hearing.

## 4.   Organization

Administrative agencies, boards, or commissions usually have a chairperson and four other members. Laws creating the regulatory body usually specify that no more than three of the five members may belong to the same political party. Appointments require Senate confirmation, and appointees are not permitted to engage in any other business or employment during their terms. They may be removed from office by the President only for inefficiency, neglect of duty, or malfeasance in office.

Regulatory agencies require staffs to carry out their duties. While each agency has its own distinctive organizational structure to meet its responsibilities, most agencies have persons performing certain functions common to all agencies. Most agencies have **quasi-legislative** and quasi-judicial functions as well as the usual executive ones. Therefore, the organizational chart of an agency usually contains all the usual duties of government. Figure 8-2 shows an organizational chart outlining the usual functions and duties of most agencies.

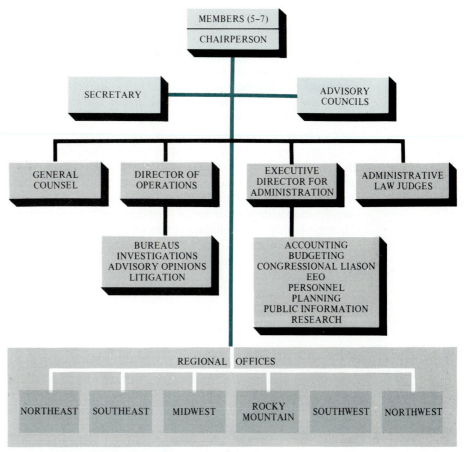

**FIGURE 8-2**
Organizational Chart of Typical Agency, Board, or Commission.

The chairperson is designated by the President and is the presiding officer at agency meetings. The chairperson usually belongs to the same political party as the President, and while an equal in voting, is somewhat more important than the other members because of visibility and the power to appoint staff. For example, the chairman of the Federal Reserve Board is often in the news while the other members are relatively unknown.

The secretary is responsible for the minutes of agency meetings and is legal custodian of its records. The secretary usually signs orders and official correspondence and is responsible for publication of all actions in the *Federal Register*. The secretary also coordinates the activities of the agency with others involved in the regulatory process.

Advisory councils are persons not employed by the agency but interested in its mission. Persons serving on councils are usually selected because of their expertise. For example, the Consumer Product Safety Commission has an advisory council in poison-prevention packaging and another on flammable fabrics. These councils provide for interaction between regulators and regulatees.

The office of **general counsel** is so important in many agencies that the appointment usually requires Senate approval. The general counsel is the chief law officer and legal adviser. He or she represents the agency in court and often makes the decision as to whether or not a suit will be filed, or what other remedies will be pursued. The general counsel has significant impact on policy and is often as powerful as a commissioner or board member.

Some laws authorize a member of the executive branch of government to perform functions similar to the general counsel and to work with administrative agencies in order to keep at least a semblance of the separation of powers concept. This is true when the agency is primarily a quasi-judicial one dealing with allegations of illegal activity. For example, the secretary of labor is charged with enforcing the Occupational Safety and Health Act. As such, he or she is given wide discretion in bringing charges and settling cases before the Occupational Safety and Health Review Commission. The relative authority of each is discussed in the case which follows.

# CUYAHOGA VALLEY RAILWAY COMPANY v. UNITED TRANSPORTATION UNION et al.

106 S.Ct. 286 (1985)

PER CURIAM: The Secretary of Labor is authorized to inspect work sites to uncover noncompliance with the Occupational Safety and Health Act 2. If, as a result of such an inspection, the Secretary discovers a violation of the Act, he is authorized to issue a citation to the employer fixing a reasonable time for the abatement of the violation, and assessing a penalty for the violation. The employer then has 15 days in which to contest the citation. Similarly, employees have 15 days in which to challenge as unreasonable "the period of time fixed in the citation for the abatement of the violation." The statute and rules of the Occupational Safety and Health Review Commission also permit affected employees to participate as parties in any hearing in which the employer contests the citation.

If an employer contests the citation, and the Secretary intends to seek its enforcement, the Secretary must file a complaint with the Commission within 20 days, and the employer must file an answer within 15 days. Once these pleadings are filed, a hearing to determine the validity of the citation will be held before an Administrative Law Judge, with discretionary review by the Commission.

In the present case, the Secretary cited Cuyahoga Valley Railway Company for a violation of the Act. Cuyahoga contested the citation, the Secretary filed a complaint with a Commission, and Cuyahoga filed an answer. Respondent United Transportation Union, which represents Cuyahoga employees, properly moved to intervene in the proceedings. At the hearing, however, the Secretary moved to vacate the citation on the ground that the Federal Railway Administration, not the Secretary, had jurisdiction over the relevant safety conditions. Despite the Union's objection, the ALJ granted the Secretary's motion and vacated the citation. Thereafter, the Commission directed review of the ALJ's order. The Secretary promptly objected to this action, asserting that part of the citation involved matters beyond the reach of the Act and that additional portions of the citation did not warrant litigation because of the state of the evidence....Some six years later, the Commission rejected this submission and remanded the case to the ALJ for consideration of the union's objections.

The Court of Appeals for the Sixth Circuit affirmed the Commission's holding that it could review the Secretary's decision to withdraw a citation. The court recognized that the Secretary "has the sole authority to determine whether to prosecute" a violation of the Act. Here, however, the court found that the Secretary "had already made the decision to prosecute by filing a complaint and that complaint had been answered at the time the Secretary attempted to withdraw the citation." Because the "adversarial process was well advanced at the time the Secretary attempted to withdraw the citation," the court reasoned that the Commission, "as the adjudicative body, had control of the case and the authority to review the Secretary's withdrawal of the citation."

Contrary to the Sixth Circuit's decision, eight other courts of appeals have held that the Secretary has unreviewable discretion to withdraw a citation charging an employer with violating the Occupational Health and Safety Act. We agree with the decisions of these courts.

It is apparent that the Court of Appeals' decision is inconsistent with the detailed statutory scheme which contemplates that the rights created by the Act are to be protected by the Secretary.

It is also clear that enforcement of the Act is the sole responsibility of the Secretary. It is the Secretary, not the Commission, who sets the substantive standards for the work place, and only the Secretary has the authority to determine if a citation should be issued to an employer for unsafe working conditions. A necessary adjunct of that power is the authority to withdraw a citation and enter into settlement discussions with the employer. The Commission's function is to act as a neutral arbiter and determine whether the Secretary's citations should be enforced over employee or union objections. Its authority plainly does not extend to overturning the Secretary's decision not to issue or to withdraw a citation.

The Sixth Circuit's conclusion that the Commission can review the Secretary's decision to withdraw a citation would discourage the Secretary from seeking voluntary settlements with employers in violation of the Act, thus unduly hampering the enforcement of the Act.

Such a procedure would also allow the Commission to make both prosecutorial decisions and to serve as the adjudicator of the dispute, a commingling of roles that Congress did not intend. Indeed, the Commission itself was created to avoid giving the Secretary both prosecutorial and adjudicatory powers.

The other courts of appeals to address this problem have recognized the distinct roles of the Secretary and the Commission and accordingly have acknowledged that the Secretary's decision to withdraw a citation against an employer of the Act is not reviewable by the Commission. Based on these considerations, the judgment of the Court of Appeals is [*Reversed.*]

The executive director for administration is the chief operating official of an agency, and supervises usual administrative functions such as accounting, budgeting, and personnel. Research and planning are usually supervised by the executive director, also. Since agencies spend a great deal of time lobbying with Congress, most of them have a legislative liaison which is under the executive director for administration.

*Administrative law judges* perform the adjudicative fact-finding functions. They hear cases of alleged law violations and apply the law to the facts. The members of the agency board or commission only hear appeals from the decisions of the administrative law judges. The judges are organizationally separate from the rest of the agency so that the quasi-judicial function will be performed impartially. Administrative law judges use prior decisions or precedent. In addition, they must follow the procedural rules of the agency as well as its policy directives.

The duties and suborganization of the director of operations vary greatly from agency to agency. These operating bureaus are assigned specific areas of activity. For example, at the EPA, one group will be concerned with clean air and another with water problems.

Regional offices investigate alleged violations of the law. In addition, they usually have an educational function. Many regional offices have their own administrative law judges and special legal counsel.

## 5.   Influencing Agency Decisions

As discussed in section 3, agencies adopt rules and regulations as part of their quasi-legislative function and decide controversies in the performance of the quasi-judicial function. Due process of law requires that before a rule or regulation may be adopted by an agency, interested parties be given notice of the proposed rules and an opportunity to express their views on them. Statutes require that agencies give public notice of proposed rules and that they hold public hearings on them.

At public hearings, interested parties are allowed to present evidence in support of, or in opposition to, a proposed rule or regulation. As a result, the best means of influencing a quasi-legislative decision of an administrative agency is to participate in the adoption process.

What alternatives are available to a party unhappy with either rules and regulations that have been adopted or with the quasi-judicial decisions? What are the powers of courts in reviewing decisions of administrative agencies? What chance does one aggrieved by an agency's decision have in obtaining a reversal of the decision? How much deference is given to an agency's decisions? Answers to these questions must be clearly understood if one is to really appreciate the role of administrative agencies in our system. The principles and issues are somewhat different depending upon whether the court is reviewing either a rule or a regulation or a quasi-judicial decision. Judicial review of agency decisions is discussed in the sections that follow. However, it should be recognized that judicial review may sometimes be available even in cases where there was no hearing before the administrative agency. A federal statute known as the Hobbs Act grants judicial review in the Courts of Appeal from all final orders of federal administrative agencies.

In addition to the direct court-imposed constraints on agency action, more subtle ones exist. These include potential lawsuits against individual administrators, and political pressures. The subject of lawsuits against agency personnel is discussed in section 11.

Agencies are not politically responsible, in the sense that they are elected by the people. However, it is clear that they react, sometimes dramatically, to the force of public opinion. For example, in the late 1970s OSHA changed much of its emphasis and efforts from nit-picking safety concerns to major health problems because of public criticism.

Letters designed to obtain action or a change in policy to agencies from citizens may be effective. These are probably even more effective if directed to a member of Congress, who in turn asks the agency for an official response or explanation. At various times, a given agency may find itself bombarded with official congressional hearings inquiring into its activities. Such investigations may actually result in a budget cutback or change in the agency's authority. Just the threat of such a proceeding is often sufficient to cause a review of administrative policy. Finally, even without hearings, it is evident that agencies have often reevaluated policies and changed their posture due to adverse criticism from the media.

# JUDICIAL REVIEW OF AGENCY DECISIONS

## 6.   Introduction

Each branch of government has some control over the administrative process. The executive branch normally appoints the top officials of an agency with the advice and consent of the legislative branch. In addition, the executive branch makes budget recommendations to the legislature and has veto power over its statutes. The legislature can review and control administrative activity by abolishing the agency, enacting specific legislation contrary to rules adopted by the agency, more explicitly defining limitations on the agency's activities, providing additional procedural requirements for the agency's adjudications, or limiting appropriations of funds to the agency.

The courts also check on administrative bodies by using judicial review of their actions. Just as laws enacted by the legislature must be within its power as established by the Constitution or be void, rules and regulations promulgated by an administrative body must be within the confines of its grant of power from the legislature, or a court will find them void. However, once having determined that an act of the legislature is constitutional or a rule of an agency is authorized, the courts will not inquire into its wisdom or effectiveness. An unwise or ineffectual law may be corrected by political action at the polls; an unwise rule or regulation adopted by an agency may be corrected by the legislature that gave the agency power to make the rule in the first place. In the sections which follow, court functions in reviewing agency activities will be discussed in more detail. Keep in mind that the principles and issues differ somewhat depending upon whether the court reviews either a rule or regulation on one hand or a quasi-judicial decision on the other.

## 7.   Judicial Review of Agency Rule Making

The rule-making function in the administrative process is essentially legislative in character. Administrative agencies are usually created by enactments of the legislature in which the legislative branch is generally said to delegate certain responsibility or quasi-legislative power to the agency. Some courts have taken the view that the legislature cannot delegate its lawmaking function at all, but have concluded that authorizing an administrative agency to "fill in the details" of legislation is valid as not being an exercise of the legislative power. Other courts have stated that the legislature can delegate part of its function to an agency as long as certain constitutional safeguards are met. The difference is largely a matter of semantics.

There are two basic issues in litigation challenging the validity of a rule made by an administrative agency. First, is the delegation valid, and second, has the agency exceeded its authority? Delegations of quasi-legislative authority to administrative agencies are subject to two constitutional limitations. First, a delegation must be definite, or it will violate due process. Definiteness means that the delegation must be set forth with sufficient clarity so that all concerned, and especially reviewing courts, will be able to ascertain the extent of the agency's authority. For many reasons, broad language has been held sufficiently definite to meet this test. For example, the term "unfair methods of competition" has been held to be sufficiently definite to meet the requirements of due process.

A very similar limitation to the definiteness requirement on the exercise of quasi-legislative authority is the requirement that the power of administrative agencies to make rules be limited. The limited-power concept means that delegations must contain standards by which a court can determine whether the limitations have been exceeded. The standards set must meet certain minimum requirements before the agency in question is validly empowered to act in a certain area, and the rules promulgated by the agency must follow these standards and limitations imposed by the law establishing the agency, if they are to be upheld. Also, procedural safeguards must exist to control arbitrary administrative action and any administrative abuse of discretionary power.

Just as broad language has been approved as being sufficiently definite for a delegation to be valid under the due process clause, so also have broad standards been approved to meet the limited-power test since the 1930s. Today, it is generally agreed that delegations of authority to make rules may be in very broad language. For example, the delegation of authority to make such rules as the "public interest, convenience and necessity may require" is subject to a valid standard. Delegations that include criteria that are as concrete as the "subject area field and factors involved permit" will be held valid, since the law now recognizes that practical considerations often make definite standards impossible. In fact, some cases have held that on a challenge of unconstitutional delegation of legislative authority, the court's inquiry should focus on procedural safeguards rather than on statutory standards.

Although it is highly unlikely that a court would hold a delegation invalid because of indefiniteness or lack of standards, courts do find that agencies have exceeded their authority from time to time. Delegation of quasi-legislative power usually involves grants of substantial discretion to the board or agency involved. It must be kept in mind that the delegation of discretion is to the agency and not the courts. Therefore courts cannot interfere with the discretion given to the agency and cannot substitute their judgment for that of the agency. Courts will hold that an agency has exceeded its authority if an analysis of legislative intent confirms the view that the agency has gone beyond that intent, however noble its purposes may be. The following case is typical of those in which an agency adopted a role for good reason, but it was found to be beyond the authority of the agency.

---

# BOARD OF GOVERNORS v. DIMENSION FIN. CORP.
106 S.Ct. 681 (1986)

Section 2(c) of the Bank Holding Company Act of 1956 defines "bank" as any institution "which (1) accepts deposits that the depositor has a legal right to withdraw on demand, and (2) engages in the business of making commercial loans." In response to the increase in the number of arguably uncovered "nonbank banks"—such as institutions offering customers "NOW" accounts, and institutions offering "commercial loans substitutes" such as certificates of deposit and commer-

cial paper—the Federal Reserve Board amended its "Regulation Y" in 1984 to redefine a "bank" as any institution that (1) accepts deposits that "as a matter of practice" are payable on demand and (2) engages in the business of making "any loan other than a loan to an individual for personal, family, household, or charitable purposes," including "the purchase of retail installment loans or commercial paper, certificates of deposit, bankers' acceptances, and similar money market instruments." The Court of Appeals set aside the regulation.

BURGER, J.:...The Bank Holding Company Act of 1956, vests broad regulatory authority in the Board over bank holding companies "to restrain the undue concentration of commercial banking resources and to prevent possible abuses related to the control of commercial credit."...

The Board amended its definition of "demand deposit" primarily to include within its regulatory authority institutions offering NOW accounts. A NOW account functions like a traditional checking account—the depositor can write checks that are payable on demand at the depository institution. The depository institution, however, retains a seldom exercised but nevertheless absolute right to require prior notice of withdrawal. Under a literal reading of the statute, the institution—even if it engages in full scale commercial lending—is not a "bank" for the purposes of the Holding Company Act because the prior notice provision withholds from the depositor any "legal right" to withdraw on demand. The Board in its amended definition closes this loophole by defining demand deposits as a deposit, not that the depositor has a "legal right to withdraw on demand," but a deposit that "as a matter of practice is payable on demand."

In determining whether the Board was empowered to make such a change, we begin, of course, with the language of the statute. If the statute is clear and unambiguous "that is the end of the matter, for the court, as well as the agency, must give effect to the unambiguously expressed intent of Congress." The traditional deference courts pay to agency interpretation is not to be applied to alter the clearly expressed intent of Congress.

Application of this standard to the Board's interpretation of the "demand deposit" element of § 2(c) does not require extended analysis. By the 1966 amendments to

§ 2(c), Congress expressly limited the Act to regulation of institutions that accept deposits that "the depositor has a legal right to withdraw on demand." The Board would now define "legal right" as meaning the same as "a matter of practice." But no amount of agency expertise—however sound may be the result—can make the words "legal right" mean a right to do something "as a matter of practice." A *legal* right to withdraw on demand means just that: a right to withdraw deposits without prior notice or limitation. Institutions offering NOW accounts do not give the depositor a legal right to withdraw on demand; rather, the institution itself retains the ultimate legal right to require advance notice of withdrawal. The Board's definition of "demand deposit," therefore, is not an accurate or reasonable interpretation of § 2(c).

Section 2(c) of the Act provides that, even if an institution accepts deposits that the depositor has a legal right to withdraw on demand, the institution is not a bank unless it "engages in the business of making commercial loans." Under Regulation Y, "commercial loan" means "any loan other than a loan to an individual for personal, family, household, or charitable purposes," including "the purchase of retail installment loans or commercial paper, certificates of deposit, bankers' acceptances, and similar money market instruments."

The purpose of the amended regulation is to regulate as banks institutions offering "commercial loan substitutes," that is, extensions of credit to commercial enterprises through transactions other than the conventional commercial loan....

As the Board's characterization of these transactions as "commercial loan substitutes" suggests, however, money market transactions do not fall within the commonly accepted definition of "commercial loans." The term "commercial loan" is used in the financial community to describe the direct loan from a bank to a business customer for the purpose of providing funds needed by the customer in its business. The term does not apply to, indeed is used to distinguish, extensions of credit in the open market that do not involve close borrower-lender relationships. These latter money market transactions undoubtedly involve the indirect extension of credit to commercial entities but, because they do not entail the face-to-face negotiation of credit between borrower and lender, are not "commercial loans."...

The statute by its terms, however, exempts from regulation *all* institutions that do not engage in the business of making commercial loans. The choice of this general language demonstrates that,...Congress intended to exempt the class of institutions not making commercial loans. Furthermore, the legislative history supports this plain reading of the statute. Nothing in the statutory language or the legislative history, therefore, indicates that the term "commercial loan" meant anything different from its accepted ordinary commercial usage. The Board's definition of "commercial loan," therefore, is not a reasonable interpretation of § 2(c)....

Without doubt there is much to be said for regulating financial institutions that are the functional equivalent of banks. NOW accounts have much in common with traditional payment-on-demand checking accounts; indeed we recognize that they generally serve the same purpose. Rather than defining "bank" as an institution that offers the functional equivalent of banking services, however, Congress defined with specificity certain transactions that constitute banking subject to regulation. The statute may be imperfect, but the Board has no power to correct flaws that it perceives in the statute it is empowered to administer. Its rulemaking power is limited to adopting regulations to carry into effect the will of Congress as expressed in the statute.

If the Bank Holding Company falls short of providing safeguards desirable or necessary to protect the public interest, that is a problem for Congress, and not the Board or the courts, to address. Numerous proposals for legislative reform have been advanced to streamline the tremendously complex area of financial institution regulation. Our present inquiry, however, must come to rest with the conclusion that the action of the Board in this case is inconsistent with the language of the statute for here, "[o]nce the meaning of an enactment is discerned...the judicial process comes to an end." [*Affirmed.*]

## 8. Review of Adjudications: Procedural Aspects

The exercise of quasi-judicial functions by administrative agencies is very common. Critics say that an agency acts as prosecutor, finder of facts, and judge. However, similar to the current attitude on delegation of legislative power, judicial power may be generally granted to an administrative agency if the power is restricted by procedural safeguards preventing its abuse. The right to a jury trial does not exist in either formal or informal hearings conducted by administrative bodies.

Judicial review of agencies' adjudications by its very nature is quite limited. Legislatures have delegated authority to agencies because of their expertise and knowledge, and courts usually exercise restraint and resolve doubtful issues in favor of an agency. For example, courts reviewing administrative interpretations of law do not always decide questions of law for themselves. It is not unusual for a court to accept an administrative interpretation of law as final if it in the record is warranted and has a rational basis in law. Administrative agencies are frequently called upon to interpret the statute governing an agency, and an agency's construction is persuasive to courts. However, courts frequently replace administrative holdings with their own interpretations of law.

Administrative agencies develop their own rules of procedure unless mandated otherwise by an act of the legislature. These procedures are far less formal than judicial procedures, because one of the functions of the administrative process is to decide issues expeditiously. To proceed expeditiously usually means, for example, that administrative agencies are not restricted by the strict rules of evidence used by courts. Such agencies cannot ignore all rules, but they can use some leeway. They cannot, for example, refuse to permit any cross-examination or unduly limit it. Because an agency "is frequently the accuser, the prosecutor, the judge and the jury," it must remain alert to observe accepted standards of fairness. Reviewing courts are, therefore, alert to ensure that the true substance of a fair hearing is not denied to a party to an administrative hearing. However, the inordinate delay common in administrative hearings is a legitimate cause of public concern.

In reviewing the procedures of administrative agencies, courts are not empowered to substitute their judgment or their own procedures for those of the agency. Judicial responsibility is limited to ensuring consistency with statutes and compliance with the demands of the Constitution for a fair hearing. The latter is based on the due process clause. Due process usually requires a hearing by an agency, but on occasion sanctions may be imposed prior to the hearing.

The principle that federal administrative agencies should be free to fashion their own rules of procedure and pursue methods of inquiry permitting them to discharge their duties grows out of the view that administrative agencies and administrators will be familiar with the industries they regulate. Thus, they will be in a better position than courts or legislative bodies to design procedural rules adapted to the peculiarities of the industry and the tasks of the agency involved.

Important procedural aspects of the broad area of judicial review of administrative action are those of standing to sue and **exhaustion of remedies.** Standing to sue involves two important issues. First, the question is asked, is the action or decision of the agency subject to judicial review? Not all administrative decisions are reviewable. The Federal Administrative Procedure Act provides for judicial review except where "(1) statutes preclude judicial review or (2) agency action is committed to agency discretion by law." Few statutes actually preclude judicial review, and preclusion of judicial review by inference is rare. It is most likely to occur when an agency decides not to undertake action to enforce a statute. For example, prison inmates ask the Food and Drug Administration (FDA) to ban the use of lethal injections to carry out the death penalty. It refused to do so. The Supreme Court held that this decision of the FDA was not subject to judicial review. Congress may commit an issue only to an agency's discretion by failing to include a meaningful standard against which courts may judge the agency's exercise of discretion.

The second issue is whether or not the plaintiff in any particular case is able to obtain judicial review. It is generally required that the plaintiff be "an aggrieved party" before he or she is allowed judicial review. This subject was discussed as a part of Chapter 4. It is clear that persons who may suffer economic loss due to an agency's action have standing to sue. Recent decisions have expanded the group of persons with standing to sue to include those who have noneconomic interests such as First Amendment rights. The second procedural aspect, exhaustion of remedies, is discussed in the next section.

## 9.  Exhaustion of Remedies

The doctrine of exhaustion of remedies recognizes that in reviewing administrative decisions, courts should not decide in advance of a hearing that it will not be conducted fairly by the agency in question. In general (although there are exceptions), courts refuse to review administrative actions until a complaining party has exhausted all the administrative remedies and procedures available to him or her for redress. Judicial review is only available for final actions by an agency. Preliminary orders such as a decision to file a complaint are not reviewable. Otherwise, the administrative system would be denied important opportunities to make a factual record, to exercise its discretion, or to apply its expertise in its decision making. Also, exhaustion allows an agency to discover and correct its own errors, and thus it helps to dispense with any reason for judicial review. Exhaustion clearly should be required in those cases involving an area of the agency's expertise or specialization; it should require no unusual expense. It should also be required when the administrative remedy is just as likely as the judicial one to provide appropriate relief. The doctrine of exhaustion of remedies avoids the premature interruption of the administrative process. In general, it is probably more efficient for that purpose to go forward without interruption.

However, when there is nothing to be gained from the exhaustion of administrative remedies, and when the harm from the continued existence of the administrative ruling is great, the courts have not been reluctant to discard this doctrine. This is especially true when very fundamental constitutional guarantees such as freedom of speech or press are involved or when the administrative remedy is likely to be inadequate. Also, probably no court would insist upon exhaustion when the agency is clearly acting beyond its jurisdiction (because its action is not authorized by statute, or the statute authorizing it is unconstitutional), or where it would result in irreparable injury (such as great expense) to the petitioner. Finally, an exception to the doctrine is fraud. If an agency is acting fraudulently, immediate access to the court is appropriate.

A doctrine similar to exhaustion of remedies is known as *primary jurisdiction*. "Exhaustion" applies where a claim is cognizable in the first instance by an administrative agency alone. "Primary jurisdiction" applies where a claim is originally cognizable in the courts. It comes into play whenever enforcement of the claim requires the resolution of issues which, under a regulatory scheme, have been placed within the special competence of an administrative body. In such a case, the judicial process is suspended pending referral of such issues to the administrative body for its views. Primary jurisdiction ensures uniformity and consistency in dealing with matters entrusted to an administrative body. The doctrine is invoked when referral to the agency is preferable because of its specialized knowledge or expertise in dealing with the matter in controversy. Statutes such as those guaranteeing equal employment opportunity that create a private remedy for dollar damages sometimes require resort to an administrative agency as a condition precedent to filing suit. Some of these are federal statutes which require referral to state agencies. In these cases, referral must occur, but the right to sue is not limited by the results of the administrative decision.

## 10. Review of Agency's Determination of Facts

When it reviews the findings of fact made by an administrative body, a court presumes them to be correct. A court of review examines the evidence by analyzing the record of the agency's proceedings. It upholds the agency's findings and conclusions on questions of fact if they are supported by substantial evidence in the record. In other words, the record must contain material evidence from which a reasonable person might reach the same conclusion as did the agency. If substantial evidence in support of the decision is present, the court will not disturb the agency's findings, even though the court itself might have reached a different conclusion on the basis of other conflicting evidence also in the record. The determination of credibility of the witnesses who testify in quasi-judicial proceedings is for the agency to determine and not the courts.

Thus, it is apparent that on review courts do not (1) reweigh the evidence, (2) make independent determinations of fact, or (3) substitute their view of the evidence for that of the agency. However, courts do determine if there is substantial evidence to support the action taken. But in their examination of the evidence, all that is required is evidence sufficient to convince a reasonable mind to a fair degree of certainty. Thus, substantial evidence is that which a reasonable mind might accept as adequate to support the conclusion. When a case involves the special expertise of the agency, even more deference is paid to the agency's decisions as held in the following case.

# BALTIMORE GAS & ELEC. v. NATURAL RES. DEF. COUNCIL
103 S.Ct. 2246 (1983)

The National Environmental Policy Act (NEPA) requires federal agencies to consider the environmental impact of any major federal action. The Nuclear Regulatory Commission (NRC) adopted a series of generic rules relating to the environmental effect of a nuclear power plant's fuel cycle. In these rules, the NRC decided that licensing boards should assume that the permanent storage of certain nuclear wastes would have no significant environmental impact (the so-called zero-release assumption) and thus should not affect the decision whether or not to license a particular nuclear power plant. The NRC had computed the resources used by nuclear power plants (front-end activities) and the effluents released by them (back-end activities) in making the zero-release assumption. These computations were set forth in a table, Table S-3, adopted by the NRC.

The Court of Appeals held that the rules were arbitrary and capricious and inconsistent with NEPA because the NRC had not factored the consideration of uncertainties surrounding the zero-release assumption into the licensing process in such a manner that the uncertainties could potentially affect the outcome of any decision to license a plant.

O'CONNOR, J.:...We are acutely aware that the extent to which this Nation should rely on nuclear power as a source of energy is an important and sensitive issue. Much of the debate focuses on whether development of nuclear generation facilities should proceed in the face of uncertainties about their long-term effects on the environment. Resolution of these fundamental policy questions lies, however, with Congress and the agencies to which Congress has delegated authority, as well as with state legislatures and, ultimately, the populace as a whole. Congress has assigned the courts only the limited, albeit important, task of reviewing agency action to determine whether the agency conformed with controlling statutes....

Administrative decisions should be set aside in this context, as in every other, only for substantial procedural or substantive reasons as mandated by statute—not simply because the court is unhappy with the result reached.

The controlling statute at issue here is the National Environmental Policy Act. NEPA has twin aims. First, it places upon an agency the obligation to consider every significant aspect of the environmental impact of a proposed action. Second, it ensures that the agency will inform the public that it has indeed considered environmental concerns in its decisionmaking process. Congress in enacting NEPA, however, did not require agencies to elevate environmental concerns over other appropriate considerations. Rather, it required only that the agency take a "hard look" at the environmental consequences before taking a major action. The role of the courts is simply to ensure that the agency has adequately considered and disclosed the environmental impact of its actions and that its decision is not arbitrary or capricious.

In its Table S-3 Rule here, the Commission has determined that the probabilities favor the zero-release assumption, because the Nation is likely to develop methods to store the wastes with no leakage to the environment....The Commission recognized, however, that the geological, chemical, physical and other data it relied on in making this prediction were based, in part, on assumptions which involve substantial uncertainties. Again, no one suggests that the uncertainties are trivial or the potential effects insignificant if time proves the zero-release assumption to have been seriously wrong. After confronting the issue, though, the Commission has determined that the uncertainties concerning the development of nuclear waste storage facilities are not sufficient to affect the outcome of any individual licensing decision.

It is clear that the Commission, in making this determination, has made the careful consideration and disclosure required by NEPA. The sheer volume of proceedings before the Commission is impressive. Of far greater importance, the Commission's Statement of Consideration announcing the final Table S-3 Rule shows that it has digested this mass of material and disclosed all substantial risks. The Statement summarizes the major uncertainty of long-term storage in bedded-salt repositories, which is that water could infiltrate the repository as a result of such diverse factors as geologic faulting, a meteor strike, or accidental or deliberate intrusion by man. The Commission noted that the probability of intrusion was small, and that the plasticity of salt would tend to heal some types of intrusions. The Commission also found the evidence "tentative but favor-

able" that an appropriate site could be found....

Given this record and the Commission's statement, it simply cannot be said that the Commission ignored or failed to disclose the uncertainties surrounding its zero-release assumption.

Congress did not enact NEPA, of course, so that an agency would contemplate the environmental impact of an action as an abstract exercise. Rather, Congress intended that the "hard look" be incorporated as part of the agency's process of deciding whether to pursue a particular federal action....

...NEPA does not require agencies to adopt any particular internal decision-making structure. Here, the agency has chosen to evaluate generically the environmental impact of the fuel cycle and inform individual licensing boards, through the Table S-3 rule, of its evaluation. The generic method chosen by the agency is clearly an appropriate method of conducting the hard look required by NEPA. The environmental effects of much of the fuel cycle are not plant specific, for any plant, regardless of its particular attributes, will create additional wastes that must be stored in a common long-term repository. Administrative efficiency and consistency of decision are both furthered by a generic determination of these effects without needless repetition of the litigation in individual proceedings, which are subject to review by the Commission in any event.

The Court of Appeals...concluded that the Commission...violated NEPA by failing to factor the uncertainty surrounding long-term storage into Table S-3 and precluding individual licensing decisionmakers from considering it.

The Commission's decision to affix a zero value to the environmental impact of long-term storage would violate NEPA, however, only if the Commission acted arbitrarily and capriciously in deciding generically that the uncertainty was insufficient to affect any individual licensing decision. In assessing whether the Commission's decision is arbitrary and capricious, it is crucial to place the zero-release assumption in context. Three factors are particularly important. First is the Commission's repeated emphasis that the zero-risk assumption—and, indeed, all of the Table S-3 rule—was made for a limited purpose....

Second, the Commission emphasized that the zero-release assumption is but a single figure in an entire Table, which the Commission expressly designed as a risk-averse estimate of the environmental impact of the fuel cycle....A reviewing court should not magnify a single line item beyond its significance as only part of a larger Table.

Third, a reviewing court must remember that the Commission is making predictions, within its area of special expertise, at the frontiers of science. When examining this kind of scientific determination, as op-

posed to simple findings of fact, a reviewing court must generally be at its most deferential.

With these three guides in mind, we find the Commission's zero-release assumption to be within the bounds of reasoned decisionmaking required by the APA....

In sum, we think that the zero-release assumption—a policy judgment concerning one line in a conservative Table designed for the limited purpose of individual licensing decisions—is within the bounds of reasoned decisionmaking. It is not our task to determine what decision we, as Commissioners, would have reached. Our only task is to determine whether the Commission has considered the relevant factors and articulated a rational connection between the facts found and the choice made. Under this standard, we think the Commission's zero-release assumption, within the context of Table S-3 as a whole, was not arbitrary and capricious....[*Reversed.*]

The findings of an administrative body are not set aside unless the record clearly precludes the decision of the administrative body. The decision of an agency will be affirmed even if the court believes it to be erroneous, if a reasonable person could have reached the conclusion stated. It is the function of an agency to pass upon the weight to be accorded to the evidence and to make the choice, if necessary, between varying inferences which might be drawn therefrom. The possibility of drawing either of two inconsistent inferences from the evidence does not prevent an agency from drawing one of them. Courts, however, do not always agree with the administrative determination, and sometimes they set aside a finding because it is not supported by substantial evidence.

For the courts to exercise their function of limited review, an agency must provide a record which sets forth the reasons and basis for its decision. If this record shows that the agency did not examine all relevant data and that it ignored issues before it, a court may set aside the agency's decision because such a decision is arbitrary and capricious. Agencies cannot assume their decisions. They must be based on evidence, and the record must support the decision.

## 11. Damage Suits

In such a litigious society as ours, it is not surprising that agencies and administrators sometimes are sued for dollar damages by those subject to their administrative rules, regulations, and decisions. Such suits may involve allegations that government officials have violated the constitutional rights of citizens. For example, it has been held that a violation of the Fourth Amendment by federal agents gives rise to a cause of action for damages.

Agencies and officials that are sued usually assert a defense known as sovereign or governmental **immunity.** They simply contend that they cannot be sued. At common law, governmental bodies at both the federal and state levels had this immunity defense. The theory was that public assets and the income from general taxation could not be used for the sole benefit of a private individual. It was thought that paying a tort claim for damages would be such a private use of public funds. Damage claims therefore were considered an illegal diversion of funds from public to private purposes.

In addition, immunity was extended to public officials for two reasons: (1) It would be an injustice, particularly in the absence of bad faith, to subject a public official to liability for discretion poorly exercised if his or her position requires exercising discretion. (2) The threat of liability would deter public officials from performance of their duties, and they would not act with the decisiveness required for the public good.

Today, Congress and most state legislatures have passed laws eliminating sovereign immunity as a defense in most tort cases. Just as the defense of charitable immunity was eliminated because charities could purchase liability insurance the same as any other organization, sovereign immunity was eliminated because governmental bodies could include funds in their budgets to pay legitimate claims for injuries caused by government employees.

The federal law waiving tort liability is known as the Federal Tort Claims Act. The law authorizes suits for damages against the United States "for injury or loss of property, or personal injury or death caused by the negligent or wrongful act or omission of any employee of the Government while acting within the scope of his office or employment," under circumstances where the United States, if a private person, would be liable to the claimant in accordance with the law of the place where the act or omission occurred."

The statute lists several exceptions to this broad waiver of immunity. In other words the statute reaffirms and retains sovereign immunity in certain cases. Of great importance to the administrative process and to administrators is the section providing that there shall be no liability for "any claim...based upon the exercise or performance or the failure to exercise or perform a discretionary function or duty on the part of a federal agency or an employee of the Government, whether or not the discretion involved be abused."

This exception is known as the "discretionary function" exception. For it to be applicable, the conduct creating the alleged tort liability must involve an element of judgment or choice. Thus the discretionary function exception will not apply when a federal statute, regulation, or policy specifically prescribes a course of action that a government employee must follow. If an employee must adhere to a direction and has no judgment or choice, the exception is not applicable and there is no sovereign immunity.

In addition, if there is an element of judgment, courts must determine if it is the kind of judgment that the discretionary function exception was designed to cover. Congress intended to prevent judicial "second-guessing" of legislative and administrative decisions grounded in social, economic, and political policy in tort actions in court. The exception protects only governmental actions and decisions based on considerations of public policy. In summary, the discretionary function rule retains sovereign immunity if the action challenged in the tort case involves the permissible exercise of policy judgment. Therefore, it is apparent that not all acts rising out of regulatory activities are covered by the discretionary function exception. For example, the Supreme Court held that there could be liability for licensing an oral polio vaccine that caused polio. The law directed the agency to take certain steps; had it not done so, there would be liability because no discretion was involved. Failure to act in accordance with specific statutory mandates can result in liability.

The leading case in this area involved tort suits against the FAA for negligently certifying airplanes for operation without actually inspecting them. Such activity was declared to be immune from tort suit. The decision to "spot-check" planes was discretionary because it represented a policy decision to achieve airline safety within a limited budget. The FAA had no liability for mere mistakes in judgment, whether the mistake is one of fact or one of law. Damage suits cannot be used as a means to review an agency's discretionary decisions.

The immunity defense is often limited because government officials should not ignore with impunity the limitations which controlling law places on their powers. Immunity only protects officials from conduct that is within the scope of their duties and responsibilities.

As a general rule, hearing examiners and administrative law judges have absolute immunity. Judges have immunity because of the special nature of their responsibilities. Hearing examiners and administrative judges serve a similar function. They exercise independent judgment on the evidence, and they must be free of pressure from the parties. Therefore, persons performing in adjudicatory functions within a government agency are entitled to immunity from damage suit liabilities.

Public prosecutors also have been granted absolute immunity because of the importance of their function and the need to prevent harassment of them by persons charged with crime. The prosecutor's role would likely provoke retaliation unless the immunity were absolute. Therefore, the courts have concluded that an agency's officials who perform functions analogous to those of a prosecutor and who are responsible for the decision to initiate or to continue a proceeding are also entitled to absolute immunity from damage claims. In addition, an agency's attorney who presents evidence in an agency hearing has absolute immunity from suits based on the introduction of such evidence.

Legal remedies are available within the agency and within the courts to provide a sufficient check on the activities of such officials of agencies. The quasi-judicial function of government agencies shares enough of the characteristics of the judicial process for those agency officials to have the same immunity as their counterparts in the judicial process. The risk of an unconstitutional act by agency officials is clearly outweighed by the importance of preserving their independent judgment.

## 12.  Equal Access to Justice

The Equal Access to Justice Act, which took effect October 1, 1982, requires Uncle Sam to pay the legal costs of small businesses, nonprofit groups, and most individuals who can show they were unjustly treated by the federal government. Prior to the enactment of this law, small companies often were reluctant to take on the U.S. government because of litigation costs. The government was at a great advantage because of the number of attorneys and other resources it has. This law enables the "little guy" to fight the bureaucracy. It should be recognized that awards for legal expenses aren't available to just anyone. Congress limited eligibility to persons whose net worth doesn't exceed $1 million and businesses with no more than $5 million net worth and 500 employees. Charitable and religious tax-exempt organizations qualify if they have 500 or fewer employees. Also, the law grants legal fees only to parties that overcome the government's position in court, administrative proceedings, or in a settlement. Even then, the government agency isn't required to pay if it can show that its original decision was "substantially justified." The word "substantially" means to be justified in substance or in the main, not justified to a high degree. The action must be justified to a degree that could satisfy a reasonable person, and must have reasonable basis in both law and fact. For the position of the government to be substantially justified, so that the award of attorneys' fees under the Equal Access to Justice Act is not appropriate, the government's position must be more than merely undeserving of sanctions for frivolity.

The Equal Access to Justice Act is not being used very extensively. During the first nineteen months under the law, the government lost 12,000 lawsuits, but there were only thirty applications for legal fees. Under the law, courts may order the federal government to pay attorneys' fees and other legal costs if the agency has acted without "substantial justification." Most of the time the government's position meets this test.

### 13.  Common Criticisms

The independent regulatory agencies and the administrative process are subjected to a great deal of criticism. (See Table 8-2, which summarizes many of the common criticisms.) They are often charged with being inefficient and ineffective. Many complaints about the administrative process are directly related to its vastness and size. This vastness permeates all levels of government—federal, state, and local. In a real sense, bureaucracy and bureaucrats are the actual rulers of the country.

Of course, one of the major criticisms of the fourth branch of government is its high cost. This is discussed in the next section.

### 14.  Cost of Regulation

Regulation is a form of taxation. It directly increases the cost of government. But these direct costs of regulation are only a small fraction of the indirect costs. Regulation significantly adds to the cost of doing business, and these costs are passed on to the taxpaying, consuming public. The consumer, for whose protection many regulations are adopted, pays both the direct cost of regulation (in taxes) and the indirect cost (when purchasing products and services).

The existence of a governmental agency usually forces a business subject to the agency's jurisdiction to create a similar bureaucracy within its own organization to deal with the agency. For example, the existence of EEOC has caused most large corporations to designate affirmative action employees; they assist the company in complying with the laws, rules, and regulations enforced by EEOC. Whenever a bureaucracy exists, firms dealing with it must have internal groups with responsibilities that are the mirror image of the agency.

Other costs the public must absorb result from agency regulations that inhibit competition and innovation. Regulation has protected existing companies by creating a barrier to entry into a market. Regulation tends to protect "cozy competition" to the extent that, quite often, the parties that object the most to deregulation are the businesses being regulated.

Perhaps the most disturbing additional cost to the business community is the cost of paperwork. The burden of the paperwork involved in filing applications, returns, reports, and forms is overwhelming and a major cost of doing business. In a recent year, it was estimated that 2 billion forms had to be filled out and filed by business because of bureaucratic red tape—at a cost in excess of $20 billion.

Historically, there was little or no cost-benefit analysis when new rules and regulations were proposed. Government has tended only to assess the benefits accruing from a .cleaner environment, safer products, healthier working conditions, and so on, in deciding to embark upon vast new regulatory programs. The primary focus of policy making by way of such social

**TABLE 8-2**    Common Criticisms of Administrative Agencies

**Relating to personnel**

1    Government has difficulty in hiring and retaining the best-qualified people. Salaries are often not competitive, and advancement is often slower than in the private sector. Also, some people are overqualified for their positions.
2    The reward system usually doesn't make a significant distinction between excellent, mediocre, and poor performances. There are few incentives to improve productivity and job performance.
3    It is very difficult, if not impossible, to discharge unsatisfactory employees. Transfers of employees are easier to accomplish than discharges.
4    The **peter principle,** which holds that people are promoted to their level of incompetence, is obviously present in many administrative agencies.
5    Personnel in many top positions are selected for political reasons. They often lack the necessary expertise to run an effective organization.

**Relating to procedures**

1    Delay in the decision-making process is quite common. There often is no reason to expedite decisions, and a huge backlog of cases is common in agencies such as EEOC.
2    The administrative process is overwhelmed with paperwork and with meetings.
3    Rules and regulations are often written in complex legal language—"legalese"—which laypeople cannot understand.
4    There is often a lack of enforcement procedures to follow up actions taken to ensure compliance.
5    The administrative process can be dictatorial; there may be too much discretionary power, often unstructured and unchecked, placed in many bureaucratic hands. Formal as well as informal administrative action can amount to an abuse of power.

**Relating to substance**

1    There are so many agencies making rules and regulations directed at the business community that the rules and regulations often overlap and are in conflict.
2    Some agencies are accused of "sweetheart regulations," or favoring the industry or industries they regulate over the public interest. This may arise as a result of the "revolving door" relationship. Regulators are often persons who had former high executive positions in the industries they regulate. The reverse is also true: people in high-paying jobs in certain industries often had been regulators in those very industries.
3    Many actions for illegal conduct end with only consent orders. A business accused of a violation agrees not to violate the law in the future without admitting any past violation. Such actions have little deterrent effect on others, and no punishment is imposed for illegal conduct.
4    The volume of rules adopted by agencies is beyond the ability of the business community to absorb. In 1987, the *Federal Register* contained over 40,000 pages—down from 80,000 in 1980, but still extremely high.
5    Enforcement of some laws varies over time. For example, OSHA, as a part of its reversal of a de-regulatory trend, recently fined Chrysler $1.6 million. The vacillation can be seen in the following:

**OSHA Penalties**
**Penalties set by OSHA for record-keeping violations**

| FISCAL YEAR | | FISCAL YEAR | |
| --- | --- | --- | --- |
| 1980 | $22,826 | 1984 | $    21,950 |
| 1981 | 14,166 | 1985 | 23,061 |
| 1982 | 15,990 | 1986 | 1,445,915 |
| 1983 | 9,561 | 1987* | 1,681,000 |

*6 months
Source: Occupational Safety and Health Administration

regulation has not been on balancing the costs of the programs with their potential benefits. The public, and especially consumers, have frequently been forced to pay for many things they did not want or need in the sense that the cost far exceeded the benefits. Moreover, the law does not generally require cost-benefit analysis, as the case which follows illustrates.

# AMERICAN TEXTILE MANUFACTURERS INSTITUTE, INC. v. DONOVAN

101 S.Ct. 2478 (1981)

OSHA promulgated a standard strictly limiting occupational exposure to cotton dust, an airborne particle produced during the manufacture of cotton products, exposure to which induces a serious and potentially disabling disease, byssinosis, also known as "brown lung" disease. Petitioners, representing the interests of the cotton industry, challenged the validity of the "cotton dust standard" in the Court of Appeals. They contended that the Occupational Safety and Health Act requires OSHA to demonstrate that its standard reflects a reasonable relationship between the costs and benefits associated with the Standard. The Court of Appeals upheld the Standard and ruled that the Act does not require OSHA to compare costs and benefits. The U.S. Supreme Court granted certiorari.

BRENNAN, J.:...The principal question presented in this case is whether the Occupational Safety and Health Act requires the Secretary, in promulgating a standard pursuant to § 6(b)(5) of the Act, to determine that the costs of the standard bear a reasonable relationship to its benefits. Relying on § 6(b)(5) and 3(8) of the Act, petitioners urge not only that OSHA must show that a standard addresses a significant risk of material health impairment, but also that OSHA must demonstrate that the reduction in risk

of material health impairment is significant in light of the costs of attaining that reduction. Respondents on the other hand contend that the Act requires OSHA to promulgate standards that eliminate or reduce such risks "to the extent such protection is technologically and economically feasible." To resolve this debate, we must turn to the language, structure, and legislative history of the Occupational Safety and Health Act.

The starting point of our analysis is the language of the statute itself. § 6(b)(5) of the Act provides:

**The Secretary, in promulgating standards dealing with toxic materials or harmful physical agents under this subsection, shall set the standard which most adequately assures, _to the extent feasible_, on the basis of the best available evidence, that no employee will suffer material impairment of health or functional capacity even if such employee has regular exposure to the hazard dealt with by such standard for the period of his working life.**

Although their interpretations differ, all parties agree that the phrase "to the extent feasible" contains the critical language in § 6(b)(5) for purposes of this case.

The plain meaning of the word "feasible" supports respondents' interpretation of the statute. According to Webster's Third New International Dictionary of the English

Language, "feasible" means "capable of being done, executed, or effected." Thus, § 6(b)(5) directs the Secretary to issue the standard that "most adequately assures… that no employee will suffer material impairment of health," limited only by the extent to which this is "capable of being done." In effect then, as the Court of Appeals held, Congress itself defined the basic relationship between costs and benefits, by placing the "benefit" of worker health above all other considerations save those making attainment of this "benefit" unachievable. Any standard based on a balancing of costs and benefits by the Secretary that strikes a different balance than that struck by Congress would be inconsistent with the command set forth in § 6(b)(5). Thus, cost-benefit analysis by OSHA is not required by the statute because feasibility analysis is….

The legislative history of the Act, while concededly not crystal clear, provides general support for respondents' interpretation of the Act. The congressional reports and debates certainly confirm that Congress meant "feasible" and nothing else in using that term. Congress was concerned that the Act might be thought to require achievement of absolute safety, an impossible standard, and therefore insisted that health and safety goals be capable of economic and technological accomplishment. Perhaps most telling is the absence of any indication whatsoever that Congress intended OSHA to conduct its own cost-benefit analysis before promulgating a toxic material or harmful physical agent standard. The legislative history demonstrates conclusively, that Congress was fully aware that the Act would impose real and substantial costs of compliance on industry, and believed that such costs were part of the cost of doing business….

Not only does the legislative history confirm that Congress meant "feasible" rather than "cost-benefit" when it used the former term, but it also shows that Congress understood that the Act would create substantial costs for employers, yet intended to impose such costs when necessary to create a safe and healthful working environment. Congress viewed the costs of health and safety as a cost of doing business. Senator Yarborough, a cosponsor of the Williams bill, stated: "We know the costs would be put into consumer goods but that is the price we should pay for the 80 million workers in America."

Other members of Congress voiced similar views. Nowhere is there any indication that Congress contemplated a different balancing by OSHA of the benefits of worker health and safety against the costs of achieving them. Indeed Congress thought that the *financial costs* of health and safety problems in the workplace were as large or larger than the *financial costs* of eliminating these problems. In its statement of findings and declaration of purpose encompassed in the Act itself, Congress announced that "personal injuries and illnesses arising out of work situations impose a substantial burden upon, and are a hindrance to, interstate commerce in terms of lost production, wage loss, medical expenses, and disability compensation payment."

When Congress passed the Occupational Safety and Health Act in 1970, it chose to place pre-eminent value on assuring employees a safe and healthful working environment, limited only by the feasibility of achieving such an environment. We must measure the validity of the Secretary's actions against the requirements of that Act. For "the judicial function does not extend to substantive revision of regulatory policy. That function lies elsewhere—in Congressional and Executive oversight or amendatory legislation." Accordingly, the judgment of the Court of Appeals is…[*Affirmed.*]

At first glance, the application of cost-benefit analysis to the administrative process would seem to make sense. However, on closer examination, it is obvious that in many cases it is not possible to weigh the costs against the benefits of regulation.

How do you apply cost-benefit analysis to a rule dealing with human life? How much dollar benefit is to be assigned to a life in measuring it against the cost? Assume that a Department of Transportation rule requiring air bags in all new automobiles sold adds a cost of $800 to each car. Assume also that it saves 50,000 lives per year. Is the cost worth the benefit? Your answer may depend on whether you are one of the 50,000 or not. Cost-benefit analysis becomes ethically awkward when there is an attempt to place a dollar value on things not usually bought and sold, such as life, health, or mobility.

## REVIEW QUESTIONS

1  For each term in the left-hand column, match the most appropriate description in the right-hand column:

(1) CPSC

(a) Protects the public from anticompetitive behavior and unfair and deceptive business practices; a law enforcement agency

(2) EPA

(b) Licenses and regulates the nuclear energy industry

(3) FCC

(c) Protects the public against unreasonable risks of injury associated with consumer products

(4) FTC

(d) Seeks to prevent discrimination in employment based on race, color, religion, sex, or national origin, and other unlawful employment practices

(5) FDA

(e) Regulates interstate and foreign communications by means of radio, television, wire, cable, and satellite

(6) EEOC

(f) Ensures all workers a safe and healthy work environment

(7) NLRB

(g) Enforces the federal securities laws which regulate sale of securities to the investing public

(8)  NRC

(9)  OSHA

(10)  SEC

(h)  Administers laws to prohibit distribution of adulterated, misbranded, or unsafe food and drugs

(i)  Conducts union certification elections and holds hearings on unfair labor practice complaints

(j)  Administers all laws relating to the environment, including laws on water pollution, air pollution, solid wastes, pesticides, toxic substances, etc.

**2**   A liquor control board suspended a liquor license because a clerk sold a twelve-pack of beer to a sixteen-year-old. The customer looked "old," and the drinking age was eighteen. There was no evidence of previous violations. Will a court reverse the decision? Why, or why not?

**3**   The FTC issued an administrative complaint against several major oil companies alleging unfair methods of competition. After failing to get the FTC to dismiss the complaint, the oil companies brought a separate action against the FTC in federal court asserting that the FTC had issued the complaint without having reason to believe that the companies were violating the law. They sought an order to require the FTC to withdraw the complaint. The gist was that political pressure for a public explanation of the gasoline shortages of 1973 forced the FTC to issue the complaint despite insufficient investigation. Should the case be dismissed? Why?

**4**   Harvey, a school teacher of limited means, had a dispute with a federal administrative agency. When the matter was not resolved before the agency, Harvey appealed to a federal court. The court found all of the issues for Harvey satisfactorily and observed that the government officials had been arbitrary and capricious. Harvey paid his attorney $10,000 to handle the case. Is he entitled to recover this loss from the government? Explain.

**5**   The EPA discovered that a chemical company was dumping toxic waste into a local river. The agency conducted a hearing with proper notice to the chemical company and found the company to be in violation of EPA's regulations. A heavy fine was imposed. The company appealed to the court, contending that the hearing had denied it its right to a trial by jury. Is it correct? Why, or why not?

**6**   Leonard's, Inc., was charged with violating a rule of an administrative agency. A hearing was conducted by an administrative law judge. The judge found the company guilty. The rules of the agency provided for a review by the full commission, but rather than seek such a review, Leonard's filed a case in the courts to enjoin further agency action. Is Leonard's entitled to an injunction? Why, or why not?

**7**   Joe owned a tract of real estate across the street from a major shopping center. The lot was at an intersection of a main road leading to the shopping center, and Joe wanted to build a service station on the property. The property was zoned for single-family residences. Joe filed a request to have the zoning classification changed to commercial. The zoning board denied the request, and Joe filed suit. He contended that the present and best use of the property was for commercial purposes. The zoning board contended that there needed to be a buffer between the shopping center and the residential area, and the only appropriate buffer was the street. What was the decision? Why?

**8** Lawyers and legally trained persons are highly visible and important in most administrative agencies. Why do these agencies require so many legally trained personnel to accomplish their goals? Explain.

**9** The law creating the EPA states that its purpose is to establish rules and regulations to "promote a healthful environment." Pursuant to this delegation of authority, the agency adopted a regulation that made it unlawful to manufacture or to utilize power plant equipment that allowed emissions "detrimental to the atmosphere." Consumers Power Company was charged with violating the agency rule. It challenged the constitutionality of the rule. What was the result? Why?

**10** Hershel filed a claim for workers' compensation, alleging that he received a knee injury which arose out of and in the course of his employment. The employer contended that Hershel's knee had been hurt in a touch football game. The hearing examiner denied the claim. Hershel then filed suit against the employer and the hearing examiner, contending that there was collusion between them in the denial of his claim. The hearing examiner moved to dismiss the lawsuit. What was the result? Why?

**11** The Reagan administration, when it took office, rescinded the requirement by the National Highway Traffic Safety Administration that all new cars sold after September 1982 include air bags. Several automobile insurance companies filed suit, challenging the rescission of the air-bag rule. The rule had been rescinded on the belief that it was an example of excessive governmental regulation. After the air-bag order was issued, was its rescission on such grounds proper? Why, or why not?

**12** To bring destabilizing competition among dairy farmers under control, a federal law authorizes the secretary of agriculture to issue milk market orders setting the minimum prices that handlers (those who process dairy products) must pay to producers (dairy farmers) for their milk products. Ultimate consumers of milk brought suit, challenging milk market orders. Should the case be dismissed? Why, or why not?

**13** A congressman filed an administrative complaint with the Federal Election Commission, alleging various violations of the Federal Election Campaign Act by several different groups that made campaign contributions. Dissatisfied with the progress of the FEC's investigation, he filed suit against the FEC in federal district court, seeking to compel agency action. The court found that the agency action was "arbitrary and capricious." Does this entitle him to an award of attorney's fees under the Equal Access to Justice Act? Why, or why not?

**14** Plaintiffs purchased state lottery tickets and were winners along with seventy-six others. The state had advertised that $1,750,000 would be the prize, but it only distributed $744,471. Plaintiff sued the lottery director, alleging fraud in the conduct of the lottery. The Illinois lottery law provides for administrative hearings upon complaints charging violations of the lottery law or of regulations thereunder. It also allows any party adversely affected by a final order to determination of the administrative agency to seek judicial review. Must the plaintiffs exhaust their administrative remedies? Why or why not?

# *Part Three*
# CONTRACTS AND TORTS

# Chapter

# 9

# Contract Law and Private Enterprise

## CHAPTER PREVIEW

Millions of new contracts are formed daily in the United States. Both businesspeople and consumers alike make contractual agreements. Over the years, no other area of the law has been as important as the law of contracts in supporting the private enterprise system.

The making of contracts is basic to the understanding of the legal environment of business. Labor unions and managers make collective bargaining agreements, which are contracts (Chapter 17). Antitrust law prohibits contracts that restrain trade (Chapters 22–24). Corporations can act only through contracts made by their agents (Chapters 12–13). In securities law (Chapter 19), consumer protection (Chapter 20), and debtor protection (Chapter 21), the government regulates the contractual process. Security agreements that protect creditors are contracts (Chapter 21). A major cause of action in product liability cases is breach of contract (Chapter 11). Even the Constitution has a clause that prohibits the states from "impairing the Obligation of Contracts" (Chapter 6).

There are five basic elements of a contract: offer, acceptance, consideration, capacity of parties, and legality of purpose. A substantial part of this chapter focuses on these elements and how they come together to form contracts. However, before discussing the formation of contracts, we must develop the role of contract law in the private enterprise system and consider various classifications of contracts.

Sections of this chapter also discuss other contract law topics, such as the significance of written contracts, the interpretation of contracts, the rights of third parties to contracts, and the performance of contracts. The concluding section outlines trends in contract law.

A special area of contract law covers the sale of goods. *Goods* are tangible, movable personal property, a category that covers everything from airplanes to flea collars. It does not, however, include services and real estate. Contracts for the sale of goods are covered by the Uniform Commercial Code, a special body of law adopted in every state except Louisiana. This chapter recognizes many instances in which the law treats sales of goods differently from other types of contracts.

Important contract terms include accord and satisfaction, assignment, bilateral contract, capacity, consideration, duress, executory contract, firm offer, fraud, implied contract, parol evidence rule, promissory estoppel, quasi-contract, rescission, specific performance, statute of frauds, third-party beneficiary, and voidable contract.

## 1.   Contract Law and Its Place in Private Enterprise

When is the last time you entered a contract? Was it last month when you signed an apartment or dorm lease? If so, you must be very hungry. This is because one enters a contract when buying a meal or a snack from the vending machine. Actually, most people contract daily for a great variety of goods and services that they purchase or lease. The rules of contract law underlie the private enterprise system at every turn.

A **contract** is a legally enforceable promise. It need not usually be a formal, written document, and those who make a contract do not have to use the word "contract" nor recognize that they have made a legally enforceable promise. Still, the rules of contract law apply. If the expectations of the parties to a contract are not met, these rules affect legal negotiations or a lawsuit. For instance, contract law says that a restaurant "promises" that its food is fit to eat. Should the restaurant serve a meal that gives the buyer food poisoning, it would now be liable for the injury caused by breaking its promise.

Contract law enables people to make private agreements legally enforceable. Enforceability of agreements is desirable because it gives people the certainty they need to rely on promises contained in agreements. For instance, a shirt manufacturer in Los Angeles must know that it can rely on the promise of a store in Boston to pay for a thousand specially manufactured shirts. The manufacturer is more likely to agree to sew the shirts if it can enforce payment from the buyer, if necessary, under the law of contracts.

In an important sense, then, the law of contracts is vital for our private enterprise economy. It helps make buyers and sellers willing to do business together. Contract law is not as needed in the economy of the Soviet Union, where the state controls all buying and selling relationships. It is also less needed in countries such as Japan, where centuries of tradition regulate business arrangements. But in the United States the law of contracts promotes certainty that agreements will be kept and permits reliance on promises. It encourages the flow of commerce.

## 2. Sources of Contract Law

Most of the contract law outlined in this chapter is common law (see Chapter 1). The courts have developed principles controlling contract formation, performance, breach, and remedies in countless cases that come to us today in the form of precedents. This judge-made law affects many types of contracts, including real property, service, employment, and general business contracts.

Another source of contract law is legislation. Various states have enacted parts of the common law, sometimes modifying it. The Uniform Commercial Code's coverage of the sale of goods is an example of how the legislation may modify the common law of contracts. The making of contracts in specific industries, such as the insurance industry, is also often controlled by legislation.

## 3. Classification of Contracts

### EXECUTORY AND EXECUTED CONTRACTS

We use a number of terms to help classify contracts. Mastery of these terms provides an important basis for further understanding of the topic. For instance, an **executory contract** (or term of a contract) is one which the contracting parties have not yet performed. An **executed contract** (or term) is one which the parties have performed.

### EXPRESS AND IMPLIED CONTRACTS

Many contracts arise from discussions in which parties actually discuss the promised terms of their agreement. These are called **express contracts.** A negotiated purchase of land for construction of a manufacturing plant is an example of an express contract. There are also **implied contracts** which arise from the conduct or actions of the parties, rather than by words. For instance, seeking professional services at a doctor's office implies a contractual agreement to pay the going rate for services even though no express promise to pay is made.

### UNILATERAL AND BILATERAL CONTRACTS

One classification of contracts concerns those that are unilateral and those that are bilateral. A **unilateral contract** involves a present act given in return for a promise of future performance. A loan of money in return for a promise to repay at interest illustrates the unilateral contract. Another example is catching a bank robber in return for the promise of a reward. In **bilateral contracts** each party makes a promise to perform for the other: Greshman promises to deliver a deed to the land on October 31; Gomez promises to pay Greshman $50,000 for the land on that date. When it is unclear whether the parties to an agreement intend a unilateral or a bilateral contract, courts usually presume that the contract is bilateral.

### VOID CONTRACTS

**Void contracts** are really not contracts at all. They are agreements which lack an essential contractual element. Often this element is legality of purpose. For example, in states where gambling is illegal, a bet on a football game is void. This usually means that a court will take no action when parties do not live up to the betting agreement. The opposite of a void contract is a **valid** one, which contains all the proper elements of a contract.

### VOIDABLE CONTRACTS

A **voidable contract** binds one of the parties to an agreement but gives the other party the option of withdrawing from it. Contracts based on fraud or misrepresentation are two important examples of voidable contracts. **Fraud** involves an intentional misstatement of material (important) fact that induces one to rely justifiably to his or her injury. Intentionally calling a zircon a diamond and persuading someone to purchase it on that basis is a fraud. Sometimes, failures to disclose a material fact can also be a fraud, e.g., as when a landowner sells a buyer land, knowing that the buyer wishes to build a home on it, and does not disclose that the land is underwater during the rainy season. The defrauded party can withdraw from the contract. **Misrepresentation** is simply a misstatement without intent to mislead. However, a contract entered into through misrepresentation is still voidable by the innocent party.

Other examples of voidable contracts are those induced by duress or undue influence. **Duress** means force or threat of force. The force may be physical or, in some instances, economic. **Undue influence** occurs when one is taken advantage of unfairly through a contract by a party who misuses a position of relationship or legal confidence. Contracts voidable because of undue influence often arise when persons weakened by age or illness are persuaded to enter into a disadvantageous contract by a family member or other person.

## QUASI-CONTRACT

When one party is unjustly enriched at the expense of another, the law may imply a duty on the first party to pay the second, even though there is no contract between the two parties. The doctrine which requires this result is **quasi-contract.**

If a debtor overpays a creditor $5,000, the debtor can force the creditor to return that amount by suing under quasi-contract. It would be an unjust enrichment to allow the creditor to keep the $5,000. Likewise, when John has paid taxes on land, thinking that he owns it, and Mary comes along with a superior title (ownership) to the land and has John evicted, quasi-contract requires that Mary reimburse John for the taxes paid.

Note that quasi-contract is not an answer to every situation in which no contract exists. Over the years, courts have come to apply quasi-contract in a fairly limited number of cases based on unjust enrichment.

## 4.   Remedies for Breach of Contract

A party that does not live up to the obligation of contractual performance is said to **breach** the contract. There are several remedies available for a breach of contract. Figure 9-1 summarizes these remedies, which include negotiated settlement, arbitration, various damage awards, **specific performance,** and **rescission.**

The victim of a contract breach must *mitigate* compensatory and consequential damages when possible. To mitigate damages requires the victim to take reasonable steps to reduce them. Example: when a tenant breaches a house lease by moving away before the lease expires, the landlord must mitigate damages by renting the house to another willing and suitable tenant if such a person is available.

Trial litigation for breach of contract is fairly rare. By far the most common remedy for breach of contract is the *negotiated settlement*. The parties voluntarily reach an agreement to resolve the breach of contract. There are several reasons for this fact. First, trial litigation is time-consuming and very expensive. No matter who ultimately wins a lawsuit, both sides will lose the valuable productive effort of employees required to participate in the litigation. If at all possible, it is better to reach a mutual settlement of a breach of contract and to avoid trial litigation. Second, litigation inevitably causes hard feelings between parties and can destroy valuable business relationships. Since the parties may need to continue to do business with each other, it is best to settle a breach of contract rather than litigate it. Finally, in a trial situation one party wins and the other loses. When millions of dollars are at stake, it may be better to compromise and settle a breach of contract rather than risk losing everything in a trial. The wisdom of compromise and settlement in such situations is emphasized by the fact that juries are often

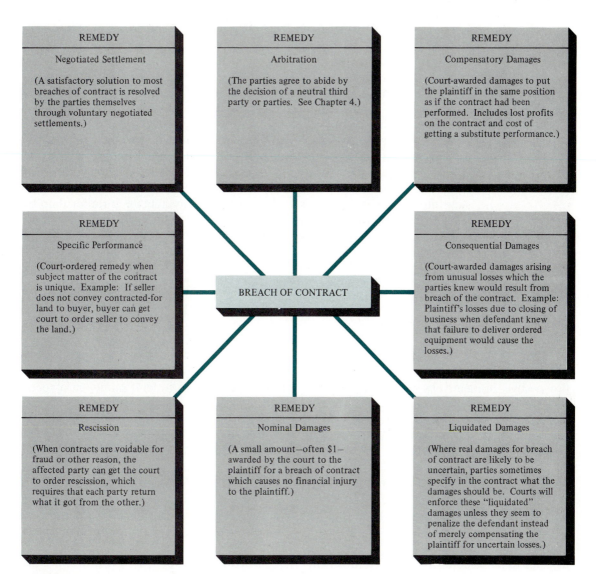

**FIGURE 9-1**
Remedies for Breach of Contract.

ignorant of business practices, which tends to make their verdicts in business matters unpredictable.

For example, Westinghouse Electric Corp. failed to honor contracts calling for it to deliver uranium to a number of utility companies operating nuclear reactors. A sudden, worldwide tripling of prices by uranium producers caused Westinghouse to be unable to afford uranium to supply to the utility companies. When more than fifteen companies sued

Westinghouse, Westinghouse reached settlements totaling over $700 million. Not one of the cases ever went to trial.

## 5.  Offer To Contract

The contractual agreement begins with an offer made to an offeree (the person to whom the offer is made). An *offer* contains a specific promise and a specific demand. "I will pay $15,000 for that electrical transformer" promises $15,000 and demands a specific transformer in return. An offeror (person making the offer) must intend to make the offer, but courts measure intent objectively, that is, by how others reasonably see it rather than by what the offeror thinks he or she means. Still, as the following case illustrates, there can be confusion over what is and what is not an offer.

---

# PIONEER REALTY AND LAND CO. v. MORTGAGE PLUS, INC.
346 N.W.286 (N.D. 1984)

---

Prospective homebuyers applied for mortgages with Mortgage Plus. At the time of application, Kocourek, the Mortgage Plus loan officer, told the home buyers that its interest rate was 11½ percent. While the applications were being processed, Mortgage Plus raised its rate and refused to honor the 11½ percent rate. The homebuyers then got their loans elsewhere and had to pay more than 11½ percent. They sued Mortgage Plus, claiming that Mortgage Plus breached its offer to lend money to qualified buyers at 11½ percent. The trial court determined that Mortgage Plus and the homebuyers did not enter into any agreements binding Mortgage Plus to provide the loans at the 11½ percent interest rate.

VANDE WALLE, J.: On appeal, the plaintiffs raised a number of issues of which we conclude our answer to the following single issue is dispositive: Whether or not the district court erred by failing to find that a binding obligation to lend money at a specified interest rate and discount points existed between Mortgage Plus and the loan applicants.

The district court determined that Mortgage Plus and the loan applicants represented in this lawsuit did not enter into any oral or written agreements binding Mortgage Plus to provide home-loan funding at a specified interest rate and discount point fee.

Having reviewed the record in this case, we conclude that there is sufficient evidence to support the trial court's finding that Mortgage Plus did not enter binding agreements with the loan applicants to provide home-loan funding at a specified interest rate and discount point fee. It is undisputed that Kocourek quoted home-loan funding to be available, at the time the loan applications were submitted, at an interest rate of 11½ percent together with a fee of two or three discount points. However, there is evidence upon which the district court could find, as it did, that Kocourek's quotations did not constitute a binding agreement or commitment to provide funds at the quoted rates.

Kocourek testified that, in his opinion, at no time did he commit, orally or in writing, to provide home-loan money to any applicant at a specified interest rate or discount points.

The substance of the loan applicant's testimony was that Kocourek quoted the interest rate and discount points in effect at the time the loan applications were filed, but not necessarily the rates that would be in effect when the loans closed. In that regard, Jean Foltz [a plaintiff] testified:

"Q. When you met with him [Kocourek], did you discuss interest rates and points?

"A. Yes, we did.

"Q. What did Mr. Kocourek say to you at that time?

"A. The rate at that time was eleven-and-a-half, and three points."

Each of the loan applicants signed the following written statement during the time that their loan applications were being processed by Mortgage Plus:

**I/We the undersigned who have applied for the mortgage loan on the above property do agree that the loan will bear the maximum interest rate in effect at the time of closing but in no event will the interest rate be less than that in effect at the time of application.**

At no time did any of the loan applicants receive a written commitment from Mortgage Plus relative to the interest, discount points, or date of closing on the loan application requests....[*Affirmed.*]

### DEFINITENESS OF TERMS

Under the common law of contracts, contractual terms must be definite and specific. An offer to employ at a "reasonable salary" cannot be the basis for a contract because of *indefiniteness*. Most advertisements and catalog price quotes are considered too indefinite to form the basis for a contract unless they are specific about the quantity of goods being offered.

However, under the Uniform Commercial Code (UCC), contracts for the sale of goods can leave open nonquantity terms to be decided at a future time. An agreement for the sale of 500 cameras will bind the parties even though they leave open the price to be decided on delivery in six months.

### TERMINATION OF OFFER

Once an offer is made, when does it terminate if the offeree does not accept it? Table 9-1 lists several common instances showing when an offer may terminate.

## 6.  Acceptance of Offer

*Acceptance* of an offer is necessary to a binding contract. An offer to enter into a bilateral contract is accepted by the offeree's making the required promise. When Toni offers Aaron certain widgets for $2,500 to be deliv-

**TABLE 9-1** When an Offer Terminates

1  By provision in the offer: "This offer terminates at noon Friday."
2  By lapse of a reasonable period of time if the offer fails to specify a time: What is "reasonable" depends on the circumstances.
3  By rejection of the offer: "Thank you, but I do not want the widgets you are offering." A *counteroffer* is also a rejection: "Your offer of $10,000 for the land is too low. I will sell it to you for $12,500."
4  By revocation of the offer: "I regret to inform you that I am withdrawing my offer."
5  By destruction of the subject matter: The widgets are destroyed by fire before the offer of their sale has been accepted.
6  By the offeror's death or insanity: Offeror dies before the offer has been accepted.
7  By the contractual performance becoming illegal: The State Department declares that sales of certain computers to the Soviet Union are illegal. This terminates an offer to sell the computers to a Soviet trading company.

ered by November 30 on ninety-day credit terms, and Aaron accepts, Aaron is promising to pay $2,500 on ninety-day credit terms.

Unilateral contracts are accepted by performing a requested act, not by making a promise. A company's offer of a $2,500 reward for information leading to the conviction of anyone vandalizing company property is not accepted by promising to provide the information. Only the act of providing information accepts such an offer.

### DEPOSITED ACCEPTANCE RULE

When does the acceptance become binding on the offeror? Unless the offer itself specifies a particular moment, the acceptance usually binds the parties when the offeree dispatches it. Since the offeree frequently mails the acceptance, the acceptance becomes binding when it is "deposited" with the postal service—hence, the *deposited acceptance rule*.

The importance of the deposited acceptance rule is that the offeror cannot revoke the offer once the offeree has accepted it. An added significance is that an offeror's revocation is not effective until the offeree actually receives it. Thus, a deposited acceptance creates a binding contract even though a revocation is also in the mail.

### MIRROR IMAGE RULE

For an acceptance to create a binding contract, standard contract law requires that the acceptance must "mirror" the offer, that is, must match it exactly. If the acceptance changes the terms of the offer or adds new terms, it is not really an acceptance. It is a counteroffer.

The UCC has changed the **mirror image rule** with regard to merchants contracting for the sale of goods. An acceptance between merchants creates a binding contract even though it proposes new or different terms. The new or different terms become part of the contract unless: (1) the offer expressly limits acceptance to the original terms, (2) the proposed terms materially (importantly) alter the contract, or (3) the offeror rejects the proposed terms.

### SILENCE NOT ACCEPTANCE

In general, an offeror's failure to reject an offer does not imply acceptance. Another way to say this is that silence is not acceptance. The offeree has no usual duty to reply to the offer, even if the offer states that the offeror will treat silence as acceptance.

There are major exceptions to this rule. For instance, parties may have a contract that specifies that future shipments of goods be made automatically unless the offeree expressly rejects them. Many book- and record-club contracts operate in this manner.

A related doctrine looks at the parties' prior *course of dealing*—the way they have done business in the past. Silence may well imply acceptance if the parties previously dealt with each other by having the buyer take shipments from the seller unless the buyer notified the seller in advance not to ship.

Finally, the UCC says that a contract may arise from the *conduct* of a buyer and seller of goods. Emphasis is placed on how the parties act rather than on a formal offer and acceptance of terms.

## 7. Voluntary Consent to Contracts

To be enforceable, a contract must be voluntarily made. The previously discussed doctrines of fraud, misrepresentation, duress, and undue influence show that a contract is voidable when both parties do not reach it through a voluntary, knowing consent.

What happens when each party misunderstands something very basic and material about a contract? Such a situation goes right to the heart of whether there has been a "voluntary" consent to a contract. When there is *mutual mistake* as to a material fact inducing a contract, rescission is appropriate. The test of materiality is whether the parties would have contracted had they been aware of the mistake. If they would not have contracted, the mistaken fact is material.

There is a difference between a mutual or bilateral mistake and a unilateral mistake. A *unilateral mistake* arises when only one of the parties to a contract is wrong about a material fact. Suppose that Royal Carpet Co. bids $8.70 per yard for certain carpet material instead of $7.80 per yard as it had intended. If the seller accepts Royal Carpet's bid, a contract results even though there was a unilateral mistake. As the following case shows, a party who has made a contractual promise because of a unilateral mistake cannot in most instances withdraw from it.

# LIBBY, McNEIL & LIBBY v. UNITED STEELWORKERS

809 F.2d 1432 (9th Cir. 1987)

THOMPSON, J.:...Libby, McNeil & Libby, Inc. ("Libby") sought a judgment declaring that its collective bargaining agreement with United Steelworkers of America ("the Union") did not obligate it to provide "Rule of 65" benefits in its pension plan. [Under the Rule of 65, employees whose jobs are discontinued and who have at least twenty years of service would be eligible for certain benefits provided that their age plus years of service equal or exceed 65.] Libby contended it had never agreed to include these benefits, and if it had, it had done so by mistake. The magistrate found that Libby and the Union had mutually agreed that Libby's pension plan would be amended to contain whatever pension benefits American Can Company provided in its pension plan. American Can's plan contained Rule of 65 benefits, and, therefore, Libby was required to provide the same benefits. Judgment was entered accordingly. Libby appeals and we affirm.

The Union represented employees at Libby's can manufacturing plant in Sacramento, California. From 1974 until the plant closed in 1983, the Union negotiated collective bargaining agreements with Libby every three years. In 1974, Libby agreed to "duplicate" the pension plan previously negotiated by the Union with American Can Company. In 1977, although negotiations between the Union and Libby preceded the Union's negotiations with American Can, Libby agreed that if American Can modified its plan, Libby would modify its plan "in a similar manner." Subsequently, as part of its 1977 collective bargaining agreement, American Can modified its plan to include a Rule of 65 pension benefit. In 1980, after

collective bargaining negotiations, Libby reiterated that it had "the same pension plan as that of the American Can Company," and that if American Can modified its plan, Libby would adopt the "same modifications."

Libby argues that it did not intend to adopt the Rule of 65. To buttress this assertion, Libby contends its 1977 agreement to modify the plan in a "similar manner" is not tantamount to an agreement to incorporate unequivocally all American Can pension plan modifications. To ascertain the intended meaning of the arguably ambiguous "similar" term in the 1977 agreement booklet, the magistrate considered the circumstances surrounding the agreement's execution, the parties' preceding negotiations, and their subsequent conduct. The magistrate found that Libby intended to duplicate all provisions and modifications of the American Can plan. A review of the record reveals that the magistrate's findings are not clearly erroneous.

Libby also raises a claim of unilateral mistake. Libby argues that even if the Rule of 65 had been incorporated into the 1977–80 agreement, it is not obligated to provide the benefit to employees who became eligible after 1980 because it entered the 1980 negotiations under the mistaken belief that the Rule of 65 was not part of the contract. Under California law, the unilateral mistake of one party is ground for relief where the other party "knew or had reason to know" of the mistake. Libby argues that the magistrate substituted an improper "should have known" inquiry for the proper "reason to know" standard.

Libby's unilateral mistake argument

fails. After carefully weighing the evidence, the magistrate found that during the 1980 negotiations, the Union reasonably believed Libby knew about the Rule of 65. This finding is not clearly erroneous and precludes Libby's claim of unilateral mistake. If the Union believed Libby knew about the Rule of 65, the Union could not "know or have reason to know" Libby was ignorant of the Rule. [*Affirmed.*]

## 8. Consideration in the Contract

Courts will not enforce contractual promises unless they are supported by **consideration.** Before Robert can enforce a promise made by Peter, Robert must have given consideration, that is, assumed a legal obligation to Peter or surrendered a legal right. In a bilateral contract, each party promises something to the other. The binding promises are the consideration. In a unilateral contract, the consideration of one party is a promise; the consideration of the other party is performance of an act. When it is not clear whether there is consideration to support a promise, a court will often examine a transaction as a whole.

### CONSIDERATION MUST BE BARGAINED FOR

An important part of consideration is that it must be *bargained for*. Sometimes the parties to an agreement specify an insignificant consideration in return for a great one, for example, a promise of $1 in return for a promise to convey 40 acres of land. In such situations a court must decide whether the party promising to convey the land really bargained for the $1 or merely promised to make a gift. Promises to make gifts are not binding, because no bargained-for consideration supports the promise.

Similarly, *prior consideration* is no consideration. For instance, after many years of working at Acme Co., Bigman retires as vice-president for financial planning. The company's board of directors votes him a lifetime pension of $3,000 per month "for services rendered." One year later the board terminates his pension. If Bigman sues for breach of contract, he will lose. He gave no consideration to support the promise of a pension. The past years of service were not "bargained for" by the company's board when they granted the pension. The board merely promised to give an unenforceable gift to Bigman.

### AGREEMENT NOT TO SUE IS CONSIDERATION

Where reasonable grounds for a lawsuit exist, an agreement not to sue is consideration to support a promise. If First Bank agrees not to sue Maria, who has failed to repay a student loan, in return for the promise of Maria's parents to repay the loan, First Bank has given consideration. It has promised to surrender its legal right to sue Maria.

Likewise, suppose that a consulting firm bills a client $5,000 for fifty hours' work at $100 per hour. The client disputes the bill and contends that the consulting firm worked only twenty-five hours and should get only $2,500. If the two parties compromise the bill at $3,500 for thirty-five hours, this agreement binds them both. Each has surrendered the right to have a court determine exactly what amount is owed. Such an agreement and the payment of the $3,500 is an **accord and satisfaction.**

### PERFORMANCE OF PRE-EXISTING OBLIGATION IS NOT CONSIDERATION

A party to an agreement does not give consideration by promising to do something which he or she is already obligated to do. For example, suppose a warehouse owner contracts to have certain repairs done for $20,000. In the middle of construction, the building contractor demands an additional $5,000 to complete the work. The owner agrees, but when the work is finished he gives the contractor only $20,000. If the contractor sues, he will lose. The owner's promise to pay an extra $5,000 is not supported by consideration. The contractor is under a pre-existing obligation to do the work for which the owner promises an additional $5,000.

If the contractor promised to do something he was not already obligated to do, there would be consideration to support the promise of the additional $5,000. Promising to modify the repair plans illustrates such new consideration.

### WHEN NO CONSIDERATION IS NECESSARY

The pre-existing obligation rule discussed above does not apply to a sale-of-goods contract. The UCC states that parties to a sale-of-goods contract may make binding modifications to it without both parties giving new consideration. If a buyer of widgets agrees to pay a seller an additional $5,000 over and above the amount already promised, the buyer is bound, although the seller gives only the consideration (widgets) that she is already obligated to give.

Under the UCC, the rules of consideration also do not apply to a **firm offer.** A firm offer exists when a merchant offering goods promises in writing that the offer will not be revoked for a period not to exceed three months. This promise binds the merchant, although the offeree buyer gives no consideration to support it. With offers not involving sales of goods by a merchant, a promise not to revoke an offer must be supported by the offeree's consideration to be binding. Such an arrangement is called an *option.*

An important exception to the rule requiring consideration to support a promise is the doctrine of **promissory estoppel.** This doctrine arises when a promisee justifiably relies on a promisor's promise to his or her economic injury. The promisor must know that the promisee is likely to rely on the promise. As the next case illustrates, promissory estoppel is becoming an increasingly used doctrine when the facts of a business relationship do not amount to an express or implied contract.

# ESQUIRE RADIO & ELECTRONICS v. MONTGOMERY WARD

804 F.2d 787 (2nd Cir. 1986)

Esquire Radio & Electronics (Esquire) helped develop and import consumer electronics products for Montgomery Ward & Co. (Ward). Ward issued import orders to foreign manufacturers for products and spare parts. The orders were shipped to Esquire, which inventoried both products and spare parts for Ward's buy back. Although this arrangement continued for many years, the buy back terms were never expressly set forth. In 1984, Ward terminated its relationship with Esquire and refused to buy Esquire's existing spare parts inventory. Esquire sued and won in the trial court. Ward appealed.

PIERCE, J.: . . . Notwithstanding the absence of a written agreement, courts applying New York law recognize other enforceable obligations, including oral contracts, implied contracts, and promissory estoppel. In our view, the doctrine of promissory estoppel applies to the facts of this case.

The doctrine of promissory estoppel, as set forth in § 90 of the Restatement of Contracts and as adopted in New York, has three principal requirements: "a clear and unambiguous promise; a reasonable and foreseeable reliance by the party to whom the promise is made; and an injury sustained by the party asserting the estoppel by reason of his reliance."

Here, all three elements are present. As noted above, there was evidence that, on several critical occasions, Ward clearly and unambiguously promised to repurchase accumulated spare parts inventories. The evidence showed that in the 1960s, Fisher, a Ward manager, assured Esquire that Ward would purchase the spare parts and that in

the meantime Esquire should consider such inventories as being held on Ward's account. Similarly, at a meeting of executives and managers from both companies in the early 1970s, Esquire specifically expressed its concerns regarding the costs and risks of mounting inventories, and Ward, this time through Senior Vice President Dean Lewis, explicitly advised Esquire not to "concern yourself about the size of the inventory. We will buy the parts." In fact, in 1975, Ward's Parts Specialist, Harris Asher, unilaterally approached Esquire's Sales Vice President, Maffei, to induce Esquire to increase spare parts inventories regarding certain cassette recorders. When Maffei responded that he was concerned about the potential costs of such accumulations, Asher replied, "I don't know what you are concerned about. We are going to buy them from you anyway. We are going to use them." Certainly these specific, clear and unambiguous statements at the very least "suffice[d] to create a factual question" as to whether Ward had promised to repurchase accumulated spare parts during the tenure of the buy-back arrangement. Thus the question of whether there was such a promise was properly submitted to the jury.

We draw the same conclusion as to whether Esquire reasonably and foreseeably relied on Ward's repurchase promises. At the meeting during the early 1970s, Ward's Senior Vice President, Lewis, not only promised that Ward would purchase Esquire's inventories; he also urged Esquire to continue accumulating inventories as it had been doing throughout the period of the buy-back arrangement. While it is true that at that meeting Ward declined to adopt Esquire's proposal that accumulated inventories be stored in Ward's newly opened National Parts Center in Berkeley, Illinois, we think it significant that Ward's stated reason for declining was not that it wished Esquire to bear the risks that spare parts might not be needed, but that the Berkeley facility could not accommodate the size of the accumulated inventory. Further, in 1975, Asher, Ward's Parts Specialist, not only promised that Ward would buy Esquire's inventories but specifically sought to induce Esquire to accumulate more inventories in reliance on that promise: "You ought to carry more and not be so tight on the quantities." Certainly, based on this evidence the jury rationally could conclude that, over the years, Ward induced Esquire to accumulate spare parts by making several specific promises to repurchase such parts, and that Esquire reasonably and foreseeably relied on such promises.

Finally, we think it is clear that Esquire sustained injury by reason of its reliance on Ward's promises. Esquire continued to accu-mulate extensive spare parts inventories after repeated assurances by Ward that it would repurchase the inventory, which by the time of termination, exceeded $1.2 million paid by Esquire to Ward for the parts plus shipment costs, including the 5 percent fee charged by the Ward trading company. The bulk of spare parts inventory valuation evidence came from Esquire documents prepared in the ordinary course of business, and admitted in accordance with applicable rules of evidence. Based on this evidence, the jury awarded Esquire what it paid for the spare parts ($1,241,340.95), excluding any benefit of the bargain profit that Esquire would have realized had Ward not repudiated.

Having affirmed the judgment as to spare parts shipments lacking written purchase agreements on the theory of promissory estoppel, we need not reach the question of whether the judgment might equally be affirmed on the basis of implied or oral contract. [*Affirmed.*]

---

Note in the *Montgomery Ward* case that the court apparently did not believe that Ward's assurances that it would buy the spare parts amounted to an implied-in-fact contract. Promissory estoppel usually arises when there is no contract.

## 9.  Capacity of Parties To Contract

**Capacity** refers to a person's ability to be bound by a contract. Courts have traditionally held three classes of persons to lack capacity to be bound by contractual promises: minors (also called "infants"), intoxicated persons, and mentally incompetent persons.

### MINORS

In most states, a minor is anyone under age 18. Minors usually cannot be legally bound to contractual promises unless those promises involve *necessaries of life* such as food, clothing, shelter, medical care, and—in some states—education. Even for necessaries, minors often cannot be sued for the contract price, only for a "reasonable" value. In a number of states, courts will hold a minor who has misrepresented his or her age to contractual promises.

A contract into which a minor has entered is voidable at the election of the minor. The minor can *disaffirm* the contract and legally recover any consideration which has been given an adult, even if the minor cannot return the adult's consideration. On the other hand, the adult is bound by the contract unless the minor elects to disaffirm it.

A minor may disaffirm a contract anytime before reaching the age of majority (usually 18) and for a reasonable time after reaching majority. If the minor fails to disaffirm within a reasonable time after reaching majority, the minor is said to *ratify* the contract. Upon ratification, the minor loses the right to disaffirm.

### INTOXICATED AND MENTALLY INCOMPETENT PERSONS

Except when a court has judged an adult to be mentally incompetent, she or he does not lose capacity to contract simply because of intoxication or mental impairment. In most cases involving adult capacity to contract, courts measure capacity by whether the adult was capable of understanding the nature and purpose of the contract. Obviously, the more complex a contractual transaction gets, the more likely a court is to decide that an intoxicated or mentally impaired person lacks capacity to contract.

## 10. Illegal Contracts

A basic requirement of a valid contract is legality of purpose. A "contract" to murder someone is hardly enforceable in a court of law. Contracts which require commission of a crime or tort or which violate accepted standards of behavior (*public policy*) are void. Table 9-2 gives common examples of illegal contracts.

**TABLE 9-2**  Examples of Illegal Contract

1  Gambling agreements (except where permitted)
2  Certain contracts made on Sunday (in about half the states)
3  Contracts for usurious interest (see Chapter 21)
4  Professional contracts made by unlicensed persons in which a regulatory statute requires licensing
5  Contracts which unreasonably restrain trade (see Chapters 22 to 24)
6  Many contracts which attempt to limit negligence liability of a seller of goods or services to the public (called *exculpatory contracts*)
7  Unconscionable contracts involving a sale of goods under the UCC (usually applied when a difference in bargaining power or education leads a merchant to take unreasonable advantage of a consumer)
8  Other contracts prohibited by statute or against public policy

**EFFECT OF ILLEGALITY ON A CONTRACT**

Illegality makes a contract void. Courts will generally take no action on a void contract, and they will leave the parties to the contract where they have put themselves. As the next case shows, this fact means that a plaintiff can get no damages for breach of an illegal contract.

# MASON v. HOSTA

199 Cal. Rptr. 859 (1984)

Plaintiff Mason, a hospital administrator, made an agreement with defendant Hosta, a medical doctor. Mason agreed to contact other medical hospital administrators on behalf of Hosta and try to persuade them to use Hosta's emergency room services. For each hospital client Mason referred to Hosta, Hosta was to pay Mason $250. After three years, Hosta stopped making referral payments to Mason because he claimed the contract violated the Business and Professions Code. Mason sued under the contract for the unpaid amount owed for his referrals on behalf of the defendant. The trial court denied the plaintiff's motion for summary judgment. On appeal, the California Court of Appeal determined that the contract was illegal under the Business and Professions Code.

MERRICK, J.: The subject contract provides for payments to [Mason] by [Hosta] as compensation for [Mason's] soliciting, referring and procuring clients on [Hosta's] behalf. It is precisely this sort of referral fee to which the prohibition of Business and Professions Code § 650 is directed. Performance of the subject contract violates the statute. "It is well established in California that a con-

tract which requires the performance of unlawful acts is unenforceable." Civil Code § 1550 provides that a lawful object is essential to the very existence of a valid contract. Similarly, Civil Code § 1607 states that the consideration for a promise must be lawful. Civil Code § 1608 provides that if any part of a single consideration for one or more objects, or of several considerations for a single object, is unlawful, the entire contract is void. Lastly a purported agreement in direct violation of the terms of the express prohibition in a statute is void.

No matter how subtly disguised, or ingeniously interpreted, the subject contract, by its terms, and the performance required of defendant/respondent thereunder, violates § 650 of the Business and Professions Code. Further it is an attempt to thwart the legislative design and public policy to proscribe illegal and unethical contracts providing for the payment by licensed physicians of consideration as compensation and inducement to non-licensees for the referral of patients, clients or customers.

We find the trial court correctly granted [Hosta's] Motion for Summary Judgment. [*Its judgment is affirmed.*]

There are several exceptions to the general rule that courts will take no action on an illegal contract. A contract may have both legal and illegal provisions to it. In such a case, courts will often enforce the legal provisions and refuse to enforce the illegal ones. For instance, a contract providing services or leasing goods sometimes contains a provision excusing the service provider or lessor from liability for negligently caused injury. Courts usually will not enforce this provision but will enforce the rest of the contract.

Often, courts will allow an innocent party to recover payment made to a party who knows (or should know) that a contract is illegal. For example, courts will allow recovery of a payment for professional services made by an innocent person to a person who is unlicensed to provide such services.

Finally, in some cases courts may allow a person to recover compensation under quasi-contract for services performed on an illegal contract. Recovery may be allowed where an otherwise qualified professional lets his or her license expire and provides services to a client before renewing the license.

## 11. When Contracts Should Be in Writing

Some people have the impression that contracts have to be in writing to be enforceable. In most instances, this is not so. However, it is true that certain contracts must be in writing (or at least evidenced by writing) to be enforceable.

The law requiring that certain contracts be in writing is the **statute of frauds.** Designed to prevent frauds arising from oral contracts, the original English statute is more than 300 years old. Today, every state has its own statute of frauds. Business-related provisions require the following contracts to be in writing: (1) contracts for the sale of an interest in land, (2) collateral contracts to pay the debt of another person, (3) contracts which cannot be performed within one year, and (4) sale-of-goods contracts for $500 or more.

### CONTRACTS FOR THE SALE OF AN INTEREST IN LAND

Sales of interests in land are common contracts covered by the statute of frauds. Although "sales of interests in land" covers a contract to sell land, it includes much more. Interests in land include contracts for mortgages (see Chapter 21), mining rights, easements (rights to use another's land, such as the right to cross it with electric power wires), and leases of longer than one year. However, a contract to insure land or to erect a building is not an interest in land.

The doctrine of *part performance* creates an exception to the requirement that sales of interests in land must be in writing. When a buyer of land has made valuable improvements in it, or where the buyer is in possession of it and has paid part of the purchase price, even an oral contract to sell is enforceable.

### COLLATERAL CONTRACTS TO PAY THE DEBT OF ANOTHER

A collateral promise is a secondary one. It is not Janet's promise to pay Joan's debt, which is an original or primary promise. A collateral contract arises only from Janet's promise to pay Joan's debt if Joan does not. Under the statute of frauds only collateral contracts must be in writing. The following case illustrates the difference between a collateral and an original promise.

---

# GARLAND CO., INC. v. ROOFCO CO.

809 F.2d 546 (8th Cir. 1987)

---

BOWMAN, J.:...George Rasor, the president and principal stockholder of the Roofco Company, appeals from a judgment holding him personally liable to the Garland Company, a supplier of materials used in Roofco's business. Rasor contends that his oral promise to pay Roofco's debt to Garland falls within the Statute of Frauds and therefore is unenforceable. We disagree and affirm the judgment of the District Court.

Garland sold $48,517 worth of roofing materials to Roofco. Roofco failed to pay. In conversations between Rasor and Garland, Rasor personally guaranteed that he would pay the debt. When after some nine months the debt remained unpaid, Garland brought suit to enforce the oral promise. As an affirmative defense, Rasor invoked the Missouri Statute of Frauds, asserting that since his promise was not in writing it was not enforceable. Garland countered, arguing that Rasor's promise was an original promise and thus was not within the Statute of Frauds. The District Court found for Garland and entered judgment against Rasor for the amount of the debt.

Under Missouri law, "It is well established that a promise which is original as between the promisee and the promisor, as opposed to one which is collateral to the primary obligation of a third party, is not barred by the Statute of Frauds." In *Diehr v.*

*Carey* the court restated a three-part test to determine whether a promise is properly characterized as original or collateral.

**[T]he tests to be applied to determine whether an agreement is an original undertaking, and not within the statute of frauds, are laid down as follows: (1) Credit must be given by the promisee to the promisor alone; and (2) the leading or main purpose of the promisor in making the promise must be to gain some advantage for himself, rather than to become the mere guarantor or surety of another's debt, and (3) the promise must be supported by a consideration beneficial to the promisor.**

This test long has been part of Missouri law and has been given wide application in Missouri cases.

The District Court properly applied the three-part Missouri test to the present case and found: (1) following Rasor's promise to pay Roofco's debt, Garland had extended further credit to Rasor alone; (2) Rasor, as principal shareholder and president of Roofco, had a unique and personal interest in Garland's credit extensions (in the form of delay in filing suit) which allowed Roofco to continue its operations and to realize money from several jobs; and (3) Rasor received beneficial consideration in the form of Garland's grant of credit extensions to Roofco and of Garland's forbearance from levying on a performance bond when absent such forbearance, Roofco's name would have been removed from a list of approved contractors.

Rasor argues that the District Court erred in concluding that benefit to a corporation may be found to be sufficient consideration to support a promise made by a stockholder and officer of the corporation. As a matter of Missouri law, however, this argument appears to be incorrect. In any event, we cannot say that the District Court's

determination of this point of state law is unsupported by authority or lacking in reasoned analysis.

Having reviewed the record, we are satisfied that none of the findings of the District Court is clearly erroneous. Under Missouri law, these findings amply support the District Court's ultimate conclusion that Rasor's promise was original and thus not within the Statute of Frauds. Accordingly, the judgment of the District Court is [*Affirmed.*]

---

**CONTRACTS WHICH CANNOT BE PERFORMED WITHIN ONE YEAR**

The statute of frauds applies to a contract which the parties cannot perform within one year after its making. Courts usually interpret the one-year requirement to mean that the contract must specify a period of performance longer than one year. Thus, an oral contract for services which last twenty months is not enforceable. But an oral contract for services to be completed "by" a date twenty months away is enforceable. The difference is that the latter contract can be performed within one year, even if it actually takes longer than that to perform it.

As interpreted by the courts, the statute of frauds applies only to executory contracts which the parties cannot perform within a year. Once one of the parties has executed her performance for the other, she can enforce an oral multiyear contract.

**SALE OF GOODS OF $500 OR MORE**

Under the UCC, the statute of frauds covers sales of goods of $500 or more. Modifications to such contracts are also included. Table 9-3 lists exceptions to the writing requirement for sale-of-goods contracts.

**TABLE 9-3**  Exceptions to Statute-of-Frauds Requirement for Oral Sale-of-Goods Contracts

1  Contract for goods specially manufactured for the buyer on which the seller had begun performance
2  Contract for goods for which payment has been made and accepted or which have been received and accepted
3  Contract for goods in which the party being sued admits in court or pleadings that the contract has been made
4  Contract for goods between merchants in which the merchant sued has received a written notice from the other merchant confirming the contract and in which merchant sued does not object to the confirmation within ten days

#### OTHER CONTRACTS REQUIRED TO BE IN WRITING

In addition to the basic contracts covered by the statute of frauds, other contracts must be in writing in various states. Most states require insurance policies to be written. Several states demand written estimates in contracts for automobile repair.

#### NATURE OF THE REQUIRED WRITING

In some states, the statute of frauds requires that the actual contract between the parties must be in writing. However, most states merely require that the contract be *evidenced* by writing and be signed by the party to be held. This requirement means that the party being sued must have signed a note, memorandum, or another written form short of a formal contract which describes with reasonable certainty the terms of the oral agreement. As Table 9-3 indicates with regard to a sale of goods between merchants, the writing need not always be by the party sued. Under certain circumstances, it may be by the suing party.

## 12. The Parol Evidence Rule

Like the statute of frauds, the **parol evidence rule** influences the form of contracts. This rule states that parties to a complete and final written contract cannot introduce oral evidence in court which changes the intended meaning of the written terms.

The parol evidence rule applies only to evidence of oral agreements made at the time of or prior to the written contract. It does not apply to oral modifications coming after the parties have made the written contract (although the statute of frauds may apply).

Suppose that Chris Consumer wants to testify in court that a merchant of an Ultima Washing Machine gave him an oral six-month warranty on the machine, even though the $450 written contract specified "no warranties." If the warranty was made after Chris signed the contract, he may testify about its existence. Otherwise, the parol evidence rule prevents him from testifying about an oral agreement which changes the terms of the written contract.

An exception to the parol evidence rule allows evidence of oral agreement which merely explains the meaning of written terms without changing the terms. Also, oral evidence which changes the meaning of written terms can be given if necessary to prevent fraud.

## 13. Interpretation of Contracts

If each party is satisfied with the other's performance under a contract, there is no problem with interpreting the contract's terms. But when disagreement about contractual performance exists, often interpretation of the terms becomes necessary. Courts have devised several rules to assist in interpreting contracts.

Common words are given their usual meaning. "A rose is a rose is a rose," said the poet, and a court will interpret this common word to refer to a flower. However, if the word has a particular *trade usage*, courts will give it that meaning. In a contract in the wine trade, the term "rose" would not refer to a flower at all but to a type of wine.

Some words have special legal meanings. A party to a contract had best appreciate that courts give legal terms their legal meaning. The buyer of radios may think that a contractual phrase calling for "delivery to the buyer on November 20" means that the seller will take the radios to the buyer's place of business, but it does not.

"Delivery" is a legal term referring to the transfer of possession from the seller to the buyer. It does not make the seller responsible for "shipping" the radios to the buyer. Furthermore, the UCC says that when the contract states no place for delivery, the place of delivery is the seller's place of business. The buyer will have to take delivery of the radios at the seller's place of business on November 20. Because some terms have both common and legal meanings, a person should have an attorney examine contracts drawn up by others.

Many businesses today use printed form contracts. Sometimes the parties to one of these printed contracts type or handwrite additional terms. What happens when the typed or handwritten terms contradict the printed terms? What if the printed terms of a contract state "no warranties" but the parties have written in a ninety-day warranty? In such a case, courts interpret handwritten terms to control typed terms and typed terms to control printed ones. The written warranty will be enforced since the writing is the best evidence of the parties' true intention.

Another rule is that when only one of the parties drafts (draws up) a contract, courts will interpret ambiguous or vague terms against the party that drafts them. As the following case shows, courts often apply this rule to insurance contracts.

---

# STATE FARM MUTUAL AUTOMOBILE INSURANCE COMPANIES v. QUEEN

688 P.2d 935 (Mont. 1984)

---

Rhonda R. Queen was sued for injuries received in an accident by the passenger of an automobile she was driving. Queen was insured by State Farm Mutual Automobile Insurance Company, and she demanded that the company defend her under the insurance policy. State Farm asked the court to order that Queen's accident was not covered by her insurance policy since (1) she did not own the automobile involved in the accident,

(2) the policy covered only the first-named insured in nonowned automobiles, and (3) she was the second-named insured under the policy. Agreeing with State Farm, the court so ordered. The order was appealed.

MORRISON, J.: The following issue was certified to this Court by the Circuit Court of Appeals: Must this policy be construed to provide coverage for Rhonda Queen while driving a non-owned automobile, on the ground that the policy is ambiguous as to whether Gary Queen, Rhonda Queen, or both, are the first-named insured?

The policy question affords coverage for the use of "non-owned automobiles" to "the first person named in the declaration." The policy declaration lists the following as insureds:

> **Queen, Gary A. and Rhonda R.**
> **Box 145**
> **Rt. 2**
> **Ronan, MT 59864**

The insurer is responsible for the language which the policy contains. Whenever a contract of insurance is drawn so that it is fairly susceptible to two constructions, one favorable to the insured and the other favorable to the insurer, the one favorable to the insured will be adopted.

There are several different ways that State Farm could have listed the persons in the declaration so that the first person listed would present no ambiguity. The names could have been listed as: Gary Queen, Rhonda Queen. Less clear but perhaps sufficient to avoid an ambiguity would be: Gary Queen and Rhonda Queen. Though the names are here coupled, Gary Queen's name does appear first. However, in the instant policy, the first-named is simply "Queen." Following the last name the names Gary and Rhonda are coupled. This would seem to indicate an intention on the part of State Farm to grant no preference to one of the individuals as a first-named insured entitled to coverage on non-owned automobiles.

One test for determining whether a policy is capable of more than one construction is whether different persons looking at the writing in light of its purpose cannot agree upon its meaning. This case is a perfect illustration. The dissenters think the policy clearly shows Gary Queen as the first person named in the declaration. The three members of the Court signing this opinion think that the last name of the couple is the first name listed in the declaration and the first two names are coupled together making both parties first named in the declaration. We have seven Supreme Court Justices, who frequently review insurance policy language, closely divided in interpretation. What more need be said?

In conclusion, the declaration sheet of the insurance policy contains an ambiguity which must be construed against the maker of the policy. We find there is coverage for Rhonda Queen. [*Reversed and remanded.*]

---

## 14.  Assignment of Contracts

Electronics, Inc., sells 250 radios on credit at $20 apiece to Radio Land Retail. Electronics then sells its rights under the contract to Manufacturers' Credit Co. When payment is due, can Manufacturers' Credit legally collect the $5,000 owed to Electronics by Radio Land? This transaction is controlled by the law of **assignment,** which is a transfer (generally a sale) of rights under a contract. Figure 9-2 shows the transaction and introduces important terms.

There is an important exception to the rule that assignees are subject to assignors' defenses. Under the UCC, an assignee, called a *holder in due course* who takes an assignment of rights through a *negotiable instrument* or *document,* will not be subject to the personal contract defenses of an assignor. To be negotiable, an instrument or document must be signed by the obligor (the party bound by legal obligation) and must contain certain language.

When an assignor assigns rights, he or she makes an implied warranty that the rights are valid. If the assignee is unable to enforce the rights against the obligor because of illegality, incapacity, or breach of contract, the assignee can sue the assignor. But the assignor does not guarantee that the obligor is able to pay the claim.

### NOTICE OF ASSIGNMENT

When an assignment is made, an assignee should notify the obligor immediately. Otherwise, the obligor may perform for the obligee-assignor. If Radio Land pays Electronics before being notified of the assignment by Manufacturers' Credit, Radio Land cannot be held liable to Manufacturers' Credit.

A dishonest or careless assignor may assign the same contract rights to two different assignees. Notification of the obligor is especially important in this situation. In most states, the law says that the first assignee to notify the obligor has priority no matter which assignee receives the first assignment of rights.

**FIGURE 9-2**
Assignment Diagram.

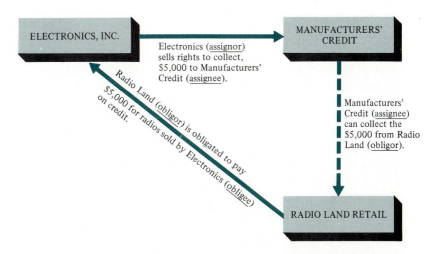

ELECTRONICS, INC.

Electronics (assignor) sells rights to collect, $5,000 to Manufacturers' Credit (assignee).

MANUFACTURERS' CREDIT

Radio Land (obligor) is obligated to pay $5,000 for radios sold by Electronics (obligee) on credit.

Manufacturers' Credit (assignee) can collect the $5,000 from Radio Land (obligor).

RADIO LAND RETAIL

### CONTRACTS WHICH CANNOT BE ASSIGNED

Although most contracts can be assigned, certain ones cannot. An assignment that increases the burden of performance to the obligor cannot be assigned. For instance, a right to have goods shipped to the buyer's place of business cannot be assigned by an Atlanta buyer to a Miami buyer if a New York seller has to ship the goods to Miami instead of Atlanta. Similarly, a *requirements contract* to supply a retail buyer with all the radios needed cannot be assigned because it depends upon the buyer's personal situation.

Most states regulate the assignment of wages. They limit the amount of wages which a wage earner can assign. This protects wage earners and their families.

A party to a contract cannot assign (delegate) performance of duties under a contract when performance depends on the character, skill, or training of that party. Otherwise, duties under a contract can be assigned as well as rights.

## 15. Contracts Benefiting a Third Party

The performance of a contract may benefit persons who are not parties to the contract. Such persons are called **third-party beneficiaries.** In general, persons who are not parties to a contract have no rights to sue to enforce the contract or to obtain damages for breach of contract. As the next case illustrates, however, a third-party beneficiary can sue if the parties to the contract intended to benefit that person.

# BRIDGMAN v. CURRY
398 N.W.2d 167 (Iowa 1986)

Plaintiffs Thomas and Ann Bridgman sold their farm to John and Edna Curry. The contract of sale obligated the Currys to make annual payments to the plaintiffs. The Currys later assigned four-sixths of the farm to the four defendants Stevens, Fike, Greene, and Bibo. The assignment contract stated that these four defendants agreed "to be bound by the terms of the Bridgman contract." When the Currys failed to pay the Bridgmans and filed for bankruptcy, the plaintiffs sued the defendants.

WOLLE, J.:...From the inception of this action the plaintiffs have contended that they are third-party beneficiaries of the joint venture contract and acceptance agreement under which the assignee defendants Stevens, Fike, Greene, and Bibo agreed to be bound by the terms and conditions of the plaintiffs' contract with Currys. The assignee defendants responded and the trial court found, that the assignments "were not entered into for plaintiffs' benefit." The trial court held that the plaintiffs were "gratuitous beneficiaries of such assignments" who had no right to enforce the assignee defendants' promises to perform the Bridgman-Curry contract. We disagree.

The decisive factor in determining whether a party may bring an action to enforce a contract between other parties is the intent of the contracting parties themselves. We recently emphasized the importance of the intent of the contracting parties, particularly the promise, in *Khabbaz v. Swartz,* where we stated: In order to enforce a contract, the third-party beneficiary must show that the contract was made for his express benefit....This test for determining when third-party beneficiaries may enforce contracts between other parties is consistent with the test of the Restatement (Second) of Contracts (1981), which in § 302 provides:

**Unless otherwise agreed between promisor and promisee, a beneficiary of a promise is an intended beneficiary if recognition of a right to performance in the beneficiary is appropriate to effectuate the intention of the parties and either:**

**(a) the performance of the promise will satisfy an obligation of the promisee to pay money to the beneficiary; or**

**(b) the circumstances indicate that the promisee intends to give the beneficiary the benefit of the promised performance.**

Section 304 then provides:

**A promise in a contract creates a duty in the promisor to any intended beneficiary to perform the promise, and the intended beneficiary may enforce the duty.**

Under the test in *Khabbaz,* as well as the Restatement black-letter rules, the plaintiffs in this case are intended beneficiaries who have the right to enforce the promises the assignee defendants made to the Currys. Their joint venture contract, as well as their acceptance of the assignment, specifically provided that the assignees were to be bound by the terms of "the Bridgman contract." Currys obviously intended that the assignee defendants, as joint venturers with Currys, would be obligated to share with them the burden of paying amounts due under the Bridgman-Curry contract. They thereby intended that plaintiffs be benefited to that extent. Our cases firmly establish that intended beneficiaries, like the plaintiffs here, may enforce an agreement between promisees like the Currys and promisors like the assignee defendants who have agreed to make the promisees' debt their own. [*Affirmed.*]

### CREDITOR, DONEE, AND INCIDENTAL BENEFICIARIES

If Susan owes Bob $1,000 and she performs services for Frank, she may contract to have Frank pay Bob $1,000. In such an instance, Bob is a third-party **creditor beneficiary** of the contract between Susan and Frank. Bob can sue Frank if there is a breach of the contract and can also sue Susan, since she still owes him $1,000.

When the performance under a contract is meant as a gift to a third party, that person is a **donee beneficiary.** Donee beneficiaries can sue the party that owes them a performance under a breached contract, but they cannot sue the party that contracted to make them a gift. The beneficiary of a life insurance policy is usually a donee beneficiary.

An **incidental beneficiary** is a third party that unintentionally benefits from a contract. The incidental beneficiary has no rights under a contract.

## 16.   Performance of Contracts

At the time parties reach agreement under a contract, the *duty of performance* becomes binding. Each party must perform the consideration promised to the other. Failure to perform breaches the contract.

### CONDITIONS IN CONTRACTS

Parties often put **conditions** in a contract that affect its performance. If something must take place in the future before a party has a duty to perform, it is called a **condition precedent.** For example, a building developer may contract to buy certain land "when the city of Euphoria annexes it." The annexation is a condition precedent to the developer's duty to purchase the land.

A **condition subsequent** excuses contractual performance if some future event takes place. A marine insurance policy that terminates shipping loss coverage "if war is declared" contains a condition subsequent.

Under *concurrent conditions* each party's contractual performance is triggered by the other party's tendering (offering) performance. In a contract for the purchase of land, the performing obligations of the seller and buyer are concurrent conditions. The significance of a concurrent condition is that a party must offer to perform before legally holding the other party for nonperformance. The land buyer must offer to pay for the land before suing the seller for failing to perform.

The conditions discussed above may be express or implied. Express conditions are set forth in the contract. Implied conditions do not appear in the contract but are implied by law.

### LEVELS OF CONTRACT PERFORMANCE

A party to a contract may not always perfectly perform duties under it. The more complex a contract is, the more difficult it is for a party to complete every aspect of performance. Courts generally recognize three levels of specific performance.

*Complete performance* recognizes that a contracting party has fulfilled every duty required by the contract. Payment of money, for example, is a contractual duty of performance which a party can perform completely. A party that performs completely is entitled to a complete performance by the other party and may sue to enforce this right.

*Substantial performance* represents a less-than-complete performance. A contracting party has honestly attempted to perform but has fallen short. Because of the complexity of building contractors' work, they often are able to reach substantial performance but not complete performance. One who substantially performs is entitled to the price promised by the other less that party's damages.

*Material breach* is a level of performance below what is reasonably acceptable. A party that has materially breached a contract cannot sue the other party for performance and is liable for damages arising from the breach.

## 17.   Discharge of Contracts

A party to a contract is *discharged* when the party is released from all further obligation of performance. Of course, complete performance discharges a party to a contract. Table 9-4 lists other events which create discharge.

### IMPOSSIBILITY OF PERFORMANCE

One event which discharges a party's obligation of performance deserves special attention. A party is discharged because of *impossibility of performance*.

If the subject matter of the contract is destroyed, the contract becomes impossible to perform. When a contract exists for the sale of a building, and the building burns, the seller is discharged from performance. Likewise, when there is a contract for personal services, and the party promising the services becomes ill or dies, the party receives discharge from performance.

The party that promised performance which becomes illegal is also discharged because of impossibility of performance. Mere increased difficulty or reduced profitability, however, does not constitute impossibility of performance.

Finally, under the UCC a party to a sale-of-goods contract receives discharge from performance because of **commercial impracticability.** The "impracticability" standard is not as difficult to meet as the "impossibility" standard. What constitutes impracticability of performance depends upon the circumstances of the situation. For instance, a manufacturer may be discharged from an obligation to make goods for a buyer when the manufacturer's major source of raw materials is unexpectedly interrupted. But if the raw materials are reasonably available from another supplier, the manufacturer may not receive discharge because of impracticability.

**TABLE 9-4**   Events Which Discharge a Party to a Contract

1   Complete performance
2   Occurrence of a condition subsequent
3   Nonoccurrence of a condition precedent
4   Material breach by the other party
5   Legal surrender of the right to enforce performance (waiver)
6   Mutual agreement to rescind
7   Expiration of the statute of limitations for enforceability
8   Novation (the substitution by agreement of one party for another on a contract)
9   Impossibility of performance

## 18. Trends in Contract Law

This chapter has given you an appreciation of the influence of contract law on private commercial transactions. To this end, the discussion has centered on the rules of contract law. Legal enforceability of contractual agreements provides an important framework for promoting certainty and efficiency in commercial dealings.

In general, however, trends in contract law do not affect the basic rules discussed in this chapter. Other chapters in the book develop many of the trends that affect contract law today. They deal with specific types of contracts or the use of contracts in particular situations. Still, several trends which are not mentioned elsewhere deserve attention here.

### TRENDS AFFECTING CONTRACTUAL RELATIONSHIPS BETWEEN BUSINESSES

As commercial transactions have grown increasingly complex, courts and legislatures have created more and more exceptions to traditional, fairly inflexible requirements of contract formation. These exceptions reflect an attempt to accommodate law to the actual reality of business dealings. For instance, UCC provisions on modification of contracts without consideration, open-ended contract terms, and contract formation by course of dealing are exceptions to traditional rules.

Similarly, courts have demonstrated greater willingness in recent years to grant damages based on one party's reasonable reliance on another's promises instead of merely on the party's expectations under a formal contract. This development reflects attempts to conform law to actual behavior in a complicated business world.

Increasingly, businesses are taking contracts to court. A study by University of Wisconsin law professor Mark Galanter shows a 258 percent rise in contract disputes filed in federal courts between 1960 and 1986. By 1986 contract disputes represented 18.7 percent of all civil cases filed in federal courts, the largest single category of cases. Professor Galanter attributes this growth in contract litigation to businesses suing each other over contractual performance.

Finally, as previously mentioned, many contracting parties do not seek legal enforcement of breached agreements. Often, parties use arbitration, mediation, and negotiation when business problems arise under contracts. They avoid the time-consuming, expensive, and uncertain litigation process.

### TRENDS AFFECTING CONTRACTUAL RELATIONSHIPS BETWEEN BUSINESSES AND EMPLOYEES

A recent statistic asserts that more than half of the country's biggest corporations now have employment contracts for top management. This figure represents a 50 percent increase since 1982. Contract negotiation is becoming increasingly important for many executives.

Most lower-level workers still do not have express contracts with their employers. Employers may terminate the employment of these workers at will (see Chapter 15). However, courts in growing numbers have been willing to take statements made by employers in personnel manuals and other documents and use them as a basis for implying contract rights for employees.

### TRENDS AFFECTING CONTRACTUAL RELATIONSHIPS BETWEEN BUSINESSES AND CONSUMERS

A major trend in contract law has been the passage of many statutes affecting contracts between businesses and consumers. Government has stepped in at both the federal and state levels to protect consumers as they make contracts with businesses. Chapter 20 and 21 discuss protection of consumers and debtors.

One recent development affecting business and consumer contracts has been enactment of "plain English" statutes in several states. These statutes require that standard business and consumer form contracts be written in a clearly understandable way. Drafters of such contracts must avoid legal expressions not ordinarily comprehended by consumers. More than thirty states have related statutes directed specifically at insurance contracts. A number of federal laws affecting readability also apply to specific types of contracts.

## 19.  Contractual Ethics

The federal government spends more than $200 billion a year in contracts for goods and services from private businesses. Recent scandals involving the bidding of these contracts have raised substantial issues of contractual ethics. Business students must be aware that when businesses fail to act ethically, legal regulations are often imposed to force business conduct into line with what society finds acceptable. Already the federal government is considering changes in the laws regulating government contracts.

In general, ethical concerns are increasingly reflected in how courts decide contractual disputes. Although the traditional rules of contract law are still very important, they cannot always be used to predict what courts will do when one party acts in *bad faith* or violates the *expectations* that another party brings to a business arrangement. For instance, the *Wall Street Journal* has reported a "boom" of lawsuits against banks for bad faith. Believing that banks are going to loan them money, customers sue when the banks eventually refuse to lend, and the customers are unable to obtain funding elsewhere. Even when there are no express contracts requiring banks to make loans, juries have held banks liable. In another variation of the bad faith lawsuit, banks are sued when they reduce levels of ongoing lending, causing their business customers to collapse financially. In spite of express contracts permitting banks to cut back lending, some juries have found them liable for doing so.

Involved in all such lawsuits are not only legal issues but also the ethical values that society holds regarding appropriate business practices. Business persons sometimes argue that jurors do not understand business dealings, and this is likely true. At the same time, however, juries may also be operating from a different set of ethical expectations than a segment of the business community. When this happens large verdicts against business defendants may surprise the business community.

Eventually, ethical values may provide the basis for legal rules. In contract law the growing use of promissory estoppel and implied contract doctrine shows the willingness of courts to make binding business arrangements that in the past would have been unenforceable without an express contract. It is easy to understand these changes in terms of the good faith expectations of the parties to business arrangements and in light of society's evolving ethical standards.

## REVIEW QUESTIONS

**1** For each term in the left-hand corner column, match the most appropriate description in the right-hand column:

| | |
|---|---|
| (1) Accord and satisfaction | (a) A recovery based on unjust enrichment |
| (2) Assignment | (b) A merchant's written promise to hold open an offer |
| (3) Bilateral contract | (c) A contract which binds one party but which allows the other party to withdraw legally |
| (4) Condition precedent | (d) A future uncertain event which must occur before performance is due |
| (5) Executory contract | (e) A level of contractual performance which is below what is reasonably acceptable |
| (6) Firm offer | (f) Settlement and payment of a disputed debt by mutual agreement |
| (7) Material breach | (g) The doctrine that prohibits use of oral evidence to alter or vary the terms of certain written contracts |
| (8) Parol evidence rule | (h) A contract the consideration for which is a binding promise given by each party |

(9) Quasi-contract

(10) Rescission
(11) Voidable contract

(i) A remedy which requires that each party return what it got from the other
(j) A transfer of contractual rights
(k) A contract which the parties have not yet performed

**2** Why is the law of contracts vital to the private enterprise system?

**3** Gustavson contracts with Sanders to buy 51 percent of the stock of Gimlet Corporation. When Sanders breaches the contract, Gustavson sues for specific performance. Is specific performance an appropriate remedy under these circumstances? Explain.

**4** Most contractual disputes are resolved by negotiated settlement. Explain why.

**5** Condor Equipment Company offers to sell Snappy Jack Biscuits, Inc., a dough-cutting machine. The offer states: "This offer expires Friday noon." On Thursday morning, the sales manager for Condor calls the president of Snappy Jack and explains that the machine has been sold to another purchaser. Discuss whether Condor has legally revoked its offer to Snappy Jack.

**6** Fielding Bros. offers to ship six furnaces to Central City Heating and Cooling Co. for $4,500 cash. Central City accepts on the condition that Fielding give 120 days' credit. Has a contract resulted? Explain.

**7** Goldman, an appliance wholesaler, signs an agreement with the Cool-It Corporation for 250 air-conditioners. The order price is left open and is to be decided in three months when the air-conditioners are delivered. Has a binding contract resulted? Would your answer be different if the parties specified the price but left open the quantity term until delivery?

**8** Hunt signs an equipment lease contract with Edwards Rental. The contract contains a clause stating: "Lessor disclaims all liability arising from injuries caused by use of this equipment." Because the equipment has been improperly serviced by Edwards Rental, Hunt is injured while using it. If Hunt sues, will the disclaimer clause likely be enforced? Explain.

**9** Elegante Haberdashery telephones an order to Nordic Mills for 500 men's shirts at $15 each. Each shirt will carry the Elegante label and have the Elegante trademark over the pocket. After the shirts are manufactured, Elegante refuses to accept delivery of them and raises the statute of frauds as a defense. Discuss whether this defense applies to these facts.

**10** Gus contracts to buy a used car from Cars Galore, Inc. The printed contract specifies "no warranties." But Gus and the sales manager of Cars handwrite into the contract a ninety-day guarantee on the transmission. If the transmission fails after sixty days, is there a warranty protecting Gus or not?

**11** Franchetti Rifle Distributors assigns a $20,000 claim against Top Gun, Inc., to the Zenith Collection Agency. When Zenith sues Top Gun, Top Gun asserts that it rejected a shipment of rifles from Franchetti, out of which the claim arose, because they had defective trigger guards. Explain whether Top Gun can properly assert its defense against plaintiff Zenith.

**12** The Store Owners Association at the Clearcreek Mall hires City Security Service to patrol the mall's parking lot after dark. Nancy Boggins, owner of the Shoe Attic at the mall, is mugged one night while the security guard is making an unauthorized visit to a friend's house. Can Nancy successfully sue City Security? Does it change your answer if Nancy is not a member of the Store Owners Association?

**13**  Bryan Developers signs a contract to purchase certain real estate for $256,000 "if the property is annexed by the city of Carnesville within one year." What type of condition is the quoted language? What is its legal effect?

**14**  Ace Contracting constructs an office building for Realty Enterprises. Realty's tenants quickly find a number of minor problems with the plumbing and insulation of the new building. When Realty contacts Ace about bringing its work up to standard, Ace promises to correct the problems, but never does. Can Realty rescind the contract? What are Realty's legal remedies?

**15**  In the mid-1970s, a tripling of prices by an illegal cartel of uranium producers caused Westinghouse Electric Corp. to default on uranium delivery contracts to a number of utility companies. The companies sued, and Westinghouse settled. If the case had gone to trial, what defense might Westinghouse have raised to excuse its nonperformance under the contracts?

# *Chapter*
# *10*

# Torts in the Business Environment

## CHAPTER PREVIEW

The word "tort" means "wrong." Legally, a tort is a civil wrong other than a breach of contract. Most torts involve injuries to persons or property. These injuries may be crimes as well as torts, but the doctrine of tort itself is civil rather than criminal. The usual remedy for a tort is court-granted damages. Behavior that constitutes a tort is called *tortious* behavior. One who commits a tort is a *tortfeasor*.

This chapter divides torts into three main categories: intentional torts, negligence torts, and strict liability torts. Intentional torts involve deliberate actions that cause injury. Negligence torts involve injury following a failure to use "reasonable care." Strict liability torts impose legal responsibility for injury even though a liable party neither intentionally nor negligently causes the injury.

Important to torts are the concepts of duty and causation. One is not liable for another's injury unless he or she has a *duty* toward the person injured. And, of course, there is usually no liability for injury unless one has *caused* the injury. We explain these concepts under the discussion of negligence, where they are most relevant.

This chapter also covers the topic of damages. The topic concerns the business community because the size of damage awards, frequently against businesses, has risen greatly in recent years. The chapter concludes with consideration of policy trends that are developing in tort law.

There are a great number of significant terms in this chapter. They include assault and battery, assumption of risk, cause in fact, comparative responsibility, contributory negligence, conversion, copyright, defamation, duty, false imprisonment, infliction of mental distress, intentional interference with contractual relations, invasion of privacy, patent, proximate causation, punitive damages, respondent superior, strict liability, trademark, trade secret, and trespass.

## 1.  The Development of Tort Law

### NINETEENTH CENTURY

Prior to 1800, much of the law of personal-property injury was founded on the doctrine of **trespass.** When we think of trespass now, we think mainly of trespass to land. In the past, however, the doctrine was used by any plaintiff who had sustained an injury to person or property due to the act of the defendant. And the trespass doctrine was a strict liability one. The fact that the defendant was not at fault nor could have reasonably avoided the accident was usually irrelevant.

The trespass doctrine as applied to personal injury, however, was the doctrine of an uncomplicated age and of a simple people. At that time, any injury done by another invited swift revenge if the law did not impose itself between the actor and the injured. But in the 1800s, as populations expanded and social and economic life became more complex, values and attitudes grew more sophisticated. The law changed to meet these changing conditions, and the doctrine of negligence emerged. No longer was one liable for reasonably unavoidable injury inflicted upon the person of another. Instead, liability would be imposed only when the actor was at fault and had failed to act as a "reasonable man."

Economic realities in the 1800s help explain the widespread acceptance of the new negligence doctrine. Many judges apparently considered that the strict liability of trespass would threaten the struggling infant industries of the time, putting an end to the socially valuable production of machined goods. The courts thus extended negligence law and defenses into areas of employer-employee relations, products liability, and accidents arising from business activity.

Nineteenth-century negligence doctrine is sometimes viewed as achieving a type of distributive justice that removed legal liability from nonnegligent business persons. It transferred the risk of injury from the nonnegligent to the victims of negligent behavior, providing a type of "subsidy" for business development. This view, however, is not the only one; many economics-inclined scholars disagree with it. They argue that in cases where the negligence doctrine was developing, the courts simply were allocating accident losses and property rights in the most economically efficient manner possible.

Whichever view is most accurate, it remains undeniable that courts in the 1800s fashioned numerous tort principles which left injury losses on accident victims. In addition to negligence doctrine, the courts created the defense of **contributory negligence,** which barred plaintiffs from any recovery if their own fault contributed to their injuries. Another court-created doctrine, the **assumption-of-risk** defense, barred plaintiffs from recovery when they knowingly submitted themselves to hazardous conditions created by the carelessness of others.

Another barrier courts placed in the way of plaintiff recovery was the doctrine of **proximate causation.** Not only did plaintiffs have to prove that their injuries actually were caused by negligence, they also had to establish that their injuries "foreseeably" arose from (were proximately caused by) the negligence (see section 16). Courts regarded questions of proximate cause as "matters of law." Judges dismissed many negligence claims upon the basis that the alleged facts showed no proximate cause.

### TWENTIETH CENTURY

Beginning in the twentieth century, the pendulum started to swing back. The courts (and legislatures) acted in many situations to distribute accident losses away from injured victims. In the workplace, the passage of workers' compensation statutes accomplished this goal (see Chapter 15). In product-related accidents, the courts arrived at tort reform through a series of developments which culminated in strict tort liability—which requires no proof of fault—for the sale of defective products (see Chapter 11). Also, the harsh application of contributory negligence has been eased (see section 17).

Even the application of negligence doctrine has changed. Today, many courts consider questions of proximate cause as issues which plaintiff-sympathetic juries, rather than judges, should resolve. Also, in recent years courts have expanded the scope of **duty,** which encompasses those to whom one owes reasonable care (nonnegligence) (see section 13).

What has caused these changes in tort law in the twentieth century? Economic conditions are chiefly responsible. The infant industries of the nineteenth century have grown into healthy maturity. Business no longer needs the liability protection it required a hundred years ago. Courts and legislatures also follow the mood of the country. To a significant extent, the public has demanded that tort laws be reformed to relieve injured individuals of potentially catastrophic accident losses.

Note that the rapid development of tort law has chiefly concerned negligence and strict liability. Changes in intentional tort law have been more gradual, although they have also taken place.

# INTENTIONAL TORTS

An important element in the following torts is *intent,* as we are dealing with *intentional* torts. "Intent" is usually defined as the desire to bring about certain results. But in some circumstances the meaning is even broader, including not only desired results but also results which are "substantially likely" to result from an action. Recently, employers who knowingly exposed employees to toxic substances without warning them of the dangers have been sued for committing the intentional tort of battery. The employers did not desire their employees' injuries, but these injuries were "substantially likely" to result from the failure to warn.

The following sections explain the basic types of intentional torts. Table 10-1 lists these torts.

## 2.   Assault and Battery

An **assault** is the placing of another in immediate apprehension for his or her physical safety. "Apprehension" has a broader meaning than "fear." It includes the expectation that one is about to be physically injured. The person who intentionally creates such apprehension in another is guilty of the tort of assault. Many times a battery follows an assault. A **battery** is an illegal touching of another. As used here, "illegal" means that the touching is done without justification and without the consent of the person touched. The touching need not cause injury.

A store manager who threatens an unpleasant customer with a wrench is probably guilty of assault. Actually hitting the customer with the wrench would constitute battery.

**TABLE 10-1**   Types of Intentional Torts

Assault and battery
Intentional infliction of mental distress
Invasion of privacy
False imprisonment
Trespass
Conversion
Defamation
Common law business torts
Statutory competitive torts
Constitutional torts

### 3.   Intentional Infliction of Mental Distress

Intentional **infliction of mental distress** is a battery to the emotions. It arises from outrageous, intentional conduct which carries a strong probability of causing mental distress to the person at whom it is directed. Usually, one who sues on the basis of an intentional infliction of mental distress must prove that the defendant's outrageous behavior caused not only mental distress, but also physical symptoms, such as headaches or sleeplessness. The following case shows how this tort can occur in an employment relationship.

# FORD v. REVLON
734 P.2d 580 (Ariz. 1987)

A supervisor made repeated sexual advances toward an employee. The employee complained to management, but she was advised "to forget the matter." Nine months later, the employee filed an official charge of sexual harassment and asked for protection from her supervisor. She was told the supervisor would be "closely monitored." Finally, thirteen months after the initial harassment, the employer Revlon issued a letter of censure to the supervisor. Four months later, the employee, who had developed high blood pressure and chest pains, attempted suicide. That same month, the employer fired the supervisor. The employee then sued the supervisor and the employer. The trial court held the employer liable for intentional infliction of emotional distress. When the court of appeals reversed that decision, the Arizona Supreme Court granted certiorari.

CAMERON, J.:...The Restatement of Torts recognizes that conduct which is extreme and outrageous may cause severe emotional distress for which one may be subject to liability. The Restatement also states that the tort of emotional distress inflicted intentionally or recklessly is recognized as a separate and distinct basis of tort liability. There is no need to show elements of other torts such as assault and battery. We have followed this standard for liability. More specifically, intentional infliction of emotional distress is often based upon claims of sexual harassment. The failure of an employer to promptly investigate complaints of sexual harassment is significant in making a determination to impose liability on an employer for its supervisors' acts of sexual harassment.

Elements of the tort of intentional infliction of emotional distress have been set out by this court, relying upon the language of the Restatement of Torts. The three required elements are: first, the conduct by the defendant must be "extreme" and "outrageous"; second, the defendant must either intend to cause emotional distress or recklessly disregard the near certainty that such distress will result from his conduct; and third, severe emotional distress must indeed occur as a result of defendant's conduct.

We believe that the conduct of Revlon met these requirements. First, Revlon's conduct can be classified as extreme or outrageous. Ford made numerous Revlon managers aware of Braun's activities at company functions. Ford did everything that could be done, both within the announced policies of Revlon and without, to bring this matter to Revlon's attention. Revlon ignored her and the situation she faced, dragging the matter out for months and leaving Ford without redress. Here is sufficient evidence that Revlon acted outrageously.

Second, even if Revlon did not intend to cause emotional distress, Revlon's reckless disregard of Braun's conduct made it nearly certain that such emotional distress would in fact occur. Revlon knew that Braun had subjected Ford to physical assaults, vulgar remarks, that Ford continued to feel threatened by Braun, and that Ford was emotionally distraught, all of which led to manifestations of physical problems. Despite Ford's complaints, Braun was not confronted for nine months, and then only upon Ford's demand for a group meeting. Another three months elapsed before Braun was censured. Revlon not only had actual knowledge of the situation but it also failed to conduct promptly any investigation of Ford's complaint.

Third, it is obvious that emotional distress did occur. Ample evidence, both medical and otherwise, was presented describing Ford's emotional distress. Ford testified about her emotional distress and her development of physical complications caused by her stressful work environment. The evidence convinced the jury, which found that emotional distress had occurred.

We also note that Revlon had set forth a specific policy and several guidelines for the handling of sexual harassment claims and other employee complaints, yet Revlon recklessly disregarded these policies and guidelines. Ford was entitled to rely on the policy statements made by Revlon. Once an employer proclaims a policy, the employer may not treat the policy as illusory. We hold that Revlon's failure to take appropriate action in response to Ford's complaint of sexual harassment by Braun constituted the tort of intentional infliction of emotional distress. [*The decision of the court of appeals is reversed.*]

---

In the business world, many examples of infliction of mental distress come about from the efforts of creditors to extract payment from their debtors. Frequent, abusive, threatening phone calls by creditors might provide the basis for a claim of intentional infliction of mental distress. As torts go, this one is of fairly recent origin. It is a judge-made tort, which furnishes a good example of how the courts are becoming increasingly sensitive to the range of injuries for which compensation is appropriate. In some states, courts have gone so far as to establish liability for carelessly inflicted mental distress, such as the distress of a mother who sees her child negligently run down by a delivery truck.

## 4. Invasion of Privacy

The tort of **invasion of privacy** is one that is still in the early stages of legal development. As the statutes and court cases recognize it, the tort at present comprises three principal invasions of personal interest. An invasion of any one of these areas of interest is sufficient to trigger liability.

Most commonly, liability will be imposed on a defendant who appropriates the plaintiff's name or likeness for his or her own use. Many advertisers and marketers have been required to pay damages to individuals when pictures of them have been used without authorization to promote products, or when their names and identities have been used without permission for promotional purposes. Before using anyone's picture or name, an advertiser must obtain a proper release from that person to avoid possible liability. Appropriating another's name and identity in order to secure credit is an additional example of this invasion-of-privacy tort.

A second invasion of privacy is the defendant's intrusion upon the plaintiff's physical solitude. Illegal searches or invasions of home or possessions, illegal wiretapping, and persistent and unwanted telephoning can provide the basis for this invasion-of-privacy tort. In one case, a woman even recovered damages against a photographer who entered her sickroom and snapped a picture of her. Employers who enter their employees' homes without permission have also been sued successfully for invasions of privacy. If the invasion of privacy continues, it may be enjoined by the court. Jacqueline Kennedy Onassis sought and obtained an injunction which forbade a certain photographer from getting too close to her and her children. Under this tort, the invasion of physical solitude must be highly objectionable to a reasonable person.

The third invasion of personal interest which gives rise to the invasion-of-privacy tort is the defendant's public disclosure of highly objectionable, private information about the plaintiff. A showing of such facts can be the basis for a cause of action, even if the information is true. Thus, publishing in a newspaper that the plaintiff does not pay his or her debts has been ruled to create liability for the defendant creditor. Communicating the same facts to a credit reporting agency or the plaintiff's employer usually does not impose liability, however. In these cases, there has been no disclosure to the public in general. Also, the news media are protected under the First Amendment when they publish information about public officials and other public figures.

## 5. False Imprisonment and Malicious Prosecution

Claims of **false imprisonment** stem most frequently in business from instances of shoplifting. This tort is the intentional unjustified confinement of a nonconsenting person. Although most states have statutes which permit merchants or their employees to detain customers suspected of shoplifting, this detention must be a reasonable one. The unnecessary use of force, lack of reasonable suspicion of shoplifting, or an unreasonable length of confinement can cause the merchant to lose the statutory privilege. The improperly detained customer is then able to sue for false imprisonment. Allegations of battery are also usually made if the customer has been touched.

The tort of **malicious prosecution** is often called "false arrest." Malicious prosecution arises from causing someone to be arrested criminally without proper grounds. It occurs, for instance, when the arrest is accomplished simply to harass someone. In Albany, New York, a jury awarded a man $200,000 for malicious prosecution. His zipper had broken, leaving open his fly, and a store security guard had him arrested for indecent exposure even after he explained that he had not noticed the problem.

## 6.   Trespass

To enter another's land without consent or to remain there after being asked to leave constitutes the tort of **trespass.** A variation on the trespass tort arises when something (such as particles of pollution) is placed on another's land without consent. Although the usual civil action for trespass asks for an injunction to restrain the trespasser, the action may also ask for damages.

Union pickets walking on company property (in most instances), customers refusing to leave a store after being asked to do so, and unauthorized persons entering restricted areas are all examples of trespass. Note that trespass is often a crime as well as a tort. Intentional wrongdoing is frequently criminal.

## 7.   Conversion

**Conversion** is the wrongful and unlawful exercise of dominion (power) and control over the personal property of another. Conversion deprives the proper owner of lawful rights in the property. The deprivation may be either temporary or permanent, but it must constitute a serious invasion of the owner's rights. Abraham Lincoln once convinced an Illinois court that a defendant's action in riding the plaintiff's horse for fifteen miles was not sufficiently serious to be a conversion since the defendant had returned the horse in good condition. The plaintiff had left the horse with the defendant to be stabled and fed.

Conversion arises often in business situations. Stealing property or purchasing stolen property (even innocently) is a conversion. Failing to return properly acquired property at the designated time, delivering property to the wrong party, and destruction and alteration of property are all conversions if the deprivation of ownership rights is serious or long-lasting. Even if she or he intends to return it, one who converts is absolutely liable for any damage done to property. A warehouse operator who improperly transfers stored goods from a designated to a nondesignated warehouse is absolutely liable when a tornado destroys the goods, or when a thief steals them.

## 8.  Defamation

**Defamation** is the publication of untrue statements about another which hold up that individual's character or reputation to contempt and ridicule. "Publication" means that the untruth must be made known to third parties. If defamation is oral, it is called **slander.** Written defamation, or defamation published over radio or television, is termed **libel.**

False accusations of dishonesty or inability to pay debts frequently bring on defamation suits in business relationships. Sometimes, such accusations arise during the course of a takeover attempt by one company of another through an offering to buy stock. In a recent instance, the chairman of one company called the chairman of a rival business "lying, deceitful, and treacherous" and charged that he "violated the standards by which decent men do business." If untrue, these remarks provide a good example of defamation of character. Punitive or punishment damages, as well as actual damages, may be assessed in defamation cases.

Individuals are not the only ones who can sue for defamation. A corporation can also sue for defamation if untrue remarks discredit the way the corporation conducts its business. Untruthfully implying that a company's entire management is dishonest or incompetent defames the corporation.

Because of the First Amendment, special rules regarding defamation apply to the news media. These media are not liable for the defamatory untruths they print about public officials and public figures unless plaintiffs can prove that the untruths were published with "malice" (evil intent, that is, the deliberate intent to injure) or with "reckless disregard for the truth." Public figures are those who have consciously brought themselves to public attention.

Does the malice standard apply to nonmedia as well as media defendants? The Supreme Court faced this issue in the following case.

# DUN & BRADSTREET, INC. v. GREENMOSS BUILDERS, INC.

105 S.Ct. 2939 (1985)

Dun & Bradstreet issued a false credit report to plaintiff's creditors indicating that the plaintiff had filed a voluntary petition for bankruptcy. The report grossly misrepresented plaintiff's assets and liabilities. Dun & Bradstreet thereafter issued a corrective notice, but the plaintiff was dissatisfied with the notice and filed a defamation suit in Vermont State Court alleging injury to reputation. When the jury awarded compensatory and punitive damages to the plaintiff, the trial court granted Dun & Bradstreet's motion for a new trial. The Vermont Supreme Court reversed the trial court. The United States Supreme Court granted certiorari on the issue of whether or not the Constitution requires a showing of "actual malice" before damages can be awarded against a nonmedia defendant.

POWELL, J.: In *New York Times Co. v. Sullivan*...the Supreme Court for the first time held that the First Amendment limits the reach of state defamation laws. That case concerned a public official's recovery of damages for the publication of an advertisement criticizing police conduct in a civil rights demonstration. As the Court noted, the advertisement concerned "one of the major public issues of our time." Noting that "freedom of expression upon public questions is secured by the First Amendment," and that "debate on public issues should be uninhibited, robust, and wide-open," the Court held that a public official cannot recover damages for defamatory falsehood unless he proves that the false statement was made with "'actual malice'—that is, with

knowledge that it was false or with reckless disregard of whether it was false or not." In later cases, all involving public issues, the Court extended this same constitutional protection to libels of public figures, and in one case suggested in a plurality opinion that this constitutional rule should extend to libels of any individual so long as the defamatory statements involved a "matter of public or general interest."...

In *Gertz v. Robert Welch, Inc.*, we held that the fact that expression concerned a public issue did not by itself entitle the libel defendant to the constitutional protections of *New York Times*. These protections, we found, were not "justified solely by reference to the interest of the press and broadcast media in immunity from liability." Rather, they represented "an accommodation between [First Amendment] concern[s] and the limited state interest present in the context of libel actions brought by public persons." In libel actions brought by private persons we found the competing interests different. Largely because private persons have not voluntarily exposed themselves to increased risk of injury from defamatory statements and because they generally lack effective opportunities for rebutting such statements, we found that the State possessed a "strong and legitimate...interest in compensating private individuals for injury to reputation." Balancing this stronger state interest against the same First Amendment interest at stake in *New York Times*, we held that a State could not allow recovery of presumed and punitive damages absent a showing of "actual malice." Nothing in our opinion, however, indicated that this same balance would be struck regardless of the type of speech involved.

We have never considered the *Gertz* balance obtains when the defamatory statements involve no issue of public concern. To make this determination, we must employ the approach approved in *Gertz* and balance the State's interest in compensating private individuals for injury to their reputation against the First Amendment interest in protecting this type of expression. This state interest is identical to the one weighed in Gertz. There we found that it was "strong and legitimate."...

The First Amendment interest, on the other hand, is less important than the one weighed in *Gertz*. We have long recognized that not all speech is of equal First Amendment importance. It is speech on "matters of public concern" that is "at the heart of the First Amendment's protection." [S]peech on matters of purely private concern is of less First Amendment concern. As a number of state courts, including the court below, have recognized, the role of the Constitution in regulating state libel law is far more limited when the concerns that activated *New York Times* and *Gertz* are absent. In such a case,

[t]here is no threat to the free and robust debate of public issues; there is no potential interference with a meaningful dialogue of ideas concerning self-government; and there is no threat of liability causing a reaction of self-censorship by the press. The facts of the present case are wholly without the First Amendment concerns with which the Supreme Court of the United States has been struggling.

While such speech is not totally unprotected by the First Amendment, its protections are less stringent. In *Gertz*, we found that the state interest in awarding presumed and punitive damages was not "substantial" in view of their effect on speech at the core of First Amendment concern. This interest however, is "substantial" relative to the incidental effect these remedies may have on speech of significantly less constitutional interest....In light of the reduced constitutional value of speech involving no matters of public concern, we hold that the state interest adequately supports awards of presumed and punitive damages—even absent a showing of "actual malice." [*The court then decided that Dun & Bradstreet's credit report did not concern a public issue. Affirmed.*]

---

Plaintiffs' verdicts in defamation cases are often overturned by appellate courts. Because of the constitutional protection given to speech and the media, appellate judges reexamine trial evidence very closely to determine whether the necessary elements of defamation had been proven.

There are two basic defenses to a claim of defamation. One defense is that the statements made were true. *Truth* is an absolute defense. The second defense is that the statements arose from *privileged communications*. For example, statements made by legislators, judges, attorneys, and those involved in lawsuits are privileged under many circumstances.

Nearly one-third of all defamation suits are currently brought by employees against present and former employers. Often these suits arise when employers give job references on former employees who have been discharged for dishonesty. As a result, many employers will now not give job references, or will only say that former employees did work for them.

## 9.   Business Torts

The label *business torts* is admittedly a vague one. It embraces several different kinds of torts which involve intentional interference with business relations.

### INJURIOUS FALSEHOOD

**Injurious falsehood,** sometimes called **trade disparagement,** is a common business tort. It consists of the publication of untrue statements that disparage the plaintiff's ownership of property or its quality. General disparagement of the plaintiff's business may also provide basis for liability. As a cause of action, injurious falsehood is similar to defamation of character. It differs, however, in that it usually applies to the plaintiff's property or business rather than character or reputation. The requirements of proof are also somewhat different. Defamatory remarks are presumed false unless the defendant can prove their truth. But in disparagement cases the plaintiff must establish the falsity of the defendant's statements. The plaintiff must also show actual damages arising from the untrue statements.

As an example of injurious falsehood, consider the cases filed by a major home products company. The complaints alleged that the defendants had distributed handouts which associated the company's familiar emblem of moon and stars with satanism—the worship of the devil. At the heart of this tort is the interference with the company's future sales.

### INTENTIONAL INTERFERENCE WITH CONTRACTUAL RELATIONS

A second type of business tort is **intentional interference with contractual relations.** Inducing employees to breach contracts with their employers can bring liability to third parties. Recently, a brokerage firm in New Orleans sued a competitor and obtained a judgment for several hundred thousand dollars because the competitor had induced a number of the firm's employees to break their employment contracts. In another suit, a jury awarded Pennzoil over $10 billion against Texaco for persuading Getty Oil to breach an agreement of merger with Pennzoil. After Texaco filed for bankruptcy, Pennzoil accepted a settlement of around $3 billion.

Lawsuits for interfering with contractual relations are not limited to those involving employee contracts. As the following case shows, however, suits to recover damages for such interference are not always successful.

# WELCH v. BANCORP MANAGEMENT ADVISORS, INC.

675 P.2d 172 (Or. 1984)

The plaintiff executed a contract with a real estate investment trust (the Trust). The Trust agreed to finance a real estate development plan by the plaintiff. In return it would receive interest on the money borrowed and half of the net profit when the property sold. An Investment Committee comprised of employees of the banks that supplied the Trust with funds for such ventures had an agreement with the Trust to act as an agent for the Trust by providing investment advice. Upon advice from the Investment Committee, the Trust breached the contract with the plaintiff and refused to loan him any money. The plaintiff sued the Investment Committee in tort for intentional interference with a contractual relationship between the Trust and the plaintiff. He argued that the Investment Committee was primarily motivated by the interest of the banks involved instead of the interest of the Trust.

CARLSON, J.: We hold that the privilege of a financial adviser is analogous to the qualified privilege of a corporate officer or employee. An agent acting as financial adviser is thus privileged to interfere with or induce breach relations with third parties, as long as the agent's actions are within the scope of his employment and taken with an intent to further the best interests of the principal. If this two-prong test is met, it is immaterial that the agent or another principal also profits by the advice. However, where an agent-financial adviser acts against the best interests of the principal or acts solely for his own benefit, he is liable in tort for harm done to the other contracting party.

We turn now to the facts of this case. Applying the two-prong test set out above, there is no evidence that the Investment Committee acted outside the scope of its authority in advising the Trust. In fact, in paragraph XI of the first count of plaintiff's Fifth Amended Complaint, he asserts that defendant's actions were within the scope of their actual and apparent authority.

As for the second prong, we find that there is no genuine issue of material fact to dispute that the advice given by the Investment Committee to the Trust was given with the intent to benefit the Trust....

The evidence in defendant's exhibits was enough for the trial judge to determine that the Investment Committee was acting in the best interests of the Trust. The evidence when viewed in the light most favorable to plaintiff, shows that defendants did meet their burden of proving that they acted within the scope of their authority as advisers to the Trust and that they acted to benefit the Trust, even if they benefited the banks as well. The trial judge applied the correct legal analysis.... [*Reversed.*]

## OBTAINING TRADE SECRETS

Another variety of business tort arises from wrongfully obtaining a rival's trade secrets. The Fifth Circuit Court of Appeals has defined a **trade secret** as "any formula, pattern, device, or compilation of information which is used in one's business, and which gives him an opportunity to obtain an advantage over competitors who do not know or use it." Information which is general knowledge cannot be a trade secret.

Many times employees who leave their employment to go into competition with their employers are accused of misappropriating trade secrets. An employee may draw upon the general knowledge, skills, and experience he or she has gained in working for a former employer, but it is a tort for the employee to use specific customer lists, documents, or other trade secrets gained through previous employment. In addition to obtaining provable damages, someone whose trade secrets have been misappropriated will usually ask the court to enjoin the defendant from using trade secrets in competition with the plaintiff.

For a trade secret to remain a trade secret, a business must take active steps to keep the information confidential. A major soft-drink manufacturer once withdrew from a consumer market of 400 million people in India rather than reveal the secret of its cola-based mixture, as demanded by the Indian government.

A final common law business tort involves *unfair competition*. It includes "palming off" a competitor's goods as one's own, and misappropriating trademarks. In addition to being a common law tort, unfair competition also includes several statutory torts. A statutory tort, of course, is one created by statute. For instance, violation of the antitrust laws is a tort under the Clayton Act (see Chapter 24). The next two sections discuss statutory torts of unfair competition involving trademarks, false advertising, patents, and copyrights.

## 10.  Trademarks and False Advertising: the Lanham Act

**TRADEMARKS**

The law of trademarks covers trademarks, service marks, certification marks, and collective marks. A **trademark** is any mark, word, picture, or design which attaches to goods to indicate their source. If the mark is associated with a service, it is a *service mark*. A *certification mark* is used by someone other than its owner to certify the quality, point of origin, or other characteristic of goods or services. Use of a *collective mark* represents membership in a certain organization or association. McDonald's golden arches, the words and design of Coca-Cola, the Good Housekeeping Seal of Approval, the prancing horse of Ferrari, and the "union label" are all marks of one kind or another. In the discussion which follows, all marks are termed trademarks.

The common law protects the use of trademarks, but since the *Lanham Act* of 1946, the principal protection has come from federal law. Trademark law recognizes that property rights extend beyond ownership of actual goods to the intangible aspects of goodwill which trademarks represent. In forbidding misappropriation of trademarks, the law prevents misappropriation of a company's goodwill and reputation. It protects both the company that owns the mark and the buyer of goods or services who relies upon it.

To acquire the protection of the Lanham Act, a trademark must be registered on the Principal Register. Only a mark in current use on goods and services in interstate commerce may be registered. In addition, the mark must be uniquely distinctive and nondescriptive. A mark which merely describes a use or characteristic of the product cannot generally be registered. A quick-order restaurant could not register the trademark "Fast Food."

Unauthorized use of a registered trademark constitutes the competitive tort of **infringement.** Infringement exists not only when the exact trademark is copied but also when the mark used resembles the protected trademark enough to confuse the public. The Lanham Act provides that any person who infringes on another's registered trademark in selling or advertising goods or services is liable for damages and subject to injunction. In instances of willful infringement, a court may award triple damages. Wendy's International, Inc. forced dozens of retailers to remove thousands of "Where's the beef?" T-shirts from their shelves. The shirts' manufacturer lacked the fast-food chain's permission to use the trademarked slogan.

A growing problem in recent years has been the deliberate counterfeiting of products. Levi jeans, Rolex watches, and other well-known brand products have been copied and sold. The U.S. International Trade Commission estimated that the volume of counterfeiting tripled between 1978 and 1983.

Now Congress has made deliberate counterfeiting a felony, punishable by jail terms and substantial fines. It is also a federal crime to traffic knowingly in goods containing a counterfeit mark.

To maintain a trademark, the owner must prevent its misuse and unauthorized use. If the public comes to think that a registered trademark represents a general class of goods, rather than a single brand, registration and the right to sue for trademark infringement may be lost. For instance, employees of a popular cola beverage have been instructed always to ask for it at a restaurant by its famous trademarked name. If the restaurant brings a competitor's cola beverage instead of the one ordered, the employees are instructed to object strenuously to the substitution for the trademarked brand. It is all part of the attempt to preserve the uniqueness of the trademark. Table 10-2 gives examples of trademarks which have lost their uniqueness due to general use.

## FALSE ADVERTISING

A tort related to but different from trademark infringement is the competitive tort of **false advertising.** Section 43(a) of the Lanham Act establishes an action for civil damages for any false description or representation of

**TABLE 10-2**   Trademarks Lost Due To General Use

---

Aspirin
Cellophane
Thermos
Monopoly (the game)
Escalator

---

one's goods or services which may damage a competitor. This action need not involve trademark infringement.

There are many different kinds of false advertising which are actionable under the Lanham Act. For an advertiser to represent its product as "California redwood" when the wood is actually red oak might invite a tort action by anyone legitimately associated with the redwood industry. To portray a picture of a competitor's product as one's own, as in an advertisement, is actionably false if the two products are not identical.

Section 43(a) applies only to false representations made about the defendant's own goods or services. It does not apply to false statements made about the plaintiff's goods or services. Falsehoods of the latter kind are actionable under the common law tort of disparagement.

## 11.   Patents and Copyrights

#### PATENTS

In the last century, a government official urged that the Patent Office be closed because there was nothing left to invent. Today, however, inventors file approximately 100,000 new patent applications every year. When granted, **patents** give their holders a seventeen-year legal monopoly over the use and licensing of new processes, products, machines, and other combinations of matter. Design patents can be obtained for shorter time periods. Underlying the grant of patents is the belief that the law should encourage invention by granting inventors exclusive rights for a limited duration to the profits of their efforts.

To be patentable, inventions must be *nonobvious, novel,* and *useful.* They also must be tangible applications of an idea. Discovery of a new fact about the universe does not in itself allow the discoverer to patent all future uses of that fact. Only when that fact is specifically applied through design of a new machine or process may it be patented.

Federal patent law permits the holder of a patent to bring a statutory tort action against anyone who infringes on the patent. The principal issues in most patent cases are: (1) whether or not the patent is valid and (2) whether or not the defendant has infringed the patent. The plaintiff in patent cases usually seeks remedies of injunction and damages. Triple damages are available against defendants found guilty of "willful and wanton" infringement.

Interestingly, having a patent properly registered with the Patent Office does not conclusively establish its validity. It only creates a presumption of validity. In a large percentage of cases involving patents, courts find the patents either to be invalid or otherwise unenforceable. However, that percentage is smaller than before 1982 when the Court of Appeals for the Federal Circuit was created. That court now handles all patent infringement appeals.

New technologies lead to new issues of patent law. Of especial current concern is the patentability of computer programs. In *Diamond v. Diehr and Lutton,* the Supreme Court held that a process for curing rubber did not become unpatentable simply because it incorporated a computer program. On the other hand, computer applications of mathematical formulas are not patentable. Another issue of present significance to patent law involves the extent to which new "genetically engineered" life forms can be patented. The Supreme Court has ruled that under some circumstances patent law does apply to protect the inventors of such life forms.

### COPYRIGHTS

**Copyright** law protects authors rather than inventors. An author creates works of a literary, dramatic, musical, graphic, choreographic, audio, or visual nature. Ranging from printed material to photographs to records and motion pictures, these works receive automatic federal protection under the Copyright Act of 1976 from the moment the author creates them. The copyright allows the holder to control the reproduction, display, distribution, and performance of a protected work. The copyright runs for the author's lifetime, plus fifty additional years.

Although copyright protection is automatic, a tort action for copyright infringement cannot be begun unless the author has properly filed copies of the protected work with the Copyright Office. And one who infringes on a copyright cannot be held liable for actual or statutory damages unless a copyright symbol or notice accompanies the protected work. When the author has observed the proper formalities, however, she or he may recover actual or statutory damages, attorney's fees, and any profits which the infringer has made. Illegally reproduced copies may also be seized, and willful copyright violations are criminal offenses.

The law permits a fair use of copyrighted work for teaching, research, and reporting purposes. In the next case, the Supreme Court considers whether videotaping television programs for home use violates the copyright laws.

# SONY CORP. OF AMERICA v. UNIVERSAL CITY STUDIOS, INC.

104 S.Ct. 774 (1984)

Sony Corporation manufactures home videotape recorders (VTRs). Universal City Studios owns the copyrights on some of the television programs that are broadcast on the public airwaves. Universal brought an action against Sony Corp. alleging that VTR customers had recorded some of Universal's work that infringed on their copyrights, and Universal claimed that Sony was liable for this infringement because it marketed the VTRs. The federal district court denied relief, holding that noncommercial home use was not a copyright infringement. The Court of Appeals reversed the district court decision, and Sony appealed.

STEVENS, J.: The respondents and Sony both conducted surveys of the way the Betamax machine was used by several hundred owners during a sample period in 1978. Although there were some differences in the surveys, they both showed that the primary use of the machine for most owners was "time-shifting"—the practice of recording a program to view it once at a later time, and thereafter erasing it. Time-shifting enables viewers to see programs they otherwise would miss because they are not at home, are occupied with other tasks, or are viewing a program on another station at the time of a broadcast that they desire to watch....

[U]nauthorized uses of a copyrighted work are not necessarily infringing. An unlicensed use of the copyright is not an infringement unless it conflicts with one of the specific exclusive rights conferred by the copyright statute. Moreover, the definition of exclusive rights in § 106 of the present Act is prefaced by the words "subject to §§ 107 through 118." Those sections describe a variety of uses of copyrighted material that "are not infringements of copyright notwithstanding the provisions of § 106." The most pertinent in this case is § 107, the legislative endorsement of the doctrine of "fair use."

That section identifies various factors that enable a Court to apply an "equitable rule of reason" analysis to particular claims of infringement. Although not conclusive, the first factor requires that "the commercial or nonprofit character of an activity" be weighed in any fair use decision. If the Betamax were used to make copies for a commercial or profit-making purpose, such use would presumptively be unfair. The contrary presumption is appropriate here, however, because the District Court's findings plainly establish that time-shifting for private home use must be characterized as a noncommercial, nonprofit activity. Moreover, when one considers the nature of a televised copyrighted audiovisual work, and that time-shifting merely enables a viewer to see such a work which he had been invited to witness in its entirety free of charge, the fact that the entire work is reproduced, does not have its ordinary effect of militating against a finding of fair use.

This is not, however, the end of the inquiry because Congress has also directed us to consider "the effect of the use upon the potential market for or value of the copyrighted work." The purpose of copyright is to create incentives for creative effort. Even copying for noncommercial purposes may impair the copyright holder's ability to obtain the rewards that Congress intended him to have. But a use that has no demonstrable effect upon the potential market for, or the value of, the copyrighted work need not be prohibited in order to protect the author's incentive to create. The prohibition of such noncommercial uses would merely inhibit access to ideas without any countervailing benefit.

Thus, although every commercial use of copyrighted material is presumptively an unfair exploitation of the monopoly privilege that belongs to the owner of the copyright, noncommercial uses are a different matter. A challenge to a noncommercial use of a copyrighted work requires proof either that the particular use is harmful, or that if it should become widespread, it would adversely affect the potential market for the copyrighted work. Actual present harm need not be shown; such a requirement would leave the copyright holder with no defense against predictable damage. Nor is it necessary to show with certainty that future harm will result. What is necessary is a showing by a preponderance of the evidence that some meaningful likelihood of future harm exists. If the intended use is for commercial gain, that likelihood may be presumed. But if it is for a noncommercial purpose, the likelihood must be demonstrated.

In this case, respondents failed to carry their burden with regard to home time-shifting. The District Court described respondents' evidence as follows:

**Plaintiffs' experts admitted at several points in the trial that the time-shifting without librarying would result in "not a great deal of harm." Plaintiffs' greatest concern about time-shifting is with "a point of important philosophy that transcends even commercial judgment." They fear that with any Betamax usage, "invisible boundaries" are passed: "the copyright owner has lost control over his program."**

Later in its opinion, the District Court observed: "Most of plaintiffs' predictions of harm hinge on speculation about audience viewing patterns and ratings, a measurement system which Sidney Sheinberg, MCA's president, calls a 'black art' because of the significant level of imprecision involved in the calculations."

There was no need for the District Court to say much about past harm: "Plaintiffs have admitted that no actual harm to their copyrights has occurred to date."

On the question of potential future harm from time-shifting, the District Court offered a more detailed analysis of the evidence. It rejected respondents' "fear that persons 'watching' the original telecast of a program will not be measured in the live audience and the ratings and revenues will decrease," by observing that current measurement technology allows the Betamax audience to be reflected. It rejected respondents' prediction "that live television or movie audiences will decrease as more people watch Betamax tapes as an alternative," with the observation that "[t]here is no factual basis for [the underlying] assumption." It rejected respondents' "fear that time-shifting will reduce audiences for telecast reruns," and concluded instead that "given current market practices, this should aid plaintiffs rather than harm them." And it declared that respondents' suggestion "that theater or film rental exhibition of a program will suffer because of time-shift recording of that program" lacks merit.

When these factors are all weighed in the "equitable rule of reason" balance, we must conclude that this record amply supports the District Court's conclusion that home time-shifting is fair use. In light of the findings of the District Court regarding the state of the empirical data, it is clear that the Court of Appeals erred in holding that the statute as presently written bars such conduct. [*Reversed.*]

---

Recently, Congress has granted copyright protection to the designs of integrated circuits. These circuits are designed into silicon chips used in computers and other electronic equipment. The new law gives ten years of copyright protection to any chips designed since July 1, 1983.

## 12.   Constitutional Torts

Section 1983 of the Civil Rights Act of 1871 creates tort liability for any public official or employee who injures a person by depriving him or her of constitutionally guaranteed rights. Through interpretation, the Supreme Court has extended this liability to municipal (city) governments that support such behavior by "custom, practice, or policy." An example of constitutionally guaranteed rights—called "civil rights"—is the Fourteenth Amendment's right not to be deprived of life, liberty, or property without due process.

Most Section 1983 cases have involved police misconduct—usually false arrest, physical abuse, or failure to protect prisoners in custody. However, other areas of potential liability exist (see Table 10-3). Injured persons may sue municipal governments and their employees for actual damages and attorneys' fees. Employees may have to pay *punitive* (punishment) *damages* as well.

As with many other types of tort cases, the number of cases filed annually doubled. Even judges are not immune from the reach of Section 1983. In 1984, the Supreme Court ruled that it applied to a judge who wrongfully jailed two men who were unable to post bond for misdemeanors which were not jailable offenses.

**TABLE 10-3**   Areas of Potential Liability Involving Section 1983

1   Unfavorable recommendations of former government employees
2   Use of zoning for political or discriminatory purposes
3   Failure to award contracts to lowest bidders (in some instances)
4   Discharge of government employees
5   Failure to train and supervise public employees
6   Use of permit, inspection, or licensing procedures for political, harassing, or discriminatory purposes

# NEGLIGENCE

The second major field of tort liability involves behavior which causes an unreasonably great risk of injury. This field of tort is called negligence. In the United States, more lawsuits allege negligence than any other single cause of action.

A complaint for negligence must show four elements (see Table 10-4). The following sections discuss these elements.

## 13. Duty of Care

A critical element of the negligence tort is duty. Without a duty to another person, one does not owe that person reasonable care. Accidental injuries occur daily for which people other than the victim have no responsibility, legally or otherwise.

Duty usually arises out of a person's conduct or activity. A person doing something has a duty to use reasonable care and skill around others to avoid injuring them. Whether one is driving a car or manufacturing a product, she or he has a duty not to injure others by unreasonable conduct.

Usually, a person has no duty to avoid injuring others through nonconduct. There is no general duty requiring a sunbather at the beach to warn a would-be surfer that a great white shark is lurking offshore, even if the sunbather has seen the fin. There is moral responsibility, but no legal duty present.

Where there is a special relationship between persons, the situation changes. A person in a special relationship with another may have a duty to avoid unreasonable nonconduct. A business renting surfboards at the beach would probably be liable for renting a board to a customer who was attacked by a shark if it knew the shark was nearby and failed to warn the customer. The "special business relationship" between the two parties creates a duty to warn and makes the business potentially liable for nonconduct (failing to warn).

**TABLE 10-4**   Elements of Negligence

1   Existence of a duty of care owed by the defendant to the plaintiff
2   Unreasonable behavior which breaches the duty
3   Causation of the plaintiff's injury by the defendant's behavior:
   a   Cause in fact
   b   Proximate causation
4   An actual injury

In recent years, negligence cases against business for nonconduct have grown dramatically. Most of these cases have involved failure to protect customers from crimes. The National Crime Prevention Institute estimates that such cases have increased tenfold since the mid-1970s. In probably the most famous case to date, singer Connie Francis settled with a Long Island motel for $1,475,000. She alleged that the motel was negligent for failing to protect her from an attack she suffered in her room.

## 14.   Unreasonable Behavior

At the core of negligence is the unreasonable behavior which breaches the duty of care that the defendant owes to the plaintiff. The problem is how do we separate reasonable behavior which causes accidental injury from unreasonable behavior which causes injury? Usually a jury determines this issue, but negligence is a mixed question of law and fact. Despite the trend for judges to let juries decide what the standard of reasonable care is, judges also continue to be involved in the definition of negligence. A well-known definition by Judge Learned Hand states that negligence is determined by "the likelihood that the defendant's conduct will injure others, taken with the seriousness of the injury if it happens, and balanced against the interest which he must sacrifice to avoid the risk."

In some negligence cases, there is a strong suspicion that the defendant failed to use reasonable care, but the plaintiff may have great difficulty in proving exactly what the defendant did. Suppose that a barrel rolled off an upper story of the defendant's warehouse and struck the plaintiff on the head. No one seems to know how the barrel came to fall from the warehouse. A negligence doctrine which aids a plaintiff in situations such as these is called **res ipsa loquitur.** Meaning "the thing speaks for itself," res ipsa loquitur applies when a plaintiff can show that the item which caused the injury was within the sole control of the defendant and that the injury typically would not have occurred unless the defendant were negligent.

When the plaintiff's case shows these circumstances, the burden of proof shifts from the plaintiff to the defendant. Instead of the plaintiff having to prove that the defendant's conduct was unreasonable, the defendant must now prove that he or she followed reasonable standards. In our hypothetical case, the barrel was in the sole control of the defendant, and barrels do not normally roll off buildings unless someone is negligent. Res ipsa loquitur is appropriate for this case.

A special type of aggravated negligence is "willful and wanton" negligence. Although this does not reveal intent, it does show an extreme lack of due care. Negligent injuries inflicted by drunk drivers show willful and wanton negligence. The significance of this type of negligence is that the injured plaintiff can recover punitive damages as well as actual damages.

## 15.   Cause in Fact

Before a person is liable to another for negligent injury, the person's failure to use reasonable care must actually have "caused" the injury. This observation is not so obvious as it first appears. A motorist stops by the roadside to change a tire. Another motorist drives past carelessly and sideswipes the first as he changes the tire. What caused the accident? Was it the inattention of the second motorist, or the fact that the first motorist had a flat tire? Did the argument that the second motorist had with her boss before getting in the car cause the accident, or was it the decision of the first motorist to visit one more client that afternoon? In a real sense, all these things caused the accident. Chains of causation stretch out infinitely.

Still, in a negligence suit the plaintiff must prove that the defendant actually caused the injury. The courts term this **cause in fact.** In light of the many possible ways to attribute accident causation, how do courts determine if a plaintiff's lack of care, in fact, caused a certain injury? They do so very practically. Courts leave questions of cause in fact almost entirely to juries as long as the evidence reveals that a defendant's alleged carelessness could have been a substantial, material factor in bringing about an injury. Juries then make judgments about whether a defendant's behavior in fact caused the harm.

A particular problem of causation arises where the carelessness of two or more tortfeasors contributes to cause the plaintiff's injury, as when two persons are wrestling over control of the car which strikes the plaintiff. Tort law handles such cases by making each tortfeasor *jointly and severally* liable for the entire judgment. The plaintiff can recover only the amount of the judgment, but she or he may recover it wholly from either of the tortfeasors, or get a portion of the judgment from each.

A variation of the joint tortfeasor situation occurs when one of two or more persons is guilty of negligence and the plaintiff cannot identify the specific tortfeasor. In the next case, the Michigan Supreme Court faces this problem.

# ABEL v. ELI LILLY AND CO.
343 N.W.2d 164 (Mich. 1984)

Plaintiffs brought suit against several companies that had previously manufactured diethylstilbestrol (DES), a drug taken by the mothers of the plaintiffs to prevent miscarriages during pregnancy. The plaintiffs, all women, developed cancer, usually while in their twenties, and claimed it was the result of the DES taken by their mothers. The plaintiffs also maintained that the defendants knew or should have known that DES contained a cancer-causing agent. Because of the lapse in time from the period when the mothers took DES until the cancer developed in their daughters, many of the plaintiffs could not identify which manufacturer of DES supplied the drug to their mothers. Therefore, the plaintiffs sued all manufacturers of DES that supplied the drug during a specific time period in the area where their mothers lived.

WILLIAMS, C.J.: Defendants correctly assert that the threshold requirement of any products liability action is identification of the injury-causing product and its manufacturer. The plaintiff must produce evidence of a defect which caused the accident and trace that defect into the hands of the defendant.

It is undisputed that all the plaintiffs in this action will not be able to meet the identification requirement. Paragraph 16 of the Thirteenth Amendment Complaint reads: "[S]ome of the plaintiffs will be unable to identify the specific defendant that manufactured the injury-producing drug that was sold to their mothers in spite of all good-faith efforts to determine same."

Despite this hiatus in the pleadings, defendants recognize that plaintiffs would still have set forth a cause of action if their factual situation meets the requirements of the theory of alternative liability. Also called "clearly established double fault and alternative liability," this procedural device shifts the burden of proof on the element of causation in fact to the defendants once an innocent plaintiff demonstrates that all defendants acted tortiously, but only one unidentifiable defendant caused plaintiff's injury. If the defendants cannot meet this burden and exculpate themselves, joint and several liability will be imposed.

Defendants assert that plaintiffs' reliance on alternative liability is totally unsupportable by the pleaded facts of the present case. In order to evaluate this claim, we must explore the theory of alternative liability as it has developed in the jurisprudence of this state.

The doctrine of alternative liability first received formal recognition in the case of *Summers v. Tice*....In that case, plaintiff was injured by one shot during a hunting expedition. Plaintiff sued both of his hunting companions, claiming that both negligently shot at him, although he was unable to determine which one fired the specific shot that injured him.

The *Summers* court agreed, as a preliminary matter, that both defendants were at fault in having acted negligently toward the plaintiff. The court also recognized that plaintiff had failed to meet his traditional burden regarding cause in fact. Only one shot had injured plaintiff; both defendants could not have shot it. Since the most the plaintiff could prove was a 50% probability that either one of the defendants was more likely than the other to have caused the injury, plaintiff had failed to establish that either one of the defendants was more likely than the other to have caused the injury.

The court then decided—as a matter of policy—that it was preferable that the two wrongdoers, both of whom had acted negligently toward the plaintiff and had created the situation wherein plaintiff was injured, should bear the burden of absolving themselves rather than leaving the innocent plaintiff remediless. Therefore, the court placed the burden of proof on the issue of causation in fact upon the defendants.

This rule is now embodied in 2 Restatement Torts, 2d 433B(3), pp. 441–442. Commentary to the Restatement agrees that the reason for the exception to traditional rules is to prevent the injustice of allowing proved wrongdoers to escape liability for an injury inflicted upon an innocent plaintiff "merely because the nature of their conduct and the resulting harm has made it difficult or impossible to prove which of them has caused the harm...."

[T]he policy underlying the theory of alternative liability has been adopted in this state. We now formally express our approval of the theory of alternative liability....

In sum, alternative liability will be applied in cases in which all defendants have acted tortiously, but only one unidentifiable defendant caused plaintiff's injury. If a plaintiff brings all the possible defendants into court and establishes the other elements of the underlying cause of action, the court should equitably shift an onerous burden of causation in fact to the defendants. If the defendants are unable to exonerate themselves, joint and several liability results.

Plaintiffs, [also] seek to proceed on the traditional theory of concert of action. This theory, although not developed to ease plaintiff's traditional burden of proof of causation, may have that effect. If plaintiffs can establish that all defendants acted tortiously pursuant to a common design, they will all be held liable for the entire result.

The concept is perhaps most clearly illustrated in the racing context. If three drivers join in a drag race, as a result of which one pedestrian is injured, all three may be held liable. Thus a legal fiction is created: all three drivers are found to be the cause in fact, although only one driver may have actually struck the pedestrian....

Unlike the procedural device of alternative liability, a concert of action case does not require that the plaintiff be unable to identify the specific defendant who caused his injury in fact. The plaintiff is usually able to make that determination. Such identification does not preclude liability on a concert of action theory.

Here plaintiffs have alleged that defendants acted together in negligently manufacturing and promoting drugs which were ineffective and dangerous, were inadequately tested, and were distributed without sufficient warnings. These allegations are sufficient to withstand summary judgment....Those plaintiffs who have alleged that a specific manufacturer caused their injuries are not precluded from this cause of action. [*Affirmed.*]

---

Other courts have handled DES cases differently. In *Sindell v. Abbott Laboratories* the California Supreme Court adopted what it called the *"market share theory."* When the plaintiff could not identify which defendant in fact manufactured the DES which injured her, the court held all defendants liable according to the percentage of the market they had at the time the plaintiff's mother took the drug.

## 16. Proximate Causation

It is not enough that a plaintiff suing for negligence prove that the defendant caused an injury in fact. The plaintiff also must establish proximate causation. "Proximate cause" is, perhaps, more accurately termed "legal cause." It represents the proposition that those engaged in activity are legally liable only for the *foreseeable* risk which they cause.

Defining proximate causation in terms of foreseeable risk creates further problems about the meaning of the word *foreseeable*. In its application, foreseeability has come to mean that the plaintiff must have been one whom the defendant could reasonably expect to be injured by a negligent act. For example, it is reasonable to expect, thus foreseeable, that a collapsing hotel walkway should injure those on or under it. But many courts would rule as unforeseeable that someone a block away, startled upon hearing the loud crash of the walkway, should trip and stumble into the path of an oncoming car. The court would likely dismiss that person's complaint against the hotel as failing to show proximate causation.

Another application of proximate cause doctrine requires the injury to be caused *directly* by the defendant's negligence. Causes of injury which intervene between the defendant's negligence and the plaintiff's injury can destroy the necessary proximate causation. Some courts, for instance, would hold that it is not foreseeable that an owner's negligence in leaving keys in a parked car should result in an intoxicated thief who steals the car, crashing and injuring another motorist. These courts would dismiss for lack of proximate cause a case brought by the motorist against the car's owner.

The torts scholar William Prosser urges that we not try to force the doctrine of proximate causation into a rigid logical structure. He says that at the basis of the doctrine is "social policy": the view of nineteenth-century courts that economic activity was valuable and that those engaged in it required insulation from liability for all but the most direct and immediate consequences of their negligence.

Although tort law still requires that the plaintiff prove proximate causation, courts today treat the doctrine somewhat differently than they did a hundred years ago. Today the trend is for courts not to dismiss cases on the basis of lack of proximate cause. The trend is to let plaintiff-sympathetic juries determine this issue.

## 17. Defenses to Negligence

There are two principal defenses to an allegation of negligence: contributory negligence and assumption of risk. Both these defenses are *affirmative defenses,* which means that the defendant must specifically raise these defenses to take advantage of them. When properly raised and proved, these defenses limit or bar the plaintiff's recovery against the defendant. The defenses are valid even though the defendant has actually been negligent.

### CONTRIBUTORY NEGLIGENCE

As originally applied, the contributory negligence defense absolutely barred the plaintiff from recovery if the plaintiff's own fault contributed to the injury "in any degree, however slight." The trend today, however, in the great majority of states is to offset the harsh rule of contributory negligence with the doctrine of comparative responsibility (also called comparative negligence and comparative fault). Under comparative principles, the plaintiff's contributory negligence does not bar recovery. It merely compares the plaintiff's fault with the defendant's and reduces the damage award propor-

plaintiff's fault with the defendant's and reduces the damage award proportionally. Under comparative responsibility, injury damages of $100,000 would be reduced by the jury to $80,000 if the jury determined that the plaintiff's own fault contributed 20 percent to the injury.

The following case illustrates contributory negligence and comparative responsibility. Can you tell from the Florida Supreme Court's decision why contributory negligence is an affirmative defense?

# INSURANCE COMPANY OF NORTH AMERICA v. PASAKARNIS

415 So.2d 447 (Fla. 1984)

John Menninger ran a red light and caused an accident hitting Richard Pasakarnis' jeep. Pasakarnis was thrown from the jeep and injured. He sued Menninger. The defendant argued, as an affirmative defense, that the injury would not have occurred if Pasakarnis had used his seat belt. The trial court granted the plaintiff's motion to strike the "seat belt defense," and the jury found the defendant 100 percent responsible for the accident.

ALDERMAN, C.J.: [The issue to be decided is] whether Florida courts should consider seat belt evidence as bearing on comparative negligence or mitigation of damages.

In *Hoffman v. Jones*, we decided that contributory negligence as a complete bar to a plaintiff's action was unjust. We reasoned that contemporary conditions must be met with contemporary standards which are realistic and better calculated to obtain justice among all parties involved, based upon the circumstances, and stated that it was inequitable to vest an entire accidental loss on one of the parties whose negligent conduct combined with the negligence of another to produce the loss. The best argument in favor of comparative negligence we found was that it simply provided a more equitable system of determining liability. We stated that in the field of tort law, the most equitable result to be achieved is to equate liability with fault. In adopting the doctrine of comparative negligence, we explained that under this theory a plaintiff is prevented from recovering *"only that proportion of his damages for which he is responsible."*

[We] hold that the "seat belt defense" is viable in Florida. The seat belt has been proven to afford the occupant of an automobile a means whereby he or she may minimize his or her personal damages prior to occurrence of the accident.

As we have already expressly acknowledged..., automobile collisions are foreseeable as are the so-called "second collisions" with the interior of the automobile. The seat belt has been a safety device required by the federal government for nearly twenty years. In a 1982 study by the United States Department of Transportation, National Highway Safety Administration Technical Report entitled the "Effectiveness and Efficiency of Safety Belt and Child Restraining Usage," it is reported that the evidence for the effectiveness of safety belts in reducing deaths and injury severity is substantial and unequivocal. In view of the importance of the seat belt as a safety precaution available for a plaintiff's protection, failure to wear it under certain circumstances may be a pertinent factor for the jury to consider in deciding whether plaintiff exercised due care for his or her own safety. We agree...that:

**[T]he failure to expend the minimal effort required to fasten an available safety device which has been put there specifically in order to reduce or avoid injuries from a subsequent accident is, on the very face of the matter, obviously pertinent and thus should be deemed admissible in an action for damages, part of which would not have been sustained if the seat belt had been used.**

Those jurisdictions adopting the "seat belt defense" have considered three different approaches: (1) plaintiff's nonuse is negligent per se; (2) in failing to make use of an available seat belt, plaintiff has not complied with a standard of conduct which a reasonable prudent man would have pursued under similar circumstances, and therefore he may be found contributorily negligent; and (3) by not fastening his seat belt, plaintiff may, under the circumstances of a particular case, be found to have acted unreasonably and in disregard of his or her best interests and, therefore, should not be able to recover those damages which would not have occurred if his or her seat belt had been fastened.

Because Florida does not by statute require the use of available seat belts, we reject the rule that failure to wear a seat belt is negligence per se as have the majority of jurisdictions. We also reject the second approach because contributory negligence is applicable only if plaintiff's failure to exercise due care causes, in whole or in part, the accident rather than enhancing the severity of the injuries. Rather, we adopt the third approach. Nonuse of the seat belt may or may not amount to failure to use reasonable care on the part of the plaintiff. Whether it does depends on the particular circumstances of the case. Defendant has the burden of pleading and proving that the plaintiff did not use an available and operational seat belt, that the plaintiff's failure to use the seat belt was unreasonable under the circumstances, and that there was a causal relationship between the injuries sustained by the plaintiff and plaintiff's failure to buckle up. If there is competent evidence to prove that the failure to use an available and operational seat belt produced or contributed substantially to producing at least a portion of plaintiff's damages, then the jury should be permitted to consider this factor, along with all other facts in evidence, in deciding whether the damages for which defendant may otherwise be liable should be reduced. Nonuse of an available seat belt, however, should not be considered by the triers of fact in resolving the issue of liability unless it has been alleged and proved that such nonuse was a proximate cause of the accident....[*Remanded.*]

---

Adoption of the comparative negligence principle seems to lead to more frequent and larger awards for plaintiffs. This was the conclusion of a study by the Illinois Insurance Information Service for the year following that state's adoption of comparative negligence.

#### ASSUMPTION OF RISK

If contributory negligence involves failure to use proper care for one's own safety, the assumption-of-the-risk defense arises from the plaintiff's knowing and willing undertaking of an activity made dangerous by the negligence of another. When professional hockey first came to this country, many spectators injured by flying hockey pucks sued and recovered for negligence. But as time went on and spectators came to realize that attending a hockey game meant that one might occasionally be exposed to flying hockey pucks, courts began to allow the defendant owners of hockey teams to assert that injured spectators had assumed the risk of injury from a speeding puck.

Assumption of the risk may be implied from the circumstances, or it can arise from an express agreement. Many businesses attempt to relieve themselves of potential liability by having employees or customers agree contractually not to sue for negligence, that is, to assume the risk. Some of these contractual agreements are legally enforceable, but many will be struck down by the courts as being against public policy, especially where a business possesses a vastly more powerful bargaining position than does its employee or customer.

It is important to a successful assumption-of-the-risk defense that the assumption was voluntary. Entering a hockey arena while knowing the risk of flying pucks is a voluntary assumption of the risk. Courts have often ruled, however, that people who imperil themselves while attempting to rescue their own or others' property from a risk created by the defendant have not assumed the risk voluntarily. A plaintiff who is injured while attempting to save his possessions from a fire negligently caused by the defendant is not subject to the assumption-of-the-risk defense.

A voluntary assumption of risk usually bars the plaintiff from any recovery for the defendant's negligence. Contrast this with the situation in many states where the plaintiff's contributory negligence merely reduces the recovery for negligent injury. Because assumption-of-the-risk and contributory negligence defenses in practical application frequently are very similar, this result appears unfair.

# STRICT LIABILITY IN TORT

**Strict liability** is a catchall phrase for the legal responsibility for injury-causing behavior which is neither intentional nor negligent. There are various types of strict liability torts, some of which are more "strict" than others. What ties them together is that they all impose legal liability, regardless of the intent or fault of the defendant. The next two sections discuss these torts and tort doctrines.

## 18.  Respondeat Superior

Any time an employee is liable for tortious acts in the "scope of employment," the employer is also liable. This is because of the tort doctrine of **respondeat superior** ("let the master reply").

The reason for respondeat superior is that the employee is advancing the interests of the employer when the tortious act occurs. If the employee were not doing the work, the employer would have to do it. Therefore, the employer is just as liable as the employee when the employee acts tortiously in carrying out the work. In a sense, the employer has set the employee in motion and is responsible for the employee's acts.

Most respondeat superior cases involve employee negligence. Note, however, that the employer is strictly liable once the employee's fault is established. And it does not matter that the employer warned the employee against the tortious behavior. Because Mary's employer told her to be careful while delivering pizzas does not prevent him from being liable when Mary runs a red light and has an accident.

Some respondeat superior cases involve an employee's intentional tort. If a store's service representative strikes a customer during an argument over the return of merchandise, the store will be liable under respondeat superior. But if the argument concerns football instead of the return of merchandise, the store will not be liable. The difference is that the argument over football is not within the scope of employment.

Usually, the only defense the employer has to the strict liability of respondeat superior is that the employee was outside the scope of employment. Sometimes this defense is made using the language **frolic and detour.** An employee who is on a frolic or detour is no longer acting for the employer. If Mary has delivered her employer's pizzas and is driving to see a friend when an accident occurs, the employer is not liable.

An employer who must pay for an employee's tort under respondeat superior may legally sue the employee for reimbursement. In practice, this seldom happens because the employer carries insurance. Occasionally, an insurer who has paid a respondeat superior claim will sue the employee who caused the claim.

### 19. Other Strict Liability Torts

In most states, the courts impose strict liability in tort for types of activities they call "ultrahazardous." Transporting and using explosives and poisons fall under this category, as does keeping dangerous wild animals. Injuries caused from artificial storage of large quantities of liquid also can bring strict liability on the one who stores. In one unfortunate instance, a 2-million-gallon vat of molasses burst and drowned a number of passersby in a nearby street. Regardless of whose fault or intent it was, the vat owner is strictly liable in this situation because of ultrahazardous activity.

The majority of states impose strict liability upon tavern owners for injuries to third parties caused by their intoxicated patrons. The acts imposing this liability are called *dram shop acts.* Because of the public attention given in recent years to intoxicated drivers, there has been a tremendous increase in dram shop act cases.

Common carriers, transportation companies licensed to serve the public, are also strictly liable for damage to goods being transported by them. Common carriers, however, can limit their liability in certain instances through contractual agreement, and they are not liable for: (1) acts of God, such as natural catastrophes; (2) action of an alien enemy; (3) order of public authority, such as authorities of one state barring potentially diseased fruit shipments from another state from entering their state; (4) the inherent nature of the goods, such as perishable vegetables; and (5) misconduct of the shipper, such as improper packaging.

A major area today of strict liability law is *strict tort liability* for defective products. Sellers of such products are liable without fault to any injured user. Chapter 11 covers product liability in detail. Note that many scholars do not consider this liability as being *strict,* in the truest legal sense of the word.

Under workers' compensation statutes, employers are strictly liable for accidental injuries their employees suffer which arise "out of and in the course of employment." Chapter 15 discusses the workers' compensation system.

## 20.  Damages

A noted legal scholar concludes that "the crucial controversy in personal injury torts today" is in the area of damages. This is because the average personal injury award has been increasing at nearly double the rate of inflation. For dramatic examples of the size of awards or settlements in some recent cases, take note of Table 10-5. The size of damage awards is largely deter-

**TABLE 10-5**   Recent Damage Awards or Settlements in Tort Cases

| Defendant Company | Event Causing Injury | Award or Settlement in Millions of Dollars |
|---|---|---|
| A. H. Robins | Product (Dalkon Shield) | 233 |
| Arco | Ship sinking | 51 |
| Cargill Inc. | Interference with contractual relations | 16 |
| Cessna Aircraft Corp. | Product (airplane) | 29 |
| Chevron | Toxic fumes | 15 |
| Dow Chemical | Product (Bendectine) | 120 |
| Hyatt Corp. | Skywalk collapse | 120 |
| MGM | Hotel fire | 75 |
| Seven chemical companies | Product (Agent Orange) | 180 |
| Stouffer Corp. | Hotel fire | 48 |
| Texaco | Interference with contractual relations | 10,530 |
| Wyeth Laboratories | Drug (suppository) | 22 |

mined by juries, but judges also play a role in damages, especially in damage instructions to the jury and in deciding whether to approve substantial damage awards.

### COMPENSATORY DAMAGES

Most damages awarded in tort cases compensate the plaintiff for injuries suffered. The purpose of damages is to make the plaintiff whole again, at least financially. There are three major types of loss which potentially follow tort injury and which are called "compensatory damages." They are: (1) past and future medical expenses, (2) past and future economic loss (including property damage and loss of earning power), and (3) past and future pain and suffering. Compensatory damages may also be awarded for loss of limb, loss of consortium (the marriage relationship), and mental distress.

Calculation of damage awards creates significant problems. Juries frequently use state-adopted life expectancy tables and present-value discount tables to help them determine the amount of damages to award. But uncertainty about the life expectancy of injured plaintiffs and the impact of inflation often make these tables misleading. Also, awarding damages for pain and suffering is an art rather than a science. These awards measure jury sympathy as much as they calculate compensation for any financial loss. The recent dramatic increases in the size of damage awards helps underline the problems in their calculation. One result is that many individuals and businesses are underinsured for major tort liability.

### PUNITIVE DAMAGES

Compensatory damages are not the only kind of damages. There are also *punitive damages*. By awarding punitive damages, courts or juries punish defendants for committing intentional torts and for negligent behavior considered "gross" or "willful and wanton." The key to the award of punitive damages is the defendant's motive. Usually the motive must be "malicious," "fraudulent," or 'evil." Increasingly, punitive damages are also awarded for dangerously negligent conduct which shows a conscious disregard for the interests of others. These damages punish those who commit aggravated torts, and act to deter future wrongdoing. Because they make an example out of the defendant, punitive damages are sometimes called **exemplary damages.**

Presently, there is much controversy about how appropriate it is to award punitive damages against corporations for their economic activities. Especially when companies fail to warn of known danger created by their activities, or when cost-benefit decisions are made at the risk of substantial human injury, courts are upholding substantial punitive damage awards against companies. Yet, consider that these damages are a windfall to the injured plaintiff who has already received compensatory damages. And instead of punishing guilty management for wrongdoing, punitive damages may end up punishing innocent shareholders by reducing their dividends.

Many court decisions also overlook a very important consideration about punitive damages. Most companies carry liability insurance policies which reimburse them for "all sums which the insured might become legally obligated to pay." This includes reimbursement for punitive damages. Instead of punishing guilty companies, punitive damages may punish other companies who have to pay increased insurance premiums, and may punish consumers, who ultimately pay higher prices. As a matter of public policy, several states prohibit insurance from covering punitive damages, but the great majority of states permit such coverage. This fact severely undermines arguments for awarding punitive damages against companies for their economic activities.

Consider also that an award of punitive damages greatly resembles a criminal fine. Yet the defendant who is subject to these criminal-type damages lacks the right to be indicted by a grand jury and cannot assert the right against self-incrimination. In addition, the defendant is subject to a lower standard of proof than in a criminal case. Might a defendant in a tort suit challenge an award of punitive damages on a constitutional basis?

Finally, note that the United States is the only country in the world where punitive damages are regularly awarded.

### STRUCTURED SETTLEMENTS

A major response to the growing size of damage awards is the rapid spread of **structured settlements** of damages in personal-injury cases. For example, a Florida court awarded two children $18 million. Negligent derailment of several tank cars had released poisonous gases which injured the children and killed their parents. Instead of paying the children a lump sum, the railroad negotiated a structured settlement for them. Also known as a periodic payment or protected settlement, the structured settlement usually takes the form of a guaranteed annuity for the plaintiff's lifetime. The annuity purchased for the children in the Florida case could be worth as much as $52 million during their lives, although it only cost the railroad $11.5 million.

Already a tort reform movement in this country has persuaded many states to change some tort doctrines. These states have eliminated (or modified) joint and several liability, limited damages for the pain and suffering of personal injury, and significantly reduced the circumstances that warrant punitive damages. Many business lobbying groups are also urging Congress to federalize tort reform.

Much of the pressure to reform tort law arises because of business concern over product liability. Specific tort reforms being urged in product liability are discussed in the next chapter.

# REVIEW QUESTIONS

**1** For each term in the left-hand column, match the most appropriate description in the right-hand column:

(1) Assumption of risk

(2) Comparative negligence

(3) Copyright

(4) Defamation

(5) Duty

(6) Proximate causation

(7) Punitive damages

(8) Respondeat superior

(9) Trademark

(10) Trespass

(a) The liability of an employer for an employee's torts

(b) Damages which punish a defendant for wrongdoing

(c) Knowingly encountering a dangerous condition caused by another

(d) The legal cause of an injury, which is determined by the "foreseeability" test

(e) Reduction of plaintiff's damages by the amount that plaintiff's own carelessness caused the injury

(f) The legal right of an author to control reproduction or performance of a literary, musical, or graphic work

(g) Publication of harmful, untrue statements about another

(h) The legal responsibility of a person, which arises out of conduct, to act (or not act) in a certain way toward others

(i) The tort of entering another's land without consent

(j) A mark, word, picture, or design which attaches to goods to indicate their source

**2** Discuss the basic change in accident-loss distribution in the twentieth century.

**3** In recent months, homeowners downwind from International Cement Company have had clouds of cement dust settle on their property. Trees, shrubbery, and flowers have all been killed. The paint on houses has also been affected. Explain what tort cause of action these homeowners might pursue against International.

**4** You are concerned because several of your employees have recently broken their employment contracts and left town. Investigation reveals that your competitor in a nearby city has paid bonuses to your former employees to persuade them to break their contracts. Discuss what legal steps you can take against your competitor.

**5** Acme Airlines attempts to get control of Free Fall Airways by making a public offer to buy its stock from shareholders. Free Fall's president advises the shareholders in a letter that Acme's president is "little better than a crook" and "can't even control his own company." Analyze the potential liability of Free Fall's president for these remarks.

**6**   The Stillwater Record Corporation discovers that a number of retail stores are selling counterfeit copies of its popular line of environmental records and tapes. Discuss Stillwater's legal rights against the retailers and the counterfeiter.

**7**   Total Truck Renter, Inc., ran advertising that showed both its trucks and the trucks of its biggest competitor. Tricks of photography were used to make Total's trucks appear larger than the competitor's. Actually, the trucks were all of similar size. Is what Total has done legally acceptable? Discuss.

**8**   Bartley signs a storage contract with Universal Warehouses. The contract specifies that Bartley's household goods will be stored at Universal's midtown storage facility while he is out of the country on business. Later, without contacting Bartley, Universal transfers his goods to a suburban warehouse. Two days after the move, a freak flood wipes out the suburban warehouse and Bartley's goods. Is Universal liable to Bartley? Explain.

**9**   Carlos delivers pizza for Mama Mia's Pizza Parlor. One of his employer's rules is that delivery employees are never to violate posted speed limits. While traveling 50 miles per hour in a 30-mile-per-hour speed zone, Carlos negligently crashes into a city bus. Is Mama Mia's liable for the injuries caused by Carlos? Discuss.

**10**   Through no one's fault, a sludge dam of the Phillips Phosphate Company breaks. Millions of gallons of sludge run off into a nearby river that empties into Pico Bay. The fishing industry in the bay area is ruined. Is Phillips Phosphate liable to the fishing industry? Explain.

**11**   An equipment manufacturer learns that a former employee has begun a competing business. Many of the same processes used by the manufacturer are also being used by the new business. Further, many of the manufacturer's customers are being contacted by the former employee. The manufacturer desires to sue its former employee. What must it prove in order to maintain a successful suit? Discuss.

**12**   State Realty owns a large apartment complex. One of its tenants has been robbed and badly beaten in the unlighted parking lot of the complex. The tenant now sues State Realty for negligently failing to maintain adequate security. Describe the basic elements of negligence and discuss how they might apply to these facts.

**13**   A jury finds liable the defendant in a tort case. It determines that the plaintiff has suffered $200,000 in damages. The jury also finds that the plaintiff's own fault contributed 25 percent to his injuries. Under a comparative negligence instruction, what amount of damages will the jury award the plaintiff?

**14**   How does the "market share" theory modify traditional rules of tort causation?

**15**   Discuss the pros and cons of punitive damage awards against corporations.

# Chapter
# *11*

# Products and Service Liability

## CHAPTER PREVIEW

Products and service liability are of special importance to managers, marketers, product designers, insurers, engineers, attorneys, accountants, health care specialists, and many other members of the business and professional communities. This chapter explains the legal theories out of which this liability arises.

*Products liability* is not a theory or cause of action upon which a lawsuit is based. It refers to all of the liabilities which sellers have for the goods they sell. After a short historical introduction, this chapter shows how liabilities arise when sellers breach legal duties relating to (1) seller conduct, (2) product quality, and (3) promises or representations. It is breach of these legal duties that constitutes the basic theories which sellers face in products liability lawsuits.

Following a discussion of the basic legal theories in product liability cases, this chapter examines concepts of product defect and injury causation that plaintiffs must prove to win such cases. Next, this chapter identifies the various defendants whom plaintiffs may sue and what their defenses are. Then it examines legislative reform, management planning for products liability, and trends.

Closely related to products liability is service liability. The final sections of this chapter focus on liability concerns of the professional and of other service providers. Malpractice and the accounting profession are highlighted.

The previous chapter on torts explained many of the significant terms used in this chapter. Important terms introduced in this chapter include caveat emptor, defect, implied warranty of merchantability, indemnification, malpractice, merchant, privity, state-of-the-art defense, statute of repose, and subrogation.

## 1.   Historical Development of Products Liability

### NEGLIGENCE

Chapter 10 discussed how tort law moved away from strict liability to embrace negligence in the 1800s. This movement was significant for the developing law of liability for injury because of defective products.

The new doctrine of negligence almost totally insulated manufacturers and retailers from being sued successfully. This result occurred because judges ruled that sellers of products owed the "reasonable man" duty only to persons with whom they had actually dealt. For a manufacturer to be liable, the manufacturer must have sold the defective product directly to the injured party. If the injured party were not the purchaser, or if the injured party had purchased the product from a retailer, the manufacturer would not have been liable for the defects. This aspect of negligence, which limited liability of sellers to those persons with whom they had entered into a contract, was called the **privity** doctrine. Although the doctrine originally arose out of contract law, it now came to be applied as well in tort cases.

### PRIVITY

The privity doctrine protected retailers in addition to manufacturers. Even if the injured party has purchased the product directly from the retailer, the retailer could seldom be found negligent. The defective product, which was frequently packaged, was the fault not of the retailer but of the manufacturer. The retailer had therefore acted as a "reasonable man." And so moral attitudes and economic conditions become embodied in law which assisted the growing industries of the nineteenth century. With the exception of cases involving "inherently dangerous" products (guns, drugs, and so on), the law placed the risk of loss upon the injured party in most instances. It was truly a time of **caveat emptor,** "let the buyer beware."

In the twentieth century, the pendulum began to swing slowly toward strict liability. As infant industries grew into healthy maturity, as the country became economically prosperous, and as products became increasingly more numerous and complex, the courts began dismantling the legal structure of products liability which had been raised in the preceding century. In its place rose the condition of **caveat venditor,** "let the seller beware."

### ABOLITION OF PRIVITY

First to go was the privity doctrine as applied to negligence law. In the famous case of *MacPherson v. Buick* in 1916, Justice Benjamin Cardozo ruled that a plaintiff could sue an automobile company even though the plaintiff had not purchased the defective automobile from the company and was not in privity of contract. Cardozo noted that the automobile company knew that the buyer (the retailer) would resell the automobile to someone like the plaintiff. He argued that "precedents drawn from the days of travel by stagecoach" must not control the "needs of life in a developing civilization."

It took nearly fifty years following the *MacPherson* case for the privity doctrine as used in negligence to collapse completely. But today no state applies privity in negligence law.

### RISE OF IMPLIED WARRANTY

Around the time of *MacPherson,* state courts across the country also began to abandon the concepts of "fault" and the "reasonable man" and to find sellers strictly liable when defective food and drink harmed consumers. Rather than use a strict liability in tort, the courts used a type of strict liability based on an "implied" warranty or guarantee which manufacturers and sellers supposedly made to those who might be affected by the food and drink. Although "warranty" and "guarantee" are words based in contract law, the courts generally did not require the presence of privity of contract between plaintiff and defendant in these cases. Instead, the courts, and in some instances the legislatures, imposed such warranties by law.

During the next half century, as the privity doctrine collapsed in negligence law, it collapsed as well in implied warranty cases involving food, drink, and drugs. Strict liability was imposed for defects in these products in increasing numbers of states. Finally, in the late 1950s and early 1960s the implied warranty doctrine expanded to cover all types of products. And in the famous case of *Henningsen v. Bloomfield Motors* in 1960, the New Jersey Supreme Court made it clear that the implied warranty could not be disclaimed by the manufacturer in an express contract where the manufacturer's bargaining power was so much greater than the purchaser's that the disclaimer could be presented on a take-it-or-leave-it basis. Other states swiftly followed this reasoning, and throughout the cases the courts continually made reference to "modern marketing conditions" and "the needs of the community."

### RETURN TO STRICT LIABILITY IN TORT

Still, the close connection of implied warranty to contract law prevented many plaintiffs from suing successfully. The difficulty of meeting various technical requirements of contract law kept many product-injured plaintiffs out of the courts. One last step remained before the full circle of products liability could be completed. The law would have to return to strict liability in tort. Then came the following case.

---

# GREENMAN v. YUBA POWER PRODUCTS, INC.
377 P.2d 897 (Calif. 1963)

---

TRAYNOR, J.: Plaintiff brought this action for damages against the retailer and the manufacturer of a Shopsmith, a combination power tool that could be used as a saw, drill, and wood lathe. He saw a Shopsmith demonstrated by the retailer and studied a brochure prepared by the manufacturer. He decided he wanted a Shopsmith for his home workshop, and his wife bought and gave him one for Christmas in 1955. In 1957 he bought the necessary attachments to use the Shopsmith as a lathe for turning a large piece of wood he wished to make into a chalice. After he had worked on the piece of wood several times without difficulty, it suddenly flew out of the machine and struck him on the forehead, inflicting serious injuries. About ten and a half months later, he gave the retailer and the manufacturer written notice of claimed breaches of warranties and filed a complaint against them alleging such breaches and negligence.

After a trial before a jury, the court ruled that there was no evidence that the retailer was negligent or had breached any express warranty and that the manufacturer was not liable for the breach of any implied warranty. Accordingly, it submitted to the jury only the cause of action alleging breach of implied warranties against the retailer and the causes of action alleging negligence and breach of express warranties against the manufacturer. The jury returned a verdict for the retailer against plaintiff and for plaintiff against the manufacturer in the amount of $65,000. The trial court denied the manufacturer's motion for a new trial and entered judgment on the verdict. The manufacturer and plaintiff appeal. Plaintiff seeks a reversal of the part of the judgment in favor of the retailer, however, only in the event that the part of the judgment against the manufacturer is reversed.

Plaintiff introduced substantial evidence that his injuries were caused by defective design and construction of the Shopsmith. His expert witnesses testified that inadequate set screws were used to hold parts of the machine together so that normal vibration caused the tailstock to the lathe to move away from the piece of wood being turned permitting it to fly out of the lathe. They also testified that there were other more positive ways of fastening the parts of the machine together, the use of which would have prevented the accident. The jury could therefore reasonably have concluded that the manufacturer negligently constructed the Shopsmith. The jury could also reasonably have concluded that statements in the manufacturer's brochure were untrue, that they constituted express warranties, and that the plaintiff's injuries were caused by their breach.

The manufacturer contends, however, that plaintiff did not give it notice of breach of warranty within a reasonable time and that therefore his cause of action for breach of warranty is barred by section 1769 of the Civil Code. Since it cannot be determined whether the verdict against it was based on the negligence or warranty cause of action or both, the manufacturer concludes that the error in presenting the warranty cause of action to the jury was prejudicial.

Section 1769 of the Civil Code provides: "In the absence of express or implied agreement of the parties, acceptance of the goods by the buyer shall not discharge the seller from liability in damages or other legal remedy for breach of any promise or warranty in the contract to sell or the sale. But, if, after acceptance of the goods, the buyer fails to give notice to the seller of the breach of any promise or warranty within a reasonable time after the buyer knows, or ought to know of such breach, the seller shall not be liable therefor."

Like other provisions of the uniform sales act, § 1769 deals with the rights of the parties to a contract of sale or a sale. It does not provide that notice must be given of the breach of a warranty that arises independently of a contract of sale between the parties. Such warranties are not imposed by the sales act, but are the product of common-law decisions that have recognized them in a variety of situations.

The notice requirement of section 1769, however, is not an appropriate one for the court to adopt in actions by injured consumers against manufacturers with whom they have not dealt. "As between the immediate parties to the sale [the notice requirement] is a sound commercial rule, designed to protect the seller against unduly delayed claims for damages. As applied to personal injuries, and notice to a remote seller, it becomes a boobytrap for the unwary. The injured consumer is seldom 'steeped in the business practice which justifies the rule,' and at least until he has had legal advice it will not occur to him to give notice to one with whom he has had no dealing." We conclude, therefore, that even if plaintiff did not give timely notice of breach of warranty

to the manufacturer, his cause of action based on the representations contained in the brochure was not barred.

Moreover, to impose strict liability on the manufacturer under the circumstances of this case, it was not necessary for plaintiff to establish an express warranty as defined in § 1732 of the Civil Code. A manufacturer is strictly liable in tort when an article he places on the market knowing that it is to be used without inspection for defects, proves to have a defect that causes injury to a human being. Recognized first in the case of unwholesome food products, such liability has now been extended to a variety of other products that create as great or greater hazards if defective.

Although in these cases strict liability has usually been based on the theory of an express or implied warranty running from the manufacturer to the plaintiff, the abandonment of the requirement of a contract between them, the recognition that the liability is not assumed by agreement but imposed by law...and the refusal to permit the manufacturer to define the scope of its own responsibility for defective products...make clear that the liability is not one governed by the law of contract warranties but by the law of strict liability in tort. Accordingly, rules defining and governing warranties that were developed to meet the needs of commercial transactions cannot properly be invoked to govern the manufacturer's liability to those injured by their defective products unless those rules also serve the purposes for which such liability is imposed.

The purpose of strict liability is to insure that the costs of injuries resulting from defective products are borne by the manufacturers that put such products on the market rather than by the injured persons who are powerless to protect themselves. Sales warranties serve this purpose fitfully at best. In the present case, for example, plaintiff was able to plead and prove an express warranty only because he read and relied on the representations of the Shopsmith's ruggedness contained in the manufacturer's brochure. Implicit in the machine's presence on the market, however, was a representation that it would safely do the jobs for which it was built. Under these circumstances, it should not be controlling whether plaintiff selected the machine because of the statement in the brochure, or because of the machine's own appearance of excellence that belied the defect lurking beneath the surface, or because he merely assumed that it would safely do the jobs it was built to do. It should not be controlling whether the de-

tails of the sales from manufacturer to retailer and from retailer to plaintiff's wife were such that one or more of the implied warranties of the sales act arose. "The remedies of injured consumers ought not to be made to depend upon the intricacies of the law of sales." To establish the manufacturer's liability it was sufficient that plaintiff proved that he was injured while using the Shopsmith in a way it was intended to be used as a result of a defect in design and manufacture of which plaintiff was not aware that made the Shopsmith unsafe for its intended use. [*Judgment affirmed.*]

---

With Justice Roger Traynor's decision in the *Greenman* case, the law in California returned to strict tort liability. State after state has followed the reasoning of this case. Today, strict tort liability is nearly universal in its application to product-related injuries. And underlying the widespread adoption of strict liability are social and economic considerations (see Table 11-1).

## THE BASIC THEORIES OF LIABILITY

### 2. Introduction

To many sellers of products, it must seem as though they are liable anytime someone is injured by one of their products. This, however, is untrue. Sellers are not insurers in the sense that they guarantee no injury will befall those who come into contact with the seller's products. Another way of put-

**TABLE 11-1**    Arguments Made for Adoption of Strict Tort Liability

1   Where sellers promote mass consumption, injured product users should not have to bear financial losses caused by defective products.
2   Sellers are better able than injured product users to spread liability losses by raising the price of products and obtaining insurance.
3   Strict tort liability will provide manufacturers with incentives for more careful product design and quality control.

ting it is to say that sellers are not absolutely responsible for all harm which follows the use of their products. Instead, they are liable only when they have breached some *legal duty* which is owed to any injured party. Such legal duties may arise: (1) because of the conduct of the seller, especially that of the manufacturer; (2) because of the quality of the product; and (3) because of promises or representations the seller has made.

## 3. Duty Based upon Conduct of the Seller: Negligence

The concepts of negligence discussed in Chapter 10 apply in products liability cases. The conduct of sellers must fulfill the duty of "ordinary and reasonable" care. Otherwise, sellers must answer in damages for negligence to those injured by their conduct.

### DUTY OF REASONABLE CARE

In products liability law, sellers owe the duty of reasonable care to all those who may come in contact with the sellers' products. The duty exists because of the sellers' act in placing their products into the stream of commerce. It is the legal reflection of society's judgment that those who make a profit by selling products must bear the expense of harm when by fault of their conduct they cause injury.

Under negligence law, however, not every sale of a defective product, or of one capable of causing injury, constitutes a failure to use reasonable care. For instance, in today's era of prepackaged goods, a retail seller of a defective product can usually not be found liable for negligence. It is not legally "reasonable" to expect that a retailer will open every can of peas to discover whether or not there is a nail in them. Nor can the manufacturing seller always be held liable for negligence for placing a defective product into the stream of commerce. An injured plaintiff must show how the manufacturer was at fault for using unreasonable design, production, or inspection standards. In light of the complexity of modern production processes, it is frequently difficult for the plaintiff actually to show this unreasonableness.

### RES IPSA LOQUITUR

Over the years, plaintiffs have used the negligence doctrine of res ipsa loquitur in appropriate circumstances to assist them in establishing breach of the duty of reasonable care. Recall that this doctrine applies when a plaintiff can prove that the "thing" causing harm was within the sole control of the defendant and that the injury would not typically have happened unless the defendant were negligent (see Chapter 10). In products liability cases which apply res ipsa loquitur, the plaintiff must show that the product defect occurred while the product was within a defendant's sole control.

This may not be difficult to show if the defect is a mouse in a soft-drink bottle. But if the defect is a crack in the bottle, a specific defendant's sole control may be harder to prove. For example, did the crack in the soft-drink bottle which exploded occur during the manufacturing process or the bottling process? Or did the retailer drop the bottle on the floor prior to shelving it?

### PROXIMATE CAUSATION

Proximate causation is also important in products liability cases. Negligent products sellers (and those who are strictly liable) are liable only for injuries that are "foreseeable." Thus, when a defective soft-drink bottle explodes in a grocery store and puts out the eye of the shopper who has just picked it up, the bottler, if at fault, will be liable, since such an injury is foreseeable. But as to the store manager who was also injured by the same explosion when the loud noise caused him to slip from a chair in which he was standing to replace a light bulb on the other side of the store, he will not likely recover from the bottler.

The ability to foresee injury, which is required by the proximate causation standard, ties in directly to the duty of the seller. For instance, in the next case the seller argued that there was no duty to give certain warnings since injury resulting from product misuse was legally unforeseeable.

# GERMANN v. F.L. SMITHE MACH. CO.
395 N.W.2d 922 (Minn. 1986)

The defendant, Smithe, sold Germann's employer a PHP 33, a hydraulic press with a detachable safety bar. During routine maintenance of the press, the safety bar was removed and not reattached. Germann, who did not know about the safety bar, sustained serious injury to his left leg when it became caught in the press. He sued the defendant and won. Asserting that it had no duty to warn Germann about the consequences of an unforeseeable misuse of its product, Smith appealed.

KELLEY, J.:...The primary issue raised in this appeal is whether Smithe had the legal duty to warn users of the dangers of using PHP 33 when the safety bar was not properly attached. The question of whether a le-gal duty to warn exists is a question of law for the court—not one for jury resolution.

Smithe contends it had no duty to provide warnings as to the unsafe operation of a machine it manufactured when it had provided a safety bar which, if properly installed and maintained, would have prevented the accident. The danger caused by the absence of the safety bar, it contends, was solely due to the neglect of Quality Park in its failure to properly maintain the safety bar in place. It relies on *Westerberg v. School District* where we noted the duty to warn rests directly on the foreseeability of the injury. Improper use of the product, however, resulting from such things as improper maintenance need not be anticipated by the manufacturer.

While not disagreeing that foreseeability of injury is the linchpin for determination whether a duty to warn exists, Germann responds that because Smithe designed the press with a removable safety bar, a design that, in fact, requires its removal for the machine's maintenance, Smithe reasonably knew or should have recognized the potentiality that the bar might not be properly replaced. Germann argues Smithe should, therefore, have warned operators, by the attachment of a warning decal or by other appropriate means, that for the safe operation of the machine, the safety bar should be properly installed and functional.

As indicated, whether there exists a duty is a legal issue for court resolution. In determining whether the duty exists, the court goes to the event causing the damage and looks back to the alleged negligent act. If the connection is too remote to impose liability as a matter of public policy, the courts then hold there is no duty, and consequently no liability. On the other hand, if the consequence is direct and is the type of occurrence that was or should have been reasonably foreseeable, the courts then hold as a matter of law a duty exists. Other issues such as adequacy of the warning, breach of duty and causation remain for jury resolution.

In some respects the facts in *Westerberg* are indistinguishable from those in the case at bar. Each case involves injury arising from the use of a machine approximately six years old. Each machine was heavily used.

Both accidents occurred as a result of faulty maintenance by the purchaser-owner-employer which caused designed safety mechanisms in each machine to fail. However, in our opinion, a distinguishing fact of significance exists. The safety lid device on the washer in *Westerberg* was installed by the manufacturer in such a manner it was only remotely foreseeable that the safety feature would be altered or allowed to fall into disrepair in a manner so as to increase any risk of injury to a user. To the contrary, in the case at bar, the safety bar was designed to be attached by the purchaser. In addition, the safety bar was detachable as the result of the machine's design. In fact, it had to be detached in order that the press might be serviced. Knowing that, Smithe could have reasonably foreseen that on a machine designed for extended and heavy use, it was almost inevitable that for maintenance purposes the safety bar would be removed, and that there was a risk it might not be properly reattached. If the safety bar was not properly reattached, there would be exposure to a user-operator of increased danger of injury of the type the safety bar had been designed to prevent. This misuse was foreseeable; it was not remote; and the danger of injury to a user because of the misuse was likewise foreseeable. Therefore, we hold Smithe had a legal duty to warn operators of the peril of running the press without a properly attached and operating safety bar. [*Affirmed.*]

## 4.   Duty Based upon Quality of the Product

If negligence law in products liability is founded upon fault in the conduct of the seller, then strict liability principles come from defects in the quality of the product. The focus in negligence is upon the behavior of the seller; in strict liability, it is upon the behavior of the product in the environment of its use. Because it is far easier to prove a product defect than it is to establish unreasonable human behavior, the enormous explosion in products liability suits during recent times can be explained in large part by the development of strict liability doctrines.

In strict products liability, the duty of the commercial seller is to avoid placing defective products into the stream of commerce. As it is currently expressed, such liability can be imposed in virtually every state under tort law or through breach of the implied warranty of merchantability, a contract doctrine.

### STRICT LIABILITY IN TORT

Since the *Greenman* decision in 1963, strict products liability in tort has swept the country. In many states, the courts have declared this doctrine to be law. In other states, the legislatures have imposed strict tort liability on sellers. There is considerable variation in the manner and extent of application of the doctrine from state to state, but the majority of states have applied strict tort liability as it is found in the Second Restatement of Torts. Students should recall that the restatement was prepared by the American Law Institute, a national body of lawyers, judges, and legal scholars whose pronouncements of the law are very influential, even though they have no official legal weight until courts or legislatures decide to apply them.

Section 402A of the Second Restatement of Torts says that anyone engaged in the business of selling a product who sells it in a "*defective condition unreasonably dangerous* to the user or consumer or to his property" is liable for injuries caused to the user or his property by the defect. The section emphasizes that such liability results even if "the seller has exercised all possible care" and despite the fact that the injured party is not in privity of contract with the seller.

The effect of 402A is to open up all sellers in the distribution chain—manufacturer, wholesaler, distributor, and retailer—to liability to the injured user or consumer. No longer can the retailer successfully defend the suit involving the nail in the can of peas by asserting the reasonableness of his or her behavior. Any seller in the chain of distribution is liable without fault for sale of a defective product causing injury.

The restatement does not take a position, however, on whether or not strict tort liability extends to protect parties other than consumers or users. Does strict liability act to protect an injured pedestrian who is hit by a car which is out of control due to a defective steering column? The definite trend among the states is to extend strict liability in tort to such *bystanders*, but several states have chosen not to protect these individuals through strict liability. In states which have not so extended strict liability, bystanders are covered only by negligence law.

Once the plaintiff establishes strict products liability in tort, the question arises as to the extent to which the plaintiff can recover damages. Presently, the majority of states permit injured parties to recover personal damages, which compensate for bodily harm, and property damages, which compensate for property other than the defective product itself, but they do not allow injured parties to recover for *economic damages* such as harm to profits or loss of goodwill. Thus, in most states a restaurant owner cannot recover from a food supplier in strict tort liability when restaurant customers suffer food poisoning from spoiled fish, even though the incident deprives the restaurant of goodwill and future profits.

### IMPLIED WARRANTY OF MERCHANTABILITY

Another theory of strict products liability arises from the **implied warranty of merchantability** which accompanies every sale of *goods* by a **merchant.** This warranty is implied by law into every contract for the sale of goods by one who is in the business of selling such goods, and it is imposed on sellers by Section 2-314 of the Uniform Commercial Code (UCC). Every state has adopted the UCC with the exception of Louisiana, and Louisiana recognizes law similar to Section 2-314.

Under the implied warranty of merchantability, it is the seller's duty to provide the buyer with a product which is *"fit for the ordinary purposes for which such goods are used."* If the product is not fit for its ordinary use, the seller is strictly liable for injury to person, property, or the product itself. This warranty also guarantees that the goods sold are properly packaged and conform to the class of goods (Grade A, Grade B, and so on) of which they are members. Such guarantees are especially important to commercial buyers who purchase for industrial use or resale. Products liability law is by no means limited only to consumer application.

The UCC permits sellers to disclaim the implied warranty of merchantability. In a written contract, for the disclaimer to be binding, the seller must either use the term "merchantability," that is, "seller disclaims all warranties of merchantability," or else use language such as "with all faults" or "as is." Language which recites merely that the seller disclaims "all warranties" does not exclude the implied warranty of merchantability.

It is important, also, to note that presently under federal law a seller cannot disclaim the implied warranty of merchantability as to the product itself in any written consumer warranty or service contract made by the seller. The disclaimer permitted by the UCC still applies in the commercial setting and in consumer transactions in which the seller is not offering a written warranty or a service contract. The UCC, however, does not permit disclaimers to limit damages for personal injuries. Nor does it allow disclaimer of damages in any situation where the court decides the disclaimer is **unconscionable.** In reading the following case, note the similarity between the doctrine of unconscionability and the doctrine of contractual illegality discussed in Chapter 9.

# HANSON v. FUNK SEEDS INTERNATIONAL

373 N.W.2d 30 (S.D. 1985)

Larry Hanson purchased seed corn from Funk Seeds International. Hanson's agent took delivery of the fifty-five bags of corn and signed a delivery receipt that stated in part: "By acceptance and use of the seed, Buyer agrees that the Company's liability and the Buyer's exclusive remedy for breach of any warranty...shall be limited in all events to a return of the purchase price of the seed." This provision was also contained on a tag attached to each bag of corn. When some of the fields planted with corn failed to grow properly, Hanson sued Funk.

HENDERSON, J.: At trial, appellant Funk attempted to introduce delivery receipts and a tag which was attached to the bags of seed delivered to appellee Hanson. These exhibits contained the warranty disclaimer and limitation of remedy provisions outlined in the facts above. The trial court, however, denied admission of these exhibits and found the provisions in question to be unconscionable. Appellant here asserts that such a determination was in error. We disagree.

The exclusion or modification of warranties and the contractual modification or limitation of remedies is permitted under SDCL 57A-2-316 and SDCL 57A-2-719, respectively. In sum, a seller may use a disclaimer clause to control his liability by reducing the manner in which he can be found to have breached; and, also, a seller may attempt to restrict the type of remedy available once a breach occurs. However, the trial court may refuse to enforce such provisions if it finds them to have been unconscionable when made and if it affords the parties a reasonable opportunity to present evidence concerning its commercial setting, purpose, and effect so as

to aid the court's decision. The trial court properly followed these procedural requirements by accepting pretrial memoranda and offers of proof at trial and correctly excluded the exhibits, determining their provisions to be unconscionable.

In reaching our determination, we are most persuaded by our past decision in *Durham v. Ciba-Geigy Corp.,*...In *Durham*, this Court stated:

**To permit the manufacturer of the pesticide to escape all consequential responsibility for the breach of contract by inserting a disclaimer of warranty and limitation of consequential damages clause, such as was used herein, would leave the pesticide user without any substantial recourse for his loss. One-sided agreements whereby one party is left without a remedy for another party's breach are oppressive and should be declared unconscionable.**

**In this case, loss of the intended crop due to ineffectiveness of the herbicide is inevitable and potential plaintiffs should not be left without a remedy. Furthermore, the purchasers of pesticides are not in a position to bargain with chemical manufacturers for contract terms more favorable than those listed on the preprinted label, nor are they in a position to test the effectiveness of the pesticide prior to purchase....**

**[P]ublic policy should not allow a chemical manufacturer to avoid responsibility for the ineffectiveness of a product which was offered for one purpose, the effective control of corn rootworm larvae.**

Although the product in *Durham* was manufactured and the product here in question, to wit, corn seed, is a product of nature, the process used in marketing both products is nearly identical so as to permit application of the considerations found relevant in *Durham*.

Appellee Hanson, like most farmers, was not in a position to bargain for more favorable contract terms, nor was he able to test the seed before the purchase. A crop failure is inevitable if the corn seed is ineffective and to enforce the provisions here in question, which would only allow the return of the purchase price, would leave appellee without any substantial recourse for his loss. In essence, appellee would be left without a remedy for another's breach. The trial court's determination that these provisions were unconscionable is therefore not in error and we uphold its decision in this regard. [*Affirmed.*]

The implied warranty of merchantability applies only to sales of *goods*, that is, tangible, movable personal property. In recent years, however, many courts have applied the implied warranty concept by analogy to home builders who are sued by home buyers. The courts call the new legal theory the *implied warranty of habitability*. Under this theory, buyers can sue commercial builder-sellers who sell houses with major construction defects.

Of the jurisdictions adopting the warranty, the majority have ruled that it applies only to sales of new housing. Most courts have also imposed privity-of-contract requirements on the enforceability of the warranty. Thus, only the original buyer may hold the builder-seller to the warranty.

### 5.   Duty Based upon Promises or Representations

A seller has an absolute duty of performance for any promises or representations he or she makes about a product when such statements become part of the basis for the bargain with the buyer. Several theories of law apply to this duty, which is of particular significance in commercial dealings.

#### EXPRESS WARRANTY

Section 2-313 of the UCC creates an *express warranty* for any promises the seller makes about a product's performance, such as: "The transmission of this tractor is guaranteed against mechanical defect for five years." This UCC section also establishes an express warranty for any factual statements describing the product. ("All moving parts are made of stainless steel.") Similarly, the seller is held to warrant expressly that a final shipment of goods will conform to any sample or model that has been furnished the buyer. None of these express warranties need use the words "warranty" or "guarantee," and express warranties cannot be disclaimed by the seller. Special federal law applies to the making of written warranties to consumers. This law is covered in Chapter 20.

Note that an express warranty places upon the seller an absolute duty of performance. That he or she has acted reasonably or that the product is fit for its ordinary use and is not defective does not protect the maker of an express warranty. If the product is not as described or if it does not perform as promised, the seller is liable.

#### MISREPRESENTATION

A duty of performance which overlaps that of express warranty places tort liability on anyone who misrepresents to the public a material fact about the character or quality of a product through advertising or labeling. This doctrine of *misrepresentation* also imposes a duty of absolute performance upon the seller. A good example of this absolute duty involves a pharmaceutical laboratory. The laboratory advertised its painkilling product as being "nonaddictive." When a patient, whose doctor prescribed the drug freely, became addicted and later died, his widow sued the drug maker. Although the court found that the laboratory was not negligent, that the product was neither defective nor unreasonably dangerous, and that the laboratory honestly believed the drug to be nonaddictive, it held the laboratory liable. The description of the drug contained the misrepresentation of a material fact and created absolute liability for the manufacturer. The doctrines of express warranty and misrepresentation warn manufacturers not to oversell products by describing them beyond their capabilities of performance.

#### IMPLIED WARRANTY OF FITNESS FOR A PARTICULAR PURPOSE

In addition to the doctrines of express warranty and misrepresentation, the law imposes absolute liability on sellers through the *implied warranty of fitness for a particular purpose.* Under UCC Section 2-315, if a purchaser relies upon a seller's skill and judgment to select a product to serve a particular mentioned purpose, the seller is liable if the product fails the purpose. At the basis of this doctrine is the purchaser's describing the purpose to the seller and the subsequent reliance upon the seller to select the proper product. Thus, if a contractor asks a manufacturer to furnish a digging machine which is capable of digging through a certain rocky soil, the manufacturer who supplies a digger is liable if it fails to cleave the soil. This is true even though the machine is not defective and is capable of digging in other kinds of softer soil. To avoid problems in which a piece of equipment is required for a particular purpose, however, the purchaser must make sure that the seller does not disclaim the implied warranty of fitness. The UCC permits such disclaimer.

## THE PLAINTIFF'S CASE

In most instances, a plaintiff must prove certain things to hold the defendant liable for products that injure (see Table 11-2). The plaintiff must

**TABLE 11-2** Necessary Elements of the Plaintiff's Products Liability Case

1 Defect must be in production or design
2 Defect must be in the hands of the defendant
3 Defect must have caused the harm
4 Defect must make the product unreasonably dangerous

prove these things whether the case involves negligence, strict tort liability, or the implied warranty of merchantability.

## 6.  Product Defect

Except where there is an absolute duty of performance (such as in express warranty), the plaintiff must establish that the product causing injury is defective before recovery is permitted. Since the great majority of plaintiffs in product liability suits cannot rely upon express warranties or similar legal theories, they must prove that the product contains a **defect.** Such proof is required whether the lawsuit focuses upon the unreasonableness of the defendant's conduct (negligence), the unreasonable dangerousness of a defect (strict tort liability), or the lack of fitness for ordinary use (implied warranty of merchantability). How the law identifies a defect assumes considerable significance to both plaintiff and defendant.

### DETERMINATION OF DEFECT

A number of factors enter into the determination of a defect. Probably the best way to summarize these factors is to say that a *product becomes defective when it does not meet the standard of safety society expects.* That the blade of a kitchen knife may slice a person's thumb, even in normal use, is to be expected, and the law does not regard the knife as defective for doing so. On the other hand, for the sharp blades of a self-propelled power mower to slice the foot of a user is a different matter. If such injury could have been avoided by adding a safety guard, the law may regard lack of the guard as a defect in the mower.

### PRODUCTION DEFECTS

For convenience, product defects can be divided into two categories: production defects and design defects. *Production defects* are generally easy to identify. The product does not meet the manufacturer's own internal production standards. Although the manufacturer may not be negligent simply because there is a production defect, such a defect usually allows the plaintiff to rely upon strict tort or implied warranty of merchantability theories of liability.

**DESIGN DEFECTS**

In contrast to the case of production defect, the *design defect* case does not involve a deviation from the manufacturer's own standards. Indeed, the product acts just as the manufacturer intended it should. Still, it has injured a plaintiff who sues. In such a case, might the manufacturer be liable because of the product's design? Here the expectations of the user and society become important.

One significant cause of products liability suits is the breakdown of products toward the end of their useful lives. Products, especially complex machinery, are hardly expected to last forever, yet when older products break down, causing injury, they are frequently considered "defective" by those injured. Lawsuits ensue.

The issue of whether product breakdown after long use means the product is defective is presently of primary concern to manufacturers. Obviously, if the breakdown, even after long product life, is due to a production flaw, the manufacturer is likely to be found liable for injuries which arise. Many manufacturers, however, have also been held liable in cases of breakdown for design defects. Courts and juries usually determine such cases on the basis of whether or not the breakdown has been premature. The prematurity question relates directly back to the reasonable expectations users have for products they purchase.

Manufacturers can often protect themselves in cases involving the performance life of products by issuing appropriate warnings; warnings should cover both the expected duration of product use and proper maintenance procedures. In some states, the legislatures have set *statutes of limitations* for the bringing of products liability suits which permit a suit to be filed, for example, only within six years following purchase. After six years, the manufacturer is not liable for injuries arising out of product use. Such statutes eliminate the long "tail" of many tort statutes of limitation which run, not from the time of purchase, but from the time of injury.

## 7.   Defect in the Hands of the Defendant

Just because a product user has been injured by a defect in the product does not mean that the manufacturer, or any particular party in the chain of distribution, is liable. A vital fact which the plaintiff must prove to win a products liability case is that the defect occurred or existed while in the hands of the defendant. As we previously mentioned, a defective crack in a beverage bottle may have occurred during manufacture or distribution, while being shelved, or when the injured user placed the warm bottle in the freezer to chill.

Engineering consultants and other expert witnesses can frequently provide testimony which will fix at what point the product became defective. Sometimes, however, expert witnesses for the plaintiff and for the defendant disagree and contradict one another. In such cases, the jury must decide whom to believe, bearing in mind that it is the obligation of the plaintiff to prove his or her case by the preponderance of the evidence.

### 8.   The Defect Must Have Caused the Harm

Chapter 10 discussed the requirement of proof of causation in a successful tort action. The same requirement applies in products liability cases based either on tort or in contract. To win a products liability case, the plaintiff must do more than establish merely that a defect in the product existed at the time of the accident. To win, the plaintiff must show a causal link between the defect and the harm. An inability to do so will usually defeat the claim. For instance, an automobile crash can hardly be attributed to a defective transmission when the automobile turned over after hitting a pothole in the road, even though the defect may have been present when the accident occurred.

   In more subtle cases, however, the causation issue can be extremely difficult to unravel. A dramatic example of this was the tragic crash in 1979 of a DC-10 jetliner immediately after takeoff. Authorities initially assigned responsibility for the accident to a sheared wing-mounting bolt found in the grass near the runway. Only after several days had passed did they change their minds and place the cause for the crash elsewhere. Instead of being defective, the bolt had merely broken under the great pressure put upon it by another mechanical failure.

   As among manufacturers, parts makers, and various subcontractors, it is extremely important to place causation for an accident like the DC-10 crash as precisely as possible. Tens of millions of dollars may be involved. Even experts, however, often disagree on whether a particular defect has caused a particular harm.

### 9.   Defect Must Make the Product Unreasonably Dangerous

Closely tied to the concept of product defect is that the defect must make the product *unreasonably dangerous*. This unreasonably dangerous element of the plaintiff's proof in strict liability cases merges completely with the proof of defect when a production flaw causes the injury. The defectively produced product *is* unreasonably dangerous if the defect causes injury.

   In cases which involve charges of unsafe design, however, the "unreasonably dangerous" doctrine becomes important. Since the injury-causing item contains no production defect, it will create liability for the manufacturer only if the court determines that the design is unreasonably dangerous. To this extent, strict liability and negligence liability for defectively designed products are very similar. Both theories focus on whether or not it is unreasonable for a product to be sold in the marketplace.

**WARNINGS**

Proper warnings which accompany a potentially dangerous product can go far toward reducing the possibility that a court might find the product unreasonably dangerous. Although many products, such as drugs, can be dangerous under certain conditions or to certain groups, these products are often useful and valuable to society. When accompanied by a warning, they can be used without risk of unreasonable danger. However, whether a warning is adequate is an issue usually left to the jury in a product liability suit. Consider the next case and note the appellate court's deference to the jury's decision about the warning's inadequacy.

# KARNS v. EMERSON ELECTRIC CO.
817 F.2d 1452 (10th Cir. 1987)

LOGAN, J.:...Defendant manufactured and sold a product called the "Weed Eater Model XR-90," a multipurpose weed-trimming and brush-cutting device. The XR-90 consists of a hand-held gasoline-powered engine connected to a long drive shaft at the opposite end of which various cutting tools may be attached.

The accident giving rise to this lawsuit occurred while Donald Pearce, then thirteen years old, was helping his uncle, Martin Karns, clean up an overgrown yard. Pearce was picking up trash while Karns operated an XR-90 with the circular saw blade attached. Pearce had stooped to pick up something approximately six to ten feet behind and slightly to the left of Karns when, according to Karns, the blade of the XR-90 struck something near the ground which caused the machine to swing violently around to Karns' left, cutting off Pearce's right arm above the elbow.

At trial, plaintiff argued that the XR-90's propensity to "kickback" when the blade strikes something it cannot cut, together with defendant's failure to provide adequate warnings concerning this phenomenon, rendered the XR-90 defective and unreasonably dangerous. Additionally, plaintiff argued that defendant's knowledge of the kickback phenomenon, and its failure to take steps to reduce the hazard, justified an award of punitive damages. The jury awarded plaintiff $1,000,000 compensatory damages and $1,000,000 punitive damages.

Since there is sufficient evidence to support plaintiff's version of the accident, we are easily persuaded that a device with an exposed metal sawblade capable of suddenly flinging itself through an uncontrolled, 180 degree arc poses a danger to bystanders like Pearce that exceeds the expectations of the ordinary consumer. Defendant argues that plaintiff failed to establish the feasibility of safer, alternative designs, or that the danger of the XR-90 as designed outweighs its utility. While evidence bearing upon design alternatives and the "state of the art" in the industry may be relevant to determining whether a product is unreasonably dangerous, such evidence is not an essential element of the plaintiff's case. Moreover, Block [the plaintiff's expert witness] did testify that the force of the kickback could be substantially reduced by reducing the speed or mass of the blade. Although such modifications would, no doubt, reduce the XR-90's effectiveness as a cutting tool, we cannot say, as a matter of law, that the utility of the machine as designed justifies the risk associated with its use. Although the existence of warnings might render an otherwise dangerous product not unreasonably so, here there was a basis for the jury to conclude that the warnings and instructions accompanying the XR-90 were inadequate to overcome its inherent danger. A list of twenty-four "Safety Rules and Precautions" appears on page three of the owner's manual accompanying the XR-90. Number fifteen states: "Keep children away. All people and pets should be kept at a safe distance from the work area, at least 30 feet, especially when using the blade." Page twelve, dealing with the brushcutter attachment, refers to the "bounce" phenomenon in the following terms:

**Cutting with a dull blade, feeding the blade too rapidly into a large diameter tree or trying to cut when the blade is turning too slowly will cause the blade to 'bounce' away from what is being cut. Always be prepared for this to happen. Always keep both feet spread apart in a comfortable stance and yet braced for the unit's 'bounce'.**

A manufacturer cannot defend on the basis that perfect compliance with its instructions would have prevented the accident when the warnings given are "unclear or inadequate to apprise the consumer of the inherent or latent danger." In addition, the effectiveness of a warning or instruction is likely to be somewhat diminished when, as here, the risk created by the product extends to bystanders who have no access to such warnings or instructions. We think the jury could reasonably have concluded that the warnings given were inadequate to apprise consumers of the XR-90's violent kickback potential. [*Affirmed*].

---

The *Germann* case in section 3 also emphasizes the importance of adequate product warnings.

In deciding whether or not a warning is necessary or how to word a warning, manufacturers often face two undesirable alternatives. The dramatic impact of a warning may affect product marketability. On the other hand, the failure to warn may subject the manufacturer to multimillion-dollar products liability suits. A company's legal staff, as well as its marketing division, must be consulted in weighing these alternatives.

When a manufacturer does decide to warn about product features or side effects, the statement must be worded precisely, or the manufacturer may be held liable even though a warning has been made. In one noted case, the label of a cleaning solvent cautioned users not to breathe the solvent's fumes and to make sure that the place of use was adequately ventilated. Nonetheless, a court held the manufacturer liable when several people were injured by the fumes. The court stated that the warning should have said explicitly that the fumes must be vented to the outside air. The people had been injured because the ventilating system was a closed circulation system which had recycled fumes back into the room.

In planning for product safety, manufacturers frequently seek to avoid products liability problems by ensuring that their products meet all relevant government standards and industry practices. Although courts will take such steps into their deliberations, many courts have ruled that the meeting of standards and industry practices by no means will bar the courts from determining products to be unreasonably dangerous. The likelihood of a product being called unreasonably dangerous is, of course, substantially less when the product meets relevant standards than when it does not.

## THE DEFENDANT'S CASE

### 10. Parties

In today's highly complex marketplace, seldom does a single firm or company bear complete responsibility for the manufacture, distribution, and sale of a product to the ultimate user. As a result, when someone's person or property is injured through use of a defective product, the damage will usually create potential liability for a number of parties (see Figure 11-1).

**FIGURE 11-1**
Possible Defendants in Product Liability.

1  Liable only in negligence or for express warranties.
2  Usually not liable for negligence; may seek indemnification from preceding seller; some states do not permit products liability actions against these parties if the manufacturer is solvent.
3  Liable only when the product defect is caused by the parts and materials supplied or the work performed by these parties.

The plaintiff in these cases usually sues all such parties to increase the chances of recovery against a guilty party that is financially able to pay the judgment. It becomes important, then, to know who may be a defendant in a products liability lawsuit.

### LESSORS

The principles of products liability had their beginnings in regular sales transactions. Conditions of the modern marketplace, however, have now led other groups besides those in the normal distribution chain of sale to be pulled within the controlling influence of these principles. Commercial lessors are one such group.

Using the rules of strict tort and warranties of merchantability or fitness for a particular purpose, courts in most jurisdictions presently impose strict liability on commercial lessors of defective products. In 1982, the Supreme Court of Rhode Island imposed strict liability on a commercial lessor. The court noted that such lessors "stand in a far better financial and technical position than lessees to insure against, prevent, or spread the costs of product-related injuries."

Note that in a technical sense both Section 402A of the Restatement and the warranty sections of the UCC apply only to the *sale* of products. In extending strict liability to commercial lessors, the courts have analogized to these rules rather than relied upon them in any absolute fashion. Thus, courts make new law, stretch old rules, and fill in existing legal gaps and ambiguities to meet what they see as changing needs of society.

### FRANCHISORS

One of the most significant developments in marketing during the past twenty-five years has been the growth of franchising. The franchisor grants the franchisee the right to manufacture, distribute, or sell a product using the trademark and name of the franchisor. As a result, almost inevitably, franchisors have become the target of products liability suits based on theories of strict tort and implied warranty. Although franchisors may not manufacture, handle, design, or require the use of a product, they frequently do retain the right to control or approve the design, and they may specify quality-control standards and conduct advertising for the trademark.

### SELLERS OF USED PRODUCTS

Sellers of used products are liable for negligence when they fail to use reasonable care in selling defective products that cause injury. However, it is not clear that they may be held strictly liable. Courts in some states favor strict liability for injury-causing, defective used products. Courts in other states do not. Whether or not courts apply strict tort liability or implied warranties of merchantability in used-product cases, sellers of such products will quickly be held liable if a used product does not live up to an express warranty.

## 11. Defendant's Defenses

As we mentioned previously, the defendant in products liability cases usually will not be held absolutely liable for injuries caused to the plaintiff. There are still certain burdens of proof, such as "defect," "unreasonable dangerousness," or "fault," which the plaintiff must meet to win the lawsuit. Also, the defendant can raise and prove various defenses, which will defeat a plaintiff's recovery (see Table 11-3). Some of the defenses can be raised only to defeat causes of action based on negligence. Other defenses also apply in strict liability cases.

### CONTRIBUTORY NEGLIGENCE

As it is modified by comparative fault principles, *contributory negligence* can be a defense in a products liability negligence action. Chapter 10 discusses this defense in its general tort context. Specifically, products liability defendants are concerned with whether or not they can raise this defense when the plaintiff attempts to hold them strictly liable. Some states do not recognize contributory negligence as a defense to strict tort or warranty liability. However, the trend is to allow defendants to raise comparative fault versions of the contributory negligence defense in products liability actions.

### ASSUMPTION OF RISK

Although states disagree over whether or not carelessness may bar a plaintiff's recovery in strict liability cases, most states permit defendants to claim that the plaintiff voluntarily assumed the risk of a defective product or that injury resulted from the plaintiff's misuse of the product. These defenses are available to defendants in negligence, strict tort, and warranty cases. For the defense of *assumption of risk* to succeed, the defendant must show that the plaintiff understood the nature of the risk and voluntarily and unreasonably assumed it. This defense is frequently used in industrial accident cases in which the plaintiff argues defective design (for example, lack of

**TABLE 11-3**   Defendant's Product Liability Defenses

1   Contributory negligence (comparative fault type)
2   Assumption of risk
3   State-of-the-art
4   Misuse

a safety guard on a machine) and the defendant can prove that the plaintiff knew the risk and assumed it.

### STATE-OF-THE-ART

Another defense is the so-called **state-of-the-art defense.** Product manufacturers, especially machine makers, frequently find themselves sued for injuries which occur during the use of a product which is twenty years old or more. Since the time an older product has been manufactured, the state of technological art may have progressed until it is now possible to manufacture a product considerably safer than the older product. Products liability defendants in situations involving older products raise the state-of-the-art defense usually when the plaintiff has alleged a defective design. The state-of-the-art defense requires that juries judge defendants by the technology feasible at the time the defendants manufactured the products in question.

### MISUSE

The defendant may also avoid liability by showing that the plaintiff deliberately misused the product. The *misuse* defense might apply when a plaintiff is injured while using a frying pan as a hammer or a power lawnmower as a hedge trimmer. As the *Germann* case in section 3 indicates, courts have been reluctant to bar the plaintiff's recovery when the manufacturer should have foreseen specific misuse. However, even when misuse is foreseeable, some states permit the defendant to raise it as an absolute defense.

## 12. Industrial Accidents Involving Products

When workers suffer job-related injuries, they receive workers' compensation from their employers. Chapter 15 discusses this workers' compensation law in detail. This chapter, however, stresses that workers' compensation is the only amount which an injured employee can get from an employer. Usually, it is only a small fraction of what a jury may have given an employee for the same injury.

As might be expected, injured employees often look to parties other than the employer in an attempt to escape the limitations of workers' compensation. Since many employees are injured while using industrial machinery, they turn to the manufacturers and sellers of this equipment for legal satisfaction of their injury claims. Products liability suits are the result.

Claims by injured employees against the manufacturers and sellers of industrial equipment now constitute a significant portion of total products liability costs. Work-related accidents account for almost half the amount paid to satisfy products liability claims. Furthermore, in many states the employer who has paid workers' compensation to an employee because of a product-related injury has the right to recover the entire amount from the manufacturer or seller if a products liability claim can be made. This right is the right of **subrogation.** Under the principles of subrogation, the employer stands in the place of the employee for the purposes of exercising the legal claim.

## 13.   Indemnification

As we discussed previously, a large group of defendants may be potentially liable in products liability cases. This group ranges from the retail seller all the way back to the manufacturer or even to the raw materials supplier. To establish the basis for liability, however, the plaintiff must be able to prove that the defect existed while the product was in the hands of a particular seller. Because several sellers in the chain of distribution may be liable to the plaintiff, what is their relationship to one another? If one seller pays the entire claim, can that seller seek recovery from other sellers in the distribution chain?

The law answers these questions through the principles of **indemnification.** As they are applied in products liability, these principles permit any seller who is compelled to pay the injured plaintiff to obtain full recovery from the party that sold the defective product to him or her. For instance, a retailer who is held liable can get indemnification from the manufacturer, provided that the defect can be traced back to the manufacturer and the retailer is without fault for failing to conduct a reasonable inspection of the product.

## 14.   Products Liability Trends

### THE LITIGATION EXPLOSION

In the past twenty years the number of products and service liability lawsuits has exploded. Responsibility for the present situation cannot be attributed to any single cause; many factors have led to it. Among them has been the increase in the number of suits brought due to the growing public awareness of the right to sue for injuries arising from defective products and carelessly rendered services. This awareness is likely to be related to certain changes in the law, which have made it easier for injured parties to recover, and to the resulting widespread coverage in the media of extraordinarily large recoveries received by plaintiffs in some lawsuits.

The Federal Interagency Task Force on Product Liability has also pinpointed the growth in number and complexity of products on the market as a reason for the increase in products liability suits. Uninformed use of such products frequently causes injury, which, in turn, leads to litigation. An estimated 33 million persons are injured and 28,000 killed each year by consumer products.

A major problem created by the litigation explosion is due to the litigation system itself. Litigation costs take up the largest part of every insurance dollar—nearly 40 percent. The lengthy formal proceedings required by the traditional adversarial process help create this situation. The eroding of many products liability defenses in recent years and the knowledge of the jury that most corporations carry liability insurance have also contributed to higher jury verdicts and greater overall costs in that area.

### MAGNUSON-MOSS ACT AND ATTORNEYS' FEES

One products liability trend of recent years has developed after passage of the Magnuson-Moss Act, which is discussed in detail in Chapter 20. One provision of the act allows a prevailing consumer to recover attorneys' fees and costs from a defendant in a products liability case. The case must arise from the defendant's breach of an express warranty or implied warranty or of a service contract.

This provision permits consumers to sue product sellers when otherwise they could not because of high legal costs. Remember that usually plaintiffs must pay their own attorneys' fees and costs. This means that in cases involving only a few hundred (or even a few thousand) dollars, it is hardly worthwhile for a plaintiff to file a lawsuit because of the expense involved.

Now under Magnuson-Moss, consumers are much more willing to bring certain lawsuits because they can recover attorneys' fees and costs. These lawsuits usually involve automobiles or major appliances which consumers have purchased and find unsatisfactory.

## 15. Legislative Revision of Products Liability

Traditionally, products liability law has been largely judge-made. It emerged out of common law in a case-by-case process over the last 150 years. Since the early 1950s, the pace of its development has accelerated. There has been much "judicial activism" as courts have evolved products liability law to accommodate what they believe are changing needs in society. Many commentators applaud this evolutionary process and view the judicial system as a "laboratory of ideas" where courts can develop new concepts and modify old ones in the best interests of society.

However, this case-by-case development imposes costs on manufacturers, insurers, and consumers. Manufacturers face uncertainty about products design and safety standards. Uncertainty also deters new products development. For insurance companies, it makes difficult rate-setting for products liability insurance. Ultimately, the costs arising from uncertainty are passed on to consumers.

### STATE REFORM

Responding to rapidly changing judge-made law and the uncertainty it creates, over half the states have enacted statutes revising products liability laws. From the viewpoint of the business community, however, these revisions have not produced satisfactory results. The problem is that product manufacturers and sellers often do business in many states. Even where states have revised products liability laws, their revisions have not been uniform on a state-by-state basis. Moreover, much reform has been on a piecemeal basis. Uncertainty still results, and businesses frequently find themselves forced to set marketing policies or insurance rates on a "worst case" basis, that is, on what the current law is in the strictest jurisdiction. But since the law is still evolving, even that approach cannot always be depended upon for long.

### FEDERAL REFORM

As of this writing, many trade association groups are lobbying Congress to enact a federal products liability law to help bring uniformity and certainty to this area. Some consumer groups and most attorney associations oppose federal enactment as an attempt to roll back the rights of injured parties, kill the "laboratory of ideas," and deprive the states of their traditional role in setting products liability policies.

We can identify several key areas of products liability revision that proponents and opponents of federal adoption are debating (see Table 11-4). In these areas, some state revision has already occurred and other state revision is possible if federal reform efforts fail.

## 16.  Management Planning for Products Liability

The best solution for a company's anxieties concerning products liability is not in legislative reform of existing laws. It lies in placing concern for prod-

**TABLE 11-4**  Possible Products Liability Reforms

---

1  Reduce the various products liability theories that apply against manufacturers to one theory similar to strict liability
2  Permit only negligence actions against retailers and wholesalers unless the product manufacturer is insolvent
3  Eliminate strict liability recovery for defective product design
4  Establish comparative negligence (fault) principles in all products liability actions
5  Bar products liability claims against sellers if products have been modified or altered by a user
6  Provide for the presumption of defense in product-design cases in which the product meets the "state-of-the-art," that is, the prevailing industry standards, at the time of product manufacture
7  Create a **statute of repose** which would specify a period (such as twenty-five years) following product sale after which plaintiffs would lose their rights to bring suits for product-related injuries
8  Reduce or eliminate punitive damage awards in most products liability cases
9  Reduce products liability awards by the amount of workers' compensation the product-injured employees have received
10  Create a no-fault alternative to litigation for injured product users who do not wish to sue

ucts liability prevention into every phase of manufacturing, from initial design through production and final sale (see Table 11-5). Until recently, few companies formally evaluated the dangers of products liability and then followed procedures to lessen them. A Conference Board study concluded that fewer than 30 percent of nearly 300 companies surveyed had full-time products liability managers at the corporate level. Yet, management planning is one of the most crucial components in reducing a manufacturer's products liability.

Although all departments of a company, especially marketing and engineering, should share an interest in the problems of potential products liability, management ultimately is one to deal effectively with these problems. For instance, a company's engineers may bear the responsibility for designing a product and developing standards for its parts, but management should decide whether to incorporate certain safety features into the product or rely upon warnings about possible product hazards. This evaluation and decision-making process must not be too informal. A formally constituted committee or products safety officer who reports to top management is desirable.

Many potential product defects can be eliminated prior to the time actual production builds up sales inventories. Thus, management must consider the extent to which preproduction testing is necessary. Lack of proper testing as well as faulty design contributes to the creation of defective products. Also, before production begins, management should be aware of what dangers may arise from product use and of how purchasers will be safeguarded from or warned about them.

Of course, quality control during production is central to preventing product defects, but merely setting standards is not enough. Management must make sure it constantly audits production to determine that standards are being observed. The key to products safety is supervision.

Before a product is released into the marketplace, management must carefully review all support documents related to the product. Such documents include buyer instructions, labeling, warranties, and even advertising. Legal advice is particularly important at this step. Leaving the review to the marketing department is risky, since that department may be more concerned with sales than with liability prevention.

## TABLE 11-5  Products Liability Prevention

1  Management involvement at all levels of planning and production
2  Formal product-safety policies
3  Product-safety officers or committees
4  Preproduction safety testing
5  Production quality controls and safety audits
6  Thorough legal review of product documents, such as labeling, warranties, and advertising
7  Product monitoring of actual consumer use
8  Product recall plans

People in management must realize that products liability prevention does not stop with sale of the product. Buyer experience with the product must be monitored. To this end, consumers might be provided with a toll-free number to call if they encounter problems in product use. Sales representatives should be instructed to forward complaints concerning product defects directly to the products safety committee or officer. The company should also make plans for product recall in case that becomes necessary.

Finally, from the beginning to the end of the manufacturing and sales processes, management must convey to all departments that the high quality of company products is a primary company objective. One way to convey this is through a formal statement of company policy, as the following excerpts from the Caterpillar Code of Ethics illustrates:

---

## PRODUCT QUALITY

---

A major Caterpillar objective is to design, manufacture, and market products of superior quality. We aim at a level of quality which, in particular, offers superiority for demanding applications. . . .

Products are engineered to exacting standards to meet users' expectations for performance, reliability, and life. Throughout the world, products are manufactured to the highest quality level commensurate with value. . . .

Product quality is constantly monitored. Our policy is to offer continuing product improvements in response to needs of customers and requirements of the marketplace.

---

Products liability prevention efforts should represent more than a practical business response to dealing with the cost of products liability and its effect on the profitability of the business. By satisfying society's ethical expectation that marketed products will be safe, a business can demonstrate that it also cares about human life and safety.

## SERVICE LIABILITY

### 17. Overview

Another component of the liability explosion in the business and professional communities is service liability. Providers of services frequently become defendants in lawsuits when the services they render cause personal or property injuries. Unlike defective products cases, however, strict liability does not generally reach cases that involve only the sale of services. For instance, the South Carolina Supreme Court ruled that strict liability did not apply in a case in which the defendant failed to remove a deteriorating valve stem from an automobile tire he installed. And an Illinois court held that an injured plaintiff could not sue in strict liability an installer of an elevator furnished by another company.

Most defective service cases are tried under negligence concepts of ordinary and reasonable care. But there are some instances in which courts have found defendants strictly liable when they sell a product and a service together. Plaintiffs have successfully sued under strict liability hairdressers who sell, then apply a hair product which causes injury. Such cases resemble those in the food preparation area where restauranteurs are subject to strict liability for injuries arising from the food they prepare and serve.

Lawyers, accountants, doctors, dentists, hospital administrators, realtors, engineers, and other professionals are held to special standards for defective services. Instead of the duty of the "reasonable person," providers of professional services must observe a higher duty—the duty of the "reasonable professional." Those who breach this duty are guilty of **malpractice.** The chief concept of malpractice, then, is professional negligence, although it also encompasses breach of contract (including the breach of confidential relationship) and even fraud.

Who determines the nature of the duty owed by professionals? Although standards of professional practice set or followed by professional groups are persuasive in determining this duty, the courts ultimately define its nature and extent. In several instances, courts have imposed liability even when the conduct of defendants was acceptable by professional standards.

The number of malpractice suits filed has grown rapidly in recent years. Many of the same factors discussed before are responsible for the rise in litigation in each area, principally the heightened awareness of potential plaintiffs of their rights to sue and the increased willingness of such parties to sue. Because of the lobbying pressure of various professional groups, several states have taken steps to limit the effects of excessive numbers of malpractice suits against one profession or another. Usually, these steps center upon submitting malpractice claims to arbitration rather than to the formal courtroom process. Some professional organizations have taken internal steps to understand the causes of and reduce the numbers of malpractice suits. For instance, the American Bar Association funded a multiyear project to study legal malpractice insurance claims. Other professional organizations present seminars aimed at reducing malpractice claims.

The next section considers what constitutes malpractice in one particular profession.

## 18. Malpractice and the Accounting Profession

The federal securities laws are the source of much potential liability for the accounting profession. Chapter 19 examines these laws. What follows here is a discussion of the common law liability of the accountant for malpractice.

In the conduct of their profession, accountants must exercise that degree of care and competence reasonably expected of members of their profession. Failure to exercise this care renders them liable for malpractice. As Table 11-6 shows, malpractice can cost accounting firms dearly. When they are guilty of malpractice against their clients, accountants are liable either for breach of contract or, in tort, for negligence or fraud. All such actions, however, are based on the injury-causing failure of proper professional care.

Accounting malpractice toward a client can arise, for instance, when accountants present a negligently prepared financial statement to the client, and the client relies on it and is injured. Malpractice also results during an audit when accountants fail to pursue evidence that a client's employee is defrauding the client.

A frequent issue in accounting malpractice cases involves the accountants' liability to parties other than their clients for breach of the duty of professional care. The starting point from which to consider this issue is the famous decision in *Ultramares Corp. v. Touche*. In that case, Justice Cardozo ruled that an accountant did not owe a duty to all parties that might foreseeably rely upon the accountant's negligent work. To hold otherwise would be to expose accountants "to a liability in an indeterminate amount for an indeterminate time to an indeterminate class."

In 1985 the New York Court of Appeals upheld the *Ultramares* decision. The court stated:

> Before accountants may be held liable in negligence to noncontractual parties who rely to their detriment on inaccurate financial reports, certain prerequisites must be satisfied: (1) the accountants must have been aware that the financial reports were to be used for a particular purpose or purposes; (2) in the furtherance of which a known party or parties was intended to rely; and (3) there must have been some conduct on the part of the accountants linking them to that party or parties, which evinces the accountant's understanding of that party or parties' reliance.

**TABLE 11-6**   Out-of-Court Malpractice Settlements By "Big Eight" Accounting Firms, 1980–1985

| Firm | Settlement Total |
|------|-----------------|
| Arthur Andersen | $137,089,359 |
| Peat Marwick Mitchell | 19,400,000 |
| Ernst & Whinney | 6,020,500 |
| Deloitte Haskins & Sells | 4,997,585 |
| Coopers & Lybrand | 4,375,850 |
| Price Waterhouse | 3,500,000 |
| Touche Ross | 2,250,000 |
| Arthur Young | 1,490,000 |

Courts in Arkansas, Indiana, Illinois, Iowa, and South Dakota in addition to New York, have recently applied the *Ultramares* approach to accountants' liability to parties other than their clients. This approach essentially requires a type of privity between the accountant and third parties before liability can be imposed.

Another approach to accountants' legal liability to third parties has been followed by courts in California, New Jersey, and Wisconsin. These courts have imposed malpractice liability on accountants under general negligence standards. Accountants arc held liable for all "foreseeable injuries," including injuries to third parties who may reasonably rely on audits prepared for accountants' clients.

Perhaps a majority of states follow a still different approach to accountants' liability. This approach is illustrated by the following case of the North Carolina Supreme Court:

# SIDBEC-DOSCO, INC. v. CHERRY, BEKAERT & HOLLAND
367 S.E.2d 609 (N.C. 1988)

The plaintiff, who was a creditor of Intercontinental Metals Corp. (IMC), alleged that it gave considerable credit to IMC based on incorrect information contained in an audit report prepared for IMC by the defendant accounting firm. When IMC failed to repay plaintiff, plaintiff sued defendant claiming damages arising from its reliance upon the incorrect audit report. The trial court dismissed plaintiff's complaint, but the court of appeals reversed. Then the North Carolina Supreme Court granted certiorari. The case excerpt begins with the consideration of the various standards under which the defendant might be held liable to third parties such as the plaintiff.

EXUM, J.:...We reject the *Ultramares* "privity or near-privity" approach...because it provides inadequately for the central role independent accountants play in the financial world. Accountants' audit opinions are increasingly relied upon by the investing and lending public in making financial decisions. The accounting profession itself has recognized as much. The Financial Accounting Standards Boards has stated that

**[m]any people base economic decisions on their relationships to and knowledge about business enterprises and thus are potentially interested in the information provided by financial reporting. Among users are owners, lenders, suppliers, potential investors and creditors, employees, management, directors, customers, financial analysts and advisors...and the public.**

Because of this heavy public reliance on audited financial information we believe an approach that protects those persons, or classes of persons, whom an accountant knows will rely on his audit opinion, but who may not otherwise be in "privity or near privity," with him is desirable.

Although the *Ultramares* approach to accountants' liability seems unduly restrictive, we also decline to adopt the "reasonably foreseeable" test because it would result in liability more expansive than an accountant should be expected to bear. Courts which extend an accountant's liability to all reasonably foreseen users of his financial information do so on the ground that there is no good reason to exempt accountants from the general rule that a negligent actor is liable for all reasonably foreseeable consequences of his negligence.

Manufacturers, and to a lesser extent designers, can limit their potential liability by controlling the number of products they release into the marketplace. Auditors, on the other hand, have no control over their exposure to liability. Moreover, as noted previously, auditors do not control their client's accounting records and processes. While, in the final analysis, an auditor renders an opinion concerning the accuracy of his client's records, he necessarily relies, in some measure, on the client for the records' contents. Because of the accountant's inability to control the distribution of his report, as well as his lack of control over some of the contents of the statements he assesses, a standard which limits his potential liability is appropriate.

A more fundamental difference between product designers and manufacturers and accountants lies in their differing expectations concerning their work product. Manufacturers and designers fully expect that their products will be used by a wide variety of unknown members of the public. Indeed, this is their hope, for with wider use will come increased profits. This is not the case when an accountant prepares an audit. An accountant performs an audit pursuant to a contract with an individual client. The client may or may not intend to use the report for other than internal purposes. It does not benefit the accountant if his client distributes the audit opinion to others. Instead, it merely exposes his work to many whom he

may have had no idea would scrutinize his efforts. We believe that in fairness accountants should not be liable in circumstances where they are unaware of the use to which their opinions will be put. Instead, their liability should be commensurate with those persons or classes of persons whom they know will rely on their work. With such knowledge the auditor can, through purchase of liability insurance, setting fees, and adopting other protective measures appropriate to the risk, prepare accordingly.

We conclude that the standard set forth in the Restatement (Second) of Torts § 552 (1977) represents the soundest approach to accountants' liability for negligent misrepresentation. It constitutes a middle ground between the restrictive *Ultramares* approach advocated by defendants and the expansive "reasonably foreseeable" approach advanced by plaintiffs. It recognizes that liability should extend not only to those with whom the accountant is in privity or near privity, but also to those persons, or classes of persons, whom he knows and intends will rely on his opinion, or whom he knows his client intends will so rely. On the other hand, as the commentary makes clear, it prevents extension of liability in situations where the accountant "merely knows of the everpresent possibility of repetition to anyone, and the possibility of action in reliance upon [the audited financial statements], on the part of anyone to whom it may be repeated." As such it balances, more so than the other standards, the need to hold accountants to a standard that accounts for their contemporary role in the financial world with the need to protect them from liability that unreasonably exceeds the bounds of their real undertaking....

Applying the Restatement test to Sidbec-Dosco's complaint, we conclude Sidbec-Dosco has stated a legally sufficient claim against defendants for negligent misrepresentation. Sidbec-Dosco alleges that when defendants prepared the audited financial statements for IMC they knew: (1) the statements would be used by IMC to represent its financial condition to creditors who would extend credit on the basis of them; and (2) plaintiff and other creditors would rely upon these statements. These allegations are sufficient to impose upon defendants a duty of care to Sidbec-Dosco under the Restatement approach as we have interpreted and adopted it herein. [*Affirmed.*]

---

If they have been hesitant to expose accountants to the possibility of third-party liability for negligence, many courts have been willing to allow *any* injured third party, foreseen or not, to sue accountants who are party to a *fraud*. Moreover, some courts do not require a showing of *intentional* misrepresentation before assessing fraud liability. They hold that gross negligence or even "blindness to the obvious" may provide sufficient evidence upon which to sustain a finding of fraud. This blurring of the distinction between professional negligence and fraud in accounting malpractice cases has helped further extend accountant malpractice liability to third parties.

Frauds can involve not only misrepresentation of facts but also, under certain circumstances, the failure to disclose facts. In one instance, an accounting firm was held liable in fraud for failing to disclose newly learned information which changed the implications of a previously released financial statement. Highly controversial at present is whether accounting firms must disclose the problems of one client to another client who does business with the first client.

## REVIEW QUESTIONS

**1** For each term in the left-hand column, match the most appropriate description in the right-hand column:

| | |
|---|---|
| (1) Caveat emptor | (a) Professional negligence |
| (2) Production defect | (b) A contractual connection |
| (3) Merchant | (c) Let the buyer beware |
| (4) Implied warranty of merchantability | (d) Legislation establishing a legal date after which no lawsuit may be begun |
| (5) Indemnification | (e) A difference between the way a manufacturer intended a product to be and the way it actually is |
| (6) Malpractice | (f) One who ordinarily sells goods in the course of business |

(7) Privity

(8) State-of-the-art defense

(9) Subrogation

(10) Statute of repose

(g) An insurer's right to be put into the legal position of an insured to whom it has paid benefits

(h) The right to recover from someone based on payment of that person's legal obligation

(i) Requires that juries judge products by the technology feasible at the time of manufacture

(j) The guarantee that a product is fit for ordinary use

**2** Products liability law has gone from caveat emptor to caveat venditor. Discuss the legal developments that have made this statement true.

**3** Why is negligence a more difficult standard than strict liability for plaintiffs to prove?

**4** Acme Tiller Company sells a tiller to Whole Earth Wholesalers, which resells the tiller to Ralph's Retail. Ralph's Retail sells the tiller to Mr. Smith. While using the tiller, Mr. Smith's assistant is injured when a defective blade bolt breaks. Discuss the potential liability of the various sellers to the assistant.

**5** Assume that when the defective blade bolt in question 4 breaks, the tiller blade flies through the window of a passing car, injuring its driver, Ms. Jones. The car then runs off the road and hits Billy Bystander. Under these facts, who will be liable to whom and under what legal theories?

**6** To what extent does the law allow a seller to disclaim an implied warranty of merchantability?

**7** A manufacturer describes its personal computer as "the best in the world." Does this description amount to an express warranty? Explain why or why not.

**8** While driving under the influence of alcohol, Joe College runs off the road and wrecks his car. As the car turns over, the protruding door latch hits the ground and the door flies open. Joe, who is not wearing his seat belt, is thrown from the car and badly hurt. Joe sues the car manufacturer, asserting that the door latch was defectively designed. Discuss the legal issues raised by these facts.

**9** An injured worker sues the Darrell Brothers Forklift Company, alleging that she was injured because the forklift she was driving lacked certain safety features. Is the plaintiff alleging a production defect or a design defect? Explain the difference between these two types of defects.

**10** While using a skinning knife, a hunter accidentally slices his leg and severs a nerve. He sues the manufacturer of the knife, alleging that the blade was defective because it was too sharp. Discuss whether or not the court is likely to hold the manufacturer liable.

**11** A new car purchaser has returned her car twelve times to the dealer for warranty work on the drive train. Still, the car does not drive properly. The purchaser wants the dealer to replace the car or grant her rescission of the purchase contract. Explain how federal law has made it more likely that the purchaser will sue the dealer under these circumstances.

**12** Your company is being sued by an injured plaintiff who alleges that the company's widget is defectively designed. Your company is able to prove that the widget meets all current government standards for widgets. The widget is also as well-designed as any other company's widget. Will your company likely win the lawsuit? Discuss.

**13** Does strict liability apply to the selling of services? Explain.

**14** What steps have been taken in recent years to help control the effects of rising numbers of malpractice suits?

**15** As president of the City National Bank, you are notified that a major borrower has defaulted on repayment of a $5 million loan and is declaring bankruptcy. Investigation uncovers that the borrower's certified financial statement, upon which City National relied in extending the loan, contains a major misstatement as to both assets and liabilities of the borrower. You now consider the possibility of a lawsuit against the accounting firm which certified the financial statement. Discuss the theories upon which such a suit might be based, and indicate what proof is needed to support each theory.

# *Part Four*
# CONDUCTING BUSINESS

# Chapter

# *12*

# Selecting the Form of Business Organization

## CHAPTER PREVIEW

As we continue to focus on the law and business portion of the legal environment of business, it is appropriate that we examine some of the fundamental legal aspects of business organizations. These aspects fall into two categories: (1) legal issues relating to setting up various forms of business organizations, and (2) issues of liability. The liability of the business organization and its owners will be discussed in the next chapter. In this chapter we will discuss the types of business organizations, their operational advantages and disadvantages, and the factors to consider when selecting one of these organizational forms.

## 1. Introduction

The question of selecting the best-suited organization for a business's purpose is of vital importance when a business is being started or when it encounters a substantial change, such as rapid growth. Therefore, the factors used to select a form or organization need to be reviewed periodically. This review should be in consultation with close advisers such as attorneys, accountants, and bankers. These people weigh the factors and costs involved and then select the organizational form deemed most suitable to the business's needs at that time. Because this selection process balances advantages against disadvantages, the decision often is to choose the least objectionable form of organization.

Prior to examining this chapter in depth, you should understand that the discussion throughout this chapter is based on the presumption that the business being analyzed is closely held. In other words, a limited number of owners of the business are involved in this selection decision. When a business is publicly held by an unlimited number of owners, the form of organization almost always is a corporation. The reason for this corporate form being utilized is that shareholders can transfer their ownership interests without interfering with the organization's management.

After having completed your study of this chapter, you should be familiar with the meaning and application of the following terms: corporation, derivative action suit, dissolution, general partnership, incorporators, joint and several liability, limited partnership, sole proprietorship, Subchapter S corporation.

## 2.  Alternatives of Organizational Forms

Business is conducted under a variety of legal forms. The three basic forms are sole proprietorships, partnerships, and corporations. Many hybrid forms take on the form of both a partnership and a corporation. These forms include the limited partnership, the professional corporation, and the Subchapter S corporation.

As the name implies, a **sole proprietorship** is a business owned by only one person. The business's property belongs to the proprietor, and any income or losses are added to or deducted from that individual's personal income for tax purposes. Any debts incurred by the organization actually are obligations of the proprietor. Because of its inherent limitation to one owner, a sole proprietorship cannot be a possible choice when more than one person wants to co-own a business.

In general, a **partnership** is created by an agreement between two or more persons to operate a business and to share profit and losses. A **corporation** is an artificial, intangible person or being which is created under the authority of a state's law. When a partnership allows some of the partners to be treated like corporate shareholders for liability purposes, these partners are said to have limited liability. They are limited partners in a **limited partnership.** The law also allows shareholders of a corporation to elect to have their organization taxed like a partnership. Such an election creates a **Subchapter S corporation.**

When considering which of these organizational alternatives is best suited for your new or changing business, the following factors must be studied: (1) advantages and disadvantages of each organizational form, (2) legal capacity of each organization, (3) creation, (4) continuity, (5) control, (6) liability, and (7) taxation. The relative importance of each of these independent factors will vary greatly depending on the size of the business. The determination of which organization is best is a weighing or balancing process that should be discussed with competent advisers.

## GENERAL FACTORS

### 3.   Advantages and Disadvantages of Partnerships

The basic law relating to partnerships is found in the Uniform Partnership Act, which has been adopted by every state except Louisiana. According to this statute, the partnership form of organization generally has the following advantages:

1   A partnership is easily formed because it is based on a contract among persons.

2   Costs of formation are not significant.

3   Partnerships are not a tax-paying entity.

4   Each partner has an equal voice in management, unless there is a contrary agreement.

5   A partnership may operate in more than one state without obtaining a license to do business.

6   Partnerships generally are subject to less regulation and less governmental supervision than are corporations.

Offsetting these advantages, the following aspects of partnerships have been called disadvantages:

1   For practical reasons, only a limited number of people can be partners.

2   A partnership is dissolved any time a partner ceases to be a partner, regardless of whether the reason is withdrawal or death.

3   Each partner's personal liability is unlimited, contrasted with the limited liability of a corporate shareholder.

4   Partners are taxed on their share of the partnership's profits, whether the profits are distributed or not. In other words, partners often are required to pay income tax on money they do not receive.

**5** In a limited partnership, the limited partners are not entitled to participate in management.

## 4. Advantages and Disadvantages of Corporations

The usual advantages of the corporate form of organization include the following:

**1** This form is the best practical means of bringing together a large number of investors.

**2** Control can be vested in those with a minority of the investment.

**3** Ownership may be divided into many unequal shares.

**4** Shareholders' liabilities are limited to their investments.

**5** This organization can have perpetual existence.

**6** In addition to being owners, shareholders may be employees entitled to benefits such as workers' compensation.

Among the frequently cited disadvantages of the corporate organization are the following:

**1** The cost of forming and maintaining a corporation, with its formal procedural requirements, is significant.

**2** License fees and franchise taxes often are assessed against corporations but not partnerships.

**3** Corporate income may be subject to double taxation.

**4** A corporation must be qualified in all states where it is conducting local or intrastate business.

**5** Generally, corporations are subject to more governmental regulation at all levels than are other forms of business.

**6** A corporation, as a legal entity, is required to be represented by an attorney in any litigation.

The case that follows provides the reasoning behind the requirement that corporations must be represented by an attorney-at-law in litigation.

# LAND MANAGEMENT v. DEPARTMENT OF ENVIR. PROTEC.

368 A.2d 602 (Me. 1977)

ARCHIBALD, J.:...The sole issue raised by this appeal is whether the presiding Justice acted properly in dismissing the plaintiff's complaint on the ground that the plaintiff was a corporation not represented by a duly admitted attorney. We conclude that the Justice below correctly dismissed the complaint, and we therefore deny the plaintiff's appeal.

The plaintiff, Land Management, Inc., is a corporation doing business in the State of Maine. On April 9, 1976, it commenced an action in the Superior Court seeking declaratory and injunctive relief against the defendants. Throughout the proceedings in the Superior Court the plaintiff was represented by its president who, admittedly, is not an attorney admitted to practice law in Maine.

All of the defendants filed motions to dismiss the plaintiff's complaint....[These were granted] solely on the basis

**that the Plaintiff Land Management, Inc. is not entitled to proceed in this action *pro se* by and through a person who is not an attorney licensed to practice law.**

In support of its position that a corporation may represent itself in Maine courts through a corporate officer who is not a duly admitted attorney, the plaintiff relies upon language found in 4 M.R.S.A. §§ 807 and 811.

4 M.R.S.A. § 807 provides:

**Unless duly admitted to the bar of this State, no person shall practice law or any branch thereof, or hold himself out to practice law or any branch thereof, within the State or before any court therein, or demand or receive any remuneration for such services rendered in this State. Whoever, not being duly admitted to the bar of this State, shall practice law or any branch thereof, or hold himself out to practice law or any branch thereof, within the State or before any court therein, or demand or receive any remuneration for such services rendered in this State, shall be punished by a fine of not more than $500 or by imprisonment for not more than three months, or by both. This section shall not be construed to apply to practice before any Federal Court by any person duly admitted to practice therein nor to a person pleading or managing his own cause in court....**

4 M.R.S.A. § 811 defines a "person" as "any individual, corporation, partnership or association."

On the basis of these statutory provisions, the plaintiff contends that since a corporation can only act through its agents, it may authorize a non-attorney to represent it in court. We do not agree with the plaintiff's assertion that the Legislature, in enacting §§ 807 and 811, intended to permit a corporation to be represented before the courts of this State by a person who is not authorized to practice law. To accept plaintiff's argument would require us to hold that a corporation may authorize a non-attorney to represent it in court, while an individual may not. We do not believe that the Legislature intended such an illogical result. The purpose of § 811 for including a corporation within the definition of the word "person" was to make it clear that a corporation, as well as anyone else, is prohibited from engaging in the unauthorized practice of law. This section modified the § 807 prohibition against unauthorized practice rather than expanding the right of individuals to represent themselves in either the Federal or State courts.

The rule that a corporation may appear in court only through a licensed attorney was stated succinctly in *Paradise v. Nowlin*, 86 Cal. App.2d 897, 195 P.2d 867 (1948):

**A natural person may represent himself and present his own case to the court although he is not a licensed attorney. A corporation is not a natural person. It is an artificial entity created by law and as such it can neither practice law nor appear or act in person. Out of court it must act in its affairs through its agents and representatives and in matters in court it can act only through licensed attorneys. A corporation cannot appear in court by an officer who is not an attorney and it cannot appear in *propria persona*.**

Sound public policy reasons also require such a rule. As stated by the Ohio Supreme Court:

**To allow a corporation to maintain litigation and appear in court represented by corporate officers or agents only would lay open the gates to the practice of law for entry to those corporate officers or agents who have not been qualified to practice law and who are not amenable to the general discipline of the court.**

There is abundant authority, both state and federal, rejecting the argument, as advanced by the plaintiff, that a corporation has the right to appear in court without the aid of a licensed attorney.

Since the plaintiff was not represented by counsel licensed to practice law, its complaint was a nullity and was properly dismissed by the presiding Justice. [*Appeal denied.*]

## 5. Legal Capacity

*Legal capacity* refers to the capacity of the organization to sue and be sued in its own name. It also refers to the organization's power to own and dispose of property as well as to enter into contracts in its own name. When an organization lacks this legal capacity, it must act through its owners as representatives of the organization rather than as a legal entity itself.

In early law, a corporation was considered a legal entity, but a partnership was not. Being a legal entity usually meant that capacity was present to sue and be sued and to hold title to and convey real and personal property in the name of the business instead of the names of the individual owners. Modern statutes on procedure allow suits by and against a partnership in the firm name. They also allow a partnership to own and dispose of real estate and personal property in the firm name. To this extent, a partnership is treated as a legal entity. Because of this modern view of partnerships, the importance of considering this factor has diminished.

## GOING INTO BUSINESS

### 6. Creating Partnerships

A partnership, which is an association of two or more persons who co-own a business for profit, is created by an agreement of the parties who are to be the owners and managers. This agreement, usually known as "Articles of Copartnership," creates the partnership (sometimes called a general partnership) between the partners. A partnership may also arise by implication from the conduct of the parties. Conduct may create a partnership even though the parties do not call themselves partners or understand the consequences of their conduct.

# LUPIEN v. MALSBENDEN
477 A.2d 746 (Me. 1984)

Plaintiff, Lupien, contracted with Cragin, who did business as York Motor Mart, for the construction of a Bradley automobile from a kit. Plaintiff paid down $4,450 of the $8,020 price. He periodically visited York Motor Mart to check on his car. Plaintiff generally dealt with the defendant Malsbenden, because Cragin was seldom present. On one occasion, Malsbenden told plaintiff to sign over ownership of his pickup truck so that the proceeds from its sale could be applied to the purchase price of the car. Malsbenden had provided plaintiff with a rental car and later with a "demo" model of the Bradley. When the plaintiff did not receive the Bradley, he sued Malsbenden for a refund of the purchase price.

Malsbenden asserts that his interest in York Motor Mart was only that of a banker. He had lent $85,000 to Cragin, without interest, to finance the Bradley portion of York Motor Mart's business. The loan was to be repaid from the proceeds of each car sold. Malsbenden testified that Bradley kits were purchased with his personal checks and admitted that he had also purchased equipment for York Motor Mart. After Cragin disappeared, the defendant had physical control of the premises of York Motor Mart. The trial court held that Malsbenden was liable as a partner.

McKUSICK, J.:...The Uniform Partnership Act defines a partnership as "an association of 2 or more persons...to carry on as co-owners a business for profit."...Whether a partnership exists is an inference of law based on established facts....A finding that the relationship between two persons constitutes a partnership may be based upon evidence of an agreement, either express or implied,

**to place their money, effects, labor, and skill, or some or all of them, in lawful commerce or business with the understanding that a community of profits will be shared....No one factor is alone determinative of the existence of a partnership....**

If the arrangement between the parties otherwise qualifies as a partnership, it is of no matter that the parties did not expressly agree to form a partnership or did not even intend to form one:

**It is possible for parties to intend no partnership and yet to form one. If they agree upon an arrangement which is a partnership in fact, it is of no importance that they call it something else, or that they even expressly declare that they are not to be partners. The law must declare what is the legal import of their agreements, and names go for nothing when the substance of the arrangement shows them to be inapplicable....**

Here the trial justice concluded that, notwithstanding Malsbenden's assertion that he was only a "banker," his "total involvement" in the Bradley operation was that of a partner. The testimony at trial, both respecting Malsbenden's financial interest in the enterprise and his involvement in day-to-day business operations, amply supported the Superior Court's conclusion. Malsbenden had a financial interest of $85,000 in the Bradley portion of York Motor Mart's operations. Although Malsbenden termed the investment a loan, significantly he conceded that the "loan" carried no interest. His "loan" was not made in the form of a fixed payment or payments, but was made to the business, at least in substantial part, in the form of day-to-day purchases of Bradley kits, other parts and equipment, and in the payment of wages. Furthermore, the "loan" was not to be repaid in fixed amounts or at fixed times, but rather only upon the sale of Bradley automobiles.

The evidence also showed that, unlike a banker, Malsbenden had the right to participate in control of the business and in fact did so on a day-to-day basis. According to

Urbin Savaria, who worked at York Motor Mart from late April through June 1980, Malsbenden during that time opened the business establishment each morning, remained present through part of every day, had final say on the ordering of parts, paid for parts and equipment, and paid Savaria's salary. On plaintiff's frequent visits to York Motor Mart, he generally dealt with Malsbenden because Cragin was not present. It was Malsbenden who insisted that plaintiff trade in his truck prior to the completion of the Bradley because the proceeds from the sale of the truck were needed to complete the Bradley. When it was discovered that the "demo" Bradley given to plaintiff while he awaited completion of his car actually belonged to a third party, it was Malsbenden who bought the car for plaintiff's use. As of three years after the making of the contract now in litigation, Malsbenden was still doing business at York Motor Mart, "just disposing of property."

Malsbenden and Cragin may well have viewed their relationship to be that of creditor-borrower, rather than a partnership. At trial Malsbenden so asserts, and Cragin's departure from the scene in the spring of 1980 deprives us of the benefit of his view of his business arrangement with Malsbenden. In any event, whatever the intent of these two men as to their respective involvements in the business of making and selling Bradley cars, there is no clear error in the Superior Court's finding that the Bradley car operation represented a pooling of Malsbenden's capital and Cragin automotive skills, with joint control over the business and intent to share the fruits of the enterprise. As a matter of law, that arrangement amounted to a partnership....[*Judgment affirmed.*]

The sharing of the net profits of a business enterprise by two persons gives rise to a presumption that a partnership exists between them, except when the share of profits is received by one of them for a special reason such as wages of an employee, as rent to a landlord, or as interest on a loan. A partnership may be considered to be between the partners and third persons when a person by his or her conduct leads third persons to believe a partnership exists and the third person acts in reliance on this conduct (partnership by estoppel). This is true even though there is in fact no partnership between the alleged partners.

A partnership is easily formed, since all that is required is an agreement between partners. The cost of formation is minimal, and the business need not qualify to do business in foreign states. One problem which frequently is a major concern in the creation of a business entity is the name to be used. Since a partnership is created by an agreement, the parties select the name. This right of selection is subject to two limitations in many states. First, a partnership may not use any word in the name, such as "company," that would imply the existence of a corporation. Second, if the name is other than that of the partners, they must give notice as to the actual identity of the partners. Failure to comply with a state's assumed-name statutes may result in the partnership's being denied access to courts, or it may result in criminal actions being brought against those operating under the assumed name.

## 7. Creating Corporations

A corporation is created by a state issuing a charter upon the application of individuals known as *incorporators*. In comparison with partnerships, corporations are more costly to form. Among the costs of incorporation are filing fees, license fees, franchise taxes, attorneys' fees, and the cost of supplies, such as minute books, corporate seals, and stock certificates. In addition to these costs of creation, there also are annual costs in continuing a corporation's operation. These recurring expenses include annual reporting fees and taxes, the cost of annual shareholders' meeting, and ongoing legal-related expenses.

The application for corporate charter, which is called the "Articles of Incorporation," must contain the proposed name of the corporation. So that persons dealing with a business will know that it is a corporation, the law requires that the corporate name include one of the following words or end with an abbreviation of them: "corporation," "company," "incorporated," or "limited." In addition, a corporate name must not be the same as, or deceptively similar to, the name of any domestic corporation or that of a foreign corporation authorized to do business in the state to which the application is made. Courts of equity may enjoin the use of deceptively similar names, and charters will be refused if the state believes that the names are deceptively similar. The corporate name is an asset and a part of goodwill. As such, it is legally protected.

In addition to the proposed corporate name, the Articles of Incorporation usually will include the proposed corporation's period of duration, the purpose for which it is formed, the number of authorized shares, and information about the initial corporate officials. Typically, a corporation will apply for a perpetual duration; however, a corporation can legally be created for a stated number of years. The corporate purpose stated in the Articles of Incorporation usually is very broad. For example, it would be better to say that a corporation is in the business of selling goods, rather than to limit this activity to either the retail or wholesale level. Stating the purpose very specifically may prohibit a growing corporation from expanding into related areas of operations.

With respect to authorized shares of stock, these Articles of Incorporation must indicate the class and value of stock and the number of shares of each class that will be sold. For example, incorporators may request that the state authorize 250,000 shares of $5 par value common stock of which 100,000 shares will be sold during the first year of operation. A corporation must pay taxes on the shares actually sold rather than on the shares authorized. If additional stock is sold after these initial 100,000 shares, the corporation must file a report and pay the extra taxes or fees.

Finally, the Articles of Incorporation must indicate the names and addresses of the initial board of directors. In other words, these directors are appointed by the incorporators until such time as the shareholders can elect a board. Also appointed and specifically named in the application is the person serving as the corporation's agent to whom legal papers, such as complaints in lawsuits, may be served. Usually, the names and addresses of those persons acting as incorporators also must be included in the Articles of Incorporation.

Once drafted, these papers are sent to the appropriate state official (usually the secretary of state) who approves them and issues a corporate charter. Notice of this incorporation usually has to be advertised in the local newspaper in order to inform the public that a new corporation has been created. The initial board of directors then meets, adopts the corporate bylaws, and approves the sale of stock. At this point, the corporation becomes operational. Sections 11 and 12 discuss issues relating to operating a corporation.

If a corporation wishes to conduct business in states other than the state of incorporation, that corporation must be licensed in these foreign states. The process of qualification usually requires payment of license fees and franchise taxes above and beyond those paid during the initial incorporation process. If a corporation fails to qualify in states where it is conducting business, the corporation may be denied access to the courts as a means of enforcing its contracts.


## 8.   Creating Limited Partnerships

A limited partnership is a hybrid between a general partnership and a corporation. This special organization has at least one general partner with unlimited liability and one or more limited partners who are comparable to shareholders of a corporation. The general partners manage the daily operations of the organization, and they are personally liable for the business' debts. The limited partners also contribute capital and share in the profits or losses, but they are not allowed to control the organization's operations. In return for foregoing this control, these limited partners incur no personal liability beyond their capital contribution with respect to the partnership's debts. It is from this limited liability of the limited partners that the organization gets its name.

Like a general partnership, a limited partnership is created by agreement. However, as in the case of a corporation, state law requires that the contents of a certificate must be recorded in a public office so that everyone may be fully advised as to the details of the organization. This certificate contains, among other matters, the following information: the name of the partnership, the character of the business, its location, the name and place of residence of each member, those who are to be the general partners and those who are to be the limited partners, the length of time the partnership is to exist, the amount of cash or the agreed value of property to be contributed by each partner, and the share of profit or compensation each limited partner shall receive.

The limited-partnership certificate is required to be recorded in the county where the partnership has its principal place of business. An additional copy has to be filed in every community where the partnership conducts business or has an office. Whenever there is a change in the information contained in the filed certificate, a new certificate must be prepared and recorded. If an accurate certificate is not on record and if the limited partnership continues its operation, the limited partners become liable as general partners. Substantial compliance with all the technical requirements of the limited-partnership law is essential if the limited partners are to be assured of their limited liability.

The terms of the limited-partnership agreement control the governance of the organization. These terms should be read carefully and understood by all general and limited partners before the agreement is signed. The following case involves the kind of issues that may arise about the interpretation of a limited-partnership agreement. Obviously the outcome of this interpretative process is vitally important to the investing limited partners.

# REILLY v. RANDERS MANAGEMENT, INC.
717 S.W.2d 422 (Tex. App. 1986)

FENDER, J.:….RMI has been the managing general partner of TRL since May 29, 1974, when TRL was first formed….

On April 29, 1980, the First Amended Limited Partnership Agreement…was adopted….

At a meeting of the partners of TRL held on March 13, 1984, RMI and CCK, the general partners, proposed to amend the First Agreement. The amendments are contained in the Second Amended Limited Partnership Agreement….The amendments are:

**1** to change the value for which newly issued units of TRL could be issued from at least $50,000.00 to at least their fair market value determined by the managing general partner of TRL on an annual basis; [and]

**2** to change the number of authorized units of TRL from 300 to an unlimited number….

At the time the Second Agreement was proposed for adoption on March 13, 1984, there were two general partners, CCK and RMI, and 17 limited partners, including appellant. The general partners owned 83.78% of the outstanding units of TRL. Appellant owns .69% of TRL. A vote was taken on the amendments and the two general partners and five limited partners voted in favor of the amendments. Eleven limited partners, including appellant, did not vote. One limited partner voted against the amendments.

The central issue in this case is whether the written consent of only 66⅔ percent of the outstanding units of TRL was required to adopt the amendments, rather than the consent of the owners of all the outstanding units of TRL. Appellant contends…that the trial court erred in granting summary judgment because as a matter of law unanimous consent was needed to adopt the amendments….Article XV of the First Agreement concerns when unanimous consent is necessary to pass an amendment. Article XV provides in relevant part:

**C. *Unanimous Consent of Limited Partners.* Subject to the provisions of ARTICLE XIV hereof, any amendment to this Agreement which would adversely affect the general liabilities of the Limited Partners, or change the method of allocation of the profits or losses or the distribution of the Partnership funds or assets shall require the consent in writing of all Limited Partners.**

**D. Two-Thirds Consent of Partners. Subject to the provisions of ARTICLE XII and XIV hereof, any other amendment to this Agreement shall require the approval in writing of Partnership Percentages aggregating sixty-six and two-thirds percent (66⅔).**

Appellant contends that unanimous consent is required under art. XV(C) to adopt the amendments because the amendments:

**1** would adversely affect the general liabilities of the limited partners; [or]

**2** would change the method of allocation of profits or losses;…

Appellees contended…that only 66⅔% vote is needed to approve and pass the new amendments.

Appellant contends that the new amendments, which allow more than 300 limited partnership units to be issued for less than $50,000.00, change the general liabilities of the limited partners and, therefore, require unanimous consent.

...The First Agreement states in subdivision E concerning the "Liability of Limited Partners" that "the Limited Partners shall have no personal liability with respect to any liabilities or obligations of the Partnership." This is in accordance with the Texas Uniform Limited Partnership Act which states in § 2 that the limited partners shall not be bound by the obligations of the partnership. A limited partner is one whose liability is limited to the amount of his or her contribution. General partners are the ones who conduct the business of the partnership and who are personally liable to creditors as in an ordinary partnership.

An amendment which would adversely affect the *general liability* of the limited partners is one that would make a limited partner liable beyond the amount of his contribution to the partnership. It is not, as appellant suggests, one which would create an unlimited right of forced capital contribution, or create a "liability" to a partnership. If the drafters had meant the word "general liability" to include capital contributions, the word "capital contributions" would have been used. The amendments do not adversely affect the general liabilities of the limited partners.

Appellant next contends that the amendments "change the method of allocation of profits and losses." Article VIII(A) states how partnership profits and losses are to be allocated and how distributions are to be made. Subdivision A, concerning allocation of profits and losses, is as follows:

**A.** *Allocation of Profits and Losses.* **The profits and losses of the Partnership as well as each Partner's separate distributive share of all taxable income, gains, losses, deductions and cred-** its of the Partnership shall be allocated to the Partners as follows:

**(1) To the Managing General Partner that portion equal to an amount which is the result of multiplying the percent of Units owned by such Managing General Partner in the Partnership times one hundred fifty percent (150%) or its percentage of the total Units in the Partnership plus 7.5% of total profits and losses, whichever is less.**

**(2) To the Limited Partners and General Partners other than the Managing General Partner, the remaining share, after subtracting that allocated to the Managing General Partner, in proportion to each such Partner's Units to total Units owned by such Partners.**

Although the wording of art. VIII of the first amended agreement was not changed, appellant contends that the method of allocation of profits and losses has been changed because the "definition" of the word "unit" as defined in art. VI(J) has been changed so that an unlimited number of units can be issued at a price to be determined by the managing general partner, whereas before the amendments, only 300 units could be issued and in no event would a unit be issued for less than $50,000.00. Appellant contends that because the profits and losses are to be allocated "in proportion to each such Partner's Units to total Units owned by such partners," then the very basis of the method of allocation is changed.

Appellant is correct in recognizing that a certain number of dollars in profits distributed by the method indicated in art. VIII(A) to, for instance, 1000 partners, is going to result in each of the partners getting a lesser amount than, for instance, if these profits were distributed to only ten partners. In other words, the more partners there are, the lesser amount each is going to get of the profits. However, when the number of partners is increased, this is not a change in the *method* of allocation of the profits and losses. Instead, this is simply a change in the *number of people* to whom the profits and losses will be allocated.

A change in the *method* of the allocation in profits and losses would be if art. VIII(A) was changed so that the managing general partner received as his share of profits and losses, a different *percentage*. Another exam- ple would be an amendment which gave the general partners a set amount rather than allocating to them their share in proportion to the total of units owned by them to the total units owned by all the partners.

We find that the method of allocation of profits and losses has not been changed.... [*Affirmed.*]

## 9.   Continuity of Organizations

One factor that should be considered when selecting the best form of orga- nization for your business purpose is the degree to which an organization's existence is tied to its owners. In essence, this factor concerns how stable is an organization's independent continuity. In this section, the dissolution of organizations is examined. This term **dissolution** refers to the legal exist- ence of the organizational form. The following paragraphs include general principles about dissolutions and statements about the impact of a dissolu- tion on a business.

A general partnership is dissolved any time there is a change in the partners. For example, if a partner dies, retires, or otherwise withdraws from the organization, the partnership is dissolved. Likewise, if a person is added as a new partner, there is a technical dissolution of the organization. Therefore, it generally is said that the partnership organization is easily dis- solved. Even if the partnership agreement provides that the partnership will continue for a stated number of years, any partner still retains the power to dissolve the organization. In other words, although liability may be imposed on the former partner for wrongful dissolution in violation of the agree- ment, the partnership nevertheless is dissolved. (Note: the principles stated in this paragraph are applicable to limited partnerships if there is a change in the general partners. A limited partner may assign his or her interest to another without dissolving the limited partnership.)

In contrast to the easily dissolved nature of a partnership, a corporation usually is formed to have perpetual existence. The law treats a corporation's existence as distinct from its owners' status as shareholders. Thus, a share- holder's death or sale of her or his stock does not affect the organizational structure of a corporation. This ability to separate management from own- ership is an often cited advantage of the corporation.

To rely on the general principles of a partnership's continuity being much more unstable than a corporation's is to be shortsighted. The more important question is: How will a dissolution of an organization affect the business of that organization? A dissolution does not necessarily destroy the business of a partnership. Dissolution is not the equivalent of terminating an organization's business activity. Termination involves the winding up or liquidating of a business; dissolution simply means the legal form of organization no longer exists. Likewise, the death of a major shareholder of a corporation has no impact on the organization's existence. However, such an event may have an adverse influence on that corporation's ability to keep old customers or attract new ones.

The solution to problems arising when a partner dies or withdraws from a partnership, or when a shareholder dies or desires to withdraw from a closely held corporation, is a *buy and sell agreement.* These agreements, which need to be entered into when the business entity is *created,* provide for the amount and manner of compensation for the interest of the deceased or withdrawing owner. In a partnership, the buy and sell provisions are usually contained in the Articles of Copartnership. In a corporation, the agreement may be between shareholders or between shareholders and the corporation itself. In the latter case, the corporation redeems the stock of the withdrawing or deceased shareholder. Buy and sell agreements frequently use formulas to compute the value of the withdrawing owner's interest and provide for the time and method of payment. In the case of death, the liquidity needed is often provided by the cash proceeds from life insurance which was taken out on the life of the deceased and made payable to the business or to the surviving partner or shareholder. Upon payment of the amount required by the buy and sell agreement to the estate of the deceased, the interest of the deceased ends, and the surviving owners continue the business. A buy and sell agreement should specify whether the agreement is a right of first refusal or whether the surviving or remaining owners must purchase the interest of the deceased or withdrawing owner.

---

# RENBERG v. ZARROW
667 P.2d 465 (Okla. 1983)

---

In 1963, the shareholders of a closely held corporation executed an agreement which provided that upon the death of any shareholder, the survivors had an option for one year from the date of death to buy a deceased shareholder's shares at a price set by the majority shareholders each year. If no price was established for a given year, the most recently set price prevailed.

Dorothy Renberg died April 22, 1978. During April of 1979, the surviving shareholders notified Dorothy's husband that they wished to purchase her shares pursuant to the buy and sell agreement. The husband refused to sell and initiated this suit to prevent the transfer of stock. The trial court enforced the agreement, and the plaintiff appealed.

HODGES, J.:...Absolute restrictions forbidding the alienation of corporate stock are invalid, but reasonable restrictions are not. The usual purpose of shareholders' agreements which restrict the sale of corporate stock is to prevent transfers to outsiders without first providing an opportunity for the shareholders to acquire the stock. The agreement evolved as a device to assure the succession in interest of persons most likely to act in harmony with the other stockholders. Stock in a corporation creates a personal relationship analogous to a partnership, and shareholders in a close corporation should have the same right to choose one's associates in a corporation as in a firm. Restrictive agreements designed to prevent sale of stock to outsiders must be strictly construed and cannot be applied to transactions which are not expressly mentioned in the agreement; nor can they be enlarged by implication.

A basic reason for buy-sell agreements is to provide methodology to determine the value of the stock. The difficulty of determining the price to be paid arises because shares of a close corporation are not traded on the open market and, therefore, the value cannot be readily ascertained. To induce shareholders to purchase decedents' shares and to provide a market for the stock, the price must be attractive. A great deal of leeway is permitted because the shares represent more than a mere interest in property.

The Sooner shareholders considered several factors other than income tax implications in the periodic revaluation of the option price. These included: the ability of the surviving shareholders to pay the purchase price; maintenance of the option price at a level which would be attractive enough to the survivors to exercise their options; and provision of a market for the shares.

Buy-sell agreements are construed to comply with the manifest intent of the parties. After parties in a close corporation agree on a price formula, the validity of the restriction on transfer does not rest on any abstract notion of intrinsic fairness of price. Before the restriction can be declared invalid, it must be shown that there is more than a mere disparity between option price and current market value. In the absence of fraud, overreaching, or bad faith, an agreement between the stockholders that upon the death of any of them, the stock may be acquired by the corporation is binding. Even a great disparity between the price specified in a buy-sell agreement and the actual value of the stock is not sufficient to invalidate the agreement. Although this agreement inured to the benefit of the Zarrows, it might very well have resulted in benefit to Dorothy had she survived. Under the actuarial tables in effect at the time of the 1963 Agreement, Dorothy stood to gain most by the agreement; she was consistently advised of the value of the stock; she and her attorney had access to Sooner's financial records; and could have called a shareholders' meeting to reassess the stock had she so desired....The language of a written contract governs the rights and obligations of the contracting parties. The courts may not rewrite a shareholders' agreement under the guise of relieving one of the parties from the apparent hardship of an improvident bargain; nor may the courts rewrite an agreement which is clear and unambiguous on its face. We agree with the trial court's finding that the stipulated price provision wherein no one knows for certain at the time the price is set whether he is to be a buyer or a seller is inherently fair and provides mutuality of risk....

A court of equity will not enforce stock transfer restrictions adopted under circumstances which indicate bad faith and inequitable treatment of stock purchasers. Because close corporations are usually family affairs, a special relationship may exist between the majority shareholder of a close corporation and a minority shareholder. If a fiduciary relationship exists, and circumstances result in the enhancement of the value of the stock which are known to the officers, directors or the majority shareholders because of their position in the corporation, but which are unknown to the minority, the officers, directors, or the majority shareholders are required to make a full disclosure to the minority. Failure to do so may amount to fraud or deceit sufficient to vitiate a sale, and entitle the minority to relief for unjust enrichment.

The relationship of brother and sister does not of itself create a fiduciary relationship between the parties. However, a majority shareholder has a fiduciary duty not to misuse his power by promoting his personal interests at the expense of the corporation, and the majority shareholder has the duty to protect the interests of the minority. Unless minority shareholders have been systematically excluded from directors and shareholders' meetings, minority stockholders in a close corporation usually have access, apart from the corporate records, to inside information which may affect the value of the stock. It has been held that absent circumstances from which fraud or unfair dealing may be inferred, an officer or director of a close corporation has no duty to volunteer information to a stockholder from whom he purchases stock.

There is no evidence that there was fraud or overreaching in connection with the buy-sell agreement. It operated equally concerning all shareholders. The fact that surviving shareholders were allowed to purchase Dorothy's shares on stated terms and conditions which resulted in purchase for less than actual value of the stock does not subject the agreement to attack as a breach of the relation of trust and confidence.... [*Affirmed.*]

## CONTROL

### 10.  In Partnerships

In every business organization, some individual or group of people will make decisions or possess control of the business. In a general partnership, unless the agreement provides to the contrary, each partner has an equal voice in the firm's affairs, with an equal right to possess partnership property for business purposes. In a limited partnership, the general partner or partners with unlimited liability are in control. Limited partners have no right to participate in management.

Partners are liable for all transactions entered into by any partner in the scope of the partnership business and are similarly liable for any partner's torts committed while she or he is acting in the course of the firm's business. Each partner is in effect both an agent of the partnership and a principal, being capable of creating both contract and tort liability for the firm and for her or his copartners, and likewise being responsible for her or his own acts. There are many technical rules concerning what acts of a partner are within the scope or course of the partnership. One such special rule is worthy of mention. A partner in a trading partnership, that is, one engaged in the business of buying and selling commodities, has the implied authority to borrow money in the usual course of business and to pledge the credit of the firm; but a partner in a nontrading partnership, such as an accounting firm, has no implied power to borrow money. In the latter case, such authority must be actual before the firm will be bound. A further discussion of the partnership's operation and liability of the partners is presented in the next chapter.

## 11. Of Large Corporations

In the corporate form of organization, legal problems created by persons in control and by those seeking control are quite numerous. In very large corporations, control by management is maintained with a very small percentage of stock ownership through the utilization of corporate records and funds to solicit proxies. Management can, at corporate expense, solicit the right to vote the stock of shareholders unable to attend the meetings at which the directors of the company are elected. An outsider must either own sufficient stock to elect the directors or must solicit proxies at his or her own expense. Although there are a few proxy fights, the management of a large corporation usually can maintain control with only a small minority of actual stock ownership.

In corporations having several hundred shareholders or more, a number of techniques are used to gain control without having a majority of the total investment. One technique is to issue classes of stock. In some states there can be nonvoting stock—the group seeking to keep control will buy voting stock while selling nonvoting stock to others. Preferred stock may be used to increase capital without losing control. For example, a group may invest $100,000 in common stock of $1 par value each. Then they will sell another $100,000 of the same common stock, requiring that for each share of common stock purchased, a $5 share of nonvoting preferred stock must be purchased. Thus, the corporation would raise $700,000, and the $100,000 original investment made by the organizing individuals would have 50 percent of the voting power. Another method of gaining and keeping control is to pool the stock of several shareholders into a voting trust so that one person gains the power, by contract, to vote all the shares in the trust.

Once again, other issues concerning corporate operations are discussed in the next chapter on liability and in Chapter 19 on investor protection. An understanding of these securities laws really is essential when a corporation's stock is being publicly traded.

## 12. Of Closely Held Corporations

Unlike the situation with a large, publicly held corporation, one shareholder (or at least a small group of shareholders) may be able to control a closely held corporation. This can result because this individual (or the group) can own an actual majority of the issued shares. This majority can control the election of a board of directors. In fact, the shareholders with the largest amount of stock often are elected to this board of directors. The directors, in turn, elect officers, who again may be the shareholders with the largest interests. The directors also establish important corporate policies, such as declaring dividends and amending the bylaws. In a very real sense, those who own a majority of a closely held corporation can rule with near absolute authority.

What are the rights of those who do not possess control in a closely held corporation—the so-called "minority interest"? To a large degree, the owners of the minority interest are subject to the whim or caprice of the majority. The majority may pay themselves salaries which use up profits and may never declare a dividend. However, the minority interest is not without some rights, because the directors and officers stand in a fiduciary relation to the corporation and to the minority shareholders if the corporation is closely held. This relation imposes a duty on directors to act for the best interests of the corporation rather than for themselves individually.

If the majority is acting illegally or is oppressive of the rights of the minority shareholders, a lawsuit known as a **derivative action** may be brought by a minority shareholder on behalf of the corporation. Such suits may seek to enjoin the unlawful activity or to collect damages for the corporation. For example, contracts made between the corporation and an interested director or officer may be challenged. The burden is on the director or officer (who may be the majority shareholder) to prove good faith and inherent fairness in such transactions if a suit is commenced.

A derivative suit cannot be used as a means of harassing management. Therefore, these actions generally cannot begin until all possible means to solve the problem within the corporate organization have been exhausted. Generally, a minority shareholder must first demand that the board of directors institute a suit to protect the corporation. However, a formal demand on the board is excused if the demand would be futile, such as when the directors are accused of the wrongdoing. In these situations, companies may appoint a disinterested committee to decide when a derivative suit filed on behalf of the company is in the organization's best interest. An independent committee balancing between the rights of the aggrieved shareholders and the needs of management may be subject to judicial review.

The basic difficulty of owning a minority interest in a closely held corporation arises from the fact that there is no ready market for the stock should the shareholder desire to dispose of it. Of course, if there is a valid buy and sell agreement, then there is a market for the stock. Thus, buy and sell agreements are absolutely essential in closely held corporations. Although shareholders have the right to attend meetings and vote for directors, they may be constantly outvoted. They have a right to any dividends that are declared but no right to have them declared. They also have a preemptive right, which is to purchase their proportionate share of any new stock issue, but they may not be interested in investing more money when no dividends are being paid. Therefore, as a practical matter, the majority may be able to increase their percentage of ownership further.

The minority shareholder has a right to inspect the books and records of the company, but at a proper time and place; and the books may not have much meaning without entries and account balances being analyzed by an expert.

Finally, minority shareholders have the right to their proportionate share of assets on dissolution, but they have no right to dissolution, except that they may seek it in a court of equity under circumstances that will cause a court to step in to protect creditors and the corporation.

# LIABILITY FACTORS

## 13. Liability Factors: Partnerships

All partners in a general partnership and the general partners in a limited partnership are treated the same for liability purposes. These partners have unlimited liability for their organization's debts. In other words, these partners' personal assets, which are not associated with the partnership, may be claimed by the partnership's creditors. From a creditor's perspective, this personal liability of each partner extends to the organization's entire debt, not just to a pro rata share. These partners are *jointly and severally liable* for the partnership's obligations. For example, assume that a general partnership has three partners and that it owes a creditor $300,000. If it is necessary to collect the debt, this creditor can sue all three partners jointly for the $300,000. As an alternative, the creditor can sue any one partner or any combination of two for the entire $300,000. Between the partners, anyone who has to pay the creditor more than her or his pro rata share of the liability usually can seek contribution from the remaining partners.

A more in-depth discussion of partners' liability is presented in the next chapter. There you will see that personal liability may arise from (1) breach of a contract, (2) commitment of a tort, (3) failure to perform a public duty, or (4) violation of a statute. The degree of liability placed on the individual partner may vary depending on the occurrence of each of these events.

The limited partnership as a hybrid for liability purposes has been mentioned previously. The Uniform Limited Partnership Act, which has been adopted or revised by every state except Louisiana, governs the rights and duties of the general and limited partners. Under this statute, a limited partner is viewed as lending money to the business organization for a percentage of the profits rather than for a fixed return such as interest. Because the limited partner is treated as a creditor, there are several restrictions placed on the activities of this party. For example, contributions to the firm may be in cash or property but not services. Surnames of the limited partner may not be used in the partnership's name unless there is a general partner with the same name. If a limited partner's name is used in the firm's name, that partner will become personally liable to unsuspecting creditors. Also, limited partners may not participate in management without incurring unlimited liability. In some states, this participation may not even be indirect, as by managing the partnership through a corporate general partner. However, limited partners do not lose their limited liability by showing an interest in the firm or by making suggestions, as occurred in the following case.

# TRANS-AM BUILDERS, INC. v. WOODS MILL, LTD.
210 S.E.2d 866 (Ga. 1974)

STOLZ, J.:...The litigation before us arose out of the construction of an apartment complex involving Trans-Am Builders, Inc., as general contractor (appellant) and Woods Mill, Ltd., a limited partnership (appellee) with a number of individuals as limited partners and The Baier Corporation as the general partner....

During the construction of the project, financial difficulties arose, resulting in appellant's either abandoning or being removed from the project. Suits and countersuits were filed. However, there is but one issue before us, that is, have the limited partners conducted themselves in such a manner as to "take part in the control of the business" and thus become liable as a general partner?...

Code Ann. § 75-411 provides as follows: **(1) A limited partner shall have the same rights as a general partner to (a) Have the partnership books kept at the principal place of business of the partnership, and at all times to inspect and copy any of them. (b) Have on demand true and full information of all things affecting the partnership, and a formal account of partnership affairs whenever circumstances render it just and reasonable. (c) Have dissolution and winding up by decree of court. (2) A limited partner shall have the right to receive a share of the profits or other compensation by way of income, and to the return of his contribution....**

The evidence before us reveals that the limited partners (with one exception) held at least two meetings after it became apparent that the project was in financial difficulty. At these meetings the situation was presented by a representative of the general partner, discussions were participated in, and additional money was raised to meet financial obligations. At least one of the limited partners went to the project and went over it with the appellant's superintendent, and "obnoxiously" complained and objected to the way the work was being conducted, but there is nothing to indicate that he gave any directions which may have been followed by the plaintiff's superintendent....The appellant contends that these actions violated Code Ann. § 75-411, *supra,* and that the limited partners thus became general partners. The trial judge held otherwise and sustained the limited partners' motion for summary judgment, from which judgment the plaintiff appeals....

It is well established that just because a man is a limited partner in an enterprise he is not by reason of that status precluded from continuing to have an interest in the affairs of the partnership, from giving advice and suggestions to the general partner or his nominees, and from interesting himself in specific aspects of the business. Such casual advice as limited partners may have given to [the employees] can hardly be said to be interference in day-to-day management. Certainly common sense dictates that in times of severe financial crisis all partners in such an enterprise, limited or general will become actively interested in any effort to keep the enterprise afloat and many abnormal problems will arise that are not under any stretch of the imagination mere day-to-day matters of managing the partnership business. This is all that occurred in this instance....

It would be unreasonable to hold that a limited partner may not advise with the general partner and visit the partnership business, particularly when the project is confronted with a severe financial crisis. [*Judgment affirmed.*]

---

In an attempt to modernize and clarify the law of limited partnership, a Revised Uniform Limited Partnership Act has been prepared and proposed to the states for adoption. A majority of the states has adopted this revised act. In these states there is a substantial change in the liability of a limited partner who participates in control of the business. The liability of a general partner is imposed on a limited partner who participates in the control of the business only if the third party has had knowledge of the participation. In addition, this revised act clarifies that a limited partner does not participate in the control of the business by (1) being an agent or employee of the business, (2) consulting with or advising a partner with respect to the partnership, (3) acting as surety of the limited partnership, (4) approving or disapproving of an amendment to the certificate, and (5) voting on matters such as dissolution, sale of assets, or a change of name.

## 14.   Liability Factors: Corporations

Traditionally, it has been said that the investors in a corporation have limited liability but those in a partnership have unlimited liability. This generalization is too broad and needs qualification. To be sure, someone investing in a company listed on the New York Stock Exchange will incur no risk greater than the investment, and the concept of limited liability certainly applies. However, if the company is a small, closely held corporation with limited assets and capital, it will be difficult for it to obtain credit on the strength of its own net worth standing alone. As a practical matter, shareholders will usually be required to add their own individual liability as security for debts. For example, if the XYZ Company seeks a loan at a local bank, the bank often will require the owners, X, Y, and Z, to personally guarantee repayment of the loan. This is not to say that shareholders in closely held corporations do not have some degree of limited liability. Shareholders have limited liability for contract-like obligations which are imposed as a matter of law (such as taxes). Liability also is limited when the corporate obligation results from torts committed by company employees while doing company business.

Even in these situations, the mere fact of corporate existence does not mean the shareholders will have liability limited to their investment. When courts find that the corporate organization is being misused, the corporate entity can be disregarded. This event has been called "piercing the corporate veil." When this veil of protection has been pierced, the shareholders are treated like partners who have unlimited liability for their organization's debts.

Courts have identified several situations in which the corporate veil can be pierced. First, the corporate entity may be used to defraud or avoid an otherwise valid obligation. For example, if A sold B a business and A agreed not to compete with B for two years, but if, in violation of the contract, A organized a corporation and competed with B, the contract would have been breached. Second, the corporation may be used to evade a statute. For example, if a state law provides that a person may not hold more than one liquor license at a time, this law cannot be circumvented by forming multiple corporations. Third, the corporate entity may be disregarded when one corporation is organized, controlled, and conducted in a manner that makes it an instrument of another corporation. In such circumstances, one corporation is said to be the "alter ego" of another. It must be recognized that the mere relationship of a parent corporation with a subsidiary is not enough by itself to justify piercing the corporate veil. Subsidiaries are often formed in order to limit the liability of the parent corporation. The alter-ego theory, by which the corporate veil can be pierced, may also be used to impose personal liability upon corporate officers and stockholders. If the corporate entity is disregarded by the principals themselves, so that there is such a unity of ownership and interest that separateness of the corporation has ceased to exist, the alter-ego doctrine will be followed and the corporate veil will be pierced. The following case illustrates that courts are not limited to these three factors when they decide whether or not to disregard a corporation's separate identity.

---

# CASTLEBERRY v. BRANSCUM
721 S.W.2d 270 (Tex. 1986)

SPEARS, J.: Joe Castleberry sued Texan Transfer, Inc. and Byron Branscum and Michael Byboth, individually, on a promissory note signed by the corporation for Castleberry's shares in the closely held corporation. The jury found that Branscum and Byboth used Texan Transfer as a sham to perpetrate a fraud. Based on the jury findings, the trial court rendered judgment against Texan Transfer, disregarding its corporate fiction to hold both Byboth and Branscum individually liable. The court of appeals reversed...We reverse the court of appeals judgment and affirm the trial court, because under the applicable law there was some evidence to support the jury's verdict,...and disregarding the corporate fiction is a fact question for the jury.

*Disregarding the Corporate Fiction*

The corporate form normally insulates shareholders, officers, and directors from liability for corporate obligations; but when these individuals abuse the corporate privilege, courts will disregard the corporate fiction and hold them individually liable. We disregard the corporate fiction, even though corporate formalities have been observed and corporate and individual property have been kept separately, when the corporate form has been used as part of a basically unfair device to achieve an inequitable result.

Specifically, we disregard the corporate fiction:

**(1)** when the fiction is used as a means of perpetrating fraud;

**(2)** where a corporation is organized and operated as a mere tool or business conduit of another corporation;

**(3)** where the corporate fiction is resorted to as a means of evading an existing legal obligation;

**(4)** where the corporate fiction is employed to achieve or perpetrate monopoly;

**(5)** where the corporate fiction is used to circumvent a statute; and

**(6)** where the corporate fiction is relied upon as a protection of crime or to justify wrong.

Many Texas cases have blurred the distinction between alter ego and the other bases for disregarding the corporate fiction and treated alter ego as a synonym for the entire doctrine of disregarding the corporate fiction. However,...alter ego is only one of the bases for disregarding the corporate fiction: "where a corporation is organized and operated as a mere tool or business conduit of another corporation."

Alter ego applies when there is such unity between corporation and individual that the separateness of the corporation has ceased and holding only the corporation liable would result in injustice. It is shown from the total dealings of the corporation and the individual, including the degree to which corporate formalities have been followed and corporate and individual property have been kept separately, the amount of financial interest, ownership and control the individual maintains over the corporation, and whether the corporation has been used for personal purposes. Alter ego's rationale is: "if the shareholders themselves disregard the separation of the corporate enterprise, the law will also disregard it so far as necessary to protect individual and corporate creditors."

The basis used here to disregard the corporate fiction, a sham to perpetrate a fraud, is separate from alter ego. It is sometimes confused with intentional fraud; however, "[n]either fraud nor an intent to defraud need be shown as a prerequisite to disregarding the corporate entity; it is sufficient if recognizing the separate corporate existence would bring about an inequitable result."...Thus, we held that note holders could disregard the corporate fiction without showing common-law fraud or deceit when the circumstances amounted to constructive fraud. In *Tigrett v. Pointer,* the Dallas Court of Appeals disregarded the corporate fiction, stating correctly that "[w]hether [the individual] misled them or subjectively intended to defraud them is immaterial... [f]or the action was so grossly unfair as to amount to constructive fraud."

To prove there has been a sham to perpetrate a fraud, tort claimants and contract creditors must show only constructive fraud. We distinguished constructive from actual fraud in *Archer v. Griffith:*

**Actual fraud usually involves dishonesty of purpose or intent to deceive, whereas constructive fraud is the breach of some legal or equitable duty which, irrespective of moral guilt, the law declares fraudulent because of its tendency to deceive others, to violate confidence, or to injure public interests.**

Because disregarding the corporate fiction is an equitable doctrine, Texas takes a flexible fact-specific approach focusing on equity....Dean Hildebrand, a leading authority on Texas corporation law, stated well the equitable approach: "When this [disregarding the corporate fiction] should be done is a question of fact and common sense. The court must weigh the facts and consequences in each case carefully, and common sense and justice must determine [its] decision."...[The court then reviewed the evidence and concluded.]

...A jury could find that Byboth and Branscum manipulated a closely-held corporation, Texan Transfer, and formed competing businesses to ensure that Castleberry did not get paid. Castleberry had little choice but to sell his shares back to the corporation. While this evidence may be no evidence of intentional fraud, constructive fraud, not intentional fraud, is the standard for disregarding the corporate fiction on the basis of a sham to perpetrate a fraud.

In determining if there is an abuse of the corporate privilege, courts must look through the form of complex transactions to the substance. The variety of shams is infinite, but many fit this case's pattern: a closely held corporation owes unwanted obligations; it siphons off corporate revenues, sells off much of the corporate assets, or does other acts to hinder the on-going business and its ability to pay off its debts; a new business then starts up that is basically a continuation of the old business with many of the same shareholders, officers, and directors.... [*We reverse the court of appeals' judgment and affirm the trial court's judgment.*]

# TAXATION FACTORS

### 15.   Taxation Factors: Partnerships

A partnership, whether of a general or limited nature, is not a taxable entity. The fact that this type of organization pays no income tax does not mean that the profits of the partnership are free of income tax. A partnership files an information return which allocates to each individual partner his or her proportionate share of profits or losses from operations, dividend income, capital gains or losses, and other items which would affect the income tax owed by a partner. Partners then report their share of such items on their individual income tax returns, irrespective of whether they have actually received the items.

This aspect of a partnership becomes advantageous to the partners if the organization suffers a net loss. The pro rata share of this loss is allocated to each partner, and it can be used to reduce these partners' personal taxable income. However, by this same reasoning the partnership organization becomes disadvantageous if any profits made are retained by the organization for expansion purposes. Suppose a partnership which has three equal partners has $30,000 in net income. If this money is kept by the partnership, there still is a constructive distribution of $10,000 to each partner for tax purposes. Assuming that these partners are in a 28 percent personal income tax bracket, they each would have to pay $2,800 in taxes even though they actually received nothing from the partnership.

During the eighties, limited partnerships have been used to finance real estate development, theatrical productions, professional sport teams, and other projects that require large amounts of capital. The limited partners' interest in these limited partnerships have been traded in ways similar to trading stock in publicly held corporations. When thousands of limited partners are involved, *master limited partnerships* have been formed.

The distributions of income to the limited partners from a master limited partnership are tax-free until such distributions exceed the limited partners' original investment. However, the 1986 tax law prohibits limited partners from taking deductions of the master limited partnerships' losses. Congress is studying the possibility of treating these master limited partnerships as corporations for taxation purposes.

### 16.   Taxation Factors: Corporations

Unlike partnerships, corporations must pay income taxes on their earnings. The corporate tax rates may be changed by Congress. These changes relate to the condition of our economy and the impact desired on employment and economic growth. In August 1986, Congress enacted a tax-reform law, which lowered both individual and corporate tax rates. The lower rates were offset by the elimination of certain deductions and credits, such as the investment tax credit. The following table sets forth these tax rates, beginning in 1987:

## Corporate Tax Rates

| $ of Income | Tax Rate |
| --- | --- |
| 0–50,000 | 15 percent |
| 50–75,000 | 25 percent |
| Over 75,000 | 34 percent |

An additional 5 percent tax, up to $11,750, is imposed on corporate taxable income over $100,000. Corporations with taxable income of at least $335,000 will pay a flat rate of 34 percent.

The fact that there is a separate corporate income tax may work as an advantage. For example, if the corporation makes a profit which is to be retained by the corporation for growth needs, no income is allocated to the shareholders. In other words, these shareholders will not have their personal taxable income increased as would a partner in a similar situation. Also, the corporate rate may be lower than the individual rates.

In the past, the most often cited advantage of the corporate organizational form was the sheltering of taxable income. In general, the employees of a corporation could defer from taxes much more income than could employees of a proprietorship, partnership, or limited partnership. Therefore, whenever a business became very successful, there were strong incentives to become a corporation. As of 1984, these incentives have been removed by Congress. Indeed, for the purposes of sheltering income from taxes, all business organizations are treated essentially equally. Thus, the factor of the amount that can be paid into profit-sharing and pension plans is no longer of major importance when deciding which organization is the best for a particular business.

Now we turn to some tax disadvantages of the corporation. Suppose a corporation suffers a loss during a given tax year. The existence of the corporate tax works as a disadvantage, since this loss cannot be distributed to the shareholders in order to reduce their personal tax liability. Indeed, a net operating loss to a corporation can be used only to offset corporate income earned in other years. And the allocation of such a loss can be carried back only for three years and carried forward for fifteen years. (Note: There are many different rules concerning specialized carryover situations. The Internal Revenue Code should be examined prior to relying on the general rule just stated.) Perhaps a greater disadvantage of the corporate tax occurs when a profit is made and the corporation wishes to pay a dividend to its shareholders. The money used to pay this dividend will have been taxed at the corporate level. It is then taxed again because the shareholder must take the amount of the dividend into his or her own personal income. The rate of this second tax depends on the personal tax rate of the shareholder receiving the dividend. This situation has been called the *double tax* on corporate income. A similar situation of "double taxation" occurs when a corporation is dissolved and its assets are distributed to shareholders as capital gains. This next section presents a discussion which indicates that the "double tax" may not be as big a disadvantage as it first seems.

## 17. Avoiding Double Taxation

There are at least five techniques for avoiding at least part of the problem caused by the double taxation of corporate income. First of all, reasonable salaries paid to corporate officials may be deducted in computing the taxable income of the business. Thus, in a closely held corporation in which all or most shareholders are officers or employees, this technique may avoid double taxation of substantial portions of income. As might be suspected, the Internal Revenue Code disallows a deduction for excessive or unreasonable compensation and treats such payments as dividends. Therefore, the determination of the reasonableness of corporate salaries is often a tax problem in that form of organization.

Second, corporations provide expense accounts for many employees including shareholder-employees. These are used to purchase travel, food, and entertainment. When so used, the employee, to some extent, has compensation which is not taxed. In an attempt to close this tax loophole, the law limits deductions for business meals and entertainment to 80 percent of the cost. Meal expenses and entertainment are deductible only if the expenses are directly related to or associated with the active conduct of a trade or business. For a deduction, business must be discussed directly before, during, or directly after the meal. Additionally, meal expenses are not deductible to the extent the meal is lavish or extravagant. Thus, it is apparent that the use of the expense account to avoid taxation of corporate income is subject to numerous technical rules and limitations.

Third, the capital structure of the corporation may include both common stock and interest-bearing loans from shareholders. For example, assume that a company needs $100,000 cash to go into business. If $100,000 of stock is issued, no expense will be deducted. However, assume that $50,000 worth of stock is purchased by the owners, and $50,000 is lent to the company by them at 10 percent interest. In this case, $5,000 interest each year is deductible as an expense of the company and thus subject to only one tax as interest income to the owners. Just as in the case of salaries, the Internal Revenue Code has a counteracting rule relating to corporations that are undercapitalized. If the corporation is undercapitalized, interest payments will be treated as dividends and disallowed as deductible expenses.

The fourth technique for avoiding double taxation, at least in part, is simply not to pay dividends and to accumulate the earnings. The Internal Revenue Service seeks to compel corporations to distribute those profits not needed for a business purpose, such as growth. When a corporation retains earnings in excess of $250,000, there is a presumption that these earnings are being accumulated to avoid a second tax on dividends. If the corporation cannot rebut this presumption, an additional tax of 27½ percent is imposed on the first $100,000 unreasonably accumulated in excess of $250,000. For undistributed earnings above this amount, the penalty tax equals 38½ percent of the unreasonable accumulation.

Fifth, there is a special provision in the Internal Revenue Code that allows small, closely held business corporations to be treated as partnerships for income tax purposes and thereby avoid having a tax assessed on the corporate income itself. These Subchapter S corporations cannot have over thirty-five shareholders, each of whom must elect to be taxed as a partnership, that is, to have the corporate income allocated to the shareholders annually in computing their income for tax purposes, whether actually paid out or not. The permissible number of shareholders has been increased in recent years from ten to thirty-five to encourage greater use of the Subchapter S election. There are many technical rules of tax law involved in Subchapter S corporations, but as a rule of thumb, this method of organization has distinct advantages for a business operating at a loss because the loss is shared and immediately deductible on the returns of the shareholders. It is also advantageous for businesses capable of paying out net profits as earned. In the latter case, the corporate tax is avoided. If net profits must be retained in the business, Subchapter S tax treatment is disadvantageous because income tax is paid on earnings not received, and there is a danger of double taxation to the individual because undistributed earnings which have been taxed once are taxed again in the event of the death of a shareholder. Thus, it is evident that the theoretical advantage of using the Subchapter S corporation to avoid double taxation of corporate income must be heavily qualified.

## REVIEW QUESTIONS

**1** Identify the terms in the left-hand column by matching each with the appropriate statement in the right-hand column:

(1) Partnership

(2) Proprietorship

(a) A business owned by one person who is personally liable for all losses

(b) An artificial being created by a state

(3) Limited partnership

(4) Corporation

(5) Legal capacity

(6) Buy and sell agreement

(7) Subchapter S corporation

(8) Accumulated earnings tax

(c) Imposed when a corporation fails to justify not paying dividends from earnings

(d) Created when shareholders elect to be treated as partners for tax purposes

(e) Created by an agreement between two or more persons who agree to share profits and losses

(f) Provides for compensation to a deceased or withdrawing owner of a business in return for that owner's interest

(g) The ability of an organization to sue or to own property

(h) Exists when some partners are treated like shareholders for liability purposes

**2** An injured worker filed for unemployment compensation. His former corporate employer challenged the claim before the appropriate state agency. The president of the corporation and its sole shareholder attended the proceedings and sought to cross-examine the claimant and argue the case. The agency refused to allow him to do so since he was not a licensed attorney. Was the agency action correct? Explain.

**3** Sam was employed by George to sell and service boilers. He was paid 50 percent of the net profit of each sale. Are Sam and George partners? Why or why not?

**4** Lewis and Tabor signed a written agreement to operate a dairy farm. This contract required Tabor to furnish the cows and the labor and Lewis to provide the land and the milking equipment. These parties also agreed to share the proceeds or losses equally. Their agreement specifically stated that these parties were not partners but that Tabor was leasing Lewis' land and equipment. Are these parties actually partners? Why or why not?

**5** Alvin Volkman contacted David McNamee about obtaining advice on a residential construction project. McNamee informed Volkman that he (McNamee) was going into business with Phillip Carroll. Later Volkman was introduced to Carroll, who responded, "I am happy we will be working with you." Volkman signed a contract with DP Associates, and he assumed the organization's name was taken from the first letter of David McNamee's and Phillip Carroll's names. In fact, there had been no actual agreement between McNamee and Carroll to go into business together. A dispute arose between Volkman and DP Associates. When a resolution was not reached, Volkman sued DP Associates as a partnership and McNamee and Carroll, individually, as partners. Carroll sought to be dismissed from this lawsuit since he was not in business with McNamee. May an individual who is not officially a partner be held liable as though he were a partner? Explain.

**6** First Wyoming Savings and Loan Association filed a complaint seeking to enjoin the First National Bank of Lander from changing its name to First Wyoming Bank—

Lander. The basis of this complaint against First National Bank was that First Wyoming S&L had established a trade name in the words "First Wyoming." It was claimed that the use of the name "First Wyoming Bank—Lander" would result in confusion and deception to the general public of Fremont County. Has First Wyoming S&L established a secondary meaning in its trade name "First Wyoming" so as to authorize injunctive relief? Why or why not?

**7** Michal, Walter, Olga, and Harold executed and recorded a certificate to establish the River Bend Limited Partnership. One was listed as general partner, and the others were listed as limited partners. This certificate was signed and acknowledged by all the partners before a notary. It was not sworn to, however. Are all partners liable as general partners? Why or why not?

**8** Richard and his son Robert each raised potatoes on their own land. The potatoes are stored together, and the parties advertised together under the name Richard and Son. The profit from the sale of the potatoes was split evenly. A major loss was incurred by Robert as a result of spraying the potatoes with the wrong spray. Must Richard share in the loss? Why or why not?

**9** Libby and Gloria have formed a limited partnership, with Gloria agreeing to be the general partner. This partnership has purchased supplies from Carl. Carl has received a promissory note signed on behalf of the partnership as payment. If the partnership is unable to pay this note, can Carl hold Gloria personally liable? Explain.

**10** The plaintiffs entered into a series of contracts involving coal excavations with Doral Coal Company and Dean Coal Company. Robert W. William, defendant, was president of both coal companies. When royalty payments owed were not made by the corporations as agreed, plaintiffs canceled the agreements and filed suit against the defendant individually. They contended that the defendant was personally liable because he was the sole shareholder of each corporation. Is the defendant liable? Why or why not?

**11** List and explain four techniques used to avoid the double taxation of corporate income in closely held corporations.

**12** Curtis sold feed to a corporation. He was given a corporate check that was returned by the bank for insufficient funds. When the corporation failed to cover the check, he sued the directors and sought to hold them personally liable for the check. Give examples of factors that would justify a decision for the plaintiff.

**13** Albert Anderson and Barbara Brinson wish to enter into the business of manufacturing fine furniture. Which form of business organization would you recommend in each of the following situations? Explain each of your answers.

   **a** Brinson is a furniture expert, but she has no funds. Anderson knows nothing about such production, but he is willing to contribute all the money needed to start the business.
   **b** The furniture manufacturing process requires more capital than either Anderson or Brinson can raise together. However, they wish to maintain control of the business.
   **c** The production process can be very dangerous, and a large tort judgment against the business is foreseeable.
   **d** Sales will be nationwide.
   **e** A loss is expected for the first several years.

# Chapter

# *13*

# Liability of Business Organizations and Managers

## CHAPTER PREVIEW

When a contract is breached, a tort is committed, or a law is violated, issues of liability immediately arise. Is the business entity liable? Is the person involved liable? If there is liability, to whom? If payment is made to one person, is there a right of contribution or indemnity from another? These issues are, in part, answered by the law of agency. Other answers are found in the law of partnerships and corporations. Still others are found in various statutes and in case law. The sections which follow will discuss some of the more important legal theories used to impose liability on various kinds of businesses and those who operate them. You should understand the meaning and application of the following terms: actual authority, agency, agent, apparent authority, master, principal, ratification, and servant.

# GENERAL AGENCY PRINCIPLES

### 1. Terminology

Because individuals by themselves cannot accomplish all they desire every person has asked for help and has been asked for help. From the perspective of a business organization, nothing can be accomplished without the aid of others. Indeed, a partnership and a corporation must act through its owners and employees. This nature of interdependency makes the law of agency very important today. The term **agency** is applicable to the situation when one person acts on behalf of another. A **principal** is the person or organization who controls the activities of an **agent,** the person or organization acting on behalf of the principal. These parties may be individuals, partnerships, corporations, or other types of organizations.

The relationship between a principal and agent is fiduciary in nature. Fiduciaries occupy a special position of trust and confidence. Therefore, principals and agents owe to one another the duty of loyalty and honesty. This fiduciary concept of the agency is of major importance when examining the liability of business organization managers.

Typically the terms "principal" and "agent" are used whenever the factual situation involves the negotiation or performance of a contract. If the circumstances involve a tort or personal injury, the term **master** is technically more correct than principal and the term **servant** is more accurate than agent. In either case, the agent or servant usually will have encountered a *third party* who often raises questions about holding the principal (master) or agent (servant) or both liable.

In general, the third party who has signed a contract with an agent wants the principal to be bound to the contract. In other words, the third party wants to have the principal liable instead of the agent. Likewise, when a third party is injured by a servant, that third party usually wants to recover from the master because the master has a "deeper pocket." In order for contractual liability to pass from the agent to the principal, the law requires the agent to act within the scope of the authority granted. Similarly, the master becomes liable for a servant's torts only when the servant is acting within the scope of employment.

### 2. Actual Authority

**Actual authority** may take two basic forms. First, a principal can *express* directions or instructions to an agent. This expression of authority may be in a written or oral form; however, for the purposes of clarity, it is almost always better to have a written expression of authority. Second, actual authority may be *implied* from the conduct of the parties, from customary practices, or from the factual situation. In essence, implied authority is necessary for an agent to carry out the express authority granted.

The third parties who negotiate and contract with agents have the burden of proving that actual authority existed. Anyone dealing with an agent should not act negligently with regard to the agent's implied authority. Nor should the third party blindly trust the agent's statements concerning authority. At all times third parties must use reasonable diligence in determining if the agent is acting within the scope of his authority. In order to do this, the third party must ascertain, usually from the principal, the nature and extent of the agent's authority.

### 3. Apparent Authority

The term **apparent authority,** sometimes called "ostensible authority," refers to situations in which no actual authority exists, but in which the law binds the principal as if it did. The law does so if the principal, by his or her conduct, has led third persons to believe that the agent has authority and that they should rely on the belief. Ostensible authority is when a principal, intentionally or through carelessness, causes or allows another to believe the agent possesses authority. Liability of the principal for the ostensible agent's acts rests on the doctrine of estoppel. Its essential elements are representation by the principal, justifiable reliance thereon by the third party, and change of position or injury resulting from such reliance.

In addition to being the basis of liability when an agent lacks actual authority, apparent authority can expand an actual agent's authority beyond that granted by the principal. In other words, apparent authority may exist in a person who is not an agent, or it may increase the actual authority of an agent. In either of these situations, an agent cannot create her or his own apparent authority. This type of authority must be based on the principal's words or conduct; it cannot be based on anything the agent says or does.

Probably the typical situation in which apparent authority is found to exist is when the actual authority is terminated, but notice of this fact is not given to third parties. Cancellation of actual authority does not automatically terminate the apparent authority created by prior transactions. Because apparent authority may survive the termination of an agency relationship, the principal should give notice of termination to third parties.

### 4. Ratification

A principal is also liable for unauthorized contracts if he or she is found to have ratified the contract. Conduct that indicates an intention to adopt an unauthorized transaction will constitute **ratification.** For example, an expression of approval to the agent or performance of the contract will constitute a ratification. For a valid ratification to occur, the principal must: (1) have capacity to do what the agent has done, (2) be known to the third party, and (3) have full knowledge of the facts.

First, since ratification relates to the time of the agent's actions, both the principal and agent must be capable of that action at that time. Furthermore, they must maintain their capacity until the ratification actually occurs.

Second, an agent's act may be ratified only when the agent has acted as an agent. A person who professes to act for himself in his own name does nothing that can be ratified, even though he intends at the time to let another have the benefit of his acts. In other words, the third party has to have known about the existence of the principal at the time the unauthorized actions occurred.

Third, in general, a principal cannot be held to have ratified an agent's unauthorized acts if he lacks full knowledge of all the material facts associated with the agent's actions. When the principal expressly ratifies unauthorized acts and shows no desire to learn all the facts, he may not deny liability on the ground that he has been ignorant of all important information. However, when ratification is implied from the principal's conduct, a lack of full knowledge may become a defense against liability. The following case illustrates this requirement of the principal having full knowledge prior to a valid ratification occurring.

---

## PERKINS v. PHILBRICK
443 A.2d 73 (Me. 1982)

---

WATHEN, J.:....The issue raised by this appeal is whether defendant's forged signature on settlement drafts and a release form can effectuate a settlement and bar defendant's underlying tort claim against plaintiff. We hold that it cannot and deny the appeal.

In 1976 the parties were involved in an automobile accident in which defendant was injured. He hired an attorney to press his claim against plaintiff, and the attorney entered into communications with plaintiff's insurer. In late 1976, in a conversation with the attorney, the insurer's claims adjuster offered to settle defendant's claim for $26,000. The attorney replied that he would have to discuss the offer with his client. In January 1977 without prior discussion with his client the attorney told the adjuster that the settlement was acceptable. The insurer prepared drafts together with a release and inadvertently mailed them to the defendant. Two of the drafts received by the defendant were payable jointly to him and his attorney and one was payable to him and Blue Cross/Blue Shield. Defendant gave the unsigned documents to his attorney explaining that he did not want to settle for that amount. Defendant neither signed nor authorized the endorsement of any draft or the release. The two drafts payable jointly to defendant and his attorney were subsequently presented for payment bearing defendant's purported endorsement. The release form was not immediately returned to the insurer. When, after numerous calls, the claims adjuster visited the attorney's office, he was given the release purportedly signed by defendant. Sometime in February or March of 1977 the attorney gave defendant between $7,000 and $7,800 which he claimed was part of a $10,000 advance by the insurer. Throughout this period defendant took an active interest in the progress of his claim without learning that the drafts and release had been signed and presented.

In 1979 defendant, represented by his present attorney, commenced suit against plaintiff in Superior Court, seeking damages for his injury in the 1976 accident. Plaintiff then filed this action seeking a declaratory judgment that her obligation to defendant had been discharged when the drafts issued by her insurance company were paid by the bank and the executed release form was received by the insurer. The presiding justice did not issue a declaratory judgment but instead denied plaintiff's request. He based his order on his findings that defendant had neither accepted the settlement nor authorized anyone including his attorney to do so for him by signing the release. These factual findings are undisputed, and we find no settlement has been effectuated under these circumstances....

The parties' briefs focus solely upon the legal principles of authority and ratification applicable to defendant's endorsement forged by his attorney. Dealing with the issue as thus framed, we find a long established principle in Maine and many other jurisdictions that "an attorney clothed with no other authority than that arising from his employment in that capacity has no power to compromise and settle or release and discharge his client's claim." In the absence of authority, the mere fact that the release was signed with defendant's name does not constitute a bar to defendant's tort action.

Neither does the payment of the settlement draft over defendant's forged endorsement effect a settlement of the underlying claim. "Any unauthorized signature is wholly inoperative as that of the person whose name is signed, unless he ratifies it or is precluded from denying it." Thus, the forgery of defendant's name, even if accomplished by his attorney, was not an acceptance of the draft according to its terms as "a release of all claims for damages."

Plaintiff argues that even if the forgeries cannot effectuate a settlement, defendant is bound by them because he ratified the purported settlement by accepting what he thought was an advance. We conclude, as did the Superior Court, that no ratification occurred which would bar defendant's underlying tort action.

For ratification of an agent's actions to occur, it is necessary that all material facts be known by the principal.... The record in this case plainly shows that defendant did not have knowledge of the forgery when he accepted the advance from the attorney; therefore the court correctly concluded that ratification had not occurred. [*Affirmed.*]

---

A ratification may be expressed by the principal, or it may be implied from the principal's conduct. Any conduct that clearly indicates the principal's intention to approve the agent's actions will be a ratification. Accepting the benefits of the unauthorized acts definitely is a ratification. If the principal knows what the agent has done, and if she or he makes no objection within a reasonable time, a ratification results by operation of law. The issue of what is a reasonable time is a factual one for a jury to resolve.

## AGENCY AND CONTRACT LIABILITY

### 5. Introduction

In contractual situations, the ultimate purpose of an agency is to have the agent negotiate and reach an agreement with the third party. Although the contract is made by these two parties, typically they each desire to have the liability run between the principal and third party. That is, in general it is desired and expected of all parties for the principal to be substituted for the agent. If everything works, the principal and third party become liable to each other, and the agent is not liable on the contract.

This basic concept of substituting a principal for an agent is not as simple as it may seem. There are three different positions a principal may occupy from the third party's perspective. First, a principal is *disclosed* when his existence and identity are known to the third party. In essence, this is the type of principal presumed for the above discussion. Second, a principal may be completely *undisclosed*. This situation arises when the third party thinks he is dealing only with the agent who is representing himself. In order to be undisclosed, a principal's identity and existence are concealed. Finally, a principal may occupy an in-between position. When the third party knows that a principal exists but does not know that principal's actual identity, the principal is said to be *partially disclosed*. The three situations involving the types of principals are shown in Figure 13-1.

The liability issues among all three parties to an agent-negotiated contract depend on the type of principal involved. The next three sections discuss these liability issues. For the sake of simplifying these issues, an undisclosed and partially disclosed principal will be treated the same. Therefore, whenever the word *undisclosed* is used, it includes the term *partially disclosed* unless the material indicates otherwise.

### 6. Liability of Principals

In determining the liability of a principal, it is necessary to decide two things. First, is the concern with the liability of the principal to the agent or to the third party? Second, is the principal disclosed or undisclosed?

**TO AGENTS**

Regardless of the type of principal involved, the principal is obligated to hold the agent free from liability if the agent acts within the scope of actual

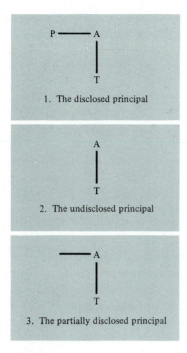

**FIGURE 13-1**
Positions a Principal May Occupy from a Third Party's Perspective.

authority granted. This obligation is known as the principal's duty to indemnify the agent. However, the principal is not liable to protect the agent from liability if the agent exceeds the actual authority and no ratification has occurred. Note that because of the reasons discussed in section 4, an undisclosed principal cannot ratify an agent's unauthorized acts. For ratification to be valid, an agent must act as an agent which is not the case when the principal is undisclosed.

### TO THIRD PARTIES

When the principal is disclosed, that principal becomes contractually bound to the third party if the agent acts with actual or apparent authority or if the principal ratifies an agent's unauthorized actions. In essence, this legal statement supports the concept of substituting the principal for the agent for liability purposes.

   If the principal is undisclosed, the principal becomes liable to third parties for contracts negotiated by agents with actual authority if the contract is the type that can be transferred to the undisclosed principal. In essence, this transferability requirement prevents an agent from shifting responsibility of performance to the undisclosed principal if the third party had contracted for the personal services of the agent. However, in the typical sale of commercial products transaction, the transferability of the contract generally is not restricted. Note that the stated rule on the undisclosed principal's liability is limited to situations where an agent acts with actual authority. Because of the nature of the undisclosed principal's position, an agent of that principal cannot have apparent authority and ratification by the principal cannot occur.

## 7. Liability of Agents

As in the case of principals, the liability of agents is determined by the agents' relationships with principals and third parties. Again the status of the agent's principal is significant.

### TO PRINCIPALS

Agents owe various duties to their principals. Many of these duties are based on the contract of employment, and others are implied by law from the nature of the relationship. Since the relationship is a fiduciary one, there is an implied duty of loyalty to the principal. This duty of loyalty requires that agents avoid conflicts of interest. A conflict of interest exists if an agent undertakes a business venture that competes or interferes in any manner with the business of the employer. In addition, an agent may not make a contract for himself or herself that should have been made for the principal. Agents cannot enter into contracts on behalf of the principal with themselves as the other party. Agents may deal with themselves only if they obtain permission of the principal, after full disclosure of all facts materially influencing the situation. Transactions violating the duty of loyalty may always be rescinded by the principal, even if the agent acted for the best interests of his or her principal and the contract was as favorable as could be obtained elsewhere. If an agent violates this duty of loyalty through a conflict of interest, the principal may rescind the contract. Moreover, a principal is entitled to treat any profit realized by the agent in violation of this duty as belonging to the principal. Such profits include rebates, bonuses, commissions, or divisions of profits received by the agent.

Violations of the duty of loyalty often involve improper use of confidential information. Confidential information or trade secrets may include formulas, customer lists, processes, and business data. Trade secrets are known only to a few persons, and efforts to protect them are required if they are to be protected by law. The law prohibits employees from using trade secrets in competition with the employer or from making them public. Industrial espionage is a major problem for high-technology industries. The law in all its aspects is available to assist employers in protecting these trade secrets. Theft of them is a crime. Courts will enjoin the improper use of them and may award damages for violations of the duty of loyalty. Of course, many important property interests are also protected by laws on patents and copyrights. Infringement suits are common, and there is extensive litigation to protect property rights based on the creation of new products and ideas.

---

# J & K COMPUTER SYSTEMS, INC. v. PARRISH
642 P.2d 732 (Utah 1982)

HOWE, J.: Plaintiff, J & K Computer Systems, Inc., brought this action seeking to recover damages from and enjoin its former employees Douglas T. Parrish and A. Chris Chlarson, and a corporation formed by them, Dynamic Software Corporation, from using or disclosing certain of plaintiff's confidential computer programs....

The trial court found for the plaintiff, awarded it $7,500 damages and enjoined the defendants and all persons associated with them from further use of the computer programs....Defendants appeal.

J & K was originally formed...by John Robertson and Keith Blake in 1976 to develop, market and install computer software. In March 1978, they hired Parrish as a computer programmer.

In the months that followed, Parrish developed an open-item/balance forward accounts receivable program which would be usable on the IBM System 34. After the program was developed, it was installed by Parrish at the Arnold Machinery Company in Salt Lake City....

In May 1979, Parrish's brother-in-law, Chlarson, was hired as a trainee by J & K and was assigned to work under his direction. Chlarson also entered into an employment agreement similar to the contract between Parrish and J & K prohibiting the disclosure of J & K's computer programs. Two months later, in May 1979, Parrish voluntarily left the employ of J & K and entered into an agreement with Arnold Ma-

chinery Company whereby Parrish would provide Arnold Machinery with programming services....

In June 1979, Chlarson voluntarily left J & K and began working with Parrish. Later that month, they formed Dynamic Software Corporation with Parrish as president and Chlarson as secretary-treasurer. The record shows that in July 1979, Parrish made an electronic copy of the accounts receivable program which J & K had installed at Arnold Machinery Company. This copy was made on a magnetic disk which Parrish then gave to Chlarson so that Chlarson could become familiar with it. Chlarson took the disk to the IBM 34 Computer workroom in the IBM building in Salt Lake City, and there began to work with the programs contained thereon. While Chlarson was working with the disk, an employee of J & K saw one of its programs displayed on the screen of the computer terminal. The employee then advised his employer who thereafter, upon advice of legal counsel, went back to the computer room at IBM. Plaintiff retrieved from the garbage can two printouts of the programs which had been displayed and discarded by Chlarson. Those programs were similar to the J & K accounts receivable program and serve as the basis for this lawsuit.

Defendants assail the judgment of the trial court awarding the plaintiffs damages and injunctive relief claiming that the accounts receivable programs were not confidential or trade secrets. There is no dispute that the plaintiff regarded the programs which it developed and used in its business as proprietary. The employment contracts which Parrish and Chlarson signed specified that the computer programs were "valuable, special and unique assets" of plaintiff's business. An expert witness…gave testimony which supports the finding that the programs are trade secrets.…

A trade secret includes any formula, patent, device, plan or compilation of information which is used in one's business and which gives him an opportunity to obtain an advantage over competitors who do not know it.

It is a well recognized principle that our law will afford protection to the inventor of a special process or trade secret. With the evidence recited above before it, the trial court could have reasonably determined that J & K's accounts receivable program was secret and worthy of protection by the law. Defendants assert that the accounts receivable program was revealed to certain customers and therefore not protectable. The record, however, shows that the plaintiff en-

deavored to keep its accounts receivable program secret. Plaintiff's employees and customers were informed of the secret nature of the program. The program was marked with the following legend: "Program Products Proprietary To J & K Computer Systems, Inc., Salt Lake City, Utah. Authorized Use By License Agreement Only." That a few of the plaintiff's customers had access to the program does not prevent the program from being classified as a trade secret where the plaintiff was attempting to keep the secret and the program is still unavailable to the computer trade as a whole.

Defendants next contend that it is unlawful to enjoin them from using their skills, training and experience which they have gained in the computer programming business.…Defendants were not enjoined by the order of the trial court from using their general knowledge, skills, memory or experience. They were, however, enjoined from using the proprietary accounts receivable program which the plaintiff had developed.… [*Affirmed.*]

---

In addition to, or as a result of, these fiduciary duties owed, an agent must act within the scope of the actual authority granted. An agent may exceed actual authority and still contractually bind a disclosed principal to a third party if there is apparent authority. In such situations, the principal may recover from the agent for any performance the principal may have owed to the third party. If the disclosed principal ratifies the unauthorized acts of an agent, that agent has no liability to the principal.

### TO THIRD PARTIES

In general, agents do not become personally liable to third parties since the principal is substituted for the agent. However, there are three situations when an agent and third party are contractually bound to one another. First, if the agent has represented an undisclosed principal, the agent is personally liable on the contract. The third party has no one other than the agent to hold liable. The agent remains liable to the third party until that time when the principal is disclosed, and the third party elects to hold the principal, and not the agent, liable.

The second situation arises whenever the agent agrees to be liable personally or when the agent has failed to sign a document in a representative capacity. When an agent works for a truly undisclosed principal, no representative capacity will be indicated. However, if the agent for a disclosed or partially disclosed principal fails to indicate his agency capacity clearly, that agent becomes personally liable to the third party.

A third instance of an agent's becoming bound personally to a third party occurs when the agent has exceeded actual and apparent authority. Whenever an agent negotiates with a third party, that agent implicitly promises he or she has authority to make the contract involved. If that promise is breached, the agent is liable to the third party.

### 8.  Liability of Third Parties

The law always is concerned about the mutuality of contractual obligations. One party should not be bound to a contract if the other party is not bound also. The third party is liable, therefore, to the principal when the principal is liable to the third party. Likewise, the third party becomes contractually bound to the agent when that agent is bound to the third party.

**TO PRINCIPALS**

A third party is bound to a disclosed principal on contracts negotiated by an agent who had either actual or apparent authority and also on contracts negotiated by an unauthorized agent if the disclosed principal ratifies the agreement. A third party is liable to an undisclosed principal on contracts negotiated by an agent with actual authority if the contract can be transferred to the principal.

**TO AGENTS**

Generally, a third party does not become personally liable to the agent because the principal is substituted for the agent. However, the third party may be bound to an agent (1) who represents an undisclosed principal, (2) who fails to indicate a representative capacity, (3) who agrees to be personally liable, or (4) who exceeds the authority granted by a principal.

## AGENCY AND TORT LIABILITY

### 9.  Basic Concepts

In addition to the contract liability issues arising out of an agency, questions of liability for injuries to a third party's person or property may be present. Recall that when the liability issue is based on torts, courts will use the terms master and servant as well as principal and agent. The typical situation involving tort liability occurs when an employment arrangement results in injury to a third party. The issue usually involves determining who is liable for the third party's injury—the employee (servant)* or the employer (master). The following general statements present the guidelines used in determining tort liability:

1 The party committing the tort (wrong) is liable for the damage done.

2 A master is liable for the torts of servants who were acting within the scope of their employment.

3 The party hiring an independent contractor usually is not liable for the torts of that independent contractor.

## 10. Respondeat Superior

A principal is liable for the torts of an agent. And an employer is liable for the torts of an employee if the agent or employee acts within the scope of his or her employment or is working for the employer. Likewise, a partnership and the individual parties have tort liability for torts of a partner or of an employee when the torts are committed within the scope of the partnership business. This liability is created by respondeat superior.

The doctrine of respondeat superior imposes vicarious liability on those (masters) who actually have not committed any tort. This concept of vicarious liability is based on the public policy of placing responsibility on the party who is most capable of paying for the damage done. This principle has been referred to as the *deep pocket* theory of liability. In essence, the doctrine of respondeat superior provides that the cost of doing business should include liability for injuries to persons and property which are caused by employees within the scope of employment. Thus, the business, rather than just the injured victim or the employee, bears the cost of these injuries. However, remember that an employee is liable for the torts committed. The fact that the employer also may be liable does not excuse the wrongdoer.

---

# SANFORD v. KOBEY BROS. CONST. CORP.
689 P.2d 724 (Colo. App. 1984)

---

BERMAN, J.: Plaintiffs, Andrew M. and Olivia M. Sanford, appeal the judgment of the trial court holding defendant Kobey Brothers Construction Corp. (Kobey Broth-ers) liable to plaintiffs in the amount of $8,905.59 and holding co-defendant Harris Kobey not jointly or severally liable....

Kobey Brothers constructed a home for

the plaintiffs in the Cherry Hills North area of Englewood, Colorado. For various reasons, the foundation was incompatible with the soil, resulting in heaving and damage to the home. Plaintiffs sued both Harris Kobey and Kobey Brothers for negligent construction and breach of express and implied warranties. The trial court found no individual liability on the part of Harris Kobey, but found Kobey Brothers liable for damages arising from the negligent reduction of the "void space" between the foundation and interior basement walls, as well as from certain other work negligently performed. The trial court measured plaintiffs' damages by the cost to repair the injuries caused by the improperly reduced void space and other errors attributable to Kobey Brothers.

Plaintiffs first contend that the trial court erred in not finding Harris Kobey personally liable for his allegedly negligent acts. They argue the trial court improperly applied the doctrine of *respondeat superior* as a shield barring personal liability and *sua sponte* looked unsuccessfully for reasons to "pierce the corporate veil" instead of simply attributing to Harris Kobey personal responsibility for his negligent acts. We agree that Kobey should be held personally liable.

Neither the doctrine of *respondeat superior* nor the fiction of corporate existence bars imposition of individual liability for individual acts of negligence, even when the individual is acting in a representative capacity. Rather, a servant may be held personally liable for his individual acts of negligence, as also may an officer, director, or agent of a corporation for his or her tortious acts, regardless of the fact that the master or corporation also may be vicariously liable. Thus, if Harris Kobey personally committed any negligent act, judgment should also have entered against him personally.

The record reveals that Harris Kobey did personally commit the negligent act causing the major portion of damages attributable to Kobey Brothers. The trial court found that the reduction in size of the "void space" from the specified three inches to the improper one and one-half inches constituted negligence. Harris Kobey admitted three times on the witness stand that he personally and solely authorized the reduction, and in fact did so arbitrarily. Accordingly, joint and several liability for the entire judgment should have entered against Harris Kobey....[*Reversed.*]

---

The concept of vicarious liability is an expanding one. In the twentieth century, juries and courts have enlarged the definition of scope of employment and thus have increased the total risk of businesses of all types. This is especially true now that the automobile and truck play a major role in the conduct of business.

Principals may also have tort liability based on apparent authority. For example, a trade association was held to have liability under the antitrust laws if its personnel were involved in the violations. Likewise, a principal is liable for an agent's fraud even though the agent acts solely to benefit himself or herself, if the agent has apparent authority.

Under the apparent authority theory, liability is based upon the fact that the agent's position facilitates the consummation of the fraud, in that from the point of view of the third person the transaction seems regular on its face and the agent appears to be acting in the ordinary course of business.

It should be noted that everyone performing a service is not necessarily a servant or agent of an employer. Work is sometimes performed by an independent contractor. Whether a person is a servant or an independent contractor is determined by the degree of control the employing party exercises. More control indicates a master-servant relationship. Less control is associated with a proprietor-independent contractor relationship. In essence, an independent contractor has the power to control the details of the work performed.

As a general rule, the person hiring an independent contractor is not personally liable for the contracts or torts of the independent contractor. In other words, general agency principles, including the doctrine of respondeat superior, are not applicable in the typical situation involving an independent contractor.

Liability based on tort theories is so important that it was the subject matter of Chapter 10.

# LIABILITY OF ORGANIZATIONS

### 11. Introduction

The law of agency principles makes it clear that principals (masters) may have liability for their agents' (servants') actions. Therefore, when the principal (master) is a business, that organization also may have liability due to its employees' acts. This liability may be based on contract or tort law theories. In addition to these agency concepts of liability, the next two sections illustrate that organizations also may be (1) criminally liable, or (2) civilly liable for violating a statute or for acting contrary to public policy.

### 12. Criminal Liability

Most statutes provide for penalties to be imposed upon those who violate their provisions. If a statute imposes fines or incarceration as a penalty, the law is criminal, and for a court to find a violation there must be proof beyond a reasonable doubt.

The fiction of the corporate entity creates some difficult problems insofar as criminal law is concerned. A corporation cannot be imprisoned, although in theory a death penalty of sorts could be imposed simply by the domiciliary state dissolving it. Corporations act only through agents, and while it is possible to imprison the agents in many instances, this would not be satisfactory punishment for the corporate entity. It is, of course, possible to punish a corporation by imposing a fine.

Proving the commission of a crime by a corporation is often as difficult as imposing a meaningful penalty. "Crime" is usually defined in terms of intentional commission of some prohibited act, often with the *specific* intent to do so. How can an artificial being with no mind have criminal intent? The law has generally resolved this problem by imputing to the corporation the guilty intent of an agent, if the agent was authorized and acting within the scope of his or her employment at the time he or she committed the crime. Many cases have equated "acquiescence" by the company in the wrongful conduct with authority to commit the illegal act.

There are a number of laws about which business organizations must be concerned in our legal environment. Among those providing criminal sanctions are the Foreign Corrupt Practices Act (Chapter 14), the securities acts (Chapter 19), and antitrust laws (Chapters 22–24), and the environmental laws (Chapter 25).

## 13. Civil Liability

In addition to criminal penalties, business organizations may become liable to pay money damages or for some equitable relief. In the area of torts there are numerous examples of organizations having to pay large sums of money to injured third parties. One issue of tort liability that has received much attention and has been extensively litigated is the question of when an organization becomes liable for the punitive damages awarded by a jury.

One theory has been to follow the general rules of vicarious liability under the doctrine of respondeat superior and hold the organization liable for the punitive damages. The more modern view seeks to determine the blameworthiness of the organization for the injury. This view has been called the *complicity rule* and is discussed in the following case.

---

# MERCURY MOTOR EXPRESS, INC. v. SMITH

393 So.2d 545 (Fla. 1981)

---

ALDERMAN, J.:…Richard Welch, an employee of the petitioner, Mercury Motors Express, while driving a tractor-trailer for his employer, lost control of the vehicle, drove off the road, and hit David J. Faircloth, Jr., causing his death. Respon-

dent, the personal representative of the decedent's estate and the plaintiff in the trial court, alleged that Welch, "while acting in the scope of his employment with the Defendant, MERCURY MOTORS EXPRESS, INC.," was "driving and operating the said vehicle while under the influence of alcohol to the extent that his ability to drive was impaired and did so in a reckless and negligent manner and at an excessive rate of speed, with a willful and wanton disregard for the life and safety of others...." Mercury Motors does not dispute these factual allegations, and for the purpose of our review, we accept them as true. When the case was tried, the jury awarded the plaintiff $400,000 compensatory and $250,000 punitive damages. Mercury Motors paid the compensatory damage award and appealed only the punitive damage judgment. In a brief opinion, the district court said that the legal issue presented "is whether a corporate employer and Interstate Commerce Commission permit holder can be liable in punitive damages for the willful and wanton misconduct of its employee while acting within the scope of his employment and operating a tractor and trailer leased by the corporate employer and operated under its permit." The district court, concluding that "a jury may assess punitive damages against a corporate employer when its employee, acting within the scope of his employment, has been guilty of willful and wanton misconduct, such as in this case," affirmed the award of punitive damages. We quash the decision of the district court and hold that, in the absence of some fault on the part of the corporate employer, it is not punitively liable for the willful and wanton misconduct of its employees.

We begin our analysis of this case by affirming the long-established Florida rule that "the liability of a corporate master for punitive or exemplary damages for wanton or malicious torts committed by an agent or servant is no different from the liability of an individual master under the same circumstances." The fact that the employer in this case is a corporation rather than a natural person is not legally significant....

Plaintiff effectually argues that under the doctrine of respondeat superior, an employer without fault on his part will always be vicariously liable for punitive damages for the willful and wanton misconduct committed by his employees within the scope of their employment. We reject this argument....

We conclude that the principles of law which should be applied in this and in other similar respondeat superior cases are as follows: (1) An employer is vicariously liable for *compensatory* damages resulting from the negligent acts of employees committed within the scope of their employment even if the employer is without fault. This is based upon the long-recognized public policy that victims injured by the negligence of employees acting within the scope of their employment should be compensated even though it means placing vicarious liability on an innocent employer. (2) Punitive damages, however, go beyond the actual damages suffered by an injured party and are imposed only as a punishment of the defendant and as a deterrent to others. (3) Before an employer may be held vicariously liable for punitive damages under the doctrine of respondeat superior, there must be some fault on his part. (4) Although the misconduct of the employee, upon which the vicarious liability of the employer for punitive damages is based, must be willful and wanton, it is not necessary that the fault of the employer, independent of his employee's conduct, also be willful and wanton. It is sufficient that the plaintiff allege and prove some fault on the part of the employer which foreseeably contributed to the plaintiff's injury to make him vicariously liable for punitive damages.

Applying these principles, we hold that there is no basis for the punitive damage award against the defendant employer. The plaintiff alleges no fault on the part of the employer and relies entirely upon the master-servant relationship to make the employer vicariously liable for punitive damages. The district court should have re- versed the punitive damage judgment. [*Reversed and remanded.*]

In addition to the tort liability it may face, a business may owe dollar damages to injured parties because of illegal conduct by its officers, agents, or other employees. Conduct may be illegal either because it violates a statute or because it is contrary to public policy. Many statutes provide legal rights to injured parties to recover the damages caused by a business organization. In a civil action, investors can seek to recover their investment when the organization has violated any of the securities laws (Chapter 19), labor laws (Chapters 17 and 18), antitrust laws (Chapters 22–24), or environmental laws (Chapter 25). The law of employment also provides for civil remedies if a worker is discharged in violation of equal employment opportunities (Chapter 17). Indeed, a breach of any contract by a business can result in the wronged party seeking monetary damages.

In recent years, courts increasingly have imposed liability upon a business even though the organization has not violated a statute. The basis of this liability is the fact that a business may have acted contrary to public policy. For example, such issues have arisen in cases concerned with the right of an employer to discharge an employee. Public-policy considerations are very important when an employee is not protected by either a collective bargaining agreement or another contract that provides a stated term of employment. Employees who lack these protections traditionally have been called *employees at will*, since the employer can terminate the employment relationship at any time for any reason.

Although the employment-at-will doctrine still exists today, there is a growing movement by courts to vest workers with certain rights and to require business organizations to justify firing a worker. This justification requirement is especially important when the discharge appears to deny an employee the opportunity to exercise a legal right. Such rights may include (1) serving on a jury, (2) filing a workers' compensation claim, (3) refusing to give perjured testimony, (4) refusing to commit an illegal or unethical act, and (5) assisting in the investigation of the organization's wrongful acts.

# PALMATEER v. INTERNATIONAL HARVESTER CO.
421 N.E.2d 876 (Ill. 1981)

SIMON, J.: The plaintiff, Ray Palmateer, complains of his discharge by International Harvester Company (IH). He had worked for IH for 16 years, rising from a unionized job at an hour rate to a managerial position on a fixed salary. Following his discharge,

Palmateer filed a…complaint against IH, alleging…that he had suffered a retaliatory discharge. According to the complaint, Palmateer was fired both for supplying information to local law-enforcement authorities that an IH employee might be involved in a violation of the Criminal Code of 1961 and for agreeing to assist in the investigation and trial of the employee if requested. The circuit court of Rock Island County ruled the complaint failed to state a cause of action and dismissed it; the appellate court affirmed….We granted Palmateer leave to appeal to determine the contours of the tort of retaliatory discharge approved in *Kelsay v. Motorola, Inc.* (1978), 74 Ill.2d 172.

In *Kelsay* the plaintiff was discharged in retaliation for filing a worker's compensation claim. The court noted that public policy strongly favored the exercise of worker's compensation rights; if employees could be fired for filing compensation claims, that public policy would be frustrated.…

With *Kelsay,* Illinois joined the growing number of States recognizing the tort of retaliatory discharge. The tort is an exception to the general rule that an "at-will" employment is terminable at any time for any or no cause. This general rule is a harsh outgrowth of the notion of reciprocal rights and obligations in employment relationships—that if the employee can end his employment at any time under any condition, then the employer should have the same right.…

Recent analysis has pointed out the shortcomings of the mutuality theory. With the rise of large corporations conducting specialized operations and employing relatively immobile workers who often have no other place to market their skills, recognition that the employer and employee do not stand on equal footing is realistic. In addition, unchecked employer power, like unchecked employee power, has been seen to present a distinct threat to the public pol-

icy carefully considered and adopted by society as a whole. As a result, it is now recognized that a proper balance must be maintained among the employer's interest in operating a business efficiently and profitably, the employee's interest in earning a livelihood, and society's interest in seeing its public policies carried out.

By recognizing the tort of retaliatory discharge, *Kelsay* acknowledged the common law principle that parties to a contract may not incorporate in it rights and obligations which are clearly injurious to the public.…But the Achilles heel of the principle lies in the definition of public policy. When a discharge contravenes public policy in any way the employer has committed a legal wrong. However, the employer retains the right to fire workers at will in cases "where no clear mandate of public policy" is involved: But what constitutes clearly mandated public policy?

There is no precise definition of the term. In general, it can be said that public policy concerns what is right and just and what affects the citizens of the State collectively. It is to be found in the State's constitution and statutes and, when they are silent, in its judicial decisions. Although there is no precise line of demarcation dividing matters that are the subject of public policies from matters purely personal, a survey of cases in other States involving retaliatory discharges shows that a matter must strike at the heart of a citizen's social rights, duties, and responsibilities before the tort will be allowed. Thus, actions for retaliatory discharge have been allowed where the employee was fired for refusing to violate a statute. It has also been allowed where the employee was fired for refusing to evade jury duty, for engaging in statutorily protected union activities, and for filing a claim under a worker's compensation statute.

The action has not been allowed where the worker was discharged in a dispute over a company's internal management system, where the worker took too much sick leave, where the worker tried to examine the company's books in his capacity as a shareholder, where the worker impugned the company's integrity, where the worker refused to be examined by a psychological-stress evaluator, where the worker was attending night school, or where the worker improperly used the employer's Christmas fund.

The cause of action is allowed where the public policy is clear, but is denied where it is equally clear that only private interests are at stake. Where the nature of the interest at stake is muddled, the courts have given conflicting answers as to whether the protection of the tort action is available.... 

It is clear that Palmateer has here alleged that he was fired in violation of an established public policy. The claim is that he was discharged for supplying information to a local law-enforcement agency that an IH employee might be violating the Criminal Code, for agreeing to gather further evidence implicating the employee, and for intending to testify at the employee's trial, if it came to that....There is no public policy more basic, nothing more implicit in the concept of ordered liberty than the enforcement of a State's criminal code.

There is no public policy more important or more fundamental than the one favoring the effective protection of the lives and property of citizens.

Public policy favors the exposure of crime and the cooperation of citizens possessing knowledge thereof is essential to effective implementation of that policy. Persons acting in good faith who have probable cause to believe crimes have been committed should not be deterred from reporting them by the fear of discharge. Public policy favors Palmateer's conduct in volunteering information to the law-enforcement agency. Once the possibility of crime was reported, Palmateer was under a statutory duty to further assist officials when requested to do so. Public policy thus also favors Palmateer's agreement to assist in the investigation and prosecution of the suspected crime.

The foundation of the tort of retaliatory discharge lies in the protection of public policy, and there is a clear public policy favoring investigation and prosecution of criminal offenses. Palmateer has stated a cause of action for retaliatory discharge.... [*Reversed.*]

## LIABILITY OF MANAGERS

### 14. Partners

The general laws of agency apply to partnerships. Each partner, in effect, is an agent of the organization and both a principal and an agent with respect to all fellow partners. As such, every partner owes the duty of loyalty to the partnership and to the other partners. When conducting business, each partner is obligated to exercise good faith and to contemplate the well-being of the organization and the partners. Any time one partner tries to take advantage of a business opportunity for his own personal benefit, he becomes personally liable for damages, since he has broken his fiduciary duty.

With respect to contractual liability, the principles of authority and ratification are applicable to the partnership and its partners. In general, the implied authority of a partner is greater than that of a general agent. Among the common implied powers are the following: to compromise, adjust, and settle claims or debts owed by or to the partnership; to sell goods in the regular course of business and to make warranties; to buy property within the scope of the business for cash or upon credit; to buy insurance; to hire employees; to make admissions against interest; to enter into contracts within the scope of the partnership; and to receive notices. A partner in a trading partnership, i.e., one engaged in buying and selling commodities, has the implied authority to borrow money in the usual course of business and to pledge the credit of the firm; but a partner in a nontrading partnership, such as an accounting firm, has no implied power to borrow money. In the latter case, such authority must be actual before the firm will be bound. A partner entering into such a contract is personally liable on it.

With respect to torts, a partner has the power to impose liability on the partnership through the doctrine of respondeat superior. As we discussed in the previous chapter, partners are jointly and severally liable for the debts of their partnership. Therefore, each partner potentially is liable for the torts of every other partner. If a partnership has liability because of a tort of a partner, the organization has the right to collect its losses from the partner at fault. Likewise, any partner who has liability due to another partner's tort can seek contribution from the partner at fault. However, if the injured third party collects directly from the guilty partner, that partner cannot seek contribution from the other partners.

In addition to the agency principles, creating contract and tort liability on partners, an act in violation of a statute or an act contrary to public policy may make the partners liable for monetary damages to third parties. Criminal liability may be imposed on the individual partners as well.

## 15.   Corporate Officers and Directors—in General

The liability of corporate directors is most frequently based on a violation of the fiduciary duty of loyalty owed to the corporation. A director occupies a position of trust and confidence in the corporation and cannot, by reason of his or her position, directly or indirectly derive any personal benefits not enjoyed by the corporation or the shareholders. The duty of loyalty and the duty to act in good faith prohibit directors from acting with a conflict of interest. The most common violation of this duty occurs when a director enters into a contract with or personally deals with the corporation. Since all officers enter into contracts of employment, alleged violations of this duty are quite common. In all circumstances, the director or officer must fully disclose his or her conflict of interest to the corporation. If he or she fails to do so, the contract may be rescinded.

At common law, such a contract was voidable unless it was shown to be (1) approved by a disinterested board, and (2) "fair" to the corporation, in that its terms were as favorable as those available from any other person. Under some modern statutes, the transaction is valid if (1) it is approved, with knowledge of the material facts, by a vote of disinterested directors or shareholders; and (2) the director can show it to be "fair."

The good-faith requirement is also lacking when a director or officer takes an opportunity for him or herself that the corporation should have had. A director is required to first present all possible corporate opportunities to the corporation. Only after an informed determination by the disinterested directors that the corporation should not pursue such opportunities can a director pursue them for personal benefit. In a closely held corporation, this fiduciary duty of loyalty and good faith extends to the other shareholders and even to the other officers.

Directors are also liable for failure to exercise due care. In its simplest terms, the duty of care is synonymous with a duty not to be negligent. The standard may be stated in a variety of ways, but the most common says that a director must exercise that degree of care that an ordinarily prudent person would exercise in managing his or her own personal affairs.

Since many directors are not actively engaged in the day-to-day operation of the business, the law recognizes that they must rely on others for much of the information used in decision making. In performing duties, a director is entitled to rely on information, opinions, reports, and statements of others. These include officers and employees whom the director reasonably believes to be reliable and competent in the matters presented. A director may also rely on legal counsel, public accountants, and other expert professionals. Finally, a director may also rely on committees of the board if they act within the designated authority and if he or she reasonably believes they merit confidence. A director does not fulfill his or her duties and does not act in good faith if he or she has knowledge that would cause the reliance to be unwarranted.

These requirements allow directors to use their best business judgment without incurring liability for honest mistakes. Directors must make difficult policy decisions, and they should not have liability if their decisions are based on information that later turns out to be false.

The Caterpillar code recognizes that the duties owed by the board of directors is to the company and to shareholders. However, all decisions are to take the public interest into account. The code provides:

## BOARD STEWARDSHIP

Law and logic support the notion that boards of directors are constituted to represent shareholders—the owners of the enterprise. We have long held the view that Caterpillar board members can best meet their responsibilities of stewardship to shareholders if they are elected solely by them—and not appointed by governments, labor unions, or other non-owner groups.

Board composition and board deliberations should be highly reflective of the public interest. We believe that is a basic, inseparable part of stewardship to shareholders.

### 16. Corporate Officers and Directors—Contracts and Torts

The officers and directors of a corporation may become personally liable for breach of a contract or for commitment of a tort. Liability usually is based on the general legal principles of agency previously discussed. This liability of officials usually is owed to the corporation; however, under certain circumstances the liability may extend to shareholders and to third parties.

Under the law of contracts, a corporate official does not become personally bound on agreements negotiated as long as he or she signs in a representative capacity and does not exceed the authority granted to him. If the corporation's identity and existence are undisclosed, the official is liable to the third party.

The tort liability of corporate officers and directors is based on principles of fault. For example, an official who participates in fraudulent conduct by the corporation has personal liability to the damaged third party on the common law tort theories just like any other agent or servant. The following case illustrates that corporate officers are not free from liability just because they act on behalf of their corporation.

# MISSISSIPPI PRINTING v. MARIS, WEST & BAKER
492 So.2d 977 (Miss. 1986)

GRIFFIN, J.: This defamation action was instigated by Mississippi Printing Company, Inc., a Greenwood, Mississippi, corporation engaged primarily in the business of printing, against Maris, West & Baker, Inc., an advertising agency incorporated in Mississippi and located in Jackson. Also named as defendants were the president of the corporation, the executive vice president, and an employee serving as production manager.

The complaint stated that Maris, West & Baker maliciously, and with the intent to defame and damage the reputation and business of Mississippi Printing Company, wrote a letter to the Better Business Bureau in Jackson which contained libelous statements....

At the conclusion of the trial, the lower court directed a verdict in favor of the three individual defendants,...

The jury returned a verdict against Mississippi Printing Company...

The subject of this lawsuit was a letter written by the three individual defendants named to the Better Business Bureau in Jackson, and circulated to several of Mississippi Printing Company's clients. The letter contained accusations that Mississippi Printing Company "centered around very unbusinesslike conduct," deliberately destroyed client material, was careless, and engaged in unethical conduct by contacting Maris, West & Baker's clients when Mississippi Printing was not awarded a particular bid.

The truth or falsity of the allegations contained in the letter was properly submitted to the jury for its determination of the corporation's liability. However, we are of the opinion the lower court erred in directing a verdict in favor of the corporate officers and agent.

The question of whether the officers and agents of a corporation may be held personally liable when they participate in defamatory conduct has not been addressed by this Court. However, the general rule is well established that when a corporate officer directly participates in or authorizes the commission of a tort, even on behalf of the corporation, he may be held personally liable.

The potentially libelous letter was signed by the corporation's president, the executive vice president, and the production manager. Each signed in their official capacities on Maris, West & Baker stationery. It is clear that the individuals named participated directly in the publication of the letter.

It is true that the case was properly presented to the jury as to Maris, West & Baker, Inc., however we find and hold that it was error to direct a verdict in favor of the individual defendants, and that it was not harmless error under Rule 11, Miss. Sup.Ct. Rules. Therefore, the case should be retried as to the individual defendants and the corporation....[*Reversed and remanded.*]

The liability of directors for negligence in the management of the corporation is to the corporation. Since no duty runs to third-party creditors, there is no liability to them or to shareholders. Of course, a shareholder may enforce this liability through a derivative suit—one brought by a shareholder on behalf of the corporation.

### 17.   Corporate Officers and Directors—Violation of Statutes

There are several statutes that impose liability on directors and officers. For example, directors or officers may be liable for failure to pay federal withholding and social security taxes for corporation employees if they have responsibility in that area. Likewise, a director or officer is subject to third-party liability for aiding a corporation in such acts as patent, copyright, or trademark infringements, unfair competition, antitrust violations, violation of laws relating to discrimination, or violations of securities laws. Many of these matters are covered in subsequent chapters.

Just as employees are liable for their own torts, they are responsible for their own crimes. And, as employers are liable for torts committed while employees are acting in the course of their employment, employers may also be held culpable for the business-related crimes of their employees. For example, suppose that the chief of marketing of ABC, Inc., enters into a price-fixing arrangement with two major competitors of ABC. Clearly both the chief and ABC are guilty of a violation of the Sherman Act, discussed in Chapter 23, and both could be fined. The chief also could be imprisoned. But what about the officers of ABC who are superiors of the chief of marketing, who have no knowledge of the chief's wrongdoing, and who are only indirectly connected to it by reason of their executive position and overall company responsibilities? Are they also guilty? Technically, such persons are not the employer of the chief of marketing—ABC is. Therefore, it would appear that the doctrine of respondeat superior would not apply to such top officials. However, they sometimes are prosecuted criminally. The issue in the following case was whether the chief executive officer of a corporation was properly convicted of a crime when he had no direct connection with its commission.

# UNITED STATES v. PARK
95 S.Ct. 1903 (1975)

Acme Markets, Inc., a large national retail food chain, and Park, its chief executive officer, were charged with violating the Federal Food, Drug, and Cosmetic Act. They had allegedly allowed interstate food shipments being held in their Baltimore warehouse to be exposed to contamination by rodents. While Acme pleaded guilty, Park entered a plea of not guilty.

Park admitted that all of Acme's employees were in a sense under his general direction but contended that the company had an "organizational structure for responsibilities for certain functions according to which different phases of its operations were assigned to individuals who, in turn, have staff and departments under them." He identified those persons responsible for sanitation and claimed that he had been informed that a vice president was investigating the situation in Baltimore when it was called to the company's attention by FDA. Park stated that he did not "believe that there was anything [he] could have done more construc-

tively than what [he] found was being done." However Park admitted that providing sanitary conditions for food was something that he was "responsible for" but argued that it was one of many phases of the company that he assigned to "dependable subordinates."

The court instructed the jury that it was not necessary for Park to have personally participated in the situation to be convicted, so long as he had "a responsible relationship to the issue." The conviction was reversed by the Court of Appeals on the ground that the jury instructions should have required a finding of "wrongful action." The Supreme Court granted certiorari.

BURGER, J.:...The question presented [is] whether "the manager of a corporation, as well as the corporation itself, may be prosecuted under the Federal Food, Drug, and Cosmetic Act of 1938 for the introduction of misbranded and adulterated articles into interstate commerce." In *Dotterweich* a jury...had convicted Dotterweich, the corporation's president and general manager. The Court of Appeals reversed the conviction on the ground that only the drug dealer, whether corporation or individual, was subject to the criminal provisions of the Act, and that where the dealer was a corporation, an individual connected therewith might be held personally only if he was operating the corporation "as his 'alter ego.'"

In reversing the judgment of the Court of Appeals and reinstating Dotterweich's conviction, this Court looked to the purposes of the Act and noted that they "touch phases of the lives and health of the people which, in the circumstances of modern industrialism, are largely beyond self-protection." It observed that the Act is of "a now familiar type" which "dispenses with the conventional requirement for criminal conduct—awareness of some wrongdoing. In the interest of the larger good it puts the burden of acting at hazard upon a person otherwise innocent but standing in responsible relation to a public danger."

Central to the Court's conclusion that individuals other than proprietors are subject to the criminal provisions of the Act was the reality that "the only way in which a corporation can act is through the individuals who act on its behalf."

The cases reveal that in providing sanctions which reach and touch the individuals who execute the corporate mission—and this is by no means necessarily confined to a single corporate agent or employee—the Act imposes not only a positive duty to seek out and remedy violations when they occur but also, and primarily, a duty to implement measures that will insure that violations will not occur. The requirements of foresight and vigilance imposed on responsible corporate agents are beyond question demanding, and perhaps onerous, but they are no more

stringent than the public has a right to expect of those who voluntarily assume positions of authority in business enterprises whose services and products affect the health and well-being of the public that supports them....

[The Court then turned to respondent's argument that the instructions to the jury were defective because they suggested that a finding of guilt could be justified solely because of respondent's corporate position.]

Reading the entire charge satisfies us that the jury's attention was adequately focused on the issue of respondent's authority with respect to the conditions that formed the basis of the alleged violations. Viewed as a whole, the charge did not permit the jury to find guilt solely on the basis of respondent's position in the corporation; rather, it fairly advised the jury that to find guilt it must find respondent "had a responsible relation to the situation," and "by virtue of his position...had authority and responsibility" to deal with the situation. The situation referred to could only be "food...held in unsanitary conditions in a warehouse with the result that it consisted, in part, of filth or...may have been contaminated with filth."...

The record in this case reveals that the jury could not have failed to be aware that the main issue for determination was not respondent's position in the corporate hierarchy, but rather his accountability, because of the responsibility and authority of his position, for the conditions which gave rise to the charges against him.

We are satisfied that the Act imposes the highest standard of care and permits conviction of responsible corporate officials who, in light of this standard of care, have the power to prevent or correct violations of its provisions....[*Reversed.*]

Whereas the Court intimated above that the jury's finding of guilty was not based solely on the respondent's position in the corporate hierarchy (and would be improper if it were), that conclusion is difficult to accept. It is hard to imagine a case where the chief executive officer of a large corporation would not have a "responsible relation" and "by virtue of his position" not have "authority and responsibility" to deal with almost any situation which might arise in the conduct of the business.

In one recent case, the officers of a corporation were convicted of murder. The company used cyanide in its processes, and steps had not been taken to protect workers from cyanide poisoning. In another case, three corporate officials received 20-year prison sentences for failing to warn employees of unsafe working conditions which resulted in the death of an employee. In perhaps the most publicized case on corporate officers' criminal liability, two executives of the Beech-Nut Nutrition Corporation were given prison sentences plus large fines for allowing their company to sell apple juice labeled "100% pure" when in fact little or no apple juice was in the container. Later, the Beechnut convictions were reversed on technical grounds.

From these cases it is clear there is a trend toward holding top company officials responsible for crimes, even though they are only indirectly involved. This is particularly true when public welfare statutes are violated, making certain acts criminal because they endanger the public health, safety, or general welfare. Conviction of such crimes usually does not require proof of an intent to commit the acts outlawed.

## 18. Ethical Considerations

The fiduciary duties which the director, officer, or other employee owes the corporation—especially the duty of loyalty—can often present difficult ethical as well as legal questions.

In the past, it has been all too common for corporate officers to engage in bribery, price-fixing, illegal campaign contributions, tax evasion, fraud, kickbacks, and bid rigging to further their business interests. Obviously, such blatant illegality could not hide behind any "duty of loyalty," for it violates not only the law, but also contemporary ethical ideas of what is "right" and "good." True loyalty to a corporation would entail seeing that the corporation operated within the law. Often, ethical standards are embodied in the law, thus ensuring that the principled corporation is not put at a disadvantage in competing with those less scrupulous. For example, every United States firm doing business in a foreign country is prohibited from bribing public officials. Each corporate management has a responsibility under the Foreign Corrupt Practices Act, as discussed in section 9 of chapter 14, to ensure adequate internal controls to prevent business bribes to foreign officials. Management further must take corrective action if violations are discovered. Various laws prohibit bribes and kickbacks in the

United States. Caterpillar's Code of Ethics regarding these matters is consistent with both the statutes and generally accepted ethical norms.

## RELATIONSHIPS WITH PUBLIC OFFICIALS

In dealing with public officials, as with private business associates, Caterpillar will utilize only ethical commercial practices. We won't seek to influence sales of our products (or other events impacting on the company) by payments of bribes, kickbacks, or other questionable inducements.

Caterpillar employees will take care to avoid involving the company in any such activities engaged in by others. We won't advise or assist any purchaser of Caterpillar products, including dealers, in making or arranging such payments. We will discourage dealers from engaging in such practices.

Payments of any size to induce public officials to fail to perform their duties—or to perform them in an incorrect manner—are prohibited. Company employees are also required to make good faith efforts to avoid payment of gratuities or "tips" to certain public officials, even where such practices are customary. Where these payments are as a practical matter unavoidable, they must be limited to customary amounts; and they may be made only to facilitate correct performance of the officials' duties.

## REVIEW QUESTIONS

**1** Test your knowledge and understanding by matching the term in the left-hand column with the appropriate statement in the right-hand column.

| | |
|---|---|
| (1) Implied authority | (a) Approval of an agent's unauthorized acts |
| (2) Apparent authority | (b) Doctrine that creates vicarious liability on the master |
| (3) Ratification | (c) Standard by which managers' decisions are judged |
| (4) Undisclosed principal | (d) A type of actual authority |
| (5) Respondeat superior | (e) The fundamental obligation owed by all agents to their principals |
| (6) Fiduciary | (f) The authority that is created by the principal from the third party's perspective |
| (7) Business judgment rule | (g) Exists when a third party does not know of a principal's existence |

(8) Duty of loyalty

**2** Jinks became acquainted with Gene Frye, who drove a new Ford Thunderbird automobile which had an Arrington & Blount dealer tag. Frye gave Jinks one of his business cards which showed that he was a "sales counselor" for Arrington & Blount. Jinks and his wife visited Arrington and Blount Ford and talked with Frye about purchasing a 1971 Ford station wagon. After negotiations, an agreement was reached and the purchase price was paid in two installments. When the title was not forthcoming as Frye had promised, Jinks contacted Arrington and Blount Ford. Jinks was told that Frye had been fired and that the 1971 Ford station wagon had been stolen by Frye. Therefore, the dealership demanded that Jinks return the automobile. Jinks surrendered possession of the car, but he filed suit for a refund of the purchase price. Did Frye have implied authority to bind Arrington and Blount Ford? Explain.

**3** Plaintiff sued to enforce a land sales contract. It provided that the plaintiff would be allowed to trade one purchased lot for a 2-acre parcel of the plaintiff's choice as soon as the property was developed for sale. Defendant contended that its salesperson, Walsh, lacked authority to agree to trade commercial property for residential property. Although the agent had no actual authority to do so, is the principal bound by this contract term agreed to by its agent? Why or why not?

**4** Ward contracted to sell 3,000 bushels of soybeans to Pillsbury to be delivered in January. In January, Ward had harvested only 2,000 bushels which left him 1,000 bushels short. Ward hired Bullock to deliver the 2,000 bushels that Ward had. Due to heavy rain that made unloading difficult,

(h) Type of relationship based on trust and confidence

Bullock and Pillsbury agreed to extend the delivery date. Pillsbury informed Ward that an extension-of-time agreement would be sent, but Ward never was told why the delivery was postponed. Ward refused to sign the extension agreement, and he claimed the sales contract was cancelled since Pillsbury refused to accept delivery in January. This position allowed Ward to avoid having to purchase the 1,000 bushels of soybeans he was short at an increased market price. Assuming that Bullock was an agent of Ward, can a principal ratify his agent's unauthorized action when he, as the principal, was unaware of all the circumstances? Explain.

**5** Klepp Wood Flooring is a contractor engaged in the business of installing wood floors in gymnasiums. Butterfield, an architect, invited Klepp to bid on a job. After the bid was received, Butterfield accepted the bid, but no formal contract was signed. Klepp completed the work and billed Butterfield. Butterfield refused to pay and told Klepp for the first time that the gym was owned by an undisclosed principal. Klepp sued Butterfield for the work performed. What was the result? Why?

**6** Roy Laccoarce was driving his truck on his return home from Roseburg when it went out of control and injured Stanfield. Roy worked for his parents, and consequently Stanfield sued both Roy and his parents. Although the evidence as to the primary purpose for Roy's trip to Roseburg was conflicting, at least one purpose was to pick up supplies for various businesses owned by Roy's parents. Was Roy acting within the scope of his employment? Why or why not?

**7** Tammy was shopping in Save-a-Lot Grocery Store when Stewart, an employee, brushed Tammy's ankle with a grocery cart. A short time later, while still shopping, Tammy told Stewart that he should say "Excuse me," and then people would get out of his way. Stewart then punched Tammy in the face, knocking her to the floor. If Tammy sues Save-a-Lot, should she collect for her injuries? Explain.

**8** Murphy slipped and fell on a sidewalk at a Holiday Inn motel which was operated by the Betsy-Len Motor Corporation. In order to recover for his injuries, Murphy sued Holiday Inns, Inc. Murphy contended that through its franchise agreement, Holiday Inns, Inc. had such control over the Betsy-Len Motor Corporation that these parties were master and servant. Holiday Inns, Inc. argued that it had no liability since it did not exercise sufficient control over Betsy-Len Motor Corporation to create a master-servant relationship. Did the franchise agreement provide Holiday Inns, Inc. sufficient control over Betsy-Len to make Holiday Inns, Inc. liable as a master? Why or why not?

**9** The two shareholders of Bonanza, Inc., which operated a shopping center, each owned 50 percent of the stock. Hunt was president and manager of the business. Sampson was secretary but inactive. Hunt purchased Sampson's stock for $75,000. At the time of the sale, Hunt did not inform Sampson of: (1) additional leases that had been obtained, (2) a commitment for financing of a third phase of the development, and (3) the sale of part of the stock to three doctors. When Sampson learned these facts, he sued to recover the difference between the selling price and the fair market value of the stock at the time of the sale. Did Hunt breach the fiduciary duties owed to Sampson? Explain.

**10** Taylor and Terry agreed to operate a business called the Christian Book Center, Inc. Each owned 50 percent of the corporate stock. From the business' inception, Taylor was the corporate president. An argument occurred over the operations of the business. Thereafter, Taylor told Terry that he was "out of business." A short time later, a promissory note that the corporation owed became due. Rather than discussing a possible extension of this note with Terry, Taylor allowed the corporation to default. At a foreclosure sale, Taylor purchased the assets of the corporation and continued the operation in his own name. Terry was not informed of the default or foreclosure sale. When he learned of Taylor's actions, he sued. What was the result? Why?

**11** Agatha, Alicia, and Hilary operated the AAH Family Health Spa. Agatha and Hilary paid themselves salaries of $18,000 a year, but they paid Alicia only $5,000 annually. Agatha and Hilary sold spa membership to their families at below the normal rate. They also refused to discuss partnership affairs with Alicia. Does Alicia have a cause of action against Agatha and Hilary? Explain.

**12** A patient sued Dr. Flynn for medical malpractice. Dr. Flynn, who is a partner in a medical partnership, sought contributions from his partners. He contended that his negligence, if any, occurred in the course of the partnership's business. Is Dr. Flynn entitled to contributions from his partners? Why or why not?

**13** Plaintiffs, residents of a housing development built by Milzoco Builders, Inc., sued the president, vice president, and secretary of the corporation as individuals. The plaintiffs allege that due to faulty planning, their homes were built in an area that is often flooded by the drainage of the other areas of the development and that the defendants were negligent in constructing the development. Can these officers be held personally liable? Why or why not?

**14**   An injured workman brought an action to enforce a worker's compensation award against a bankrupt corporation. The corporation failed to carry workers' compensation insurance. Since the employee was unable to recover from the bankrupt corporation, he brought an action against the officers and directors of the corporation. What was the result? Why?

# Chapter
# *14*

# International Business Transactions

### 1. Introduction

As we move toward a global economy where countries grow more economically interdependent on each other, some understanding of the international legal environment is essential for students of business. International business affects almost every individual in the United States. For instance, the typical American consumer who purchases a Japanese television has an indirect role in international trade. Several international trade participants, from the Japanese manufacturer to the local American retailer, played a part in the sale of the television to the customer in the United States.

International business activities generate more than one-third of the U.S. gross national product (GNP). The global impact of international business also is staggering. More than two hundred multinational businesses have sales in excess of $1 billion per year. Virtually all Fortune 500 companies are engaged in international trade, as are most major foreign business enterprises and many smaller domestic firms. As a firm expands beyond a single country and its business activities cross national borders, the need for the firm's managers to understand the evolving international business marketplace is of paramount importance.

The international legal environment of business does not consist of a cohesive body of uniform principles. It contains elements of United States domestic law, the law of other countries, multilateral, bilateral and regional agreements or treaties, and customary international law. Meaningful issues for firms engaging in international business transactions presented in this chapter include: (1) methods of transacting international business; (2) risks involved in international trade; (3) international organizations and agreements affecting trade; and (4) protection of domestic industries in a world market.

This chapter will introduce the following terms and concepts: the act of state doctrine, dumping, economic boycotts, export controls, expropriation, joint ventures, letters of credit, nationalization, retaliatory trade practices, and sovereign immunity. Moreover, many international organizations and agreements will be explained.

# METHODS OF TRANSACTING INTERNATIONAL BUSINESS

A United States business that wants to engage in international trade is presented with an almost limitless array of possibilities. Choosing a method of doing business in foreign countries requires understanding not only the factors normally involved in selecting an organization and operating a business domestically, but also demands an appreciation of the international trade perspective. The business enterprise form used in the movement of goods, technology, and services across national borders may be either direct foreign sales, licensing agreements, or direct foreign investment depending upon the country, type of export, and amount of export involved in the particular transaction.

## 2.  Foreign Sales

The simplest, least risky approach for a manufacturer to use when trying to penetrate foreign markets is to sell goods directly to buyers located in other countries. However, with foreign sales, increased uncertainty over the ability to enforce the buyer's promise to pay for goods often requires that more complex arrangements for payment be made than with the usual domestic sale. Commonly, an **irrevocable letter of credit** is used to ensure payment. Transactions using such a letter involve, in addition to a seller and buyer, an **issuing bank** in the buyer's country. The buyer obtains a commitment from the bank to advance (pay) a specified amount (i.e., the price of the goods) upon receipt from the carrier, of a **bill of lading,** stating that the goods have been shipped. The issuing bank's commitment to pay is given, not to the seller directly, but to a **confirming bank** located in the United States from which the seller obtains payment. The confirming bank forwards the bill of lading to the issuing bank in order to obtain reimbursement of the funds that have been paid to the seller. The issuing bank releases the bill of lading to the buyer after it has been paid, and with the bill of lading the buyer is able to obtain the goods from the carrier. Use of a letter of credit in the transaction thus reduces the uncertainties involved. The buyer need not pay the seller for goods prior to shipment, and the seller can obtain payment for the goods immediately upon shipment.

### 3.  Licenses or Franchises

In appropriate circumstances, a domestic firm may choose to grant a foreign firm the means to produce and sell its product. The typical method for controlling these transfers of information is the **license** or **franchise** contract. In this manner, intangible property rights, such as patents, copyrights, trademarks, or manufacturing processes, are transferred in exchange for royalties in the foreign country. A licensing arrangement allows the international business to enter a foreign market without any direct foreign investment. Licensing often is used as a transitional technique for firms expanding international operations since the risks are greater than with exporting but considerably less than with direct foreign investment.

### 4.  Direct Foreign Investment

As a business increases its level of international trade, it may find that creation of a **foreign subsidiary** is necessary. Most countries will permit a foreign firm to conduct business only if a national (individual or firm) of the host country is designated as its legal representative. Since this designation may create difficulties in control and result in unnecessary expense, the usual practice for multinational corporations is to create a foreign subsidiary in the host country. The form of subsidiary most closely resembling a U.S. corporation is known as a *societé anonyme (S.A.)* or, in German-speaking countries, an *Aktiengesellschaft (A.G.)*. Other forms of subsidiaries may also exist that have characteristics of limited liability of the owners and fewer formalities in their creation and operation.

Creation of a foreign subsidiary may pose considerable risk to the domestic parent firm. The 1983 incident in Bhopal, India, where hundreds of people were killed and thousands injured as a result of toxic gas leaks from a chemical plant, resulted in lawsuits against both the Indian subsidiary corporation and Union Carbide, the parent firm in the United States. Such is the magnitude of the problem that Union Carbide offered $350 million to settle these claims.

In many instances, however, the only legal or political means a firm has to invest directly in a foreign country is to engage in a **joint venture** with an entity from that host country. A host country's participant may be a private enterprise or, especially in developing countries, a government agency or government-owned corporation. Many foreign countries favor joint ventures because they allow local individuals and firms to participate in the benefits of economic growth and lessen the risk of foreign domination of local industry. Many of the developing countries require that the local partner have majority equity control of the venture and also insist on joint ventures with government participation. For example, mineral resources are considered to be owned by the foreign state; thus, extraction or production of these resources depends upon participation of a state agency.

# RISKS INVOLVED IN INTERNATIONAL TRADE

### 5.  Expropriation and Nationalization

If a domestic firm is involved in a foreign country to the extent of locating assets there (whether through branches, subsidiaries, joint ventures, or otherwise), it may be subject to the ultimate legal and political risk of international business activity—expropriation. **Expropriation,** as used in the context of international law, is the seizure of foreign-owned property by a government. When the owners are not fairly compensated, the expropriation is also considered to be a **confiscation** of property. Usually, the expropriating government also assumes ownership of the property, so the process includes **nationalization** as well. In the United States, the counterpart of expropriation is called the power of eminent domain. This power of all governments to take private property is regarded as inherent, yet it is subject to restraints upon its exercise. Our Constitution (as well as the constitutions of most states) prohibits the government from seizing private property except for "public purposes" and upon the payment of "just compensation." These Constitutional safeguards are limited, however, to the taking of property by the states or the federal government. Questions arise, then, as to the legal recourse against a foreign government that has taken over ownership of property within its jurisdiction.

Of course, constitutional or statutory safeguards against expropriation may exist in other countries as well as in the United States. However, the extent of such protection varies widely. Treaties (or other agreements) between the United States and other countries may provide additional protection against uncompensated takings of property. It is customary for international law to recognize the right of governments to expropriate the property of foreigners only when accompanied by "prompt, adequate and effective compensation." This standard is followed by most industrialized countries; however, developing countries and socialist countries have increasingly rejected this standard in favor of a *national* standard whereby absolute supremacy is asserted with regard to nationalizations in general and compensation in particular.

## 6. Sovereign Immunity and the Act of State Doctrine

Nationalization of American assets accompanied by unsatisfactory offers of compensation has led aggrieved parties to file lawsuits in the United States to seek satisfactory compensation. Two distinct but related doctrines pose serious obstacles for recovery in these situations: the **act of state doctrine** and the **doctrine of sovereign immunity.** Both doctrines demonstrate a policy of respect for the autonomy of foreign states and, if applied, lead to judicial abstention in disputes between U.S. firms and foreign countries.

### ACT OF STATE

The Supreme Court outlined the act of state doctrine more than ninety years ago in *Underhill v. Hernandez* and held that "[e]very sovereign State is bound to respect the independence of every other sovereign State, and the courts of one country will not sit in judgment on the acts of the government of another done within its own territory." The act of state doctrine also has constitutional underpinnings and recognizes that it is the President's responsibility to conduct foreign policy. The doctrine is the federal judiciary's response to foreign policy tensions that can be created when an American court sits in judgment of a foreign state's governmental affairs within that country's borders.

The doctrine has undergone some modification over the past century. Several exceptions to the doctrine have been recognized. The Supreme Court has held that the doctrine should not be extended to foreign governments acting in a commercial capacity and "should not be extended to include the repudiation of a purely commercial obligation owed by a foreign sovereign or by one of its commercial instrumentalities." This interpretation recognizes that governments also may act in a private or commercial capacity and, when doing so, will be subjected to the same rules of law as are applicable to private individuals. Of course, a nationalization of assets probably will be considered an act in the "public interest."

Congress outlined its narrow interpretation of the act of state doctrine in the Hickenlooper Amendment to the *Foreign Assistance Act of 1964*. The amendment directs that the act of state doctrine shall *not* be applied by the courts in cases when property is confiscated in violation of international law, unless the President decides that application of the doctrine is necessary. Federal courts, however, have not received this provision enthusiastically and have applied it only to cases in which the property has returned to the United States.

The party moving for the application of the doctrine has the burden of proving that the doctrine is appropriate and, as the following case demonstrates, there are limits to when the doctrine may be utilized.

---

# THE REPUBLIC OF THE PHILIPPINES v. FERDINAND E. MARCOS

862 F.2d 1355 (9th Cir. 1988)

---

The Republic of the Philippines (the Republic) brought a civil suit against its former President, Ferdinand Marcos, and his wife Imelda (the Marcoses), asserting claims under the Racketeer Influenced and Corrupt Organizations Act (RICO) and other applicable law. The district court entered a preliminary injunction enjoining the Marcoses from disposing of any of their assets except the payment of attorney fees and normal living expenses. The Marcoses appealed.

NOONAN, J.: Contrary to the contention of the Marcoses, the complaint, as interpreted by the district court, sufficiently alleges a RICO offense. The Republic alleges that the Marcoses and the other defendants arranged for the investment in real estate in Beverly Hills, California of $4 million fraudulently obtained by the Marcoses; that the Marcoses arranged for the creation of two bank accounts in the name of Imelda Marcos at Lloyds Bank of California totaling over $800,000 also fraudulently obtained by the Marcoses; and that the Marcoses transported into Hawaii money, jewels, and other property worth over $7 million also fraudulently obtained by them.... The gravamen of the Republic's entire case is the allegation that the Marcoses stole public money....

Before determining whether issuance of an injunction was appropriate we must consider two defenses which, if accepted, would block trial of the case the Marcoses maintain. First, that their acts are insulated because they were acts of state not reviewable by our courts, and second, that any adjudication of these acts would involve the investigation of political questions beyond our courts' competence.

The classification of certain acts as "acts of state" with the consequence that their validity will be treated as beyond judicial review is a pragmatic device, not required by the nature of sovereign authority and inconsistently applied in international law. The purpose of the device is to keep the judiciary from embroiling the courts and the country in the affairs of the foreign nation whose acts are challenged. Minimally viewed, the classification keeps a court from making pronouncements on matters over which it has no power: maximally interpreted, the classification prevents the embarrassment of a court offending a foreign government that is "extant at the time of suit."

The "continuing vitality" of the doctrine depends on its capacity to reflect the proper distribution of functions between the judicial and political branches of the government on matters bearing upon foreign relations....

As a practical tool for keeping the judicial branch out of the conduct of foreign affairs, the classification of "act of state" is not a promise to the ruler of any foreign country that his conduct, if challenged by his own country after his fall, may not become the subject of scrutiny in our courts. No estoppel exists insulating a deposed dictator from accounting. No guarantee has been granted that immunity may be acquired by an ex-chief magistrate invoking the magic words "act of state" to cover his or her past performance...

In the instant case the Marcoses offered no evidence whatsoever to support the classification of their acts as acts of state. The burden of proving acts of state rested upon them. They did not undertake the proof....

Bribetaking, theft, embezzlement, extortion, fraud, and conspiracy to do these things are all acts susceptible of concrete proof that need not involve political questions. The court, it is true, may have to determine questions of Philippine law in determining whether a given act was legal or illegal. But questions of foreign law are not beyond the capacity of our courts. The court will be examining the acts of the president of a country whose immediate political heritage is from our own. Although sometimes criticized as a ruler and at times invested with extraordinary power, Ferdinand Marcos does not appear to have had the authority of an absolute autocrat. He was not the state, but the head of the state, bound by the laws that applied to him. Our courts have had no difficulty in distinguishing the legal acts of a deposed ruler from his acts for personal profit that lack a basis in law....[*Affirmed.*]

## DOCTRINE OF SOVEREIGN IMMUNITY

Although inextricably related to the act of state doctrine, the doctrine of sovereign immunity differs fundamentally in its operation. This judicially developed doctrine provides that a foreign sovereign is immune from suit in the United States. By contrast, the act of state doctrine does not immunize anyone from suit but merely concerns the limits for determining the application and validity of a rule of law. The act of state doctrine may be relevant whether or not the sovereign nation is a direct party in the lawsuit. Under the doctrine of sovereign immunity, the foreign sovereign claims to be immune from suit entirely based on its status as a state.

Until approximately 1952, this notion was absolute. From 1952 until 1976, U.S. courts adhered to a *restrictive theory* under which immunity existed with regard to sovereign or public acts but not with regard to private or commercial acts. In 1976, Congress enacted the *Foreign Sovereign Immunities Act* that codifies this restrictive theory and rejects immunity for commercial acts carried on in the United States or having direct effects in this country. The case which follows illustrates the application of a foreign sovereign's immunity from suit in this country.

# TRANSAMERICAN STEAMSHIP v. SOMALI DEMOCRATIC REPUBLIC
767 F.2d 998 (D.C. Cir. 1985)

An American shipper, Transamerican Steamship, brought suit against the Somali Democratic Republic (SDR) for losses, totaling approximately $10,000 per day, when the government detained its ship over a dispute involving the emergency shipment of 40,000 tons of corn by the Agency for International Development. The shipment was part of a $20 million famine relief program to ameliorate widespread starvation and malnutrition in Somalia. The lawsuit centered around actions taken by SDR to protect the interests of the Somali Shipping Agency (Agency) in the controversy.

TAMM, J.: The Foreign Sovereign Immunities Act of 1976 (FSIA) grants foreign sovereigns immunity from suit in the United States unless one of the specified statutory exceptions applies. If an exception applies, [the law] confers subject matter jurisdiction on the district courts to hear claims against foreign states. The purpose of the FSIA is to facilitate suits in United States courts arising from the commercial conduct of foreign sovereigns....

Thus, a foreign state may not invoke sovereign immunity in any case in which the foreign state has implicitly or explicitly waived its immunity or where the claim arises from commercial activities by the foreign state....In accordance with the restrictive view of sovereign immunity reflected in FSIA, the burden of proof in establishing the inapplicability of these exceptions is upon the party claiming immunity.... Transamerican argues that SDR's actions were not governmental, but clearly commercial in character....

The proper inquiry is whether the embassy acted in a sovereign or essentially private capacity. SDR argues that its actions were diplomatic in character, undertaken to...promote friendly relations with Transamerican and, presumably, the United States. Although the embassy certainly could be viewed as "protecting" the interests of the Agency, its conduct exceeded the bounds of ordinary diplomatic behavior....We therefore conclude that the SDR has not sustained its burden of proving the inapplicability of the exception and that the Somali government has participated in commercial activity in the United States. The district court thus has subject matter jurisdiction over Transamerican's claims against the SDR.... [*Affirmed in part and reversed in part.*]

## 7.   Export Controls

Another risk involved in doing business abroad is **export controls** placed on the sale of certain U.S. goods and technology abroad. The United States controls the export of strategic goods and technology abroad to Soviet bloc nations and countries engaged in or supporting international terrorism. The United States' export control system currently is regulated by the Department of State and the Department of Commerce, pursuant to authority provided under the *Export Administration Act* and the *Arms Export Control Act.* The Department of Defense also plays a key role in determining the technology to be controlled as does the United States Customs Service in the enforcement of the controls. Significant criminal and administrative sanctions may be imposed upon corporations and individuals convicted of violating the law.

As a means of preventing the diversion of strategic items to prohibited destinations, U.S. export controls have been confused, fragmented, and often contradictory. Moreover, these controls pose a serious risk for a business engaged in international trade. Over the past decade these controls have become an extremely controversial topic in the international business community. Export controls make successful business deals more difficult for exporters. Foreign buyers may be reluctant to trade with an American exporter due to the red tape involved in obtaining governmental approval to export certain high-tech products like computers. They also run the risk that the United States may not permit an American company to honor a contract to export goods when its political relationship with the United States worsens. For instance, in 1986 President Reagan imposed economic sanctions on Libya, after determining that Libyan-sponsored terrorism had been directed against the United States. The sanctions prohibited the performance of contractual obligations by U.S. companies or their foreign subsidiaries, including the export of goods and technology to Libya.

The case which follows demonstrates the uncertainty faced by foreign buyers and the economic costs generated on U.S. firms and their foreign subsidiaries by the sudden imposition of export controls.

# DRESSER INDUSTRIES, INC. AND DRESSER (FRANCE) S.A. v. BALDRIDGE
549 F.Supp. 108 (D.C. 1982)

Dresser France, a French corporation owned and operated by Dresser Industries (a United States manufacturing corporation), signed a contract with Creusot-Loire, a French company and V/O Machinoimport, a Soviet agency, for the delivery of 21 gas compressors for use in building the oil and gas pipeline currently being constructed be-

tween the Soviet Union and Western Europe. Dresser France's manufacture of the compressors is based on technology obtained from Dresser Industries, pursuant to a licensing agreement between those two entities. In response to Soviet behavior concerning Poland, the Commerce Department thereafter issued regulations under the Export Administration Act forbidding export to the Soviet Union of U.S.-origin commodities and technical data and non-U.S.-origin commodities and technical data by U.S.-owned or controlled foreign firms for oil and gas transmission and refinement. The French government required the French subsidiary, Dresser (France), to abide by the contract and export the compressors from France to the Soviet Union. Since both the foreign subsidiary and the U.S.-parent firm, Dresser Industries, had violated U.S. export controls, the Commerce Department announced that sanctions would be levied against them.

GREEN, J.: This action was filed by plaintiffs, Dresser Industries, Inc., and Dresser (France) S.A., seeking injunctive relief preventing defendants, the Secretary of Commerce and other officials of the Department of Commerce, from imposing sanctions on Dresser (France) for violating regulations prohibiting the export of certain goods to the Soviet Union....

The factors which the Court must consider when presented with an application for injunctive relief are...(1) whether the movant has made a strong showing that it is likely to prevail on the merits of the case, (2) whether the movant has shown that without such relief, it will be injured irreparably, (3) whether the issuance of an injunction would substantially harm other parties interested in the proceedings, and (4) where the public interest lies.

At this juncture, upon the record that thus far has been established, it cannot be said that plaintiffs have made a strong showing that they are likely to prevail on the merits. Moreover, in light of the continuing availability of administrative remedies in the ongoing proceedings before the agency, the Court cannot find that irreparable harm necessarily will fall upon the plaintiffs if the extraordinary injunctive relief sought is not granted....

Most acutely evident to all those involved in this case is the potential for profound harm that could inure to the United States should injunctive relief issue. The regulations that lie at the heart of this dispute, which prohibit the export of certain goods and technology to the Soviet Union, particularly those goods sought for the construction of the gas pipeline between that country and Western Europe were promulgated as part of a major foreign policy exercise. The purpose of this foreign policy action was to effectuate the response of the United States to certain events which have transpired over the past year in Poland, creating a political situation in that country which this country's leadership has declared unacceptable and which has shown no substantial sign of reversal to previous conditions. Accordingly, the United States has a grave interest in its ability to enforce these regulations which are, in its view, essential to the accomplishment of important foreign policy objectives. As the relief plaintiffs seek would only serve to benefit them and those doing business with them, to the potentially serious detriment of the United States, it cannot be doubted that the public interest does not lie with a grant of the injunction requested by plaintiffs....[*So Ordered.*]

---

The *Coordinating Committee for Multilateral Export Controls* (COCOM) is an organization created by the major Western nations ( Japan and NATO, with the exception of Iceland) to limit on a multilateral basis the flow of strategic exports to the Soviet Union, Eastern European countries, North Korea, Vietnam, and the People's Republic of China. COCOM carries out its function by developing standards for controls, drawing up lists of controlled items, considering individual exceptions from the controls, and coordinating enforcement efforts between member states.

Unfortunately, since COCOM operates as an informal and voluntary organization, there has been no consensus on what constitutes acceptable technology transfer to the East or on enforcement systems to control more effectively the unauthorized transfers. The 1987 revelations that a Toshiba Corporation subsidiary violated COCOM controls and illegally sold the Soviet Union tools to make superquiet submarine propellers, costing the United States billions of dollars in submarine technology, has raised the issue of needed reforms in COCOM to the forefront. The United States responded to the Toshiba case by imposing, as part of the *Omnibus Trade and Competitiveness Act of 1988*, mandatory sanctions against Toshiba and comprehensive penalties aimed at punishing present and future COCOM violators to ensure compliance by foreign companies with COCOM controls.

## 8.  International Economic Boycotts

Another problem in international business is the risk of an **economic boycott** initiated by one or more countries as an additional weapon against a common enemy. The Arab countries engaged in such a boycott immediately prior to the creation of Israel in 1948 and the first Arab-Israeli war. The Arab boycott of Israel has assumed three basic forms: primary, secondary and tertiary. The primary boycott is the refusal by Arab states and their nationals to trade with Israel or its nationals. In 1950, the Arab boycott was extended to a secondary level to include the refusal by Arab states to trade with third parties which contribute to Israel's economic and military strength. Finally, in 1954, the Arabs expanded the boycott to a tertiary level to forbid utilization of materials, equipment, or services of an ostracized business by a non-blacklisted firm in its exports or ventures in an Arab country.

By use of the Export Administration Act and the Internal Revenue Code, the United States has adopted antiboycott laws aimed at prohibiting a U.S. company or person from participating in or cooperating with an international boycott without approval of the U.S. government. The law, aimed primarily at containing the Arab boycott, requires the disclosure of any requests to participate in a boycott or requests to furnish information about the religion or nationality of employees, suppliers, or customers.

The following case shows that firms cannot use the first amendment protection of free speech to escape the requirements of this law.

# BRIGGS & STRATTON CORP. v. BALDRIGE
728 F.2d 915 (7th Cir. 1984)

Companies which did business with Arab countries and who were forbidden by the Export Administration Act and regulations promulgated thereunder to respond to questions asked by the Arab boycott offices pursuant to the Arabs' trade boycott of Israel brought action attacking the constitutionality of those provisions. The companies contended that their proposed answers are entitled to the full measure of protection afforded by the First Amendment: that is, that the boycott responses should be considered "traditional" rather than "commercial" speech. The district court entered summary judgment in favor of the government.

ESCHBACH, J.: Many Arab countries are engaged in a long-standing trade boycott of Israel. As one means of policing their boycott, the Arabs, through their boycott offices, send questionnaires to companies they suspect are violating the terms of the boycott. Companies are typically questioned about their relationship with Israel, Israeli firms, and other companies that do business with Israel. The Arabs have in the past blacklisted companies which do not return completed questionnaires, although failure to reply does not always result in this sanction. The appellants received such questionnaires. A portion of their business depends on access to the Arab states. The appellants wanted to respond to the questionnaires in order to avoid the possibility of being blacklisted. This they were forbidden to do, however, by the Export Administration Act.... The appellants concede that their desire to answer the questionnaires is motivated by economics: through this lawsuit, appellants hope to avoid the disruption of

trade relationships that depend on access to the Arab states. However, they advance three arguments for defining their speech as noncommercial.

First, the appellants argue that each question on the boycott questionnaire is implicitly an allegation that they have engaged in conduct or maintained relationships contrary to the Arabs' boycott principles. They assert that they have a right to answer the questionnaires in an effort to promote the truth about their business relationships. Thus, the appellants contend, their proposed answers are not "related solely to the interests of the speaker and its audience." However, the appellants' interest in disseminating truthful information cannot be distinguished in this instance from their economic interests. We do not understand appellants to be arguing that they would be interested in answering the questionnaires if truthful answers would result in the imposition of economic sanctions. Rather, their interest is in maintaining their advantageous commercial relationships, and any interest in promoting truth is directly proportional to the economic result it would achieve.

The appellants next argue that their proposed communications are attempts to influence the political decisions of a sovereign government, and as such should be fully protected. The appellants reason that the questionnaires are sent to companies by the Arabs in an attempt to enforce their economic boycott of Israel. The decision to boycott Israel is itself a political decision, as is the decision to blacklist those who do not comply with boycott principles. Therefore, the appellants argue, their answers to the questionnaires should be viewed as attempts to influence political decision-making.

Despite appellants' attempts to color their communications with a protected interest in political speech, this argument must also fail. The appellants are free to communicate their views about the relative merits of the Arabs' political decisions directly to the Arabs if they choose, so long as in doing so they do not furnish information about business relationships with boycotted countries or blacklisted persons in violation of the Act. However, the appellants do not seek to answer the questionnaire in order to influence the Arabs' decision to conduct or enforce a trade boycott with Israel. The Arabs' policy in conducting their boycott is irrelevant to appellants' answers. They wish through their answers only to show that the boycott's sanctions should not be applied to them, because they have not violated its terms.

Finally, the appellants argue that the presence of economic motivation alone is not enough to show that speech is commercial. We need not disagree, but it does not follow, of course, that all economically-motivated speech is fully protected noncommercial speech. The commercial speech doctrine was created to afford a measure of First Amendment protection to speech, such as appellants', pertaining to traditionally-regulated commercial activity....[W]e hold that the appellants' proposed communications are commercial speech. [*Affirmed.*]

---

### 9. Foreign Corrupt Practices Act

Following widespread disclosure of scandalous payments by domestic firms to officials of foreign governments, Congress enacted the *Foreign Corrupt Practices Act* (FCPA) in 1977. The law is designed to stop bribery of foreign officials and to prohibit U.S. citizens and companies from making payments to foreign officials whose duties are not "essentially ministerial or clerical" for the purpose of obtaining business.

This statute has two principal requirements: (1) financial records and accounts must be kept "which, in reasonable detail, accurately and fairly reflect the transactions and dispositions of assets" of the business, and (2) the business must "devise and maintain a system of internal accounting controls sufficient to provide reasonable assurances" that transactions are being carried out in accordance with management's authorization. These provisions are intended to correct the previously widespread practice of accounting for bribes as commission payments, payments for services, or other normal business expenses, and then illegally deducting the payments on income tax returns.

Many legal observers criticized FCPA for creating a significantly chilling effect on U.S. companies seeking business in many developing countries where under-the-table payments to government officials are an accepted practice. Indeed, many civil servants are expected to supplement their salaries in this manner. The U.S. prohibition of such payments is perceived as an attempt to impose American standards of morality in other parts of the world, and it has caused resentment and discrimination against American businesses. Moreover, the FCPA puts U.S. firms at a competitive disadvantage with businesses in other countries that are not operating under similar constraints.

As a result of intensive lobbying by the American business community, Congress amended the FCPA in 1988 in an effort to eliminate ambiguity and uncertainty over what constitutes improper conduct. While the law still prohibits bribery and corruption, the amendments establish clearer standards for firms to follow in overseas operations. The amendments limit criminal liability for violations of accounting standards to those who "knowingly" circumvent accounting controls or falsify records of corporate payments and transactions. The amendments also clarify the level of detail required in such record keeping and should improve compliance by businesses and enforcement by the government. Moreover, under the new law otherwise prohibited payments to foreign officials may be defended if they were legal under the written laws of the host country or if they cover "reasonable and bona fide" expenses associated with the promotion of the product and the completion of the contract.

Under the 1988 amendments, criminal penalties for companies violating the FCPA have been increased to a maximum of $2 million and individuals may be fined up to $100,000 and/or five years in prison.

## 10. Antitrust Laws

The U.S. antitrust laws, discussed in detail in Chapters 20 and 21, represent the legal embodiment of our nation's commitment to free markets and the competitive process. Perhaps no other aspect of our legal system has generated as much recent controversy and ill will abroad as the application of our antitrust laws to conduct occurring beyond the borders of the United States. To protect the welfare of the U.S. consumer, however, the government's enforcement efforts must sometimes reach foreign defendants. The U.S. attitude toward the extraterritorial application of domestic antitrust law is that conduct that has a direct, substantial, and foreseeable impact on domestic trade or commerce, no matter where it occurs, will be subject to scrutiny. Domestic firms, foreign subsidiaries of domestic firms, and foreign firms that violate domestic antitrust law in the United States or abroad may be subject to antitrust enforcement actions.

In November 1988, the Department of Justice issued new *Antitrust Enforcement Guidelines for International Operations* to provide international businesses with general guidance on how the government analyzes certain commonly occurring international issues affecting its enforcement decisions. The guidelines recognize that "considerations of comity among nations—the notion that foreign nations are due deference when acting within their legitimate spheres of authority—properly play a role in determining" when to apply U.S. antitrust laws. Under the guidelines, "the Department considers whether significant interests of any foreign sovereign would be affected and asserts jurisdiction only when the Department concludes it would be reasonable to do so." This rule involves a balancing of interests of the United States along with those of the foreign state to determine whether application of our law is warranted.

# INTERNATIONAL ORGANIZATIONS AND AGREEMENTS AFFECTING TRADE

## 11. The United Nations

The *United Nations* (UN) is the paramount international political organization in terms of representation and scope of activities.

The *International Court of Justice* (ICJ), or "World Court," is the judicial branch of the UN. It sits at The Hague in the Netherlands and consists of fifteen judges representing all of the world's major legal systems. The judges are elected by the UN's General Assembly and the Security Council after having been nominated by national groups, not governments. No more than one judge may be a national of any country. Since it began functioning in 1946, the ICJ has rendered, on average, only one contested decision per year and one advisory opinion every two years. Obviously, there has been widespread reluctance to resort to the ICJ as a forum for resolving international disputes. An often misunderstood aspect of the ICJ's jurisdiction to hear and decide disputes is the provision that only *countries* have access to the court. Private persons or corporations may not directly present claims before the court. Further, only countries that have submitted to the court's jurisdiction may be parties. Some countries have presented claims to the ICJ on behalf of their aggrieved nationals, but no device exists in U.S. law by which a firm or individual can compel the U.S. government to press a claim on its behalf before the ICJ.

The *United Nations Commission on International Trade Law* (UNCITRAL) was created in 1966 in an effort to develop standardized commercial practices and agreements. One of the documents drafted by UNCITRAL is the *Convention on the International Sale of Goods* (CISG) which has been ratified by the United States and ten other nations. CISG, which went into force in 1988, is a multilateral treaty that applies to international transactions, much as Article 2 of the Uniform Commercial Code applies to domestic transactions. The agreement covers "the formation of the contract of sale and the rights and obligations of the seller and the buyer arising from such a contract" between parties whose places of business are in different nations.

The *United Nations Conference on Trade and Development* (UNCTAD) is a permanent organ of the General Assembly. It was created in 1964 to deal with international trade reform and redistribution of income through trade. It works primarily on behalf of developing countries; to date, UNCTAD has achieved little notable success.

## 12.   The European Community

Perhaps the most significant recent development affecting international business is the historic attempt by the European countries to promote and achieve economic unity by 1992. Created by the *Treaty of Rome* in 1957, the *European Community* (EC or Common Market) includes 12 member countries: Belgium, Denmark, France, West Germany, Greece, Ireland, Italy, Luxembourg, the Netherlands, Portugal, Spain, and the United Kingdom. The EC is a truly supranational entity possessing the equivalent of its own legislative, executive, and judicial branches. The treaty is the primary source of EC law. It allocates authority among four institutions: (1) the *European Parliament* (or Assembly), made up of members from each state elected by direct universal suffrage; (2) the *Court of Justice,* composed of 11 judges appointed for six years by agreement among the member states; (3) the *Council,* made up of representatives from the governments (primarily the foreign ministers); and (4) the *Commission,* consisting of individuals appointed to 4-year terms who must remain independent of their governments and the Council.

The EC's objectives include the free movement of goods, services, labor, professions, transportation, and capital between member states. While the Europeans are not expected to erase their cultural or national differences and create a unified nation, the EC demonstrates an understanding that Europe may achieve a greater voice in worldwide decision making and more autonomy from the United States as a single economic force. EC members have reduced or removed tariffs, quotas, and other barriers to trade with each other while individual national trade barriers with nonmember states have been retained. By reducing trade barriers between each other, EC members have not only opened up their markets but have saved billions of dollars on red tape as well.

Although the creation of a single market of 320 million people is well underway, much of the 1992 agenda may be difficult, if not impossible, to achieve. The political disharmony in Europe between conservatives favoring a free-market economy and liberals supporting governmental intervention and partnership may endanger achievement of economic unity. These political strains undoubtedly will influence the resolution of a variety of other issues critical to unification such as disputes over the deregulation of industry, the unification of taxes, and the development of a common currency throughout Europe.

A recent Dun & Bradstreet survey of 5,000 U.S. companies indicates that 11 percent of the companies plan to start exporting to Europe soon, so the implications of the 1992 agenda could be far-reaching. The common market purchases $600 billion worth of U.S. goods and services each year and is America's largest foreign market. American companies are investing approximately $20 billion a year on new plants and equipment and spending over $2 billion a year on acquiring European companies. The drive to reduce international trade barriers is expected to energize European rivals to established U.S. multinationals. Moreover, Europe's initiative to integrate its economy is expected to lead to the imposition of additional tariffs or duties on U.S. exports and to increase pressure on U.S. firms to manufacture their products in Europe. At the very least, American exporters will have to improve their distribution and marketing operations and upgrade their service programs to survive in this new atmosphere.

## 13.   U.S.-Canada Free Trade Accord

Following the lead of the European Community, the United States and Canada signed in 1988 the *U.S.-Canada Free Trade Agreement.* The pact will phase out all tariffs and quotas between the two nations by 1999. Described by experts as "the most important U.S. trade agreement in the past 20 years," the accord also guarantees equal treatment for individuals and businesses that invest across the border and removes restrictions on the sale of farm products, oil, gas, electricity, and commercial services.

Economists have predicted that the free trade agreement will increase the gross national product for the United States by $44 billion a year and an extra $12 billion a year for Canada. The free-trade pact provides momentum and opportunities for more American businesses to explore expansion of their operations into Canada. President Bush has endorsed "a new North American compact" to expand trade with Mexico as well. Although implementing this idea appears to be several years away, there are powerful incentives for integration of the North American market. The population of North America is 355 million, 10 percent greater than the European Community, and the fastest-growing country economically is Mexico.

## 14.   General Agreement on Tariffs and Trade

The *General Agreement on Tariffs and Trade* (GATT) is a series of over 100 international agreements and protocols subscribed to by approximately ninety countries, including the United States. GATT attempts to prohibit discrimination in import regulations and prevent the establishment of import quotas through the mechanism of *most-favored nation* status. Under this provision, each member of GATT is obligated to treat all other GATT members at least as well as it treats the country that receives the most favorable treatment regarding imports or exports. In other words, no country is to give special trading advantages to others. An additional provision specifies that imports will be treated no worse than domestic products with regard to internal taxation or regulation.

GATT, unfortunately, has little administrative machinery and has little real power over violators. Nevertheless, GATT has managed to eliminate tariffs of any real consequence and can claim some of the credit for the impressive growth in international trade since its creation in 1947.

GATT members presently are in the midst of negotiations, the so-called "Uruguay Round" expected to last until 1990, to push the world's trading partners toward freer markets. These negotiating "rounds" generally occur every five or ten years and create an opportunity for members to examine new problems and solutions to international trade. The United States, a longtime critic of foreign barriers to American farm exports, is campaigning for a more open agricultural trade policy in this round.

### 15. Other Organizations and Agreements

The *Council for Mutual Economic Aid* (COMECON) is the Soviet-bloc counterpart to the EC. COMECON members include Bulgaria, Cuba, Czechoslovakia, East Germany, Hungary, Poland, Rumania, and the Soviet Union. The staged purpose of COMECON is to coordinate the development efforts of its members, raise the standard of industrialization and increase the productivity of its members, and to further economic cooperation among its members. Dominated by the Soviet Union, COMECON has been weakened in its supranational structure by the increasing unwillingness of some member countries to accept the roles delegated to them.

A number of other regional organizations exist that have not achieved the degree of success of the EC or COMECON. They include the Latin America Free Trade Association, the Central American Common Market, the East African Economic Community, and the Economic Community of West African States. In addition, many narrowly based international organizations exist, such as the International Labour Organization, the International Monetary Fund, the International Civil Aviation Organization, and the Organization of Petroleum Exporting Countries.

## PROTECTING DOMESTIC INDUSTRIES IN A WORLD MARKET

### 16. Restrictions on Imports

Although the number of exports from the United States has grown over the past several years, imports to America have continued to swell; this creates a persistent, negative balance of trade with other countries. The 1986 trade deficit was $169.8 billion, an increase of $21.3 billion over the previous year. By comparison, the entire trade deficit five years earlier was only $39.8 billion. Over the period from 1950–1985, the United States' share of world exports to other countries has declined from 21 percent to less than 13 percent. This critical situation led Congress to enact the *Omnibus Trade and Competitiveness Act of 1988* to obtain for U.S. businesses more open, equitable, and reciprocal foreign markets.

The premise of this new law, which has been the subject of much debate, is that the United States can use access to its huge market as a lever to pry open foreign markets for its products and set a forceful example to the world. The law toughens the federal response to unfair foreign trade practices and provides federal relief for import-damaged U.S. industries. It also requires the U.S. Trade Representative to conduct investigations of countries that maintain numerous trade barriers and to name nations with large trade surpluses. It calls for negotiations with those nations to facilitate a more equitable trade balance and provides the President with the authority to retaliate against violators of trade agreements or other "unjustifiable" foreign trade practices.

## 17. Piracy and Counterfeit Goods

One of the major threats to U.S. competitiveness is the trade in counterfeit and pirated goods. Consumers often purchase brand-name merchandise unaware that it may be counterfeit. Lost sales from the unauthorized use of U.S. patents, trademarks, and copyrights is estimated at $20 billion annually and over 750,000 domestic jobs are believed to be affected. Moreover, there is the additional cost for American business through lost goodwill towards the owner due to the often inferior quality of the counterfeit product.

Despite the lack of an international agreement on the subject of counterfeiting, some relief is available to distressed businesses. The *Paris Convention on Industrial Property* provides for the "application of special measures with respect to articles bearing infringing marks when quick and effective action is necessary." Trademarks, however, are not defined in the Paris Convention and their enforcement is left primarily to each state's law. In 1984, the United States passed the *Trademark Counterfeiting Act* which provides for extensive criminal penalties for product counterfeiting. As a part of the *Omnibus Trade and Competitiveness Act of 1988* the government has tightened protection for intellectual property and eased the standards a manufacturer must satisfy in order to halt the importation of patent-infringing products. The law requires the United States Trade Representative "to identify and initiate cases against 'priority' countries with trading practices that infringe on U.S. intellectual property rights."

## 18. Antidumping Laws

**Dumping** is the practice of selling foreign goods in one country at less than the comparable price in the country from which the goods are being exported. Since the practice of dumping potentially may create an unfair economic advantage (especially when a foreign market may be protected against reciprocal competition from domestic firms), Congress has limited it through several antidumping statutes. Current antidumping legislation is found in the *Trade Agreements Act of 1979*. This statute establishes a two-part test for triggering additional import duties on the goods being dumped. First, the Secretary of the Treasury must determine that a class or kind of merchandise is being or is likely to be sold in the United States at *"less than fair value"* (LTFV). In LTFV determinations, the price for which the goods are being sold in the United States is compared with the price for which the goods are being sold in the country of origin. The second provision requires that the International Trade Commission (part of the Department of Commerce) determine that a domestic industry is being materially injured or threatened or that establishment of domestic industry is being materially retarded. When both determinations prove affirmative, an additional duty will be imposed upon the goods in an amount by which their foreign value exceeds the domestic price. Obviously, the question of what is "material" is crucial to these determinations, but the statute does not define the term.

The Omnibus Trade and Competitiveness Act of 1988 has tightened existing antidumping laws by authorizing the Commerce Department to prevent circumvention of additional duties by shipments through third countries and requires expedited investigations of certain products from multiple offenders of antidumping laws.

### 19.   Suing Foreign Firms in the United States

As foreign products and technology are imported into the United States, disputes may arise over either the terms of contract or the performance of the goods. In order to sue a foreign firm in the United States, the Supreme Court recently has held that the plaintiff must establish "minimum contacts" between the foreign defendant and the forum court. The plaintiff must demonstrate that exercise of personal jurisdiction over the defendant "does not offend traditional notions of fair play and substantial justice."

Once the plaintiff decides to sue in the United States, he also must comply with the terms of the *Hague Service Convention* when serving the foreign defendant notice of the lawsuit. The Hague Service Convention is a multilateral treaty that was formulated "to provide a simpler way to serve process abroad, to assure that defendants sued in foreign jurisdictions would receive actual and timely notice of suit, and to facilitate proof of service abroad." Thirty-two countries, including the United States, have ratified or acceded to the Convention. The primary requirement of the agreement is to require each nation to establish a central authority to process requests for service of documents from other countries. "Once the central authority receives the request in proper form, it must serve the documents by a method prescribed by the internal law of the receiving state or by a method designated by the requester and compatible with that law."

As the following case demonstrates, the plaintiff also may serve process on a foreign corporation by merely serving its domestic subsidiary in the United States.

---

# VOLKSWAGENWERK AKTIENGESELLSCHAFT v. SCHLUNK
108 S.Ct. 2104 (1988)

---

After his parents were killed in an automobile accident, the respondent filed a wrongful death action in an Illinois court, alleging that defects in the automobile designed and sold by Volkswagen of America, Inc. (VWoA), in which the parents were driving, caused or contributed to their deaths. When VWoA's answer denied that it had designed or assembled the vehicle, respondent amended his complaint to add as defendant petitioner here (VWAG), a German corporation which is the sole owner of VWoA. Respondent attempted to serve the amended complaint on VWAG by serving VWoA as VWAG's agent. VWAG moved to quash the service on the grounds that it could be served only in accordance with the Hague Service Convention, and that respondent had not complied with the Convention's requirements. The court denied the motion and VWAG appealed.

O'CONNOR, J.: This case involves an attempt to serve process on a foreign corporation by serving its domestic subsidiary which, under state law, is the foreign corporation's involuntary agent for service of process. We must decide whether such service is compatible with the Convention on Service Abroad of Judicial and Extrajudicial Documents in Civil and Commercial Matters, (Hague Service Convention), [1969]....

The Hague Service Convention is a multilateral treaty that was formulated in 1964 by the Tenth Session of the Hague Conference of Private International Law. The Convention revised parts of the Hague Conventions on Civil Procedure of 1905 and 1954. The revision was intended to provide a simpler way to serve process abroad, to assure that defendants sued in foreign jurisdictions would receive actual and timely notice of suit, and to facilitate proof of service abroad....

The primary innovation of the Convention is that it requires each state to establish a central authority to receive requests for service of documents from other countries. Once a central authority receives a request in the proper form, it must serve the documents by a method prescribed by the internal law of the receiving state or by a method designated by the requester and compatible with that law. The central authority must then provide a certificate of service that conforms to a specified model. A state also may consent to methods of service within its boundaries other than a request to its central authority....

VWAG protests that it is inconsistent with the purpose of the Convention to interpret it as applying only when the internal law of the forum requires service abroad. One of the two stated objectives of the Convention is "to create appropriate means to ensure that judicial and extrajudicial documents to be served abroad shall be brought to the notice of the addressee in sufficient time." The Convention cannot assure adequate notice, VWAG argues, if the forum's internal law determines whether it applies. VWAG warns that countries could circumvent the Convention by defining methods of service of process that do not require transmission of documents abroad. Indeed, VWAG contends that one such method of service already exists and that it troubled the Conference: *notification au parquet.*

*Notification au parquet* permits service of process on a foreign defendant by the deposit of documents with a designated local official. Although the official generally is supposed to transmit the documents abroad to the defendant, the statute of limitations begins to run from the time that the official receives the documents, and there allegedly is no sanction for failure to transmit them....

The parties make conflicting representations about whether foreign laws authorizing *notification au parquet* command the transmittal of documents for service abroad within the meaning of the Convention. The final report is itself somewhat equivocal. It says that, although the strict language of Article 1 might raise a question as to whether the Convention regulates *notification au parquet,* the understanding of the drafting Commission, based on the debates, is that the Convention would apply. Although this statement might affect our decision as to whether the Convention applies to *notification au parquet,* an issue we do not resolve today, there is no comparable evidence in the negotiating history that the Convention was meant to apply to substituted service on a subsidiary like VWoA, which clearly does not require service abroad under the forum's internal law. Hence neither the language of the Convention nor the negotiating history contradicts our interpretation of the Convention, according to which the internal law of the forum is presumed to determine whether there is occasion for service abroad....

Where service on a domestic agent is valid and complete under both state law and the Due Process Clause, our inquiry ends and the Convention has no further implications. Whatever internal, private communications take place between the agent and a foreign principal are beyond the concerns of this case. The only transmittal to which the Convention applies is a transmittal abroad that is required as a necessary part of service. And, contrary to VWAG's assertion, the Due Process Clause does not require an official transmittal of documents abroad every time there is service on a foreign national. Applying this analysis, we conclude that this case does not present an occasion to transmit a judicial document for service abroad within the meaning of Article 1. Therefore the Hague Service Convention does not apply, and service was proper. The judgment of the Appellate Court is [*Affirmed.*]

## 20. International Arbitration

International businesses now are focusing on the need for new methods of resolving international commercial disputes and, as a result, are frequently resorting to the use of arbitration. The advantages of arbitration in domestic transactions, previously discussed in Chapter 4, are more pronounced in national transactions where differences in languages and legal systems make litigation costs still more costly.

The *United Nations Convention on the Recognition and Enforcement of Foreign Arbitral Awards* (New York Convention), which has been adopted in over fifty countries, encourages the use of arbitration in commercial agreements made by companies in the signatory countries. Under the New York Convention it is easier to compel arbitration, where previously agreed upon by the parties, and to enforce the arbitrator's award once a decision has been reached. Most international arbitration occurs in Geneva, London, New York, Paris, and Stockholm where arbitration organizations have developed rules for conducting the arbitration hearings.

Once the parties to a commercial transaction have agreed to arbitrate disputes between them, the U.S. courts are reluctant to disturb that agreement.

---

# MITSUBISHI MOTORS v. SOLER CHRYSLER-PLYMOUTH
473 U.S. 614 (1985)

The petitioner, a Japanese corporation that manufactures automobiles, is the product of a joint venture between Chrysler International; S.A. (CISA), a Swiss corporation; and another Japanese corporation. The petitioner's aim is to distribute through Chrysler dealers outside the continental United States automobiles manufactured by Mitsubishi. Respondent, a Puerto Rican corporation, entered into distribution and sales agreements with CISA. The sales agreement contained a clause providing for arbitration by the Japan Commercial Arbitration Association of all disputes arising out of certain articles of the agreement or for the breach thereof. Thereafter, when attempts to work out disputes arising from a slackening of the sale of new automobiles failed, petitioner withheld shipment of automobiles to respondent, which disclaimed responsibility for them. Petitioner then brought an action in federal district court under the federal Arbitration Act seeking an order to compel arbitration of the disputes in accordance with the arbitra-

tion clause. Respondent filed an answer and counterclaims, asserting causes of action under the Sherman Act and other statutes. The district court ordered arbitration of most of the issues, including the federal antitrust issues, raised in the complaint and counterclaims. Despite the doctrine uniformly followed by the Courts of Appeals, that rights conferred by the antitrust laws are inappropriate for enforcement by arbitration, the district court held that the international character of the undertaking in question required enforcement of the arbitration clause even as to the antitrust claims. The Court of Appeals reversed insofar as the District Court ordered submission of the antitrust claims to arbitration.

BLACKMUN, J.:...The first task of a court asked to compel arbitration of a dispute is to determine whether the parties agreed to arbitrate that dispute. The court is to make this determination by applying the "federal substantive law of arbitrability, applicable to any arbitration agreement within the coverage of the Act." And that body of law counsels

**that questions of arbitrability must be addressed with a healthy regard for the federal policy favoring arbitration....The Arbitration Act establishes that, as a matter of federal law, any doubts concerning the scope of arbitrable issues should be resolved in favor of arbitration....**

That is not to say that all controversies implicating statutory rights are suitable for arbitration....By agreeing to arbitrate a statutory claim, a party does not forego the substantive rights afforded by the statute; it only submits to their resolution in an arbitral, rather than a judicial, forum. It trades the procedures, and opportunity for review of the courtroom for the simplicity, informality, and expedition of arbitration.... Having made the bargain to arbitrate, the party should be held to it unless Congress itself has evinced an intention to preclude a waiver of judicial remedies for the statutory rights at issue. Nothing, in the meantime, prevents a party from excluding statutory claims from the scope of an agreement to arbitrate....

We now turn to consider whether Soler's antitrust claims are nonarbitrable even though it has agreed to arbitrate them....We conclude that concerns of international comity, respect for the capacities of foreign and transnational tribunals, and sensitivity to the need of the international commercial system for predictability in the resolution of disputes require that we enforce the parties' agreement, even assuming that a contrary result would be forthcoming in a domestic context.

...[T]his Court had recognized the utility of forum-selection clauses in international transactions. In *The Bremen,* an American oil company, seeking to evade a contractual choice of an English forum and,

by implication, English law, filed a suit in admiralty in a United States District Court against the German corporation which had contracted to tow its rig to a location in the Adriatic Sea. Notwithstanding the possibility that the English court would enforce provisions in the towage contract exculpating the German party which an American court would refuse to enforce, this Court gave effect to the choice-of-forum clause. It observed:

**The expansion of American business and industry will hardly be encouraged if, notwithstanding solemn contract, we insist on a parochial concept that all disputes must be resolved under our laws and in our courts....We cannot have trade and commerce in world markets and international waters exclusively on our terms, governed by our laws, and resolved in our courts....**

Again, the Court emphasized:

**A contractual provision specifying in advance the forum in which disputes shall be litigated and the law to be applied is...an almost indispensable precondition to achievement of the orderliness and predictability essential to any international business transaction....**

**A parochial refusal by the courts of one country to enforce an international arbitration agreement would not only frustrate these purposes, but would invite unseemly and mutually destructive jockeying by the parties to secure tactical litigation advantages....[It would] damage the fabric of international commerce and trade, and imperil the willingness and ability of businessmen to enter into international commercial agreements....**

The judgment of the Court of Appeals is affirmed in part and reversed in part, and the cases are remanded for further proceedings consistent with this opinion. [*So ordered.*]

## REVIEW QUESTIONS

**1** Define the following terms.
**a** nationalization
**b** expropriation
**c** sovereign immunity
**d** dumping
**e** irrevocable letter of credit
**f** bill of lading

**2** Describe the several ways in which a U.S. firm may conduct business abroad.

**3** What are the main provisions of the Foreign Corrupt Practices Act?

**4** What is the European Community? What does it do? Explain.

**5** When do the antidumping provisions of the United States law apply? Explain.

**6** Explain the act of state doctrine.

**7** Describe how U.S. export controls may impede international trade for an American business.

**8** What is GATT? What issues are being debated in the Uruguay round?

**9** What risks do American businesses face in complying with the Arab boycott?

**10** Describe how U.S. antitrust laws influence international business operations. What provisions are contained in the new guidelines?

**11** How may foreign counterfeit goods affect American business?

**12** What are the advantages to an arbitration clause in a contract involving international trade?

**13** What are some of the inherent dangers of regional trading blocs? Do the EC and the U.S.-Canada Free Trade Accord pose risks to free trade? Explain.

# *Part Five*
# PROTECTING EMPLOYEES

# *Chapter*
# *15*

# Worker Protection

## CHAPTER PREVIEW

Worker protection laws developed only in this century. Prior to 1900, workers had very little or no protection from dangerous job conditions, low pay, and the risk of firing. Today, however, many statutes protect the worker. They are part of a trend which will be likely to continue and grow.

This chapter addresses two primary issues of worker protection: job safety (including the handling of work-related injuries) and financial security. The Occupational Safety and Health Administration is the federal agency most responsible for job safety. When accidental employee injuries do occur in the course of employment, state workers' compensation laws impose strict liability on employers for death or disability benefits, medical expenses, and wage losses.

The Fair Labor Standards Act protects children in the workplace by limiting the types of employment children can have at various ages. This act also sets minimum-wage and overtime requirements on employers and is the first major federal act aimed at increasing workers' financial security.

Passed in the 1930s, the unemployment compensation law is one part of the Social Security Act. The other part is the employer-employee funding of retirement, disability, and health insurance programs. Together, they mark a major step in worker protection.

Private pension plans have helped to advance the financial retirement security of millions of workers. This chapter covers the Employee Retirement Income Security Act, which is the major federal law regulating private pension plans.

Concluding the chapter is a discussion of trends limiting employment-at-will, the right of employers to discharge most employees without regard to job security. These trends shed light on the larger picture of worker protection.

Important terms of this chapter include course of employment, defined benefit plan, defined contribution plan, discharge for proper cause, employment-at-will, exclusive remedy rule, fellow-servant rule, individual retirement account, minimum wage, qualified pension plan, and vested rights.

## 1. The Occupational Safety and Health Act

### IN GENERAL

Congress adopted the *Occupational Safety and Health Act* (OSHA) in 1970 to ensure safe and healthful working conditions for practically every employee in the United States. Special health and safety laws in such industries as construction, maritime, and coal mining had been previously adopted, but such far-reaching legislation as OSHA, with an impact of such magnitude on business, had never been considered at the national level.

OSHA requires that employers furnish to each employee a place of employment that is free from recognized hazards that are causing or are likely to cause death or serious physical harm. It also requires that the employer comply with occupational safety and health standards established under the act by the secretary of labor. This is done through an agency called The Occupational Safety and Health Administration (also known as OSHA). To accomplish its mission, OSHA investigators conduct unannounced inspections. During any investigation, an employer as well as an employee has the right to accompany the inspectors or have a representative do so. Remember that the Supreme Court has ruled that employers can require OSHA inspectors to produce a search warrant before they begin an inspection. Employers also, as required by regulations, must keep and preserve records relating to accidents and injuries.

OSHA regulates employees as well as employers. It requires that each employee comply with occupational safety and health standards and all rules, regulations, and orders issued under it which are applicable to his or her own actions and conduct.

The secretary of labor issues standards for healthful and safe employment. The Occupational Safety and Health Review Commission reviews citations of violations and proposed penalties. Orders of this commission are, of course, reviewable by a federal Court of Appeals, as in the case of other federal administrative agencies. The most significant aspect of OSHA is its approach to enforcement by unannounced inspections. Inspections of businesses may be made either on the initiative of the department itself or upon the request of an employee or employees' representative. Inspections must be made during regular working hours and at other reasonable times within reasonable limits and in a reasonable manner. No advance notice of inspections can be given. Employees' representatives have the right to participate in walk-around inspections, and such representatives get compensation from the employer for the time involved. If an inspection reveals a violation, the employer receives a citation. If the violation presents a threat of serious or immediate harm, the secretary of labor can go into a federal district court and get a temporary injunction to restrain the danger. Having received a citation, the employer is next informed of the penalty. If the employer decides to contest the citation or penalty, it may appeal through the review commission and then into the federal court system.

In certain cases, OSHA regulations permit employees a right of "self-help." Because the act itself does not mention a self-help remedy, the following case challenged the remedy's legality.

# WHIRLPOOL CORPORATION v. MARSHALL

100 S.Ct 883 (1980)

STEWART, J.: The Occupational Safety and Health Act of 1970 (Act) prohibits an employer from discharging or discriminating against any employee who exercises "any right afforded by" the Act. The Secretary of Labor (Secretary) has promulgated a regulation providing that, among the rights that the Act so protects, is the right of an employee to choose not to perform his assigned task because of a reasonable apprehension of death or serious injury coupled with a reasonable belief that no less drastic alternative is available. The question presented in the case before us is whether this regulation is consistent with the Act.

The petitioner company maintains a manufacturing plant in Marion, Ohio, for the production of household appliances. Overhead conveyors transport appliance components throughout the plant. To protect employees from objects that occasionally

fall from these conveyors, the petitioner has installed a horizontal wire mesh guard screen approximately 20 feet above the plant floor.

Maintenance employees of the petitioner spend several hours each week removing objects from the screen, replacing paper spread on the screen to catch grease drippings from the material on the conveyors, and performing occasional maintenance work on the conveyors themselves. To perform these duties, maintenance employees usually are able to stand on the iron frames, but sometimes find it necessary to step onto the steel mesh screen itself.

In 1973 the company began to install heavier wire in the screen because its safety had been drawn into question. Several employees had fallen partly through the old screen, and on one occasion an employee had fallen completely through to the plant floor below but had survived.

On June 28, 1974, a maintenance employee fell to his death through the guard screen in an area where the newer, stronger mesh had not yet been installed. Following this incident, the petitioner effectuated some repairs and issued an order strictly forbidding maintenance employees from stepping on either the screens or the angle-iron supporting structure.

On July 7, 1974, two of the petitioner's maintenance employees, Virgil Deemer and Thomas Cornwell, met with the plant maintenance superintendent to voice their concern about the safety of the screen. The superintendent disagreed with their view.... Later,...Deemer contacted an official of the regional OSHA office and discussed the guard screen.

The next day, Deemer and Cornwell reported for the night shift at 10:45 P.M. Their foreman, after himself walking on some of the angle-iron frames, directed the two men to perform their usual maintenance duties on a section of the old screen. Claiming that the screen was unsafe, they refused to carry out this directive. The foreman then sent them to the personnel office, where they were ordered to punch out without working or being paid for the remaining six hours of the shift. The two men subsequently received written reprimands, which were placed in their employment files.

A little over a month later, the Secretary filed suit in the United States District Court for the Northern District of Ohio, alleging that the petitioner's actions against Deemer and Cornwell constituted discrimination in violation of...the Act.

Following a bench trial, the District Court found that the two employees had "refused to perform the cleaning operation because of a genuine fear of death or serious bodily harm," that the danger presented had been "real and not something which

[had] existed only in the minds of the employees," that the employees had acted in good faith, and that no reasonable alternative had realistically been open to them other than to refuse to work. The District Court nevertheless denied relief, holding that the Secretary's regulation was inconsistent with the Act and therefore invalid.

The Court of Appeals for the Sixth Circuit reversed the District Court's judgment.... [The] question, as stated at the onset of this opinion, is whether the Secretary's regulation authorizing employee "self-help" in some circumstances is permissible under the Act....

The Act itself creates an express mechanism for protecting workers from employment conditions believed to pose an emergent threat of death or serious injury....

[T]he Secretary is obviously correct when he acknowledges in his regulation that, "as a general matter, there is no right afforded by the Act which would entitle employees to walk off the job because of potential unsafe conditions at the workplace." By providing for prompt notice to the employer of an inspector's intention to seek an injunction against an imminently dangerous condition, the legislation obviously contemplates that the employer will normally respond by voluntarily and speedily eliminating the danger. And in the few instances where this does not occur, the legislative provisions authorizing prompt judicial action are designed to give employees full protection in most situations from the risk of injury or death resulting from an imminently dangerous condition at the worksite.

As this case illustrates, however, circumstances may sometimes exist in which the employee justifiably believes that the express statutory arrangement does not sufficiently protect him from death or serious injury. Such circumstances will probably not often occur, but such a situation may arise when (1) the employee is ordered by his employer to work under conditions that the employee reasonably believes pose an imminent risk of death or serious bodily injury, and (2) the employee has reason to believe that there is not sufficient time or opportunity either to seek effective redress from his employer or to apprise OSHA of the danger....

[T]he Secretary has exercised his rule-making power...and has determined that, when an employee in good faith finds himself in such a predicament, he may refuse to expose himself to the dangerous condition, without being subjected to "subsequent discrimination" by the employer....

The regulation clearly conforms to the fundamental objective of the Act—to prevent occupational deaths and serious injuries.... The Act does not wait for an employee to die or become injured. It authorized the promulgation of health and safety standards and the issuance of citations in the hope that these will act to prevent deaths or injuries from ever occurring....

The regulation accords no authority to government officials. It simply permits private employees of a private employer to avoid workplace conditions that they believe pose grave dangers to their own safety. The employees have no power under the regulation to order their employer to correct the hazardous condition or to clear the dangerous workplace of others. Moreover, any employee who acts in reliance on the regulation runs the risk of discharge or reprimand in the event a court subsequently finds that he acted unreasonably or in bad faith....

For these reasons we conclude that [the regulation] was promulgated by the Secretary in the valid exercise of his authority under the Act. Accordingly, the judgment of the Court of Appeals is affirmed. [*Affirmed.*]

---

### TRENDS

In the 1970s, OSHA came under much criticism from industry groups. Its safety regulations were long and difficult to understand and apply. Many people considered OSHA inspectors to be biased against business and too quick to issue citations. The number of workers injured annually failed to go down and in some instances actually rose.

OSHA has tried a different approach in the 1980s. Its focus has changed somewhat from safety to health. Instead of an inflexible concern over the number of knotholes in ladders and the height of fire extinguishers from the floor, OSHA has devoted attention to workers' exposure to chemical and other health hazards. It has issued regulations limiting exposure to lead, asbestos, cotton dust, noise, and other potential causes of disability and disease. In 1986, OSHA put into effect a hazardous substance, right-to-know standard. The rule requires chemical manufacturers, distributors, and importers to assess the hazards of their chemicals and pass along that information to their buyers. In addition every employer must identify and list hazardous substances in the workplace, obtain material safety data sheets for each substance, and train workers in the proper use of hazardous substances.

A second change in OSHA has been a careful targeting of its resources. It presently concentrates inspections on industries which offer the greatest threat to worker health and safety (see Table 15-1). It has virtually eliminated inspections of certain employers, including insurance companies, retail stores, and other white-collar and service businesses, where the potential for danger to employees is low. To increase operating efficiency, OSHA has begun a program which allows approved labor-management committees to conduct workplace inspections and keep records. These committees free agency inspectors for other duties.

A final change in OSHA has been the effort to be seen as a helper of business, rather than its enemy. OSHA inspectors have been ordered to offer more help in correcting workplace hazards. The agency has also begun programs which exempt certain employers from regular OSHA inspections when they maintain exceptional safety records.

There are critics of the changes in OSHA. Union leaders have criticized OSHA as attempting to accommodate businesses instead of protecting workers. They point to a decline in the number of OSHA inspections initiated by workers' complaints. They view the significant reduction in the number of employers who contest OSHA complaints as evidence that OSHA is not pursuing cases concerning serious safety violations. Partly as a result of these criticisms, OSHA recently has begun to prosecute more vigorously those businesses that underreport workplace accidents in required reports to OSHA. Several major corporations have received large fines.

## 2. Workers' Compensation Acts

**INTRODUCTION**

Around the turn of the century, the tort system was largely replaced in the workplace by a series of workers' compensation acts. These statutes were enacted at both the state and federal level, and they imposed a type of strict liability on employers for accidental workplace injuries suffered by their em-

**TABLE 15-1**   Most and Least Dangerous Industries According to Days Lost to Occupational Injury or Illness*

| Most Dangerous | Least Dangerous |
|---|---|
| 1   Truck transportation | 1   Communications |
| 2   Railroad equipment | 2   Chemical products |
| 3   Meat packing | 3   Aircraft |
| 4   Lumber and wood products | 4   Electrical equipment |
| 5   Newspapers | 5   Petroleum refining |
| 6   Rail transportation | 6   Textile products |
| 7   Water transportation | 7   Apparel making |
| 8   Paper products | 8   Pipeline transportation |
| 9   Government | 9   Motor-vehicle products |
| 10   Air transportation | 10   Natural gas production |

*Data from National Safety Council.

ployees. The clear purpose of these statutes was to remove financial losses of injury from workers and redistribute them onto employers and ultimately onto society. The following two sections examine present workers' compensation acts.

## HISTORY

Workers' compensation laws are state statutes designed to protect employees and their families from the risks of accidental injury, death, or disease resulting from their employment. They were passed because the common law did not give adequate protection to employees from the hazards of their work. At common law, anyone was liable in tort for damages resulting from injuries caused to another as a proximate result of negligence. If an employer acted unreasonably and his or her carelessness was the proximate cause of physical injury suffered by an employee, the latter could sue and recover damages from the employer. However, the common law also provided the employer with the means of escaping this tort liability in most cases. It provided three defenses: (1) assumption of the risk, (2) contributory negligence, and (3) the fellow-servant rule.

For example, assume that employer E knowingly instructed workers to operate dangerous machinery not equipped with any safety devices, even though it realized injury to them was likely. W, a worker, had his arm mangled when it was caught in the gears of one of these machines. Even though E was negligent in permitting this hazardous condition to persist, if W were aware of the dangers which existed, he would be unable to recover damages because he knowingly *assumed the risk* of his injury. In addition, if the injury were caused by contributory negligence of the employee as well as the negligence of the employer, the action was defeated. And if the injury occurred because of the negligence of another employee, the negligent employee, rather than the employer, was liable because of the fellow-servant rule.

The English Parliament passed a workers' compensation statute in 1897. Today all states have such legislation, modeled to a greater or lesser degree on the English act. These laws vary a great deal from state to state as to the industries subject to them, the employees they cover, the nature of the injuries or diseases which are compensable, the rates of compensation, and the means of administration. In spite of wide variances in the laws of the states in this area, certain general observations can be made about them.

## THE WORKERS' COMPENSATION SYSTEM

State workers' compensation statutes provide a system to pay workers or their families if the worker is accidentally killed or injured or incurs an occupational disease while employed. To be compensable, the death, illness, or injury must arise out of and in the course of the employment. Under these acts, the negligence or fault of the employer in causing an on-the-job injury is not an issue. Instead, these laws recognize the fact of life that a certain number of injuries, deaths, and diseases are bound to occur in a modern industrial society as a result of the attempts of businesses and their employees to provide the goods and services demanded by the consuming public.

This view leads to the conclusion that it is fairer for the consuming public to bear the cost of such mishaps rather than to impose it on injured workers. Workers' compensation laws create strict liability for employers of accidentally injured workers. Liability exists regardless of lack of negligence or fault, provided the necessary association between the injuries and the business of the employer is present. The three defenses the employer had at common law are eliminated. The employers, treating the costs of these injuries as part of the costs of production, pass them on to the consumers who created the demand for the product or service being furnished.

Workers' compensation acts give covered employees the right to certain cash payments for their loss of income due to accidental, on-the-job injuries. In the event of a married employee's death, benefits are provided for the surviving spouse and minor children. The amount of such awards usually is subject to a stated maximum and is calculated by using a percentage of the wages of the employee. If the employee suffers permanent, partial disability, most states provide compensation both for injuries which are scheduled in the statute and those which are nonscheduled. As an example of the former, a worker who loses a hand might be awarded 100 weeks of compensation at $95 per week. Besides scheduling specific compensation for certain specific injuries, most acts also provide compensation for nonscheduled ones based upon the earning power the employee lost due to his or her injury. In addition to the above payments, all statutes provide for medical benefits.

As the result of inflation, many states have increased the amounts payable as workers' compensation benefits. However, the amounts paid in most states are substantially inadequate to provide a decent standard of living for injured workers. For example, even some of the more generous of these provide only about $100 per week for periods of temporary total disability and around $25,000 for death benefits.

In some states, employers have a choice of covering their workers' compensation risk with insurance or of being self-insured (that is, paying all claims directly) if they can demonstrate their capability to do so. Approximately 20 percent of compensation benefits are paid by self-insurers. In other states, employers pay into a state fund used to compensate workers entitled to benefits. In these states, the amounts of the payments are based on the size of the payroll and the experience of the employer in having claims filed against the system by its employees.

Workers' compensation laws are usually administered exclusively by an administrative agency called the industrial commission or board, which has quasi-judicial powers. Of course, the ruling of such boards is subject to review by the courts of the jurisdiction in the same manner as the actions of other administrative agencies.

## TESTS FOR DETERMINING WORKERS' COMPENSATION

The tests for determining whether an employer must pay workers' compensation to an employee are simply: (1) *"Was the injury accidental?"* and (2) *"Did the injury arise out of and in the course of employment?"* Because workers' compensation laws benefit workers, courts interpret them liberally to favor workers.

In recent years, cases have tended to expand employers' liability. For instance, courts have held that heart attacks (as well as other common ailments in which the employee has had either a preexisting disease or a physical condition likely to lead to the disease) are compensable as "accidental injuries." One ruling approved an award to a purchasing agent who became mentally ill because she was exposed to unusual work, stresses, and strains. Her "nerve-racking" job involved a business whose sales grew over sixfold in ten years. Factors contributing to her "accidental injury" included harsh criticism by her supervisor, long hours of work, and inability to take vacations due to the requirements of her position.

Likewise, the courts have been liberal in upholding awards which have been challenged on the ground that the injury did not arise "out of and in the course of employment." Courts routinely support compensation awards for almost any accidental injury which employees suffer while traveling for their employers. A recent Minnesota Supreme Court decision upheld a lower court award of compensation to a bus driver. On a layover during a trip, the driver had been shot accidentally in a tavern parking lot following a night on the town.

However, as the following case shows, not every workplace injury arises out of employment.

# UNITED PARCEL SERVICE v. FETTERMAN
336 S.E.2d 892 (Va. 1985)

PER CURIAM: The question presented in this workers' compensation case is whether the claimant, a parcel delivery service employee, sustained an accidental injury arising out of the employment when he strained his back while bending over to tie his shoe.

Randall F. Fetterman sustained a lumbosacral strain on March 19, 1984, during the course of his employment as a driver for United Parcel Service of America. The claimant's duties included loading, unloading, and delivering packages weighing an average of 35 pounds.

On the day in question, the claimant was unloading packages from his truck. He was reaching across the rear of the truck and pulling parcels to place them on a hand cart when he noticed that his right shoe was untied. He raised his foot to the back of the truck, bent over to tie the shoe, and felt acute pain in his lower back.

At the hearing level, a deputy commissioner denied the claim for compensation.

She decided that the injury did not meet the requirement of arising out of the employment because it could not fairly be traced to the employment as a contributing proximate cause and it did not follow as a natural incident of the work. The hearing commissioner concluded that the claimant's conduct in bending over to tie his shoe was not a risk of the employment but, rather, was merely coincidental with the employment.

Upon review, the full Commission unanimously decided the claim was compensable. The Commission disagreed with the deputy's reasoning and opined that "the work environment certainly had something to do with the manner in which the employee went about tying his shoe and this was no doubt necessary for him to continue his work." On appeal, the employer and its insurance carrier contend the Commission erred. We agree.

An accident arises out of the employment when there is a causal connection between the claimant's injury and the conditions under which the employer requires the work to be performed. Under this test, an injury arises "out of" the employment when it has followed as a natural incident of the work and has been a result of the exposure occasioned by the nature of the employment. Excluded is an injury which comes from a hazard to which the employee would have been equally exposed apart from the employment. The causative danger must be peculiar to the work, incidental to the character of the business, and not independent of the master-servant relationship. The event must appear to have had its origin in a risk connected with the employment, and to have flowed from that source as a rational consequence.

Applying these principles to the present case, we hold this injury did not arise out of the claimant's employment. Under these circumstances, the act of bending over to tie the shoe was unrelated to any hazard common to the workplace. In other words, nothing in the work environment contributed to the injury. Every person who wears laced shoes must occasionally perform the act of retying the laces. The situation of a loose shoelace confronting the claimant was wholly independent of the master-servant relationship.

For these reasons, the award appealed from will be reversed and the application will be dismissed. [*Reversed* and *dismissed*.]

---

The outcome of this case is not obvious. Before the employer appealed to the Virginia Supreme Court, the workers' compensation board had granted the employee compensation. Suppose the employee had argued that his carrying an especially large package had caused him to stumble over his shoelaces. Then, does the untied lace arise out of employment? In another state, an employee received compensation for a back injury related to his decision to kill a roach on his employer's ceiling.

### EXCLUSIVE REMEDY RULE

Recently, some courts have been liberal in their interpretations of the **exclusive remedy rule.** This rule, which is written into all compensation statutes, states that an employee's sole remedy against an employer for workplace injury or illness shall be workers' compensation. In the past few years, courts in several important jurisdictions have created exceptions to this rule (see Table 15-2). Note that these exceptions recognize in part that workers' compensation laws do not adequately compensate badly injured workers.

Since workers' compensation laws apply only to accidentally injured workers, the exclusive remedy rule does not protect employers who intentionally injure workers. But the issue arises as to how "intentional" such an injury has to be. What if an employer knowingly exposes employees to a chemical which may cause illness in some employees over a long term?

#### EXCLUSIONS FROM WORKERS' COMPENSATION COVERAGE

Even though all states have some form of workers' compensation, the statutes exclude certain types of employment from their coverage. Generally, domestic and agricultural employees are not covered. In addition, the law may not provide compensation for specified kinds of accidents or diseases. In about one-half the states, the statutes are compulsory. In the other half, employers may elect to be subject to the act or to lawsuits by employees or their survivors for damages. If the latter course is chosen, an employee seeking compensation for injuries must prove they resulted proximately from the negligence of the employer, as at common law, however, the case is *not* subject to the common-law defenses. In negligence, there is no statutory limit to the amount of damages recoverable.

#### THE FUTURE OF STATE WORKERS' COMPENSATION

Currently, many problems confront the state workers' compensation system. Fifty separate nonuniform acts make up the system. Many acts exclude from coverage groups such as farm workers, government employees, and employees of small businesses. Many state legislatures have enacted changes in their compensation laws. However, states which have broadened coverage and increased benefits have greatly boosted the cost of doing business within their borders. This discourages new businesses from locating within these states and encourages those already there to move out.

In the last decade, workers' compensation payments have tripled. Many workers exaggerate their injuries to get compensation. On the other hand,

#### TABLE 15-2  Exceptions to the Exclusive Remedy Rule*

1  Employee sues manufacturer of a product which causes work-related injury
2  Employee sues fellow employee who causes work-related injury
3  Employee sues insurer who breaches a duty to warn employer of dangerous work conditions
4  Employee sues employer who intentionally inflicts injury, including mental distress, or who intentionally conceals a dangerous work condition
5  Employee sues employer who is in a "dual capacity" with employee. Example: Employer manufactured product which injured employee in the workplace
6  Employee sues employer who fraudulently conceals an employee's medical condition caused by exposure to workplace conditions

*Not all exceptions exist in all states.

compensation payments to seriously injured workers are often inadequate, and this has led to attempts to get around the exclusive remedy rule.

As our national economy moves from a manufacturing to a service emphasis, the nature of injuries suffered under workers' compensation programs begins to change. In particular, the number of mental-stress claims rises. The National Council on Compensation Insurance states that these claims have increased fivefold in the past five years. Problems of proving (or disproving) mental-stress claims bring new concerns for the workers' compensation system.

A major problem concerns slowly developing, occupational diseases. Many toxic chemicals cause cancer and other diseases only after workers have been exposed to them over many years. Often it is difficult or impossible for workers or their survivors to recover workers' compensation for such diseases. A university-conducted study released in 1984 showed that only about one-third of the average losses caused by asbestos diseases was compensated.

One solution to the problems confronting the workers' compensation system would be federal reform. Those advocating such reform have put forth several plans, but Congress has shown little inclination so far to adopt a uniform federal act. However, as the next section reveals, there are already federal compensation acts covering certain segments of the work force.

## 3.  Federal Compensation Acts

Congress has enacted several statutes which extend liability to certain kinds of employers for injuries, diseases, and deaths arising out of the course of employment. Railroad workers and other transportation workers are covered by the *Federal Employers Liability Act* (FELA). This statute does not provide for liability without fault, as in the case of workers' compensation, but it greatly increases the chances of a worker's winning a lawsuit against her or his employer by eliminating the defenses the employer would have had at common law. In a suit for damages based upon the negligence of the officers, agents, or employees of an employer, the contributory negligence of the injured employee does not prevent recovery. If it is present, however, the comparative responsibility rule reduces damages in proportion to the amount of the employee's negligence. This rule does not apply when the employer's violation of a statute enacted for the safety of the employee has contributed to the injury. Also, the common-law defense of assumption of the risk is not available to an employer.

The act further provides that a term in a contract of employment which attempts to exempt a covered employer from liability or prevent enforcement of the FELA is void. In addition, the legal rights of a deceased employee which are created by the statute survive for the benefit of the surviving spouse and children. Although fault of the employer must be proved for an employee to recover for injuries under FELA, and a regular lawsuit must be filed in court, the act provides the worker with a distinct advantage over many workers' compensation systems. There is no limit or ceiling to the amount an employee can recover for injuries. It is clear that juries often are sympathetic to the injured worker, and verdicts in six or seven figures are not unusual. The Jones Act gives maritime employees the same rights against their employers as railway workers have against theirs under FELA.

Other federal statutes require awards for on-the-job injuries or deaths of certain employees without regard to the fault of the employer, which is in the manner of state workers' compensation laws. These federal statutes provide formulas to use in computing the amounts of the awards for various kinds and degrees of disability, along with upper and lower limits for such awards. One statute is the Longshoremen's and Harbor Workers' Compensation Act. Congress extended this act to cover workers of private employers on United States defense bases.

## 4.   Wages and Hours of Work

### GENERALLY

Statutes setting **minimum wages** per hour and maximum hours of work exist on both the state and the federal level. Early state legislation of this type mainly concerned labor by children and women. At first, employers successfully attacked such legislation as being an unconstitutional invasion of the freedom of contract. Today we recognize that state governments possess the power to enact statutes of this type for social and economic purposes. Approximately 70 percent of the states have minimum-wage laws.

The federal government also regulates wages and hours. The *Fair Labor Standards Act* (FLSA), which was originally enacted in 1938, has been amended several times to increase the minimum wage, decrease maximum hours, and broaden its coverage. Originally, FLSA required covered employers to pay their employees at least 25 cents an hour for a regular workweek of forty-four hours, to pay such employees at least time and one-half for all work performed over the forty-four-hour week, and to keep certain records for each worker which would demonstrate compliance or noncompliance with the act. It also restricted the use of child labor. The Supreme Court held the statute to be a constitutional exercise of the power of Congress under the commerce clause.

### MINIMUM WAGE

At the time of this book's writing, the minimum hourly wage is generally $3.35. The standard workweek is forty hours, with overtime pay at a rate of not less than one and one-half times the employee's regular rate of pay. Although this regular rate may not be less than the minimum wage, it can be and usually is more. If it is, the time and one-half is the higher rate. For example, an employee whose hourly rate is $4 receives $6 per hour for overtime. The wage and overtime provisions apply whether an employee is paid on a time, piece, job, incentive, or other basis. The FLSA does *not* require sick pay, holidays off, vacations, overtime pay for weekend or holiday work, or a limit on the hours of work for employees who are sixteen years of age or older.

## COVERAGE

Not all types of employment were covered by the original FLSA, nor are they today. However, the amendments have expanded coverage greatly, along with the minimum wage, so that now it protects most workers. Although there are still some exempt businesses, their number is decreasing, and the trend is to require the minimum wage for all. Categories of persons who are presently not covered include many who do not need the protection such as those engaged in the practice of a profession, managerial and supervisory personnel, and outside salespeople. Most of the time, persons engaged in such employment earn incomes far in excess of the FLSA minimums anyway. Also not covered are certain workers employed by small farms and small businesses such as "mom and pop" retail establishments and other small independent stores which are intrastate in operation.

In addition, messengers, handicapped workers, and full-time students employed in similar service operations, institutions of higher education, or agriculture may be paid lower minimum wages, provided the employer first obtains special certificates from the administrator of the Wage and Hour Division of the Department of Labor. As the next case shows, the minimum wage also does not apply to individuals in training when the employer gains no benefit from the training itself.

# DONOVAN v. TRANS WORLD AIRLINES, INC.
726 F.2d 415 (1984)

PER CURIAM: The Secretary of Labor appeals from a final judgment entered in the District Court for the Western District of Missouri ruling that flight attendant trainees who had trained at Trans World Airlines, Inc.'s (TWA) Breech Training Academy were not "employees" for the purposes of the Fair Labor Standards Act (FLSA) during the first four weeks of training and, consequently, were not covered by the minimum wage and reporting provisions of the FLSA. We affirm.

For many years TWA, a major commercial air carrier, chose to train all TWA flight attendants at its Breech Training Academy (Academy) located in Overland Park, Kansas. Flight attendant positions were highly desirable and TWA received literally thousands of applications each year. In an effort to keep the cost of training flight attendants down, TWA tried to predict the number of flight attendant vacancies that would arise. Based on those determinations, TWA carefully selected its prospective trainees from a large group of applicants.

Although not officially required to do so, most flight attendant trainees resided in dormitory-like accommodations located on the Academy grounds. During the disputed four-week training period, the trainees neither received nor expected any wages or monetary compensation from TWA. However, TWA did provide meals, lodging, ground transportation, and health and accident insurance during the training periods.

Trainees attended approximately forty hours of classes per week. About one-half of the training was devoted to the safety and emergency instruction required by the Federal Aviation Administration. TWA also provided instruction in subjects such as aviation history, grooming, personal and public communications, physical fitness, foreign currencies, and food and liquor preparation. The District Court found that although much of this instruction was geared to TWA passenger service and equipment, "much of that training could be utilized in service on other airlines and in other fields of endeavor."

At no time prior to completion of the training course were trainees permitted to work on regular commercial flights or to supplement the work of regular flight attendants. Although completion of the training course qualified trainees as flight attendants, TWA did not guarantee that all successful trainees would be hired upon graduation.

The District Court concluded that TWA flight attendant trainees were not "employees" within the meaning of the relevant provisions of the FLSA because TWA received no immediate benefit from their efforts during training.

Whether or not an individual is an "employee" within the meaning of the FLSA is a legal determination rather than a factual one.

After careful examination of the record, we conclude that the district court's determination is correct. Accordingly, we affirm on the basis of the district court's analysis. [*Affirmed*]

---

One proposal to amend minimum-wage coverage would allow employers to pay teenagers less than minimum wage. This proposal is in response to widespread teenage unemployment, especially in the cities. The theory is that if employers could pay less than minimum wage, they would hire more teenagers. Unions, however, oppose a reduction in the minimum wage.

### CHILD LABOR

Besides its wage and hour provisions, FLSA contains sections which regulate the employment of child labor outside agriculture. Under these, eighteen is the minimum age for employment in occupations which are declared *hazardous* by the secretary of labor. These include such jobs as working in areas that involve exposure to radioactivity, operating various kinds of dangerous machinery, mining, and roofing. Otherwise, the basic minimum age for employment is sixteen, at which age children may be employed in any nonhazardous work.

The employment of fourteen- and fifteen-year-olds is limited to certain occupations such as sales and clerical work, under specific conditions of work, for limited hours, and outside school time only. Children under fourteen may not be employed, except for a few jobs which are specifically exempt. For example, children employed in agriculture outside of school hours, children employed by their parents in nonhazardous occupations, child actors, and newspaper deliveries are exempt. State laws on child labor must also be followed if they are more strict than the federal standards.

### PENALTIES AND REMEDIES

Willful violations of the provisions of the Fair Labor Standards Act may be prosecuted criminally by the attorney general. Violators may be punished by a fine of up to $10,000 for the first offense and, for subsequent offenses, a fine of up to $10,000 or imprisonment for up to six months, or both. Violators of the child-labor provisions can be fined a civil penalty of up to $1,000 for each violation. The act also empowers the federal district courts to issue injunctions restraining violations of it.

Finally, employees who are injured by a violation may bring a civil suit against their employer and recover unpaid wages or overtime compensation and an equal amount as "liquidated" damages, plus reasonable attorneys' fees and costs of the action. However, if the employer shows the court that she or he acted in good faith and had reasonable grounds to believe that she or he was not violating the law, the court may, in its discretion, award no liquidated damages, or limit them. The administrator of the Wage and Hour Division of the Department of Labor may supervise the payment of back wages, or the secretary of labor may, upon the written request of an employee, bring suit for back pay due the employee. In 1987, a federal court ordered a Texas utility company to pay employees $7.6 million in back overtime pay.

## 5.  Unemployment Compensation

### GENERALLY

Unemployment compensation is a federal-state program which provides for payments for temporary periods to workers who are unemployed through no fault of their own. It is a classic example of the use of the federal taxing power as a tool to pressure the states into adopting legislation deemed desirable by the federal government. The Social Security Act of 1935 imposed a federal tax on the wages paid by all employers who were not exempt. However, the act provided that taxed employers were entitled to a credit of up to 90 percent of this tax for any contributions they made to an approved state unemployment insurance plan. Although only Wisconsin had an unemployment compensation law in 1935, all the states enacted such statutes shortly after the Social Security Act.

The federal policy to encourage state unemployment insurance was a result of the mass unemployment in the depression during the 1930s. Then, millions were out of work for long periods, with about 25 percent of the labor force being unemployed. Partly, this mass unemployment was due to a self-feeding cycle. As workers were laid off, they lost their purchasing power and could consume less. Less consumption meant less need for production, so employers had to lay off more workers who lost their purchasing power and could consume less. Production continued to fall, so more workers became unemployed.

A major goal of unemployment compensation, besides the humanitarian one, was to break this vicious cycle.

### REQUIREMENTS OF THE LAW

Today, the basic standard of the federal unemployment law imposes a tax on any person who pays $1,500 of wages during any three-month period of the current or preceding year. The tax is on the first $7,000 of wages at a 1990 rate of 6.2 percent. Up to 90 percent of this tax may be deducted for amounts paid to a state unemployment compensation fund.

The federal law grants a series of exemptions from the unemployment tax. Among the exempted are agricultural labor for certain small farming operations, family labor, labor for the United States government or for a state, and labor for a religious, charitable, or educational organization. The states may provide for wider coverage if they desire.

Only workers in a covered business can collect unemployment compensation, and then only if they meet certain tests. If they qualify, they draw payments as a matter of right, regardless of financial position, since need is not a factor. The laws require them either to have worked for a certain minimum number of weeks in a covered industry or to have earned a certain minimum amount of wages. These times and amounts vary from state to state. Generally, a worker must wait one week before applying and must register with the state employment agency and be ready, willing, and able to undertake suitable employment.

The maximum period during which benefits are payable varies from state to state and generally has ranged from twenty-six to thirty-nine weeks. The maximum amount of weekly payments for unemployment also varies widely. Usually it is computed as a percentage of the highest quarterly earnings in a base period.

All states have adopted **experience rating systems** which excuse employers who have a good record of maintaining stable employment from paying part or all of the state unemployment tax. Such systems have been adopted as a result of the provision which allows employers a credit against the federal tax not only for amounts paid the state but also for such amounts as they are excused from paying because of a good experience rating. Thus, businesses with a good rating pay less in unemployment taxes than ones with a higher unemployment experience.

As a result of the credit permitted by the experience rating system, the average unemployment tax rate nationwide has been considerably less than that provided for in the law. Experience rating has given employers the incentive to attempt to control their unemployment record and detect fraudulent claims filed by former employees. On the minus side, it means that taxes will be lower during times when the economy is in good condition and higher when general conditions are bad.

### DISQUALIFICATION FROM RECEIVING COMPENSATION

State laws usually disqualify persons from receiving unemployment compensation for: (1) voluntarily leaving the job without good cause, (2) being discharged for misconduct, and (3) refusing suitable work while unemployed. In the following case, the Supreme Court considers whether federal law permits Missouri to deny unemployment compensation to women who voluntarily leave their jobs due to pregnancy.

# WIMBERLY v. LABOR AND INDUS. RELATIONS COM'N
107 S.Ct. 821 (1987)

Petitioner Wimberly was on pregnancy leave from her job under her employer's policy that she would be rehired only if a position were available. When she wanted to return to work, she was told there were no positions available. She then applied for unemployment compensation and was denied it on the basis of a Missouri statute that denied compensation to one who has left work "voluntarily without good cause attributable to his work or to his employer." The Missouri Supreme Court upheld the validity of the Missouri statute, denying the petitioner's claim that the statute violated the Federal Unemployment Tax Act. The United States Supreme Court granted certiorari.

O'CONNOR, J.: The Federal Unemployment Tax Act (Act)…enacted originally as Title IX of the Social Security Act in 1935…envisions a cooperative federal-state program of benefits to unemployed workers. The Act establishes certain minimum federal standards that a State must satisfy in order for a State to participate in the program. The standard at issue in this case, § 3304(a)(12), mandates that "no person shall

be denied compensation under such State law solely on the basis of pregnancy or termination of pregnancy."

Apart from the minimum standards reflected in § 3304(a), the Act leaves to state discretion the rules governing the administration of unemployment compensation programs. State programs, therefore, vary in their treatment of the distribution of unemployment benefits, although all require a claimant to satisfy some version of a three-part test. First, all States require claimants to earn a specified amount of wages or to work a specified number of weeks in covered employment during a one-year base period in order to be entitled to receive benefits. Second, all States require claimants to be "eligible" for benefits, that is, they must be able to work and available for work. Third, claimants who satisfy these requirements may be "disqualified" for reasons set forth in state law. The most common reasons for disqualification under state unemployment compensation laws are voluntarily leaving the job without good cause, being discharged for misconduct, and refusing suitable work.

The treatment of pregnancy-related terminations is a matter of considerable disparity among the States. Most States regard leave on account of pregnancy as a voluntary termination for good cause. Some of these States have specific statutory provisions enumerating pregnancy-motivated termination as good cause for leaving a job, while others, by judicial or administrative decision, treat pregnancy as encompassed within larger categories of good cause such as illness or compelling personal reasons. A few States, however, like Missouri, have chosen to define "leaving for good cause" narrowly. In these States, all persons who leave their jobs are disqualified from receiving benefits unless they leave for reasons directly attributable to the work or to the employer.

Petitioner does not dispute that the Missouri scheme treats pregnant women the same as all other persons who leave for reasons not causally connected to their work or their employer, including those suffering from other types of temporary disabilities. She contends, however, that § 3304(a)(12) is not simply an antidiscrimination statute, but rather that it mandates preferential treatment for women who leave work because of pregnancy. According to petitioner, § 3304(a)(12) affirmatively requires States to provide unemployment benefits to women who leave work because of pregnancy when they are next available and able to work, regardless of the State's treatment of other similarly situated claimants.

Contrary to petitioners' assertions, the plain import of the language of § 3304(a)(12) is that Congress intended only to prohibit States from singling out pregnancy for unfavorable treatment. The text of the statute provides that compensation shall not be denied under state law "solely on the basis of pregnancy." The focus of this language is on the basis for the State's decision, not the claimant's reason for leaving her job. Thus, a State could not decide to deny benefits to pregnant women while at the same time allowing benefits to persons who are in other respects similarly situated: the "sole basis" for such a decision would be on account of pregnancy. On the other hand, if a State adopts a neutral rule that incidentally disqualifies pregnant or formerly pregnant claimants as part of a larger group, the neutral application of that rule cannot readily be characterized as a decision made "solely on the basis of pregnancy." For example, under Missouri law, *all* persons who leave work for reasons not causally connected to the work or the employer are disqualified from receiving benefits. To apply this law, it is not necessary to know that petitioner left because of pregnancy: all that is relevant is that she stopped work for a reason bearing no causal connection to her work or her employer. Because the State's decision could have been made without ever knowing that petitioner had been pregnant, pregnancy was not the "sole basis" for the decision under a natural reading of § 3304(a)(12)'s language....

Because § 3304 (a)(12) does not require States to afford preferential treatment to women on account of pregnancy, the judgment of the Missouri Supreme Court is affirmed. [*It is so ordered.*]

---

Most states disqualify workers from receiving unemployment compensation if they are on strike because of a labor dispute. Sometimes, strikes affect workers who are not themselves on strike. In such cases, the workers can get unemployment compensation.

## 6. Social Security

### IN GENERAL

Social Security is a federal program for providing income when a family's earnings are reduced or stopped because of retirement, disability, or death. Under Social Security's Medicare provisions, hospital and medical insurance help protect persons who are sixty-five and older from high health-care costs. Every month, 36 million people receive Social Security benefits, which represent 27 percent of all expenditures made by the federal government.

Congress enacted the first Social Security Act in 1935. At first, it covered only certain workers in commerce and industry and provided them only with retirement benefits. Since then, a number of amendments have increased the kind and dollar amount of benefits to what they are today. These amendments have also greatly increased the number of persons covered so that now most self-employed persons, employees of nonprofit corporations, household and farm employees, federal employees, members of the armed forces, the clergy, and others are included also. Currently, nine out of ten workers in the United States are earning Social Security protection, and approximately one out of seven persons receives monthly Social Security checks.

The Social Security law requires that during their working years, covered employees, their employers, and self-employed persons pay Social Security taxes to the federal government. Employers must deduct their employees' share of the contribution to the Social Security system from their wages, match those payments, and send the combined amount to the IRS. Self-employed persons pay their tax each year when filing their individual income tax returns. Generally, employers must file an Employer's Quarterly Tax Return with the IRS and deposit Social Security taxes with an authorized commercial bank or Federal Reserve Bank at various times, usually at least once per month, depending on the amount of undeposited taxes at the time. A penalty is imposed for failure to make required deposits when due, without reasonable cause. Earnings of workers are taxable even if they are receiving Social Security benefits at the time.

Employers must keep all records pertaining to employment taxes for inspection by the IRS for a period of at least four years after the taxes are due or are paid. These records must include such things as the names, addresses, occupations, and Social Security numbers of the employees paid; the amounts and dates of the payments made to them; the period of their employment; duplicate copies of tax returns filed; and the dates and amounts of deposits made.

### CRITICISMS AND PROBLEMS OF THE SOCIAL SECURITY SYSTEM

In recent years, concern has grown over the financial health of the Social Security system. It appears underfunded, in spite of the fact that the amount of wages subject to Social Security tax, as well as its rates, have increased dramatically. In 1989, the tax was paid on the first $48,000 of personal income, an amount that was $29,700 in 1981. For 25 percent of all employees, Social Security tax is larger than federal income tax, and for small businesses it is the largest federal tax. The rates of taxation will rise gradually, at least through 1990 (see Table 15-3).

Critics of the system point to the fact that much of the burden of paying for increasing Social Security benefits is being imposed on the younger workers of today, at a time when many of them are raising families and attempting to purchase homes. The work force appears to be leveling off due to the trend toward zero population growth in the country. However, the number of Social Security beneficiaries will be increasing due to longer life expectancies and, at the turn of the century, to the retirement of persons born during the period after World War II, that is, the "baby boom" generation. The Congressional Budget Office estimates that between now and the year 2005 the number of Social Security beneficiaries will climb 22 percent while the number of workers will grow only 14 percent.

In 1983, Congress amended the Social Security Act to raise the retirement age for receiving full benefits. Beginning in the year 2000, the current retirement age of 65 will begin to rise. For persons born in 1960 and later, the retirement age will be 67. However, early retirement at reduced benefits will be available. That option may also be exercised at present.

Congress also has made taxable up to 50 percent of Social Security benefits for retirees whose incomes exceed a certain amount. Previously, all Social Security benefits were nontaxable. Even with these changes, however, there is still concern about the solvency of the Social Security system. In light of soaring medical costs, the Medicare trust fund of the Social Security system, which pays for retirement health costs, faces severe financial problems in the near future.

## 7.  Private Pension Plans: Incentives and Protection

Economic security in retirement has been a national policy goal for much of this century. The Social Security system is a good example. Encouragement

**TABLE 15-3**    Rates of Social Security Taxation Through 1990*

| Year | Employee and Employer, Each | Self-employed |
|------|------------------------------|---------------|
| 1986 | 7.15% | 14.30% |
| 1987 | 7.15% | 14.30% |
| 1988 | 7.51% | 15.02% |
| 1989 | 7.51% | 15.02% |
| 1990 | 7.65% | 15.30% |

*The amount of income to which the tax applies will also likely rise, but Congress has not yet set it.

of private pension plans is another part of this policy. In the past decade, the number of employer-established private retirement plans has more than doubled. Some 60 million employees are currently covered by private plans.

The law provides incentives for businesses and individuals to create private pension plans. It also protects employees who are part of such plans.

### INCENTIVES FOR PENSION PLANS: THE "QUALIFIED" PLAN

There are many types of pension plans (as well as profit-sharing arrangements). One of the motivations for such plans, of course, is a genuine interest by a business in the retirement future of all its employees, along with a desire to attract and retain high-quality workers. Some plans have resulted mainly from union pressure and collective-bargaining agreements. In addition, those persons in control of a business have a personal interest in assuring their own financial futures.

A major financial incentive to the formation of private pension plans is favorable income tax treatment. If an employer has instituted a **qualified pension plan,** as defined by the Internal Revenue Code, it can claim income tax deductions from contributions made to fund the plan, and fund earnings from investments are not taxable. Employees need pay personal income tax only on payments received after retirement. Such payments often receive special retirement income treatment and come at a time when other sources of income are lower, putting the retired person in a lower tax bracket. Basically, to qualify for this special treatment, a plan must cover either a certain percentage of all employees (usually 70 percent) or cover classifications of employees which do not discriminate in favor of management (officers or highly compensated employees) or shareholders, as determined by the IRS.

### EMPLOYEE RETIREMENT INCOME SECURITY ACT

Qualification of a pension plan by the IRS does not ensure that it is a good plan for employees. Prior to 1974, plans were sometimes improperly funded, and the money in them was irresponsibly invested. In other cases, many employees lacked **vested rights** (rights which cannot be taken away) in their company's pension plan. If they were discharged prior to retirement, they received no pension.

In 1974, Congress passed the *Employee Retirement Income Security Act* (ERISA) to protect employee rights in private pension plans. The act applies to both **defined benefit plans** and **defined contribution plans** (often called money-purchase plans). Defined benefit plans usually guarantee employees a certain retirement income based on years of service and salary or wage level. Actuarial calculations determine employers' funding obligations with such a plan. Under a defined contribution plan, employers contribute a percentage of an employee's pay (often 5 to 10 percent) to the pension fund. Retirement income is determined by the total of these contributions plus investment return.

The defined contribution plan allows employers to budget pension costs in advance. Because of this and because ERISA regulates funding requirements for defined benefit plans very heavily, the majority of employers favor defined contribution plans.

### PENSION BENEFIT GUARANTY CORPORATION

An important provision of ERISA requires **plan termination insurance coverage** for all defined benefit plans. The idea is to make the plans pay annual premiums to insure the benefits to participants in the event that the plan is terminated and its assets are not sufficient to meet its obligations. The act creates the Pension Benefit Guaranty Corporation (PBGC) to provide this insurance. It ensures that vested benefits will be paid up to established maximums. The employer, not just the separate pension plan itself, is also made liable to reimburse PBGC for the insured benefits it pays, up to 30 percent of the employer's net worth. Without this requirement, claims could be made only against the pension trust's assets, but not against the employer when the pension trust failed.

### THE FIDUCIARY OBLIGATION

Another aspect of ERISA is also designed to protect the assets of pension plans. Strict rules require plan **fiduciaries** (those who are placed in a position of trust and confidence with regard to another's assets) to exercise the degree of care that a prudent person would in handling his or her own affairs in the management of a fund's assets. Anyone who has any such control, as well as one who gives investment advice for a fee, is included in the act's definition of a fiduciary. Also, transactions between the plan and a party with a conflicting interest, like the employer, are forbidden. Under this rule, a loan between the plan and employer is prohibited, as is a sale of property between them. Investments by a plan in the securities of the employer are generally limited to 10 percent.

### VESTING

ERISA also ensures employees' rights to benefits under pension plans. The law states that benefits from an employee's own contributions (if any) to a plan are fully and immediately vested when the contributions are made. Benefits from an employer's plan contributions must begin vesting before retirement under one of several ERISA standards. The most common standard selected by employees provides for full employee vesting after ten years of service. Another standard establishes a gradual five- to fifteen-year vesting.

### RECORD-KEEPING AND REPORTING REQUIREMENTS

The record-keeping and reporting requirements under ERISA are substantial. The years of service and percentage of vesting of benefits of each participant must be recorded. If vested employees terminate before retirement, the plan administrator must furnish both the IRS and the Department of Labor with information on their vested benefits. A booklet (approved by the Department of Labor) must be prepared for distribution to plan participants. It must include a detailed plan description and a summary, understandable by the average participant. A very detailed annual report must be filed with the department and made available for examination by plan participants and for public inspection. The plan report generally must include financial statements, an opinion on them by an independent certified accountant, information on the plan's investments, assets, and transactions, and other data which are specified in great detail by the act.

### SIMPLIFIED EMPLOYEE PENSIONS

The Revenue Act of 1978 permits employers to set up **simplified employee pensions.** This change was designed to appeal to employers, particularly smaller businesses, who do not wish to set up a full-blown pension plan of their own because of the expense and complications involved. Under this plan, employers can contribute up to a specified amount of an employee's income to an **individual retirement account** (IRA) for each employee. The contributions (including interest or other income from their investment) are not taxable to the employees until they begin drawing from their account in retirement, which can start anytime after age fifty-nine and one-half without penalty. Employees select their own investment vehicle when they open their IRAs. The approved list includes banks, savings and loans, credit unions, insurance companies, and mutual funds. The fact that the employee decides where the IRA is invested should result in greatly reduced liability risk on the part of the employer. The IRA belongs to the employee, so it vests immediately. Also, the fund goes along with the employee who changes jobs, and it continues to accumulate.

Businesses which adopt the simplified employee pensions plan may deduct contributions from their income tax. However, to qualify they must meet certain requirements. For example, all covered employees must receive the same *percentage* contribution. The percentage rate of contribution may be changed from year to year (for all workers), or, in a bad year, the employer may decide to make no contributions at all.

### INDIVIDUAL RETIREMENT ACCOUNTS

Any person under age seventy and one-half can set up and fund an individual retirement account. Within limits set by ERISA, the person can invest the IRA funds. IRA contributions up to $2000 annually are fully deductible from presently taxable income if the person is not covered by an employment retirement plan. For persons already covered by employment retire ment plans (or whose spouses are covered), there are substantial limits on deductibility of IRA contributions at higher income levels.

Because the purpose of IRAs is to provide retirement income, there are substantial tax penalties for early withdrawal of funds. Withdrawals can be made without penalty beginning at age fifty-nine and one-half. If death occurs prior to that age, distributions can also be made to survivors without penalty. Along with pension plans, IRAs have helped reduce demands for an expanded Social Security program.

### ERISA TRENDS

Most observers consider ERISA a success. Over 30 million Americans participate in more than 500,000 private pension plans. These plans hold assets of over $500 billion. Because of its success, ERISA might be amended to include retirement medical insurance. This step would help prop up the Social Security Medicare program, which could become insolvent if medical costs continue to rise and Congress fails to provide additional funding.

Even with its success, ERISA also faces problems. More than 1,000 private pension plans have fallen into insolvency, and the PBGC is operating at a deficit to meet the obligations of these plans to retired employees. One solution, which PBGC has proposed to Congress, is to raise the annual insurance premium which employers with defined benefit plans currently pay to PBGC.

A major problem of ERISA is the amount of paperwork required of employers who maintain pension plans. These employers must keep records and make reports to three separate governmental agencies: PBGC, the Labor Department, and the Treasury Department (IRS). Many smaller businesses cannot afford to do this and do not have pension plans. Only 15 percent of businesses with fewer than 25 employees cover their work force with a pension plan. A proposed solution would centralize authority in one agency, probably PBGC, thus reducing the paperwork burden.

## 8.  Workers' Privacy

Individual privacy is such an important part of individual freedom that both legal and ethical questions regarding privacy are bound to multiply in the computer age. While debate continues concerning the need for further federal privacy legislation, many states have passed their own privacy-related statutes. Several states guarantee workers access to their job personnel files and restrict disclosure of personal information to third parties.

Concerns for individual privacy also contributed to passage of the 1988 Employee Polygraph Protection Act. Under this federal law private employers generally are forbidden from using lie dectector tests while screening job applicants. Current employees may not be tested randomly, but may be tested as a result of a specific incident or activity that causes economic injury or loss to an employer's business. The act permits testing of job applicants by private security companies and allows testing both job applicants and current employees of companies that manufacture or sell controlled substances. The Labor Department may seek fines of up to $10,000 against employers who violate the act. Employees are also authorized to sue employers under the act.

Another important privacy concern involves drug testing. At present there is no uniform law regarding the drug testing of employees. Many private companies conduct such testing. However, at least six states have placed some limits on a private company's right to test for drugs.

Public employees are protected from some drug testing by the fourth amendment's prohibition against "unreasonable" searches. However, exactly when drug tests are unreasonable is subject to much debate in the courts. In general, public employees may be tested when there is a proper suspicion that employees are using illegal drugs that impair working ability or violate employment rules. Courts have also upheld drug testing as part of required annual medical exams.

## 9. Trends in Worker Protection

### PLANT CLOSING NOTICE

In 1988 Congress passed the Worker Adjustment and Retraining Notification Act. This act specifies circumstances under which employers must give advance notice of plant closings or layoffs.

Under the act any employer with 100 or more employees must give 60 days notice to affected employees and local government officials before closing any plant or "operating unit." In cases of employee layoffs when a plant is not closed, an employer must give notice if one-third of a plant's work force (or at least 500 employees, whichever is less) are laid off.

The act exempts an employer from giving notice when the closing or layoff was caused by "not reasonably foreseeable circumstances," such as floods or earthquakes. An employer also need not give notice when doing so will keep it from getting new capital or new business that might enable it to postpone the closing or layoff.

The act authorizes the federal courts to fine an employer who violates the act. The Labor Department may also require violators to pay up to 60 days' back pay and benefits to employees not given proper notice.

## LIMITATIONS ON EMPLOYMENT AT WILL

Historically, unless employees contracted for a definite period of employment (such as for one year), employers were able to discharge them without reason at any time. This is called the **employment-at-will** doctrine.

During the 1930s, employers began to lose this absolute right to discharge employees whenever they desired. The Labor-Management Relations Act prohibited employers from firing employees for union activities. Now, many federal laws limit employers in their right to terminate employees, even at-will employees (see Table 15-4). Some states have also prohibited employers by statute from discharging employees for certain reasons, such as for refusing to take lie-detector examinations.

Courts, too, have begun limiting the at-will doctrine. Under contract theory, several courts have stated that at-will employment contracts (which are not written and are little more than the agreement to pay for work performed) contain an implied promise of good faith and fair dealing by the employer. This promise, implied by law, can be broken in certain cases by unjustified dismissal of employees. As the following case illustrates, other courts have ruled that an employer's publication of personnel handbooks can change the nature of at-will employment.

**TABLE 15-4**   Federal Statutes Limiting Employment-at-will Doctrine

| Statute | Limitation on Employee Discharge |
| --- | --- |
| 1  Labor-Management Relations Act | Prohibits discharge for union activity or for filing charges under the act |
| 2  Fair Labor Standards Act | Forbids discharge for exercising rights guaranteed by minimum wage and overtime provisions of the act |
| 3  Occupational Safety and Health Act | Prohibits discharge for exercising rights under the act |
| 4  Civil Rights Act | Makes illegal discharge based on race, sex, color, religion, or national origin |
| 5  Age Discrimination in Employment Act | Forbids age-based discharge of employees aged forty to seventy |
| 6  Employee Retirement Income Security Act | Prohibits discharge to prevent employees from getting vested pension rights |
| 7  Clean Air Act | Prevents discharge of employees who cooperate in proceedings against employer for violation of the act |
| 8  Clean Water Act | Prevents discharge of employees who cooperate in proceedings against employer for violation of the act |
| 9  Consumer Credit Protection Act | Prohibits discharge of employees due to garnishment of wages for any one indebtedness |
| 10  Judiciary and Judicial Procedure Act | Forbids discharge of employees for service on federal grand or petit juries |

# SMALL v. SPRING INDUSTRIES, INC.
357 S.E.2d 452 (S.C. 1987)

HARWELL J.: Respondent Small sued appellant Springs Industries, Inc. (Springs) for breach of contract. After Small had been employed at Springs for five years, the company issued an employee handbook and distributed it to all of its employees. Springs later issued a bulletin to all employees setting forth in full the handbook's termination procedure. This handbook and bulletin provided for a four-step disciplinary process which consisted of a verbal reprimand, a written warning, a final written warning, and discharge. Small was discharged after only one written warning. The trial judge allowed the jury to determine whether or not the employee handbook, the bulletin, and oral assurances by Small's supervisors that Springs would always follow the handbook's four-step discharge process, altered the otherwise at-will employment relationship. The jury found for Small and returned a verdict of $300,000 actual damages for breach of the employment contract. Springs appeals.

Small's employment record at Springs is less than impressive. Her record is replete with absences and injuries. Nonetheless, Springs' employee handbook provides a four-step discharge policy for all of its employees. The handbook does contain an exception to this four part process: "[S]ome offenses, such as fighting, drunkenness, and others of an equally serious nature, will lead to immediate discharge without the usual four-step procedure being followed." At trial, Small's boss testified that he had never had any disciplinary problems with Small; she had never come to work intoxicated; and she had never created any fights or disputes.

Under the common law, a trial court should submit to the jury the issue of existence of a contract when its existence is questioned and the evidence is either conflicting or admits of more than one inference. It was for the jury to decide whether or not Springs reasonably could have determined that Small's actions constituted a serious offense which could result in discharge without the four-step process. The jury obviously determined that a contract was established and that Small's action could not have fallen into the "serious offense" category. Since Springs admittedly failed to follow its own discharge policy, the jury allowed Small to recover for breach of contract. In a law action that is tried by a jury, our jurisdiction extends only to correcting errors of law. We will not disturb a factual finding made by the jury unless there is no evidence in the record which reasonably supports the jury's findings.

Springs contends that no employment contract was established and, therefore, Small remained an at-will employee who could be terminated without notice for any reason. Small acknowledges the validity of the at-will employment rule but she contends that Springs altered this relationship and became contractually bound by the employee handbook, bulletin, and oral assurances of her supervisors. Springs contends that no employment contract was established because there was no mutuality or "meeting of the minds" between the parties; the writings did not contain the necessary elements of an employment contract; and the writings lacked reciprocal rights, duties, and obligations.

Springs' analysis might be valid if it were applied to a bilateral contract or agreement. The employment agreement in this case, like most employment agreements, was a unilateral agreement. Springs made an offer or promise to hire Small in return for specified benefits and wages. Small accepted this offer by performing the act on which the promise was impliedly or expressly based. Springs' promise constituted the terms of the employment agreement. Small's action or forebearance in reliance on Springs' promise was sufficient consideration to make the promise legally binding. There was no contractual requirement that Small do anything more than perform the act on which the promise was predicated in order to legally bind Springs.

If an employer wishes to issue policies, manuals, or bulletins as purely advisory statements with no intent of being bound by them and with a desire to continue under the employment at will policy, he certainly is free to do so. This could be accomplished merely by inserting a conspicuous disclaimer or provision into the written document. It is patently unjust to allow an employer to couch a handbook, bulletin, or other similar material in mandatory terms and then allow him to ignore these very policies as "a gratuitous, nonbinding statement of general policy" whenever it works to his disadvantage. Assuredly, the employer would view these policies differently if it were the employee who failed to follow them.

Springs contends that employers will stop providing handbooks, bulletins, and similar materials if they are bound by them. If company policies are not worth the paper on which they are printed, then it would be better not to mislead employees by distributing them. Due to the potential for gross inequality in a situation such as the one in the case at bar, a majority of states has determined that a handbook can alter the employment status. South Carolina, as a progressive state which wishes to see that both employer and employee are treated fairly, now joins those states. We hold that a jury can consider an employee handbook, along with other evidence, in deciding whether the employer and employee had a limiting agreement on the employee's at-will employment status. [*Affirmed in part as to the existence of a contract. Reversed in part as to the amount of damages.*]

---

Many contract and tort exceptions to employment at will have involved one of three types of employer behavior: (1) discharge of employee for performance of an important public obligation (such as jury duty); (2) discharge of employee for reporting employer's alleged violations of law (called "whistle blowing"); and (3) discharge of employee for exercising statutory rights. Most of the cases that limit at-will employment state that the employer has violated "public policy." What does it mean to say that an employer has violated public policy? Is it a court's way of saying that most people no longer support the employer's right to do what it did?

Limitations on employment-at-will doctrine show continued development of worker protection. Instead of dealing with worker safety and financial security, they concern a related issue: job security. It may be part of a trend which could ultimately lead to some type of broad, legally guaranteed job security. Many nations have much stricter laws promoting an employee's right to job security than does the United States. In recent years, unions have increasingly focused on job-security issues in their bargaining with employers.

## REVIEW QUESTIONS

**1** For each term in the left-hand column, match the most appropriate description in the right-hand column:

(1) Course of employment

(2) Defined benefit plan

(3) Defined contribution plan

(4) Discharge for proper cause

(5) Employment at will

(6) Exclusive remedy rule

(7) Fellow-servant rule

(8) Minimum wage

(a) The law which states that an employee may only recover workers' compensation against an employer for an accidental injury.

(b) A common-law doctrine which held that an employer was not liable when one employee injured another.

(c) The legal concept that an employer may fire at any time an employee who is not under contract.

(d) A pension system which guarantees employees a certain retirement income based on years of service and salary.

(e) A pension system under which an employer pays a certain percentage of an employee's wage or salary to a fund but does not guarantee a certain level of retirement income.

(f) The pursuing of the employer's interest under the employer's direction.

(g) The firing of someone for failing to follow orders, tardiness, and so on, which makes that person ineligible for unemployment compensation.

(h) Rights which cannot legally be taken away.

(9) Qualified pension plan

(10) Vested rights

(i) The lowest legal pay an employer can give for certain types of employment.

(j) A retirement income program under which employers can claim income tax deductions for contributions made to fund the program.

**2**  You are the owner of a small smelting plant. An employee informs you that an OSHA inspector has just arrived in the plant parking lot. Must you allow the inspector entrance to the plant? If OSHA issues your company a citation for violating its standards, what happens then? Discuss.

**3**  How did the assumption-of-risk, contributory-negligence, and fellow-servant doctrines make it difficult in the 1800s for injured employees to sue their employers for job-related accidents?

**4**  If Corgel fails to wear a hard hat as required by his employer and is injured by a falling screwdriver, can he recover workers' compensation from the employer?

**5**  Discuss exceptions to the exclusive-remedy rule. Why are ever greater numbers of injured employees trying to avoid the impact of the rule?

**6**  A railroad employee falls from a moving train and suffers back injury. Can the employee recover under workers' compensation? Explain.

**7**  While preparing her income tax return, Corrine Smythe finds that she worked 2,500 hours in 1987 in her job as a picker-packer. Her hourly wage was $8 and her employer paid her a total of $20,000 during the year. Suddenly, Smythe realizes that her employer has violated the Fair Labor Standard Act. Explain and tell what remedies she has under the act.

**8**  The foreman of a work crew employed by the Zenith Roof Company asks the company to hire his sixteen-year-old nephew as a roofer's assistant during the summer. How should the company respond to this request? Explain.

**9**  What tax incentive is there for businesses to have a low turnover of employees? Explain.

**10**  Claudia's employer fired her for theft of office supplies. Marco quit his job in hopes of becoming a writer. Are either of these two persons entitled to unemployment compensation?

**11**  Discuss the problems facing the Social Security system.

**12**  Consider defined benefit pension plans and defined contribution pension plans. From a financial viewpoint, which type will an employer usually prefer? An employee? Discuss.

**13**  Weitz, a retired industrial worker, gets $750 monthly under a defined benefit pension plan. He learns that his former employer is bankrupt and that there is not enough money in the pension plan to continue paying his benefits. What will likely happen to Weitz's retirement income?

**14**  Roebuck Manufacturing, a small equipment firm, has only thirty-five employees. Because of the expense and complication of setting up a regular defined benefit or contribution plan, it has not set up a pension plan for its employees. Then it learns of the "simplified employee pension." Discuss the advantages of this type of pension plan for a firm like Roebuck Manufacturing.

**15** Turner was employed by the Apco Textile Company. He injured his back and missed a substantial period of work. When he sought workers' compensation, he was fired. Can he sue Apco for damages? Explain.

*Chapter*

# 16

# Discrimination in Employment

## CHAPTER PREVIEW

This chapter examines laws which require employers to give equal job opportunities to various groups. The laws prohibit discrimination based on race, sex, color, religion, and national origin. In many instances, they also forbid discrimination arising from age or handicap.

Note in your study that discrimination can be illegal even when it is *not* intentional. For example, a company's hiring policies which apply equally to all job applicants are illegal if they discriminate disproportionately and are not related directly to job performance. Realize that the courts, not the employer, will decide whether hiring policies are job-related.

At the federal level, the Equal Employment Opportunity Commission investigates and prosecutes complaints of illegal job discrimination. Employees can also often file discrimination charges with state agencies. When these regulatory bodies do not resolve differences between employees and their employer, the employees can take complaints of discrimination into the courts.

Key terms in this chapter are affirmative action, bona fide occupational qualifications, comparable worth, disparate impact, disparate treatment, paper fortress, pattern and practice cases, reverse discrimination, Section 1981, and seniority system.

## 1. Historical Development of Employment Discrimination Law

"That all men are created equal" was one of the "self-evident" truths recognized by the Founding Fathers in the Declaration of Independence. However, equality among all our citizens clearly has been an ideal rather than a fact. The Constitution itself recognizes slavery by saying that slaves should count as "three-fifths of all other Persons" for determining population in House of Representatives elections. And, of course, that all *men* are created equal says nothing about women, who did not even get a constitutionally guaranteed right to vote until 1920.

Nowhere have effects of inequality and discrimination been felt more acutely than in the area of job opportunity. Historically, common law permitted employers to hire and fire virtually at will, unless restrained by contract or statute. Under this system, white males came to dominate the job market in their ability to gain employment and their salaries and wages.

Although the Civil Rights Act of 1866 contains a provision which plaintiffs now widely use in employment discrimination cases, such use is recent. Passage of labor law in the 1920s and 1930s marks the first significant federal limitation on the relatively unrestricted right of employers to hire and fire. Then, in connection with the war effort, President Roosevelt issued executive orders in 1941 and 1943 requiring a clause prohibiting racial discrimination in all federal contracts with private contractors. Subsequent executive orders in the 1950s established committees to investigate complaints of racial discrimination against such contractors. Affirmative action requirements on federal contracts followed from executive orders of the 1960s.

The most important statute eliminating discriminatory employment practices, however, is the federal Civil Rights Act of 1964, as amended by the Equal Employment Opportunity Act of 1972.

## 2. The Civil Rights Act: General Provisions

The provisions of Title VII of the Civil Rights Act of 1964 apply to employers with fifteen or more employees. They also cover labor unions and certain others (see Table 16-1). The major purpose of these laws is to eliminate job discrimination against employees, job applicants, or union members based on race, color, religion, sex, or national origin. Discrimination for any of these reasons is a violation of the law, except that employers, employment agencies, and labor unions can discriminate on the basis of religion, sex, or national origin where these are **bona fide occupational qualifications (bfoq)** reasonably necessary to normal business operations. Title VII also permits discrimination if it results unintentionally from a seniority or merit system.

**TABLE 16-1**  Employers and Others Covered by Title VII

1  Private employers with fifteen or more employees
2  Labor unions with fifteen or more members
3  Employment agencies
4  State and local governments (but elected officials are not covered)
5  Public and private educational institutions
6  Federal government (in most instances)

The types of employer action in which discrimination is prohibited include: (1) discharge, (2) refusal to hire, (3) compensation, and (4) terms, conditions, or privileges of employment. Employment *agencies* are prohibited from either *failing to refer* or from *actually referring* an individual for employment on the basis of race, color, religion, sex, or national origin. This prohibition differs from the law binding *employers*, where it is unlawful only to fail or refuse to hire on discriminatory grounds—the affirmative act of hiring for a discriminatory reason is apparently not illegal. For example, assume that a contractor with a government contract seeks a qualified black engineer and requests an employment agency to refer such an individual. The agency complies with the request, and a black is referred and hired. Unless a white applicant was discriminated against, the employer probably did not commit an unlawful practice; but the employment agency, by referring an individual on the basis of his color, unquestionably *did* commit an unlawful practice under Title VII.

Employers, unions, and employment agencies are prohibited from discriminating against an employee, applicant, or union member because he or she has made a charge, testified, or participated in an investigation or hearing under the act, or otherwise opposed any unlawful practice.

Note that regarding general hiring, referrals, advertising, and admissions to training or apprenticeship programs, Title VII allows discrimination only on the basis of religion, sex, or national origin and only where these considerations are bona fide occupational qualifications. For example, it is legal for a Baptist church to refuse to engage a Lutheran minister. EEOC guidelines on sex discrimination consider sex to be a bona fide occupational qualification, for example, where it is necessary for authenticity or genuineness in hiring an actor or actress. The omission of *race* and *color* from this exception must mean that Congress does not feel these two factors are ever bona fide occupational qualifications.

Additional exemptions exist with respect to laws creating preferential treatment for veterans and hiring based on professionally developed ability tests that are not designed or intended to be used to discriminate. Such tests must bear a relationship to the job for which they are administered, however.

### 3. Enforcement Procedures

**GENERALLY**

The Civil Rights Act of 1964 created the Equal Employment Opportunity Commission. This agency has the primary responsibility of enforcing the provisions of the act. The EEOC is composed of five members, not more than three of whom may be members of the same political party. They are appointed by the President, with the advice and consent of the Senate, and serve a five-year term. In the course of its investigations, the Equal Employment Opportunity Commission has broad authority to hold hearings, obtain evidence, and subpoena and examine witnesses under oath.

Under the Equal Employment Opportunity Act of 1972, the EEOC can file a civil suit in federal district court and represent a person charging a violation of the act. However, it must first exhaust efforts to settle the claim. Remedies which may be obtained in such an action include reinstatement with back pay for the victim of an illegal discrimination and injunctions against future violations of the act by the defendant. Since discrimination complaints can take years to litigate to a conclusion, the size of back pay awards is often substantial (see Table 16-2).

In enacting Title VII, Congress made it clear that it did not intend to preempt states' fair employment laws. Where state agencies begin discrimination proceedings, the EEOC must wait sixty days before it starts action. Furthermore, if a state law provides relief to a discrimination charge, the EEOC must notify the appropriate state officials and wait sixty days before continuing action.

An employee must file charges of illegal discrimination with the EEOC within 180 days after the alleged unlawful practice occurred. If the EEOC does not act within a certain time period, the employee may personally file a civil action in federal district court against the employer.

**TABLE 16-2**  Selected Recent Awards in Employee Discrimination Cases

| Defendant | Plaintiff(s) | Award or Settlement |
|---|---|---|
| University of Minnesota | 250 female faculty members | $40 million, plus $2 million attorneys' fees |
| General Motors | Women and minorities | $42.5 million |
| Nabisco | 8,000 women | $5 million |
| Leeway Motor Freight | Eighty-two black employees | $2.8 million |
| Federated Department Stores | Three employees | $2.3 million, plus attorney fees |
| Burlington Northern, Inc. | 4,000 black employees | $10 million |
| Kemper Group | Female employees | $3 million |
| State Farm | Black employees | $4 million |
| Northwest Airlines | Female employees | $52.2 million |
| Geneva Tire and Rubber Company | Two female employees | $118,000, plus $138,000 attorney's fees |
| Alabama Power Company | Black employees | $1.7 million |

**LITIGATION**

To win a Title VII civil action, a plaintiff must initially show that actions taken by the employer were likely based on an illegally discriminatory basis, such as race. Generally, the plaintiff must prove either disparate (unequal) treatment or disparate impact. In proving **disparate treatment** the plaintiff must convince the court that the employer *intentionally* discriminated against the plaintiff. In a **disparate impact** case the plaintiff must prove that the employer's policies had a discriminatory effect on a group protected by Title VII. The employer can defeat the plaintiff's claim by showing that the policies used are job-related and based on business necessity. However, the plaintiff may still prove a violation by establishing that other policies would serve the legitimate interests of the employer without having undesirable discriminatory effects. In the following case the Supreme Court explains disparate treatment and disparate impact. It then extends disparate impact theory to apply to subjective as well as to objective employer evaluations of employees.

---

# WATSON v. FORT WORTH BANK & TRUST
108 S.Ct. 2777 (1988)

---

Petitioner Clara Watson worked for the respondent Fort Worth Bank & Trust. After she was denied four different promotions by her supervisors, all of whom were white, she filed a discrimination charge with the EEOC. Exhausting her administrative remedies, she filed suit in federal district court. Both the district court and the court of appeals ruled that Ms. Watson must prove intentional discrimination. These courts ruled that subjective promotion policies could not be tested under disparate impact theory. Ms. Watson petitioned the Supreme Court for a writ of certiorari. Certiorari was granted.

O'CONNOR, J.:…Several of our decisions have dealt with the evidentiary standards that apply when an individual alleges that an employer has treated that particular person less favorably than others because of the plaintiff's race, color, religion, sex, or na-

tional origin. In such "disparate treatment" cases, which involve "the most easily understood type of discrimination," the plaintiff is required to prove that the defendant had a discriminatory intent or motive. In order to facilitate the orderly consideration of relevant evidence, we have devised a series of shifting evidentiary burdens that are "intended progressively to sharpen the inquiry into the elusive factual question of intentional discrimination." Under the scheme, a prima facie case is ordinarily established by proof that the employer, after having rejected the plaintiff's application for a job or promotion, continued to seek applicants with qualifications similar to the plaintiff's. The burden of proving a prima facie case is "not onerous," and the employer in turn may rebut it simply by producing some evidence that it had legitimate, nondiscriminatory reasons for the decision. If the defendant carries this burden of production, the plaintiff must prove by a preponderance of all the evidence in the case that the legitimate reasons offered by the defendant were a pretext for discrimination....

In *Griggs v. Duke Power Co.,* this Court held that a plaintiff need not necessarily prove intentional discrimination in order to establish that an employer has violated... [Title VII]: In certain cases, facially neutral employment practices that have significant adverse effects on protected groups have been held to violate the Act without proof that the employer adopted those practices with a discriminatory intent. The factual issues and the character of the evidence are inevitably somewhat different when the plaintiff is exempted from the need to prove intentional discrimination. The evidence in these "disparate impact" cases usually focuses on statistical disparities, rather than specific incidents, and on competing explanations for those disparities....

This Court has repeatedly reaffirmed the principle that some facially neutral employment practices may violate Title VII even in the absence of a demonstrated discriminatory intent. We have not limited this principle to cases in which the challenged practice served to perpetuate the effects of pre-Act intentional discrimination. Each of our subsequent decisions, however, involved standardized employment tests or criteria.... In contrast, we have consistently used conventional disparate-treatment theory, in which proof of intent to discriminate is required, to review hiring and promotion decisions that were based on the exercise of personal judgment or the application of inherently subjective criteria....

The parties present us with stark and uninviting alternatives. Petitioner contends that subjective selection methods are at least as likely to have discriminatory effects as are the kind of objective tests at issue in Griggs and our other disparate impact cases. Furthermore, she argues, if disparate impact analysis is confined to objective tests, employers will be able to substitute subjective criteria having substantially identical effects, and Griggs will become a dead letter. Respondent and the United States (appearing as amicus curiae) argue that conventional disparate treatment analysis is adequate to accomplish Congress' purpose in enacting Title VII. They also argue that subjective selection practices would be so impossibly difficult to defend under disparate impact analysis that employers would be forced to adopt numerical quotas in order to avoid liability....

We are persuaded that disparate impact analysis is in principle no less applicable to subjective employment criteria than to objective or standardized tests. In either case, a facially neutral practice, adopted without discriminatory intent, may have effects that are indistinguishable from intentionally discriminatory practices. It is true, to be sure, that an employer's policy of leaving promotion decisions to the unchecked discretion of lower level supervisors should itself raise no inference of discriminatory conduct. Especially in relatively small businesses like respondent's, it may be customary and quite reasonable simply to delegate employment decisions to those employees who are most familiar with the jobs to be filled and with the candidates for those jobs. It does not follow, however, that the particular supervisors to whom this discretion is delegated always act without discriminatory intent. Furthermore, even if one assumed that any such discrimination can be adequately policed through disparate treatment analysis, the problem of subconscious stereotypes and prejudices would remain. In this case, for example, petitioner was apparently told at one point that the teller position was a big responsibility with "a lot of money...for blacks to have to count." Such remarks may not prove discriminatory intent, but they do suggest a lingering form of the problem that Title VII was enacted to combat. If an employer's undisciplined system of subjective decisionmaking has precisely the same effects as a system pervaded by impermissible intentional discrimination, it is difficult to see why Title VII's proscription against discriminatory actions should not apply. In both circumstances, the employer's practices may be said to "adversely affect [an individual's] status as an employee, because of such individual's race, color, religion, sex, or national origin." We conclude, accordingly, that subjective or discretionary employment practices may be analyzed under the disparate impact approach in appropriate cases.

Having decided that disparate impact analysis may in principle be applied to subjective as well as to objective practices, we turn to the evidentiary standards that should apply in such cases. It is here that the concerns raised by respondent have their greatest force. Respondent contends that a plaintiff may establish a prima facie case of disparate impact through the use of bare statistics, and that the defendant can rebut this statistical showing only by justifying the challenged practice in terms of "business necessity" or "job relatedness."

We do not believe that disparate impact theory need have any chilling effect on legitimate business practices. We recognize, however, that today's extension of that theory into the context of subjective selection practices could increase the risk that employers will be given incentives to adopt quotas or to engage in preferential treatment. Because Congress has so clearly and emphatically expressed its intent that Title VII not lead to this result, we think it imperative to explain in some detail why the evidentiary standards that apply in these cases should serve as adequate safeguards against the danger that Congress recognized. Our previous decisions offer guidance, but today's extension

of disparate impact analysis calls for a fresh and somewhat closer examination of the constraints that operate to keep that analysis within its proper bounds.

First, we note that the plaintiff's burden in establishing a prima facie case goes beyond the need to show that there are statistical disparities in the employer's work force. The plaintiff must begin by identifying the specific employment practice that is challenged. Although this has been relatively easy to do in challenges to standardized tests, it may sometimes be more difficult when subjective selection criteria are at issue....

Once the employment practice at issue has been identified, causation must be proved; that is, the plaintiff must offer statistical evidence of a kind and degree sufficient to show that the practice in question has caused the exclusion of applicants for jobs or promotions because of their membership in a protected group. Our formulations, which have never been framed in terms of any rigid mathematical formula, have consistently stressed that statistical disparities must be sufficiently substantial that they raise such an inference of causation....

Nor are courts or defendants obliged to assume that plaintiff's statistical evidence is reliable. "If the employer discerns fallacies or deficiencies in the data offered by the plaintiff, he is free to adduce countervailing evidence of his own"....

A second constraint on the application of disparate impact theory lies in the nature of the "business necessity" or "job relatedness" defense. Although we have said that an employer has "the burden of showing that any given requirement must have a manifest relationship to the employment in question," such a formulation should not be interpreted as implying that the ultimate burden of proof can be shifted to the defendant. On the contrary, the ultimate burden of proving that discrimination against a protected group has been caused by a specific employment practice remains with the plaintiff at all times. Thus, when a plaintiff has made out a prima facie case of disparate impact, and when the defendant has met its burden of producing evidence that its employment practices are based on legitimate business reasons, the plaintiff must "show that other tests or selection devices, without a similarly undesirable racial effect, would also serve the employer's legitimate interest in efficient and trustworthy workmanship."...

In the context of subjective or discretionary employment decisions, the employer will often find it easier than in the case of standardized tests to produce evidence of a "manifest relationship to the employment in question." It is self-evident that many jobs, for example those involving managerial responsibilities, require personal qualities that have never been considered amenable to standardized testing. In evaluating claims that discretionary employment practices are insufficiently related to legitimate business purposes, it must be borne in mind that "[c]ourts are generally less competent than employers to restructure business practices, and unless mandated to do so by Congress they should not attempt it."...In sum, the high standards of proof in disparate impact cases are sufficient in our view to avoid giving employers incentives to modify any normal and legitimate practices by introducing quotas or preferential treatment....The judgment of the Court of Appeals is vacated, and the case is remanded for further proceedings consistent with this opinion. [*It is so ordered.*]

---

Even though the employer's practices do not have a disparate impact on minorities, a plaintiff may also prove his or her case by showing: (1) that he or she belongs to a minority, (2) that he or she applied and was qualified for a job for which the employer was seeking applicants, (3) that despite his or her qualifications, he or she was rejected, and (4) that the job remained open and the employer continued to seek applicants from persons with the plaintiff's qualifications. Here, too, the employer can prevail by showing a legitimate nondiscriminatory reason for the plaintiff's rejection. For example, an employer would not be expected to fill the position of cashier with an applicant who had a prior record of embezzlement.

### CURRENT TRENDS

In recent years, the EEOC has reduced the number of *pattern and practice* cases it chooses to file. Based on statistical profiles of employer work forces by race and sex, these cases show bias through statistical imbalances rather than discriminatory intent. However, the EEOC has continued to prosecute individual complaints vigorously. Note that private plaintiffs can still maintain pattern and practice cases and that a change in presidential administration might cause the EEOC once again to involve itself in such cases on a large scale.

### 4. Discrimination on the Basis of Race or Color

The integration of blacks into the mainstream of American society was the primary objective of the Civil Rights Act of 1964. Title VII, which deals with employment practices, was recognized by Congress as being the key to achieving this goal. Without equal employment opportunities, blacks can hardly enjoy other guaranteed rights, such as access to public accommodations.

Title VII prohibits discriminatory employment practices based on race or color which involve *recruiting*, *hiring*, and *promotion* of employees. Of course, intentional discrimination in these matters is illegal, but as previously stated, policies with disparate impact are also forbidden. Such discrimination arises from an employer's policies or practices which apply equally to everyone but which discriminate in greater proportion against minorities and have no relation to job qualification. Table 16-3 gives examples of disparate impact on race. Often at issue in disparate impact cases is whether a discriminatory policy or practice relates to job qualification. Courts require proof, not mere assertion, of job relatedness before upholding an employer's discriminatory personnel test or other practice.

The law also prohibits discrimination in *employment conditions* and *benefits*. EEOC decisions have found such practices as the following to be violations: permitting racial insults in the work situation; maintaining all-white or all-black crews for no demonstrable reasons; providing better housing for whites than blacks; and granting higher average Christmas bonuses to whites than blacks for reasons that were not persuasive to the Commission.

### 5. Discrimination on the Basis of National Origin

Title VII's prohibition against national origin discrimination protects Hispanics and other ethnic groups in the population. Discrimination concerning the speaking of a native language is a frequent source of national-origin lawsuits.

For instance, courts have ruled illegal an employer's rule against speak-

**TABLE 16-3**    Examples of Disparate Impact on Race

1   Denying employment to unwed mothers where minorities have a higher rate of illegitimate births than whites
2   Refusing to hire people because of poor credit rating when minorities are disproportionately affected
3   Refusing to hire people with arrest records when minorities have higher arrest rates than whites
4   Giving hiring priority to relatives of present employees when minorities are underrepresented in the work force
5   Using discriminatory personnel tests which have no substantial relation to job qualification

ing Spanish during working time without the employer's showing a business need to understand all conversations between Hispanic employees. On the other hand, some courts have held that if jobs require contact with the public, requirements that employees speak some English *may* be a bona fide occupational qualification.

Direct foreign investment in the United States has doubled and redoubled in recent years. This increasing investment has presented some unusual issues of employment discrimination law. For instance, many commercial treaties with foreign countries give foreign companies operating in the United States the right to hire executive-level employees "of their choice." Does this mean that foreign companies in the United States can discriminate as to their managerial employees on a basis forbidden under Title VII? In 1982, the Supreme Court partially resolved this issue by ruling that the civil rights laws applied to a Japanese company which did business through a subsidiary incorporated in this country.

## 6. Discrimination on the Basis of Religion

As was noted, religious corporations, associations, or societies can discriminate in all their employment practices on the basis of religion, but not on the basis of race, color, sex, or national origin. Other employers cannot discriminate on the basis of religion in employment practices, and they must make reasonable accommodation to the religious needs of their employees if it does not result in undue hardship to them. In the following case, the Supreme Court provided guidance on how far employers must go reasonably to accommodate religious needs of their workers.

---

# TRANS WORLD AIRLINES, INC. v. HARDISON
97 S.Ct. 2264 (1977)

---

WHITE, J.:...Petitioner Trans World Airlines (TWA) operates a large maintenance and overhaul base in Kansas City, Mo....[R]espondent Larry G. Hardison was hired by TWA to work as a clerk in the Stores Department at its Kansas City base. Because of its essential role in the Kansas City operation, the Stores Department must operate 24 hours per day, 365 days per year, and whenever an employee's job in that department is not filled, an employee must be shifted from another department or a supervisor must cover the job, even if the work in other areas may suffer.

Hardison, like other employees at the Kansas City base, was subject to a seniority system contained in a collective-bargaining agreement that TWA maintains with petitioner International Association of Machinists and Aerospace Workers (IAM)....

In the spring of 1968 Hardison began to study the religion known as the Worldwide Church of God. One of the tenets of that religion is that one must observe the Sabbath by refraining from performing any work from sunset on Friday until sunset on Saturday....Hardison was asked to work Saturdays when a fellow employee went on vacation. TWA agreed to permit the union to seek a change of work assignments for Hardison, but the union was not willing to violate the seniority provisions set out in the collective-bargaining contract, and Hardison had insufficient seniority to bid for a shift having Saturdays off.

A proposal that Hardison work only four days a week was rejected by the company. Hardison's job was essential and on weekends he was the only available person on his shift to perform it. To leave the position empty would have impaired Supply Shop functions, which were critical to airline operations; to fill Hardison's position with a supervisor or an employee from another area would simply have undermanned another operation; and to employ someone not regularly assigned to work Saturdays would have required TWA to pay premium wages.

When an accommodation was not reached, Hardison refused to report for work on Saturdays. A transfer to the twilight shift proved unavailing since that schedule still required Hardison to work past sundown on Fridays. After a hearing, Hardison was discharged on grounds of insubordination for refusing to work during his designated shift.

Hardison, having first invoked the administration remedy provided by Title VII, brought this action for injunctive relief in the United States District Court against TWA and IAM, claiming that his discharge by TWA constituted religious discrimination in violation of Title VII....Hardison's claim of religious discrimination rested on 1967 EEOC guidelines requiring employers "to make reasonable accommodations to the re-ligious needs of employees" whenever such accommodation would not work an "undue hardship," and on similar language adopted by Congress in the 1972 amendments to Title VII.

After a bench trial, the District Court ruled in favor of the defendants....As the District Court construed the Act, TWA had satisfied its "reasonable accommodation" obligations, and any further accommodation would have worked an undue hardship on the company.

The Eighth Circuit Court of Appeals reversed the judgment for TWA....The Court of Appeals held that TWA had not made reasonable efforts to accommodate Hardison's religious needs under the 1967 EEOC guidelines in effect at the time the relevant events occurred. In its view, TWA had rejected three reasonable alternatives, any one of which would have satisfied its obligation without undue hardship. First, within the framework of the seniority system, TWA could have permitted Hardison to work a four-day week, utilizing in his place a supervisor or another worker on duty elsewhere. That this would have caused other shop functions to suffer was insufficient to amount to undue hardship in the opinion of the Court of Appeals. Second—according to the Court of Appeals, also within the bounds of the collective-bargaining contract—the company could have filled Hardison's Saturday shift with other available personnel competent to do the job, of which the court said there were at least 200. That this would have involved premium overtime pay was not deemed an undue hardship. Third, TWA could have arranged a "swap between Hardison and another employee either for another shift or for the Sabbath days." In response to the assertion that this would have involved a breach of the seniority provisions of the contract, the court noted that it had not been settled in the courts whether the required statutory accommodation to religious needs stopped short of transgressing seniority rules....

We disagree with the Court of Appeals in all relevant respects....Any shift or change was impossible within the seniority framework and the union was not willing to violate the seniority provision set out in the contract to make a shift or change. As the record shows, Hardison himself testified [TWA] was willing, but the union was not, to work out a shift or job trade with another employee....

Hardison and the EEOC insist that the statutory obligation to accommodate religious needs takes precedence over both the collective-bargaining contract and the seniority rights of TWA's other employees. We agree that neither a collective-bargaining contract nor a seniority system may be employed to violate the statute, but we do not believe that the duty to accommodate requires TWA to take steps inconsistent with the otherwise valid agreement....Without a clear and express indication from Congress, we cannot agree with Hardison and the EEOC that an agreed-upon seniority system must give way when necessary to accommodate religious observances....

Had TWA nevertheless circumvented the seniority system by relieving Hardison of Saturday work and ordering a senior employee to replace him, it would have denied the latter his shift preference so that Hardison could be given his....There were no volunteers to relieve Hardison on Saturdays, and to give Hardison Saturdays off, TWA would have had to deprive another employee of his shift preference at least because he did not adhere to a religion that observed the Saturday Sabbath.

Title VII does not contemplate such un-equal treatment. The repeated, unequivocal emphasis of both the language and the legislative history of Title VII is on eliminating discrimination in employment, and such discrimination is proscribed when it is directed against majorities as well as minorities....It would be anomalous to conclude that by "reasonable accommodation" Congress meant that an employer must deny the shift preferences of some employees, as well as deprive some of them of their contractual rights, in order to accommodate or prefer the religious needs of others, and we conclude that Title VII does not require an employer to go that far....

[A]bsent a discriminatory purpose, the operation of a seniority system cannot be an unlawful employment practice even if the system has some discriminatory consequences....

To require TWA to bear more than a [slight] cost in order to give Hardison Saturdays off is an undue hardship. Like abandonment of the seniority system, to require TWA to bear additional costs when no such costs are incurred to give other employees the days off that they want would involve unequal treatment of employees on the basis of their religion....While incurring extra costs to secure a replacement for Hardison might remove the necessity of compelling another employee to work involuntarily in Hardison's place, it would not change the fact that the privilege of having Saturdays off would be allocated according to religious beliefs....

In the absence of clear statutory language or legislative history to the contrary, we will not readily construe the statute to require an employer to discriminate against some employees in order to enable others to observe their Sabbath. [*Reversed.*]

In another case, the Supreme Court let stand a lower-court ruling that an employee cannot be required to pay union dues if she or he has religious objections to unions. There, it held that a union had violated the Civil Rights Act by forcing the company to fire a Seventh Day Adventist who did not comply with a collective-bargaining agreement term that all employees must pay union dues. This was despite the union's contention that it had made "reasonable accommodation" to the worker's religious needs by offering to give any dues paid by him to charity.

### 7.   Discrimination on the Basis of Sex

CIVIL RIGHTS ACT

Historically, states have enacted many laws designed to supposedly protect women. For example, many states by statute have prohibited the employment of women in certain occupations such as those which require lifting heavy objects. Others have barred women from working during the night or more than a given number of hours per week or day. A federal district court held that a California state law which required rest periods for women only was in violation of Title VII. Some statutes prohibit employing women for a specified time after childbirth. Under EEOC guidelines, such statutes are not a defense to a charge of illegal sex discrimination and do not provide an employer with a bona fide occupational qualification in hiring standards. Other EEOC guidelines forbid employers: (1) to classify jobs as male or female and (2) to advertise in help-wanted columns that are designated male or female, unless sex is a bona fide job qualification. Similarly, employers may not have separate male and female seniority lists.

Table 16-4 gives examples of prohibited acts of sex discrimination under Title VII.

Whether sex is a bona fide occupational qualification (and discrimination is thus legal) has been raised in several cases. The courts have tended to consider this exception narrowly. In the following instances involving hiring policy, *no* bona fide occupational qualification was found to exist: a rule re-

**TABLE 16-4**   *Examples of Illegal Sex Discrimination*

1   A radio station's refusing to hire a female newscaster because "news coming from a woman sounds like gossip"
2   A bank's allowing males but not females to smoke at their desks
3   A utility company's allowing women to retire at age fifty, while requiring men to wait until age fifty-five
4   A company's failing to promote women to overseas positions because foreign clients were reluctant to do business with women
5   A hospital's firing a pregnant x-ray technician for health reasons instead of giving her a leave of absence
6   A company's failure to stop repeated, offensive sexual flirtations on the part of some of its employees

quiring airline stewardesses, but not stewards, to be single; a policy of hiring only females as flight-cabin attendants; a rule against hiring females with preschool-age children, but not against hiring males with such children; and a telephone company policy against hiring females as switchmen because of the alleged heavy lifting involved in the job. In this latter instance, the court held that for a bona fide occupational qualification to exist, there must be "reasonable cause to believe, that is, a factual basis for believing, that all or substantially all women would be unable to perform safely and efficiently the duties of the job involved." The Supreme Court has indicated that for such a qualification to exist, sex must be provably relevant to job performance.

As previously discussed, Title VII prohibits discrimination against protected employees in compensation, terms, conditions, or privileges of their employment. But does Title VII apply to prevent protected employees from being harassed by co-workers when there is no form of economic discrimination? In the following sex discrimination case, the Supreme Court addresses this issue.

# MERITOR SAVINGS BANK v. VINSON
477 U.S. 57 (1986)

Mechelle Vinson brought a Title VII action against her former employer, the Meritor Savings Bank. She claimed that during her employment at the bank she had been sexually harassed by her supervisor Sidney Taylor. She admitted to having sexual intercourse with Taylor over a several-year period out of fear of losing her job. She finally requested sick leave and was eventually dismissed for abuse of the sick leave policy. Then she brought this lawsuit. At the trial her supervisor denied all of her claims.

Without resolving the conflicting testimony, the district court denied Vinson relief under Title VII. The district court determined that since the sexual relationship was voluntary, and had nothing to do with her continued employment, there was no illegal discrimination. It further found that since Vinson had not notified the bank of the alleged harassment, the bank could not in any

event be held liable for the supervisor's actions. When the court of appeals reversed the district court, the bank petitioned the Supreme Court for certiorari. Certiorari was granted. In the opinion that follows, the bank is the petitioner and Vinson is the respondent.

REHNQUIST, J.:...Respondent argues, and the Court of Appeals held, that unwelcome sexual advances that create an offensive or hostile working environment violate Title VII. Without question, when a supervisor sexually harasses a subordinate because of the subordinate's sex, that supervisor "discriminate[s]" on the basis of sex. Petitioner apparently does not challenge this proposition. It contends instead that in prohibiting discrimination with respect to "compensation, terms, conditions, or privileges" of employment, Congress was concerned with what petitioner describes as "tangible loss" of "an economic character," not "purely psychological aspects of the workplace environment." In support of this claim petitioner observes that in both the legislative history of Title VII and this Court's Title VII decisions, the focus has been on tangible, economic barriers erected by discrimination.

We reject petitioner's view. First, the language of Title VII is not limited to "economic" or "tangible" discrimination. The phrase "terms, conditions, or privileges of employment" evinces a congressional intent "to strike at the entire spectrum of disparate treatment of men and women" in employment. Petitioner has pointed to nothing in the Act to suggest that Congress contemplated the limitation urged here.

Second, in 1980 the EEOC issued Guidelines specifying that "sexual harassment," as there defined, is a form of sex discrimination prohibited by Title VII. As an "administrative interpretation of the Act by the enforcing agency," those guidelines, "while not controlling upon the courts by reason of their authority, do constitute a body of experience and informed judgment to which courts and litigants may properly resort for guidance." The EEOC Guidelines fully support the view that harassment leading to noneconomic injury can violate Title VII....

The question remains, however, whether the District Court's ultimate finding that respondent "was not the victim of sexual harassment" effectively disposed of respondent's claim. The Court of Appeals recognized, we think correctly, that this ultimate finding was likely based on one or both of two erroneous views of the law. First, the District Court apparently believed that a claim for sexual harassment will not lie absent an economic effect on the complainant's employment. Since it appears that

the District Court made its findings without ever considering the "hostile environment" theory of sexual harassment, the Court of Appeals' decision to remand was correct....

Petitioner contends that even if this case must be remanded to the District Court, the Court of Appeals erred in one of the terms of its remand. Specifically, the Court of Appeals stated that testimony about respondent's "dress and personal fantasies," which the District Court apparently admitted into evidence, "had no place in this litigation." The apparent ground for this conclusion was that respondent's voluntariness in submitting to Taylor's advances was immaterial to her sexual harassment claim. While "voluntariness" in the sense of consent is not a defense to such a claim, it does not follow that a complainant's sexually provocative speech or dress is irrelevant as a matter of law in determining whether he or she found particular sexual advances unwelcome. To the contrary, such evidence is obviously relevant....

Although the District Court concluded that respondent had not proved a violation of Title VII, it nevertheless went on to consider the question of the bank's liability. Finding that "the bank was without notice" of Taylor's alleged conduct, and that notice to Taylor was not the equivalent of notice to the bank, the court concluded that the bank therefore could not be held liable for Taylor's alleged actions. The Court of Appeals took the opposite view, holding that an employer is strictly liable for a hostile environment created by a supervisor's sexual advances, even though the employer neither knew nor reasonably could have known of the alleged misconduct. The court held that a supervisor, whether or not he possesses the authority to hire, fire, or promote, is necessarily an "agent" of his employer for all Title VII purposes, since "even the appearance" of such authority may enable him to impose himself on his subordinates....

This debate over the appropriate standard for employer liability has a rather abstract quality about it given the state of the record in this case. We do not know at this stage whether Taylor made any sexual advances toward respondent at all, let alone whether those advances were unwelcome, whether they were sufficiently pervasive to constitute a condition of employment, or whether they were "so pervasive and so long continuing...that the employer must have become conscious of [them]."

We therefore decline the parties' invitation to issue a definitive rule on employer liability, but we do agree that Congress wanted courts to look to agency principles for guidance in this area. While such common-law principles may not be transferable in all their particulars to Title VII, Congress' decision to define "employer" to include any "agent" of an employer surely evinces an intent to place some limits on the acts of employees for which employers under Title VII are to be held responsible. For this reason, we hold that the Court of Appeals erred in concluding that employers are always automatically liable for sexual harassment by their supervisors. For the same reason, absence of notice to an employer does not necessarily insulate that employer from liability.

Finally, we reject petitioner's view that the mere existence of a grievance procedure and a policy against discrimination, coupled with respondent's failure to invoke that procedure, must insulate petitioner from liability....Petitioner's general nondiscrimination policy did not address sexual harassment in particular, and thus did not alert employees to their employer's interest in correcting that form of discrimination. Moreover, the bank's grievance procedure apparently required an employee to complain first to her supervisor, in this case Taylor....Petitioner's contention that respondent's failure should insulate it from liability might be substantially stronger if its procedures were better calculated to encourage victims of harassment to come forward.

In sum, we hold that a claim of "hostile environment" sex discrimination is actionable under Title VII, that the District Court's findings were insufficient to dispose of respondent's hostile environment claim, and that the District Court did not err in admitting testimony about respondent's sexually provocative speech and dress. As to employer liability, we conclude that the Court of Appeals was wrong to entirely disregard agency principles and impose absolute liability on employers for the acts of their supervisors, regardless of the circumstances of a particular case.

Accordingly, the judgment of the Court of Appeals reversing the judgment of the District Court is affirmed, and the case is remanded for further proceedings consistent with this opinion. [*It is so ordered.*]

---

**PREGNANCY DISCRIMINATION ACT**

The Pregnancy Discrimination Act amended the Civil Rights Act in 1978. Under it, employers can no longer discriminate against women workers who become pregnant or give birth. Thus, employers with health or disability plans must cover pregnancy, childbirth, and related medical conditions in the same manner as other conditions are covered. The law covers unmarried as well as married pregnant women. It also states that an employer cannot force a pregnant women to stop working until her baby is born, provided she is still capable of performing her duties properly. And, the employer cannot specify how long a leave of absence must be taken after childbirth. Coverage for abortion is not required by the statute, unless an employee carries to term and her life is endangered, or she develops medical complications because of an abortion. If a woman undergoes an abortion, though, all other benefits provided for employees, such as sick leave, must be provided to her.

Note that sex discrimination applies to discrimination against men as well as against women. For example, under the Pregnancy Discrimination Act the Supreme Court ruled unlawful an employer's health insurance plan that covered the pregnancies of female employees but did not cover the pregnancies of male employees' wives.

### EQUAL PAY ACT

Other federal legislation which pertains to sex discrimination in employment includes the *Equal Pay Act of 1963.* Presently administered by the EEOC, the act prohibits an employer from discriminating on the basis of sex in the payment of wages for equal work performed. For jobs to be equal, they must require "equal skill, effort, and responsibility" and must be performed "under similar working conditions." Discrimination is allowed if it arises from a **seniority system,** a merit system, a piecework production system, or on any factor other than sex.

The focus of Equal Pay Act cases is whether the male and female jobs being compared involve "equal" work. Courts have recognized that *equal* does not mean *identical*, it means *substantially* equal. Thus, courts have ruled "equal" the work of male barbers and female beauticians and of male tailors and female seamstresses. Differences in male and female job descriptions will not totally protect employers against charges of equal pay infractions. The courts have held that "substantially equal" work done on different machines would require the employer to compensate male and female employees equally.

In 1983, the Supreme Court ruled that discriminatory male and female pay differences can also be illegal under Title VII. In *County of Washington v. Gunther,* the Court decided that plaintiffs can use evidence of such pay differences to help prove intentional sex discrimination, even where the work performed is not "substantially equal." Relying on the *Gunther* case, several lower courts have held that women must be paid equally with men who perform comparable work. For instance, a federal district court ruled that the state of Washington discriminated against secretaries (mostly women) by paying them less than maintenance and other personnel (mostly men). The **comparable worth** theory is highly controversial and has not yet been upheld by the Supreme Court.

# EMPLOYMENT PRACTICES WHICH MAY BE CHALLENGED

### 8. Testing and Educational Requirements

Employers have used a number of tools to help them find the right person for the right job in hiring and promoting employees. Among these are interviews, references, minimum educational requirements (such as a high school diploma), and personnel tests. Obviously, interviewers can be biased, even if they try not to be. One study indicated that interviewers tended to select tall men for sales positions because interviewers *subconsciously* related height with potential sales success. References may not be so reliable, either. A previous employer's letter may reflect personal biases against an applicant that were not related to job performance.

At the other extreme, an employer may give a poor employee a top recommendation because of sympathy or fear of a lawsuit in case the letter is somehow obtained by the employee. Advocates of personnel tests in the selection process feel they are very valuable in weeding out the wrong persons for a job and picking the right ones. They believe reliance on tests results eliminates biases which interviewers or former employers who give references may have.

As a result of court decisions and government enforcement guidelines, however, many companies have eliminated or sharply reduced testing as an employment tool, because compliance is too costly and time-consuming. Even if companies obtain what appears to be proper evidence that a given test is valid, the threat of a court challenge with its costs and bad publicity would still exist.

### 9. Height and Weight Requirements

Minimum or maximum height or weight job requirements apply equally to all job applicants, but if they have the effect of screening out applicants on the basis of race, national origin, or sex, the employer must demonstrate that such requirements are validly related to the ability to perform the work in question. For example, maximum size standards would be permissible, even if they favored women over men, if the available work space were too small to permit larger persons to perform the duties of the job properly. Most size requirements have dictated minimum heights or weights, often based on a stereotyped assumption that a certain amount of strength probably was necessary for the work that smaller persons might not have. In one case, a 5-foot, 5-inch, 130-pound Hispanic won a suit against a police department on the basis that the department's 5-foot, 8-inch minimum height requirement discriminated against Hispanics, who often are shorter than that standard. Later, he was hired when he passed the department's physical agility examination, which included dragging a 150-pound body 75 feet and scaling a 6-foot wall.

In the following case, the Supreme Court considered the legality of Alabama's statutory minimum height and weight requirements for prison guards, along with a Board of Corrections regulation which expressly limited prison jobs to men.

---

# DOTHARD v. RAWLINSON
97 S.Ct. 2720 (1977)

Appellee Rawlinson, a 22-year-old college graduate whose major had been correctional psychology, applied for employment as a "correctional counselor" (prison guard) in Alabama. When her application was rejected because she failed to meet the minimum 120-pound weight requirement of an Alabama Statute, which also established a height minimum of 5 feet, 2 inches, Rawlinson filed a charge with the Equal Employment Opportunity Commission and ultimately brought a class action against appellant corrections officials alleging violations of the Civil Rights Act. The suit challenged: (1) the height and weight requirements of the Alabama Statute; and (2) "Regulation 204" of the Alabama Board of Corrections, which provided that only males could be assigned as correctional counselors to maximum security institutions for "contact positions" (positions requiring close physical proximity to inmates). A three-judge district court decided in appellee's favor, and the Supreme Court agreed to hear the appeal of the correctional officials.

STEWART, J.:...Like most correctional facilities in the United States, Alabama's prisons are segregated on the basis of sex. Currently the Alabama Board of Corrections operates four major all-male penitentiaries.

[T]hese are maximum security institutions. Their inmate living quarters are for the most part large dormitories, with communal showers and toilets that are open to the dormitories and hallways. The Draper and Fountain penitentiaries carry on extensive farming operations, making necessary a large number of strip searches for contraband when prisoners re-enter the prison building.

A correctional counselor's primary duty within these institutions is to maintain security and control of the inmates by continually supervising and observing their activities....

The gist of the claim that the statutory height and weight requirements discriminate against women does not involve an assertion of purposeful discriminatory motive. It is asserted, rather, that these facially neutral qualification standards work in fact disproportionately to exclude women from eligibility for employment by the Alabama Board of Corrections. We dealt in [other cases] with similar allegations that facially neutral employment standards disproportionately excluded Negroes from employment, and those cases guide our approach here....

When the height and weight restrictions are combined, Alabama's statutory standards would exclude 41.13% of the female population while excluding less than one percent of the male population....

[W]e cannot say that the District Court was wrong in holding that the statutory height and weight standards had a discriminatory impact on women applicants....

We turn, therefore, to the appellants' argument that they have rebutted the prima facie case of discrimination by showing that the height and weight requirements are job related. These requirements, they say, have a relationship to strength, a sufficient but unspecified amount of which is essential to effective job performance as a correctional counselor. In the District Court, however, the appellants produced no evidence correlating the height and weight requirements with the requisite amount of strength thought essential to good job performance. Indeed, they failed to offer evidence of any kind in specific justification of the statutory standards.

If the job-related quality that the appellants identify is bona fide, their purpose could be achieved by adopting and validating a test for applicants that measures strength directly. Such a test, fairly administered, would fully satisfy the standards of Title VII because it would be one that "measure[s] the person for the job and not the person in the abstract." But nothing in the present record even approaches such a measurement.

For the reasons we have discussed, the District Court was not in error in holding that Title VII of the Civil Rights Act of 1964, as amended, prohibits application of the statutory height and weight requirements to Rawlinson and the class she represents.

Unlike the statutory height and weight requirements, Regulation 204 explicitly discriminates against women on the basis of their sex. In defense of this overt discrimination, the appellants rely on § 703(e) of Ti-

tle VII, which permits sex-based discrimination "in those certain instances where... sex...is a bona fide occupational qualification reasonably necessary to the normal operation of that particular business or enterprise."

The District Court rejected the bona fide occupational qualification (bfoq) defense, relying on the virtually uniform view of the federal courts that § 703(e) provides only the narrowest of exceptions to the general rule requiring equality of employment opportunities....The Federal courts have agreed that is it impermissible under Title VII to refuse to hire an individual woman or man on the basis of stereotyped characterizations of the sexes....

In the particular factual circumstances of this case, however, we conclude that the District Court erred in rejecting the State's contention that Regulation 204 falls within the narrow ambit of the bfoq exception.

The environment in Alabama's penitentiaries is a peculiarly inhospitable one for human beings of whatever sex. Indeed, a federal district court has held that the conditions of confinement in the prisons of the State, characterized by "rampant violence" and a "jungle atmosphere," are constitutionally intolerable. The record in the present case shows that because of inadequate staff and facilities, no attempt is made in the four maximum security male penitentiaries to classify or segregate inmates according to their offense or level of dangerousness.... Consequently, the estimated 20% of the male prisoners who are sex offenders are scattered throughout the penitentiaries' dormitory facilities....

In the usual case, the argument that a particular job is too dangerous for women may appropriately be met by the rejoinder that it is the purpose of Title VII to allow the individual woman to make that choice for herself. More is at stake in this case, however, than an individual woman's decision to weigh and accept the risks of employment in a "contact" position in a maximum security male prison.

The essence of a correctional counselor's job is to maintain prison security. A woman's relative ability to maintain order in a male, maximum security, unclassified penitentiary of the type Alabama now runs could be directly reduced by her womanhood....In a prison system where violence is the order of the day, where inmate access to guards is facilitated by dormitory living arrangements, where every institution is understaffed, and where a substantial portion of the inmate population is composed of sex offenders mixed at random with other prisoners, there are few visible deterrents to inmate assaults on women custodians....

There was substantial testimony from experts on both sides of this litigation that the use of women as guards in "contact" positions under the existing conditions in Alabama maximum security male penitentiaries would pose a substantial security problem, directly linked to the sex of the prison guard. On the basis of that evidence, we conclude that the District Court was in error in ruling that being male is not a bona fide occupational qualification for the job of correctional counselor in a "contact" position in an Alabama male maximum security penitentiary. [*The judgment is accordingly affirmed in part and reversed in part, and the case is remanded to the District Court for further proceedings consistent with this opinion. It is so ordered.*]

Even though the Supreme Court found that sex was a bona fide occupational qualification in *Rawlinson*, note that the bfoq exception is narrowly interpreted.

## 10.   Appearance Requirements

Employers often have set grooming standards for their employees. Those regulating hair length of males or prohibiting beards or mustaches have been among the most common. Undoubtedly, motivation for these rules stems from the feeling of the employer that the image it projects to the public through its employees will be adversely affected if their appearance is not "proper." It is unclear whether appearance requirements are legal or illegal, since there have been rulings both ways. Refusing to hire applicants because of a company policy prohibiting "handlebar" and "Fu Manchu" mustaches and bushy hairstyles was found illegal. Although the policies appeared neutral on their face, it was held that they had a disparate impact against blacks.

In another case, a black employee argued that he was wrongfully fired for breaking a company rule prohibiting beards. Dermatologists testified that the plaintiff had a condition called "razor bumps" (which occurs when the tightly curled facial hairs of black men become ingrown from shaving) and that the only known cure was for him not to shave. Although the federal appeals court found that the plaintiff was prejudiced by the employer's regulation, it held in favor of the company, ruling that its "slight racial impact" was justified by the "business purpose" it served. However, a conflicting opinion in still another case upheld an employee's right to wear a beard because of razor bumps.

## 11. Affirmative Action Programs and Reverse Discrimination

### AFFIRMATIVE ACTION

Since the 1940s, a series of presidential executive orders have promoted nondiscrimination and **affirmative action** by employers who contract with the federal government. The authority for these orders rests with the President's executive power to control the granting of federal contracts. As a condition to obtaining such contracts, employers must agree contractually to take affirmative action to avoid unlawful discrimination in recruitment, employment, promotion, training, rate of compensation, and layoff of workers.

The affirmative action requirement means that federally contracting employers must actively recruit members of minority groups being underused in the work force. That is, employers must hire members of these groups when there are fewer minority workers in a given job category than one could reasonably expect, considering their availability. In many instances, employers must develop written affirmative action plans and set goals and timetables for bringing minority (or female) work forces up to their percentages in the available labor pool.

The Labor Department administers executive orders through its Office of Federal Contract Compliance Programs (OFCCP). The OFCCP can terminate federal contracts with employers who do not comply with its guidelines and can make them ineligible for any future federal business. For instance, it required Uniroyal, Inc., to give its female employees an estimated $18 million in back pay to compensate for past employment discrimination. The alternative was elimination of $36 million of existing federal contracts and ineligibility for future federal business.

In the early 1980s, the Labor Department eased OFCCP regulations on 75 percent of the firms which do business with the federal government. Firms with fewer than 250 employees and federal contracts of under $1 million no longer must prepare written affirmative action plans for hiring women and minorities. The OFCCP has also begun to limit its use of back-pay awards to specific individuals who can show an actual loss due to violation of OFCCP guidelines.

### REVERSE DISCRIMINATION

Not all affirmative action programs are imposed on employers by the government. Many employers have adopted programs voluntarily or through collective-bargaining agreements with unions. Sometimes these affirmative action programs have subjected employers to charges of **reverse discrimination** when minorities or women with lower qualifications or less seniority than white males are given preference in employment or training. Even though such programs are intended to remedy the effects of present or past discrimination or other barriers to equal employment opportunity, white males have argued that the law does not permit employers to discriminate against *them* on the basis of race or sex any more than it allows discrimination against minorities or women.

In *United Steelworkers of America v. Weber*, the Supreme Court ruled legal under Title VII a voluntary affirmative action plan between an employer and a union. The plan required that at least 50 percent of certain new work trainees be black. The Court noted that the plan did not require that white employees be fired or excluded altogether from advancement. It was only a temporary measure to eliminate actual racial imbalance in the work force.

The *Weber* case provoked much controversy. Some scholars questioned whether the Supreme Court might reverse *Weber* or limit its application. In further upholding affirmation action against charges of reverse discrimination, the next case seems to answer those questions.

# JOHNSON v. SANTA CLARA COUNTY TRANSPORTATION AGENCY
107 S. Ct. 1442 (1987)

The district court ruled that the Agency had violated Title VII. When the court of appeals reversed, the Supreme Court granted certiorari.

BRENNAN, J.:...In December 1978, the Santa Clara County Transit District Board of Supervisors adopted an Affirmative Action Plan (Plan) for the County Transportation Agency. The Plan implemented a County Affirmative Action Plan, which had been adopted, declared the County, because "mere prohibition of discriminatory practices is not enough to remedy the effects of past practices and to permit attainment of an equitable representation of minorities, women and handicapped persons." Relevant to this case, the Agency Plan provides that, in making promotions to positions within a traditionally segregated job classification in which women have been significantly underrepresented, the Agency is authorized to consider as one factor the sex of a qualified applicant.

In reviewing the composition of its work force, the Agency noted in its Plan that women were represented in numbers far less than their proportion of the county labor force in both the Agency as a whole and in five of seven job categories. Specifically, while women constituted 36.4% of the area labor market, they composed only 22.4% of Agency employees. Furthermore, women working at the Agency were concentrated largely in EEOC job categories traditionally held by women: women made up 76% of Office and Clerical Workers, but only 7.1% of Agency Officials and Administrators, 8.6% of Professionals, 9.7% of Technicians, and 22% of Service and Maintenance workers. As for the job classification relevant to this case, none of the 238 Skilled Craft

Worker positions was held by a woman. The Plan noted that this underrepresentation of women in part reflected the fact that women had not traditionally been employed in these positions, and they had not been strongly motivated to seek training or employment in them "because of the limited opportunities that have existed in the past for them to work in such classifications."

The assessment of the legality of the Agency Plan must be guided by our decision in [*United Steelworkers of America v. Weber*]. In that case, the Court addressed the question whether the employer violated Title VII by adopting a voluntary affirmative action plan designed to "eliminate manifest racial imbalances in traditionally segregated job categories."…

We upheld the employer's decision to select less senior black applicants over the white respondent, for we found that taking race into account was consistent with Title VII's objective of "break[ing] down old patterns of racial segregation and hierarchy." As we stated:

**It would be ironic indeed if a law triggered by a Nation's concern over centuries of racial injustice and intended to improve the lot of those who had 'been excluded from the American dream for so long' constituted the first legislative prohibition of all voluntary, private, race-conscious efforts to abolish traditional patterns of racial segregation and hierarchy.…**

We noted that the plan did not "unnecessarily trammel the interests of the white employees," since it did not require "the discharge of white workers and their replacement with new black hirees." Nor did the plan create "an absolute bar to the advancement of white employees," since half of those trained in the new program were to be white. Finally we observed that the plan was a temporary measure, not designed to maintain racial balance, but to "eliminate a manifest racial imbalance." As Justice BLACK-

MUN's concurrence made clear, *Weber* held that an employer seeking to justify the adoption of a plan need not point to its own prior discriminatory practices, nor even to evidence of an "arguable violation" on its part. Rather, it need only point to a "conspicuous…imbalance in traditionally segregated job categories." Our decision was grounded in the recognition that voluntary employer action can play a crucial role in furthering Title VII's purpose of eliminating the effects of discrimination in the workplace, and that Title VII should not be read to thwart such efforts.…

In reviewing the employment decision at issue in this case, we must first examine whether that decision was made pursuant to a plan prompted by concerns similar to those of the employer in *Weber*. Next, we must determine whether the effect of the plan on males and non-minorities is comparable to the effort of the plan in that case.…

In evaluating the compliance of an affirmative action plan with Title VII's prohibition on discrimination, we must be mindful of "this Court's and Congress' consistent emphasis on 'the value of voluntary efforts to further the objectives of the law.'" The Agency in the case before us has undertaken such a voluntary effort, and has done so in full recognition of both the difficulties and the potential for intrusion on males and non-minorities. The Agency has identified a conspicuous imbalance in job categories traditionally segregated by race and sex. It has made clear from the outset, however, that employment decisions may not be justified solely by reference to this imbalance, but must rest on a multitude of practical, realistic factors. It has therefore committed itself to annual adjustment of goals so as to provide a reasonable guide for actual hiring and promotion decisions. The Agency earmarks no positions for anyone; sex is but one of several factors that may be taken into account in evaluating qualified applicants for a position. As both the Plan's language and its manner of operation attest, the Agency has no intention of establishing a work force whose permanent composition is dictated by rigid numerical standards.

We therefore hold that the Agency appropriately took into account as one factor the sex of Diane Joyce in determining that she should be promoted to the road dispatcher position. The decision to do so was made pursuant to an affirmative action plan that represents a moderate, flexible, case-by-case approach to effecting a gradual improvement in the representation of minorities and women in the Agency's work force. Such a plan is fully consistent with Title VII, for its embodies the contribution that voluntary employer action can make in eliminating the vestiges of discrimination in the workplace. [*Accordingly, the judgment of the Court of Appeals is affirmed.*]

---

The EEOC has issued guidelines intended to protect employers who set up affirmative action plans. This indicates that Title VII is not violated if an employer determines that there is a reasonable basis for concluding that such a plan is appropriate, and the employer takes "reasonable" affirmative action. For example, if an employer discovers that it has a job category where one might expect to find more women and minorities employed than are actually in its work force, the employer has a reasonable basis for affirmative action.

In an affirmative action move intended to help minority-owned businesses, Congress passed the 1977 Public Works employment plan. This requires that 10 percent of the work on federally funded local public works projects be performed by minority contractors or subcontractors. Contractor groups attacked the 10 percent requirement as an unconstitutional form of reverse discrimination, in violation of the Fifth and Fourteenth Amendments. However, in 1980 the Supreme Court upheld validity of the requirement.

## 12. Seniority Systems

Seniority systems give priority to those employees who have worked longer for a particular employer, or in a particular line of employment of the employer. Employers may institute seniority systems on their own, but in a union shop they are usually the result of collective bargaining. Their terms are spelled out in the agreement between the company and the union. Seniority systems often determine the calculation of vacation, pension, and other fringe benefits. They also control many employment decisions such as the order in which employees may choose shifts or qualify for promotions or transfers to different jobs. They also are used to select the persons to be laid off when an employer is reducing its labor force. As a result of seniority, the last hired are usually the first fired. Decisions based on seniority have been challenged in recent years as violating the laws relating to equal employment opportunity. Challenges often arose when recently hired members of minority groups were laid off during periods of economic downturn. Firms with successful affirmative action programs often lost most of their minority employees.

Section 703(h) of the Civil Rights Act of 1964 provides that, notwithstanding other provisions in the act, it is not an unlawful employment practice for an employer to apply different employment standards under a bona fide (good faith) seniority system if the differences are not the result of an *intention* to discriminate. In *Memphis Fire Dept. v. Stotts* the Supreme Court ruled that discrimination resulting from application of a seniority system was lawful even when it affected minorities hired or promoted by affirmative action.

## OTHER STATUTES AND DISCRIMINATION IN EMPLOYMENT

### 13. Civil Rights Act of 1866

An important federal law which complements Title VII of the 1964 Civil Rights Act is the Civil Rights Act of 1866. One provision of that act, known as *Section 1981*, provides that "all persons...shall have the same right to make and enforce contracts...as enjoyed by white citizens." Since union memberships and employment relationships involve contracts, Section 1981 bans racial discrimination in these areas.

The courts have interpreted Section 1981 as giving a private plaintiff most of the same protections against racial discrimination that the 1964 Civil Rights Act provides. In addition, there are at least two advantages to the plaintiff who files a suit based on Section 1981. First, there are no procedural requirements for bringing such a suit, while there are a number of fairly complex requirements plaintiffs must follow before bringing a private suit under Title VII. For instance, they must file charges of discrimination with the EEOC within 180 days after the illegal practice occurs, or they will lose their rights.

By using Section 1981, a plaintiff can immediately sue an employer in federal court but need not worry about losing rights if he or she fails to do so within 180 days. A second advantage to Section 1981 is that under it the courts can award damages to aggrieved plaintiffs. Although it permits recovery of back pay, Title VII does not allow for the assessment of damages. As a practical matter, parties alleging discrimination usually proceed under both Section 1981 and Title VII.

Note that Section 1981 does not cover discrimination based on sex, religion, national origin, age, or handicap. As interpreted by the courts, this section applies only to *racial* discrimination. However, what is race? The Supreme Court has held that being of Arabian or Jewish ancestry constitutes "race" as protected by Section 1981. The Court stated that when the law was passed in the 19th century the concept of race was much broader than it is today. Race then included the descendants of a particular "family, tribe, people, or nation." A question to consider is has the Court opened the door for a white job applicant to sue a black employer for discrimination under Section 1981?

## 14. Discrimination on the Basis of Age

Neither the Civil Rights Act nor the Equal Employment Opportunity Act forbids discrimination based on age. In 1967, however, Congress passed the Age Discrimination in Employment Act, which protects persons between forty and sixty-five years old from job discrimination against them because of their age. The act is enforced by the EEOC.

In 1986, Congress amended the act to prohibit mandatory retirement of employees at any age. Firefighters and police officers may still be forced into retirement under certain circumstances until 1993. Bona fide executives and high policymakers of private companies who will have pensions of at least $27,000 per year also can be forced into early retirement. The statute invalidates retirement plans and labor contracts that call for retirement in violation of the act.

In one case under the act, Standard Oil Company of California agreed to pay $2 million in back wages to 160 employees who had been laid off and were over forty. Thus, if persons over forty are just as qualified as younger workers to handle their jobs, they usually must be kept. To cut costs, some companies have discriminated against older, higher-ranking, and higher-paid employees by replacing them with younger, lower-salaried persons who are equally competent to handle the job. This cost-cutting is also illegal. One decision awarded three former department store executives $2.3 million for such discrimination. In another case, a firm transferred a sixty-year-old man to a job that required him to stand for long periods. When he died, his widow, arguing that the transfer was a subterfuge to induce him to retire, obtained a judgment against the firm for $750,000 in damages for illegal age discrimination.

An important area of age discrimination litigation exists when age is a bona fide occupational qualification. It is recognized that as people grow older their physical strength, agility, reflexes, hearing, and vision tend to diminish in quality. However, this generally provides no legal reason for discriminating against older persons as a class. Although courts will uphold job-related physical requirements if they apply on a case-by-case basis, they frequently find as illegal those policies which prohibit the hiring of persons beyond a maximum age, or which establish a maximum age beyond which employees are forced to retire for physical reasons. Thus, one court ruled that a mandatory retirement age of sixty-five was illegally discriminatory as applied to the job of district fire chief. To the contrary, another court ruled that the airlines could impose a maximum age for hiring a new pilot in light of a Federal Aviation Administration-mandated retirement age for pilots.

Courts have disagreed on whether remedies for violation of the act include, in addition to reinstatement and wages lost, damages for the psychological trauma of being fired or forced to resign illegally. One federal district court awarded $200,000 to a victim of age discrimination who was an inventor and scientist, for the psychological and physical effects suffered from being forced into early retirement at age sixty. Also awarded were out-of-pocket costs of $60,000 and attorney's fees of $65,000. Note that "willful" violations of the act entitle discrimination victims to *double damages.*

Since the 1978 amendments to the act, age discrimination claims have grown rapidly. In recent years, they have more than doubled in number.

## 15.   Discrimination on the Basis of Handicaps

To promote and expand employment opportunities for handicapped persons, both in the public and private sectors, Congress enacted the Rehabilitation Act of 1973. This statute requires each department and agency in the executive branch of the federal government to have an approved affirmative action plan for the hiring, placement, and advancement of qualified handicapped individuals. And under Section 503 of the Rehabilitation Act, every employer doing business with the federal government under a contract for over $2,500 must take affirmative action to hire and advance qualified handicapped persons at all levels, including executive. Section 503 affects about one-half the businesses in the United States and the twelve million or so employable handicapped persons in the population.

A handicapped person protected by the act is anyone with a physical or mental impairment which substantially limits a major life activity (such as a blind, deaf, paraplegic, or mentally retarded person), or one who has a *record of* such an impairment (this would include a rehabilitated mental patient or a person with a history of cancer or heart condition). *All* such handicapped persons are not covered, however. An individual must be "qualified," or capable of performing a particular job, with reasonable accommodation to his or her handicap. And an amendment to the act specifically provides that the term "handicapped individual" does not include any individual who is an alcoholic or drug abuser.

Both contractors and subcontractors must make "reasonable accommodation" to the physical and mental limitations of handicapped employees or applicants, unless it can be shown that such would involve an "undue hardship" to them. The cost of any necessary workplace accommodation and availability of alternatives bear upon the issue of undue hardship.

The Department of Labor's Office of Federal Contract Compliance Programs can enforce Section 503 of the act by forcing settlements of claims of discrimination by handicapped workers. Claims may be settled by hiring the claimants with payment of back wages and retroactive seniority, or the like. In an extreme case, the government contract with the offending employer can be terminated.

Section 504 of the Rehabilitation Act prohibits discrimination against a handicapped person under any program receiving federal financial assistance. Section 504 applies to a great many state and local government programs that receive federal grants. Private organizations receiving federal assistance are also affected. Although the next case was brought under Section 504, it has significance as well for private employers under Section 503. For the first time, the Supreme Court rules that a contagious disease can make one a "handicapped person."

# SCHOOL BOARD OF NASSAU COUNTY, FLA. v. ARLINE
107 S.Ct. 1123 (1987)

BRENNAN, J.: Section 504 of the Rehabilitation Act of 1973...prohibits a federally funded state program from discriminating against a handicapped individual solely by reason of his or her handicap. This case presents the questions whether a person afflicted with tuberculosis, a contagious disease, may be considered a "handicapped individual" within the meaning of § 504 of the Act, and, if so, whether such an individual is "otherwise qualified" to teach elementary school.

From 1966 until 1979 respondent Gene Arline taught elementary school in Nassau County, Florida. She was discharged in 1979 after suffering a third relapse of tuberculosis within two years. After she was denied relief in state administrative proceedings, she brought suit in federal court, alleging that the School Board's decision to dismiss

her because of her tuberculosis violated § 504 of the Act.

In her trial memorandum, Arline argued that it was "not disputed that the [School Board dismissed her] solely on the basis of her illness. Since the illness in this case qualified the Plaintiff as a 'handicapped person' it is clear that she was dismissed solely as a result of her handicap in violation of § 504." The District Court held, however, that although there was "[n]o question that she suffers a handicap," Arline was nevertheless not "a handicapped person under the terms of that statute." The court found it "difficult...to conceive that Congress intended contagious diseases to be included within the definition of a handicapped person." The court then went on to state that, "even assuming" that a person with a contagious disease could be deemed a handicapped person, Arline was not "qualified" to teach elementary school.

The Court of Appeals reversed, holding that "persons with contagious diseases are within the coverage of § 504," and that Arline's condition "falls…neatly within the statutory and regulatory framework" of the Act. The court remanded the case "for further findings as to whether the risks of infection precluded Mrs. Arline from being 'otherwise qualified' for her job and, if so, whether it was possible to make some reasonable accommodation for her in that teaching position" or in some other position. We granted certiorari, and now affirm.

In enacting and amending the Act, Congress enlisted all programs receiving federal funds in an effort "to share with handicapped Americans the opportunities for an education, transportation, housing, health care, and jobs that other Americans take for granted." To that end, Congress not only increased federal support for vocational rehabilitation, but also addressed the broader problem of discrimination against the handicapped by including § 504, an antidiscrimination provision patterned after Title VI of the Civil Rights of 1964. Section 504 of the Rehabilitation Act reads in pertinent part:

**No otherwise qualified handicapped individual in the United States, as defined in § 706(7) of this title, shall, solely by reason of his handicap, be excluded from participation in, be denied the benefits of, or be subjected to discrimination under any program or activity receiving Federal financial assistance....**

In 1974 Congress expanded the definition of "handicapped individual" for use in § 504 to read as follows:

**[A]ny person who (i) has a physical or mental impairment which substantially limits one or more of such person's major life activities, (ii)** **has a record of such an impairment, or (iii) is regarded as having such an impairment.**

The amended definition reflected Congress' concern with protecting the handicapped against discrimination stemming not only from simple prejudice, but from "archaic attitudes and laws" and from "the fact that the American people are simply unfamiliar with and insensitive to the difficulties confront[ing] individuals with handicaps."

Petitioners concede that a contagious disease may constitute a handicapping condition to the extent that it leaves a person with "diminished physical or mental capabilities," Brief for Petitioners 15, and concede that Arline's hospitalization for tuberculosis in 1957 demonstrates that she has a record of a physical impairment. Petitioners maintain, however, Arline's record of impairment is irrelevant in this case, since the School Board dismissed Arline not because of her diminished physical capabilities, but because of the threat that her relapses of tuberculosis posed to the health of others.

We do not agree with petitioners that, in defining a handicapped individual under § 504, the contagious effects of a disease can be meaningfully distinguished from the disease's physical effects on a claimant in a case such as this. Arline's contagiousness and her physical impairment each resulted from the same underlying condition, tuberculosis. It would be unfair to allow an employer to seize upon the distinction between the effects of a disease on others and the effects of a disease on a patient and use that distinction to justify discriminatory treatment.

Nothing in the legislative history of § 504 suggests that Congress intended such a result. That history demonstrates that Congress was as concerned about the effect of an impairment on others as it was about its effect on the individual.

Allowing discrimination based on the contagious effects of a physical impairment would be inconsistent with the basic purpose of § 504, which is to ensure that handicapped individuals are not denied jobs or other benefits because of the prejudiced attitudes or the ignorance of others. By amending the definition of "handicapped individual" to include not only those who are actually physically impaired, but also those who are regarded as impaired and who, as a result, are substantially limited in a major life activity, Congress acknowledged that society's accumulated myths and fears about disability and disease are as handicapping as are the physical limitations that flow from actual impairment. Few aspects of a handicap give rise to the same level of public fear and misapprehension as contagiousness.... The remaining question is whether Arline is otherwise qualified for the job of elementary school teacher. To answer this question in most cases, the District Court will need to conduct an individualized inquiry and make appropriate findings of fact. Such an inquiry is essential if § 504 is to achieve its goal of protecting handicapped individuals from deprivations based on prejudice, stereotypes, or unfounded fear, while giving appropriate weight to such legitimate concerns of grantees as avoiding exposing others to significant health and safety risks....

We hold that a person suffering from the contagious disease of tuberculosis can be a handicapped person within the meaning of the § 504 of the Rehabilitation Act of 1973, and that respondent Arline is such a person. We remand the case to the District Court to determine whether Arline is otherwise qualified for her position. [*The judgment of the Court of Appeals is affirmed.*]

---

The *Arline* case is especially important because of the spread of AIDS. As of now, there are cases pending in the federal court system brought by employees with AIDS against their former employers.

### 16. Other Federal Legislation

Other federal legislation dealing with employment discrimination includes the National Labor Relations Act. The NLRB has ruled that appeals to racial prejudice in a collective-bargaining representation election constitute an unfair labor practice. The NLRB has also revoked the certification of unions which practice discriminatory admission or representation policies. Additionally, employers have an obligation to bargain with certified unions over matters of employment discrimination. Such matters are considered "terms and conditions of employment" and are thus mandatory bargaining issues. Note that the reverse discrimination issue in the *Weber* case (p. 490) arose because of an affirmative action plan in a collective-bargaining contract.

Finally, various other federal agencies may prohibit discriminatory employment practices under their authorizing statutes. The Federal Communications Commission, for example, has prohibited employment discrimination by its licensees (radio and TV stations) and has required the submission of affirmative action plans as a condition of license renewal.

## 17. State Discrimination Laws

Federal laws concerning equal employment opportunity specifically permit state laws which impose additional duties and liabilities. In recent years, fair employment practices legislation has been introduced and passed by many state legislatures. At the time the federal Equal Employment Opportunity Act became effective, forty states had such laws, but their provisions varied considerably. A typical state act makes it an unfair employment practice for any employer to refuse to hire or otherwise discriminate against any individual because of his or her race, color, religion, national origin, or ancestry. If employment agencies or labor organizations discriminate against an individual in any way because of one of the foregoing reasons, they are also guilty of an unfair employment practice. State acts usually set up an administrative body, generally known as the Fair Employment Practices Commission, which has the power to make rules and regulations and hear and decide charges of violations filed by complainants.

In addition, many states have enacted equal pay statutes similar to the federal one, but these have not proved to be very effective.

## 18. Avoiding Unfounded Discrimination Claims

Much unintentional discrimination, even intentional discrimination, does occur in employment situations. But most employers strive to obey equal employment laws. These employers still face discrimination claims, however, including many made by unsatisfactory employees who have been discharged or disciplined. How can employers protect themselves from unfounded discrimination claims in such instances? The best protection is a system of adequate documentation. Sometimes called the **paper fortress,** this documentation consists of job descriptions, personnel manuals, and employee personnel files.

Before handing anyone an employment application, the employer should insist that the person carefully study a job description. A well-written job description will help potential applicants eliminate themselves from job situations for which they lack interest or qualification. Applicant self-elimination helps employers later avoid having to dismiss disinterested or unqualified employees, which can lead to discrimination claims.

Once a new employee is hired, the employer should give the employee a personnel manual. This manual should include information about employee benefits and should also outline work rules and job requirements. The employer should go over the manual with the employee and answer any questions. Clear identification of employer expectations and policies helps provide a defense against discrimination claims if subsequent discipline or discharge of the employee becomes necessary. The employer should ask that the employee sign a form indicating receipt of the manual and the employer's explanation of its contents.

The employer should enter this form, with all other documentation relevant to an employee's work history, in the employee's personnel file. Regular written evaluations of employee performance should also be entered in the personnel file. A chronological record of unsatisfactory work performance is a very useful defense against an unjustified claim of employment discrimination following discipline or discharge.

Another piece of documentation which helps justify employer decisions in light of equal employment law is the written warning. Anytime an employee breaks a work rule or performs unsatisfactorily, the employer should issue the employee a written warning and should place a duplicate in the personnel file. The warning should explain specifically where the employee went wrong, that is, what work rule the employee violated, and it should give the employee the opportunity to place a letter of explanation in the personnel file. Employers should either have an employee sign that he or she has received a warning, or else note in the personnel file that the employee has received a copy of it.

Congress did not intend for equal employment laws to prevent employers from discharging unsatisfactory employees. Whatever the employee's race, sex, religion, or ethnic background, the employer should not hesitate to terminate the employee for unacceptable performance. In an actual termination conversation, however, the employer should provide the employee with specific reasons for discharge, taken from the personnel file. The employee should also be encouraged to succeed in other employment.

In combating unfounded discrimination claims, an adequate system of documentation is vital. However, other things are also important, such as having a specific company policy coupled with an effective employment program promoting nondiscrimination. Caterpillar has such a policy in its Code of Ethics.

## AN EFFECTIVE EMPLOYMENT PROGRAM

We aspire to a high standard of excellence in human relationships. Specifically, we intend to select and place employees on the basis of qualifications for the work to be performed—without discrimination in terms of race, religion, national origin, color, sex, age, or handicap unrelated to the task at hand.

## REVIEW QUESTIONS

**1** For each term in the left-hand column, match the most appropriate description in the right-hand column:

(1) Affirmative action

(a) Selection of employees for hire or promotion in a pattern significantly different from that of racial minorities or women available in the pool of job applicants

(2) Comparable worth

(b) Documentation including job descriptions, personnel manuals, and employee personnel files

(3) Paper fortress

(c) Job-related employment characteristics based on sex or religion

(4) Seniority system

(d) A theory under which employees are paid equally based on jobs which are dissimilar but are rated equally

(5) Reverse discrimination

(e) Taking active steps to seek out and employ groups traditionally underrepresented in the work force

(6) Discrimination in effect

(f) A system to give priority to those employees who have worked longer for a particular employer

(7) Bfoqs

(g) Prohibits contractual discrimination based on race

(8) Section 1981

(h) Employment discrimination against white males

**2** Historically, employers could discriminate against employees and job applicants for any reason. Discuss the series of legal developments that changed this historic right of employers in the employment discrimination area.

**3** Jennings Company, which manufactures sophisticated electronic equipment, hires its assembly employees on the basis of applicants' scores on a standardized mathematics aptitude test. It has been shown that those who scored higher on the test almost always perform better on the job. However, it has also been demonstrated that the use of the test in hiring employees has the effect of excluding blacks and other minority groups. Is this practice of the Jennings Company prohibited by the Civil Rights Act of 1964?

**4** Martel, a competent male secretary to the president of ICU, is fired because the new president of the company believes it is more appropriate to have a female secretary.

**a** Has a violation of the law occurred?

**b** Assume that a violation of the law has occurred and Martel decides to take an extended vacation after he is fired. Upon his return seven months later, Martel files suit in federal district court against ICU, charging illegal discrimination under the Civil Rights Act of 1964. What remedies will be available to him under the act?

**5** A male supervisor at Star Company makes repeated offensive sexual remarks to female employees. The employees complain to higher management, which ignores the complaints. If the company does not discharge or otherwise penalize the employee, has it violated Title VII? Discuss.

**6** The Acme Corporation has a hiring policy of giving preference to the relatives of present company employees. Does this policy violate Title VII? Explain what you need to know to answer this question fully.

**7** ADCO, an advertising agency, asks an employment agency to refer females to it who might be suitable to play the role of Mother Nature in a TV commercial ADCO is preparing. The agency referred five women to ADCO, one of whom is selected for the part. Has either ADCO or the employment agency violated the Civil Rights Act?

**8** Muscles-Are-You, Inc., a bodybuilding spa targeted primarily toward male bodybuilders, refuses to hire a woman for the position of executive director. The spa's management states that the executive director must have a "macho" image to relate well with the spa's customers. Discuss whether it is likely that the spa has violated Title VII.

**9** Ortega, an employee of ABC, Inc., recently joined a church which forbids working on Saturdays, Sundays, and Mondays. Ortega requests that his employer change his work schedule from eight-hour days, Monday through Friday, to ten-hour days, Tuesday through Friday. Ortega's request is refused because the employer is in operation only eight hours per day, five days a week. After a month during which Ortega fails to work on Mondays, he is fired, since the employer says that "only a full-time employee would be acceptable" for Ortega's position. What are Ortega's legal rights, if any?

**10** Assume that the degree of job difficulty for secretaries and maintenance personnel is approximately the same. If your state pays secretaries (mostly women) an average salary which is $2,000 below that of maintenance personnel (mostly men), has it violated employment discrimination laws?

**11** Tartel, Inc., had been guilty of flagrant discrimination against blacks in its hiring, promotion, and compensation of employees before the Civil Rights Act of 1964 was passed. After the act, Tartel decided to remedy the situation and place blacks in 50 percent of all new openings created by expansion, or by the retirement, resignation, or death of persons in its almost exclusively white work force. Discuss the legality of Tartel's action.

**12** Your company has traditionally hired males to do its assembly-line work. The assembly-line positions include some jobs which require lifting and some that do not. Males are rotated between these jobs as all male workers are on the same pay scale. The company has recently started to hire females for the assembly line, but they work only in nonlifting positions. For this reason, they are paid a lower wage scale than the men. The women employees sue. Discuss the considerations a court deciding the case should take into account.

**13** Cantrell, the controller of Xylec's, Inc., was forced to retire at age fifty-eight due to a general company policy. Although Cantrell has a company pension of $50,000 per year, she believes that her lifestyle will soon be hampered due to inflation, since the pension provides for no cost-of-living increases. What are Cantrell's rights, if any?

**14** The owner of Harold's Restaurant refuses to hire a job applicant because he is Hispanic. Can the job applicant immediately sue the owner in federal district court? Explain.

**15** Ralph Torrison is a systems analyst for the Silicon Corporation, a major defense contractor. When Ralph's co-workers learn that he has AIDS, six of them quit work immediately. Fearing that additional resignations will delay production, the company discharges Ralph. Discuss whether or not the company has acted legally.

**16** You have just been hired as personnel manager of a medium-sized corporation. Discuss what steps you can take to shield your company from unfounded claims of employment discrimination.

# Chapter
# *17*

# Right to Union Activity

## CHAPTER PREVIEW

This chapter and the next cover the topic of labor law and the rights of workers to bargain collectively. The subject matter is labor-management relations; the goal of labor law is successful collective bargaining. Collective bargaining is the process by which labor and management negotiate and reach agreements on matters of importance to both. This chapter emphasizes the rights of workers to engage in union activity.

Basic statutes are considered which have been enacted by Congress to regulate labor-management relations. The next chapter examines various violations of these laws and the sanctions which may be imposed for such violations. Most of the legal principles involved in labor law have been developed at the federal level because of the need for national uniformity. The National Labor Relations Board has the primary responsibility for enforcing these statutes, and special attention should be paid to this very important administrative agency.

This chapter introduces the following terms used in labor law: closed shop, collective bargaining, eighty-day cooling-off period, Landrum-Griffin Act, right-to-work law, Taft-Hartley Act, unfair labor practices, union shop, Wagner Act, and yellow-dog contract.

## 1.  Introduction

Various statutes governing labor-management relations have been enacted by Congress to provide a framework in which management and labor can collectively make decisions on issues of importance to both. Such issues include wages to be paid workers, hours to be worked, and other terms and conditions of employment. This framework also recognizes that the public has an important stake in a workable system of **collective bargaining,** since it benefits not only employers and employees but the public interest as well. Because collective bargaining can only be successful if the bargaining power of the parties is equal, most laws regulating labor-management relations seek to equalize this bargaining power. As a result, some laws add to the bargaining position of labor while others add to that of management.

The law encourages workers to join together and bargain as a group with employers: labor laws generally require employers to bargain with unions. The depth of this policy requirement is demonstrated by cases holding that the management of a successor company is required to bargain with the union representing its predecessor's employees. This encouragement of union activity is the logical result of the inequality of bargaining power between any single employee and a business.

Unions have had a significant impact on wages, hours, and conditions of employment, not only in unionized industries but also in those which are not. In companies without unions, many of the goals of unions have been met in order to avoid unionization. At the present time, approximately 14 percent of the non-farm, private-sector work force is unionized. Approximately 33 percent of such workers were unionized two decades ago. The opposite trend prevails in the government sector. In the last two decades union membership by government workers has risen from 11 percent to 33 percent.

The major federal laws which govern labor-management relations are briefly described in Table 17-1 and are discussed in more detail later in this chapter.

# FEDERAL LAWS BEFORE 1935

## 2.  Clayton Act

The first federal statute of any importance to the labor movement was the Clayton Act of 1914. It contained two sections relating to labor. The first attempted to prohibit federal courts from enjoining activities such as strikes and picketing in disputes over terms or conditions of employment. This provision was narrowly construed by the Supreme Court and has had little

## TABLE 17-1   Federal Laws Governing Labor-Management Relations

| Year | Statute | Summary of Major Provisions |
|---|---|---|
| 1914 | Clayton Act | 1  Exempted union activity from the antitrust laws |
| 1926 | Railway Labor Act | 1  Governs collective bargaining for railroads and airlines |
|  |  | 2  Created the National Mediation Board to conduct union elections and mediate differences between employers and unions |
| 1932 | Norris-LaGuardia Act | 1  Outlawed yellow-dog contracts |
|  |  | 2  Prohibited federal courts from enjoining lawful union activities, including picketing and strikes |
| 1934 | Wagner Act (National Labor Relations Act) | 1  Created the National Labor Relations Board (NLRB) |
|  |  | 2  NLRB to conduct union certification elections |
|  |  | 3  Outlawed certain conduct by management as unfair to labor (unfair labor practices) |
|  |  | 4  Authorized NLRB to hold hearings on unfair labor practices and correct wrongs resulting therefrom |
| 1947 | Taft-Hartley Act | 1  Outlawed certain conduct by unions as unfair labor practices |
|  |  | 2  Provided for an eighty-day cooling-off period in strikes which imperil national health or safety |
|  |  | 3  Allowed states to enact right-to-work laws |
|  |  | 4  Created the Federal Mediation and Conciliation Service to assist in settlement of labor disputes |
| 1959 | Landrum-Griffin Act (Labor Management Reporting and Disclosure Act—LMRDA) | 1  Bill of Rights for union members |
|  |  | 2  Requires reports to the Secretary of Labor |
|  |  | 3  Added to the list of unfair labor practices |

impact. The second section stated that antitrust laws regulating anticompetitive contracts did not apply to labor unions or their members in lawfully carrying out their legitimate activities. This exemption covered legitimate union practices. A union that seeks by agreement with a nonlabor party to reduce competition for the benefit of such a party may be guilty of an antitrust violation.

To illustrate the labor union antitrust exemption, assume that a union and several employers enter into a collective-bargaining agreement that restricts the hours of operation of the employers. Such an agreement is immune from attack under the Sherman Antitrust Act. The national labor policy immunizes from the Sherman Act union-employer agreements on when, and on how long, employees must work.

### 3.  Railway Labor Act

In 1926, Congress enacted the Railway Labor Act which encouraged collective bargaining in the railroad industry to resolve labor disputes that might otherwise disrupt transportation. The act, which provided a means for dealing with labor disputes, was later extended to airlines; it applies to both air and rail transportation today. It established the three-member National Mediation Board, which must designate the bargaining representative for any given bargaining unit of employees in the railway or air transport industries. The Board generally does this by holding representation elections. The Railway Labor Act also outlawed certain **unfair labor practices** such as refusing to bargain collectively.

In 1951, Congress amended the Railway Labor Act to permit the union shop. A union shop permits a union and an employer to require all employees in the bargaining unit to join the union as a condition of continued employment. The act does not permit a union to spend an objecting employee's dues to support political causes, however. The use of money for political purposes is unrelated to the desire of Congress to prevent *free riders*—those who get the benefits of the union without paying a fair share of the costs. There are other expenditures of dues that are improper. For example, the courts have held that the dues of nonunion members may not be used to pay for (1) litigation that does not involve the negotiation of agreements or the settlement of employee grievances, (2) general organizing efforts, and (3) publications not related to bargaining. The test is whether or not an expenditure is necessarily or reasonably incurred for the purpose of performing the duties of an exclusive representative of the employees in dealing with the employer on labor-management issues.

The National Mediation Board, unlike the National Labor Relations Board (NLRB), has no judicial power to hold hearings and issue cease and desist orders. Willful violations of the Railway Labor Act are punishable through criminal proceedings initiated by the Department of Justice in the regular federal court system. However, convictions are almost impossible to obtain because it is difficult to prove beyond any reasonable doubt that the commission of a given unfair labor practice was intentional.

When the parties to a dispute over proposed contract terms in the transportation industry cannot reach an agreement concerning rates of pay or working conditions, the National Mediation Board must attempt mediation of their differences. If mediation does not resolve their differences, the Board encourages voluntary arbitration. If the parties refuse arbitration and the dispute is likely to disrupt interstate commerce substantially, the Board informs the President, who then appoints a special emergency board. This emergency board also lacks any judicial power, but it encourages the parties to reach an agreement by investigating the dispute and publishing its findings of fact and recommendations for settlement. During the investigation, which lasts thirty days, and for an additional thirty days after the report is issued, business is conducted without interruption. The parties, however, have no duty to comply with the special board's proposals. Thus, if no new collective-bargaining agreement is reached after the sixty-day period, lockouts by management and strikes by workers become legal.

In several cases since 1940, the Railway Labor Act has failed to resolve major disputes, necessitating special action by the President or the Congress. The transportation industry frequently has had its labor problems presented to the government for solution because the procedures of the Railway Labor Act are not such that all disputes can be resolved without irreparable damage to the public. It should be noted that the provisions previously discussed apply to assisting employers and unions in arriving at a collective-bargaining agreement where none currently is in force. The act requires compulsory arbitration of disputes concerning interpretation of existing contracts between the parties. This requirement is peculiar to the transportation industry.

The Railway Labor Act allows collective bargaining contracts to require union membership as a condition of employment. If an employee is engaged in engine, train, yard, or hostling service, the union membership requirement may be met by membership in any national union representing similar workers. The fact that a worker need not belong to the union that represents him does not mean that the union to which he does belong may become involved on his behalf, even in a grievance hearing. The following case explains the rationale of this limitation.

# LANDERS v. NATIONAL R.R. PASSENGERS CORP.
108 S.Ct. 1440 (1988)

Landers (petitioner), an engineer employed by Amtrak, belonged to the United Transportation Union (UTU) rather than to the Brotherhood of Locomotive Engineers (BLE). BLE represented all Amtrak Engineers for collective-bargaining purposes.

Landers requested that the UTU be allowed to represent him at a company level disciplinary hearing. When his request was denied, he represented himself, was suspended for thirty days and then brought suit contending that his rights under the Railway Labor Act had been violated. The lower courts denied any relief.

WHITE, J.:...Petitioner contends that § 2, Eleventh, of the Railway Labor Act, provides railroad operating employees with a right to be represented by a "minority" union (*i.e.,* a union other than their collective-bargaining representative) at company-level grievance or disciplinary proceedings.

Section 2, Eleventh (a), permits a railroad and a union "duly designated and authorized to represent [its] employees" to enter into a union-shop agreement requiring "as a condition of continued employment, that...all employees shall become members of the labor organization representing their craft or class." An employee engaged in "engine, train, yard, or hostling service" may satisfy the requirement of membership in a labor organization, however, by "holding or acquiring membership in any one of the labor organizations, national in scope, organized in accordance with this chapter and admitting to membership employees of a craft or class in any of said services." It is not disputed in this action that § 2, Eleventh (c), permits petitioner to satisfy the union-shop provision of the BLE-Amtrak collective-bargaining agreement by holding membership in the UTU.

Neither § 2, Eleventh, nor any other provision of the Railway Labor Act expressly addresses what role, if any, a minority union is entitled to play in company-level grievance and disciplinary proceedings....

We are unwilling to read into the Railway Labor Act a right to minority union participation in company-level grievance and disciplinary proceedings that Congress declined to put there. That Congress expressly provided railroad employees with the right to the representative of their choice in Adjustment Board proceedings, but did not do so with regard to any earlier phase of the dispute resolution process, is persuasive evidence that Congress did not believe that the participation of minority unions or other outsiders in company-level proceedings was necessary to accomplish the purposes of the Act.

Indeed, the statutory purpose of "providing for the prompt and orderly settlement of all disputes growing out of grievances or out of the interpretation or application of agreements covering rates of pay, rules, or working conditions," might often be frustrated if employees could demand to be heard through the representative of their choice at grievance and disciplinary proceedings conducted on the employer's property. For example, many disputes might be resolved less expeditiously, or not at all, if employees had a statutory right to be represented at the company level by minority unions, which do not have the same established relationship with the employer as do official bargaining representatives or the same familiarity with how similar disputes have been resolved in the past.

In addition, a minority union might use the grievance and disciplinary proceedings to undermine the position of the bargaining representative and thereby destabilize labor-management relations. A majority union's prosecution of employee grievances and defense of employee disciplinary charges "complement its status as exclusive bargaining representative by permitting it to participate actively in the continuing administration of the contract." As Professor Cox has recognized, if the bargaining representative is instead prevented from exercising control over the presentation of grievances, the opportunity arises for "dissident groups, who may belong to rival unions,...to press aggressively all manner of grievances, regardless of their merit, in an effort to squeeze the last drop of competitive advantage out of each grievance and to use the settlement even of the most trivial grievances, as a vehicle to build up their own prestige." In such circumstances, "the settlement of grievances could become the source of friction and competition and a means for creating and perpetuating employee dissatisfaction instead of a method of eliminating it." The same potential for friction and competition exists, of course, when minority unions are allowed to participate in disciplinary proceedings such as those at issue here.

We find no merit in petitioner's contention that the right of railroad operating employees to be represented by minority unions at company-level grievance and disciplinary proceedings is implicit in § 2, Eleventh (c)....

There is no reason to believe that petitioner will suffer any appreciable prejudice if he cannot be represented by the UTU at grievance and disciplinary proceedings conducted on the Amtrak property. It is appropriate to assume that petitioner's interests will be adequately represented by the BLE, which owes the same duty of fair representation to all members of the bargaining unit regardless of their union affiliation. Moreover, if the dispute cannot be resolved at the company level, petitioner may be heard by the Adjustment Board through the representative of his choice. [*Affirmed.*]

### 4.  Norris-LaGuardia Act

In 1932 the Norris-LaGuardia Act was passed by Congress. The first major provision of the Norris-LaGuardia Act made **yellow-dog contracts** (those forbidding union membership) unenforceable. The second listed specific acts of persons and organizations participating in labor disputes which were not subject to federal court injunctions. These included (1) striking or quitting work, (2) belonging to a labor organization, (3) paying strike or unemployment benefits to participants in a labor dispute, (4) publicizing the existence of a labor dispute or the facts related to it (including picketing), (5) peaceably assembling to promote their interests in a labor dispute, and (6) agreeing with others or advising or causing them to do any of the above acts without fraud or violence. These acts are given a liberal interpretation, as is illustrated by the following case which had its roots in international politics rather than in labor relations.

# JACKSONVILLE BULK TERMINALS, INC. v. INTERNATIONAL LONGSHOREMEN'S ASSOC.
102 S.Ct. 2673 (1982)

After former President Carter announced certain trade restrictions with the Soviet Union because of its intervention in Afghanistan, the defendant union announced that its members would not handle any cargo bound to, or coming from, the Soviet Union. When an affiliated local union refused to load certain goods (not included in the presidential embargo) bound for the Soviet Union, the employer of the union brought suit against the international union, its officers and agents, and the local union. The employer alleged that the union's work stoppage violated the terms of a collective-bargaining agreement which contained a no-strike clause and a provision requiring arbitration of disputes. The district court granted a preliminary injunction pending arbitration. The court reasoned that the political motivation behind the work stoppage rendered inapplicable § 4 of the Norris-LaGuardia Act, which prohibits injunctions against strikes "in any case involving or growing out of any labor dispute."

MARSHALL, J.: Section 4 of the Norris-LaGuardia Act provides in part:

**No court of the United States shall have jurisdiction to issue any restraining order or temporary or permanent injunction in any case involving or growing out of any labor dispute to prohibit any person or persons participating or interested in such dispute…from doing, whether singly or in concert, any of the following acts:**

**(a) Ceasing or refusing to perform any work or to remain in any relation of employment.**

Congress adopted this broad prohibition to remedy the growing tendency of federal courts to enjoin strikes by narrowly construing the Clayton Act's labor exemption from the Sherman Act's prohibition against conspiracies to restrain trade. This Court has consistently given the anti-injunction provisions of the Norris-LaGuardia Act a broad interpretation, recognizing exceptions only in limited situations where necessary to accommodate the Act to specific federal legislation or paramount congressional policy.

The *Boys Markets* exception,…is relevant to our decision today. In *Boys Markets*, this Court…held that, in order to accommodate the anti-injunction provisions of Norris-LaGuardia to the…strong federal policy favoring arbitration, it was essential to recognize an exception to the anti-injunction provisions for cases in which the employer sought to enforce the union's contractual obligation to arbitrate grievances rather than to strike over them.…

The Employer argues that the Norris-LaGuardia Act does not apply in this case because the political motivation underlying the Union's work stoppage removes this controversy from that Act's definition of a "labor dispute."…

At the outset, we must determine whether this is a "case involving or growing out of any labor dispute" within the meaning of § 4 of the Norris-LaGuardia Act. Section 13(c) of the Act broadly defines the term labor dispute to include "any controversy concerning terms or conditions of employment."

The Employer argues that the existence of political motives takes this work stoppage controversy outside the broad scope of this definition. This argument, however, has no basis in the plain statutory language of the Norris-LaGuardia Act or in our prior interpretations of that Act. Furthermore, the argument is contradicted by the legislative history of not only the Norris-LaGuardia Act but also the 1947 amendments to the National Labor Relations Act (NLRA).

An action brought by an employer against the union representing its employees to enforce a no-strike pledge generally involves two controversies. First, there is the "underlying dispute," which is the event or condition that triggers the work stoppage. This dispute may or may not be political, and it may or may not be arbitrable under the parties' collective-bargaining agreement. Second, there is the parties' dispute over whether the no-strike pledge prohibits the work stoppage at issue. This second dispute can always form the basis for federal court jurisdiction, because § 301(a) gives federal courts jurisdiction over "suits for violation of contracts between an employer and a labor organization."

It is beyond cavil that the second form of dispute—whether the collective-bargaining agreement either forbids or permits the union to refuse to perform certain work—is a "controversy concerning the terms or conditions of employment." This § 301 action was brought to resolve just such a controversy. In its complaint, the Employer did not seek to enjoin the intervention of the Soviet Union in Afghanistan, nor did it ask the District Court to decide whether the Union was justified in expressing disapproval of the Soviet Union's actions. Instead, the Employer sought to enjoin the Union's decision not to provide labor, a decision which the Employer believed violated the terms of the collective-bargaining agreement. It is this contract dispute, and not the political dispute, that the arbitrator will resolve, and on which the courts are asked to rule.

The language of the Norris-LaGuardia Act does not except labor disputes having their genesis in political protests. Nor is there any basis in the statutory language for the argument that the Act requires that *each* dispute relevant to the case be a labor dispute. The Act merely requires that the case involve "any" labor dispute. Therefore, the plain terms of § 4(a) and § 13 of the Norris-LaGuardia Act deprive the federal courts of the power to enjoin the Union's work stoppage in this § 301 action, without regard to whether the Union also has a nonlabor dispute with another entity.

The conclusion that this case involves a labor dispute within the meaning of the Norris-LaGuardia Act comports with this Court's consistent interpretation of that Act. Our decisions have recognized that the term "labor dispute" must not be narrowly construed because the statutory definition itself is extremely broad and because Congress deliberately included a broad definition to overrule judicial decisions that had unduly restricted the Clayton Act's labor exemption from the antitrust laws....

The critical element in determining whether the provisions of the Norris-LaGuardia Act apply is whether "the employer-employee relationship is the matrix of the controversy." In this case, the Employer and the Union representing its employees are the disputants, and their dispute concerns the interpretation of the labor contract that defines their relationship. Thus, the employer-employee relationship is the matrix of this controversy....

This case, brought by the Employer to enforce its collective-bargaining agreement with the Union, involves a "labor dispute" within any common-sense meaning of that term. Were we to ignore this plain interpretation and hold that the political motivation underlying the work stoppage removes this controversy from the prohibitions of the Norris-LaGuardia Act, we would embroil federal judges in the very scrutiny of "legitimate objectives" that Congress intended to prevent when it passed that Act. The applicability not only of § 4, but of all of the procedural protections embodied in that Act, would turn on a single federal judge's perception of the motivation underlying the concerted activity.

In essence, the Employer asks us to disregard the legislative history of the Act and to distort the definition of a labor dispute in order to reach what it believes to be an "equitable" result. The Employer's real complaint, however, is not with the Union's political objections to the conduct of the Soviet Union, but with what the Employer views as the Union's breach of contract. The Employer's frustration with this alleged breach of contract should not be remedied by characterizing it as other than a labor dispute....In the past, we have consistently declined to constrict Norris-LaGuardia's broad prohibitions except in narrowly defined situations where accommodation of that Act to specific congressional policy is necessary. We refuse to deviate from that path today.

In conclusion, we hold that an employer's § 301 action to enforce the provisions of a collective-bargaining agreement allegedly violated by a union's work stoppage involves a "labor dispute" within the meaning of the Norris-LaGuardia Act, without regard to the motivation underlying the union's decision not to provide labor. [*Affirmed.*]

Although the Norris-LaGuardia Act greatly restricts the use of injunctions in labor disputes, it does not prohibit them altogether. An injunction may be issued to enjoin illegal strikes, such as ones by public employees. When unlawful acts are threatened, they may be enjoined also. These unlawful acts must cause substantial, irreparable damage. The situation must be such that public authorities who have the duty to protect the employer's property cannot furnish adequate protection or are unwilling to do so. In addition, one seeking an injunction in a labor dispute must meet the test of a stringent, clean-hands rule. No restraining order will be granted to any person who has failed to comply with any obligation imposed by law or who has failed to make every reasonable effort to settle the dispute.

The Norris-LaGuardia Act restricts the use of federal court injunctions in labor disputes; it does not limit the jurisdiction of state courts in issuing them. The Supreme Court has upheld the jurisdiction of a state court to enjoin a union's work stoppage and picketing in violation of a no-strike clause in its collective-bargaining agreement.

# THE WAGNER ACT

## 5.   General Summary

The labor movement received its greatest stimulus for growth with the enactment in 1935 of the National Labor Relations Act (*Wagner Act*). Noting that a major cause of industrial strife was the inequality of bargaining power between employees and employers, the act stated that its policy was to protect by law the right of employees to organize and bargain collectively and to encourage the "friendly adjustment of industrial disputes."

The Wagner Act accomplishes this policy by providing that the right of employees to bargain collectively is a fundamental right. Section 7 of the law provides:

> Employees shall have the right to self organization, to form, join, or assist labor organizations, to bargain collectively through representatives of their own choosing, and to engage in concerted activities for the purpose of collective bargaining or other mutual aid or protection.

In summary, the Wagner Act did the following:

1   Created the National Labor Relations Board (NLRB) to administer the act.

2   Provided for selection by employees through NLRB-supervised elections of a union with exclusive power to act as their collective-bargaining representative.

3   Outlawed certain conduct by employers which generally had the effect of either preventing the organization of employees or emasculating their

unions where they did exist. These forbidden acts were defined as "unfair labor practices" and are discussed in Chapter 18 in detail.

**4**   Authorized the NLRB to conduct hearings on unfair labor practice allegations and, if unfair practices were found to exist, take corrective action including issuing cease and desist orders and awarding dollar damages to unions and employees.

## 6.   The NLRB

Today, the NLRB has five members appointed by the President, with the advice and consent of the Senate, who serve staggered terms of five years each. The President designates one member to serve as chairman. In addition, there is a General Counsel of the Board who supervises Board investigations and serves as prosecutor in cases before the Board. The General Counsel supervises operations of the NLRB so that the Board itself may perform its quasi-judicial function of deciding unfair labor practice cases free of bias. As part of this function, the Board has full authority over the Division of Administrative Law Judges. The administrative law judges are responsible for the initial conduct of hearings in unfair labor practice cases. The General Counsel is appointed by the President, with the advice and consent of the Senate, for a term of four years. The General Counsel has final authority in investigation of charges, issuance of complaints, and prosecution of such complaints, as well as the dismissal of charges.

The General Counsel also is responsible for the conduct of representation elections, since the Board has delegated this function to its regional directors, subject to a review of their actions. (The Board still determines policy questions, such as what types of employers and groups of employees are covered by the labor law.) In addition, the General Counsel is responsible for seeking court orders requiring compliance with the Board's orders, and represents the Board in miscellaneous litigation.

Congress gave the NLRB jurisdiction over any business "affecting commerce," with a few exceptions. However, certain employers and employees are specifically exempt from NLRB jurisdiction. These include employees of federal and state governments, political subdivisions of the states, and persons subject to the Railway Labor Act. Also excluded are independent contractors, individuals employed as agricultural laborers or domestic servants in a home, and those employed by their spouse or a parent. Finally, supervisors are not considered employees. This supervisor exception excludes all employees properly classified as "managerial." For example, university professors who control admissions, hire and fire faculty, and participate in budget preparation are supervisors, and they are not covered by the act. Professors who have no power to act in these areas are covered.

The supervisor or managerial exception raises difficult issues when applied to persons having access to confidential information. The mere fact that a person has access to confidential information of an employer does not make the person a supervisor. Only those persons with access to confidential information of the employer concerning labor relations are exempt. This labor-relations connection means that persons who serve in a confidential capacity to persons who formulate, determine, or effectuate labor policy are not covered by the act.

The NLRB has never been able to exercise fully the powers given it because of budget and time constraints. It has limited its own jurisdiction to business of a certain size. Table 17-2 lists these businesses.

As a result of the NLRB's policy, federal laws do not cover many small employers who are subject to applicable state law on labor relations and common law principles. Of course the Board may decide to take jurisdiction over any business that affects interstate commerce.

Each year the NLRB handles over 50,000 cases of all kinds. About two-thirds involve unfair labor practice charges. Most of these are filed by unions or workers against employers, but one-third involve charges against unions.

## 7. NLRB Sanctions

The Wagner Act directs the Board, upon finding that a person has committed an unfair labor practice, to issue an order requiring him or her to cease and desist such practices. The Board is also authorized to order corrective

**TABLE 17-2**  NLRB Assumes Jurisdiction of the Following

1. Nonretail operations with an annual outflow or inflow across state lines of at least $50,000
2. Retail enterprises with a gross volume of $500,000 or more a year
3. Enterprises operating office buildings if the gross revenues are at least $100,000 per year
4. Transportation enterprises furnishing interstate services
5. Local transit systems with an annual gross volume of at least $250,000
6. Newspapers which subscribe to interstate news services, publish nationally syndicated features, or advertise nationally sold products and have a minimum annual gross volume of $250,000
7. Communication enterprises which operate radio or television stations or telephone or telegraph services with a gross volume of $100,000 or more per year
8. Local public utilities with an annual gross volume of $250,000 per year or an outflow or inflow of goods or services across state lines of $50,000 or more per year
9. Hotel and motel enterprises which serve transient guests and gross at least $500,000 in revenues per year
10. All enterprises whose operations have a substantial impact on national defense
11. Nonprofit hospitals
12. Private universities and colleges

action if necessary to overcome any injury caused by the unfair labor practice. Such orders are subject only to limited judicial review. On such a review, the Board's order will not be disturbed unless it can be shown that it is an obvious attempt to achieve ends contrary to the policies of the law. The NLRB has no independent power to enforce its orders. If necessary, it seeks enforcement in the United States Courts of Appeal.

To illustrate the corrective action that may be taken, consider the example of an employee who has been discharged wrongfully. The NLRB may order the reinstatement of that employee with back pay and restoration of full seniority rights. In fact, even a purchaser of a business who acquires and operates it knowing that the seller discharged an employee in violation of the Wagner Act may be ordered by the NLRB to reinstate the employee with back pay. The NLRB may require an employer to bargain collectively with the appropriate union, or vice versa. It may order an employer to post notices at the plant assuring employees that it will no longer commit a particular unfair labor practice of which it has been found guilty. If an employer or union has committed an unfair labor practice which may have influenced the outcome of a representation election, the NLRB may set aside the election and hold another one free of such improper pressures on the employees.

At one time, the NLRB was willing to certify a union that lost an election if the employer was guilty of unfair labor practices to such an extent that the employer's conduct could be described as outrageous and pervasive. In 1984, the courts reversed this policy, and today the NLRB will not certify a union that loses an election. It will set aside the election and require the employees to vote again. A nonmajority bargaining order departs from the national policy of employee free choice. The law requires a union election victory or some other concrete proof of majority assent to union representation. At the present time, unions lose the majority of certification and decertification elections. This negative trend has developed since the late 1970s.

### 8.   NLRB Elections

An employer may recognize voluntarily that its workers desire to have a certain union represent them and agree to bargain with the union. In the absence of such voluntary recognition, the selection of a union as collective-bargaining representative is made by a majority of the employees voting "in a unit appropriate for such purposes." Elections are by secret ballot and are supervised by the NLRB. The Board decides what unit of employees is appropriate for purposes of collective bargaining and therefore which employees are entitled to vote in the election. It may select the total employer unit, craft unit, plant unit, or any subdivision of the plant.

Obviously, how the Board exercises its discretion in this regard may be crucial to the outcome of a given election. If all 100 workers at one plant operated by an employer desire to organize but 400 out of 500 at another of the employer's plants do not, designation of the total employer unit as appropriate would ensure that both plants would remain nonunion. The Board may deny some employees the right to vote, as the case that follows illustrates.

---

# N.L.R.B. v. ACTION AUTOMOTIVE, INC.
105 S.Ct. 984 (1985)

---

BURGER, C.J.: We granted certiorari to decide whether the National Labor Relations Board may exclude from a collective-bargaining unit employees who are relatives of the owners of a closely held corporation that employs them, without a finding that the employees receive special job-related benefits.

Respondent, Action Automotive, Inc., is a retail automobile parts and gasoline dealer with stores in a number of Michigan cities. Action Automotive is a closely held corporation owned equally by three brothers, Richard, Robert, and James Sabo. The Sabo brothers are actively involved in the daily operations of the business. They serve as the corporation's officers, make all policy decisions, and retain ultimate authority for the supervision of every department.

In March 1981, the Retail Store Employees Union, Local 40 (the Union), filed with the Board a petition requesting that a representation election be held among Action Automotive's employees. Action Automotive and the Union agreed to elections in two bargaining units—one consisting of employees at the company's nine retail stores, and the other comprising clerical employees at the company's headquarters. The elections were held on May 29, 1981, and the Union received a plurality of votes in each unit; enough ballots were challenged by each side, however, to place the outcome of

the elections in doubt. We are concerned only with the Union's challenge to the ballots of Diane and Mildred Sabo.

Diane Sabo is the wife of Action Automotive's president and one-third owner, Richard Sabo. She works as a general ledger clerk at the company's headquarters in Flint, Michigan. She resides with her husband and both work at the same office. Unlike other clerical workers, she works part-time and receives a salary. She also is allowed to take breaks when she pleases, and she often spends her break in her husband's office.

Mildred Sabo is the mother of the three Sabo brothers who own and manage Action Automotive. She is employed as a full-time cashier at the company's store in Barton, Michigan. Mildred Sabo lives with James Sabo, Secretary-Treasurer of the corporation, and she regularly sees or telephones her other sons and their families. She earns 25 cents per hour more than any other cashier, but she is also one of the company's most experienced cashiers.

In light of these facts, the Board's hearing officer concluded that Diane Sabo's interests are different from those of other clerical employees in the company's headquarters, and that Mildred Sabo's "interests are more closely aligned with management than with the employees of Action Automotive." He reached this conclusion without finding that Diane and Mildred Sabo enjoy special job-related benefits. Believing that such a finding was not a prerequisite to excluding the two women from the bargaining units, the hearing officer recommended that the union's challenge to their ballots be sustained.

The Board adopted the hearing officer's recommendations and, after all qualified votes were counted, certified the Union as the exclusive bargaining representative for the two units. When Action Automotive refused to bargain, the Union filed charges with the Board. The Board...ordered the company to bargain with the Union.

The United States Court of Appeals for the Sixth Circuit denied enforcement of the Board's order.

Section 9(b) of the Act vests in the Board authority to determine "the unit appropriate for the purposes of collective bargaining." The Board's discretion in this area is broad, reflecting Congress' recognition of the need for flexibility in shaping the bargaining unit to the particular case. The Board does not exercise this authority aimlessly; in defining bargaining units, its focus is on whether the employees share a community of interest. A cohesive unit—one relatively free of conflicts of interest—serves the Act's purpose of effective collective bargaining, and prevents a minority interest group from being submerged in an overly large unit.

The Board has long hesitated to include the relatives of management in bargaining units because their interests are sufficiently distinguished from those of the other employees....

...The Board considers a variety of factors in deciding whether an employee's familial ties are sufficient to align his interests with management and thus warrant his exclusion from a bargaining unit.

For instance, a relevant consideration is whether the employee resides with or is financially dependent on a relative who owns or manages the business; such an employee is typically excluded from the unit. The greater the family involvement in the ownership and management of the company, the more likely the employee-relative will be viewed as aligned with management and hence excluded. The Board, of course, is always concerned with whether the employee receives special job-related benefits such as high wages or favorable working conditions. When other criteria satisfy the Board that the employee-relative's interests are aligned with management, however, he may be excluded from the unit even though he enjoys no special job-related benefits.

Our review is limited to whether the Board's practice of excluding some close relatives who do not enjoy special job-related benefits has a reasonable basis in law. In reviewing the Board decisions, we consistently yield to the Board's reasonable interpretations and applications of the Act. Indeed, the Board's orders defining bargaining units are "rarely to be disturbed."

The Board's policy regarding family members...is a reasonable application of its "community of interest" standard. Close relatives of management, particularly those who live with an owner or manager, are likely to get a more attentive and sensitive ear to their day-to-day and long-range work concerns than would other employees. And it is reasonable for the Board to assume that the family member who is significantly dependent on a member of management will tend to equate his personal interests with the business interests of the employer. The very presence at union meetings of close relatives of management could tend to inhibit free expression of views and threaten the confidentiality of union attitudes and voting....

We are not prepared to second-guess the Board's informed judgment that a bargaining unit's community of interest may be diluted by circumstances other than divergent job-related benefits....

The Board, in applying its general policy to the facts of this case, did not abuse its discretion. Diane Sabo resides with her husband, the president and one-third owner of Action Automotive; Mildred Sabo, the mother of the three owners, lives with one of her sons. All three owners are closely related and actively involved in running the business on a day-to-day basis. Diane Sabo works at the same office with her husband and occasionally takes her coffee breaks in his office. Mildred Sabo has daily contacts

with her sons. Certainly their participation in the collective-bargaining units would be viewed with suspicion by other employees. On these facts, the Board could reasonably conclude that Diane and Mildred Sabo's interests are more likely to be aligned with the business interests of the family than with the interests of the employees.

We hold that the Board did not exceed its authority in excluding from collective-bargaining units close relatives of management, without a finding that the relatives enjoy special job-related privileges. The judgment of the Court of Appeals is [*Reversed.*]

---

## PETITIONS

Before a representation election is conducted by the NLRB, a petition for such an election must be filed with the Board by either an employee, labor organization, or employer. If the petition is filed by either an employee or labor organization, it must allege either (1) that a substantial number of employees want a collective-bargaining representative but their employer refuses to recognize their representative, or (2) that a substantial number of employees assert that the union which has been certified by the Board or which the employer currently recognizes as their bargaining representative is no longer such. "Substantial" has been interpreted to mean that at least 30 percent of the employees must support the petition.

An employer may file a petition for selection of an initial representative without making and proving any allegations of fact. However, an employer who files a petition for an election to invalidate certification of an incumbent union must show that it doubts, in good faith, the continued support of the union by a majority of the employees.

The NLRB investigates a petition, and if it determines that there is an issue to be voted upon, it directs that a representation election be held by a secret ballot. After the results are tallied, the Board certifies either that no union has been selected by a majority of the employees or that a given one has. In some cases, two or more unions compete to qualify as the legal representative of the bargaining unit.

As was noted, employees may withdraw authority from a previously designated bargaining representative by secret ballot. If at least 30 percent of those in a bargaining unit allege that they desire their union's authority to be rescinded, the Board must hold an election to that effect. However, after any valid election has been conducted by the NLRB, another is not permitted for one year. Also, if an election has resulted in Board certification of a union, no new election may take place within one year of the certification. Also, an election is not allowed within the term of a collective-bargaining agreement or three years after it has been signed, whichever period is shorter.

**CARDS**

A union seeking to represent employees may solicit cards from them indicating their willingness for the union to represent them. An employer may then recognize the union as the bargaining agent for its employees if the cards are signed by a majority of the employees. An employer, however, is not required to recognize the union based on a majority card showing and always has the option to insist on an election. However, once an employer recognizes the union—no matter how informally—the employer is bound by the recognition and loses the right to seek an election. For example, in one case a company president agreed upon accepting the cards to recognize the union if the majority of the employees had signed. He then acknowledged that the cards indeed represented a majority. The courts held that it was with that acknowledgment that the bargain was sealed and the company committed to recognize the union.

Cards also may be used as a substitute for an election if certain conditions are met. The NLRB may issue a bargaining order based on such cards if the cards are unequivocal and clearly indicate that the employee signing the card is authorizing the union to represent him or her. The general counsel of the NLRB is not required to prove that the employees had read or understood the cards. If a card states on its face that it authorizes collective bargaining, it will be counted for that purpose unless there is clear proof that the employee was told that it would not be used for that purpose.

Most cards simply request an election because of the belief that peer pressure may cause workers who do not actually favor the union to sign the cards. The secret ballot of the election process ensures freedom of choice for the workers. An employer is entitled to insist upon an election as the refusal to accept a union based on cards is not an unfair labor practice.

# THE TAFT-HARTLEY ACT

## 9. Major Provisions

The Wagner Act opened the door for the rapid growth of the union movement. From 1935 to the end of World War II, the strength and influence of unions grew by leaps and bounds. Where, prior to the Wagner Act, employers had the greater advantage in bargaining power, by 1946 many persons felt the pendulum had shifted and that unions with their ability to call nationwide, crippling strikes had the better bargaining position.

As an attempt to balance the scale, the Labor-Management Relations Act of 1947 (the *Taft-Hartley Act*) was enacted to amend the Wagner Act. Its purposes were to ensure the free flow of commerce by eliminating union practices which burden commerce and to provide procedures for avoiding disputes which jeopardize the public health, safety, or interest. It recognized that both parties to collective bargaining need protection from wrongful interference by the other and that employees sometimes need protection from the union itself.

In attempting to balance bargaining power, the Taft-Hartley Act did the following;

**1** Created the Federal Mediation and Conciliation Service to assist in the settlement of labor disputes.

**2** Restricted the right of unions to insist on a union membership.

**3** Attempted to give employers freedom of speech in labor-management relations.

**4** Provided for an *eighty-day cooling-off period* in strikes which imperil the national health or safety.

**5** Allowed suits for breach of contract against a union.

**6** Outlawed certain conduct by unions as **unfair labor practices** (see Chapter 18).

The Federal Mediation and Conciliation Service has a staff of trained specialists who work with the parties to a labor dispute in an attempt to resolve differences. These mediators often become public figures, as in the case of the mediator involved in the baseball strike and the one involved in the air traffic controller strike.

## 10. Union Membership and Dues

The second major change brought about by the Taft-Hartley Act was its provision which outlawed the **closed shop** but permitted the union shop in those states which did not outlaw it by enacting **right-to-work legislation.** In a closed-shop contract, the employer agrees that it will *not* hire any person who is *not* a member of the union. In a union-shop contract, the employer agrees to require membership in the union after an employee has been hired as a condition of his or her continued employment. Under the Taft-Hartley Act, such a requirement may not be imposed until the thirtieth day after employment begins. In addition, an employer may not compel union membership of an employee (1) if membership was not available on the same terms and conditions applicable to other members, or (2) if the employee's membership was denied or terminated for reasons other than failure to pay dues and fees. In states that allow union-security agreements, nonunion workers must pay dues, but they cannot be discharged for failing to abide by union rules or policies. The dues or their equivalent, called agency fees, can only be used for collective-bargaining activities. These dues are to prevent free riders while prohibiting compulsory unionism. The case which follows indicates that the same rules apply to workers covered by the Railway Labor Act.

# COMMUNICATIONS WORKERS OF AMERICA v. BECK
108 S.Ct. 2641 (1988)

The National Labor Relations Act (NLRA) permits an employer and a union to enter into an agreement requiring all employees in the bargaining unit to pay union dues or an equal amount in agency fees as a condition of continued employment, whether or not the employees become union members. Such an agreement was in effect in this case. Respondents, bargaining-unit employees who chose not to become union members, filed suit challenging their union's (CWA) use of the agency fees for purposes other than collective bargaining, contract administration, or grievance adjustment hereinafter referred to as "collective-bargaining activities." They alleged that expenditure of their fees on activities such as organizing the employees of other employers, lobbying for labor legislation, and participating in social, charitable, and political events violated the union's duty of fair representation. The District Court and the Court of Appeals held for plaintiffs.

BRENNAN, J.:…Added as part of the 1947 Labor Management Relations Act, or Taft-Hartley Act, § 8(a)(3) makes it an unfair labor practice for an employer "by discrimination in regard to hire or tenure of employment…to encourage or discourage

membership in any labor organization." The section contains two provisos without which all union security clauses would fall within this otherwise broad condemnation: the first states that nothing in the Act "preclude[s] an employer from making an agreement with a labor organization…to require as a condition of employment membership therein" 30 days after the employee attains employment, the second, limiting the first, provides:

**[N]o employer shall justify any discrimination against an employee for nonmembership in a labor organization (A) if he has reasonable grounds for believing that such membership was not available to the employee on the same terms and conditions generally applicable to other members, or (B) if he has reasonable grounds for believing that membership was denied or terminated for reasons other than the failure…to tender the periodic dues and the initiation fees uniformly required as a condition of acquiring or retaining membership.**

Taken as a whole, § 8(a)(3) permits an employer and a union to enter into an agreement requiring all employees to become union members as a condition of continued employment, but the "membership" that may be so required has been "whittled down to its financial core." The statutory question presented in this case, then, is whether this "financial core" includes the obligation to support union activities beyond those germane to collective bargaining, contract administration, and grievance adjustment. We think it does not.

Although we have never before delineated the precise limits § 8(a)(3) places on the negotiation and enforcement of union security agreements, the question the parties proffer is not an entirely new one. Over a quarter century ago we held that § 2, Eleventh of the Railway Labor Act (RLA) does not permit a union, over the objections of nonmembers, to expend compelled agency fees on political causes. Because the NLRA and RLA differ in certain crucial respects, we have frequently warned that decisions construing the latter often provide only the roughest of guidance when interpreting the former. Our decision..., however, is far more than merely instructive here; we believe it is controlling, for § 8(a)(3) and § 2, Eleventh are in all material respects identical. Indeed, we have previously described the two provisions as "statutory equivalents," and with good reason, because their nearly identical language reflects the fact that, in both, Congress authorized compulsory unionism only to the extent necessary to ensure that those who enjoy union-negotiated benefits contribute to their cost.... We think that it is clear that Congress intended the same language to have the same meaning in both statutes.

Both the structure and purpose of § 8(a)(3) are best understood in light of the statute's historical origins. Prior to the enactment of the Taft-Hartley Act of 1947, § 8(a)(3) of the Wagner Act of 1935 (NLRA) permitted majority unions to negotiate "closed shop" agreements requiring employers to hire only persons who were already union members. By 1947, such agreements had come under increasing attack, and after extensive hearings Congress determined

that the closed shop and the abuses associated with it "created too great a barrier to free employment to be longer tolerated." The 1947 Congress was equally concerned, however, that without such agreements, many employees would reap the benefits that unions negotiated on their behalf without in any way contributing financial support to those efforts.... Thus, the Taft-Hartley Act was

**intended to accomplish twin purposes. On the one hand, the most serious abuses of compulsory unionism were eliminated by abolishing the closed shop. On the other hand, Congress recognized that in the absence of a union-security provision "many employees sharing the benefits of what unions are able to accomplish by collective bargaining will refuse to pay their share of the cost."**

The legislative solution embodied in § 8(a)(3) allows employers to enter into agreements requiring all the employees in a given bargaining unit to become members 30 days after being hired as long as such membership is available to all workers on a nondiscriminatory basis, but it prohibits the mandatory discharge of an employee who is expelled from the union for any reason other than his or her failure to pay initiation fees or dues. As we have previously observed, Congress carefully tailored this solution to the evils at which it was aimed:

**The legislative history clearly indicates that Congress intended to prevent utilization of union security agreements for any purpose other than to compel payment of union dues and fees. Thus Congress recognized the validity of unions' concerns about 'free riders,' *i.e.*, employees who receive the benefits of union representation but are unwilling to contribute their *fair share* of financial support to such union, and gave unions the power to contract to meet *that problem* while withholding from unions the power to cause the discharge of employees for**

**any other reason." Indeed, "Congress' decision to allow union-security agreements *at all* reflects its concern that...the parties to a collective bargaining agreement be allowed to provide that there be no employees who are getting the benefits of union representation without paying for them." [The court then reviewed the legislative history of § 2. Eleventh of the RLA.]**

In *Street* we concluded "that § 2, Eleventh contemplated compulsory unionism to force employees to share the costs of negotiating and administering collective agreements, and the costs of the adjustment and settlement of disputes," but that Congress did not intend "to provide the unions with a means for forcing employees, over their objection, to support political causes which they oppose." Construing the statute in light of this legislative history and purpose, we held that although § 2, Eleventh on its face authorizes the collection from nonmembers of "periodic dues, initiation fees, and assessments...*uniformly required* as a condition of acquiring or retaining membership" in a union, this authorization did not "vest the unions with unlimited power to spend exacted money." We have since reaffirmed that "Congress' essential justification for authorizing the union shop" limits the expenditures that may properly be charged to nonmembers under § 2, Eleventh to those "necessarily or reasonably incurred for the purpose of performing the duties of an exclusive bargaining representative." Given the parallel purpose, structure, and language of § 8(a)(3), we must interpret that provision in the same manner. Like § 2, Eleventh, § 8(a)(3) permits the collection of "periodic dues and initiation fees uniformly required as a condition of acquiring or retaining membership" in the union, and like its counterpart in the RLA, § 8(a)(3) was designed to remedy the inequities posed by "free riders" who would otherwise unfairly profit from the Taft-Hartley Act's abolition of the closed shop. In the face of such statutory congruity, only the most compelling evidence could persuade us that Congress intended the nearly identical language of these two provisions to have different meanings. Petitioners have not proffered such evidence here....

We conclude that § 8(a)(3), like its statutory equivalent, § 2, Eleventh of the RLA, authorizes the exaction of only those fees and dues necessary to "performing the duties of an exclusive representative of the employees in dealing with the employer on labor-management issues." Accordingly, the judgment of the Court of Appeals is [*Affirmed.*]

---

One of the sections of the Taft-Hartley Act most distasteful to unions is 14(b), which outlaws the union shop in states which have adopted a right-to-work law. Right-to-work laws prohibit agreements requiring membership in a labor organization as a condition of continued employment of a person who was not in the union when hired. Approximately twenty states have right-to-work laws today. Workers in these states who do not belong to a union may not be required to pay representation fees to the union that represents the employees. However, such workers are subject to the terms of the collective-bargaining agreement, and the union must handle their grievances, if any, with management.

A union has the power to discipline its members and impose fines. However, unions may not fine employees who are not members or who resign. A union constitution may not prohibit resignations. Taft-Hartley has eliminated compulsory union membership through a closed shop and as a result, a union may not fine former members who have resigned.

---

# PATTERN MAKERS' LEAGUE OF NORTH AMERICA v. N.L.R.B.

105 S.Ct. 3064 (1985)

---

POWELL, J.: The Pattern Makers' League of North America, AFL-CIO (the League), a labor union, provides in its constitution that resignations are not permitted during a strike or when a strike is imminent. The League fined 10 of its members who, in violation of this provision, resigned during a strike and returned to work. The National Labor Relations Board held that these fines were imposed in violation of § 8(b)(1)(A) of the National Labor Relations Act. We granted a petition for a writ of certiorari in order to decide whether § 8(b)(1)(A) reasonably may be construed by the Board as prohibiting a union from fining members who have tendered resignations invalid under the union constitution.

    The League is a national union composed of local associations (locals). In May 1976, its constitution was amended to provide that:

**No resignation or withdrawal from an Association, or from the League, shall be accepted during a strike or lockout, or at a time when a strike or lockout appears imminent.**

    This amendment, known as League Law 13, became effective in October 1976, after being ratified by the League's locals. On May 5, 1977, when a collective-bargaining agreement expired, two locals began an economic strike against several manufacturing companies in Rockford, Illinois and Beloit,

Wisconsin. Forty-three of the two locals' members participated. In early September 1977, after the locals formally rejected a contract offer, a striking union member submitted a letter of resignation to the Beloit association. He returned to work the following day. During the next three months, 10 more union members resigned from the Rockford and Beloit locals and returned to work. On December 19, 1977, the strike ended when the parties signed a new collective-bargaining agreement. The locals notified 10 employees who had resigned that their resignations had been rejected as violative of League Law 13. The locals further informed the employees that, as union members, they were subject to sanctions for returning to work. Each was fined approximately the equivalent of his earnings during the strike.

    The Rockford-Beloit Pattern Jobbers' Association (the Association) had represented the employers throughout the collective-bargaining process. It filed charges with the Board against the League and its two locals, the petitioners. Relying on § 8(b)(1)(A), the Association claimed that levying fines against employees who had resigned was an unfair labor practice. Following a hearing, an Administrative Law Judge found that the petitioners had violated § 8(b)(1)(A) by fining employees for returning to work after tendering resignations. The Board agreed that § 8(b)(1)(A) prohibited the union from imposing sanctions on the 10 employees....

The United States Court of Appeals for the Seventh Circuit enforced the Board's order....

We granted a petition for a writ of certiorari to resolve the conflict between the Courts of Appeals over the validity of restrictions on union members' right to resign. The Board has held that such restrictions are invalid and do not justify imposing sanctions on employees who have attempted to resign from the union. Because of the Board's "special competence" in the field of labor relations, its interpretation of the Act is accorded substantial deference. The question for decision today is thus narrowed to whether the Board's construction of § 8(b)(1)(A) is reasonable....

Section 7 of the Act grants employees the right to "refrain from any or all concerted...activities...." This general right is implemented by § 8(b)(1)(A). The latter section provides that a union commits an unfair labor practice if it "restrains or coerces employees in the exercise" of their § 7 rights. When employee members of a union refuse to support a strike (whether or not a rule prohibits returning to work during a strike), they are refraining from concerted activity." Therefore, imposing fines on these employees for returning to work "restrains" the exercise of their § 7 rights. Indeed, if the terms "refrain" and "restrain or coerce" are interpreted literally, fining employees to enforce compliance with any union rule or policy would violate the Act.

Despite this language from the Act, the Court in *NLRB v. Allis-Chalmers* held that § 8(b)(1)(A) does not prohibit labor organizations from fining current members. In *NLRB v. Textile Workers,* the Court found as a corollary that unions may not fine former members who have resigned lawfully....We decide today whether a union is precluded

from fining employees who have attempted to resign when resignations are prohibited by the union's constitution.

Section 8(b)(1)(A) allows unions to enforce only those rules that "impair no policy Congress has imbedded in the labor laws...." The Board has found union restrictions on the right to resign to be inconsistent with the policy of voluntary unionism implicit in § 8(a)(3). We believe that the inconsistency between union restrictions on the right to resign and the policy of voluntary unionism supports the Board's conclusion that League Law 13 is invalid.

Closed shop agreements, legalized by the Wagner Act in 1935, became quite common in the early 1940's. Under these agreements, employers could hire and retain in their employ only union members in good standing. Full union membership was thus compulsory in a closed shop; in order to keep their jobs, employees were required to attend union meetings, support union leaders, and otherwise adhere to union rules. Because of mounting objections to the closed shop, in 1947—after hearings and full consideration—Congress enacted the Taft-Hartley Act. Section 8(a)(3) of that Act effectively eliminated compulsory union membership by outlawing the closed shop. The union security agreements permitted by § 8(a)(3) require employees to pay dues, but an employee cannot be discharged for failing to abide by union rules or policies with which he disagrees.

Full union membership thus no longer can be a requirement of employment. If a new employee refuses formally to join a union and subject himself to its discipline, he cannot be fired. Moreover, no employee can be discharged if he initially joins a union, and subsequently resigns. We think it noteworthy that § 8(a)(3) protects the employment rights of the dissatisfied member, as well as those of the worker who never assumed full union membership. By allowing employees to resign from a union at any time, § 8(a)(3) protects the employee whose views come to diverge from those of his union.

League Law 13 curtails this freedom to resign from full union membership. Nevertheless, the petitioners contend that League Law 13 does not contravene the policy of voluntary unionism imbedded in the Act. They assert that this provision does not interfere with workers' employment rights because offending members are not discharged, but only fined. We find this argument unpersuasive, for a union has not left a "worker's employment rights inviolate when it exacts his entire paycheck in satisfaction of a fine imposed for working." Congress in 1947 sought to eliminate completely any requirement that the employee maintain full union membership. Therefore, the Board was justified in concluding that by restricting the right of employees to resign, League Law 13 impairs the policy of voluntary unionism.

The Board has the primary responsibility for applying "the general provisions of the Act to the complexities of industrial life." Where the Board's construction of the Act is reasonable, it should not be rejected "merely because the courts might prefer another view of the statute." In this case, two factors suggest that we should be particularly reluctant to hold that the Board's interpretation of the Act is impermissible. First, in related cases this Court invariably has yielded to Board decisions on whether fines imposed by a union "restrain or coerce" employees. Second, the Board consistently has construed § 8(b)(1)(A) as prohibiting the imposition of fines on employees who have tendered resignations invalid under a union constitution. Therefore, we conclude that the Board's decision here is entitled to our deference. [*Affirmed.*]

## 11.  Free Speech

Employers had complained that the Wagner Act violated their right of free speech. To meet this objection, Congress added the following provision:

> 8(c) The expressing of any views, argument, or opinion, or the dissemination thereof, whether in written, printed, graphic, or visual form, shall not constitute or be evidence of an unfair labor practice under any of the provisions of this Act, if such expression contains no threat of reprisal or force or promise of benefit.

This provision gives employers limited free speech, at best. It is difficult to make statements that cannot be construed as a threat or a promise. For example, if an employer predicts dire economic events as a result of unionization, such may be an illegal threat if the employee has it within his or her power to make the prediction come true. Whether particular language is coercive or not often depends on the analysis of the total background of facts and circumstances in which it was uttered. To be forbidden, the statements of an employer need not be proved to have been coercive in fact but only to have had a reasonable tendency to intimidate employees under the circumstances. At the present time, the NLRB takes the position that misleading statements will not automatically cancel election results, nor will inadvertent errors overturn elections. The purpose of this approach is to advance free speech by both sides.

An employer's threats to withdraw existing benefits of employees if they unionize is not speech protected by Section 8(c). For example, in one case the officer of a firm noted in a speech to employees of a plant where an election was forthcoming that the business could supply the same product from one of its nonunion plants. The NLRB held that this statement constituted a threat to provide better and more jobs at nonunion plants, and it set aside the election, which the union had lost. In another case, an illegal threat was ruled to be implied from management comments shortly before a representation election warning that annual pay raises would be subject to collective bargaining and thus delayed by a union victory. However, mere predictions and prophecies are protected. For example, an employer's speeches and handbills during the union's organizational campaign stated its intention to fight the union in every legal way possible and to "deal hard" with the union at arm's length if it were voted in, and warned that employees could be permanently replaced if the union called an economic strike. This language was held to fall within the protection of Section 8(c). The right of free speech guaranteed by the Taft-Hartley Act applies to labor unions as well as employers. However, there is a rule prohibiting either side from making election speeches on company time to massed assemblies of employees within twenty-four hours before an election.

## 12.  Eighty-Day Cooling-off Period

The provision of the Taft-Hartley Act calling for an eighty-day "cooling-off period" after certain procedures that have been followed begins, "Whenever in the opinion of the President of the United States, a threatened or actual strike or lockout affecting an entire industry or substantial part thereof engaged in trade, commerce, transportation, transmission, or communication among the several states or with foreign nations, or engaged in the production of goods for commerce, will, if permitted to occur or to continue, imperil the national health or safety, he may appoint a board...." Thus the procedure starts with the President, recognizing the emergency characteristics of a strike, appointing a board of inquiry to obtain facts about the strike. The board then makes a study of the strike and reports back to the President. If the board finds that the national health or safety is indeed affected by the strike, then the President, through the attorney general, goes to the federal court for an injunction ordering the union to suspend the strike (or company to suspend the lockout) for eighty days. During the eighty-day period, the Federal Mediation Service works with the two parties to try to achieve an agreement. If during this time the reconciliation effort fails, the presidential board holds new hearings and receives the company's final offer. The union members are then allowed to vote on this final proposal by the company. If they vote for the new proposal, the dispute is over and work continues as usual. If they vote against the proposal, the workers may again be called out on strike. At this point, the strike may continue indefinitely until the disagreement causing it is resolved by collective bargaining, or unless there is additional legislation by Congress to solve the problem. Experience has shown that many disputes are settled during the eighty-day period. The injunction provided for in the Taft-Hartley Act may not be used for all strikes but is limited to "national emergency" strikes. These must involve national defense or key industries or must have a substantial effect on the economy.

### 13. Suits Against Unions

Section 301 of the Taft-Hartley Act provides that suits for breach of a contract between an employer and a labor organization can be filed in the federal district courts, without regard to the amount in question. A labor organization is responsible for the acts of its agents and may sue or be sued. Any money judgment against it is enforceable only against its assets and not against any individual member. Moreover, individuals cannot be sued for actions such as violating no-strike provisions of a collective-bargaining contract. Thus, an employer may enforce a no-strike clause in a collective-bargaining agreement by obtaining an injunction against the union, or it may recover money damages from the union if it breaches such a contract clause. In addition, employees may sue their union and recover the money damages they suffer because of an illegal strike. If a union activity is both an unfair labor practice and a breach of a collective-bargaining agreement, the NLRB's authority is not exclusive and does not destroy the jurisdiction of courts under Section 301 of the Taft-Hartley Act.

## THE LANDRUM-GRIFFIN ACT

### 14. As a "Bill of Rights"

The Landrum-Griffin Act, or Labor-Management Reporting and Disclosure Act (LMRDA) was passed in 1959 as a result of the widespread corruption, violence, and lack of democratic procedures in some labor unions that were revealed in congressional hearings conducted in the 1950s. Its requirements provide for union reform and a "bill of rights" for union members. LMRDA gives union members the following rights:

**1** To nominate candidates, to vote in elections, to attend membership meetings, and to have a voice in business transactions, subject to reasonable union rules and regulations

**2** To have free expression in union meetings, business discussions, and conventions subject to reasonable rules and regulations

**3** To vote on an increase of dues or fees

**4** To sue and testify against the union

**5** To receive written, specific charges; to be given a reasonable time for defense; and to be accorded a full and fair hearing before any disciplinary action is taken by the union against them except for nonpayment of dues

**6** To be given a copy of the collective-bargaining agreement that they work under, upon request

The rights and remedies granted to union members by this statute are in addition to any other rights members may have under other laws or under union constitutions and bylaws. In the event that a member's rights are violated, the statute allows him or her to bring civil actions for damages, including an injunction.

The case which follows is typical of those brought to protect the rights of the rank-and-file union members to control their union. In this case, the Secretary of Labor filed suit under the Landrum-Griffin Act, challenging the validity of an international union rule which limited eligibility for local union office to certain members.

# LOCAL 3489 UNITED STEELWORKERS OF AMERICA v. USERY

97 S.Ct. 611 (1977)

BRENNAN, J.: The Secretary of Labor brought this action in the District Court under § 402(b) of the Labor, Management Reporting and Disclosure Act of 1959 (LMRDA) to *invalidate* the 1970 election of officers of Local 3489, United Steelworkers of America. The Secretary alleged that a provision of the Steelworkers' International constitution, binding on the Local, that limits eligibility for local union office to members who have attended at least one-half of the regular meetings of the Local for three years previous to the election (unless prevented by union activities or working hours), violated § 401(e) of the LMRDA. The District Court dismissed the complaint, finding no violation of the Act. The Court of Appeals for the Seventh Circuit reversed. We granted certiorari to resolve a conflict among Circuits over whether the Steelworkers' constitutional provision violates § 401(e)....

The LMRDA does not render unions powerless to restrict candidacies for union office. The injunction in § 401(e) that "every member in good standing shall be eligible to be a candidate and to hold office" is made expressly "subject to reasonable qualifications uniformly imposed." But "Congress plainly did not intend that the authorization... of 'reasonable qualifications...' should be given a broad reach. The contrary is implicit in the legislative history of the section and in its wording...." The basic objective of Title IV of the LMRDA is to guarantee "free and democratic" union elections modeled on "political elections in this country" where "the assumption is that voters will exercise common sense and judgment in casting their ballots."...

Whether a particular qualification is "reasonable" within the meaning of § 401(e) must therefore "be measured in terms of its consistency with the Act's command to unions to conduct 'free and democratic' union elections."...

We conclude that here the antidemocratic effects of the meeting-attendance rule outweigh the interests urged in its support. An attendance requirement that results in the exclusion of 96.5% of the members from candidacy for union office hardly seems to be a "reasonable qualification" consistent with the goal of free and democratic elections. A requirement having that result obviously severely restricts the free choice of the membership in selecting its leaders.

Petitioners argue that...a member can assure himself of eligibility for candidacy by attending some 18 brief meetings over a three-year period. In other words, the union would have its rule treated not as excluding a category of member from eligibility, but simply as mandating a procedure to be followed by any member who wishes to be a candidate.

Even examined from this perspective, however, the rule has a restrictive effect on union democracy. In the absence of a permanent "opposition party" within the union, opposition to the incumbent leadership is likely to emerge in response to particular issues at different times, and member interest in changing union leadership is therefore likely to be at its highest only shortly before elections. Thus it is probable that to require that a member decide upon a potential candidacy at least 18 months in advance of an election when no issues exist to prompt that decision may not foster but discourage candidacies and to that extent impair the general membership's freedom to oust incumbents in favor of new leadership.

Nor are we persuaded by petitioners' argument that the Secretary has failed to show an antidemocratic effect because he has not shown that the incumbent leaders of the union became "entrenched" in their offices as a consequence of the operation of the attendance rule. The reasons for leaderships becoming entrenched are difficult to isolate. The election of the same officers year after year may be a signal that antidemocratic election rules have prevented an effective challenge to the regime, or might well signal only that the members are satisfied with their stewardship; if elections are uncontested, opposition factions may have been denied access to the ballot, or competing interests may have compromised differences before the election to maintain a front of unity....Congress did not saddle the courts with the duty to search out and remove improperly entrenched union leaderships. Rather, Congress chose to guarantee union democracy by regulating not the results of a union's electoral procedure, but the procedure itself. Congress decided that if the elections are "free and democratic," the members themselves are able to correct abuse of power by entrenched leadership. Procedures that unduly restrict free choice among candidates are forbidden without regard to their success or failure in maintaining corrupt leadership.

Petitioners next argue that the rule is reasonable within § 401(e) because it encourages attendance at union meetings, and assures more qualified officers by limiting election to those who have demonstrated an interest in union affairs, and are familiar with union problems. But the rule has plainly not served these goals. It has obviously done little to encourage attendance at meetings, which continue to attract only a handful of members. Even as to the more limited goal of encouraging the attendance of potential dissident candidates, very few members, as we have said, are likely to see themselves as such sufficiently far in advance of the election to be spurred to attendance by the rule....

We therefore conclude that Congress, in guaranteeing every union member the opportunity to hold office, subject only to "reasonable qualifications," disabled unions from establishing eligibility qualifications as sharply restrictive of the openness of the union political process as is petitioners' attendance rule....[*Affirmed.*]

---

Some other restrictions relating to union elections have been upheld. In the case which follows, the union was concerned about outside financial support for candidates in union elections. Note that union candidates are given less protection and have more restrictions placed upon them than do candidates for public office.

---

# UNITED STEELWORKERS OF AMERICA v. SADLOWSKI
102 S.Ct. 2339 (1982)

---

A union amended its constitution to include an "outsider rule." This rule prohibits candidates for union office from accepting campaign contributions from nonmembers. It also creates a committee to enforce the rule and makes the committee's decisions final and binding. Plaintiff is a union member who had been an unsuccessful candidate for union office before adoption of the rule. He had received much of the financial support for his campaign from sources outside the union. He filed suit claiming that the rule violated the "freedom of speech and assembly" provision of Section 101(a)(2) of the LMRDA. The Court of Appeals held that the "outsider" rule was illegal.

MARSHALL, J.:...Section 101(a)(2) is contained in Title I of the LMRDA, the "Bill of Rights of Members of Labor Organizations." It provides:

**_Freedom of speech and assembly._—Every member of any labor organization shall have the right to meet and assemble freely with other members;**

and to express any views, arguments, or opinions; and to express at meetings of the labor organization his views, upon candidates in an election of the labor organization or upon any business properly before the meeting, subject to the organization's established and reasonable rules pertaining to the conduct of meetings: *Provided,* That nothing herein shall be construed to impair the right of a labor organization to adopt and enforce reasonable rules as to the responsibility of every member toward the organization as an institution and to his refraining from conduct that would interfere with its performance of its legal or contractual obligations.

We must decide whether this statute is violated by a union rule that prohibits candidates for union office from accepting campaign contributions from individuals who are not members of the union.

At the outset, we address respondents' contention that this case can be resolved simply by reference to First Amendment law. Respondents claim that § 101(a)(2) confers upon union members rights equivalent to the rights established by the First Amendment. They further argue that in the context of a political election, a rule that placed substantial restrictions on a candidate's freedom to receive campaign contributions would violate the First Amendment. Thus, a rule that substantially restricts contributions in union campaigns must violate § 101(a)(2). We are not persuaded by this argument. In light of the legislative history, we do not believe that § 101(a)(2) should be read as incorporating the entire body of First Amendment law, so that the scope of protections afforded by the statute coincides with the protections afforded by the Constitution.... There is absolutely no indication that Congress intended the scope of § 101(a)(2) to be identical to the scope of the First Amendment. Rather, Congress' decision to include a proviso covering "reasonable" rules refutes

that proposition. First Amendment freedoms may not be infringed absent a compelling governmental interest. Even then, any government regulation must be carefully tailored, so that rights are not needlessly impaired. Union rules, by contrast, are valid under § 101(a)(2) so long as they are reasonable; they need not pass the stringent tests applied in the First Amendment context.

To determine whether a union rule is valid under the statute, we first consider whether the rule interferes with an interest protected by the first section of § 101(a)(2). If it does, we then determine whether the rule is "reasonable" and thus sheltered by the proviso to § 101(a)(2). In conducting these inquiries, we find guidance in the policies that underlie the LMRDA in general and Title I in particular. First Amendment principles may be helpful, although they are not controlling. We must look to the objectives Congress sought to achieve, and avoid "placing great emphasis upon close construction of the words." The critical question is whether a rule that partially interferes with a protected interest is nevertheless reasonably related to the protection of the organization as an institution.

Applying this form of analysis here, we conclude that the outsider rule is valid. Although it may limit somewhat the ability of insurgent union members to wage an effective campaign, an interest deserving some protection under the statute, it is rationally related to the union's legitimate interest in reducing outsider interference with union affairs.

An examination of the policies underlying the LMRDA indicates that the outsider rule may have some impact on interests that Congress intended to protect under § 101(a)(2). Congress adopted the freedom of speech and assembly provision in order to promote union democracy. It recognized that democracy would be assured only if union members are free to discuss union policies and criticize the leadership without fear of reprisal. Congress also recognized that this freedom is particularly critical, and deserves vigorous protection, in the context of election campaigns. For it is in elections that members can wield their power, and directly express their approval or disapproval of the union leadership.

The interest in fostering vigorous debate during election campaigns may be affected by the outsider rule. If candidates are not permitted to accept contributions from persons outside the union, their ability to criticize union policies and to mount effective challenges to union leadership may be weakened. Restrictions that limit access to funds may reduce the number of issues discussed, the attention that is devoted to each issue, and the size of the audience reached.

Although the outsider rule does affect rights protected by the statute, as a practical matter the impact may not be substantial. Respondents...suggest that incumbents have a large advantage because they can rely on their union staff during election campaigns. Challengers cannot counter this power simply by seeking funds from union members; the rank-and-file cannot provide sufficient support. Thus, they must be permitted to seek funds from outsiders. In fact, however, the rank-and-file probably can provide support. The USWA is a very large union whose members earn sufficient income to make campaign contributions. Requiring candidates to rely solely on contributions from members will not unduly limit their ability to raise campaign funds. Uncontradicted record evidence discloses that challengers have been able to defeat incumbents or administration-backed candidates, despite the absence of financial support from nonmembers....

Although the outsider rule may implicate rights protected by § 101(a)(2), it serves a legitimate purpose that is clearly protected under the statute. The union adopted the rule because it wanted to ensure that nonmembers do not unduly influence union affairs. USWA feared that officers who received campaign contributions from nonmembers might be beholden to those individuals and might allow their decisions to be influenced by considerations other than the best interests of the union. The union wanted to ensure that the union leadership remained responsive to the membership. An examination of the policies underlying the LMRDA reveals that this is a legitimate purpose that Congress meant to protect....

We hold that USWA's rule prohibiting candidates for union office from accepting campaign contributions from nonmembers does not violate § 101(a)(2). Although it may interfere with rights Congress intended to protect, it is rationally related to a legitimate and protected purpose, and thus is sheltered by the proviso to § 101(a)(2). We reverse the decision below and remand for further proceedings consistent with this opinion. [*It is so ordered.*]

---

The LMRDA protects rank and file union members. It does not protect job security or tenure of union officers or employees. For example, the courts have held that after a union election, the winner may remove appointive union officials. Union leaders may select staff members with compatible views.

## 15. LMRDA Reporting Requirements

The act also contains several provisions concerning the Secretary of Labor and reports required of unions. The purpose of these reports is to reveal practices detrimental to union members. For example, each union must adopt a constitution and bylaws and file them with the Secretary of Labor, together with the following information:

1 The name and address of the union office and the place where records are kept

2 The names and titles of officers

3 The amount of initiation fees required

4 The amount of dues charged

5 A detailed statement of procedures for (a) qualification for office, (b) levying fees, (c) insurance plans, (d) disbursement of funds, (e) audits, (f) selection of officers, (g) removal of officers, (h) determining bargaining demands, (i) fines, (j) approval of contracts, (k) calling strikes, and (l) issuance of work permits

In addition, yearly financial reports must be filed which indicate:

1 Assets and liabilities

2 Receipts and sources of funds

3 Salaries of officers

4 Loans to members greater than $250

5 Loans to business enterprises

6 Other disbursements

Note that the above reports do not concern the operation of union welfare and pension plan funds, which involve a great deal more money than union treasuries. The Welfare and Pension Plans Disclosure Act of 1958 (as amended in 1962), also known as the Teller Act, governs such funds. This act requires filing with the Secretary of Labor a description of every employee pension and welfare plan covered by it as well as annual reports detailing the operations of the funds. The act also gives the Secretary broad investigative and enforcing powers.

The Landrum-Griffin Act also requires reports on trusteeships. A trusteeship is a method of supervision or control whereby a labor union suspends the autonomy otherwise available to a subordinate body under its constitution and bylaws. In this report, the union must state the names and addresses of subordinate organizations, the date of establishing trusteeship, and the reasons for establishing the trusteeship.

In addition to the foregoing reports, union employees and officials must file a yearly report with the Secretary of Labor containing information on possible areas of conflict of interest, such as stock holdings in companies with which the union has dealings and payments personally received from employers. Employers must file yearly reports with the Secretary reporting payments made to unions or union officials. Employers must also report payments made to consultants engaged to deal with unions. Reports made to the Secretary of Labor become public information and may be used as the basis of criminal proceedings.

## 16. Internal Union Activities

The Landrum-Griffin Act provides an elaborate system of regulation of internal union activities. These regulations cover union election procedures, management of union funds, trusteeships, and union personnel. The Secretary of Labor is given power to investigate alleged violations of any of the regulations and may institute criminal proceedings through the Attorney General.

The act requires that elections be held at minimum regular intervals to promote democracy. National unions must hold elections at least every five years, locals every three years, and intermediate bodies every four years. Elections must be by secret ballot of members, or of delegates chosen by secret ballot of members. Every candidate for union office must have access to membership lists. The union must provide adequate safeguards to ensure a fair election, and every candidate is given the right to post observers at the polls and counting place. All candidates must have equal opportunity to run for office without penalty or punishment by the organization. Union funds may not be used by any candidate in his or her campaign.

The act also recognizes the fiduciary responsibility of officers of unions. All clauses in union constitutions which attempt to provide that union officers do not have liability for wrongful conduct are void as against public policy. A member of a union may sue for funds mishandled by union officers after he or she has exhausted union proceedings, and the member will be repaid the cost of bringing suit.

The act makes embezzlement of union funds a federal crime. The penalty is imprisonment for up to five years or a fine of up to $10,000, or both. Every union employee who handles funds must be bonded. No union may lend more than $2,000 to a union employee or official. Any person who willfully violates either of these two provisions is subject to imprisonment for one year or a fine of up to $10,000, or both. Unions are not permitted to pay the fines imposed on their officers or employees who are convicted of violating the act. However, the propriety of payments to cover legal fees in lawsuits is judged on an individual basis.

The Landrum-Griffin Act also makes it a federal offense to engage in extortionate picketing. This is picketing to force an employer to pay money to union officials or other individuals for their own personal use rather than for the benefit of the union membership generally.

## 17. Labor Law and Government Employees

Perhaps the most difficult problems in the labor field today involve government employees. Should such employees have the right to form unions and to bargain collectively with the government units that employ them? If collective bargaining fails to reach satisfactory agreements, should government employees have the right to strike? The clear-cut trend in the law is to answer the first question affirmatively and the second negatively. Today, unions or employee organizations exist at all levels of government. As noted at the beginning of this chapter, approximately one-third of all government workers are organized today. A union without the right to strike may be viewed as a "paper tiger." Without the right to strike, the power of public-employee unions is much less than that of unions in the private sector.

The right to strike is denied to government workers because such strikes affect the public more adversely than those by employees in the private sector. Strikes by police, firefighters, teachers, sanitation workers, transportation workers, and other public employees who perform vital services obviously can be directly and immediately detrimental to the health, safety, and welfare of those whom they serve.

Collective bargaining in public employment varies throughout the country. States vary from having no laws granting bargaining rights to public employees to having statutes with broad guarantees. A few states even give some public employees the right to strike. Unions of public workers are pressing for legislation that would give them the choice of striking or turning to binding arbitration if a dispute cannot be resolved. Other unions advocate the expansion of the present Wagner and Taft-Hartley Acts to cover state and local employees.

The difficulties of collective bargaining in the public sector are multiplied by the problem of funds needed to meet labor's demands, since one of the most significant differences between public and private labor relations is that there is no "bottom line" for cost in governmental bodies as there is in private corporations. Frequently, public officials have neither the funds to meet labor's demands nor the power to raise taxes without the consent of the voters. A school board may be very willing to grant pay increases, but unless voters will agree to the tax increases required, the money to do so is simply not available. For example, the faculty of Florida's state colleges and universities bargained for a raise of 10 percent. The legislature refused to fund it. In such a case, the collective-bargaining agreement must give way to the constitutional provisions on state funding. A possible solution to this dilemma is to integrate the bargaining process with the budgetary process.

It is expected that the number of public employees represented by unions will continue to grow. However, few of these will have the right to strike. Employees performing essential services are not likely to be granted this right, even though it is basic to the whole concept of unions. Employees performing nonessential services may acquire the right to strike, or, in some cases, actions will not be taken to stop such strikes even if they are technically illegal. The more important the job, the less likely a strike will be tolerated.

## REVIEW QUESTIONS

**1** Identify the federal statute which accomplished each of the following:
  **a** Exempted union activity from the antitrust laws
  **b** Created the National Labor Relations Board (NLRB)
  **c** Allowed states to enact right-to-work laws
  **d** Outlawed certain conduct by management as unfair to labor (unfair labor practices)
  **e** Governed collective bargaining for railroads and airlines
  **f** Prohibited federal courts from enjoining lawful union activities, including picketing and strikes
  **g** Established bill of rights for union members
  **h** Provided for an eighty-day cooling-off period in strikes which imperil national health or safety
  **i** Outlawed yellow-dog contracts
  **j** Created the Federal Mediation and Conciliation Service

**2** Two labor unions enter into an agreement with an employer that no union member should work for another company that is a competitor of the employer. The employer is the largest firm in its industry, and the other company is a new firm. Is the agreement exempt from the antitrust laws? Why or why not?

**3** Which of the following expenditures would be proper for a union collecting dues from nonmembers?
  **a** Political contributions
  **b** Convention expenses
  **c** Officers' salaries
  **d** Official publications
  **e** Social events
  **f** General organizing efforts

**4** Assume that a company has a collective-bargaining agreement that includes a no-strike clause during its terms. Despite this, the union calls a strike. No violence has resulted from the strike. Will the Norris-LaGuardia Act prevent a *state court* from issuing an injunction that enforces the contract and orders the strike to cease? Explain.

**5** Except for the members of the National Labor Relations Board, what position connected with the NLRB has the most power and responsibility? Briefly describe these powers and responsibilities.

**6** Albert owns a small retail store with seven full- and part-time employees. One employee is fired for advocating that the employees form a union. If the employee files a complaint of an unfair labor practice with the NLRB, what will be the result? Why?

**7** A railroad seeks a preliminary injunction in a federal court against secondary picketing by a union that represents railroad employees. Does the federal court have jurisdiction to enter the injunction? Why or why not?

**8** A union obtains authorization cards from a majority of employees and demands that it be recognized as the collective-bargaining representative. The employer suggests that the union petition the NLRB for an election. The union files a charge of unfair labor practice based on the refusal to bargain. Is the employer guilty? Explain.

**9** The general counsel of the NLRB issues a bargaining order based on union authorization cards. The authorization cards are unequivocal and clearly state that the employee authorize the union to represent him or her. The employer contends that the employees were orally told that signing the cards would only result in an election. Will the bargaining order be set aside? Why or why not?

**10** Pat lives in a state that has enacted a right-to-work law. The company which employs her has recognized the United Clerical Workers (UCW) as the bargaining representative of its workers. The union has sought to collect union dues or their equivalent from Pat. Is she required to pay them? Why or why not?

**11** ABC Company's employees vote by 51 percent in an election to have American Confederation act as their collective-bargaining representatives. Only four months later, 60 percent of the employees become disenchanted with American Confederation and wish to oust it. May they do so? Explain.

**12** The president of your company is writing a speech to give to the workers prior to a union representation election. What advice would you give relative to the contents of the speech?

**13** Sterling lays off all of its production employees and goes out of business. Fall River acquires Sterling's plant, real property, equipment, and remaining inventory. It reopens the plant and hires employees, a majority of which had worked formerly for Sterling. The union that had represented Sterling now contends that it is the authorized union of Fall River's employees. Is it correct? Explain.

**14** The Amalgamated Lead Workers' Union (AML) suspects that antiunion persons are infiltrating its ranks to overthrow the union. Accordingly, its board proposes a rule, which the membership adopts, that only those who have belonged to the union for at least two years will be eligible for union office. Walter, who has been in AML for only eighteen months, files a petition to run for president, but it is refused because of the two-year requirement. Walter files suit, challenging the rule. What will be the result? Why?

**15** The garbage collectors in Metropolis are city employees. They are represented by a union. Negotiations with the city manager have broken down and the garbage collectors have gone on strike. The city manager has notified all employees that anyone who does not return to work within twenty-four hours will be discharged. Those who do not return are then replaced with new employees. Will a court order the discharged workers to be rehired? Why or why not?

## Chapter 18

# Unfair Labor Practices

## CHAPTER PREVIEW

The previous chapter introduced you to labor law. It emphasized that the Wagner Act declared certain practices by management to be unfair to labor unions and workers. The Taft-Hartley Act later declared certain practices by unions to be unfair and illegal. The Landrum-Griffin Act later added to both lists. This chapter discusses these unfair labor practices in detail.

As you study this chapter, keep in mind that the law encourages collective bargaining. It seeks to give employees a free choice in choosing whether or not to be represented by a union. The responsibility for determining whether or not a party has committed an unfair labor practice is with the NLRB, and its rules and decisions are given great deference. As you read this chapter, recognize how easy it is for both management and labor to commit an unfair labor practice.

The following additional legal terms are introduced in this chapter: compulsory-bargaining issue, concerted activities, constructive discharge, featherbedding, hot-cargo contract, organizational picketing, secondary boycott, voluntary-bargaining issue, work rules, and Wright-Line Doctrine.

## 1. Introduction

The term "unfair labor practice" was originally used to describe practices by management that were unfair to workers and their unions. The Wagner Act listed five general categories of such violations. A later amendment added a sixth. These are summarized in Table 18-1.

**TABLE 18-1**   Unfair Labor Practices by Employers

1  Interference with efforts of employees to form, join, or assist labor organizations, or to engage in concerted activities for mutual aid or protection
2  Domination of a labor organization or contribution of financial or other support to it
3  Discrimination in hiring or tenure of employees for reason of union affiliation
4  Discrimination against employees for filing charges or giving testimony under the act
5  Refusal to bargain collectively in good faith with a duly designated representative of the employees
6  Agreeing with a labor organization to engage in a secondary boycott

An activity may be, and often is, a violation of more than one of the listed unfair labor practices. Indeed, most violations constitute interference with the right to engage in concerted activity (the first category). For example, retaliation against a union leader for filing charges would constitute a violation of both the first and fourth categories.

If management is guilty of an unfair labor practice, the NLRB has a broad range of remedies to use in eliminating the impact of the violation. If a union has lost a representation election, it may order a new one. If an employee has been wronged, for example, by a wrongful discharge, the Board can order the employee rehired with back pay. The NLRB has the capability of righting wrongs that have occurred.

As we noted in the prior chapter, the Taft-Hartley Act declared that certain actions by unions are also unfair labor practices. The Landrum-Griffin Act also expanded the list of unfair labor practices. The sections which follow give examples of violations by both parties—management and labor. The discussion of unfair labor practices by unions begins with section 10 of this chapter.

## 2.   Interference with Efforts of Employees to Form or Join Labor Organizations

In part, the first unfair labor practice listed is for an employer to interfere with the efforts of employees to form, join, or assist labor organizations. This is a catchall intended to guarantee the right to organize and to join a labor union. It clearly prohibits "scare" tactics such as threats by employers to fire those involved in organizing employees, or threats to cut back on employee benefits if employees succeed in unionizing. In addition, less obvious activities are outlawed, such as requiring job applicants to state on a questionnaire whether they would cross a picket line in a strike, unless the questionnaire contains an assurance by the employer against reprisal. In one typical case, the company personnel director questioned two employees on break about both the whereabouts of a union meeting and if the union was paying employees to sign authorization cards. These questions were a coercive interrogation and an unfair labor practice. An employer cannot engage in conduct calculated to erode employee support for the union.

Retaliation for union activity is discussed more fully in section 4 of this chapter. However, keep in mind that not every act of retaliation is an unfair labor practice. For example, the filing of a lawsuit may or may not be an unfair labor practice depending on the outcome of the lawsuit. The First Amendment protects persons filing lawsuits and employers have the right to seek local judicial protection from tortious conduct during labor disputes. Therefore, the filing and prosecution of a well-founded lawsuit may not be enjoined as an unfair labor practice, even if it was initiated by the plaintiff's desire to retaliate against the defendant for exercising rights protected by the Wagner Act.

Although it is not unlawful to prosecute a meritorious action, the same is not true of suits based on insubstantial claims—suits that lack a "reasonable basis." Such suits are not within the scope of First Amendment protection. As a result, the NLRB may halt a state-court suit if it lacks a reasonable basis in fact or law and there is a retaliatory motive present.

### CONFERRING BENEFITS

Even the conferring of benefits by an employer may be an unfair labor practice. In one case, the employer reminded its employees by a letter sent two weeks before a representation election that the company had just instituted a "floating holiday" which they could take on their birthdays. The letter also announced a new system for computing overtime during holiday weeks, which had the effect of increasing wages for those weeks, and a new vacation schedule which let employees extend their vacations by sandwiching them between two weekends. The union lost the election, but the Supreme Court set it aside. It held that it was an unfair labor practice for the employer to engage in conduct immediately favorable to employees which is undertaken with the express purpose of impinging upon their freedom of choice for or against unionization and is reasonably calculated to have that effect. The danger inherent in well-timed increases in benefits is the suggestion of a fist inside the velvet glove. Employees are not likely to miss the inference that the source of benefits now conferred is also the source from which future benefits must flow and which may dry up if it is not obliged.

### WORK RULES

Company **work rules** often negatively affect workers' attempts to organize and join a union. These work rules may prohibit wearing buttons or insignia on work clothes. Unless the employer can establish a valid reason for such rules, they cannot be used to stop the wearing of union buttons or insignia. To punish a worker for violating such a work rule would constitute an unfair labor practice. Similarly, "no solicitation on the premises" rules which go beyond the actual necessity of the employer based on health, safety, or the like are not enforceable to stop workers from organizing.

A rule which prohibits solicitation during "working time" is presumptively valid, but a rule which bans solicitation during "working hours" is presumptively invalid. It is an unfair labor practice to prohibit union activity and solicitation on company property during the employees' own time. The employer need not permit it when the employee is supposed to be working.

In one case, the NLRB held that a hospital's rule prohibiting solicitation by its employees at all times "in any area of the hospital which is accessible to or utilized by the public" was presumed to be invalid except in "immediate patient areas." These were defined as places such as patients' rooms, operating rooms, and places where patients receive treatment. The Supreme Court agreed with the Board that the hospital had not justified its rule as applied to its cafeteria, gift shop, and the lobbies and entrances on its first floor. However, union solicitation in the presence or within the hearing of patients in corridors and sitting rooms that adjoined patients' rooms and operating and treatment rooms might have an adverse effect on their recovery. Thus, the no-solicitation rule was not an unfair labor practice as applied to such areas, in addition to the "immediate patient-care areas."

Of course, the Wagner Act does not guarantee the rights of employees to solicit for *any* cause on an employer's property. Solicitation must be protected by Section 7 as involving collective bargaining or an activity engaged in for other mutual aid or protection.

### WRITTEN AND ORAL STATEMENTS MADE TO EMPLOYEES

A difficult aspect is presented in those cases in which an employer is accused of an unfair labor practice as a result of something he has said or written. Such allegations may conflict with First Amendment guarantees of freedom of speech and the press. Moreover, as noted in Chapter 17, the Taft-Hartley Act provides that the expression of views, arguments, or opinions is not evidence of an unfair labor practice if it contains no threats of reprisal or promises of benefits.

An employer may even predict that the consequences of unionization will be unfavorable if she or he does so in a way which contains no threat. The statement that "it is our definite view that if the union were to come in here, it would work to your serious harm" has been held privileged and noncoercive. However, if the employer predicts dire economic events as a result of unionization, such may be an illegal threat if he has it within his power to make the prediction come true.

It is extremely difficult to draw a clear-cut line between those statements of employers which are coercive and those which are noncoercive and thus privileged. Interpretations of the Board have varied with its membership over the years.

### 3. Interfering with Concerted Activities

The first half of the first unfair labor practice refers to interference with efforts to form, join, or assist labor organizations. The second half covers "**concerted activities** for mutual aid or protection." A violation of the second half does not have to involve a union. It protects any group of employees acting for mutual aid and protection. This protection is limited, however, when an exclusive bargaining representative has already been chosen. It does not protect individuals in other unions.

Concerted activity may directly involve a union and may involve issues of importance to the workers and their union. The phrase is given a liberal interpretation in order to create a climate that encourages unionization, collective bargaining, and all that may flow therefrom. For example, some employees refused to work after a heated grievance meeting. They followed their supervisors onto the workroom floor and continued to argue loudly until they were ordered a second time to resume work. The employer issued letters of reprimand alleging insubordination. This was an unfair labor practice. The employees were engaged in a protected activity. The protection of employee conduct at grievance meetings is extended to a brief "cooling-off period" following an employer's termination of such a meeting. Protection of employees' participation in the meetings themselves would be seriously threatened if the employer could at any point call an immediate halt to the operation of the law simply by declaring the meeting ended.

The case which follows illustrates the extent to which the law protects workers in concerted activities.

# EASTEX, INC. v. N.L.R.B.
98 S.Ct. 2505 (1978)

Employees of the petitioner corporation sought to distribute a four-section union newsletter in nonworking areas of petitioner's plant during nonworking time. The second section encouraged employees to write their legislature to oppose incorporation of the state "right-to-work" statute into a revised state constitution. The third section criticized a presidential veto of an increase in the federal minimum wage and urged employees to register to vote to "defeat our enemies and elect our friends." Representatives of petitioner refused to permit the requested distribution of the newsletter because of the content of its second and third sections. The union then filed an unfair labor practice charge with the NLRB. The Board ruled that petitioner's refusal constituted an unfair labor practice. The Board's cease and desist order was enforced by the Court of Appeals, and the Supreme Court granted certiorari.

POWELL, J.:...The question presented here is whether...distribution of the newsletter is the kind of concerted activity that is protected from employer interference by §§ 7 and 8(a)(1) of the National Labor Relations Act....

Section 7 provides that "employees shall have the right...to engage in... concerted activities for the purpose of collective bargaining or other mutual aid or protection...." Petitioner contends that the activity here is not within the "mutual aid or protection" language because it does not relate to a "specific dispute" between employees and their own employer "over an issue which the employer has the right or power to affect." In support of its position, petitioner asserts that the term "employees" in § 7 refers only to employees of a particular employer, so that only activity by employees on behalf of themselves or other employees of the same employer is protected. Petitioner also argues that the term "collective bargaining" in § 7 "indicates a direct bargaining relationship whereas 'other mutual aid or protection' must refer to activities of a similar nature...." Thus, in petitioner's view, under § 7 "the employee is only protected for activity within the scope of the employment relationship." Petitioner rejects the idea that § 7 might protect any activity that could be characterized as "political," and suggests that the discharge of an employee who engages in any such activity would not violate the Act.

We believe that petitioner misconceives the reach of the "mutual aid or protection" clause. The "employees" who may engage in concerted activities for "mutual aid or protection" are defined by the Act to "include any employee, and shall not be limited to the employees of a particular employer, unless the Act explicitly states otherwise...."

This definition was intended to protect employees when they engage in otherwise proper concerted activities in support of employees of employers other than their own. In recognition of this intent, the Board and the courts long have held that the "mutual aid or protection" clause encompasses such activity. Petitioner's argument on this point ignores the language of the Act and its settled construction.

We also find no warrant for petitioner's view that employees lose their protection under the "mutual aid or protection" clause when they seek to improve terms and conditions of employment or otherwise improve their lot as employees through channels outside the immediate employee-employer relationship. The 74th Congress knew well enough that labor's cause often is advanced on fronts other than collective bargaining and grievance settlement within the immediate employment context. It recognized this fact by choosing, as the language of § 7 makes clear, to protect concerted activities for the somewhat broader purpose of "mutual aid or protection" as well as for the narrower purposes of "self-organization" and "collective bargaining." Thus, it has been held that the "mutual aid or protection" clause protects employees from retaliation by their employers when they seek to improve working conditions through resort to administrative and judicial forums, and that employees' appeals to legislators to protect their interests as employees are within the scope of this clause. To hold that activity of this nature is entirely unprotected—irrespective of location or the means employed—would leave employees open to retaliation for much legitimate activity that could improve their lot as employees. As this could "frustrate the policy of the Act to protect the right of workers to act together to better their working conditions," we do not think that Congress could have intended the protection of § 7 to be as narrow as petitioner insists....

The Board determined that distribution of the second section urging employees to write their legislators to oppose incorporation of the state "right-to-work" statute into a revised state constitution, was protected because union security is "central to the union concept of strength through solidarity" and "a mandatory subject of bargaining in other than right-to-work states." The newsletter warned that incorporation could affect employees adversely "by weakening unions and improving the edge business has at the bargaining table." The fact that Texas already has a "right-to-work" statute does not render employees' interest in this matter any less strong, for, as the Court of Appeals noted, it is "one thing to face a legislative scheme which is open to legislative modification or repeal" and "quite another thing to face the prospect that such a scheme will be frozen in a concrete constitutional mandate." We cannot say that the Board erred in holding that this section of the newsletter bears such a relation to employees' interest as to come within the guarantee of the "mutual aid or protection" clause.

The Board held that distribution of the third section, criticizing a presidential veto of an increase in the federal minimum wage and urging employees to register to vote to "defeat our enemies and elect our friends," was protected despite the fact that petition-

er's employees were paid more than the vetoed minimum wage. It reasoned that the "minimum wage inevitably influences wage levels derived from collective bargaining, even those far above the minimum," and that "concern by petitioner's employees for the plight of other employees might gain support for them at some future time when they might have a dispute with their employer." We think that the Board acted within the range of its discretion in so holding. Few topics are of such immediate concern to employees as the level of their wages. The Board was entitled to note the widely recognized impact that a rise in the minimum wage may have on the level of negotiated wages generally, a phenomenon that would not have been lost on petitioner's employees. The union's call, in the circumstances of this case, for these employees to back persons who support an increase in the minimum wage, and to oppose those who oppose it, fairly is characterized as concerted activity for the "mutual aid or protection" of petitioner's employees and of employees generally.

In sum, we hold that distribution of both the second and the third sections of the newsletter is protected under the "mutual aid or protection" clause of § 7....[*The judgment of the Court of Appeals therefore is affirmed.*]

---

### WORK RULES

Concerted activities often involve the refusal to follow work rules. If the employer has a rule with which the workers disagree, it is not uncommon for several of them to refuse to comply. Is it permissible to discipline such employees, or is discipline in such cases an unfair labor practice? The answer is often unclear and depends upon the facts in each case.

For example, a typical work rule used in industry is that a worker may not leave work without permission. In one case, the employer discharged seven employees for violating this rule. The employees on a particularly cold day had walked off the job from an uninsulated machine shop which on that day had no heat. On other occasions, protests had been made about the poor heat. The employees claimed to have acted as a group in protest against unfit working conditions, hoping that their concerted action would cause the employer to heat the shop properly. The employer justified the discharge action by claiming that the men left work without permission. The NLRB ruled that the action of the employees was protected concerted activity and that their discharge amounted to an unfair labor practice. The Supreme Court agreed and noted that employees do not

> …necessarily lose their right to engage in concerted activities…merely because they do not present a specific demand upon their employer to remedy a condition which they find objectionable. The language of the law is broad enough to protect concerted activities whether they take place before, after, or at the same time such a demand is made.…Having no bargaining representative and no established procedures…the men took the most direct course to let the company know they wanted a warmer place in which to work.

However, in another case the Supreme Court held that it was not an unfair labor practice for a company to fire certain employees who picketed the company's store, against union advice. There, the union had investigated charges that the company was racially discriminating against employees and had invoked the contract grievance procedure under the collective-bargaining agreement by demanding that the joint union-management Adjustment Board be convened "to hear the entire case." The discharged employees had begun picketing the company because they felt that the grievance procedure being utilized was inadequate. In upholding the NLRB's decision, the court ruled that the law recognizes the principle of exclusive representation. Therefore, concerted activities by a minority of employees to bargain with their employer over issues of employment discrimination are not protected by the Wagner Act. Such employees may not bypass their exclusive bargaining representative.

### INTERVIEWS

The concerted-activity concept has been expanded in recent decisions. In one case, an employer was investigating theft by employees. One employee asked that a union representative be present during her interview. She was refused. The Supreme Court held that the employee had a right to representation when there was a perceived threat to her employment security. The presence of a representative assures other employees in the bargaining unit that they too can obtain aid and protection if they wish when there appears to be a threat to their job security. Refusing the assistance at the interview was an unfair labor practice.

A few years later, a nonunion employee sought to have a union representative present at an investigatory interview. The courts held that the employee had a right to this assistance. Just as a union member has this right, so does a nonunion employee. The right to representation is derived from the protection afforded to concerted activity for mutual aid or protection, not from a union's right to act as an employee's exclusive representative for the purpose of collective bargaining.

### SOLE EMPLOYEE AS CONCERTED ACTIVITY

The right to engage in concerted activity has been expanded to cover the actions of a sole employee under certain circumstances. If an employee has a grievance which may affect other workers, that employee has rights protected by the concerted-activity language of the first unfair labor practice.

---

# N.L.R.B. v. CITY DISPOSAL SYSTEMS, INC.
104 S.Ct. 1505 (1984)

---

James Brown, a truck driver, was employed by City Disposal Systems, Inc., which hauls garbage for the city of Detroit. He was discharged when he refused to drive a truck that he honestly and reasonably believed to be unsafe because of faulty brakes. The collective-bargaining agreement provided: "the Employer shall not require employees to take out on the streets or highways any vehicle that is not in safe operating condition or equipped with safety appliances prescribed by law. It shall not be a violation of the Agreement where employees refuse to operate such equipment unless such refusal is unjustified."

Brown filed a grievance with the union, but the union declined to process it. He then filed an unfair labor practice charge challenging his discharge. The NLRB found that Brown was discharged for refusing to operate the truck and that the discharge was an unfair labor practice. It found that an employee who acts alone in asserting a contract right is nevertheless engaged in concerted activity. He was ordered reinstated with back pay. The Court of Appeals reversed, holding that there was no concerted activity.

BRENNAN, J.:...The question to be decided is whether Brown's honest and reasonable assertion of his right to be free of the obligation to drive unsafe trucks constituted "concerted activity" within the meaning of § 7 of the National Labor Relations Act.

The Administrative Law Judge (ALJ)... held that an employee who acts alone in asserting a contractual right can nevertheless be engaged in concerted activity within the meaning of § 7:

**When an employee makes complaints concerning safety matters which are embodied in a contract, he is acting not only in his own interest, but is attempting to enforce such contract provisions in the interest of all the employees covered under the contract. Such activity we have found to be concerted and protected under the Act, and the discharge of an individual for engaging in such activity to be in violation of Section 8(a)(1) of the Act.**

Section 7 of the NLRA provides that "employees shall have the right to...join or assist labor organizations, to bargain collectively through representatives of their own choosing, and to engage in other concerted activities for the purpose of collective bargaining or other mutual aid or protection." The NLRB's decision in this case applied the Board's longstanding *"Interboro* doctrine," under which an individual's assertion of a right grounded in a collective-bargaining agreement is recognized as "concerted activity" and therefore accorded the protection of § 7. The Board has relied on two justifications for the doctrine: First, the assertion of a right contained in a collective-bargaining agreement is an extension of the concerted action that produced the agreement, and second, the assertion of such a right affects the rights of all employees covered by the collective-bargaining agreement.

The question for decision today is whether the Board's application of § 7 to Brown's refusal to drive truck No. 244 is reasonable. Several reasons persuade us that it is.

Neither the Court of Appeals nor respondent appears to question that an employee's invocation of a right derived from a collective-bargaining agreement meets § 7's requirement that an employee's action be taken "for purposes of collective bargaining or other mutual aid or protection."...A single employee's invocation of such rights affects all the employees that are covered by the collective-bargaining agreement. This type of generalized effect,...is sufficient to bring the actions of an individual employee within the "mutual aid or protection" standard, regardless of whether the employee has his own interests most immediately in mind....

The invocation of a right rooted in a collective-bargaining agreement is unquestionably an integral part of the process that gave rise to the agreement. That process—beginning with the organization of a union, continuing into the negotiation of a collective-bargaining agreement, and extending through the enforcement of the agreement—is a single, collective activity. Obviously, an employee could not invoke a right grounded in a collective-bargaining agreement were it not for the prior negotiating activities of his fellow employees. Nor would it make sense for a union to negotiate a collective-bargaining agreement if individual employees could not invoke the rights

thereby created against their employer. Moreover, when an employee invokes a right grounded in the collective-bargaining agreement, he does not stand alone. Instead, he brings to bear on his employer the power and resolve of all his fellow employees. When, for instance, James Brown refused to drive a truck he believed to be unsafe, he was in effect reminding his employer that he and his fellow employees, at the time their collective-bargaining agreement was signed, had extracted a promise from City Disposal that they would not be asked to drive unsafe trucks. He was also reminding his employer that if it persisted in ordering him to drive an unsafe truck, he could reharness the power of that group to ensure the enforcement of that promise. It was just as though James Brown was reassembling his fellow union members to reenact their decision not to drive unsafe trucks. A lone employee's invocation of a right grounded in his collective-bargaining agreement is, therefore, a concerted activity in a very real sense.

Furthermore, the acts of joining and assisting a labor organization, which § 7 explicitly recognizes as concerted, are related to collective action in essentially the same way that the invocation of a collectively bargained right is related to collective action. When an employee joins or assists a labor organization, his actions may be divorced in time, and in location as well, from the actions of fellow employees. Because of the integral relationship among the employees' actions, however, Congress viewed each employee as engaged in concerted activity. The lone employee could not join or assist a labor organization were it not for the related organizing activities of his fellow employees. Conversely, there would be limited utility in forming a labor organization if other employees could not join or assist the organization once it is formed. Thus, the formation of a labor organization is integrally related to the activity of joining or assisting such an organization in the same sense that the negotiation of a collective-bargaining agreement is integrally related to the invocation of a right provided for in the agreement. In each case, neither the individual activity nor the group activity would be complete without the other.

The *Interboro* doctrine is also entirely consistent with the purposes of the Act, which explicitly include the encouragement of collective bargaining and other "practices fundamental to the friendly adjustment of industrial disputes arising out of differences as to wages, hours, or other working conditions."...Moreover, by applying § 7 to the actions of individual employees invoking their rights under a collective-bargaining agreement, the *Interboro* doctrine preserves the integrity of the entire collective-bargaining process; for by invoking a right grounded in a collective-bargaining agreement, the employee makes that right a real-

ity, and breathes life, not only into the promises contained in the collective-bargaining agreement, but also into the entire process envisioned by Congress as the means by which to achieve industrial peace....

The NLRB's *Interboro* doctrine recognizes as concerted activity an individual employee's reasonable and honest invocation of a right provided for in his collective-bargaining agreement. We conclude that the doctrine constitutes a reasonable interpretation of the Act. Accordingly, we accept the Board's conclusion that James Brown was engaged in concerted activity when he refused to drive truck No. 244. We therefore reverse the judgment of the Court of Appeals and remand the case for further proceedings consistent with this opinion, including an inquiry into whether respondent may continue to defend this action on the theory that Brown's refusal to drive truck No. 244 was unprotected, even if concerted. [*It is so ordered.*]

---

### 4.   Discharge and Other Forms of Retaliation

One of the primary techniques used by management to discourage unionization and to interfere with the right of workers to engage in concerted union activity is either to threaten to "fire" the workers or actually to discharge them if the union wins the election. Retaliation and the threat of retaliation are clearly unfair labor practices. However, the issues are often much more complicated. Is it an unfair labor practice to discharge a union organizer who is also an unsatisfactory employee? What is the effect of an employer's assisting others in making it impossible for the worker to continue his or her employment?

The latter issue was involved in the following case.

# SURE-TAN, INC. v. N.L.R.B.
104 S.Ct. 2803 (1984)

After a union was certified, the employer sent a letter to the Immigration and Naturalization Service (INS), asking it to check the immigration status of five named employees. After a short investigation, INS agents discovered that each of the five employees listed in the letter was a Mexican national working illegally in the United States. They were arrested and later accepted the INS grant of voluntary departure as a substitute for deportation. The administrative law judge (ALJ) and the NLRB found that the employer had in effect discharged the employees for voting for and supporting the union. The Court of Appeals affirmed.

O'CONNOR, J.:…We…determine whether the National Labor Relations Board (NLRB or Board) may properly find that an employer engages in an unfair labor practice by reporting to the Immigration and Naturalization Service (INS) certain employees known to be undocumented aliens in retaliation for their engaging in union activity, thereby causing their immediate departure from the United States.…

We consider the predicate question whether the NLRA should apply to unfair labor practices committed against undocumented aliens. The Board has consistently held that undocumented aliens are "employees" within the meaning of § 2(3) of the Act.…

Accepting the premise that the provisions of the NLRA are applicable to undocumented alien employees, we must now address the more difficult issue whether, under the circumstances of this case, petitioners committed an unfair labor practice by reporting their undocumented alien employees to the INS in retaliation for participating in union activities. Section 8(a)(3) makes it an unfair labor practice for an employer "by discrimination in regard to hire or tenure of employment or any term or condition of employment to encourage or discourage membership in any labor organization." The Board…has long held that an employer violates this provision not only when, for the purpose of discouraging union activity, it directly dismisses an employee, but also when it purposefully creates working conditions so intolerable that the employee has no option but to resign—a so-called "constructive discharge."

Petitioners do not dispute that the antiunion animus element of this test was, as expressed by the lower court, "flagrantly met." The record is replete with examples of Sure-Tan's blatantly illegal course of conduct to discourage its employees from supporting the Union. Petitioners contend, however, that their conduct in reporting the undocumented alien workers did not force the workers' departure from the country; instead, they argue, it was the employees' status as illegal aliens that was the actual "proximate cause" of their departure.

This argument is unavailing. According to testimony by an INS agent before the ALJ, petitioners' letter was the sole cause of the investigation during which the employees were taken into custody. This evidence was undisputed by petitioners and amply supports ALJ's conclusion that "but for petitioners' letter to Immigration, the discriminatees would have continued to work indefinitely."…

We observe that the Board quite properly does not contend that an employer may never report the presence of an illegal alien employee to the INS....The reporting of any violation of the criminal laws is conduct which ordinarily should be encouraged, not penalized. It is only when the evidence establishes that the reporting of the presence of an illegal alien employee is in retaliation for the employee's protected union activity that the Board finds a violation of § 8(a)(3). Absent this specific finding of anti-union animus, it would not be an unfair labor practice to report or discharge an undocumented alien employee....[*Reversed and Remanded to permit formulation by the Board of an appropriate remedial order.*]

---

In cases involving mixed motivation for discharge, the NLRB follows a procedure known as the **Wright-Line Doctrine.** Under this doctrine, the NLRB's General Counsel first introduces evidence that makes a prima facie showing sufficient to support the inference that the employer's opposition to protected conduct was a "motivating factor" in the employer's discharge decision. The NLRB can find an unfair labor practice based solely on the general counsel's proof of a prima facie case of discrimination. This is possible if the employer does not come forward with any evidence to support its allegations that the discharge has been for legitimate business reasons.

Once this prima facie case is established, the burden shifts to the employer to demonstrate that the same action would have taken place even in the absence of the protected conduct. The Board retains the burden to prove retaliatory discharge by a preponderance of the evidence.

The case which follows is typical of those involving mixed motivation for discharge and the application of the Wright-Line Doctrine. Note that the employer does not have the burden of proving that an unfair labor practice has not occurred. The weighing by the NLRB includes a careful consideration of the employer's "good" reason as well as of the general counsel's evidence of improper motive.

---

# N.L.R.B. v. TRANSPORTATION MANAGEMENT CORP.
103 S.Ct. 2469 (1983)

---

The National Labor Relations Board found that Transportation Management Corp. (TMC) has discharged Santillo, one of TMC's bus drivers, for union activity. Santillo had attempted to organize TMC drivers and convince them to join the Teamsters' Union. TMC contended that Santillo was dismissed for leaving his keys in the bus and taking unauthorized breaks. The administrative law judge (ALJ) found that the asserted reasons for the discharge could not withstand scrutiny. While acknowledging that Santillo had engaged in some unsatisfactory conduct, the ALJ was not persuaded that Santillo would have been fired had it not been for his union activities.

In conducting the hearing, the Board followed a procedure known as the Wright-Line Doctrine. The Court of Appeals held that this doctrine should not be followed.

WHITE, J.:…The National Labor Relations Act (NLRA or Act) makes unlawful the discharge of a worker because of union activity, but employers retain the right to discharge workers for any number of other reasons unrelated to the employee's union activities. When the General Counsel of the National Labor Relations Board (Board) files a complaint alleging that an employee was discharged because of his union activities, the employer may assert legitimate motives for his decision. In *Wright Line*, 251 N.L.R.B. 1083 (1980), the National Labor Relations Board reformulated the allocation of the burden of proof in such cases. It determined that the General Counsel carried the burden of persuading the Board that an anti-union animus contributed to the employer's decision to discharge an employee, a burden that does not shift, but that the employer, even if it failed to meet or neutralize the General Counsel's showing, could avoid the finding that it violated the statute by demonstrating by a preponderance of the evidence that the worker would have been fired even if he had not been involved with the Union. The question presented in this case is whether the burden placed on the employer in *Wright Line* is consistent with the NLRA which provides that the Board must prove an unlawful labor practice by a "preponderance of the evidence."…

Employees of an employer covered by the NLRA have the right to form, join, or assist labor organizations. It is an unfair labor practice to interfere with, restrain, or coerce the exercise of those rights or by discrimination in hire or tenure "to encourage or discourage membership in any labor organization."

Under these provisions it is undisputed that if the employer fires an employee for having engaged in union activities and has no other basis for the discharge, or if the reasons that he proffers are pretextual, the employer commits an unfair labor practice. He does not violate the NLRA, however, if any anti-union animus that he might have entertained did not contribute at all to an otherwise lawful discharge for good cause.…

The presence of an anti-union motivation in a discharge case is not the end of the matter. An employer can escape the consequences of a violation by proving that without regard to the impermissible motivation, the employer would have taken the same action for wholly permissible reasons.

The Board's *Wright Line* decision in 1980 was an attempt to restate its analysis in a way more acceptable to the Courts of Appeals. The Board held that the General Counsel of course had the burden of proving that the employee's conduct protected by § 7 was a substantial or a motivating factor in the discharge. Even if this was the case, and the employer failed to rebut it, the employer could avoid being held in violation…by proving by a preponderance of the evidence that the discharge rested on the employee's unprotected conduct as well and that the employee would have lost his job in any event. It thus became clear, if it was not clear before, that proof that the discharge would have occurred in any event and for valid reasons amounted to an affirmative defense on which the employer carried the burden of proof by a preponderance of the evidence. The shifting burden merely requires the employer to make out what is actually an affirmative defense.…

The Court of Appeals held that the General Counsel…had the burden of showing not only that a forbidden motivation contributed to the discharge but also that the discharge would not have taken place independently of the protected conduct of the employee. The Court of Appeals was quite correct,…that throughout the proceedings, the General Counsel carries the burden of proving the elements of an unfair labor practice.…We are quite sure, however, that the Court of Appeals erred in holding that § 10(c) forbids placing the burden on the employer to prove that absent the improper motivation he would have acted in the same manner for wholly legitimate reasons.

As we understand the Board's decisions, they have consistently held that the unfair labor practice consists of a discharge or other adverse action that is based in whole or in part on anti-union animus—or as the Board now puts it, that the employee's protected conduct was a substantial or motivating factor in the adverse action. The General Counsel has the burden of proving these elements under § 10(c). But the Board's construction of the statute permits an employer to avoid being adjudicated a violator by showing what his actions would have been regardless of his forbidden motivation. It extends to the employer what the Board considers to be an affirmative defense but does not change or add to the elements of the unfair labor practice that the General Counsel has the burden of proving under § 10(c).

We assume that the Board could reasonably have construed the Act in the manner insisted on by the Court of Appeals. We also assume that the Board might have considered a showing by the employer that the adverse action would have occurred in any event as not obviating a violation adjudication but as going only to the permissible remedy, in which event the burden of proof could surely have been put on the employer. The Board has instead chosen to recognize, as it insists it has done for many years, what it designates as an affirmative defense that the employer has the burden of sustaining. We are unprepared to hold that this is an impermissible construction of the Act. The Board's construction here, while it may not be required by the Act, is at least permissible under it and in these circumstances its position is entitled to deference.

The Board's allocation of the burden of proof is clearly reasonable in this context.… The employer is a wrongdoer; he has acted out of a motive that is declared illegitimate by the statute. It is fair that he bear the risk that the influence of legal and illegal motives cannot be separated, because he knowingly created the risk and because the risk was created not by innocent activity but by his own wrongdoing.

For these reasons, we conclude that the Court of Appeals erred in refusing to enforce the Board's orders, which rested on the Board's *Wright Line* decision.

The Board was justified in this case in concluding that Santillo would not have been discharged had the employer not considered his efforts to establish a union.… The Board's finding that Santillo would not have been fired even if the employer had not had an anti-union animus was supported by substantial evidence on the record considered as a whole.

Accordingly, the judgment is [*Reversed.*]

---

The NLRB has a rule regarding the discharge of supervisors. Under the rule, the discharge of a supervisor is unlawful only if it interferes with the rights of an employee. Supervisors are excluded from the definition of employee, and the employer is entitled to insist on the loyalty of supervisors. Supervisors are not free to engage in activities which would be protected if engaged in by other employees. The only exceptions to the rule are (1) to discharge a supervisor for testifying before the Board or during the grievance process, (2) to discipline a supervisor for refusing to commit an unfair labor practice, or (3) to discharge a supervisor who has hired his own pro-union crew as a pretext for terminating the former crew.

Retaliation may take other forms than discharge. It may entail a reduction of benefits. For example, several workers were on sick leave when their union commenced a strike. The company discontinued accident and sickness payments to all workers who were sick but continued to make payments to workers who were disabled by job-related injuries. This distinction constituted an unfair labor practice. The sick workers were not required to repudiate the strike, and the employer may not presume support of the strike by silence.

## 5.   Domination of a Labor Organization

Before the Wagner Act was passed, it was a fairly common practice for employers to sidetrack the desires and efforts of employees to organize by forming a "union" which was, in fact, controlled by the employer. The second unfair labor practice prohibits the domination of a labor organization by employers or their contribution of financial or other support to it, and puts an end to the use of such company unions.

Under the Wagner Act, any organization of employees must be completely independent of their employers. Neither they nor their supervisory personnel may promote or sponsor a particular organization for collective bargaining. In the case of a controversy between competing unions, employers must remain strictly neutral, unless they already have a union-shop agreement in force with one of them. This section of the law was violated when it was agreed that an employee representative plan could not be amended if the employer disapproved. Such control of the form and structure of the employeees' representative committee deprived them of the guaranteed freedom from control by their employer. It is an unfair labor practice for the employer to support a union by giving it a meeting place, providing refreshments for union meetings, permitting the union to use the employer's telephone, secretary, or copying machine, or allowing the union to keep cafeteria or vending-machine profits.

An employer's agreement to pay initiation fees and dues to a union for member employees is in violation when it is an inducement to join the union. This provision also prevents an employer from recognizing or bargaining with a union before it wins an election if there are two or more rival unions. Even when there is only one union, the employer is in violation by bargaining with it if it does not represent a majority of the employees.

## 6.   Discrimination for Union Affiliation

Under provisions designed to prevent the third unfair labor practice, an employer may neither discharge nor refuse to hire an employee either to encourage or discourage membership in any labor organization. Nor may the employer discriminate regarding any term or condition of employment for such purposes. Thus, discrimination on account of union affiliation concerning wages, hours, work assignments, promotions, vacations, and the like is also forbidden. The law does not oblige an employer to favor union members in hiring employees. It also does not restrict him or her in the normal exercise of any employer's right to select or discharge employees. However, the employer may not abuse that right by discriminatory action based on union membership or activities which encourages or discourages membership in a labor organization. A company may not go partially out of business because some of its employees have organized, nor may it temporarily close that portion of its business that has unionized. If a company closes one plant because a union is voted in, such action discourages union activity at other plants. Partial closings to "chill" unionism are unfair labor practices.

Many other examples of discrimination against union members and especially union leaders exist. In one example, a collective-bargaining agreement contained a no-strike clause, but there was no provision requiring union officials to prevent illegal work stoppages. When union members and leaders refused to cross a picket line (established by a different union), the company suspended employees who were union members for five to ten days. The employees who were union leaders were suspended twenty-five days. The court held that the employer violated Section 8(a)(3) of the Wagner Act. To justify the more severe punishment imposed upon union leaders, there must be an affirmative duty that these leaders prevent illegal work stoppages. Since the contract contained no such duty, the company's action was discriminatory on the basis of an employee's union activity.

In cases such as these, the terms of the collective-bargaining agreement are very important. The union may agree to harsher penalties for union officials as a part of the bargaining process. For example, a wildcat strike was conducted in violation of a collective-bargaining agreement. A union official was suspended for ten days while the rank and file strikers were only suspended for five days. This was not an unfair labor practice. A contract may allow for selective discipline of union officials. The parties to a collective-bargaining agreement may seek to increase the effectiveness of a no-strike clause by providing for heightened efforts on the part of union officials to avoid or reduce the disruptive effects of strikes during the contract term. Provision of harsher penalties for union officials who disobey these duties may spur union officials to honor those duties. Allowing the parties to give effect to such contractual terms furthers the strong national labor policy of substituting peaceful dispute resolution for industrial strife and the equally strong policy of freedom of contract.

## 7.   Discrimination: NLRB Proceedings

Under provisions to prevent the fourth unfair labor practice, employees are protected from being discharged or from other reprisals by their employers because they have sought to enforce their rights under the act. This prevents the NLRB's channels of information from being dried up by employers' intimidation of complainants and witnesses. An employer cannot refuse to hire a prospective employee because charges have been filed by him or her. Although supervisors are not regarded as "employees" within the meaning of the act, they have been held to be protected from discharge or reprisal for testifying in a labor proceeding.

The main defense of any employer accused of reprisal is that he or she discharged or discriminated against the employee for some reason other than filing charges or giving testimony. Thus, most often such cases boil down to trying to prove what motivated the company in pursuing its course of action. If the company can convince the NLRB that the employee was discharged because of misconduct, low production, personnel cutbacks necessitated by economic conditions, or other legitimate considerations, the company will be exonerated. Otherwise, it will be found guilty of this unfair labor practice. Please refer to the discussion in section 4 of this chapter which deals with discharge and other forms of retaliation which constitute violations of the first unfair labor practice provision. Many cases violate more than one provision. Most cases involving the fourth category also involve the first.

## 8.   The Duty to Bargain Collectively in Good Faith

It is now an unfair labor practice for both an employer and the representatives of employees to refuse to bargain collectively with each other. The Wagner Act did not define the term "to bargain collectively." Judicial decisions have added the concept "good faith" to it, so that it actually means to bargain in good faith. Thus, although an employer need not agree to any union demands, such conduct as the failure to make counterproposals to union demands may be evidence of bad faith. To comply with the requirement that they bargain collectively in good faith, employers and unions must approach the bargaining table with fair and open minds and a sincere purpose to find a basis of agreement. Refusing to meet at reasonable times with representatives of the other party, refusing to reduce agreements to writing, and designating persons with no authority to negotiate as representatives at meetings are examples of this unfair labor practice. The employer's duty to bargain collectively includes a duty to provide relevant information needed by a union for the proper performance of its duties as the employees' bargaining representative. For example, data about chemicals used by employees must be furnished so that the union and its members are aware of dangers to health. Companies cannot refuse to provide unions with job-related nonproprietary safety and health information that does not disclose personal medical records. The union has an obligation to safeguard its members' health and safety.

A more fundamental issue than good faith is also inherent in the requirement that parties bargain collectively. That issue, simply stated, is: "About what?" Must the employer bargain with the union about all subjects and all management decisions in which the union or the employees are interested? Are there subjects and issues upon which management is allowed to act unilaterally?

In answering these questions, the law divides issues into two categories—**compulsory-bargaining issues** and **voluntary-bargaining issues.** Compulsory or mandatory bargaining issues are those concerned with wages, hours, and other terms and conditions of employment. Although the parties may voluntarily consider other issues, the refusal by either to bargain in good faith on such other permissive matters is not an unfair labor practice. Nor is it an unfair labor practice to refuse to bargain over the rights of former employees. For example, an employer eliminated medical benefits to retired workers when Medicare became effective. The union demanded to negotiate. This was not a mandatory bargaining issue. If a matter does not affect employees in a working relationship, it will be a mandatory issue of bargaining only if it vitally affects the terms and conditions of employment for those working.

In recent years, one of the most difficult legal issues in labor-management relations has been the impact on collective-bargaining contracts of bankruptcy proceedings. Employers frequently seek reorganization under Section 11 of the bankruptcy laws. Since collective-bargaining agreements are "executory contracts," the bankruptcy code permits a debtor in possession of its estate or the trustee in bankruptcy to modify or cancel such contracts. The Supreme Court in 1984 in a five-to-four decision held that an employer could unilaterally cancel collective-bargaining agreements and change the wage structure of its employees without committing an unfair labor practice. The Supreme Court decision holding that a unilateral rejection or modification of a labor contract is not an unfair labor practice has been on the premise that such a rejection is a necessary part of reorganization. The dissenting justices believe that the duty to bargain collectively prohibits termination or modification unless the union is given timely notice, there is an order to meet and confer, and the agreement continues for sixty days after notice.

Subsequent to this decision, Congress has amended the bankruptcy laws to give more protection to workers. The law now requires employers filing for bankruptcy to have court approval before they repudiate a labor contract. As a result, employers seeking reorganization may unilaterally change the terms of their collective-bargaining agreement only with court approval. The terms of labor contracts remain compulsory bargaining issues. Courts before approving a petition to modify or reject a labor contract will require reasonable efforts to negotiate a voluntary modification and proof that collective bargaining cannot produce a prompt and satisfactory solution to the problem.

Classifying an issue as *compulsory* or *voluntary* is done on a case-by-case basis. For example, questions relating to fringe benefits are compulsory bargaining issues because they are "wages." The NLRB and the courts are called on to decide whether management and labor must bargain with each other on a multitude of issues, as the case which follows illustrates.

# FORD MOTOR COMPANY v. N.L.R.B.
99 S.Ct. 1842 (1979)

The petitioner, Ford Motor Company, provided its employees with in-plant cafeteria and vending-machine services. The services were managed by an independent caterer, ARA, but the petitioner had the right to review and approve the quality, quantity, and prices of the food served. When petitioner notified respondent union, which represents the employees, that the cafeteria and vending-machine prices were to be increased, the union requested bargaining over the prices and services. Petitioner refused to bargain, and the union then filed an unfair labor practice charge with the National Labor Relations Board, alleging a refusal to bargain contrary to § 8(a)(5) of the National Labor Relations Act (NLRA). Taking the view that in-plant food prices and services are "other terms and conditions of employment," the NLRB sustained the charge and ordered petitioner to bargain. The Court of Appeals enforced the order, and the Supreme Court granted certiorari.

WHITE, J.:...Because the "classification of bargaining subjects as 'terms or conditions of employment' is a matter concerning which the Board has special expertise," its judgment as to what is a mandatory bargaining subject is entitled to considerable deference....

Of course, the judgment of the Board is subject to judicial review; but if its construction of the statute is reasonably defensible, it should not be rejected merely because the courts might prefer another view of the statute....

Construing and applying the duty to bargain and the language of § 8(d), "other terms and conditions of employment," are tasks lying at the heart of the Board's function. With all due respect to the courts of appeals that have held otherwise, we conclude that the Board's consistent view that in-plant food prices and services are mandatory bargaining subjects is not an unreasonable or unprincipled construction of the statute and that it should be accepted and enforced.

It is not suggested by petitioner that an employee should work a full 8-hour shift without stopping to eat. It reasonably follows that the availability of food during working hours and the conditions under which it is to be consumed are matters of deep concern to workers, and one need not strain to consider them to be among those "conditions" of employment that should be subject to the mutual duty to bargain. By the same token, where the employer has chosen, apparently in his own interest, to make available a system of in-plant feeding facilities for his employees, the prices at which food is offered and other aspects of this service may reasonably be considered among those subjects about which management and union must bargain. The terms and conditions under which food is available on the job are plainly germane to the "working environment." Furthermore, the company is not in the business of selling food to its employees, and the establishment of in-plant food prices is not among those "managerial decisions, which lie at the core of entrepreneurial control." The Board is in no sense attempting to permit the Union to usurp managerial decisionmaking; nor is it seeking to regulate an area from which Congress intended to exclude it....

As illustrated by the facts of this case, substantial disputes can arise over the pricing of in-plant supplied food and beverages. National labor policy contemplates that areas of common dispute between employers and employees be funneled into collective bargaining. The assumption is that this is preferable to allowing recurring disputes to fester outside the negotiation process until strikes or other forms of economic warfare occur.

The trend of industrial practice supports this conclusion. In response to increasing employee concern over the issue, many contracts are now being negotiated that contain provisions concerning in-plant food services....Although not conclusive, current industrial practice is highly relevant in construing the phrase "terms and conditions of employment."

Ford nevertheless argues against classifying food prices and services as mandatory bargaining subjects because they do not "vitally affect" the terms and conditions of employment within the meaning of the standard assertedly established by *Allied Chemical*

*and Alkali Workers v. Pittsburgh Plate Glass Co.*, and because they are trivial matters over which neither party should be required to bargain.

There is no merit to either of these arguments. First, Ford has misconstrued *Pittsburgh Plate Glass*. That case made it clear that while § 8(d) normally reaches "only issues that settle an aspect of the relationship between the employer and employees... matters involving individuals outside the employment relationship...are not wholly excluded."...As for the argument that in-plant food prices and service are too trivial to qualify as mandatory subjects, the Board has a contrary view, and we have no basis for rejecting it. It is also clear that the bargaining-unit employees in this case considered the matter far from trivial since they pressed an unsuccessful boycott to secure a voice in setting food prices. They evidently felt, and common sense also tells us, that even minor increases in the cost of meals can amount to a substantial sum of money over time....

Ford also argues that the Board's position will result in unnecessary disruption because any small change in price or service will trigger the obligation to bargain. The problem it is said, will be particularly acute in situations where several unions are involved, possibly requiring endless rounds of negotiations over issues as minor as the price of a cup of coffee or a soft drink....

The Board apparently assumes that, as a practical matter, requests to bargain will not be lightly made. Moreover, problems created by constantly shifting food prices can be anticipated and provided for in the collective-bargaining agreement. Furthermore, if it is true that disputes over food prices are likely to be frequent and intense, it follows that more, not less, collective bargaining is the remedy. This is the assumption of national labor policy, and it is soundly supported by both reason and experience.

Finally, Ford asserts that to require it to engage in bargaining over in-plant food service prices would be futile because those prices are set by a third-party supplier, ARA. It is true that ARA sets vending machine and cafeteria prices, but under Ford's contract with ARA, Ford retains the right to review and control food services and prices. In any event, an employer can always affect prices by initiating or altering a subsidy to the third-party supplier such as that pro-

vided by Ford in this case, and will typically have the right to change suppliers at some point in the future. To this extent the employer holds future, if not present, leverage over in-plant food services and prices.

We affirm, therefore, the Court of Appeals' judgment upholding the Board's determination in this case that in-plant food services and prices are "terms and conditions of employment" subject to the mandatory bargaining under § 8(a)(5) and 8(d) of the National Labor Relations Act. [*Affirmed.*]

---

A party to labor negotiations may present a demand relating to a nonmandatory bargaining issue as long as its resolution is not a condition precedent to the resolution of mandatory bargaining issues. Tying a voluntary bargaining issue to a compulsory bargaining issue results in a failure to bargain in good faith and is in effect an unfair labor practice.

Courts tend to defer to the special expertise of the NLRB in classifying collective-bargaining subjects, especially in the area of "terms or conditions of employment." The courts have affirmed Board rulings holding that issues such as union dues checkoff, health and accident insurance, safety rules, merit pay increases, incentive-pay plans, Christmas and other bonuses, stock purchase plans, pensions, paid vacations and holidays, the privilege of hunting on a reserved portion of a paper company's forest preserve, proposals for effective arbitration and grievance procedures, and no-strike and no-lockout clauses are compulsory-bargaining issues. Industry practice is a major factor in many decisions.

The Board has recently changed its policy on the issue of whether the employer can unilaterally transfer operations from a unionized facility to an unorganized facility during the term of a collective-bargaining agreement. In 1982, the Board held that a unilateral transfer is an unfair labor practice. In 1984, the Board held that an employer does not violate the Wagner Act by relocating the work of a bargaining unit without the union's consent so long as the employer is willing to bargain in good faith over the proposed change. An employer may not unilaterally institute changes before reaching a good-faith impasse in bargaining. Although an employer may not modify the terms and conditions of the contract without the union's consent, if the contract does not specifically prohibit the change, then the only obligation is to bargain in good faith on the issue.

Remember that neither the employer nor the union is required to make concessions to the other concerning a mandatory subject of bargaining. The law only demands that each negotiate such matters in good faith with the other before making a decision and taking unilateral action. If the parties fail to reach an agreement after discussing these problems, each may take steps which are against the wishes and best interests of the other party. For example, the employer may refuse to grant a wage increase requested by the union, and the union is free to strike.

### 9. Agreeing with a Union to Engage in a Secondary Boycott

The unfair labor practice by employers of agreeing with a union to engage in a **secondary boycott** was not one forbidden under the Wagner Act. Moreover secondary boycotts were and are legal under the Railway Labor Act. Taft-Hartley attempted to limit the use by unions subject to its provisions of the secondary boycott as an indirect weapon in a campaign to organize employees. It was an unfair labor practice for a union to induce the *employees* of an employer to strike, or engage in a concerted refusal to use, handle, or work on any goods or to perform any services, in order to force the employer to stop doing business with any other person. For example, assume that employer A sells supplies to manufacturer B, which are transported by trucking firm C, whose employees are nonunion. This Taft-Hartley provision makes it illegal for either a union attempting to organize the employees of C or the union representing the employees of A to induce the employees of A to strike or refuse to load C's trucks with supplies in order to require A to stop shipping its goods by C. This represents a swing of the pendulum back from the Norris-LaGuardia Act's and the Railway Labor Act's liberalization of the use of secondary boycotts toward the policy of the law as it existed before those acts. Then, secondary boycotts were viewed as illegal combinations in restraint of trade under the Sherman Act or as illegal conspiracies under the common law.

Taft-Hartley, however, was not successful in eliminating all secondary boycotts. Loopholes appeared in its proscriptions. For example, a **hot-cargo contract** in which an *employer* voluntarily agrees with a union not to handle, use, or deal in non-union-produced goods of another person, was held to be legal. The union was prevented only from inducing the *employees* of the employer to strike or otherwise act to force their employer not to handle such goods. The Landrum-Griffin Act plugged this loophole and outlawed hot-cargo contracts and participation in secondary boycotts. Its amendment to Taft-Hartley made it an unfair labor practice for any labor organization and any *employer* to enter into any contract or agreement whereby such employer agrees to refrain from handling, using, selling, transporting, or otherwise dealing in any of the products of any other employer, or to cease doing business with any other person. The secondary boycott provisions as they pertain to unions are discussed further in section 11 of this chapter.

# UNFAIR LABOR PRACTICES BY UNIONS

## 10.   Introduction

The Wagner Act did not contain any provisions relating to unfair labor practices by labor unions. It was, in effect, one-sided. The Taft-Hartley Act covered the missing side by declaring that certain conduct or activities by labor unions also were unfair labor practices and thus illegal. Six such activities were specified. The Landrum-Griffin Act in 1959 added two additional unfair labor practices by unions to those declared illegal by the Taft-Hartley Act.

Table 18-2 summarizes the actions and omissions by unions which are unfair labor practices:

**TABLE 18-2**   Unfair Labor Practices by Unions

1   Restraining or coercing an employee to join a union or an employer in selecting representatives to bargain with the union
2   Causing or attempting to cause the employer to discriminate against an employee who is not a union member, unless there is a legal union-shop agreement in effect
3   Refusing to bargain with the employer if it is the NLRB-designated representative of the employees
4   Striking, picketing, and engaging in secondary boycotts for illegal purposes
5   Charging new members excessive or discriminatory initiation fees when there is a union-shop agreement
6   Causing an employer to pay for work not performed ("**featherbedding**")
7   Picketing to require an employer to recognize or bargain with a union which is not currently certified as representing its employees in certain cases
8   Agreeing with an employer to engage in a secondary boycott

Numbers 1, 4, 5, 7, and 8 are discussed in subsequent sections. (Number 3 is the union duty to bargain in good faith. It was discussed in section 8 with the same duty of employers.) The second unfair practice by unions recognizes that if a legal union-shop agreement is in effect, a labor organization may insist that the employer observe its terms.

## 11.   Restraining or Coercing an Employee into Joining a Union

This unfair labor practice includes misconduct by unions directed toward employees and employers. Also forbidden are any attempts by a union to influence an employer in selecting its representatives to bargain with the union. Most allegations of unfair labor practices filed against unions are brought under this provision. The law makes it illegal for a union to restrain or coerce employees in the exercise of their rights to bargain collectively, just as it is an unfair labor practice by employers to interfere with the same rights. Employees also are guaranteed the right to *refrain* from union activities unless required by a legal union-shop agreement in force between their employer and a labor organization. In the following case, the employer refused to bargain with a union which had won a representation election on the grounds that prior to the election the union had violated this provision.

# N.L.R.B. v. SAVAIR MANUFACTURING COMPANY
94 S.Ct. 495 (1973)

DOUGLAS, J.: The National Labor Relations Board...conducted an election by secret ballot among the production and maintenance employees of respondent at the request of the Mechanics Educational Society of America (the Union)....The Union won the election by a vote of 22–20.

Respondent filed objections to the election, but...the Board certified the Union as the representative of the employees in that unit. Respondent, however, refused to bargain. The Union thereupon filed an unfair labor practice charge...alleging that respondent had violated § 8(a)(1) and (5) of the Act. The Board sustained the allegations and ordered respondent to bargain with the Union. The Court of Appeals denied enforcement of the order....

It appeared that prior to the election, "recognition slips" were circulated among employees. An employee who signed the slip before the election became a member of the union and would not have to pay what at times was called an "initiation fee" and at times a "fine." If the Union was voted in, those who had not signed a recognition slip would have to pay....Under the by-laws of the Union, an initiation fee apparently was

not to be higher than $10; but the employees who testified at the hearing (1) did not know how large the fee would be and (2) said that their understanding was that the fee was a "fine" or an "assessment."

One employee, Donald Bridgeman, testified that he signed the slip to avoid paying the "fine" if the union won. He got the message directly from an employee picked by the union to solicit signatures on the "slips." So did Thomas Rice, another employee....

Whatever his true intentions, an employee who signs a recognition slip prior to an election is indicating to other workers that he supports the Union. His outward manifestation of support must often serve as a useful campaign tool in the Union's hands to convince other employees to vote for the Union, if only because many employees respect their co-workers' views on the unionization issue. By permitting the Union to offer to waive an initiation fee for those employees signing a recognition slip prior to the election, the Board allows the Union to buy endorsements and paint a false portrait of employee support during its election campaign.

That influence may well have been felt

here for, as noted, there were 28 who signed up with the Union before the election petition was filed with the Board and either seven or eight more who signed up before the election. We do not believe that the statutory policy of fair elections…permits endorsements, whether for or against the Union, to be bought and sold in this fashion.

In addition, while it is correct that the employee who signs a recognition slip is not legally bound to vote for the Union and has not promised to do so in any formal sense, certainly there may be some employees who would feel obligated to carry through on their stated intention to support the Union. And on the facts of this case, the change of just one vote would have resulted in a 21–21 election rather than a 22–20 election.

Any procedure requiring a "fair" election must honor the right of those who oppose a union as well as those who favor it. The Act is wholly neutral when it comes to that basic choice. By § 7 of the Act employees have the right not only to "form, join, or assist" unions but also the right "to refrain from any or all of such activities." An employer who promises to increase the fringe benefits by $10 for each employee who votes

against the union, if the union wins the election, would cross the forbidden line under our decisions.…

The Board in its supervision of union elections may not sanction procedures that cast their weight for the choice of a union and against a nonunion shop or for a nonunion shop and against a union.

In the *Exchange Parts* case we said that although the benefits granted by the employer were permanent and unconditional, employees were "not likely to miss the inference that the source of benefits now conferred is also the source from which future benefits must flow and which may dry up if it is not obliged." If we respect, as we must, the statutory right of employees to resist efforts to unionize a plant, we cannot assume that unions exercising powers are wholly benign towards their antagonists whether they be nonunion protagonists or the employer. The failure to sign a recognition slip may well seem ominous to nonunionists who fear that if they do not sign they will face a wrathful union regime, should the union win. That influence may well have had a decisive impact in this case where a change of one vote would have changed the result. [*Affirmed.*]

---

The second part of this provision prohibits a union from restraining or coercing an employer in the selection of its representatives for collective bargaining. The provision is violated if a union refuses to bargain with a proper representative of the employer and yet threatens a strike if bargaining does not succeed. However, if a strike called by a union is for economic purposes to obtain certain contractual terms and is not based on the refusal to deal with the employer's representative, the strike is not considered to be coercion of the employer.

Union fines levied against union-member supervisors sometimes run afoul of this provision. If a union were able to retaliate against supervisors who negotiate with the union or take part in grievance proceedings, management would be coerced in the selection of its representatives. However, supervisors who are not engaged in collective bargaining, grievance adjust ment, or some other closely related activity such as contract interpretation are still subject to union discipline and fines. Union discipline is an unfair labor practice only when it may adversely affect the supervisor's future conduct in performing labor-management related duties, and only when the supervisor is disciplined for behavior while he or she performs such duties. An employer is not restrained or coerced in the selection of its representatives because a union member must accept union expulsion or other discipline to continue in a supervisory position. Since union members have a right to resign from a union at any time and avoid imposition of union discipline, the employer may require that its representatives leave the union.

### 12. Causing an Employer To Discriminate Against a Nonunion Member

As noted in the prior chapter, the Taft-Hartley Act made union-security contracts calling for a closed shop illegal, even if both employer and employees are in favor of one. However, if a legal union-shop agreement is in effect, a labor organization may insist that the employer observe its terms. But even when a legal union-shop contract is in effect, the law prohibits a union from attempting to cause an employer to discriminate against an employee who has been denied membership or had his or her membership terminated for some reason other than failure to pay the dues and initiation fees uniformly required of all members. And, even if an employee is a member, the union may not cause the employer to discriminate against him or her for not following union rules. This prohibition was designed to prevent the use of the union shop as a means of intimidating employees who were at odds with union officials over their policies.

### 13. Secondary Boycotts and Other Illegal Strikes and Picketing

It is an unfair labor practice for a union to threaten, coerce, or restrain third persons not parties to a labor dispute for the purpose of causing the third person to cease using, selling, handling, transporting, or otherwise dealing in the products of any other producer, or to cease doing business with any other person. The purpose of this law restricting most strikes and picketing to the employer with which the union actually has a labor dispute, protects neutral parties from serious economic injury or even ruin.

Activities such as passing out handbills may be legal because they are not considered as coercive as picketing. The case which follows allowed some pressure on neutral but interested third parties by unions.

# DeBARTOLO CORP. v. FLA. GULF COAST BLDG. & CONST.
108 S.Ct. 1392 (1988)

DeBartolo Corp. operates a shopping mall in Tampa, Florida. The High Construction Company (High) was building a department store in the mall for Wilson, one of 85 mall tenants. A union had a dispute with High over alleged substandard wages and fringe benefits. In order to encourage the other mall businesses to influence the conduct of Wilson and High, the union distributed handbills asking mall customers not to shop at any of the stores in the mall "until the Mall's owner publicly promises that all construction at the Mall will be done using contractors who pay their employees fair wages and fringe benefits." The handbills' message was that "the payment of substandard wages not only diminishes the working person's ability to purchase with earned, rather than borrowed, dollars, but it also undercuts the wage standard of the entire community." The handbills made clear that the union was seeking a consumer boycott against the other mall tenants, not a secondary strike by their employees. The union peacefully distributed the handbills without any accompanying picketing or patrolling.

DeBartolo filed a complaint alleging that the Union was guilty of violating § 8(b)(4)(ii)B which forbids a union to "threaten, coerce, or restrain" any person to cease doing business with another person. The NLRB upheld the complaint but the Court of Appeals reversed.

WHITE, J.:...The case turns on whether handbilling such as involved here must be held to "threaten, coerce, or restrain any person" to cease doing business with another, within the meaning of § 8(b)(4)(ii)(B). We note first that "inducing or encourag-

ing" employees of the secondary employer to strike is proscribed by § 8(b)(4)(i). But more than mere persuasion is necessary to prove a violation of § 8(b)(4)(ii): that section requires a showing of threats, coercion, or restraints.

There is no suggestion that the leaflets had any coercive effect on customers of the mall. There was no violence, picketing, or patrolling and only an attempt to persuade customers not to shop in the mall.

The Board nevertheless found that the handbilling "coerced" mall tenants and explained in a footnote that "appealing to the public not to patronize secondary employers is an attempt to inflict economic harm on the secondary employers by causing them to lose business. As the case law makes clear, such appeals constitute 'economic retaliation' and are therefore a form of coercion." Our decision in *Tree Fruits,* however, makes untenable the notion that *any* kind of handbilling, picketing, or other appeals to a secondary employer to cease doing business with the employer involved in the labor dispute is "coercion" within the meaning of § 8(b)(4)(ii)(B) if it has some economic impact on the neutral. In that case, the union picketed a secondary employer, a retailer, asking the public not to buy a product produced by the primary employer. We held that the impact of this picketing was not coercion within the meaning of § 8(b)(4) even though, if the appeal succeeded, the retailer would lose revenue.

*NLRB v. Retail Store Employees,* 100 S.Ct. 2372, (1980) (*Safeco*), in turn, held that consumer picketing urging a general boycott of a secondary employer aimed at causing him to sever relations with the union's real antagonist was coercive and forbidden by § 8(b)(4). It is urged that *Safeco* rules this case because the union sought a general boycott of all tenants in the mall. But picketing is qualitatively different from other modes of communication, and *Safeco* noted that the picketing there actually threatened the neutral with ruin or substantial loss. As Justice STEVENS pointed out in his concurrence in *Safeco*, picketing is "a mixture of conduct and communication" and the conduct element "often provides the most persuasive deterrent to third persons about to enter a business establishment." Handbills containing the same message, he observed, are "much less effective than labor picketing" because they "depend entirely on the persuasive force of the idea."...

In *Tree Fruits*, we could not discern with the "requisite clarity" that Congress intended to proscribe all peaceful consumer picketing at secondary sites. There is even less reason to find in the language of § 8(b)(4)(ii), standing alone, any clear indication that handbilling, without picketing, "coerces" secondary employers. The loss of customers because they read a handbill urging them not to patronize a business, and not because they are intimidated by a line of picketers, is the result of mere persuasion, and the neutral who reacts is doing no more than what its customers honestly want it to do....

The Board's reading of § 8(b)(4) would make an unfair labor practice out of any kind of publicity or communication to the public urging a consumer boycott of employers other than those (with whom the union has a primary dispute). On the facts of this case, newspaper, radio, and television appeals not to patronize the mall would be prohibited; and it would be an unfair labor practice for unions in their own meetings to urge their members not to shop in the mall. Nor could a union's handbills simply urge not shopping at a department store because it is using a nonunion contractor, although the union could safely ask the store's customers not to buy there because it is selling mattresses not carrying the union label. It is difficult, to say the least, to fathom why Congress would consider appeals urging a boycott of a distributor of a nonunion product to be more deserving of protection than nonpicketing persuasion of customers of other neutral employers such as that involved in this case.

Neither do we find any clear indication in the relevant legislative history that Congress intended § 8(b)(4)(ii) to proscribe peaceful handbilling, unaccompanied by picketing, urging a consumer boycott of a neutral employer....

In our view, interpreting § 8(b)(4) as not reaching the handbilling involved in this case is not foreclosed either by the language of the section or its legislative history.... [*Affirmed.*]

---

Another example of illegal secondary activity occurs when a union induces the employees of an employer to strike or engage in a concerted refusal to use, handle, or work on any goods or to perform any services, to force the employer to stop doing business with some third person. As previously noted, if employer A sells supplies to manufacturer B, which are transported by trucking firm C, whose employees are nonunion, it is illegal for either a union attempting to organize the employees of C or the union representing the employees of A to induce the employees of A to strike or refuse to load C's trucks with supplies to require A to stop shipping its goods by C. Similarly, it is forbidden for the union of X's employees in the course of a dispute with X to induce any employees of Y to strike to coerce Y to stop buying the products of X. Likewise, it would be a violation for the union of X's employees to induce them not to work on goods produced by "scab" labor at the nonunion plant of Z, to induce X to use union-made goods instead.

It is also an unfair labor practice for both the employer involved and the union to enter into a hot-cargo contract. A hot-cargo contract is one in which an employer voluntarily agrees with a union that the employees should not be required by their employer to handle or work on goods or materials going to, or coming from, an employer designated by the union as "unfair." Such goods are said to be "hot cargo." These clauses were common in trucking and construction. The law thus forbids an employer and a labor organization to make an agreement whereby the employer agrees to stop doing business with any other employer.

It is also an unfair labor practice for a union to threaten or to coerce an employer to recognize or bargain with one union if another one has been certified as the representative of its employees. This provision was made to protect employers (and their employees) from the destructive rivalry between unions competing to be the bargaining representative of employees in a unit where they had already chosen one.

Jurisdictional strikes are also unfair labor practices. A jurisdictional strike is one forcing an employer to assign work to employees in one craft union rather than another. Since the dispute is between the two unions and not with the employer, the law requires that such disputes be submitted to the NLRB by the unions. Note that it is not a violation for a union certified by the Board to represent the employees performing the particular work involved to force the employer to assign it to them.

## 14. Requiring Employees to Pay Excessive Fees

The unfair labor practice of requiring employees to pay excessive fees was included in the law to protect employees who were required to join a union as a condition of employment by reason of a union-shop agreement. It prohibits the charging of an excessive or discriminatory initiation fee as a requirement of becoming a member of the union.

Since the employees (especially *new* employees) have no choice about membership and no bargaining power, the law requires that the dues and fees be reasonable and not discriminatory. For example, in one case a union raised its initiation fee to $500 from the former $50 for all new employees who received a certain minimum starting salary. This fee was held to be excessive and discriminatory.

## 15.   Causing an Employer to Pay for Work Not Performed

Designating the unfair labor practice of requiring an employer to pay for work that is not performed as illegal was meant to prevent featherbedding. It is quite limited in actual operation. The issue is: What are "services not performed or not to be performed"? Make-work rules have been approved by the courts as being outside the prohibition of this provision. It is not violated as long as some services are performed, even if they are of little or no actual value to the employer. In one such case, the Supreme Court held that it was permissible for a musicians' union to require a theater to employ a local orchestra to play overtures at intermissions as a condition of its consent to local appearances of traveling big-name bands. And in another decision, the Court approved the insistence by a union that newspaper publishers who used advertising mats as molds for metal castings from which to print advertisements pay union printers for setting up in type duplicates of these advertisements. The payments were found to be for work actually done, in spite of the fact that the duplicates were not used and ordinarily were just melted down.

## 16.   Picketing When Not Certified

The seventh provision makes it illegal for union picketing to require an employer to recognize or bargain with the union if it is not currently certified as the duly authorized collective-bargaining representative, in certain cases. The purpose is to reinforce the effectiveness of the election procedures employed by the NLRB by outlawing certain tactics used by unions backed by only a minority of the employees of a particular employer. Thus, picketing to force an employer to recognize an uncertified union has become illegal in the following cases:

**1**   When the employer lawfully has recognized another union as the collective-bargaining representative of its employees

**2**   When a valid representation election has been conducted by the NLRB within the past twelve months

**3**   When picketing has been conducted for a reasonable time, not in excess of thirty days, without a petition for a representation election being filed with the NLRB

Under item 3, however, the act does not prohibit so-called "informational" picketing. That is, picketing or publicity to truthfully advise the public (including consumers) that an employer has a nonunion business is not prohibited, unless the effect of the picketing is to induce employees of another person to observe the picket line.

Certain kinds of **organizational picketing** have been made unfair by the Landrum-Griffin Act. Before, it was possible for a minority union to picket an employer for recognition as the collective-bargaining representative of its employees, when it was illegal for the employer to accept it as such. Though Congress felt that unions should be able to publicize the fact that certain employers are nonunion, it also felt that unions should not be permitted to attempt to force employers to violate the law. Purely recognitional picketing under the circumstances stated above is illegal. Purely informational picketing probably is legal.

The fact is, however, that often picketing has both purposes. Such dual-purpose picketing under the facts stated in cases 1 or 2 listed above is literally unlawful. However, dual-purpose picketing in case 3 is probably legal unless it inhibits deliveries of goods to the employer being picketed, or the like. Even if it does, the NLRB has ruled that such interruptions must be substantial enough to curtail the employer's business. The rules concerning the application of this provision of the statute have not been clearly enunciated by the NLRB (which has taken several positions) or the courts.

This part of the act also prohibits picketing by an uncertified union (in the situations enumerated) in order to force the *employees* of an employer to select that union as their collective-bargaining representative. When a charge of a violation is filed and there is reasonable cause to believe it is true, the proper officer of the Board must seek a temporary injunction restraining further violation until the NLRB disposes of the matter.

## 17. The Union's Duty of Fair Representation

None of the federal labor laws contains an *express* provision which requires a union to fairly represent the employees in a collective-bargaining unit after it has been certified as their exclusive bargaining representative. However, Supreme Court rulings have imposed an *implied* duty of fair representation on unions under both the Railway Labor Act and the National Labor Relations Act. Section 9(a) of the NLRA states the "Representatives designated or selected for the purposes of collective bargaining by the *majority* of the employees in a unit appropriate for such purposes, shall be the *exclusive* representative of *all* the employees in such unit for the purposes of collective bargaining in respect to rates of pay, wages, hours of employment, or other conditions of employment...." [*Emphasis added.*] A similar provision is found in the Railway Labor Act. Thus, bargaining by a single employee with the employer concerning that employee's terms or conditions of employment is not permitted, even if the employee voted against the union. Collectively-bargained agreements, through the union and for the benefit of the group, are substituted by the act for employment contracts negotiated separately by individual employees. Because of the union's position as the *exclusive* representative, the Supreme Court has reasoned that the union must exercise fairly the power given it by statute on behalf of all for whom it acts.

In negotiating a collective-bargaining agreement with the employer, the union has an implied "duty of fair representation" to act reasonably, with honesty of purpose, and in good faith. The union can prove that it has met this duty by showing that its motives in settling for the terms in the contract which finally results have not been improper. The union is required to represent all the employees in the bargaining unit, including those who are nonunion, impartially and without hostile discrimination. A union has a great deal of discretion in bargaining and may work to obtain different terms for different employees or subgroups of employees, provided it does not have an improper motive for doing so.

The duty of fair representation not only applies to the *negotiation* of a collective-bargaining agreement, but also to the *administration* of the agreement while it is in effect. That is, unions must also fairly represent employees in disputes with the employer regarding the *interpretation* and *application* of the terms of an existing contract. The law does not grant unions the same exclusive power in the processing of grievances as it does in negotiating contracts. Section 9(a) of the NLRA states that: "any individual employee or a group of employees shall have the right at any time to present grievances to their employer and to have such grievances adjusted, without the intervention of the bargaining representative, as long as the adjustment is not inconsistent with the terms of a collective bargaining contract...then in effect: *Provided...*, that the bargaining representative has been given an opportunity to be present at such adjustment." However, most collective-bargaining agreements provide that the union has final control over their grievance-arbitration processes.

An employee may file suit in state court against the union and its representatives for damages resulting from breach of their duty of fair representation in processing his or her grievance against the employer. Unions must act honestly and in good faith in processing grievances as well as in negotiating collective-bargaining agreements. A union may not process a grievance in an arbitrary, indifferent, or careless manner. For example, failure to investigate a grievance probably would be arbitrary. However, even if a union violates its duty of fair representation, the damages attributable solely to the employer's breach of contract are its sole responsibility and are not charged to the union. The union is liable to the employee only for increases (if any) in those damages caused by its refusal to process the grievance. Thus, the award assessed against it may not be substantial. Some authorities feel that the current labor laws do not provide penalties severe enough to deter unions from breaching their duty of fair representation.

The cases in which unions have been found guilty of breaching the duty of fair representation include failing to file a grievance of an employee within the time permitted by a collective-bargaining agreement; failing to present all available evidence in favor of an employee's case; and failure to notify the employee of the time of an arbitration hearing, knowing that no other witnesses would testify in his or her behalf.

# REVIEW QUESTIONS

**1**  A firm parks a cart filled with groceries in the area where employees are casting ballots against the union. Is this an unfair labor practice? Why or why not?

**2**  A company representative orders an employee to remove his van from an employee parking lot unless he removes from the side of the van a 4-foot by 6-foot sign endorsing a candidate for president of the union local. The company has a rule which prohibits on company property vehicles displaying "any type of large sign or banner, political or otherwise." Vehicles with bumper stickers, window stickers, or similar ornamentation or devices commonly displayed on automobiles are allowed. Did the company commit an unfair labor practice? Why or why not?

**3**  Union members select a new chairman. The employer notifies the new chairman that he will not be allowed the same privileges that had been granted the former chairman. Among the privileges taken are four hours of paid time per day to conduct union business. Is this change of policy an unfair labor practice? Why or why not?

**4**  Two months after the conclusion of a union strike against a country club, the club's president invites the regular, full-time employees who had worked during the strike to an "appreciation party." The work schedules of at least three employees are adjusted so that they can attend the party. Employees who participated in the strike, and therefore are not invited, work for the club at the party, which cost approximately $4,000. Is the club guilty of an unfair labor practice? Why or why not?

**5**  An airline treats union flight attendants who worked during a strike more favorably than those who stayed on strike. In addition, trainees are given job preference over employees with more seniority. Are these unfair labor practices? Why or why not?

**6**  Sally, a supervisor for May Candy Company, orders Will, a worker, to come into her office for an interview regarding alleged serious breaches of company rules. Will complies, and when the interview confirms Will's misconduct, he is fired. Will and the union file charges of unfair labor practices with the NLRB against the May Candy Company because a union representative was not present during the interview. What should be the result? Why?

**7**  Burger King issues a ban on its employees' wearing any button on their uniforms. Only items using the Burger King logo can be worn by employees. Some counter employees want to wear union buttons. When they are not allowed to do so, they file a complaint with the NLRB, alleging that an unfair labor practice has been committed. Is the ban on buttons an unfair labor practice? Why or why not?

**8**  Deering Milliken is a holding company for several separately incorporated textile mills. The company informs the workers that if the union wins an NLRB election, the plant will be closed. When the workers vote for union representation, the board of directors liquidates the corporation, sells all plant machinery and equipment, and lays off their entire work force. Is this an unfair labor practice? Why or why not?

**9**  A chemical manufacturer is asked to provide the union representing its employees with the generic names of all substances used and produced at the manufacturer's plant. The union also requests information concerning occupational illness and accident data related to workers' compensation claims. The company refuses to furnish the information. Is this refusal an unfair labor practice? Why or why not?

**10** For many years, the employer gave all employees a Christmas turkey. The practice continued after a union was certified. For economic reasons, the employer decides to cancel the practice. The union alleges that cancellation is an unfair labor practice and that cancellation cannot be unilateral. The turkeys are not mentioned in the collective-bargaining agreement. Is the employer guilty of an unfair labor practice. Why or why not?

**11** A union prevails in an NLRB election. The employer challenges it on the ground that a union agent made threatening statements to employees one hour before the election. The evidence establishes that the union agent said that if anyone helped the employer in a strike, he would be made an example of, and noted that during the last strike an individual who opposed the union was still in the hospital. Should the election be set aside? Why or why not?

**12** Four employees solicit union authorization cards from other employees. They inform those people solicited that union initiation fees will be waived if the cards are signed. Is this a ground for setting aside a union election victory? Explain.

**13** Helton, a waitress at Johnson's restaurant, is fired because of her efforts to organize a union. Later, Helton and others picket the restaurant and distribute leaflets. Johnson files a suit for damages and injunctive relief against Helton in state court. It alleges that Helton had harassed customers, blocked access to the restaurant, created a threat to public safety, and libeled the restaurant by false statements in the leaflets. Is filing the lawsuit in the state court an unfair labor practice which the NLRB can stop? Why or why not?

**14** Safeco Title Insurance Co. underwrites real estate title insurance and does business with several title insurance companies that derive over 90 percent of their gross incomes from the sale of Safeco insurance policies. After contract negotiations between Safeco and the union reached an impasse, the employees go on strike. The union pickets each of the title companies, urging customers to support the strike by canceling their Safeco policies. Is the union's picketing an unfair labor practice? Why or why not?

**15** Ed is discharged for allegedly stealing property from his employer. He asks his union to have him reinstated because his discharge violates the collective-bargaining agreement in force. However, the union does not investigate the incident until it is too late to file a request for arbitration under the collective-bargaining agreement. Assuming that Ed is innocent of the charges, does he have any rights against the union? Explain.

# *Part Six*
# PROTECTING PARTIES TO TRANSACTIONS

# Chapter
## *19*

# Investor Protection

## CHAPTER PREVIEW

Chapter 12 contained a discussion of legal factors that should be considered when creating a business organization. This chapter can be viewed as a continuation of that topic as well as a continuation of Chapter 13 on the managers' liability. A clear understanding of securities regulation is essential if managers are to avoid the liability, both civil and criminal, discussed in this chapter. This chapter is also designed to acquaint investors with the laws designed to protect them.

This chapter examines the broad legal meaning given to the word **security.** In addition, federal and state securities laws are discussed. Such laws at the federal level regulate the sale of securities in interstate commerce as well as the operation of national securities exchanges. The following sections should give the reader an understanding of two major federal securities laws—the Federal Securities Act of 1933 and the Federal Securities Exchange Act of 1934. At the end of the chapter, states' securities laws, often called **blue-sky laws,** are described. These laws regulate the sale of securities in intrastate commerce.

As you study this chapter, remember that the regulation of securities began as part of the program to help the United States overcome the great depression of the early 1930s. You should also realize that these securities laws are designed to give potential investors sufficient information so that they can make intelligent investment decisions based on factual information rather than on other less certain criteria.

By the end of this chapter, you should be familiar with the meaning and application of the following terms: blue-sky laws, controlling person, insider, issuer, prospectus, registration statement, scienter, security, seller, shelf registration, tippee, and underwriter.

## 1.  Definition of Security

Because the objective of securities laws is to protect uninformed people from investing their money without sufficient data, the term security has a very broad definition. Indeed, the federal securities laws provide the following definition:[1]

> "Security" means any note, stock, treasury stock, bond, debenture, evidence of indebtedness, certificate of interest of participation in any profit-sharing agreement, collateral-trust certificate, preorganization certificate or subscription, transferable share, investment contract, voting-trust certificate, certificate of deposit for a security, fractional undivided interest in oil, gas, or other mineral rights, or in general, any interest or instrument commonly known as a "security", or any certificate of interest or participation in, temporary or interim certificate for receipt for, guarantee of, or warrant or right to subscribe to or purchase, any of the foregoing.

As this definition indicates, the term security includes much more than corporation stock. A security exists when one person invests money and looks to others to manage the money for profit. The securities laws apply to every investment contract in which a person receives some evidence of indebtedness or a certificate of interest or participation in a profit-sharing agreement. As a result, sales of oil-well interests, whiskey receipts, interests in limited partnerships, margin sales of coins, and even savings and loan investments come within the scope of securities laws. Courts seek positive answers to the following three questions when determining whether a person has purchased a security. (1) Is the investment in a common venture? (2) Is the investment premised on a reasonable expectation of profits? (3) Will these profits be derived from the entrepreneurial efforts of others?

Many courts adopted the *sale of business doctrine* to remove a sale of stock from the scope of the securities laws. In essence, these courts ruled that a purchaser of 100 percent of a corporation's stock does not rely on the efforts of others to make a profit. The following case illustrates that this sale of business doctrine does not provide an absolute exemption from the securities laws. This case also stands for the proposition that when an instru-

---

[1] 15 U.S.C.A. § 77b(1).

ment is labeled as "stock" and possesses the characteristics typically associated with stock, it is a security regardless of the economic substance of the sales transaction.

---

# LANDRETH TIMBER COMPANY v. LANDRETH

105 S.Ct. 2297 (1985)

---

POWELL, J.:...This case presents the question whether the sale of all of the stock of a company is a securities transaction subject to the antifraud provisions of the federal securities laws (the Acts).

Respondents Ivan K. Landreth and his sons owned all of the outstanding stock of a lumber business they operated in Tonasket, Washington. The Landreth family offered their stock for sale through both Washington and out-of-state brokers. Before a purchaser was found, the company's sawmill was heavily damaged by fire. Despite the fire, the brokers continued to offer the stock for sale. Potential purchasers were advised of the damage, but were told that the mill would be completely rebuilt and modernized.

Samuel Dennis, a Massachusetts tax attorney, received a letter offering the stock for sale. On the basis of the letter's representations concerning the rebuilding plans, the predicted productivity of the mill, existing contracts, and expected profits, Dennis became interested in acquiring the stock. He talked to John Bolten, a former client who had retired to Florida, about joining him in investigating the offer. After having an audit and an inspection of the mill conducted, a stock purchase agreement was negotiated, with Dennis the purchaser of all of the common stock in the lumber company. Ivan Landreth agreed to stay on as a consultant for some time to help with the daily opera-

tions of the mill. Pursuant to the terms of the stock purchase agreement, Dennis assigned the stock he purchased to B & D Co., a corporation formed for the sole purpose of acquiring the lumber company stock. B & D then merged with the lumber company, forming petitioner Landreth Timber Co. Dennis and Bolten then acquired all of petitioner's Class A stock, representing 85% of the equity, and six other investors together owned the Class B stock, representing the remaining 15% of the equity.

After the acquisition was completed, the mill did not live up to the purchasers' expectations. Rebuilding costs exceeded earlier estimates, and new components turned out to be incompatible with existing equipment. Eventually, petitioner sold the mill at a loss and went into receivership. Petitioner then filed this suit seeking rescission of the sale of stock and $2,500,000 in damages, alleging that respondents had widely offered and then sold their stock without registering it as required by the Securities Act of 1933. Petitioner also alleged that respondents had negligently or intentionally made misrepresentations and had failed to state material facts as to the worth and prospects of the lumber company, all in violation of the Securities Exchange Act of 1934.

Respondents moved for summary judgment on the ground that the transaction was not covered by the Acts because under the so-called "sale of business" doctrine, petitioner had not purchased a "security" within the meaning of those Acts. The District Court granted respondents' motion and dismissed the complaint for want of federal jurisdiction. It acknowledged that the federal statutes include "stock" as one of the instruments constituting a "security," and that the stock at issue possessed all of the characteristics of conventional stock. Nonetheless, it joined what it termed the "growing majority" of courts that had held that the federal securities laws do not apply to the sale of 100% of the stock of a closely held corporation.

...The District Court ruled that the stock could not be considered a "security" unless the purchaser had entered into the transaction with the anticipation of earning profits derived from the efforts of others. Finding that managerial control of the business had passed into the hands of the purchasers, and thus, that the transaction was a commercial venture rather than a typical investment, the District Court dismissed the complaint.

The United States Court of Appeals for the Ninth Circuit affirmed the District Court's application of the sale of business doctrine....Because the Courts of Appeals are divided over the applicability of the federal securities laws when a business is sold by the transfer of 100% of its stock, we granted certiorari....

It is axiomatic that the starting point in every case involving construction of a statute is the language itself. [The Court then reviewed the definition of security quoted in the text above.]

...This definition is quite broad and includes both instruments whose names alone carry well-settled meaning, as well as instruments of more variable character [that] were necessarily designated by more descriptive terms, such as "investment contract" and instrument commonly known as a "security." The face of the definition shows that "stock"

is considered to be a "security" within the meaning of the Acts....

...However, the fact that instruments bear the label "stock" is not of itself sufficient to invoke the coverage of the Acts. Rather, we concluded that we must also determine whether those instruments possess some of the significant characteristics typically associated with stock, recognizing that when an instrument is both called "stock" and bears stock's usual characteristics, a purchaser justifiably [may] assume that the federal securities laws apply. We identified those characteristics usually associated with common stock as (i) the right to receive dividends contingent upon an apportionment of profits; (ii) negotiability; (iii) the ability to be pledged or hypothecated; (iv) the conferring of voting rights in proportion to the number of shares owned; and (v) the capacity to appreciate in value....

It is undisputed that the stock involved here possesses all of the characteristics we identified...as traditionally associated with common stock. Indeed, the District Court so found. Moreover,...the context of the transaction involved here—the sale of stock in a corporation—is typical of the kind of context to which the Acts normally apply. It is thus much more likely here...that an investor would believe he was covered by the federal securities laws. Under the circumstances of this case, the plain meaning of the statutory definition mandates that the stock be treated as "securities" subject to the coverage of the Acts....

We also perceive strong policy reasons for not employing the sale of business doctrine under the circumstances of this case. By respondents' own admission, application of the doctrine depends in each case on whether control has passed to the purchaser. It may be argued that on the facts of this case, the doctrine is easily applied, since the transfer of 100% of a corporation's stock normally transfers control. We think even that assertion is open to some question, however, as Dennis and Bolten had no intention of running the sawmill themselves. Ivan Landreth apparently stayed on to manage the daily affairs of the business....

More importantly, however, if applied to this case, the sale of business doctrine would also have to be applied to cases in which less than 100% of a company's stock was sold. This inevitably would lead to difficult questions of line-drawing. The Acts' coverage would in every case depend not only on the percentage of stock transferred, but also on such factors as the number of purchasers and what provisions for voting and veto rights were agreed upon by the parties....

In sum, we conclude that the stock at issue here is a "security" within the definition of the Acts, and that the sale of business doctrine does not apply. The judgment of the United States Court of Appeals for the Ninth Circuit is therefore [*Reversed.*]

Despite the broad definition of a security, the Supreme Court has made it clear that federal securities laws are not designed to provide a remedy for all fraudulent transactions. In recent years, the Court has held that securities laws do not necessarily apply (1) to a compulsory pension plan into which the employee is not required to make contributions, or (2) to certificates of deposit insured by the federal government. In the first instance, the Court found that the employee was protected by the Employee Retirement Income Security Act, and in the second situation it found that the customer was insured by the Federal Deposit Insurance Corporation. In these areas where "an investor" is protected by other means, protection provided by the securities laws is less essential.

## 2.   Securities and Exchange Commission

The Securities and Exchange Commission (SEC), which was created in 1934, is responsible for administering the federal securities laws. The materials discussed in Chapter 8 on administrative agencies generally apply to the SEC. The SEC consists of five commissioners appointed by the President for a five-year term. In addition to these commissioners, the SEC employs staff personnel such as lawyers, accountants, security analysts, security examiners, and others.

The SEC has both quasi-legislative and quasi-judicial powers. Using its quasi-legislative power, it has adopted rules and regulations relating to financial and other information which must be furnished to the Commission. It also has rules prescribing information which must be given to potential investors. The SEC also regulates the various stock exchanges, utility holding companies, investment trusts, and investment advisers.

The SEC is involved in a variety of investigations and rule-making activities. Typical of these are the following:

**1**  Investigating insider trading and stock manipulation, especially that connected with takeover attempts and rumors

**2**  Investigating the leakage of information (factual and false) that can significantly affect stock prices

**3**  Studying and investigating numerous examples of suspected insider trading

**4**  Adopting rules that govern which shareholder-proposed resolutions must be submitted for a vote at corporate annual meetings. For example, the SEC requires that a shareholder must have invested $1,000 for at least one year before submitting a proposal. A proposal must get at least 5 percent of the vote the first time before it can be resubmitted

**5**  Adopting rules that require members of the New York Stock Exchange to monitor trading at their firms for possible violations of securities laws

**6**  Adopting rules that standardize the information that may be advertised concerning mutual funds so that investors have a better chance to compare these funds

**7**  Adopting rules that require publicly held companies to disclose when and why they change auditors

## FEDERAL SECURITIES ACT OF 1933: GOING PUBLIC

### 3.  General Provisions

The Federal Securities Act of 1933 was enacted by Congress to regulate the initial sale of securities to the public. This law makes it illegal to use the mails or any other interstate means of communication or transportation to sell securities without disclosing certain financial information to potential investors. The following sections discuss several aspects of the Federal Securities Act of 1933 in detail, including who is regulated, what documents are required, which transactions are exempted, when civil and criminal liability exists, and what defenses are available. As you read, remember that this law applies only to the initial sale of the security. Subsequent transfers of securities are governed by the Federal Securities Exchange Act of 1934, discussed in sections 11 through 16.

In essence, the 1933 Act requires the disclosure of information to the potential investor or other interested party. The information given must not be untrue or even misleading. If this information is not accurate, liability is imposed upon those responsible. The Federal Securities Act of 1933 recognizes three sanctions for violations. There is the criminal punishment, the equitable remedy of an injunction, and civil liability, which may be imposed in favor of injured parties in certain cases. Proof of an intentional violation usually is required before criminal or civil sanctions are imposed. However, proof of negligence will support an injunction.

## 4.  Parties Regulated

The Federal Securities Act of 1933 regulates anyone who is involved with or who promotes the initial sale of securities. Typically, involved parties may include issuers, underwriters, controlling persons, and sellers. An **issuer** is the individual or business organization offering a security for sale to the public. An **underwriter** is anyone who participates in the original distribution of securities by selling such securities for the issuer or by guaranteeing their sale. (Often securities brokerage firms or investment bankers have acted as underwriters with respect to a particular transaction.) A **controlling person** is one who controls or is controlled by the issuer, such as a major stockholder of a corporation. Finally, a **seller** is anyone who contracts with a purchaser or who exerts a substantial role which causes the purchase transaction to occur.

These parties who participate in or promote a sale of securities from an issuer to the public are subject to the Federal Securities Act of 1933, which protects a person from being defrauded by false or nonexistent information. The initial reading of the previous paragraph may not indicate the broad meaning given to the words "issuer," "underwriter," "controlling person," and "seller." However, the following case illustrates the wide application of the 1933 Act.

# JUNKER v. CRORY
650 F.2d 1349 (5th Cir. 1981)

James Junker owned 162 shares of stock in Reco Investment Corporation. These shares were equal to 16.2 percent of the 1,000 shares Reco had outstanding. Reco became heavily indebted to another corporation known as Road Equipment Company, Inc. In order to resolve Reco's poor financial condition, Frederick Heisler, a lawyer for Reco, suggested and strongly recommended that Reco be merged into Road. Due to what he believed was an unreasonably low ap-

praised value of Reco's stock, Junker voted against the proposed merger. However, the remaining shareholders of Reco approved the merger plan, and it was accomplished. Later, Junker discovered some negative news about Road's financial condition. This information was not revealed at the shareholders' meeting when the merger vote was taken. Junker sued Frederick Heisler, alleging a violation of the 1933 Securities Act. Heisler defended the suit by arguing he had no duty to reveal additional information. The district court ruled in Junker's favor, and Heisler appealed.

RUBIN, J.:...Heisler...was not an officer, director or shareholder in either Reco or Road. According to the trial court's findings, he acted as attorney or agent for both corporations....Finding no state law cause of action on which to ground Heisler's liability to Junker, we turn to the federal securities law claims.

The trial court held Heisler liable for violation of the 1933 Act....

To recover..., the plaintiff must establish that the defendant as a seller of a security misrepresented or failed to state material facts to the plaintiff in connection with the sale....

A merger may amount to a purchase or sale of a security for purposes of the federal securities laws. Thus, the exchange of Junker's Reco shares for stock in Road pursuant to the merger qualifies Junker as a purchaser of Road stock.

Because a purchaser may recover...only from his immediate seller, our inquiry focuses on whether Heisler's role in the merger transaction constituted him a seller for purposes of that section. Mere participation in the events leading up to the transaction is insufficient to constitute one a seller of a security. Only those in privity with the purchaser or those "whose participation in the buy-sell transaction is a substantial factor in causing the transaction to take place" are classified as sellers....

We held in *Croy v. Campbell,* 624 F.2d 709 (5th Cir. 1980), that an attorney whose connection with the sale was limited to advising the purchaser on its tax consequences was not a seller. The attorney in *Croy* did not attempt to persuade the plaintiffs to make the purchase; he made no representations to them concerning the operational aspects of the project in which the plaintiffs ultimately invested. In determining that his involvement was insufficient to constitute a proximate cause of the sale, we noted, "this conclusion should not be interpreted to mean that a lawyer who participates in the transaction can never be a seller...."

Heisler's role in bringing about the merger in this case differed significantly from the relatively inactive part played by the lawyer in *Croy.* According to Heisler's testimony, he initially suggested the possibility of a merger. The minutes of the Reco shareholders' meeting at which the merger was discussed reflect that Heisler attended as...proxy and advanced the merger as the solution to Reco's financial problems. He also prepared the merger documents. Thus, unlike the attorney in *Croy,* Heisler did attempt to persuade the Reco shareholders to make the purchase of Road stock pursuant to the merger. He also made representations at the Reco shareholders' meeting regarding his investigation into possible sales of Reco property and the feasibility of a liquidation of Reco as compared with the merger. The evidence of Heisler's involvement in the effort to bring about the merger supports the trial court's finding that he was a key participant in the transaction. His role was not that of a passive advisor as was that of the attorney in *Croy;* rather, he was an active negotiator in the transaction, acting as agent-in-fact as well as attorney-at-law, implementor not counsellor. Therefore, we agree with the trial court's conclusion that Heisler's actions brought him within the scope of the seller definition....

Having determined that Heisler's actions constituted him a seller...we also conclude that his representations made to the Reco shareholders at the shareholders' meeting amounted to an oral communication containing misstatements or omissions of material facts relevant to the merger transaction....Therefore, we conclude that

Heisler did not satisfy the burden of proof required to establish that, exercising reasonable care, he could not have been aware of the material misstatements and omissions in

his presentation at the Reco shareholders' meeting....

For these reasons the judgment in Junker's favor is [*Affirmed.*]

---

In a recent Supreme Court opinion (see section 9 below), the meaning of the "seller" under the 1933 Act was discussed. The Court wrote that merely being a "substantial factor" in causing the sale of illegal securities does not render an individual liable as a "seller." However, the Court failed to provide specific guidance for when someone would and would not be liable as a seller. Recently, the SEC announced its position regarding lawyers' liability as sellers. Lawyers who prepare materials to be used by a client in the sale of securities are not sellers unless these lawyers also engage in direct solicitation of potential buyers.

## 5.   Documents Involved

In regulating the initial sale of securities, the Federal Securities Act of 1933 should be viewed as a disclosure law. In essence, this law requires that securities subject to its provisions be registered prior to any sale and that a prospectus be furnished to any potential investor prior to any sale being consummated. Thus, an issuer of securities who complies with the federal law must prepare (1) a *registration statement,* and (2) a *prospectus.*

### REGISTRATION STATEMENT

The Federal Securities Act of 1933 contains detailed provisions relating to the registration of securities and describes which selling activities are permitted at the various stages of the registration process. There are three distinct periods during the registration process: (1) the pre-filing period, (2) the waiting period, and (3) the posteffective period. A registration becomes effective at the expiration of the waiting period, twenty days after it is filed, unless the SEC gives notice that it is not in proper form or unless the SEC accelerates the effective date. Any amendment filed without the Commission's consent starts the twenty-day period running again.

During the pre-filing period, it is legal for the issuer of a security to engage in preliminary negotiations and agreements with underwriters. It is illegal to sell a covered security during this period. Offers to sell and offers to buy securities also are prohibited during this pre-filing period.

During the waiting period, it is still illegal to sell a security subject to the act. However, it is not illegal to make an offer to buy or an offer to sell. Written offers to sell must conform to the prospectus requirements, but oral offers are permissible. Since contracts to sell are still illegal, offers cannot be accepted during the waiting period. As a result of these waiting periods, sellers may solicit offers for later acceptance also.

Many offers during the waiting period are made in advertisements called "tombstone ads." These ads are brief announcements identifying the security and stating its price, by whom orders will be executed, and from whom a prospectus may be obtained. Almost any issue of *The Wall Street Journal* contains such ads. Offers may also be made during the waiting period by use of a statistical summary, a summary prospectus, or a preliminary prospectus. These techniques allow dissemination of the facts that are to be ultimately disclosed in the formal prospectus.

### PROSPECTUS

During the posteffective period, securities may be sold. A prospectus must be furnished to any interested investor, and it must conform to the statutory requirements. Like the registration statement, the prospectus contains financial information related to the issuer. Indeed, the prospectus contains the same essential information contained in the registration statement. The prospectus supplies the investor with sufficient facts (including financial information) so that he or she can make an intelligent investment decision. The SEC has adopted rules relating to the detailed requirements of the prospectus. The major requirements are detailed facts about the issuer and financial statements, including balance sheets and statements of operations of the issuer.

Theoretically, any security may be sold under the act, provided the law and the rules and regulations enacted under it are followed. The law does not prohibit the sale of worthless securities. An investor may "foolishly" invest his or her money, and a person may legally sell the blue sky if the statutory requirements are met. In fact, the prospectus must contain the following in capital letters and boldface type:

> THESE SECURITIES HAVE NOT BEEN APPROVED OR DISAPPROVED BY THE SECURITIES AND EXCHANGE COMMISSION NOR HAS THE COMMISSION PASSED UPON THE ACCURACY OR ADEQUACY OF THIS PROSPECTUS. ANY REPRESENTATION TO THE CONTRARY IS A CRIMINAL OFFENSE.

### 6.  Shelf Registration

Regarding initial sale of securities to the public, the most significant development in some time has been the SEC's relaxation of disclosure requirements. This trend is not a change in the 1933 law, but it is a new direction for the rules and regulations issued by the SEC pursuant to the 1933 Act.

Rule 415 of the SEC, which provides for **shelf registration** of securities, allows companies to submit a single, comprehensive disclosure statement describing their long-term financing plans. These disclosure statements permit companies to sell securities whenever rapidly changing market conditions appear most favorable. Due to Rule 415, the issuer of securities to the public no longer has to prepare a prospectus for the SEC's review every time it plans to sell securities.

Under SEC Rule 415 as modified, companies with less than $150 million in stock held by investors unaffiliated with the company can no longer use the shelf-registration method of selling securities to the public. The Rule 415 limitations are designed to protect investors who may not be able to get adequate financial data about these smaller, little-known companies in the short time between the announcement of a shelf issue and its sale.

## 7. Exemptions

Some statutory provisions exempt certain transactions, and others exempt certain securities from registration requirements. Provisions that exempt certain transactions limit the application of the law to transactions in which a security is sold in a public offering by the issuer, an underwriter, a controlling person, or a seller. Transactions by a securities dealer (as distinguished from an issuer or an underwriter) are exempt after forty days have elapsed from the effective date of the first public offer. If a company offers the security with no prior registration statements, this period is ninety days. This exemption allows a dealer to enter into transactions in securities after a minimum period has elapsed. In addition, brokers' transactions executed on any exchange or in the over-the-counter market are exempt.

### PRIVATE SALES TRANSACTIONS

Perhaps the most difficult issue in determining whether a sale is an exempt transaction is the concept of a public offering. Private sales are exempt. Sales to the general public are not. In determining whether or not a sale is being made to the general public, the SEC will examine: (1) the number of offerees, (2) their knowledge about the company in which they are investing, (3) the relationship between the offeror and offeree, (4) whether the security remains in the hands of the offeree or is resold, and (5) the amount of advertising involved. The issuer has the burden of proof to show that the sale is private and not public.

### SPECIALIZED SECURITIES

The law also exempts certain securities from its coverage. These include securities subject to regulation by governmental agencies other than the SEC, such as securities of banks and savings and loan institutions and intrastate offerings. The intrastate exemption covers securities that are offered and sold only to persons who reside within the state of incorporation. If the issuer is unincorporated, the purchasers must reside within the state of its residence and place of business. If the sale is to a resident planning to resell to a nonresident, the intrastate exemption is lost. The same is true if the mails or interstate systems of communication are used to sell the security. Remember that even if the sale is exempt under federal law, it is probably subject to a similar state law. Commercial paper arising out of current transactions with a maturity not exceeding nine months and securities issued by not-for-profit corporations are also exempt.

### SIZE OF OFFERING

The SEC can create additional exemptions. Typically, these exemptions depend on the dollar amount of securities sold and on who the investor-purchasers are. Furthermore, the exemptions change from time to time. In recent years, the SEC's trend has been to exempt larger offerings to help businesses raise capital. Currently, any business may sell up to $500,000 in securities during a twelve-month period without registering the offering, according to the 1933 Act's requirements. The amount of this exemption increases to $5 million if the issuer believes that there are no more than thirty-five investor-purchasers who lack the sophistication to acquire and evaluate information about the security being sold.

No general advertising or solicitation is permitted in association with exempt transactions. Furthermore, all parties involved in the initial sales of securities from the issuer remain subject to the federal laws' antifraud and civil liability provisions. States also may require compliance with their securities laws, regardless of any applicable federal disclosure exemptions. Finally, the securities sold in these exempt transactions are restricted. In other words, before these securities can be resold, registration requirements must be satisfied unless the resale is part of another exempt transaction.

Table 19-1 summarizes the exemptions provided in the 1933 Securities Act and regulations issued by the SEC.

**TABLE 19-1**   Exemptions

| Exempt Securities | Exempt Transactions |
|---|---|
| 1   Securities up to $1.5 million in value during a twelve-month period (Regulation A) | 1   Securities dealers' and brokers' transactions |
| 2   Securities subject to governmental regulation other than the SEC (banks, savings and loan, not-for-profit corporations, etc.) | 2   Private offering (not available to general public) |
| 3   Securities sold only intrastate | 3   $500,000 per twelve-month period for any business |
| | 4   $5,000,000 per twelve-month period if there are thirty-five or fewer nonaccredited investors |
| | 5   Unlimited offering if there are thirty-five or fewer nonaccredited investors who have expertise to evaluate investment opportunity |

### 8. Criminal Liability

Under the Federal Securities Act of 1933, both civil and criminal liability may be imposed for violations. Criminal liability results from a willful violation of the Act, or fraud in *any* offer or sale of securities. Fraud also occurs when any material fact is omitted, causing a statement to be misleading. The penalty is a fine up to $10,000 or five years in prison or both. Fraud in the sale of an exempt security is also a criminal violation if the mail is used or if an instrumentality of interstate commerce such as the telephone has been used.

The law requires that violations be willful. "Willful" means with intent to defraud. The government can meet its burden by proving that a defendant deliberately closed his or her eyes to facts he or she had a duty to see, or recklessly stated as facts things of which he or she was ignorant. The willfulness requirement can be satisfied by mere "proof of representation which due diligence would have shown to be untrue." In discussing the state of mind required for a criminal conviction of a lawyer or an accountant under the statute, one court observed:

> In our complex society the accountant's certificate and the lawyer's opinion can be instruments for inflicting pecuniary loss more potent than the chisel or the crowbar. Of course, Congress did not mean that any mistake of law or misstatement of fact should subject an attorney or an accountant to criminal liability simply because more skillful practitioners would not have made them. But Congress equally could not have intended that men holding themselves out as members of these ancient professions should be able to escape criminal liability on a plea of ignorance when they have shut their eyes to what was plainly to be seen or have represented a knowledge they knew they did not possess.

A person accused of intentionally violating the 1933 Act usually cannot escape criminal liability by arguing that a nonexempt transaction involving the exchange of misinformation technically was outside the 1933 Act's scope. For example, the Supreme Court held that a pledge of stock as collateral for a bank loan was a sale of a security, and if the value of the stock was misrepresented, the person pledging the stock could be found guilty of a crime under the statute. A pledge of stock as security for a loan is a disposition of a security for value.

### 9. Civil Liability

This portion of the chapter discusses three sections of the Federal Securities Act of 1933 that directly apply to civil liability of parties involved in issuing securities. The first section of importance (Section 11 of the Act) deals with registration statements; the second (Section 12 of the Act) relates to prospectuses and oral and written communication; and the third (Section 17 of the Act) concerns fraudulent interstate transactions.

### SECTION **11**: REGISTRATION STATEMENT

The civil liability provision dealing with registration statements imposes liability on the following persons in favor of purchasers of securities:

**1** Every person who signed the registration statement

**2** Every director of the corporation or partner in the partnership issuing the security

**3** Every person who, with his or her consent, is named in the registration statement as about to become a director or partner

**4** Every accountant, engineer, or appraiser who assists in the preparation of the registration statement or its certification

**5** Every underwriter

The persons mentioned in the preceding paragraph are liable if the registration statement (1) contains untrue statements of material facts, (2) omits material facts required by statute or regulation, or (3) omits information which if not given makes the facts stated misleading. This latter situation describes the factual situation of a statement containing a half-truth, which has the net effect of being misleading. The test of accuracy and materiality is as of the date the registration statement becomes effective.

The SEC and the courts have attempted to define materiality. The term *material* limits information concerning those matters as to which an average prudent investor ought reasonably to be informed before purchasing the security registered. What are "matters as to which an average prudent investor ought reasonably to be informed?" They are matters which such an investor needs to know before he or she can make an intelligent, informed decision whether or not to buy the security. As a result, a material fact is one which if correctly stated or disclosed would have deterred or tended to deter the average prudent investor from purchasing the securities in question. The term does not cover minor inaccuracies or errors in matters of no interest to investors. Facts that tend to deter a person from purchasing a security are those that have an important bearing upon the nature or condition of the issuing corporation or its business.

A plaintiff-purchaser need not prove reliance on the registration statement in order to recover, but proof of actual knowledge of the falsity by the purchaser is a defense. Knowledge of the falsity by a defendant need not be proved, but except for an issuer, reliance on an expert such as an accountant is a defense. For example, a director may defend a suit based on a false financial statement by showing reliance on a CPA.

### SECTION **12**: PROSPECTUS AND OTHER COMMUNICATIONS

This section of the 1933 Act is divided into two parts. Whereas Section 11 creates liability for those responsible for a false or misleading registration statement, the first subsection of Section 12 imposes liability on those who offer or sell securities which are not registered with the SEC. This liability exists regardless of the intent or conduct of those who fail to comply with the registration requirements. Thus, liability traditionally has been imposed against violators even though they lacked any wrongful intent.

In the following case, the Supreme Court approved the defendant's argument that the plaintiff was equally responsible for the failure to register the securities sold. This case appears to be a movement away from the traditional strict liability for failure to file the required registration statement.

# PINTER v. DAHL
108 S.Ct. 2063 (1988)

BLACKMUN, J.:...The question presented by this case...[is] whether the common-law *in pari delicto* defense is available in a private action brought under § 12(1) of the Securities Act of 1933 for the rescission of the sale of unregistered securities....

The controversy arises out of the sale prior to 1982 of unregistered securities (fractional undivided interests in oil and gas leases) by petitioner Billy J. "B.J." Pinter to respondents Maurice Dahl and Dahl's friends, family, and business associates. Pinter is an oil and gas producer in Texas and Oklahoma, and a registered securities dealer in Texas. Dahl is a California real estate broker and investor, who, at the time of his dealings with Pinter, was a veteran of two unsuccessful oil and gas ventures. In pursuit of further investment opportunities, Dahl employed an oilfield expert to locate and acquire oil and gas leases. This expert introduced Dahl to Pinter. Dahl advanced $20,000 to Pinter to acquire leases, with the understanding that they would be held in the name of Pinter's Black Gold Oil Company and that Dahl would have a right of first refusal to drill certain wells on the leasehold properties. Pinter located leases in

Oklahoma, and Dahl toured the properties, often without Pinter, in order to talk to others and get a feel for the properties. Upon examining the geology, drilling logs, and production history assembled by Pinter, Dahl concluded, in the words of the District Court, that "there was no way to lose."

After investing approximately $310,000 in the properties, Dahl told the other respondents about the venture. Except for Dahl and respondent Grantham, none of the respondents spoke to or met Pinter or toured the properties. Because of Dahl's involvement in the venture, each of the other respondents decided to invest about $7,500.

Dahl assisted his fellow investors in completing the subscription-agreement form prepared by Pinter. Each letter-contract signed by the purchaser stated that the participating interests were being sold without the benefit of registration under the Securities Act....

When the venture failed and their interests proved to be worthless, respondents brought suit against Pinter in the United States District Court for the Northern District of Texas, seeking rescission under § 12(1) of the Securities Act for the unlawful sale of unregistered securities.

In a counterclaim, Pinter alleged that Dahl, by means of fraudulent misrepresentations and concealment of facts, induced Pinter to sell and deliver the securities. Pinter averred that Dahl falsely assured Pinter that he would provide other qualified, sophisticated, and knowledgeable investors with all the information necessary for evaluation of the investment. Dahl allegedly agreed to raise the funds for the venture from those investors, with the understanding that Pinter would simply be the "operator" of the wells. Pinter also asserted, on the basis of the same factual allegations, that Dahl's suit was barred by the equitable defenses of estoppel and *in pari delicto*.

The District Court, after a bench trial, granted judgment for respondent- investors....

A divided panel of the Court of Appeals for the Fifth Circuit affirmed. The court...held that Dahl's involvement in the sales to the other respondents did not give Pinter an *in pari delicto* defense to Dahl's recovery. The court concluded that the defense is not available in an action under § 12(1) because that section creates "a strict liability offense" rather than liability based on intentional misconduct....

The equitable defense of *in pari delicto,* which literally means "in equal fault," is rooted in the common-law notion that a plaintiff's recovery may be barred by his own wrongful conduct. Traditionally, the defense was limited to situations where the plaintiff bore at least substantially equal responsibility for his injury and where the parties' culpability arose out of the same illegal act....

We feel that the Court of Appeals' notion that the *in pari delicto* defense should not be allowed in actions involving strict liability offenses is without support in history or logic. The doctrine traditionally has been applied in any action based on conduct that transgresses statutory prohibitions....

Our task...is to determine whether... recognition of the defense is proper in a suit for rescission brought under § 12(1) of the Securities Act. All parties in this case, as well as the Commission, maintain that the defense should be available. We agree, but find it necessary to circumscribe the scope of its application.

...A defendant cannot escape liability unless, as a direct result of the plaintiff's own actions, the plaintiff bears at least substantially equal responsibility for the underlying illegality. The plaintiff must be an active, voluntary participant in the unlawful activity that is the subject of the suit....Unless the degrees of fault are essentially indistinguishable or the plaintiff's responsibility is clearly greater, the *in pari delicto* defense should not be allowed, and the plaintiff should be compensated....

A purchaser's knowledge that the securities are unregistered cannot, by itself, constitute equal culpability, even where the investor is a sophisticated buyer who may not necessarily need the protection of the Securities Act....

The primary purpose of the Securities Act is to protect investors by requiring publication of material information thought necessary to allow them to make informed investment decisions concerning public offerings of securities in interstate commerce. The registration requirements are the heart of the Act, and § 12(1) imposes strict liability for violating those requirements. Liability under § 12(1) is a particularly important enforcement tool, because in many instances a private suit is the only effective means of detecting and deterring a seller's wrongful failure to register securities before offering them for sale.

In our view, where the § 12(1) plaintiff is primarily an investor, precluding suit would interfere significantly with effective enforcement of the securities laws and frustrate the primary objective of the Securities

Act. The Commission, too, takes this position. Because the Act is specifically designed to protect investors, even where a plaintiff actively participates in the distribution of unregistered securities, his suit should not be barred where his promotional efforts are incidental to his role as an investor. Thus, the *in pari delicto* defense may defeat recovery in a § 12(1) action only where the plaintiff's role in the offering or sale of nonexempted, unregistered securities is more as a promoter than as an investor.

Whether the plaintiff in a particular case is primarily an investor or primarily a promoter depends upon a host of factors, all readily accessible to trial courts. These factors include the extent of the plaintiff's financial involvement compared to that of third parties solicited by the plaintiff, the incidental nature of the plaintiff's promotional activities, the benefits received by the plaintiff from his promotional activities, and the extent of the plaintiff's involvement in the planning stages of the offering (such as whether the plaintiff has arranged an underwriting or prepared the offering materials). We do not mean to suggest that these factors provide conclusive evidence of culpable promotional activity, or that they constitute an exhaustive list of factors to be considered. The courts are free, in the exercise of their sound discretion, to consider whatever facts are relevant to the inquiry.

Given the record in this case, we cannot ascertain whether Pinter may successfully assert an *in pari delicto* defense against Dahl's § 12(1) claim. The District Court's findings in this case are not adequate to determine whether Dahl bears at least substantially equal responsibility for the failure to register the oil and gas interests or to distribute the securities in a manner that conformed with the statutory exemption, and whether he was primarily a promoter of the offering. The findings indicate, on the one hand, that Dahl may have participated in initiating the entire investment, and that he loaned money to Pinter and solicited his associates' participation in the venture, but, on the other hand, that Dahl invested substantially more money than the other investor-respondents, expected and received no commission for his endeavors, and drafted none of the offering documents. Furthermore, the District Court made no findings as to who was responsible for the failure to register or for the manner in which the offering was conducted. Those findings will be made on the remand of this case for further proceedings. [*Judgment vacated and remanded.*]

---

The second subsection of Section 12 imposes liability on sellers who use a prospectus or make communications (by mail, telephone, or other instrumentalities of interstate commerce) that contain an untrue statement of material facts required to be stated or necessary to make statements not misleading. Like under Section 11, the plaintiff does not have to prove reliance on the false or misleading prospectus or communication. Nor does the plaintiff have to establish that the defendant intended the deception.

Purchasers of such securities may sue for their actual damages. If the purchaser still owns the securities and he can prove a direct contractual relationship with the seller, the remedy of rescission and a refund of the purchase price is also available.

**SECTION 17: FRAUDULENT TRANSACTIONS**

This provision concerning fraudulent interstate transactions prohibits the use of any instrument of interstate communication in the offer or sale of any securities when the result is (1) to defraud, (2) to obtain money or property by means of an untrue or misleading statement, or (3) to engage in a business transaction or practice that may operate to defraud or deceive a purchaser.

The requirement that a defendant-seller must act with the intent (**scienter**) to deceive or mislead in order to prove a Section 17 violation has caused much controversy over the years. In 1980, the Supreme Court resolved this issue by announcing the following decision with respect to the SEC seeking injunctive relief. You should realize that this decision is limited to the remedy of an injunction, since Section 17 does not explicitly provide for the private remedy of monetary damages. Note that the 1, 2, 3 referred to in this case is the same 1, 2, and 3 as mentioned above.

# AARON v. SECURITIES AND EXCHANGE COMMISSION
100 S.Ct. 1945 (1980)

Peter Aaron was the managerial employee of a registered broker-dealer firm. Two employees of this firm, Schreiber and Jacobson, gave false information about Lawn-A-Mat Chemical & Equipment Corporation in order to induce clients to invest in Lawn-A-Mat common stock. After being informed of his brokers' wrongful actions, Aaron failed to prevent these brokers, under his direct supervision, from continuing to make false and misleading statements in promoting Lawn-A-Mat common stock.

The SEC filed a complaint seeking to enjoin Aaron from aiding and abetting continuous violations of Section 17(a) of the 1933 Securities Act.

STEWART, J.: The issue in this case is whether the Securities and Exchange Commission (Commission) is required to establish scienter as an element of a civil enforcement action to enjoin violations of § 17(a) of the Securities Act of 1933 (1933 Act)....

Following a bench trial, the District Court found that the petitioner had violated and aided and abetted violations of 17(a)...and enjoined him from future violations of these provisions. The District Court's finding of past violations was based upon its factual finding that the petitioner had intentionally failed to discharge his supervisory responsibility to stop Schreiber and Jacobson from making statements to prospective investors that the petitioner knew to be false and misleading....

The Court of Appeals for the Second Circuit affirmed the judgment. Declining to reach the question whether the petitioner's conduct would support a finding of scienter, the Court of Appeals held instead that when the Commission is seeking injunctive relief, "proof of negligence alone will suffice" to establish a violation of § 17(a)....

We granted certiorari to resolve the conflict in the federal courts as to whether the Commission is required to establish scienter—an intent on the part of the defendant to deceive, manipulate, or defraud—as element of a Commission enforcement action to enjoin violations of § 17(a)....

Section 17(a), which applies only to sellers, provides:

**It shall be unlawful for any person in the offer or sale of any securities by the use of any means or instruments of transportation or communication in interstate commerce or by the use of the mails, directly or indirectly—**

**(1) to employ any device, scheme, or artifice to defraud, or**

**(2) to obtain money or property by means of any untrue statement of a material fact or any omission to state a material fact necessary in order to make the statements made, in the light of the circumstances under which they were made, not misleading, or**

**(3) to engage in any transaction, practice, or course of business which operates or would operate as a fraud or deceit upon the purchaser....**

The issue here is whether the Commission in seeking injunctive relief...for violations of § 17(a)...is required to establish scienter. Resolution of that issue could depend upon (1) the substantive provisions of § 17(a)... or (2) the statutory provisions authorizing injunctive relief "upon a proper showing"...

In determining whether proof of scienter is a necessary element of a violation of § 17(a), there is less precedential authority in this Court to guide us, but the controlling principles are well settled. Though cognizant that "Congress intended securities legislation enacted for the purpose of avoiding frauds to be construed 'not technically and restrictively but flexibly to effectuate its remedial purposes,'" the Court has also noted that "generalized references to the 'remedial purposes'" of the securities laws "will not justify reading a provision 'more broadly than its language and the statutory scheme reasonably permit.'" Thus, if the language of a provision of the securities laws is sufficiently clear in its context and not at odds with the legislative history, it is unnecessary "to examine the additional considerations of 'policy'...that may have influenced the lawmakers in their formulation of the statute."

The language of § 17(a) strongly suggests that Congress contemplated a scienter requirement under § 17(a)(1), but not under § 17(a)(2) or § 17(a)(3). The language of § 17(a)(1), which makes it unlawful "to employ any device, scheme, or artifice to defraud," plainly evinces an intent on the part of Congress to proscribe only knowing or intentional misconduct. Even if it be assumed that the term "defraud" is ambiguous, given its varied meanings at law and in equity, the terms "device," "scheme" and "artifice" all connote knowing or intentional practices....

By contrast, the language of § 17(a)(2), which prohibits any person from obtaining money or property "by means of any untrue statement of a material fact or any omission to state a material fact," is devoid of any suggestion whatsoever of a scienter requirement....

Finally, the language of § 17(a)(3), under which it is unlawful for any person "to engage in any transaction, practice, or course of business which *operates* or *would operate* as a fraud or deceit," (emphasis added) quite plainly focuses upon the *effect* of particular conduct on members of the investing public, rather than upon the culpability of the person responsible....

It is our view, in sum, that the language of § 17(a) requires scienter under § 17(a)(1), but not under § 17(a)(2) or § 17(a)(3). Although the parties have urged the Court to adopt a uniform culpability requirement for the three subparagraphs of § 17(a), the language of the section is simply not amenable to such an interpretation. This is not the first time that this Court has had occasion to emphasize the distinctions among the three subparagraphs of § 17(a). In *United States v. Naftalin*, 99 S.Ct. 2077, the Court noted that each subparagraph of § 17(a) "proscribes a distinct category of misconduct. Each succeeding prohibition is meant to cover additional kinds of illegalities—not to narrow the reach of the prior sections." Indeed, since Congress drafted § 17(a) in such a manner as to compel the conclusion that scienter is required under one subparagraph but not under the other two, it would take a very clear expression in the legislative history of congressional intent to the contrary to justify the conclusion that the statute does not mean what it so plainly seems to say....

Accordingly, when scienter is an element of the substantive violation sought to be enjoined, it must be proven before an injunction may issue. But with respect to those provisions such as § 17(a)(2) and § 17(a)(3), which may be violated even in the absence of scienter,...there is nothing in the legislative history of either provision to suggest a contrary legislative intent.

This is not to say, however, that scienter has no bearing at all on whether a district court should enjoin a person violating or about to violate § 17(a)(2) or § 17(a)(3). In cases where the Commission is seeking to enjoin a person "*about* to engage in any acts or practices which...*will* constitute" a violation of those provisions, the Commission must establish a sufficient evidentiary predicate to show that such future violation may occur. An important factor in this regard is the degree of intentional wrongdoing evident in a defendant's past conduct. Moreover, as the Commission recognizes, a district court may consider scienter or lack of it as one of the aggravating or mitigating factors to be taken into account in exercising its equitable discretion in deciding whether or not to grant injunctive relief. And the proper exercise of equitable discretion is necessary to ensure a "nice adjustment and reconciliation between the public interest and private needs."

For the reasons stated in this opinion, we hold that the Commission is required to establish scienter as an element of a civil enforcement action to enjoin violations of § 17(a)(1) of the 1933 Act....We further hold that the Commission need not establish scienter as an element of an action to enjoin violations of § 17(a)(2) and § 17(a)(3) of the 1933 Act. The Court of Appeals affirmed the issuance of the injunction in this case in the misapprehension that it was not necessary to find scienter in order to support an injunction under any of the provisions in question. Accordingly, the judgment of the Court of Appeals is vacated, and the case is remanded to that court for further proceedings consistent with this opinion. [*So ordered.*]

## 10.   Defenses

The Federal Securities Act of 1933 recognizes several defenses that may be used to avoid liability. Lack of materiality is a common defense. Determining whether or not a particular fact is material depends on the facts and the parties involved.

The statute of limitations is a defense for both civil and criminal liability. The basic period is one year. The statute does not start to run until the discovery of the untrue statement or omission. Or it does not start to run until the time such discovery would have been made with reasonable diligence. In no event may a suit be brought more than three years after the sale.

A defense similar to the statute of limitations is also provided. This statute provides that if the person acquiring the security does so after the issuer has made generally available an earnings statement covering at least twelve months after the effective date of the registration statement, then this person must prove actual reliance on the registration statement. However, this defense has little applicability in most cases.

A very important defense for experts such as accountants is the due diligence defense. The law provides that no person is liable who shall sustain the burden of proof that "as regards any part of the registration statement purporting to be made upon his authority as an expert that he had, after reasonable investigation, reasonable ground to believe and did believe, at the time such part of the registration statement became effective, that the statements therein were true and that there was no omission to state a material fact required to be stated therein or necessary to make the statements therein not misleading." In determining whether or not an expert such as an accountant has made a reasonable investigation, the law provides that the standard of reasonableness is that required of a prudent person in the management of his or her own property. The burden of proof of this defense is on the expert, and the test is as of the time the registration statement became effective. The due diligence defense, in effect, requires proof that a party was not guilty of fraud or negligence.

To better understand the materials concerning civil liability under the Federal Securities Act of 1933, study Table 19-2. It is intended as a summary of Sections 11, 12, and 17.

# FEDERAL SECURITIES EXCHANGE ACT OF 1934: BEING PUBLIC

## 11.   General Coverage

Whereas the Federal Securities Act of 1933 deals with original offerings of securities, the Federal Securities Exchange Act of 1934 regulates transfers of securities after the initial sale. The 1934 Act, which created the SEC, also deals with regulation of security exchanges, brokers, and dealers in securities.

It is illegal to sell a security on a national exchange unless a registration is effective for the security. Registration under the 1934 Act differs from registration under the 1933 Act. Registration under the former requires filing prescribed forms with the applicable stock exchange and the SEC. As a

**TABLE 19-2**   Civil Liability under the 1933 Act

| Section of 1933 Act | Purpose of Section | Plaintiff's Required Proof of Defendant's Scienter | Defendant's Defense |
|---|---|---|---|
| Section 11 | Creates liability for false or misleading registration statements | Not required to prove defendant's intent to deceive | 1  Proof of no false or misleading information is a defense<br>2  Proof that plaintiff knew of false or misleading nature of information is a defense<br>3  Except for issuer, proof of reliance on an expert (attorney, accountant, etc.) is a defense<br>4  Proof of good faith is *not* a defense. |
| Section 12 | 1  Creates liability for failing to file a required registration statement<br>2  Creates liability for false or misleading prospectus | 1  Not required to prove defendant's intent to deceive<br><br>2  Not required to prove defendant's intent to deceive | 1  *In pari delicto;* the plaintiff was equally at fault for failing to file the registration statement<br>2  Same as Section 11, above |
| Section 17 | In an interstate transaction it is:<br>1  unlawful to employ device, scheme, or artifice to defraud<br>2  unlawful to obtain money or property by untrue statement or omission of material fact<br>3  unlawful to engage in events which operate or would operate as a fraud or deceit | 1  Required to prove defendant's intent to deceive<br>2  Not required to prove defendant's intent to deceive<br>3  Not required to prove defendant's intent to deceive | 1  Proof of no intent to deceive is a defense; good faith is a defense<br>2  Proof of no material misstatement of omission is a defense; good faith is *not* a defense<br>3  Proof of no involvement in unlawful activities is a defense; good faith is *not* a defense |

general rule, all equity securities held by 500 or more owners must be registered if the issuer has more than $1 million in gross assets. This rule picks up issues traded over the counter and applies to securities that might have qualified under one of the exemptions under the 1933 Act.

Provisions relating to stockbrokers and dealers prohibit the use of the mails or any other instrumentality of interstate commerce to sell securities unless the broker or the dealer is registered. The language is sufficiently broad to cover attempted sales as well as actual sales. Brokers and dealers must keep detailed records of their activities and file annual reports with the SEC.

The SEC requires that issuers of registered securities file periodic reports as well as report significant developments which would affect the value of the security. For example, the SEC requires companies to disclose foreign payoffs or bribes to obtain or retain foreign business operations. Businesses must disclose their minority hiring practices and other social data that may be of public concern. Business has been forced by the SEC to submit certain shareholder proposals to all shareholders as a part of proxy solicitation. When a new pension law was enacted, the SEC required that financial reports disclose the law's impact on the reporting business. SEC activity concerning information corporations must furnish to the investing public is almost limitless. As a result, SEC regulations are of paramount significance to all persons concerned with the financial aspects of business. This area of regulation directly affects the accounting profession. Since the SEC regulates financial statements, the Commission frequently decides issues of proper accounting and auditing theory and practices.

How the Federal Securities Exchange Act of 1934 affects the business person, the accountant, the lawyer, the broker, and the investor is seen in the following sections. These sections cover some fundamental concepts of this law, such as civil liability in general and insider transactions in particular, as well as criminal violations and penalties under the 1934 Act.

## 12.   Section 10(b) and Rule 10b-5

Most of the litigation under the Federal Securities and Exchange Act of 1934 is brought under Section 10(b) of the Act and Rule 10b-5 promulgated by the SEC pursuant to the Act. Section 10(b) and Rule 10b-5 declare that it is unlawful to use the mails or any instrumentality of interstate commerce or any national securities exchange to defraud *any person* in connection with the *purchase or sale* of any security. They provide a private remedy for defrauded investors. This remedy may be invoked against "any person" who indulges in fraudulent practices in the purchase or sale of securities. In actual practice, defendants in such cases tend to fall into four general categories: (1) insiders; (2) broker-dealers; (3) corporations whose stock is purchased or sold by plaintiffs; and (4) those, such as accountants, who "aid and abet" or conspire with a party who falls into one of the first three categories.

Section 10(b) and Rule 10b-5 are usually referred to as the antifraud provisions of the Act. A plaintiff seeking damages under the provisions must establish (1) the existence of a material misrepresentation or omission made in connection with the purchase or sale of a security, (2) the culpable state of mind of the defendant, (3) his or her reliance and due diligence, and (4) damage as a result of the reliance. Materiality under the 1934 Act is the same as materiality under the 1933 Act. Liability under Rule 10b-5 requires proof of scienter and not proof of simple negligence. It also requires proof of a practice that is manipulative and not merely corporate mismanagement.

One of the most difficult issues concerning materiality arises in preliminary merger negotiations. What should management respond when asked about merger possibilities? The following case involves the Supreme Court's examination of this issue.

# BASIC INCORPORATED v. LEVINSON
108 S.Ct. 978 (1988)

BLACKMUN, J.:...This case requires us to apply the materiality requirement of § 10(b) of the Securities Exchange Act of 1934 and the Securities and Exchange Commission's Rule 10b-5, promulgated thereunder, in the context of preliminary corporate merger discussions....

Prior to December 20, 1978, Basic Incorporated was a publicly traded company primarily engaged in the business of manufacturing chemical refractories for the steel industry. As early as 1965 or 1966, Combustion Engineering, Inc., a company producing mostly alumina-based refractories, expressed some interest in acquiring Basic, but was deterred from pursuing this inclination seriously because of antitrust concerns it then entertained. In 1976, however, regulatory action opened the way to a renewal of Combustion's interest. The "Strategic Plan," dated October 25, 1976, for Combustion's Industrial Products Group included the objective: "Acquire Basic Inc. $30 million."

Beginning in September 1976, Combustion representatives had meetings and telephone conversations with Basic officers and directors, including petitioners here, concerning the possibility of a merger. During 1977 and 1978, Basic made three public statements denying that it was engaged in merger negotiations. On December 18,

1978, Basic asked the New York Stock Exchange to suspend trading in its shares and issued a release stating that it had been "approached" by another company concerning a merger. On December 19, Basic's board endorsed Combustion's offer of $46 per share for its common stock, and on the following day publicly announced its approval of Combustion's tender offer for all outstanding shares.

Respondents are former Basic shareholders who sold their stock after Basic's first public statement of October 21, 1977, and before the suspension of trading in December 1978. Respondents brought a class action against Basic and its directors, asserting that the defendants issued three false or misleading public statements and thereby were in violation of § 10(b) of the 1934 Act and of Rule 10b-5. Respondents alleged that they were injured by selling Basic shares at artificially depressed prices in a market affected by petitioners' misleading statements and in reliance thereon.

...On the merits...the District Court granted summary judgment for the defendants. It held that, as a matter of law, any misstatements were immaterial: there were no negotiations ongoing at the time of the first statement, and although negotiations were taking place when the second and third statements were issued, those negotiations were not "destined, with reasonable certainty, to become a merger agreement in principle."

The United States Court of Appeals for the Sixth Circuit…reversed the District Court's summary judgment and remanded the case. The court reasoned that while petitioners were under no general duty to disclose their discussions with Combustion, any statement the company voluntarily released could not be so incomplete as to mislead. In the Court of Appeals' view, Basic's statements that no negotiations were taking place, and that it knew of no corporate developments to account for the heavy trading activity, were misleading. With respect to materiality, the court rejected the argument that preliminary merger discussions are immaterial as a matter of law, and held that "once a statement is made denying the existence of any discussions, even discussions that might not have been material in absence of the denial are material because they make the statement made untrue."…

We granted certiorari to resolve the split among the Courts of Appeals as to the standard of materiality applicable to preliminary merger discussions.…

The 1934 Act was designed to protect investors against manipulation of stock prices. Underlying the adoption of extensive disclosure requirements was a legislative philosophy: "There cannot be honest markets without honest publicity. Manipulation and dishonest practices of the market place thrive upon mystery and secrecy." This Court repeatedly has described the fundamental purpose of the Act as implementing a philosophy of full disclosure.…

The Court previously has addressed various positive and common-law requirements for a violation of § 10(b) or of Rule 10b-5. The Court also explicitly has defined a standard of materiality under the securities laws, see *TSC Industries, Inc. v. Northway, Inc.*, 426 U.S. 438, 96 S.Ct. 2126, 48 L.Ed.2d 757 (1976), concluding in the proxy-solicitation context that "[a]n omitted fact is material if there is a substantial likelihood that a reasonable shareholder would consider it important in deciding how to vote." Acknowledging that certain information concerning corporate developments could well be of "dubious significance," the Court was careful not to set too low a standard of materiality; it was concerned that a minimal standard might bring an overabundance of information within its reach, and lead management "simply to bury the shareholders in an avalanche of trivial information—a result that is hardly conducive to informed decisionmaking." It further explained that to fulfill the materiality requirement "there must be a substantial likelihood that the disclosure of the omitted fact would have been viewed by the reasonable investor as having significantly altered the 'total mix' of information made available." We now expressly adopt the *TSC Industries* standard of materiality for the § 10(b) and Rule 10b-5 context.

The application of this materiality standard to preliminary merger discussions is not self-evident. Where the impact of the corporate development on the target's fortune is certain and clear, the *TSC Industries* materiality definition admits straightforward application. Where, on the other hand, the event is contingent or speculative in nature, it is difficult to ascertain whether the "reasonable investor" would have considered the omitted information significant at the time. Merger negotiations, because of the ever-present possibility that the contemplated transaction will not be effectuated, fall into the latter category.

Petitioners urge upon us a Third Circuit test for resolving this difficulty. Under this approach, preliminary merger discussions do not become material until "agreement-in-principle" as to the price and structure of the transaction has been reached between the would-be merger partners. By definition, then, information concerning any negotiations not yet at the agreement-in-principle stage could be withheld or even misrepresented without a violation of Rule 10b-5....

[The Court examined the rationale used to support the agreement-in-principle theory of materiality and concluded with the following statement.]

We...find no valid justification for artificially excluding from the definition of materiality information concerning merger discussions, which would otherwise be considered significant to the trading decision of a reasonable investor, merely because agreement-in-principle as to price and structure has not yet been reached by the parties or their representatives.

Even before this Court's decision in *TSC Industries*, the Second Circuit had explained the role of the materiality requirement of Rule 10b-5, with respect to contingent or speculative information or events, in a manner that gave that term meaning that is independent of the other provisions of the Rule. Under such circumstances, materiality "will depend at any given time upon a balancing of both the indicated probability that the event will occur and the anticipated magnitude of the event in light of the totality of the company activity." *SEC v. Texas Gulf Sulphur Co.*, 401 F.2d, at 849. Interestingly, neither the Third Circuit decision adopting the agreement-in-principle test nor petitioners here take issue with this general standard. Rather, they suggest that with respect to preliminary merger discussions, there are good reasons to draw a line at agreement on price and structure.

In a subsequent decision, the late Judge Friendly, writing for a Second Circuit panel, applied the *Texas Gulf Sulphur* probability/

magnitude approach in the specific context of preliminary merger negotiations. After acknowledging that materiality is something to be determined on the basis of the particular facts of each case, he stated:

**Since a merger in which it is bought out is the most important event that can occur in a small corporation's life, to wit, its death, we think that inside information, as regards a merger of this sort, can become material at an earlier stage than would be the case as regards lesser transactions—and this even though the mortality rate of mergers in such formative stages is doubtless high.**

*SEC v. Geon Industries, Inc.*, 531 F.2d 39, 47–48 (CA2 1976). We agree with that analysis.

Whether merger discussions in any particular case are material therefore depends on the facts. Generally, in order to assess the probability that the event will occur, a factfinder will need to look to indicia of interest in the transaction at the highest corporate levels. Without attempting to catalog all such possible factors, we note by way of example that board resolutions, instructions to investment bankers, and actual negotiations between principals or their intermediaries may serve as indicia of interest. To assess the magnitude of the transaction to the issuer of the securities allegedly manipulated, a factfinder will need to consider such facts as the size of the two corporate entities and of the potential premiums over market value. No particular event or factor short of closing the transaction need be either necessary or sufficient by itself to render merger discussions material.

As we clarify today, materiality depends on the significance the reasonable investor would place on the withheld or misrepresented information. The fact-specific inquiry we endorse here is consistent with the approach a number of courts have taken in assessing the materiality of merger negotiations. Because the standard of materiality we have adopted differs from that used by both courts below, we remand the case for reconsideration of the question whether a grant of summary judgment is appropriate on this record. [*Remanded.*]

The concept of fraud under Section 10(b) encompasses not only untrue statements of material facts, but also the failure to state material facts necessary to prevent statements actually made from being misleading. In other words, a half-truth that misleads is fraudulent. Finally, failure to correct a misleading impression left by statements already made, or silence where there is a duty to speak, gives rise to a violation of Rule 10b-5 because it is a form of "aiding and abetting." Although there is no general duty on the part of all persons with knowledge of improper activities to report them, a duty to disclose may arise from the fact of a special relationship or set of circumstances, such as an accountant certifying financial statements.

The application of Section 10(b) and Rule 10b-5 applies to all sales of any security if the requisite fraud exists and the interstate aspect is established. The rule requires that those standing in a fiduciary relationship disclose all material facts before entering into transactions. This means that an officer, a director, or a controlling shareholder has a duty to disclose all material facts. Failure to do so is a violation and, in effect, fraudulent. Privity of contract is not required for a violation, and lack of privity of contract is no defense.

Liability under Rule 10b-5 may be imposed on an accountant even though he or she performs only an unaudited write-up. An accountant is liable for errors in financial statements contained in a prospectus or other filed report even though unaudited if there are errors he or she knew or should have known. Even when performing an unaudited write-up, an accountant must undertake at least a minimal investigation into the figures supplied to him or her and cannot disregard suspicious circumstances.

A plaintiff in a suit under Rule 10b-5 must prove damages. The damages of a defrauded purchaser are usually "out-of-pocket" losses or the excess of "what was paid" over the value of "what was received." Courts in a few cases have used the "benefit of the bargain" measure of damages and awarded the buyer the difference between what he or she paid and what the security was represented to be worth. A buyer's damages are measured at the time of purchase.

Computation of a defrauded seller's damages is more difficult. A defrauding purchaser usually benefits from an increase in the value of the securities, while the plaintiff seller loses this increase. Courts do not allow defrauding buyers to keep these increases in value. Therefore, the measure of the seller's damages is the difference between the fair value of all that the seller received and the fair value of what he or she would have received had there been no fraud, except where the defendant received more than the seller's loss. In this latter case, the seller is entitled to the defendant's profit. As a result, defendants lose all profits flowing from the fraudulent conduct.

Plaintiffs under Rule 10b-5 are also entitled to consequential damages. These include lost dividends, brokerage fees, and taxes. In addition, courts may order payment of interest on the funds. Punitive damages are not permitted as they are in cases of common-law fraud based on state laws. This distinction results from the language of the statute which limits recoveries to "actual damages."

As a general rule, attorneys' fees are not recoverable. This is consistent with the rule in most litigation. However, in class action suits, the attorneys can collect their fees out of the recovery. These fees in a class action suit will often exceed the usual hourly rate and will often be close to or equal to the contingent fee rate (one-third of the recovery).

## 13.   Insider Transactions

Section 16, one of the most important provisions of the Federal Securities Exchange Act of 1934, concerns insider transactions. An **insider** is any person (1) who owns more than 10 percent of any security, or (2) who is a director or an officer of the issuer of the security. Section 16 and SEC regulations require that insiders file, at the time of the registration or within ten days after becoming an insider, a statement of the amount of such issues of which they are the owners. The regulations also require filing within ten days after the close of each calendar month thereafter, if there has been any change in such ownership during such month (indicating the change). There are exemptions to the insider rules for executors or administrators of estates, and odd-lot dealers are also generally exempt.

The reason for prohibiting insiders from trading for profits is to prevent the use of information that is available to an insider but not to the general public. Because the SEC cannot determine for certain when nonpublic information is improperly used, Section 16 creates a presumption that any profit made within a six-month time period is illegal. These profits are referred to as *short-swing profits*. Thus, if a director, officer, or principal owner realizes profits on the purchase and sale of a security within a six-month period, the profits inure and belong to the company or to the investor who purchased it from or sold it to an insider, resulting in the insider's profit and investor's loss. The order of the purchase and sale is immaterial. The profit is calculated on the lowest price in and highest price out during any six-month period. Unlike the required proof of intent to deceive under Section 10(b), the short-swing profits rule of Section 16 does not depend on any misuse of information. In other words, short-swing profits by insiders, regardless of the insiders' state of mind, are absolutely prohibited.

Insider rules are rigidly applied in ordinary sale and purchase transactions. However, courts have held that the provisions do not apply to certain "unorthodox" transactions that are not within the intent of the law. For example, it has been held that if a purchaser did not own 10 percent of the total stock prior to the purchase, then the purchase and later sale within six months was not subject to the law.

## 14. Nonpublic Information

The SEC's concern for trading based on nonpublic information goes beyond the Section 16 ban on short-swing profits. Indeed, a person who is not technically an insider but who trades securities without disclosing nonpublic information may violate Section 10(b) and Rule 10b-5. The SEC takes the position that the profit obtained as the result of a trader's silence concerning information that is not freely available to everyone is a manipulation or deception prohibited by Section 10(b) and Rule 10b-5. In essence, the users of nonpublic information are treated like insiders if they can be classified as a *tippee,* or a *temporary insider.*

A tippee is a person who learns of nonpublic information from an insider. A tippee is liable for the use of nonpublic information, because an insider should not be allowed to do indirectly what he cannot do directly. In other words, a tippee is liable for trading or passing on information that is nonpublic.

The use of nonpublic information for financial gain has not been prohibited entirely. For example, in one case, a financial printer had been hired to print corporate takeover bids. An employee of the printer was able to deduce the identities of both the acquiring companies and the companies targeted for takeover. Without disclosing the knowledge about the prospective takeover bids, the employee purchased stock in the target companies and then sold it for a profit immediately after the takeover attempts were made public. He was indicted and convicted for having violated Section 10(b) and Rule 10b-5. The Supreme Court reversed, holding that the defendant had no duty not to reveal the nonpublic information, since he was not in a fiduciary position with respect to either the acquiring or the acquired companies.

In another case the United States Supreme Court further narrowed a tippee's liability. The Court ruled that a tippee becomes liable under Section 10(b) only if the tipper breaches a fiduciary duty to the business organization or fellow shareholders. Therefore, if the tipper communicated nonpublic information for reasons other than personal gain, neither the tipper nor the tippee could be liable for a securities violation.

These two Supreme Court cases have made it more difficult for the SEC to control the use of nonpublic information. Despite these court-created loopholes in the SEC's efforts, this agency has been successful in convincing district and appellate courts that a person should be considered to be a temporary insider if that person conveys nonpublic information which was to have been kept confidential. This philosophy has become known as the *misappropriation theory* of insider trading.

In the following case, the Supreme Court failed to support or reject the misappropriation theory since it was evenly divided. Nevertheless the facts of this case provide the typical situation that the SEC wishes to control in order to restore and maintain the public's confidence in the securities exchanges.

# CARPENTER v. U.S.
108 S.Ct. 316 (1987)

WHITE, J.:...Petitioners Kenneth Felis and R. Foster Winans were convicted of violating § 10(b) of the Securities Exchange Act of 1934 and Rule 10b-5....Petitioner David Carpenter, Winans' roommate, was convicted for aiding and abetting....

In 1981, Winans became a reporter for the Wall Street Journal (the Journal) and in the summer of 1982 became one of the two writers of a daily column, "Heard on the Street." That column discussed selected stocks or groups of stocks, giving positive and negative information about those stocks and taking "a point of view with respect to investment in the stocks that it reviews." Winans regularly interviewed corporate executives to put together interesting perspectives on the stocks that would be highlighted in upcoming columns, but, at least for the columns at issue here, none contained corporate inside information or any "hold for release" information. Because of the "Heard" column's perceived quality and integrity, it had the potential of affecting the price of the stocks which it examined. The District Court concluded on the basis of testimony presented at trial that the "Heard" column "does have an impact on the market, difficult though it may be to quantify in any particular case."

The official policy and practice at the Journal was that prior to publication, the contents of the column were the Journal's confidential information. Despite the rule, with which Winans was familiar, he entered into a scheme in October 1983 with Peter Brant and petitioner Felis, both connected with the Kidder Peabody brokerage firm in New York City, to give them advance information as to the timing and contents of the "Heard" column. This permitted Brant and Felis and another conspirator, David Clark, a client of Brant, to buy or sell based on the probable impact of the column on the market. Profits were to be shared. The conspirators agreed that the scheme would not affect the journalistic purity of the "Heard" column, and the District Court did not find that the contents of any of the articles were altered to further the profit potential of petitioners' stock-trading scheme. Over a four-month period, the brokers made prepublication trades on the basis of information given them by Winans about the contents of some 27 Heard columns. The net profits from these trades were about $690,000.

In November 1983, correlations between the "Heard" articles and trading in the Clark and Felis accounts were noted at Kidder Peabody and inquiries began. Brant and Felis denied knowing anyone at the Journal and took steps to conceal the trades. Later, the Securities and Exchange Commission began an investigation. Questions were met by denials both by the brokers at Kidder Peabody and by Winans at the Journal. As the investigation progressed, the conspirators quarreled, and on March 29, 1984, Winans and Carpenter went to the SEC and revealed the entire scheme. This indictment and a bench trial followed. Brant, who had pled guilty under a plea agreement, was a witness for the Government.

The District Court found, and the Court of Appeals agreed, that Winans had knowingly breached a duty of confidentiality by misappropriating prepublication information regarding the timing and contents of the "Heard" columns, information that had been gained in the course of his employment under the understanding that it would not be revealed in advance of publication and that if it were, he would report it to his employer. It was this appropriation of confidential information that underlay...the securities laws...counts. With respect to the § 10(b) charges, the courts below held that the deliberate breach of Winans' duty of confidentiality and concealment of the scheme was a fraud and deceit on the Journal. Although the victim of the fraud, the Journal, was not a buyer or seller of the stocks traded in or otherwise a market participant, the fraud was nevertheless considered to be "in connection with" a purchase or sale of securities within the meaning of the statute and the rule. The courts reasoned that the scheme's sole purpose was to buy and sell securities at a profit based on advance information of the column's contents. The courts below rejected petitioners' submission...that criminal liability could not be imposed on petitioners under Rule 10b-5 because "the newspaper is the only alleged victim of fraud and has no interest in the securities traded."...

The Court is evenly divided with respect to the convictions under the securities laws and for that reason affirms the judgment below on those counts....[*Affirmed.*]

---

While the facts of the preceding case have received substantial media attention, the importance of the SEC's victory in this case has been overshadowed by the events that led to the Ivan Boesky case. The magnitude of Mr. Boesky's trading with nonpublic information is evidenced by his consent to pay $100,000,000 in illegal profits. Mr. Boesky also was sentenced to three years in prison after pleading guilty to 10(b) violations. With the cooperation of Mr. Boesky, the SEC and the Justice Department have brought numerous cases of illegal trading against individuals and brokerage firms. The largest case to date (through 1988) resulted in the firm of Drexel Burnham Lambert, Inc. pleading guilty to six felonies and paying $650,000,000 in fines and illegal profits.

The SEC has been trying to curb "insider" transactions, but historically it has been difficult because of a limited civil sanction. Historically, the "insider" has been liable only to return the profit illegally gained. In 1984, President Reagan signed into law authority for the SEC to seek a civil penalty of three times the illegal profits. In 1988, then President Reagan signed legislation that further increased the penalties for trading with nonpublic information. Under this law, companies that fail to prevent these violations by employees may be civilly liable for treble damages. It is anticipated that the SEC will use these increased penalties to further its campaign against the use of inside information.

Because of the increased SEC enforcement, corporations' interest in insiders' use of nonpublic information is very high. The following statement from Caterpillar's Code of Ethics illustrates an appropriate corporate policy on the use and nonuse of inside information.

## INSIDE INFORMATION

Inside information may be defined as information about Caterpillar which isn't known to the investing public. Such information may have value—for example, certain financial data, technical materials, and future plans. Those with access to such information are expected to treat it confidentially, and in a fashion which avoids harm to Caterpillar.

Inside information may or may not be "material." Information is "material" if there is substantial likelihood that a reasonable investor would consider it important in making an investment decision about Caterpillar.

Those who have "material" inside information are expected to refrain from using it for personal gain. For example, they are required to refrain from personal trading of Caterpillar stock until the information has become public...or until it's no longer "material."

The preceding pertains to both: (1) all corporate officers; and (2) those who, by reason of their jobs, possess such information.

While Caterpillar may hire individuals who have knowledge and experience in various technical areas, we don't wish to employ such persons as a means of gaining access to trade secrets of others. New employees are asked not to divulge such trade secrets.

The concept of "inside information" extends outside the company, and requires ethical judgments by people involved. Beyond other conflict of interest rules which may apply, a Caterpillar employee having access to confidential company information that could affect the price of a supplier's, customer's or customer's stock shouldn't trade in such stock.

## 15. Additional Civil Liability

Section 18 of the Securities Exchange Act of 1934 imposes liability on a theory of fraud on any person who shall make or cause to be made any false and misleading statements of material fact in any application, report, or document filed under the act. This liability favors both purchasers and sellers. Plaintiffs must prove scienter (knowingly making a false statement), reliance on the false or misleading statement, and damage. Good faith is a defense. Good faith exists when a person acts without knowledge that the statement is false and misleading. In other words, freedom from fraud is a defense under an action predicated on Section 18. There is no liability under this section for simple negligence.

In addition to Section 18, the securities laws include many provisions that require reports to be filed with the SEC. These reporting provisions do not lead to a civil remedy for inaccurate reporting. This result is due in part to the specific civil remedy provided in Section 18.

Section 14(e) of the Act prohibits fraudulent, deceptive, or manipulative acts or practices in connection with tender offers. This provision has been interpreted in the same way as Section 10(b). For a violation to occur, there must be a misrepresentation or nondisclosure of a material fact—in other words, fraud must be proven. Unfairness is not a violation.

# SCHREIBER v. BURLINGTON NORTHERN, INC.
105 S.Ct. 2458 (1985)

In December, 1982, Burlington Northern, Inc., made a hostile tender offer for El Paso Gas Co. Although a majority of El Paso's shareholders subscribed, Burlington did not accept the tendered shares. In January 1983, Burlington and El Paso announced "a new and friendly takeover agreement." Burlington rescinded the December tender offer and substituted a new tender offer. This January tender offer was soon oversubscribed by the shareholders. The rescission of the first tender offer caused a reduced payment to those shareholders who had tendered during the first offer, because those shareholders who retendered were subject to substantial proration. Plaintiff (petitioner) filed suit on behalf of herself and similarly situated shareholders, alleging that Burlington, El Paso, and members of El Paso's board had violated Section 14(e) of the Securities Exchange Act of 1934, which prohibits "fraudulent, deceptive or manipulative acts or practices...in connection with any tender offer." She alleged that Burlington's withdrawal of the first tender offer, coupled with the substitution of the January offer, was a "manipulative" distortion of the market for El Paso stock. The District Court dismissed the suit, and the Court of Appeals affirmed.

BURGER, J.:...We are asked in this case to interpret § 14(e) of the Securities Exchange Act. The starting point is the language of the statute. Section 14(e) provides:

**It shall be unlawful for any person to make any untrue statement of a material fact or omit to state any material fact necessary in order to make the statements made, in the light of the circumstances under which they are made, not misleading, or to engage in any fraudulent, deceptive or manipulative acts or practices, in connection with any tender offer or request or invitation for tenders, or any solicitation of security holders in opposition to or in favor of any such offer, request, or invitation. The Commission shall, for the purposes of this subsection, by rules and regulations define, and prescribe means reasonably designed to prevent, such acts and practices as are fraudulent, deceptive, or manipulative.**

Petitioner relies on a construction of the phrase, "fraudulent, deceptive or manipulative acts or practices." Petitioner reads the phrase "fraudulent, deceptive or manipulative acts or practices" to include acts which, although fully disclosed, "artificially" affect the price of the takeover target's stock. Petitioner's interpretation relies on the belief that § 14(e) is directed at purposes broader than providing full and true information to investors.

Petitioner's reading of the term "manipulative" conflicts with the normal meaning of the term. We have held in the context of an alleged violation of § 10(b) of the Securities Exchange Act:

**Use of the word 'manipulative' is especially significant. It is and was virtually a term of art when used in connection with the securities markets. It connotes intentional or willful conduct** *designed to deceive or defraud* **investors by controlling or artificially affecting the price of securities.**

Other cases interpreting the term reflect its use as a general term comprising a range of misleading practices:

**The term refers generally to practices, such as wash sales, matched orders, or rigged prices, that are intended to mislead investors by artificially affecting market activity.... Section 10(b)'s general prohibition of practices deemed by the SEC to be 'manipulative'—in this technical sense of artificially affecting market activity in order to mislead investors—is fully consistent with the fundamental purpose of the 1934 Act "to substitute a philosophy of full disclosure for the philosophy of** *caveat emptor....***" ...Indeed, nondisclosure is usually essential to the success of a manipulative scheme....No doubt Congress meant to prohibit the full range of ingenious devices that might be used to manipulate securities prices. But we do not think it would have chosen this 'term of art' if it had meant to bring within the scope of § 10(b) instances of corporate mismanagement such as**

**this, in which the essence of the complaint is that shareholders were treated unfairly by a fiduciary.**

The meaning the Court has given the term "manipulative" is consistent with the use of the term at common law, and with its traditional dictionary definition.

She argues, however, that the term manipulative takes on a meaning in § 14(e) that is different from the meaning it has in § 10(b). Petitioner claims that the use of the disjunctive "or" in § 14(e) implies that acts need not be deceptive or fraudulent to be manipulative. But Congress used the phrase "manipulative or deceptive" in § 10(b) as well, and we have interpreted "manipulative" in that context to require misrepresention....

All three species of misconduct, *i.e.*, "fraudulent, deceptive or manipulative," listed by Congress are directed at failures to disclose. The use of the term "manipulative" provides emphasis and guidance to those who must determine which types of acts are reached by the statute; it does not suggest a deviation from the section's facial and primary concern with disclosure or Congressional concern with disclosure which is the core of the Act.

Our conclusion that "manipulative" acts under § 14(e) require misrepresentation or nondisclosure is buttressed by the purpose and legislative history of the provision. Section 14(e) was originally added to the Securities Exchange Act as part of the Williams Act. "The purpose of the Williams Act is to insure that public shareholders who are confronted by a cash tender offer for their stock will not be required to respond without adequate information."...

Nowhere in the legislative history is there the slightest suggestion that § 14(e) serves any purpose other than disclosure, or that the term "manipulative" should be read as an invitation to the courts to oversee the substantive fairness of tender offers; the quality of any offer is a matter for the marketplace.

To adopt the reading of the term "manipulative" urged by petitioner would not only be unwarranted in light of the legislative purpose but would be at odds with it. Inviting judges to read the term "manipulative" with their own sense of what constitutes "unfair" or "artificial" conduct would inject uncertainty into the tender offer process. An essential piece of information—whether the court would deem the fully disclosed actions of one side or the other to be "manipulative"—would not be available until after the tender offer had closed. This uncertainty would directly contradict the expressed Congressional desire to give investors full information.

Congress' consistent emphasis on disclosure persuades us that it intended takeover contests to be addressed to shareholders. In pursuit of this goal, Congress, consistent with the core mechanism of the Securities Exchange Act, created sweeping disclosure requirements and narrow substantive safeguards. The same Congress that placed such emphasis on the shareholder choice would not at the same time have required judges to oversee tender offers for substantive fairness. It is even less likely that a Congress implementing that intention would express it only through the use of a single word placed in the middle of a provision otherwise devoted to disclosure.

We hold that the term "manipulative" as used in § 14(e) requires misrepresentation or nondisclosure. It connotes "conduct designed to deceive or defraud investors by controlling or artificially affecting the price of securities." Without misrepresentation or nondisclosure, § 14(3) has not been violated.

Applying that definition to this case, we hold that the actions of respondents were not manipulative. The amended complaint fails to allege that the cancellation of the first tender offer was accompanied by any misrepresentation, nondisclosure or deception. The District Court correctly found, "All activity of the defendants that could have conceivably affected the price of El Paso shares was done openly."…[*Affirmed.*]

## 16. Criminal Liability

The 1934 Act provides for criminal sanctions for willful violations of its provisions or the rules adopted under it. Liability is imposed for false material statements in applications, reports, documents, and registration statements. The penalty is a fine not to exceed $100,000 or five years in prison, or both. Corporations may be fined up to $500,000. Due to the emphasis the SEC has placed on the unlawful use of nonpublic information (see section 14 above), Congress passed and President Reagan signed legislation that increased the criminal sanctions for insider trading. Today, individuals found guilty of this violation face up to a $1,000,000 fine and 10 years in prison. Corporations may be fined up to $2,500,000 for insider trading violations.

Failure to file the required reports and documents makes the issuer subject to a $100 forfeiture per day. A person cannot be convicted if he or she proves that he or she has no knowledge of a rule or regulation, but, of course, lack of knowledge of a statute is no defense.

Criminal liability is important for officers and directors. It is also important for accountants. Accountants have been found guilty of a crime for failure to disclose important facts to shareholder-investors. Compliance with generally accepted accounting principles is not an absolute defense. The critical issue in such cases is whether the financial statements as a whole fairly present the financial condition of the company and whether they accurately report operations for the covered periods. If they do not, the second issue is whether the accountant acted in good faith. Compliance with generally accepted accounting principles is evidence of good faith, but such evidence is not necessarily conclusive. Lack of criminal intent is the defense usually asserted by accountants charged with a crime. They usually admit mistakes or even negligence but deny any criminal wrongdoing. Proof of motive is not required.

In the case of *United States v. Natelli,* 527 F.2d 311 (1975), the U.S. Court of Appeals for the Second Circuit had occasion to discuss the element of criminal intent and the role of the jury in deciding if it exists. It noted that the failure to follow sound accounting practice is evidence that may prove criminal intent. It said in part:

> It is hard to prove the intent of a defendant. Circumstantial evidence, particularly with proof of motive, where available, is often sufficient to convince a reasonable man of criminal intent beyond a reasonable doubt. When we deal with a defendant who is a professional accountant, it is even harder, at times, to distinguish between simple errors of judgment and errors made with sufficient criminal intent to support a conviction, especially when there is no financial gain to the accountant other than his legitimate fee....
>
> ...The arguments Natelli makes in this court as evidence of his innocent intent were made to the jury and presented fairly. There is no contention that Judge Tyler improperly excluded any factual evidence offered....
>
> ...We reject the argument of insufficiency as to Natelli, our function being limited to determining whether the evidence was sufficient for submission to the jury. We hold that it was.
>
> ...There are points in favor of Natelli, to be sure, but these were presented to the jury and rejected.

From the foregoing, it is clear that great deference is given to the findings of fact by the jury in criminal cases.

As with issues of civil liability, most cases involving potential criminal liability are litigated under Section 10(b) and Rule 10b-5.

# CONSIDERATIONS BEYOND THE FEDERAL SECURITIES LAWS

## 17.   State "Blue Sky" Laws

In addition to understanding the federal securities laws discussed in the previous sections, every person dealing with the issuance of securities should be familiar with state securities regulations. Throughout their history, these laws commonly have been referred to as **"blue sky" laws**—probably because they were intended to protect the potential investor from buying "a piece of the attractive blue sky" (worthless or risky securities) without financial and other information about what was being purchased. The "blue sky" laws can apply to securities subject to federal laws as well as those securities exempt from the federal statutes. It is clearly established that the federal laws do not preempt the existence of state "blue sky" laws. Due to their broad application, any person associated with issuing or thereafter transferring securities should survey the "blue sky" laws passed by the various states.

Although the existence of federal securities laws has influenced state legislatures, enactment of "blue sky" laws has not been uniform. Indeed, states typically have enacted laws that contain provisions similar to either (1) the antifraud provisions, (2) the registration of securities provisions, (3) the registration of securities brokers and dealers provisions, or (4) a combination of these provisions of the federal laws. To bring some similarity to the various "blue sky" laws, a Uniform Securities Act was proposed for adoption by all states beginning in 1956. Since that time, the Uniform Securities Act has been the model for "blue sky" laws. A majority of states have used the uniform proposal as a guideline when enacting or amending their "blue sky" laws.

### REGISTRATION REQUIREMENTS

Despite the trend toward uniformity, state laws still vary a great deal in their methods of regulating both the distribution of securities and the practices of the securities industry within each state. For example, state regulations concerning the requirements of registering securities vary widely. States have chosen one of the following types of regulations: (1) registration by notification or (2) registration by qualification. Registration by notification allows issuers to offer securities for sale automatically after a stated time period expires, unless the administrative agency takes action to prevent the offering. This is very similar to the registration process under the Federal Securities Act of 1933. Registration by qualification usually requires a more detailed disclosure by the issuer. Under this type of regulation, a security cannot be offered for sale until the administrative agency grants the issuer a license or certificate to sell securities.

In an attempt to resolve some of this conflict over the registration procedure, the drafters of the Uniform Securities Act may have compounded the problem. This act adopts the registration by notification process for an issuer who has demonstrated stability and performance. Registration by qualification is required by those issuers who do not have a proven record and who are not subject to the Federal Securities Act of 1933. In addition, the Uniform Securities Act created a third procedure—registration by coordination. For those issuers of securities who must register with the SEC, duplicate documents are filed with the state's administrative agency. Unless a state official objects, the state registration becomes effective automatically when the federal registration statement is deemed effective.

### EXEMPTIONS

To further compound the confusion about "blue sky" laws, various exemptions of the securities or transactions have been adopted by the states. Four basic exemptions from "blue sky" laws have been identified. Every state likely has enacted at least one and perhaps a combination of these exemptions. Among these common four are the exemption (1) for an isolated transaction, (2) for an offer or sale to a limited number of offerees or purchasers within a stated time period, (3) for a private offering, and (4) for a sale if the number of holders after the sale does not exceed a specified number.

This second type of exemption probably is the most common exemption since it is part of the Uniform Securities Act. Nevertheless, states vary on whether the exemption applies to offerees or to purchasers. There also is great variation on the maximum number of such offerees or purchasers involved. That number likely ranges between five and thirty-five, depending on the applicable "blue sky" law. The time period for the offers or purchases, as the case may be, also may vary; however, twelve months seems to be the most common period.

Usually the applicable time limitation is worded to read, for example, "*any* twelve-month time period." In essence, this language means that each day starts a new time period running. For example, assume a security is exempt from "blue sky" registration requirements if the issuer sells (or offers to sell) securities to no more than thirty-five investors during any twelve-month period. Furthermore, assume the following transactions occur, with each investor being a different person or entity:

On February 1, 1989, issuer sells to five investors.

On June 1, 1989, issuer sells to ten investors.

On September 1, 1989, issuer sells to ten investors.

On December 1, 1989, issuer sells to five investors.

On March 1, 1990, issuer sells to five investors.

On May 1, 1990, issuer sells to ten investors.

Only thirty investors are involved during the twelve-month period following February 1, 1989. However, forty investors are purchasers during the twelve months following June 1, 1989. Therefore, this security and the transactions involved are not exempt from the "blue sky" law. Civil as well as criminal liability may result for failure to comply with applicable legal regulations.

Although "blue sky" laws may cause confusion due to their variation, ignorance of the state legal requirements is no defense. This confusion is furthered when the business person considers the applicability of federal securities laws as well as the variety of "blue sky" laws. To diminish this confusion, any person involved in the issuance or subsequent transfer of securities should consult with lawyers and accountants as well as other experts who have a working knowledge of securities regulations.

## 18. Ethical Considerations

Because of the importance of complying with the financial reporting and disclosure requirements of the securities laws, many companies have developed explicit policies recognizing the legal and social obligations involved. Caterpillar's Code of Ethics, for example, includes the following statements:

## ACCOUNTING RECORDS AND FINANCIAL REPORTING

Accounting is called the "universal language" of business. Therefore, those who rely on the company's records—investors, creditors, and other decision makers and interested parties—have a right to information that is timely and true.

The integrity of Caterpillar accounting and financial records is based on validity, accuracy, and completeness of basic information supporting entries to the company's books of account. All employees involved in creating, processing, or recording such information are held responsible for its integrity.

Every accounting or financial entry should reflect exactly that which is described by the supporting information. There must be no concealment of information from (or by) management, or from the company's independent auditors.

Employees who become aware of possible omission, falsification, or inaccuracy of accounting and financial entries, or basic data supporting such entries, are held responsible for reporting such information. These reports are to be made as specified by corporate procedure.

A basic premise of Caterpillar's financial reporting is that conservatism in determining earnings is in the best long-term interests of the company and its shareholders. This means the accounting practices followed by Caterpillar are those which minimize: (1) the possibility of overstating reported earnings; and (2) the likelihood of having unexpected or extraordinary adjustments in future periods.

## DISCLOSURE OF INFORMATION

In a free society, institutions flourish and businesses prosper not only by customer acceptance of their products and services, but also by public acceptance of their conduct.

Therefore, the public is entitled to a reasonable explanation of operations of a business, especially as those operations bear on the public interest. Larger economic size logically begets an increased responsibility for such public communication.

In pursuit of these beliefs, the company will:

1  Respond to public inquiries—including those from the press and from governments—with answers that are prompt, informative, and courteous.
2  Keep investors, securities trading markets, employees, and the general public informed about Caterpillar on a timely, impartial basis.

## REVIEW QUESTIONS

**1**  Identify the terms in the left-hand column by matching each with the appropriate statement in the right-hand column.

(1) Registration statement

(a) An advertisement made during the waiting period. It announces the security, its price, by whom orders will be executed, and from whom a prospectus may be obtained.

(2) Prospectus

(b) A participant in the distribution of a security who guarantees the sale of an issue.

(3) Tombstone ad

(c) The individual or business organization that offers a security for sale.

(4) Insider

(d) The document that contains financial and other information. It must be filed with the SEC prior to any sale of a security.

(5) Issuer

(e) A party who controls or is controlled by the issuer.

(6) Controller person

(f) A person who owns more than 10 percent of a security of an issuer or who is a director of an officer of an issuer.

(7) Underwriter

(8) Seller

(g) Any person who contracts with a purchaser or who exerts a substantial role which causes a purchase transaction to occur.

(h) A document or pamphlet that includes the essential information contained in the registration statement. It is filed with the SEC and made available to potential investors.

**2** W. J. Howey Company and Howey-in-the-Hills Service, Inc., are Florida corporations under common control and management. Howey Company offers to sell to the public its orange grove, tree by tree. Howey-in-the-Hills Service, Inc., offers these buyers a contract wherein the appropriate care, harvesting, and marketing of the oranges would be provided. Most of the buyers who sign the service contracts were nonresidents of Florida who had very little knowledge or skill needed to care for and harvest the oranges. These buyers are attracted by the expectation of profits. Is a sale of orange trees by the Howey Company and a sale of services by Howey-in-the-Hills Service, Inc., a sale of a security? Why or why not?

**3** Under the provisions of the Federal Securities Act of 1933, there are three important time periods concerning when securities may be sold or offered for sale. Name and describe these three time periods.

**4** In an attempt to increase issuers' flexibility in raising capital, the SEC has adopted Rule 415 on shelf registration. Explain the meaning and purpose of shelf registration. What is the applicability of Rule 415?

**5** Patrick, a promoter for a newly organized corporation, begins to solicit purchasers of the corporation's stock. The corporation does not limit the number of potential shareholders, but it does not plan to sell more than $400,000 worth of securities. What is Patrick's responsibility under the provisions of the Federal Securities Act of 1933 with respect to registering this offering?

**6** To secure a loan, Rubin pledges stock which he represents as being marketable and worth approximately $1.7 million. In fact, the stock is nonmarketable and practically worthless. He is charged with violating the Federal Securities Act of 1933. He claims that since no sale occurred, he is not guilty. Is he correct? Why or why not?

**7** A securities brokerage firm hires a public accounting firm to conduct audits and prepare financial statements for filing with the SEC. The brokerage firm fails and sues the accounting firm, alleging that the accounting firm breached its duty owed to customers by conducting an improper audit and certification. Is the law requiring such audits and reports a basis of a suit for damages? Why or why not?

**8** Section 10(b) of the Federal Securities Exchange Act of 1934 and Rule 10b-5 are of fundamental importance in the law of securities regulations. What is the main purpose of this section and rule?

**9** Santa Fe wants to merge under the Delaware "short-form" merger statute and obtains independent appraisal values of the stock. The company complies with the statute and sends to each minority shareholder an information statement containing the appraisal values of the assets. It offers the minority shareholders $150 per share (the appraisal value was $125) for their stock. Respondents, minority shareholders, do not pursue their appraisal remedy in the state courts. Instead, they file suit under Rule 10b-5, claiming that Santa Fe used a device to defraud and that the information statement failed to reveal that the stock was actually worth $772 per share. Did Santa Fe violate Rule 10b-5? Explain.

**10**  Donna, a corporate director, sold 100 shares of stock in her corporation on June 1, 1985. The selling price was $10.50 a share. Two months later, after the corporation had announced substantial losses for the second quarter of the year, Donna purchases 100 shares of the corporation's stock for $7.25 a share. Are there any problems with Donna's sale and purchase? Explain.

**11**  Lund is the chief executive officer and chairman of the board of Verit Company. Horowitz is the chief executive officer and chairman of the board of P&F. To solicit investment funds, Horowitz tells Lund about P&F's opportunity to participate in a Las Vegas gambling casino. Horowitz requests investment capital from Verit. After learning of these unannounced plans, Lund purchases 10,000 shares of P&F's stock. Three days later, P&F's plans to participate in the casino joint venture are announced, and the stock doubles in price. Lund sells his shares at a substantial profit. The SEC sues Lund for violating Section 10(b) of the Federal Securities Exchange Act of 1934. Did Lund illegally use nonpublic information to gain a profit? Explain.

**12**  When given an ethical choice, should an executive of a company select the accounting practice that states income conservatively (low) or liberally (high)?

**13**  Eric Ethan, president of Inside-Outside Sports Equipment Company, has access to information which is not available to the general investor. What standard should Eric Ethan apply in deciding whether this information is so material as to prevent him from investing in his company prior to the information's public release?

# Chapter
## 20

# Consumer Protection

## CHAPTER PREVIEW

There have been more consumer protection laws passed since World War II than in the 175 years preceding the war. Two key factors seem primarily responsible for this rapid expansion of legal regulation. First, most of the past several decades has been a time of rising affluence, when the public has been willing to absorb costs of additional legal regulation. These costs inevitably come in the form of higher prices for goods and services. Second, the organization of well-financed consumer lobbying groups has led to legislative responses favorable to consumer interests.

Recent trends toward a more cautious federal approach to consumer protection reveal the conservative, market-oriented philosophy of a Republican administration. At the state level, however, consumer protection regulation continues to be increasingly active. Even at the federal level, there are a great number of existing laws which continue to be enforced. Many provide remedies which allow injured consumers to sue law violators.

This chapter divides consumer protection into federal and state laws. At the federal level, the Federal Trade Commission (FTC) is the primary regulatory agency. It enforces statutes which prohibit unfair and deceptive trade practices, various credit abuses, and misleading warranties.

At the state level, all states have laws to prohibit unfair and deceptive acts and practices. State attorneys general usually administer these laws, which greatly resemble the federal FTC Act. The states also have a variety of consumer protection laws regulating specific businesses such as auto repair shops and health spas.

Significant terms in this chapter include bait-and-switch promotion, consumer, investigative consumer report, corrective advertising, industry guide, legal clinics, redlining, respondent, and trade practice regulation.


## 1. Who is a Consumer?

The laws discussed in this chapter protect consumers. Who is a **consumer?** Consider the following case.

---

# ANDERSON v. FOOTHILL INDUSTRIAL BANK
674 P.2d 232 (Wyo. 1984)

---

Appellants Glen and Marlene Anderson contracted with the United States Postal Service to deliver mail on a route. The Andersons borrowed $27,500 from appellee Foothill Industrial Bank for start-up expenses in establishing the mail delivery route. The Andersons sued the Foothill Industrial Bank while refinancing the loan, claiming that the bank had failed to comply with Wyoming's Uniform Consumer Credit Code (UCCC) and the federal Truth-in-Lending Act by misrepresenting the annual percentage rate of the loan and other acts.

ROONEY, C.J.: These allegations of appellants are premised on the fact of the loan being a consumer loan and not a commercial loan. The U.C.C.C. applies only to consumer loans and not to commercial loans. A consumer loan is defined in 40-14-304, W.S. 1977, as follows:

**(a) Except with respect to a loan primarily secured by an interest in land, 'consumer loan' is a loan made by a person regularly engaged in** the business of making loans in which: (i) The debtor is a person other than an organization; (ii) The debt is incurred primarily for a personal, family, household or agricultural purpose; (iii) Either the debt is payable in installments or a loan finance charge is made; and (iv) Either the principal does not exceed twenty-five thousand dollars ($25,000.00) or the debt is secured by an interest in land.

Considering the evidence in this case in accordance with the foregoing, we find that it established the loan to be a commercial loan and not a consumer loan as a matter of fact. Appellant Glen Anderson inquired of three lendors in an attempt to secure the money for his mail route business. He told the loan officer at Person-to-Person that the money was to be used to "buy a mail route." At First Wyoming Bank, he said that it was to be used to operate a truck or otherwise engage in the mail route. He told the representative of appellee Foothill Industrial Bank that it was for a down payment on a truck and for start-up expenses. He did not require a loan until he decided to go into the mail route business. The debt was not "incurred primarily for a personal, family, household...purpose" as required by 40-14-304, W.S. 1977, supra. Although part of the proceeds of the loan were used to pay off that due on a second mortgage on appellants' residence, the testimony was that prudent lending practice would require such

pay off with transfer of the collateral if the loan were made for the purpose of financing another enterprise. The thrust of all of the evidence was that the debt was "incurred primarily" for the purpose of entering a mail route business and not for a personal family or household purpose. It was not a consumer loan....[*Affirmed.*]

According to the *Anderson* case, consumers are natural (rather than corporate) persons who incur debt "primarily for personal, family, or household purposes." Most of the statutes in this chapter define "consumer" similarly.

Although the Federal Trade Commission Act protects businesses as well as consumers, the consumer protection mission of the Federal Trade Commission (FTC) is promoted by a special bureau called the Bureau of Consumer Protection. This body within the FTC is the regulatory center for federal consumer protection. The next sections examine activities of the FTC and the Bureau of Consumer Protection.

# FEDERAL CONSUMER PROTECTION

### 2.   The Federal Trade Commission

Created in 1914, the FTC is an "independent" regulatory agency charged with keeping competition free and fair, and with protecting consumers. The FTC obeys its mandate to promote competition through enforcement of the antitrust laws discussed in Chapters 22 to 24. It achieves its consumer protection goal by trade-practice regulation under that section of the FTC Act which prohibits using "unfair or deceptive acts or practices in commerce." It also administers several other consumer protection acts covered in this chapter and Chapter 21 (see Table 20-1). In the final analysis, promoting competition and protecting consumers overlap considerably. A highly competitive economy produces better goods and services at lower prices, while **trade practice regulation** ensures fair competition by preventing those who would deceive consumers from diverting trade from those who compete honestly.

The FTC furthers consumer protection through trade practice regulation in several ways. For instance, it advises firms that request it as to whether a proposed practice is unfair or deceptive. Although not legally binding, an **advisory opinion** furnishes a good idea about how the FTC

**TABLE 20-1**   Consumer Protection Laws the FTC Administers

| Laws | Duties |
| --- | --- |
| FTC Act | To regulate unfair or deceptive acts or practices |
| Fair Packaging and Labeling Act | To prohibit deceptive labeling of certain consumer products and require disclosure of certain important information |
| Equal Credit Opportunity Act | To prevent discrimination in credit extension based on sex, age, race, religion, national origin, marital status, and receipt of welfare payments |
| Truth-in-Lending Act | To require that suppliers of consumer credit fully disclose all credit terms before an account is opened or a loan made |
| Fair Credit Reporting Act | To regulate the consumer credit reporting industry |
| Magnuson-Moss Warranty Act | To require the FTC to issue rules concerning consumer product warranties |
| Fair Debt Collection Practices Act | To prevent debt-collection agencies from using abusive or deceptive collection practices |

views the legality of a given trade practice. Sometimes the FTC also issues **industry guides,** which specify the agency's view of the legality of a particular industry's trade practices. Like advisory opinions, industry guides are informal and not legally binding. The Bureau of Consumer Protection plays the major role in issuing advisory opinions and industry guides on trade regulation issues.

In its function of protecting consumers, however, the FTC goes far beyond merely advising businesses about the legality of trade practices. It also prosecutes them for committing unfair or deceptive trade practices. Such prosecutions arise in one of two related ways. First, the Bureau of Consumer Protection may allege that an individual or company, called a **respondent,** has violated Section 5 of the FTC Act, which prohibits *unfair or deceptive acts or practices.* Over the years, the FTC's administrative law judges and the commissioners who review decisions of the judges have derived a body of quasi-judicial interpretations as to what constitutes unfair and deceptive acts.

Prosecutions may also arise from allegations under Section 5 that a respondent's actions violate a trade regulation rule of the FTC. At the recommendation of the Bureau of Consumer Protection, the five-member Commission adopts trade regulation rules in exercising its quasi-legislative power. These rules are formal interpretations of what the FTC regards as unfair or deceptive, and they have the force and effect of law. The rules usually deal with a single practice in a single industry, and they cover all firms in the affected industry. Examples of trade regulation rules include required disclosures of the "R" value for siding and insulation and the familiar warning on cigarette packages and in ads.

Alleged trade practice violations may come to the attention of the Bureau of Consumer Protection in a variety of ways. A business executive may complain about another's acts that injure competition, or a consumer may direct the attention of the Bureau to unfair or deceptive acts of a business. Such complaints are filed informally, and the identity of the complainant is not disclosed. A letter signed by a complaining party provides a basis for proceedings if it identifies the offending party, contains all the evidence which is the basis for the complaint, and states the relief desired. Of course, other government agencies, Congress, or the FTC itself may discover business conduct alleged to be illegal. For instance, the Bureau of Consumer Protection maintains a special media monitoring unit which examines the media for trade practice violations.

The chief legal tools of the Bureau are the consent order and the cease and desist order. As discussed in Chapter 8, under the consent-order procedure, a party "consents" to sign an order which restrains the promotional activity deemed offensive and agrees to whatever remedy, if any, the Bureau imposes. Most cases brought by the Bureau are settled by this procedure.

If a party will not accept a consent order, it will be prosecuted before an administrative law judge. If the party is found guilty, the judge issues a cease and desist order prohibiting future violations. Parties may appeal cease and desist orders to the full five-member commission and from there to the court of appeals if legal basis for further appeal is present.

## 3.   FTC Penalties and Remedies

CIVIL FINES

The basic penalty for trade practice violations under the FTC Act is a civil fine of not more than $10,000 per violation. The punishment function of finding violators is only an incidental one, as the FTC's main purpose is to prevent and deter trade practice violations.

To obtain fines, either the FTC or the Justice Department must ask the federal court to assess them. The exception is when companies agree to fines as part of a consent order. Fines may be assessed in three distinct situations: (1) for a violation of a consent or cease and desist order, (2) for a violation of a trade regulation rule, and (3) for a knowing violation of prior FTC orders against others.

This last situation requires some explanation. In 1975, Congress amended the FTC Act to permit the FTC to assess fines against parties who knowingly did what others had been ordered to stop in the past. The main purpose in this change in the law was to be fair to firms who had been ordered to stop a certain practice but whose competitors continued to do it. As changed, the law allows assessment of fines against such competitors once they know of the illegality of their practice. To establish knowledge, the FTC can mail copies of its orders against a respondent to other firms in a respondent's industry. Then, any further instance of the practice would be a knowing violation. In one penalty action, the FTC assessed a $100,000 fine against a toy manufacturer who knowingly continued a practice which the FTC had ordered another manufacturer to cease.

The FTC Act provides that "each separate violation of…an order shall be a separate offense." It also states that in the case of a violation through continuing failure to obey an order, each day the violation continues is a separate offense. Because of these provisions, the total fine against a violator may be considerably more than $10,000. As the following case illustrates, there can be disagreement about what constitutes a separate violation under the act.

---

# UNITED STATES v. READER'S DIGEST ASSOCIATION, INC.
662 F.2d 955 (1981), cert. denied.

---

Following an investigation in 1970 of the direct-mail solicitation campaigns of the Reader's Digest (Digest), the FTC notified the Digest that the company's sweepstakes promotions were "unfair and deceptive." In 1971 the Digest agreed to accept a consent order which barred it from "using or distributing simulated checks…or issuing or distributing any confusingly simulated item of value." In 1973 and 1975, the Digest engaged in four bulk-mailing sweepstakes promotions which featured "travel checks" and "cash-convertible bonds." Upon the advice of the FTC, the Justice Department filed an action in 1975 seeking penalties for violation of the consent order. In 1978 the district court granted the Justice Department's motion for a summary judgment. Following further discovery proceedings, the district court concluded in 1980 that the Digest had been guilty of over 17 million violations of the Act, one for each letter distributed in the bulk mailings. The court assessed a penalty of $1,750,000 and the Digest appealed.

HUNTER, J.: The Digest challenges the district court's assessment of a $1,750,000 penalty for its violation of the consent order. The company's first assertion is that the trial court erroneously determined the number of violations of the order. It argues that each bulk mailing, and not, as the district court concluded, "each individual distribution of a Travel Check or Cash Convertible Bond," constituted a separate violation of the order. The Digest also maintains that the district court's calculation of the $1,750,000 penalty was based upon an improper analysis of the factors [previously] set forth by this court….For the reasons given below, we disagree.

In determining the number of violations of the consent order, we must examine the applicable provisions of the statute, and the order itself. The statute provides, in pertinent part, that a violator of an FTC cease and desist order "shall forfeit and pay to the United states a civil penalty of not more than $10,000 for *each* violation." [*Emphasis added.*] The statute further provides that "[e]ach separate violation of such an order shall be a separate offense." Turning to the applicable terms of the consent order, the Digest was prohibited from "[u]sing or distributing simulated checks, currency, 'new car certificates'; or using or distributing *any* confusingly simulated item of value." Juxtaposing the language of the statute and the order, we reach the same conclusion as the district court—the distribution of *any* simulated item of value comprised a separate violation of the order. Thus, each mailing of an individual travel check or cash convertible bond constituted a distinct violation of the consent order, punishable by a penalty not to exceed $10,000.

Our holding that each letter included as part of a mass mailing constitutes a separate violation is also predicated upon our belief that it is consistent with the legislative purpose underlying the penalty provision of the statute. As the Supreme Court held in *ITT Continental Baking*, "Congress was concerned with avoiding a situation in which the statutory penalty would be regarded by potential violators of FTC orders as nothing more than an acceptable cost of violation, rather than as a deterrence to violation." Adopting the Digest's position that one bulk mailing—no matter how large—comprises only one violation would eviscerate any punitive or deterrent effect of FTC penalty proceedings.

We also reject the Digest's contention that "logic" dictates that it could not have committed so many violations as to have exposed it to a potential penalty amounting to billions of dollars. Although our holding with respect to the number of violations does give rise to the possibility of enormous potential liability, any penalty actually imposed by a district court would be subject to the limitation of judicial discretion....

In determining the size of the penalty to be assessed against the Digest, the district court took five factors into consideration: (1) the good or bad faith of the defendants; (2) the injury to the public; (3) the defendant's ability to pay; (4) the desire to eliminate the benefits derived by a violation; and (5) the necessity of vindicating the authority of the FTC. The Digest does not challenge the district court's reliance on these factors; rather, it asserts that the court evaluated three of the factors improperly: good faith; public injury; and benefits derived by a violation. We will review each of these contentions below.

The record clearly supports the district court's conclusion that the Digest did not act in good faith when it disseminated the travel checks and cash-convertible bonds. Although the FTC informed the Digest as early as April 13, 1973, that it considered the travel checks to be violative of the consent order, the Digest nonetheless proceeded to complete its promotional campaign by mailing millions of additional travel checks between April 13 and June 30, 1973. The Digest now maintains that these additional mailings simply reflected the lag time required by the logistics of bulk mailing. We reject this argument, and agree with the district court's conclusion that the course of conduct engaged in by the Digest between April 13 and June 30, 1973 "[did] not reflect a good faith effort to comply."...

Turning to the second factor at issue, public injury, the Digest asserts that the record is devoid of evidence of consumer confusion or deception. But this argument fails for the same reason that it did with respect to the construction of the consent order—proof of actual confusion or deception is not required. As the district court observed, "[t]he principal purpose of a cease and desist order is to prevent material having a capacity to confuse or deceive from reaching the public...[t]hus, whenever such promotional items reach the public, that *in and of itself* causes harm and injury." The trial court had already determined that the travel check and cash-convertible bond possess the capacity to deceive; accordingly, the Government was not obligated to adduce evidence of specific injuries to consumers.

Finally, with respect to the benefits derived by the violation, the district court concluded that the Digest received "substantial benefits from the violative distributions." We find ample support for the court's conclusion. The district court found that the Digest obtained more than $5,000,000 in gross subscription revenues from the travel check and cash-convertible bond promotions. The travel check campaign ranked among the top three of all the company's promotions. Thus, the district court properly rejected the Digest's contention that it received no particular benefit from the violative mailings.

In sum, we conclude that the district court carefully considered the relevant factors prior to assessing the $1,750,000 penalty upon the Digest. We hold that there was no abuse of discretion by the district court....Therefore, the judgment of the district court will be affirmed. [*Affirmed.*]

---

**OTHER REMEDIES**

In addition to assessing penalty fines, the FTC has broad powers to fashion appropriate remedies to protect consumers in trade regulation cases. One remedy the FTC uses to accompany some of its orders is **corrective advertising.**

When a company has advertised deceptively, the FTC can require it to run ads that admit the prior errors and correct the erroneous information. The correction applies to a specific dollar volume of future advertising. The theory is that the future advertising, however truthful itself, will continue to be deceptive unless the correction is made because it will remind consumers of the prior deceptive ads. Corrective ads have forced admissions that a mouthwash does not reduce cold symptoms or prevent sore throats, that an oil-treatment product cannot decrease gasoline consumption, and that an aspirin-based drug cannot relieve tension.

Other remedies the FTC may use in its orders, or may seek to impose by court action under certain circumstances, include: (1) recission of contracts (each party must return what has been obtained from the other), (2) refund of money or return of property, (3) payment of damages to consumers, and (4) public notification of trade practice violations. When it is in the public interest, and when harm from an illegal practice is substantial and likely to continue, the FTC may ask the federal court to grant temporary or even permanent injunctions to restrain violators.

## 4.  Traditional Trade Practice Regulation

The FTC conducts trade practice regulation under its power to determine "unfair or deceptive acts or practices in commerce." Most of its cases have focused on deceptive practices. Often, as the following discussion reveals, proof of traditional deception relies more on a showing of legalistically inaccurate promotional language, rather than on consumer injury.

### PRICE MISREPRESENTATIONS

One common type of advertising traditionally attacked by the FTC makes prospective purchasers believe they will be getting a "good deal" in terms of price if they buy the product in question. For example, a seller of goods was ordered to refrain from advertising its products for sale using a price comparison in which its actual price was compared to a higher "regular" price or a manufacturer's list price. The Commission ruled that it is deceptive to refer to "regular price" unless the defendant has usually sold the items at the price recently in the regular course of business. Also, it was held deceptive to refer to the "manufacturer's list price" when that list price is not the ordinary and customary retail sales price of the item in the locality. This is in spite of the fact that manufacturers themselves suggest the retail prices to which the seller may compare its lower selling price. In ordering enforcement of the Commission's cease and desist order, the Court of Appeals said: "We do not understand the Commission to hold that use of the term 'manufacturer's list price' is unlawful per se; rather it is unlawful only if it is not the usual and customary retail price in the area."

Similar to price representations which offer "free" goods for the purchase of others is a **bait-and-switch promotion.** Here, the seller intends to use a product advertised at a low price only as bait to capture the interest of consumers and then switch their attention from it to products which the baiter really has desired to sell from the beginning.

### PERFORMANCE MISREPRESENTATIONS

Besides involving misleading price representations, deceptive practices may result from fraudulent, false, or misleading advertising or other representations concerning the performance capability of goods or services being sold. False representations of the composition, quality, character, or source of products, by misbranding or otherwise, have been barred as deceptively misleading. For example, lumber dealers have been barred from advertising under names such as "California white pine" and "Western white pine" when their products were inferior to genuine "white pine," even though these terms were accepted and understood in the trade. Other cases falling into this category of violation are ones in which a seller suggested that a beauty aid "restored natural moisture necessary for a lively healthy skin," a claim which was false, and one in which cigars made of domestic tobacco were labeled "Havana."

False statements which misrepresent either a product or its price have also been ruled unfair or deceptive. Typical of these is one in which a product is endorsed by one who is misrepresented to be a "doctor" or "scientific expert." Disparaging the goods of others in an attempt to promote the sale of one's own is also an unfair practice. For example, the FTC restrained a manufacturer of stainless-steel cooking utensils from publishing questions such as the following: "Do you know that aluminum pans may be full of the most deadly bacteria known to science?" "Did you ever find maggots in your aluminum pans?"

#### TRUTHFUL YET DECEPTIVE ADS

Other cases have involved no actual misstatement but representations which, while true in themselves, were intended to mislead. Using a word while having a hidden or unusual interpretation in mind for the purpose of promoting sales is an example. If a manufacturer states that its product is "guaranteed for life," most people would probably believe that the guarantee was to run for the life of the purchaser. However, Parker Pen Company used this phrase in its advertising with the undisclosed intention that the lives in question were those of the pens they manufactured, thus making the guarantee worthless. Parker was restrained from making such "guarantees."

Using the technique of product-name simulation is also unfair. This occurs when a manufacturer or seller uses either the same name or one that is deceptively similar to another product of another manufacturer which has acquired consumer acceptance. This conduct, whether undertaken with the intent of exploiting the goodwill of a competitor or not, may confuse consumers. If the name selected is close enough to that of the established product, its use may be restrained by the FTC as being deceptive.

Even silence by a seller may result in deception of consumers, and the Commission may require that positive disclosures be made before further sales of the goods in question are permissible. For example, nondisclosure that books published were abridged or condensed was ruled as deceptive. In addition, distributing secondhand or rebuilt goods without indicating them as such and selling foreign goods without disclosing their origin have been restrained by the Commission in its efforts to protect consumers from unfair or deceptive trade practices.

Table 20-2 gives recent examples of FTC deceptive trade practice cases. Most of these cases are "traditional" in nature.

### 5.   Policy Trends at the FTC

#### GENERALLY

After the 1970s, the consumer activist decade at the FTC, the 1980s has brought a more restrained effort at consumer protection by the agency. During the 1970s, the FTC began broad-scale use of its rule-making powers. It passed or proposed sweeping rules on thermal insulation, eyeglasses, the funeral industry, franchising, business opportunities, vocational schools, food labeling, used cars, and children's advertising. These rules threw many affected businesses into such turmoil that Congress, prompted by heavy lobbying, acted to restrain the FTC.

In the 1980s, the FTC has backed away from its earlier enthusiasm for rule making. Prior to final adoption, the proposed food labeling and

**TABLE 20-2**  Recent FTC Deceptive Practice Cases

| Company | Order |
|---|---|
| American Home Products | Must not give the impression that pain relievers are something other than aspirin when they are not. Must disclose presence of aspirin when company's product is contrasted with another product containing aspirin. Required to prove claims of product superiority with two controlled clinical studies. |
| California-Texas Oil Co. | Must not make unsubstantiated claims about gasoline additives improving fuel mileage. Cannot use language that additives improve mileage "up to" 15 percent unless an appreciable number of consumers can achieve that performance under normal conditions. |
| General Nutrition, Inc. | Must pay $600,000 for health research due to alleged false and unsubstantiated claims that its dietary supplement "Healthy Greens" was effective in reducing cancer risk. |
| Heatcool | Company must run twelve months of corrective ads stating that its products "do not insulate better than comparable glass storm windows." |
| Kingsbridge Media & Marketing, Inc. | Must pay $1.1 million into an account to provide consumer refunds. Action based on defendants' claims that diet pills would induce weight loss while sleeping and without exercise or dieting. |
| Sears | Must cease and desist from making claims that Lady Kenmore dishwashers eliminate the need for scraping and prerinsing dishes. Cannot make claims for *any* major home appliance unless reliable substantiating evidence is available. |
| Standard Financial Management Corp. | Must pay $1.5 million into a fund to provide consumer refunds due to misrepresentation of value and investment potential of coins it sold. |

children's advertising rules were withdrawn from consideration. Under the Reagan FTC, the Bureau of Consumer Protection focused its enforcement efforts on a case-by-case approach to regulation, rather than on rule making. And in line with the theory that the marketplace itself can cure many types of deceptive practices, the Reagan FTC substantially reduced the number of deceptive trade practice cases from the levels of previous administrations.

Another development of the 1970s which has continued vitality in the 1980s is the FTC's **ad substantiation program.** It is now an unfair and deceptive trade practice for sellers to make affirmative claims about their products which they cannot prove. The claims themselves may even be true, but it is illegal to make them if there is no proof to support them. Thus, the FTC required a manufacturer of weight-loss tablets to prove claims that consumers could lose weight without restricting caloric intake. When the manufacturer could not substantiate the ads, it had to discontinue them. Occasionally, the FTC has applied ad substantiation to claims made by an entire industry, rather than to the claims of a specific advertiser.

One 1970s trend at the FTC which continues into the 1980s is the trade regulation emphasis on disclosure to consumers. For instance, the Commission forced a major encyclopedia company to disclose in its advertising that salespersons would call on anyone who returned response coupons. The Commission termed it "deceptive" for the company to fail to make this disclosure. The emphasis on disclosure underscores the belief that informed consumers can "regulate" many trade practices by voting with their dollars, if they possess sufficient information.

In recent years, the FTC has grappled with advertising problems presented by radio and television. The following case illustrates that in electronic media ads the FTC can go beyond words to analyze "aural-visual" imagery.

# AMERICAN HOME PRODUCTS CORP. v. F.T.C.
695 F.2d 681 (1982)

The Federal Trade Commission (FTC) ruled that American Home Products (AHP) engaged in deceptive advertising in violation of the Federal Trade Commission Act. AHP falsely claimed that Anacin had a unique pain-killing formula that was superior in effectiveness to all other nonprescription analgesics, when, in reality, Anacin's sole pain-killing component was merely aspirin. AHP appealed the Commission's ruling.

ADAMS, J.: A. The Standard of Review of Findings of Deceptiveness

The Federal Trade Commission Act directs that "[t]he findings of the Commission as to the facts, if supported by evidence, shall be conclusive." It is "clear that properly interpreted, the statute requires review by the substantial evidence in the record as a whole standard." This standard "does not permit the reviewing court to weigh the evidence, but only to determine that there is in the record 'such relevant evidence as a rea-sonable mind might accept as adequate to support a conclusion.'"

This deferential standard with respect to Commission findings of fact applies to the findings here. Although "in the last analysis the words 'deceptive practices' set forth a legal standard and they must get their final meaning from judicial construction," a Commission finding that advertisements are deceptive or tend to mislead "is obviously an impressionistic determination more closely akin to a finding of fact than a conclusion of law."

*Colgate-Palmolive* explained that the "Commission is often in a better position than are courts to determine when a practice is deceptive within the meaning of the Act. This Court has frequently stated that the Commission's judgment is to be given weight by reviewing courts. This admonition is especially true with respect to allegedly deceptive advertising since the finding of a § 5 violation in this field rests so heavily on inference and pragmatic judgment."

The Commission's familiarity with the expectations and beliefs of the public, acquired by long experience, is especially crucial when, as with the advertisements proscribed by Parts I(B) and III of the Order in this case, "the alleged deception results from an omission of information instead of a statement."

B. How Advertising is to be Interpreted

"[T]he tendency of the advertising to deceive must be judged by viewing it as a whole, without emphasizing isolated words or phrases apart from their context." The impression created by the advertising, not its literal truth or falsity, is the desideratum....

In the present proceeding, the Commission analyzed not only the words used, but also, with respect to the television advertisements, the messages conveyed through the "aural-visual" pattern. The Commission's right to scrutinize the visual and aural imagery of advertisements follows from the principle that the Commission looks to the impression made by the advertisements as a whole. Without this mode of examination, the Commission would have limited recourse against crafty advertisers whose deceptive messages were by means other than, or in addition to, spoken words. In *Standard Oil Co. of California v. FTC*, the court upheld a Commission finding "that the predominant visual message was misleading, and that it was not corrected or contradicted by the accompanying verbal message in advertisements." *Colgate-Palmolive* also supports the Commission's right to look beyond spoken words to the message conveyed visually. According to *Colgate-Palmolive,* "even if an advertiser has himself conducted a test, experiment or demonstration which he honestly believes will prove a certain product claim, he may not convey to television viewers the false impression that they are seeing the test, experiment or demonstration for themselves, when they are not because of the undisclosed use of mock-ups."... [*Modified.*]

---

### DECEPTION GUIDELINES

Traditionally, the concept of deceptive trade practices includes all practices which have a "tendency or capacity" to mislead consumers. No actual harm to any specific group of consumers needs to be shown. As of this writing, the courts have not changed the "tendency or capacity standard." The FTC, however, has.

In its standard, the FTC has said that it will use three tests to determine whether to take action against trade practices. First, the FTC must conclude that the ad is "likely to mislead consumers." Second, misled consumers must be "acting reasonably in the circumstances." Third, the practice must be "material"; that is, it must potentially affect consumers' purchasing decisions.

In explaining its standard, the FTC noted that certain practices are unlikely to deceive consumers acting reasonably. Generally, the FTC will not bring advertising cases based on subjective claims (taste, feel, appearance, smell) or on correctly stated opinion claims. It will also not pursue cases involving obviously exaggerated or puffing claims.

Under the guidelines, the FTC will likely ignore technically deceptive practices which cannot be shown to affect consumers' purchase decisions, such as an ad which falsely claims the "best prices in town." Although the

FTC retains the authority to conclude on its own evaluation whether a practice affects consumers' decision making (is material), the guidelines will probably cause it to turn increasingly to outside evidence provided by consumer testing.

## 6. Introduction to Federal Credit Regulations

In addition to the FTC Act, the FTC administers several other consumer protection statutes as well. One of them, the Fair Debt Collection Practices Act, is discussed in Chapter 21 on debtor-creditor relations. Most of the other FTC-administered statutes concern credit regulation.

As the large number of credit cards in the average consumer's wallet indicates, credit buying has truly become a national pastime. Credit financing of consumer contracts has jumped astronomically in recent years. At the close of World War II, consumer credit outstanding amounted to only $2.5 billion, a figure which had changed little since the 1920s. Today, however, consumer credit debt has soared above the $350 billion mark. Both in absolute terms and as a percentage of GNP, credit debt has grown steadily since World War II. Considering the importance of credit buying to the consumer and business, it is no surprise that a number of laws regulating credit extension has been passed. The laws discussed in the following sections cover nondiscrimination in credit extension, the collection of information for credit reports, and the standardized disclosure of credit charges.

## 7. Equal Credit Opportunity Act

In 1975, Congress passed the Equal Credit Opportunity Act (ECOA). The ECOA's purpose is to prevent discrimination in credit extension. In an economy in which credit availability is so important, the ECOA is a logical extension in a vital consumer area of the antidiscrimination laws found in the employment field.

### ECOA PROHIBITIONS

This act prohibits discrimination based on sex, marital status, race, color, age, religion, national origin, or receipt of welfare in any aspect of a consumer credit transaction. Although the ECOA forbids discrimination on the basis of all these different categories, it is aimed especially at preventing sex discrimination. As the divorce rate climbs, the age of first marriage grows later, and more women enter the work force, it is expected that sex discrimination in credit extension will increasingly become a subject for litigation.

The law prohibits one to whom the act applies from discouraging a consumer from seeking credit based on sex, marital status, or any other of the enumerated categories. A married woman, for example, cannot be denied the right to open a credit account separate from her husband's or in her maiden name. Unless the husband will be using the account or the consumer is relying on her husband's credit, it is illegal even to ask if the consumer is married. It is also illegal to ask about birth-control practices or childbearing plans or to assign negative values on a credit checklist to the fact that a woman is of childbearing age.

The ECOA applies to all businesses which regularly extend credit, including financial institutions, retail stores, and credit-card issuers. It also affects automobile dealers, real estate brokers, and others who steer consumers to lenders. And as the following case indicates, many courts are ruling that ECOA covers consumer leasing situations, which may substitute in place of credit-based sales.

## BROTHERS v. FIRST LEASING
724 F.2d 789 (1984)

Patricia Ann Brothers attempted to lease an automobile in her own name from the defendant, First Leasing. Even though Brothers did not intend to lease the car jointly with her husband, First Leasing required her to provide information concerning her husband's financial history and required him to sign the application. First Leasing rejected Brothers' application because her husband had previously filed for bankruptcy. Brothers sued First Leasing, claiming the denial of her application constituted discrimination on the basis of sex or marital status under the Equal Credit Opportunity Act (ECOA). The federal district court held that the lease was not covered by the ECOA, and it dismissed the action.

REINHARDT, J.: The issue, then, is whether the ECOA applies only to the Truth in Lending Act or to the Consumer Leasing Act as well....

Preliminarily, we note that there is nothing in the literal language or the legislative history of the CLA, or of the ECOA, including the 1976 amendments, that sug-

gests that the ECOA does not apply to the CLA. We also note that in interpreting other titles of the Consumer Credit Protection Act, we have found an examination of the purpose of the particular title to be crucial to our decision.

"The purpose of the ECOA is to eradicate credit discrimination waged against women, especially married women whom creditors traditionally refused to consider for individual credit." Congress reaffirmed the goal of antidiscrimination in credit in the 1976 amendments to the ECOA by adding race, color, religion, national origin, and age to sex and marital status as characteristics that may not be considered in deciding whether to extend credit.

In enacting and amending the ECOA, Congress recognized that a prohibition against discrimination in credit provides a much-needed addition to the previously existing strict prohibitions against discrimination in employment, housing, voting, education, and numerous other areas. The ECOA is simply one more tool to be used in our vigorous national effort to eradicate invidious discrimination "root and branch" from our society.

In view of the strong national commitment to the eradication of discrimination in our society, we see no reason why Congress would have wanted to subject the leasing of durable consumer goods to regulation under the disclosure provisions of the Consumer Credit Protection Act, but to exclude those transactions from the scope of the antidiscrimination provisions of that Act. Certainly, abolishing discrimination in the affording of credit is at least as important as compelling the disclosure of information regarding finance charges. To conclude that discrimination in consumer leasing transactions is exempt from the ECOA simply because Congress did not add express language covering consumer leases when it amended the ECOA for entirely unrelated reasons would be inconsistent with the broad purpose of the statute and the liberal construction we must give it. It is far more reasonable to conclude that Congress thought that an express amendment was unnecessary because the ECOA on its face applies to all credit transactions and, therefore, the language already in the Act was broad enough to cover consumer leases.

In enacting the Consumer Leasing Act [CLA], Congress explicitly recognized the "recent trend toward leasing automobiles and other durable goods for consumer use as an alternative to installment credit sales." Prospective lessors run extensive credit checks on consumer lease applicants just as they do in the case of credit sales applicants. The problems of persons discriminated against with respect to credit under the Truth in Lending Act and the CLA are for the most part identical. Therefore, inter-

preting "credit transactions" so that the ECOA applies to lease transactions, as well as to credit sales and loans, is essential to the accomplishment of the Act's antidiscriminatory goal.

We turn now to an analysis of the statutory scheme. The CLA is a part of a comprehensive act regulating numerous financial transactions. The ECOA is a later part of that same comprehensive statute. We must view the umbrella act, the Consumer Credit Protection Act, as a whole and not as separate unrelated parts. We must also treat the amendments to the statute as if they were adopted as part of the original enactment. When the ECOA is examined in that light, it becomes evident that it applies to all transactions covered by Title I of the Consumer Credit Protection Act. The statutory scheme is wholly inconsistent with the view that the ECOA applies to one part of Title I, the Truth in Lending Act, but not to another, the CLA. Moreover, any doubt as to this point is removed when we consider the fact that the CLA was enacted and codified as a subchapter of the Truth in Lending Act, and not as a separate measure.

Finally, to interpret the term "credit transactions" narrowly, so as to exclude consumer leases would nullify Congress' use of flexible language necessary "to insure the effective application of legislative policy to changing circumstances." We hold only that Congress intended to make the ECOA's anti-discrimination provisions applicable to all transactions covered by the Consumer Credit Protection Act, whether those transactions were covered under the initial form of the Act or as a result of the subsequent amendments.... [*Reversed and remanded.*]

---

**RESPONSIBILITIES OF THE CREDIT EXTENDER**

In basing a credit decision on the applicant's income, the credit extender must consider alimony, child support, and maintenance payments as income, although the likelihood of these payments being actually made may be considered as well. The credit extender must also tell an applicant that she need not disclose income from these sources unless she will be relying on that income to obtain credit. In calculating total income, those subject to the law must include income from regular part-time jobs and public assistance programs.

Information on accounts used by both spouses must be reported to third parties, such as credit reporting agencies, in the names of both spouses. This provision of the law helps women establish a credit history and enables a woman who separates from her husband to obtain credit in her own right.

To date, much of the litigation surrounding the ECOA concerns the requirement that *specific* reasons be given a consumer who is denied credit. Several cases have imposed liability upon credit extenders who have failed to provide any reasons for credit denial or who merely informed the consumer that she had failed to achieve a minimum score on a credit rating system. Other cases have dealt with age and race discrimination. The government filed an action recently against a large consumer finance company which made extension of credit to the elderly conditional upon their obtaining credit life insurance. It has also been established that the practice of **redlining,** that is, refusing to make loans at all in certain areas where property values are low, can discriminate on the basis of race in granting mortgage credit.

### ECOA REMEDIES AND PENALTIES

Private remedies for violation of the ECOA are recovery of actual damages, punitive damages up to $10,000, and attorney's fees and legal costs. Actual damages can include recovery for embarrassment and mental distress. Punitive damages can be recovered even in the absence of actual damages. In addition to private remedies, the government may bring suit to enjoin violations of the ECOA and to assess civil penalties. In one case, the FTC assessed a $200,000 civil penalty against a major national oil company. The FTC charged that the company practiced race and sex discrimination by using ZIP codes as a factor in deciding whether to extend credit and by failing to consider women's alimony and child support income.

## 8.  The Fair Credit Reporting Act

In 1988 the five largest companies in the credit reporting industry issued almost a half-billion reports. These reports covered not only consumers seeking credit but also persons seeking jobs or insurance. Although most of the information contained in such reports is accurate, the harm caused by occasionally inaccurate information and the potential for undue invasion of privacy led Congress to pass the Fair Credit Reporting Act (FCRA). FCRA applies to anyone who prepares or uses a credit report in connection with (1) extending credit, (2) selling insurance, or (3) hiring or firing an employee. The law regulates credit reports on consumers but not those on businesses.

### CONSUMER RIGHTS UNDER FCRA

The law gives individual consumers certain rights whenever they are rejected for credit, insurance, or employment because of an adverse credit report. These rights include: (1) the right to be told the name of the agency making the report, (2) the right to require the agency to reveal the information given in the report, and (3) the right to correct the information or at least give the consumer's version of the facts in dispute.

This law does have one important limitation. It provides that a report containing information solely as to transactions or experiences between the consumer and the person making the report is not a "consumer report" covered by the act. To illustrate this limitation, assume that a bank is asked for information about its credit experience with one of its customers. If it reports only as to its own experiences, the report is not covered by the act. The act is designed to cover credit reporting agencies which obtain information from several sources, compile it, and furnish it to potential creditors. If the bank passed along any information it had received from an outside source, then its credit report would be subject to the provision of the act. Also, if the bank gave its opinion as to the creditworthiness of the customer in question, it would come under the act. The limitation is restricted to information relating to transactions or experiences, and the information furnished must be of a factual nature if the exception in the law is to be applicable.

Many businesses can avoid the pitfalls of being a credit reporting agency, but most businesses will be subject to the "user" provisions of this law. The "user" provision requires that consumers who are seeking credit for personal, family, or household purposes be informed if their application is denied because of an adverse credit report. They must also be informed of the source of the report and the fact that they are entitled to make a written request within sixty days as to the nature of the information received. If they request the information in the report, they are entitled to receive it so that they may challenge the accuracy of the negative aspects of its contents.

### INVESTIGATIVE CONSUMER REPORTS

The act also contains a provision on **investigative consumer reports.** These are reports on a consumer's character, general reputation, mode of living, and so on, obtained by personal interviews in the consumer's community. No one may obtain such a report unless at least three days' advance notice is given the consumer that such a report will be sought. The consumer has the right to be informed of the nature and scope of any such personal investigation. Reports which are intended to be covered by this act are those usually conducted for insurance companies and employment agencies.

### OBSERVING REASONABLE PROCEDURES

In making investigations and collecting information, credit reporting agencies must observe *reasonable procedures,* or they will be liable to consumers. For example, when a consumer investigative report contained false information about a consumer's character—including rumored drug use, participation in demonstrations, and eviction from prior residences—a court found liability against the credit reporting agency. The agency's investigator had obtained the information from a single source, a person with a strong bias against the consumer, and he failed to double-check it. However, if an agency follows reasonable procedures, it is not liable to a consumer, even if it reports false information. Furthermore, several courts have ruled that the FCRA preempts state law. This prevents consumers from filing libel actions against agencies which report false information.

### FCRA PENALTIES AND REMEDIES

Anyone who violates the FCRA is civilly liable to an injured consumer. For instance, as the next case shows, a business that seeks a credit report for an improper reason may be liable under the FCRA.

# ZAMORA v. VALLEY FED. SAV. & LOAN ASS'N
811 F.2d 1368 (10th Cir. 1987)

PER CURIAM: This is an appeal from a judgment of the United States District Court for the District of Colorado upholding a jury verdict of $61,500 actual damages for violation of the Fair Credit Reporting Act (FCRA). The FCRA provides for damages when a credit report user willfully and knowingly obtains a credit report under false pretenses for an impermissible purpose.

On appeal, defendant argues that the district court erred (1) in ruling that the FCRA does not permit an employer to obtain a credit report on the spouse of an employee for "employment purposes"; (2) in

relying for its definition of false pretenses on the permissible purposes listed in 15 U.S.C. § 1681b, to the exclusion of the willful and knowing requirement; and (3) in denying defendant's motion for a new trial of remittitur because the damages were clearly excessive and punitive in nature. We affirm.

Plaintiff's wife was employed by defendant as a loan officer. When she married the plaintiff, the defendant, through one of its vice-presidents, William P. Inscho, Jr., obtained a credit report on plaintiff from the Mesa County Credit Bureau (credit bureau). Inscho represented to the credit bureau that the report was to be used for "employment purposes." At the time the report was requested, plaintiff's wife was being considered for a branch manager position. The credit report indicated, among other things, an unpaid telephone bill, which plaintiff disputed. Because defendant's request for the credit report started an effort to collect the telephone bill, plaintiff learned of the request, plaintiff's wife confronted Inscho, and Inscho admitted requesting the credit report. Plaintiff then filed this action, claiming that defendant knowingly and willfully obtained a credit report on plaintiff under false pretenses for "employment purposes" in violation of the FCRA. The district court granted plaintiff's motion for partial summary judgment and ruled that a credit report cannot be obtained on the spouse of an employee for "employment purposes."

The issue of whether defendant willfully and knowingly obtained the credit report on plaintiff under false pretenses was presented to the jury. The jury found for plaintiff and awarded actual damages of $61,500. Defendant filed a motion for new trial.... The district court denied the motion and subsequently entered its final judgment. Defendant appealed.

Defendant first maintains that the FCRA permits an employer to obtain a credit report on a spouse of an employee being considered for a security-sensitive position, so long as the intended purpose and actual use of the report is to evaluate the employee's trustworthiness for the position. We disagree. [The FCRA] sets forth an exclusive list of permissible purposes for which a consumer credit report may be obtained. Section 1681b(3) (B) permits a consumer reporting agency to furnish a consumer report for "employment purposes." "The term 'employment purposes' when used in connection with a consumer report means a report used for the purpose of evaluating a consumer for employment, promotion, reassignment or retention as an employee." The

FCRA defines a consumer as "an individual."

Nothing in the FCRA indicates that a consumer credit report for "employment purposes" may be obtained on any person other than the actual individual whose employment is being considered. By enacting the FCRA, Congress intended to prevent invasions of consumers' privacy. Permitting a user of consumer reports to obtain information on a spouse for "employment purposes" would violate the right to privacy Congress intended to protect.

Defendant argues that the district court erred in its definition of false pretenses by relying on the permissible purposes for obtaining a consumer report listed in § 1681b, to the exclusion of the willful and knowing requirement. We disagree. The district court properly defined false pretenses, and there is ample evidence in the record from which the jury could conclude that defendant knew a request for spousal information was not permissible....

Whether a consumer report has been obtained under false pretenses will ordinarily be determined by reference to the permissible purposes for which consumer reports may be obtained, as enumerated in § 1681b. A consumer reporting agency may only issue a report for the purposes listed in § 1681(b). Accordingly, if a user requests information for a purpose not permitted by § 1681b while representing to the reporting agency that the report will be used for a permissible purpose, the user may be subject to civil liability for obtaining information under false pretenses.

In this case defendant's vice president, William P. Inscho, Jr., informed the credit agency it sought information on plaintiff for "employment purposes." A credit bureau employee testified that he would not have provided defendant the credit report had he known defendant's actual purpose for seeking the report. But defendant appears to further contend that civil liability should not be imposed, because defendant did not knowingly and willfully seek information not permitted under the FCRA. This contention must also fail. The testimony at trial indicated that both Inscho, Jr. and another vice-president of the bank, William P. Inscho, Sr., knew the permissible purposes for obtaining consumer reports. Both are vice-presidents of defendant, a savings and loan which does frequent consumer checks and which has a compliance officer, an in-house attorney, to ensure compliance with federal statutes, such as the FCRA....Inscho, Jr. trained employees on making credit report requests at one of defendant's branches. The credit bureau employee testified that all credit bureau employees knew they could not access the records of a spouse when checking the credit of an individual. Plaintiff's wife, who was one of defendant's loan officers, testified that a credit report could not be obtained on a spouse if the spouse was not listed on the loan application. She testified that Inscho, Sr. admitted to her that the request was a mistake and attempted to rectify the mistake by offering her a bottle of wine.

From this evidence the jury could reasonably find that defendant knowingly and willfully obtained the consumer report under false pretenses. Because the jury's findings are not clearly erroneous, the findings are conclusively binding on appeal. [*Affirmed.*]

---

The government may also assess civil and criminal penalties against FCRA violators in certain instances.

### 9.   The Truth-in-Lending Act

The Truth-in-Lending Act authorized the Federal Reserve Board to adopt regulations "to assure a meaningful disclosure of credit terms so that the consumer will be able to compare more readily the various credit terms available to him and avoid the uninformed use of credit." As previously mentioned, the FTC enforces these regulations.

#### TRUTH-IN-LENDING COVERAGE

The Truth-in-Lending Act covers all transactions in which: (1) the lender is in the business of extending credit in connection with a loan of money, a sale of property, or the furnishing of services; (2) the debtor is a natural person, as distinguished from a corporation or business entity; (3) a finance charge may be imposed; and (4) the credit is obtained primarily for personal, family, household, or agricultural purposes. It covers loans secured by real estate, such as mortgages, as well as unsecured loans and loans secured by personal property. Disclosure is necessary whenever a buyer pays in four installments or more.

Truth-in-Lending imposes a duty on all persons regularly extending credit to private individuals to inform them fully of the cost of the credit. It does not regulate the charges which are imposed.

### FINANCE CHARGE AND ANNUAL PERCENTAGE RATE

The Truth-in-Lending philosophy of full disclosure is accomplished through two concepts, namely, the **finance charge** and the **annual percentage rate** (APR). The borrower uses these two concepts to determine the amount he or she must pay for credit and what the annual cost of borrowing will be in relation to the amount of credit received. Theoretically, a debtor armed with this information will be better able to bargain for credit and choose one creditor over the other.

The finance charge is the sum of all charges payable directly or indirectly by the debtor or someone else to the creditor as a condition of the extension of credit. Included in the finance charge are interest, service charges, loan fees, points, finder's fees, fees for appraisals, credit reports or investigations, and life and health insurance required as a condition of the loan.

Among the costs frequently paid by debtors which are not included in the finance charge are recording fees and taxes, such as a sales tax, which are not usually included in the listed selling price. These are items of a fixed nature, the proceeds of which do not go to the creditor. Other items of cost not included are title insurance or abstract fees, notary fees, and attorney's fees for preparing deeds.

The law requires that the lender disclose the finance charge, expressing it as an annual percentage rate, and specifies the methods for making this computation. The purpose is to ensure that all credit extenders calculate their charges in a uniform fashion. This enables consumers to make informed decisions about the cost of credit.

### FINANCING STATEMENT

The finance charge and annual percentage rate are made known to borrowers by use of a financing statement. This statement must be given to the borrower before credit is extended and must contain, in addition to the finance charge and the annual percentage rate, the following information:

**1** Any default or delinquency charges that may result from a late payment

**2** Description of any property used as security

**3** The total amount to be financed, including a separation of the original debt from finance charges

As the following case indicates, the financing statement must disclose certain terms more conspicuously than others.

# HERRERA v. FIRST NORTHERN SAVINGS & LOAN ASSN.
805 F.2d 896 (10th Cir. 1986)

Plaintiffs Manuel and Lupe Herrera entered into a real estate loan agreement with defendant First Northern Savings & Loan Association. The defendant gave plaintiffs the disclosure statement required by the Truth-in-Lending Act (TILA), which is part of the Consumer Credit Protection Act. Plaintiffs later sued defendant for numerous alleged violations of TILA and asked for statutory damages under § 1640 of the Act. When the district court granted a summary judgment in favor of the plaintiffs, defendant appealed.

HOLLOWAY, J.:...Plaintiffs and defendant entered into a real estate loan agreement, evidenced by a promissory note secured by a mortgage on the Herreras' real property. Pursuant to this agreement, First Northern, in its ordinary course of business, extended credit to the Herreras, jointly and severally, as husband and wife, and imposed a finance charge. First Northern provided the Herreras with a TILA disclosure statement entitled "NOTICE TO CONSUMER REQUIRED BY LAW," which disclosed among other things the interest charged, expressed as an "annual percentage rate."

The Herreras sued First Northern alleging numerous violations of TILA and Regulation Z, and sought to recover statutory damages, reasonable attorney's fees and costs. Plaintiffs sought summary judgment, which was granted. The court held that defendant's disclosure of the "annual percentage rate" on its TILA disclosure statement did not fulfill the "more conspicuously" mandate of Parts 226.6(a) and 226.8(b)(2) of Regulation Z, and therefore, violated the

Act. It found that while the term "annual percentage rate" appeared on the "Notice to Consumer Required by Federal Law" in all capital letters, over 30 other terms and phrases appeared on this disclosure statement printed in the identical size, style and boldness of type in the capitalized format. The court granted plaintiffs a single statutory penalty of $1,000 to be divided between them, costs of $20.16, and attorney's fees of $1,930.00. This appeal...followed.

First Northern contends that the district court erred in granting summary judgment in favor of plaintiffs for three principal reasons: (1) that genuine issues as to material facts existed regarding the sufficiency of the "annual percentage rate" disclosure which precluded summary judgment; (2) that in any event the "annual percentage rate" disclosure was properly shown so as to meet the § 226.6(a) requirements; and (3) that even if there was a violation of the Act, defendant is not liable because of the "bona fide error" and "informed use of credit" defenses.

Plaintiffs contend that First Northern's TILA disclosure statement violates § 226.6(a) of Regulation Z as a matter of law because the term "annual percentage rate" is not printed "more conspicuously" than other terminology required by the Consumer Credit Protection Act. Section 226.6(a) of the Regulation states in pertinent part:

**The disclosures required to be given by this part shall be made clearly, conspicuously, in meaningful sequence, in accordance with the further requirements of this section, and at**

**the time and in the terminology prescribed in applicable sections....[Where the terms "finance charge" and "annual percentage rate" are required to be used, they shall be printed more conspicuously than other terminology required by this part.]**

The validity of this provision in the Regulation is not questioned and only the issue of violation of it here is involved. It is unnecessary for plaintiffs to show any actual damage in order to recover for TILA violations under § 1640. On the disclosure statement, the term "annual percentage rate" is printed in all capital letters in boldface type. However, § 226.6(a) of the Regulation requires that the APR be printed "more conspicuously" than other required terms. However, as the district court concluded, over 30 other terms and phrases appearing on the disclosure statement are also printed in capital letters, in the identical size, style and boldness of type as the "annual percentage rate". Thus, the APR disclosure does not meet the § 226(a) mandate.

Defendant argues that there is a genuine issue as to whether the "annual percentage rate" is "more conspicuously" shown and that the issue of "conspicuousness" is one on which reasonable minds could differ, precluding summary judgment. We disagree. We hold that reasonable minds cannot differ with the ruling that the disclosure statement fails to meet the § 226.6(a) mandate.

Moreover, the district court's conclusion comports with the underlying policies of the Truth-in-Lending Act. The Act was passed "to assure a meaningful disclosure of credit terms so that the consumer will be able to compare more readily the various credit terms available to him and avoid the uninformed use of credit." The most important disclosures mandated are those on which consumers can compare competing loans—

the finance charge and annual percentage rate. Regulation Z, by which the Federal Reserve Board specified the disclosures helpful to informed borrowing, reflects the Act's concern with the cost of credit by requiring the annual percentage rate and finance charge to be printed more conspicuously than other terms. The rule facilitates comparison shopping for credit and stresses the cost of credit for the consumer.

Defendant asserts that its failure, if any, to disclose the annual percentage rate "more conspicuously" was unintentional and resulted from a bona fide error, so that it is relieved from liability under § 1640(c) of TILA. We agree with the district court that the defense does not apply here.

While defendant correctly points out that two different interpretations of § 1640(c) emerged in the 1970s—one view construing it to apply only to mistakes of a clerical or mathematical nature and the other construing § 1640(c) more broadly to encompass good faith efforts at compliance—Congress resolved this issue when it amended the Act by the Truth-in-Lending Simplification and Reform Act of 1980. Congress clearly stated in its amendment of § 1640(c) that "[e]xamples of a bona fide error include, but are not limited to clerical, calculation, computer malfunction and programming, and printing errors, *except that an error of legal judgment with respect to a person's obligations under this subchapter is not a bona fide error.*"

Defendant's violation was not clerical, mathematical, or due to printing or computer errors. It was perhaps an "error of legal judgment," a belief that it had complied with the Act. However defendant's failure to adopt a disclosure statement which complied with TILA and Regulation Z requirements, even if in good faith, is not excusable under § 1640(c). The district court correctly rejected this defense.

Finally, defendant contends that because plaintiffs received the benefit of the "informed use of credit" which concerned Congress, it is not liable for any damages. As noted, no showing of actual damages is required in order for plaintiff to recover the statutory penalty. A proven violation of the disclosure requirements is presumed to injure the borrower by frustrating the purpose of permitting consumers to compare various available credit terms. [*Affirmed.*]

---

The court in the *Herrera* case awarded the plaintiffs a $1,000 statutory penalty, $1,930 in attorney's fees, and $20 in costs. A question arises: Why did the defendant savings and loan association pursue this case all the way to the court of appeals? Was it because the defendant had disclosed APRs to many other consumers on the same printed form?

### PENALTIES AND REMEDIES UNDER TRUTH-IN-LENDING

There are both civil and criminal penalties for violation of Truth-in-Lending. The civil liability provisions make creditors liable to debtors for an amount equal to twice the finance charge, but not less than $100 nor more than $1,000, plus the costs and attorney's fees required to collect it. Creditors may avoid liability in the event they make an error, provided they notify the debtor within sixty days after discovering the error and also correct the error. In this connection, the law allows for corrections in favor of the debtor only. Creditors cannot collect finance charges in excess of those actually disclosed.

The Truth-in-Lending Act also gives debtors the right to rescind or cancel certain transactions for a period of three business days from the date of the transactions or from the date they are given the notice of their right to rescind, whichever is later. For example, consumers may generally cancel transactions in which they give a security interest on their principal residence if they do so within the three-day period. If the transaction is rescinded, the borrower has no liability for any finance charge, and the security which he or she has given is void.

### TRUTH-IN-LENDING TRENDS

In 1980, Congress passed the Truth-in-Lending Simplification Act. Two changes from the original act stand out. First, the law eliminates statutory penalties based on purely technical violations of the act. It restricts such penalties to failures to disclose credit terms that are of *material* importance in credit comparisons. Second, the Simplification Act requires the Federal Reserve Board to issue model disclosure forms. These are particularly important to small businesses that cannot afford legal counsel to help prepare such forms. Proper use of the forms proves compliance with the Simplification Act.

Studies conducted by the FTC show that many of those involved in credit extension, such as home builders and realtors, fail to make required

Truth-in-Lending disclosures in their advertising. In several instances, the FTC has successfully undertaken programs to educate these businesses about their disclosure obligations under Truth-in-Lending.

## 10.   The Magnuson-Moss Warranty Act

Not all federal consumer protection laws involve deceptive trade practices or credit abuses. This section concerns federal regulation or express warranties. Remember from Chapter 11 that an express warranty makes a statement about a product or a promise about its performance. Many, perhaps most, problems that consumers have with the products they buy come from breaches of warranty.

Historically, one of the major problems with consumer warranties was that they contained highly technical legal language. Consumers did not understand that this language often placed severe limitations on their rights to exercise warranties. Many express warranties even actually deprived consumers of rights, such as the rights furnished by implied warranties. Yet at the same time, manufacturers used consumer warranties promotionally to show that their products were "guaranteed."

In 1975, Congress passed the Magnuson-Moss Warranty Act to help correct warranty problems with consumer products. The law covers **express consumer warranties.** Warranties on such goods must disclose the terms of the warranty in simple and readily understood language. If a product costs more then $10, the warranty must be labeled "full" or "limited." The FTC has the responsibility to prepare regulations to accomplish the goals of the law.

Products covered by a *full* warranty must be repaired or replaced by the seller without charge and within a reasonable time in the event there is a defect. Manufacturers cannot impose requirements on buyers to obtain the repairs or replacements unless the requirements are reasonable. The law does not require manufacturers to give any warranty, but if one is given, its nature and extent must be in language that can be understood by the buyer. If a warranty is to be *limited,* the limitation must be conspicuous so that buyers are not misled. If a written warranty is given, there can be no disclaimer of implied warranties, although consequential damages may be limited.

To aid consumers in making intelligent purchase selections, sellers must make warranty information available to buyers prior to purchase. The information must be conspicuously displayed in association with the warranted product. The FTC has taken action against several sellers who have failed to observe this requirement.

The Magnuson-Moss Act also encourages sellers to set up informal dispute-settlement procedures to handle complaints made under the warranty. Although not requiring such procedures, the act requires that if they exist, consumers must pursue them prior to filing a lawsuit.

As a result of the law, many sellers have eliminated their warranties or have opted for the limited warranty. Some companies, rather than become involved with all the law's requirements, have stopped giving warranties. But the warranties which remain are more useful to consumers than before Magnuson-Moss.

# STATE CONSUMER PROTECTION

### 11.    State Consumer Fraud Legislation

A Justice Department study released in 1982 identifies fraud as a major problem in our economic system. "Consumer fraud is a serious and pervasive phenomenon which continues to plague the American marketplace," the study stated. In the last twenty-five years, all states have passed legislative acts to help deal with this problem.

Generally termed Unfair and Deceptive Acts and Practices (UDAP) statutes, these acts often resemble the FTC Act. They prohibit fraudulent, deceptive, and unconscionable trade practices. They seek to deter merchants from engaging in such practices and provide remedies to ensure that consumers will recover for damages and suffering.

Typically, a state's attorney general will administer a UDAP statute, although special agencies are sometimes used. These public authorities often have power to make rules and conduct investigations. If they uncover fraudulent activities, they can impose a variety of remedies (see Table 20-3). Remedies imposed by public authorities (public remedies) constitute the basic means of UDAP enforcement in most states.

In the last half of the 1980s, state attorneys general began coordinating enforcement activity in multiple states through the National Association of Attorneys General. Among other results, this enforcement activity has won a $16-million settlement from Chrysler Corporation for odometer fraud

**TABLE 20-3**    Public UDAP Remedies

1   Injunctions prohibiting offensive practices
2   Restitution forcing fraudulent merchants to reimburse their victims
3   Civil penalties which must be paid to the state
4   Revocation of licenses and other forms of permission to do business within a state
5   Court appointment of a receiver who handles the defendant's assets and runs the
     defendant's business to benefit injured consumers
6   Criminal fines and/or imprisonment
7   Assessment of court costs or cost of the fraud investigation

*Not all states permit every remedy.

**TABLE 20-4**   Private UDAP Remedies*

1   Recovery of actual losses
2   Recovery of triple damages or a set minimum amount
3   Assessment of punitive damages
4   Assessment of attorney's fees and costs
5   Authorization of class actions by injured consumers
6   Injunctions prohibiting offensive practices
7   Rescission which frees consumers from deceptive arrangements and requires reimbursement of deposits or prepayments

*Not all states permit every remedy.

and a $4-million settlement from Minolta Corporation for manipulating retail camera prices. It has also forced reevaluation of various airline and car rental advertising practices.

To assist state enforcement efforts through public remedies, UDAP statutes provide a number of private remedies that injured consumers themselves can seek from dishonest merchants (see Table 20-4). Private litigation offers a powerful deterrent to consumer fraud and allows consumers to gain compensation for their injuries.

### STATE REGULATION OF SPECIFIC BUSINESSES

Recently, states have begun amending UDAP statutes or passing new legislation to regulate specific businesses. For instance, several states specifically regulate the auto-repair industry. This regulation came as a result of a United States Department of Transportation undercover study which concluded that consumers waste 53 percent of every dollar spent on auto repairs.

Another specific business targeted by state consumer protection statutes is apartment leasing. A number of states prohibit lessors from retaining consumers' security deposits on apartments unless they follow clearly outlined procedures. Door-to-door sales firms and health spas are also regulated in many states.

States have imposed a variety of procedures for controlling fraud in specific businesses. *Escrow accounts* restrict a seller's ability to get or keep money until he or she has given satisfactory performance. Failure to perform means that the escrow agent (frequently a bank) will return part or all of a consumer's payment. *Bonding* provides a compensation fund for consumers. *Industry pools,* adopted in Hawaii for travel agencies, establish an industry-funded "pool," which is used to compensate defrauded consumers. *Registration* permits easy location of firms by public authorities. *Licensing* requires special training or competence before doing business.

Still other consumer protection regulations serve to prevent fraud or to limit losses in specific situations. *Mandatory disclosures* require merchants to provide certain written information before a sale becomes final. *Plain*

*English* rules require consumer contract provisions to be written in a simply understood fashion. *Cooling-off periods* allow consumers a few days to cancel door-to-door sales agreements. *Limited duration* establishes a maximum length for service contracts and thus limits a consumer's future financial obligations. *Limited prepayments* limit the amount a merchant can require consumers to pay in advance.

Increasingly, state (and federal) pressure on specific businesses is forcing them to adopt procedures for mediating or arbitrating disputes with dissatisfied consumers. For instance, consumers who have engine problems with General Motors cars can turn to their local Better Business Bureau for arbitration. Arbitration decisions are binding on GM, although consumers retain the right to go into court if they disagree with the decisions. Most other car manufacturers also have arbitration-type procedures to resolve consumer dissatisfaction problems.

# CONSUMER PRIVACY ETHICS AND THE FUTURE OF CONSUMERISM

## 12.  Consumer Privacy

As society becomes more complex, as population growth creates overcrowding, and as the technology of information gathering becomes more sophisticated, the need for privacy increases. In recent years, the law has come to recognize the invasion of privacy as a tort (see Chapter 10) and even to extend a constitutional right of privacy. For example, a constitutional right of privacy has been asserted by the Supreme Court under the First and Fourth Amendments in cases involving the freedom of association, the possession in the home of pornographic materials, and the use of contraceptive devices. Most of the laws and cases which apply the concepts of privacy protect the individual from being overwhelmed by the intrusive power of the government and other large organizations, including businesses. Many laws directly affect us as "consumers," and almost all apply to protect us in our personal, rather than public, lives. Consumer protection regulation and privacy laws, then, have very much in common.

Several of the consumer protection laws discussed in this chapter contain provisions protecting personal privacy. Under the Fair Credit Reporting Act, for example, a potential employer, insurer, or creditor must inform the consumer that an investigative report is being obtained on him or her. This notice allows the consumer to terminate the contemplated transaction, thus ending the legitimate business reason for the report and preventing the report from being obtained legally.

One of the chief threats to individual privacy comes from the government and governmental agencies which investigate individuals or which collect information from individuals. Several federal statutes are directed specifically at this problem. The Privacy Act of 1974 places constraints on how certain kinds of information collected by the federal government can be used and limits those to whom the information may be released. It also provides a tort cause of action against those who violate the act. A second statute, the Right to Financial Privacy Act of 1978, requires all government agencies seeking depositor records from banks and other financial institutions to notify depositors of this fact. The individual depositor then has fourteen days to challenge an agency's legal basis for seeking the records. Depositors are allowed to sue the government agencies or financial institutions which fail to comply with the statute for actual and punitive damages, plus attorney's fees.

### 13. Ethical Considerations

Individual privacy is such an important part of individual freedom that both legal and ethical questions regarding privacy are bound to multiply in the computer age. While debate continues concerning the need for further federal privacy legislation, many states have passed their own privacy-related statutes. Several states guarantee workers access to their job personnel files and restrict disclosure of personal information to third parties. Almost half the states forbid businesses from requiring lie-detector tests as a condition of employment, although employers can still ask job applicants to submit voluntarily to the tests. Other state laws prohibit illegal interception of computer communications and regulate the privacy of data transmitted on cable television networks.

Responding to privacy issues, hundreds of companies have adopted privacy sections in their codes of ethics. Most of these sections concern personnel information. The following is an example from the Caterpillar Code of Ethics.

### PRIVACY OF INFORMATION ABOUT EMPLOYEES

Information needed for administration of payrolls, benefit plans, and labor agreements—and for compliance with laws—has resulted in collection, by Caterpillar, of an increasing amount of personal data. We seek to minimize intrusiveness, and maximize fairness and confidentiality of such data.

Personal data will contain only such individually identifiable information as is necessary for business purposes and compliance with law. Such information is to be handled confidentially and securely. Company access to such information is limited to those who have legitimate, pertinent business purposes.

Entries to employee data files are to be factual, job-related, and accurate. Any information found to be in error will be corrected or eliminated. Company data about an employee will be made available, on request, to that employee...excepting for special, sensitive files such as those pertaining to career planning and litigation.

---

## 14.   Policy Trends: the Future of Consumerism

Consumerism and the litigation it breeds seem to be here to stay. The slowdown in the appearance of new consumer protection regulation should by no means, however, be taken as an end to the importance of consumer protection in general. As the laws discussed in this chapter indicate, there is substantial consumer regulation already enacted. And, as these existing laws are further implemented, their impact on the business community will be likely to continue to grow.

In a quiet way, a recent change in the marketing of legal services may also give a boost to the consumer movement. Low-cost assistance provided by **legal clinics,** which specialize in routine, high-volume services, is enabling many individuals to pursue consumer complaints which would previously have been too expensive for them to pursue.

Large chains like Sears and H&R Block are also beginning to open their facilities for use by attorneys who provide inexpensive legal advice. In addition, legal advertising is on the increase and probably will contribute significantly to the public's awareness of the availability of legal remedies for common consumer problems.

The increasing number of lawyers is one factor which will ensure that the amount of consumer litigation does not diminish. There are now approximately 600,000 lawyers in the United States, twice as many as practiced twenty years ago. We have three times as many lawyers per capita as England and twenty times as many as Japan.

Prepaid legal plans for workers and other developments will also help ensure a healthy future for consumerism. Millions of workers and their dependents are presently covered by prepaid legal plans. General Motors has recently covered its 400,000 employees with a legal service plan called for in a collective-bargaining contract.

Finally, the number of legal "hot lines," which provide legal advice by telephone, is growing rapidly. In several states, CIGNA Corp. offers credit-card holders unlimited telephone consultations for a low monthly fee.

## REVIEW QUESTIONS

**1** For each term in the left-hand column, match the most appropriate description in the right-hand column:

(1) Bait-and-switch

(a) A person who buys something for personal, family, or household use.

(2) Consumer

(b) A report prepared on someone's personal life, as well as credit status.

(3) Corrective advertising

(c) A private person against whom an agency takes administrative action.

(4) Consumer investigative report

(d) The practice of generally refusing credit to persons who live in certain areas.

(5) Industry guides

(e) Another name for FTC consumer protection activity.

(6) Redlining

(f) The practice of attracting consumers to a store by advertising a specific product and then criticizing that product to persuade them to purchase another, higher-priced product.

(7) Legal clinics

(g) Advertising which contains a message that counters prior deceptive advertising.

(8) Respondent

(h) Law firms which specialize in inexpensive, mass legal services.

(9) Trade practice regulation

(i) Informal, nonbinding FTC guidelines on a trade group's business practices.

**2** The Mosquito-No Company claims that its electronic mosquito repellent will "eliminate all mosquito problems within a one-half acre area." The Federal Trade Commission doubts that this claim is correct. What will the FTC likely demand that the company do?

**3** List the penalties and remedies available to the FTC for use against a business that has violated the FTC Act.

**4** Jane Thomas applies for automobile financing at Kenwood Cars, Inc., a used-car dealership. The dealership obtains a credit report on her. On the basis of this report, the dealership denies her credit. The manager informs her that she will have to get her husband to cosign her application if she wants dealership financing. She refuses, and sues Kenwood Cars, Inc., under the ECOA. What was the result and why?

**5** The ABC Department Store refuses credit to Mary Jane. Mary Jane has a good job and no debts. She cannot understand the refusal. What would you suggest Mary Jane do? Explain.

**6** A potential employer requests information about a former employee of yours. Without complying with the requirements of the Fair Credit Reporting Act, can you tell the potential employer that the former employee:
  a Was often late to work?
  b Was caught drunk on the job?
  c Has a general reputation in your community as a troublemaker? Explain.

**7** Wes Tomic takes out a $50,000 loan with First Bank to open a small electronics business. Shortly after signing the final loan papers, Tomic finds out that he could have gotten his financing elsewhere at a lower interest rate. He then realizes that First Bank never furnished him a Truth-in-Lending financing disclosure form. Does he have rights against the bank under the Truth-in-Lending Act? Discuss.

**8** Under the Truth-in-Lending Act, what is a "finance charge?" What charges are and are not included as finance charges?

**9** Discuss various legal remedies granted consumers under state UDAP statutes.

**10** Mr. Jones, a black school principal, applies for a mortgage loan at a bank. After examining the application, the bank politely but firmly refuses the loan, explaining that property values in Mr. Jones's neighborhood are too low to support the amount he is seeking. Might Mr. Jones have some course of action against the bank? Under what law?

**11** Discuss how privacy is protected by the various laws covered in this chapter.

**12** Jan has a problem with the engine of his new Chevrolet. If the car dealer refuses to take care of the problem under the warranty, what can Jan do? Consider that he cannot afford to hire an attorney.

**13** Discuss trends that suggest that the impact of consumer protection laws on the business community may continue to grow.

*Chapter*

*21*

# Creditor and Debtor Protection

## CHAPTER PREVIEW

In a private enterprise economy based on freedom of contract, there will always be creditors and debtors. Each group has legal rights. The problem is how to balance rights between creditors and debtors while keeping a fairly run economy. For instance, creditors can no longer put a debtor into prison for failure to pay debts, but creditors can seize a debtor's wages and property, a topic covered in Chapter 4.

This chapter discusses the laws that protect creditors and debtors. Creditor protection includes: (1) artisan's and mechanic's liens, which give unpaid creditors a claim against personal and real property which they have carried, stored, repaired, or improved; (2) bulk transfer law, which protects creditors when a merchant debtor sells a major part of its inventory out of the ordinary course of its business; (3) suretyship, which covers the legal rules applying when one promises to perform for a creditor if a debtor does not; (4) secured transactions in personal property, which covers Article 9 of the Uniform Commercial Code; and (5) secured transactions in real property, which focuses on mortgages.

Debtor protection includes: (1) usury laws, which regulate maximum interest rates on loans; (2) limitation on debt collection, which considers the

Fair Debt Collection Practices Act; (3) the Bankruptcy Act, which specifies when debtors can have their debts discharged or adjusted; and (4) special consumer-debtor protection, which covers abolishment of the holder-in-due-course doctrine and the power of consumers to revoke credit-card charges.

Important terms in this chapter are artisan's lien, attachment, bulk transfer, contribution, financing statement, foreclosure, liquidation, mechanic's lien, real estate mortgage, perfection, purchase-money security interest, reimbursement, reorganization, right of redemption, surety, and usury.

# CREDITOR PROTECTION

## 1. Introduction

Many laws protect creditors. As used in the following sections, a **creditor** is one who lends money or extends credit for goods or services.

In a private enterprise economy it is extremely important to all consumers that creditors have legal protection. First, legal protection makes creditors more willing to lend money and extend credit. Second, if there were no legal protection of creditors, they would have to charge higher interest and prices to all consumers to cover the greater losses suffered because of the lack of legal protection. The conclusion is that the creditor protection laws discussed in the following sections benefit consumers as well as creditors.

## 2. Artisan's Liens

A *lien* is an obligation for payment of money—also called a "security interest"—which attaches to property as a result of statute, common law, equity, or contract. Usually the property can be sold to satisfy the lien if the lien holder is not paid. Among others, there are tax liens, judgment liens, mortgage liens (see section 7), Article 9 liens (see section 6), mechanic's liens (see section 3) and **artisan's liens.**

Today, statutes in every state create artisan's liens. These liens are a class of liens which protect those who store, carry, or repair the goods of another for a price. For instance, if a common carrier, such as the railroad, is not paid for shipping and storing goods, it may sell the goods to satisfy the obligation. Likewise, failure to pay for repair of a television allows the person who performed the repairs to sell the television to satisfy the debt owed. In both instances, the creditor can sell the property because of the artisan's lien. Generally, the statute requires the creditor to give notice to the debtor before a sale takes place. Any surplus from the sale after the debt is paid must be returned to the debtor.

Usually, an artisan's lien lasts only as long as the creditor has possession of the property. Surrender of the property to the debtor means that the creditor loses the lien if someone buys the property from the debtor or legally seizes it. However, some statutes permit the creditor to record the artisan's lien with the proper records office. If the creditor records the lien, it has priority even against third parties who legally acquire it from the debtor. In fact, an artisan's lien is commonly superior to all claims on the property.

### 3.  Mechanic's Liens

Almost any contract for the improvement of real property creates a **mechanic's lien** in favor of the person who improves the property. For instance, a contractor who constructs a building has a lien on it for payment of what is owed. A landscaper, an architect, and a roofing repairer also have mechanic's liens for services rendered. These are all persons who contract directly with an owner to improve real property and who are known as "contractors."

Mechanic's liens also protect those who provide services or material to contractors who improve real property. These persons include building material suppliers and those hired by a contractor to work on the property. Note that these persons, called "subcontractors," contract with the primary contractor rather than with the property owner.

Mechanic's lien statutes usually specify that a lien must be recorded within sixty to ninety days following completion of work or delivery of materials to establish priority over third parties, such as mortgagees or buyers of the property. Subcontractors must also record within this period to be able to exercise a lien against the property owner, although contractors often have two to three years to record against the property owner. The difference in treatment between contractors and subcontractors arises because property owners may not know of the existence of the latter group. The mechanic's lien is lost if it is not recorded within the specified time periods.

Two problems deserve special comment. First, real estate purchasers should always check the records office for mechanic's liens. This check is part of the title search, which is routine for most real estate sales. But a title search cannot detect very recent mechanic's liens, because of the sixty- to ninety-day period allowed for recording them against third parties. Real estate purchasers should therefore try to determine whether any improvements or repairs have been made on the property within this statutory time period.

The second problem concerns the property owner. It is quite possible for the owner to pay a building contractor for work performed but the contractor to fail to pay material suppliers or workers. These suppliers or workers can exercise mechanic's liens against the property. The owner will have to pay again to avoid foreclosure of the liens. Of course, in these situations the building contractor is often uncooperative, unavailable, or bankrupt.

Property owners can protect themselves from this problem in several ways. It is often possible for an owner to get subcontractors, and even contractors, to *waive* (legally give up) their rights to mechanic's liens. Alternatively, an owner should get from the contractor a sworn statement listing all subcontractors. The owner can then pay the subcontractors directly or demand proof of payment for materials or services before paying the contractor.

An owner may rely upon the truthfulness of the contractor's sworn statement concerning the identity of and amount owed to subcontractors. If an owner gets a proper sworn statement, subcontractors who are not listed or who are listed for a smaller amount than they are owed can look for payment only to the contractor with whom they dealt.

## 4.   Bulk Transfers

Bob Jackson, owner of Acme Hardware, is in financial trouble. His major creditor, First Bank, has refused to renew his loan and is requiring a $75,000 payment which he cannot meet. Several smaller creditors have called recently and demanded payment of long-overdue accounts. The significant possibility of lawsuits and bankruptcy hang over him. The only real asset he has left is the inventory of his store.

After considering his increasingly slim chances of staying in business, he phones the owner of City Hardware, a neighboring competitor, and offers to sell his entire inventory for a very reasonable price. His offer is quickly accepted. Later that week, Bob Jackson leaves town. He takes with him the $55,000 he got for his inventory and leaves no forwarding address.

When merchants get into financial difficulty, the last asset they have is often the inventory and equipment of their businesses. Sometimes they sell this asset to a competitor and neglect to pay their creditors. A special body of law addresses this problem. It is the law of bulk transfers found in Article 6 of the Uniform Commercial Code.

Article 6 defines a **bulk transfer** as a transfer (usually a sale) out of the ordinary course of business of all or a major part of the inventory (or inventory and equipment) of a merchant. Inventory is the stock that a merchant holds for resale. Note that the sale must be "out of the ordinary course of business" and that it must constitute a "major part" of the inventory. Regular sales to a merchant's customers are not included within the meaning of bulk transfer.

Creditor protection under Article 6 places a notice requirement on bulk buyers, that is, on those who buy a major part of a merchant's inventory out of the ordinary course of business. A bulk buyer must get from the merchant a schedule of the inventory sold and a sworn list of the merchant's creditors. The bulk buyer can rely upon the accuracy of this list. The buyer must then notify the listed creditors, personally or by registered mail, that a bulk sale will take place. Notice must be given at least ten days before the bulk buyer takes possession of the inventory or pays for it. Table 21-1 tells what information the bulk buyer must provide to the creditors.

The notice requirement of Article 6 gives a merchant's creditors plenty of time to stop a bulk sale by throwing the merchant into bankruptcy or otherwise protecting themselves. Should a bulk buyer fail to give required notice, the merchant's creditors can seize the inventory property from the bulk buyer and sell it to satisfy their debts. In the example which introduced this section, City Hardware may lose the hardware inventory it purchased to the creditors of Bob Jackson.

Some states require the bulk buyer to apply proceeds of a bulk sale to satisfy the merchant's creditors. In these states, failure to apply proceeds to the merchant's debts creates personal liability on the bulk buyer for the value of the inventory property.

## 5. Suretyship

### INTRODUCTION

A savings and loan association bonds its employees for "faithful performance." If an employee embezzles money, the S&L can recover its loss from the bonding company. A retail store having a new warehouse built requires the builder to get a construction bond. If the builder fails to complete the warehouse when promised, the store can demand payment of this construction bond. A bank insists that a student's parents endorse her education loan note. If she does not repay the loan, the bank can get payment from the parents.

**TABLE 21-1**   Bulk Buyer's Notice Requirements to Creditors of Seller

1   That a bulk transfer is about to be made
2   The names and business addresses of the bulk buyer and seller
3   Whether or not the seller's debts are to be paid in full from the proceeds of the sale
    If the debts are not to be paid in full from the sale proceeds, the bulk buyer must further state:
4   The location and description of the property to be transferred and the estimated total of the seller's debts
5   The address where the schedule of property and list of creditors may be inspected
6   The sale price and the time and place for payment

    If the transfer of property is to satisfy an existing debt, this must be stated instead.

These situations all involve the law of suretyship, which is important in many commercial transactions. A **surety** is one who promises to perform some obligation upon breach or default of performance by another person. The parties to a suretyship are a *debtor* who owes a performance, a *creditor* to whom the performance is owed, and a surety who will have to perform if the debtor does not. Figure 21-1 illustrates this three-part relationship in the example of a student loan.

A suretyship is a contractual arrangement. The consideration given which binds the surety may come from one of several sources; for example, the debtor may pay the surety (the construction bond is an example), or the creditor may provide some other consideration to the surety (agreeing to extend an education loan to the surety's child).

If the surety signs the contract between the creditor and debtor, it is a true suretyship contract. The student-loan note endorsed by a parent is an example. Where the surety is not a party to the creditor-debtor contract, but contracts separately, the resulting arrangement is a *guaranty*. The construction bond is a guaranty, since the bonding company does not sign the building contract between the builder and the owner. The builder contracts separately with the bonding company. Usually, the law treats suretyship and guaranty contracts in identical fashion, so the rest of this discussion will call all such contracts "suretyship contracts."

Unless they state otherwise, suretyship contracts are *unconditional*. This means that once the debtor fails to perform, the creditor can immediately demand performance from the surety. *Conditional* suretyship contracts require that the creditor meet some condition before being entitled to the surety's performance. Often, the condition is that the creditor sue the debtor and get a judgment before demanding payment from the surety.

Once all conditions are properly met, the surety must perform. However, since commercial suretyship arrangements are frequently very complex, there may be dispute over the nature of the surety's required performance. The following case illustrates this.

**FIGURE 21-1**
Suretyship Arrangement for a $10,000 Education Loan.

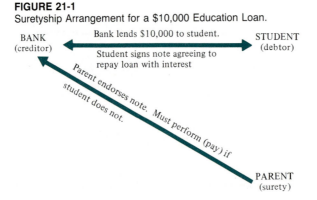

# NEW HAMPSHIRE INS. CO. v. GRUHN
670 P.2d 941 (Nev. 1983)

PER CURIAM: Appellant New Hampshire Insurance Company issued a surety bond to The Realatorium, a mortgage company, in which it undertook to "pay all damages suffered by any person… by reason of any fraud, dishonesty, misrepresentation or concealment of material facts." In this lawsuit, the trial court found that The Realatorium was guilty of fraudulent misrepresentation. The trial court awarded the plaintiffs $5,000 in punitive damages and ordered the insurance company to pay the punitive damage award "forthwith."

The company contends that its liability under the bond does not include an obligation to indemnify against punitive damages. The contention is correct, and we reverse, vacating the order requiring the insurance company to pay the $5,000 punitive sum.

To determine the scope of the coverage, we look to the language and purpose of the bond, and in doing so, to that of the statute. NRS 645B.030(2) provides that the surety is obligated to "pay all damages suffered." The language of the bond was identical to that of the statute. The trial judge held that "all damages" included punitive damages which were awarded against the mortgage company. It does not. One does not "suffer" punitive damages. The policy behind punitive damages is to punish the wrongdoer for his conduct and to deter others from acting in a similar fashion. For this reason punitive damages are not awarded to compensate the plaintiff for harm incurred.

Apart from the wording of the statute, a bond is required in order to provide a minimum source of funds for those who have suffered compensable losses. We have already noted that where claims against a bond are asserted by more than one party, and that bond is insufficient to satisfy all claims in full, each claimant is entitled to a pro rata share of the bond proceeds. It is doubtful that the legislature intended for this pool to be diluted with awards for punitive damages at the expense of reducing the pro rata share of those claimants who have suffered pecuniary loss. Moreover, it is incumbent upon the party whose conduct was so outrageous as to merit punishment by means of punitive damages to bear the burden of paying the award. Only then will the goal of punishment and deterrence be effectuated. This policy would be thwarted if the tortfeasor is able to skirt the award by passing the liability on to a surety. It cannot be said that the legislature intended to provide a means whereby a tortfeasor could avoid the penalty of paying punitive damages by allowing satisfaction to be sought from a surety. The purpose of NRS 645B.030 is to protect the public and not to protect the mortgage company.

Since the plaintiff does not "suffer" punitive damages within the meaning of NRS 645B.030(2), the order requiring New Hampshire Insurance Company to pay the $5,000 punitive sum to the Gruhns is [*reversed and vacated.*]

Being a surety can expose one to a great deal of liability, although the consideration given the surety for undertaking the risk may be small or nothing. The defenses which the surety can raise when the creditor demands performance are thus very important.

### DEFENSES AVAILABLE TO SURETY

Chapter 9 discussed defenses to an allegation of breach of contract. These defenses include *fraud, duress, illegality, lack of consideration, proper performance, mistake,* and *impossibility of performance.* Regarding these defenses, the basic rule in suretyship situations is that any time defenses are available to the debtor, they are also available to the surety. When the creditor demands that the surety perform, it is possible then for the surety to escape liability by establishing that the creditor defrauded the debtor, that the creditor did not perform properly for the debtor, or that some other defense exists.

The surety may also raise defenses which are not available to the debtor. If the creditor releases the debtor from liability, the surety is generally released as well. Likewise, if the creditor knows or learns of facts which increase the surety's risk, but fails to warn the surety (for example, if a bank fails to tell the bonding company that a bank employee had previously stolen money from the bank), the surety can later assert this to avoid liability. Also, recall from Chapter 9 that if a suretyship contract is not in writing, the surety can raise the statute of frauds as a defense.

If the creditor and debtor modify their contract so as to increase the risk to the surety, it discharges the surety from liability. Typical modifications which may release the debtor include substituting one debtor for another and legally changing the amount, place, or time of the debtor's payments.

Historically, any modification of the debtor's duties gave the surety a defense. In most states today, however, the modification must *materially increase* the risk to the surety, especially if the surety is a commercial insurance or bonding company. A "material" increase is one that is important or significant to the assumed risk.

Certain defenses available to the debtor cannot be raised by the surety. For example, the debtor's *infancy* or *incapacity* will not prevent the surety from being liable, although the debtor can assert these defenses if sued. The reason for this is obvious: the creditor may insist on having a surety to begin with because of the debtor's age or lack of capacity.

### RIGHTS AVAILABLE TO THE SURETY

Even if the surety is liable because of the debtor's failure to perform the contract properly, the surety has certain rights and remedies. For instance, the right of **set off** permits the surety to reduce the amount owed to the creditor. The sum can be reduced by any amount which the creditor owes the surety arising out of some other transaction.

In most cases, the rights of reimbursement and subrogation will be even more valuable to the surety. **Reimbursement,** or indemnity, refers to the duty of the debtor to reimburse the surety when the surety has had to pay the creditor. The surety may sue to enforce this right, although often the debtor has no money.

When the surety has performed for the debtor, the surety has the same rights against the debtor that the creditor had. Another way of saying this is that the surety has a right of subrogation. If the creditor is holding the debtor's property as collateral for a debt, the subrogation right will entitle the surety to the collateral when he or she pays the debt to the creditor. Should the creditor defeat the surety's subrogation right by returning the collateral to the debtor, the surety's obligation to the creditor reduces by an amount equal to the collateral's value.

### CO-SURETYSHIP

Sometimes more than one surety guarantees the same obligation of a debtor. This arrangement is called co-suretyship. Co-sureties share *joint and several liability*. The creditor whose debtor defaults on a $20,000 loan may recover the amount from either or both of the co-sureties, although, of course, the creditor may collect only $20,000 in all.

Co-sureties have the same rights of reimbursement and subrogation that single sureties have. In addition, they have the right of **contribution.** If both guarantee the $20,000 loan, and the creditor collects that amount from only one of them, the one who paid can recover $10,000 from the other co-surety.

A creditor who releases co-surety A from liability destroys co-surety B's right of contribution against co-surety A. As a result, the law reduces co-surety B's liability by the amount of the destroyed right of contribution. The next case examines this rule.

# KEYSTONE BANK v. FLOORING SPECIALISTS, INC.
518 A.2d 1179 (Pa. 1986)

A corporation borrowed money from the Keystone bank. As representatives of the corporation, the president Philip McCosby and vice president Anthony DeRubeis signed a promissory note for the amount owed. In their personal capacities, the president and vice president (and their wives) also signed a surety clause in the note, thus guaranteeing payment if the corporation defaulted on the debt. When the corporation failed to pay, the bank sued and got judg-ment liens against the real property owned by the sureties. Subsequently, the bank re-leased its lien against certain real property owned by the corporate president and his wife so they could sell it. When the bank sought a writ of execution against the home of the corporate vice president and his wife, these persons asserted that the bank's re-lease of the lien against the co-sureties' property discharged them from liability. Both the trial and appellate courts ruled against the DeRubeises. The Pennsylvania Supreme Court granted certiorari.

NIX, J.: The issue in this appeal is whether the appellants, who were two of four co-guarantors on a negotiable promissory note, were discharged from their obligations because the creditor had released from the effect of its judgment lien certain property belonging to the other guarantors....

At common law a surety was discharged of his obligation if and to the extent that the creditor voluntarily released the principal debtor from liability, unless the surety consented to such release or the creditor expressly reserved his rights against the surety. Also, if the creditor, without the surety's consent or without having reserved his rights against the surety, made a binding commitment to extend the time for the principal to pay the debt, such an act had the effect of discharging the surety's obligation.

Another important element in the common law of suretyship was the well-settled rule that, if a creditor surrendered or impaired collateral which served as security for the principal's debt, the surety was discharged from his obligation to the extent that the collateral would have produced funds sufficient to pay the debt in whole or in part. As with the other suretyship defenses, if the surety consented to the creditor's surrender, release or impairment of collateral there would be no discharge of the surety's obligation.

Each of the foregoing common law grounds for the discharge of a surety addressed situations in which the creditor, without the consent of the surety or without a reservation of rights, committed some act which prejudiced the surety's rights or increased the risk of the surety's undertaking. For example, a release of the principal debtor from liability undercuts the surety's right to seek reimbursement from the former; a binding extension of time for paying the debt frustrates and delays the surety's opportunity to have the transaction liquidated; and a release or impairment of collateral defeats in whole or part the surety's right to look to such security for recourse should he have to pay the principal debt.

Where, as in the case at bar, there are several sureties for the principal's unpaid debt, each surety owes to his co-sureties a duty to pay his proportional share of their common debt. Should one of the co-sureties have to pay more than his proportional share of the debt, one of the rights incidental to his co-suretyship is the right to enforce contribution from the other sureties for the excess.

In the same way that a surety can be discharged from his obligation to the creditor because of transactions between the creditor and the principal debtor which prejudice the surety's rights, so too can one surety be discharged because of prejudicial transactions between the creditor and another surety for the same debt. That is because where there are several co-sureties each of them is in legal effect, as against the others, a principal for his proportion of the debt and a surety for the rest of it....In connection with the premise, it has also been held that if the creditor releases collateral obtained from one of several co-sureties to secure the debt, such release can impair the other sureties' right to resort to such collateral to enforce their rights of contribution, and that if the release has such an effect, the other co-sureties will be entitled to a...discharge of their obligations [to the extent of that impairment]....

Although we conclude that the DeRubeises, as co-sureties with the McCosbys, had the right to raise the "impairment of collateral" defense because of Keystone's release of the judgment lien on the McCosby property, the question of whether that release actually prejudiced the appellants' rights of contribution, or to what extent, cannot be determined from the record before us. All we have before us in that regard are the appellants' assertion that the sale of the McCosby property could have, or did, produce proceeds sufficient to satisfy the McCosbys' proportional share of the debt, and the counter-assertion by Keystone that the five thousand dollars ($5,000.00) paid to it by the McCosbys was the most it could have gotten under the circumstances. The trial court's opinion does not address this important factual issue which must be resolved before a decision can be made.

Accordingly, we hereby reverse the orders of the Superior Court, and remand the instant case to the trial court for further proceedings consistent with this opinion and for the entry of an appropriate judgment. [*Reversed and remanded.*]

## 6.   Secured Transactions in Personal Property

A **secured transaction** occurs when a debtor puts up personal property as collateral to ensure repayment of a loan or an extension of credit. If the debtor does not repay, the creditor may seize and sell the property to satisfy the debt. Secured transactions are extremely important to the smooth running of our economic system. Banks and other financial institutions are much more willing to lend money when valuable property secures the loan. Manufacturers are more likely to extend credit to retailers—and retailers are more likely to sell on credit to consumers—when their risk is secured by more than a simple promise to pay.

Article 9 of the Uniform Commercial Code controls secured transactions nationwide, except in Louisiana. It applies to *personal property* (as opposed to real property). The various types of personal property, which are very important to Article 9, are set out in Table 21-2.

**TABLE 21-2**   Types of Personal Property Covered by Article 9

1   Tangible property
  a   Consumer goods: those bought for personal or family use
  b   Inventory: goods bought for resale or lease
  c   Equipment: goods bought for use in a business (does not include inventory)
  d   Farm products: crops, livestock, or supplies produced or used in a farming operation
2   Intangible property
  a   Account: any right to payment for leased or sold goods or services
  b   General intangible: personal property such as royalty rights, copyrights, and patent rights
3   Documentary property
  a   Instruments: certificates of deposit, promissory notes, checks, and other negotiable instruments
  b   Documents of title: documents which represent ownership rights to goods held by a warehouse, freight carrier, or other keeper of property

## WHY HAVE A SECURED INTEREST?

If a debtor fails to repay a loan or credit, the creditor can always sue the debtor, get a judgment, and, if necessary, sell the debtor's property to satisfy the judgment. Why then is it desirable to have a security interest? There are two main reasons.

First, if the creditor has a proper security interest in personal property and the debtor defaults in payment, the creditor can simply seize the personal property and sell it to satisfy the debt. This bypasses the complicated, expensive litigation process.

Second, a secured creditor often has priority over many other parties who may also want the property which has the security interest on it. Judgment creditors, lien holders, trustees in bankruptcy, and buyers of the property are all worthy opponents of a secured creditor. The *rules of priority,* which are discussed later, determine whether the secured creditor will triumph over these opponents. Note, however, that the unsecured creditor has no priority at all.

## ATTACHMENT OF A SECURITY INTEREST

To be enforceable, a security interest in the property must first attach. **Attachment** occurs when three elements are present:

**1**   There must be an *agreement* that there should be a security interest. This agreement is usually in writing and signed by the debtor. Often, it is part of a sales or credit contract.

**2**   The creditor must give *value* to the debtor. Goods sold on credit or money from a loan is the usual form of value given by the creditor.

**3**   The debtor must have *rights in the property,* which is collateral for the security interest.

The next case considers what it means for the debtor to have rights in the collateral.

---

# FIRST NATIONAL BANK OF SANTA FE v. QUINTANA
733 P.2d 858 (N.M. 1987)

---

Manesas and Archuleta entered into an agreement to buy a restaurant and equipment from a restauranteur. The First National Bank of Santa Fe loaned them $59,000 and took out a security agreement on the equipment that they intended to get from the restauranteur. A financing statement was filed. When the buyers did not go through with their purchase of the restaurant and equipment, the defendant, Dan

Quintana, bought it. He then entered a contract to sell the restaurant and equipment to Manesas and Archuleta, who took possession of the restaurant and equipment. Manesas and Archuleta never paid either the bank or Quintana. Quintana seized the restaurant and equipment from them, and the bank sued Quintana for the equipment and damages, alleging priority under a perfected security agreement.

WALTERS, J.:...The trial court granted partial summary judgment on the bank's claim, further ruling that the bank was entitled, at its election, either to judgment against Quintana for the value of the collateral or for repossession of the collateral. Pursuant to that order, the bank elected to receive the value of the collateral.

We do not agree with the bank that its security interest attached to the collateral, thereby placing it in a position superior to that of Quintana. In order for a security interest to attach, there must be an agreement that it attach, value must be given, and the debtor must have rights in the collateral.

The Bank erroneously relies on *Morton Booth Co. v. Tiara Furniture, Inc.*...as authority for its contention that the Manesas and Archuletas acquired "rights in the collateral" sufficient to effectuate attachment.

Where the debtor acquires possession of the collateral pursuant to a contract which grants the debtor an interest other than mere possession, the debtor has obtained rights in the collateral so as to allow the security interest to attach. But as the court in *Morton Booth* correctly observed, "[M]ere possession of goods is not enough under the Code to demonstrate that the debtor had 'rights' in the collateral."

We agree with Quintana that the purchase agreement between Quintana and the Manesas and Archuletas contained a condition precedent which was never performed; therefore, as a matter of law, the contract was never consummated.

Manesas and Archuletas failed to comply with the initial requirements of the contract, i.e., payment of the full $29,000 required under the purchase agreement, which would have given them more than mere possession of the equipment. Naked possession of collateral provides an insufficient acquisition of rights in it upon which the bank's security interest might attach. As a matter of law, the bank had neither a valid security interest in the collateral, nor a claim against the property of Quintana, much less a perfected security interest superior to Quintana's claimed landlord's lien. [*We reverse and remand for dismissal of the bank's complaint.*]

---

It seems obvious that the debtor cannot put up property to secure a loan when he or she has no rights to that property. Yet, Article 9 permits a security interest in *after-acquired property*, property in which the debtor has no rights when the security interest initially attaches but which is acquired at a future date. An example is when a bank lends a merchant money to buy inventory, and the security agreement contains an after-acquired property clause. Any inventory goods which the merchant later acquires become subject to the bank's security interest. Article 9 says that as soon as the merchant acquires the property and has rights in it, the bank's security interest immediately attaches.

### PERFECTION OF A SECURITY INTEREST

Attachment alone seldom gives a secured creditor maximum priority over others who want the secured property. **Perfection** must also take place. The creditor perfects the security interest in one of several ways.

Attachment does give perfection when the creditor has a **purchase-money security interest** in consumer goods. A purchase-money interest arises when the credit or loan extended is used to acquire the property which is subject to the security interest. Most often this type of perfection is found in credit sales of retail goods. A merchant who sells a television on credit obtains a perfected security interest in the television through mere attachment of the security interest.

**Possession** is an alternate means of establishing perfection of a security interest. The pawnbroker is a good example of a creditor who has a perfected security interest through possession. Note that the interest remains perfected only as long as possession exists. An exception is that a secured party that perfects by possession continues to have perfection for twenty-one days when releasing negotiable instruments or documents back to the debtor so the debtor can obtain his or her payment.

A special type of possession is *field warehousing*. Field warehousing enables a creditor to possess inventory goods even though they remain at the debtor's place of business. For a small sum, the creditor rents a portion of the debtor's business premises and temporarily hires one of the debtor's employees. The secured goods are placed in the rented area and roped off from the rest of the debtor's premises. Signs are posted to indicate the creditor's possession.

The legal test for possession by field warehousing is whether the creditor has *sole dominion and control* over the secured property. As used here, "dominion" means the right to possess. Field warehousing of inventory is sometimes necessary because inventory that is in the debtor's possession can be sold free and clear of any security interest to buyers in the ordinary course of the debtor's business.

The last method for getting perfection is by filing a **financing statement** in the appropriate records office. A proper financing statement is signed by the debtor and secured creditor, gives their addresses, and contains an adequate description of the secured property. An "adequate description" is one that informs others as to which of the debtor's properties are covered by the security interest. The appropriate place for filing the financing statement varies according to the state.

Sometimes a debtor in possession of secured property sells it or transforms it into something else. Thus, a retailer might sell secured inventory and get paid for it, or a manufacturer might take secured raw materials and turn them into finished products. In these situations, payments for inventory or finished products from raw materials are called *proceeds*. A secured creditor continues to have a perfected security interest in finished products from raw materials if a financing statement covers proceeds. Even if there is no mention of proceeds, the perfected security interest in proceeds continues for ten days. A slightly different provision is made for cash or check proceeds.

The law requires perfection to obtain maximum priority for the secured creditor. This is because perfection gives notice to other creditors and parties of the existence of the secured interest. Certainly, possession by the creditor gives notice that there may be a security interest in property. A financing statement provides notice by being publicly available. As to purchase-money security interests in consumer goods, one suspects that with widespread consumer credit sales almost any consumer goods may be subject to security interests.

## PRIORITIES OF SECURITY INTERESTS

Article 9 contains many rules regarding priorities of security interests. The best way to illustrate these priorities is through a series of examples:

**1** John and Mary each hold an attached security interest in the same property. Neither has perfected. The interest which attached first has priority.

**2** First Bank has an attached (but not perfected) security interest in Farmer Brown's prize bull. Judgment creditor Smith, who had lent money to Farmer Brown, gets a writ of execution and seizes the bull. First Bank sues to recover the bull. First Bank loses. It has no priority over other creditors of the debtor.

**3** First Bank has an attached (but not perfected) security interest in Acme Manufacturers' bottling equipment. Second Bank has a security interest in the same equipment which is both attached and perfected. Even if First Bank's interest attaches first, Second Bank has priority because a perfected interest prevails over a merely attached one.

**4** In example 3, suppose that both First Bank and Second Bank have perfected security interests. The first to perfect has priority.

**5** TV Barn sells a television on credit to John Consumer and perfects its purchase-money security interest through attachment alone. TV Barn has priority over John's judgment creditors and a trustee in bankruptcy. It does not have priority over a television repairperson's lien, or over a neighbor who does not know of the security interest and buys the set from John in good faith.

**6** In example 5, if TV Barn had perfected by filing a financing statement, it would have priority over the claim of John's neighbor. It would not have priority over liens of repair, storage, or transportation, because these liens always triumph over Article 9 security interest.

**7** First Bank has perfected its security interest in Computer Retail's inventory by filing a finance statement. Mary buys a computer out of this inventory. So long as she buys it as a customer in Computer Retail's *ordinary course of business,* she takes it free and clear of the security interest.

**8** In example 7, another computer store which bought Computer Retail's entire stock would be subject to First Bank's security interest. This sale is not in the ordinary course of Computer Retail's business.

**9** Best Builder Corp. gets a $50,000 loan from Second Bank. Second Bank takes possession of and holds as secured collateral a $75,000 promissory note which a client owes Best Builder. Later, Second Bank returns the promissory note to Best Builder so that it can collect payment of the note from its client. For a twenty-one-day period following release of the note for collection, Second Bank continues to have priority over judgment creditors of Best Builder or a trustee in bankruptcy. The bank does not have priority over someone who buys the note from Best Builder in good faith, for value, and without actual notice of Second Bank's perfected security interest.

**10** Note that in example 9, Second Bank's priority is limited to $50,000, the value it has lent to Best Builder. A judgment creditor or trustee in bankruptcy could get the remaining $25,000 represented by the promissory note.

**11** First Bank perfects its security interest in inventory belonging to Hernandez's Department Store. Later, Imperial Chair Mfg. perfects a purchase-money security interest in chairs it sells to Hernandez's, and Imperial notifies First Bank of its perfected interest. When Hernandez's goes bankrupt, First Bank seizes the inventory, including the chairs. Imperial sues to recover the chairs. As long as Imperial perfected its purchase-money security interest and gave First Bank notice before Hernandez's received the chairs, Imperial has priority. This result is an exception to the rule that the first to perfect has priority.

**12** In example 11, if the purchase-money collateral were equipment, a different rule would apply. Imperial has priority over First Bank as long as it perfects its interest within ten days after Hernandez receives the equipment. No notice to First Bank is required.

**13** Venture Capital, Inc., sets up a field warehouse on certain inventory of its debtor, Associated Manufacturers. When Associated goes into bankruptcy, the trustee seizes this inventory and Venture sues to recover it. As long as Venture has sole dominion and control over the field-warehouse inventory, it has priority over the trustee, judgment creditors, or a buyer of the inventory.

Article 9 covers other types of priority, but the listed examples cover most priority situations.

**RIGHTS UPON DEFAULT**

If the debtor fails to repay a loan or pay for goods or services sold on credit, the debtor is in *default* under the contract. At this point, the secured creditor may repossess the collateral, if it is in the debtor's possession, and sell it. The creditor may also propose to the debtor that the creditor keep the collateral property in satisfaction of the debt owed. However, when the collateral is consumer goods, and 60 percent of the cash price or loan has been repaid, the secured creditor must sell the goods within ninety days.

If the collateral is accounts receivable, instruments, or documents, the creditor may collect whatever comes due on the collateral. For instance, a bank with a security interest in a merchant's accounts receivable could, upon default, notify the merchant's debtors to pay their accounts directly to the bank.

In selling collateral in its possession, a secured creditor may sell the collateral in any "commercially reasonable manner." If possible, the secured creditor must notify the debtor of the time and place of a public sale or the time after which a private sale will be made.

The secured creditor applies the proceeds gotten from sale of the collateral in the following order: (1) expenses of the creditor in repossessing and selling the property; (2) satisfaction of the debt owing the creditor; (3) satisfaction of debt owing to holders of subordinate security interests (such as one whose security interest was perfected after that of the selling secured creditor); and (4) return of what remains, if anything, to the debtor. Note that the debtor continues to be liable to the creditor if proceeds from sale of the collateral do not satisfy the debt owed.

Failure to sell the collateral in a commercially reasonable manner, or violation of some other Article 9 procedure concerning handling of the collateral, can cause the creditor problems. It can make it impossible for the creditor to recover the rest of the debt should sale proceeds not cover all indebtedness. Or the creditor may be liable to the debtor for failing to return a reasonable surplus in such situations. In cases involving a consumer, there is a statutory penalty which the consumer can seek against a creditor who fails to comply with Article 9 requirements regarding default.

## 7. Secured Transactions in Real Property

More families in the United States own homes than in any other major country of the world. Few families would be able to own homes, however, were lenders unwilling to lend major sums for home purchase. Lenders, in turn, are willing to make such loans only because they can secure them. The usual method of securing home-purchase loans is the **real estate mortgage.**

**LIEN AND TITLE THEORY**

Most commonly, the real estate mortgage places a **lien** against the home or business property purchased with the loan given. If the debtor, called the *mortgagor,* fails to repay the loan, the creditor, or *mortgagee,* can foreclose the mortgage and sell the property. In a few states, the mortgagor grants **title** (ownership) to the mortgagee subject to the condition of repayment of the loan. When the mortgagor pays off the loan, title returns to the mortgagor.

#### PROMISSORY NOTE AND MORTGAGE DEED

The mortgage arrangement usually consists of a *promissory note* and a *mortgage deed.* The note promises repayment of the loan at a fixed or variable interest rate. The mortgagee must file the mortgage deed, which is the legal document establishing the security interest, in the appropriate records office. Failure to file and record means that the security interest is not perfected against third parties who buy the property from the mortgagor. The mortgagee also lacks protection against later mortgagees who record their mortgage deeds first.

Recall from Chapter 9 that a mortgage must be in writing to be enforceable. The statute of frauds requires it because a mortgage is considered a sale of an interest in land.

#### RIGHTS AND DUTIES OF MORTGAGOR AND MORTGAGEE

The mortgage agreement specifies many of the rights and duties of the mortgagor and mortgagee. The law imposes others. Table 21-3 sets out a list of common rights and duties of mortgagor and mortgagee.

For the mortgagee, the most important right is the right of **foreclosure.** If the mortgagor defaults in repaying the loan, the mortgagee can cut off the debtor's rights to the property (foreclose) and sell the property to satisfy the debt. The usual procedure is for the mortgagee to sue in an equity court to get foreclosure. The court will then order the property sold.

If there is more-than one mortgage on the property, the first mortgage must be completely satisfied by proceeds from the foreclosure sale before any money goes to satisfy subsequent mortgages. Then, any surplus amount goes to the mortgagor. The buyer at a foreclosure sale takes the property free and clear of the subsequent mortgages.

**TABLE 21-3**   Rights and Duties of Mortgagor and Mortgagee

| Mortgagor | Mortgagee |
|---|---|
| 1  Retains possession of the property | 1  Has a lien against the property in most states |
| 2  May lease the property and keep all rents | 2  Has priority over all claims except tax liens if mortgagee records properly |
| 3  Can sell the property | 3  Can sell mortgage rights to a third party |
| 4  Must pay taxes on and insure the property | 4  Can foreclose the mortgage if the mortgagor defaults |
| 5  Cannot "waste" the property, that is, reduce its value through exploitation or failure to maintain | 5  Must terminate lien or return title when mortgagor repays loan |
| 6  Can redeem the property | |

Foreclosure usually results when the mortgagor does not meet the scheduled monthly payments under the mortgage note. It can happen, however, when the mortgagor fails to pay taxes. Many mortgage agreements have *due-on-sale* clauses. If the mortgagor sells the property, the entire remaining balance of the loan is due. Mortgagees place due-on-sale clauses in mortgage agreements so they can force renegotiation of interest rates when the property is sold. However, exercise of the due-on-sale clause can lead to foreclosure if renegotiation is unsuccessful.

A significant right of the mortgagor is the common law **right of redemption** (also called "equity of redemption"). When the mortgagor has defaulted on the mortgage agreement, and before an equity court orders the property sold, the mortgagor can redeem it or get it back free of the lien. The mortgagor must pay the entire debt owed, plus interest and costs. Even after a foreclosure sale, most states grant the mortgagor a statutory right to redeem the property for a period of time, often one year.

**SALE OF MORTGAGED PROPERTY**

In the United States, homes are resold every five years on the average. Most of these homes have mortgages on them. The law permits mortgagors to sell their mortgaged property, subject to provisions such as the due-on-sale clause.

Most buyers of mortgaged property assume the mortgage. An *assumption of mortgage* occurs when the new buyer agrees to accept liability for making the mortgage payments and complying with other mortgage provisions. If proceeds from a foreclosure sale are not enough to pay the mortgage debt, the buyer who assumes the mortgage is personally liable for the deficiency.

Since the original mortgagor remains as a surety on the mortgage debt, the mortgagee can recover the deficiency from him or her if the buyer does not pay it. However, several states prohibit mortgage lenders from recovering deficiencies on purchase-money residential mortgages.

If a buyer of mortgaged property does not assume the mortgage, the property is still *subject* to the mortgage. Should the mortgagor not meet the payments, the mortgagee can foreclose against the property in the hands of the buyer.

# DEBTOR PROTECTION

## 8.   Introduction

Mounting credit debts and swings of the economy between boom and recession cause many debtors to be unable to repay their debts on time. Several laws protect debtors when this happens. These laws recognize that creditors should not be allowed to take advantage of debtors. They attempt to balance fairness to individual debtors against the benefits produced by an efficient market system. Appreciate, then, that laws protecting individual debtors can raise the cost of goods and services to everyone, since creditors who face bad debts or increased costs of debt collection will spread these costs to their other customers.

The next four sections discuss laws which: (1) limit the interest a creditor may charge to a debtor, (2) regulate the methods of legitimate debt collection, (3) discharge debtors from their debts, and (4) allow debtors to assert certain defenses against third parties. Note that some of these laws protect only consumer debtors; others protect business debtors as well.

## 9.   Usury

The law has traditionally attempted to protect debtors by limiting the amount of interest that may be charged upon borrowed money or for the extension of the maturity of a debt. Contracts by which the lender is to receive more than the maximum legal rate of interest are *usurious*. **Usury** laws usually provide for criminal penalties and, in addition, may deny a lender the right to collect any usurious interest. However, a few states permit recovery of interest at the legal rate.

The usury laws of most states are better known for permitting exceptions to the general principles than for applying them. Debtors who need the protection of usury laws usually find that their creditors are legally entitled to charge far in excess of the stated legal maximum rate because of some statutory exception. For example, it is not usurious in most states to collect the legal maximum interest in advance or to add a service fee that is no larger than reasonably necessary to cover the costs of making the loan—such as inspection, legal, and recording fees. Both of these practices have the effect of increasing the actual rate of interest paid.

A seller of goods may also add a finance or carrying charge on long-term credit transactions in addition to the maximum interest rate. A different means of avoiding usury is to have a "credit" price that differs from the "cash" price. Another is to charge extra interest for delinquent payments. Some states permit special lenders such as pawnshops, small loan companies, or credit unions to charge in excess of the otherwise legal limit. In addition, as the next case shows, usury statutes often apply only to consumer, rather than to business, loans.

# RADFORD v. COMMUNITY AND INVESTMENT CORP.

312 S.E.2d 292 (Va. 1984)

Ronald Radford operated a sole proprietorship known as "Radford Wallcovering." His wife Ginger Radford had no interest in the business. When the couple were unable to pay tax owed on their joint individual income tax returns, they took out a loan with defendant finance company. Mr. Radford supplied defendant with the written statement that "Money obtained from Community Mortgage will be used for business purposes." In fact, some of the money was used to satisfy taxes, with the remainder being spent for personal needs. When it turned out that more tax was owed than thought, the Radfords took out a second loan. They signed the following statement: "This loan is to satisfy Federal Bus. taxes." The Radfords were unable to repay the loaned amount, and the defendant sought to foreclose a lien against the Radfords' home that secured the second loan. To stop a foreclosure sale, the Radfords filed suit claiming the loans were usurious. The defendant argued that the loan was a business loan and thus was not usurious under Virginia statute. The trial court dismissed the suit. Radfords appealed.

RUSSELL, J.:...The parties stipulate that the note in issue, bearing interest at an annual percentage rate of 19.67, is usurious unless the loan is exempt from the usury laws by Code §6.1-330.44. In 1979, that section exempted from the usury laws loans which were made "for the acquisition or conduct of a business or investment as sole proprietor, owner, joint venturers or owners provided that the initial amount of the loan is five thousand dollars or more." In 1979,

the statute contained additional provisions which stated:

**For the purposes of this section, if a borrower shall represent in his own handwriting the purposes of the loan, such representation shall be conclusive and binding upon him.**

**For the purposes of this section, unless a loan is for family, household, or personal purposes (which shall not include a passive or active investment), it shall be deemed to be for business or investment purposes within the meaning of this section.**

The usury laws serve a beneficial public purpose and are to be liberally construed with a view to advance the remedy and suppress the mischief. "[T]he usury statutes represent a clarification of the public policy of the state that usury is not to be tolerated, and the court should therefore be chary in permitting this policy to be thwarted."

Usury, when pleaded, must be shown by clear and cogent proof, but the introduction in evidence of a contract expressly providing for a greater rate of interest than the law allows will establish a prima facie case. Thereupon, the burden shifts to the opposing party to go forward with evidence which would bring the transaction within an exception to the usury laws, or to show some other valid reason to avoid their application.

In determining whether a transaction is usurious, the court has both the right and the duty to probe behind the written instruments and to examine all facts and circumstances which shed light on the true nature of the transaction. In the case before us, the evidence shows that the second loan subsumed the first, that all borrowed funds were to be used to pay the borrower's personal income tax liabilities and normal personal household expenses, and that these facts were clearly understood by both borrowers and lenders before the second loan was made.

In defense of Radfords' prima facie showing of usury, the lender points to Mrs. Radford's handwritten note: "This loan is to satisfy Federal Bus. taxes." But the writing is an insufficient shield. As the trial court correctly held, it is not "conclusive and binding" on Mr. Radford because it is not in his handwriting. Although it constitutes an admission by him and is conclusive as to Mrs. Radford, it is an admission only as to the facts it recites. These are not sufficient to bring the loan within Code § 6.1-330.44.

The lender argues that the payment of "federal business taxes" is tantamount to the "acquisition or conduct of a business or investment," the area in which Code § 6.1-330.44 provides an exemption from the usury laws. We do not agree. Since the usury laws must be liberally construed, it follows that exemptions therefrom must be strictly construed, in order to "advance the remedy and suppress the mischief." It was plain to the lender that the loan proceeds were not to be used as working capital of the business, nor to establish a reserve out of which future taxes would be paid when due. Out of the proceeds of the first loan, $10,500.00 was turned over to the borrowers for unspecified use, and was actually used to pay family and household expenses, at a time when the lender believed that the borrowers' tax liability amounted to only $3,420.00. Before the second loan was made, the lender was fully aware of the disposition made of the proceeds of the first loan. When the second loan was made to retire it, the first loan was a personal family debt, entirely unrelated to the conduct of business. The proceeds of the second loan were expressly devoted to the repayment of the first loan and to the satisfaction of recorded liens for past due personal income taxes assessed against Mr. and Mrs. Radford as individuals.

Expert testimony at trial established that the taxes were personal obligations of the Radfords: "That's an individual income tax return. The tax liability would adhere to the individuals regardless of what happened to the business." All of their property, real and personal, was subject to the tax liens, whether used in business operations or not. The I.R.S. was under no obligation to exhaust business assets before levying on personal assets to satisfy the liens. The "federal business taxes" referred to in Mrs. Radford's handwritten note were in fact, and were known by the lender to be, family and personal obligations of the Radfords. Accordingly, neither Mrs. Radford's handwritten statement nor the evidence of surrounding circumstances establishes that the loan was for any purpose other than "family, household, or personal purposes." The lender thus failed to overcome the Radfords' prima facie showing of usury.

For the foregoing reasons, the decree appealed from will be reversed, the temporary injunction continued in effect, and the cause remanded to the circuit court for further proceedings not inconsistent with this opinion. [*Reversed and remanded.*]

When usury is suspected, courts examine very carefully the details and true intent of a transaction. For example, a court may decide that a transaction is a usurious "sale," even though the contract calls it a "lease."

Supporters of an unrestricted marketplace advocate legislation to abolish interest rate limits on consumer credit. They have proposed several plans to Congress.

## 10. Debt Collection

In a consumer-credit-oriented economy, the collection of bad debts is very important. At present, there are more than 5,000 collection agencies in the United States engaged in collecting unpaid accounts, judgments, and other bad debts. Annually, creditors turn over bills totaling more than $5 billion for collection to such agencies.

### FAIR DEBT COLLECTION PRACTICES ACT

Due to complaints that some debt-collection agencies used techniques of harassment, deception, and personal abuse to collect debts, Congress in 1978 passed the Fair Debt Collection Practices Act (FDCPA). The act covers only *consumer* debt collections. It applies to agencies and individuals whose primary business is the collection of consumer debts for others. It also applies to the Internal Revenue Service and attorneys who collect consumer debts on behalf of their clients. Creditor collection efforts are exempt from the act.

One of the first actions of a debt collector will usually be to locate the debtor. This action, known as "skip-tracing," may require that the collector contact third parties who know of the debtor's whereabouts. The FDCPA permits the collector to contact third parties, such as neighbors or employers, but it limits the way in which this contact may be carried out. The collector may not state that the consumer owes a debt nor contact any given third party more than once, except in very limited circumstances. When the collector knows that an attorney represents the debtor, the collector may not contact any third parties, except the attorney, unless the attorney fails to respond to the collector's communication.

Having located the debtor, the collector will next seek to get payment on the overdue account. However, the FDCPA restricts methods that can be used in the collection process. Table 21-4 outlines these restrictions.

### FDCPA REMEDIES AND ENFORCEMENT

If the consumer debtor desires to stop the debt collector from repeatedly contacting him or her about payment, the debtor need only notify the collector in writing of this wish. Any further contact by the collector following such notification violates the act. The collector's sole remedy now is to sue

**TABLE 21-4** FDCPA'S Restrictions on Collection Methods of Collection Agencies

The collector cannot:
1 Physically threaten the debtor
2 Use obscene language
3 Represent himself or herself as an attorney unless it is true
4 Threaten debtor with arrest or garnishment unless the collector can legally take such action and intends to do so
5 Fail to disclose his or her identity as a collector
6 Telephone before 8:00 A.M. or after 9:00 P.M. in most instances
7 Telephone repeatedly with intent to annoy
8 Place collect calls to the debtor
9 Use any "unfair or unconscionable means" to collect the debt

the debtor. Violations of the FDCPA entitle the debtor to sue the debt collector for actual damages, including damages for invasion of privacy and infliction of mental distress, plus court costs and attorney's fees. In the absence of actual damages, the court may still order the collector to pay the debtor up to $1,000 for violations. Class action suits, as well as individual ones, are permitted under the act.

### STATE LAWS REGULATING DEBT COLLECTION

Congress specified that the FDCPA does not preempt state laws regulating debt collections so long as they are more strict than FDCPA standards. As the following case illustrates, these laws may apply to debt collections by *creditors* as well as by collection agencies.

# JACKSONVILLE STATE BANK v. BARNWELL
481 So.2d 863 (Ala. 1985)

Plaintiff Barnwell borrowed money from the defendant bank to purchase a mobile home. He put up the mobile home as collateral. Later, it burned in a fire. The home was not covered by insurance. When Barnwell failed to make further payments on his debt, the bank began a series of telephone calls to him. The bank placed between twenty-eight and thirty-five calls to Barnwell at home and work. His supervisor reprimanded him about the calls, and he requested that the bank not call him at work. The calls continued. Then the bank sent an agent to Barnwell's place of employment. The agent caused a commotion and called Barnwell vulgar names in front of his fellow employees. Barnwell became anxious and had to be hospitalized. He sued the bank for, among other things, invasion of privacy. When the jury returned a verdict against the bank, the bank appealed.

HOUSTON, J.:...Alabama recognizes that a person has an actionable right to be free from the invasion of privacy. The debtor-creditor aspect of this right has been characterized as:

**the wrongful intrusion into one's private activities in such a manner as to outrage or cause mental suffering, shame or humiliation to a person of ordinary sensibilities....**

The court has previously recognized the right of a creditor to take reasonable action to pursue a debtor and collect a debt. Where the creditor takes actions which exceed the bounds of reasonableness, however, the debtor has an action against the creditor for injuries suffered.

We find the tendencies of the evidence in this case, when viewed in a light most favorable to the plaintiff, support a finding that the bank far exceeded the bounds of reasonableness in its efforts to collect the Barnwell debt. Twenty-eight to thirty-five phone calls to one's home and place of employment fall within the realm of a "systematic campaign of harassment"...Furthermore, Trevino's remarks at Barnwell's

place of employment, as the bank's agent, unequivocally constitute coarse, inflammatory, malicious, and threatening language.

The bank contends that no evidence was presented suggesting Trevino was an agent of the bank. To the contrary, Trevino was given a letter of authorization by the bank which stated the bearer was authorized by the bank to repossess Barnwell's automobiles and would be protected by the bank from any and all claims arising from the repossession. Likewise, Barnwell testified that Trevino introduced himself by commenting, "I work for Jacksonville State Bank." Further, the record shows Trevino added, "I'm authorized to use whatever force is necessary to get the car." None of this testimony was objected to at trial. Under these facts, an issue of fact was created concerning whether Trevino was an agent of the bank and whether he was acting within the scope of that agency in his encounters with Barnwell.

In any event, the record raises issues of fact regarding whether the actions of the bank, independent of Trevino's, constituted a campaign of harassment and were beyond the bounds of reasonableness, giving rise to liability for invasion of privacy....

Based on the foregoing, the judgments entered by the trial court are due to be, and they are hereby, affirmed. [*Affirmed.*]

## 11.   Bankruptcy

In 1978, Congress revised the federal bankruptcy laws. This marks the first time in over fifty years that these laws have been substantially revised. Since the 1978 Bankruptcy Act became effective, the number of bankruptcies has skyrocketed. Personal bankruptcies climbed from 228,000 in 1979 to over twice that number in 1984. Although a recession prompted part of that increase, the Federal Reserve Board of Atlanta estimated that, nationwide, as much as 75 percent of the increase was due to the liberal provisions of the new law. Annually, the courts discharge more than $6 billion of nonmortgage consumer debt.

Although the force of the consumer movement helped prompt the new changes in the bankruptcy laws, the laws apply to both consumers and businesses. Under the present laws, corporations and partnerships cannot be discharged of their debts, but all individuals, whether consumers or entrepreneurs, can be.

A principal change in the new laws has been the institution of a bankruptcy court. Previously, most bankruptcy proceedings were handled by legal officials appointed under the authority of the federal district court. Because the new federal bankruptcy judges do not have lifetime appointments, there is serious question as of this writing about the constitutionality of their creation

## BANKRUPTCY PROCEEDINGS

Bankruptcy proceedings begin upon the filing of either a voluntary or involuntary petition to the court. A *voluntary petition* is one filed by the debtor; an *involuntary petition* is filed by one or more creditors of the debtor. The creditors who sign the involuntary petition must be owed at least $5,000. If the court finds in an involuntary proceeding that the debtor is *unable to pay his or her debts as they mature,* the court will order "relief" against the debtor. Relief may also be ordered if someone has been appointed to control the debtor's property (for example, a receiver) within the previous 120 days for the purpose of satisfying a judgment of other lien.

Two alternatives are possible in a bankruptcy proceeding against an individual. The individual's property either will be **liquidated** and the debts discharged, or the debts will be *adjusted.* An individual who has secured debts (mortgages, security interests against personal property, and so on) of less than $350,000 and unsecured debts of under $100,000 can have his or her debts adjusted by the court. The amount and repayment schedule of the debts will be arranged by the court to permit the debtor to repay the creditors. Creditors cannot require the court to adjust the debts. The decision must be that of the debtor. Most debtors choose to have their debts discharged and their property liquidated, rather than to seek an adjustment, since they remain obligated to pay a portion of adjusted debts.

Even when a debtor's property is liquidated, federal law exempts a substantial portion of the property from the liquidation process. Individual states, however, may reduce the amounts of the federal exemptions through legislation.

Corporations and partnerships can also have all their assets liquidated and distributed to creditors. However, especially for large businesses, an alternative to liquidation is **reorganization.** A main part of the reorganization is a plan that is proposed by the business and considered by a committee of creditors prior to court approval. The plan rearranges the business's liabilities and equities (ownership assets). Parts of the business may be sold, and always the existing ownership interests in the business are reduced. In effect, the creditors often become owners in the business. The number of bankruptcy reorganizations nearly tripled between 1980 and 1987.

### TRUSTEE IN BANKRUPTCY

The **trustee** in bankruptcy is an important person in the bankruptcy proceeding. The trustee is someone elected by the creditors to represent the debtor's estate in taking possession of and liquidating (selling off) the debtor's property. Broad powers are granted to the trustee. The trustee can: (1) affirm or disaffirm contracts with the debtor which are yet to be performed; (2) set aside fraudulent conveyances, that is, transfers of the debtor's property for inadequate consideration or for the purpose of defrauding creditors; (3) void certain transfers of property by the debtor to creditors which prefer some creditors over others; (4) sue those who owe the debtor some obligation; and (5) set aside statutory liens against the debtor's property which take effect upon the beginning of bankruptcy proceedings. With the court's authorization, the trustee also can run the debtor's business during the liquidation process.

### CREDITOR PRIORITY

Under bankruptcy laws, certain creditors receive priority over others in the distribution of a debtor's assets. The law divides creditors into priority classes, as set forth in Table 21-5. The amounts owing to each creditor class must be satisfied fully before the next lower class of priority can receive anything. Note that secured creditors who hold mortgages or Article 9 security interests in the debtor's property usually have priority over the bankruptcy creditor classes.

### TABLE 21-5   Priority of Bankruptcy Creditors

1  Creditors with claims that arise from the costs of preserving and administering the debtor's estate (such as the fee of an accountant who performs as audit of the debtor's books for the trustee)
2  Creditors with claims that occur in the ordinary course of the debtor's business after a bankruptcy petition has been filed
3  Employees who are owed wages earned within ninety days, or employee benefits earned within 180 days of the bankruptcy petition (limited to $2,000 per employee)
4  Consumers who have paid deposits or prepayments for undelivered goods or services (limited to $900 per consumer)
5  Government (for tax claims)
6  Creditors who have other claims (general creditors)

## DISCHARGE

From the debtor's point of view, the purpose of bankruptcy is to secure a *discharge* of further obligation to the creditor. Certain debts, however, cannot be discharged in bankruptcy. They include those arising from taxes, alimony and child support, intentional torts (including fraud), breach of fiduciary duty, liabilities arising from drunken driving, government fines, and debts not submitted to the trustee because the creditor has lacked knowledge of the proceedings. Education loans which become due within five years of the filing of the bankruptcy petition are also nondischargeable.

In addition to having certain debts denied discharge, the debtor may fail to receive a discharge from *any* of his or her debts if the courts find that the debtor has concealed property, falsified or concealed books of record, refused to obey court orders, failed to explain satisfactorily any losses of assets, or been discharged in bankruptcy within the prior six years. As mentioned previously, corporations and partnerships as legal entities cannot receive a discharge of their debts. Of course, the individuals behind these businesses can always form a new corporation or partnership.

## TRENDS IN BANKRUPTCY

A major bankruptcy trend in recent years has been the increasing frequency with which large businesses have gone through bankruptcy reorganization. Some see this trend as a management strategy of even financially healthy businesses for avoiding potential liabilities or forcing renegotiation of burdensome contracts. For instance, the Manville Corporation entered bankruptcy reorganization to attempt to force a favorable settlement of the thousands of asbestos-related lawsuits which it faces. Another reason for this trend is that the 1978 revision of the bankruptcy laws has made it easier for existing management to take a business through reorganization while staying in control of the business. Texaco, Inc., chose reorganization following the multibillion-dollar judgment obtained against it by Pennzoil.

Other companies have sought reorganization to relieve themselves of obligations imposed by collective-bargaining contracts with unions. After the Supreme Court ruled in 1984 that bankruptcy did affect performance of collective-bargaining contracts, Congress changed the law. Now, bankruptcy reorganization can reject a collective-bargaining contract only if the union has refused to accept necessary contractual modifications "without good cause," and, on balance, the court decides that the situation "clearly favors" rejection.

Another important bankruptcy development affects a consumer's ability to get a discharge of debts through liquidation. Congress amended the law in 1984 to give courts power to refuse to allow consumers to seek the relief of discharge when relief would amount to a "substantial abuse" of the bankruptcy process.

This change in the law recognizes a problem of the bankruptcy process. Historically, consumers with few assets, but well-paying jobs, could get discharged of their debts by surrendering their few assets to liquidation. Creditors argued that debt discharge was unfair in this situation since credit is usually extended to consumers based on their ability to repay out of future earned income.

With the change in the law, courts can deny consumers a discharge of debts through liquidation. When liquidation and discharge relief would be a "substantial abuse," a consumer's only bankruptcy relief will be an adjustment of debts. In this type of relief, the court can consider a consumer's future earning power in deciding what percentage of the consumer's debts must be repaid. It is likely that courts will find that a substantial abuse exists when consumers can reasonably pay for debts out of future income.

## 12. Additional Protection for Consumer-Debtors

A lawsuit is not always an adequate remedy for an injured party to a contract. For instance, it is usually not practical for consumers to sue a seller of goods or services over breaches of contract involving only a few hundred dollars. Attorney's fees are high, and small claims' court awards are difficult to enforce. From consumers' viewpoints, it would be better if they could simply refuse to pay for unsatisfactory products or services. However, many times consumers have already paid for what they obtained or promised to pay.

If consumers have already paid for products or services, they have little recourse except to initiate legal proceedings when others refuse to perform their contractual obligations properly. But what occurs in a situation in which consumers have signed credit agreements and have merely *promised* to pay? It appears that consumers can simply refuse to pay until the obligations owed them have been performed satisfactorily. In the past, however, this was not usually the case.

### THE HOLDER-IN-DUE-COURSE DOCTRINE AND ITS ABOLISHMENT

Until fairly recently, most credit contracts contained clauses which stated that consumers agreed not to assert any contractual defenses against third parties. These clauses meant that if a merchant sold a consumer's credit contract to a collection agency, the agency could legally collect the contract price from the consumer in spite of the fact that the merchant had breached the contract, or had even defrauded the consumer. In addition to a credit agreement, many times the consumer had also signed a promissory note. (A promissory note is an easily transferrable, special type of commercial instrument or paper.) Because of the **holder-in-due-course** doctrine, third parties who bought notes and other forms of commercial paper could usually enforce them free of all personal defenses the consumer might have against the merchant, such as that purchased goods were defective or were never delivered.

In the mid-1970s, the FTC acted to protect consumers who made purchases on credit. It adopted a rule which abolishes the holder-in-due-course concept and which declares illegal contract provisions cutting off defenses against third parties. The rule applies only to *consumer* transactions. The rule also specifies that the consumer-debtor's right to assert claims and defenses against collection agencies, banks, and other third parties must actually be set forth in any installment credit contract used to finance retail purchases.

### REJECTION OF DISPUTED CREDIT-CARD CHARGES

A related law now protects consumers in instances in which credit-card charges have been made and contractual disputes arise. Under the federal Fair Credit Billing Act, a consumer can withhold from any credit-card payments the amount of a disputed charge made to a seller of goods or services. This right applies to any charge of more than $50 when the charge is made in the consumer's home state or within 100 miles of his or her home. The procedure requires that the consumer first attempt to resolve the contractual dispute with the seller. When this fails, the consumer can send the bank which issues the credit card a written notice of the problem which states that negotiations have been unfruitful. The consumer can then withhold the amount of the disputed charge from credit-card payments to the bank.

As a practical matter, banks recredit a consumer's account for the amount of a disputed charge (if it has been already deducted) and charge back against the seller's bank. The seller's bank then charges back against the seller. The seller might sue the consumer, but once again, litigation costs make such a course of action unlikely in cases which involve relatively small amounts of money.

# REVIEW QUESTIONS

**1**  For each term in the left-hand column, match the most appropriate description in the right-hand column:

(1) Lien

(2) Attachment

(3) Bulk transfer

(4) Foreclosure

(a) The sale of all or most of the inventory of a merchant out of the ordinary course of business.

(b) A legal claim against property to secure a debt or obligation.

(c) The lending of money at an illegal interest rate.

(d) A security interest in property arising from the credit extended to buy the property.

(5) Liquidation

(6) Real estate mortgage

(7) Perfection

(8) Purchase-money security interest

(9) Surety

(10) Usury

(e) Occurs when a security agreement exists, the creditor has given value to the debtor, and the debtor has rights in the collateral.

(f) The cutting off of a debtor's rights in property.

(g) A security interest in land.

(h) One who gives a collateral promise to answer for another's debt.

(i) In bankruptcy, the selling off of a debtor's property to get cash to pay the creditors.

(j) This is usually necessary before the secured creditor has priority over other creditors.

**2** Arrow Sales recently had built a new warehouse. A roofing subcontractor contacts the warehouse manager and demands $15,000 in payment for his work and materials. The manager responds that Arrow Sales had no contract with the roofing subcontractor and that all subcontractors must look to the general contractor for payment. When told that the general contractor has filed for bankruptcy, the manager replies that Arrow Sales paid the general contractor in full for the work and that all subcontractors will have to get paid from the general contractor's estate. Is the manager correct? Explain.

**3** To set yourself up in business, you are considering buying the inventory of a local hardware store which is going out of business. What must you be sure to do before paying for the inventory or taking delivery of it?

**4** First Bank promotes its bonded teller to vice president. If First Bank forgets to notify the bonding company of the promotion and the new vice president embezzles money, is the bank still protected by the bond? Explain.

**5** If Smith guarantees a $20,000 debt and Smyth guarantees $10,000 of the same debt, what is Smith's right of contribution against Smyth if Smith has to pay the entire $20,000?

**6** Under what circumstances is it possible to perfect a security interest by attachment alone?

**7** Clela buys a car from Adam's Auto Company. Adam's inventory was subject to a security interest held by Second Bank. If Adam's does not repay its loan to Second Bank, can Second Bank recover the car from Clela? Explain.

**8** If Eli takes mortgaged property "subject to the mortgage," will he be liable if a foreclosure sale of the property later fails to pay off the debt which the mortgage secured?

**9** Why is it true that the usury laws of most states are better known for permitting exceptions to general usury principles than for applying them?

**10** Discuss the FDCPA's restrictions on collection methods of collection agencies.

**11**   The Zenith Credit Bureau telephones Dan and his family almost daily about payment of a $3,500 debt which Dan owes to Equipment Suppliers, Inc. The phone calls are causing stress for Dan's family. Dan cannot afford to pay the debt at present, and he needs a listed telephone number for his business. Is there anything Dan can do legally to stop the calls from Zenith?

**12**   Willson Manufacturing, Inc., has gone into bankruptcy liquidation. Bankruptcy creditors include employees, suppliers, the electric utility, and the government (for back income tax). In what order will these various creditors be paid out of the debtor's estate?

**13**   Targett Company manufactures pharmaceuticals. Recently, one of its drugs has been found to cause birth defects. Hundreds of lawsuits have been filed against Targett. Amounts claimed in damages against Targett exceed insurance limits. The lenders who finance Targett are becoming nervous. Its stock prices have fallen on the stock exchange. Targett is considering bankruptcy relief. What relief is available other than liquidation? Why might it be attractive to Targett's management? Explain.

**14**   Sims borrows money from a local finance company to help send her daughter to college. The loan contract Sims signs contains a clause that waives any defenses she may have against the finance company if the contract is assigned to a third party. Discuss the legality of this clause.

**15**   Susan joins a newly opened exercise spa. She pays the annual $200 membership fee with her bank credit card. One week later, the spa locks its doors and goes out of business. Repeated phone calls and letters to the spa's management, which demand a refund of her money go unanswered. What is now Susan's best course of legal action for getting back her $200?

# *Part Seven*
# PROTECTING SOCIETY

# Chapter
# 22

# Protecting Competition

## CHAPTER PREVIEW

This chapter and the next two chapters discuss antitrust laws. These are laws intended to make our competitive economic system work. The goal is workable competition and all of the benefits that are intended to flow from it.

This chapter introduces the basic statutes designed to protect competition: the Sherman Antitrust Act of 1890 and the Clayton Act of 1914. It also discusses activities that are exempt from the antitrust laws, such as those required by state governments.

There are three major sanctions available to enforce the antitrust laws. First, it is a crime to violate many of the provisions. Second, courts of equity may use the injunction remedy either to prevent violations or to correct the impact of past violations. Last and most important, persons who suffer injury as a result of noncompliance may sue wrongdoers for **triple damages.** As you study this chapter, keep in mind the great importance of this triple damage remedy and the fact that antitrust cases frequently involve millions of dollars. These remedies are enforced by the Department of Justice, the Federal Trade Commission, and private individuals.

One of the important distinctions in this chapter is the distinction between violations that are **per se illegal** and those that are subject to the **rule of reason.** The concept of per se illegality means that proof of an activity is proof of a violation without any evidence of its economic impact. The following terms are introduced in this chapter: *Illinois Brick* Doctrine, monopoly, *Noerr-Pennington* Doctrine, nolo contendere, *Parker v. Brown* Doctrine, per se illegality, restraint of trade, rule of reason, Sherman Act, state action exemption, and triple damages.

## 1.   The Meaning of Antitrust

A **trust** is a fiduciary relationship concerning property in which one person, known as the **trustee,** holds legal title to property for the benefit of another, known as the **beneficiary.** The trustee has the duty to manage and preserve the property for the use and enjoyment of the beneficiary. Trusts are generally legal, and the so-called *antitrust laws* are not aimed at trusts which serve legitimate and socially desirable purposes, such as promoting education or caring for spendthrift or incompetent children.

In the last part of the nineteenth century, the trust device was used extensively to gain monopolistic control of different types of business. Through it, a group of corporations having the same type of business could unite in following common business policies and eliminate competition among themselves by controlling production, dividing the market, and establishing price levels. The trust device allowed all or at least a majority of the stock of several companies to be transferred to a trustee. Stockholders were issued trust certificates which named them as beneficiaries of the trust and entitled them to dividends declared on the stock they had transferred. The trustee then was in a position to control the operation and policy making of all the companies, since it held the stock and could vote for directors of its own choosing in each. Technically, the companies were still separate businesses, but in substance they were united under one guiding hand.

The first statutes attempting to control monopolistic combinations were enacted about the time this trust device was in vogue; hence, these laws came to be known as antitrust laws, although they were aimed at protecting the public from any type of monopoly or activity in restraint of trade. The term "antitrust laws" is used to describe all laws that attempt to regulate competition. The goal of such laws is to ensure that our competitive economic system works and achieves its goals of lower prices, product innovation, and equitable distribution of real income among consumers and the factors of production. In other words, the antitrust laws are designed to ensure a system of workable competition.

## 2.   Statutes Involved

There are several statutes involved in the field of antitrust law. The basic statute is the **Sherman Antitrust Act** of 1890. Prior to that time, states had enacted the first antitrust laws. These proved to be largely ineffective in preventing monopolistic practices, for a number of reasons. Among these were lack of enforcement facilities and the fact that **monopolies** were really a national problem. The federal government entered the scene in 1887 with the enactment of the Interstate Commerce Act (ICA) to control the railroads, where the obvious danger of monopoly had first appeared. This was followed in 1890 by the Sherman Act, which Congress passed under its constitutional authority to regulate interstate commerce.

The Sherman Act attacks two types of anticompetitive business behavior to further the policy of preserving competition. Section 1 covers contracts, combinations, and conspiracies in restraint of trade or commerce. Contracts in restraint of trade usually result from words, but combinations usually result from conduct. A conspiracy is usually established by words, followed by some act carrying out the plan of the conspiracy.

Section 2 of the act is directed at monopoly and the attempts to monopolize any part of interstate or foreign commerce. The law supplies a means to break up existing monopolies and to prevent others from developing. It is directed at single firms and does not purport to cover shared monopolies or **oligopolies.**

In 1914, Congress decided that the Sherman Act was too general and that it needed to be made more specific. It enacted the *Clayton Act,* which is actually an amendment to the Sherman Act. The Clayton Act contains several important sections, many of which were later amended. In this text, we will review the provisions and the appropriate amendments in the chapters and sections, as indicated:

|  | Clayton Act Section | Subject Matter | Text Coverage |
|---|---|---|---|
| Section 2 | As amended by the Robinson-Patman Act (1936) | Price discrimination | Chapter 24; sections 2–9 |
| Section 3 |  | Tying and exclusive contracts | Chapter 24; sections 10–13 |
| Section 4 |  | Triple damage suits | Chapter 22; section 8 and 9 |
| Section 7 | As amended by the Celler-Kefauver Amendment (1950) | Mergers and acquisitions | Chapter 24; sections 14–20 |
| Section 8 |  | Interlocking directorates | Chapter 24; section 2 |

In 1914, Congress also passed the Federal Trade Commission Act (FTC Act). This act created the Federal Trade Commission (FTC). The FTC was created to have an independent administrative agency charged with keeping competition free and fair. It enforces the Clayton Act provisions on price discrimination, tying and exclusive contracts, mergers and acquisitions, and interlocking directorates. In addition, it enforces Section 5 of the FTCA.

This act originally made "unfair methods of competition" in commerce unlawful. The Wheeler-Lea amendments of 1938 added that "unfair or deceptive acts or practices in commerce" were also unlawful under Section 5. The role of the FTC in antitrust enforcement will be discussed in Chapter 24.

### 3. Exemptions to the Sherman Act

There are numerous business activities that are exempt from the Sherman Act. Some of these exemptions were created by the original statute; others were allowed by the Clayton Act and other amendments, and still others by the courts. Each of these exemptions is based upon some other form of regulation and a policy that overrides the goals of the Sherman Act. Among activities and businesses for which there are statutory exceptions are insurance companies, farmers' cooperatives, shipping, milk marketing, and investment companies. Activities required by state law are exempt. In addition, normal activities of labor unions are exempt. These exemptions are narrowly construed and do not mean that every activity of a firm is necessarily exempted simply because most activities are exempted. For example, it has been held that an agreement between an insurance company and a pharmaceutical organization which regulates the price of prescription drugs given to policyholders of the insurance company was not exempt—it was not the business of insurance that was involved in the transaction. It is the business of insurance that is exempt and not the business of insurance companies. Similarly, the courts have eliminated from exemptions people who belong to organizations but do not actually participate in the industry declared to be exempt. Likewise, a union would forfeit its exemption when it agreed with one set of employers to impose a certain wage scale on other employer-bargaining units. It is only the usual and legitimate union activity that is exempt.

### 4. The State Action Exemption

In a 1943 case known as *Parker v. Brown,* the Supreme Court created a **state action exemption** to the Sherman Act. This state action exemption, usually referred to as the **Parker v. Brown Doctrine,** was based on the reasoning that the Sherman Act does not apply to state government. Since that time, numerous cases have attempted to define the limits of this exemption. Although the courts are still deciding cases and adding to the body of law applicable to the doctrine of *Parker v. Brown,* several principles limiting its application are evident. They may be summarized as follows:

1 When a state acts in its sovereign capacity, it is immune from federal antitrust scrutiny.

**2**   Although municipalities are state subdivisions, they do not enjoy the deference due a state. A municipality will be immune from antitrust liability only if it acts as an instrumentality of the state, through which the state has clearly and affirmatively chosen to implement its policies.

**3**   When a state agency or subdivision claims immunity from federal law, it must first identify a clearly expressed state policy that authorizes its actions. The legislation must contain an affirmative showing of intent to replace competition with regulation, though it need do no more than authorize the challenged conduct.

**4**   So long as the resulting anticompetitive activities are a foreseeable consequence of state delegation, the state policy of replacing competition with regulation has been clearly articulated. The party claiming the state action defense must show that the legislature contemplated the complained-of action.

**5**   A state need not actively supervise a municipality, since a municipality, unlike a private party, has no incentive to act other than in the public interest. When the challenged actor is a private party, both foreseeability and supervision must be demonstrated.

Notwithstanding the aforesaid limitations, there are many state laws which do create immunity from antitrust sanctions, not only for the state, but also for private parties that comply with state laws. When a state acting in its sovereign capacity seeks to limit competition and replace it with regulations supervised and enforced by the state, *Parker v. Brown* will prevent antitrust liability. For example, Kansas City, Missouri, granted an exclusive license to one company to provide ambulance services. This was held to be a valid state action. The city established the ambulance system pursuant to state authority, and it clearly expressed state policy.

In another case, an unsuccessful candidate for admittance to the Arizona Bar alleged a conspiracy by the Bar examiners in violation of the Sherman Act. He contended that the grading scale was dictated by the number of new attorneys desired rather than by the level of competition and answers on the exam. The courts held that this activity was exempt from the Sherman Act. The grading of bar examinations is, in reality, conduct of the Arizona Supreme Court and thus exempt. Action by the courts is just as immune as actions by the legislature.

### 5.   The Noerr-Pennington Doctrine

Another exemption from the Sherman Act is known as the **Noerr-Pennington Doctrine.** This doctrine exempts from the antitrust laws concerted efforts to lobby government officials, regardless of the anticompetitive purposes. The doctrine is applicable even though the activity to be influenced is a commercial enterprise. The doctrine is based on the First Amendment. For example, Budget Rent-A-Car filed suit against Hertz and National Rent-A-Car because the defendants lobbied officials at three state-owned airports to limit the number of car-rental operations. They lobbied for restrictions that would have made it more difficult for Budget to compete. For example, they sought a restriction that would require equal fees for all agencies. They also requested that nationwide reservation systems be required, and that each firm have a specified number of years' experience at a specified number of airports. This lobbying was exempt from the Sherman Act. The Noerr-Pennington Doctrine is based on the free flow of information and the First Amendment right to petition government for a redress of grievances. The doctrine does not have a commercial exception, and it applies to attempts to influence government on behalf of business.

Attempts to influence nongovernmental bodies, such as associations that set standards within an industry, are not protected by this exception. For example, a federal court in 1987 held that, by virtue of the Noerr-Pennington Doctrine, attempts to influence private associations which set product-safety standards that are often incorporated into state and local statutes are not immune from antitrust scrutiny.

# SANCTIONS

## 6. The Criminal Sanction

The Sherman Act as amended by the Clayton Act recognizes four separate legal sanctions. First, it is a federal crime to violate the Sherman Act. Second, violations may be enjoined by the courts. Third, injured parties may collect triple damages. Finally, any property owned in violation of Section 1 of the act that is being transported from one state to another is subject to seizure by and forfeiture to the United States. This last remedy has rarely been used.

In addition to these sanctions, the law allows the government to demand information from suppliers, consumers, and target companies in noncriminal investigations. The data obtained may be used to establish proof of market share or other relevant statistics. The information may then be used to obtain injunctions.

The punishment imposed by the criminal law may be a fine, imprisonment, or both, for any person or corporation that violates its provisions. Although originally such violations were only misdemeanors, today crimes under the Sherman Act are felonies. An individual found guilty may be fined up to $100,000 and imprisoned up to three years. A corporation found guilty may be fined up to $1 million for each offense.

In criminal cases, the defendant has three possible pleas to enter to an indictment charging a violation—"guilty," "not guilty," or "**nolo contendere.**" This last plea of "no contest" allows sentencing just as if the defendant had pleaded or been found guilty. It has the advantage to a defendant of avoiding the cost of trial and the effect of a guilty plea or finding in a subsequent civil suit. Criminal convictions create **prima facie** cases for triple damages, but this effect can be avoided by the nolo contendere plea. Acceptance of nolo contendere pleas (the plea is not a matter of right, but discretionary with the trial court) tends to discourage triple damage suits because of the difficulties private parties face in proving Sherman Act violations. The cost of investigation and preparation of antitrust suits is usually substantial, and, therefore, private litigants benefit greatly from either a guilty plea or a conviction. As a result, the government today often opposes pleas of nolo contendere.

The criminal sanction has historically been the least used of Sherman Act remedies. However, in recent years it has been used more often. In 1987, the Justice Department had 150 grand juries looking into allegations of criminal **price-fixing** and bid-rigging in industries that ranged from defense contracting and gasoline retailing to soft-drink and kosher food preparation. As a general rule, it is used in price-fixing cases when there is proof of specific intent to restrain trade or to monopolize. If a firm has been charged civilly and found guilty, the government is required to bring criminal charges if the evidence suggests continuing violations. Many first-offense cases are handled civilly rather than criminally. However, criminal prosecution is likely to result if practices similar to those engaged in have been held to be a violation in a prior case. Action undertaken with knowledge of a prior decision will supply the requisite criminal intent.

Criminal prosecutions under the Sherman Act do require proof of criminal intent. There is no presumption of wrongful intent. The major use of the criminal sanction is in price-fixing cases. For example, criminal cases have been brought against road builders of interstate highways because of rigged bids and against various real estate firms for fixing the price of real estate commissions. These criminal cases were brought to deter others from similar practices.

## 7. The Injunction

The Sherman Act empowers courts to grant injunctions at the request of the government or a private party that will prevent and restrain violations or continued violations of its provisions. An injunction may prevent anticompetitive behavior or it may even force a breakup of a corporation. For example, it was used to split the former American Telephone & Telegraph Company (Ma Bell) into eight organizations—one national company for long-distance telephone service and seven regional companies for local service. The remedy is also used to prevent acquisitions and stop practices that are deemed to be anticompetitive.

The injunction remedy is frequently used when the success of a criminal prosecution is doubtful. It takes less proof to enjoin an activity (preponderance of the evidence only) than it does to convict of a crime (**beyond a reasonable doubt**). There have been cases involving this remedy even after an acquittal in a criminal case. In effect, the court ordered the defendant not to do something which it had been found innocent of doing.

Under Section 16 of the Clayton Act, private parties "threatened with loss or damage by a violation of the antitrust laws" may seek injunctive relief. This private remedy is in addition to suits for triple damages. To obtain an injunction, a private party must prove a threat of an antitrust injury—an injury of the type the antitrust laws were designed to prevent. These are the same types of injuries that may result in triple damages. As the case which follows illustrates, loss of profits due to increased competition is not such an injury.

---

# CARGILL, INC. v. MONFORT OF COLORADO, INC.
107 S.Ct. 484 (1986)

---

BRENNAN, J.:...Under § 16 of the Clayton Act, private parties "threatened with loss or damage by a violation of the antitrust laws" may seek injunctive relief. This case presents two questions: whether a plaintiff seeking relief under § 16 must prove a threat of antitrust injury, and, if so, whether loss or damage due to increased competition constitutes such injury....

Monfort operates in both the market for fed cattle (the input market) and the market for fabricated beef (the output market). These markets are highly competitive, and the profit margins of the major beef packers are low. The current markets are a product of two decades of intense competition, during which time packers with modern integrated plants have gradually displaced packers with separate slaughter and fabrication plants.

Monfort is the country's fifth-largest beef packer. Petitioner Excel Corporation (Excel), one of the two defendants below, is the second-largest packer. Excel operates five integrated plants and one fabrication plant. It is a wholly owned subsidiary of Cargill, Inc., the other defendant below, a large privately owned corporation with more than 150 subsidiaries in at least 35 countries.

On June 17, 1983, Excel signed an agreement to acquire the third-largest packer in the market, Spencer Beef, a division of the Land O'Lakes agricultural cooperative. Spencer Beef owned two integrated plants and one slaughtering plant. After the acquisition, Excel would still be the second-largest packer, but would command a market share almost equal to that of the largest packer, IBP, Inc. (IBP).

Monfort brought an action under § 16 of the Clayton Act, to enjoin the prospective merger. Its complaint alleged that the acquisition would "violate Section 7 of the Clayton Act because the effect of the proposed acquisition may be substantially to lessen competition or tend to create a monopoly in several different ways...." Monfort described the injury that it allegedly would suffer in this way:

**(f) *Impairment of plaintiff's ability to compete*. The proposed acquisition will result in a concentration of economic power in the relevant markets which threatens Monfort's supply of fed cattle and its ability to compete in the boxed beef market....**

The District Court held that Monfort's allegation of "price-cost 'squeeze'" that would "severely narrow" Monfort's profit margins constituted an allegation of antitrust injury. It also held that Monfort had shown that the proposed merger would cause this profit-squeeze to occur, and that the merger violated § 7 of the Clayton Act.

On appeal, Excel argued that an allegation of lost profits due to a "price-cost squeeze" was nothing more than an allegation of losses due to vigorous competition, and that losses from competition do not constitute antitrust injury.... The Court of Appeals held that Monfort's allegation of a "price-cost squeeze" was not simply an allegation of injury from competition; in its view, the alleged "price-cost squeeze" was a claim that Monfort would be injured by what the Court of Appeals "considered to be a form of predatory pricing in which Excel will drive other companies out of the market by paying more to its cattle suppliers and charging less for boxed beef that it sells to institutional buyers and consumers."

This case requires us to decide, at the outset, a question we have not previously addressed: whether a private plaintiff seeking an injunction under § 16 of the Clayton Act

must show a threat of antitrust injury. To decide the question, we must look first to the source of the antitrust injury requirement, which lies in a related provision of the Clayton Act, § 4.

Like § 16, § 4 provides a vehicle for private enforcement of the antitrust laws. Under § 4, "any person who shall be injured in his business or property by reason of anything forbidden in the antitrust laws may sue therefor in any district court of the United States..., and shall recover threefold the damages by him sustained, and the cost of suit, including a reasonable attorney's fee." In *Brunswick Corp. v. Pueblo Bowl-O-Mat, Inc.*, we held that plaintiffs seeking treble damages under § 4 must show more than simply an "injury causally linked" to a particular merger; instead, "plaintiffs must prove *antitrust* injury, which is to say injury of the type the antitrust laws were intended to prevent and that flows from that which makes the defendants' acts unlawful."...

This reasoning in *Brunswick* was consistent with the principle that "the antitrust laws...were enacted for 'the protection of *competition*, not *competitors*.'"...

Section 16 of the Clayton Act provides in part that "any person, firm, corporation, or association shall be entitled to sue for and have injunctive relief...against threatened loss or damage by a violation of the antitrust laws...." It is plain that § 16 and § 4 do differ in various ways. For example, § 4 requires a plaintiff to show actual injury, but § 16 requires a showing only of "threatened" loss or damage; similarly, § 4 requires a showing of injury to "business or property," while § 16 contains no such limitation. Although these differences do affect the nature of the injury cognizable under each section, under both § 16 and § 4 the plaintiff must still allege an injury of the type the antitrust laws were designed to prevent....

The wording concerning the relationship of the injury to the violation of the antitrust laws in each section is comparable. Section 4 requires proof of injury "by reason of anything forbidden in the antitrust laws"; § 16 requires proof of "threatened loss or damage by a violation of the antitrust laws." It would be anomalous, we think, to read the Clayton Act to authorize a private plaintiff to secure an injunction against a threatened injury for which he would not be entitled to compensation if the injury actually occurred.

There is no indication that Congress intended such a result. Indeed, the legislative history of § 16 is consistent with the view that § 16 affords private plaintiffs injunctive relief only for those injuries cognizable under § 4....

Sections 4 and 16 are thus best understood as providing complementary remedies for a single set of injuries. Accordingly, we conclude that in order to seek injunctive relief under § 16, a private plaintiff must allege threatened loss or damage "of the type the antitrust laws were designed to prevent and that flows from that which makes defendants' acts unlawful." We therefore turn to the question of whether the proposed merger in this case threatened respondent with antitrust injury....

Monfort's claim is that after the merger, Excel would lower its prices to some level at or slightly above its costs in order to compete with other packers for market share. Excel would be in a position to do this because of the multiplant efficiencies its acquisition of Spencer would provide. To remain competitive, Monfort would have to lower its prices; as a result, Monfort would suffer a loss in profitability, but would not be driven out of business. The question is whether Monfort's loss of profits in such circumstances constitutes antitrust injury....

*Brunswick* holds that the antitrust laws do not require the courts to protect small businesses from the loss of profits due to continued competition, but only against the loss of profits from practices forbidden by the antitrust laws. The kind of competition that Monfort alleges here, competition for increased market share, is not activity forbidden by the antitrust laws. It is simply, as petitioners claim, vigorous competition. To hold that the antitrust laws protect competitors from the loss of profits due to such price competition would, in effect, render illegal any decision by a firm to cut prices in order to increase market share. The antitrust laws require no such perverse result, for "it is in the interest of competition to permit dominant firms to engage in vigorous competition, including price competition."

The logic of *Brunswick* compels the conclusion that the threat of loss of profits due to possible price competition following a merger does not constitute a threat of antitrust injury.

We hold that a plaintiff seeking injunctive relief under § 16 of the Clayton Act must show a threat of antitrust injury, and that a showing of loss or damage due merely to increased competition does not constitute such injury. The record below does not support a finding of antitrust injury, but only of threatened loss from increased competition. Because respondent has therefore failed to make the showing § 16 requires, we need not reach the question of whether the proposed merger violates § 7. [*Reversed and remanded.*]

---

Many antitrust cases are settled by agreement of the government and the defendants. In the past, it was sometimes alleged that political considerations played a part in such settlements. Therefore, the law now requires that all contacts between government and company officials, except for those between the lawyers involved, be reported when a proposed negotiated settlement of an antitrust case is made public. In addition, out-of-court settlements must be approved by the court, and the judge must find that the settlement is in the national interest before it can be approved. In the case involving AT&T, the trial judge balked at accepting the settlement agreed upon by the parties. It was later approved after some modifications.

## 8.   Triple Damages

The third remedy (created by the Clayton Act amendment in 1914) affords relief to persons injured by another's violation of the Sherman Act. Such victims are given the right, in a civil action, to collect three times the damages they have suffered, plus court costs and reasonable attorney's fees. Normally, the objective of awarding money damages to individuals in a private lawsuit is to place them in the position they would have enjoyed, as nearly as this can be done with money, had their rights not been invaded. The triple damage provisions of the antitrust laws, however, employ the remedy of damages to punish a defendant for a wrongful act in addition to compensating the plaintiff for actual injury. Today it is perhaps the most important remedy of all, because it allows one's competitors as well as injured members of the general public to enforce the law if government fails to do so.

In recent years, there have been several developments relating to triple damages. After the Supreme Court held that, under the Sherman Act, foreign governments are persons, Congress by statute provided that foreign nations may sue only for actual damages when they have purchased products for which prices have been fixed. The Court had also held that local governments and nonprofit organizations may be sued under the law. In response, Congress in 1984 passed the Local Government Antitrust Act. It provides that no antitrust damages may be recovered from any local government, or official, or employee acting in an official capacity. It also prohibits the collection of damages from any person based on official action directed by a local government or official acting in an official capacity.

The law authorizes the attorney general of a state to file triple damage suits on behalf of the citizens of a state. Such suits are similar to a class action suit. For example, either the consumers involved or the attorney general on their behalf may sue for triple damages when consumers have paid higher prices for products and the higher prices resulted from antitrust violations. Damages under the antitrust laws are not limited to commercial losses or to those of a competitive nature. The term "property" is given a broad definition and includes anything of a material value, including money.

The triple damage remedy is perhaps the most important of all the sanctions available. Successful triple damage suits may impose financial burdens on violators far in excess of any fine that could be imposed as a result of a criminal prosecution. This significant liability may be far in excess of the damages caused by any one defendant, because the liability of defendants is based on tort law and is said to be joint and several. For example, assume that ten companies in an industry conspire to fix prices and that the total damages caused by the conspiracy equal $100 million. Also, assume that nine of the defendants settle out of court for $25 million. The remaining defendant, if the case is lost, would owe $275 million (3 × 100 − 25). The case which denied any right of contribution in such circumstances follows. It should be noted that Congress is considering legislation to change this decision because of its impact on a few companies which face liabilities approaching a billion dollars.

# TEXAS INDUSTRIES, INC. v. RADCLIFF MATERIALS
101 S.Ct. 2061 (1981)

BURGER, C. J.: This case presents the question whether the federal antitrust laws allow a defendant, against whom civil damages, costs, and attorneys' fees have been assessed, a right to contribution from other participants in the unlawful conspiracy on which recovery was based....

Petitioner and the three respondents manufacture and sell ready-mix concrete in the New Orleans, La., area. In 1975, the Wilson P. Abraham Construction Corp., which had purchased concrete from petitioner, filed a civil action...naming petitioner as defendant; the complaint alleged that petitioner and certain unnamed concrete firms had conspired to raise prices in violation of § 1 of the Sherman Act....The complaint sought treble damages plus attorneys' fees under § 4 of the Clayton Act....

Through discovery, petitioner learned that Abraham believed respondents were the other concrete producers that had participated in the alleged price-fixing scheme. Petitioner then filed a third-party complaint

against respondents seeking contribution from them should it be held liable in the action filed by Abraham. The District Court dismissed the third-party complaint holding that federal law does not allow an antitrust defendant to recover in contribution from co-conspirators....

On appeal, the Court of Appeals for the Fifth Circuit affirmed....

The common law provided no right to contribution among joint tortfeasors. In part, at least, this common-law rule rested on the idea that when several tortfeasors have caused damage, the law should not lend its aid to have one tortfeasor compel others to share in the sanctions imposed by way of damages intended to compensate the victim. Since the turn of the century, however, 39 states and the District of Columbia have fashioned rules of contribution in one form or another, 10 initially through judicial action and the remainder through legislation. Because courts generally have acknowledged that treble-damages actions under the antitrust laws are analogous to common-law actions sounding in tort, we are urged to follow this trend and adopt contribution for antitrust violators....

Proponents of a right to contribution advance concepts of fairness and equity in urging that the often massive judgments in antitrust actions be shared by all the wrongdoers. In the abstract, this position has a certain appeal: collective fault, collective responsibility. But the efforts...to invoke principles of equity presuppose a legislative intent to allow parties violating the law to draw upon equitable principles to mitigate the consequences of their wrongdoing....

The proponents of contribution also contend that, by allowing one violator to recover from co-conspirators, there is a greater likelihood that most or all wrongdoers will be held liable and thus share the consequences of the wrongdoing. It is argued that competition would thus promote more vigorous private enforcement of the antitrust laws and thereby deter violations, one of the important purposes of the treble-damages action under § 4 of the Clayton Act. Independent of this effect, a right to contribution may increase the incentive of a single defendant to provide evidence against co-conspirators so as to avoid bearing the full weight of the judgment. Realization of this possibility may also deter one from joining an antitrust conspiracy.

Respondents...opposing contribution point out that an even stronger deterrent may exist in the possibility, even if more remote, that a single participant could be held fully liable for the total amount of the judgment. In this view, each prospective co-conspirator would ponder long and hard before engaging in what may be called a game of "Russian roulette."...

The parties...also discuss at length how a right to contribution should be structured and, in particular, how to treat problems that may arise with the allocation of damages among the wrongdoers and the effect of settlements. Dividing or apportioning damages among a cluster of co-conspirators presents difficult issues, for the participation of each in the conspiracy may have varied. Some may have profited more than others; some may have caused more damage to the injured plaintiff. Some may have been "leaders" and others "followers"; one may be a "giant," others "pygmies." Various formulae are suggested: damages may be allocated according to market shares, relative profits, sales to the particular plaintiff, the role in the organization and operation of the conspiracy, or simply pro rata, assessing an equal amount against each participant on the theory that each one is equally liable for the injury caused by collective action....

The contentions advanced indicate how views diverge as to the "unfairness" of not providing contribution, the risks and tradeoffs perceived by decisionmakers in business, and the various patterns for contribution that could be devised. In this vigorous debate over the advantages and disadvantages of contribution and various contribution schemes, the parties...have paid less attention to a very old question: whether courts have the power to create such a cause of action absent legislation and, if so, whether that authority should be exercised in this context.

A right to contribution may arise in either of two ways: first, through the affirmative creation of a right of action by Congress, either expressly or by clear implication; or, second, through the power of federal courts to fashion a federal common law of contribution.

There is no allegation that the antitrust laws expressly establish a right of action for contribution. Nothing in these statutes refers to contribution, and if such a right exists it must be by implication. Our focus, as it is in any case involving the implication of a right of action, is on the intent of Congress. Congressional intent may be discerned by looking to the legislative history and other factors, e.g., the identity of the class for whose benefit the statute was enacted, the overall legislative scheme, and the traditional role of the States in providing relief.

Petitioner readily concedes that "there is nothing in the legislative history of the Sherman Act or the Clayton Act to indicate that Congress considered whether contribution was available to defendants in antitrust actions." Moreover, it is equally clear that the Sherman Act and the provision for treble-damages actions under the Clayton Act were not adopted for the benefit of the participants in a conspiracy to restrain trade.... The very idea of treble damages reveals an intent to punish past, and to deter future, unlawful conduct, not to ameliorate the liability of wrongdoers. The absence of any reference to contribution in the legislative history or of any possibility that Congress was concerned with softening the blow on joint wrongdoers in this setting makes examination of other factors unnecessary. We therefore conclude that Congress neither expressly nor implicitly intended to create a right to contribution. If any right to contribution exists, its source must be federal common law.

There is, of course, "no general federal common law." Nevertheless, the Court has recognized the need and authority in some limited areas to formulate what has come to be known as "federal common law." These instances are "few and restricted," and fall into essentially two categories: those in which a federal rule of decision is "necessary to protect uniquely federal interests," and those in which Congress has given the courts the power to develop substantive law....

The antitrust laws were enacted pursuant to the power of Congress under the Commerce Clause, Art. I, § 8, cl. 3, to regulate interstate and foreign trade, and the case law construing the Sherman Act now spans nearly a century. Nevertheless, a treble-damages action remains a private suit involving the rights and obligations of private parties. Admittedly, there is a federal interest in the sense that vindication of rights arising out of these congressional enactments supplements federal enforcement and fulfills the objects of the statutory scheme. Notwithstanding that nexus, contribution among antitrust wrongdoers does not involve the duties of the Federal Government, the distribution of powers in our federal system, or matters necessarily subject to federal control even in the absence of statutory authority. In short, contribution does not implicate "uniquely federal interest" of the kind that oblige courts to formulate federal common law.

[The court then reviewed the Sherman and Clayton Acts and the remedies provided.] We are satisfied that neither the Sherman Act nor the Clayton Act confers on federal courts the broad power to formulate the right to contribution sought here.

The policy questions presented by petitioner's claimed right to contribution are far reaching. In declining to provide a right to contribution, we neither reject the validity of those arguments nor adopt the views of those opposing contribution. Rather, we recognize that, regardless of the merits of the conflicting arguments, this is a matter for Congress, not the courts, to resolve....

Because we are unable to discern any basis in federal statutory or common law that allows federal courts to fashion the relief urged by petitioner, the judgment of the Court of Appeals is...[*Affirmed.*]

### 9.    The Illinois Brick Doctrine

Who is entitled to collect triple damages? Is everyone in the chain of distribution entitled to use Section 4 of the Clayton Act and recover damages? The leading case on this point involved a company called Illinois Brick. The case has become so well known in antitrust law that the legal principle which it announced is simply referred to as the **Illinois Brick Doctrine.** This doctrine announced that courts generally restrict the recovery of triple damages to direct purchasers, and they do not allow recoveries by indirect purchasers.

# ILLINOIS BRICK CO. v. ILLINOIS
97 S.Ct. 2061 (1977)

The State of Illinois and several of its local entities brought suit for triple damages against Illinois Brick Co., a manufacturer of concrete blocks. Illinois Brick sold concrete blocks to many companies who, in turn, had sold them to general contractors from whom the plaintiff had purchased them as part of completed buildings. The complaint alleged that the defendant was a part of a price-fixing conspiracy in violation of Section 1 of the Sherman Act.

The defendant moved for a summary judgment on the ground that indirect purchasers cannot recover triple damages. It relied on the case of *Hanover Shoe, Inc., v. United Shoe Machinery Corp.*, 392 U.S. 481 (1968) which had held that a direct purchaser could collect triple damages even though the price increase due to price-fixing had been passed on. The case had held that evidence of injury to indirect purchasers was not admissible or, in other words, there was no pass-on defense in triple damage cases. The district court granted the motion, and the Court of Appeals reversed. The Supreme Court granted certiorari.

WHITE, J.:...In this case we once again confront the question whether the overcharged direct purchaser should be deemed for purposes of Section 4 to have suffered the full injury from the overcharge, but the issue is presented in the context of a suit in which the plaintiff, an indirect purchaser, seeks to show its injury by establishing pass-on by the direct purchaser and in which the antitrust defendants rely on Hanover Shoe's rejection of the pass-on theory. Having decided that in general a pass-on theory may not be used defensively by an antitrust violator against a direct purchaser plaintiff, we must now decide whether that theory may be used offensively by an indirect purchaser plaintiff against an alleged violator. We hold that it may not and we REVERSE.

We reach this result in two steps. First, we conclude that whatever rule is to be adopted regarding pass-on in antitrust damage actions, it must apply equally to plaintiffs and defendants....Second, we decline to abandon the construction given Section 4 in *Hanover Shoe*—that the overcharged direct purchaser, and not others in the chain of manufacture of distribution, is the party "injured in his business or property" within the meaning of the section—in the absence of a convincing demonstration that the Court was wrong in *Hanover Shoe* to think that the effectiveness of the antitrust treble-damage action would be substantially reduced by adopting a rule that any party in the chain may sue to recover the fraction of the overcharge allegedly absorbed by it.

The parties in this case agree that however Section 4 is construed with respect to the pass-on issue, the rule should apply equally to plaintiffs and defendants—that an indirect purchaser should not be allowed to use a pass-on theory to recover damages from a defendant unless the defendant would be allowed to use a pass-on defense in a suit by a direct purchaser...We...agree for two reasons.

First, allowing offensive but not defensive use of pass-on would create a serious risk of multiple liability for defendants....

Second, the reasoning of *Hanover Shoe* cannot justify unequal treatment of plaintiffs and defendants with respect to the permissibility of pass-on arguments. The principal basis for the decision in *Hanover Shoe* was the Court's perception of the uncertainties and difficulties in analyzing price and output decisions "in the real economic world rather than an economists' hypothetical model," and on the costs to the judicial system and the efficient enforcement of antitrust laws of attempting to reconstruct those decisions in the courtroom. This perception that the attempt to trace the complex economic adjustments to a change in the cost of a particular factor of production would greatly complicate and reduce the effectiveness of already protracted treble-damage proceedings applies with no less force to the assertion of pass-on theories by plaintiffs than to the assertion by defendants. However "long and complicated" the proceed-

ings would be when defendants sought to prove pass-on, they would be equally so when the same evidence was introduced by plaintiffs. Indeed, the evidentiary complexities and uncertainties involved in the defensive use of pass-on against a direct purchaser are multiplied in the offensive use of pass-on by a plaintiff several steps removed from the defendant in the chain of distribution. The demonstration of how much of the overcharge was passed on by the first purchaser must be repeated at each point at which the price-fixed goods changed hands before they reached the plaintiff....

We thus decline to construe Section 4 to permit offensive use of a pass-on theory against an alleged violator that could not use the same theory as a defense in an action by direct purchasers....

We are left, then, with two alternatives: either we must overrule *Hanover Shoe* (or at least narrowly confine it to its facts), or we must preclude respondents from seeking to recover on their pass-on theory. We choose the latter course....

Permitting the use of pass-on theories under Section 4 essentially would transform treble-damage actions into massive efforts to apportion the recovery among all potential plaintiffs that could have absorbed part of the overcharge—from direct purchasers to middlemen to ultimate consumers. However appealing this attempt to allocate the overcharge might seem in theory, it would add whole new dimensions of complexity to treble-damage suits and seriously undermine their effectiveness....

It is true that...the *Hanover Shoe* rule denies recovery to those indirect purchasers who may have been actually injured by antitrust violations. Of course, as Mr. Justice Brennan points out in dissent, "from the deterrence standpoint, it is irrelevant to whom damages are paid, so long as some one redresses the violation." But Section 4 has another purpose in addition to deterring violators and depriving them of "the fruits of their illegality," it is also designed to compensate victims of antitrust violations for their injuries. *Hanover Shoe* does further the goal of compensation to the extent that the direct purchaser absorbs at least some and often most of the overcharge. In view of the considerations supporting the *Hanover Shoe* rule, we are unwilling to carry the compensation principle to its logical extreme by attempting to allocate damages among all "those within the defendant's chain of distribution," especially because we question the extent to which such an attempt would make individual victims whole for actual injuries suffered rather than simply depleting the overall recovery in litigation over pass-on issues. Many of the indirect purchasers barred from asserting pass-on claims under the *Hanover Shoe* rule have such a small stake in the lawsuit that even if they were to recover as part of a class, only a small fraction would be likely to come forward to collect their damages.

And given the difficulty of ascertaining the amount absorbed by any particular indirect purchaser, there is little basis for believing that the amount of the recovery would reflect the actual injury suffered. [*Reversed.*]

---

The *Illinois Brick* decision continues to require further interpretation and application. Several courts have held that *Illinois Brick* does not preclude consumers from suing manufacturers who allegedly conspire with middlemen to fix retail prices. These courts recognize that the claim is not based on pass-through damages but is instead a form of retail price-fixing.

Not every case fits into the *Illinois Brick* mold. In one instance, an employee sued for wrongful discharge for refusing to participate in a Sherman Act violation. The employee had standing to sue because the damage problems of the pass-on theory are not present in such cases. The case which follows illustrates another exception to *Illinois Brick*.

---

# BLUE SHIELD OF VIRGINIA v. McCREADY
102 S.Ct. 2540 (1982)

---

As a county employee in Virginia from 1975 to 1978, McCready received partial compensation in the form of coverage under a prepaid health plan purchased from Blue Shield. This health plan provided reimbursement for a portion of any outpatient psychotherapy administered by *psychiatrists*. The plan did not reimburse for treatment by *psychologists* unless supervised by and billed through a physician.

McCready submitted several claims to Blue Shield. These claims were denied because they were not billed through a physician. He then filed a class action on behalf of all Blue Shield subscribers denied reimbursement for psychological services, alleging that Blue Shield and the Neuropsychiatric Society of Virginia, Inc., had engaged in unlawful conspiracy to exclude psychologists from receiving compensation under Blue Shield plans in violation of the Sherman Act, Section 1. Plaintiff sought triple damages. Defendants contended that plaintiff was not in the class of persons entitled to triple damages.

The district court held that McCready had no standing under Section 4 to maintain her suit and that only psychologists could sue. Thus, while McCready clearly had suffered an injury by being denied reimbursement, this injury was "too indirect and remote to be considered 'antitrust injury.'"

The United States Court of Appeals reversed, holding that McCready had alleged an injury within the meaning of Section 4 of the Clayton Act and had standing to maintain the suit. The court recognized that the goal of the alleged conspiracy was the exclusion of clinical psychologists from some segment of the psychotherapy market. But it held that the Section 4 remedy was available to any person "whose property loss is directly or proximately caused by" a violation of the antitrust laws, and that McCready's loss was not "too remote or indirect to be covered by the Act."

BRENNAN, J.:…Section 4 of the Clayton Act provides a treble-damages remedy to "*any person* who shall be injured in his business or property *by reason of anything* forbidden in the antitrust laws." On its face, § 4 contains little in the way of restrictive language. And the lack of restrictive language reflects Congress' "expansive remedial purpose" in enacting § 4: Congress sought to create a private enforcement mechanism that would deter violators and deprive them of the fruits of their illegal actions, and would provide ample compensation to the victims of antitrust violations. As we have recognized, the statute does not confine its protection to consumers, or to purchasers, or to competitors, or to sellers.…The Act is comprehensive in its terms and coverage, protecting all who are made victims of the forbidden practices by whomever they may be perpetrated.

Consistent with the congressional purpose, we have refused to engraft artificial limitations on the § 4 remedy. Two recent cases illustrate the point. *Pfizer Inc. v. India* afforded the statutory phrase "any person" its "naturally broad and inclusive meaning," and held that it extends even to an action brought by a foreign sovereign. Similarly, *Reiter v. Sonotone Corp.* rejected the argument that the § 4 remedy is available only to redress injury to commercial interests. In that case we afforded the statutory term "property" its "naturally broad and inclusive meaning," and held that a consumer has standing to seek a § 4 remedy reflecting the increase in the purchase price of goods that was attributable to a price-fixing conspiracy. In sum, in the absence of some articulable consideration of statutory policy suggesting a contrary conclusion in a particular factual setting, we have applied § 4 in accordance with its plain language and its broad remedial and deterrent objectives. But drawing on statutory policy, our cases have acknowledged two types of limitation on the availability of the § 4 remedy to particular classes of persons and for redress of particular forms of injury. We treat these limitations in turn.

In *Hawaii v. Standard Oil Co.*, 92 S. Ct. 885 (1972), we held that § 4 did not authorize a State to sue in its *parens patriae* capacity for damages to its "general economy." Noting that a "large and ultimately indeterminable part of the injury to the 'general economy'…is no more than a reflection of injuries to the 'business or property' of consumers, for which they may recover themselves under § 4," we concluded that "even the most lengthy and expensive trial could not...cope with the problems of double recovery inherent in allowing damages" for injury to the State's quasi-sovereign interests.

In *Illinois Brick Co. v. Illinois*, 97 S.Ct. 2061 (1977), similar concerns prevailed. *Hanover Shoe v. United Shoe Mach.*, 88 S.Ct. 2224 (1968), had held that an antitrust defendant could not relieve itself of its obligation to pay damages resulting from overcharges to a direct-purchaser plaintiff by showing that the plaintiff had passed the amount of the overcharge on to its own customers. *Illinois Brick* was an action by an indirect purchaser claiming damages from the antitrust violator measured by the amount that had been passed on to it. Relying in part on *Hawaii v. Standard Oil Co., supra*, the Court found unacceptable the risk of duplicative recovery engendered by allowing both direct and indirect purchasers to claim damages resulting from a single overcharge by the antitrust defendant. The Court found that the splintered recoveries and litigative burdens that would result from a rule requiring that the impact of an overcharge be apportioned between direct and indirect purchasers could undermine the active enforcement of the antitrust laws by private actions. The Court concluded that direct purchasers rather than indirect purchasers were the injured parties who as a group were most likely to press their claims with the vigor that the § 4 treble-damages remedy was intended to promote.

The policies identified in *Hawaii* and *Illinois Brick* plainly offer no support for petitioner here. Both cases focused on the risk of duplicative recovery engendered by allowing every person along a chain of distribution to claim damages arising from a single transaction that violated the antitrust laws. But permitting respondent to proceed in the circumstances of this case offers not the slightest possibility of a duplicative exaction from petitioners. McCready has paid her psychologist's bills; her injury consists of Blue Shield's failure to pay her. Her psychologist can link no claim of injury to himself arising from his treatment of McCready; he has been fully paid for his service and has not been injured by Blue Shield's refusal to reimburse her for the cost of his services. And whatever the adverse effect of Blue Shield's actions on McCready's employer, who purchased the plan, it is not the employer as purchaser, but his employees as subscribers, who are out of pocket as a consequence of the plan's failure to pay benefits.

It is petitioners' position that McCready's injury is too "fortuitous," "incidental," and "remote" from the alleged violation to provide the basis for a § 4 action....

We do not think that because the goal of the conspirators was to halt encroachment by psychologists into a market that physicians and psychiatrists sought to preserve for themselves, McCready's injury is rendered "remote." The availability of the § 4 remedy to some person who claims its benefit is not a question of the specific intent of the conspirators. Here the remedy cannot reasonably be restricted to those competitors whom the conspirators hoped to eliminate from the market....

Section 4 of the Clayton Act provides a remedy to "any person" injured "by reason of" anything prohibited in the antitrust laws. We are asked in this case to infer a limitation on the rule of recovery suggested by the plain language of § 4. But having reviewed our precedents and, more importantly, the policies of the antitrust laws, we are unable to identify any persuasive rationale upon which McCready might be denied redress under § 4 for the injury she claims. The judgment of the Court of Appeals is [*Affirmed.*]

## 10. Proof of Sherman Act Violations

Plaintiffs seeking triple damages must satisfy the interstate commerce element to have a Sherman Act claim. They must allege facts which show that the activity is either in interstate commerce or that it has a substantial effect on interstate commerce. A plaintiff need not allege and prove a change in the volume of interstate commerce but only that the activity had a substantial and adverse or not insubstantial effect on interstate commerce. In a recent case involving the medical profession, it was held that the Sherman Act is applicable to staff privileges at a hospital. The impact on interstate commerce is readily apparent.

Difficulties may arise in proving the existence of a contract, combination, or conspiracy among competitors when they indulge in cooperative action to control the market in some fashion. Must an actual oral or written offer and acceptance be established? If the market behavior of competitors is consciously parallel, will it be implied that they are conspiring together? If one party reacts to another's conduct, does this prove a conspiracy? In the case that follows, there was evidence that a manufacturer terminated a distributor in response to other distributors' complaints about price-cutting. Is this sufficient to prove a conspiracy in violation of Section 1 of the Sherman Act? If there is evidence that tends to prove that a manufacturer and others had a conscious commitment to a common silence designed to achieve an unlawful objective, the issue becomes one of fact for a jury.

---

# MONSANTO CO. v. SPRAY-RITE SERVICE CORP.
104 S.Ct. 1464 (1984)

POWELL, J.: This case presents a question as to the standard of proof required to find a vertical price-fixing conspiracy in violation of § 1 of the Sherman Act.

Petitioner Monsanto Company manufactures chemical products, including agricultural herbicides. By the late 1960's, the time at issue in this case, its sales accounted for approximately 15% of the corn herbicide market and 3% of the soybean herbicide market. In the corn herbicide market, the market leader commanded a 70% share. In the soybean herbicide market, two other competitors each had between 30% and 40% of the market. Respondent Spray-Rite Service Corporation was engaged in the wholesale distribution of agricultural chemicals from 1955 to 1972. Spray-Rite was essentially a family business, whose owner and president, Donald Yapp, was also its sole salaried salesman. Spray-Rite was a discount operation, buying in large quantities and selling at a low margin.

Spray-Rite was an authorized distributor of Monsanto herbicides from 1957 to 1968. In October...1968 Monsanto declined to renew Spray-Rite's distributorship. At that time, Spray-Rite was the tenth largest out of approximately 100 distributors of Monsanto's primary corn herbicide. Ninety percent of Spray-Rite's sales volume was devoted to herbicide sales, and 16% of its sales were of Monsanto products. After Monsanto's termination, Spray-Rite continued as a herbicide dealer until 1972. It was able to purchase some of Monsanto's products from other distributors, but not as much as it desired or as early in the season as it needed. Monsanto introduced a new corn herbicide in 1969. By 1972, its shares of the corn herbicide market had increased to approximately 28%. Its share of the soybean herbicide market had grown to approximately 19%.

Spray-Rite brought this action under § 1 of the Sherman Act. It alleged that Monsanto and some of its distributors conspired to fix the resale prices of Monsanto herbicides. Its complaint further alleged that Monsanto terminated Spray-Rite's distributorship, adopted compensation programs and shipping policies, and encouraged distributors to boycott Spray-Rite in furtherance of this conspiracy. Monsanto denied the allegations of conspiracy, and asserted that Spray-Rite's distributorship had been terminated because of its failure to hire trained salesmen and promote sales to dealers adequately.

The case was tried to a jury. The District Court instructed the jury that Monsanto's conduct was *per se* unlawful if it was in furtherance of a conspiracy to fix prices. In answers to special interrogatories, the jury found that the termination of Spray-Rite was pursuant to a conspiracy between Monsanto and one or more of its distributors to set resale prices....

The jury awarded $3.5 million in damages, which was trebled to $10.5 million.

The Court of Appeals for the Seventh Circuit affirmed. It held that there was sufficient evidence to satisfy Spray-Rite's burden of proving a conspiracy to set resale prices. The court stated that "proof of termination following competitor complaints is

sufficient to support an inference of concerted action."...

In substance, the Court of Appeals held that an antitrust plaintiff can survive a motion for a directed verdict if it shows that a manufacturer terminated a price-cutting distributor in response to or following complaints by other distributors....We reject the statement by the Court of Appeals for the Seventh Circuit of the standard of proof required to submit a case to the jury in distributor-termination litigation, but affirm the judgment under the standard we announce today.

This Court has drawn two important distinctions that are at the center of this and any other distributor-termination case. First, there is the basic distinction between concerted and independent action—a distinction not always clearly drawn by parties and courts. Section 1 of the Sherman Act requires that there be a "contract, combination... or conspiracy" between the manufacturer and other distributors in order to establish a violation. Independent action is not proscribed. A manufacturer of course generally has a right to deal, or refuse to deal, with whomever it likes, as long as it does so independently. (Colgate Doctrine)

Under *Colgate*, the manufacturer can announce its resale prices in advance and refuse to deal with those who fail to comply. And a distributor is free to acquiesce in the manufacturer's demand in order to avoid termination.

The second important distinction in distributor-termination cases is that between concerted action to set prices and concerted action on nonprice restrictions. The former have been *per se* illegal since the early years of national antitrust enforcement. The latter are judged under the rule of reason, which requires a weighing of the relevant circumstances of a case to decide whether a restrictive practice constitutes an unreasonable restraint on competition.

It is of considerable importance that independent action by the manufacturer, and concerted action on non-price restrictions, be distinguished from price-fixing agreements, since under present law the latter are subject to per se treatment and treble damages. On a claim of concerted price-fixing, the antitrust plaintiff must present evidence sufficient to carry its burden of proving that there was such an agreement. If an inference of such an agreement may be drawn from highly ambiguous evidence, there is a considerable danger that the doctrine enunciated in *Colgate* will be seriously eroded.

The flaw in the evidentiary standard adopted by the Court of Appeals in this case is that it disregards this danger. Permitting an agreement to be inferred merely from the existence of complaints, or even from the fact that termination came about "in response to" complaints, could deter or penalize perfectly legitimate conduct. As Monsanto points out, complaints about price-cutters "are natural—and from the manufacturer's perspective, unavoidable—reactions by distributors to the activities of their rivals." Such complaints, particularly where the manufacturer has imposed a costly set of nonprice restrictions, "arise in the normal course of business and do not indicate illegal concerted action." Moreover, distributors are an important source of information for manufacturers. In order to assure an efficient distribution system, manufacturers and distributors constantly must coordinate their activities to assure that their product will reach the consumer persuasively and efficiently. To bar a manufacturer from acting solely because the information upon which it acts originated as a price complaint would create an irrational dislocation in the market. In sum, "to permit the inference of concerted action on the basis of receiving complaints alone and thus to expose the defendant to treble damage liability would both inhibit management's exercise of independent business judgment and emasculate the terms of the statute."

Thus, something more than evidence of complaints is needed. There must be evidence that tends to exclude the possibility that the manufacturer and nonterminated distributors were acting independently. As Judge Aldisert has written, the antitrust plaintiff should present direct or circumstantial evidence that reasonably tends to prove that the manufacturer and others "had a conscious commitment to a common scheme designed to achieve an unlawful objective."

Applying this standard to the facts of this case, we believe there was sufficient evidence for the jury reasonably to have concluded that Monsanto and some of its distributors were parties to an "agreement" or "conspiracy" to maintain resale prices and terminate price-cutters. In fact there was substantial *direct* evidence of agreements to maintain prices....

We conclude that the Court of Appeals applied an incorrect standard to the evidence in this case. The correct standard is that there must be evidence that tends to exclude the possibility of independent action by the manufacturer and distributor. That is, there must be direct or circumstantial evidence that reasonably tends to prove that the manufacturer and others had a conscious commitment to a common scheme designed to achieve an unlawful objective. Under this standard, the evidence in this case created a jury issue as to whether Spray-Rite was terminated pursuant to a price-fixing conspiracy between Monsanto and its distributors. The judgment of the court below is affirmed. [*It is so ordered.*]

## 11.   The Rule of Reason and Per Se Illegality

The **rule of reason** as applied to the Sherman Act was enunciated in the case of *Standard Oil Co. v. United States.*[1] The court in that case held that contracts or conspiracies in **restraint of trade** were illegal only if they constituted *undue* or *unreasonable* restraints of trade, and that only *unreasonable* attempts to monopolize were covered by the Sherman Act. As a result, acts which the statute prohibits may be removed from the coverage of the law by a finding that they are *reasonable*. The rule of reason gives flexibility and definition to the law. The rule does not open the field of antitrust inquiry to any argument in favor of a challenged restraint that may fall within the realm of reason. Instead, it focuses directly on the challenged restraint's impact on competitive conditions. The fact that prices fixed are reasonable is no defense. Monopolistic practices that promote trade are still illegal.

The *test of reasonableness* is whether challenged contracts or acts are unreasonably restrictive of competitive conditions. Unreasonableness can be based either: (1) on the nature or character of the contracts or (2) on surrounding circumstances giving rise to the inference or presumption that they were intended to restrain trade and enhance prices. Under either branch of the test, the inquiry is confined to a consideration of impact on competitive conditions. If an agreement promotes competition, it may be found legal. If it suppresses or destroys competition, it is unreasonable and illegal.

For purposes of the rule of reason, Sherman Act violations may be divided into two categories. Some agreements or practices are so plainly anticompetitive and so lacking in any redeeming virtues that they are conclusively presumed to be illegal without further examination under the rule of reason. These agreements have such a pernicious effect on competition that elaborate inquiry as to the precise harm they may cause or a business excuse for them are unnecessary. They are said to be illegal per se. It is not necessary to examine them to see if they are reasonable. They are conclusively presumed to be unreasonable. Of course, the other category consists of agreements and practices that are illegal only if they impose an unreasonable restraint upon competitors.

The concept of per se illegality simplifies proof in cases in which it is applied. When an activity is illegal per se, courts are not required to conduct a complicated and prolonged examination of the economic consequences of the activity to determine whether it is unreasonable. If it is illegal per se, proof of the activity is proof of a violation and proof that it is in restraint of trade.

The most common example of an agreement that is illegal per se is one that fixes prices. In other words, an unreasonable contract or combination in restraint of trade is established by simply proving the existence of a price-fixing agreement. Similar contracts to those fixing the price at which con-

---

[1]221 U.S. 1 (1911).

spirators sell their product have been held unreasonable per se. Thus, agreements among competitors to divide up territories, to fix the market price of a product or service they are buying, or to limit the supply of a commodity are outlawed without proof of any unreasonable effects. Group boycotts are usually held to be illegal per se. In studying antitrust cases, you should note those activities to which the illegal per se concept is applied and those to which the rule of reason is applied. Courts develop this distinction on a case-by-case basis, as is done in the following case.

# CATALANO, INC. v. TARGET SALES, INC.
100 S.Ct. 1925 (1980)

Plaintiffs, beer retailers, brought suit alleging that their wholesalers had engaged in an unlawful conspiracy to restrain trade by refusing to sell beer unless plaintiffs paid cash in advance or at the time of the delivery. The wholesalers had an agreement that none of them would grant short-term credit although such credit had been extended in the past. Plaintiffs requested the trial court to declare the case one of "per se" illegality. The trial court refused and the plaintiffs appealed.

PER CURIAM: In construing and applying the Sherman Act's ban against contracts, conspiracies, and combinations in restraint of trade, the Court has held that certain agreements or practices are so "plainly anticompetitive," and so often lack…any redeeming virtue, that they are conclusively presumed illegal without further examination under the rule of reason generally applied in Sherman Act cases.

A horizontal agreement to fix prices is the archetypal example of such a practice. It has long been settled that an agreement to fix prices is unlawful per se. It is no excuse that the prices fixed are themselves reasonable. In *United States v. Socony-Vacuum Oil Co.*, 310 U.S. 150, 60 (1940), we held that an agreement among competitors to engage in

a program of buying surplus gasoline on the spot market in order to prevent prices from falling sharply to be unlawful without any inquiry into the reasonableness of the program, even though there was no direct agreement on the actual prices to be maintained. In the course of the opinion, the Court made clear that "the machinery employed by a combination for price-fixing is immaterial."

"Under the Sherman Act a combination formed for the purpose and with the effect of raising, depressing, fixing, pegging, or stabilizing the price of a commodity in interstate or foreign commerce is illegal per se."…

It is virtually self evident that extending interest-free credit for a period of time is equivalent to giving a discount equal to the value of the use of the purchase price for that period of time. Thus, credit terms must be characterized as an inseparable part of the price. An agreement to terminate the practice of giving credit is thus tantamount to an agreement to eliminate discounts, and thus falls squarely within the traditional per se rule against price fixing. While it may be that the elimination of a practice of giving variable discounts will ultimately lead in a competitive market to corresponding decreases in the invoice price, that is surely not necessarily to be anticipated. It is more realistic to view an agreement to eliminate credit sales as extinguishing one form of competition among the sellers. In any event, when a particular concerted activity entails an obvious risk of anticompetitive impact with no apparent potentially redeeming value, the fact that a practice may turn out to be harmless in a particular set of circumstances will not prevent its being declared unlawful per se....

Thus, under the reasoning of our cases, an agreement among competing wholesalers to refuse to sell unless the retailer makes payment in cash either in advance or upon delivery is "plainly anticompetitive." Since it is merely one form of price fixing, and since price-fixing agreements have been adjudged to lack any "redeeming virtue," it is conclusively presumed illegal without further examination under the rule of reason.

Accordingly, the judgment of the Court of Appeals is reversed, and the case is remanded for further proceedings consistent with this opinion. [*It is so ordered.*]

## 12.  Enforcement

The antitrust laws are enforced by: (1) the Department of Justice, (2) the FTC, and (3) private parties. The Department of Justice alone has the power to bring criminal proceedings. The Department shares power with the FTC and private parties in civil proceedings. The civil proceedings may use either the injunctive remedy or the triple damage remedy.

A separate division of the Justice Department deals with antitrust. The Antitrust Division is headed by an assistant attorney general, appointed by the President and confirmed by the Senate. The Antitrust Division is essentially a large law office with several hundred lawyers whose basic function is litigation. It conducts investigations as well as tries and settles cases. By statute, the Division has the power to subpoena information and discover documents. Grand juries are routinely impaneled to assist the Division in gathering evidence when the criminal sanction is likely to be used.

Chapter 23 discusses the role of the Federal Trade Commission in enforcing the antitrust laws and especially the unfair methods of competition provision of the FTC Act. Previous sections dealing with the triple damage remedy have covered the role of private persons in the enforcement process.

Antitrust enforcement by state government is rapidly expanding. As previously noted, a state attorney general may bring triple damage suits under the Sherman Act as well as suits for an injunction. In addition, state legislators have enacted antitrust laws that cover both products and services. These laws cover intrastate activities and are designed to prevent loss of competition in local communities. For example, recent cases have involved agreements by golf course operators to fix the price of green fees and golf cart rentals. Another case involved a real estate subdivider whose contracts of sale required that his real estate firm be used as the broker on a subsequent sale. For several years, the federal government awarded grants to aid state governments in antitrust enforcement. The impact of such local enforcement is likely to be much greater in the future.

## REVIEW QUESTIONS

**1** For each term in the left-hand column, match the most appropriate description in the right-hand column:

(1) Nolo contendere

(2) *Noerr-Pennington* Doctrine

(3) Per se illegality

(4) State action exemption

(5) The rule of reason

(6) *Illinois Brick* Doctrine

(a) Only direct purchasers from a price-fixer are entitled to collect triple damages.

(b) A rule that states that contracts or conspiracies are illegal only if they constitute undue or unreasonable restraints of trade, or if they unreasonably attempt to monopolize.

(c) Certain acts, in themselves, are unreasonable and, therefore, illegal under the Sherman Act.

(d) Concerted efforts to lobby governmental bodies are exempt from the antitrust laws.

(e) The antitrust laws do not cover activities mandated by state and local laws.

(f) A plea of "no contest" to a charge of a criminal violation of the law.

**2** A city used federal funds to build a sewage-treatment facility. It refused to supply sewage-treatment services to neighboring towns, but it did supply services to landowners who agreed to be annexed to the city. Neighboring towns brought suit under the Sherman Act. What was the result? Why?

**3** Three rating bureaus that represent common carriers in five southeastern states provided a forum for carriers to discuss and agree on rates for intrastate transportation of commodities. These rates are then proposed to the various state public-service commissions for approval. The United States instituted action to enjoin this activity. The defendants asserted the state action exemption. What was the result? Why?

**4** The National Basketball Association and the National Basketball Players Association entered into a collective-bargaining agreement. The agreement limits to one year the period during which a team has exclusive rights to negotiate with and sign draftees. It permits a salary cap, under which a team that has reached its maximum allowable team salary may sign a first-round draft choice only to a one-year contract for $75,000. It also prohibits the use of player corporations, which had been formed by players to enter into contracts with teams. Wood filed suit, alleging that the agreement violates the Sherman Act. Is he correct? Why, or why not?

**5** A complaint alleges that private individuals conspired with city officials to legalize the operation of poker clubs in certain areas of a city. The conspiracy was allegedly carried out by advocating the adoption of a local zoning ordinance which authorized the clubs in a specified area. What defense will likely be asserted? Explain.

**6** The four largest real estate brokers in Atlanta conspired to fix real estate commissions. They were indicted by a federal grand jury and ultimately entered a plea of nolo contendere. The usual commission rate prior to the conspiracy was 5 percent. The agreed-upon rate was 7 percent.

   **a** What punishment may be imposed on the individuals involved?

   **b** If the brokers are incorporated, what punishment may be imposed?

   **c** If a suit for triple damages is filed, what proof is required? Explain.

   **d** Assume that you had sold your house for $150,000 during the period the conspiracy was in effect. How much could you collect from your broker who was involved?

**7** A former employee alleges that his employer and other lithograph label manufacturers conspired to fix prices, allocate customers, and boycott anyone who interfered with their plans. As a result, he is forced to leave his job for refusing to participate in the scheme. He claims he is unable, after his resignation, to find another job in the label industry. He sues for triple damages under Section 4 of the Clayton Act. The defendants contend that the plaintiff lacks standing to sue. What is the result? Why?

**8** A group of gasoline dealers, through concerted action, refuses to sell gasoline to the general public for several days. The purpose of the action is to influence the government to raise the maximum retail price of gasoline. When charged with an antitrust violation, they contend that they are exercising their right of free speech and that it is exempt from the antitrust law for activities aimed at influencing the government. Are they guilty? Why, or why not?

**9** Assume that a Sherman Act violation is not illegal per se. What is the significance of this legal conclusion? Explain.

**10** The plaintiff operates a motion-picture theater in a neighborhood shopping center. It files suit against film distributors because they restrict first-run motion pictures to downtown theaters. The jury finds the defendant not guilty of restraining competition. The plaintiff contends that the court should have held the defendant guilty as a matter of law. Is he correct? Why or why not?

*Chapter*

# 23

# Sherman Act Enforcement

## CHAPTER PREVIEW

Chapter 22 introduced you to the Sherman Act and the sanctions which may be used to enforce its provisions. This chapter illustrates typical violations under both Sherman Act provisions. The sections illustrating activities in restraint of trade (Section 1 of the Sherman Act) cover in detail such illegal contracts, combinations, and conspiracies as price-fixing, both horizontal and vertical, and concerted activities among competitors. Price-fixing is said to be horizontal when it is done among competitors, and vertical when a manufacturer fixes a price for either its wholesalers or retailers.

The latter portions of this chapter discuss Section 2 of the Sherman Act, which deals with monopoly and attempts to monopolize. These cases are brought either by the government or by a competitor seeking triple damages. As you study this chapter, keep in mind the importance of the distinction between the rule of reason and per se illegality. Also, note that many of the cases seek triple damages.

The following terms are introduced in this chapter: Colgate Doctrine, consignment, fee schedule, price-fixing, resale price-maintenance, and vertical price-fixing.

## 1. Activities in Restraint of Trade

Section 1 of the Sherman Act is directed at contracts, combinations, and conspiracies in restraint of trade. An express agreement is not required to create a contract in restraint of trade. Such contracts may be implied. For example, discussion of price with one's competitors taken together with conscious parallel pricing would establish a violation.

Joint activities by two or more persons that may constitute a contract, combination, or conspiracy in restraint of trade are limitless. The most common form of violation is price-fixing. Agreements relating to territories of operation as well as any other agreement among competitors may be a violation. For example, an agreement by several competitors to buy exclusively from a single supplier is a violation of Section 1. Competition is required when buying as well as when selling. A group boycott may be a violation, even though the victim is just one merchant whose business is so small that its destruction makes little difference to the economy. An attempt to extend the monopolistic economic power of a patent or copyright to unrelated products or services may be a violation. Providing credit to one corporation on the condition that products be purchased from a separate corporation likewise may be illegal.

The acceptance of an invitation to participate in a plan that is in restraint of interstate commerce is sufficient to establish an unlawful conspiracy. Circumstantial evidence may be used to prove a conspiracy. For example, the simultaneous price increases by three major cigarette producers at a time of declining sales were admissible evidence without direct proof of communication among them.

The sections which follow illustrate typical Section 1 cases. The usual remedy is a suit for triple damages. However, some of the examples involve criminal violations and others are cases involving injunctions.

## 2. Price-fixing

Price-fixing agreements among competitors are illegal per se. The term "price-fixing" is not given a literal interpretation. For example, if partners set the price of their goods or services, they have engaged in "price-fixing," but not the type envisioned by the Sherman Act. The price-fixing covered by the Sherman Act is that which threatens free competition. It is no defense to a charge of price-fixing that the prices fixed are fair or reasonable. It also is no defense that price-fixing is engaged in by small competitors to allow them to compete with larger competitors. The per se rule makes price-fixing illegal whether the parties to it have control of the market or not, and whether or not they are trying to raise or lower the market price. It is just as illegal to fix a low price as it is to fix a high price. It is just as illegal to fix the price of services as it is to fix the price of goods. Maximum fee agreements are therefore just as illegal as minimum fee agreements in the service sector. Price-fixing in the service sector has been engaged in by professional persons as well as by service workers, such as automobile and TV repair workers, barbers, and refuse collectors. For many years it was contended that persons performing services were not engaged in trade or commerce. It was also contended that there was a "learned profession" exception to the Sherman Act.

In the mid-1970s, the Supreme Court rejected these arguments and held that the Sherman Act covered services, including those performed by the learned professions such as attorneys at law.

# GOLDFARB ET UX. v. VIRGINIA STATE BAR ET AL.
95 S.Ct. 2004 (1975)

BURGER, J.: We granted certiorari to decide whether a minimum fee schedule for lawyers published by the Fairfax County Bar Association and enforced by the Virginia State Bar violates § 1 of the Sherman Act, 15 U.S.C. § 1....

In 1971 petitioners, husband and wife, contracted to buy a home in Fairfax County, Virginia. The financing agency required them to secure title insurance; this required a title examination, and only a member of the Virginia State Bar could legally perform that service. Petitioners therefore contacted a lawyer who quoted them the precise fee suggested in a minimum fee schedule published by respondent Fairfax County Bar Association; the lawyer told them that it was his policy to keep his charges in line with the minimum fee schedule which provided for a fee of 1% of the value of the property involved. Petitioners then tried to find a lawyer who would examine the title for less than the fee fixed by the schedule. They sent letters to 36 other Fairfax County lawyers requesting their fees. Nineteen replied and none indicated that he would charge less than the rate fixed by the schedule; sev-

eral stated that they knew of no attorney who would do so.

The fee schedule the lawyers referred to is a list of recommended minimum prices for common legal services. Respondent Fairfax County Bar Association published the fee schedule although, as a purely voluntary association of attorneys, the County Bar has no formal power to enforce it. Enforcement has been provided by respondent Virginia State Bar which is the administrative agency through which the Virginia Supreme Court regulates the practice of law in that State; membership in the State Bar is required in order to practice in Virginia. Although the State Bar has never taken formal disciplinary action to compel adherence to any fee schedule, it has published reports condoning fee schedules and has issued two ethical opinions indicating fee schedules cannot be ignored. The most recent opinion states that "evidence that an attorney *habitually* charges less than the suggested minimum fee schedule adopted by his local bar association raises a presumption that such lawyer is guilty of misconduct...."

Because petitioners could not find a lawyer willing to charge a fee lower than the schedule dictated, they had their title examined by the lawyer they had first contacted. They then brought this class action against the State Bar and the County Bar alleging that the operation of the minimum fee schedule, as applied to fees for legal services relating to residential real estate transactions, constitutes price fixing in violation of § 1 of the Sherman Act. Petitioners sought both injunctive relief and damages.

[The Court then reviewed the decisions of the lower courts which had resulted in a denial of relief to petitioners.]

We...are thus confronted for the first time with the question of whether the Sherman Act applies to services performed by attorneys in examining titles in connection with financing the purchase of real estate.

...The County Bar argues that because the fee schedule is merely advisory, the schedule and its enforcement mechanism do not constitute price fixing. Its purpose, the argument continues, is only to provide legitimate information to aid member lawyers in complying with Virginia professional regulations. Moreover the County Bar contends that in practice the schedule has not had the effect of producing fixed fees. The facts found by the trier belie these contentions.... The fee schedule was enforced through the prospect of professional discipline from the State Bar, and the desire of attorneys to comply with announced professional norms, the motivation to conform was reinforced by the assurance that other lawyers would not compete by underbidding. This is not merely a case of an agreement that may be inferred from an exchange of price information, for here a naked agreement was clearly shown, and the effect on prices is plain.

Moreover, in terms of restraining competition and harming consumers like petitioners, the price-fixing activities found here are unusually damaging. A title examination is indispensable in the process of financing a real estate purchase, and since only an attorney licensed to practice in Virginia may legally examine a title, consumers could not turn to alternative sources for the necessary service. All attorneys, of course, were practicing under the constraint of the fee schedule....These factors coalesced to create a pricing system that consumers could not realistically escape. On this record respondent's activities constitute a classic illustration of price fixing.

The County Bar argues that Congress never intended to include the learned professions within the terms "trade or commerce" in § 1 of the Sherman Act, and therefore the sale of professional services is exempt from the Act. No explicit exemption or legislative history is provided to support this contention, rather the existence of state regulation seems to be its primary basis. Also, the County Bar maintains that competition is inconsistent with the practice of a profession because enhancing profit is not the goal of professional activities; the goal is to provide services necessary to the community. That, indeed, is the classic basis traditionally advanced to distinguish professions from trades, businesses, and other occupations, but it loses some of its force when used to support the fee control activities involved here.

In arguing that learned professions are not "trade or commerce" the County Bar seeks a total exclusion from antitrust regulation. Whether state regulation is active or dormant, real or theoretical, lawyers would be able to adopt anticompetitive practices with impunity. We cannot find support for the proposition that Congress intended any such sweeping exclusion. The nature of an occupation, standing alone, does not provide sanctuary from the Sherman Act, nor is the public service aspect of professional practice controlling in determining whether § 1 includes professions. Congress intended to strike as broadly as it could in § 1 of the

Sherman Act, and to read into it so wide an exemption as that urged on us would be at odds with that purpose.

The language of § 1 of the Sherman Act, of course, contains no exception.... Indeed, our cases have specifically included the sale of services within § 1. Whatever else it may be, the examination of a land title is a service; the exchange of such a service for money is "commerce" in the most common usage of that word. It is no disparagement of the practice of law as a profession to acknowledge that it has this business aspect, and is subject to § 1 of the Sherman Act.... In the modern world it cannot be denied that the activities of lawyers play an important part in commercial intercourse, and that anticompetitive activities by lawyers may exert a restraint on commerce.

In *Parker v. Brown* 317 U.S. 341 (1943), the Court held that an anticompetitive marketing program "which derived its authority and efficacy from the legislative command of the state" was not a violation of the Sherman Act because the Act was intended to regulate private practices and not to prohibit a State from imposing a restraint as an act of government. Respondent State Bar and respondent County Bar both seek to avail themselves of this so-called state action exemption....

The threshold inquiry in determining if an anticompetitive activity is state action of the type the Sherman Act was not meant to proscribe is whether the activity is required by the State acting as sovereign. Here we need not inquire further into the state action question because it cannot fairly be said that the State of Virginia through its Supreme Court Rules required the anticompetitive activities of either respondent. Respondents have pointed to no Virginia statute requiring their activities....[*Reversed and remanded.*]

---

As a result of the foregoing case, the cost of legal services for real estate transactions was reduced significantly in the area involved. Price competition in the service sector is lowering such prices, and the threat of triple damage suits is forcing the abandonment of price-fixing activities by many groups which had actively engaged in them prior to 1975.

Some professional groups have attempted to avoid laws restricting price-fixing through the use of ethical standards. Others have attempted to determine the price of services indirectly by using formulas and relative value scales. For example, some medical organizations have determined that a given medical procedure would be allocated a relative value on a scale of one to ten. Open-heart surgery might be labeled a nine and an appendectomy a three. All members of the profession would then use these values in determining professional fees. Such attempts have been uniformly held to be illegal.

The case which follows is typical of those in which an ethical standard came into conflict with the Sherman Act's ban on limiting competition. While such ethical standards are not illegal per se, they are nevertheless anticompetitive and a violation of the Sherman Act. While not a form of price-fixing, the ethical standards in this case prevented price competition.

# NATIONAL SOCIETY OF PROFESSIONAL ENGINEERS v. UNITED STATES

98 S.Ct. 1355 (1978)

STEVENS, J.: This is a civil antitrust case brought by the United States to nullify an association's canon of ethics prohibiting competitive bidding by its members. The question is whether the canon may be justified under the Sherman Act, 15 U.S.C. Section 1 et seq., because it was adopted by members of a learned profession for the purpose of minimizing the risk that competition would produce inferior engineering work endangering the public safety. The District Court rejected this justification without making any findings on the likelihood that competition would produce the dire consequences foreseen by the association. The Court of Appeals affirmed. We granted certiorari,…we affirm.…

The charges of a consulting engineer may be computed in different ways. He may charge the client a percentage of the cost of the project, may set his fee at his actual cost plus overhead plus a reasonable profit, may charge fixed rates per hour for different types of work, may perform an assignment for a specific sum, or he may combine one or more of these approaches. Suggested fee schedules for particular types of services in certain areas have been promulgated from time to time by various local societies. This case does not, however, involve any claim that the National Society has tried to fix specific fees, or even a specific method of calculating fees. It involves a charge that the members of the Society have unlawfully agreed to refuse to negotiate or even to discuss the question of fees until after a prospective client has selected the engineer for a particular project. Evidence of this agreement is found in Section 11(c) of the Society's Code of Ethics, adopted in July 1964.

The District Court found that the Society's Board of Ethical Review has uniformly interpreted the "ethical rules against competitive bidding for engineering services as prohibiting the submission of any form of price information to a prospective customer which would enable that customer to make a price comparison on engineering services." If the client requires that such information be provided, then Section 11(c) imposes an obligation upon the engineering firm to withdraw from consideration for that job. The Society's Code of Ethics thus "prohibits engineers from both soliciting and submitting such price information," and seeks to preserve the profession's "traditional" method of selecting professional engineers. Under the traditional method, the client initially selects an engineer on the basis of background and reputation, not price.

In 1972 the Government filed its complaint against the Society alleging that members had agreed to abide by canons of ethics prohibiting the submission of competitive bids for engineering services and that, in consequence, price competition among the members had been suppressed and customers had been deprived of the benefits of free and open competition. The complaint prayed for an injunction terminating the unlawful agreement.

In its answer the Society admitted the essential facts alleged by the Government and…in defense…averred that the standard set out in the Code of Ethics was reasonable because competition among professional engineers was contrary to the public interest. It was averred that it would be cheaper and easier for an engineer "to design and specify inefficient and unnecessarily expensive structures and methods of construction." Accordingly, competitive pressure to offer engineering services at the lowest possible price would adversely affect the quality of engineering. Moreover, the practice of awarding engineering contracts to the lowest bidder, regardless of quality, would be dangerous to the public health, safety and welfare. For these reasons, the Society claimed that its Code of Ethics was not an "unreasonable restraint of interstate trade or commerce." (The lower courts held that the canon was a per se violation of Section 1 and illegal without regard to claimed or possible benefits.)

[After reviewing the rule of reason the court continued.]

Price is the "central nervous system of the economy," and an agreement that "interferes with the setting of price by free market forces" is illegal on its face. In this case we are presented with an agreement among competitors to refuse to discuss prices with potential customers until after negotiations have resulted in the initial selection of an engineer. While this is not price fixing as such, no elaborate industry analysis is required to demonstrate the anticompetitive character of such an agreement. It operates as an absolute ban on competitive bidding, applying with equal force to both complicated and simple projects and to both inexperienced and sophisticated customers. As the District Court found, the ban "impedes the ordinary give and take of the market place" and substantially deprives the customer of "the ability to utilize and compare prices in selecting engineering services." On its face, this agreement restrains trade within the meaning of Section 1 of the Sherman Act....

The Sherman Act does not require competitive bidding; it prohibits unreasonable restraints on competition. Petitioner's ban on competitive bidding prevents all customers from making price comparisons in the initial selection of an engineer, and im-

poses the Society's views of the costs and benefits of competition on the entire market place. It is this restraint that must be justified under the Rule of Reason, and petitioner's attempt to do so on the basis of the potential threat that competition poses to the public safety and the ethics of its profession is nothing less than a frontal assault on the basic policy of the Sherman Act.

The Sherman Act reflects a legislative judgment that ultimately competition will not only produce lower prices, but also better goods and services. "The heart of our national economic policy long has been faith in the value of competition." The assumption that competition is the best method of allocating resources in a free market recognizes that all elements of a bargain—quality, service, safety, and durability—and not just the immediate cost, are favorably affected by the free opportunity to select among alternative offers. Even assuming occasional exceptions to the presumed consequences of competition, the statutory policy precludes inquiry into the question whether competition is good or bad.

The fact that engineers are often involved in large-scale projects significantly affecting the public safety does not alter our analysis. Exceptions to the Sherman Act for potentially dangerous goods and services would be tantamount to a repeal of the statute. In our complex economy the number of items that may cause serious harm is almost endless—automobiles, drugs, foods, aircraft components, heavy equipment, and countless others, cause serious harm to individuals or to the public at large if defectively made. The judiciary cannot indirectly protect the public against this harm by conferring monopoly privileges on the manufacturers....

In sum, the Rule of Reason does not support a defense based on the assumption that competition itself is unreasonable.... [*Affirmed.*]

## 3. Resale Price Maintenance: Vertical Price-Fixing

Manufacturers frequently seek to control the ultimate retail price for their products. These efforts result in part from the desire to maintain a high-quality product image, the assumption being that a relatively high price establishes quality. These efforts are also based on a desire to maintain adequate channels of distribution. If one retailer is selling a product at prices significantly below those of other retailers, there is a strong likelihood that the other retailers will not continue to carry the product.

At one time, retail price maintenance was based on state fair trade laws. Congress had authorized states to enact fair trade laws as an exception to the Sherman Act. These fair trade laws allowed manufacturers to enter into contracts with one or more retailers, setting the minimum price for products. The provisions of these contracts were then binding on all sellers in that state, and in effect nonsigners of the contract could not sell below the agreed-upon price without being in breach of contract. In the 1970s, the fair trade exception to the Sherman Act was repealed, and state fair trade laws and the contracts entered into pursuant to them were thus illegal.

Although most **resale price-maintenance** schemes run afoul of the Sherman Act, it is possible for a manufacturer to effectively control the resale price of its products. The primary method of legally controlling the retail price is for a manufacturer to simply announce its prices and refuse to deal with those who fail to comply. This practice is commonly referred to as the **Colgate Doctrine.** The Colgate Doctrine recognizes that independent action by a manufacturer is not a per se violation of the Sherman Act. The *Monsanto* case on page 703 illustrated that although price-fixing is illegal per se, there must be concerted action and not simply a refusal to deal with distributors who do not comply with the announced price policy. The Colgate Doctrine will justify resale price-maintenance only if there is no coercion or pressure other than the announced policy and its implementation. If the manufacturer sits down with the distributor or retailer and gets an agreement that the parties will comply, then there is a violation of Section 1 of the Sherman Act. The Colgate Doctrine only allows the announcement of prices and refusal to deal with those who do not comply.

Other methods of maintaining retail prices have been attempted. For example, real estate leases and equipment leases sometimes contain provisions allowing the lessor to set the prices to be charged by the lessee. Such leases are illegal because there is usually coercion present. Another example of attempted retail price maintenance is the use of a **consignment** contract. In a consignment, the consignor retains title to the property and the consignee has possession. The consignee is paid a commission if he or she sells the property. Since the property belongs to the consignor, she or he is entitled to determine the price for its product. Art objects and racehorses are frequently sold on consignment. However, the consignment technique may not be used to subvert the antitrust laws.

Not every consignment of common goods which attempts to control retail price is illegal. For example, a bakery consigned its products to wholesalers under an arrangement by which the bakery fixed the wholesale prices to be paid by retailers who receive the goods from the distributors. This was not a violation. The prices were wholesale prices, and the bakery bore the burden of risk during the consignment period.

Whether or not **vertical price-fixing** should be illegal per se has been a matter of debate among economists and politicians. There is a possibility that a vertical restraint imposed by a single manufacturer or wholesaler may stimulate interbrand competition as it reduces intrabrand competition. Nevertheless, Congress in 1984 adopted a resolution condemning vertical price-fixing. The resolution indicated Congress' attitude that vertical price-fixing is just as bad as horizontal price-fixing and, therefore, should be illegal per se. Since Congress has spoken, vertical price-fixing is now just as illegal as horizontal price-fixing.

### 4. Other Vertical Restraints

Sometimes one competitor complains to a manufacturer about the conduct of another competitor, especially when that conduct consists of lowering prices to the extent that the complaining competitor cannot compete. Is it legal for a manufacturer to impose restraints on one competitor at the request of the other? Is such conduct illegal per se or is it subject to the rule of reason? Is there a difference between restraints that are directed at price and those that are not? The case which follows discusses these issues.

# BUSINESS ELECTRONICS CORPORATION v. SHARP ELECTRONICS CORPORATION
108 S.Ct. 1515 (1988)

SCALIA, J.:...In 1968, petitioner (Business Electronics Corporation) became the exclusive retailer in the Houston, Texas area of electronic calculators manufactured by respondent Sharp Electronics Corporation. In 1972, respondent appointed Gilbert Hartwell as a second retailer in the Houston area. During the relevant period, electronic calculators were primarily sold to business customers for prices up to $1000....Petitioner's retail prices were often below respondent's suggested retail prices and generally below Hartwell's retail prices, even though Hartwell too sometimes priced below respondent's suggested retail prices. Hartwell complained to respondent on a number of occasions about petitioner's prices. In June 1973, Hartwell gave respondent the ultimatum that Hartwell would terminate his dealership unless respondent ended its relationship with petitioner within 30 days. Respondent terminated petitioner's dealership in July 1973.

Petitioner brought suit…alleging that respondent and Hartwell had conspired to terminate petitioner and that such conspiracy was illegal *per se* under § 1 of the Sherman Act….[The District Court found in favor of the petitioner but the Fifth Circuit Court of Appeals reversed.] It held that, to render illegal *per se* a vertical agreement between a manufacturer and a dealer to terminate a second dealer, the first dealer "must expressly or impliedly agree to set its prices at some level, though not a specific one. The distributor cannot retain complete freedom to set whatever price it chooses."

Section 1 of the Sherman Act provides that "every contract, combination in the form of trust or otherwise, or conspiracy, in restraint of trade or commerce among the several States, or with foreign nations, is declared to be illegal." Since the earliest decisions of this Court interpreting this provision, we have recognized that it was intended to prohibit only unreasonable restraints of trade. Ordinarily, whether particular concerted action violates § 1 of the Sherman Act is determined through case-by-case application of the so-called rule of reason—that is, "the factfinder weighs all of the circumstances of a case in deciding whether a restrictive practice should be prohibited as imposing an unreasonable restraint on competition." Certain categories of agreements, however, have been held to be *per se* illegal, dispensing with the need for case-by-case evaluation. We have said that *per se* rules are appropriate only for "conduct that is manifestly anticompetitive," that is, conduct "'that would always or almost always tend to restrict competition and decrease output,'"…

Although vertical agreements on resale prices have been illegal *per se* since 1911, we have recognized that the scope of *per se* illegality should be narrow in the context of vertical restraints.…

We refused to extend *per se* illegality to vertical nonprice restraints, specifically to a manufacturer's termination of one dealer pursuant to an exclusive territory agreement with another. We noted that especially in the vertical restraint context "departure from the rule-of-reason standard must be based on demonstrable economic effect rather than…upon formalistic line drawing." We concluded that vertical nonprice restraints had not been shown…to justify *per se* illegality. Rather, we found, they had real potential to stimulate interbrand competition, "the primary concern of antitrust law."

Moreover, we observed that a rule of *per se* illegality for vertical nonprice restraints was not needed or effective to protect *intra* brand competition. First, so long as interbrand competition existed, that would provide a "significant check" on any attempt to exploit intrabrand market power. In fact, in order to meet that interbrand competition, a manufacturer's dominant incentive is to lower resale prices. Second, the *per se* illegality of vertical restraints would create a perverse incentive for manufacturers to integrate vertically into distribution, an outcome hardly conducive to fostering the creation and maintenance of small businesses.…

There has been no showing here that an agreement between a manufacturer and a dealer to terminate a "price cutter," without a further agreement on the price or price levels to be charged by the remaining dealer, almost always tends to restrict competition and reduce output.…

Any agreement between a manufacturer and a dealer to terminate another dealer who happens to have charged lower prices can be alleged to have been directed against the terminated dealer's "price cutting." In the vast majority of cases, it will be extremely difficult for the manufacturer to convince a jury that its motivation was to ensure adequate services, since price cutting and some measure of service cutting usually go hand in hand. Accordingly, a manufacturer that agrees to give one dealer an exclusive territory and terminates another dealer pursuant to that agreement, or even a manufacturer that agrees with one dealer to terminate another for failure to provide contractually-obligated services, exposes itself to the highly plausible claim that its real motivation was to terminate a price cutter. Moreover, even vertical restraints that do not result in dealer termination, such as the initial granting of an exclusive territory or the requirement that certain services be provided, can be attacked as designed to allow existing dealers to charge higher prices....

We cannot avoid this difficulty by invalidating as illegal *per se* only those agreements imposing vertical restraints that contain the word "price," or that affect the "prices" charged by dealers....As the above discussion indicates, all vertical restraints...have the potential to allow dealers to increase "prices" and can be characterized as intended to achieve just that. In fact, vertical nonprice restraints only accomplish the benefits identified...because they reduce intrabrand price competition to the point where the dealer's profit margin permits provision of the desired services....The manufacturer often will want to ensure that its distributors earn sufficient profit to pay for programs such as hiring and training additional salesmen or demonstrating the technical features of the product....

In resting our decision upon the foregoing economic analysis, we do not ignore common-law precedent concerning what constituted "restraint of trade" at the time the Sherman Act was adopted. But neither do we give that pre-1890 precedent the dispositive effect some would. The term "restraint of trade" in the statute, like the term at common law, refers not to a particular list of agreements, but to a particular economic consequence, which may be produced by quite different sorts of agreements in varying times and circumstances....

The Sherman Act adopted the term "restraint of trade" along with its dynamic potential. It invokes the common law itself, and not merely the static content that the common law had assigned to the term in 1890. If it were otherwise, not only would the line of *per se* illegality have to be drawn today precisely where it was in 1890, but also case-by-case evaluation of legality (conducted where *per se* rules do not apply) would have to be governed by 19th-century notions of reasonableness. It would make no sense to create out of the single term "restraint of trade" a chronologically schizoid statute, in which a "rule of reason" evolves with new circumstances and new wisdom, but a line of *per se* illegality remains forever fixed where it was.

Of course the common law, both in general and as embodied in the Sherman Act, does not lightly assume that the economic realities underlying earlier decisions have changed, or that earlier judicial perceptions of those realities were in error. It is relevant, therefore, whether the common law of restraint of trade ever prohibited as illegal *per se* an agreement of the sort made here, and whether our decisions under § 1 of the Sherman Act have ever expressed or necessarily implied such a prohibition....

[The court reviewed previous decisions concerning the analysis used under § 1 of the Sherman Act and concluded as follows:] In sum, economic analysis supports the view, and no precedent opposes it, that a vertical restraint is not illegal *per se* unless it includes some agreement on price or price levels. Accordingly, the judgment of the Fifth Circuit is [*Affirmed.*]

### 5. Concerted Activities by Competitors

Concerted activities among competitors take a variety of forms and appear in diverse circumstances. Some arise out of a desire to protect a channel of distribution or a marketing system. Others result from attempts to keep marginal competitors in business, which is, in fact, one goal of the antitrust laws. Thus, some cases dealing with concerted activities actually involve conflicts between various competing goals of the antitrust laws.

In the next case, the concerted activity among competitors took the form of an exchange of price information. Economic theory was used to support the assumption that prices would be more unstable and lower if the information had not been exchanged. Conduct directed at price stabilization is per se anticompetitive.

# UNITED STATES v. CONTAINER CORPORATION OF AMERICA
89 S.Ct. 510 (1969)

DOUGLAS, J.: This is a civil antitrust action charging a price-fixing agreement in violation of § 1 of the Sherman Act....

The case as proved is unlike any other price decisions we have rendered. There was here an exchange of price information but no agreement to adhere to a price schedule....There was here an exchange of information concerning specific sales to identified customers, not a statistical report on the average cost to all members, without identifying the parties to specific transactions....While there was present here, as in *Cement Manufacturers Protective Assn. v. United States* 268 U.S. 588, an exchange of prices to specific customers, there was absent the controlling circumstance, *viz.*, that cement manufacturers, to protect themselves from delivering to contractors more cement than was needed for a specific job and thus receiving a lower price, exchanged price information as a means of protecting their legal rights from fraudulent inducements to deliver more cement than needed for a specific job.

Here all that was done was a request by each defendant from its competitor for information as to the most recent price charged or quoted, whenever it needed such information and whenever it was not available from another source. Each defendant on receiving that request furnished the data with the expectation that he would be furnished reciprocal information when he wanted it. That concerted action is of course sufficient to establish the combination or conspiracy, the initial ingredient of a violation of § 1 of the Sherman Act.

There was of course freedom to withdraw from the agreement. But the fact remains that when a defendant requested and received price information, it was affirming its willingness to furnish such information in return.

There was to be sure an infrequency and irregularity of price exchanges between the defendants; and often the data was available from the records of the defendants or from the customers themselves. Yet the essence of the agreement was to furnish price information whenever requested.

Moreover, although the most recent price charged or quoted was sometimes fragmentary, each defendant had the manuals with which it could compute the price charged by a competitor on a specific order to a specific customer.

Further, the price quoted was the current price which a customer would need pay in order to obtain products from the defendant furnishing the data.

The defendants account for about 90% of the shipment of corrugated containers from plants in the southeastern United States. While containers vary as to dimensions, weight, color, and so on, they are substantially identical, no matter who produces them, when made to particular specifications. The prices paid depend on price alternatives. Suppliers when seeking new or additional business or keeping old customers, do not exceed a competitor's price. It is common for purchasers to buy from two or more suppliers concurrently. A defendant supplying a customer with containers would usually quote the same price on additional orders, unless costs had changed. Yet where a competitor was charging a particular price, a defendant would normally quote the same price or even a lower price.

The exchange of price information seemed to have the effect of keeping prices within a fairly narrow ambit. Capacity has exceeded the demand from 1955 to 1963, the period covered by the complaint, and the trend of corrugated container prices has been downward. Yet despite this excess capacity and the downward trend of prices, the industry has expanded in the Southeast from 30 manufacturers with 49 plants to 51 manufacturers with 98 plants. An abundance of raw materials and machinery makes entry into the industry easy with an investment of $50,000 to $75,000.

The result of this reciprocal exchange of prices was to stabilize prices though at a downward level. Knowledge of a competitor's price usually meant matching that price. The continuation of some price competition is not fatal to the Government's case. The limitation or reduction of price competition brings the case within the ban, for…interference with the setting of price by free market forces is unlawful *per se*. Price information exchanged in some markets may have no effect on a truly competitive price. But the corrugated container industry is dominated by relatively few sellers. The product is fungible and the competition for sales is price. The demand is inelastic, as buyers place orders only for immediate, short-run needs. The exchange of price data tends toward price uniformity. For a lower price does not mean a larger share of the available business but a sharing of the existing business at a lower return. Stabilizing prices as well as raising them is within the ban of § 1 of the Sherman Act. As we said in *United States v. Socony Vacuum Oil Co.,* "in terms of market operations stabilization is but one form of manipulation." The inferences are irresistible that the exchange of price information has had an anticompetitive effect in the industry, chilling the vigor of price competition.…

Price is too critical, too sensitive a control to allow it to be used even in an informal manner to restrain competition. [*Reversed.*]

Typical of the cases involving concerted activities was a 1981 suit filed against the National Association of Broadcasters, charging that its "over-commercialization" rules improperly regulated the amount and format of advertising on television in violation of the Sherman Act. The code had the effect of curtailing and restricting the quantity of broadcast time available for television advertising and the number and format of advertisements that could be broadcast. The challenged rules put varying limits on the amount of "nonprogram material" aired every hour. In prime time, the hourly limit was nine and one-half minutes, plus thirty seconds for promotional announcements. At other times, it was generally sixteen minutes; however, children's shows were allowed nine and one-half minutes on weekends and twelve minutes during the week. Other rules limited the number of consecutive announcements and the number of interruptions within programs. A consent decree was entered stopping the practice. The rules on the number of broadcasts were not per se violations. However, a rule prohibiting more than one product being advertised in a commercial lasting less than sixty seconds was a per se violation.

In 1984, the televising of college football games was the subject matter of a significant antitrust suit. It was filed by two football powers, the University of Georgia and the University of Oklahoma, against the National Collegiate Athletic Association (NCAA). The NCAA had adopted a plan to limit television of college football games in order to prevent adverse effect on game attendance. The number of television games was limited, as was the number of appearances by any one school. Television receipts were divided among participating schools. The Supreme Court held that the agreements were a violation of the Sherman Act and a form of price-fixing, as well as a group boycott. The plan raised prices and reduced output without regard to consumer preference. The plan was basically anticompetitive, and there was no evidence to justify its existence.

Competitors sometimes attempt to share some activities or join together in the performance of a function. Joint research efforts to find a cure for cancer or to find substitutes for gasoline would seem to provide significant benefits to society. A sharing of technology may be beneficial also. Joint efforts in other areas may reduce costs and improve efficiency. For example, several professional football teams share the information of a college scouting organization. Joint operations may violate the Sherman Act.

## 6. Agreements Relating to Territory

Territorial agreements may be either horizontal or vertical. A horizontal agreement would be entered into by competing businesses for the purpose of giving each an exclusive territory. For example, if all Oldsmobile dealers in state X agreed to allocate to each an exclusive territory, a horizontal arrangement would exist. It would be illegal per se under the Sherman Act.

This is true even if the arrangement is made by a third party. For example, an agreement among competing cable television operators to divide the market in Houston, Texas, was a per se violation even though the agreement required city council approval.

A vertical agreement is one between a manufacturer and a dealer or distributor. It assigns the dealer or distributor an exclusive territory, and the manufacturer agrees not to sell to other dealers or distributors in that territory in exchange for an agreement by the dealer that it will not operate outside the area assigned. Such agreements are usually part of a franchise or license agreement, and while they are not per se violations, they may nevertheless be illegal. The case which follows explains why such agreements are subject to the rule of reason.

# CONTINENTAL T.V., INC. v. GTE SYLVANIA, INC.
97 S.Ct. 2549 (1977)

GTE (Sylvania), in order to improve its market position, limits the number of retail franchises granted for any given area. It requires each franchisee to sell its television sets only from the location or locations at which it is franchised. At one time, Sylvania had distributed its television sets through wholesalers. Its plan to distribute through franchised retailers rather than through wholesalers was developed after it suffered a significant reduction in its market share. It was decided that only aggressive and competent retailers should be allowed to sell its televisions. However, franchisees were not given exclusive territories.

This suit was brought by one of the franchised retailers (Continental) after Sylvania had granted an additional franchise within approximately 1 mile of Continental's place of business. Sylvania had also denied petitioner a franchise in another area. These decisions ruptured the franchiser-franchisee relationship between the parties and ultimately resulted in a lawsuit by Sylvania to recover money owed by Continental. Conti-

nental, in defense, alleged a violation of Section 1 of the Sherman Act.

The trial judge rejected Sylvania's jury instruction that the location restriction was illegal only if it unreasonably restrained or oppressed competition. Instead, the court instructed the jury that it was a per se violation if Sylvania attempted to restrict the locations from which the retailers resold merchandise purchased from it. The jury found for Continental and assessed triple damages. The Court of Appeals reversed, holding that the restriction should be judged under the rule of reason. The Supreme Court granted certiorari.

POWELL, J.:...Franchise agreements between manufacturers and retailers frequently include provisions barring the retailers from selling franchised products from locations other than those specified in the agreements. This case presents important questions concerning the appropriate antitrust analysis of these restrictions under Section 1 of the Sherman Act…and the Court's decision in *United States v. Arnold, Schwinn & Co.*, 388 U.S. 365, (1967).

We turn first to Continental's contention that Sylvania's restriction on retail locations is a per se violation of Section 1 of the Sherman Act as interpreted in Schwinn.

…[In Schwinn] the Court proceeded to articulate the following "bright line" per se rule of illegality for vertical restrictions: "Under the Sherman Act, it is unreasonable without more for a manufacturer to seek to restrict and confine areas or persons with whom an article may be traded after the manufacturer has parted with dominion over it." But the Court expressly stated that the rule of reason governs when "the manufacturer retains title, dominion, and risk with respect to the product and the position and function of the dealer in question are, in fact, indistinguishable from those of an agent or salesman of the manufacturer."…

In the present case, it is undisputed that title to the television sets passed from Sylvania to Continental. Thus, the Schwinn per se rule applies unless Sylvania's restriction on location falls outside Schwinn's prohibition against a manufacturer's attempting to restrict a "retailer's freedom as to where and to whom it will resell the products."… The language of Schwinn is clearly broad enough to apply to the present case.…

Both Schwinn and Sylvania sought to reduce but not to eliminate competition among their respective retailers through the adoption of a franchise system.…The Schwinn franchise plan included a location restriction similar to the one challenged here. These restrictions allowed Schwinn and Sylvania to regulate the amount of competition among their retailers by preventing a franchisee from selling franchised products from outlets other than the one covered by the franchise agreement.…

Sylvania argues that if Schwinn cannot be distinguished, it should be reconsidered.… We are convinced that the need for clarification of the law in this area justifies reconsideration. Schwinn itself was an abrupt and largely unexplained departure from *White Motor Co. v. United States*, 372 U.S. 253, (1963), where only four years earlier the Court had refused to endorse a per se rule for vertical restrictions. Since its announcement, Schwinn has been the subject of continuing controversy and confusion, both in the scholarly journals and in the federal courts.…In our view, the experience of the past 10 years should be brought to bear on this subject of considerable commercial importance.

The traditional framework of analysis under § 1 of the Sherman Act is familiar and does not require extended discussion. § 1 prohibits "every contract, combination… or conspiracy, in restraint of trade or commerce." Since the early years of this century a judicial gloss on this statutory language has established the "rule of reason" as the prevailing standard of analysis. Under this rule, the fact-finder weighs all of the circumstances of a case in deciding whether a restrictive practice should be prohibited as imposing an unreasonable restraint on competition.

Per se rules of illegality are appropriate only when they relate to conduct that is manifestly anticompetitive. As the Court explained in *Northern Pac. R. Co. v. United States*, 356 U.S. 1,5, (1958), "there are certain agreements or practices which because of their pernicious effect on competition and lack of any redeeming virtue are conclusively presumed to be unreasonable and therefore illegal without elaborate inquiry as to the precise harm they have caused or the business excuse for their use."

In essence, the issue before us is whether Schwinn's per se rule can be justified under the demanding standards of Northern Pac. R. Co. We turn now to consider Schwinn in light of Northern Pac. R. Co....

The market impact of vertical restrictions is complex because of their potential for a simultaneous reduction of intrabrand competition and stimulation of interbrand competition. Significantly, the Court in Schwinn did not distinguish among the challenged restrictions on the basis of their individual potential for intrabrand harm or interbrand benefit....The pivotal factor was the passage of title: All restrictions were held to be per se illegal where title had passed, and all were evaluated and sustained under the rule of reason where it had not.

...Nonsale transactions appear to be excluded from the per se rule, not because of a greater danger of intrabrand harm or a greater promise of interbrand benefit, but rather because of the Court's unexplained belief that a complete per se prohibition would be too "inflexible."...

Vertical restrictions promote interbrand competition by allowing the manufacturer to achieve certain efficiencies in the distribution of his products. These "redeeming virtues" are implicit in every decision sustaining vertical restrictions under the rule of reason. Economists have identified a number of ways in which manufacturers can use such restrictions to compete more effectively against other manufacturers. For example, new manufacturers and manufacturers entering new markets can use the restrictions in order to induce competent and aggressive retailers to make the kind of investment of capital and labor that is often required in the distribution of products unknown to the consumer. Established manufacturers can use them to induce retailers to engage in promotional activities or to provide service and repair facilities necessary to the efficient marketing of their products. Service and repair are vital for many products, such as automobiles and major household appliances.

The availability and quality of such services affect a manufacturer's goodwill and the competitiveness of his product. Because of market imperfections such as the so-called "free rider" effect, these services might not be provided by retailers in a purely competitive situation, despite the fact that each retailer's benefit would be greater if all provided the services than if none did.

Economists also have argued that manufacturers have an economic interest in maintaining as much intrabrand competition as is consistent with the efficient distribution of their products. Although the view that the manufacturer's interest necessarily corresponds with that of the public is not universally shared, even the leading critic of vertical restrictions concedes that Schwinn's distinction between sale and nonsale transactions is essentially unrelated to any relevant economic impact. Indeed, to the extent that the form of the transaction is related to interbrand benefits, the Court's distinction is inconsistent with its articulated concern for the ability of smaller firms to compete effectively with larger ones. Capital requirements and administrative expenses may prevent smaller firms from using the exception for nonsale transactions.

We conclude that the distinction drawn in Schwinn between sale and nonsale transactions is not sufficient to justify the application of a per se rule in one situation and a rule of reason in the other. The question remains whether the per se rule stated in Schwinn should be expanded to include nonsale transactions or abandoned in favor of a return to the rule of reason. We have found no persuasive support for expanding the per se rule....

We revert to the standard articulated in *Northern Pac. R. Co,* and reiterated in *White Motor,* for determining whether vertical restrictions must be "conclusively presumed to be unreasonable and therefore illegal without elaborate inquiry as to the precise harm they have caused or the business excuse for their use." Such restrictions, in varying forms, are widely used in our free market economy. As indicated above, there is substantial scholarly and judicial authority supporting their economic utility. There is relatively little authority to the contrary. Certainly, there has been no showing in this case, either generally or with respect to Sylvania's agreements, that vertical restrictions have or are likely to have a "pernicious effect on competition" or that they "lack...

any redeeming virtue." Accordingly, we conclude that the per se rule stated in Schwinn must be overruled....

In sum, we conclude that the appropriate decision is to return to the rule of reason that governed vertical restrictions prior to Schwinn. When anticompetitive effects are shown to result from particular vertical restrictions they can be adequately policed under the rule of reason, the standard traditionally applied for the majority of anticompetitive practices challenged under § 1 of the Act. [*Affirmed.*]

---

A vertical territorial restriction may be illegal and may result in the awarding of triple damages. If a plaintiff can establish that the interbrand market structure is such that intrabrand competition is a critical source of competitive pressure on price, a plaintiff may recover triple damages. The plaintiff is required to show the nature and effect of the territorial restriction were it to adversely affect market competition.

# MONOPOLY

## 7. Section 2: The Rationale

Competition tends to keep private markets working in ways that are socially desirable. It encourages an efficient allocation of resources, stimulates efficiency and product innovation, and may even encourage the conservation of scarce resources. Competition also tends to limit private economic power and substitutes individual decisions for government regulation. Of course, a competitive system that allows easy entry and withdrawal from the marketplace is consistent with individual freedom and economic opportunity. Therefore, it is not surprising that the Sherman Act attacks monopoly and attempts to monopolize.

In *United States v. Aluminum Company of America*[1] Circuit Judge Learned Hand commented on the purposes and philosophy of Section 2 of the Sherman Act. In holding that Alcoa was guilty of a violation of Section 2 for

---

[1]148 F.2d 416 (1945).

having intentionally acquired and maintained control of over 90 percent of the domestic "virgin" ingot market in aluminum, even though Alcoa had not misused such monopoly power to obtain exorbitant profits, Judge Hand said:

> ...it is no excuse for "monopolizing" a market that the monopoly has not been used to extract from the consumer more than a "fair" profit. The Act has wider purposes. Indeed, even though we disregard all but economic considerations, it would by no means follow that such concentration of producing power is to be desired, when it has not been used extortionately. Many people believe that possession of unchallenged economic power deadens initiative, discourages thrift and depresses energy; that immunity from competition is a narcotic, and rivalry is a stimulant, to industrial progress; that the spur of constant stress is necessary to counteract an inevitable disposition to let well enough alone. Such people believe that competitors, versed in the craft as no consumer can be, will be quick to detect opportunities for saving and new shifts in production, and be eager to profit by them. In any event the mere fact that a producer, having command of the domestic market, has not been able to make more than a "fair" profit, is no evidence that a "fair" profit could not have been made at lower prices....True, it might have been thought adequate to condemn only those monopolies which could not show that they had exercised the highest possible ingenuity, had adopted every possible economy, had anticipated every conceivable improvement, stimulated every possible demand. No doubt, that would be one way of dealing with the matter, although it would imply constant scrutiny and constant supervision, such as courts are unable to provide. Be that as it may, that was not the way that Congress chose; it did not condone "good trusts" and condemn "bad" ones; it forbade all. Moreover, in so doing, it was not necessarily actuated by economic motives alone. It is possible, because of its indirect social or moral effect, to prefer a system of small producers, each dependent for his success upon his own skill and character, to one in which the great mass of those engaged must accept the direction of a few....

Judge Hand indicated that, besides the economic reasons behind the Sherman Act's proscription of monopoly,

> ...there are others, based upon the belief that great industrial consolidations are inherently undesirable, regardless of their economic results. In the debates in Congress Senator Sherman himself...showed that among the purposes of Congress in 1890 was a desire to put an end to great aggregations of capital because of the helplessness of the individual before them....Throughout the history of these statutes it has been constantly assumed that one of their purposes was to perpetuate and preserve, for its own sake and in spite of possible cost, an organization of industry in small units, which can effectively compete with each other....

In 1958, Justice Black in *Northern Pacific Ry. Co. v. United States*, 356 U.S. 1, discussed the purpose of the Sherman Act. He stated in part:

The Sherman Act was designed to be a comprehensive charter of economic liberty aimed at preserving free and unfettered competition as the rule of trade. It rests on the premise that the unrestrained interaction of competitive forces will yield the best allocation of our economic resources, the lowest prices, the highest quality and the greatest material progress, while at the same time providing an environment conducive to the preservation of our democratic political and social institutions.

## 8.   Section 2: The Approach

Under Section 2, it is a violation for a firm to: (1) monopolize, (2) attempt to monopolize, or (3) conspire to monopolize any part of interstate or foreign commerce. Attempts to monopolize cases require proof of intent to destroy competition or achieve monopoly power. This is most difficult and, as a result, there have been few cases concerning attempts to monopolize. A conspiracy to monopolize requires proof of specific intent to monopolize and at least one overt act to accomplish it. Proof of monopoly power or even that it was attainable is not required. This conspiracy theory is usually joined with the allegation of actual monopoly in most cases.

A firm has violated Section 2 if it followed a course of conduct through which it obtained the power to control price or exclude competition. The mere possession of monopoly power is not a violation. There must be proof that the power resulted from a deliberate course of conduct or proof of intent to maintain the power by conduct. Proof of deliberateness is just as essential as is proof of the power to control price to exclude competition.

Section 2 Sherman Act cases require proof of market power—the power to affect the price of the firm's products in the market. Whether such power exists is usually determined by an analysis of the reaction of buyers to price changes by the alleged monopolist seller. Such cases require a definition of the relevant market and a study of the degree of concentration within the market. Barriers to entry are analyzed, and the greater the barriers, the greater the significance of market share. The legal issues in such cases require structural analysis.

In defining the relevant market, the courts examine both product market and geographic market. A relevant market is the smallest one wide enough so that products from outside the geographic area or from other producers in the same area cannot compete with those included in the defined relevant market. In other words, if prices are raised or supply is curtailed within a given area while demand remains constant, will products from other areas or other products from within the area enter the market in enough quantity to force a lower price or increased supply?

Some monopoly cases involve homogeneous products, whereas others involve products for which there are numerous substitutes. For example, aluminum may be considered a product that is generally homogeneous. If a firm has 90 percent of the virgin aluminum market, a violation would be established. However, if a firm had 90 percent of the Danish coffee cake market, the decision is less clear, because numerous products compete with Danish coffee cakes as a breakfast product. The relevant product is often difficult to define because of differences in products, substitute products, product diversification, and even product clusters.

Section 2 cases may involve a variety of proofs and many different forms of economic analysis. The degree of market concentration, barriers to entry, structural features such as market shares of other firms, profit levels, the extent to which prices respond to changes in supply and demand, whether or not a firm discriminates in price between its customers, and the absolute size of the firm are all factors usually considered by courts in monopoly cases. In addition, courts examine the conduct of the firm. How did it achieve its market share? Was it by internal growth or acquisition? Does the firm's current conduct tend to injure competition? These and other issues are important aspects in any finding of the existence of monopoly power. Note that in the case which follows the illegal conduct was the failure to cooperate with a competitor. This conduct was designed to eliminate the competitor, and it resulted in liability for triple damages.

# ASPEN SKIING CO. v. ASPEN HIGHLANDS SKIING CORP.
105 S.Ct. 2847 (1985)

The plaintiff, Highlands, owns one of the four major mountain facilities for downhill skiing at Aspen, Colorado. It filed a triple damage suit against the defendant, which owns the other three major facilities, alleging a violation of Section 2 of the Sherman Act. In the early years of Aspen skiing, there were three major facilities operated by three independent companies, including these parties. Each competitor offered both its own tickets for daily use of a mountain and an interchangeable six-day, all-Aspen ticket, which provided convenience to skiers who wanted flexibility as to what mountain they might ski each day. The defendant acquired the second of the three original facilities and opened a fourth. It also offered a weekly multiarea ticket which covered only its mountains, but eventually the all-Aspen ticket outsold the multiarea tickets.

Over the years, the method for allocation of revenues from the all-Aspen ticket to the competitors developed into a system based on random-sample surveys to determine the number of skiers who used each mountain. However, for the 1977–1978 season, plaintiff was required to accept a fixed percentage of the ticket's revenues as a condition of defendant's participation. When plaintiff refused to accept a lower percentage for the next season—considerably below its historical average, based on usage—defendant discontinued its sale of the all-Aspen tickets. Instead, the defendant sold six-day tickets which covered only its own mountains, and took additional actions that made it extremely difficult for plaintiff to market its own multiarea package to replace the joint offering. Plaintiff's share of the market declined steadily thereafter.

The case was tried by a jury which rendered a verdict finding Aspen Ski Company guilty of the § 2 violation and calculating Highlands' actual damages at $2.5 million and tripled them to $7.5 million plus costs and attorney's fees. The Court of Appeals affirmed.

STEVENS, J.:...In a private treble damages action, the jury found that petitioner Aspen Skiing Company (Ski Co.) had monopolized the market for downhill skiing services in Aspen, Colorado. The question presented is whether that finding is erroneous as a matter of law because it rests on an assumption that a firm with monopoly power has a duty to cooperate with its smaller rivals in a marketing arrangement in order to avoid violating § 2 of the Sherman Act....

The Court of Appeals held that the multi-day, multi-area ticket could be characterized as an "essential facility" that Ski Co. had a duty to market jointly with Highlands.... It held that there was sufficient evidence to support a finding that Ski Co.'s intent in refusing to market the 4-area ticket, "considered together with its other conduct," was to create or maintain a monopoly....

The court noted that by "refusing to cooperate" with Highlands, Ski Co. "became the only business in Aspen that could offer a multi-day multi-mountain skiing experience;" (and) that the refusal to offer a 4-mountain ticket resulted in "skiers' frustration over its unavailability."...

In this Court, Ski Co. contends that even a firm with monopoly power has no duty to engage in joint marketing with a competitor, that a violation of § 2 cannot be established without evidence of substantial exclusionary conduct, and that none of its activities can be characterized as exclusionary....

The central message of the Sherman Act is that a business entity must find new customers and higher profits through internal expansion—that is, by competing successfully rather than by arranging treaties with its competitors. Ski Co., therefore, is surely correct in submitting that even a firm with monopoly power has no general duty to engage in a joint marketing program with a competitor. Ski Co. is quite wrong, however, in suggesting that the judgment in this case rests on any such proposition of law. For the trial court unambiguously instructed the jury that a firm possessing monopoly power has no duty to cooperate with its business rivals.

The absence of an unqualified duty to cooperate does not mean that every time a firm declines to participate in a particular cooperative venture, that decision may not have evidentiary significance, or that it may not give rise to liability in certain circumstances. The absence of a duty to transact business with another firm is, in some respects, merely the counterpart of the independent businessman's cherished right to select his customers and his associates. The high value that we have placed on the right to refuse to deal with other firms does not mean that the right is unqualified.

In *Lorain Journal v. United States,* 72 S.Ct. 181, (1951), we squarely held that this right was not unqualified. Between 1933 and 1948 the publisher of the Lorain Journal, a newspaper, was the only local business disseminating news and advertising in that Ohio town. In 1948, a small radio station was established in a nearby community. In an effort to destroy its small competitor, and thereby regain its "pre-1948 substantial monopoly over the mass dissemination of all news and advertising," the Journal refused to sell advertising to persons that patronized the radio station.

In holding that this conduct violated § 2 of the Sherman Act, the Court dispatched the same argument raised by the monopolist here:

**The publisher claims a right as a private business concern to select its customers and to refuse to accept advertisements from whomever it pleases. We do not dispute that general right. But the word "right" is one of the most deceptive of pitfalls; it is so easy to slip from a qualified meaning in the premise to an unqualified one in the conclusion. Most rights are qualified. The right claimed by the publisher is neither absolute nor exempt from regulation. Its exercise as a purposeful means of monopolizing interstate commerce is prohibited by the Sherman Act. The operator of the radio station, equally with the publisher of the newspaper, is entitled to the protection of that Act. *In the absence of any purpose to create or maintain a monopoly,* the act does not restrict the long recognized right of trader or manufacturer engaged in an entirely private business, freely to exercise his own independent discretion as to parties with whom he will deal.**

The Court approved the entry of an injunction ordering the Journal to print the advertisements of the customers of its small competitor....

The qualification on the right of a monopolist to deal with whom he pleases is not so narrow that it encompasses no more than the circumstances of *Lorain Journal.* In the actual case that we must decide, the monopolist did not merely reject a novel offer to participate in a cooperative venture that had been proposed by a competitor. Rather, the monopolist elected to make an important change in a pattern of distribution that had originated in a competitive market and had persisted for several years.... It continued to provide a desirable option for skiers when the market was enlarged to include four mountains, and when the character of the market was changed by Ski Co.'s acquisition of monopoly power. Moreover, since the record discloses that interchangeable tickets are used in other multi-mountain areas which apparently are competitive, it seems appropriate to infer that such tickets satisfy consumer demand in free competitive markets.

Ski Co.'s decision to terminate the all-Aspen ticket was thus a decision by a monopolist to make an important change in the character of the market....

Since the jury was unambiguously instructed that Ski Co.'s refusal to deal with Highlands "does not violate § 2 if valid business reasons exist for that refusal," we must assume that the jury concluded that there were no valid business reasons for the refusal. The question then is whether that conclusion finds support in the record.

The question whether Ski Co.'s conduct may properly be characterized as exclusionary cannot be answered by simply considering its effect on Highlands. In addition, it is relevant to consider its impact on consumers and whether it has impaired competition in an unnecessarily restrictive way. If a firm has been "attempting to exclude rivals on some basis other than efficiency," it is fair to characterize its behavior as predatory. It is, accordingly, appropriate to examine the effect of the challenged pattern of conduct on consumers, on Ski Co.'s smaller rival, and on Ski Co. itself....

The evidence supports a conclusion that consumers were adversely affected by the elimination of the 4-area ticket. In the first place, the actual record of competition between a 3-area ticket and the all-Aspen ticket in the years after 1967 indicated that skiers demonstrably preferred four mountains to three. Highlands' expert marketing witness testified that many of the skiers who come to Aspen want to ski the four mountains, and the abolition of the 4-area pass made it more difficult to satisfy that ambition. A consumer survey undertaken in the 1979–1980 season indicated that 53.7% of the respondents wanted to ski Highlands, but would not; 39.9% said that they would not be skiing at the mountain of their choice because their ticket would not permit it....

The adverse impact of Ski Co.'s pattern of conduct on Highlands is not disputed in this Court. Expert testimony described the extent of its pecuniary injury....Highlands' share of the relevant market steadily declined after the 4-area ticket was terminated. The size of the damages award also confirms the substantial character of the effect of Ski Co.'s conduct upon Highlands.

Perhaps most significant, however, is the evidence relating to Ski Co. itself, for Ski Co. did not persuade the jury that its conduct was justified by any normal business purpose....

That conclusion is strongly supported by Ski Co.'s failure to offer any efficiency justification whatever for its pattern of conduct....

Although Ski Co.'s pattern of conduct may not have been as "'bold, relentless, and predatory'" as the publisher's actions in *Lorain Journal,* the record in this case comfortably supports an inference that the monopolist made a deliberate effort to discourage its customers from doing business with its smaller rival. The sale of its 3-area, 6-day ticket, particularly when it was discounted below the daily ticket price, deterred the ticket holders from skiing at Highlands....

Because we are satisfied that the evidence in the record, construed most favorably in support of Highlands' position, is adequate to support the verdict under the instructions given by the trial court, the judgment of the Court of Appeals is [*Affirmed.*]

---

As previously noted, proof of monopoly power alone is not enough. Some monopolies are lawful. If monopoly power is "thrust upon" a firm or if it exists because of a patent or franchise, there is no violation of Section 2 if the firm does not engage in conduct that has the effect or purpose of protecting, enforcing, or extending the monopoly power. The power must either have been acquired or used in ways that go beyond normal, honest industrial business conduct for a violation to exist. In other words, the power must have been *deliberatively* acquired or used. A firm is guilty of monopolization when it acquires or maintains monopoly power by a course of deliberate conduct that keeps other firms from entering the market or from expanding their share of it. Deliberativeness is not difficult to prove in most cases.

Conduct that proves deliberativeness may be anything in restraint of trade. For example, predatory conduct would prove deliberativeness. Conduct which is exclusionary in purpose and effect will also do so. For example, if a firm through its leases tends to exclude its competitors from a market, the case is made, even though the conduct is less than predatory. In some cases, the courts have concluded that proof of monopoly power creates a prima facie case. If the firm seeks to deny that power was deliberately achieved or maintained, it may rebut the presumption by proving that power is attributable solely to a reason that is not illegal or against public policy. For example, proof that power arose from a patent or franchise would rebut the presumption.

Monopolistic conduct is often described as predatory. "Predatory" means that a firm seeks to advance its market share by injuring its actual or potential competitors by means other than improved performance. It may be for the purpose of driving out competitors, for keeping them out, or for making them less effective. Pricing policies are frequently examined for proof of predatory conduct. Profit-maximizing pricing; limit pricing, whereby the price is limited to levels that tend to discourage entry; and the practice of price discrimination all may tend to prove monopoly power and predatory conduct.

# ETHICAL CONSIDERATIONS

## 9.  Formal Code of Ethics

The antitrust violations discussed in this chapter raise several ethical questions which are coextensive with or complementary to the legal issues involved. Is it ethical to develop or to enforce a code of professional ethics running counter to the requirements of the law? What are the ethical implications of retaining corporate executive officers who are found guilty of price-fixing?

The first question—can a code of ethics be unethical?—must be answered affirmatively. It is clear that a law can be unethical, such as one stating that all people of a certain race may not own property or have civil rights, or that human slaves may be bought and sold. One can imagine scores of examples of possible laws which would violate commonly accepted ideas of what is right. But one hopes that a democratic approach to creation of law prevents such "unethical" law, or stated another way, that the law encourages or at least tolerates ethical behavior.

A code of ethics derived by any group to affect or control the conduct of group members is akin to private law. It is the group's opinion of proper conduct within the group's domain. It is possible for any code of conduct, even one labeled a code of ethics, to sanction acts contrary to law or to the ethics of society as a whole. Thus, we see professional groups in both the *Goldfarb* and *National Society of Professional Engineers* cases discussed in section 2 laying down standards of professional conduct which are anticompetitive in the extreme. By preventing price competition, the conduct encouraged as "ethical" for both attorneys and engineers amounted to unreasonable restraints of trade in violation of Section 1 of the Sherman Act. One suspects that these "ethical" approaches to "professional competition" were designed and used less to protect the public from shoddy work and more to protect the professionals from the rigors of the marketplace. Whether or not a conscious decision has been made to avoid the obligations imposed by law or ethics, a group's code which abrogates standards established by society at large is subject to legal challenge, social criticism, or both.

## 10.   Informal Codes of Ethics

Whether or not a corporation creates a formal code of ethics, it has one. If found nowhere else, a code is established by the activities encouraged (or condoned by inaction) in the corporate hierarchy. The ethical attitudes and sensitivities of the corporation's leaders appear to be crucial in determining the ethical character of a corporation. Consider, for example, why price-fixing by competitors in industry has been so common. An alarmingly high percentage of both large and small businesses has engaged in price-fixing at various times in the more than ninety years it has been a crime. Companies prominent both nationally and in their respective industries have been convicted of it. Some have even been regular, repeat offenders. It has been estimated that price-fixing costs consumers $60 billion annually. Like other crimes committed for corporate rather than direct personal gain, price-fixing has soiled businesses' general reputation and depressed public confidence in executives. So why have price-fixing violations continued?

Until recently, the profits to be made through price-fixing were often high compared to the risks of being caught or the penalties imposed. Today's threat of triple damage actions together with greater criminal fines and the likelihood of prison terms may counterbalance the economic incentives to conspire with competitors. Of course, many factors contribute to price-fixing, including similarities of products sold, degree of price competition, profit margins, the industry's production capacity, character of market demand, and the level in the corporation where prices are determined. The most important determinant may be whether the company treats price-fixing as improper conduct. Is there emphasis on short-run returns and an uncaring attitude about how those profits are achieved? Is there formal, or even informal, training about what market conduct is approved and what is prohibited by the company? Are executives or other employees convicted of price-fixing discharged or allowed to resign, or are they welcomed back to the corporate bosom with open arms? If employees who violate the law "on behalf of" the corporation are treated differently from those who violate the law "against" the corporation (embezzlement), a message is being sent through the corporate structure that criminal conduct on behalf of the company will be tolerated.

If a company were serious about not price-fixing, it would act as though it meant it by imposing corporate penalties for price-fixing. Law compliance programs and training to help employees deal with ethical dilemmas would also affirm the corporation's attitude toward misconduct. However, a real threat to job security for price-fixers might go further than any educational program or code of ethics ever could. Giving lip service to corporate integrity while at the same time tolerating unlawful conduct to reach a profit on the bottom line signifies either corporate hypocrisy or blindness. Either leads one to the conclusion that the company is ethically insensitive.

## 11. Caterpillar Code of Competition

As an illustration of a corporate statement concerning competitive conduct, the following detailed provision of the Caterpillar code is included. It should be noted that Caterpillar appears to be using United States law to establish ethical norms for its conduct throughout the world.

## COMPETITIVE CONDUCT

Fair competition is fundamental to the free enterprise system. We support laws prohibiting restraints of trade, unfair practices, or abuse of economic power. And we avoid such practices everywhere—including areas of the world where laws don't prohibit them.

In large companies like Caterpillar, particular care must be exercised to avoid practices which seek to increase sales by any means other than fair merchandising efforts based on quality, design features, productivity, price, and product support.

In relationships with competitors, dealers, suppliers, and customers, Caterpillar employees are directed to avoid arrangements restricting our ability to compete with others—or the ability of any other business organization to compete freely and fairly with us, and with others.

There must be no arrangements or understandings, with competitors, affecting prices, terms upon which products are sold, or the number and type of products manufactured or sold—or which might be construed as dividing customers or sales territories with a competitor.

In the course of our business, we may sell engines and other items to companies which are also competitors in other product areas. Related information from such customers will be treated with the same care we would expect Caterpillar data to be accorded, in a similar situation.

Relationships with dealers are established in the Caterpillar dealership agreements. These embody our commitment to fair competitive practices, and reflect customs and laws of various countries where Caterpillar products are sold. Our obligations under these agreements are to be scrupulously observed.

Caterpillar aims to increase its sales—to excel and lead. We intend to do this through superior technical skill, efficient operations, sound planning, and effective merchandising.

We believe that fair competition is good for the marketplace, customers and Caterpillar.

# REVIEW QUESTIONS

**1** Doctors in a county medical society fix *maximum* fees to be charged patients for various medical services. Arizona files suit to enjoin the use of maximum fee schedules. What is the result? Why?

**2** National associations of repossessors establish fee schedules to be used in charging for their services. Repossessors are hired by lenders such as automobile dealers to take possession of items that are bought with loans that are later defaulted. The Justice Department looks to enjoin the use of the fee schedules. What is the result? Why?

**3** Members of a real estate brokers' association vote to raise their commission rate from 6 to 7 percent. The bylaws of the association provided for expulsion of any member charging less than the agreed-upon commission. If broker X continues to charge 6 percent, can she be expelled legally? Why or why not?

**4** Auto manufacturers enter into contracts with their dealers, who are the only persons eligible to bid on "company cars" (new automobiles which had been used only by manufacturers' employees). They agree that the dealers will not bid on such cars for the purpose of reselling them to used-car dealers in other towns. Are the contracts violations of the Sherman Act? Why or why not?

**5** The *Kansas City Star* publishes the only major daily newspapers in Kansas City. It terminates its existing contracts with independent carriers and uses instead its employees who sell and deliver newspapers. No newspapers are sold at wholesale. As a result, the newspaper has a monopoly of the distribution of newspapers. Is this a Sherman Act violation? Why or why not?

**6** A New York statute provided that liquor retailers must charge at least 112 percent of the wholesaler's "posted" bottle price in effect at the time the retailer sells or offers to sell the item. The law did not provide for active supervision by the state itself. A retailer challenges the validity of the state law.

   **a** What theory will support the challenge?

   **b** What defense will be asserted? Decide the case.

**7** The American Society of Anesthesiologists has an ethical standard which prevents its member doctors from working for salaries at hospitals. It insists on fee-for-service arrangements. Is such a standard a violation of the Sherman Act? Explain.

**8** There was a contract between the manufacturer of paint and a retailer of paint in which they agreed not to compete on the retail level. Is this a per se violation of the Sherman Act? Why or why not?

**9** Assume that all the producers of a product agree to limit their advertising budgets to 10 percent of gross sales. The resultant savings is used to reduce the price of the product to the consumer. Is the agreement legal? Explain.

**10** An association of real estate brokers which operated a multiple-listing service deny membership to part-time brokers. Zippy files suit against the association, contending the denial is a violation of the antitrust laws. What is the result? Why?

**11** Standard Oil enters into exclusive-supply contracts with the operators of 5,937 independent retail service stations in seven western states. In these contracts, the dealers agree to purchase from Standard Oil not only all of their requirements for petroleum products but also all of their tubes, tires, and batteries. Are these "T.B.A," contracts illegal? Why or why not?

**12**  A shopping center leases a service-station location to a major oil company. The lease contains a provision that the lessor would not lease any other part of the shopping center for use as a service station. Does the lease violate the Sherman Act? Why or why not?

**13**  A buying association for small- and medium-sized regional supermarket chains allocates territories to its members in which they have exclusive or de factor exclusive licenses to sell the association's private-label brands, and a veto over admission of new members. No price-fixing was involved. It was contended that such practices actually increase competition by enabling members of the association to compete successfully with larger regional and national chains. Is

this arrangement a violation of the Sherman Act? Why or why not?

**14**  A newspaper publisher produces the only paper serving a three-county area. It informs all of its advertisers that they must boycott the local radio station before the newspaper will sell them advertising space. Is this a Sherman Act violation? Why or why not?

**15**  The government files a civil suit under Section 2 of the Sherman Act claiming Grinnell Corporation has a monopoly over the central station hazard-detecting devices. These are security devices to prevent burglary and to detect fires. They involve electronic notification of the police and fire departments at a central location. Grinnell, through three separate companies, controls 87 percent of that business. It argues that it faces competition from other modes of protection from burglary, and therefore it does not have monopoly power. Does Grinnell violate the Sherman Act? Why or why not?

# *Chapter*
# *24*

# Clayton Act and FTC Act Enforcement

## CHAPTER PREVIEW

In 1914, Congress decided to make the Sherman Act more specific. It did so by enacting the Clayton Act. This chapter is primarily concerned with three provisions of the Clayton Act—Section 2 on price discrimination, Section 3 on tying and exclusive contracts, and Section 7 on mergers and acquisitions. There will also be a brief discussion of Section 8 on interlocking directorates.

Also in 1914 Congress adopted the FTC Act which created the FTC as an administrative agency to assist the Justice Department in enforcing the antitrust laws. This chapter will discuss this role of the FTC.

Section 2 of the Clayton Act, which deals with the subject of price discrimination, was amended in 1936 by a statute known as the Robinson-Patman Act. The materials in this chapter dealing with price discrimination are based on that statute. The basic goal of the Robinson-Patman amendment is to ensure that all retailers can buy a manufacturer's goods at the same price.

Section 3 of the Clayton Act seeks to preserve competition by limiting special contractual arrangements whereby the effect may be to lessen competition substantially. These special arrangements include contracts which

seek to connect one product with another, contracts which contain reciprocal arrangements in which each party is a buyer and a seller, and provisions
foreclosing buying or selling with others. These latter exclusive-dealing contracts are quite common. In studying the material in this chapter, keep in
mind that most violations are subject to the rule of reason, and it is only
when coercion or force is present that per se violations may occur.

Section 7 covers a very important area of antitrust—acquisition of one
business by another. Such acquisitions may lead to monopoly power or may
only involve a lessening of competition. They can make the goals of our
competitive economic system difficult to attain.

There are thousands of acquisitions each year, and many involve very
large businesses. The extent to which Section 7 is enforced varies from time
to time, and its enforcement or lack thereof often has significant economic
consequences.

The following legal terms are introduced in this chapter: Bank Merger
Acts, conglomerate merger, consolidation, exclusive dealing, failing-
company doctrine, geographic extension merger, geographic market, good-
faith meeting of competition, greenmail, Herfindahl-Hirschman Index, horizontal merger, interlocking directorates, market extension merger, merger
guidelines, potential-entrant doctrine, predatory pricing, price discrimination, product extension merger, product market, reciprocal dealing,
Robinson-Patman amendment, shark repellent, tender offer, tying contract,
vertical merger, and white knight.

## 1.  Introduction

After it had been in effect for a time, the Sherman Act was criticized as being inadequate. For one thing, it did little to prevent practices which only
tended to reduce competition or which were simply conducive to creating
monopolies. As interpreted with the rule of reason, the Sherman Act did
not apply to situations likely to lead to the destruction of competition but
which fell short of an actual monopoly or combination in unreasonable restraint of trade. Also, the rule of reason and lack of specificity in the
Sherman Act practically required that courts decide each alleged violation
on its own merits on a case-by-case basis. There were a few interpretations
by the courts that were contrary to the will of Congress. For example, the
Supreme Court held that the law did apply to labor unions.

The foregoing factors led to the passage of the Clayton Act and the
Federal Trade Commission Act in 1914. One purpose of the Clayton Act
was to exclude labor unions along with nonprofit agricultural organizations
from the scope of antitrust legislation. The Federal Trade Commission
(FTC) was created as the expert agency in the antitrust field to enforce the
antitrust laws.

The Clayton Act declares that certain enumerated practices in commerce are illegal. These are practices that might adversely affect competition but which are not clear violations of the Sherman Act. The enumerated practices do not have to actually injure competition to be wrongful; they are outlawed if their effect may substantially lessen competition or tend to create a monopoly. The Clayton Act makes it possible to attack many practices in their incipiency which, if continued, eventually could destroy competition or create monopoly.

The sections of the Clayton Act discussed in detail later in this chapter are:

Section 2—price discrimination

Section 3—tying and exclusive contracts

Section 7—mergers and acquisitions

Section 8 of the Clayton Act also has antitrust significance as it is aimed at **interlocking directorates.** It prohibits a person from being a member of the board of directors of two or more corporations at the same time, when one of them has capital, surplus, and undivided profits which total more than $1 million, and where elimination of competition by agreement between such corporations would amount to a violation of any of the antitrust laws.

As corporations have tended to diversify and as the number of conglomerates has increased substantially, it has not been difficult to find some form of competition between two companies which are ostensibly involved in quite different fields. For example, a director on the board of a business which manufactures aluminum who also served on the board of a steel company was found to be in violation, even though the companies are in different industries, because aluminum and steel compete under certain circumstances.

Violations of the original Clayton Act were not crimes, and the act contained no sanction for forfeiture of property. However, it did provide that the Justice Department might obtain injunctions to prevent violations. Those persons injured by a violation could obtain injunctive relief in their own behalf and, in addition, were given the right to collect three times the damages they suffered plus court costs and reasonable attorney's fees. The discussion in Chapter 22 relating to triple damage suits was based on Section 4 of the Clayton Act.

The Clayton Act expanded Sherman Act provisions by allowing private individuals to obtain injunctions in cases of threatened loss due to violations of any of the antitrust laws. It also greatly eased the burden of proof which normally must be shouldered by a plaintiff in triple damage suits. A final decision in favor of the United States to the effect that a defendant has violated the antitrust laws was made prima facie evidence of such violation. This means that if a business is found to be guilty of a Sherman Act violation, a suit for triple damages need not prove violation of the law other than by showing a copy of the court order which finds the defendant guilty.

## CLAYTON ACT—SECTION 2

### 2. Historical Perspective

Section 2 of the Clayton Act as originally adopted in 1914 declared that it is unlawful for a seller to discriminate in the price that is charged to different purchasers of commodities when the effect of this may be to lessen competition substantially or to create a monopoly in any line of commerce. However, "discrimination in price…on account of differences in the grade, quality, or quantity of the commodity sold, or that makes only due allowance for differences in the cost of selling or transportation…" was not illegal. This latter provision so weakened Section 2 that it was very difficult if not impossible to prevent **price discrimination.**

In the 1920s and early 1930s, various techniques such as quantity discounts were used by large-volume retailers, especially chain stores, to obtain more favorable prices than those available to smaller competitors. In addition to obtaining quantity discounts, some large businesses created subsidiary corporations that received brokerage allowances as wholesalers. Another method used by big business to obtain price advantages was to demand and obtain larger promotional allowances than were given to smaller businesses. The prevalence of the foregoing practices led to the enactment in 1936 of the *Robinson-Patman amendment* to Section 2 of the Clayton Act. This statute attempted to eliminate the advantage that a large buyer could secure over a small buyer solely because of the large buyer's quantity-purchasing ability. The legal principles in the sections which follow are based on the Robinson-Patman amendment.

### 3. Predatory Pricing

The Robinson-Patman amendment made it a crime for a seller to sell at lower prices in one geographic area than elsewhere in the United States to eliminate competition or a competitor, or to sell at unreasonably low prices to drive out a competitor. The statutory language declared **predatory pricing** to be illegal.

Predatory pricing means pricing below marginal cost by a company willing and able to sustain losses for a prolonged period to drive out competition. (It is assumed that the price will later be increased when the competitor is destroyed.) Predatory pricing also involves charging higher prices on some products to subsidize below-cost sales of other products or cutting prices below cost on a product in just one area to wipe out a small local competitor.

Historically, price-cutting was generally deemed predatory when a price was below total costs, including long-term fixed costs. However, some economists have argued that pricing is predatory only if companies slash prices below average variable costs—the short-run expenditures such as labor and materials—needed to produce some more units of a product. With long-term fixed costs excluded, prices legally can be cut to a much lower level without the price-cutter being guilty of predatory conduct.

Today a prima facie case of predatory pricing is established by proof that a price is below average variable costs. Such pricing is proof of anticompetitive conduct, unless evidence of justification is admitted to show some other reason for the low price. If a price is below average total costs but above average variable costs, a plaintiff must offer proof that the price has been predatory. Only when prices are below average variable costs is a prima facie case established. As a result of the variable-cost test, many cases which allege predatory pricing do not succeed.

There are several recognized exceptions to the laws prohibiting sales below cost. For example, sales for legitimate purposes such as for liquidation of excess, obsolete, or perishable merchandise, may be legal even if the prices used are below unit cost.

## 4.  Price Discrimination

The goal of the Robinson-Patman amendment is to ensure equality of price to all customers of a seller of commodities for resale when the result of unequal treatment may be to lessen competition substantially or tend to create a monopoly in any line of commerce or injure competition with any person. An injury to competition may be established by showing an injury to a single competitor who is victimized by the discrimination provided there is predatory intent. If there is no proof of predatory intent, price discrimination may not be demonstrated solely by the showing of injury to a single competitor. It is a violation to knowingly receive a benefit of such discrimination. Therefore, the law applies to both buyers and sellers. It is just as illegal to receive the benefit of price discrimination as it is to give a lower price to one of two buyers. In price-discrimination cases, a determination of fact is required to establish the relevant market and the probable anticompetitive effects of the discrimination. The relevant market determination has two aspects—product market and geographic market.

The Robinson-Patman amendment forbids any person engaged "in commerce" to discriminate in price when the goods involved are for resale. It does not apply to a sale by a retailer to consumers. The term "commerce" is defined as "trade...among the several states and with foreign nations...." This means that the Robinson-Patman amendment extends only to transactions in goods in interstate commerce; it does not extend to transactions that only affect intrastate commerce. In addition, the law is applicable only to the sale of commodities. It does not cover contracts that involve the sale of services or the sale of advertising such as television time.

The law protects competitors from one another. As a general rule, there is no exemption for state purchases to compete with private enterprise. However, the Nonprofit Institutions Act provides that the Robinson-Patman amendment does not apply to purchases of supplies for their own use by schools, colleges, universities, public libraries, churches, hospitals, and charitable institutions not operated for profit. This exemption is limited to goods purchased for their own use. If the goods are resold, there is no governmental exemption.

---

# JEFFERSON CTY. PHARMACEUTICAL ASS'N v. ABBOTT LABS.
103 S.Ct. 1011 (1983)

---

POWELL, J.:...The issue presented is whether the sale of pharmaceutical products to state and local government hospitals for resale in competition with private retail pharmacies is exempt from the proscriptions of the Robinson-Patman Act.

Petitioner, a trade association of retail pharmacists and pharmacies doing business in Jefferson County, Alabama, commenced this action in 1978...as the assignee of its members' claims. Respondents are 15 pharmaceutical manufacturers, the Board of Trustees of the University of Alabama, and the Cooper Green Hospital Pharmacy. The University operates a medical center, including hospitals, and a medical school. Located in the University's medical center are two pharmacies. Cooper Green Hospital is a county hospital, existing as a public corporation under Alabama law.

The complaint seeks treble damages and injunctive relief...for alleged violations of § 2(a) and (f) of the Clayton Act, as amended by the Robinson-Patman Act

(the Act). Petitioner contends that the respondent manufacturers violated § 2(a) by selling their products to the University's two pharmacies and to Cooper Green Hospital Pharmacy at prices lower than those charged petitioner's members for like products. Petitioner alleges that the respondent hospital pharmacies knowingly induced such lower prices in violation of § 2(f) and sold the drugs to the general public in direct competition with privately owned pharmacies....

The District Court held that "government purchases are...beyond the intended reach of the Robinson-Patman Price Discrimination Act, at least with respect to purchases for hospitals and other traditional governmental purposes." The Court of Appeals affirmed....

The issue here is narrow. We are not concerned with sales to the federal government, nor with state purchases for use in traditional governmental functions. Rather, the issue before us is limited to state purchases for the purpose of competing against private enterprise—with the advantage of discriminatory prices—in the retail market.

The courts below held, and respondents contend, that the Act exempts all state purchases. Assuming, without deciding, that Congress did not intend the Act to apply to state purchases for consumption in traditional governmental functions, and that such purchases are therefore exempt, we conclude that the exemption does not apply where a State has chosen to compete in the private retail market.

The Robinson-Patman Act by its terms does not exempt state purchases....Moreover, as the courts below conceded, the statutory language—"persons" and "purchasers"—is sufficiently broad to cover governmental bodies....

We do not perceive any reason to construe the word "person" in that Act any differently than we have in the Clayton Act, which it amends, and it is undisputed that the Clayton Act applies to states. In sum, the plain language of the Act strongly suggests that there is no exemption for state purchases to compete with private enterprise.

The plain language of the Act is controlling unless a different legislative intent is apparent from the purpose and history of the Act. An examination of the legislative purpose and history here reveals no such contrary intention.

Our cases have been explicit in stating the purposes of the antitrust laws, including the Robinson-Patman Act. On numerous occasions, this Court has affirmed the comprehensive coverage of the antitrust laws and has recognized that these laws represent "a carefully studied attempt to bring within them every person engaged in business whose activities might restrain or monopolize commercial intercourse among the states."

It has been said, of course, that the antitrust laws, and Robinson-Patman in particular, are to be construed liberally, and that the exceptions from their application are to be construed strictly. The Court has recognized, also, that Robinson-Patman "was enacted in 1936 to curb and prohibit all devices by which large buyers gained discriminatory preferences over smaller ones by virtue of their greater purchasing power." Because the Act is remedial, it is to be construed broadly to effectuate its purposes.

The legislative history falls far short of supporting respondents' contention that there is an exemption for state purchases of "commodities" for "resale."...We find no legislative intention to enable a State, by an unexpressed exemption, to enter private competitive markets with congressionally approved price advantages.

"A general application of the Robinson-Patman Act to all combinations of business and capital organized to suppress commercial competition is in harmony with the spirit and impulses of the times which gave it birth." The legislative history is replete with references to the economic evil of large organizations purchasing from other large organizations for resale in competition with the small, local retailers. There is no reason, in the absence of an explicit exemption, to think that congressmen who feared these evils intended to deny small businesses, such as the pharmacies of Jefferson County, Alabama, protection from the competition of the strongest competitor of them all. To create an exemption here clearly would be contrary to the intent of Congress.

We hold that the sale of pharmaceutical products to state and local government hospitals for resale in competition with private pharmacies is not exempt from the proscriptions of the Robinson-Patman Act. [*Reversed.*]

The Robinson-Patman amendment gives the FTC jurisdiction and authority to regulate quantity discounts. It also proscribes certain hidden or indirect discriminations by sellers in favor of certain buyers. Section 2(c) prohibits an unearned brokerage commission related to a sale of goods. For example, it is unlawful to pay or to receive a commission or discount on sales or purchases except for actual services rendered. Section 2(d) outlaws granting promotional allowances or payments on goods bought for resale unless such allowances are available to all competing customers. For example, a manufacturer who gives a retailer a right to purchase three items for the price of two as part of a special promotion must give the same right to all competitors in the market. Section 2(e) prohibits giving promotional facilities or services on goods bought for resale, unless they are made available to all competing customers. The act does not expressly require that any anticompetitive effects be demonstrated to prove a violation of these provisions.

## 5.   Proof Required

Price discrimination is not illegal per se. Only those differences in prices that may adversely affect competition are prohibited. A plaintiff seeking triple damages because of price discrimination must prove that the effect of the discrimination is to injure, destroy, or prevent competition with any person who grants or knowingly receives the benefit of the discrimination, or with customers of either of them. A plaintiff seeking damages for a Robinson-Patman violation must prove actual injury attributable to the violation. It is not enough to prove a price differential, as there are no automatic damages.

---

# J. TRUETT PAYNE CO. v. CHRYSLER MOTORS CORP.
101 S.Ct. 1923 (1981)

---

Plaintiff, petitioner, a former automobile dealer, brought suit against Chrysler alleging that defendant's "sales incentive" programs over a certain period violated the Robinson-Patman amendment. Under its programs, defendant paid a bonus to its dealers if they exceeded their sales quotas. Plaintiff alleged that its quotas were higher than those of its competitors and that to the extent it failed to meet its quotas, and to the extent its competitors met their lower quotas it received fewer bonuses. The net effect to plaintiff was that it paid more for its automobiles than did its competitors. Plaintiff sought as damages the amount of the price difference multiplied by the number of petitioner's purchases. The defendant maintained that the sales incentive programs were nondiscriminatory, and that they did not injure petitioner or adversely affect competition. The jury returned a verdict for the plaintiff which the court trebled. The Court of Appeals reversed, finding that the plaintiff had failed to introduce substantial evidence of injury attributable to the programs, much less substantial evidence of the amount of such injury, as was required in order to recover triple damages under § 4 of the Clayton Act.

REHNQUIST, J.:...The question presented in this case is the appropriate measure of damages in a suit brought under § 2(a) of the Clayton Act, as amended by the Robinson-Patman Act.

Petitioner first contends that once it has proved a price discrimination in violation of § 2(a) it is entitled at a minimum to so-called "automatic damages" in the amount of the price discrimination. Petitioner concedes that in order to recover damages it must establish cognizable injury attributable to an antitrust violation and some approximation of damage. It insists, however, that the jury should be permitted to infer the requisite injury and damage from a showing of a substantial price discrimination....We disagree.

By its terms § 2(a) is a prophylactic statute which is violated merely upon a showing that "the effect of such discrimination *may be* substantially to lessen competition." As our cases have recognized, the statute does not "require that the discriminations must in fact have harmed competition." Section 4 of the Clayton Act, in contrast, is essentially a remedial statute. It provides treble damages to "any person who *shall be injured* in his business or property by reason of anything forbidden in the antitrust laws...." To recover treble damages, then, a plaintiff must make some showing of actual injury attributable to something the antitrust laws were designed to prevent....It must prove more than a violation of § 2(a), since such proof establishes only that injury may result.

Our decision here is virtually governed by our reasoning in *Brunswick Corp. v. Pueblo Bowl-O-Mat, Inc.,* 97 S. Ct. 690, (1977). There we rejected the contention that the mere violation of § 7 of the Clayton Act, which prohibits mergers which *may* substantially lessen competition, gives rise to a damage claim under § 4. We explained that "to recover damages [under § 4] respondents must prove more than that the petitioner violated § 7, since such proof established only that injury may result."

Likewise in this case, proof of a violation does not mean that a disfavored purchaser has been actually "injured" within the meaning of § 4.

Petitioner next contends that even though it may not be entitled to "automatic damages" upon a showing of a violation of § 2(a), it produced enough evidence of actual injury to survive a motion for a directed verdict....[After reviewing the evidence the court remanded the case so that the Court of Appeals could consider the sufficiency of plaintiff's evidence of injury.] [*So ordered.*]

---

Plaintiffs can satisfy the injury requirement of the Robinson-Patman amendment in one of two ways. First, they may use a market analysis to show a substantial possibility of injury to competition. Second, they may prove actual injury to a competitor coupled with predatory intent.

Proof of injury to a sole competitor is not enough. If there is no proof of injury to competition, there must be proof of predatory intent. Proof of predatory intent may be by circumstantial evidence.

## 6.  Levels of Competition

Robinson-Patman cases vary somewhat, depending on the level of competition. Courts recognize primary-level cases (competition among sellers); secondary-level cases (competition among customers of sellers); and third-level cases (when there is a wholesaler between the manufacturer and the retailer). Figure 24-1 illustrates these levels.

In primary-level cases, proof of an adverse competitive effect is required. Primary-level cases usually involve territorial price discrimination—the charging of different prices by a multimarket seller in different geographic areas—to drive out its direct competitors. For example, a frozen pie maker was sued for triple damages when it sold pies for a lower price to retail outlets only in the Salt Lake City market to increase its share of that market.

In secondary-line competition cases, it is presumed that competition is adversely affected if directly competing customers of manufacturers and producers are charged different prices. Note, this establishes the violation but not the injury. Secondary line cases require proof that both buyers compete in the same geographic area.

Cases have expanded the lines of competition to include injuries to competitors of the customer of the buyer. In the case which follows, there were actually four levels in the distribution system.

**FIGURE 24-1**
Levels of Competition: Robinson-Patman Violation Analysis.

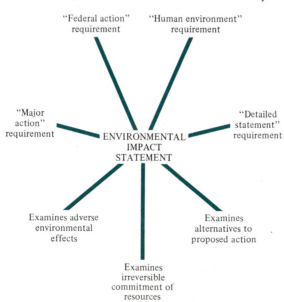

# PERKINS v. STANDARD OIL COMPANY OF CALIFORNIA

89 S.Ct. 1871 (1969)

Plaintiff, Perkins, brought suit for triple damages under Section 2 of the Clayton Act as amended by the Robinson-Patman amendment. He alleged that Standard Oil was guilty of price discrimination in two ways: (1) that it sold gasoline to its own branded dealers at prices lower than it sold to plaintiff and (2) that it sold gasoline at a lower price to another oil company, which in turn sold it to a wholesaler, who in turn sold it to a competitor of the plaintiff at a price that was still lower than the price paid by the plaintiff for similar gasoline. The jury awarded plaintiff $432,404.57, which when tripled gave plaintiff $1,297,213.71. The Court of Appeals reversed. The issue on this appeal is whether or not the second type of price discrimination which was alleged is within the coverage of the act.

BLACK, J.:...We disagree with the Court of Appeals conclusion that § 2 of the Clayton Act, as amended by the Robinson-Patman Act, does not apply to the damages suffered by Perkins as a result of the price advantage granted by Standard to Signal, then by Signal to Western, then by Western to Regal. The Act, in pertinent part, provides:

**(a)It shall be unlawful for any person engaged in commerce...either directly or indirectly, to discriminate in price between different purchasers of commodities of like grade and quality... where the effect of such discrimination may be substantially to lessen competition or tend to create a monopoly in any line of commerce, or to injure, destroy, or prevent competition with any person who either grants or knowingly receives the benefit of such discrimination, or with customers of either of them....**

The Court of Appeals read this language as limiting "the distributing levels on which a supplier's price discrimination will be recognized as potentially injurious to competition." According to that court, the coverage of the Act is restricted to injuries caused by an impairment of competition with (1) the seller ["any person who...grants...such discrimination"], (2) the favored purchaser ["any person who...knowingly receives the benefit of such discrimination"] and (3) customers of the discriminating seller or favored purchaser ["customers of either of them"]. Here, Perkins' injuries resulted in part from impaired competition with a customer (Regal) of a customer (Western Hyway) of the favored purchaser (Signal). The Court of Appeals termed these injuries "fourth level" and held that they were not protected by the Robinson-Patman Act. We conclude that this limitation is wholly an artificial one and is completely unwarranted by the language or purpose of the Act.

In *FTC v. Fred Meyer, Inc.,* 390 U.S. 341 (1968), we held that a retailer who buys through a wholesaler could be considered a "customer" of the original supplier within the meaning of § 2(d) of the Robinson-Patman Act, a section dealing with discrimination in promotional allowances which is closely analogous to § 2(a) involved in this case. In *Meyer,* the Court stated that to read "customer" narrowly would be wholly untenable when viewed in light of the purposes of the Robinson-Patman Act. Similarly, to read "customer" more narrowly in this section than we did in the section involved in *Meyer* would allow price discriminators to avoid the sanctions of the Act by the simple expedient of adding an additional link to the distribution chain. Here, for example, Standard supplied gasoline and oil to Signal. Signal, allegedly because it furnished Standard with part of its vital supply of crude petroleum, was able to insist upon a discriminatorily lower price. Had Signal then sold its gas directly to the Regal stations, giving Regal stations a competitive advantage, there would be no question, even under the decision of the Court of Appeals in this case, that a clear violation of the Robinson-Patman Act had been committed. Instead of selling directly to the retailer Regal, however, Signal transferred the gasoline first to its subsidiary, Western Hyway, who in turn supplied the Regal stations. Signal owned 60% of the stock of Western Hyway; Western in turn owned 55% of the stock of the Regal stations. We find no basis in the language or purpose of the Act for immunizing Standard's price discriminations simply because the product in question passed through an additional formal exchange before reaching the level of Perkins' actual competitor. From Perkins' point of view, the competitive harm done him by Standard is certainly no less because of the presence of an additional link in this particular distribution chain from the producer to the retailer. Here Standard discriminated in price between Perkins and Signal, and there was evidence from which the jury could conclude that Perkins was harmed competitively when Signal's price advantage was passed on to Perkins' retail competitor Regal. These facts are sufficient to give rise to recoverable damages under the Robinson-Patman Act....[*Verdict and judgment reinstated.*]

## 7. Defenses

The statute recognizes certain exceptions or defenses:

**1** Price differentials based on differences in the cost of manufacture, sale, or delivery of commodities are permitted (cost-justification defense).

**2** Sellers may select their own customers in bona fide transactions and not in restraint of trade.

**3** Price changes may be made in response to changing conditions, such as actual or imminent deterioration of perishable goods, obsolescence of seasonal goods, distress sales under court process, or sales in good faith in discontinuance of business in the goods concerned (changing conditions defense).

**4** A seller in good faith may meet the equally low price of a competitor (**good-faith meeting-of-competition** defense).

When a plaintiff has introduced proof of differential pricing of the same kind of goods by the defendant and proves that requisite injury to competition resulted, he or she has established a prima facie case. The cost justification defense may be used to overcome the prima facie case of price discrimination established by a plaintiff. The burden of showing cost justification is upon the person charged with a violation. The cost justification defense has proved largely illusory in practice. Because of the complexities in determining what is "cost," this defense very rarely was successful in the past. One obvious problem is that of bringing forth acceptable evidence of cost. As a practical matter, proof of cost involves both direct costs and indirect costs. Indirect costs are based on assumptions, and accountants may make different ones. Therefore, there are disputes over the technique to determine actual cost, and proof of it is difficult, if not impossible. The status of the act is such that only the most prosperous and patient business firms can afford pursuit of this often illusory defense.

## 8. Good-Faith Meeting-of-Competition Defense

A very important affirmative defense justifying price discrimination is the good-faith meeting of competition. Section 2(b) of the Robinson-Patman amendment permits a defendant to demonstrate that a given price discrimination was not unlawful by "showing that his lower price or the furnishing of services or facilities to any purchaser or purchasers was made in good faith to meet an equally low price of a competitor, or the services or facilities furnished by a competitor." This defense may be established by proof of a price reduction to meet a competitor's price. It may also be established by proof that price was not increased in one market to meet competition in that market when prices were raised in other markets. In other words, the defense may result from active conduct (lowering prices), or it may be passive (not increasing prices).

"Good faith" is not easily defined. It is a flexible and pragmatic, not a technical or doctrinaire, concept. The standard of good faith is simply the standard of the prudent businessperson responding fairly to what he or she reasonably believes is a situation of competitive necessity. The facts and circumstances in each case govern its interpretation and application. Thus, the same method of meeting competition may be consistent with an inference of good faith in some circumstances, inconsistent with such an inference in others.

Although the term "good faith" cannot be quantified, it is clear that this defense cannot be established when the purpose of a seller's price discrimination is to eliminate competition. The seller may offer discriminatory prices to customers whether or not it has done business with them in the past, but these discriminatory prices must not knowingly be lower than those offered by competitors.

The timing of the price offers must be such that it is apparent they are made to meet an individual competitive situation and are not part of a general system of competition. The seller must have knowledge of the prices it is meeting, to the extent that a reasonable person would believe a lower price was necessary. Actual knowledge of a competitor's exact price is not required.

The overriding consideration concerning the good-faith requirement is the motive of the discriminating seller. The good-faith concept should be used solely to test the seller's adherence to the basic objectives of the meeting-competition proviso: facilitating price reductions in genuine response to competitive market pressures to equalize a competitive opportunity.

The good-faith meeting-of-competition defense is available to buyers as well as sellers. The buyers' liability is based on the sellers' liability, and as the next case shows, if the seller has a defense, so does the buyer.

# GREAT ATLANTIC & PACIFIC TEA CO., INC. v. F.T.C.
99 S.Ct. 925 (1979)

STEWART, J.:…The question presented in this case is whether the petitioner, the Great Atlantic and Pacific Tea Company (A&P), violated Section 2(f) of the Robinson-Patman Act, by knowingly inducing or receiving illegal price discriminations from the Borden Company (Borden).

The alleged violation was reflected in a 1965 agreement between A&P and Borden under which Borden undertook to supply "private label" milk to more than 200 A&P stores in a Chicago area that included portions of Illinois and Indiana. This agreement resulted from an effort by A&P to achieve cost savings by switching from the sale of "brand label" milk (milk sold under the brand name of the supplying dairy) to the sale of "private label" milk (milk sold under the A&P label).

To implement this plan, A&P asked Borden, its longtime supplier, to submit an offer to supply under private label certain of A&P's milk and other dairy product requirements. After prolonged negotiations, Borden offered to grant A&P a discount for switching to private label milk provided A&P would accept limited delivery service. Borden claimed that this offer would save A&P $410,000 a year compared to what it had been paying for its dairy products. A&P however, was not satisfied with this offer and solicited offers from other dairies. A competitor of Borden, Bowman Dairy, then submitted an offer which was lower than Borden's.

At this point, A&P's Chicago buyer contacted Borden's chain store sales manager and stated, "I have a bid in my pocket. You [Borden] people are so far out of line it is not even funny. You are not even in the ball park." When the Borden representative asked for more details, he was told nothing except that a $50,000 improvement in Borden's bid "would not be a drop in the bucket."

Borden was thus faced with the problem of deciding whether to rebid. A&P at the time was one of Borden's largest customers in the Chicago area. Moreover, Borden had just invested more than five million dollars in a new dairy facility in Illinois. The loss of the A&P account would result in underutilization of this new plant. Under these circumstances, Borden decided to submit a new bid which doubled the estimated annual savings to A&P, from $410,000 to $820,000. In presenting its offer, Borden emphasized to A&P that it needed to keep

A&P's business and was making the new offer in order to meet Bowman's bid. A&P then accepted Borden's bid after concluding that it was substantially better than Bowman's.

[The FTC filed a complaint against A&P charging that it had violated Section 2(f) of the Robinson-Patman Act by knowingly inducing or receiving price discrimination from Borden. The Commission found that Borden had discriminated in price between A&P and its competitors, that the discrimination had been injurious to competition, and that A&P had known or should have known that it was the beneficiary of unlawful price discrimination. The Commission rejected A&P's defenses that the Borden bid had been made to meet competition and was cost justified. The Court of Appeals affirmed holding that as a matter of law A&P could not successfully assert a meeting competition defense because it, unlike Borden, had known that Borden's offer was better than Bowman's. The Supreme Court granted certiorari.]

The Robinson-Patman Act was passed in response to the problem perceived in the increased market power and coercive practices of chain stores and other big buyers that threatened the existence of small independent retailers. Notwithstanding this concern with buyers, however, the emphasis of the Act is in Section 2(a), which prohibits price discriminations by sellers. Indeed, the original Patman Bill as reported by Committees of both Houses prohibited only seller activity, with no mention of buyer liability. Section 2(f) of the Act, making buyers liable for inducing or receiving price discriminations by sellers, was the product of a belated floor amendment near the conclusion of the Senate debates.

As finally enacted, § 2(f) provides: "That it shall be unlawful for any person engaged in commerce, in the course of such commerce, knowingly to induce or receive a discrimination in price which is prohibited by this section."

Liability under § 2(f) thus is limited to situations where the price discrimination is one "which is prohibited by this section." While the phrase "this section" refers to the entire § 2 of the Act, only subsections (a) and (b) dealing with seller liability involved discriminations in price. Under the plain meaning of § 2(f), therefore, a buyer cannot be liable if a prima facie case could not be established against a seller or if the seller has an affirmative defense. In either situation, there is no price discrimination "prohibited by this section." The legislative history of § 2(f) fully confirms the conclusion that buyer liability under § 2(f) is dependent on seller liability under § 2(a)....

Thus, a buyer cannot be held liable under § 2(f) if the lower prices received are justified by reason of one of the seller's affirmative defenses.

The petitioner, relying on this plain meaning of § 2(f) argues that it cannot be liable under § 2(f) if Borden had a valid meeting competition defense. The respondent, on the other hand, argues that the petitioner may be liable even assuming that Borden had such a defense. The meeting competition defense, the respondent contends, must in these circumstances be judged from the point of view of the buyer. Since A&P knew for a fact that the final Borden bid beat the Bowman bid, it was not entitled to assert the meeting competition defense even though Borden may have honestly believed that it was simply meeting competition. Recognition of a meeting competition defense for the buyer in this situation, the respondent argues, would be contrary to the basic purpose of the Robinson-Patman Act to curtail abuses by large buyers.

The short answer to these contentions of the respondent is that Congress did not provide in § 2(f) that a buyer can be liable even if the seller has a valid defense. The clear language of § 2(f) states that a buyer can be liable only if he receives a price discrimination "prohibited by this section." If a seller has a valid meeting competition defense, there is simply no prohibited price discrimination....

Because both the Commission and the Court of Appeals proceeded on the assumption that a buyer who accepts the lower of two competitive bids can be liable under Section 2(f) even if the seller has a meeting competition defense, there was not a specific finding that Borden did in fact have such a defense. But it quite clearly did.

The test for determining when a seller has a valid meeting competition defense is whether a seller can "show the existence of facts which would lead a reasonable and prudent person to believe that the granting of a lower price would in fact meet the equally low price of a competitor." "A good faith belief, rather than absolute certainty, that a price concession is being offered to meet an equally low price offered by a competitor is sufficient to satisfy the Robinson-Patman's Section 2(b) defense." Since good faith, rather than absolute certainty, is the touchstone of the meeting competition defense, a seller can assert the defense even if it has unknowingly made a bid that in fact not only met but beat his competition.

Under the circumstances of this case, Borden did act reasonably and in good faith when it made its second bid....

Since Borden had a meeting competition defense and thus could not be liable under Section 2(b), the petitioner who did no more than accept the offer cannot be liable under Section 2(f). [*Accordingly, the judgment is Reversed.*]

### 9.  The Future of Section 2

The FTC is the sole governmental agency that now brings actions to enforce the Robinson-Patman amendment. It brings very few cases, and it has recently encouraged repeal of the law. This lack of enforcement results, in part, from the opinion of many economists that the Robinson-Patman amendment has resulted in higher prices than would exist in a more competitive market. Moreover, there is evidence that the statute offers little economic protection to small businesses; rather, it promotes high prices, restricts entry, and encourages inefficiency in the distribution of goods. Some commissioners of the FTC believe that the underlying philosophy of the amendment is no longer relevant and that the law is unpoliceable. Violations are probably an everyday occurrence.

Enforcement by way of triple damage suits by victims of price discrimination has also been greatly reduced in recent years as a result of two judicial decisions. First, the decision which holds that the statute does not apply to intrastate businesses but only to businesses engaged in interstate commerce has eliminated a significant percentage of all total cases. Second, the holding that a plaintiff must prove actual damages and that proof of price-differential is insufficient proof of damages as a practical matter has discouraged many cases. It is very difficult today to collect triple damages based on Robinson-Patman violations. The lack of effective private enforcement may eventually lead to the repeal of this law that many people believe is outdated.

# THE CLAYTON ACT—SECTION 3

### 10. Tying Arrangements—Generally

Section 3 of the Clayton Act makes it unlawful for a person engaged in commerce to lease or sell commodities or to fix a price charged on the condition that the lessee or purchaser should not use or deal in the commodities of a competitor(s) of the lessor or seller when the effect may be to substantially lessen competition or tend to create a monopoly in any line of commerce. The same issues concerning the relevant market and probable anticompetitive effects are involved in determining a violation of Section 3 of the Clayton Act as in a case of alleged price discrimination under Section 2. Under Section 3, the law covers tying contracts, reciprocal dealings, and exclusive arrangements.

A **tying contract** is one in which a commodity is sold or leased for use only on condition that the buyer or lessee purchase a different product or service from the seller or lessor. The arrangement tying a product may even be to a loan of money. Tying arrangements may be violations of both Section 1 of the Sherman Act and Section 3 of the Clayton Act. Although most tying arrangements are subject to the rule of reason, some tying arrangements are illegal without proof of anticompetitive effects. They are unreasonable in and of themselves (a per se violation) whenever (1) a party has sufficient economic power with respect to the tying product to restrain free competition appreciably in the market for the tied product; (2) some coercion is shown; and (3) a "not insubstantial" amount of interstate commerce is affected.

The per se rule for tying contracts does allow a defendant to justify undertaking the tie. A tie-in may be justified if it is implemented for a legitimate purpose and if a no less restrictive alternative is available.

A common form of tying arrangements is known as *full-line forcing*. In full-line forcing, the buyer or lessee is compelled to take a complete product line from the seller. Under these arrangements, the buyer cannot purchase only one product of the line. A typical illegal agreement under this concept is one in which a gasoline company requires its dealers to purchase a stated amount of regular gasoline and premium-priced gasoline in order to obtain no-lead gasoline. Another example is when an automobile manufacturer requires that only its radios be sold with its new cars.

## 11.  Reciprocal Dealings

A **reciprocal-dealing arrangement** exists when two parties face each other as both buyer and seller. One party offers to buy the other's goods but only if the second party buys other goods from the first party. For example, if one party is both a food wholesaler and a provider of goods used in processing foods, food processors may be faced by a reciprocal requirement. The first party may agree to buy the processor's products only if the processor buys the processing goods from it.

Reciprocity cases are quite similar to tying cases, and courts treat them in a similar manner. In each case, one side of a transaction has special power in the marketplace. It uses this power to force those with whom it deals to make concessions in another market. In tying arrangements, a seller with economic power forces the purchaser to purchase something else to obtain the desired item. In reciprocal dealings, a buyer with economic power forces a seller to buy something from it to sell its goods. In both cases, the key is the extension of economic power in one market to another market. Thus, the standard for judging reciprocal arrangements is the same as the standard for judging tie-in arrangements, as previously discussed. A reciprocal arrangement may be a per se violation if it is coercive and not justified by legitimate business objectives for which there is no better alternative.

Most cases involving reciprocity threaten foreclosure only of small percentages of any market. Nevertheless, courts apply the per se rule. Reciprocity cases are complicated by the fact that they can occur without an actual agreement. A seller may buy from a would-be customer in the hope that doing so will create goodwill and will lead eventually to sales. It is a natural thing for a seller to show appreciation by purchasing from its buyers.

## 12.  Exclusive Dealings

An **exclusive-dealings** contract contains a provision that one party or the other (buyer or seller) will deal only with the other party. For example, a seller of tomatoes agrees to sell only to Campbell Soup. A buyer of coal may agree to purchase only from a certain coal company. Such agreements tend to foreclose a portion of the market from competitors.

A similar arrangement is known as a *requirements contract*. In a requirements contract, a buyer agrees to purchase all of its needs of a given contract from the seller during a certain period of time. The buyer may be a manufacturer who needs the raw materials or parts agreed to be supplied, or it may be a retailer who needs goods for resale. In effect, the buyer is agreeing not to purchase any of the product from competitors of the seller.

Franchise contracts often require that the franchisee purchase all of its equipment and inventory from the franchiser as a condition of the agreement. These provisions are commonly inserted because of the value of the franchiser's trademark and the desire for quality control to protect it. For example, Baskin-Robbins ice cream may require its franchisees to purchase all of their ice cream from Baskin-Robbins. The legitimate purpose is to maintain the image of the franchise and the product. Customers expect the same ice cream from every retail operation. Such agreements, while anticompetitive, are legal, because the legitimate purpose outweighs the anticompetitive aspects.

However, a franchiser is not able to license its trademark in such a manner that it can coerce franchisees to give up all alternate supply sources, because such agreements are unreasonable restraints of trade. The quality-control aspect is not present for items such as packaging materials and food items in which special ingredients or secret formulas are not involved; thus, the purpose of the "exclusive source of supply" provision is only to limit competition. Although franchise agreements are not per se violations, they are subject to the rule of reason.

Exclusive contracts and requirements contracts are less likely to harm competition than are tying contracts. Such contracts may add competition by eliminating uncertainties and the expense of repeated contracts. However, the courts tend to give per se violation treatment to exclusive contracts if they substantially affect commerce. In one case involving less than 1 percent of the coal market, the court concluded that the contract was legal because the small percentage of foreclosures did not actually or potentially cause a substantial reduction of competition. As a result of these decisions, we do not have full per se illegality in this area, but neither do we have full economic inquiry as to the impact of a given contract.

## 13.  Ethics and Section 3

Caterpillar has a special part of its ethics code which deals with the relationship with suppliers. Reciprocity is forbidden, and exclusive dealings are rare. The specific statement is as follows. Note that compliance with this standard will probably prevent any legal problems from occurring.

## RELATIONSHIPS WITH SUPPLIERS

Caterpillar's supplier relationships are a vital, highly-valued aspect of our worldwide operations. These relationships are based on a commitment to deal fairly and reasonably.

We aim at creation and maintenance of long-lasting company-supplier relationships. But as a general rule, neither Caterpillar nor a supplier should be overly dependent on the other, from a long-term standpoint.

Selection of suppliers and purchase of materials and services are determined by evaluations of quality, cost/price benefit, delivery capability, service, and maintenance of adequate supply sources. Other things being equal, our intention is to buy from sources as near to the using facility as possible.

Supplier competitiveness for Caterpillar business is encouraged throughout the world...as is company-supplier cooperation toward maximizing the value of Caterpillar products. No supplier is asked to buy Caterpillar products in order to compete for business, or continue as a supplier.

Suppliers may trade with Caterpillar's competitors and still merit our purchases. Further, Caterpillar personnel shall avoid arrangements or understandings prohibiting a supplier from selling products in competition with us, except where: (1) the supplier makes the product with tooling or materials owned by Caterpillar or (2) the product is one in which the company has a proprietary interest which has been determined to be legally protectable. Such an interest might arise from an important contribution by Caterpillar to the concept, design, application, or manufacturing process.

# THE CLAYTON ACT—SECTION 7

## 14. Introduction

A business may acquire other businesses in a variety of ways. For example, two corporations may join together and create a third corporation, with the two original companies being dissolved. This is technically known as a **consolidation.** One business may acquire and absorb another business, with the acquired business being dissolved. This is technically known as a *merger.* Another method for one company to acquire another is for the former to purchase a controlling interest in the stock of the latter. The subsidiary is controlled by the parent company's electing the board of directors and controlling policy. When the stock of a company is controlled, both companies continue to exist, and no dissolution occurs. A fourth method of acquisition is for one business to purchase the assets of another. The selling company then ceases to continue its former business activities, and the purchased assets are integrated into the buying company.

In the material which follows, technical consolidations, mergers, and other acquisitions are generally referred to as mergers. Mergers are usually classified as *horizontal, market extension, vertical, or conglomerate.* A **horizontal merger** usually combines two businesses in the same field or industry. The acquired and acquiring companies have competed with each other, and the merger reduces the number of competitors and leads to greater concentration in the industry. The term **market extension merger** describes an acquisition in which the acquiring company extends its markets. This market extension may be either in new products (**product extension**) or in new areas (**geographic extension**). For example, if a brewery which did not operate in

New England were to acquire a New England brewery, this would be a geographic market extension merger.

A **vertical merger** brings together a company which is the customer of the other in one of the lines of commerce in which the other is a supplier. Such a combination ordinarily removes, or has the potential to remove, the merged customer from the market as far as other suppliers are concerned. It also may remove a source of supply if the acquiring company is a customer of the acquired one. A **conglomerate merger** is one in which the businesses involved neither compete nor are related as customer and supplier in any given line of commerce. Some people consider product extension and geographic extension mergers to be conglomerate ones with many characteristics of horizontal ones. In any event, there is a great deal of similarity in the legal principles applied to market extension and to conglomerate mergers.

Theoretically, a merger or acquisition may be challenged under the Sherman Act. A horizontal merger would amount to a violation of the Sherman Act if it were a combination in unreasonable restraint of trade, if it were to result in monopolization of a line of commerce, or if it were an attempt to monopolize. A Sherman Act case requires detailed economic analysis of markets and market structure as well as the characteristics of the firms involved in a merger. Since Section 7 cases require less-detailed proof and analysis, the Sherman Act is seldom used to prevent a merger.

A great deal of merger litigation involves banks. Such mergers are subject to both the Sherman Act and the Clayton Act. In addition, they are subject to the provision of the *Bank Merger Acts* of 1960 and 1966. Under these laws, bank mergers are illegal unless they are approved by one of the agencies which regulates banks. If a merger involves a national bank, the approval of the comptroller of the currency is required. If the banks involved in a merger are state banks that are members of the Federal Reserve System, the approval of the Federal Reserve Board is necessary. Other mergers of banks insured by the Federal Deposit Insurance Corporation require approval of that agency.

If a bank merger is approved by one of the three appropriate regulatory agencies, it may nevertheless be challenged under the antitrust laws by the Justice Department within thirty days. The filing of a suit by the Justice Department stops the merger until the case is decided.

## 15.   General Principles

As originally enacted in 1914, the Clayton Act covered horizontal mergers. In 1950, Congress passed the *Celler-Kefauver* amendment, which substantially broadened the coverage. First of all, this amendment plugged a loophole, in that the original Section 7 only prohibited certain acquisitions of stock by one corporation of another. Technically, the same end could be accomplished and was permitted under it through an acquisition of assets. Therefore, the acquisition of assets was also prohibited. Second, the Celler-Kefauver amendment prohibited all acquisitions in which the effect lessened competition substantially in any line of commerce in any section of the country. Thus, the amendment added vertical and conglomerate mergers to the coverage of Section 7. In 1980, Congress expanded coverage by substituting "person" for "corporation," and included not only businesses engaged in interstate commerce, but businesses engaged in activities which affect commerce. The word "person" includes sole proprietorships and partnerships.

The language of Section 7 neither adopts nor rejects any particular tests for measuring relevant markets. Both the product market and geographic market of the companies involved are factual issues to be considered by the courts. In determining the relevant "line of commerce" (product market) and the relevant "section of the country" (geographic market) affected by the merger in question, the actual outcome of the litigation is frequently decided. The more narrowly the product line or geographic area is defined, the greater the impact a merger or acquisition will have on competition. Thus, the relevant market decision frequently determines the issue as to the probable anticompetitive effects of the merger. It is also obvious that a decision which enlarges the line of commerce may be equally important in establishing that a merger is *not* anticompetitive. Trial courts and reviewing courts frequently disagree as to what constitutes relevant markets in any given case. Reviewing courts today give great deference to trial court findings on these issues.

In addition to determining the relevant market affected by a given merger, courts must also find that within that market the effect of the merger "may be substantially to lessen competition, or to tend to create a monopoly" before a violation is established. Some cases have held that a small percentage increase in market share is sufficient to establish the prohibited effect. The degree of market concentration prior to the merger and the relative position of the merged parties are important factors in such cases. Where there has been a history of tendency toward concentration in an industry, slight increases in further concentration are prohibited because of the policy of the law to curb such tendencies in their incipiency. The following case illustrates the great uncertainty that exists as to the legality of many mergers and acquisitions. Note that the law deals with probabilities and is designed to arrest anticompetitive tendencies at their incipiency.

# UNITED STATES v. VON'S GROCERY CO.
384 U.S. 270 (1966)

The United States brought an action which charged that the acquisition by Von's Grocery Company of Shopping Bag Food Stores violated Section 7 of the Clayton Act. After the district court refused the request of the government for a temporary injunction, Von's immediately took over Shopping Bag's capital stock and assets. Then, after hearing the evidence, the district court entered judgment for the defendants, ruling as a matter of law that there was "not a reasonable probability" that the acquisition would tend "substantially to lessen competition" or tend to "create a monopoly." The government appealed.

BLACK, J.:...The record shows the following facts relevant to our decision. The market involved here is the retail grocery market in the Los Angeles area. In 1958 Von's retail sales ranked third in the area and Shopping Bag's ranked sixth. In 1960 their sales together were 7.5% of the total two and one-half billion dollars of retail groceries sold in the Los Angeles market each year. For many years before the merger both companies had enjoyed great success as rapidly growing companies. From 1948 to 1958 the number of Von's stores in the Los Angeles area practically doubled from 14 to 27, while at the same time the number of Shopping Bag's stores jumped from 15 to 34. During that same decade, Von's sales increased fourfold and its share of the market almost doubled, while Shopping Bag's sales multiplied seven times and its share of the market tripled. The merger of these two highly successful, expanding and aggressive competitors created the second largest grocery chain in Los Angeles with sales of almost $172,488,000 annually. In addition the findings of the District Court show that the number of owners operating a single store in the Los Angeles retail grocery market decreased from 5,365 in 1950 to 3,818 in 1961. By 1963, three years after the merger, the number of single-store owners had dropped still further to 3,590. During roughly the same period from 1953 to 1962 the number of chains with two or more grocery stores increased from 96 to 150. While the grocery business was being concentrated into the hands of fewer and fewer owners, the small companies were continually being absorbed by the larger firms through mergers. According to an exhibit prepared by one of the Government's expert witnesses, in the period from 1949 to 1958 nine of the top 20 chains acquired 126 stores from their smaller competitors. Figures of a principal defense witness...illustrate the many acquisitions and mergers in the Los Angeles grocery industry from 1953 through 1961 including acquisitions made by Food Giant, Alpha Beta, Fox and Mayfair, all among the 10 leading chains in the area. Moreover, a table prepared by the Federal Trade Commission appearing in the Government's reply brief, but not a part of the record here, shows that acquisitions and mergers in the Los Angeles retail grocery market have continued at a rapid rate since the merger. These facts alone are enough to cause us to conclude contrary to the District Court that Von's Shopping Bag merger did violate § 7. Accordingly, we reverse....

Like the Sherman Act in 1890 and the Clayton Act in 1914, the basic purpose of the 1950 Celler-Kefauver Bill was to prevent economic concentration in the American economy by keeping a large number of small competitors in business. In stating the purposes of the bill, both of its sponsors, Representative Celler and Senator Kefauver, emphasized their fear, widely shared by other members of Congress, that this concentration was rapidly driving the small businessman out of the market. The period from 1940 to 1947, which was at the center of attraction throughout the hearings and debates on the Celler-Kefauver Bill, had been characterized by a series of mergers between large corporations and their smaller competitors resulting in the steady erosion of the small independent business in our economy....

The facts of this case present exactly the threatening trend toward concentration which Congress wanted to halt. The number of small grocery companies in the Los Angeles retail grocery market had been declining rapidly before the merger and continued to decline rapidly afterwards. This rapid decline in the number of grocery store owners moved hand in hand with a large number of significant absorptions of the small companies by the larger ones. In the midst of this steadfast trend toward concentration, Von's and Shopping Bag, two of the most successful and largest companies in the area, jointly owning 66 grocery stores, merged to become the second largest chain in Los Angeles. This merger cannot be defended on the ground that one of the companies was about to fail or that the two had to merge to save themselves from destruction by some larger and more powerful competitor. What we have on the contrary is simply the case of two already powerful companies merging in a way which makes them even more powerful than they were before. If ever such a merger would not violate § 7, certainly it does when it takes place in a market characterized by a long and continuous trend toward fewer and fewer owner-competitors, which is exactly the sort of trend which Congress, with power to do so, declared must be arrested.

Appellee's primary argument is that the merger between Von's and Shopping Bag is not prohibited by § 7 because the Los Angeles grocery market was competitive before the merger, has been since, and may continue to be in the future. Even so, § 7 "requires not merely an appraisal of the immediate impact of the merger upon competition, but a prediction of its impact upon competitive conditions in the future; this is what is meant when it is said that the amended § 7 was intended to arrest anticompetitive tendencies in their 'incipiency.'" It is enough for us that Congress feared that a market marked at the same time by both a continuous decline in the number of small businesses and a large number of mergers would, slowly but inevitably, gravitate from a market of many small competitors to one dominated by one or a few giants, and competition would thereby be destroyed. Congress passed the Celler-Kefauver Bill to prevent such a destruction of competition. Our cases since the passage of that bill have faithfully endeavored to enforce this congressional command. We adhere to them now....Since appellees have been on notice of the anti-trust charge from almost the beginning...we not only reverse the judgment below but direct the District Court to order divestiture without delay. [*Reversed.*]

[Two of the Justices issued a strong dissent from the majority opinion above, stating in effect that the court was holding that the existence of certain superficial facts which were unrelated to any actual anticompetitive effects lead to a conclusion that the merger violated Section 7, per se. They argued that there should be demonstrated at least a reasonable probability of a substantial reduction in competition before a merger is outlawed, and that an examination of the economic facts in the relevant market did not establish such a probability in the *Von's Grocery* case.]

The Reagan administration followed a policy of limited application of Section 7. It allowed numerous mergers and acquisitions of large companies involving billions of dollars to go unchallenged. Its only concern was with a few horizontal acquisitions. The extend to which the Bush administration will use the principles of Section 7 is unclear.

### 16.   Special Doctrines

The law recognizes two special doctrines in the merger area. These are commonly referred to as the *potential-entrant doctrine* and *the failing-company doctrine*. The **potential-entrant doctrine** recognizes that there may be injury to competition as the result of a loss of a potential competitor. Of course, potential competitors that actually join a market increase competition. In addition, the mere presence of a potential competitor may affect a market by influencing the conduct of those actually competing. For example, the existence of a potential entrant may inhibit price increases. Actual competitors may price their goods just below the level that would attract the potential entrants to the market.

The potential-entrant doctrine finds that the prohibited effect may exist when an acquisition or merger involves a potential entrant into a market. An acquisition of a competitor by a potential competitor is thus illegal when the effect may be to substantially lessen competition. The potential-entrant doctrine has been used to prevent product extension mergers as well as geographic extension mergers. The potential-entrant doctrine is applied not only because if entry does occur there is an additional competitor, but also because the mere presence of a potential competitor at the edge of the market has positive effects on those companies actually competing.

In the 1920s, the Supreme Court created a **failing-company exception** to the law restricting mergers. It held that when a company is failing, the statutory prohibitions on anticompetitive mergers are set aside. The company in the case in which the exception was decided had in one year turned a surplus of $4 million into a deficit of $4.4 million.

The failing-company doctrine allows for special approval of mergers that would otherwise be unlawful. There are three general conditions which must be met. First, the acquisition candidate must be on the brink of bankruptcy. Second, corporate reorganization under Chapter 11 of the bankruptcy laws must not be a viable alternative. Finally, the doctrine requires proof that there is no other merger partner that would raise fewer antitrust problems.

Historically, the courts have been quite strict in interpreting the failing-company doctrine. They have required clear and convincing proof of the foregoing conditions. However, the Justice Department and the FTC have been more lenient in deciding which cases to oppose. The Justice Department's attitude has always been to recognize the doctrine and not to challenge those involving companies in serious financial difficulty. It has tended to consider the long-term prospects of a company, and if the future looks bleak, it has tended not to challenge the acquisition of a failing company.

As more and more companies have diversified and acquired subsidiaries, the failing-company doctrine has been applied to failing divisions and failing subsidiaries. If a company is about to close down an operation and a competitor is willing to take it over, society is probably better off if the law allows the sale or divestiture of the division rather than have it no longer exist as an economic unit. A sale which increases concentration is preferable to the death of the unit. At least the employees would still have jobs, and a new owner may be able to restore the division or organization to a profitable entity.

## 17.   Enforcement

Section 7 of the Clayton Act is enforced by the Justice Department, the FTC, and individuals and affected firms. It is both a tool to prevent hostile takeovers and a law that is enforced by government. The basic remedy used by the Justice Department is the injunction. The FTC may prevent a merger by use of a cease and desist order, or it may order a divestiture through a decision which finds unfair methods of competition.

The injunction is a major sanction used by government and individuals in the merger field. A preliminary injunction prevents consummation of a merger until all legal issues are resolved. Preliminary injunctions are issued whenever there is a strong likelihood that the merger is illegal if there is potential for serious injury to the public from the proposed merger. After a trial, a preliminary injunction either is made permanent or is dissolved. If it is dissolved, the parties are free to proceed with the merger.

The injunction remedy is also used after mergers have been consummated. Such mandatory injunctions may require a divestiture of a merged firm or even a sale of stock in the event there is only partial ownership. Sometimes an acquisition or merger is challenged many years after it was consummated. While an acquisition of stock or assets may be perfectly legal at that time, it later may become illegal because it "threatens to ripen into a prohibited effect" of substantially lessening competition. The test of illegality is the time of the challenge.

The remedy of triple damages, in effect, allows one's competitors and other individuals directly affected to enforce the antimerger provisions of the Clayton Act. There have been numerous triple damage suits brought by one competitor against another and by a takeover candidate against its "suitor." Such suits may seek damages because of inadequate prices or for the costs of fending off a hostile takeover.

The FTC looks at market share as an important indication of anticompetitive effects of mergers. Other factors considered are barriers to entry and technological changes. If the barriers to entry are low, market share is less important. The FTC has indicated that it will give great weight to the Justice Department guidelines, which are discussed in more detail in Section 19.

The FTC also examines the companies involved. Market power is more important than market share. Market share may understate competitive significance. For example, a firm with a small market share may have unique competitive potential. Since mergers may improve the efficiency of a firm, this factor is considered in deciding whether or not to challenge an acquisition. However, if the challenge is made, increased efficiency is no defense. The failing-division as well as the failing-company doctrine are also considered by the FTC. The fact that a company or a part of one may go out of business is obviously a factor to consider, unless someone else seeks to take it over and keep it as a competitor.

Most cases involving Section 7 are settled by agreement. Many consent decrees in merger cases contain an arrangement that the company involved will not acquire any other firm for a stated period of time. Such decrees frequently provide that the divesting company will not engage in a certain line of business for a stated period, as well. The usual number of years in such cases is ten, although some have been for as long as twenty.

The Justice Department has used Section 7 of the Clayton Act as a basis for attacking foreign acquisitions. For example, it was used to prevent the Gillette Company from acquiring a German manufacturer of electric razors. The theory was that the German company was a potential competitor in the domestic shaving instrument market. Thus, the power of United States courts applies to foreign as well as to domestic mergers.

## 18. Tender Offers

It should be recognized that many acquisitions and mergers are not the result of a mutual agreement. Many takeovers are, in fact, hostile, at least insofar as the management of the acquired firms is concerned. Hostile takeovers occur as a result of **tender offers** by the acquiring firm to the shareholders of the acquired firm. The management of the firm to be acquired often objects to the takeover, for very obvious reasons. Hostile takeovers usually result in wholesale changes in management, and existing management is simply fighting for survival. Moreover, if roadblocks are placed in the path of a merger, the price may be raised and other offerors may even enter the picture. It is common for existing management to contend that an offering price is too low even though the offering price is substantially in excess of current market price. Existing management frequently raises legal objections to a proposed takeover, even though the Justice Department and the FTC do not.

To discourage hostile takeovers, a variety of techniques have been developed and are being adopted by various corporations and state governments interested in protecting local businesses. Among the techniques are the following:

**1** *Fair pricing bylaws:* These require that all shareholders be paid the same price for their stock in the event of a takeover.

**2** *Staggered terms for directors:* These bylaws make it more difficult to gain control of the board of directors. Since fewer directors are elected each year, more votes are required to elect a director.

**3** *Special stock issues:* These give special voting rights to a limited group of shareholders likely to oppose a takeover.

**4** *Stronger voting guidelines:* These require a large percentage of all shareholders to approve a merger or takeover. Some of these percentages are as high as 95 percent.

**5** *Golden parachutes:* These contracts protect executives by guaranteeing them cash settlements equal to several years' salaries if a takeover occurs.

**6** *Corporate restructuring:* Corporations sometimes take "poison pills," in the form of increased debt, to avoid a takeover. The debt may be used to buy back stock. Valuable units are also sometimes sold to make a business less attractive.

These techniques have been described as **shark repellents,** because the company attempting a hostile takeover is viewed as a shark. They are needed by existing management, because the price offered is usually significantly higher than the existing market price of the stock. The fair-price bylaw stops someone from buying majority control at one price and paying a lower price or not purchasing the shares of other shareholders. The proposal for staggered terms for directors is designed to prevent someone from buying 5 percent or 10 percent of a company's stock and threatening a proxy fight unless management agrees to buy back the raider's stock at a premium. This latter technique is often described as **greenmail** to indicate that it is, in fact, a form of blackmail by which individuals or companies force someone to pay them off to avoid a takeover.

The *golden parachute* phenomenon does not prevent many mergers and acquisitions. However, it does give management the security of knowing that it will be well rewarded financially if a takeover occurs. There have been so many agreements providing golden parachutes in recent months that the SEC is seriously considering rules that limit such agreements. Under the terms of some agreements, a corporate president may receive several million dollars in the event the business is taken over by another organization. Some agreements call for the opening of the parachute on less than a total change of ownership and management.

Another technique used to fight takeovers is often referred to as the **white knight.** The white knight is another firm that makes a competing offer at a price significantly higher than the tender offer. The white knight is a friendly takeover candidate, and its presence creates a bidding war. The use of the white knight is in recognition that the company is likely to lose its independence, and, therefore, the best arrangement is a friendly rather than a hostile buyer.

Another technique used to discourage hostile takeovers is known as the *lockup.* In a lockup, the target company agrees either to sell part of its stock or part of its company to an acquirer of its choice. The lockup usually involves a white knight, and it frequently means that the most attractive part of the company is gone, thus discouraging the hostile takeover. The net effect of a lockup is to favor one bidder over another and to stack the deck in favor of one. Sometimes the lockup simply involves an option to someone to purchase a significant portion of the business.

Congress is considering several means of curbing unfriendly takeovers. Some people contend that the antitrust laws should be tightened to restrict unfriendly takeovers as a predatory practice. Others contend that the employees should be given the power to veto unfriendly takeovers. Finally, there is substantial support for new laws prohibiting greenmail. In some recent situations, greenmail has rewarded certain individuals and companies they control with windfall profits of $30 million to $40 million. A buyer can achieve such a windfall by acquiring a substantial block of stock and forcing management to rebuy it at a premium. One of the notable examples of greenmail in recent years involved Walt Disney. In this situation, one group made millions of dollars and significantly depressed the value of Disney stock in the process.

## 19. FTC Premerger Notification

The application of Section 7 to any given merger is discretionary with the Justice Department and the FTC. Both have issued guidelines as to which mergers are likely to be challenged, but they have reserved the right to bring action against mergers and acquisitions they feel will probably lessen competition or tend to create a monopoly. To assist in enforcement, the FTC, pursuant to a 1976 statute, has adopted a premerger notification rule. This rule requires that prior notice be given to the Justice Department and to the FTC of all pending mergers subject to the rule. Once the notice is given in advance of the acquisition, either agency may institute appropriate action to prevent it.

The application of the premerger notification rules are determined by the size of the firms involved and the size of the transaction. The rules cover transactions involving at least 15 percent of either the assets or the voting securities of the firm to be acquired when the value of the purchase exceeds $15 million. The value of the assets is determined by fair market value, not by book value. The value of the securities is current value, not par value.

If we assume that the transaction is within the required size, we find that the premerger rules are applied if the acquiring party has either annual net sales or total assets of $100 million or more, and if the acquired firm is engaged in manufacturing and has annual net sales or total assets of $5 million or more. If the acquired firm is not engaged in manufacturing, the rule applies if the acquired firm has total assets of $5 million, irrespective of the size of sales. To prevent avoidance of the rules by having the smaller firm acquire the larger, the rules are also applicable whenever an acquired firm has annual sales of $10 million or more and the acquiring firm has annual sales of $100 million or more.

The notification requires a brief description of the proposed acquisition, the amount of securities or assets being acquired, and the manner of acquisition. It will include the sales information, broken down by industry, product class, and product. Copies of all SEC filings, together with market information and facts relative to other acquisitions by both firms, must be submitted.

## 20. Justice Department Merger Guidelines

In 1982, the Justice Department issued new **merger guidelines.** The guidelines are designed primarily to indicate when the Justice Department is likely to challenge a merger. These latest guidelines are more permissive than the ones announced in the 1960s, and most of their attention is directed at horizontal acquisitions. Under the new guidelines, the legality of vertical and conglomerate mergers is judged solely on their impact on future direct competition. Horizontal mergers are examined for the post-merger market concentration and the increase in concentration resulting from the merger.

An index known as the **Herfindahl-Hirschman Index** (HHI) is used to test the legality of horizontal acquisitions. The index is computed by squaring the market share of each firm in a market and adding the results. If the sum is 1,000 or less, the merger probably will not be challenged, as the market is considered to be unconcentrated, having the equivalent of at least ten equally sized firms. If the sum is between 1,000 and 1,800, a careful examination of the moderately concentrated market will be made to determine if acquisition is likely to harm competition. Harm will likely be found if the merger adds 100 points to the index. If less than fifty points are added, the Justice Department is unlikely to challenge the merger. The amount a merger will add is equal to twice the product of the merging firms' market share.

Notwithstanding the foregoing use of the HHI, the Justice Department is likely to challenge the merger of any firm with 1 percent of the market with the leading firm if the latter has 35 percent or more of the total market and is approximately twice as large as the second largest firm. In addition to examining market concentration and market share, the Justice Department also examines ease of entry, the nature of the product, conduct of firms in the market, and market performance in deciding if a merger will be challenged. Keep in mind that the HHI is only a guide and a general prediction of which mergers and acquisitions will actually be challenged. A sample HHI calculation is shown in Table 24-1.

In 1984, the Justice Department revised the merger guidelines to clarify some aspects of them. The revision explains the techniques to be used in defining and measuring a market. It also lists the factors that may affect the significance of concentration and market-share data in evaluating horizontal mergers. The guidelines also indicate that foreign competition will be included in the relevant market data, even though there are important quotas. Import quotas are treated as a separate factor to be considered.

The revised guidelines indicate that if entry into a market is so easy that existing competitors could not succeed in raising prices for any significant

**TABLE 24-1**   Example of HHI Calculation

Assumptions: In a market of ten firms, with market shares as stated, Firm No. 4 seeks to merge with Firm No. 8.

| Firm No. | Assumed Market Share | Premerger Index | Assumed Merger of No. 4 + No. 8 Index |
|---|---|---|---|
| 1 | 20 | 400 | 400 |
| 2 | 18 | 324 | 324 |
| 3 | 16 | 256 | 256 |
| 4 | 12 | 144 | 289 |
| 5 | 10 | 100 | 100 |
| 6 | 8 | 64 | 64 |
| 7 | 6 | 36 | 36 |
| 8 | 5 | 25 | -- |
| 9 | 3 | 9 | 9 |
| 10 | 2 | 4 | 4 |
| | Increase of +120 | 1,362 | 1,482 |

Note that the increase in the index is equal to the product of the market share of the merging firms times 2 ($12 \times 5 \times 2 = 120$).

period of time, the Department is unlikely to challenge mergers in that market. The Department is more likely to challenge a merger in the following circumstances:

**1**   Firms in the market previously have been found to have engaged in horizontal collusion in regard to price, territories, and customers, and the characteristics of the market have not changed appreciably since the most recent finding.

**2**   One or more of the following types of practices are adopted by substantially all of the firms in the market: (a) mandatory delivered pricing; (b) exchange of price or output information in a form that could assist firms in setting or enforcing an agreed price; (c) collective standardization of product variables on which the firms could compete; and (d) price protection clauses.

**3**   The firm to be acquired has been an unusually disruptive and competitive influence in the market.

Two other items of the revised guidelines are worthy of note. First, the Department recognizes that increased efficiency is generally desirable. Some mergers that otherwise might be challenged may be reasonably necessary to achieve significant net efficiencies. If the parties to the merger establish by clear and convincing evidence that a merger will achieve such efficiencies, those efficiencies will be considered in deciding whether to challenge the merger. Efficiency claims will be rejected if comparable savings can reasonably be achieved through other means.

Second, the guidelines recognize the failing-company doctrine and note that it has been ambiguous. The guidelines indicate that the Justice Department is unlikely to challenge an anticompetitive merger in which one of the merging firms is allegedly failing when: (1) the allegedly failing firm probably would be unable to meet its financial obligations in the near future; (2) it probably would not be able to reorganize successfully in bankruptcy; and (3) it has made unsuccessful good-faith efforts to elicit reasonable acquisition offers that would keep it in the market and pose a less severe danger to competition. Similarly, the "failure" of a division is an important factor affecting the likely competitive effect of a merger.

## THE FEDERAL TRADE COMMISSION ACT

### 21.   Introduction

The FTC was created in 1914 to have an "independent" administrative agency charged with keeping competition free and fair. It enforces the

Clayton Act provisions on price discrimination, tying and exclusive contracts, mergers and acquisitions, and interlocking directorates. In addition, it enforces Section 5 of the Federal Trade Commission Act. This act originally made "unfair methods of competition" in commerce unlawful. The *Wheeler-Lea amendments* of 1938 added that "unfair or deceptive acts or practices in commerce" were also unlawful under Section 5. The FTC has broad, sweeping powers and a mandate to determine what methods, acts, or practices fall within the vague category of being "unfair or deceptive" and are thus unlawful. Such decisions are made on a case-by-case basis. A discussion of unfair methods of competition follows in the next section. Since unfair or deceptive acts or practices were prohibited to protect consumers and not competition, they were discussed in Chapter 20, which deals with consumer protection. That chapter also discussed many of the other consumer protection statutes for which the FTC has enforcement responsibility.

The FTC issues trade regulation rules which deal with business practices in an industry. For example, the FTC has said the American Medical Association must allow doctors to advertise. The FTC also periodically issues "trade practice rules and guides," sometimes referred to as industry guides. These rules are the FTC's informal opinion of legal requirements applicable to a particular industry's practices. Although compliance with the rules is voluntary, they provide the basis for the informal and simultaneous abandonment by industry members of practices thought to be unlawful. *Guidelines* are administrative interpretations of the statutes which the Commission enforces, and they provide guidance to both the FTC staff and businesspeople evaluating the legality of certain practices. Guidelines deal with a particular practice and may cut across industry lines.

The primary function of the FTC is to prevent illegal business practices rather than to punish violations. It prevents wrongful actions by use of cease and desist orders. Whereas violations of these orders may be punished by a fine of $10,000 per day, with each day being a new violation, the punishment factor is only incidental to the FTC's primary prevention role. As noted in Chapter 8 on administrative law, most FTC cases are settled by consent orders. In such cases, the respondent need not admit a law violation but agrees *not* to do the complained-of act in the future.

## 22.   Unfair Methods of Competition

Although the original Section 5 of the FTC Act outlawed unfair methods of competition in commerce and directed the FTC to prevent the use of such, it offered no definition of the specific practices which were unfair. The term "unfair methods of competition" was designed by Congress as a flexible concept, the exact meaning of which could evolve on a case-by-case basis. It can apply to a variety of unrelated activities. It is generally up to the FTC to determine what business conduct is "unfair." Great deference is given to the FTC's opinion as to what constitutes a violation and to the remedies it desires to correct anticompetitive behavior. To decide whether challenged business conduct is "unfair" as a method of competition or as a commercial practice, the Commission asks three major questions if there is no deception or antitrust violation involved:

**1**  Does the conduct injure consumers significantly?

**2**  Does the conduct offend an established public policy? (Conduct may offend public policy even though not previously unlawful.)

**3**  Is the conduct oppressive, unscrupulous, immoral, or unethical?

Answering any one of these questions affirmatively could lead to a finding of unfairness. The Supreme Court has declared that the Commission can operate "like a court of equity" in considering "public values" to establish what is unfair under Section 5.

Business conduct in violation of any provision of the antitrust laws may also be ruled illegal under Section 5 of the FTC Act. Further, anticompetitive acts or practices which *fall short* of transgressing the Sherman or Clayton Acts may be restrained by the FTC as being "unfair methods of competition."

If a business practice is such that it is doubtful that the evidence is sufficient to prove a Sherman or Clayton Act violation, the FTC may nevertheless proceed and find that the business practice is unfair. Thus, business practices which could not be prevented in a judicial proceeding may be stopped by FTC cease and desist orders.

In FTC cases, the concepts of per se illegality and the rule of reason are used to determine the elements of proof required. While proof of relevant markets may be required, the FTC looks at the reality of the situation to see if elaborate market analysis is required. In the case which follows, the court did not require the FTC to examine the effects on the three-county market in great detail. The court more or less simply recognized that the markets for dental services tend to be localized.

---

# F.T.C. v. INDIANA FEDERATION OF DENTISTS
106 S.Ct. 2009 (1986)

---

WHITE, J.: This case concerns commercial relations among certain Indiana dentists, their patients, and the patients' dental health care insurers.... 

Since the 1970's, dental health insurers... have attempted to contain the cost of dental treatment by, among other devices, limiting payment of benefits to the cost of the "least expensive yet adequate treatment" suitable to the needs of individual patients. Implementation of such cost-containment measures, known as "alternative benefits" plans, requires evaluation by the insurer of the diagnosis and recommendation of the treating dentist....In order to carry out such evaluation, insurers frequently request dentists to submit, along with insurance claim forms requesting payment of benefits, any dental x rays that have been used by the dentist in examining the patient....Typically, claim forms and accompanying x rays are reviewed by...dental consultants, who are licensed dentists....The dental consultant may recommend that the insurer approve a claim, deny it, or pay only for a less expensive course of treatment.

Such review of diagnostic and treatment decisions has been viewed by some dentists as a threat to their professional independence and economic well-being. In the early 1970's, the Indiana Dental Association... initiated an aggressive effort to hinder insurers' efforts to implement alternative benefits plans by enlisting member dentists to pledge not to submit x rays in conjunction with claim forms. The Association's efforts met considerable success...

By the mid-1970's, fears of possible antitrust liability had dampened the Association's enthusiasm for opposing the submission of x rays to insurers. In 1979, the Association...consented to a Federal Trade Commission order requiring them to cease and desist from further efforts to prevent member dentists from submitting x rays.... In 1976, a group of such dentists formed the Indiana Federation of Dentists, respondent in this case, in order to continue to pursue the Association's ploy of resisting insurers' requests for x rays. The Federation... immediately promulgated a "work rule" forbidding its members to submit x rays to dental insurers in conjunction with claim forms. Although the Federation's membership was small, numbering less than 100, its members were highly concentrated in and around three Indiana communities: Anderson, Lafayette, and Fort Wayne. The Federation succeeded in enlisting nearly 100% of the dental specialists in the Anderson area, and approximately 67% of the dentists in and around Lafayette. In the areas of its strength, the Federation was successful in continuing to enforce the Association's prior policy of refusal to submit x rays to dental insurers.

In 1978, the Federal Trade Commission issued a complaint against the Federation, alleging in substance that its efforts to prevent its members from complying with insurers' requests for x rays constituted an unfair method of competition in violation of § 5 of the Federal Trade Commission Act. Following lengthy proceedings...the Commission ruled that the Federation's policy constituted a violation of § 5 and issued an order requiring the Federation to cease and desist from further efforts to organize dentists to refuse to submit x rays to insurers. The Commission based its ruling on the conclusion that the Federation's policy of requiring its members to withhold x rays amounted to a conspiracy in restraint of trade that was unreasonable and hence unlawful under...§ 1 of the Sherman Act. The Commission found that...the Federation's policy had had the actual effect of eliminating such competition among dentists and preventing insurers from obtaining access to x rays in the desired manner. These findings of anticompetitive effect, the Commission concluded, were sufficient to establish that the restraint was unreasonable even absent proof that the Federation's policy had resulted in higher costs to the insurers and patients than would have occurred had the x rays been provided....

The Federation sought judicial review of the Commission's order in the United States Court of Appeals for the Seventh Circuit, which vacated the order on the ground that it was not supported by substantial evidence.

The issue is whether the Commission erred in holding that the Federation's policy of refusal to submit x rays to dental insurers for use in benefits determinations constituted an "unfair method of competition," unlawful under § 5 of the Federal Trade Commission Act....

In the case now before us, the sole basis of the FTC's finding of an unfair method of competition was the Commission's conclusion that the Federation's collective decision to withhold x rays from insurers was an unreasonable and conspiratorial restraint of trade in violation of § 1 of the Sherman Act. Accordingly, the legal question before us is whether the Commission's factual findings, if supported by evidence, make out a violation of Sherman Act § 1.

[After finding that the evidence supported the Commission's findings, the court continued...]

The question remains whether these findings are legally sufficient to establish a violation of § 1 of the Sherman Act—that is, whether the Federation's collective refusal to cooperate with insurers' requests for x rays constitutes an "unreasonable" restraint of trade. Under our precedents, a restraint may be adjudged unreasonable either because it fits within a class of restraints that has been held to be "*per se*" unreasonable, or because it violates what has come to be known as the "Rule of Reason," under which the "test of legality is whether the restraint imposed is such as merely regulates and perhaps thereby promotes competition or whether it is such as may suppress or even destroy competition."...We have been slow to condemn rules adopted by professional associations as unreasonable *per se,* and, in general, to extend *per se* analysis to restraints imposed in the context of business relationships where the economic impact of certain practices is not immediately obvious. Thus, as did the FTC, we evaluate the restraint at issue in this case under the Rule of Reason rather than a rule of *per se* illegality.

Application of the Rule of Reason to these facts is not a matter of any great difficulty. The Federation's policy takes the form of a horizontal agreement among the participating dentists to withhold from their customers a particular service that they desire— the forwarding of x rays to insurance companies along with claim forms. "While this is not price fixing as such, no elaborate industry analysis is required to demonstrate the anticompetitive character of such an agreement." A refusal to compete with respect to the package of services offered to customers, no less than a refusal to compete with respect to the price term of an agreement, impairs the ability of the market to advance social welfare by ensuring the provision of desired goods and services to consumers at a price approximating the marginal cost of providing them. Absent some countervailing procompetitive virtue—such as, for example, the creation of efficiencies in the operation of a market or the provision of goods and services, such an agreement limiting consumer choice by impeding the "ordinary give and take of the market place," cannot be sustained under the Rule of Reason. No credible argument has been advanced for the proposition that making it more costly for the insurers and patients who are the dentists' customers to obtain information needed for evaluating the dentists' diagnoses has any such procompetitive effect....

In this case, we conclude that the finding of actual, sustained adverse effects on competition in those areas where IFD dentists predominated, viewed in light of the reality that markets for dental services tend to be relatively localized, is legally sufficient to support a finding that the challenged restraint was unreasonable even in the absence of elaborate market analysis.

The factual findings of the Commission regarding the effect of the Federation's policy of withholding x rays are supported by substantial evidence, and those findings are sufficient as a matter of law to establish a violation of § 1 of the Sherman Act, and, hence, § 5 of the Federal Trade Commission Act....[*Reversed.*]

# REVIEW QUESTIONS

**1** For each term in the left-hand column, match the most appropriate description in the right-hand column:

(1) Horizontal merger

(a) When an individual is a member of the board of directors of two or more competing corporations at the same time.

(2) Conglomerate merger

(b) When a commodity is sold or leased for use only on condition that the buyer or lessee purchase certain additional products or services from the seller or lessor.

(3) Requirements contract

(c) A contract whereby a buyer agrees not to purchase an item or items of merchandise from competitors of the seller.

(4) Full-time forcing

(d) A buyer agrees to purchase all of his or her business needs of a product from the seller during a certain period.

(5) Predatory pricing

(e) The administrative equivalent of a court injunction, which is issued by an administrative agency with quasi-judicial powers to restrain future violations of the law.

(6) Exclusive-dealing contract

(f) An arrangement that exists when two parties face each other as both buyer and seller.

(7) Reciprocal dealing

(g) To sell at prices below average variable cost to close out competition.

(8) Tying contract

(h) A doctrine which allows an acquisition to proceed because the company to be acquired would likely to go out of business because of financial difficulty.

(9) Cease and desist order

(i) Techniques used to prevent hostile takeovers.

(10) Interlocking directorate

(j) Contracts requiring payment of large salaries to corporate officials in the event the firm is acquired and the officials are replaced.

(11) Shark repellents

(k) A form of tying arrangement in which the buyer or lessee is compelled to take a complete product line from the seller as a condition of being permitted to purchase the main product of the line.

(12) Potential-entrant doctrine

(l) A merger which combines two businesses which formerly competed with each other in a particular line of commerce.

(13) Vertical merger

(m) A merger which brings together a customer in a line of commerce and a supplier.

(14) Failing-company doctrine

(n) A merger in which the businesses that are combined neither compete nor are related as customer and supplier in any given line of commerce.

(15) Golden parachute

(o) A doctrine that makes certain acquisitions illegal if the acquiring company might enter the product or geographic market of the acquired company and compete with it were it not for the acquisition.

**2**  Copp Paving Company sues Gulford for triple damages, alleging a violation of the Robinson-Patman amendment. Copp operates an asphaltic concrete "hotplant" in California. The plant manufactures asphalt for surfacing highways, including interstate highways, in California. Its whole operation is in intrastate commerce. Does the complaint allege a valid claim? Why, or why not?

**3**  Alice, who recently received a degree in business, has been named general sales manager of a building materials manufacturer. She calls a meeting of the sales force, and among other matters Alice makes the following statement: "We will cut prices so low our competitors will be cut off at the knees." If this policy is carried out, will any law be violated? Explain.

**4**   In the same situation as question 3, Alice later calls on the corporation's most important customer. While informing this customer of its special importance, Alice said: "To you, Larry, and to you alone, the price we charge will always be below cost." If this policy is carried out, will it be in violation of any law? Explain.

**5**   A class action suit is brought against defendant corporation for alleged violations of Section 1 of the Sherman Act, stemming from *tying arrangements* included in fast-food franchise agreements. Under the tie-in, potential franchisees are required to purchase a specified amount of cooking equipment and other items at a higher cost than competitors' products. What will be the result? Why?

**6**   A cemetery sells bronze markers for grave sites. It learns that it is paying $10 per marker more than a local monument dealer. It sues the manufacturer for triple damages and offers proof of the price differential and that it has purchased 1,000 markers. How much is it entitled to collect? Why?

**7**   The American Medical Association adopts a code of ethics which prohibits all advertising by physicians. Included in the prohibition are ads that indicate that physicians will make house calls. The FTC challenges the ethical rules under Section 5 of the FTC Act. What is the result? Why?

**8**   A department store solicits and receives contributions from vendors toward the cost of the store's one-hundredth anniversary celebration. The store gives the vendors no direct promotional services for vendors' products. Is the store in violation of Section 2 of the Clayton Act as amended? Why or why not?

**9**   Weinberg is on the board of directors of both Sears Roebuck & Company and B.

F. Goodrich. Sears and Goodrich each have capital, surplus, and undivided profits in excess of $1 million. They compete with each other on the retail level in ninety-seven communities in the sale of appliances, hardware, automotive supplies, sporting goods, tires, radios, television sets, and toys. Is Weinberg acting illegally? Why or why not?

**10**   In 1984, Standard Oil of California acquired the Gulf Oil Corporation for $13.4 billion, and it also acquired the Getty Oil Company for $10.1 billion. The Justice Department and the FTC decided not to challenge the acquisition. Could these mergers still be challenged? Explain.

**11**   In an industry, there were ten competitors, each with the following market shares:

| | |
|---|---|
| 1–20% | 6–10% |
| 2–18% | 7–8% |
| 3–16% | 8–5% |
| 4–15% | 9–3% |
| 5–12% | 10–1% |

Number 7 decides to merge with number 9. Will the merger be challenged under the 1982 guidelines? Explain.

**12**   Plaintiff operate a frozen dessert pie plant in Salt Lake City, Utah. The defendants market fruit pies nationally on a greater scale than the plaintiff. The defendants sell pies cheaper in the Salt Lake City market than elsewhere. Is this a Robinson-Patman violation? Why or why not?

**13**   Maxwell House, Inc. (the second-largest producer of coffee in the United States, with 36 percent of the United States market), proposes to merge with Yuban, Inc. (the tenth-largest producer of coffee in the United States, with 5 percent of the United States market). The coffee-producing industry is highly concentrated—the four largest firms have 76 percent of the United States market. Maxwell House has agreed to this merger, despite the fact that Yuban has suffered financial losses in seven of the last ten years and for the past four years consecutively. Is it likely that the merger will be challenged? Explain.

**14**  Coca-Cola entered into an agreement to buy Dr. Pepper, and Pepsi-Cola entered into an agreement to purchase 7-Up. The proposed acquisitions would give Coca-Cola and Pepsi-Cola 80 percent of the domestic soft-drink market. Royal Crown challenges the acquisition. Will the FTC stop the mergers? Why or why not?

**15**  The Brown Shoe franchise agreement provides that the retail franchisees will restrict their purchases of shoes to the Brown Shoe lines. In return, the retail operators will be given valuable benefits that are not granted to retail operators who do not execute the agreement. Can the FTC stop the use of the Brown Shoe franchise agreement as an unfair trade practice? Why or why not?

# Chapter

# 25

# Environmental Laws and Pollution Control

## CHAPTER PREVIEW

This chapter examines environmental laws and pollution control. Note that environmental regulation remains the single most expensive area of government's regulation of the business community. Over the next decade, industry will spend several hundred billion dollars on pollution control.

We can separate environmental laws into three main divisions: (1) government's regulation of itself, (2) government's regulation of business, and (3) suits by private individuals. Table 25-1 illustrates this breakdown.

Administering environmental laws at the federal level is the Environmental Protection Agency (EPA). Since many of the laws provide for joint federal-state enforcement, the states also have strong environmental agencies. Policies are set at the federal level, and the states devise plans to implement them.

Important terms in this chapter include: bubble concept, emissions reduction banking, environmental impact statement, manifest system, public and private nuisance, point source, prevention of significant deterioration, primary and secondary air quality standards, scoping, and Superfund.

**TABLE 25-1**   Pollution Control Laws

*Government's Regulation of Itself*
  National Environmental Policy Act
  State environmental policy acts
*Government's Regulation of Business*
  Clean Air Act
  Clean Water Act
  Noise Control Act
  Pesticide control acts
  Solid Waste Disposal Act
  Toxic Substances Control Act
  Natural Resource Conservation and Recovery Act
  Other federal, state, and local statutes
*Suits by Private Individuals*
  Public and private nuisance
  Strict liability for ultrahazardous activity
  Negligence
  Trespass
  Citizen enforcement provisions of various statutes

## 1.  The National Environmental Policy Act

The way government regulates the environmental impact of its decision making interests the business community greatly. The federal government, for instance, pays private enterprise over $40 billion annually to conduct studies, prepare reports, and carry out projects. In addition, the federal government is by far the nation's largest landholder, controlling one-third of the entire area of the United States. Private enterprise must rely on governmental agencies to issue permits and licenses to explore and mine for minerals, graze cattle, cut timber, or conduct other business activities on government property. Thus, any congressional legislation which influences the decision making concerning federal funding or license granting also affects business. Such legislation is the *National Environmental Policy Act* (NEPA).

NEPA became effective in 1970. The act is divided into two titles. Title I establishes broad policy goals and imposes specific duties on all federal agencies, and Title II sets up the *Council on Environmental Quality* (CEQ). As the CEQ's role under NEPA consists mainly in gathering and assessing information, issuing advisory guidelines, and making recommendations to the President on environmental matters, this section will center on Title I.

### THE ENVIRONMENTAL IMPACT STATEMENT

Title I of NEPA imposes specific "action-forcing" requirements on federal agencies. The most important requirement demands that all federal agencies prepare an **environmental impact statement** (EIS) prior to taking certain actions. An EIS must be included "in every recommendation or report on proposals for legislation and other major Federal actions significantly affecting the quality of the human environment." This EIS is a "detailed statement" that estimates the environmental impact of the proposed action. Any discussion of such action and its impact must contain information on adverse environmental effects which cannot be avoided, any irreversible use of resources necessary, and available alternatives to the action (see Figure 25-1).

There have been hundreds of cases that interpret the EIS requirements. In the following case, the Supreme Court decides whether psychological fear caused by the risk of accident at a nuclear power plant is an "environmental effect."

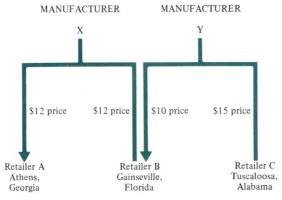

1. X and Y are primary level competitors. Y's sale to B is a primary line violation.
2. A, B, and C are secondary level competitors. Y's sale to B is also a secondary line violation.
3. If the retailers A, B, and C each purchased the goods through a wholesaler, they would be considered thrid-level competitors, and the price discrimination would be a third-line violation.

**FIGURE 25-1**

# METROPOLITAN EDISON COMPANY v. PEOPLE AGAINST NUCLEAR ENERGY
103 S.Ct. 1556 (1983)

Metropolitan Edison Company decided to reopen its TMI-1 plant at Three Mile Island, Pennsylvania, after it had been shut down when a serious accident damaged the reactor. People Against Nuclear Energy (PANE), an association of Three Mile Island-area residents, sued, claiming that the Nuclear Regulatory Commission failed to consider the psychological harm that reopening the plant and exposing the community to the risk of a nuclear accident might cause.

REHNQUIST, J.: Section 102(C) of NEPA directs all federal agencies to "include in every recommendation or report on proposals for legislation and other major Federal actions significantly affecting the quality of the human environment, a detailed statement by the responsible official on—(i) the environmental impact of the proposed action, [and] (ii) any adverse environmental effects which cannot be avoided should the proposal be implemented...."

To paraphrase the statutory language in light of the facts of this case, where an agency action significantly affects the quality of the human environment, the agency must evaluate the "environmental impact" and any unavoidable adverse environmental effects of its proposal. The theme of section 102 is sounded by the adjective "environmental": NEPA does not require the agency to assess every impact or effect of its proposed action, but only the impact or effect on the environment. If we were to seize the word "environmental" out of its context and give it the broadest possible definition, the words "adverse environmental effects" might embrace virtually any consequence of a governmental action that someone thought "adverse." But we think the context of the statute shows that Congress was talking about the physical environment—the world around us, so to speak. NEPA was designed to promote human welfare by alerting governmental actors to the effect of their proposed actions on the physical environment....

Our understanding of the congressional concerns that led to the enactment of NEPA suggests that the terms "environmental effect" and "environmental impact" in section 102 be read to include a requirement of a reasonably close causal relationship between a change in the physical environment and the effect at issue. The issue before us, then, is how to give content to this requirement. This is a question of first impression in this Court.

The federal action that affects the environment in this case is permitting renewed operation of TMI-1. The direct effects on the environment of this action include release of low-level radiation, increased fog in the Harrisburg area (caused by operation of the plant's cooling towers), and the release of warm water into the Susquehanna River. The NRC has considered each of these effects in its EIS, and again in the EIA. Another effect of renewed operation is a risk of a nuclear accident. The NRC has also considered this effect.

PANE argues that the psychological health damage it alleges "will flow directly from the risk of [a nuclear] accident." But a risk of an accident is not an effect on the physical environment. A risk is, by definition, unrealized in the physical world. In a causal chain from renewed operation of TMI-1 to psychological health damage, the element of risk and its perception by PANE's members are necessary middle links. We believe that the element of risk lengthens the causal chain beyond the reach of NEPA.

Risk is a pervasive element of modern life; to say more would belabor the obvious. Many of the risks we face are generated by modern technology, which brings both the possibility of major accidents and opportunities for tremendous achievements. Medical experts apparently agree that risk can generate stress in human beings, which in turn may rise to the level of serious health damage. For this reason among many others, the question whether the gains from any technological advance are worth its attendant risks may be an important public policy issue. Nonetheless, it is quite different from the question whether the same gains are worth a given level of alteration of our physical environment or depletion of our natural resources. The latter question rather than the former is the central concern of NEPA.

Time and resources are simply too limited for us to believe that Congress intended to extend NEPA as far as the Court of Appeals has taken it. The scope of the agency's inquiries must remain manageable if NEPA's goal of "ensur[ing] a fully informed and well considered decision," is to be accomplished.

If contentions of psychological health damage caused by risk were cognizable under NEPA, agencies would, at the very least, be obliged to expend considerable resources developing psychiatric expertise that is not otherwise relevant to their congressionally assigned functions. The available resources may be spread so thin that agencies are unable adequately to pursue protection of the physical environment and natural resources. As we said in another context "[w]e cannot attribute to Congress the intention to...open the door to such obvious incongruities and undesirable possibilities."...[*Reversed.*]

### COUNCIL ON ENVIRONMENTAL QUALITY GUIDELINES

Several regulatory guidelines issued by the CEQ have made the EIS more useful. One guideline directs the federal agencies to engage in **scoping.** Scoping requires that even before EIS preparation, agencies must designate which environmental issues of a contemplated action are most significant. It encourages impact statements to focus on more substantial environmental concerns and reduce the attention devoted to trivial issues. It also allows other agencies and interested parties to participate in the scoping process. This helps ensure that formal impact statements will address matters regarded as most important.

Another guideline directs that EISs be "clear, to the point, and written in plain English." This deters the use of technical jargon and helps those reading impact statements to understand them. The CEQ has also limited the length of impact statements, which once ran to more than 1,000 pages, to 150 pages, except in unusual circumstances.

### CRITICISMS OF THE EIS

Critics of NEPA and the CEQ guidelines raise several issues in regard to the current EIS process. Some critics point out that the present process fails to consider the economic injury caused by abandoning or delaying projects. They also contend that those preparing EISs are forced to consider far too many alternatives to proposed federal action without regard to their economic reasonableness. Other critics maintain that most impact statements are too descriptive and not sufficiently analytical. They fear that the EIS is "a document of compliance rather than a decision-making tool." A final general criticism of the EIS process notes the limits of its usefulness. As follow-ups on some EISs have shown, environmental factors are often so complex that projections concerning environmental effects amount to little more than guesswork.

Although NEPA applies only to federal actions, many states have enacted similar legislation to assist their decision making. Many interpretive problems found on the national level are also encountered at the state level. In addition, as the states frequently lack the resources and expertise of the federal government, state EISs are often even less helpful in evaluating complex environmental factors than are those prepared by federal agencies.

# GOVERNMENT'S REGULATION OF BUSINESS

## 2. Introduction

More and more companies are hiring environmental managers to deal with environmental compliance issues. This trend reflects the continuing importance of the government's regulation of private enterprise and its impact on the environment. Congress may fine-tune environmental acts, but the national commitment to a cleaner environment is here to stay.

For businesses which have borne the enormous expense of environmental cleanup, there is one bright note. When adjusted for inflation, real spending for pollution control is beginning to decline. The reason for the decline is that much of the initial expense of pollution control equipment has already been met.

## 3. The Environmental Protection Agency

The modern environmental movement began in the 1960s. As it gained momentum, it generated political pressure which forced government to reassess its role in environmental issues. One of the first steps taken at the federal level in response to this pressure was the establishing of the *Environmental Protection Agency* (EPA) in 1970. At the federal level, the EPA coordinates public control of private action as it affects the environment.

Today, the EPA is an enormous bureaucracy with a number of major responsibilities (see Table 25-2). Most importantly, it administers federal laws which concern pollution of the air and water, solid waste and toxic sub-

**TABLE 25-2**  Responsibilities of the EPA

1  Conducting research on the harmful impact of pollution
2  Gathering information about present pollution problems
3  Assisting states and local governments in controlling pollution through grants, technical advice, and other means
4  Advising the CEQ about new policies needed for protection of the environment
5  Administering federal pollution laws

stance disposal, pesticide regulation, and radiation. The following sections examine these laws.

## 4.  The Clean Air Act: Basic Structure

In 1257, Queen Eleanor of England was driven from Nottingham Castle because of harsh smoke from the numerous coal fires in London. Coal had come into widespread use in England during this time after the cutting of forests for fuel and agricultural purposes. By 1307, a royal order prohibited coal burning in London's kilns under punishment of "grievous ransoms." This early attempt at controlling air pollution does not appear, however, to have been very effective. As recently as the London smog of 1952, 4,000 people died of air-pollution-related causes, including coal smoke.

The key federal legislation for controlling air pollution in the United States is the Clean Air Act. This legislation directs the EPA administrator to establish air quality standards and to see that these standards are achieved according to a definite timetable. So far, the administrator has set primary and secondary air quality standards for particulates, carbon monoxide, sulfur dioxide, nitrogen dioxide, hydrocarbons, and lead. **Primary standards** are those necessary to protect public health. **Secondary standards** guard the public from other adverse air pollution effects such as injury to property, vegetation, and climate, and damage to esthetic values. In most instances, primary and secondary air quality standards are identical.

Governmental regulation of private action under the Clean Air Act is a joint federal and state effort. The EPA sets standards and the states devise implementation plans, which the EPA must approve, to carry them out. The states thus bear principal responsibility for enforcing the Clean Air Act, with the EPA providing standard setting, coordinating, and supervisory functions. However, the EPA may also participate in enforcement. The administrator can require the operator of any air pollution source to keep such records and perform such monitoring or sampling as the EPA deems appropriate. In addition, the EPA has the right to inspect these records and data. Various criminal and civil penalties and fines back up the Clean Air Act. In addition, industries that do not obey cleanup orders face payment to the EPA; payment amounts to the economic savings they realize from their failure to install and operate proper antipollution equipment.

### AIR POLLUTION SOURCES

For control purposes, the Clean Air Act amendments divide air pollution sources into two categories: *stationary* and *mobile* (transportation). Under the state implementation plans, major stationary polluters, such as steel mills and utilities, must reduce their emissions to a level sufficient to bring down air pollution to meet primary and secondary standards. Polluters follow timetables and schedules in complying with these requirements. To achieve designated standards, they install a variety of control devices, including wet collectors (scrubbers), filter collectors, tall stacks, electrostatic precipitators, and afterburners. New stationary pollution sources, or modified ones, must install the best system of emission reduction which has been adequately demonstrated. Under the act's provision, citizens are granted standing to enforce compliance with these standards.

The act requires both stationary and mobile sources to meet a timetable of air pollution standards for which control technology may not exist at the time. This "technology-forcing" aspect of the act is unique to the history of governmental regulation of business, yet it has been upheld by the Supreme Court.

# UNION ELECTRIC CO. v. E.P.A.
427 U.S. 246 (1975)

MARSHALL, J.: Petitioner is an electric utility company servicing the St. Louis metropolitan area, large portions of Missouri, and parts of Illinois and Iowa. Its three coal-fired generating plants in the metropolitan St. Louis area are subject to the sulfur dioxide restrictions in the Missouri implementation plan. Petitioner did not seek review of the Administrator's approval of the plan within 30 days, as it was entitled to do under § 307(b)(1) of the Clean Air Act, but rather applied to the appropriate state and county agencies for variances from the emission limitations affecting its three plants. Petitioner received one-year variances, which could be extended upon reapplication. The variances on two of petitioner's three plants had expired and petitioner was applying for extensions when, on May 31, 1974, the Administrator notified petitioner that sulfur dioxide emissions from its plants violated the emission limitations contained in the Missouri plan. Shortly thereafter petitioner filed a petition in the Court of Appeals for the Eighth Circuit for review of the Administrator's 1972 approval of the Missouri implementation plan.

Section 307(b)(1) allows petitions for review to be filed in an appropriate court of appeals more than 30 days after the Administrator's approval of an implementation plan only if the petition is "based solely on grounds arising after such 30th day." Petitioner claimed to meet this requirement by asserting that various economic and technological difficulties had arisen more than 30 days after the Administrator's approval and that these difficulties made compliance with the emission limitations impossible....

We reject at the outset petitioner's suggestion that claim of economic or technological infeasibility may be considered upon a petition for review based on new information and filed more than 30 days after approval of an implementation plan even if such a claim could not be considered by the Administrator in approving a plan or by a court in reviewing a plan challenged within the original 30-day appeal period. In pertinent part § 307(b)(1) provides:

**A petition for review of the Administrator's action in approving or promulgating any implementation plan under section 110...may be filed only in the United States Court of Appeals for the appropriate circuit. Any such petition shall be filed within 30 days from the date of such promulgation or approval, or after such**

**date if such petition is based solely on grounds arising after such 30th day.**

Regardless of when a petition for review is filed under § 307(b)(1), the court is limited to reviewing "the Administrator's action in approving...[the] implementation plan...." Accordingly, if new "grounds" are alleged they must be such that, had they been known at the time the plan was presented to the Administrator for approval, it would have been an abuse of discretion for the Administrator to approve the plan. To hold otherwise would be to transfer a substantial responsibility in administering the Clean Air Act from the Administrator and the state agencies to the federal courts.

Since a reviewing court—regardless of when the petition for review is filed—may consider claims of economic and technological infeasibility only if the Administrator may consider such claims in approving or rejecting a state implementation plan, we must address ourselves to the scope of the Administrator's responsibility. The Administrator's position is that he has no power whatsoever to reject a state implementation plan on the ground that it is economically or technologically infeasible, and we have previously accorded great deference to the Administrator's construction of the Clean Air Act. After surveying the relevant provisions of the Clean Air Amendments of 1970 and their legislative history, we agree that Congress intended claims of economic and technological infeasibility to be wholly foreign to the Administrator's consideration of a state implementation plan.

As we have previously recognized, the 1970 Amendments to the Clean Air Act were a drastic remedy to what was perceived as a serious and otherwise uncheckable problem of air pollution. The Amendments place the primary responsibility for formulating pollution control strategies on the States, but nonetheless subject the States to strict minimum compliance requirements. These requirements are of a "technology-forcing character" and are expressly designed to force regulated sources to develop pollution control devices that might at the time appear to be economically or technologically infeasible.

This approach is apparent on the face of § 110(a)(2). The provision sets out eight criteria that an implementation plan must satisfy, and provides that if these criteria are met and if the plan was adopted after reasonable notice and hearing, the Administrator "shall approve" the proposed state plan. The mandatory "shall" makes it quite clear that the Administrator is not to be concerned with factors other than those specified, and none of the eight factors appears to permit consideration of technological or economic infeasibility.

Our conclusion is bolstered by recognition that the Amendments do allow claims of technological and economic infeasibility to be raised in situations where consideration of such claims will not substantially interfere with the primary congressional purpose of prompt attainment of the national air quality standards. Thus, we do not hold that claims of infeasibility are never of relevance in the formulation of an implementation plan or that sources unable to comply with emission limitations must inevitably be shut down.

Perhaps the most important forum for consideration of claims of economic and technological infeasibility is before the state agency formulating the implementation plan. So long as the national standards are met, the State may select whatever mix of control devices it desires, and industries with particular economic or technological problems may seek special treatment in the plan itself. Moreover, if the industry is not exempted from, or accommodated by, the original plan, it may obtain a variance, as petitioner did in this case; and the variance, if granted after notice and a hearing, may be submitted to the EPA as a revision of the plan....

...Technology forcing is a concept somewhat new to our national experience and it necessarily entails certain risks. But Congress considered those risks in passing the 1970 Amendments and decided that the dangers posed by uncontrolled air pollution made them worth taking. Petitioner's theory would render that considered legislative judgment a nullity, and that is a result we refuse to reach. [*Affirmed.*]

Technology-forcing does not always succeed. It is neither always possible nor always feasible to force new technological developments. In recognizing this fact, developers of the Clean Air Act have allowed the EPA in many instances to grant *compliance waivers* and *variances* from its standards.

### 5. The Clean Air Act: Policy Trends

In the past few years, the EPA has moved to make its regulatory practices more economically efficient. All new pollution control rules are now subjected to cost-benefit analysis. The EPA has also developed specific policies to achieve air pollution control in an economically efficient manner.

THE BUBBLE CONCEPT

Traditionally, the EPA has regulated each individual pollution emission **point source** (such as a smokestack) within an industrial plant or complex. Increasingly, however, the EPA is encouraging the states, through their implementation plans, to adopt an approach called the **bubble concept.** Under the bubble concept, each plant complex is treated as if it were encased in a bubble. Instead of each pollution point source being licensed for a limited amount of pollution emission, the pollution of the plant complex as a whole is the focus of regulation. Businesses may suggest their own plans for cleaning up multiple sources of pollution within the entire complex, as long as the total pollution emitted does not exceed certain limits. This approach permits flexibility in curtailing pollution and provides businesses with economic incentives to discover new methods of control. The following case shows that the Supreme Court has upheld the EPA's authority to approve the bubble concept, even in states where pollution exceeds air quality standards.

# CHEVRON, U.S.A., INC. v. NATURAL RESOURCES DEFENSE COUNCIL
104 S.Ct. 2778 (1984)

The Clean Air Act Amendments of 1977 impose certain requirements on states that have standards established by the EPA, including the requirement that such "nonattainment" states establish a permit program regulating "new or modified major stationary sources" of air pollution. A permit may be issued only after stringent conditions are met. In 1981, the EPA ruled that the term "stationary source" included treating an entire plant as a single stationary source. Thus, an existing plant could modify the equipment on only one of several pollution-emitting devices in a single plant without meeting the permit conditions as long as the total emissions within the "bubble" did not increase. The National Resources Defense Council filed a petition for a review of the EPA "bubble" policy. The Court of Appeals determined that while the Clean Air Act did not explicitly define "stationary sources," the plantwide or "bubble" definition was "inappropriate" as applied to the nonattainment program.

STEVENS, J.: When a court reviews an agency's construction of the statute which it administers, it is confronted with two questions. First, always, is the question whether Congress has directly spoken to the precise question at issue. If the intent of Congress is clear, that is the end of the matter, for the court, as well as the agency, must give effect to the unambiguously expressed intent of Congress. If, however, the court determines Congress has not directly addressed the precise question at issue, the court does not simply impose its own construction on the statute, as would be necessary in the absence of

an administrative interpretation. Rather, if the statute is silent or ambiguous with respect to the specific issue, the question for the court is whether the agency's answer is based on a permissible construction of the statute.

"The power of an administrative agency to administer a congressionally created...program necessarily requires the formulation of policy and the making of rules to fill any gap left, implicitly or explicitly, by Congress." If Congress has explicitly left a gap for the agency to fill, there is an express delegation of authority to the agency to elucidate a specific provision of the statute by regulation. Such legislative regulations are given controlling weight unless they are arbitrary, capricious, or manifestly contrary to the statute. Sometimes the legislative delegation to an agency on a particular question is implicit rather than explicit. In such a case, a court may not substitute its own construction of a statutory provision for a reasonable interpretation made by the administrator of an agency....

In light of these well-settled principles it is clear that the Court of Appeals misconceived the nature of its role in reviewing the regulations at issue. Once it determined, after its own examination of the legislation, that Congress did not actually have an intent regarding the applicability of the bubble concept to the permit program, the question before it was not whether in its view the concept is "inappropriate" in the general context of a program designed to improve air quality, but whether the Administrator's view that it is appropriate in the context ofthis particular program is a reasonable one. Based on the examination of the legislation and its history, we agree with the Court of Appeals that Congress did not have a specific intention on the applicability of the bubble concept in these cases, and conclude that the EPA's use of that concept here is a reasonable policy choice for the agency to make....

Our review of the EPA's varying interpretations of the word "source"—both before and after the 1977 Amendments—convince us that the agency primarily responsible for administering this important legislation has consistently interpreted it flexibly—not in a sterile textual vacuum, but in the context of implementing policy decisions in a technical and complex arena. The fact that the agency has from time to time changed its interpretation of the term source does not, as respondents argue, lead us to conclude that no deference should be accorded the agency's interpretation of the statute. An initial agency interpretation is not instantly carved in stone. On the contrary, the agency, to engage in informed rulemaking, must consider varying interpretations and wisdom of its policy on a continuing basis. Moreover, the fact that the agency has adopted different definitions in different contexts adds force to the argu-

ment that the definition itself is flexible, particularly since Congress has never indicated any disapproval of a flexible reading of the statute....

Judges are not experts in the field, and are not part of either political branch of the Government. Courts must, in some cases, reconcile competing political interests, but not on the basis of the judges' personal policy preferences....

When a challenge to an agency construction of a statutory provision, fairly conceptualized, really centers on the wisdom of the agency's policy, rather than whether it is a reasonable choice within a gap left open by Congress, the challenge must fail. In such a case, federal judges—who have no constituency—have a duty to respect legitimate policy choices made by those who do. The responsibilities for assessing the wisdom of such policy choices and resolving the struggle between competing views of the public interest are not judicial ones: "Our Constitution vests such responsibilities in the political branches."

We hold that the EPA's definition of the term "source" is a permissible construction of the statute which seeks to accommodate progress in reducing air pollution with economic growth....[*The judgment of the Court of Appeals is reversed.*]

---

**EMISSIONS REDUCTION BANKING**

A number of states are now developing EPA-approved plans for **emissions reduction banking.** Under such plans, businesses can cut pollution beyond what the law requires and "bank" these reductions for their own future use or to sell to other companies as emission offsets. Eventually, we may be headed for a "marketable rights" approach to pollution control, where the right to discharge a certain pollutant would be auctioned off to the highest bidder. This approach would promote efficiency by offering to those who have the greatest need for pollution rights the opportunity to obtain them by bidding highest for them.

### PREVENTION OF SIGNIFICANT DETERIORATION

Another important policy of the Clean Air Act is the **prevention of signif-icant deterioration.** Under this policy, pollution emission is controlled, even in areas where the air is cleaner than prevailing primary and secondary air quality standards require. In some of these areas, the EPA permits construc-tion of new pollution emission sources according to a strictly limited scheme. In other areas, it allows no new pollution emission at all. Critics of this pol-icy argue that it prevents industry from moving into southern and western states, where air quality is cleaner than standards require.

### THE PERMITTING PROCESS

One of the most controversial issues involving the Clean Air Act concerns the delay and red tape caused by the permitting process. Before a business can construct new pollution emission sources, it must obtain the necessary environmental permits from the appropriate state agency. Today, the esti-mated time needed to acquire the necessary permits to build a coal-fired electrical-generating plant is five to ten years. This is nearly twice the length of time it took in the early 1970s. The formalities of the permitting process, the lack of flexibility in state implementation plans, the requirement that even minor variations in state implementation plans be approved by the EPA—all of these factors contribute to delay. Both the EPA and Congress are considering ways to streamline the permitting process.

In spite of the controversy generated by the Clean Air Act, evidence indicates that the overall air quality in the United States is steadily improv-ing. The 16,000 quarts of air we each breathe daily are cleaner and health-ier in most places than they were a decade ago. Yet an estimated 80 million persons in the United States still breathe air that violates one or more pri-mary air-quality standards. Note, also, that air pollution is an international problem and that not all countries of the world have, or can afford, our air-quality standards. This situation exists especially in developing nations of the world, which are striving to reach our standard of living.

### RECOGNITION OF NEW AIR POLLUTANTS

In drawing up air-quality standards in the 1970s, the EPA regulated only six pollutant groups. Since that time, however, environmental scientists have discovered scores of other potentially dangerous air pollutants, including as-bestos, formaldehyde, and benzene. Partially in response to lawsuits by en-vironmental organizations, the EPA has been forced to recognize that the Clean Air Act applies to these pollutants. As of this writing, the exact role of EPA in regulating many of these pollutants has not been determined.

An environmental problem about which there is growing awareness is indoor air pollution. Paints, cleaning products, furniture polishes, gas fur-naces, and stoves all emit pollutants that can be harmful to human health. Radioactive radon seeping into homes and buildings from the ground has now been recognized as a major health hazard. Some studies have found that indoor levels of certain pollutants far exceed outdoor levels, whether at work or home. Although the Clean Air Act does not apply to such pollution, the possibility of new regulation covering indoor pollution is always a possibility.

## 6. The Clean Water Act

Business enterprise is a major source of water pollution in the United States. Almost one-half of all water used in this country is for cooling and condensing purposes in connection with industrial activities. The resulting discharge into our rivers and lakes sometimes takes the form of heated water, called thermal effluents. In addition to thermal effluents, industry also discharges chemical and other effluents into the nation's waterways.

The principal federal law regulating water pollution is the *Clean Water Act*. As with the Clean Air Act, the Clean Water Act is administered primarily by the states in accordance with EPA standards. If the states do not fulfill their responsibilities, however, the federal government, through the EPA, can step in and enforce the law. The Clean Water Act applies to all navigable waterways, intrastate as well as interstate. As the following case shows, the term "navigable" has been interpreted very broadly.

---

# QUIVIRA MINING COMPANY v. E.P.A.
765 F.2d 126 (1985)

---

The EPA issued permits to Quivira Mining Company and Homestake Mining Company that limited these companies' rights to discharge pollutants into Arroyo del Puerto and San Mateo Creek. The companies challenged the EPA's power to regulate discharges into these nearly dry "gullies," asserting that the EPA could only regulate discharges into "navigable waters" under the Clean Water Act.

SAFFELS, District Judge.: It is the national goal of the Clean Water Act to eliminate the discharge of pollutants into navigable waters. The term "navigable waters" means "the waters of the United States, including the territorial seas." In *United States v. Earth Sciences, Inc.*... this court noted that the Clean Water Act is designed to regulate to the fullest extent possible sources emitting pollution into rivers, streams and lakes. "The touchstone of the regulatory scheme is that those needing to use the waters for waste distribution must seek and obtain a permit to discharge that waste, with the quantity and quality of the discharge regulated." It is the intent of the Clean Water Act to cover, as much as possible, all waters of the United States instead of just some.

The extent of the Clean Water Act's coverage of discharges of pollution is illustrated by a review of some of the cases which have been before the United States Court of Appeals for the Tenth Circuit. In

*Ward v. Coleman,*...the court found that Boogie Creek, a tributary of the Arkansas River, is a navigable water of the United States for purposes of the Clean Water Act because the Arkansas River is navigable in fact. In *United States v. Earth Sciences, Inc.,*...the court found the Rito Seco to be a "water of the United States," although it is not navigable in fact nor does it transport any goods or materials, and although it is located entirely in Costilla County, Colorado. There, the facts were that the stream supported trout and some beaver, the water collected in the reservoirs was used for agricultural irrigation, and the resulting products were sold into interstate commerce. The court stated, "It seems clear Congress intended to regulate discharges made into every creek, stream, river or body of water that in any way may affect interstate commerce. Every court to discuss the issue has used a commerce power approach and agreed upon that interpretation." In *United States v. Texas Pipe Line Co.,* the court found that the Clean Water Act covered oil spilled into an unnamed tributary of Caney Creek, which discharges into Clear Boggie Creek, itself a tributary of the Red River.

This court's findings in *Earth Sciences* and *Texas Pipe Line* compel a finding herein affirming the decision of the EPA. Substantial evidence here supports the Administrator's findings that both the Arroyo del Puerto and San Mateo Creek are waters of the United States. Substantial evidence before the Administrator supports his finding that during times of intense rainfall, there can be a surface connection between the Arroyo del Puerto, San Mateo Creek and navigable-in-fact streams. Further, the record supports the finding that both the Arroyo del Puerto and San Mateo Creek flow for a period after the time of discharge of pollutants into the waters. Further, the flow continues regularly through underground aquifers fed by the surface flow of the San Mateo Creek and Arroyo del Puerto into navigable-in-fact streams. The court finds that the impact on interstate commerce is sufficient enough to satisfy the commerce clause. And, as noted above, it was the clear intent of Congress to regulate waters of the United States to the fullest extent possible under the commerce clause. [*Affirmed.*]

---

The Clean Water Act sets goals to eliminate water pollution. Principally, these goals are to make the nation's waterways safe for swimming and other recreational use and clean enough for the protection of fish, shellfish, and wildlife. The law sets strict deadlines and strong enforcement provisions, which must be followed by industry, municipalities, and other water polluters. Enforcement of the Clean Water Act revolves around its permit discharge system. Without being subject to criminal penalties, no polluter can discharge pollutants from any point source (that is, a pipe) without a permit, and municipal as well as industrial dischargers must obtain permits. The EPA has issued guidelines for state permit programs and has approved those programs that meet the guidelines.

Under the Clean Water Act, industries have a two-step sequence for cleanup of industrial wastes discharged into rivers and streams. The first step requires polluters to install best practicable technology (BPT). The second demands installation of best available technology (BAT). Various timetables apply in achieving these steps, according to the type of pollutant being discharged. In 1984, the EPA announced application of the bubble concept to water pollution in the steel industry.

In addition to the Clean Water Act, the EPA administers two other acts related to water pollution control. One, the Marine Protection, Research, and Sanctuaries Act of 1972, requires a permit system for the discharge or dumping of various material into the seas. The other is the Safe Water Drinking Act of 1974, which has forced the EPA to set maximum drinking-water contaminant levels for certain organic and inorganic chemicals, pesticides, and microbiological pollutants.

The Clean Water Act and other current statutes do not reach one important type of water pollution: *non-point source* pollution. Much water pollution comes not from industrial and municipal point source discharges, but from runoffs into streams and rivers. These runoffs often contain agricultural fertilizers and pesticides as well as oil and lead compounds from streets and highways. In 1987, Congress authorized $400 million for the National Non-Point Source Pollution Program to study the problem.

## 7. The Noise Control Act

The Preamble to the Constitution establishes as a constitutional purpose the assurance of "domestic tranquillity." This phrase has been legally defined as the state or character of being quiet, or "quietness." Nearly two hundred years since the Constitution's ratification, however, our society is noisier than ever, despite the fact that excessive noise has been implicated not only in causing deafness but also in contributing to high blood pressure, heart disease, stress, and emotional disturbance. The EPA estimates that some seventy million Americans presently live with neighborhood noise levels sufficiently high to cause annoyance and dissatisfaction. A recent Census Bureau survey reports that street noise was the most frequently mentioned neighborhood problem.

To combat the growing effects of noise pollution, Congress passed the *Noise Control Act of 1972*. In the opening sections of the act, Congress lists as the major sources of noise transportation vehicles and equipment, machinery, appliances, and other products used in commerce. The act aims at controlling the noise emission of these manufactured items rather than at limiting outside noise levels.

Under the act, the EPA must set limits on noise emission for any product which is identified as a major source of noise or which falls into certain specified categories. In setting these standards, the EPA must consider the noise levels necessary to protect public health and welfare, the best available technology, and the cost of compliance. The EPA has set or proposed standards for trucks, motorcycles, buses, air compressors, rock drills and pavement breakers, bulldozers, front-end loaders, power mowers, and air conditioners.

Most of the standards will take effect over a several-year period and apply only to new products. Manufacturers of these products are held to warrant to purchasers that their products comply with the standards, and no state or local government may enact or enforce noise emission levels which differ from them. For any product which the EPA determines emits noise capable of adversely affecting the public welfare or which is sold on the basis of its effectiveness in reducing noise, the agency must require that notice of this product's noise level be given to each prospective purchaser.

The act prohibits: (1) commercial distribution by a manufacturer of a product not complying with designated noise levels, (2) the removal from a product of a required noise control device, (3) the use of the product after removal, (4) the distribution of a product without a required notice of noise level and removal of this notice, and (5) the importation of a product not in compliance with designated noise levels. The EPA enforces these prohibitions through both criminal and civil remedies. It may also require manufacturers to maintain records and conduct tests of their products.

In the early 1980s, implementation and enforcement of the Noise Control Act slowed considerably. It remains to be seen whether noise control in the future will gain a significant role in environmental regulation.

### 8. The Pesticide Control Acts

Pests, especially insects and mice, destroy over 10 percent of all crops grown in the United States, causing several billion dollars of damage annually. In many underdeveloped countries, however, a much greater percentage of total crop production is lost to pests, as high as 40 to 50 percent in countries such as India. Perhaps the principal reason for our lower rate of crop loss is that the United States uses more pesticides per acre than any other country.

The widespread, continual application of pesticides presents environmental problems, however. Not only is it dangerous to wildlife, particularly birds and fish, but it may eventually threaten our agricultural capacity itself. Rapidly breeding pests gradually become immune to the application of pesticides, and researchers may not always be able to invent new poisons to kill them.

Federal regulation of pesticides is accomplished primarily through two statutes: the *Federal Insecticide, Fungicide, and Rodenticide Act of 1947,* as amended, and the *Federal Environmental Pesticide Control Act of 1972* (FEPCA). Both statutes require the registration and labeling of agricultural pesticides, although FEPCA coverage extends to the application of pesticides as well.

Under the acts, the administrator of the EPA is directed to register those pesticides which are properly labeled, which meet the claims made as to their effectiveness, and which will not have unreasonable adverse effects on the environment. The phrase "unreasonable adverse effects on the environment" is defined as "any unreasonable risk to man or the environment, taking into account the economic, social, and environmental costs and benefits of the use of any pesticide." In addition to its authority to require registration of pesticides, the EPA classifies pesticides for either general use or restricted use. In the latter category, the EPA may impose further restrictions that require application only by a trained applicator or with the approval of a trained consultant.

The EPA has a variety of enforcement powers to ensure that pesticide goals are met, including the power to deny or suspend registration. In the 1980s, the EPA has used this power and banned several pesticides suspected of causing cancer.

There are two chief criticisms of pesticide control: one coming from affected businesses; the other, from the environmental movement. Pesticide manufacturers complain that the lengthy, expensive testing procedures required by the FEPCA registration process delay useful pesticides from reaching the market and inhibit new research. On the other hand, many in the environmental movement contend that our country's pesticide control policy is hypocritical in that the FEPCA does not apply to pesticides which United States manufacturers ship to foreign countries. Companies can sell overseas what they cannot sell in this country.


## 9. The Solid Waste Disposal Act

Pollution problems cannot always be neatly categorized. For instance, solid waste disposal processes often create pollution in several environmentally related forms. When solid waste is burned, it can cause air pollution and violate the Clean Air Act. When dumped into rivers, streams, and lakes, solid waste can pollute the water beyond amounts permitted under the Clean Water Act. Machinery used in solid waste disposal can also be subject to the regulation of the Noise Control Act.

By all accounts, solid waste pollution problems during the last twenty-five years have grown as the pollution has risen and as we have become more affluent and productive. Currently, total solid wastes produced yearly in the United States exceed 5 billion tons, or almost 25 tons for every individual in the population. Half this amount is agricultural waste, another third is mineral waste, and the remainder is industrial, institutional, and residential waste. Some wastes are toxic and hazardous, while others stink or attract pests. All present disposal problems of significant proportion.

The Solid Waste Disposal Act represents the primary federal effort in solid waste control. Congress recognized in this act that the main responsibility for nontoxic waste management rests with regional, state, and local management and limited the federal role in this area. Under this act, the federal role in nontoxic waste management is limited mainly to promoting research and providing technical and financial assistance to the states.

In responding to solid waste disposal problems, state and local governments have taken a variety of approaches. These include developing sanitary landfills, requiring that solid waste be separated into categories that facilitate disposal and recycling, and granting tax breaks for industries using recycled materials. A report by the Council of State Governments noted that there are over a thousand community recycling centers and that over a hundred cities and countries have waste-to-energy facilities. Nine states with 25 percent of the nation's population have beverage container deposit laws, the so-called "bottle bills."

Some companies have incorporated waste disposal provisions into their codes of ethics, as the following excerpt from the Caterpillar Code of Ethics illustrates.

---

## WASTE DISPOSAL

Proper means for disposal of municipal and industrial wastes are essential to society. For example, continued operation of Caterpillar facilities depends upon availability of landfills and contract services for disposal.

When practical, Caterpillar reuses or recycles byproducts of manufacturing processes. But in some cases, reuse and recycling aren't practical. It then becomes necessary that waste materials be handled and disposed of in a manner consistent with the public interest, as expressed in applicable laws and regulations.

Aside from government regulations, we shall make certain that disposition of Caterpillar wastes is carried out in a manner consistent with the ethical business practices set forth in the Code. When contractors are involved, they should demonstrate necessary technical competence, maintain a high level of performance, and otherwise meet Caterpillar standards regarding long-lasting supplier relationships.

---

In 1976, Congress amended the Solid Wastes Disposal Act with the *National Resource Conservation and Recovery Act*. The next section discusses this act and other statutes related to toxic wastes.

### 10.   Toxic and Hazardous Substances: Introduction

According to the opinion research organization Yankelovich, Skelly and White, the control of toxic and hazardous chemicals "ranks first" on the public's list of where the government's regulation of industry is needed. In the last several years, regulation of such chemicals has been expanding rapidly. We can divide public control of private action in this area into three categories: (1) regulation of the use of toxic chemicals, (2) regulation of toxic and hazardous waste disposal, and (3) regulation of toxic and hazardous waste cleanup.

## 11.  Toxic Substances Control Act

Even as the Clean Air and Water Acts are slowly beginning to diminish many types of air and water pollution, attention is being drawn to another environmental problem which is potentially the most serious of all: toxic substances. Hardly a day passes without the news media reporting some new instance of alleged threat to human health and well-being from one or another of the chemical substances so important to manufacturing, farming, mining, and other aspects of modern life.

Threats to human welfare from toxic substances are not new to history. Some people suggest that poisoning from lead waterpipes and drinking vessels may have depleted the ranks of the ruling class of ancient Rome and thus contributed to the downfall of the Roman Empire. More recently, some think that the "mad hatters" of the nineteenth-century fur and felt trades likely suffered brain disorders from inhaling the vapors of mercury used in their crafts. Today, however, the presence of toxic substances in the environment is made more serious by the fact that over 70,000 industrial and agricultural chemical compounds are in commercial use, and new chemicals, a significant percentage of which are toxic, are being introduced into the marketplace at the rate of over 1,000 substances annually.

To meet the special environmental problems posed by the use of toxic chemicals, Congress in 1976 enacted the *Toxic Substances Control Act* (TSCA). Prior to passage of the TSCA, there was no coordinated effort to evaluate effects of these chemical compounds. Some of these compounds are beneficial to society and present no threat to the environment. Some, however, are both toxic and long-lasting, a fact which in the past has been uncovered only after these compounds were introduced into wide use and became important to manufacturing and farming. The primary purpose of the TSCA is to force an early evaluation of suspect chemicals before they become economically important.

The EPA collects information under TSCA sections which require that manufacturers and distributors report to the EPA any information they possess which indicates that a chemical substance presents a "substantial risk" of injury to health or to the environment. The TSCA further demands that the EPA be given advance notice before the manufacture of new chemical substances or the processing of any substance for a significant new use. Based on the results of its review, the EPA can take action to stop or limit introduction of new chemicals if they threaten human health or the environment with unreasonable risks.

The law also authorizes the EPA to require manufacturers to test their chemicals for possible harmful effects. Since not all the 70,000 chemicals in commerce can be tested simultaneously, the EPA has developed a priority scheme for selecting substances for testing based on whether or not the chemicals cause cancer, birth defects, or gene mutations.

In view of the beneficial role that many chemical substances play in all aspects of production and consumption, Congress directed the EPA through the TSCA to consider the economic and social impact, as well as the environmental one, of its decisions. In this respect the TSCA is unlike the Clean Air Act, which requires that certain pollution standards be met without regard for economic factors.

## 12. Natural Resource Conservation and Recovery Act

The congressional Office of Technology Assessment reports that more than a ton of hazardous waste per citizen is dumped annually into the nation's environment. A major environmental problem has been how to ensure that the generators of toxic wastes dispose of them safely. In the past, there have been instances where even some otherwise responsible companies have placed highly toxic wastes in the hands of less-than-reputable disposal contractors.

To help ensure proper handling and disposal of hazardous and toxic wastes, Congress in 1976 amended the Solid Waste Disposal Act by the *Resource Conservation and Recovery Act* (RCRA). Under the RCRA, a generator of wastes has two primary obligations. The first is to determine whether its wastes qualify as hazardous under RCRA. The second is to see that such wastes are properly transported to a disposal facility which has an EPA permit or license.

The EPA lists a number of hazardous wastes, and a generator can determine if a nonlisted waste is hazardous in terms of several chemical characteristics specified by the EPA. The RCRA accomplishes proper disposal of hazardous wastes through the **manifest system.** This system requires a generator to prepare a manifest document which designates a licensed facility for disposal purposes. The generator then gives copies of the manifest to the transporter of the waste. After receiving hazardous wastes, the disposal facility must return a copy of the manifest to the generator. In this fashion, the generator knows the waste has received proper disposal.

Failure to receive this manifest copy from the disposal facility within certain time limits requires the generator to notify the EPA. Under RCRA, the EPA has various investigatory powers. The act also prescribes various recordkeeping requirements and assesses penalties for failure to comply with its provisions.

As amended in 1986, RCRA is moving the handling of toxic wastes away from burial on land to treatments that destroy or permanently detoxify wastes. By 1990, RCRA requirements will cost business an estimated $20 billion annually.

## 13. The Superfund

After passage of TSCA and RCRA in 1976, regulation of toxic and hazardous substances was still incomplete. These acts did not deal with problems of the cleanup costs of unsafe hazardous waste dumps or spills, which are often substantial. Many dump sites are abandoned and date back as far as the nineteenth century. Even current owners of unsafe dump sites are frequently financially incapable of cleaning up hazardous wastes. The same applies to transporters and others who cause spills or unauthorized discharges of hazardous wastes.

In 1980, Congress created the *Comprehensive Environmental Response, Compensation, and Liability Act* to address these problems. Known as the **Superfund,** this act has allotted billions of dollars for environmental cleanup of dangerous hazardous wastes. Taxes on the petroleum and chemical industries finance most of the fund.

The act requires anyone who releases unauthorized amounts of hazardous substances into the environment to notify the government. Whether it is notified or not, the government has the power to order those responsible to clean up such releases. Refusal to obey can lead to a suit for reimbursement for any cleanup monies spent from the Superfund plus punitive damages of up to triple the cleanup costs. The government can also recover damages for injury done to natural resources. To date, the biggest Superfund case involved Shell Oil and the United States Army. These parties agreed to clean up a site outside Denver. Total costs may exceed $1 billion.

The Superfund imposes a type of strict liability on those responsible for unauthorized discharges of hazardous wastes. Thus, no negligence need be proved. An additional strict liability falls on generators of hazardous wastes. They are strictly liable for *any* illegal discharge of hazardous waste as long as they have a contractual relationship with the responsible parties. For example, a chemical company whose transporter of wastes causes an unauthorized release of toxic chemicals, or whose disposal facility dumps chemicals illegally, is strictly liable for any resulting injury.

Finally, take note that both the Clean Air Act and the Clean Water Act also contain provisions related to government suits to recover costs for the cleanup of toxic chemicals. Suits under the Superfund and other acts are growing rapidly (see Table 25-3) and will be a major area of environmental litigation in coming years. The U.S. Office of Technology Assessment esti-

### TABLE 25-3  Recent Hazardous Waste Settlements

| Company | Amount | Location |
| --- | --- | --- |
| Alcoa | $5.6 million | Greenup, IL |
| Diamond Shamrock | $12 million | Newark, NJ |
| Occidental | $30 million | Niagara Falls, NY |
| Shell Oil (and United States Army) | Up to $1 billion | Denver, CO |
| Ten companies | $50 billion | Baton Rouge, LA |
| Waste Management | $10.5 million | Vickery, OH |
| Westinghouse | $90 million | Bloomington, IN |

mates that it will require as much as $500 billion during the next 50 years to clean up the nation's hazardous waste sites.

As responsible parties engage in Superfund-required cleanup, they try to pass on the costs to others, often their insurers. In the future insurers may specifically refuse to cover pollution risks in their policies. Some courts, however, have interpreted existing policies to cover waste-cleanup costs as insured-against "damages" arising from an "occurrence," which includes an "accidental" discharge of pollutants.

### 14.   Radiation

In 1979, the nuclear power plant accident at the Three Mile Island installation in Pennsylvania and subsequent evacuation of thousands of nearby residents focused the nation's attention on the potential hazards of radiation pollution. Although no single piece of legislation comprehensively controls radiation pollution and no one agency is responsible for administering legislation in this technologically complex area, overall responsibility for such control rests with the Nuclear Regulatory Commission. The EPA, however, does have general authority to conduct testing and provide technical assistance in the area of radiation pollution control. Also, the Clean Air Act, the Federal Water Pollution Control Act, and the Ocean Dumping Act all contain sections applicable to radiation discharges into the air and water.

## SUITS BY PRIVATE INDIVIDUALS

### 15.   Introduction

Achieving environmental goals requires coordinated strategy and implementation. As private citizens, individuals and groups of individuals lack both the power and foresight necessary to control pollution on a broad scale. There is a role, however, for the private control of private action in two principal areas.

First, most of the environmental laws, such as the Clean Air and Water Acts, contain "citizen enforcement" provisions. These provisions grant private individuals and groups the standing to sue to challenge failures to comply with the environmental laws. In many instances, private citizens can sue polluters directly to force them to cease violating the law. Private citizens also have standing to sue public agencies (for example, the EPA) to require them to adopt regulations or implement enforcement against private polluters which the environmental laws require. Between 1984 and 1987, citizen-enforcement actions, especially actions against polluters, grew rapidly.

A second area of private control of private action lies in tort law and its state codifications. When pollution directly injures private citizens, they may sue offending polluters under various theories of tort law. Thus, the traditional deterrence of tort law contributes to private control of private action. The next section further develops tort law's role in pollution control.

## 16. Tort Theories and Pollution

Examination of tort law and pollution control reveals little understanding of the interdependence between ourselves and our environment. Instead, tort theories, as they have been applied to environmental problems, focus on the action of one person (or business) as it injures the health or interferes with the property rights of another. In other words, tort law attacks the pollution problem by using the established theories of nuisance, negligence, and trespass.

### NUISANCE

The principal tort theory used in pollution control has been that of nuisance. The law relating to nuisance is somewhat vague, but in most jurisdictions the common law has been put into statutory form. Several common elements exist in the law of nuisance in most states. To begin with, there are two types of nuisances: public and private.

A **public nuisance** arises from an act which causes inconvenience or damage to the public in the exercise of rights common to everyone. In the environmental area air, water, and noise pollution can all constitute a public nuisance if they affect common rights. More specifically, industrial-waste discharge which kills the fish in a stream may be held a public nuisance, since fishing rights are commonly possessed by the public. Public-nuisance actions may be brought only by a public official, not private individuals, unless the latter have suffered some special damage to their persons or property as a result of the public nuisance.

Any unreasonable use of one's property which causes substantial interference with the enjoyment or use of another's land establishes a common law **private nuisance.** The unreasonableness of the interference is measured by a balancing process in which the character, extent, and duration of harm to the plaintiff is weighed against the social utility of the defendant's activity and its appropriateness to its location. Since society needs industrial activity as well as natural tranquillity, people must put up with a certain amount of smoke, dust, noise, and polluted water if they live in concentrated areas of industry. But what may be an appropriate industrial use of land in a congested urban area may be a private nuisance if it occurs in a rural or residential location.

Take note that the proving of nuisance does not demand that a property owner be found negligent. An unreasonable use of one's land does not mean that one's *conduct* is unreasonable.

### OTHER TORT DECISIONS

Private plaintiffs in pollution cases frequently allege the applicability of tort doctrines other than that of nuisance. These doctrines, however, do overlap that of nuisance, which is really a field of tort liability rather than a type of conduct.

One such doctrine is that of trespass. A defendant is liable for trespass if, without right, she or he intentionally enters land in possession of another, or causes something to do so. The entrance is considered intentional if the defendant knew that it was substantially certain to result from her or his conduct. Thus, airborne particles which fall on a plaintiff's property can constitute a trespass. In recent years, many courts have merged the theories of nuisance and trespass to such an extent that before plaintiffs can recover for a particle trespass, they must prove that the harm done to them exceeds the social utility of the defendant's enterprise.

Negligence doctrine is sometimes used by private plaintiffs in environmental pollution cases. The basis for the negligence tort lies in the defendant's breach of his or her duty to use ordinary and reasonable care toward the plaintiff, which proximately (foreseeably) causes the plaintiff injury. A factory's failure to use available pollution-control equipment may be evidence of its failure to employ "reasonable care."

Finally, some courts recognize the applicability in pollution cases of strict liability tort doctrine. This tort liability arises when the defendant injures the plaintiff's person or property by voluntarily engaging in ultrahazardous activity which necessarily involves a risk of serious harm that cannot be eliminated through the exercise of the utmost care. No finding of fault, or failure of reasonable care, on the defendant's part is necessary. This doctrine has been employed in situations involving the use of poisons, such as in crop dusting and certain industrial work, the storage and use of explosives, and the storage of water in large quantities in a dangerous place.

Increasing numbers of private plaintiffs are suing companies for pollution-related harm. In one recent case, a chemical company settled with three plaintiffs for $2.7 million.

### DAMAGES

An important issue in pollution-related tort cases concerns what damages are recoverable. Exposure to pollution frequently does not cause immediate harm. It merely increases the potential for harm (that is, disease). The next case examines what damages are recoverable in such an instance.

# AYERS v. JACKSON TOWNSHIP
525 A.2d 287 (N.J. 1987)

STEIN, J.: In this case we consider the application of the New Jersey Tort Claims Act (the Act)... to the claims asserted by 339 residents of Jackson Township against that municipality.

The litigation involves claims for damages sustained because plaintiffs' well water was contaminated by toxic pollutants leaching into the Cohansey Aquifer from a landfill established and operated by Jackson Township. After an extensive trial, the jury found that the township had created a "nuisance" and a "dangerous condition" by virtue of its operation of the landfill, that its conduct was "palpably unreasonable,"—a prerequisite to recovery under [the act]—and that it was the proximate cause of the contamination of plaintiffs' water supply. The jury verdict resulted in an aggregate judgment of $15,854,392.78, to be divided among the plaintiffs in varying amounts. The jury returned individual awards for each of the plaintiffs that varied in accordance with such factors as proximity to the landfill, duration and extent of the exposure to contaminants, and the age of the claimant.

The verdict provided compensation for three distinct claims of injury: $2,056,480 was awarded for emotional distress caused by the knowledge that they had ingested water contaminated by toxic chemicals for up to six years; $5,396,940 was awarded for the deterioration of their quality of life during the twenty months when they were deprived of running water, and $8,204,500 was awarded to cover the future cost of annual medical surveillance that plaintiffs' expert testified would be necessary because of plaintiffs' increased susceptibility to cancer and other diseases. The balance of the verdict, approximately

$196,500, represented miscellaneous expenses not involved in this appeal.

The Appellate Division upheld that portion of the judgment awarding plaintiffs damages for impairment of their quality of life. It reversed the award for emotional distress, concluding that such damages constituted "pain and suffering" for which recovery is barred by [the Act]. The Appellate Division also set aside the $8,204,500 award for medical surveillance expenses, concluding that it is "impossible to say that defendant has so significantly increased the 'reasonable probability' that any of the plaintiffs will develop cancer so as to justify imposing upon defendant the financial burden of lifetime medical surveillance for early clinical signs of cancer."

In addition, the Appellate Division affirmed the trial court's dismissal of plaintiffs' claim for damages for their enhanced risk of disease....

We granted plaintiffs' petition for certification to review the adverse portions of the Appellate Division decision, and granted defendant's cross-petition to review the affirmance of the damage award for impairment of plaintiffs' quality of life...

We now consider each of the plaintiffs' damage claims in the context of the evidence adduced at trial and the legal principles that should inform our application of the Tort Claims Act....

The trial court charged the jury that plaintiffs' claim for "quality of life" damages encompassed "inconveniences, aggravation, and unnecessary expenditure of time and effort related to the use of the water hauled to their homes, as well as to other disruption in their lives, including disharmony in the family unit." The aggregate jury verdict on this claim was $5,396,940. This represented an average award of slightly over $16,000 for each plaintiff.

In the Appellate Division and before this Court, defendant argues that this segment of the verdict is barred by the New Jersey Tort Claims Act, which provides:

**No damages shall be awarded against a public entity or public employee for pain and suffering resulting from any injury; provided, however, that this limitation on the recovery of damages for pain and suffering shall not apply in cases of permanent loss of a bodily function, permanent disfigurement or dismemberment where the medical treatment expenses are in excess $1,000.00.**

Defendant contends that the legislative intent in restricting damages for "pain and suffering" was to encompass claims for all "non-objective" injuries, unless the statutory threshold of severity of injury or expense of treatment is met. The township asserts that the inconvenience, aggravation, effort and disruption of the family unit that resulted from the loss of plaintiff's water supply was but a form of "pain and suffering" and therefore uncompensable under the Act.

The Appellate Division rejected the township's contention, concluding that there was a clear distinction between

**the subjectively measured damages for pain and suffering, which are not compensable by the Tort Claims Act, and those which objectively affect quality of life by causing an interference with the use of one's land through inconvenience and the disruption of daily activities.**

We agree with the Appellate Division's conclusion. The Tort Claims Act's ban against recovery of damages for "pain and suffering resulting from any injury" is intended to apply to the intangible, subjective feelings of discomfort that are associated with personal injuries. It was not intended to bar claims

for inconvenience associated with the invasion of a property interest. As the trial court's charge explained, plaintiffs sought damages to compensate them for the multiple inconveniences associated with a lack of running water. Although the disruption of plaintiffs' water supply is an "injury" under the Act, the interest invaded here, the right to obtain potable running water from plaintiffs' own wells, is qualitatively different from "pain and suffering" related to a personal injury.

The jury verdict awarded plaintiffs damages for emotional distress in the aggregate amount of $2,056,480. The individual verdicts ranged from $40 to $14,000.

Many of the plaintiffs testified about their emotional reactions to the knowledge that their well-water was contaminated. Most of the plaintiffs' testimony on the issue of emotional distress was relatively brief and general. Typically, their testimony did not indicate that the emotional distress resulted in physical symptoms or required medical treatment…

We acknowledge that our cases no longer require proof of causally-related physical impact to sustain a recovery for emotional distress. Nevertheless, we reject plaintiffs' assertion that the Tort Claims Act's limitation against recovery for "pain and suffering resulting from any injury" does not apply to claims based on emotional distress.

The term "pain and suffering" is not defined in the Act. The Comment to [the Act] describes the limitation on damages for pain and suffering as reflecting "the policy judgment that in view of the economic burdens presently facing public entities a claimant should not be reimbursed for non-objective types of damages, such as pain and suffering, except in aggravated circumstances.…" We are in full accord with the conclusion of the Appellate Division that the subjective symptoms of depression, stress, health concerns, and anxiety described by the plaintiffs and their expert witness constitute "pain and suffering resulting from any injury" as the phrase is used in [the Act].

The New Jersey Tort Claims Act bars the recovery of such damages. Accordingly, we affirm the Appellate Division's reversal of that portion of the jury verdict awarding damages for emotional distress.

No claims were asserted by plaintiffs seeking recovery for specific illnesses caused by their exposure to chemicals. Rather, they claim damages for the enhanced risk of future illness attributable to such exposure. They also seek to recover the expenses of annual medical examinations to monitor their physical health and detect symptoms of disease at the earliest possible opportunity....

Our disposition of this difficult and important issue requires that we choose between two alternatives, each having a potential for imposing unfair and undesirable consequences on the affected interests. A holding that recognizes a cause of action for unquantified enhanced risk claims exposes the tort system, and the public it serves, to the task of litigating vast numbers of claims for compensation based on threats of injuries that may never occur. It imposes on judges and juries the burden of assessing damages for the risk of potential disease, without clear guidelines to determine what level of compensation may be appropriate. It would undoubtedly increase already escalating insurance rates.

On the other hand, denial of the enhanced-risk cause of action may mean that some of these plaintiffs will be unable to obtain compensation for their injury. [T]hose who contract diseases in the future because of their exposure to chemicals in their well water may be unable to prove a causal relationship between such exposure and their disease.

In deciding between recognition or nonrecognition of plaintiffs' enhanced-risk claim, we feel constrained to choose the alternative that most closely reflects the legislative purpose in enacting the Tort Claims Act. In our view, the speculative nature of an unquantified enhanced risk claim, the difficulties inherent in adjudicating such claims, and the policies underlying the Tort Claims Act argue persuasively against the recognition of this cause of action....

The claim for medical surveillance expenses stands on a different footing from the claim based on enhanced risk. It seeks to recover the cost of periodic medical examinations intended to monitor plaintiffs' health and facilitate early diagnosis and treatment of disease caused by plaintiffs' exposure to toxic chemicals....

Compensation for reasonable and necessary medical expenses is consistent with well-accepted legal principles. It is also consistent with the important public health interest in fostering access to medical testing for individuals whose exposure to toxic chemicals creates an enhanced risk of disease. The value of early diagnosis and treatment for cancer patients is well-documented....

Accordingly, we hold that the cost of medical surveillance is a compensable item of damages where the proofs demonstrate, through reliable expert testimony predicated upon the significance and extent of exposure to chemicals, the toxicity of the chemicals, the seriousness of the diseases for which individuals are at risk, the relative increase in the chance of onset of disease in those exposed, and the value of early diagnosis, that such surveillance to monitor the effect of exposure to toxic chemicals is reasonable and necessary....

For the reasons stated in this opinion, the judgment of the Appellate Division is [*affirmed in part and reversed in part.*]

If a resident later develops disease caused by exposure to the toxic pollutants, could the resident still sue the town and recover damages? Note that the *Ayers* case was brought under the New Jersey Tort Claims Act because the defendant was a governmental body. Under common law negligence, the residents could have recovered damages for pain and suffering injury. Still a problem even under common law is whether damages can be awarded when negligence causes potential future harm rather than immediate injury. Courts in several states have permitted recovery of damages for the *fear* that plaintiffs *might* contract cancer in the future due to the defendant's torts.

## 17.   Trends

### INTRODUCTION

A *Wall Street Journal*/NBC News survey conducted in 1987 suggests strong nationwide support for environment cleanup. A 61 percent majority favored more government regulation of the environment. Only 6 percent thought there should be less environmental regulation.

Cleanup efforts mean environmental regulation, and after being much criticized in the early 1980s, the EPA has shown renewed commitment to achieving regulatory goals. Criminal prosecutions of environmental law violators have increased. The EPA is paying new attention to the presence of toxic chemicals in the air and water. It also has a new administrator to lead it.

Meanwhile, researchers almost daily report new instances of how technological civilization affects life on our planet. For every allegation of pollution-caused environmental harm, however, there are usually countertheories raised, which maintain that the harm is not as significant as alleged, or else argue that the harm arises from causes unrelated to industrial pollution. Lack of unanimous scientific opinion on many environmental issues underscores their great complexity. It also reveals a key controversy at the heart of environmental regulation: *How much certainty of harm is required to justify regulatory intervention?*

### ACID RAIN

The concern over *acid rain* illustrates the problem. In the eastern United States and Canada, rain with a high acid content is killing fish in lakes and posing a significant threat to forests and certain crops. Considerable theory and research points to midwestern industrial sulfur emissions as causing acid rain problems. Pressure is mounting in Congress to legislate limitations on these emissions. On the other hand, other scientific opinion warns against overly hasty legislative "solutions" to acid rain. It points out that much acid rain is caused naturally.

## OZONE

In 1987, representatives from forty-five nations met and agreed to limit production and use of chlorofluorocarbons. Scientists have asserted that these manufactured chemicals used in aerosol spray cans and refrigeration are destroying the *ozone layer* of the upper atmosphere. Destruction of ozone could lead to hundreds of thousands of cases of cataracts and skin cancer in humans, plus unknown serious damage to animal and plant life.

As of this writing the EPA has required chlorofluorocarbon manufacturers to reduce the production of the chemical by 50 percent by mid-1998. In the meantime some companies are taking their own steps. DuPont Co., the world's largest producer of chlorofluorocarbons, has promised a complete phaseout of the chemical.

Research has recently identified other chemicals that may be at work in destroying the ozone layer. These include methane and bromine compounds.

## GREENHOUSE EFFECT

Overshadowing acid rain and ozone destruction as future pollution concern is increasing atmospheric concentrations of carbon dioxide. The National Academy of Sciences notes that global carbon dioxide levels have increased 6 percent since 1960. The increase is due largely to the burning of fossil fuels such as oil and coal.

Higher carbon dioxide levels will likely lead to warmer global temperatures, the so-called *greenhouse effect*. Changing climate patterns and rising sea levels are possible results. But the timing and magnitude of the greenhouse effect is hotly debated. Is regulatory intervention justified? Will the United States join with other nations seeking to limit the growth of fossil-fuel consumption? These are some of the questions which the business students of the 1990s will quite possibly face during their business careers. Present answers to these questions are unknown. Only one conclusion is clear-cut: We possess immense technological power today to change the environment for better and for worse, both intentionally and inadvertently.

## 18. The Dilemma of Environmental Ethics

No responsible member of the business community believes that the natural environment is a proper dumpsite for unlimited amounts of manufacturing, mining, agricultural, and consumer pollutants. The dilemma of environmental ethics is much more complex. It concerns the level of proof required before a business should take steps to reduce the environmental impact of a certain practice.

Merely waiting for regulation to prohibit a business practice is not always environmentally ethical. This is especially true since both lobbying and time-consuming litigation can delay regulation, even when a practice may cause considerable environmental harm. At the same time, scientific knowledge about environmental effects is seldom certain. A business owes it to its owners, its employees, and the community generally not to stop production every time some group alleges environmental harm.

What then is the answer to the dilemma of environmental ethics? It does not lie in legal proofs. Rather, it comes from business commitment to practices that minimize environmental harm. As part of this commitment, a business must ensure that it pays careful attention to potential environmental issues, even when the law does not so require. It must also share information about both environmental and economic impacts with regulators and the public. Only in open, frank dialogue inside the business and with the outside community will a business know ethically when to reduce the environmental impact of a certain practice.

## REVIEW QUESTIONS

**1**   For each term in the left-hand column, match the most appropriate description in the right-hand column:

| | |
|---|---|
| (1) EIS | (a) An unreasonable use of one's land which interferes with the use or enjoyment of another's land. |
| (2) Point source | (b) Treating several point sources at a plant as one source. |
| (3) Prevention of significant deterioration | (c) A process which must be followed by federal agencies before undertaking major actions which significantly affect the environment. |
| (4) Superfund | (d) A smokestack, pipe, or other opening which discharges pollution. |
| (5) Nuisance | (e) The Comprehensive Environmental Response, Compensation, and Liability Act. |
| (6) Bubble concept | (f) The tracking process for toxic waste disposal. |
| (7) Manifest system | (g) Air pollution levels necessary to protect human health. |

(8)   Primary air-quality standards

(h) The policy of preventing additional pollution in certain areas which have air cleaner than required by primary standards.

**2**   Discuss why the way government regulates the environmental impact of its decision making is of significant interest to the business community.

**3**   Your firm has been hired to build a large government facility near a residential neighborhood. A committee of residents has been formed to oppose the building. You have been asked to assist in writing the EIS. What factors must your EIS take into consideration?

**4**   Outline criticisms of the EIS process. Why are state EISs often less helpful in evaluating complex environmental factors than are those prepared by federal agencies?

**5**   The Avila Timber Company has asked for and been granted permission by the Department of the Interior to cut 40 acres of timber from the 10,000-acre Oconee National Forest. Prior to the actual logging, a local environmental group files suit in federal district court, contending that the De partment of Interior has not filed an EIS. Can the group challenge the department's action? Analyze whether an EIS should be filed, in light of the facts given.

**6**   An EIS prepared for the Army Corps of Engineers by a private consulting firm concludes that the value of the farmland which will be submerged by a proposed dam is greater than the navigational benefits which the dam will bring. Is the Corps prohibited from building the dam because of this conclusion? Discuss.

**7**   What does it mean to say that the Clean Air Act is "technology-forcing"? What happens when an industry cannot meet the technological standards set by the EPA?

**8**   The Akins Corporation wishes to build a new smelting facility in Owens County, an area where air pollution exceeds primary air standards. What legal difficulties may they face? What solutions might you suggest for these difficulties?

**9**   What is the difference between "effluents" and "emissions"?

**10**   What is the difference between an individual point-source approach and a bubble-policy approach to dealing with factory pollution? For the factory owner, what are the advantages of employing the bubble concept?

**11**   Bug Control Incorporated desires to produce a new pesticide for control of fire ants. Before beginning manufacture, what process must it follow under the pesticide control acts?

**12**   Your company has decided to produce a new chemical which has great promise in manufacture of synthetic fabrics. It is recognized that if this chemical is used incorrectly or disposed of improperly, there may be risk to human health or to the environment. What steps must your company take prior to actual production to avoid legal difficulties with the EPA?

**13**   As a manufacturer of paints, you need to dispose of certain production byproducts which are highly toxic. Discuss the process which the law requires you to follow in disposing of these products.

**14**   An abandoned radioactive waste site is discovered by local authorities. The waste came from a company which manufactured radium watch faces and which is now out of business. Who will pay to clean up these radioactive wastes? Discuss.

# Appendix 1

## THE CONSTITUTION OF THE UNITED STATES OF AMERICA

We the People of the United States, in Order to form a more perfect Union, establish Justice, insure domestic Tranquility, provide for the common defence, promote the general Welfare, and secure the Blessings of Liberty to ourselves and our Posterity, do ordain and establish this Constitution for the United States of America.

### Article I

**SECTION 1**

All legislative Powers herein granted shall be vested in a Congress of the United States, which shall consist of a Senate and House of Representatives.

**SECTION 2**

The House of Representatives shall be composed of Members chosen every second Year by the People of the several States, and the Electors in each State shall have the Qualifications requisite for Electors of the most numerous Branch of the State Legislature.

No Person shall be a Representative who shall not have attained to the Age of twenty five Years, and been seven Years a Citizen of the United States, and who shall not, when elected, be an Inhabitant of that State in which he shall be chosen.

Representatives and direct Taxes shall be apportioned among the several States which may be included within this Union, according to their respective Numbers, which shall be determined by adding to the whole Number of free Persons, including those bound to Service for a Term of Years, and excluding Indians not taxed, three fifths of all other Persons. The actual Enumeration shall be made within three Years after the first Meeting of the Congress of the United States, and within every subsequent Term of ten Years, in such Manner as they shall by Law direct. The Number of Representatives shall not exceed one for every thirty Thousand, but each State shall have at Least one Representative; and until such enumeration shall be made, the State of New Hampshire shall be entitled to chuse three, Massachusetts eight, Rhode Island and Providence Plantations one, Connecticut five, New-York six, New Jersey four, Pennsylvania eight, Delaware one, Maryland six, Virginia ten, North Carolina five, South Carolina five, and Georgia three.

When vacancies happen in the Representation from any State, the Executive Authority thereof shall issue Writs of Election to fill such Vacancies.

The House of Representatives shall chuse their Speaker and other Officers; and shall have the sole Power of Impeachment.

### SECTION 3

The Senate of the United States shall be composed of two Senators from each State, chosen by the Legislature thereof, for six Years; and each Senator shall have one Vote.

Immediately after they shall be assembled in Consequence of the Election, they shall be divided as equally as may be into three Classes. The Seats of the Senators of the first Class shall be vacated at the Expiration of the second Year, of the second Class at the Expiration of the fourth Year, and of the third Class at the Expiration of the sixth Year, so that one third may be chosen every second Year; and if Vacancies happen by Resignation, or otherwise, during the Recess of the Legislature of any State, the Executive thereof may make temporary Appointments until the next Meeting of the Legislature, which shall then fill such Vacancies.

No Person shall be a Senator who shall not have attained to the Age of thirty Years, and been nine Years a Citizen of the United States, and who shall not, when elected, be an Inhabitant of that State for which he shall be chosen.

The Vice President of the United States shall be President of the Senate, but shall have no Vote, unless they be equally divided.

The Senate shall chuse their other Officers, and also a President pro tempore, in the Absence of the Vice President, or when he shall exercise the Office of President of the United States.

The Senate shall have the sole Power to try all Impeachments. When sitting for that Purpose, they shall be on Oath or Affirmation. When the President of the United States is tried, the Chief Justice shall preside: And no Person shall be convicted without the Concurrence of two thirds of the Members present.

Judgment in Cases of Impeachment shall not extend further than to removal from Office, and disqualification to hold and enjoy any Office of honor, Trust or Profit under the United States: but the Party convicted shall nevertheless be liable and subject to Indictment, Trial, Judgment and Punishment, according to Law.

### SECTION 4

The Times, Places and Manner of holding Elections for Senators and Representatives, shall be prescribed in each State by the Legislature thereof: but the Congress may at any time by Law make or alter such Regulations, except as to the Places of chusing Senators.

The Congress shall assemble at least once in every Year, and such Meeting shall be on the first Monday in December, unless they shall by Law appoint a different Day.

## SECTION 5

Each House shall be the Judge of the Elections, Returns and Qualifications of its own Members, and a Majority of each shall constitute a Quorum to do Business; but a smaller Number may adjourn from day to day, and may be authorized to compel the Attendance of absent Members, in such Manner, and under such Penalties as each House may provide.

Each House may determine the Rules of its Proceedings, punish its Members for disorderly Behaviour, and, with the concurrence of two thirds, expel a Member.

Each House shall keep a Journal of its Proceedings, and from time to time publish the same, excepting such Parts as may in their Judgment require Secrecy; and the Yeas and Nays of the Members of either House on any question shall, at the Desire of one fifth of those Present, be entered on the Journal.

Neither House, during the Session of Congress, shall, without the Consent of the other, adjourn for more than three days, nor to any other Place than that in which the two Houses shall be sitting.

## SECTION 6

The Senators and Representatives shall receive a Compensation for their Services, to be ascertained by Law, and paid out of the Treasury of the United States. They shall in all Cases, except Treason, Felony and Breach of the Peace, be privileged from Arrest during their Attendance at the Session of their respective Houses, and in going to and returning from the same; and for any Speech or Debate in either House, they shall not be questioned in any other Place.

No Senator or Representative shall, during the Time for which he was elected, be appointed to any civil Office under the Authority of the United States, which shall have been created, or the Emoluments whereof shall have been encreased during such time; and no Person holding any Office under the United States, shall be a Member of either House during his Continuance in Office.

## SECTION 7

All Bills for raising Revenue shall originate in the House of Representatives; but the Senate may propose or concur with Amendments as on other Bills.

Every Bill which shall have passed the House of Representatives and the Senate, shall, before it become a Law, be presented to the President of the United States; If he approve he shall sign it, but if not he shall return it, with his Objections to that House in which it shall have originated, who shall enter the Objections at large on their Journal, and proceed to reconsider it. If after such Reconsideration two thirds of that House shall agree to pass the Bill, it shall be sent, together with the Objections, to the other House, by which it shall likewise be reconsidered, and if approved by two thirds of that House, it shall become a Law. But in all such Cases the Votes of both Houses shall be determined by Yeas and Nays, and the Names of the Persons voting for and against the Bill shall be entered on the Journal of each House respectively. If any Bill shall not be returned by the President within ten Days (Sundays excepted) after it shall have been presented to him, the Same shall be a Law, in like Manner as if he had signed it, unless the Congress by their Adjournment prevent its Return, in which Case it shall not be a Law.

Every Order, Resolution, or Vote to which the Concurrence of the Senate and House of Representatives may be necessary (except on a question of Adjournment) shall be presented to the President of the United States; and before the Same shall take Effect, shall be approved by him, or being disapproved by him, shall be repassed by two thirds of the Senate and House of Representatives, according to the Rules and Limitations prescribed in the Case of a Bill.

### SECTION 8

The Congress shall have Power to lay and collect Taxes, Duties, Imposts and Excises, to pay the Debts and provide for the common Defence and general Welfare of the United States; but all Duties, Imposts and Excises shall be uniform throughout the United States;

To borrow Money on the credit of the United States;

To regulate Commerce with foreign Nations, and among the several States, and with the Indian Tribes;

To establish an uniform Rule of Naturalization, and uniform Laws on the subject of Bankruptcies throughout the United States;

To coin Money, regulate the Value thereof, and of foreign Coin, and fix the Standard of Weights and Measures;

To provide for the Punishment of counterfeiting the Securities and current Coin of the United States;

To establish Post Offices and post Roads;

To promote the Progress of Science and useful Arts, by securing for limited Times to Authors and Inventors the exclusive Right to their respective Writings and Discoveries;

To constitute Tribunals inferior to the supreme Court;

To define and punish Piracies and Felonies committed on the high Seas, and Offenses against the Law of Nations;

To declare War, grant Letters of Marque and Reprisal, and make Rules concerning Captures on Land and Water;

To raise and support Armies, but no Appropriation of Money to that Use shall be for a longer Term than two Years;

To provide and maintain a Navy;

To make Rules for the Government and Regulation of the land and naval Forces;

To provide for calling forth the Militia to execute the Laws of the Union, suppress Insurrections and repel Invasions;

To provide for organizing, arming, and disciplining, the Militia, and for governing such Part of them as may be employed in the Service of the United States, reserving to the States respectively, the Appointment of the Officers, and the Authority of training the Militia according to the discipline prescribed by Congress;

To exercise exclusive Legislation in all Cases whatsoever, over such District (not exceeding ten Miles square) as may, by Cession of particular States, and the Acceptance of Congress, become the Seat of the Government of the United States, and to exercise like Authority over all Places purchased by the Consent of the Legislature of the State in which the Same shall be, for the Erection of Forts, Magazines, Arsenals, dock-Yards, and othe needful buildings;—And

To make all Laws which shall be necessary and proper for carrying into Execution the foregoing Powers, and all other Powers vested by the Constitution in the Government of the United States, or in any Department or Officer thereof.

### SECTION 9

The Migration or Importation of such Persons as any of the States now existing shall think proper to admit, shall not be prohibited by the Congress prior to the Year one thousand eight hundred and eight, but a Tax or Duty may be imposed on such Importation, not exceeding ten dollars for each Person.

The Privilege of the Writ of Habeas Corpus shall not be suspended, unless when in Cases of Rebellion or Invasion the public Safety may require it.

No Bill of Attainder or ex post facto Law shall be passed.

No Capitation, or other direct, Tax shall be laid, unless in Proportion to the Census or Enumeration herein before directed to be taken.

No Tax or Duty shall be laid on Articles exported from any State.

No Preference shall be given by any Regulation of Commerce or Revenue to the Ports of one State over those of another: nor shall Vessels bound to, or from, one State, be obliged to enter, clear, or pay Duties in another.

No Money shall be drawn from the Treasury, but in Consequence of Appropriations made by Law; and a regular Statement and Account of the Receipts and Expenditures of all public Money shall be published from time to time.

No Title of Nobility shall be granted by the United States: And no Person holding any Office of Profit or Trust under them, shall, without the Consent of the Congress, accept of any present, Emolument, Office, or Title, of any kind whatever, from any King, Prince, or foreign State.

### SECTION 10

No State shall enter into any Treaty, Alliance, or Confederation; grant Letters of Marque and Reprisal; coin Money; emit Bills of Credit; make any Thing but gold and silver Coin a Tender in Payment of Debts; pass any Bill of Attainder, ex post facto Law, or Law impairing the Obligation of Contracts, or grant any Title of Nobility.

No State shall, without the Consent of the Congress, lay any Imposts or Duties on Imports or Exports, except what may be absolutely necessary for executing its inspection Laws: and the net Produce of all Duties and Imposts, laid by any State on Imports or Exports, shall be for the Use of the Treasury of the United States; and all such Laws shall be subject to the Revision and Controul of the Congress.

No State shall, without the Consent of Congress, lay any Duty of Tonnage, keep Troops, or Ships of War in time of Peace, enter into any Agreement or Compact with another State, or with a foreign Power, or engage in War, unless actually invaded, or in such imminent Danger as will not admit of delay.

## Article II

### SECTION 1

The executive Power shall be vested in a President of the United States of America. He shall hold his Office during the Term of four Years, and, together with the Vice President, chosen for the same Term, be elected, as follows:

Each State shall appoint, in such Manner as the Legislature thereof may direct, a Number of Electors, equal to the whole Number of Senators and Representatives to which the State may be entitled in the Congress: but no Senator or Representative, or Person holding an Office or Trust or Profit under the United States, shall be appointed an Elector.

The Electors shall meet in their respective States, and vote by Ballot for two Persons, of whom one at least shall not be an Inhabitant of the same State with Themselves. And they shall make a List of all the Persons voted for, and of the Number of Votes for each; which List they shall sign and certify, and transmit sealed to the Seat of the Government of the United States, directed to the President of the Senate. The President of the Senate shall, in the Presence of the Senate and House of Representatives, open all the Certificates, and the Votes shall then be counted. The Person having the greatest Number of Votes shall be the President, if such Number be a Majority of the whole Number of Electors appointed; and if there be more than one who have such Majority, and have an equal Number of Votes, then the House of Representatives shall immediately chuse by Ballot one of them for President; and if no Person have a Majority, then from the five highest on the List the said House shall in like Manner chuse the President. But in chusing the President, the Votes shall be taken by States, the Representation from each State having one Vote; A quorum for this Purpose shall consist of a Member or Members from two thirds of the States, and a Majority of all the States shall be necessary to a Choice. In every Case, after the Choice of the President, the Person having the greatest Number of Votes of the Electors shall be the Vice President. But if there should remain two or more who have equal Votes, the Senate shall chuse from them by Ballot the Vice President.

The Congress may determine the Time of chusing the Electors, and the Day on which they shall give their Votes; which Day shall be the same throughout the United States.

No Person except a natural born Citizen, or a Citizen of the United States, at the time of the Adoption of this Constitution, shall be eligible to the Office of President; neither shall any Person be eligible to that Office who shall not have attained to the Age of thirty five Years, and been fourteen Years a Resident within the United States.

In Case of the Removal of the President from Office, or of his Death, Resignation, or Inability to discharge the Powers and Duties of the said Office, the Same shall devolve on the Vice President, and the Congress may by Law provide for the Case of Removal,

Death, Resignation or Inability, both of the President and Vice President, declaring what Officer shall then act as President, and such Officer shall act accordingly, until the Disability be removed, or a President shall be elected.

The President shall, at stated Times, receive for his Services, a Compensation, which shall neither be encreased nor diminished during the Period for which he shall have been elected, and he shall not receive within that Period any other Emolument from the United States, or any of them.

Before he enter on the Execution of his Office, he shall take the following Oath or Affirmation:—"I do solemnly swear (or affirm) that I will faithfully execute the Office of President of the United States, and will to the best of my Ability, preserve, protect and defind the Constitution of the United States."

**SECTION 2**
The President shall be Commander in Chief of the Army and Navy of the United States, and of the Militia of the several States, when called into the actual Service of the United States; he may require the Opinion, in writing, of the principal Officer in each of the executive Departments, upon any Subject relating to the Duties of their respective Offices, and he shall have Power to grant Reprieves and Pardons for Offences against the United States, except in Cases of Impeachment.

He shall have Power, by and with the Advice and Consent of the Senate, to make Treaties, providing two thirds of the Senators present concur; and he shall nominate, and by and with the Advice and Consent of the Senate, shall appoint Ambassadors, other public Ministers and Consuls, Judges of the supreme Court, and all other Officers of the United States, whose Appointments are not herein otherwise provided for, and which shall be established by Law: but the Congress may be Law vest the Appointment of such inferior Officers, as they think proper, in the President alone, in the Courts of Law, or in the Heads of Departments.

The President shall have Power to fill up all Vacancies that may happen during the Recess of the Senate, by granting Commissions which shall expire at the End of their next Session.

**SECTION 3**
He shall from time to time give to the Congress Information of the State of the Union, and recommend to their Consideration such Measures as he shall judge necessary and expedient; he may, on extraordinary Occasions, convene both Houses, or either of them, and in Case of Disagreement between them, with Respect to the Time of Adjournment, he may adjourn them to such Time as he shall think proper; he shall receive Ambassadors and other public Ministers; he shall take Care that the Laws be faithfully executed, and shall Commission all the Officers of the United States.

**SECTION 4**
The President, Vice President and all civil Officers of the United States, shall be removed from Office on Impeachment for, and Conviction of, Treason, Bribery, or other high Crimes and Misdemeanors.

# Article III

### SECTION 1

The judicial Power of the United States, shall be vested in one supreme Court, and in such inferior Courts as the Congress may from time to time ordain and establish. The Judges, both of the supreme and inferior Courts, shall hold their Offices during good Behaviour, and shall, at stated Times, receive for their Services, a Compensation, which shall not be diminished during their Continuance in Office.

### SECTION 2

The judicial Power shall extend to all Cases, in Law and Equity, arising under this Constitution, the Laws of the United States, and Treaties made, or which shall be made, under their Authority;—to all Cases affecting Ambassadors, other public Ministers and Consuls;—to all Cases of admiralty and maritime Jurisdiction;—to Controversies to which the United States shall be a Party;—to Controversies between two or more States;—between a State and Citizens of another State;—between Citizens of different States;—between Citizens of the same State claiming Lands under Grants of different States, and between a State, or the Citizens thereof, and foreign States, Citizens or Subjects.

In all Cases affecting Ambassadors, other public Ministers and Consuls, and those in which a State shall be Party, the supreme Court shall have original Jurisdiction. In all the other Cases before mentioned, the supreme Court shall have appellate Jurisdiction, both as to Law and Fact, with such Exceptions, and under such Regulations as the Congress shall make.

The Trial of all Crimes, except in Cases of Impeachment, shall be by Jury; and such Trial shall be held in the State where the said Crimes shall have been committed; but when not committed within any State, the Trial shall be at such Place or Places as the Congress may by Law have directed.

### SECTION 3

Treason against the United States, shall consist only in levying War against them, or in adhering to their Enemies, giving them Aid and Comfort. No Person shall be convicted of Treason unless on the Testimony of two Witnesses to the same overt Act, or on Confession in open Court.

The Congress shall have Power to declare the Punishment of Treason, but no Attainder of Treason shall work Corruption of Blood, or Forfeiture except during the Life of the Person attainted.

# Article IV

### SECTION 1

Full Faith and Credit shall be given in each State to the public Acts, Records, and judicial Proceedings of every other State. And the Congress may by general Laws prescribe the Manner in which such Acts, Records and Proceedings shall be proved, and the Effect thereof.

### SECTION 2

The Citizens of each State shall be entitled to all Privileges and Immunities of Citizens in the several States.

A Person charged in any State with Treason, Felony, or other Crime. who shall flee from Justice, and be found in another State, shall on Demand of the executive Authority of the State from which he fled, be delivered up, to be removed to the State having Jurisdiction of the Crime.

No Person held to Service or Labour in one State, under the Laws thereof, escaping into another, shall, in Consequence of any Law or Regulation therein, be discharged from such Service or Labour, but shall be delivered up on Claim of the Party to whom such Service or Labour may be due.

### SECTION 3

New States may be admitted by the Congress into this Union; but no new State shall be formed or erected within the Jurisdiction of any other State; nor any State be formed by the Junction of two or more States, or Parts of States, without the Consent of the Legislatures of the States concerned as well as of the Congress.

The Congress shall have Power to dispose of and make all needful Rules and Regulations respecting the Territory or other Property belonging to the belonging to the United States; and nothing in this Constitution shall be so construed as to Prejudice any Claims of the United States, or of any particular State.

### SECTION 4

The United States shall guarantee to every State in this Union a Republican Form of Government, and shall protect each of them against Invasion; and on Application of the Legislature, or of the Executive (when the Legislature cannot be convened) against domestic Violence.

## Article V

The Congress, whenever two thirds of both Houses shall deem it necessary, shall propose Amendments to this Constitution, or, on the Application of the Legislatures of two thirds of the several States, shall call a Convention for proposing Amendments, which, in either Case, shall be valid to all Intents and Purposes, as Part of this Constitution, when ratified by the Legislatures of three fourths of the several States, or by Conventions in three fourths thereof, as the one or the other Mode of Ratification may be proposed by the Congress; Provided that no Amendment which may be made prior to the Year One thousand eight hundred and eight shall in any Manner affect the first and fourth

Clauses in the Ninth Section of the first Article; and that no State, without its Consent, shall be deprived of its equal Suffrage in the Senate.

## Article VI

All Debts contracted and Engagements entered into, before the Adoption of this Constitution, shall be as valid against the United States under this Constitution, as under the Confederation.

This Constitution, and the Laws of the United States which shall be made in Pursuance thereof; and all Treaties made, or which shall be made, under the Authority of the United States, shall be the supreme Law of the Land; and the Judges in every State shall be bound thereby, any Thing in the Constitution or Laws of any State to the Contrary notwithstanding.

The Senators and Representatives before mentioned, and the Members of the several State Legislatures, and all executive and judicial Officers, both of the United States and of the several States, shall be bound by Oath or Affirmation, to support this Constitution; but no religious Test shall ever by required as a Qualification to any Office or public Trust under the United States.

## Article VII

The Ratification of the Conventions of nine States, shall be sufficient for the Establishment of this Constitution between the States so ratifying the Same.

## Amendment I [1791]

Congress shall make no law respecting an establishment of religion, or prohibiting the free exercise thereof; or abridging the freedom of speech, or the press; or the right of the people peaceably to assemble, and to petition the Government for a redress of grievances.

## Amendment II [1791]

A well regulated Militia, being necessary to the security for a free State, the right of the people to keep and bear Arms, shall not be infringed.

## Amendment III [1791]

No Soldier shall, in time of peace be quartered in any house, without the consent of the Owner, nor in time of war, but in a manner to be prescribed by law.

### Amendment IV [1791]

The right of the people to be secure in their persons, houses, papers, and effects, against unreasonable searches and seizures, shall not be violated, and no Warrants shall issue, but upon probable cause, supported by Oath or affirmation, and particularly describing the place to be searched, and the persons or things to be seized.

### Amendment V [1791]

No person shall be held to answer for a capital, or otherwise infamous crime, unless on a presentment or indictment of a Grand Jury, except in cases arising in the land or naval forces, or in the Militia, when in actual service in time of War or public danger; nor shall any person be subject for the same offense to be twice put in jeopardy of life or limb; nor shall be compelled in any criminal case to be a witness against himself, nor be deprived of life, liberty, or property, without due process of law; nor shall private property be taken for public use, without just compensation.

### Amendment VI [1791]

In all criminal prosecutions, the accused shall enjoy the right to a speedy and public trial, by an impartial jury of the State and district wherein the crime shall have been committed, which district shall have been previously ascertained by law, and to be informed of the nature and cause of the accusation; to be confronted with the Witnesses against him; to have compulsory process for obtaining witnesses in his favor, and to have the Assistance of counsel for his defence.

### Amendment VII [1791]

In Suits at common law, where the value in controversy shall exceed twenty dollars, the right of trial by jury shall be preserved, and no fact tried by a jury, shall be otherwise re-examined in any Court of the United States, than according to the rules of the common law.

### Amendment VIII [1791]

Excessive bail shall not be required, nor excessive fines imposed, nor cruel and unusual punishments inflicted.

## Amendment IX [1791]

The enumeration in the Constitution, of certain rights, shall not be construed to deny or disparage others retained by the people.

## Amendment X [1791]

The powers not delegated to the United States by the Constitution, nor prohibited by it to the States, are reserved to the States respectively, or to the people.

## Amendment XI [1798]

The Judicial power of the United States shall not be construed to extend to any suit in law or equity, commenced or prosecuted against one of the United States by Citizens of another State, or by Citizens or Subjects of any Foreign State.

## Amendment XII [1804]

The Electors shall meet in their respective states and vote by ballot for President and Vice-President, one of whom, at least, shall not be an inhabitant of the same state with themselves; they shall name in their ballots the person voted for as President, and in distinct ballots the person voted for as Vice-President, and they shall make distinct lists of all persons voted for as President, and of all persons voted for as Vice-President, and of the number of votes for each, which lists they shall sign and certify, and transmit sealed to the seat of the government of the United States, directed to the President of the Senate;—The President of the Senate shall, in the presence of the Senate and House of Representatives, open all the certificates and the votes shall then be counted;—The person having the greatest number of votes for President, shall be the President, if such number be a majority of the whole number of Electors appointed; and if no person have such majority, then from the persons having the highest numbers not exceeding three on the list of those voted for as President, the House of Representatives shall choose immediately, be ballot, the President. But in choosing the President, the votes shall be taken by states, the representation from each state having one vote; a quorum for this purpose shall consist of a member or members from two-thirds of the states, and a majority of all the states shall be necessary to a choice. And if the House of Representatives shall not choose a President whenever the right of choice shall devolve upon them, before the fourth day of March next following, then the Vice-President shall act as President. The person having the greatest number of votes as Vice-President, shall be the Vice-President, if such number be a majority of the whole number of Electors appointed, and if no person have a majority, then from the two highest numbers on the list, the Senate shall choose the Vice-President; a quorum for the purpose shall consist of two-thirds of the whole number of Senators, and a majority of the whole number shall be necessary to a choice. But no person constitutionally ineligible to the office of President shall be eligible to that of the Vice-President of the United States.

## Amendment XIII [1865]

### SECTION 1
Neither slavery nor involuntary servitude, except as a punishment for crime whereof the party shall have been duly convicted, shall exist within the United States, or any place subject to their jurisdiction.

### SECTION 2
Congress shall have power to enforce this article by appropriate legislation.

## Amendment XIV [1868]

### SECTION 1
All persons born or naturalized in the United States, and subject to the jurisdiction thereof, are citizens of the United States and of the State wherein they reside. No State shall make or enforce any law which shall abridge the privileges or immunities of citizens of the United States; nor shall any State deprive any person of life, liberty, or property, without due process of law; nor deny to any person within its jurisdiction the equal protection of the laws.

### SECTION 2
Representatives shall be appointed among the several States according to their respective numbers, counting the whole number of persons in each State, excluding Indians not taxed. But when the right to vote at any election for the choice of electors for President and Vice President of the United States, Representatives in Congress, the Executive and Judicial officers of a State, or the members of the Legislature thereof, is denied to any of the male inhabitants of such State, being twenty-one years of age, and citizens of the United States, or in any way abridged, except for participation in rebellion, or other crime, the basis of representation therein shall be reduced in the proportion which the number of such male citizens shall bear to the whole number of male citizens twenty-one years of age in such State.

### SECTION 3
No person shall be a Senator or Representative in Congress, or elector of President and Vice President, or hold any office, civil or military, under the United States, or under any State, who, having previously taken an oath, as a member of Congress, or as an officer of the United States, or as a member of any State legislature, or as an executive or judicial officer of any State, to support the Constitution of the United States, shall have engaged in insurrection or rebellion against the same, or given aid or comfort to the enemies thereof. But Congress may by a vote of two-thirds of each House, remove such disability.

**SECTION 4**

The validity of the public debt of the United States, authorized by law, including debts incurred for payment of pensions and bounties for services in suppressing insurrection or rebellion, shall not be questioned. But neither the United States nor any State shall assume or pay any debt or obligation incurred in aid of insurrection or rebellion against the United States, or any claim for the loss or emancipation of any slave; but all such debts, obligations and claims shall be held illegal and void.

**SECTION 5**

The Congress shall have power to enforce, by appropriate legislation, the provisions of this article.

## Amendment XV [1870]

**SECTION 1**

The right of citizens of the United States to vote shall not be denied or abridged by the United States or by any State on account of race, color, or previous condition of servitude.

**SECTION 2**

The Congress shall have power to enforce this article by appropriate legislation.

## Amendment XVI [1913]

The Congress shall have power to lay and collect taxes on incomes, from whatever source derived, without apportionment among the several States, and without regard to any census or enumeration.

## Amendment XVII [1913]

The Senate of the United States shall be composed of two Senators from each State, elected by the people thereof, for six years; and each Senator shall have one vote. The electors in each State shall have the qualifications requisite for electors of the most numerous branch of the State legislatures.

When vacancies happen in the representation of any State in the Senate, the executive authority of such State shall issue writs of election to fill such vacancies: *Provided*, That the legislature of any State may empower the executive thereof to make temporary appointments until the people fill the vacancies by election as the legislature may direct.

This amendment shall not be so construed as to affect the election or term of any Senator chosen before it becomes valid as part of the Constitution.

## Amendment XVIII [1919]

**SECTION 1**

After one year from the ratification of this article the manufacture, sale, or transportation of intoxicating liquors within, the importation thereof into, or the exportation thereof from the United States and all territory subject to the jurisdiction thereof for beverage purposes is hereby prohibited.

**SECTION 2**

The Congress and the several States shall have concurrent power to enforce this article by appropriate legislation.

**SECTION 3**

This article shall be inoperative unless it shall have been ratified as an amendment to the Constitution by the legislatures of the several States, as provided in the Constitution, within seven years from the date of the submission hereof to the States by the Congress.

## Amendment XIX [1920]

The right of citizens of the United States to vote shall not be denied or abridged by the United States or by any State on account of sex.

Congress shall have power to enforce this article by appropriate legislation.

## Amendment XX [1933]

**SECTION 1**

The terms of the President and Vice President shall end at noon on the 20th day of January, and the terms of Senators and Representatives at noon on the 3d day of January, of the years in which such terms would have ended if this article had not been ratified; and the terms of their successors shall then begin.

**SECTION 2**

The Congress shall assemble at least once in every year, and such meeting shall begin at noon on the 3d day of January, unless they shall by law appoint a different day.

**SECTION 3**

If, at the time fixed for the beginning of the term of the President, the President elect shall have died, the Vice President elect shall become President. If a President shall not have been chosen before the time fixed for the beginning of his term, or if the President elect shall have failed to qualify, then the Vice President elect shall act as President until a President shall have qualified; and the Congress may be law provide for the case wherein neither a President elect nor a Vice President elect shall have qualified, declaring who shall then act as President, or the manner in which one who is to act shall be selected, and such person shall act accordingly until a President or Vice President shall have qualified.

### SECTION 4

The Congress may by law provide for the case of the death of any of the persons from whom the House of Representatives may choose a President whenever the right of choice shall have devolved upon them, and for the case of the death of any of the persons from whom the Senate may choose a Vice President whenever the right of choice shall have devolved upon them.

### SECTION 5

Sections 1 and 2 shall take effect on the 15th day of October following the ratification of this article.

### SECTION 6

This article shall be inoperative unless it shall have been ratified as an amendment to the Constitution by the legislatures of three-fourths of the several States within seven years from the date of its submission.

## Amendment XXI [1933]

### SECTION 1

The eighteenth article of amendment to the Constitution of the United States is hereby repealed.

### SECTION 2

The transportation or importation into any State, Territory, or possession of the United States for delivery or use therein of intoxicating liquors, in violation of the laws thereof, is hereby prohibited.

### SECTION 3

This article shall be inoperative unless it shall have been ratified as an amendment to the Constitution by conventions in the several States, as provided in the Constitution, within seven years from the date of the submission hereof to the States by the Congress.

## Amendment XXII [1951]

### SECTION 1

No person shall be elected to the office of the President more than twice, and no person who has held the office of President, or acted as President, for more than two years of a term to which some other person was elected President shall be elected to the office of the President more than once. But this Article shall not apply to any person holding the office of President when this Article was proposed by the Congress, and shall not prevent any person who may be holding the office of President, or acting as President, during the term within which this Article becomes operative from holding the office of President or acting as President during the remainder of such term.

**SECTION 2**

This article shall be inoperative unless it shall have been ratified as an amendment to the Constitution by the legislatures of three-fourths of the several States within seven years from the date of its submission to the States by the Congress.

## Amendment XXIII [1961]

**SECTION 1**

The District constituting the seat of Government of the United States shall appoint in such manner as the Congress may direct:

A number of electors of President and Vice President equal to the whole number of Senators and Representatives in Congress to which the District would be entitled if it were a State, but in no event more than the least populous State; they shall be in addition to those appointed by the States, but they shall be considered, for the purposes of the election of President and Vice President, to be electors appointed by a State; and they shall meet in the District and perform such duties as provided by the twelfth article of amendment.

**SECTION 2**

The Congress shall have power to enforce this article by appropriate legislation.

## Amendment XXIV [1964]

**SECTION 1**

The right of citizens of the United States to vote in any primary or other election for President or Vice President, for electors for President or Vice President, or for Senator or Representative in Congress, shall not be denied or abridged by the United States or any State by reason of failure to pay any poll tax or other tax.

**SECTION 2**

The Congress shall have power to enforce this article by appropriate legislation.

## Amendment XXV [1967]

**SECTION 1**

In case of the removal of the President from office or of his death or resignation, the Vice President shall become President.

**SECTION 2**

Whenever there is a vacancy in the office of the Vice President, the President shall nominate a Vice President who shall take office upon confirmation by a majority vote of both Houses of Congress.

**SECTION 3**

Whenever the President transmits to the President pro tempore of the Senate and the Speaker of the House of Representatives his written declaration that he is unable to discharge the powers and duties of his office, and until he transmits to them a written declaration to the contrary, such powers and duties shall be discharged by the Vice President as Acting President.

**SECTION 4**

Whenever the Vice President and a majority of either the principal officers of the executive departments or of such other body as Congress may by Law provide, transmit to the President pro tempore of the Senate and the Speaker of the House of Representatives their written declaration that the President is unable to discharge the powers and duties of his office, the Vice President shall immediately assume the powers and duties of the office as Acting President.

Thereafter, when the President transmits to the President pro tempore of the Senate and the Speaker of the House of Representatives his written declaration that no inability exists, he shall resume the powers and duties of his office unless the Vice President and a majority of either the principal officers of the executive department or of such other body as Congress may by law provide, transmit within four days to the President pro tempore to the Senate and the Speaker of the House of Representatives their written declaration that the President is unable to discharge the powers and duties of his office. Thereupon Congress shall decide the issue, assembling within forty-eight hours for that purpose if not in session. If the Congress, within twenty-one days after receipt of the latter written declaration, or, if Congress is not in session, within twenty-one days after Congress is required to assemble, determines by two-thirds vote of both Houses that the President is unable to discharge the powers and duties of his office, the Vice President shall continue to discharge the same as Acting President; otherwise, the President shall resume the powers and duties of his office.

## Amendment XXVI [1971]

**SECTION 1**

The right of citizens of the United States, who are eighteen years of age or older, to vote shall not be denied or abridged by the United States or by any State on account of age.

**SECTION 2**

The Congress shall have power to enforce this article by appropriate legislation.

# Appendix 2

## THE SHERMAN ACT AS AMENDED (EXCERPTS)

### 1  Trusts, etc., in Restraint of Trade Illegal; Exception of Resale Price Agreements; Penalty

Every contract, combination in the form of trust or otherwise, or conspiracy, in restraint of trade or commerce among the several States, or with foreign nations, is declared to be illegal. Every person who shall make any contract or engage in any combination or conspiracy declared by sections 1 to 7 of this title to be illegal shall be deemed guilty of a felony, and, on conviction thereof, shall be punished by fine not exceeding one million dollars or by imprisonment not exceeding three years, or by both said punishments, in the discretion of the court.

### 2  Monopolizing Trade a Felony; Penalty

Every person who shall monopolize, or attempt to monopolize, or combine or conspire with any other person or persons, to monopolize any part of the trade or commerce among the several States, or with foreign nations, shall be deemed guilty of a felony, and, on conviction thereof, shall be punished by fine not exceeding one million dollars if a corporation, or, if any other person, one hundred thousand dollars or by imprisonment not exceeding three years, or by both said punishments, in the discretion of the court.

### 16  Judgments—Prima Facie Evidence

(a)  A final judgment or decree heretofore or hereafter rendered in any civil or criminal proceeding brought by or on behalf of the United States under the antitrust laws to the effect that a defendant has violated said laws shall be prima facie evidence against such defendant in any action or proceeding brought by any other party against such defendant under said laws or by the United States under section 15a of this title, as to all matters respecting which said judgment or decree would be an estoppel as between the parties thereto: *Provided,* That this section shall not apply to consent judgments or decrees entered before any testimony has been taken or to judgments or decrees entered in action 15a of this title.

# Appendix 3

## THE CLAYTON ACT AS AMENDED (EXCERPTS)

### Section 2

(a) It shall be unlawful for any person engaged in commerce, in the course of such commerce, either directly or indirectly, to discriminate in price between different purchasers of commodities of like grade and quality, where either or any of the purchases involved in such discrimination are in commerce, where such commodities are sold for use, consumption, or resale within the United States or any Territory thereof or the District of Columbia or any insular possession or other place under the jurisdiction of the United States, and where the effect of such discrimination may be substantially to lessen competition or tend to create a monopoly in any line of commerce, or to injure, destroy, or prevent competition with any person who either grants or knowingly receives the benefit of such discrimination, or with customers of either of them: *Provided,* That nothing herein contained shall prevent differentials which make only due allowance for differences in the cost of manufacture, sale, or delivery resulting from the differing methods or quantities in which such commodities are to such purchasers sold or delivered: *Provided, however,* That the Federal Trade Commission may, after due investigation and hearing to all interested parties, fix and establish quantity limits, and revise the same as it finds necessary, as to particular commodities or classes of commodities, where it finds that available purchasers in greater quantities are so few as to render differentials on account thereof unjustly discriminatory or promotive of monopoly in any line of commerce; and the foregoing shall then not be construed to permit differentials based on differences in quantities greater than those so fixed and established: *And provided further,* That nothing herein contained shall prevent persons engaged in selling goods, wares, or merchandise in commerce from selecting their own customers in bona fide transactions and not in restraint of trade: *And provided further,* That nothing herein contained shall prevent price changes from time to time where in response to changing conditions affecting the market for or the marketability of the goods concerned, such as but not limited to actual or imminent deterioration of perishable goods, obsolescence of seasonal goods, distress sales under court process, or sales in good faith in discontinuance of business in the goods concerned.

### BURDEN OF REBUTTING PRIMA-FACIE CASE OF DISCRIMINATION

(b)   Upon proof being made, at any hearing on a complaint under this section, that there has been discrimination in price or services or facilities furnished, the burden of rebutting the prima-facie case thus made by showing justification shall be upon the person charged with a violation of this section, and unless justification shall be affirmatively shown, the Commission is authorized to issue an order terminating the discrimination: *Provided, however,* That nothing herein contained shall prevent a seller rebutting the prima-facie case thus made by showing that his lower price or the furnishing of services or facilities to any purchaser or purchasers was made in good faith to meet an equally low price of a competitor, or the services or facilities furnished by a competitor.

### PAYMENT OR ACCEPTANCE OF COMMISSION, BROKERAGE OR OTHER COMPENSATION

(c)   It shall be unlawful for any person engaged in commerce, in the course of such commerce, to pay or grant, or to receive or accept, anything of value as a commission, brokerage, or other compensation, or any allowance or discourt in lieu thereof, except for services rendered in connection with the sale or purchase of goods, wares, or merchandise, either to the other party to such transaction or to an agent, representative, or other intermediary therein where such intermediary is acting in fact for or in behalf, or is subject to the direct or indirect control, of any party to such transaction other than the person by whom such compensation is so granted or paid.

### PAYMENT FOR SERVICES OR FACILITIES FOR PROCESSING OR SALE

(d)   It shall be unlawful for any person engaged in commerce to pay or contract for the payment of anything of value to or for the benefit of a customer of such person in the course of such commerce as compensation or in consideration for any services or facilities furnished by or through such customer in connection with the processing, handling, sale, or offering for sale of any products or commodities manufactured, sold, or offered for sale by such person, unless such payment or consideration is available on proportionally equal terms to all other customers competing in the distribution of such products or commodities.

### FURNISHING SERVICES OR FACILITIES FOR PROCESSING, HANDLING, ETC.

(e)   It shall be unlawful for any person to discriminate in favor of one purchaser against another purchaser or purchasers of a commodity bought for resale, with or without processing, by contracting to furnish or furnishing, or by contributing to the furnishing of, any services or facilities connected with the processing, handling, sale, or offering for sale of such commodity so purchased upon terms not accorded to all purchasers on proportionally equal terms.

### KNOWINGLY INDUCING OR RECEIVING DISCRIMINATORY PRICE

(f)   It shall be unlawful for any person engaged in commerce, in the course of such commerce, knowingly to induce or receive a discrimination in price which is prohibited by this section.

## Section 3

It shall be unlawful for any person engaged in commerce, in the course of such commerce, to lease or make a sale or contract for sale of goods, wares, merchandise, machinery, supplies, or other commodities, whether patented or unpatented, for use, consumption, or resale within the United States or any Territory thereof or the District of Columbia or any insular possession or other place under the jurisdiction of the United States, or fix a price charged therefor, or discount from, or rebate upon, such price, on the condition, agreement, or understanding that the lessee or purchaser thereof shall not use or deal in the goods, wares, merchandise, machinery, supplies, or other commodities of a competitor or competitors of the lessor or seller, where the effect of such lease, sale, or contract for sale or such condition, agreement, or understanding that the lessee or purchaser thereof shall not use or deal in the goods, wares, merchandise, machinery, supplies, or other commodities of a competitor or competitors of the lessor or seller, where the effect of such lease, sale, or contract for sale or such condition, agreement, or understanding may be to substantially lessen competition or tend to create a monopoly in any line of commerce.

## Section 7

No person engaged in commerce or in any activity affecting commerce shall acquire, directly or indirectly, the whole or any part of the stock or other share capital and no person subject to the jurisdiction of the Federal Trade Commission shall acquire the whole or any part of the assets of another person engaged also in commerce or in any activity affecting commerce, where in any line of commerce or in any activity affecting commerce, where in any line of commerce or in any activity affecting commerce in any section of the country, the effect of such acquisition may be substantially to lessen competition, or to tend to create a monopoly.

No person shall acquire, directly or indirectly, the whole or any part of the stock or other share capital and no person subject to the jurisdiction of the Federal Trade Commission shall acquire the whole or any part of the assets of one or more persons engaged in commerce or in any activity affecting commerce, where in any line of commerce or in any activity affecting commerce in any section of the country, the effect of such aquisition, of such stocks or assets, or of the use of such stock by the voting or granting of proxies or otherwise, may be substantially to lessen competition, or to tend to create a monopoly.

This section shall not apply to persons purchasing such stock solely for investment and not using the same by voting or otherwise to bring about, or in attempting to bring about, the substantial lessening of competition. Nor shall anything contained in this section prevent a corporation engaged in commerce or in any activity affecting commerce from causing the formation of subsidiary corporations for the actual carrying on of their immediate lawful business, or the natural and legitimate branches of extensions thereof, or from owning and holding all or a part of the stock of such subsidiary corporations, when the effect of such formation is not to substantially lessen competition.

Nor shall anything herein contained be construed to prohibit any common carrier subject to the laws to regulate commerce from aiding in the construction of branches or short lines so located as to become feeders to the main line of the company so aiding in such construction or from acquiring or owning all or any part of the stock of such branch lines, nor to prevent any such common carrier from acquiring and owning all or any part of the stock of a branch or short line constructed by an independent company where there is no substantial competition between the company owning the branch line so constructed and the company owning the main line acquiring the property or an interest therein, nor to prevent such common carrier from extending any of its lines through the medium of the acquisition of stock or otherwise of any other common carrier where there is no substantial competition between the company extending its lines and the company whose stock, property, or an interest therein is so acquired.

Nothing contained in this section shall be held to affect or impair any right heretofore legally acquired: *Provided,* That nothing in this section shall be held or construed to authorize or make lawful anything heretofore prohibited or made illegal by the antitrust laws, nor to exempt any person from the penal provisions thereof or the civil remedies therein provided.

Nothing contained in this section shall apply to transactions duly consummated pursuant to authority given by the Civil Aeronautics Board, Federal Communications Commission, Federal Power Commission, Interstate Commerce Commission, the Securities and Exchange Commission in the exercise of its jurisdiction under section 79j of this title, the United States Maritime Commission, or the Secretary of Agriculture under any statutory provision vesting such power in such Commission, Secretary, or Board.

## Section 8

No private banker or director, officer, or employee of any member bank of the Federal Reserve System or any branch thereof shall be at the same time a director, officer, or employee of any other bank, banking association, savings bank, or trust company organized under the National Bank Act or organized under the laws of any State or of the District of Columbia, or any branch thereof, except that the Board of Governors of the Federal Reserve System may by regulation permit such service as a director, officer, or employee of not more than one other such institution or branch thereof; but the foregoing prohibition shall not apply in the case of any one or more of the following or any branch thereof:

(1) A bank, banking association, savings bank, or trust company, more than 90 per centum of the stock of which is owned directly or indirectly by the United States or by any corporation of which the United States directly or indirectly owns more than 90 per centum of the stock.

(2) A bank, banking association, savings bank, or trust company which has been placed formally in liquidation or which is in the hands of a receiver, conservator, or other official exercising similar functions.

(3) A corporation, principally engaged in international or foreign banking or banking in a dependency or insular possession of the United States which has entered into an agreement with the Board of Governors of the Federal Reserve System pursuant to sections 601 to 604a of Title 12.

(4)   A bank, banking association, savings bank, or trust company, more than 50 per centum of the common stock of which is owned directly or indirectly by persons who own directly or indirectly more than 50 per centum of the common stock of such member bank.

(5)   A bank, banking association, savings bank, or trust company not located and having no branch in the same city, town, or village as that in which such member bank or any branch thereof is located, or in any city, town, or village contiguous or adjacent thereto.

(6)   A bank, banking association, savings bank, or trust company not engaged in a class or classes of business in which such member bank is engaged.

(7)   A mutual savings bank having no capital stock . . .

No person at the same time shall be a director in any two or more corporations, any one of which has capital, surplus, and undivided profits aggregating more than $1,000,000, engaged in whole or in part in commerce, other than banks, banking associations, trust companies, and common carriers subject to the Act to regulate commerce, approved February fourth, eighteen hundred and eighty-seven, if such corporations are or shall have been theretofore, by virtue of their business and location of operation, competitors, so that the elimination of competition by agreement between them would constitute a violation of any of the provisions of any of the antitrust laws. The eligibility of a director under the foregoing provision shall be determined by the aggregate amount of the capital, surplus, and undivided profits, exclusive of dividends declared but not paid to stockholders, at the end of the fiscal year of said corporation next preceding the election of directors, and when a director has been elected in accordance with the provisions of this Act is shall be lawful for him to continue as such for one year thereafter.

When any person elected or chosen as a director or officer or selected as an employee of any bank or other corporation subject to the provisions of this Act is eligible at the time of his election or selection to act for such bank or other corporation in such capacity his eligibility to act in such capacity shall not be affected and he shall not become or be deemed amenable to any of the provisions hereof by reason of any change in the affairs of such bank or other corporation from whatsoever cause, whether specifically excepted by any of the provisions hereof or not, until the expiration of one year from the date of his election or employment.

# Appendix 4

## THE WAGNER ACT AS AMENDED (EXCERPTS)

### Section 7

Employees shall have the right to self-organization, to form, join, or assist labor organizations, to bargain collectively through representatives of their own choosing, and to engage in other concerted activities for the purpose of collective bargaining or other mutual aid or protection, and shall also have the right to refrain from any or all of such activities except to the extent that such right may be affected by an agreement requiring membership in a labor organization as a condition of employment as authorized in section 8(a)(3).

### Section 8

(a)  It shall be an unfair labor practice for an employer—

(1)  to interfere with, restrain, or coerce employees in the exercise of the rights guaranteed in section 7;

(2)  to dominate or interfere with the formation or administration of any labor organization or contribute financial or other support to it: *Provided,* That subject to rules and regulations made and published by the Board pursuant to section 6, an employer shall not be prohibited from permitting employees to confer with him during working hours without loss of time or pay;

(3)  by discrimination in regard to hire or tenure of employment or any term or condition of employment to encourage or discourage membership in any labor organization: *Provided,* That nothing in this Act, or in any other statute of the United States, shall preclude an employer from making an agreement with a labor organization (not established, maintained, or assisted by any action defined in section 8(a) of this Act as an unfair labor practice) to require as a condition of employment

membership therein on or after the thirtieth day following the beginning of such employment or the effective date of such agreement, whichever is the later, (i) if such labor organization is the representative of the employees as provided in section 9(a), in the appropriate collective-bargaining unit covered by such agreement when made; and (ii) unless following an election held as provided in section 9(e) within one year preceding the effective date of such agreement, the Board shall have certified that at least a majority of the employees eligible to vote in such election have voted to rescind the authority of such labor organization to make such an agreement: *Provided further,* That no employer shall justify any discrimination against an employee for nonmembership in a labor organization (A) if he has reasonable grounds for believing that such membership was not available to the employee on the same terms and conditions generally applicable to other members, or (B) if he has reasonable grounds for believing that membership was denied or terminated for reasons other than the failure of the employee to tender the periodic dues and initiation fees uniformly required as a condition of acquiring or retaining membership.

(4) to discharge or otherwise discriminate against an employee because he has filed charges or given testimony under this Act.

(5) to refuse to bargain collectively with the representatives of his employees, subject to the provisions of section 9(a).

(b) It shall be an unfair labor practice for a labor organization or its agents—

(1) to restrain or coerce (A) employees in the exercise of the rights guaranteed in section 7: *Provided,* That this paragraph shall not impair the right of a labor organization to prescribe its own rules with the respect to the acquisition or retention of membership therein; or (B) an employer in the selection of his representatives for the purposes of collective bargaining or the adjustment of grievances;

(2) to cause or attempt to cause an employer to discriminate against an employee in violation of subsection (a)(3) or to discriminate against an employee with respect to whom membership in such organization has been denied or terminated on some ground other than his failure to tender the periodic dues and the initiation fees uniformly required as a condition of acquiring or retaining membership;

(3) to refuse to bargain collectively with an employer, provided it is the representative of his employees subject to the provisions of section 9(a);

(4) (i) to engage in, or to induce or encourage any individual employed by any person engaged in commerce or in an industry affecting commerce to engage in, a strike or a refusal in the course of his employment to use, manufacture, process, transport, or otherwise handle or work on any goods, articles, materials, or commodities or to perform any services; or (ii) to threaten, coerce, or restrain any person engaged in commerce or in an industry affecting commerce, where in either case an object thereof is—

 (A) forcing or requiring any employer or self-employed person to join any labor or employer organization or to enter into any agreement which is prohibited by section 8(e);

(B)   forcing or requiring any person to cease using, selling, handling, transport-ing, or otherwise dealing in the products of any other producer, processor, or manufacturer, or to cease doing business with any other person, or forcing or requiring any other employer to recognize or bargain with a labor orga-nization as the representative of his employees unless such labor organiza-tion has been certified as the representative of such employees under the provisions of section 9: *Provided,* That nothing contained in this clause (B) shall be construed to make unlawful, where not otherwise unlawful, any primary strike or primary picketing;

(C)   forcing or requiring any employer to recognize or bargain with a particular labor organization as the representative of his employees if another labor organization has been certified as the representative of such employees under the provisions of section 9;

(D)   forcing or requiring any employer to assign particular work to employees in a particular trade, craft, or class rather than to employees in another labor organization or in another trade, craft, or class, unless such employer is fail-ing to conform to an order or certification of the Board determining the bar-gaining representative for employees performing such work:

*Provided,* That nothing contained in this subsection (b) shall be construed to make unlawful a refusal by any person to enter upon the premises of any employer (other than his own employer), if the employees of such employer are engaged in a strike rati-fied or approved by a representative of such employees whom such employer is required to recognize under this Act: *Provided further,* That for the purposes of this paragraph (4) only, nothing contained in such paragraph shall be construed to prohibit publicity, other than picketing, for the purpose of truthfully advising the public, including con-sumers and members of a labor organization, that a product or products are produced by an employer with whom the labor organization has a primary dispute and are dis-tributed by another employer, as long as such publicity does not have an effect of induc-ing any individual employed by any person other than the primary employer in the course of his employment to refuse to pick up, deliver, or transport any goods, or not to perform any services, at the establishment of the employer engaged in such distribution;

(5)   to require of employees covered by an agreement authorized under subsection (a)(3) the payment, as a condition precedent to becoming a member of such orga-nization, of a fee in an amount which the Board finds excessive or discriminatory under all the circumstances. In making such a finding, the Board shall consider, among other relevant factors, the practices and customs of labor organizations in the particular industry, and the wages currently paid to the employees affected; and

(6)   to cause or attempt to cause an employer to pay or deliver or agree to pay or deliver any money or other thing of value, in the nature of an exaction, for services which are not performed or not to be performed; and

(7)   to picket or cause to be picketed, or threaten to picket or cause to be picketed, any employer where an object thereof is forcing or requiring an employer to recognize or bargain with a labor organization as the representative of his employees, or

forcing or requiring the employees of an employer to accept or select such labor organization as their collective bargaining representative, unless such organization is currently certified as the representative of such employees:

(A)  where the employer has lawfully recognized in accordance with this Act any other labor organization and a question concerning representation may not appropriately be raised under section 9(c) of this Act.

(B)  where within the preceding twelve months a valid election under section 9(c) of this Act has been conducted, or

(C)  where such picketing has been conducted without a petition under section 9(c) being filed within a reasonable period of time not to exceed thirty days from the commencement of such picketing: *Provided,* That when such a petition has been filed the Board shall forthwith, without regard to the provisions of section 9(c)(1) or the absence of a showing of a substantial interest on the part of the labor organization, direct an election in such unit as the Board finds to be appropriate and shall certify the results thereof: *Provided further,* That nothing in this subparagraph (C) shall be construed to prohibit any picketing or other publicity for the purpose of truthfully advising the public (including consumers) that an employer does not employ members of, or have a contract with, a labor organization, unless an effect of such picketing is to induce any individual employed by any other person in the course of his employment, not to pick up, deliver or transport any goods or not to perform any services.

Nothing in this paragraph (7) shall be construed to permit any act which would otherwise be an unfair labor practice under this Section 8(b).

(c)  The expressing of any views, argument, or opinion, or the dissemination thereof, whether in written, printed, graphic, or visual form, shall not constitute or be evidence of an unfair labor practice under any of the provisions of this Act, if such expression contains no threat of reprisal or force or promise of benefit.

(d)  For the purposes of this section, to bargain collectively is the performance of the mutual obligation of the employer and the representative of the employees to meet at reasonable times and confer in good faith with respect to wages, hours, and other terms and conditions of employment, or the negotiation of an agreement, or any question arising thereunder, and the execution of a written contract incorporating any agreement reached if requested by either party, but such obligation does not compel either party to agree to a proposal or require the making of a concession: *Provided,* That where there is in effect a collective-bargaining contract covering employees in an industry affecting commerce, the duty to bargain collectively shall also mean that no party to such contract shall terminate or modify such contract, unless the party desiring such termination or modification—

(1)  serves a written notice upon the other party to the contract of the proposed termination or modification sixty days prior to the expiration date thereof, or in the event such contract contains no expiration date, sixty days prior to the time it is proposed to make such termination or modification;

(2)   offers to meet and confer with the other party for the purpose of negotiating a new contract or a contract containing the proposed modifications;

(3)   notifies the Federal Mediation and Conciliation Service within thirty days after such notice of the existence of a dispute, and simultaneously therewith notifies any State or Territorial agency established to mediate and conciliate disputes within the State or Territory where the dispute occurred, provided no agreement has been reached by that time; and

(4)   continues in full force and effect, without resorting to strike or lock-out, all the terms and conditions of the existing contract for a period of sixty days after such notice is given or until the expiration date of such contract, whichever occurs later:

The duties imposed upon employers, employees, and labor organizations by paragraphs (2), (3), and (4) shall become inapplicable upon an intervening certification of the Board, under which the labor organization or individual, which is a party to the contract, has been superseded as or ceased to be the representative of the employees subject to the provisions of section 9(a), and the duties so imposed shall not be construed as requiring either party to discuss or agree to any modification of the terms and conditions contained in a contract for a fixed period, if such modification is to become effective before such terms and conditions can be reopened under the provisions of the contract. Any employee who engages in a strike within the sixty-day period specified in this subsection shall lose his status as an employee of the employer engaged in the particular labor dispute, for the purposes of section 8, 9, and 10 of this Act, as amended, but such loss of status for such employee shall terminate if and when he is reemployed by such employer.

(e)   It shall be an unfair labor practice for any labor organization and any employer to enter into any contract or agreement, express or implied, whereby such employer ceases or refrains or agrees to cease or refrain from handling, using, selling, transporting or otherwise dealing in any of the products of any other employer, or to cease doing business with any other person, and any contract or agreement shall be to such extent unenforcible and void: *Provided,* That nothing in this subsection (e) shall apply to an agreement between a labor organization and an employer in the construction industry relating to the contracting or subcontracting of work to be done at the site of the construction, alteration, painting, or repair of a building, structure, or other work: *Provided further,* That for the purposes of this subsection (e) and section 8(b)(4)(B) the terms "any employer," "any person engaged in commerce or an industry affecting commerce," and "any person" when used in relation to the terms "any other producer, processor, or manufacturer," "any other employer," or "any other person" shall not include persons in the relation of a jobber, manufacturer, contractor, or subcontractor working on the goods or premises of the jobber or manufacturer or performing parts of an integrated process of production in the apparel and clothing industry: *Provided further,* That nothing in this Act shall prohibit the enforcement of any agreement which is within the foregoing exception.

(f)   It shall not be an unfair labor practice under subsections (a) and (b) of this section for an employer engaged primarily in the building and construction industry to make an agreement covering employees engaged (or who, upon their employment, will be engaged) in the building and construction industry with a labor organization of which building and construction employees are members (not established, maintained, or assisted by any action defined in section 8(a) of this Act as an unfair labor practice) because (1) the majority status of such labor organization has not been established under the provisions of section 9 of this Act prior to the making of such agreement, or (2) such agreement requires as a condition of employment, membership in such labor organization after the seventh day following the beginning of such employment or the effective date of the agreement, whichever is later, or (3) such agreement requires the employer to notify such labor organization of opportunities for employment with such employer, or gives such labor organization an opportunity to refer qualified applicants for such employment, or (4) such agreement specifies minimum training or experience qualifications for employment or provides for priority in opportunities for employment based upon length of service with such employer, in the industry or in the particular geographical area: *Provided,* That nothing in this subsection shall set aside the final proviso to section 8(a)3 of this Act: *Provided further,* That any agreement which would be invalid, but for clause (1) of this subsection, shall not be a bar to a petition filed pursuant to section 9(c) or 9(e).

## Section 14

(b) Nothing in this subchapter (a) shall be construed as authorizing the execution or application of agreement requiring membership in labor organization as a condition of employment in any State or Territory in which such execution or application is prohibited by State or Territorial law.

# Glossary

**Abatement**  Decrease, reduction, or diminution.

**Accord and satisfaction**  Payment of money, or other thing of value, usually less than the amount demanded, in exchange for cancellation of a debt that is uncertain in amount.

**Act of state doctrine**  A defense to suit in the courts that, if accepted, requires judicial absention based upon the notion that every nation is obligated to respect the independent acts of foreign governments.

**Actual authority**  The authority a principal expressly or implicitly gives to an agent in an agency relationship. This authority may be written, spoken, or derived from the circumstances of the relationship.

**Ad infinitum**  Without limit; endlessly.

**Adjudication**  The judicial determination of a legal proceeding.

**Administrative law**  The branch of public law dealing with the operation of the various agency boards and commissions of government.

**Ad substantiation program**  A program of the Federal Trade Commission under which the FTC demands that an advertiser substantiate any claims made in advertising. Even if the claims are not provably untrue, they are considered deceptive if they cannot be substantiated.

**Ad valorem**   According to value.

**Advisory opinion**   A formal opinion by a judge, court, regulatory agency, or law officer upon a question of law.

**Affidavit**   A sworn written statement made before an officer authorized by law to administer oaths.

**Affirmative action**   Positive steps taken in order to alleviate conditions resulting from past discrimination or from violations of a law.

**Affirmative action program**   A program designed to promote actively the position of minority workers with regard to hiring and advancement.

**Affirmative defense**   A matter which, assuming the complaint to be true, constitutes a defense to it.

**A fortiori**   Even more clearly; said of a conclusion that follows with even greater logical necessity from another which is already included in the argument.

**Agent**   The person who on behalf of a principal deals with a third party.

**Amicus curiae**   A friend of the court who participates in litigation though not a party to the lawsuit.

**Annual percentage rate**   A rate of interest that commercial lenders charge persons who borrow money. This rate is calculated in a standardized fashion required by the Truth-in-Lending Act.

**Annuity**   A contract by which the insured pays a lump sum to the insurer and later receives fixed annual payments.

**Apparent authority**   The authority that a third party in an agency relationship perceives to exist between the principal and the agent. In fact, no actual authority does exist. Sometimes also called *ostensible authority*.

**Appellant**   The party seeking review of a lower court decision.

**Appellee**   The party responding to an appeal; the winner in the trial court.

**Apportionment**   The concept used by states to divide a company's taxable income so that no one state burdens a company with an unfair tax bill.

**Arbitration**   Submission of a dispute to an extrajudicial authority for decision.

**Arguendo**   For the sake of argument.

**Artisan's lien**   The lien which arises in favor of one who has expended labor upon, or added value to, another's personal property. The lien allows the person to possess the property as security until reimbursed for the value of labor or materials. If the person is not reimbursed, the property may be sold to satisfy the claim.

**Assault and battery**  Assault: The intentional creation of immediate apprehension of injury or lack of physical safety. Battery: An intentional, unpermitted, offensive contact or touching.

**Assumption of risk**  Negligence doctrine which bars the recovery of damages by an injured party on the ground that such party acted with actual or constructive knowledge of the hazard causing the injury.

**Attachment**  The term *attachment* has three meanings. First, attachment is a method of acquiring in rem jurisdiction of a nonresident defendant who is not subject to the service of process to commence a lawsuit. By "attaching" property of the nonresident defendant, the court acquires jurisdiction over the defendant to the extent of the value of the property attached. Second, attachment is a procedure used to collect a judgment. A plaintiff may have the property of a defendant seized, pending the outcome of a lawsuit, if the plaintiff has reason to fear that the defendant will dispose of the property before the court renders its decision. Third, attachment is the event which creates an enforceable security interest under the Uniform Commercial Code (UCC). In order that a security interest attach, there must be a signed, written security agreement, or possession of the collateral by the secured party; the secured party must give value to the debtor; and the debtor must maintain rights in the collateral.

**Award**  The decision announced by an arbitrator.

**Bait-and-switch**  An illegal promotional practice in which a seller attracts consumer interest by promoting one product, the "bait," then once interest has been attracted switches it to a second, higher-priced product by making the "bait" unavailable or unattractive.

**Beneficiary**  A person entitled to the possession, use, income, or enjoyment of an interest or right to which legal title is held by another; a person to whom an insurance policy is payable.

**Beyond a reasonable doubt**  The burden of proof required in a criminal case. The prosecution in a criminal case has the burden of proving the defendant is guilty, and the jury must have no reasonable doubt about the defendant's guilt. See also *Burden of proof*.

**Bilateral contract**  An agreement which contains mutual promises, with each party being both a promisor and a promisee.

**Bill of lading**  A document issued by a carrier indicating that goods to be shipped have been received by the carrier.

**Bill of particulars**  In legal practice, a written statement furnished by one party to a lawsuit to another, describing in detail the elements upon which the claim of the first party is based.

**Biodegradable**   Capable of being decomposed by organic action.

**"Blue sky" laws**   Statutes designed to protect investors in stock and other securities by the regulation of transactions in securities, generally by requiring registration and disclosure of pertinent financial information.

**Bona fide**   In good faith; innocently; without fraud or deceit.

**Bona fide occupational qualification**   A qualification that permits discriminatory practices in employment if a person's religion, sex, or national origin is reasonably related to the normal operation of a particular business.

**Breach**   A party's failure to perform some contracted-for or agreed-upon act, or failure to comply with a duty imposed by law.

**Brief**   A written document produced by a party for a reviewing court which contains the facts, propositions of law, and argument of a party. It is in this document that the party argues the desired application of the law and any contentions as to the rulings of the lower court.

**"Bubble" concept**   A procedure by which the Environmental Protection Agency (EPA) allows a business to treat its entire plant complex as though encased in a bubble. The business suggests its own methods of cleanup, provided the total pollution does not exceed certain limits.

**Bulk transfer**   A transfer made outside the ordinary course of the transferor's business involving a major part of the business' inventory. Bulk transfers are subject to Article 6 of the UCC.

**Burden of proof**   The term *burden of proof* has two meanings. It may describe the party at a trial with the burden of coming forward with evidence to establish a fact. The term also describes the party with the burden of persuasion. This party must convince the judge or jury of the disputed facts in issue or else lose that issue. There are various degrees of proof. See also *Beyond a reasonable doubt, Preponderance of the evidence,* and *Clear and convincing proof.*

**Capacity**   Mental ability to make a rational decision which includes the ability to perceive and appreciate all relevant facts. A required element of a contract.

**Cause in fact**   The actual cause of an event; the instrument which is the responsible force for the occurrence of a certain event. A required element of a tort.

**Cause of action**   This phrase has several meanings, but it is commonly used to describe the existence of facts giving rise to a judicially enforceable claim.

**Caveat emptor**   Let the buyer beware; rule imposing on a purchaser the duty to inform him or herself as to defects in the property being sold.

**Caveat venditor**  Let the seller beware; it is the seller's duty to do what the ordinary man would do in a similar situation.

**Commercial speech**  Speech that has a business-oriented purpose. This speech is protected under the First Amendment, but this protection is not as great as that afforded to noncommercial speech.

**Common law**  That body of law deriving from judicial decisions as opposed to legislatively enacted statutes and administrative regulations.

**Comparable worth**  Jobs which, although different, produce substantially equal value for the employer.

**Comparative negligence**  A doctrine which compares the plaintiff's contributory fault with the defendant's fault and allows the jury to reduce the plaintiff's verdict by the percentage of the plaintiff's fault.

**Complaint**  In legal practice, the first written statement of the plaintiff's contentions, which initiates the lawsuit.

**Compulsory-bargaining issue**  Mandatory bargaining issue regarding wages, hours, or other terms or conditions of employment. Refusal to engage in good-faith bargaining with regard to these issues is an unfair labor practice.

**Concerted activities**  This term describes those activities involving an agreement, contract, or conspiracy to restrain trade that may be illegal under the Sherman Antitrust Act.

**Condition precedent**  An event in the law of contracts that must occur before a duty of immediate performance of the promise arises.Contracts often provide that one party must perform before there is a right to performance by the other party. For example, completion of a job is often a condition precedent to payment for that job. One contracting party's failure to perform a condition precedent permits the other party to refuse to perform, cancel the contract, and sue for damages.

**Condition subsequent**  A fact which will extinguish a duty to make compensation for breach of contract after the breach has occurred.

**Confirming bank**  The seller's bank that delivers the bill of lading to the issuing bank and obtains payment for goods shipped in international transactions. The seller then may withdraw the payment from this bank.

**Confiscation**  The seizure of property without adequate compensation.

**Conflict-of-laws principles**  Rules of law the courts use to determine which substantive law applies when there is an inconsistency between laws of different states or countries.

**Conglomerate merger**  The merger resulting when merging companies have neither the relationship of competitors nor that of supplier and customer.

**Consent order**   Any court or regulatory order to which the opposing party agrees; a contract of the parties entered upon the record with the approval and sanction of a court.

**Consideration**   An essential element in the creation of a contract obligation which creates a detriment to the promisee or a benefit to the promisor.

**Consignment**   A delivery by the owner of goods to another for disposition usually by sale by the latter.

**Consolidation**   The process by which two or more corporations are joined to create a new corporation.

**Conspiracy**   A combination or agreement between two or more persons for the commission of a criminal act.

**Constitutional law**   The legal issues that arise from interpreting the United States Constitution or a state constitution.

**Consumer**   An individual who buys goods and services for personal use rather than for business use.

**Consumer investigative report**   A report on a consumer's character, general reputation, mode of living, etc., obtained by personal interviews in the community where the consumer works or lives.

**Contingent fee**   An arrangement whereby an attorney is compensated for services in a lawsuit according to an agreed percentage of the amount of money recovered.

**Contract**   A legally enforceable promise.

**Contract clause**   The constitutional provision which prohibits states from enacting laws that interfere with existing contracts. The Supreme Court has refused to interpret this clause in an absolute manner.

**Contribution**   The right of one who has discharged a common liability to recover from another also liable, the proportionate share of the common liability.

**Contributory negligence**   A failure to use reasonable care by the plaintiff in a negligence suit.

**Controlling person**   The person who has the control of, or is controlled by, the issuer of securities in securities laws.

**Conversion**   An unlawful exercise of dominion and control over another's property which substantially interferes with property rights.

**Copyright**   The protection of the work of artists and authors which gives them the exclusive right to publish their works or determine who may publish them.

**Corrective advertising**  A Federal Trade Commission (FTC) remedy which requires companies that have advertised deceptively to run ads that admit the prior errors and correct the erroneous information.

**Counterclaim**  Any claim filed by the defendant in a lawsuit against the plaintiff in the same suit.

**Covenant**  An agreement or promise in writing by which a party pledges that something has been done or is being done. The term is often used in connection with real estate to describe the promises of the grantor of the property.

**Criminal law**  That area of law dealing with wrongs against the state as representative of the community at large, to be distinguished from civil law which hears cases of wrongs against persons.

**Damages**  Monetary compensation recoverable in a court of law.

**D.B.A.**  Doing business as

**Decree**  The decision of a court of equity.

**Defamation**  The publication of anything injurious to the good name or reputation of another.

**Defect**  Something which makes a product not reasonably safe for a use which can be reasonably anticipated.

**Defendant**  The party involved in a lawsuit that is sued; the party required to respond to the plaintiff's complaint.

**Defined benefit plan**  A money-purchase plan which guarantees a certain retirement income based on the employee's service and salary under the Employee Retirement Income Security Act. The benefits are fixed, and the contributions vary.

**Defined contribution plan**  A money-purchase plan which allows employers to budget pension costs in advance under the Employee Retirement Income Security Act. The contribution is fixed and the benefits vary.

**Demurrer**  A formal statement by the defendant that the facts alleged by the plaintiff are insufficient to support a claim for legal relief in common law pleading.

**De novo hearing**  A proceeding wherein the judge or hearing officer hears the case as if it had not been heard before.

**Deposition**  A discovery process outside the court's supervision which involves the sworn questioning of a potential witness. This oral questioning is reduced to a written form so that a record is established.

**Derivative action**  A lawsuit filed by a shareholder of a corporation on behalf of the corporation. This action is filed to protect the corporation from the mismanagement of its officers and directors.

**Dicta**  Statements made in a judicial opinion which are not essential to the decision of the case.

**Directed verdict**  A motion for a directed verdict requests that the judge direct the jury to bring in a particular verdict if reasonable minds could not differ on the correct outcome of the lawsuit. In deciding the motion, the judge will view in the light most favorable to the nonmoving party, and if different inferences may be drawn by reasonable men, then the court can not direct a verdict. In essence, a directed verdict removes the jury's discretion.

**Discovery**  Procedures by which one party to a lawsuit may obtain information relevant to the case from the other party or from third persons.

**Discrimination in effect**  The discriminatory result of policies which appear to be neutral.

**Disparate impact**  A term of employment litigation that refers to the disproportionate impact of a policy neutral on its face on some protected class (e.g. race or sex).

**Disparate treatment**  A term of employment litigation that refers to the illegal discriminatory treatment of an individual in some protected class (e.g. race or sex).

**Dissolution**  The cancellation of an agreement, thereby rescinding its binding force. A partnership is dissolved anytime there is a change in partners. A corporation's dissolution occurs when that business entity ceases to exist.

**Diversity of citizenship**  The plaintiffs filing a lawsuit must be from states different from those of the defendants. This requirement, along with over $50,000 at stake, is one method a federal district court gains jurisdiction over the subject matter of a lawsuit.

**Divestiture**  The antitrust remedy which forces a company to get rid of assets acquired through illegal mergers or monopolistic practices.

**Docket**  A book containing a brief summary of all acts done in court in the conduct of each case.

**Doctrine of abstention**  A principle used by federal courts to refuse to hear a case. When used by the federal courts, the lawsuit involved is sent to the state court system.

**Domicile**  That place that a person intends as his or her fixed and permanent legal residence; place of permanent abode, as contrasted with a residence, which may be temporary; a person can have a number of residences but only one domicile; the state of incorporation of a corporation.

**Donee beneficiary**  A third person is a donee beneficiary if the promisee who buys the promise expresses an intention and purpose to confer a benefit upon him or her as a gift.

**Double jeopardy**  A constitutional doctrine which prohibits an individual from being prosecuted twice in the same tribunal for the same criminal offense.

**Due process**  Fundamental fairness. As applied to judicial proceedings, adequate notice of a hearing and an opportunity to appear and defend in an orderly tribunal.

**Dumping**  The practice of selling foreign goods in one country at less than the comparable price in the country where the goods originated.

**Duress**  Action by a person which compels another to do what he would not otherwise do. It is a recognized defense to any act which must be voluntary in order to create liability in the actor.

**Duty**  A legal obligation imposed by the law.

**Easement**  The right of one other than the owner of land to some use of that land.

**Eighty-day cooling-off period**  A provision in the Taft-Hartley Act that allows the President to require that laborers continue working and that the laborers' representatives and management continue bargaining for at least eighty days during which it is intended that federal mediation will resolve the dispute. This provision can be utilized by the President only when there is a determination that the work stoppage is adversely affecting the national health and safety.

**Ejusdem generis**  Of the same kind or class; a doctrine of legislative interpretation.

**Embezzlement**  The fraudulent appropriation by one person, acting in a fiduciary capacity, of the money or property of another.

**Eminent domain**  Authority of the state to take private property for public use.

**Emissions-reduction banking**  The policy stating that businesses that lower pollution beyond the requirements of the law may use the additional reductions in the future.

**Employment-at-will**  A hiring for an indefinite period of time.

**En banc**  Proceedings by or before the court as a whole rather than any single judge.

**Enjoin**  To require performance or abstention from some act through issuance of an injunction.

**Environmental-impact statement**   A filing of documents required by the National Environmental Policy Act which forces governmental agencies to consider the environmental consequences of their actions.

**Equal protection**   A principle of the Fourteenth Amendment to the Constitution that individuals under like circumstances shall be accorded the same benefits and burdens under the law of the sovereign.

**Equity**   A body of law which seeks to adjust conflicting rights on the basis of fairness and good conscience. Courts of equity or chancery may require or prohibit specific acts where monetary damages will not afford complete relief.

**Escrow**   A deed, bond, or deposit which one party delivers for safekeeping by a second party who is obligated to deliver it to a third party upon the fulfillment of some condition.

**Establishment clause**   A provision in the First Amendment of the United States Constitution that prohibits the federal government from establishing any government-supported religion or church.

**Estoppel**   The legal principle that one may not assert facts inconsistent with one's own prior actions.

**Exclusive-dealing contract**   A contract under which a buyer agrees to purchase a certain product exclusively from the seller or in which the seller agrees to sell all his product production to the buyer.

**Exculpatory clause**   A provision in a contract whereby one of the parties attempts to relieve itself of liability for breach of a legal duty.

**Executed contract**   A contract which is fully accomplished or performed, leaving nothing unfulfilled.

**Executory contract**   An agreement which is not completed. Until the performance required in a contract is completed, it is executory.

**Exemplary damages**   Punitive damages. Monetary compensation in excess of direct losses suffered by the plaintiff which may be awarded in intentional tort cases where the defendant's conduct deserves punishment.

**Exhaustion of remedies**   A concept used in administrative law that requires any party to an administrative proceeding to give the administrative agency every opportunity to resolve the dispute before appealing to the court system.

**Experience rating system**   A system of sliding taxation under which employers are charged less unemployment-compensation tax as they lay off fewer workers due to economic conditions.

**Export controls**   Action taken on a national and multilateral basis to prevent the exportation of controlled goods and technology to certain destinations.

**Express consumer warranty**  Any statement of fact or promise about the performance of a product made by a seller.

**Express contract**  A contract in which parties show their agreement in words.

**Expropriation**  A foreign government's seizure of privately owned property.

**Failing company doctrine**  A merger between a failing company and a competitor may be allowed, although such a merger would be illegal if both companies were viable competitors.

**False advertising**  Untrue and fraudulent statements and representations made by way of advertising a product or a service.

**False imprisonment**  The tort of an intentional, unjustified confinement of a nonconsenting person who knows of the confinement.

**Featherbedding**  A term used in the labor laws to describe workers who are paid though they do not perform any work. Under the Taft-Hartley Act, featherbedding is an unfair labor practice by unions.

**Federalism**  A term used to describe the vertical aspect of the separation of powers. The coexistence of a federal government and the various state governments, with each having responsibilities and authorities that are distinct but overlap is called federalism.

**Federal question**  Litigation involving the application or interpretation of the federal constitution, federal statutes, federal treaties, or federal administrative agencies. The federal court system has subject-matter jurisdiction over these issues.

**Fee schedule**  A plan, usually adopted by an association, which establishes minimum or maximum charges for a service or product.

**Fellow-servant doctrine**  The doctrine which precludes an injured employee from recovering damages from his employer when the injury resulted from the negligent act of another employee.

**Felony**  A criminal offense of a serious nature, generally punishable by death or imprisonment in penitentiary; to be distinguished from a misdemeanor.

**Fiduciary**  One having a duty to act for another's benefit in the highest good faith.

**Finance charge**  Any charge for an extension of credit, which specifically includes interest, service charges, and other charges.

**Financing statement**  An established form that a secured party files with a public officer such as the Secretary of State to perfect a security interest under the Uniform Commercial Code (UCC). It is a simple form which contains basic information such as a description of the collateral, names, and addresses. It is designed to give notice that the debtor and secured party have entered into a security agreement.

**Firm offer**  An offer in signed writing by a merchant to buy or sell goods; it gives assurances that the offer will be held open as governed by the Uniform Commercial Code (UCC).

**Foreclosure**  If a mortgagor fails to perform his or her obligations as agreed, the mortgagee may declare the whole debt due and payable, and she or he may foreclose on the mortgaged property to pay the debt secured by the mortgage. The usual method of foreclosure authorizes the sale of the mortgaged property at a public auction. The proceeds of the sale are applied to the debt.

**Forum non conveniens**  The doctrine under which a court may dismiss a lawsuit in which it appears that for the convenience of the parties and in the interest of justice the action should have been brought in another court.

**Franchise**  A marketing technique whereby one party (the franchisor) grants a second party (the franchisee) the right to manufacture, distribute, or sell a product using the name or trademark of the franchisor.

**Fraud**  A false representation of fact made with intent to deceive another which is justifiably relied upon to the injury of that person.

**Free exercise clause**  A provision in the First Amendment of the United States Constitution that allows all citizens the freedom to follow or believe any religious teaching.

**Frolic and detour**  The activity of an agent or an employee who has departed from the scope of the agency and is not, therefore, a representative of his or her employer.

**Full faith and credit clause**  A provision in the United States Constitution that requires a state to recognize the laws and judicial decisions of all other states.

**Full-line forcing**  An arrangement in which a manufacturer refuses to supply any portion of the product line unless the retailer agrees to accept the entire line.

**Garnishment**  A legal proceeding whereby a creditor may collect directly from a third party who is obligated to the debtor.

**General counsel**  An individual who is responsible for coordinating all legal-related issues, such as the quasi-judicial hearings in administrative agencies. This term also is used to describe the principal lawyer of a company.

**General partnership**  A business organization wherein all owners (partners) share profits and losses, and all are jointly and severally liable for the organization's debts.

**Geographic extension merger**    A combining of companies involved with the same product or service which do not compete in the same geographical regions or markets.

**Geographic market**    The relevant section of the country affected by a merger.

**Going bare**    A professional practicing (in her or his field of expertise) without liability insurance.

**Good faith**    Honesty in dealing; innocence; without fraud or deceit.

**Good-faith meeting of competition**    A bona fide business practice which is a defense to a charge of violation of the Robinson-Patman Act. The Robinson-Patman Act is an amendment to the Clayton Act, which outlaws price discrimination that might substantially lessen competition or tend to create a monopoly. This exception allows a seller in good faith to meet the equally low price, service, or facility of a competitor. The good-faith exception cannot be established if the purpose of the price discrimination has been to eliminate competition.

**Grand jury**    A body usually of 23 persons charged with determining whether there is sufficient evidence to support having a person stand trial for criminal activity.

**Greenmail**    Forcing a corporation to buy back some of its own stock at an inflated price to avoid a takeover.

**Guardian**    One charged with the duty of care and maintenance of another person such as a minor or incompetent under the law.

**Guardian ad litem**    A guardian appointed to prosecute or defend a lawsuit on behalf of an incompetent or a minor.

**Habeas corpus**    The name of a writ which orders one holding custody of another to produce that individual before the court for the purpose of determining whether such custody is proper.

**Hearsay evidence**    Evidence of statements made or actions performed out of court which is offered to prove the truth thereof.

**Hearsay rule**    The exclusion, with certain exceptions, of hearsay evidence because of the lack of opportunity to cross-examine the original source of the evidence.

**Herfindahl-Hirschman Index**    An index used by the Justice Department to test the legality of horizontal acquisitions. The index is computed by squaring the market share of each firm in a market and adding the results.

**Holder in due course**    One who has acquired possession of a negotiable instrument through proper negotiation for value, in good faith, and without notice of any defenses to it. Such a holder is not subject to personal defenses which would otherwise defeat the obligation embodied in the instrument.

**Horizontal merger**  Merger of corporations that were competitors prior to the merger.

**Hot-cargo contract**  An agreement whereby an employer agrees to refrain from handling, using, selling, transporting, or otherwise dealing in the products of another employer or to cease doing business with any other person.

**Illinois Brick Doctrine**  The standing-to-sue requirement of the Sherman Act which requires that the plaintiff be directly injured by the defendant's violation. Damages are not passed through the channels of distribution.

**Immunity**  Status of exemption from lawsuits or other legal obligations.

**Implied in fact contract**  A legally enforceable agreement inferred from the circumstances and conduct of the parties.

**Implied warranty of merchantability**  A warranty (implied) that the goods are reasonably fit for the general purpose for which they are sold.

**Incidental beneficiary**  A person who may incidentally benefit from the creation of a contract. Such a person cannot enforce any right to incidental benefit.

**Indemnify**  To reimburse another for a loss suffered.

**Indictment**  A document issued by a grand jury formally charging a person with a felony.

**Individual retirement account**  A retirement account for persons with limited incomes that are unable to participate in a qualified pension plan.

**Industry guide**  An issue of the FTC defining the agency's view of the legality of an industry's trade practice.

**Infliction of mental distress**  An intentional tort to the emotions which causes both mental distress and physical symptoms as a result of the defendant's outrageous behavior.

**Infringement**  Unauthorized use of copyrighted or patented material.

**Injunction**  A court order directing a party to do or to refrain from doing some act.

**Injurious falsehood**  A statement or untruth which causes injury or damage to the party against whom it is made.

**In personam**  The jurisdiction of a court to affect the rights and duties of a specific individual.

**In rem**   The jurisdiction of a court to affect property rights with respect to a specific thing.

**Insider**   A person who owns 10 percent or more of a company or who is a director or officer of the company; a term used in securities law. This term also is used to describe a person possessing nonpublic information.

**Intangible property**   Something which represents value but has no intrinsic value of its own, such as a note or bond.

**Interference in contractual relations**   A business tort in which persons are induced to breach binding agreements.

**Interlocking directorates**   A situation in which the same persons are members of the board of directors of two or more corporations at the same time.

**Interpleader**   A legal procedure by which one holding a single fund subject to conflicting claims of two or more persons may require the conflicting claimants to come into court and litigate the matter between themselves.

**Interrogatory**   A written question propounded by one party to a lawsuit to another; a type of discovery procedure.

**Inter se**   Between themselves.

**Intestate**   A person who dies without a will.

**Invasion of privacy**   A tort based on misappropriation of name or likeness, intrusion upon physical solitude, or public disclosure of objectionable, private information.

**Issuer**   The term in securities law for an individual or business organization offering a security for sale to the public.

**Issuing bank**   The buyer's bank which, in international transactions, guarantees payment for goods on the condition that it receive a bill of lading stating that goods have been shipped by the seller.

**Joint tenancy**   A form of ownership in which each of two or more owners have an undivided right to possession of the property. Upon the death of an owner his or her interest passes to the surviving owners because of survivorship.

**Joint venture**   Two or more persons or business organizations agreeing to do business for a specific and limited purpose.

**Judgment**   Official adjudication of a court of law.

**Judgment notwithstanding the verdict**   The decision of a court which sets aside the verdict of a jury and reaches the opposite result.

**Judicial activist**   An activist judge tends to abide by the following judicial philosophies: (1) The political process cannot adequately handle society's difficult issues; (2) the courts can correct society's ills through the decision-making process; (3) following precedent is not crucial; and (4) "judge-made law" is often necessary to carry out the legislative intent of the law. See also *Judicial restraint.*

**Judicial restraint**   A judge who abides by the judicial restraint philosophy (1) believes that the political process, and not the courts, should correct society's ills; (2) decides an issue on a narrow basis, if possible; (3) follows precedent whenever possible; and (4) does not engage in "judge-made law," but interprets the letter of the law. See also *Judicial activist.*

**Judicial review**   The power of courts to declare laws enacted by legislative bodies and actions by the Executive to be unconstitutional.

**Jurisdiction**   The power and authority of a court or other governmental agency to adjudicate controversies and otherwise deal with matters brought before it.

**Jurisprudence**   The science of the law; the practical science of giving a wise interpretation of the law.

**Jury instruction**   A statement made by the judge to the jury informing them of the law applicable to the case which the jury is bound to accept and apply.

**Laches**   Defense to an equitable action based on the plaintiff's unreasonable delay in bringing the action.

**Legacy**   Personal property disposed of by a will. Sometimes the term is synonymous with *bequest.* The word *devise* is used in connection with real property distributed by will.

**Legal clinics**   A term referring to law firms that specialize in low-cost, generally routine legal procedures.

**Legislative history**   A technique used by courts in interpreting statutes. Courts often examine the record of the legislators' debate in an attempt to determine what was intended by the legislation.

**Letter of credit**   A document commonly used in international transactions to ensure payment and delivery of goods.

**Libel**   A defamatory written statement communicated to a third party.

**License**   A common method of controlling product or technology transfers across national borders.

**Lien**   A claim to an interest in property in satisfaction of a debt or claim.

**Limited partnership**   A partnership in which one or more individuals are general partners and one or more individuals are limited partners. The limited partners contribute assets to the partnership without taking part in the conduct of the business. Such individual are liable for the debts of the partnership only to the extent of their contributions.

**Liquidation**   The process of winding up the affairs of a business for the purpose of paying debts and disposing of assets. May be voluntary or under court order.

**Long-arm statute**   A state statute which gives extraterritorial effect to process (summons) in specified cases. It allows state courts to obtain jurisdiction in civil actions over defendants who are beyond the border of the state provided the defendants have minimum contact with the state sufficient to satisfy due process.

**Malfeasance**   Doing of some wrongful act.

**Malice**   The state of mind that accompanies the intentional doing of a wrongful act without justification or excuse.

**Malicious prosecution**   An action for recovery of damages that have resulted to person, property, or reputation from previous unsuccessful civil or criminal proceedings that were prosecuted without probable cause and with malice.

**Malpractice**   A professional's improper or negligent conduct in the performance of duties—a failure to perform one's professional duties in accordance with established professional standards.

**Mandamus**   A court order directing the holder of an office to perform his or her legal duty.

**Market extension merger**   An acquisition in which the acquiring company increases its market through product extension or geographical extension.

**Master**   The term used in an agency relationship to describe the principal (employer) involved in a tort.

**Material breach**   A substantial failure, without excuse, to perform a promise which constitutes the whole or part of a contract.

**Mayhem**   Unlawfully depriving a human being of a member of his body.

**Mechanic's lien**   A lien on real estate that is created by statute to assist suppliers and laborers in collecting their accounts and wages. Its purpose is to subject the owner's land to a lien for material and labor expended in the construction of buildings and other improvements.

**Merchant**   A person who deals in goods of the kind or otherwise by his occupation presents himself or herself as having knowledge or skill peculiar to the practice or goods involved.

**Merger**   The extinguishment of a corporate entity by the transfer of its assets and liabilities to another corporation which continues in existence.

**Merger guidelines**   Standards issued by the government to indicate which mergers are likely to be challenged under the antitrust laws.

**Minimum wage**   Minimum hourly wages, established by Congress under the Fair Labor Standards Act, to maintain the health, efficiency, and general well-being of workers.

**Ministerial duty**   An example of a definite duty regarding which nothing is left to discretion or judgment.

**Mirror image rule**   The common law rule that the terms of an acceptance must mirror exactly the terms of the offer. Any variation of terms would make the acceptance a counteroffer.

**Misdemeanor**   A criminal offense of less serious nature than a felony, generally punishable by fine or jail sentence other than in a penitentiary.

**Misfeasance**   A misdeed or trespass.

**Misrepresentation**   Any untrue manifestation of fact by word or conduct; it may be unintentional.

**Monopoly**   Exclusive control of a market by a business entity.

**Mortgage**   A transfer of an interest in property for the purpose of creating a security for a debt.

**Motion**   The process by which the parties make written or oral requests that the judge issue an order or ruling.

**Mutual mistake**   A situation in which parties to a contract reach a bargain on the basis of an incorrect assumption common to each party.


**Nationalization**   A claim made by a foreign government that it owns expropriated property.

**Negligence**   A person's failure to exercise reasonable care which foreseeably causes another injury.

**Nexus**   A logical connection.

**NLRB**   National Labor Relations Board.

**Noerr-Pennington Doctrine**   This doctrine exempts from the antitrust lawsconcerted efforts to lobby government officials regardless of the anticompetitive purposes. It is based on the First Amendment freedom of speech.

**No-fault laws**   Laws barring tort actions by injured persons against third-party tortfeasors and requiring such persons to obtain recovery from their own insurers.

**Nolo contendere**   A plea entered by the defendant in a criminal case which neither admits nor denies the crime allegedly committed but which, if accepted by the court, permits the judge to treat the defendant as guilty.

**Noscitur a sociis**   The principle that the scope of general words is delimited by specific accompanying words; a doctrine of legislative interpretation.

**Notary public**   A public officer authorized to administer oaths and certify certain documents.

**Notice**   Communication sufficient to charge a reasonable person with knowledge of some fact.

**Nuisance**   A physical condition constituting an unreasonable and substantial interference with the rights of individuals or the public at large.

**Oligopoly**   Control of the supply and price of a commodity or service in a given market by a small number of companies or suppliers.

**Option**   A contractual arrangement under which one party has for a specified time the right to buy certain property from or sell certain property to the other party. It is essentially a contract to not revoke an offer.

**Ordinance**   The legislative enactment of a city, county, or other municipal corporation.

**Organizational picketing**   Picketing by members of a union seeking to represent workers and to obtain recognition as the exclusive bargaining agent for them. Under the Landrum-Griffin Act, purely recognitional picketing under some circumstances is illegal, while purely informational picketing may be legal.

**Ownership**   The bundle of rights to possess and use property because of title to the property.

**Paper fortress**   A term referring to the documentation an employer should keep of an employee's performance.

**Pari materia, in**   Concerning the same subject matter. A rule of statutory construction that two such statutes will be construed together.

**Parker v. Brown Doctrine**   The name given to the state action exemption to the Sherman Act. See *State action exemption*.

**Parol evidence**   Legal proof based on oral statements; with regard to a document, any evidence which is extrinsic to the document itself.

**Parol-evidence rule**  Parol evidence is extrinsic evidence. In contracts, the parol-evidence rule excludes the introduction of evidence of prior written or oral agreements which may vary, contradict, alter, or supplement the present written agreement. There are several exceptions to this rule. For example, when the parties to an agreement do not intend for that agreement to be final and complete, then parol evidence is admissible.

**Partnership**  A business organization involving two or more persons agreeing to conduct a commercial venture while sharing its profits and losses.

**Patent**  To be patentable, inventions must be nonobvious, novel, and useful. A patent creates a 17-year protection period during which there is a presumption of validity if the patent is properly registered with the Patent Office.

**Per capita**  By or for each individual.

**Per curiam**  By the court; said of an opinion expressing the view of the court as a whole as opposed to an opinion authored by any single member of the court.

**Peremptory challenge**  The power granted each party to reject a limited number of potential jurors during voir dire examination. No reason for the rejection need be given.

**Perfection**  The status ascribed to security interests after certain events have occurred or certain prescribed steps have been taken, e.g., the filing of a financing statement.

**Perjury**  The giving of false testimony under oath.

**Per se**  In itself.

**Per se illegal**  Under the Sherman Act, agreements and practices are illegal only if they are unreasonable. The practices which are conclusively presumed to be unreasonable are per se illegal. If an activity is per se illegal, only proof of the activity is required, and it is not necessary to prove an anticompetitive effect. For example, price-fixing is per se illegal. See also *Rule of reason.*

**Personal property**  Physical or intangible property other than real estate.

**Peter principle**  A concept that many people are promoted to their level of incompetency.

**Petitioner**  The party filing a case in equity or a petition for writ of certiorari before a supreme court.

**Plaintiff**  The person who initiates a lawsuit.

**Plan termination insurance**  The insurance required by federal law on regulated pension plans. It protects against plan termination that leaves pension benefits underfunded.

**Pleadings**   The process by which the parties to a lawsuit present formal written statements of their contentions to create the issues of the lawsuit.

**Plenary**   Entire; complete in all respects.

**Point source**   Any source of air pollution which must be licensed under the Clean Air Act.

**Police power**   The authority a state or local government has to protect the public's health, safety, morals, and general welfare.

**Possession**   Dominion and control over property; the holding or detention of property in one's own power or command.

**Potential-entrant doctrine**   In antitrust law, a doctrine that prohibits mergers and acquisitions by a firm that is only a potential competitor in a market.

**Precedent**   A prior judicial decision relied upon as an example of a rule of law.

**Predatory pricing**   A seller lowering prices in one geographic area in order to eliminate competition.

**Preemption**   A condition when a federal statute or administrative rule governs an issue to the extent that a state or local government is prohibited from regulating that area of law.

**Prejudicial error**   An error in judicial proceedings which may have affected the result in the case.

**Preponderance**   Preponderance of the evidence means that evidence, in the judgment of the jurors, has greater weight and overcomes the opposing evidence and presumptions.

**Price discrimination**   A seller charging different purchasers different prices for the same goods at the same time.

**Price-fixing**   An agreement or combination by which the conspirators set the market price of a product or service either being sold or purchased, whether high or low.

**Prima facie**   On the face of it; thus, presumed to be true unless proved otherwise.

**Primary-air-quality standards**   The standards necessary to protect human health. Secondary-air-quality standards are stricter standards necessary to protect various environmental amenities.

**Prior restraint**   A principle applicable under the Freedom of Press and Speech clauses of the First Amendment of the United States Constitution. The courts have announced decisions that encourage governments to allow the publication or expression of thoughts rather than to restrain such thoughts in advance of their publication or expression.

**Privilege**  A special advantage accorded by law to some individual or group; an exemption from a duty or obligation generally imposed by law.

**Privileges and immunities clause**  A provision found in Article IV and the Fourteenth Amendment of the United States Constitution that prevents a state government from discriminating in favor of its citizens and against citizens from another state. This clause, while not interpreted to be absolute, has emphasized national rather than state citizenship.

**Privity**  Interest derived from successive relationship with another part; a contractual connection.

**Procedural due process**  The process or procedure assuring fundamental fairness that all citizens are entitled to under the United States Constitution.

**Procedural law**  The body of rules governing the manner in which legal claims are enforced.

**Product-extension merger**  A merger that extends the products of the acquiring company into a similar or related product but one that is not directly in competition with existing products.

**Promissory estoppel**  Court enforcement of an otherwise unbinding promise if injustice can only be avoided by enforcement of the promise. A substitute for consideration.

**Pro tanto**  So far as it goes.

**Proximate cause**  The doctrine which limits an actor's liability to consequences which could reasonably be foreseen to have resulted from the act.

**Punitive damages**  Monetary damages in excess of a compensatory award, usually granted only in intentional tort cases where defendant's conduct involved some element deserving punishment; exemplary damages.

**Purchase-money security interest**  A security interest that is taken or retained by the seller of the collateral to secure all or part of the collateral's price.

**Qualified pension plan**  A private retirement plan which gains favorable income tax treatment from the Internal Revenue Service (IRS). A qualified pension plan allows for the deduction of contributions made to fund the plan. Also, earnings from fund investments are not taxable, and employees defer personal income tax liability until payments are received after retirement. To qualify, the plan must cover a high percentage of workers (usually 70 percent) or cover classifications of employees that do not discriminate in favor of management or shareholders.

**Quantity discount**  The practice of giving a lower per unit price to businesses that buy a product in volume than to their competitors that do not.

**Quasi-contract** A quasi-contract, often referred to as an implied-in-law contract, is not a true contract. It is a legal fiction that the courts use to prevent unjust enrichment and wrongdoing. Courts permit the person who conferred a benefit to recover the reasonable value of that benefit. Nonetheless, the elements of a true contract are not present.

**Quasi-judicial** Administrative actions involving factual determinations and the discretionary application of rules and regulations.

**Quasi-legislative** This term describes the rule-making functions of administrative agencies.

**Quid pro quo** The exchange of one thing of value for another.

**Quitclaim deed** The transfer by deed of all the grantor's rights, title, and interest in property.

**Quo warranto** An action brought by the government to test the validity of some franchise, such as the privilege of doing business as a corporation. By what authority are you acting?

**Ratification** The action of a principal in an agency relationship who desires to be bound to the third party when the agent has acted without actual or apparent authority.

**Ratio decidendi** Logical basis of judicial decision.

**Real property** Land and fixtures to land.

**Reciprocal agreement** A contract in which two parties agree to mutual actions so each party can act as both a buyer and seller. The agreement violates the Clayton Act if it results in a substantial lessening of competition.

**Redlining** An act or refusal to act which results in a discriminatory practice. For example, refusing to make loans in low-income areas can discriminate against minorities in granting credit.

**Reimbursement** Restoration; to pay back or repay that expended; the act of making one whole.

**Release** The relinquishment of a right or claim against another party.

**Remand** The return of a case by an appellate court for further action by the lower court.

**Remedial statutes** Legislation designed to provide a benefit or relief to a victim of a violation of law.

**Remedy** The action or procedure that is followed in order to enforce a right or to obtain damages for injury to a right; the means by which a right is enforced or the violation of a right is prevented, redressed, or compensated.

**Reorganization** The legal process of forming a new corporation after bankruptcy or foreclosure.

**Replevin** An action for the recovery of goods wrongfully taken or kept.

**Res** A thing, object, or status.

**Res ipsa loquitur** The thing speaks for itself. A rule of evidence whereby negligence of the alleged wrongdoer may be inferred from the mere fact that the injury occurred.

**Res judicata** The doctrine which deems a former adjudication conclusive and prevents a retrial of matters decided in the earlier lawsuit.

**Resale price maintenance** Manufacturer control of a brand or trade-name product's minimum resale price.

**Rescind** To cancel or annul a contract and return the parties to their original positions.

**Rescission** The cancellation of a contract and return of the parties to the positions they would have occupied if the contract had not been made.

**Respondeat superior** The doctrine imposing liability on one for torts committed by another person who is in his or her employ and subject to his or her control.

**Respondent** The party answering a petition in equity or petition for a writ of ceriorari.

**Restraint of trade** Monopolies, combinations, and contracts that impede free competition.

**Retaliatory trade practices** Actions by aggrieved nations responding to tariffs and other unfair trade restrictions imposed by foreign governments.

**Reverse** Overturn or vacate the judgment of a court.

**Reverse discrimination** The advancement and recruitment of minority workers ahead of similarly qualified nonminority workers.

**Right of redemption** The right to buy back. A debtor may buy back or redeem his or her mortgaged property when he or she pays the debt.

**Right-to-work law** A state statute which outlaws a union-shop contract—one by which an employer agrees to require membership in the union sometime after an employee has been hired as a condition of continued employment.

**Robinson-Patman Act** The amendment to Section 2 of the Clayton Act covering price discrimination. As originally adopted, the Robinson-Patman Act outlawed price discrimination in interstate commerce that might substantially lessen competition or tend to create a monopoly.

**Rule of reason**  Under the Sherman Act, contracts or conspiracies are illegal only if they constitute an unreasonable restraint of trade or attempt to monopolize. An activity is unreasonable if it adversely affects competition. An act is reasonable if it promotes competition. The rule of reason requires that an anticompetitive effect be shown. See also *Per se illegal.*

**Sanctions**  Penalties imposed for violation of a law.

**Scienter**  With knowledge; particularly, guilty knowledge.

**Secondary boycott**  Conspiracy or combination to cause the customers or suppliers of an employer to cease doing business with that employer.

**Secured transactions**  Any credit transaction creating a security interest; an interest in real or personal property which secures the payment of an obligation.

**Security**  Under the securities law, an investment in which the investor does not participate in management.

**Seller**  In commercial law, a person who sells or contracts to sell goods.

**Seniority system**  A plan giving priority to employees based on the length of time the employee has worked for the employer. An employer may apply different standards pursuant to a good faith seniority system if the differences are not the result of an intention to discriminate.

**Separation of powers**  The doctrine which holds that the legislative, executive, and judicial branches of government function independently of one another and that each branch serves as a check on the others.

**Servant**  The person hired to act on behalf of a principal in an agency relationship.

**Set-off**  A counterclaim by defendant against plaintiff that grows from an independent cause of action and diminishes the plaintiff's potential recovery.

**Shark repellent**  Corporate action to make a threatened acquisition unattractive to the acquiring company.

**Shelf registration**  The process in securities law under SEC Rule 415 that allows an issuer to satisfy the registration-statement requirements, thereby allowing the issuer immediately to offer securities for sale.

**Sherman Act**  An 1890 congressional enactment designed to regulate anticompetitive behavior in interstate commerce.

**Simplified employee pension**  A type of pension permitted by the Revenue Act of 1978. Under this pension type employers contribute up to a specified amount to employee individual retirement accounts.

**Slander**  An oral defamatory statement communicated to a third person.

**Small claims court**  A court of limited jurisdiction, usually able to adjudicate claims up to a certain amount, such as $3000, depending on the state.

**Sole proprietorship**  The simplest form of business organization, created and controlled by one owner.

**Sovereign immunity**  A doctrine of state and international law that permits a foreign government to claim immunity from suit in the courts of other nations.

**Specific performance**  Equitable remedy which requires defendants in certain circumstances to do what they have contracted to do.

**Standing**  The doctrine that requires the plaintiff in a lawsuit to have a sufficient legal interest in the subject matter of the case.

**Standing to sue**  The requirement that a plaintiff must satisfy by demonstrating a personal interest in the outcome of litigation or an administrative hearing.

**Stare decisis**  The doctrine which traditionally indicates that a court should follow prior decisions in all cases based on substantially similar facts.

**State action exemption**  The Sherman Act exemption of the sovereign action of a state which replaces competition with regulation if the state actively supervises the anticompetitive conduct.

**State-of-the-art defense**  A defense that the defendant's product or practice was compatible with the current state of technology available at the time of the event in question.

**Status quo**  The conditions or state of affairs at a given time.

**Statute**  A legislative enactment.

**Statute of frauds**  Legislation which states that certain contracts will not be enforced unless there is a signed writing evidencing the agreement.

**Statute of repose**  A statute that applies to product liability cases. It prohibits initiation of litigation involving products more than a certain number of years (e.g., 25) following their manufacture.

**Strict liability**  The doctrine under which a party may be required to respond in tort damages without regard to such party's use of due care.

**Structured settlement**  A periodic payment of damages, usually taking the form of a guaranteed annuity.

**Subchapter S corporation**  A business organization that is formed as a corporation but, by a shareholders' election, is treated as a partnership for taxation purposes.

**Submission**    The act or process of referring an issue to arbitration.

**Subpoena**    A court order directing a witness to appear or to produce documents in his or her possession.

**Subrogation**    The right of a party secondarily liable to stand in the place of the creditor after he or she has made payment to the creditor and to enforce the creditor's right against the party primarily liable in order to obtain indemnity for him.

**Substantive due process**    The use of the due process provision of the United States Constitution to make certain that the application of a law does not unfairly deprive persons of property rights.

**Substantive law**    A body of rules defining the nature and extent of legal rights.

**Summary judgment**    A judicial determination that no genuine factual dispute exists and that one party to the lawsuit is entitled to judgment as a matter of law.

**Summons**    An official notice to a person that a lawsuit has been commenced against him or her and that he or she must appear in court to answer the charges.

**Superfund**    The Comprehensive Environmental Response, Compensation, and Liability Act of 1980.

**Supremacy clause**    Article VI, U.S. Constitution, which states that the Constitution, laws, and treaties of the United States shall be the "supreme law of the land," and shall take precedence over conflicting state laws.

**Surety**    One who incurs a liability for the benefit of another. One who undertakes to pay money in the event that his principal is unable to pay.

**Tangible property**    Physical property.

**Tender offer**    An invited public offer by a company or organization to buy shares from existing stockholders of another public corporation under specified terms.

**Testator**    One who has made a will.

**Third-party beneficiaries**    Persons who are recognized as having enforceable rights created for them by a contract to which they are not parties and for which they have given no consideration.

**Title**    Legal evidence of ownership.

**Tort**    A civil wrong other than a breach of contract.

**Trade disparagement**   The publication of untrue statements that disparage the plaintiff's ownership of property or its quality.

**Trademark**   Any word, name, symbol, or device used by a manufacturer or merchant to identify his or her goods.

**Trade practice regulation**   A term generally referring to laws that regulate competitive practices.

**Trade secret**   Any formula, pattern, machine, or process of manufacturing used in one's business which may give the user an opportunity to obtain an advantage over its competitors. Trade secrets are legally protectable.

**Treason**   Breach of allegiance to one's government, specifically by levying war against such government or by giving aid and comfort to the enemy.

**Trespass**   An act done in an unlawful manner so as to cause injury to another; an unauthorized entry upon another's land.

**Triple damages (or treble damages)**   An award of damages allowable under some statutes equal to three times the amount found by the jury to be a single recovery.

**Trust**   A fiduciary relationship whereby one party (trustee) holds legal title for the benefit of another (beneficiary).

**Trustee**   One who holds legal title to property for the benefit of another.

**Truth-in-lending**   A federal law which requires disclosure of total finance charges and the annual percentage rate for credit in order that borrowers may be able to shop for credit.

**Tying contract**   A contract which ties the sale of one piece of property (real or personal) to the sale or lease of another item of property.

**Ultra vires**   Beyond the scope of corporate powers granted in the charter.

**Unconscionable**   In the law of contracts, provisions which are oppressive, overreaching, or shocking to the conscience.

**Underwriter**   The party which, in securities law, guarantees the issuer that the securities offered for sale will be sold.

**Undue influence**   Influence of another destroying the requisite free will of a testator or donor, which creates a ground for nullifying a will or invalidating a gift. A contract will not be binding if one party unduly influences the other since the parties have not dealt on equal terms.

**Unfair labor practices**   Activities by management or labor unions which have been declared to be inappropriate by the Wagner Act and Taft-Hartley Act, respectively.

**Unilateral contract**  A contract in which no promisor receives a promise as consideration; an agreement whereby one makes a promise to do, or refrain from doing, something in return for a performance, not a promise.

**Union shop**  This term applies, in labor law, to an agreement by management and labor that all employees of a business will be or become union members. Union shops are not allowed in states with right-to-work laws.

**Usury**  A loan of money at interest above the legal rate.

**Venue**  The geographical area over which a court presides. Venue designates the court in which the case should be tried. Change of venue means to move to another court.

**Verdict**  Findings of fact by the jury.

**Vertical merger**  A merger of corporations where one corporation is the supplier of the other.

**Vertical price-fixing**  An agreement between a seller and a buyer (for example, between a manufacturer and a retailer) to fix the resale price at which the buyer will sell goods.

**Vested rights**  Rights which have become so fixed that they are not subject to being taken away without the consent of the owner.

**Voidable**  Capable of being declared a nullity, though otherwise valid.

**Void contract**  A contract which is empty, having no legal force; ineffectual, unenforceable.

**Voir dire**  The preliminary examination of prospective jurors for the purpose of ascertaining bias or interest in the lawsuit.

**Voluntary-bargaining issues**  Either party may refuse to bargain in good faith regarding matters other than wages, hours, and other terms and conditions of employment. This refusal does not constitute an unfair labor practice. An issue over which parties may bargain if they choose to do so.

**Waiver**  An express or implied relinquishment of a right.

**Warrant**  A judicial authorization for the performance of some act.

**Warranty of merchantability**  A promise implied in a sale of goods by merchants that the goods are reasonably fit for the general purpose for which they are sold.

**White-collar crime**  Violations of the law by business organizations or by individuals in a business-related capacity.

**White knight**  A slang term which describes the inducement of a voluntary acquisition when an involuntary acquisition is threatened. The voluntary acquisition group is a white knight since it saves the corporation from an unfriendly takeover.

**Workers' compensation**    A plan for the compensation for occupational diseases, accidental injuries, and death of employees which arise out of employment. Compensation includes medical expenses and burial costs and lost earnings based on the size of the family and the wage rate of the employee.

**Work rules**    A company's regulations governing the workplace, the application of which often become issues in the ability of employees to organize for their mutual benefit and protection.

**Wright-Line doctrine**    Establishes procedures for determining the burden of proof in cases involving mixed motivation for discharge.

**Writ of certiorari**    A discretionary proceeding by which an appellate court may review the ruling of an inferior tribunal.

**Writ of habeas corpus**    A court order to one holding custody of another to produce that individual before the court for the purpose of determining whether such custody is proper.

**Yellow-dog contract**    An agreement in which a worker agrees not to join a union and that discharge will result from a breach of the contract.

# INDEX

Page references in *italic* indicate tables.